GUIDE TO FEDERAL ARCHIVES

RELATING TO THE CIVIL WAR

By Kenneth W. Munden
and
Henry Putney Beers

The National Archives
National Archives and Records Service
General Services Administration

Washington: 1962

55883

NATIONAL ARCHIVES PUBLICATION NO. 63-1

Library of Congress Catalog Card No. A 62-9432

For sale by the Superintendent of Documents, U.S. Government Printing Office
Washington 25, D.C. – Price $3.00

FOREWORD

Students of the Civil War desiring to base their research in official archives have long felt the need for descriptive guides to the extant records of the two contending Governments in that war--the United States Government and the Government of the Confederate States of America.

This volume and the companion Guide to the Archives of the Government of the Confederate States of America, now being compiled, are intended to fill that need. As a part of its contribution to the centennial commemoration of the Civil War, this work is presented by the National Archives in the belief that it will meet one of the objectives of the national Civil War Centennial Commission stated by its Chairman, Allan Nevins--to "promote the publication of books and the collection of sources, which will stand as a permanent memorial of this commemoration. "

> Wayne C. Grover
> Archivist of the United States

Time................

Cypher.

6. P.m.

Office U. S. Military Telegraph,
WAR DEPARTMENT,

Washington, D. C. August 3 1864.

COPIED. WAR RECORDS 1861 1865

Lieut. Genl. Grant
City Point. Va.

I have seen your despatch in which you say "I want Sheridan put in command of all the troops in the field, with instruction to put himself South of the enemy, and follow him to the death. Wherever the enemy goes, let our troops go also." This, I think, is exactly right, as to how our forces should move. But please look over the despatches you may have received from here, ever since you made that order, and discover if you can, that there is any idea in the head of any one here, of "putting our army South of the enemy" or of following him to the death," in any direction. I repeat to you it will neither be done, nor attempted unless you watch it every day, and hour, and force it.

A. Lincoln $\frac{113}{131}$

A telegram written by President Lincoln to Lieutenant General Grant. After the message was dispatched by telegraph, the original telegram was retained by the War Department Telegraph Office. It is now in a volume of telegrams sent by President Lincoln, Mar. 10, 1864-Apr. 12, 1865, among the records of the Office of the Secretary of War (see page 249 of this Guide).

PREFACE

The compilers of this Guide proceeded on the initial assumption that the extant archives of all Federal agencies existing in the 1860's would yield information on the Civil War. As their investigation advanced they became more convinced of the validity of this assumption. The war went on for only half of the decade of the 1860's, but its aftermath brought to most agencies of the Federal Government so many new but war-related functions that postwar documentation, in its value for Civil War research, often transcends in importance the records of the war period.

This Guide, therefore, would hardly have met research needs had it described only the 1861-65 records. The structure of archives is such that they cannot in most cases be presented in terms of War and Reconstruction periods, and many series of records begun during the war continue in the postwar period. Moreover, a century's further accumulation of Federal archives has inevitably produced additional materials bearing on the Civil War. For the Government of the United States survived the Civil War and--through its judicial processes, its pensioning and memorializing programs, its investigative commissions and other boards seeking facts about the war, and its work in settling war-related claims of both domestic and foreign origin, in reestablishing relations with the Indians, and in restoring national unity--continued even into the present century to add to the documentary information about the war. This postwar documentation, indeed, serves also the purpose of resolving many questions about the Confederacy, which as a government had no opportunity to prepare final reports, settle administrative or other issues, or institute postwar inquiries.

The records of the U. S. Government are best described in terms of the agency of the Government that created them. Because most of the records with which this Guide is concerned were created during the decade of the Civil War, the information about them is presented in sections corresponding to the Government's organization in that period. The interrelationship of the functions, and consequently of the records, of the many agencies will be apparent to all who use this Guide. The general records of the Government pertinent to the investigation are described in the first section; the records of Congress, the Judiciary, the Presidency, and the executive departments and other offices are described in subsequent sections. Each section opens with a historical statement of the functions and responsibilities of the branch of the Government or the executive department or agency concerned, with emphasis on its wartime duties. Records of a general character are then described, and there follow separate descriptions of the records of component bureaus or other offices, each

usually preceded by a historical statement. Such statements are followed
by bibliographical references (suggestive rather than exhaustive), and the
descriptions of records are followed by notations of finding aids, documentary publications, and other pertinent items.

Many records of the Federal Government relate to the Confederacy.
These, of course, are described in the present Guide, but records of the
Confederacy itself will be described in the companion Guide to the Ar-
chives of the Government of the Confederate States of America. Every
effort has been made to include in this volume all pertinent archives of the
Federal Government--to produce a Guide complete and definitive. The
records described include those in the National Archives, those in Federal
Records Centers, and those in other custody. The last class includes materials still held by Federal agencies other than the National Archives and
Records Service as well as official or quasi-official materials on deposit
or available elsewhere. In the lack of adequate extant records of a given
agency, or when otherwise useful, information about accumulations of private papers is given under Records in Other Custody. Records described
under a record group number (for instance, Record Group 94) are in the
National Archives unless stated to be in a Federal Records Center. A
numerically arranged list of the record groups that contain records described in this Guide is presented as an appendix.

The authors are indebted to many staff members of the National Archives and the Federal Record Centers for invaluable assistance and cooperation in the research. It would be impossible to name them all. The
authors are especially grateful, however, for the assistance of Elizabeth
Hawthorn Buck, who not only has been their principal editor but has shared
much of the research burden. Those who have given the project their clerical support must also go unnamed, but the assistance of Mary Jane Dowd
in compiling the index is especially acknowledged. Finally--for his unfail-
ing interest, enthusiastic encouragement, and constructive suggestions--
the authors express to Bell Irvin Wiley, member of the national Civil War
Centennial Commission and distinguished Civil War historian, their deep-
felt gratitude.

Kenneth W. Munden
Henry Putney Beers

CONTENTS

Page

I. GENERAL RECORDS

OF THE

UNITED STATES GOVERNMENT

The National Archives, following the pattern established by the Department of State, maintains as a separate group certain records that relate to the activities of the Government as a whole. These include statutes, Presidential proclamations, Executive orders, international treaties and related papers, Indian treaties, and records relating to the ratification of the Constitution. Some records of the Civil War period are, of course, in that record group. As he had done since 1789 (1 Stat. 29, 68), the Secretary of State continued during the war to preserve and publish the acts and resolutions of Congress and to hold in safekeeping all treaties and Presidential proclamations. An act of Apr. 20, 1818 (3 Stat. 439), had required the Secretary to publish amendments to the Constitution when they were ratified and to certify that they had become part of the Constitution.

Record Group 11. --In the series of laws of the United States, the original enrolled public laws, private laws, and resolutions of the 37th and 38th Congresses (1861-65) are arranged chronologically in 10 large volumes. The statutes were published in newspapers currently as they were enacted, and at the end of each session they were printed in pamphlet form. Volumes containing all the statutes for the Civil War period (12 and 13 Stat.) were published in 1863 and 1866 by Little, Brown, and Co. of Boston under a contract authorized by a joint resolution of Mar. 3, 1845 (5 Stat. 798). The substance of many wartime laws is discussed elsewhere in this Guide in connection with the departmental or bureau activities that they affected.

Proclamations were signed by the President and countersigned by the Secretary of State, and they bore the imprint of the Great Seal of the United States, which the Secretary was authorized to keep. Executive orders were signed by the President but rarely bore the countersignature of the Secretary or the imprint of the seal. Proclamations were issued in connection with matters of more general interest than those treated in Executive orders. The manuscript proclamations are preserved in bound volumes; those of 1861-65 (proclamations numbered 80-148) are in 3 volumes. Proclamations issued in connection with treaties are filed with the treaties. A card index to the proclamations, with subject and numerical sections, is a useful tool. During the war many important proclamations were issued on such subjects as amnesty, the blockade of Southern ports, pardons, calls for volunteers, the reconstruction of the States that had seceded, and, of course, emancipation. Some Executive orders were also war-related, but because they concerned largely matters under the cognizance of other departments the texts did not find their way into the files of the Department of State. The file of Executive orders in that Department's records begins in 1862 and contains only nine orders through 1865. A register lists the orders chronologically; 3 index volumes provide a subject approach by the first letter of the alphabet only. More useful is the card index containing both subject and numerical sections. Proclamations were printed currently in newspapers or as broadsides, and so were Executive orders.

The texts of most proclamations and Executive orders of the war years are published in the Statutes at Large, vols. 12 and 13; in James D. Richardson, ed., A Compilation of the Messages and Papers of the Presidents, 1789-1897, vols. 5 and 6 (H. Misc. Doc. 210, 53 Cong., 2 sess., Serial 3265; Washington, 1896-99. 10 vols.); and in Edward McPherson, The Political History of the United States . . . During the Great Rebellion . . . , p. 261-307 (Washington, 1865). A list of the numbered Executive orders is in Historical Records Survey, New York City, Presidential Executive Orders, Numbered 1-8030, 1862-1938, ed. by Clifford L. Lord, Joseph E. Vaughan, and Charles E. Baker (New York, 1944); and a list of unnumbered Executive orders compiled from numerous sources is in Historical Records Survey, New Jersey, List and Index of Presidential Executive Orders (Unnumbered Series), 1789-1941, p. 26-36 (Newark, N. J., 1943). Other unlisted and unpublished Executive orders can undoubtedly be found in the records of the various departments. Information on the manuscript and printed versions of the Emancipation Proclamation is in Charles Eberstadt, Lincoln's Emancipation Proclamation (New York, 1950). See also J. M. Edelstein, "Early Editions of the Emancipation Proclamation," Library of Congress, Quarterly Journal of Current Acquisitions, 16:169-179 (Aug. 1959).

Treaties and other international agreements negotiated during the war, including unperfected treaties, Indian treaties, and postal conventions, were preserved by the Department of State. The treaties are filed numerically, and each treaty file includes the original signed treaty, the attested resolution of the Senate, the duplicate United States instrument of ratification, the exchanged instrument of ratification of the other party, the original of the certificate of protocol or procès-verbal of exchange of ratification, and the original proclamation of the treaty by the President, and sometimes drafts of treaties, full powers, memoranda, correspondence, and maps. Of the 22 treaties perfected during the war none appears to be directly war-related. The file of unperfected treaties contains instruments that were signed by the United States and the representatives of the other parties but were not subsequently ratified; consequently the documentation for a particular treaty would include some but not all of the papers mentioned. There are nine unperfected treaties for the period of the war, and two of them-- that of Aug. 12, 1861, with Russia concerning the rights of neutrals and that of Dec. 15, 1863, with the Netherlands concerning the emigration of freedmen to Surinam--bear some relationship to the war. Bilateral postal conventions are concluded by the U. S. Postmaster General and foreign postal authorities and are not submitted to the Senate for ratification. The documents are usually kept by the Post Office Department, and those of the Civil War period are described under that Department elsewhere in this

Guide. One convention with Mexico, Dec. 11, 1861, however, which was submitted to the Senate, is in the Department of State treaty series (no. 211), and in the same series (erroneously filed) is an unperfected postal convention signed with Mexico on July 31, 1861. One other postal convention, signed with Costa Rica on June 9, 1862, is in the unperfected treaty file. A card index to the unperfected treaties consists of a chronological section and a section arranged alphabetically by name of country. Document inventories of the treaty series, the unperfected treaty file, and postal conventions, compiled by the National Archives, list all the papers with each instrument and others that should be in these files but are actually filed elsewhere.

Treaties were published contemporaneously in newspapers and subsequently in the Statutes at Large. But they can be found more conveniently in William M. Malloy, comp., Treaties, Conventions, International Acts, Protocols, and Agreements Between the United States of America and Other Powers, 1776-1909 (S. Doc. 357, 61 Cong., 2 sess., Serials 5646, 5647; Washington, 1910). A chronological list of treaties is in Hunter Miller, ed., Treaties and Other International Acts of the United States, 1:63 (Washington, 1931); this compilation ceased publication when it reached the year 1863. Chronological and numerical lists of treaties are in U. S. Department of State, List of Treaties Submitted to the Senate, 1789-1934 (Department of State, Publication 765; Washington 1935).

Until 1871, following the precedent established by the British Government and the American colonial governments, the United States negotiated treaties with Indian tribes. Indian treaties were ratified by the Senate, but the signatures of the Indians were regarded as their full and final assent; consequently no ratifications were exchanged. The Indian treaty file includes the original treaties, Senate ratifications, Presidential proclamations, and sometimes copies of messages of the President to Congress, copies of letters of instruction to Indian commissioners, and journals and correspondence of the commissioners. The treaties are arranged numerically and chronologically, and a card index is available in three parts: by date, by place of signing, and by name of tribe. The index includes references to pertinent documents in the miscellaneous letters received and the domestic letters of the Department of State (Record Group 59).

Indian treaties were promulgated by publication in the session laws and the Statutes at Large. Texts of these treaties are assembled in Charles J. Kappler, comp., Indian Affairs, Laws and Treaties (vols. 1-2, S. Doc. 319, 58 Cong., 2 sess., Serials 4623, 4624; vol. 3, S. Doc. 719, 62 Cong., 2 sess., Serial 6166; Washington, 1904, 1913). A chronological list of such treaties is in National Archives, List of Documents Concerning the Negotiation of Ratified Indian Treaties, 1801-1869, comp. by John H. Martin (Special List No. 6; Washington, 1949). Those negotiated 1861-65 are Nos. 315-351, p. 126-149. This publication lists for each treaty the documents in the Records of the Bureau of Indian Affairs (Record Group 75) and the Records of the Office of the Secretary of the Interior (Record Group 48).

The Thirteenth, Fourteenth, and Fifteenth Amendments to the Constitution are referred to as the Civil War amendments because they dealt with fundamental questions of the war period. In the second session of the 36th Congress an attempt was made to employ the amending process to prevent the outbreak of war, when the proposed "Corwin amendment" was approved by Congress on Mar. 2, 1861. It prohibited any amendment to the Constitution abolishing or interfering with slavery in the States, but the secession movement was too far under way by that time to permit its ratification. Legislation adopted by Congress during the war freed Negro fugitives from the South who were the property of "rebels," abolished slavery in the District of Columbia and the Territories, and repealed the Fugitive Slave Acts. The Emancipation Proclamation was limited in effect, and its legality was disputed. The abolition of slavery by a number of border States, however, including West Virginia, Missouri, Maryland, and Tennessee, indicated that a Constitutional amendment could be ratified. Congress therefore by a joint resolution of Feb. 1, 1865 (13 Stat. 567), referred to the States a proposed amendment by which slavery was abolished in the Nation. When a sufficient number of States had ratified the Thirteenth Amendment, the Secretary of State issued a certificate of ratification on Dec. 18, 1865 (13 Stat. 774).

Though at last given his freedom, the Negro did not yet have the rights of citizenship or suffrage. Some Southern States passed acts imposing legal inferiority upon Negroes and establishing a system of labor contracts that was practically slavery. A joint resolution proposing the Fourteenth Amendment, of which the first section guaranteed the rights of citizenship, was adopted by Congress on June 16, 1866 (14 Stat. 358). Its ratification was proclaimed by the Secretary of State on July 28, 1868 (15 Stat. 708). Discriminatory laws restricting Negro suffrage in the South after the war resulted in congressional proposals, from Dec. 1865 onward, for another Constitutional amendment. Finally a joint resolution of Feb. 27, 1869 (15 Stat. 346), proposed an amendment declaring that "The right of citizens to vote shall not be denied or abridged by the United States or by any State on account of race, color, or previous condition of servitude." When the Secretary of State issued the certificate of ratification on Mar. 30, 1870 (16 Stat. 1131), the Fifteenth Amendment became a part of the Constitution.

Herman V. Ames, The Proposed Amendments to the Constitution of the United States During the First Century of Its History (American Historical Association, Annual Report, 1896, vol. 2; Washington, 1897); Joseph B. James, The Framing of the Fourteenth Amendment (Urbana, Ill., 1956); George G. Payne, comp., The Constitution of the United States of America as Amended to December 1, 1924 (Annotated) (S. Doc. 154, 68 Cong., 1 sess., Serial 8250; Washington, 1924); James G. Randall, Constitutional Problems Under Lincoln (Urbana, Ill., 1951); Howard D. Hamilton, "The Legislative and Judicial History of the Thirteenth Amendment," National Bar Journal, 9:26-134, 10:7-85 (Mar. 1951, Mar. 1952).

The records relating to the ratification of each of the amendments are in separate volumes, in which they are grouped alphabetically by name of State. They include copies of letters from the Secretary of State to the

Governors of the States, transmitting the joint resolutions of Congress and requesting action on them by the State legislatures, original letters of acknowledgment from the Governors and letters of transmittal from them with the ratifications in the form of joint resolutions of the State legislatures, and some messages of the Governors to the legislatures. Some of the ratifications are in longhand on ordinary paper, others are engrossed on parchment, and some are printed; all are certified. Rejections take the same varied forms. Communications from the Secretary of State informing Congress of the progress of ratification are also in these volumes. The certificate of ratification by which the amendment was proclaimed to be in effect through publication in newspapers and in the statutes appears not only in the volume for each amendment but in a separate file of certificates.

Texts of the joint resolutions of Congress, the resolutions of the State legislatures, the Governors' transmittal letters, and the certificates of ratification issued by the Secretary of State appear in U. S. Department of State, Documentary History of the Constitution of the United States of America, 1786-1870, comp. by Andrew H. Allen, 2:516-897 (Washington, 1894-1905. 5 vols.). The compilation does not include the ratification of every State. Delaware, for instance, did not ratify the three amendments until 1901 and did not notify the Secretary of State of its ratification until Apr. 5, 1935. Maryland did not ratify the Fourteenth Amendment until Apr. 4, 1959. The outgoing communications of the Secretary of State that are in the manuscript compilations are also copied in the domestic letters and the report books maintained by the Department of State.

II.   CONGRESS

The record of the Congress of the United States in the period of the Civil War and Reconstruction has been subjected to as close an examination by historical scholars as would seem to be possible.   The reexamination of that record here, in either its legislative or political aspects, would serve little purpose; but the largely unpublished materials described below may afford rewarding opportunities for viewing a great legislative body. Despite its vigorous opposition to many policies of the Chief Executive, despite the diminishment of its ranks by the withdrawal or expulsion of Senators and Representatives from the seceded Southern States, and despite the bitterness engendered by the war, Congress nevertheless very much conducted its "business as usual." This business is not only spread upon the journals and other printed records, long accessible to historians, but also safeguarded in the form of records never made public--although not often deliberately withheld.   The essential value of these may well lie not so much in their revealing hitherto unknown facts about Congress as in their mirroring so large a part of the general American scene in the Civil War years.

The records of the Senate are all in Record Group 46 and those of the House of Representatives are all in Record Group 233.   Although the National Archives has established Record Group 128 for the joint committees of Congress, not all of the joint records have been separated from the records of the Senate and the House.   Joint records pertinent to Civil War research are therefore divided at present among these three record groups.

The symbols (for instance, 38A-E2) occurring here and there in this description are introduced because they often are essential to finding the items mentioned.   They were devised by the National Archives to signify the particular Congress, one of the major functions by which the records are grouped, and further subdivisions corresponding in general to series or subseries.   The major functions so symbolized are as follows:

Senate:
    A.   Records of legislative proceedings.
    B.   Records of executive proceedings.
    C.   Records of impeachment proceedings.
    D.   Records of the Office of the Secretary.
House of Representatives:
    A.   Records of legislative proceedings.
    B.   Records of impeachment proceedings.
    C.   Records of the Office of the Clerk.

References specifically applicable to joint committees and committees of the Senate and the House are given below under the appropriate entries. Volumes 12 and 13 of United States Statutes at Large cover the Civil War period. The Congressional Globe (Washington, 1834-73) gives more, though occasionally less precise, details of Congressional proceedings than either the Senate or House Journal. The Tables of and Annotated Index to the Congressional Series of United States Public Documents (Washington, 1902) is a guide to the published documents of the 15th to 52d Congresses; and the Checklist of United States Public Documents, 1789-1909 (3d ed.; Washington, 1911) provides background information on the publications of Congress and lists committee publications issued

before 1910; see also Ben Perley Poore, A Descriptive Catalogue of the Government Publications of the United States, September 5, 1774-March 4, 1881 (S. Misc. Doc. 67, 48 Cong., 2 sess., Serial 2268). For information on individual members of the House and Senate see Charles Lanman, Dictionary of the United States Congress and the General Government . . . (Hartford, 1868), and Biographical Directory of the American Congress, 1774-1949 (H. Doc. 607, 81 Cong., 2 sess., Serial 11414). Edward McPherson, Clerk of the House of Representatives, undertook in 1864, "without a realizing sense of the labor it involved," his compilation, The Political History of the United States of America During the Great Rebellion . . . , which he revised the following year (Washington, 1865).

JOINT COMMITTEES OF CONGRESS

"In the period of secession and reconstruction, the decade from 1861 to 1871," McConachie wrote in his study of congressional committees, "center the most important phenomena for the study of joint committees. They flourished then because of the centralizing influence of war in demanding larger and prompter legislation; because of the economy of substituting a united inquiry for two separate investigations, especially where extensive traveling was requisite; and because of the long political accord of the two Houses, coupled with their united opposition to the policy of the Executive towards the Southern States."

The joint standing committees during the Civil War included the Committees on Enrolled Bills, the Library, and the Public Printing. The joint select committees important to Civil War research included the Joint Committee on the Conduct of the War, whose authority was to grow with the widening scope of its inquiries, and seven other joint committees authorized during or shortly after the war. In the following description, the joint standing committees are discussed first and then the joint select committees, arranged by Congress in which they were established and chronologically by the date of their authorization.

Some joint committees, not classed as either standing or select, had duties that were perfunctory or for a limited period, at the beginning and end of a session of Congress. These included the joint committees to wait upon the President to inform him that a quorum of the two Houses had assembled and was ready to receive any communication from him, or that Congress was about to adjourn. Moreover, conference committees (none of which is mentioned specifically in this Guide), composed of representatives of both Houses, had been employed from the time of the 1st Congress to reconcile or adjust differences. Their nature, as understood during the Civil War, was clarified by Vice President Hamlin in the 1st session of the 38th Congress as follows:

> Conferences are of two characters, free and simple. A free conference is that which leaves the committee of conference entirely free to pass upon any subject where the two branches have disagreed in their vote, not, however, including any action upon any subject where there has been a concurrent vote of both branches. A simple conference--perhaps it should more properly be termed a strict or a specific conference, though the parliamentary term is "simple"--is that which confines the committee of conference to the specific instructions of the body appointing it.

Also excluded from consideration in this Guide are joint select committees of the following types: those created to "report a mode for examining the votes" of the electoral college and those created to inform the President and Vice President of their election.

Lauros G. McConachie, Congressional Committees; a Study of the Origins and Development of Our National and Local Legislative Methods (New York, 1898).

Joint Standing Committees

Joint Committee on Enrolled Bills; Orville H. Browning (Ill.), chairman, 37th Cong. ; Timothy O. Howe (Wis.), chairman, 38th Cong.
This joint committee existed from 1789 to 1876. In accordance with Jefferson's manual, when a bill had passed both Houses of Congress it was delivered to this committee by the House last acting on it, to be enrolled on parchment "solidly, and all of a piece, that the blanks between the paragraphs may not give room for forgery." It then passed to the Speaker of the House, the President of the Senate, and the President, for signature. As the law directed, the bill, when approved by the President, was deposited in the State Department.
There are no records of this committee as such for the Civil War period, but its work is evidenced by the enrolled bills preserved.

Joint Committee on the Library; James A. Pearce (Md.), chairman, 37th Cong. (died Dec. 20, 1862); Jacob Collamer (Vt.), chairman, 38th Cong. (died Nov. 8, 1865).
Authorized Dec. 7, 1843.
Record Group 128. 37th and 38th Congs. --A communication from Henry Barnard, Mar. 27, 1862, concerning his nomination as a regent for the Smithsonian Institution; documents relating to the establishment of a library for the Senate (printed as S. Misc. Doc. 4, 38 Cong. , 1 sess. , Serial 1177); and the memorial of J. M. Stanley asking that Congress purchase his gallery of Indian portraits, then on exhibition at the Smithsonian Institution.
Record Group 46. 38th Cong. --Referred papers concerning remuneration to J. M. Stanley for the loss of his collection Indian portraits in the Smithsonian fire of 1865 (38A-H3); and the memorial of Henry R. School-

craft asking for an appropriation to enable him to complete his work on the Indians of the United States (38A-H25), with a letter from Mary Howard Schoolcraft to Chairman Collamer.   40th Cong. --Memorial of Mathew B. Brady asking that Congress purchase his collection of "war views and portraits," with an itemized description of it (40A-H27).

Joint Committee on the Public Printing; Henry B. Anthony (R. I.), chairman, 37th and 38th Congs.
    Authorized July 24, 1846. Sec. 12 of an act of Aug. 26, 1852 (10 Stat. 34), provided that this committee should be composed of three Senators and three Representatives, "to decide between the superintendent of the public printing and the public printer in any dispute which may arise as to the propriety of the decisions of the superintendent making deductions on account of work which the superintendent may refuse to receive, or which, in his opinion, may not be done with proper despatch, as required by law," and to pass upon the accounts of the Superintendent of Public Printing. It is of interest to note that this committee was responsible for the publication (S. Misc. Doc. 53, 39 Cong., 2 sess., Serial 1278) of the Arkansas Adjutant General's report "for the period of the late rebellion, and to November 1, 1866," which the Arkansas legislature (1867), "under disloyal control," had refused to publish.
    Record Group 46, 37th Cong. --A document (37A-E10) concerning the delay in printing the Secretary of the Treasury's 1861 report on banks. 39th Cong. --The original of the above-mentioned Arkansas Adjutant General's report (39A-H19).

Joint Select Committees

37TH AND 38TH CONGRESSES

Joint Select Committee on the Conduct of the War

    A Senate resolution of Dec. 9, 1861 (the House concurring on the following day), provided for the appointment of a joint committee of three Senators and four Representatives "to inquire into the conduct of the present war." Continuation during the recess of Congress was authorized by Senate resolution of July 16, 1862 (the House concurring). A Senate resolution of Mar. 2, 1863, authorized the committee to continue its sessions for 30 days after the close of the 37th Congress; and a Senate resolution of Jan. 20, 1864 (the House again concurring), reestablished the committee in the 38th Congress, to inquire not only "into the conduct and expenditures of the present war" but also "into all the facts and circumstances of contracts and agreements already made, or that may be made; and such contracts and agreements hereafter to be made, prior to the final report of the committee, by or with any department of the government, in any wise connected with, or growing out of, the operations of the government in suppressing the rebellion against the constituted authority." By concurrent resolution of Mar. 1-2, 1865, the life of the committee was extended for 90 days after the close of the 38th Congress. The committee was sometimes referred to as the "Joint Committee on the Conduct and Expenses of the War."
    The committee's insatiable inquisitiveness has provided a capital source of information. As Upton observed in his Military Policy of the United States:

Had the investigation been confined to transactions which had already occurred, no harm would have ensued beyond the injury done to discipline by encouraging officers to criticise their superiors with a view to securing promotion, or to the gratification of personal ill will. But a knowledge of past events by no means satisfied the committee. It pried into the present and sought to look into the future. With but little or no regard for secrecy, it did not hesitate to summon commanders of armies in the field, who were asked and encouraged to disclose the numbers of their troops and their plans of campaign.

As originally appointed, the committee consisted of Benjamin F. Wade (Ohio), Zachariah Chandler (Mich.), and Andrew Johnson (Tenn.) for the Senate; and Daniel W. Gooch (Mass.), John Covode (Pa.), George W. Julian (Ind.), and Moses F. Odell (N. Y.) for the House. When Johnson was appointed Military Governor of Tennessee, Joseph A. Wright (Ind.) replaced him. Benjamin F. Harding (Oreg.) replaced Joseph A. Wright on the committee in the 38th Congress; and Benjamin F. Loan (Mo.) replaced John Covode. Benjamin F. Wade was elected chairman at the committee's first meeting, Dec. 20, 1861.

The inquiries it undertook were usually the result of Senate or House resolutions, but some were initiated independently by the committee. The testimony and the documents exhibited are to be found in the committee's reports on the following subjects:

Treatment by the rebels at Manassas of remains of U. S. officers and soldiers; employment of Indians by the rebels (S. Rept. 41, 37 Cong., 2 sess., Serial 1125).

Battle at Fredericksburg, Va. (S. Rept. 71, 37 Cong., 3 sess., Serial 1151).

Army of the Potomac (S. Rept. 108, pt. 1, 37 Cong., 3 sess., Serial 1152).

Bull Run; Ball's Bluff (S. Rept. 108, pt. 2, 37 Cong., 3 sess., Serial 1153).

Western Department, or Missouri (S. Rept. 108, pt. 3, 37 Cong., 3 sess., Serial 1154).

Miscellaneous subjects: Hatteras Inlet expedition, Port Royal expedition, Burnside expedition, Fort Donelson, capture of New Orleans, invasion of New Mexico, Accomack expedition, Battle of Winchester (Mar. 23, 1862), Monitor and Merrimac, protecting rebel property, rebel barbarities, wounded from Front Royal (Va.), convalescent camp at Alexandria (Va.), trade in military districts, communicating the countersign, and "paymasters, returning slaves, etc." (S. Rept. 108, pt. 3, 37 Cong., 3 sess., Serial 1154).

Origin, progress, and results of the late expedition into Florida (S. Rept. 47, 38 Cong., 1 sess., Serial 1178).

Military administration at Alexandria, Va. (S. Rept. 54, 38 Cong., 1 sess., Serial 1178).

Fort Pillow massacre (S. Rept. 63, 38 Cong., 1 sess., Serial 1178; also H. Rept. 65, 38 Cong., 1 sess., Serial 1206).

Condition of returned Union prisoners (S. Rept. 68, 38 Cong., 1 sess., Serial 1178; also H. Rept. 67, 38 Cong., 1 sess., Serial 1206).

Explosion of the mine before Petersburg (S. Rept. 114, 38 Cong., 2 sess., Serial 1211).

Exchange of prisoners (S. Rept. 119, 38 Cong., 2 sess., Serial 1211).
Heavy ordnance (S. Rept. 121, 38 Cong., 2 sess., Serial 1211; also
  S. Rept. 142, pt. 2, 38 Cong., 2 sess., Serial 1213).
Army of the Potomac (S. Rept. 142, pt. 1, 38 Cong., 2 sess., Serial
  1212).
Battle of Petersburg (S. Rept. 142, pt. 1, 38 Cong., 2 sess., Serial
  1212).
Red River Expedition (S. Rept. 142, pt. 2, 38 Cong., 2 sess., Serial
  1213).
Fort Fisher Expedition (S. Rept. 142, pt. 2, 38 Cong., 2 sess., Serial
  1213).
Sherman-Johnston (S. Rept. 142, pt. 3, 38 Cong., 2 sess., Serial 1214).
Light-draught monitors (S. Rept. 142, pt. 3, 38 Cong., 2 sess., Serial
  1214).
Massacre of Cheyenne Indians (S. Rept. 142, pt. 3, 38 Cong., 2 sess.,
  Serial 1214). The reply of Gov. John Evans of the Territory of Colo-
  rado to the part of this report referring to him is in the report of the
  Joint Special Committee on the Condition of the Indian Tribes (S.
  Rept. 156, 39 Cong., 2 sess., Serial 1279, p. 78-87).
Ice contracts (S. Rept. 142, pt. 3, 38 Cong., 2 sess., Serial 1214).
Rosecrans' campaigns (S. Rept. 142, pt. 3, 38 Cong., 2 sess., Serial
  1214).
Operations against Charleston (S. Rept. 142, pt. 3, 38 Cong., 2 sess.,
  Serial 1214).
Operations in Department of the Gulf (S. Rept. 142, pt. 3, 38 Cong.,
  2 sess., Serial 1214).
Trade regulations (S. Rept. 142, pt. 3, 38 Cong., 2 sess., Serial 1214).
Battle of Cedar Mountain (S. Rept. 142, pt. 3, 38 Cong., 2 sess., Se-
  rial 1214).
Treatment of prisoners (S. Rept. 142, pt. 3, 38 Cong., 2 sess., Serial
  1214).
Treatment of rebel prisoners (S. Rept. 142, pt. 3, 38 Cong., 2 sess.,
  Serial 1214).
Exchange of prisoners (S. Rept. 142, pt. 3, 38 Cong., 2 sess., Serial
  1214); also H. Misc. Doc. 39, 38 Cong., 2 sess., Serial 1232).
Administration of Department of Arkansas (S. Rept. 142, pt. 3, 38 Cong.,
  2 sess., Serial 1214).

In response to questions put in writing to several general officers on
May 22, 1865, reports were filed with the committee by Maj. Gen. William
T. Sherman, Maj. Gen. George H. Thomas, Maj. Gen. John Pope, and
Maj. Gen. J. G. Foster. These replies were printed as an unnumbered
supplemental report (Serials 1241-1242) to S. Rept. 142, pt. 3, 38 Cong.,
2 sess. The questions put were as follows:

No. 1. Please state what positions you have held and what commands
you have exercised since the commencement of the rebellion, giving the
periods during which those commands respectively have been exercised
by you.

No. 2. Please state such particulars as you may deem necessary to
a proper understanding of the several campaigns in which you have been
engaged; setting forth the orders and instructions under which those
campaigns were conducted, and the principal orders and instructions

given by you, with such incidents and circumstances as you consider will be of interest to the public; appending to your statement copies of your reports and those of your principal subordinates, and keeping the account of each campaign by itself as far as convenient.

Other reports printed at the same time include those of Maj. Gen. Alfred Pleasanton, Maj. Gen. E. A. Hitchcock (on exchange of prisoners), Maj. Gen. P. H. Sheridan, and Brig. Gen. James B. Ricketts. There is also a "communication" of Norman Wiard "upon the subject of great guns."

The committee's journal is printed in S. Rept. 108, pt. 1, 37 Cong., 3 sess., Serial 1152, and S. Rept. 142, pt. 1, 38 Cong., 2 sess., Serial 1212. The committee adjourned sine die on May 22, 1865.

William Whatley Pierson, Jr., "The Committee on the Conduct of the War," American Historical Review, 23: 550-576 (Apr. 1918); T. Harry Williams, "The Committee on the Conduct of the War," American Military Institute, Journal, 3: 139-156 (Fall 1939), and Lincoln and the Radicals (Madison, Wis., 1941).

Record Group 128. --The complete committee papers do not appear to exist in the records of either the Senate or the House. In this record group, however, are the original manuscripts of most of the postwar reports mentioned above, specifically those of Gen. John Pope (parts 2-4 and a fragment of part 1), Maj. Gen. Alfred Pleasanton, Brig. Gen. James B. Ricketts, Maj. Gen. J. G. Foster, and Maj. Gen. P. H. Sheridan (previously printed reports of the last in lieu of a manuscript). Also in this group is the original testimony of Gen. John P. Slough, Military Governor of Alexandria, Va., and others, concerning the military administration of that city (Feb. 1864), especially the operation of the prison known as the "slave pen" and Slough's General Order 4, Nov. 21, 1862, prohibiting the "distribution of spirituous or malt liquors by sale or gift, either to officers, soldiers, or citizens."

Record Group 46. --In the records of the Senate are the original manuscripts of the following reports, the subjects of which are given above: S. Repts. 71 and 108, 37 Cong., 3 sess. (37A-D1); S. Repts. 47, 54, 63, and 68, 38 Cong., 1 sess. (38A-D1); S. Repts. 114, 119, 121, and 142, 38 Cong., 2 sess. (38A-D1).

38TH AND 39TH CONGRESSES

Joint Special Committee on the Condition of the Indian Tribes

This committee, appointed under a joint resolution of Mar. 3, 1865, consisted of Senators James R. Doolittle (Wis.), Lafayette S. Foster (Conn.), and James W. Nesmith (Oreg.), and of Representatives Lewis W. Ross (Ill.), William Higby (Calif.), William Windom (Minn.), and Asahel W. Hubbard (Iowa). In a work it considered to be "immense, covering a continent," the committee inquired into the condition of the Indian tribes and their treatment by civil and military authorities, and it submitted its report on Jan. 26, 1867. This was concerned especially with the rapid decrease in the Indian population, the causes of Indian wars, the loss of hunting grounds and destruction of game upon which the Indian subsisted, the question of the placement of the Indian Bureau under the War Department or its retention under the Interior Department, and the proposed boards of inspection. The report covers such events as the Chivington massacre (Nov. 29, 1864) and the removal of the Winnebagos and Sioux from Minnesota (1863) and affords a comprehensive view of the Indian situation at the end of the war.

There are no manuscript records of the committee. Its report was printed as S. Rept. 156, 39 Cong., 2 sess., Serial 1279.

39TH CONGRESS

Joint Select Committee on the Death of President Lincoln

Appointed under a House resolution of Dec. 5, 1865 (concurred in by the Senate on Dec. 6), "to consider and report by what token of respect and affection it may be proper for the Congress of the United States to express the sensibility of the nation to the event of the decease of their late President, Abraham Lincoln." The committee consisted of 13 Senators and one Representative from each State. By subsequent joint resolution Edwin M. Stanton was invited to "pronounce" an address "upon the life and character of Abraham Lincoln" as a fitting memorial. When Stanton, however, declined the invitation George Bancroft was selected as the orator, and he spoke on Feb. 12, 1866, before the two Houses and invited guests. (See Congressional Globe, 39 Cong., 1 sess., p. 798-805, and S. Rept. 14, 39 Cong., 1 sess., Serial 1240.)

Record Group 46. -- There are no records of the committee as such, but its original report is in the records of the Senate (39A-D2).

Joint Committee on Reconstruction

Under House resolution of Dec. 5, Senate resolution of Dec. 12, and concurring House resolution of Dec. 13, 1865, a joint committee of 15 was appointed to "inquire into the condition of the States which formed the so-called Confederate States of America, and report whether they, or any of them, are entitled to be represented in either house of Congress." (The committee was reappointed in the 2d session of the 39th Congress.) For the Senate the committee consisted of William P. Fessenden (Maine), James W. Grimes (Iowa), Ira Harris (N. Y.), Jacob M. Howard (Mich.), Reverdy Johnson (Md.), and George H. Williams (Oreg.). The House was represented by Thaddeus Stevens (Pa.); Elihu B. Washburne (Ill.), replaced by John F. Farnsworth (Ill.); Justin S. Morrill (Vt.); Henry Grider (Ky.), replaced by Elijah Hise (Ky.) upon the death of Grider; John A. Bingham (Ohio); Roscoe Conkling (N. Y.); George S. Boutwell (Mass.); Henry T. Blow (Mo.); and Andrew J. Rogers (N. J.).

Credentials of persons from "States lately in rebellion" were laid before this committee, which decided "to investigate carefully and thoroughly the state of feeling and opinion existing among the people of these States; to ascertain how far their pretended loyalty could be relied upon, and thence to infer whether it would be safe to admit them at once to a full participation in the government." The work was divided among four subcommittees that respectively investigated and reported on (1) Tennessee (including in part Andrew Johnson's military governorship); (2) Virginia, North Carolina, and South Carolina (including detailed testimony by John B. Baldwin and John Minor Botts of their visits to President Lincoln, Thomas

M. Cook's testimony on President Lincoln's mission to Richmond immediately after the evacuation, and Dorence Atwater's testimony on the burial
lists kept at Andersonville, Ga.); (3) Georgia, Alabama, Mississippi,and
Arkansas (containing Clara Barton's testimony on her work of identifying
and marking graves at Andersonville); and (4) Florida, Louisiana,and Texas.
The testimony is rich in material showing Southern social attitudes, particularly toward Yankees, freedmen, and Southern loyalists, during the
war and in the early stages of military occupation; the division of Protes-
tant church organizations (North and South) formerly national; the state of
the church during the war (many ministers testified); and operations of the
Bureau of Refugees, Freedmen, and Abandoned Lands. The majority and
minority reports and the testimony were printed as H. Rept. 30, 39 Cong.,
1 sess., Serial 1273; the majority report was printed also as S. Rept. 112,
39 Cong., 1 sess., Serial 1240.

    Record Group 128. --A few petitions referred to the committee concern-
ing restoration of the States of the former Confederacy to representation in
Congress; also the incomplete manuscript of the committee's report.

    Record Group 46. --The report of the minority, June 19, 1866, as
(first?) printed in a newspaper (39A-D2).

    Record Group 233. --Some papers of the committee (39A-F28.3).

    Records in other custody. --The manuscript of the committee's journal
is in the Columbia University Library, through circumstances related in
Benjamin B. Kendrick, The Journal of the Joint Committee of Fifteen on
Reconstruction (New York, 1914), which prints it in full. The journal was
important in the case of San Mateo County v. Southern Pacific Railroad
Company (116 U. S. 138). It relates to the genesis of the Fourteenth
Amendment.

Joint Select Committee on Retrenchment

    Authorized by concurrent resolution of July 19, 1866, "to inquire into
the expenditures in all the branches of the service of the United States, and
to report whether any, and what, offices ought to be abolished; whether any,
and what, salaries or allowances ought to be reduced; what are the methods
of procuring accountability in public officers or agents in the care and disbursement of public moneys; whether moneys have been paid out illegally;
whether any officers or agents or other persons have been or are employed
in the service without authority of law, or unnecessarily; and generally how,
and to what extent, the expenses of the service of the country may and
ought to be curtailed." The committee was composed initially of Senators
George F. Edmunds (Vt.), George H. Williams (Oreg.), and Charles R.
Buckalew (Pa.), and Representatives Robert S. Hale (N. Y.), Robert C.
Schenck (Ohio), Thomas A. Jenckes (R. I.), Samuel J. Randall (Pa.), and
John L. Thomas (Md.). Serving subsequently on the committee were Senator James W. Patterson (N. H.) and Representatives Charles H. Van Wyck
(N. Y.), Samuel J. Randall (Pa.), John A. Logan (Ill.), William B. Washburn (Mass.), Martin Welker (Ohio), George A. Halsey (N. J.), John F.
Benjamin (Mo.), and Jacob Benton (N. H.). The committee was renewed
and continued in the 40th Congress; and a joint committee with the same
powers and duties was authorized in the 41st Congress, to consider matters remaining undisposed of.

    This committee is perhaps best known for its recommendations on the
reform of the Civil Service (H. Rept. 47, 40 Cong., 2 sess., Serial 1358),

but its investigations pertaining to the Civil War included an inquiry into methods employed by the Treasury Department in printing U. S. bonds, notes, and securities (S. Rept. 273, 40 Cong., 3 sess., Serial 1362); and the investigation of a charge of the abstraction of registered bonds issued under an act of Mar. 3, 1863 (H. Rept. 23, 40 Cong., 2 sess., Serial 1357).

Record Group 128. -- Only two reports from the Treasury Department; also the original of S. Rept. 273, 40 Cong., 3 sess.

Record Group 46. -- The originals of S. Repts. 47 and 256, 41 Cong., 2 sess., and 380, 41 Cong., 3 sess. (41A-D1).

40TH CONGRESS

Joint Select Committee on Ordnance

Authorized Mar. 30, 1867, "to investigate the purchases, contracts, and experiments of the ordnance department." The committee consisted of Senators Jacob M. Howard (Mich.), Simon Cameron (Pa.), and Charles D. Drake (Mo.), and Representatives Robert C. Schenck (Ohio), John A. Logan (Ill.), and Benjamin F. Butler (Mass.). Continuation of the committee in the 2d and 3d sessions of the 40th Congress was authorized.

The committee kept "distinct and separate, as they relate specifically to the two bureaus of ordnance," its investigations of the testing and procurement of heavy guns or cannon, projectiles and ammunition for smooth-bore guns, projectiles and ammunition for rifled guns, muzzle-loading small arms and ammunition for them, breech-loading small arms and ammunition for them, and gun carriages. In the words of the preliminary report, the "importance of these inquiries will be appreciated when it is considered that during the late rebellion the purchases, contracts, and experiments made by the Ordnance Department of the army alone for the trial and supply of projectiles of this class cost the United States very nearly, if not altogether, the sum of seven millions of dollars. But more especially will it be felt when it is remembered how at Fort Fisher, Morris Island, and the many battle-fields of the Union, this arm of the service from some cause failed not only to realize the expectations of the people, but did, in fact, largely contribute to the disasters which befel [sic] us."

The committee found that certain correspondence between the Chief of Ordnance and his principal subordinates at armories and arsenals on the subjects under investigation had been destroyed "under the pretense that the whole of such correspondence was private and confidential"; it found furthermore that "for evident purposes of concealment, the Chief of Ordnance kept no record in his office of any of these transactions, and that the correspondence thus destroyed was the only written memoranda of the many official acts to which it related, and that these destroyed documents were, in fact, in form, and substance, official documents, under which the public business at said armories and arsenals was influenced and controlled."

The committee's second report (S. Rept. 266, 40 Cong., 3 sess., Serial 1362) evaluated particularly the ordnance of the Navy (Ames, Rodman, and Dahlgren guns) and presented its conclusions with respect to the ordnance departments of both the Army and the Navy; the appended testimony includes that of Horatio Ames, Norman Wiard, and Rear Adm. John A. Dahlgren. The committee reported also on the petition of Horatio Ames for compensation for guns furnished the Navy Department (S. Rept. 201,

40 Cong., 3 sess., Serial 1362); on the memorial of Norman Wiard concerning the annulment of wartime contracts with the Navy Department for the manufacture of guns (H. Rept. 6, 40 Cong., 3 sess., Serial 1388); and on Bvt. Maj. Gen. A. B. Dyer's request that formal charges be preferred against him (S. Rept. 189, 40 Cong., 2 sess., Serial 1320).

Record Group 46. -- The only extant committee paper is a petition of Norman Wiard for the abolition of government "manufactories" (40A-H27). There is also the incomplete original of the committee's preliminary report, which was printed as S. Rept. 173, 40 Cong., 2 sess., Serial 1320 (40A-D1).

42D CONGRESS

Joint Select Committee to Inquire Into the Condition of the Late Insurrectionary States

Although this committee concerned itself primarily with postwar conditions, focusing its attention upon the "Ku Klux Conspiracy" (the subtitle of its final report), the testimony it heard frequently related to wartime events or conditions. The committee was created by a joint resolution agreed to by the House on Mar. 20, 1871, and by the Senate on Apr. 17. It was composed initially of Senators John Scott (Pa.), Zachariah Chandler (Mich.), Benjamin F. Rice (Ark.), John Pool (N. C.), Daniel D. Pratt (Ind.), Francis P. Blair, Jr. (Mo.), and Thomas F. Bayard (Del.); and Representatives Luke P. Poland (Vt.), Horace Maynard (Tenn.), Glenni W. Scofield (Pa.), Burton C. Cook (Ill.), John Coburn (Ind.), Job E. Stevenson (Ohio), Charles W. Buckley (Ala.), William E. Lansing (N. Y.), Samuel S. Cox (N. Y.), James B. Beck (Ky.), Daniel W. Voorhees (Ind.), Philadelph Van Trump (Ohio), Alfred M. Waddell (N. C.), and James C. Robinson (Ill.). In the 2d session of the 42d Congress Cook, Buckley, Voorhees, and Waddell were dropped from the committee and John F. Farnsworth (Ill.), Benjamin F. Butler (Mass.), and James M. Hanks (Ark.) were added.

By the creating resolution the committee was directed "to inquire into the condition of the late insurrectionary States, so far as regards the execution of the laws and the safety of the lives and property of the citizens of the United States." It held its first meeting on Apr. 20, 1871. Its final report (S. Rept. 41, 42 Cong., 2 sess., Serials 1484-1496) consists of 13 volumes, as follows:

Part 1. Report of the committee and the views of the minority.
Part 2. Testimony taken by the committee in relation to North Carolina, and the report of the trials in the United States circuit court held at Raleigh.
Parts 3-4. Testimony taken by the committee in relation to South Carolina, and the report of the trials in the United States circuit court held at Columbia.
Parts 6-7. Testimony taken by the committee in relation to Georgia.
Parts 8-10. Testimony taken by the committee in relation to Alabama.
Parts 11-12. Testimony taken by the committee in relation to Mississippi.
Part 13. Miscellaneous testimony taken by the committee, testimony in relation to Florida, and miscellaneous documents.

Record Group 128. --The committee's journal, incomplete (Feb. 10, 17, and 19, 1872), identified as "Journal of Kuklux Committee."

Record Group 46. --The originals of the committee's reports, as follows: S. Repts. 6, 7, 15, and 41, 42 Cong., 2 sess. (42A-D1).

SENATE

The Senate of the United States was established by Article I, Section 1, of the Constitution. Until the adoption of the Seventeenth Amendment the two Senators from each State were chosen by State legislatures; this was, therefore, the practice during the Civil War. Although the Senate shares the lawmaking power with the House of Representatives, the House has the sole right to originate bills to raise revenue, and by custom the House originates general appropriation bills. Although revenue and appropriation bills originate in the House, the Senate may approve or amend them.

In addition to the legislative function, the Constitution vests certain other powers in the Senate. Section 3 of Article I provides that "The Senate shall have the sole Power to try all Impeachments," and Section 5 provides that "Each House shall be the Judge of the Elections, Returns, and Qualifications of its own Members"; thus the Senate has occasional judicial functions. Article II, which sets forth the powers of the President, vests in him the power to make treaties and to appoint certain officers of the United States but limits that power with the proviso requiring the advice and consent of the Senate.

The Senate occupied a small chamber in the Capitol until 1859, when it moved to a larger chamber in the newly constructed Senate Wing. By the outbreak of the Civil War, as now, the general structure of the Senate had changed very little since it was created. At the beginning of each Congress new members were sworn in and committees were reorganized. The chief changes in the organization of the Senate that concern those interested in Senate records are the changes that have affected the committees. An explanation of such changes during the Civil War is given below.

When secession was imminent, the South Carolina Senators in the 36th Congress--James Chesnut, Jr., and James H. Hammond--withdrew from the Senate on Nov. 10 and 11, 1860. On Jan. 21, 1861, David Levy Yulee (Fla.), Stephen R. Mallory (Fla.), Clement C. Clay, Jr. (Ala.), Benjamin Fitzpatrick (Ala.), and Jefferson Davis (Miss.) announced in the Senate their intention to withdraw, and they did so before Jan. 24. Albert G. Brown (Miss.) withdrew on Jan. 12, 1861; Alfred Iverson (Ga.) withdrew on Jan. 28; Robert Toombs (Ga.) did not occupy his seat after Feb. 4; Judah P. Benjamin and John Slidell (La.) withdrew on Feb. 4; and Alfred O. P. Nicholson (Tenn.) withdrew on Mar. 3. Although a few Senators from the seceded States returned in the 37th Congress, their seats were declared vacant by Senate resolution of Mar. 14, 1861; and the Arkansas and North Carolina Senators were expelled on July 11, 1861 (after their States had seceded in May). Virginia was represented in the Senate of the 37th Congress by Waitman T. Willey and John S. Carlile, after the withdrawal and expulsion of James M. Mason and Robert M. T. Hunter, and in the Senate of the 38th Congress by Carlile and Lemuel J. Bowden; the new State of West Virginia was represented in the 38th Congress; but the seats of Senators from the following seceded States remained vacant from the 38th Congress until the States' readmission after the war: Alabama,

Arkansas, Florida, Georgia, Louisiana, Mississippi, North Carolina, South Carolina, Tennessee, and Texas.

As Vice President of the United States, Hannibal Hamlin presided over the Senate in the 37th and 38th Congresses; in his absence the successive Presidents pro tempore of the Senate in these Congresses were Solomon Foote and Daniel Clark. Asbury Dickens and John W. Forney served successively as Secretary of the Senate.

The printed journals of the Senate for the Civil War period are in the congressional serials as follows:

Period covered	Congress and session		Serial no.
Dec. 3, 1860-Mar. 2, 1861	36	2	1077
July 4-Aug. 6, 1861	37	1	1111
Dec. 2, 1861-July 17, 1862	37	2	1116
Dec. 1, 1862-Mar. 3, 1863	37	3	1148
Mar. 4-14, 1863	37	spec.	1148
Dec. 7, 1863-July 4, 1864	38	1	1175
Dec. 5, 1864-Mar. 3, 1865	38	2	1208
Mar. 4-11, 1865	39	spec.	1208
Dec. 4, 1865-July 28, 1866	39	1	1236
Dec. 3, 1866-Mar. 2, 1867	39	2	1275

See also Henry H. Gilfry, Precedents; Decisions on Points of Order With Phraseology in the United States Senate . . . 1789-1913 (S. Doc. 1123, 62 Cong., 3 sess., Serial 6354); Journal of the Executive Proceedings of the Senate of the United States (vols. 11-14; Washington, 1887); and George H. Haynes, The Senate of the United States; Its History and Practice (Boston, 1938. 2 vols.).

Record Group 46. --The Senate records consist only of those pertaining to the official business of the Senate that were filed with the Secretary of the Senate or that remained in the hands of Senate committees and eventually were transferred to the National Archives. The records therefore do not include personal papers of the presiding officer of the Senate or of individual Senators, but the official records are useful in conjunction with the personal papers deposited elsewhere. For this reason the chairmen of standing committees and the members of select committees of the Senate in the period covered by this Guide are named below in the sections devoted to such committees.

For the three Congresses of primary concern for Civil War research (36th, 37th, and 38th) the Senate legislative proceedings consist of legislative journals (8 vols.), bills and resolutions originating in the Senate (19 ft.), and bills and resolutions originating in the House and considered in the Senate (12 ft.). The records also include the election records, pertaining to electoral votes and the credentials of Senators (4 ft.), and miscellaneous other records, including the record of yeas and nays and messages from the House of Representatives (2 ft.).

There are about 14 feet of original Senate committee reports for the three Congresses, and about 18 feet of papers of Senate committees (both standing and select). Petitions, memorials, resolutions of State legislatures, and related documents--usually but not always referred to commit-

tees--approximate another 52 feet. These records, although grouped by
subject rather than committee, are described below, together with the actual committee papers, as records of committees insofar as the committees to which they were referred can be determined. There are, however,
a good many tabled petitions and other documents, presumably never in
committee hands. Among them, for instance, are petitions expressing
alarm "that incalculable danger arises to the Army . . . from the preva-
lent use of intoxicating drinks"; urging recognition of the independence of
the Southern Confederacy; and urging an offensive and defensive alliance
with the Confederate States "for the acquisition of Mexico, Canada, and
Cuba" (38A-H25). Other petitions or memorials ordered "to lie on the
table" include the petition of Charles T. Jackson, M. D. (Feb. 28, 1863),
remonstrating against recognition of W. G. T. Morton's claim to the discovery of the anesthetic effects of ether, and resolutions of a meeting held
at the Cooper Institute, New York, Feb. 7, 1863, favoring the restoration
of Florida to the Union (37A-H29). Among other significant documents in .
this series that cannot be identified with particular committees are a copy
of a letter addressed by the Commissioners from the State of South Carolina to the President, dated Jan. 1, 1861, authenticated by R. W. Barnwell,
J. H. Adams, and J. L. Orr to be "a true copy of a letter addressed . . .
to the President today and returned by him with the above endorsement in
his own handwriting," the endorsement reading, "This paper just presented
to the President is of such a character that he declined to receive it" (36A-
G9); and authenticated copies of the original resolutions of the following
State legislatures, as transmitted to the President of the Senate, ratifying
the amendment proposing a "Fourteenth Article" to the Constitution, in each
case "ordered to lie on the table": West Virginia, New York, Pennsylvania,
Wisconsin, Rhode Island, and Ohio (39A-H17).

The President's annual messages for 1859, 1860, and 1862-64 are
in series that contain papers related to these messages as well as the
President's messages suggesting legislation and submitting specific information or documents, veto messages, and messages transmitting reports
and communications from members of the Cabinet (14 ft.). Other messages of the President, 36th-38th Congresses, include those on foreign
relations (2 ft.) and Indian relations (1 ft.) and the Executive nominations
(10 ft.). (The nominations include papers resulting from Senate committee
investigations of the fitness of persons nominated to civil and military positions in the Federal Government by President Lincoln.)

Other reports and communications (30 ft.) submitted to the Senate in
these Congresses include those from the Secretaries of State, the Treasury,
War, the Navy, and the Interior; the Postmaster General; the Commissioner
of Patents; the Commissioner of the General Land Office; and the Secretary
of the Senate.

The apparently fragmentary records of the Office of the Secretary of the
Senate for the Civil War period include his letters and related papers, a few
record books, and some printed contemporary maps. (There are, however,
many printed maps of the Civil War period in the Secretary's files of the
wartime Congresses as well as those of the 39th, 41st, and 45th Congresses.)

Finally, mention must be made of the journal of the impeachment proceedings against U. S. District Court Judge West H. Humphreys (37A-A2)
and related papers (37C-A1). Among postwar records (other than those of
committees, as described below) useful in research in the Civil War

period the record of the impeachment proceedings against Andrew Johnson ranks high. The journal of that impeachment and related papers are in the records of the Senate for the 40th Congress (2 1/2 ft.), as also are papers pertaining to the removal from office of Secretary Stanton.

National Archives, Preliminary   Harold E. Hufford and Watson G.
Inventory [No. 23] of the Records of   Caudill (Washington, 1950).
the United States Senate, comp. by

Senate Standing Committees

In early Congresses, the Senate, and the House of Representatives as well, referred each bill, joint resolution, or other matter requiring consideration to a special committee. By 1816, however, only four Senate standing committees (two of them joint) had come into existence: the Committee on Engrossed Bills, the Joint Committee on Enrolled Bills, the Joint Committee on the Library, and the Committee to Audit and Control the Contingent Expenses of the Senate. From 1816 the rule was to appoint, usually at the beginning of each session, not only these committees but 12 additional standing committees--on Claims, Commerce and Manufactures, the District of Columbia, Finance, Foreign Relations, the Judiciary, Military Affairs, the Militia, Naval Affairs, Pensions, the Post Office and Post Roads, and Public Lands. By the outbreak of the Civil War there had been added other standing committees--on Indian Affairs (1830), Patents and the Patent Office (1837), Private Land Claims (1826), Public Buildings and Grounds (1819), Revolutionary Claims (1832), and Territories (1844). A Committee on Military Affairs and the Militia had replaced the two separate committees of those names; a Committee on Commerce rather than on Commerce and Agriculture existed; and in the course of the war there were authorized additional standing committees--on Agriculture, Manufactures, Mines and Mining, and the Pacific Railroad. The number of Senate standing committees thus stood at 19 when the war began and at 23 before it ended.

Although a distinction should properly be made between papers accumulated and retained by standing committees and those referred to and (sometimes) reported back by them, the descriptions below group the papers of both kinds, by Congress, under the separate committee entries. The committees discussed in detail are entered alphabetically by their names during the Civil War; one committee established after the war is included. It has not been feasible to give the exact quantities of the records mentioned. All are in Record Group 46.

For a "Statement of the Rules   of Its Committees," 1789-1863, see
and Practice of the Senate of the   S. Misc. Doc. 42, 37 Cong., spec.
United States, in the Appointment   sess., Serial 1150.

Committee on Agriculture: John Sherman (Ohio), chairman, 38th Cong.
    Authorized Mar. 6, 1863. A committee of this name had existed previously until 1853.
    Wartime records. 38th Cong.--Views of the Commissioner of Agriculture on the expediency of taxing tobacco (38A-E1); memorials referred to the committee favoring the passage of laws to encourage foreign emigration to the United States (38A-H25).

Committee on Claims; Daniel Clark (N. H.), chairman, 37th and 38th Congs.

Authorized Dec. 10, 1816. During the Civil War, as before and after, most claims against the Government received in the Senate were referred to this committee.

Wartime records. 37th and 38th Congs.--Committee papers (37A-E1, 38A-E2), comprising opinions of the Court of Claims, especially claims on account of the seizure of cotton by the Government and its confiscation as "rebel property." Also petitions, memorials, etc., referred usually to this committee, on matters such as compensation for losses while a prisoner in 1861, for damages done to a church by U. S. troops in 1862, for a slave taken beyond the limits of Maryland, for military services rendered, and for the military use of inventions (37A-H4); as well as on matters such as compensation for property seized and confiscated under sec. 5 of an act of July 17, 1862 (12 Stat. 590), for property destroyed by soldiers, and for horses delivered to Des Moines, Iowa (38A-H3; this file contains a memorial of Mrs. Catherine Harleston, endorsed by Abraham Lincoln, for damages to her property from Union shelling).

Postwar records. 39th Cong.--Petitions, memorials, etc., referred to the committee (39A-H1), including those pertaining to compensation for property lost or destroyed by the Army, goods sold to the Army during the war, expenses incurred in raising recruits, loss of a vessel destroyed by the Confederate steamer Jamestown, property sold during the war for direct taxes, Southern property sold under the Confiscation Act, property destroyed while the owner was held prisoner on suspicion of being a Confederate spy, property of the consul of Portugal taken by General Sherman's troops at Savannah, expenditures to benefit Union officers confined in prisons at Columbia (S. C.), property taken or destroyed by the Confederacy, property destroyed in Columbia (S. C.) by U. S. forces under General Sherman, purchase of supplies for Union prisoners at Andersonville, seizure and loss of tobacco near New Orleans, the steamboat H. R. W. Hill (taken over by Commander Davis, Mississippi Squadron, June 6, 1862), property sold by direct tax commissioners in Beaufort (S. C.), appropriated cotton, and work done by Charles Forbes and others for Abraham Lincoln at the President's House (39A-H1). 40th-42d Congs.--Of the many postwar claims growing out of the Civil War that were referred to this committee, these are representative: the claim of R. W. Edmundson (clerk of the District Court, Northern District of Mississippi, and keeper of the books and records of the Land Office at Pontotoc) for expenses of moving the records from point to point "during the late rebellion" so as to safeguard them (40A-E2); petition of Dorence Atwater for compensation for preparing a list of dead soldiers at Andersonville, giving details of this work (40A-H2); petitions for compensation for boarding and nursing soldiers during the war (41A-H6); claims pertaining to the proceeds from the sale of cotton and other property captured by the "Porter Expedition" in 1864 (41A-H6); petitions of Benjamin S. Ewell for compensation for the wartime destruction of buildings and other property of the College of William and Mary at Williamsburg, Va. (41A-H6); claims of spies for the Union Army (for instance, that of R. S. M. Hunter for obtaining information about the Confederate army for General Sherman on the march from Atlanta to Savannah) (41A-H6); and papers concerning the restoration to owners of proceeds for cotton seized after June 30, 1865 (42A-E2). The main file of claims for compensation referred to the committee in the 42d Cong. (42A-H7) contains those of William L. Anderson, Rockingham Co., Va., for aiding in the escape of "loyal citizens liable to arrest and conscription by the Confederate Government," etc. (see S. Rept. 308, 42 Cong., 3 sess., Serial 1548); of Charles Baskerville, Columbus, Miss., for compensation for recovering cotton during the war; of Caleb H. Blood for expenses as U. S. Consul at Monterrey, Mexico, in 1862 and for assisting loyal refugees from Texas in 1863; of Richard Henry Garrett for losses by the burning of his barn in the capture of John Wilkes Booth (see S. Rept. 254, 42 Cong., 3 sess., Serial 1548); of George W. Hall and others for losses from seizure of the bark A One at Philadelphia on Dec. 18, 1863; of E. Lohman and Walter H. Ruth for secret service during the war by Lohman and Samuel Ruth; of many persons for cotton seized by U. S. authorities; of churches for structures or property destroyed by U. S. troops during the war; of J. W. Parish and Co. for ice furnished military hospitals in the Western States in 1863 under contract with the Medical Department; of John Potts (chief clerk of the War Department during the war), throwing light on his responsibilities as chief disbursing officer, for which he claimed compensation; and of the Winchester and Alabama Railroad for materials used by the Government during the war.

Committee on Commerce; Zachariah Chandler (Mich.), chairman, 37th and 38th Congs.

Authorized Dec. 7, 1825. Andrew Johnson was a member of this committee in the 37th Congress until his appointment in 1862 as Military Governor of Tennessee. This committee and the corresponding committee of the House, acting as a joint committee, issued a report on "Trade With Rebellious States" (H. Rept. 24, 38 Cong., 2 sess., Serial 1235).

Wartime records. 37th and 38th Congs.--Committee papers (37A-E2, 38A-E3) concerning appropriations for work on rivers and harbors, designation of Portland (Oreg.) as a port of entry, regulation of "carriage and passengers in steamships and other vessels," telegraphic communication between "the Eastern and Western Continents," pay of local inspectors of steamers, the customhouse at Portland (Maine), and salaries of customs collectors. Also the original of S. Rept. 85, 38 Cong., 1 sess., Serial 1178, on the petition of the American Shipmasters Association that the Government furnish their seamen hydrographic books and charts at slight cost (38A-D1); and petitions, memorials, etc., referred to the committee pertaining to the following subjects: erection of lighthouses and beacon lights (37A-H23), laws relating to pilots and pilotage (37A-H29), increase of salaries of lighthouse keepers (38A-H8), the cooperation of the Government with Perry M. Collins in "the construction of a continuous line of telegraph which is to connect Europe with the United States across the whole of Asia and the northwest corner of the Pacific"--Russia and England cooperating (38A-H16), the improvement of rivers and harbors (38A-H18), and the construction of ship canals (38A-H19). Also the original of the testimony heard by this committee acting jointly with the House Committee of Commerce on "Trade with Rebellious States" (38A-E3).

Postwar records. 39th Cong.--Papers concerning, among other matters, refurnishing with American registers the American vessels transferred during the war to British owners (39A-E3); also a memorial referred to the committee for restoration of lights on the Florida coast destroyed during the war (39A-H2).

Committee on the District of Columbia; James W. Grimes (Iowa), chairman,
37th and 38th Congs.
Authorized Dec. 18, 1816. A Senate resolution of Feb. 10, 1864, directed the committee to consider the expediency of providing legislation
against the exclusion of colored persons from certain railroad privileges
in the District of Columbia. The committee's inquiry "into the condition
and management of the jail in the city of Washington" was printed as S. Rept.
60, 37 Cong., 2 sess., Serial 1125; and its report on S. 108 "for the release of certain persons held to service or labor in the District of Columbia"
as S. Rept. 12 in the same serial.
Wartime records. 37th Cong.--Petitions, memorials, etc., largely referred to the committee, concerning such matters as appropriations for the
City of Washington, the employment of freedmen or "contrabands" in the
District, hospital accommodations for destitute smallpox patients, and the
opposition of the Board of Aldermen to the abolition of slavery in the District of Columbia (37A-H7). 38th Cong.--Papers relating to the Washington
Aqueduct and the Union Gaslight Co. (38A-E4); also petitions, memorials,
etc., concerning among other matters the Washington Canal, schools, and
marriage laws (38A-H6).
Postwar records. 39th Cong.--Petitions, memorials, etc., referred
to the committee concerning extension of voting irrespective of color, legislation "to put all white men who are citizens, or who have declared their
intention of becoming citizens, and residents of the District of Columbia
upon an equal footing with the Negroes," and other matters (39A-H3).
62d Cong.--Referred papers pertaining to the Lincoln Memorial (62A-J18).

Committee on Education and Labor (postwar)
This postwar committee is of interest for the Civil War primarily because of its investigations during the 48th Congress.
Postwar records. 41st Cong.--Petitions referred to the committee for
appropriations to Wilberforce University, Ohio, for the education of freedmen, touching on the history of the university and the wartime use of its
facilities (41A-H10). 48th Cong.--Original report of the committee (20 vols.,
typewritten; 48A-E7), under the chairmanship of Henry W. Blair (N. H.),
on the relations between labor and capital. This was published under the
title Report of the Committee of the Senate Upon the Relations Between Labor and Capital (Washington, 1885, 5 projected vols., only 4 published).
The testimony of Mrs. George R. Ward before the committee at Birming-
ham, Ala., on Nov. 15, 1883, constitutes, in the opinion of Douglas S.
Freeman (The South to Posterity, p. 119 ff.), "one of the most remarkable
of all the women's commentaries on the war." Her testimony (p. 1013-
1047 of vol. 17 of the original transcription) deals with the following subjects: Southern life before the Civil War, Negro superstitions, Negro mat-
rimony, religion among the Negroes, the "'scursion nuisance," "service
servants," the eve of the Civil War in the South, war prices and expedients,
"the Yankees are coming," and the aftermath of the war in the South.

Committee on Finance; William P. Fessenden (Maine), chairman, 37th and
38th Congs. (until his appointment, July 1864, as Secretary of the Treasury).
Authorized Dec. 10, 1816, as the Committee on Ways and Means; renamed Nov. 20, 1818.
Wartime records. 37th and 38th Congs.--Committee papers (37A-E4,

38A-E5), including communications from the Secretary of the Treasury on
the income tax collection, the "tax bill," and the "note bill"; papers relating to the bank loans bill; letters from the Secretary of War; a "plan for
raising money to meet the expenses of the government"; papers concerning
appropriations for the Ordnance Bureau, for the Defenses of Washington,
for the census, for carrying out the stipulations of the treaty with the Tabe-
quache band of Utah Indians of Colorado Territory (Oct. 7, 1863), and for
other purposes (including a detailed report on the 1863 organization of the
Bureau of the Register of the Treasury); papers relating to the publication
of the Congressional Globe; papers concerning losses sustained by certain
persons in Wisconsin because of the "violent resistance" to the draft at
Port Washington, Nov. 10, 1862; papers on the settlement of claims of certain land-grant railroads for transporting troops and Government stores;
papers on matters of concern to the Secretary of State, such as the claims
of Peruvian citizens, income tax on foreign consuls, and an appropriation
for suppressing the African slave trade; and papers concerning the U. S.
Mint at Philadelphia and the Nevada branch mint. Also petitions, memorials, etc., referred to the committee concerning such matters as currency, bonds, imposition or remission of duties, and taxes (37A-H6, 37A-
H27, 37A-H28, 38A-H1, 38A-H5); increase of compensation of customs
inspectors, tax assessors, steamboat inspectors, and other personnel of
executive departments (38A-H8); import duties (38A-H23) and internal
revenue (38A-H24); legislation urged by the Superintendent of Immigration
in Feb. 1865, to protect immigrants "from frauds of Boarding house
Keepers, bookers and runners of passengers for inland travel" (38A-H24);
and legislation to provide "poor white Refugees of the South, with Seed and
Farming Implements" (38A-H25).

Postwar records. 39th Cong.--Petition of Union League Club of the
City of New York (signed by Charles Butler) proposing payment to the fam-
ily of the late President Lincoln the salary for his full term of office (39A-
H19). 40th Cong.--Papers concerning the restoration of Pinckney Island,
S. C., confiscated in 1863 for nonpayment of taxes, to the heirs of Maj.
Gen. Charles Cotesworth Pinckney (40A-H27).

Committee on Foreign Relations; Charles Sumner (Mass.), chairman, 37th
     and 38th Congs.
     Authorized Dec. 10, 1816. Among other matters the committee contin-
ued during the Civil War to concern itself with the French spoliation claims,
on which it reported on Jan. 13, 1862, Jan. 20, 1863, and Apr. 4, 1864
(see particularly S. Rept. 1, 40 Cong., 1 sess., Serial 1309).

Wartime records. 37th and 38th Congs.--Petitions, memorials, etc.,
referred to the committee asking the recognition of Liberia and "Hayti,"
and favoring or opposing abrogation of the reciprocity treaty of 1854 with
Great Britain (37A-H5); other petitions concerning the reciprocity treaty
(38A-H23); and petitions for aid to Dr. D. J. Macgowan's proposed exploration of Eastern Asia (38A-H25).

Postwar records. 41st Cong.--Petitions referred to the committee for
the appointment of a commission to examine claims for damages done by the
Alabama, "other British cruisers," and armed cruisers under the flag of
the Confederate States of America (41A-H2). 42d Cong.--Petition of William B. Blanchard, who, as U. S. Consul at Melbourne, claimed to have
acted to prevent depredations by the Confederate vessel Shenandoah (42A-
H7).

Committee on Indian Affairs; James R. Doolittle (Wis.), chairman, 37th
   and 38th Congs.
      Authorized Jan. 3, 1830. The committee does not appear to have been
particularly active during the Civil War.
      Wartime records. 36th-38th Congs.--Committee papers (36A-E6,
37A-E5) on paying debts of Indian tribes, consolidating the Indian tribes of
Kansas, exempting certain chiefs and headmen of the Sioux from punishment for atrocities committed by other Sioux, and other matters. Also
petitions, memorials, etc., referred to the committee (37A-H13, 38A-H9),
including many claiming payment for damages by the Sioux in 1862 (38A-H3).

Committee on the Judiciary; Lyman Trumbull (Ill.), chairman, 37th and
   38th Congs.
      Authorized Dec. 10, 1816. Early in the Civil War the committee was
concerned (as was the corresponding committee of the House) with the memorial of the police commissioners of Baltimore, who had been arrested
and imprisoned at Fort McHenry. Other wartime concerns of the committee included confiscation legislation, the repeal of the Fugitive Slave Act,
and amendments to the Constitution. It also inquired into the conduct of
Senator John P. Hale in defending James M. Hunt, then confined in the Old
Capitol Prison (S. Rept. 5, 38 Cong., 1 sess., Serial 1178; the original
testimony, not printed, is available in 38A-D1). The committee's postwar reports on the credentials of Senators-elect (for example, S. Rept. 5,
40 Cong., 2 sess., Serial 1320, relating to Philip F. Thomas of Maryland)
are often enlightening with respect to wartime events, attitudes, and family and social relationships. S. Rept. 192, 40 Cong., 3 sess., Serial 1362,
on the credentials of Joshua Hill, claiming to be Senator-elect from Georgia, examines the question of whether that State in 1869 was entitled to representation in Congress.
      Wartime records. 37th and 38th Congs.--Committee papers (37A-E6,
38A-E6), including those pertaining to the credentials of James H. Lane
of Kansas, whose seat in the Senate was contested by Frederic P. Stanton;
credentials of claimants for Senate seats from Arkansas, with a "statement
of facts in relation to the reorganization of the State of Arkansas"; legislation sought by the Attorney General; and the committee's docket (37 Cong.,
3 sess., and 38 Cong., 1-2 sess.). Also petitions, memorials, etc., referred to the committee concerning the arrest and confinement in Fort Mc-
Henry of the Baltimore police commissioners, the abolition of the U. S.
Court for the Eastern District of Missouri, the leasing of forfeited property
in the seceded States, the failure of certain judicial officers in their duty,
the jurisdiction and sessions of certain U. S. district courts, emancipation, and the adjudication of land titles (37A-H14); the annulment of the
copyright held by M. F. Maury on scientific works prepared by him while
in the service of the U. S. Government (37A-H29); banking (37A-H1); a general uniform bankruptcy law (37A-H2 and 38A-H2); "the passage of an act
to confiscate the property of persons engaged in the present Rebellion"
(37A-H5); "freedom of the press against all unconstitutional interference of
the Administration" (37A-H9); constitutional amendments (38A-H4); increase in compensation of Federal judges and court officials (38A-H8); the
conduct of William M. Fishback during the war (38A-H25); and the admission of Senators or Representatives from Louisiana (38A-H25).
      Postwar records. 39th Cong.--Petitions, memorials, etc., referred
to the committee concerning a speedy trial for Jefferson Davis; relief of

citizens of New Orleans from certain levies assessed by Gen. B. F. Butler
in 1862; relief of citizens of New Bern, N. C., from taxes due under an ordinance of the 1865 convention of North Carolina; the enforcement of the demands of loyal creditors upon persons in the Southern States; repeal of an
act of July 2, 1862, requiring test oaths; and the establishment of a bureau
of education (urged by colored citizens of Wilmington, N. C.). There are
also petitions urging that Hannibal Hamlin be declared Constitutional President of the United States (39A-H8) and that there be a Constitutional amendment to prohibit discriminatory legislation on account of race or color (39A-
H17). 40th Cong. --Memorials referred to the committee (40A-H11), some
of which originated in the States of the former Confederacy, asking relief
from taking the loyalty oath or from civil and political disabilities or setting forth miserable conditions and asking relief; also resolutions and
memorials of the Georgia State constitutional convention (1868), the constitutional conventions of Alabama (1867) and Texas (1868-69), and the convention of the Republican Party in Mississippi (1868). 41st Cong. --Resolutions
of the State legislature of Georgia (1870) concerning the admittance of Georgia to representation in Congress (41A-H32), referred to this committee;
copies of proceedings of the State legislature of Texas (1870) concerning the
Thirteenth, Fourteenth, and Fifteenth Amendments to the Constitution
(41A-H32), also referred.

Committee on Military Affairs and the Militia; Henry Wilson (Mass.), chair-
    man, 37th and 38th Congs.
    Authorized Dec. 10, 1816, as the Committee on Military Affairs, to
which name it reverted after the Civil War. Jefferson Davis had been its
chairman in the 36th Congress. During the Civil War the committee considered and reported the enrollment bills and other military legislation
and passed on some 11,000 military appointments.
    Wartime records. 37th and 38th Congs. --Committee papers (37A-E7,
38A-E7) concerning the organization of the Signal Corps, appointment of
clerks in the War Department, indemnification of officers who lost personal
property at Hatteras Inlet, improvement of the Wisconsin and Fox Rivers
(Wis.), charges against Gen. Louis Blenker, cavalry regiments in the volunteer service, and subsistence and pay in the Army. Also wartime petitions, memorials, etc., referred to the committee (37A-H15) relating to
the establishment of a "board of health" for the Army, appointment of Jewish chaplains, exchange of prisoners, compensation for work on fortifications at St. Louis, Army rations, prohibition of the sale of intoxicating
liquors in the Army, continuation of regimental bands, construction of military roads, defenses (of Philadelphia, the Delaware River and Bay, etc.),
reestablishment of the national armory at Harper's Ferry, appropriations
to aid State militia, and other matters. There are also many referred petitions and memorials concerning the appointment of homeopathic surgeons
in the Army and Navy (37A-H10); increase in pay of private soldiers, medical cadets, paymaster clerks, and others (37A-H12); and railroads and
"telegraphs,"including the petition of P. McD. Collins concerning overland
telegraphic communication with Europe by way of Asiatic Russia (37A-H22).
Other memorials, referred to the committee in the 38th Congress (38A-H10),
pertain notably to the ambulance and hospital system, bounty, exemption of
ministers of the gospel from the draft, the enrollment act, equality of colored troops with white, exemption from military duty of the members of
various religious groups (Society of Friends, the Amana Society of Iowa,

and the Ebenezer Society of New York), the care of servicemen's orphans,
the status of colored soldiers, the construction of military roads, exchange
of captured military personnel, and the treatment of Confederate prisoners.
This file (38A-H10) contains a broadside of Laing's Battery of "Flying Artillery" (to be attached to the 10th Michigan Cavalry), offering an enlistment bounty; and the memorial of William A. Hammond, formerly Surgeon
General, dated at New York, Dec. 25, 1864, asking the Senate "to inquire
into all the circumstances connected with his recent trial and dismissal."

Still other wartime memorials referred to this committee include those
pertaining to better transportation of mails, passengers, and freight between New York and Philadelphia (38A-H15); the construction of a ship
canal around Niagara Falls (38A-H19); T. S. C. Lowe's "discoveries in
managing Balloons & other aeronautic machinery" (38A-H25); the appointment in the civil service of men honorably discharged from the Army and
Navy who had "suffered by wounds, sickness and imprisonment," with signatures by Winfield Scott, Peter Cooper, George Bancroft, M. H. Grinnell,
J. J. Astor, Jr., "and 3600 other citizens" (38A-H25; see S. Rept. 122,
38 Cong., 2 sess., Serial 1211); Solomon Andrews' "method of navigating
the air" (also 38A-H25); and pay increases for soldiers and military employees (38A-H8). Here also are the original holographic petitions of
Dr. William T. G. Morton, Jan. 1863, "for remuneration as the discov-
erer of practical anaesthesia and its use in the Army and Navy," as referred to the committee (37A-H4; see S. Rept. 89, 37 Cong., 3 sess.,
Serial 1151).

Postwar records. 39th Cong.--Papers concerning Kentucky militia
claims growing out of the war (39A-E7), among other matters; petitions of
soldiers and discharged soldiers for equalization of enlisted bounties paid
during the war (39A-H4); and the memorial of the American Freedmen's
Commission on the education of freedmen (39A-H19). Apparently not extant is the original memorial of "Miss Clara Barton, praying aid to carry
out a plan she had originated for obtaining information of missing soldiers"
(see S. Rept. 26, 39 Cong., 1 sess., Serial 1240). 40th Cong.--Several
memorials concerning the pay of officers' servants during the war (40A-H12).
41st Cong.--Petitions for settlement of claims of Kansas citizens under the
"Price Raid claims" of 1864 and claims resulting from Major General Curtis' expedition against the Indians in the same year (41A-H6); petition of
Anna Ella Carroll, writer (see S. Misc. Doc. 100, 41 Cong., 2 sess.), for
compensation for suggesting plans of operation for the armies of the United
States during the war, with copies of some of her wartime and postwar correspondence and articles (41A-H18); petition of Lorenzo Thomas, wartime
Adjutant General, throwing light on his activities in the Mississippi Valley
(41A-H18); and two memorials of Clara Barton (1869) asking release to her
of vacated buildings and surplus tools and machinery for use in the education of freedmen, with related papers (41A-H10). 63d Cong.--Referred
papers concerning the Civil War volunteer retired officers' list (63A-J57).

Committee on Naval Affairs; John P. Hale (N. H.), chairman, 37th and
      38th Congs.
Authorized Dec. 10, 1816. Its wartime chairman was appointed Minis-
ter to Spain in 1865.
Wartime records. 37th Cong.--Committee papers concerning espe-
cially the preservation of ironclad vessels from action by sea water (37A-
E8); petitions, memorials, etc., referred to the committee concerning the

location of the Naval Academy, restorations to the active list, allowances
of pay and deductions, hours of work of navy yard employees, the location
of a naval depot on the Saginaw River, the building of a "submarine war-
boat with torpedo attachment," the naval board cases of Lt. Robert B.
Riell and Capt. Francis B. Ellison, and other matters (37A-H17); other
petitions (37A-H4), including those for compensation for the burning of a
private schooner off the coast of Louisiana by order of the captain of the
U. S. S. Huntsville in Sept. 1861 and for property lost by the sinking of the
Monitor. 38th Cong.--Petitions, memorials, etc., referred to the committee concerning an increase in pay of naval service personnel and employees (38A-H8); and also (38A-H11) concerning other matters, including
questions of rank, additional allowances on construction and other naval
contracts (especially for the ironclad screw ram Dunderberg), the relief of
Paymaster Alfred A. Belknap from responsibility for money stolen from
him in New York in 1863 under extraordinary circumstances, an appropriation for testing the "double Cone Propeller" for steam vessels, allowance
of bounty for destruction of the rebel ram Arkansas, relief of responsibility for paymasters' losses, the settlement of the accounts of Edward C.
Doran (Norfolk Navy Yard paymaster whose accounts and other papers had
been seized by Southern authorities), the permanent location of a navy and
dockyard and a naval depot, the invention by S. D. Carpenter of new defense armor for war vessels, and the opening of the invention and fabrication of ordnance to public competition--a petition of Norman Wiard. In this
file (38A-H11) also is C. B. Sedgwick's letter transmitting to the Senate a
copy of the naval code prepared by him under a joint resolution of the 37th
Congress.

Among the records of the Headquarters of the Army (Record Group
108) are 15 letters sent by Gideon Welles, 1862-67, to the chairman of this
committee, the corresponding committee of the House, and the President
Pro Tempore of the Senate, relating to appropriations, legislation, and
other matters affecting the Navy Department.

Postwar records. 39th Cong.--Petition of James Tetlow for further
compensation for building tugboats for the Navy during the war (39A-H1);
petitions for awards of prize money or compensation for the capture of
Confederate vessels, with other war-related petitions (39A-H10). 40th
Cong.--Petition of Wilson D. Burlingame on behalf of the crew of the second cutter of the U. S. S. Shamrock for compensation for capturing
and sinking the Confederate ram Albemarle (40A-H2). 42d Cong.--Papers
concerning compensation to the widow of Rear Adm. John A. Dahlgren for
the Government's use of his patents during the war (42A-E11); claim of
C. W. Whitney for compensation for building the ironclad battery Keokuk
during the war (42A-H7).

Committee on Patents and the Patent Office; James F. Simmons (R. I.),
  chairman, 37th Cong.; Edgar Cowan (Pa.), chairman, 38th Cong.
  Authorized Sept. 7, 1837.
Wartime records. 36th Cong.--Petition of Samuel F. B. Morse, Jan. 1,
1861, for extension of his patents of 1840 for the "electro-magnetic telegraph" (36A-H15). 37th Cong.--Petitions, memorials, etc., concerning
Lt. D. D. Porter's quoin for pointing ordnance, the printing of the agricultural report of the Commissioner of Patents in German for the benefit of
persons of German descent in New York State and elsewhere, and other matters (37A-H18); also originals of some of the committee's reports (37A-D1).

38th Cong.--Petitions, including that of George B. Simpson for a patent on an improvement in insulating telegraph wires and another for the extension of a patent on Fisk's "metallic burial cases"(38A-H12); also a petition for extension of the patent on vulcanized India rubber granted to Charles Good-year, with remonstrances by presidents or other officers of many railroad companies, manufacturing concerns, and other businesses (38A-H13).

Committee on Pensions; Lafayette S. Foster (Conn.), chairman, 37th and 38th Congs.

Authorized Dec. 10, 1816. To this committee were referred not only petitions for pensioning survivors of earlier wars and their dependents but, in increasing numbers during and after the war, petitions relating to Civil War service.

Wartime records. 37th Cong.--Referred petitions for the granting of pensions, including among others petitions of or on behalf of the widow of John James Abert, the widow of Brig. Gen. Isaac I. Stevens (killed at the Battle of Chantilly, Sept. 1, 1862), and the mother of Maj. Theodore Talbot (37A-H19). 38th Cong.--Papers relating to bills for compensation of pension agents and for the relief of individuals (38A-E9); also petitions for pensions, including another of the widow of Abert, a petition pertaining to the work of the agent for paying pensions in New York City, and petitions to extend the benefits of the pension laws of 1861 and 1862 (38A-H14).

Postwar records. 39th Cong.--Petitions for pensions, including among many others those on behalf of sufferers from the explosion of the Allegheny Arsenal on Sept. 17, 1862 (39A-H12). 41st Cong.--Petitions for pensions on account of Civil War service, including some from those who had been on scout duty, and giving in some instances campaign details--for example, the petition of Franz Schumann, Co. K, 74th Pa. Inf. (41A-H22); also (41A-D1) the committee's original report on granting a pension to Mary Lincoln.

Many other papers on Civil War pensions, referred to this committee, are available in the records of later Congresses (see especially 64A-J64, 67A-J49, 68A-J46, 69A-J31, 70A-J36, and 71A-J50).

Committee on the Post Office and Post Roads; Jacob Collamer (Vt.), chairman, 37th and 38th Congs.

Authorized Dec. 10, 1816, as the Committee on the Post Office. Its wartime chairman had been Postmaster General in President Taylor's Cabinet.

Wartime records. 37th and 38th Congs.--Committee papers (37A-E9, 38A-E10) concerning the prewar claim of Carmick and Ramsey against the Post Office Department, the conveyance of overland mail, and the construction of a bridge across the Ohio River by the Covington and Cincinnati Bridge Co.; petitions referred to the committee to allow the New York Caucasian and "all other Democratic papers now excluded from the mails, in all the loyal States, the same privileges now enjoyed by Republican and Abolition papers" (37A-H9); other petitions or memorials (37A-H20) concerning the establishment of mail routes, abolition of the Kensington post office at Philadelphia, "postal reform," overland mail and the pony express, settlement of postmasters' accounts, and establishment of a "U. S. Residence Registry--A New Way to Find Lost Friends" (proposal of A. Watson of the Post Office Department); and still other petitions (38A-H15) pertaining to postal contracts, losses sustained in fulfilling contracts, the establishment of mail routes, and the prepayment at double rates of letters offered to route agents for mailing (with a relevant copy of United States Mail and Post Office Assistant, vol. 4, no. 3, Dec. 1863).

Committee on Public Buildings and Grounds; Solomon Foote (Vt.), chairman, 37th and 38th Congs.
Authorized Dec. 16, 1819. This committee was empowered from 1853 to act jointly with the corresponding committee of the House of Representatives. It did so in the inquiry "into the origin of the fire by which the Smithsonian Institution buildings, and the valuable deposits therein were, on Tuesday, the 24th of January [1865], in whole or in part destroyed" (S. Rept. 129, 38 Cong., 2 sess., Serial 1211).
Wartime records. 37th and 38th Congs.--Committee papers 37A-E11, 38A-E11), concerning enlargement of the Congressional Library rooms; transfer of the Superintendent of Public Buildings and Grounds from the War Department to the Interior Department and charges against the Superintendent; destitute newsboys in Washington; and the renovation of buildings and grounds.

Committee on the Public Lands; James Harlan (Iowa), chairman, 37th and 38th Congs.
Authorized Dec. 10, 1816. The wartime chairman became Secretary of the Interior in May 1865.
Wartime records. 37th and 38th Congs.--Committee papers (37A-E12, 38A-E12), including correspondence with the Commissioner of the General Land Office concerning land grants and private land claims in California, land claims in Iowa, and donation of lands for a military road and telegraph line from Appleton to Houghton, Wis.; also papers concerning grants to railroads, illegal fees taken by the register of the land office at San Francisco, and the relief of occupants of the lands of the Mission of San José, Calif. The many petitions, memorials, etc., referred to the committee include those pertaining to protection and confirmation of titles, the passage of a law "to prevent all further traffic in and monopoly of the public lands," and the sale of Reservation No. 7 in Solano County, Calif., the last with two endorsements by Abraham Lincoln, Oct. 15 and 31, 1862 (37A-H21). Other memorials relate to a bill to appropriate abandoned lands in the Southern States for the use of honorably discharged U. S. soldiers and sailors (38A-H7); appropriation of lands to endow "colleges for females," donations of land for State agricultural and other schools, sale of mineral lands in the Rocky Mountain region and aid for construction of the Northern and Central Pacific Railroads, repeal of an act of Mar. 3, 1863 (granting right of preemption to certain purchases on the Suscol Ranch, Calif.), and the survey of unsurveyed lands (38A-H16); and land grants for railroads (38A-H17).

Committee on Territories; Benjamin F. Wade (Ohio), chairman, 37th and 38th Congs.
Authorized Mar. 25, 1844. Senator Wade was also chairman of the Joint Committee on the Conduct of the War.
Wartime records. 37th Cong.--Committee papers (37A-E13) comprising the original of the message, Dec. 8, 1862, of the Governor of Utah to the Territorial legislature (S. Misc. Doc. 37, 37 Cong., 3 sess., Serial 1150) and printed papers concerning the admission of West Virginia to the Union. Also the memorial of Territory of Utah delegates in convention, Jan. 23, 1862 (signed by Daniel H. Wells), asking admission of the State of

Deseret to the Union (37A-H29).   38th Cong. --Petitions of "loyal citizens
of Virginia, " referred to this committee, to be taken directly under the protection and jurisdiction of Congress "by the formation of a territorial government or otherwise, " petitions against this, and petitions for the construction of military and wagon roads (38A-H25).

Other Committees

Senate standing committees of the war period not discussed above be-
cause their records are unavailable or irrelevant are the Committees to
Audit and Control the Contingent Expenses of the Senate, on Engrossed
Bills, on Manufactures, on Mines and Mining, on the Pacific Railroad, on
Private Land Claims, and on Revolutionary Claims.

Senate Select Committees

In the Senate, as in the House, select committees are created by resolution to consider and report upon matters beyond the authority of standing
committees or to undertake specific tasks of other kinds. The special areas
of Senate concern during the Civil War find expression, therefore, in the
work of its select committees and in that of the joint select committees of
the two Houses of Congress (see above).

All Senate select committees created toward the end of the Buchanan
administration and during the war are entered below by Congress and thereunder, with the exception of a few not treated in detail, chronologically by
date of authorization. Also included are postwar select committees of the
39th, 40th, and 41st Congresses whose records are significant to Civil War
research. As in the case of Senate standing committees, it has not been feasible to give the exact quantities of the records mentioned. All are in Record Group 46.

36TH CONGRESS

Select Committee to Inquire Into the Facts Attending the Invasion and Sei-
zure of the United States Armory at Harper's Ferry by John Brown
and His Companions

Authorized and appointed Dec. 14, 1859. The committee consisted of
James M. Mason (Va.), Jefferson Davis (Miss.), Jacob Collamer (Vt.),
Graham N. Fitch (Ind.), and James R. Doolittle (Wis.). It held confidential sessions beginning Dec. 16, 1859, and ending June 14, 1860. Its report
was printed as S. Rept. 278, 36 Cong. , 1 sess. , Serial 1040.

Records. --Papers of the committee (36A-E16), comprising its original
report with its journal; correspondence about the attendance of Hugh Forbes
as a witness, Jan. -Mar. 1860; correspondence with Thaddeus Hyatt, Jan. -
Feb. 1860; summonses and returns; correspondence with witnesses summoned and with informants (including many letters from anonymous informants); correspondence with U. S. marshals serving subpenas; newspapers
containing items about Richard Realf; and correspondence with the Governor
of Virginia about John Brown's papers.

Special Committee of Thirteen

Authorized Dec. 18, 1860, as a committee to which was referred "so much of the President's message as relates to the present agitated and distracted condition of the country, and the grievances between the slaveholding and the non-slaveholding States. " The committee was instructed "to inquire into the present condition of the country, and report by bill or otherwise. " To it were appointed, on Dec. 20, 1860, Lazarus W. Powell (Ky.), Robert M. T. Hunter (Va.), John J. Crittenden (Ky.), William H. Seward (N. Y.), Robert Toombs (Ga.), Stephen A. Douglas (Ill.), Jacob Collamer (Vt.), Jefferson Davis (Miss.), Benjamin F. Wade (Ohio), William Bigler (Pa.), Henry M. Rice (Minn.), James R. Doolittle (Wis.), and James W. Grimes (Iowa). On Dec. 31, 1860, the committee reported that it had not been able to agree upon any general plan of adjustment. Its journal is printed as S. Rept. 288, 36 Cong., 2 sess., Serial 1090.

There are no papers of the committee as such, but the original of its journal, which constituted its report, is available (36A-D1).

Select Committee on Payment of Outstanding Treasury Notes, etc.

Authorized Jan. 23, 1861, to report on a bill (H. R. 338) "to provide for the payment of outstanding treasury notes, to authorize a loan, to regulate and fix the duties on imports, and for other purposes"; appointed Jan. 24, 1861, to consist of James F. Simmons (R. I.), Robert M. T. Hunter (Va.), William Bigler (Pa.), Jacob Collamer (Vt.), and William M. Gwin (Calif.). The committee reported the bill on Feb. 1, 1861.

Records. --Copies of the House bill in question and related papers (36A-C1).

Select Committee on Certain Amendments Proposed to the Constitution by the Convention Held in Washington ("Peace Conference")

Authorized and appointed Feb. 27, 1861, to consider and report on a communication of that day from former President John Tyler, president of a convention held in Washington composed of commissioners appointed by 21 of the States "to deliberate upon the present unhappy condition of the country. " (See S. Misc. Doc. 20, 36 Cong., 2 sess., Serial 1089). On the next day the committee reported a joint resolution (S. 70) proposing certain amendments to the Constitution. This "Peace Conference," held at the invitation of the State of Virginia "to adjust the unhappy differences which now disturb the peace of the Union and threaten its continuance, " met in Washington, Feb. 4-27, 1861. The committee consisted of John J. Crittenden (Ky.), William Bigler (Pa.), John R. Thomson (N. J.), William H. Seward (N. Y.), and Lyman Trumbull (Ill.).

Records. --The original of John Tyler's communication mentioned above (36A-G9).

Other Committees

No reports or other records of the Select Committee on Inauguration of the President (appointed Feb. 14, 1861) and the Select Committee on Preservation of Order in the Galleries (appointed Mar. 8, 1861) appear to be extant.

37TH CONGRESS

Select Committee on the Construction of a Pacific Railroad

Authorized and appointed July 16, 1861, as a committee to which was referred a resolution of July 12, "That a railway from the terminus of railway communication west of the Mississippi to the Pacific Coast is at the present time demanded as a military work, and also from political considerations growing out of our present disturbances." (Both of the leading political parties in their 1860 platforms had declared in favor of building a railroad to complete rail connections between the East and the West; and the outbreak of the Civil War, bringing the necessity for closer military communication, aided the movement.) The committee consisted originally of James A. McDougall (Calif.), Samuel C. Pomeroy (Kans.), Daniel Clark (N. H.), Trusten Polk (Mo.), and Edgar Cowan (Pa.). Its continuation was authorized on Dec. 9, 1861. In the 3d session of the 37th Congress the committee was renewed and to it was referred a bill (S. 439) to amend an act of July 1, 1862 (12 Stat. 489), "to aid in the Construction of a Railroad and Telegraph Line from the Missouri River to the Pacific Ocean, and to secure to the Government the Use of the same for Postal, Military, and Other Purposes." Its chairman, James A. McDougall (Calif.), served as first chairman of the successor standing committee authorized on Dec. 22, 1863.

There are no papers of the committee as such, but the original of the referred bill, with committee notations, is available (37A-B1).

Select Committee on the Surrender of the Pensacola Navy Yard and the Destruction of Public Property at the Norfolk Navy Yard and at the Harper's Ferry Armory

Authorized July 25, 1861; appointed July 29, to consist of John P. Hale (N. H.), Andrew Johnson (Tenn.), and James W. Grimes (Iowa); continuation authorized on Dec. 9, 1861. The committee's proceedings and the evidence taken are appended to its report (S. Rept. 37, 37 Cong., 2 sess., Serial 1125); these include papers submitted by Gideon Welles concerning the Norfolk Navy Yard and the proceedings of the naval court-martial, Mar. 12, 1861, of Capt. James Armstrong, commandant of the navy yard at Warrington, Fla., at the time of its surrender.

There are no manuscript records of the committee. Its report was printed as S. Rept. 37, 37 Cong., 2 sess., Serial 1125.

Select Committee to Investigate the Charges Preferred Against Benjamin Stark

Authorized and appointed Mar. 18, 1862, to investigate the loyalty of Senator Stark of Oregon. The committee consisted of Daniel Clark (N. H.), Jacob M. Howard (Mich.), Joseph A. Wright (Ind.), Waitman T. Willey (Va.), and John Sherman (Ohio).

There are no papers of the committee as such, but the original of its report (printed as S. Rept. 38, 37 Cong., 2 sess., Serial 1125), with related papers, is available (37A-D1).

Select Committee on the National Armory and Foundry

Authorized and appointed Mar. 21, 1862, to consider a bill (S. 196) "for the establishment of a national foundry and furnace for the fabrication of cannon and projectiles for the government." Committee members were James W. Grimes (Iowa), Preston King (N. Y.), Edgar Cowan (Pa.), James Dixon (Conn.), and John B. Henderson (Mo.).

Records.--Petitions, memorials, etc., referred to the committee, urging the selection of particular sites for the armory and foundry (37A-E14, 37A-H16). These describe favorable local conditions such as available power, healthfulness, military security, and transportation facilities.

Select Committee on a Bill to Confiscate the Property and Free the Slaves of Rebels

Authorized May 6, 1862, to consider S. 151; appointed May 7, to consist of Daniel Clark (N. H.), Jacob Collamer (Vt.), Lyman Trumbull (Ill.), Edgar Cowan (Pa.), Henry Wilson (Mass.), Ira Harris (N. Y.), John Sherman (Ohio), John B. Henderson (Mo.), and Waitman T. Willey (Va.). On May 14 the committee reported a bill (S. 310) and was discharged.

No records of this committee have been found, but the originals of the resolution referred to the committee and of the bill reported are available (37A-B6, 37A-B2).

Select Committee on the Message of the H. of R. Regarding the Impeachment of West H. Humphreys

Authorized and appointed May 8, 1862, to consist of Lafayette S. Foster (Conn.), Garrett Davis (Ky.) and James R. Doolittle (Wis.). Humphreys, judge of the U. S. District Court for the several districts of Tennessee, was charged with high crimes and misdemeanors in office.

There are no records of the committee as such, but the original of its resolution of May 9, 1862, is available (37A-B6) and the journal of the impeachment proceedings and other papers are among the records of the Clerk of the Senate (see above). The record of the trial is appended to S. Journal, 37 Cong., 2 sess. (Serial 1116, p. 889-904).

Select Committee to Inquire Into the Chartering of Transport Vessels for the Banks Expedition

Under Senate resolutions of Dec. 22 and 23, 1862, a select committee of three was appointed "to inquire into and report to the Senate the facts, including brokerage, in regard to the chartering of transport vessels for the Banks expedition, the sea-worthiness of such vessels, and the character of the men employed to navigate them," and also "into the manner of the employment of transports generally by the quartermasters of the army, or by the agents of the War Department, the rates at which they were engaged, by whom, for what purpose, and for how long time." The committee consisted of James W. Grimes (Iowa), Lot M. Morrill (Maine), and Anthony Kennedy (Md.). A preliminary report (Jan. 15, 1863), with testimony, was printed as S. Rept. 75, 37 Cong., 3 sess., Serial 1151; and the final report (Feb. 9, 1863), also with testimony, as S. Rept. 84, 37 Cong., 3 sess., Serial 1151. These show the business relations of Charles Coblens of Baltimore with the

Government; the connection of Amasa C. Hall of Baltimore and Capt. Richard F. Loper of Philadelphia with chartering transport vessels; and the same with respect to Col. James Belger, quartermaster at Baltimore, and to Asst. Secretary of War John Tucker. These and other findings relate to the steamer Cecil and the steamer George Washington, "alias" Constitution, which had been selected and chartered under the authority of the Secretary of War by Cornelius Vanderbilt.

There are no papers of the committee as such, but its original reports are available (37A-D1).

Select Committee on a Commission on Military Claims Originating in the State of Virginia

Authorized and appointed Feb. 5, 1863, as a committee to which was referred a bill (S. 431) "providing for the appointment of a commission to examine and decide upon military claims originating during the present rebellion in the State of Virginia, west of the Blue Ridge, prior to the 30th of September, 1862." The committee consisted of Garrett Davis (Ky.), Daniel Clark (N. H.), John Sherman (Ohio), John S. Carlile (Va.), and John C. Ten Eyck (N. J.).

There are no papers of the committee as such, but the original of the bill upon which it reported is available (37A-B1).

Other Committees

Some Senate select committees of the 37th Congress do not appear to have reported or otherwise to have been active. These were the Committees to Consider a Bill to Promote the Efficiency of the Army (appointed July 6, 1861); on Altering and Changing the Construction of the Chamber for the Use of the Senate (appointed July 6, 1861); on a Railroad to Connect the Loyal Portions of Tennessee and North Carolina With Kentucky (appointed Dec. 23, 1861); on Submarine Cables to Connect Coastal Military and Naval Stations (appointed Dec. 23, 1861); and on the Ventilation of the Senate Chamber (appointed June 5, 1862).

38TH CONGRESS

Select Committee on Slavery and the Treatment of Freedmen

Authorized Jan. 13, 1864, "to take into consideration all propositions and papers concerning slavery and the treatment of freedmen"; appointed Jan. 14, to consist of Charles Sumner (Mass.), Jacob M. Howard (Mich.), John S. Carlile (Va.), Samuel C. Pomeroy (Kans.), Charles R. Buckalew (Pa.), Benjamin Gratz Brown (Mo.), and John Conness (Calif.). James W. Nye (Nev.) replaced Conness on Feb. 2, 1865. To the committee were referred petitions for the repeal of the Fugitive Slave Act and of all other acts for the rendition of fugitive slaves. Its report (S. Rept. 24, 38 Cong., 1 sess., Serial 1178) contains an analysis of the "fugitive clause" (Art. IV, sec. 2) of the Constitution. It reported also (S. Rept. 25, 38 Cong., 1 sess., Serial 1178) on a bill (S. 99) "to secure equality before the law in the courts of the United States."

Records. --Most of the very numerous memorials and petitions to the Senate on the general subject of slavery in the 36th and 37th Congresses were ordered "to lie on the table, "but some of them were referred to committees, including the Committee on the Judiciary, the Committee on Territories, and the Select Committee of Thirteen. During the 38th Congress memorials of this character were referred to the Select Committee on Slavery and the Treatment of Freedmen. They are all described collectively here.

These memorials concern the several major aspects of the slavery question (including the liberating of slaves in the seceded States, the abolition of slavery throughout the United States, the suppression or the reopening of the African slave trade, legislation for the protection of slavery, the repeal of the Fugitive Slave Act, advice to "drop the Negro question and attend to the business of the country" and to "dispense with all further agitation of the slavery question, " and the extension of the right of suffrage to freed slaves). They relate also to the Crittenden resolutions, the disturbed state of the country, and the "suppression of the rebellion. " These memorials came from individuals and from mass conventions, religious communities and associations, and citizens' groups often formed for petitioning purposes; from State legislative bodies and State political party conventions; and from many other groups, including even representatives of the leading railway companies. Among the memorials are not only letters or handwritten preambles to which signatures are affixed but also scrolls many feet long bearing thousands of signatures, often with the occupations or addresses of signers.

Among the memorials may be mentioned--as either representative or unusually interesting--the following: that presented by Emma Willard in the name of 14, 000 American women of several States in the East "not to allow party or sectional prejudices to prevail over the spirit of mutual conciliation"; that of members of Union Fire Company No. 1, Lancaster, Pa. , inscribed upon a colored design of the American flag, urging the passage of the Crittenden or Bigler resolutions; that signed by Susan B. Anthony and Elias Doty and 37 other citizens of Monroe County, N. Y. , for the abolition of slavery; that of the Emancipation League of Boston asking the establishment of a "bureau of emancipation, " signed by S. E. Sewall, president, and nine others including George L. Stearns and S. G. Howe, Dec. 12, 1862 (printed as S. Misc. Doc. 10, 37 Cong. , 3 sess. , Serial 1150); that of Henry Ward Beecher "and 3, 000 other citizens of the State of New York"; and that of certain "colored men" (presented by Israel Lyceum, Washington, D. C.)-- "an appeal in behalf of the elective franchise to colored people. "

The materials described are filed chronologically for the 36th and 37th Congresses (36A-H13, 37A-H25) and in part chronologically and in part by State or Territory for the 38th Congress (38A-H20, 38A-H21, 38A-H22). Also available are the incomplete original of one of the committee's reports (38A-D1) and some petitions for the confiscation of "rebel lands" and their donation to men in the Union service (38A-H7).

Select Committee on Naval Supplies

Authorized and appointed Jan. 25, 1861, "to investigate the subject of naval supplies. " The committee was composed of John P. Hale (N. H.), James W. Grimes (Iowa), and Charles R. Buckalew (Pa.). It confined itself to "recent occurrences" and was satisfied "beyond a doubt that, in the matter of naval supplies last year, the government has been grossly defrauded. "

There are no papers of the committee as such, but the damaged original of its report (printed as S. Rept. 99, 38 Cong., 1 sess., Serial 1178), including the testimony taken, is available (38A-D1).

Other Committees

The Select Committee to Examine the Condition of the Overland Mail Service (appointed Mar. 3, 1865) does not appear to have become active.

39TH CONGRESS

Select Committee on the Levees of the Mississippi

Authorized June 8, 1866, to consider the memorials from the boards of levee commissioners for the State of Louisiana and the Yazoo Valley district of the State of Mississippi asking the reconstruction of the levees on the Mississippi River; appointed June 11, to consist of Daniel Clark (N. H.), Zachariah Chandler (Mich.), Edgar Cowan (Pa.), John B. Henderson (Mo.), and Reverdy Johnson (Md.). In reaching its conclusions the committee reviewed the history of the prewar and wartime productivity of this area.

There are no manuscript records of this committee. Its report was printed as S. Rept. 126, 39 Cong., 1 sess., Serial 1240. See also S. Rept. 2, 40 Cong., 1 sess., Serial 1309.

40TH CONGRESS

Select Committee on the Message of the House of Representatives Relating to the Impeachment of Andrew Johnson

Authorized and appointed Feb. 25, 1868, to consist of Jacob M. Howard (Mich.), Lyman Trumbull (Ill.), Roscoe Conkling (N. Y.), George F. Edmunds (Vt.), Oliver P. Morton (Ind.), Samuel C. Pomeroy (Kans.), and Reverdy Johnson (Md.). The committee reported a resolution the next day. Its report of Feb. 28, 1868, "Rules and Procedure and Practice in the Senate When Sitting as a High Court of Impeachment," was printed as S. Rept. 59, 40 Cong., 2 sess., Serial 1320. See also "Proceedings of the Senate Preliminary to the Trial of Articles of Impeachment of Andrew Johnson, President of the United States," appended to S. Journal, 40 Cong., 2 sess., Serial 1315.

There are no papers of the committee as such, but its original report is available (40A-D1).

41ST CONGRESS

Select Committee on the Removal of Political Disabilities

Authorized and appointed Mar. 20, 1869, to consist of Thomas J. Robertson (S. C.), Thomas W. Osborn (Fla.), Hannibal Hamlin (Maine), Timothy O. Howe (Wis.), Orris S. Ferry (Conn.), Arthur I. Boreman (W. Va.), and George Vickers (Md.). To the committee were referred "all matters relating to the removal of disabilities under the 14th amendment of the Constitution," sec. 3 of which provided as follows:

No person shall be a Senator or Representative in Congress, or
elector of President and Vice President, or hold any office, civil or
military, under the United States, or under any State, who, having previously taken an oath, as a member of Congress, or as an officer of the
United States, or as a member of any State legislature, or as an executive or judicial officer of any State, to support the Constitution of the
United States, shall have engaged in insurrection or rebellion against
the same, or given aid or comfort to the enemies thereof. But Congress
may by a vote of two-thirds of each House, remove such disability.

To this committee were referred all previous petitions and memorials
for the removal of political disabilities. The committee reported many
bills to remove disabilities; these, after concurrence of the House of Representatives and enrollment, were presented to the President for signature.
   Records. -- The main file of petitions for removal of disabilities (41A-
H27)--arranged alphabetically by State of residence and thereunder alphabetically by name of petitioner--represents men holding public office or
otherwise prominent in public life (such as State legislators, mayors, postmasters, judges and other court officials, magistrates, bankers, overseers
of the poor, and notaries public) and includes also former officers and soldiers of the Confederate Army. Many petitions relate circumstances of allegiance to the Confederacy or give personal histories of wartime activities or
service; others indicate the petitioners' refusal of allegiance to the Confederacy. There are also many lists of names handed by Senators to the committee for favorable action, endorsements on individual applications, and
occasional protests against disability removal. A few other papers of the
same kind are in the records of the next Congress (42A-H25); and there is a
separate file of remonstrances against the removal of the political disabilities of Zebulon B. Vance and others of North Carolina (42A-E22).

Select Committee to Investigate Alleged Traffic With Rebels in Texas

Authorized Jan. 4, 1871, to investigate the arrest during the war of
Harris Hoyt "for trading with the rebels in Texas" and of Byron Sprague and
William H. Reynolds for alleged complicity with him; appointed Jan. 5, to
consist of Allen G. Thurman (Ohio), Hannibal Hamlin (Maine), Lyman Trumbull (Ill.), Timothy O. Howe (Wis.), and Waitman Willey (W. Va.).
   There are no papers of the committee as such, but the original of its report (printed as S. Rept. 377, 41 Cong., 3 sess., Serial 1443) is available
(41A-D1).

Select Committee on Alleged Outrages in the Southern States

Authorized Jan. 19, 1871, to investigate matters referred to the Senate
by the President in his messages of Jan. 13 and 17 (S. Ex. Doc. 16, 41 Cong.,
3 sess., Serial 1440); appointed Jan. 20, 1871, to consist of John Scott
(Pa.), Henry Wilson (Mass.), Zachariah Chandler (Mich.), Benjamin F.
Rice (Ark.), James W. Nye (Nev.), Thomas F. Bayard (Del.), and Francis
P. Blair, Jr. (Mo.). The first of the President's messages had presented
abstracts from military and other reports alleging the prevalence of crime
in the Southern States after 1866, and the second had communicated copies
of reports received at the War Department "relative to disloyal organizations in the State of North Carolina. " To the committee's printed report

(S. Rept. 1, 42 Cong., 1 sess., Serial 1468) are appended its journal, the exhibits, and testimony pertaining primarily to North Carolina (revealing political and social conditions in the State at the end of the war and in the immediate postwar period). The views of the minority were separately presented (S. Rept. 1, pt. 2, 42 Cong., 1 sess., Serial 1468).

There are no papers of the committee as such, but the originals of testimony taken and the minority report are available (42A-D1).

HOUSE OF REPRESENTATIVES

The United States House of Representatives was established by Article I, Section 1, of the Constitution, which provides that "All legislative Powers herein granted shall be vested in a Congress of the United States, which shall consist of a Senate and House of Representatives." Section 7 of Article I provides that "All Bills for raising Revenue shall originate in the House of Representatives; but the Senate may propose or concur with Amendments as on other Bills." No express provision vests in the House the sole power to originate general appropriation bills, but customarily such bills originate there. In addition to the legislative function, Article I, Section 2, provides that the House "shall have the sole Power of Impeachment," that is, the bringing of charges against the President and other public officials for trial before the Senate; and Section 5 provides that "Each House shall be the Judge of the Elections, Returns, and Qualifications of its own Members."

Section 2 of Article I of the Constitution, before the adoption of the Fourteenth Amendment, provided as follows:

Representatives and direct Taxes shall be apportioned among the several States which may be included within this Union, according to their respective Numbers, which shall be determined by adding to the whole Number of free Persons, including those bound to Service for a Term of Years, and excluding Indians not taxed, three fifths of all other Persons.

On July 5, 1861, the Secretary of the Interior, as required by an act of May 23, 1850 (9 Stat. 432), apportioned the representatives of the several States under the Eighth Census as follows (see H. Exec. Doc. 2, 37 Cong., 1 sess., Serial 1114):

State		State		State	
Alabama	6	Louisiana	5	Ohio	18
Arkansas	3	Maine	5	Oregon	1
California	3	Maryland	5	Pennsylvania	23
Connecticut	4	Massachusetts	10	Rhode Island	1
Delaware	1	Michigan	6	South Carolina	4
Florida	1	Minnesota	1	Tennessee	8
Georgia	7	Mississippi	5	Texas	4
Illinois	13	Missouri	9	Vermont	2
Indiana	11	New Hampshire	3	Virginia	11
Iowa	5	New Jersey	5	Wisconsin	6
Kansas	1	New York	31		
Kentucky	8	North Carolina	7		

The House of Representatives had moved on Dec. 16, 1857, from the chamber now known as Statuary Hall to a much larger chamber in the newly constructed House Wing of the Capitol. Its general organization during the Civil War conformed closely to its traditional organization from 1789. As in the Senate, important changes occurred in committee organization during the war; these are explained below in describing the records of the House committees.

Most Representatives from the seceding States withdrew from the House toward the end of the 38th Congress, and in the 37th Congress there were no Representatives from States that had seceded except that Benjamin F. Flanders and Michael Hahn represented Louisiana from Feb. 23 and 17, 1863, respectively; William G. Brown, John S. Carlile, Jacob B. Blair, Joseph E. Segar, Charles H. Upton, Lewis McKenzie, and Kellian V. Whaley represented Virginia for various periods; and George W. Bridges, Andrew J. Clements, and Horace Maynard represented Tennessee from Feb. 25, 1863, Jan. 13, 1862, and Dec. 2, 1861, respectively. Neither the 38th nor the 39th Congress included any members from the States that had seceded.

Galusha A. Grow was elected Speaker of the House of Representatives on July 4, 1861, when the 37th Congress convened; and Schuyler Colfax was elected Speaker for the 38th Congress on December 7, 1863, and again for the 39th Congress on December 4, 1865.

Clerks of the House in the 37th Congress were successively John W. Forney and Emerson Etheridge; and for the 38th Congress were successively Etheridge and Edward McPherson. McPherson continued as Clerk of the House through the 43d Congress.

The printed journals of the House for the Civil War period are in the congressional serials as follows:

Period covered	Congress and session		Serial no.
Dec. 3, 1860–Mar. 2, 1861	36	2	1091
July 4–Aug. 6, 1861	37	1	1113
Dec. 2, 1861–July 17, 1862	37	2	1126
Dec. 1, 1862–Mar. 3, 1863	37	3	1155
Dec. 7, 1863–July 4, 1864	38	1	1179
Dec. 5, 1864–Mar. 3, 1865	38	2	1215
Dec. 4, 1865–July 28, 1866	39	1	1243
Dec. 3, 1866–Mar. 2, 1867	39	2	1280

See also Hinds' Precedents of the House of Representatives of the United States (H. Doc. 355, 59   Cong., 2 sess., Serials 5182-5188; Washington, 1907-8. 8 vols.)

Record Group 233. --The records of the House of Representatives consist almost wholly of those pertaining to the official business of the House that were filed with the Clerk of the House or that were created by his Office. They include no personal papers of individual Representatives; but the official records are useful in conjunction with personal papers deposited elsewhere. For this reason the chairmen of standing committees and the members of select committees of the House in the period covered by this Guide are named below in the sections devoted to such committees.

House records available for the three Congresses spanning the Civil

War (36th, 37th, 38th) are principally the minute books (3 vols.); legislative journals (7 vols.); bills and resolutions originating in the House (34 ft.); bills and resolutions originating in the Senate and considered in the House (1 1/2 ft.); credentials of Representatives and Delegates (6 in.); originals of printed House documents (166 vols.); and reports and communications from the President and executive departments (36th Congress, 2 sess., only).

The House committee papers per se and those referred to the committees (both standing and select) are organized in two series for each Congress (ca. 88 ft. for the three above-mentioned Congresses besides 14 ft. of original committee reports); these, as well as the pertinent records of House committees of the postwar period, are described, committee by committee, below. Wartime petitions and memorials, resolutions of State legislatures, and related documents that were tabled rather than referred to committees (5 1/2 ft.) include those relating to the Crittenden Compromise (36A-H1.3); slavery (36A-H1.9); amendment of the conscription law (38A-H1.1); amendment of the Constitution to abolish slavery (38A-H1.2); bounties (38A-H1.3); claims for losses sustained by beef contractors and sutlers at the hands of Confederate troops (38A-H1.4); claims of property holders for supplies appropriated and office space leased by military authorities of the United States (38A-H1.5); establishing a uniform ambulance and hospital corps for the Army (38A-H1.6); exempting ministers and aliens from military service (38A-H1.7); increasing the pay of soldiers and sailors (38A-H1.11); pensions (38A-H1.12); granting to colored soldiers pay and allowances equal to those of white soldiers (38A-H1.13); and ships and shipbuilding (38A-H1.14).

The wartime records include also papers (4 ft.) pertaining to impeachment proceedings against John C. Watrous, judge of the U. S. District Court for the District of Texas (36B-A1), and against Andrew G. Miller (2 in.), judge of the U. S. District Court for the District of Wisconsin (38B-A1). There is also an original report on the "Astronomical and Meteorological Observations Made at the Naval Observatory During the Year 1861" (37A-K2).

Postwar but war-related House records, besides committee records (see below), include notably the papers (2 ft.) pertaining to impeachment proceedings against President Andrew Johnson, with the journal of the managers of the House (40B-A1); and papers (2 ft.) pertaining to impeachment proceedings against Richard Busteed, judge of the U. S. District Court for the District of Alabama (40B-B1, 41B-A1).

The record books of the Office of the Clerk of the House for the three Civil War Congresses (23 vols.) include bill books of House and Senate bills and resolutions, registers of bills and resolutions passed, petition books, records of orders of the day, records of committee reports, records of miscellaneous documents, the union calendar, and account books. The Clerk's letter book of outgoing correspondence, from the 33d Congress to the 1st session of the 38th Congress, is among the records of the 33d Congress(33C-C1); and his record of the membership of standing and select committees, from the 32d Congress to the 38th Congress, is among the records of the 32d Congress (32C-A9). His other wartime records include receipts for records withdrawn and, for the 36th Congress only, a subject index to House bills and resolutions. Also of possible use is the Clerk's 1-volume index to papers submitted to various committees in support of claims, pensions, and other forms of private relief, 39th-43d Congs.

(39C-C1); and his record of claims referred to the Court of Claims under the provisions of the Bowman Act of 1883 (52C-A10).

National Archives, Preliminary Inventory [No. 113] of the Records of the United States House of Representatives, 1789-1946, comp. by Buford Rowland, Handy B. Fant, and Harold E. Hufford (Washington, 1959. 2 vols.); Buford Rowland, "Recordkeeping Practices of the House of Representatives, " National Archives Accessions, 53: 1-19 (Jan. 1957).

Records of the House are restricted. The National Archives may make available for use only those records that have been printed, unless otherwise directed by law or House resolution or in writing by the Clerk of the House.

House Standing Committees

Congressional activity, particularly in the House, has been centered from the beginning in its committees. In early Congresses most of the legislative work of the House was handled by select or special committees appointed by the Speaker, but the number of standing committees at the outbreak of the Civil War stood at 34. With few exceptions the work of the standing committees was affected by the war, although to an extent less than in the case of the select committees created to deal with matters directly related to the war. In 1864 and 1865 five new standing committees were authorized, bringing the total for the war years to 39.

After the Civil War the War Claims and the Freedmen's Affairs Committees were created to deal principally or in part with the business of the House relating to the war and its aftermath; and other standing committees, in the postwar period, became involved from time to time in matters related to the Civil War.

The committees discussed below in detail are entered alphabetically by their names during the Civil War or during periods when they created records concerning the war. Although a distinction should properly be made between papers accumulated and retained by standing committees and those referred to and (sometimes) reported back by them, the descriptions given below group the papers of both kinds, by the Congress in question, under the separate sections on the committees germane to this Guide. It has not been feasible to give the exact quantities of the records mentioned. All are in Record Group 233.

Hinds' Precedents . . . , vol. 4 (59 Cong. , 2 sess., H. Doc. 355, Serial 5185); George B. Galloway, "Development of the Committee System in the House of Representatives, " American Historical Review, 65: 17-30 (Oct. 1959); Rowland, Fant, and Hufford, comps., Pre-liminary Inventory [No. 113], especially vol. 2, appendix 2, "Standing Committees of the . . . House . . ."; Edward McPherson, comp., Digested Summary and Alphabetical List of Private Claims . . . Presented to the House . . . (42 Cong. , 3d sess., H. Misc. Doc. 109, Serial 1574).

Committee on Appropriations; Thaddeus Stevens (Pa.), chairman, 39 Cong.
Authorized Mar. 2, 1865, to assume some of the burdens of the Committee of Ways and Means. The business of that committee was divided by giving appropriation bills to the new Committee on Appropriations and banking and currency bills to the new Committee on Banking and Currency.

Postwar records. 39th Cong. --Papers about the St. Louis Arsenal (39A-F2. 9); papers from or about the executive departments: Agriculture (39A-F2. 10), Interior (including numerous "Indian Papers") (39A-F2. 11), Navy (39A-F2. 12), Post Office (39A-F2. 13), State (39A-F2. 14), Treasury (39A-F2. 15), and War (39A-F2. 16); petitions, memorials, etc., concerning the reward offered for the arrest of John Wilkes Booth (39A-H2. 3). 43d Cong. --Papers concerning Mathew Brady's collection of photographs (43A-F3. 20). 46th Cong. --Papers concerning the Southern Claims Commission, that is, the Commissioners of Claims (46A-F3. 14). 48th Cong. -- Petitions, memorials, etc., concerning the Rand and Ordway collection of photographic negatives of the Civil War (48A-H3. 10). 50th Cong. --Petitions, memorials, etc., concerning headstones for graves of Union veterans (50A-H2. 6) and publication of Army and Navy records of the Civil War (50A-H2. 9). 63d Cong. --Petitions, memorials, etc., concerning the Civil War semicentennial and veterans' encampment, Vicksburg, Miss. (63A-H2. 2), and the commemoration of a half-century of Negro freedom (63A-H2. 4).

Committee of Claims; Reuben E. Fenton (N. Y.), chairman, 37th Cong.; James T. Hale (Pa.), chairman, 38th Cong.

Authorized Nov. 13, 1794. This committee had the duty to consider "all such petitions and matters or things touching claims and demands on the United States" as should be presented or referred to it by the House; and to report its "opinion thereupon, together with such propositions for relief therein" as might "seem expedient." The committee received evidence submitted by claimants of the rewards for the capture of Jefferson Davis (see H. Rept. 99, 39 Cong., 1 sess., Serial 1272; H. Misc. Doc. 82, 39 Cong., 2 sess., Serial 1302; and H. Rept. 60, 40 Cong., 2 sess., Serial 1358). In dealing with individual claims, this committee (known after the Civil War as the Committee on Claims) not only authorized the payments but actually made the appropriations of money from the Treasury.

Wartime records. 34th-39th Cong. --Minutes (34A-D3. 2). 35th-39th Congs. --Letter book (35A-D3. 4). 36th-38th Congs. --List of claims (36A-D3. 3). 36th Cong. --Claims (36A-D3. 1, 36A-G2. 1). 37th Cong. --Claims (37A-E2. 1, 37A-G1. 1). 37th and 38th Congs. --Docket (37A-E2. 3). 38th Cong. --Claims (38A-E3. 1, 38A-G2. 1).

Postwar records. 39th and 40th Congs. --Rough minutes (39A-F4. 1). 39th-42d Congs. --Minutes (39A-F4. 2). 39th Cong. --Docket (39A-F4. 3); claims (39A-H4. 1). 40th-42d Congs. --Rough minutes (40A-F4. 2). 40th and 41st Congs. --Docket (40A-F4. 3). 40th Cong. --Claims (40A-F4. 1). 41st Cong. --Claims (41A-F4. 1). 42d and 43d Congs. --Rough minutes (42A-F5. 2). 44th Cong. --Complaints and affidavits against C. F. Benjamin, clerk of the Southern Claims Commission (44A-F5. 1).

Committee of Commerce; Elihu B. Washburne (Ill.), chairman, 36th-39th Congs.

Authorized Dec. 8, 1819. The committee had the duty to consider "all such petitions and matters or things touching the commerce of the United States" as should be presented or referred to it by the House and to report its opinions on them. This committee and the corresponding committee of the Senate, acting as a joint committee, issued a report on "Trade With Rebellious States" (H. Rept. 24, 38 Cong., 2 sess., Serial 1235).

Wartime records. 36th Cong. --Claims (36A-D4. 1); papers about the

"coolie trade" (36A-D4. 2); papers about courthouses, customhouses, post
offices, and other public buildings (36A-D4. 3); papers concerning fraudulent misbranding (36A-D4. 4), lighthouses (36A-D4. 5), marine hospitals
(36A-D4. 6), ports of entry and collection districts (36A-D4. 7), the protection of female immigrants (36A-D4. 8), Provincetown Harbor (36A-D4. 9),
and other subjects (36A-D4. 10). Also petitions, memorials, etc., concerning channel, harbor, and river improvements (36A-G3. 1); claims (36A-
G3. 2); lifesaving stations and apparatus (36A-G3. 3); lighthouses, light-
vessels, and beacons (36A-G3. 4); the Revenue Cutter Service (36A-G3. 5);
and other subjects (36A-G3. 6). 37th Cong. --Claim concerning the schooner
Coiner (37A-E3. 1); and papers concerning establishment of a branch mint
in the Territory of Nevada (37A-E3. 2) and regulations on internal and coastwise commerce with the Confederate States (37A-E3. 3). Also petitions,
memorials, etc., concerning a bureau of statistics in the Interior Department (37A-G2. 1); the claim of John Saunders, master of the Baron de
Castine, a brig captured by the Alabama and converted into a cartel ship
(37A-G2. 3); other claims (37A-G2. 2); establishment of a mint in New York
City (37A-G2. 4); appointment of a solicitor of customs in New York City
(37A-G2. 5); Provincetown, Mass., Harbor (37A-G2. 6); harbor improvements (37A-G2. 7); survey for a telegraphic line "from the Amoor River to
Russian America" (37A-G2. 8); a St. Lawrence River waterway to the Great
Lakes (37A-G2. 9); and other subjects (37A-G2. 10). 38th Cong. --Papers
concerning amendment of laws on the administering of oaths by U. S. consuls abroad (38A-E4. 1), customhouse statistics of Portland (Maine) for the
year 1863 (38A-E4. 2), modification of the Steamboat Act of Aug. 30, 1852
(38A-E4. 3), and other subjects (38A-E4. 4); petitions, memorials, etc.,
concerning admeasurement of the tonnage of vessels of the United States
(38A-G3. 1), claims (38A-G3. 2), construction of a canal around Niagara
Falls (38A-G3. 3), increase in the pay of steamboat inspectors and customs
officers (38A-G3. 4), a reciprocity treaty between the United States and
Great Britain (38A-G3. 5), river and harbor improvements (38A-G3. 6),
steamship lines (38A-G3. 7), and other subjects (38A-G3. 8).

Committee for the District of Columbia; Roscoe Conkling (N. Y.), chair-
    man, 37th Cong.; Owen Lovejoy (Ill.), chairman, 38th Cong.
    Authorized Jan. 27, 1808. This committee had the duty to consider
"all such petitions and matters or things touching the said District" as
should be presented or referred to it by the House and to report its "opinion thereon, together with such propositions relative thereto" as might
seem expedient. It became known after the Civil War as the Committee
on the District of Columbia.
    Wartime records. 37th and 38th Congs. --Docket (37A-E4. 4). 37th
Cong. --Papers concerning the failure of the Bullion Bank of Washington,
D. C. (37A-E4. 1), authorization to the citizens of the District of Columbia to send a delegate to Congress (37A-E4. 2), and improvement of the
Washington Canal (37A-E4. 3); petitions, memorials, etc., concerning the
Capitol grounds (37A-G3. 1), construction of wooden hospital buildings in
Judiciary Square for Union troops (37A-G3. 2), construction of a street
railway to Georgetown (37A-G3. 3), cleaning of city streets (37A-G3. 4),
grading and paving of city streets (37A-G3. 5), and the claim of the Alexandria Canal Co. for the use of its property by Federal troops (37A-G3. 6).
38th Cong. --Docket and minutes (38A-E5. 3); papers concerning the grounds
of the Columbia Institution for the Deaf and Dumb (38A-E5. 1) and the pow-

ers of the Alexandria Canal Co. (38A-E5.2); petitions, memorials, etc.,
on various subjects (38A-G4.1). (See the committee's report to accompany
H. R. 798, "Enlisting Criminals From the Jail in the District of Columbia
in the Army and Navy of the United States, " H. Rept. 23, 38 Cong., 2 sess.,
Serial 1235.)

Committee on Education and Labor

Authorized Mar. 21, 1867. To this postwar committee were referred,
on Apr. 6, 1870, the charges made by Fernando Wood of New York against
Maj. Gen. O. O. Howard, Commissioner of the Bureau of Refugees, Freedmen, and Abandoned Lands.

Postwar records. 41st Cong. --A book of minutes relating to the investigation of charges against Howard (41A-F8.3).

Committee of Elections; Henry L. Dawes (Mass.), chairman, 37th and 38th Congs.

Authorized Apr. 13, 1789. This committee had the duty to examine and
report upon the certificates of election or other credentials of the Members
returned to serve in the House and to consider any petitions and other matters related to elections and returns that might be presented or might come
into question.

Cases of contested elections investigated by the House Committee
on Elections and the Senate Committee on the Judiciary during the
Civil War appear in the compilation
by D. W. Bartlett, Cases of Contested Elections in Congress, From
1834 to 1865, Inclusive (H. Misc.
Doc. 57, 38 Cong., 2 sess., Serial
1234). These include many claims
of Southerners that were denied for
"non-compliance with State laws
owing to existence of rebellion, "
"district within control of rebel authorities, " etc. A succeeding volume of this series, Cases of Contested Elections in the House of Representatives From 1865 to 1871, Inclusive (H. Misc. Doc. 152, 41
Cong., 2 sess., Serial 1434), includes those involving the "reorganization of State government in a
State recently in rebellion" and others involving charges of disloyalty
to the Government during the Civil
War against various Members elect.
Some cases of contested or claimed
elections throw considerable light
on local wartime affairs; among
these, cases relating to Southerners
loyal to the Union are of particular
interest (for instance, the memorial
to admit Charles Henry Foster as
Representative of the second Congressional district of North Carolina,
printed as H. Rept. 118, 37 Cong.,
2 sess., Serial 1145).

Wartime records. 34th-39th Congs. --Minutes (34A-D6.9). 36th
Cong. --Contested election cases of Francis P. Blair v. John R. Barrett,
Mo. (36A-D6.1); James S. Chrisman v. William C. Anderson, Ky. (36A-
D6.2); Samuel G. Daily v. Experience Estabrook, Territory of Nebraska
(36A-D6.3); William G. Harrison v. Henry Winter Davis, Md. (36A-D6.4);
William A. Howard v. George B. Cooper, Mich. (36A-D6.5); William P.
Preston v. J. Morrison Harris, Md. (36A-D6.6); and Amor J. Williamson
v. Daniel E. Sickles, N. Y. (36A-D6.7). 37th Cong. -- Contested election
cases of S. Ferguson Beach, Va. (37A-E5.1); John M. Butler v. William E.
Lehman, Pa. (37A-E5.2); LeGrand Byington v. William Vandever, Iowa
(37A-E5.3); Henry Foster, N. C. (37A-E5.4); John Kline v. John P. Verree,

Pa. (37A-E5.5); Frederick F. Low, Calif. (37A-E5.6); J. Sterling Morton
v. Samuel G. Daily, Territory of Nebraska (37A-E5.7); Joseph E. Segar,
Va. (37A-E5.8); and Charles H. Upton, Va. (37A-E5.9). 38th Cong.--
Contested election cases of James H. Birch v. Austin A. King, Mo. (38A-
E6.1); J. W. Crisfield v. John A. J. Creswell, Md. (38A-E6.2); José M.
Gallegos v. Francisco Perea, Territory of New Mexico (38A-E6.3); and
Hugh M. Martin v. Josiah B. Grinnell, Iowa (38A-E6.4).

Postwar records. 40th Cong.--Contested representation from the 2d
Congressional District of La. (40A-F8.1) and the case of Joseph Powell v.
Roderick R. Butler, Tenn. (40A-F8.2). 41st Cong.--Contested election
cases of Thomas P. Beard v. Stephen A. Corker, Ga. (41A-F9.2); Nathaniel
Boyden v. Francis E. Shober, N. C. (41A-F9.4); Charles S. Cameron v.
Logan H. Roots, Ark. (41A-F9.5); James T. Elliot v. Anthony A. C. Rogers,
Ark. (41A-F9.6); Benjamin F. Grafton v. John C. Conner, Tex. (41A-F9.7);
Jerome J. Hines v. William C. Sherrod, Ala. (41A-F9.8); John W. Leftwich
v. William J. Smith, Tenn. (41A-F9.9); C. A. Sheafe v. Lewis Tillman,
Tenn. (41A-F9.10); Alexander S. Wallace v. William D. Simpson, S. C.
(41A-F9.11); and John T. Zeigler v. John M. Rice, Ky. (41A-F9.12). 42d
Cong.--Contested election cases of Thomas Boles v. John Edwards, Ark.
(42A-F9.1); Christopher C. Bowen v. Robert C. De Large, S. C. (42A-
F9.2); De Witt C. Giddings v. William T. Clark, Tex. (42A-F9.4); James H.
Harris v. Sion H. Rogers, N. C. (42A-F9.6); Lewis McKenzie v. Elliott M.
Braxton, Va. (42A-F9.7); Isaac G. McKissick v. Alexander S. Wallace, S. C.
(42A-F9.8); Silas L. Niblack v. Josiah T. Walls, Fla. (42A-F9.10); B. W.
Norris v. William A. Handley, Ala. (42A-F9.11); Anthony A. C. Rogers v.
Oliver P. Snyder, Ark. (42A-F9.12); Nelson Tift v. Richard H. Whiteley,
Ga. (42A-F9.15); and G. W. Whitmore v. William S. Herndon, Tex. (42A-
F9.16).

Committees on Expenditures

Six separate committees were authorized on Mar. 30, 1816, and a seventh
was authorized on Mar. 16, 1860. The committees were to examine continuously the accounts and expenditures in the Navy Department, the Post Office (Post Office Department after about 1829), the State Department, the
Treasury Department, the War Department, the Office of the Superintendent
of Public Buildings, and the Interior Department (beginning in 1860). Despite the significance of their responsibilities, these committees left few
records of the Civil War period. Their duties were "to examine into the
state of the accounts and expenditures respectively submitted to them" and
to report whether expenditures had been legally made, whether expenditures
for claims were "supported by sufficient vouchers" and were charged to the
proper funds, and whether any changes in procedure should be adopted "to
provide more perfectly for the proper application of the public moneys, and
to secure the government from demands unjust in their character or extravagant in their amount. " The committees were also to report "from time to
time" on possible economies in Government, on any "failure to enforce the
payment of moneys which may be due to the United States, " and on any ways
"to add to the economy of the several departments and the accountability of
their officers. "

Wartime records. There are no records for the Civil War period of the
committees dealing respectively with expenditures in the Interior Department, the Post Office Department, and the State Department, or of the Committee on Expenditures on the Public Buildings. The last committee, how-

ever, made a report (H. Rept. 137, 37 Cong., 2 sess., Serial 1145) on its
1862 investigation of the Treasury and Capitol extensions and of the work
of the Bureau of Construction of the Treasury Department. The three other
committees are represented by records as follows: Committee on Expenditures in the Navy Department: 36th Cong. --A report on alleged abuses in
the Navy Department (36A-D7. 1). Committee on Expenditures in the Treasury Department: 36th Cong. --Docket, 2d sess. (36A-D8. 2); an investigation
of the "mode of expending the fund for the relief of sick and disabled seamen" (36A-D9. 1); petitions, memorials, etc., on various subjects (36A-
G6. 1). Committee on Expenditures in the War Department: 36th Cong. --
Investigation of the contract for the marble for the extension to the Capitol
(36A-D9. 1). 38th Cong. --Papers concerning improvident expenditures and
mismanagement in the War Department (38A-G6. 1).

Postwar records. Committee on Expenditures in the Treasury Department: 39th Cong. --Copies of Lt. Gen. U. S. Grant's circular telegram of
May 29, 1865, officially encouraging the resumption of the Southern export
trade, especially in cotton (39A-F8. 1). 44th Cong. --Papers concerning
captured and abandoned property (44A-F14. 1).

Committee on Foreign Affairs; John J. Crittenden (Ky.), chairman, 37th
    Cong. (died July 25, 1863); Henry Winter Davis (Md.), chairman, 38th
    Cong.; Nathaniel P. Banks (Mass.), chairman, 39th Cong.
Authorized Mar. 13, 1822. This committee had the duty to consider all
matters that concerned the "relations of the United States with foreign nations" that were referred to it by the House "and to report their opinion on
the same."

Wartime records. Only the records of the greatest pertinence are mentioned here. Even when not directly related to the war, however, the committee's records tend to show which foreign affairs were of continuing concern during the Civil War. 36th Cong. --Petitions, memorials, etc., on
the slave trade (36A-G7. 2). 37th and 38th Congs. --Minutes (37A-E6. 9);
docket (37A-E6. 10). 37th Cong. --Papers concerning damage by the Union
blockading force to the Swedish brig Admiral P. Tordenskiold (37A-E6. 7);
claim of Townsend Harris, Consul General of the United States to Japan,
for extra services to the commerce of the United States (37A-G4. 5); referred
papers on the recognition of Liberia (37A-G4. 6). 38th Cong. --Papers concerning Anglo-American friction along the Canadian border (38A-E7. 1).

Postwar records. 39th-41st Congs. --Minutes (39A-F9. 14). 39th
Cong. --Docket (39A-F9. 15); judgment of the Lord Chancellor of England in
the case of the United States v. McRae, the latter a Confederate financial
agent (39A-F9. 7); papers concerning a medal for Cornelius Vanderbilt (39A-
F9. 8). 40th Cong. --Papers concerning Confederate cotton and other property abroad (40A-F9. 4). 41st Cong. --Alabama claims (41A-F10. 1); papers
concerning the Salviati mosaic portrait of Abraham Lincoln (41A-F10. 18).
48th Cong. --Papers concerning the French and American Claims Commission (48A-F13. 8).

Committee on Freedmen's Affairs (postwar)
    Authorized Dec. 4, 1866, to consider all matters concerning freedmen
referred to it by the House. This committee succeeded to the Select Committee on Freedmen (39th Cong.), whose records it inherited. Presumably
terminated July 1, 1879.

Postwar records. 39th Cong. --Attested House resolutions of Dec. 10,

1866 (39A-F10. 1); papers on funds received by the Bureau of Refugees, Freedmen, and Abandoned Lands (39A-F10. 2); papers on the scarcity of food in South Carolina (39A-F10. 3); petitions, memorials, etc., on various subjects (39A-H11. 1). 40th Cong.--Records concerning the committee's administration (40A-F10. 1); records concerning Maj. Gen. O. O. Howard's desire for an investigation of his management of the Bureau of Refugees, Freedmen, and Abandoned Lands (40A-F10. 2); records on freedmen's affairs in Kentucky (40A-F10. 3), Mississippi (40A-F10. 4), North Carolina (40A-F10. 5), Texas (40A-F10. 6), and Virginia (40A-F10. 7); records on the National Freedman's Savings and Trust Co. (40A-F10. 8) and other subjects (40A-F10. 9); rough minutes (40A-F10. 10); petitions, memorials, etc., concerning the continuation of the Freedmen's Bureau (40A-H7. 1), emigration to Liberia (40A-H7. 2), and other subjects (40A-H7. 3). 42d Cong.--Minutes (42A-F11. 1); docket (42A-F11. 2); and referred papers concerning an appropriation to complete construction of the Georgia Infirmary in Savannah (42A-H6. 1).

In Record Group 105 (Bureau of Refugees, Freedmen, and Abandoned Lands) are some letters received by T. D. Eliot, 1867-68, when chairman of this committee.

Committee on Indian Affairs; Cyrus Aldrich (Minn.), chairman, 37th Cong. ; William Windom (Minn.), chairman, 38th Cong.
Authorized Dec. 17, 1821.
Wartime records. 37th Cong.--Papers concerning hostilities against Indians near Humboldt Bay, Calif. (37A-E7. 1), funds to conclude a treaty with the "Brulé and Yanktonai Indians" of the Territory of Dakota (37A-E7. 2), assistance to destitute New York Indians in Kansas (37A-E7. 3), claims of Delaware Indians for thefts by white men in Kansas (37A-E7. 4), relief of destitute Choctaw and Seminole Indians "driven into Kansas from Indian Territory by disloyal Indians with the aid of Confederate forces"(37A-E7. 5), Indian affairs in Minnesota as described by Bishop H. B. Whipple to the President (37A-E7. 6), expenditures of Treasury funds belonging to the Winnebago Indians (37A-E7. 7), curbing of Winnebago outrages through proceedings of a military commission sitting at South Bend in Nov. 1862 (37A-E7. 8), and the claims of certain Nemaha halfbreeds (37A-E7. 9). Also papers concerning unsettled accounts of Brigham Young, late Governor and ex officio Superintendent of Indian Affairs of the Territory of Utah (37A-E7. 11); papers about funds to conclude treaties and other aspects of Indian affairs in the Territory of Utah (37A-E7. 12); investigation, by a commission, of tribal affairs throughout the United States (37A-E7. 13); and disbursements, Southern Superintendency, for the third quarter of 1862 (37A-E7. 15). 38th Cong.--Copy of Maj. Gen. John Pope's views, Feb. 6, 1864, about Indian policy in the Department of the Northwest (38A-E8. 2).

Postwar records. 39th Cong.--Transcribed quarterly accounts, 1865 and 1866, of the Southern Superintendency and its subordinate agencies (39A-F11. 6); papers about tribal affairs in the Southern Superintendency (39A-F11. 12). 42d Cong.--Papers concerning Indian depredations in Kansas, 1860-71 (42A-F12. 2), Indian depredations in Texas (42A-F12. 3), and Indian depredations generally (42A-F12. 4).

Committee on Invalid Pensions; Alfred Ely (N. Y.), chairman, 37th Cong. ; Kellian V. Whaley (W. Va.), chairman, 38th Cong.
Authorized Jan. 10, 1831, with the duty to consider "all such matters

respecting invalid pensions"as should be referred to it by the House. Pensions from the War of 1812 were referred in practice if not by express rule to this committee until Mar. 26, 1867, when they were transferred to the Committee on Revolutionary Pensions. After the Civil War the Committee on Invalid Pensions reported all general pension legislation relating to veterans of the Civil War as well as private and special acts for the relief of Civil War soldiers. (The actual appropriation of the money was made by the Committee on Appropriations.) To the Committee on Pensions, authorized in 1880, rather than to the Committee on Invalid Pensions, were referred the pensions of all the wars of the United States other than the Civil War, but it is of interest that papers concerning pensions for Confederate veterans were being referred to the Committee on Pensions as late as the 64th Congress (64A-H19. 1).

Wartime records. 36th-45th Congs. --Minutes (36A-D12. 2). 36th Cong. --Docket (36A-D12. 3). 37th and 38th Congs. --Docket (37A-E8. 2). 38th Cong. --Docket (38A-E9. 2).

Postwar records. 39th Cong. --Docket (39A-F12. 1). 40th Cong. -- Docket (40A-F12. 3). 41st Cong. --Docket (41A-F12. 1). 42d and 43d Congs. --Docket (42A-F13. 2). 42d Cong. --Bills and resolutions referred to the committee (42A-F13. 1). 43d Cong. --Docket (43A-F13. 3); papers on committee administration etc. (43A-F13. 2); index to claimants (43A-F13. 4); referred papers concerning a bill providing for increased pensions to disabled soldiers (43A-E7. 1). 44th Cong. --Docket (44A-F18. 2). 45th Cong. -- Papers concerning transfer of certain records from the Surgeon General's Office, U. S. Army, to the Pension Office (45A-F17. 4) and to U. S. pension agents (45A-F17. 5). 46th and 47th Congs. --Press copies of outgoing correspondence (46A-F17. 3). 46th Cong. --Minutes (46A-F17. 1); docket (46A-F17. 2); record of files furnished the committee by the Pension Office (46A-F17. 4); petitions, memorials, etc., concerning administration of pension laws (46A-H11. 1), increase in pension of amputees (46A-H11. 2), pensions for soldiers who were prisoners of war (46A-H11. 3), and other subjects (46A-H11. 4). 47th and 48th Congs. --Minutes (47A-F14. 2). 47th Cong. -- Docket (47A-F14. 3); petitions, memorials, etc., concerning extension of time for filing under the Arrears of Pension Act (47A-H10. 1), pensions for Union soldiers who were prisoners of war (47A-H10. 2), a pension increase for any veteran who had lost a leg or an arm in the military service (47A-H10. 3), and other subjects (47A-H10. 4). 48th and 49th Congs. --Docket (48A-F15. 2). 48th Cong. --Minutes (48A-F15. 1); petitions, memorials, etc., concerning equalization of bounties and extension of the Arrears of Pension Act (48A-H11. 1), increase of pensions for widows and dependent relatives (48A-H11. 2), legislation to provide a minimum pension of $8 a month for all honorably discharged Union veterans (48A-H11. 3), legislation to provide pensions for ex-prisoners of war (48A-H11. 4), liberalization of pensions for various disabilities (48A-H11. 5), recommendations for general liberalization of the pension laws (48A-H11. 6), transfer of the functions of the pension agencies to the Treasury Department (48A-H11. 7), and other subjects (48A-H11. 8). 49th Cong. --Minutes (49A-F17. 2); docket (49A-F17. 3); petitions, memorials, etc., concerning equalization of bounties (49A-H10. 1), fees paid examining surgeons in pension cases (49A-H10. 2), passage of the Dependent Pension Bill over the President's veto (49A-H10.3), pensions for all honorably discharged Union veterans over 60 years of age who were manual laborers (49A-H10. 4), pensions for disabled Union veterans (49A-H10. 5), pensions for Union veterans who had been prisoners of

war (49A-H10. 6), recommendations of the Grand Army of the Republic concerning pension legislation (49A-H10. 7), repeal of the Arrears of Pension
Act (49A-H10. 8), revision of pension laws (49A-H10. 9), special taxation
to finance payment of pensions (49A-H10. 10), and other subjects (49A-
H10. 11). 50th Cong. --Minutes (50A-F17. 1); docket (50A-F17. 2); petitions,
memorials, etc., concerning equalization of bounties (50A-H12. 1), legislation to provide paid furloughs for residents of national soldiers' homes for
disabled veterans (50A-H12. 2), legislation to provide pensions for all Civil
War veterans (50A-H12. 3), pensions for Union veterans who had been prisoners of war (50A-H12. 5), pensions for veterans with various disabilities
(50A-H12. 6), removal of the time limit on applications for pension (50A-
H12. 7), and other subjects (50A-H12. 8). 51st Cong.--Minutes (51A-F17. 1);
docket (51A-F17. 2); petitions, memorials, etc., concerning Army nurse
pensions (51A-H10. 1), dependent pensions (51A-H10. 2), granting of pensions
to ex-prisoners of war (51A-H10. 3), repeal of the limitations clause of the
Arrears of Pension Act (51A-H10. 4), repeal of special limitation on pension
claims of State militiamen (51A-H10. 5), pension plans and legislation (51A-
H10. 6), and other subjects (51A-H10. 7). 52d Cong. --Minutes (52A-F21. 4);
docket (52A-F21. 5). 53d Cong. --Minutes (53A-F20. 2); docket (53A-F20. 3);
petitions, memorials, etc., concerning enactment of a service pension law
(53A-H15. 1), the forbidding of suspension of pensions without notice and
proof of fraud (53A-H15. 2), and other subjects (53A-H15. 3). 54th Cong. --
Minutes (54A-F20. 3); docket (54A-F20. 4). 55th Cong. --Minutes (55A-
F17. 2); docket (55A-F17. 3); petitions, memorials, etc., pertaining to
claims (55A-H10. 1), legislation and plans (55A-H10. 2), and other subjects
(55A-H10. 3). 56th Cong. --Petitions, memorials, etc., concerning general
pension regulations for Civil War veterans (56A-H11. 1), pensions for soldiers of the State militias of Missouri and Kentucky (56A-H11. 2), and other
subjects (56A-H11. 3). 60th Cong. --Petitions, memorials, etc., concerning
Arkansas militia and volunteers who served in the Union Army (60A-H17. 1),
disabled veterans of the Civil War (60A-H17. 3), ex-prisoners of war who
had been inmates of Confederate prisons (60A-H17. 4), the pensionable status
of Civil War veterans of the U. S. Military Telegraph Corps (60A-H17. 5),
the Sherwood bill (H. R. 7625) and similar proposals for a pension of $30
monthly to Civil War veterans (60A-H17. 6), a volunteer retired list (60A-
H17. 7), widows of Civil War veterans (60A-H17. 8), and other subjects (60A-
H17.9). 61st Cong. --Petitions, memorials, etc., concerning Army nurse
volunteers of the Civil War (61A-H14. 1), the Grand Army of the Republic
amendment to the Age Act of 1907 (61A-H14. 2), the National Tribune bill
pensioning Civil War and Mexican War veterans (61A-H14. 3), the Sherwood
bill for one-dollar-a-day pensions (61A-H14. 4), the Sulloway pension bill
(61A-H14. 5), veterans who lost limbs (61A-H14. 6), and other subjects (61A-
H14. 7). 62d Cong. --Petitions, memorials, etc., concerning deaf veterans
(62A-H15. 1), ex-prisoners of war (62A-H15. 2), maimed soldiers (62A-
H15. 3), military telegraphers (62A-H15. 4), the Sherwood pension bill (62A-
H15. 5), the Sulloway pension bill (62A-H15. 6), and other subjects (62A-
H15. 7). 69th Cong. --Petitions, memorials, etc., on pensions of Civil War
veterans and dependents.

Dockets, minutes, and other records from the 56th Congress on, although
not mentioned particularly here, are generally available.

Committee on the Judiciary; John Hickman (Pa.), chairman, 36th and 37th
   Congs.; James F. Wilson (Iowa), chairman, 38th-40th Congs.

Authorized June 3, 1813. This committee had the duty to consider "such
petitions and matters or things touching judicial proceedings" as should be
presented or be referred to it by the House and to report its "opinion thereon,
together with . . . propositions relative thereto." Printed committee reports or documents referred to the committee that exemplify its activities
during the Civil War and immediately afterward are as follows:

   Memorial of the mayor and city council of Baltimore concerning the
      suspension of the functions of the city's board of police by the U. S. Gov-
      ernment, sent by the mayor on July 25, 1861. Referred to this commit-
      tee on Aug. 1, 1861. H. Misc. Doc. 22, 37 Cong., 1 sess., Serial 1115.
   Report, Mar. 20, 1862, of inquiry into "telegraphic censorship of the
      press." H. Rept. 64, 37 Cong., 2 sess., Serial 1144.
   Report and recommendation for adoption of the resolution for the "Im-
      peachment of West H. Humphreys, Judge of the United States Dis-
      trict Court of Tennessee." H. Rept. 44, 37 Cong., 2 sess., Serial
      1144.
   Report, Jan. 20, 1863, on the Postmaster General's authority "to decide
      what newspapers may, and what shall not, be transmitted through the
      mails of the United States." H. Misc. Doc. 16, 37 Cong., 3 sess.,
      Serial 1171.

Other printed reports, in the postwar period, that should be consulted:

   Report, July 1866, in response to House resolutions of Apr. 9 and 30, 1866,
      instructing the committee "to inquire into the nature of the evidence
      implicating Jefferson Davis and others in the assassination of Presi-
      dent Lincoln; and also whether any legislation is necessary in order
      to bring such persons to a speedy and impartial trial, if it should appear
      that there was probable cause to believe that said persons, or any of
      them, are guilty of inciting, concerting, or procuring the assassination
      of the late President of the United States; and also whether any legisla-
      tion is necessary in order to bring such persons to a speedy and impar-
      tial trial for the crime of treason." H. Rept. 104, 39 Cong., 1 sess.,
      Serial 1272.
   Report, Mar. 2, 1867, with testimony about the discovery and arrest of
      John H. Surratt. H. Rept. 33, 39 Cong., 2 sess., Serial 1305.

By House resolution of Mar. 7, 1867, the Committee on the Judiciary was
authorized "to inquire into the official conduct of Andrew Johnson, Vice-Pres-
ident of the United States, discharging the present duties of the office of President of the United States, and to report to this House whether, in their opinion,
the said Andrew Johnson, while in said office, has been guilty of acts which
were designed or calculated to overthrow or corrupt the government of the
United States, or any department or officer thereof; and whether the said
Andrew Johnson has been guilty of any act, or has conspired with others
to do acts, which, in contemplation of the Constitution, are high crimes
and misdemeanors, requiring the interposition of the constitutional powers
of this House."

The report of the majority and the views of the minority, together with
the testimony taken, were printed as H. Rept. 7, 40 Cong., 1 sess., Serial
1314. The committee "spared no pains to make their investigations as

55883

complete as possible, not only in the exploration of the public archives,
but in following every indication that seemed to promise any additional
light upon the great subjects of inquiry. " In addition to its value as background for the Johnson impeachment, this document provides useful information on many aspects of Civil War military and political policy and transactions, including those pertaining to captured, abandoned, or confiscable
property; restrictions on commercial intercourse; operations of the U. S.
Military Railroads; amnesty and pardon; appointments of provisional governors; the fate of letters said to have been written by Jefferson Davis to
Confederate agents in Canada; the disposition of the Surratt papers; and,
especially, the apprehension and burial of John Wilkes Booth and the disposition of his effects, including his diary.

Publications of Congress concerning the Johnson impeachment:
H. Rept. 31, 39 Cong. , 2 sess. ,
Serial 1305; H. Rept. 7, 40 Cong.
1 sess. , Serial 1314; S. Journal,
40 Cong. , 2 sess. , appendix, Serial
1315; S. Misc. Docs. 42 and 43, 40
Cong. , 2 sess. , Serial 1319; S.
Rept. 59, 40 Cong. , 2 sess. , Serial
1320; H. Misc. Doc. 91, 40 Cong. ,
2 sess. , Serial 1350; H. Rept. 44,
40 Cong. , 2 sess. , Serial 1357; H.
Rept. 75, 40 Cong. , 2 sess. , Serial
1358. See also supplement to the
Congressional Globe entitled The
Proceedings of the Senate Sitting
for the Trial of Andrew Johnson,
40 Cong. , 2 sess. (1868).

Wartime records. 36th and 37th Congs. --Minutes (36A-D13. 12). 36th
Cong. --Docket (36A-D13. 13); papers concerning "relaxation of Federal
Laws" considered to be "coercive upon State sovereignty" (36A-D13. 8),
slavery in the Territory of New Mexico (36A-D13. 9), suppression of the
foreign slave trade (36A-D13. 10), and other subjects (36A-D13. 11); petitions, memorials, etc. , concerning the Crittenden Compromise (36A-G10.3),
fugitive slave laws (36A-G10. 4), abolition of slavery in general (36A-G10. 5)
and in the District of Columbia (36A-G10. 6), the freeing of slaves by purchase (36A-G10. 7), the slave trade (36A-G10. 8), and other subjects (36A-
G10. 9).   37th and 38th Congs. --Minutes (37A-E9. 6); docket (37A-E9. 7).
37th Cong. --Extensive original testimony on whether a telegraphic censorship of press had been established in wartime Washington, and on whether
Rep. Benjamin Wood of New York had transmitted intelligence to the Confederates (37A-E9. 8); a plan to preserve the Union (37A-E9. 2); petitions,
memorials, etc. , concerning abolition of slavery in the District of Columbia (37A-G7. 1) and in the United States (37A-G7. 2), advice to Congress "to
drop the Negro question and attend to the business of the country" (37A-G7.3),
the admission of West Virginia into the Union (37A-G7. 4), the bankruptcy
law (37A-G7. 5), claims (37A-G7. 6), an "honorable compromise" of the differences between the States (37A-G7. 7), the Crittenden Compromise (37A-
G7. 8), Federal courts and judges (37A-G7. 9), Secretary of War Floyd's
"acceptances" of certain bills of exchange presented by contractors (37A-
G7. 10), repeal of the Fugitive Slave Act (37A-G7. 11), a proposed national
convention of the States "for the peaceful adjustment of the difficulties between the North and South" (37A-G7. 12), confiscation of the property and
liberation of the slaves of persons "supporting the rebellion" (37A-G7. 13),
passage of a law calling upon all citizens (both bond and free) to aid the Government in "suppressing the rebellion" (37A-G7. 14), reduction of South
Carolina, Georgia, and part of Florida "into a territorial condition to be
colonized by Negroes freed by force of arms or by acts of Congress" (37A-

G7. 15), the proposed expulsion of Rep. Clement L. Vallandigham of Ohio from the House (37A-G7. 16), and other subjects (37A-G7. 17). 38th-40th Congs.--Minutes (38A-E10. 5). 38th Cong.--Docket (38A-E10. 6); views of Richard H. Dana, Jr., on desirable modifications of the judiciary system (38A-E10. 4); petitions, memorials, etc., on amending the Constitution to abolish slavery (38A-G10. 1), confiscating the property of persons "supporting the rebellion" (38A-G10. 2), Federal courts and judges (38A-G10.3), slavery (38A-G10. 4), and other subjects (38A-G10. 5).

Postwar records. 39th Cong.--Docket (39A-F13. 13); papers concerning civil and legal rights, especially of freedmen (39A-F13. 2); the inquiry into public affairs in Maryland begun by the Committee on Elections and continued by the Committee on the Judiciary (39A-F13. 4); papers concerning protection of Federal officials (including Provost Marshal personnel) from "local vindictiveness" (39A-F13. 7), the repair of Southern railroads (39A-F13. 8), the return of various Louisiana properties (39A-F13. 9), and the trial of Jefferson Davis for treason (39A-F13. 10); petitions, memorials, etc., concerning annexation of Virginia counties to West Virginia (39A-H14. 1) and the impeachment of President Andrew Johnson (39A-H14. 7). 40th and 41st Congs.--Minutes (40A-F13. 5), docket (40A-F13. 6). 40th Cong.--Investigation of the government in Delaware (40A-F13. 1) and Maryland (40A-F13. 2); referred papers on the impeachment of President Johnson (40A-H10. 2). 41st Cong.--Papers pertaining to collection of debts due the United States from Southern railroad corporations (41A-F13. 2); papers concerning protection of purchasers of land at tax sales under an act for the collection of taxes in the insurrectionary States (41A-F13. 11). 42d and 43d Congs.--Docket (42A-F14. 17). 42d Cong.--Papers concerning the distribution of Alabama claims funds (42A-F14. 3), enforcement of the reconstruction acts (42A-F14. 8), and removal of legal and political disabilities imposed by the Fourteenth Amendment (42A-F14. 12). 45th Cong.--Referred papers concerning settlement of the Alabama claims (45A-H11. 6).

Committee on Military Affairs; Francis P. Blair, Jr. (Mo.), chairman, 37th Cong.; Robert C. Schenck (Ohio), chairman, 38th and 39th Congs.

Authorized Mar. 13, 1822. This committee had had the duty to consider "all subjects relating to the military establishment and public defence . . . referred to them by the House, and to report their opinion thereupon; and also to report, from time to time, such measures as may contribute to economy and accountability in the said establishment."

Wartime records. 34th-36th Congs.--Minutes (34A-D12. 5). 35th and 36th Congs.--Committee clerk's calendar (35A-D12. 6). 36th Cong.--Docket (36A-D14. 8); records concerning claims (36A-D14. 1), the "outrages" on Minnesota citizens by soldiers from Fort Ridgeley (36A-D14. 2), military roads in the Territory of New Mexico (36A-D14. 3), militia in the District of Columbia (36A-D14. 4), national foundries in Alabama and Pennsylvania for the casting of cannon (36A-D14. 5), the arsenal at St. Louis (36A-D14.6), and the strengthening of Tortugas Harbor and Forts Jefferson and Taylor in the Florida Keys (36A-D14. 7); and petitions, memorials, etc., concerning claims (36A-G11. 1), arsenals and other military installations (36A-G11. 2), and other matters (36A-G11. 3). 37th Cong.--Minutes (37A-E10. 6); docket (37A-E10. 7); records concerning the pay of a retired Army officer when recalled to duty upon the outbreak of the war (37A-E10. 1), a claim for refund of a sutler's tax and for return of property seized by military authority(37A-E10. 2), the court-martial of Col. Thomas Worthington at Memphis (37A-

E10. 3), former slaves employed as servants in the Army of Kentucky (37A-
E10. 4), and other subjects (37A-E10. 5); petitions, memorials, etc. , concerning claims (37A-G8. 1), homeopathic surgeons (37A-G8. 2), the Illinois
and Michigan Canal (37A-G8. 3), repeal of legislation barring Jewish chaplains from the Army (37A-G8. 4), the Lake Michigan-Mississippi River
Canal (37A-G8. 5), Michigan troops held as prisoners of war (37A-G8. 6),
military defenses and roads (37A-G8. 7), a national armory (37A-G8. 8), the
Oswego and Erie Canals (37A-G8. 9), paymasters' compensation (37A-G8. 10),
peace and compromise of North-South difficulties (37A-G8. 11), enactment of
a law calling upon all persons (both bond and free) to aid the Government in
"suppressing the rebellion" (37A-G8. 12), abolition of slavery (37A-G8. 13),
soldiers' pay (37A-G8. 14), sutlers (37A-G8. 15), mustering out of the 1st
and 2d Regiments of the U. S. Reserve Corps (37A-G8. 16), establishment
of a professorship in German at the U. S. Military Academy (37A-G8. 17),
and other matters (37A-G8. 18). 38th Cong. --Minutes (38A-E12. 8); docket
(38A-E12. 9); records concerning the ambulance bill (38A-E12. 1), engineer
and other specialized troops (38A-E12. 2), and military justice (38A-E12. 3);
opinions of Dennis H. Mahan of the faculty of the Military Academy on the
desirability of competitive examinations for entrance and for promotion of
commissioned officers (38A-E12. 4); papers about the "bureaucratic harboring" of "rebel sympathizers" (38A-E12. 5), the pay and personnel of the
Army (38A-E12. 6) and other subjects (38A-E12. 7); petitions, memorials,
etc. , on the ambulance and hospital corps (38A-G12. 1), Gen. Robert Anderson's retirement (38A-G12. 2), bounties (38A-G12. 3), the enactment of legislation to permit Jewish chaplains in the Union forces (38A-G12. 4), claims
(38A-G12. 5), colored troops (38A-G12. 6), the conscript law (38A-G12. 7), the
southwest branch of the Pacific Railroad (38A-G12. 8), exchange and release
of Union prisoners taken by Confederate forces (38A-G12. 9), exemption of
ministers of the gospel from military service (38A-G12. 10), increase in the
pay of officers and men in the Union Army (38A-G12. 11), treatment of Confederate prisoners by Union forces (38A-G12. 12), and other matters (38A-
G12. 13).

Postwar records.   39th Cong. --Minutes (39A-F15.9); docket (39A-F15.10);
records concerning bounties for Missouri militia (39A-F15. 1), the detention of the Michigan Cavalry Regiment (39A-F15. 2), fraud in recruiting in
the Western District of New York (39A-F15. 3), the horses and equipment of
the 1st Dakota Cavalry (39A-F15. 4), the indictment of A. B. Morey for acts
allegedly committed during the occupation of Vicksburg (39A-F15. 5), payment of commutation of rations to prisoners of war for the period of their
confinement (39A-F15. 6), statistical information available in the Provost
Marshal General's Bureau (39A-F15. 7), and other subjects (39A-F15. 8);
petitions, memorials, etc. , on bounties (39A-H15. 1), the commutation
price of the Army ration (39A-H15. 2), continuation of the Veteran Reserve
Corps (39A-H15. 3), and other matters (39A-H15. 4).   40th and 41st Congs. --
Docket (40A-F15. 9).   40th Cong. --Claims (40A-F15. 1); papers on a telegraph line to link defensive posts on the Texas frontier (40A-F15. 2); and
papers concerning the court-martial at Raleigh of the Assistant Commissioner for North Carolina of the Bureau of Refugees, Freedmen, and Abandoned Lands (40A-F15. 3).   41st Cong. --Records on the granting of bounty
to honorably discharged soldiers (41A-F15. 3).   42d Cong. --Report of the
Assistant Adjutant General on the Freedmen's Bureau (42A-F17. 6); petitions,
memorials, etc. , urging the establishment of industrial homes and training
schools for orphans of Union soldiers and sailors of the Civil War (42A-

H10. 1), a grant of bounty lands to military telegraph operators in the Civil War (42A-H10. 2), a grant of bounty money and lands to soldiers and sailors of the Union Army (42A-H10. 3), increased pensions for disabled veterans of the Union Army (42A-H10. 4), and other matters (42A-H10. 5). 43dCong. -- Records concerning bounty legislation for Civil War veterans (43A-F17. 1) and relief of the State of Missouri from paying for ordnance and ordnance stores issued to it during the Civil War (43A-F17. 5). 45th Cong.--Referred papers concerning the transfer of medical records from the Provost Marshal General's Office to the Pension Office (45A-H13. 3). 46th Cong. --Records concerning the court-martial of Col. Thomas Worthington at Memphis in 1862 (46A-F21. 1) and the purchase of the papers of Generals Braxton Bragg and Leonidas Polk (46A-F21. 2); petitions, memorials, etc. , concerning equalization of bounties (46A-H14. 1) and payment of additional money to Civil War veterans to compensate for wartime inflation (46A-H14. 2). 47th Cong. --Referred papers concerning the compensation of Civil War paymasters (47A-H13. 2). 52d Cong. --Referred papers concerning preservation and marking of the battle lines at Gettysburg (52A-H15. 1). 53d Cong. -- Papers concerning medals of honor for militia and volunteer troops who offered their services in defense of Maryland and Pennsylvania in 1863 (53A-F27. 1). 60th Cong. --Papers concerning a volunteer retired list for Civil War veterans (60A-H23. 13). 61st Cong. --Officers' retired list of Civil War volunteers (61A-H22. 1). 62d Cong. --Referred papers on the incorporation of the Grand Army of the Republic (62A-H20. 1). 63d Cong. --Petitions, memorials, etc. , concerning the celebration of the 50th anniversary of the Battle of Gettysburg (63A-H10. 2), pensions to members of the Civil War Military Telegraph Corps (63A-H19. 9), and the reunion of Civil War veterans at the Vicksburg National Military Park (63A-H19. 12). 64th Cong. --Referred papers on retirement for Civil War volunteer officers (64A-H16. 2).

Committee on the Militia; Robert B. Van Valkenburgh (N. Y.), chairman, 37th and 38th Congs. ; Green Clay Smith (Ky.), chairman, 39th Cong.

Authorized Dec. 10, 1835. This committee had the duty to consider and report on all subjects connected with "organizing, arming, and disciplining the militia of the United States. " Although no committee records of the Civil War period appear to exist, the postwar records mentioned may throw light on wartime militia matters.

Postwar records. 39th-41st Cong. --Docket (39A-F16. 3). 39th Cong. -- Papers concerned with analysis and amendment of militia legislation (39A-F16. 1); correspondence with States and Territories (39A-F16. 2).

Committee on Naval Affairs; Charles B. Sedgwick (N. Y.), chairman, 37th Cong. ; Alexander H. Rice (Mass.), chairman, 38th and 39th Congs.

Authorized Mar. 13, 1822. This committee had the duty to consider and report on "all matters which concern the naval establishment" referred to it by the House; also to report, from time to time, such measures as might "contribute to economy and accountability in the said establishment. "

Robert Greenhalgh Albion, "The Naval Affairs Committees, 1816-1917," U. S. Naval Institute Proceedings, 78: 1227-1237 (Nov. 1952). The committee's printed reports during the Civil War included one on "Sites for Navy Yards"(H. Rept. 100, 38 Cong. , 1 sess. , Serial 1206) and another on marine engines "constructed and now in course of construction for the navy"(H. Rept. 8, 38 Cong. , 2 sess. , Serial 1235).

Wartime records. 37th Cong. --Papers on enlarging the waterfront of the navy yards at Boston and Philadelphia (37A-E11. 2); petitions, memorials, etc., concerning the Naval Advisory Board (37A-G9. 1), claims (37A-G9. 2), rates of pay and hours of labor in navy yards (37A-G9. 3), increase in the pay of workmen in the Washington Navy Yard (37A-G9. 4), and other matters (37A-G9. 5). 38th Cong. --Records concerning channel marking (1864) by the East Florida Expedition in and near the St. Johns River (38A-E13. 1), contractors for constructing ironclads and river or harbor batteries (38A-E13. 2), the cost of confining civilian detainees (38A-E13. 3), invitations extended to the committee (38A-E13. 4), marine engines (38A-E13. 5), the Medical Department of the Navy (38A-E13. 6), Navy commissions for civilian professors of the Naval Academy (38A-E13. 7), navy yards and depots (38A-E13. 8), pensions and retirement (38A-E13. 9), personnel (38A-E13. 10), recruiting frauds and problems (38A-E13. 11), steam-power experimentation and performance (38A-E13. 12), and the treaty of 1817 in respect to naval forces on the Great Lakes (38A-E13. 13); petitions, memorials, etc., concerning claims (38A-G13. 1), complaints of naval officers against the Naval Advisory Board (38A-G13. 2), and increase of the number of officers in the grades of commander and captain (38A-G13. 3), increase in the pay of employees of navy yards (38A-G13. 4), of paymasters (38A-G13. 5), and of the "Corps of Professors of Mathematics" (38A-G13. 6), the status of volunteer officers (38A-G13. 7), and other subjects (38A-G13. 8).

For a description of letters sent by Gideon Welles to this committee, see the Senate Committee on Naval Affairs.

Postwar records. 48th Cong. --Papers about purchasing the journals and papers of the Confederate vessel Shenandoah (48A-F23. 12); petitions, memorials, etc., on the adjudication of Civil War cases involving prize money (48A-H19. 1). 61st Cong. --Referred papers concerning the commemoration of Jefferson Davis on the silver service of the battleship Mississippi (61A-H25. 2). 62d Cong. --Records concerning Theodore R. Timby's invention of the revolving turret (62A-F28. 1).

Committee on Patents; William McKee Dunn (Ind.), chairman, 37th Cong.; Thomas A. Jenckes (R. I.), chairman, 38th and 39th Congs.

Authorized Sept. 15, 1837. Although matters pertaining to copyrights and trademarks were added later, the committee's duties during the Civil War related solely to patents.

Wartime records. 36th Cong. --Docket (36A-D16. 3). 37th Cong. --Docket (37A-E12. 3); papers concerning a charge of malfeasance against the Commissioner of Patents (37A-E12. 1), a claim for fitting up the "saloon" in the east wing of the Patent Office Building (37A-E12. 2), and expenditure of the appropriation made in 1861 for the Agricultural Bureau of the Patent Office (37A-E12. 3); petitions, memorials, etc., chiefly concerning the renewal of patents (37A-G10. 1 to 37A-G10. 8). 38th Cong. --Papers, including those referred, pertaining chiefly to renewals of patents (38A-E14. 1 to 38A-E14. 4, 38A-G14. 1 to 38A-G14. 4).

Postwar records. 39th Cong. --Docket (39A-F19. 1).

Committee on the Post Office and Post Roads; Schuyler Colfax (Ind.), chairman, 37th Cong.; John B. Alley (Mass.), chairman, 38th Cong.

Authorized Nov. 9, 1808. This committee had the duty to consider "all such petitions and matters or things touching the post office and post roads as should be presented" or referred to it by the House and to report its opinion thereon, "together with such propositions relative thereto" as might "seem expedient."

Wartime records. 37th Cong.--Petitions, memorials, etc., concerning the establishment of mail routes in States and Territories (37A-G11. 1 to 37A-G11. 15), ocean mail routes (37A-G11. 16), the sending of small parcels to soldiers by mail (37A-G11. 17), and other subjects (37A-G11. 18). 38th Cong.--Records concerning amendment of an act of March 3, 1863 (12 Stat. 708), covering the franking of official mail addressed to executive departments (38A-E15. 1), the interchange of mails between the United States and Canada (38A-E15. 2), the overland mail (especially from Atchison, Kans., to Salt Lake City, Utah) (38A-E15. 3), and other subjects (38A-E15. 4); petitions, memorials, etc., concerning abolition of the franking privilege (38A-G15. 1), claims (38A-G15. 2), establishment of postal routes (38A-G15. 3 to 38A-G15. 14), increase in the compensation of mail contractors and letter carriers (38A-G15. 15), repeal of section 4 of the "Act to provide for carrying the mails from the United States to foreign ports, and for other purposes," approved Mar. 25, 1864 (38A-G15. 16), and other matters (38A-G15. 17).

Committee on Public Buildings and Grounds; Charles R. Train (Mass.), chairman, 37th Cong.; John H. Rice (Maine), chairman, 38th and 39th Congs.

Authorized Sept. 15, 1837. This committee had the duty to consider "all subjects relating to the public edifices and grounds within the City of Washington" that might be referred to it and to report its opinion on them, "together with such propositions relating thereto" as might seem "expedient."

Wartime records. 37th Cong.--Papers concerning public works under military engineers (37A-E14. 1), extension of the Capitol and Treasury Buildings (37A-E14. 2), extension of the Library of Congress (37A-E14. 3), removal of John Plant from the Capitol police force for brutal treatment of a soldier on the Capitol grounds (37A-E14. 4), the Washington Aqueduct (37A-E14. 5), and the claim of E. Leutze for decorating the Capitol (37A-G14. 1). 38th Cong.--Papers concerning construction and improvement projects (38A-E17. 1), the membership of the committee (38A-E17. 2), occupancy of the Winder Building and leasing of office space (38A-E17. 3), salaries and personnel (38A-E17. 4), and the alleged misconduct of the chief engineer and general superintendent of the Washington Aqueduct and other persons (38A-E17. 5); petitions, memorials, etc., concerning a grant of land to the Guardian Society of the District of Columbia for a "House of Industry" and a "Widows' and Orphans' Home" (38A-G18. 1).

Postwar records. 39th Cong.--Papers concerning the White House (39A-F22. 4). 40th Cong.--Papers concerning Arlington House heirlooms of Mary Custis Lee (40A-F21. 1).

Committee on Public Expenditures; John Covode (Pa.), chairman, 37th Cong.; Calvin T. Hulburd (N. Y.), chairman, 38th and 39th Congs.

Authorized Feb. 26, 1814. This committee had the duty to examine "into the state of the several public departments, and particularly into laws making appropriations of money" and report whether the money had been disbursed "conformably with such laws." It became the committee's duty, moreover, to report on possible retrenchment in Government expenditures, on any failure to collect money due the United States, and on any procedural changes necessary to proper accountability. The notable activity of the committee during the Civil War was its investigation of the New York Customhouse, which it reported on June 15, 1864 (H. Rept. 111, 38 Cong., 1 sess., Serial 1206). It was abolished in 1880 but was revived for another two years in 1881.

Wartime records. 37th-41st Congs.--Docket (37A-E15. 1). 38th Cong. -- Correspondence and papers about the New York Customhouse investigation (38A-E18. 1).

Postwar records. 39th-41st Congs.--Minutes (39A-F23. 1).

Committee on the Public Lands; John F. Potter (Wis.), chairman, 37th Cong.; George W. Julian (Ind.), chairman, 38th Cong.

Authorized Dec. 17, 1805. From 1805 this committee had the duty to consider "all such petitions and matters or things respecting the lands of the United States" as should be presented, or referred to it by the House, and to report its opinion on them, "together with such propositions for relief therein" as might "seem expedient."

Wartime records. 34th-38th Congs.--Minutes (34A-D18. 5). 36th Cong.--Docket (36A-D21. 6). 37th Cong.--Docket (37A-E16. 13); papers pertaining to titles to lands along the Georgia-Florida boundary (37A-E16. 5) and to the Homestead Act (37A-E16. 19, 37A-G15. 4). 38th Cong.--Docket (38A-E19. 17); papers concerning titles to lands along the Georgia-Florida boundary (38A-E19. 10) and the confiscation and sale of lands abandoned by secessionists in northern Texas (38A-E19. 3).

Postwar records. 39th-42d Congs.--Minutes (39A-F24. 10). 39th Cong. -- Docket (39A-F24. 11); papers on the confirmation of titles to lands in Mississippi confiscated and sold as Confederate property (39A-F24. 2). 42d Cong. -- Petitions, memorials, etc., concerning bounties and land warrants for soldiers of the War of 1812 and the Civil War (42A-H13. 2). 48th Cong.--Petitions, memorials, etc., concerning land for honorably discharged Union veterans or their heirs (48A-H25. 9).

Committee on Roads and Canals; Robert Mallory (Ky.), chairman, 37th Cong.; Isaac N. Arnold (Ill.), chairman, 38th Cong.

Authorized Dec. 15, 1831. This committee had the duty to consider all "petitions and matters or things relating to roads and canals, and the improvement of the navigation of rivers" that were presented or referred to it by the House and to report on them, "together with such propositions relative thereto" as might "seem expedient." The committee was terminated on Apr. 9, 1869, when the Committee on Railways and Canals succeeded to its functions.

Wartime records. 37th Cong.--Petitions, memorials, etc., concerning the Illinois and Michigan Canal (37A-G18. 1) and other matters (37A-G18. 2). 38th Cong.--Petitions, memorials, etc., concerning construction of a canal around Niagara Falls (38A-G22. 1), construction of roads in the western part of the country (38A-G22. 2), construction of the St. Lawrence River Waterway Canal (38A-G22. 3), the establishment of a "through" railway line from New York to Washington (38A-G22. 4), a land grant for the Southern Minnesota Railroad (38A-G22. 5), and other matters (38A-G22. 6).

HOUSE OF REPRESENTATIVES 59

Committee on the Territories; James M. Ashley (Ohio), chairman, 37th
and 38th Congs.
Authorized Dec. 13, 1825. This committee had the duty "to examine
into the legislative, civil, and criminal proceedings of the Territories,"
and to report to the House such measure as, in its opinion, might be necessary "to secure the rights and privileges of residents and non-residents."
Wartime records. 36th–43d Congs.--Minutes (35A-D21.8). 37th
Cong.--Docket (37A-E19.5); executive message of William F. M. Arny,
Acting Governor of New Mexico, to the Legislative Assembly of the Territory, Dec. 2, 1862 (37A-E19.4); papers concerning appropriations for
the Territory of Colorado (37A-E19.1) and for the Territory of Dakota
(37A-E19.2) and a census of the Territories of Dakota and Nevada (37A-
E19.3); and petitions, memorials, etc., on various subjects (37A-G19.1).
38th Cong.--A pamphlet, Laws of the Territory of New Mexico; With the
Joint Resolutions Passed by the Legislative Assembly at the Session of
1863-64, Theodore S. Greiner, translator, printed at Albuquerque, 1864
(38A-E21.1); a proposed bill "for the relief of the citizens of Great Salt
Lake City, Territory of Utah" (38A-E21.2); petitions, memorials, etc.,
on building a capitol and prison in Dakota Territory (38A-G23.1), the construction of roads in the western territory (38A-G23.2), and salary increases for judges of the Supreme Court of Colorado Territory (38A-G23.3).

Committee on War Claims (postwar)
Authorized Dec. 2, 1873, to have jurisdiction over "all claims growing
out of any war in which the United States has been engaged," this committee
replaced the Committee on Revolutionary Claims. Like the Committee of
Claims (see above), the Committee on War Claims reported appropriations
for the payment of individual claims.
Postwar records. 42d-46th Congs.--Among the House records most
valuable for Civil War research are the records of this committee, reflecting its jurisdiction over claims ("of those citizens who remained loyal
adherents to the cause and the Government of the United States during the
war, for stores or supplies taken or furnished during the rebellion for the
use of the Army of the United States, in States proclaimed as in insurrection against the United States") presented to the Commissioners of Claims--
that is, the Southern Claims Commission. (See the Commissioners of
Claims, elsewhere in this Guide.) The committee's records include
notably the originals of the 10 annual reports of the Commissioners
of Claims, 1871-80, together with the claims rejected (42A-F29.1,
42A-F29.2, 43A-F29.2, 43A-F29.3, 44A-F37.1, 44A-F37.2, 45A-F35.1,
45A-F35.2, 46A-F35.1, 46A-F35.2). There are also a numerical list of
claims disallowed by the Commissioners, 1871-78 (42A-F29.4); a Consolidated Index of Claims Reported by the Commissioners of Claims to the
House of Representatives From 1871 to 1880 (42A-F29.5); certain barred
claims (46A-F35.3); and various dockets (43A-F29.5, 44A-F37.3, 45A-
F35.5, 46A-F35.5). 47th Cong.--Referred papers concerning payment of
"female nurses" of the Civil War (47A-H21.1). 60th Cong.--Georgia's
claim for cotton taxes collected by the Federal Government, 1862-68 (60A-
H35.1). 63d Cong.--Papers concerning the great fire at Columbia, S. C.,
in 1865 (63A-F39.1).

Committee on Ways and Means; Thaddeus Stevens (Pa.), chairman, 37th
   and 38th Congs.
   Authorized Dec. 21, 1795. From 1802 it had been the duty of this
committee "to take into consideration all such reports of the Treasury
Department, and all such propositions relative to the revenue" as might
be referred to it by the House; "to inquire into the state of the public debt
or the revenue, and of the expenditure; and to report from time to time"
its opinion thereon. It had become also the duty of the committee to report, at every session of Congress, and within 30 days after its appointment, the general appropriation bills for legislative, executive, and judicial expenses; for sundry civil expenses; for consular and diplomatic expenses; for the Army; for the Navy; for the Indian department; for invalid
and other pensions; for the support of the Military Academy; for fortifications; and for the Post Office Department, including expenses for mail
transportation by ocean steamers.
   Wartime records. 35th-37th Congs.--Minutes (35A-D22. 24). 37th
Cong.--Docket (37A-E20. 20); papers concerning the Commissioner of
Public Buildings (37A-E20. 1); communications with Members of Congress
(37A-E20. 2); papers about the contingent expenses of the Clerk of the
House of Representatives (37A-E20. 3); papers about the Court of Claims
(37A-E20. 4); papers from or about executive departments and the District
of Columbia (37A-E20. 5 to 37A-E20. 12); papers concerning domestic taxes
(37A-E20. 13), income taxes (37A-E20. 14), and the Pension Office (37A-
E20. 15); private correspondence of Thaddeus Stevens (37A-E20. 16); papers
concerning suppression of the African slave trade (37A-E20. 17), the tariff
(37A-E20. 18), and other subjects (37A-E20. 19); petitions, memorials, etc.,
concerning advice to Congress "to drop the Negro question and attend to
the business of the Country" (37A-G20. 1), national currency (37A-G20. 2),
the national debt (37A-G20. 3), Kansas and Nebraska public lands (37A-
G20. 4), establishment of a branch mint in New York City (37A-G20. 5) and
one in St. Louis (37A-G20. 6), tariff (37A-G20. 7), taxes (37A-G20. 8), and
other matters (37A-G20. 9). 38th Cong.--Docket (38A-E22. 21); papers
concerning appointments to various House committees (38A-E22. 1); attested copies of House resolutions (38A-E22. 2); claims (38A-E22. 3); papers concerning a commodity tariff or other commodity taxation (38A-
E22. 4), education (38A-E22. 5), and Government personnel (38A-E22. 6);
papers about an Academy of National Sciences (38A-E22. 7), the Attorney
General's Office (38A-E22. 8), the Commissioner of Public Buildings (38A-
E22. 9), and the Government Printing Office (38A-E22. 10); papers from or
about executive departments (38A-E22. 11 to 38A-E22. 17); papers about
tariff policy (38A-E22. 18), taxation policy (38A-E22. 19), and other subjects (38A-E22. 20); petitions, memorials, etc., concerning amendment
of the internal revenue law (38A-G24. 1), claims (38A-G24. 2), duties on
paper and the materials used in its manufacture (38A-G24. 3), a tax on dogs
(38A-G24. 4), improvement of rivers and harbors (38A-G24. 5), a duty on
wool (38A-G24. 6), the pay of assistant assessors of internal revenue (38A-
G24. 7) and of other government employees (38A-G24. 8), a branch mint at
Portland, Oreg. (38A-G24. 9), national and State banks (38A-G24. 10), the
national income tax (38A-G24. 11), certain discriminatory duties (38A-
G24. 12), the tax on the gross receipts of ships and vessels (38A-G24. 13),
other taxation (38A-G24. 14 to 38A-G24. 16), and other matters (38A-G24.17).
   Postwar records. 39th Cong.--Papers concerning direct taxes (39A-
F27. 10). 42d, 44th, and 45th Congs.--Petitions, memorials, etc., con-

cerning refund of the cotton tax (42A-H15. 9, 44A-H20. 23, 45A-H25. 27). 46th Cong. --Referred papers concerning legislation about the savings of depositors in the Freedman's Savings and Trust Co. (46A-H24. 16).

Other Committees

House standing committees of the war period not discussed above because their wartime records are unavailable or irrelevant are the Committees of Accounts; on Agriculture; on Banking and Currency; on Manufactures; on Mileage; on Mines and Mining; on the Pacific Railroad; on Private Land Claims; on Revisal and Unfinished Business; on Revolutionary Claims; on Revolutionary Pensions; and on a Uniform System of Coinage, Weights, and Measures.

House Select Committees

Select committees are created by resolution to consider matters outside the authority of House standing committees or those that require extensive investigation. The mere enumeration of the Civil War select committees suggests, therefore, the notable areas of House concern during the war. Their scope and nature, indeed, provided the House with important precedents--for example, it was established that when the Select Committee on National Armories (37th Cong.) made its report it was automatically dissolved, and that part of the report of the Select Committee on the Confiscation of Rebel Property (37th Cong.) should be ruled out because the committee had exceeded its instructions. Wartime select committees were occasionally reappointed in succeeding sessions of the same Congress or were reauthorized in the next Congress. They were usually empowered by the resolutions creating them "to send for persons and papers, and to examine witnesses. "

All House select committees created toward the end of the Buchanan administration and during the war are entered below by Congress and thereunder, with the exception of a few not treated in detail, chronologically by date of authorization. Also included are postwar select committees of the 39th, 40th, and 44th Congress whose records are significant to Civil War research. As in the case of the House standing committees, it has not been feasible to give the exact quantities of the records mentioned. All are in Record Group 233.

36TH CONGRESS

Select Committee on the Condition of the Country (Committee of Thirty-Three)

By House resolution of Dec. 4, 1860, the part of President Buchanan's message of Dec. 3 that related to "the present perilous condition of the country" was referred to a special committee consisting of one Member from each State. The following Representatives comprised this committee: Thomas Corwin (Ohio), John S. Millson (Va.), Charles F. Adams (Mass.), Warren Winslow (N. C.), James Humphrey (N. Y.), William W. Boyce (S. C.), James H. Campbell (Pa.), Peter E. Love (Ga.), Orris S. Ferry (Conn.), Henry Winter Davis (Md.), Christopher Robinson (R. I.), William G. Whiteley (Del.), Mason W. Tappan (N. H.), John L. N. Stratton (N. J.), Francis M. Bristow (Ky.), Justin S. Morrill (Vt.), Thomas A. R. Nelson

(Tenn.), William McKee Dunn (Ind.), Miles Taylor (La.), Reuben Davis (Miss.), William Kellogg (Ill.), George S. Houston (Ala.), Freeman H. Morse (Maine), John S. Phelps (Mo.), Albert Rust (Ark.), William A. Howard (Mich.), George S. Hawkins (Fla.), Andrew J. Hamilton (Tex.), Cadwallader C. Washburn (Wis.), Samuel R. Curtis (Iowa), John C. Burch (Calif.), William Windom (Minn.), and Lansing Stout (Oreg.).

The committee held a series of meetings beginning on Dec. 11, 1860, and ending on Jan. 14, 1861, when it reported "several resolutions, which do not approve action on any specific subject, but which, if adopted and approved by a vote of the House, may serve to announce principles which seem in some quarters to be questioned, while their adoption may tend to correct errors and misrepresentations that have obtained a too general belief in the southern sections of the Union." The committee was far from unanimous on the resolutions reported; seven minority reports were submitted.

The committee's journal and reports were printed as H. Rept. 31, 36 Cong., 2 sess., Serial 1104.

Records. --Committee papers (36A-D26. 2); papers referred to the committee concerning the Crittenden Compromise (36A-G23. 1), the national convention for the settlement of national difficulties (36A-G23. 2), and other subjects (36A-G23. 3).

Select Committee of Five (on the Special Message of the President)

President Buchanan's special message of Jan. 8, 1861, communicated to Congress on Jan. 9, was referred on the latter date to a special committee of five members, who were required to make immediate inquiry and report:

1. Whether any executive officer of the United States has been or is now treating or holding communication with any person or persons concerning the surrender of any forts, fortresses, or other public property of the United States, and whether any demand for such surrender has been made, when, and by whom, and what answer has been given. 2. Whether any officer of this government has at any time entered into any pledge, agreement, or understanding, with any person or persons, not to send re-enforcements to the forts of the United States in the harbor of Charleston, and the particulars of such agreement, pledge, or understanding; when, where, and with whom it was made, and on what consideration. 3. What demand for re-enforcements of the said forts has been made, and for what reason such re-enforcements have not been furnished. 4. Where the ships of the United States are now stationed, with what commands, and with what orders. 5. Whether the custom-house, post office, arsenal, and other public buildings of the United States at Charleston have been seized and are held in possession by any person or persons, and the particulars of such seizure and possession. 6. Whether any revenue cutter of the United States has been seized and is now held in possession by any person or persons, and the particulars thereof; and whether any efforts have been made by the head of the Treasury Department to recapture and recover possession of said vessel.

By a later resolution of the same day this committee was instructed also "to inquire whether any of the arms of the United States at any of the arsenals or armories have recently been removed or ordered to be removed"; and by House resolution of Jan. 26, 1861, "to inquire whether any secret organization hostile to the government of the United States exists in the District of Columbia; and if so, whether any official or employé of the city of Washington or any employés or officers of the federal government in the executive or judicial departments are members thereof?"

The committee consisted of William A. Howard (Mich.), Lawrence O'B. Branch (N. C.), Henry L. Dawes (Mass.), John Cochrane (N. Y.), and John Hickman (Pa.), replaced by John H. Reynolds (N. Y.) on Jan. 12. It completed its work on Feb. 28, 1861.

Correspondence between the Commissioners of South Carolina and President Buchanan, Dec. 1860-Feb. 1861, was referred to this committee (see H. Exec. Doc. 26, 36 Cong., 2 sess., Serial 1097, and H. Exec. Doc. 61, 36 Cong., 2 sess., Serial 1100). The reports resulting from the committee's inquiries were entitled "Militia of the United States" (H. Rept. 58, 36 Cong., 2 sess., Serial 1104), "Further Provision for Collection of Duties on Imports" (H. Rept. 59, 36 Cong., 2 sess., Serial 1104), "Alleged Hostile Organization Against the Government Within the District of Columbia" (H. Rept. 79, 36 Cong., 2 sess., Serial 1105), "Naval Force of the United States--Where Ships Are Now Stationed, etc." (H. Rept. 87, 36 Cong., 2 sess., Serial 1105), "Relative to the Correspondence Between the President and the Commissioners on the Part of the State of South Carolina" (H. Rept. 88, 36 Cong., 2 sess., Serial 1105), and "Seizure of Forts, Arsenals, Revenue Cutters, and Other property of the United States" (H. Rept. 91, 36 Cong., 2 sess., Serial 1105). The journal and general conclusions of the committee are printed as part of the last report.

Records. --Referred papers concerning the Constitution and laws of the United States (36A-G25.1), the Crittenden Compromise (36A-G25.2), the national convention for the settlement of national difficulties (36A-G25.3), and other subjects (36A-G25.4).

37TH CONGRESS

Select Committee on Government Contracts

Authorized July 8, 1861; appointed July 10. The committee had the following duties:

to ascertain and report what contracts have been made by any of the departments for provisions, supplies, and transportation; for materials, and services, or for any articles furnished for the use of government without advertising for proposals, as required by the statute of 1861; the parties to whom given; the compensation and terms thereof, and the reasons therefor. Also, where proposals were received, if contracts were awarded the lowest bidder; if not, the reason therefor. Also, whether the contracts, as let, are in accordance with the specifications inviting proposals; and if any alterations, the reason for the same. Also, whether any person or persons have any interest in the contracts thus made and awarded, or obtained the same, or profits therefrom, except the contractors.

On July 10, 1861, the committee was further instructed to inquire into the circumstances of the "hiring by the Executive" of the steamer Cataline; and other resolutions extended its field of investigation. The committee consisted of Charles H. Van Wyck (N. Y.), Elihu B. Washburne (Ill.), William S. Holman (Ind.), Reuben E. Fenton (N. Y.), Henry L. Dawes (Mass.), William G. Steele (N. J.), and James S. Jackson (Ky.). It began its inquiries in New York on Aug. 27, 1861, and continued them in subsequent sittings in that city and in Washington, Boston, New Bedford, St. Louis, Cairo, Chicago, Harrisburg, Philadelphia, Cincinnati, Indianapolis, and Wilmington. Its voluminous report of more than 2,600 printed pages (H. Rept. 2, 37 Cong., 2 sess., Serials 1142, 1143) includes its journal and the verbatim testimony. The committee believed that its "exposures of glaring abuses" had resulted in "many important reforms, which are saving large amounts of money daily; and, enlightened by their examinations, the departments have been enabled to more thoroughly scrutinize their expenditures and see where they could be reduced." Its inquiries related to the steamer Cataline; hides, tallow, and cattle; horses and wagons; arms; vessels and Navy supplies; and Army supplies. Testimony on the last subject pertained especially to transportation of troops and military supplies by railroad, purchases for the Western Department, purchases by the State of Indiana, Army shoes, Sibley tentpoles with iron tripod, fortifications of St. Louis, organization of a military force in Colorado Territory, "rotten and condemned blankets," the Quartermaster's Department at Cairo, sutlers in the Army, the inspection of horses, and frauds and irregularities in the Western Department. The hundreds of witnesses testifying included, among many other important or controversial persons, U. S. Grant, Francis P. Blair, Jr., Cornelius Vanderbilt, G. V. Fox, and M. C. Meigs.

On Feb. 26, 1862, the committee was directed to investigate receipts by Federal officers in New York City and the ownership and rents of bonded warehouses and labor contracts for the storage, hauling, delivery, etc., of foreign goods in that city; its final report (H. Rept. 49, 37 Cong., 3 sess., Serial 1173) covers these subjects. The minority report on these subjects (H. Rept. 50, 37 Cong., 3 sess., Serial 1173) discusses committee procedures and records.

Records.--Committee papers (37A-E21.1).

Select Committee on the Loyalty of Government Employees

Authorized and appointed on July 8, 1861, "to ascertain and report to the House the number of persons, with the names thereof, now employed in the several departments of the government, who are known to entertain sentiments of hostility to the government of the United States, and those who have refused to take oath to support the Constitution of the United States." The members of the committee were John F. Potter (Wis.), Sidney Edgerton (Ohio), Samuel C. Fessenden (Maine), and Edward Haight (N. Y.). It met for the first time on July 13, 1861, and almost daily thereafter until Aug. 24. After a recess it resumed its sessions on Sept. 9 and continued them from day to day until Oct. 8. During this period it investigated some 550 charges of disloyalty. It resumed its investigations with the opening of the 2d session of the 37th Congress, when it became apparent that the subject was "far from being exhausted."

The committee is discussed in   Oath . . . , p. 1-10 (Philadelphia,
Harold Melvin Hyman, Era of the   1954).

There are no manuscript records of this committee but its report is
printed as H. Rept. 16, 37 Cong., 2 sess., Serial 1144.

Select Committee on National Armories

Authorized July 10, 1861; appointed July 12, to consist of James K.
Moorhead (Pa.), John A. McClernand (Ill.), John A. Bingham (Ohio),
Francis W. Kellogg (Mich.), John L. N. Stratton (N. J.), Charles Delano
(Mass.), James S. Rollins (Mo.), William Vandever (Iowa), and John W.
Wallace (Pa.). The committee inquired into and reported on "the expedi-
ency of the establishment of a national armory west of the Alleghany moun-
tains" (H. Rept. 43, 37 Cong., 2 sess., Serial 1144), a subject to which
"Recent events" had given "a commanding importance not before possessed."
Records. --Papers referred to the committee (37A-G21. 1).

Select Committee on a General Bankrupt Law

Authorized July 15, 1861; appointed July 17, to consist of Roscoe
Conkling (N. Y.), John Hutchins (Ohio), Benjamin F. Thomas (Mass.),
John W. Noell (Mo.), and Robert McKnight (Pa.).
Records. --Papers referred to the committee (37A-G21. 2).

Select Committee on Defense of Great Lakes and Rivers

This committee, to which was referred the part of President Lincoln's
message of Dec. 3, 1861, that concerned defenses and fortifications on the
Great Lakes and rivers, was authorized on Dec. 5, 1861. It was appointed
on Dec. 11, to consist of Isaac N. Arnold (Ill.), James M. Ashley (Ohio),
John W. Noell (Mo.), Cyrus Aldrich (Minn.), Elijah Babbitt (Pa.), Elbridge
G. Spaulding (N. Y.), Bradley F. Granger (Mich.), William A. Wheeler
(N. Y.), and John F. Potter (Wis.). The committee reported on Feb. 12,
1862 (H. Rept. 23, 37 Cong., 2 sess., Serial 1144).
Records. --Papers referred to the committee (37A-G21. 3).

Select Committee on Gradual Emancipation

Authorized Apr. 7, 1862, to inquire and report on the feasibility of
gradual emancipation in Delaware, Maryland, Virginia, Kentucky, Tennessee, and Missouri, "by the people or local authorities thereof; and whether
such an object is expedient and desirable . . . and further . . . whether
colonization . . . is a necessary concomitant of their freedom." The committee was appointed Apr. 14, 1862, to consist of Albert S. White (Ind.),
Francis P. Blair, Jr. (Mo.), George P. Fisher (Del.), William E. Lehman
(Pa.), Cornelius L. L. Leary (Md.), Kellian V. Whaley (Va.), James F.
Wilson (Iowa), Samuel L. Casey (Ky.), and Andrew J. Clements (Tenn.).
Its report, which includes a bill, was printed as H. Rept. 148, 37 Cong.,
2 sess., Serial 1145.
Records. --Papers referred to the committee (37A-G21. 4).

Select Committee on the Confiscation of Rebel Property

Authorized Apr. 24, 1862; appointed Apr. 28, to consist of Abraham B. Olin (N. Y.), Thomas D. Eliot (Mass.), John W. Noell (Mo.), John Hutchins (Ohio), Robert Mallory (Ky.), Fernando C. Beaman (Mich.), and George T. Cobb (N. J.). The committee reported H. R. 471 ("to confiscate the property of rebels for the payment of the expenses of the present rebellion") and H. R. 472 ("to free from servitude the slaves of the rebels").
Records. --Papers referred to the committee (37A-G21.5).

Select Committee on a Ship Canal Around the Falls of Niagara

Authorized June 24, 1862, to consider the feasibility of a canal between Lakes Erie and Ontario on the American side; appointed June 25, to consist of Burt Van Horn (N. Y.), Harrison G. Blake (Ohio), John W. Menzies (Ky.), Rowland E. Trowbridge (Mich.), John H. Rice (Maine), William M. Davis (Pa.), and James A. Cravens (Ind.). Consideration of this enterprise had begun in 1808, and the 37th Congress select committee availed itself of reports of past committees on the subject.
There are no records of the committee as such. Its report was printed as H. Rept. 53, 37 Cong., 3 sess., Serial 1173; the original is available (37A-D3).

Select Committee to Investigate Charges Against the Hon. J. M. Ashley

Authorized Dec. 4, 1862, to investigate the official conduct of Representative James M. Ashley (Ohio) in getting for F. M. Case the appointment as surveyor general of Colorado Territory; appointed Dec. 8, to consist of Harrison G. Blake (Ohio), John W. Noell (Mo.), John P. C. Shanks (Ind.), Samuel L. Casey (Ky.), and Edward Haight (N. Y.). The committee's report was printed as H. Rept. 47, 37 Cong., 3 sess., Serial 1173.
Records. --Committee papers (37A-E21.2).

Select Committee on Interest of Government Employees in Banking Institutions Having Government Contracts or Dealing in Stocks

Authorized Dec. 22, 1862, "to inquire whether any officer or employé in any department of the government is a partner, or interested, directly or indirectly, in any banking-house, money corporation, or other business firm having contracts with the government, or dealing in stocks or other property"; appointed Dec. 23, 1862, to consist of Charles R. Train (Mass.), John A. Bingham (Ohio), Chauncy Vibbard (N. Y.), James H. Campbell (Pa.), and Cornelius L. L. Leary (Md.).
There are no records of the committee as such. Its report was printed as H. Rept. 64, 37 Cong., 3 sess., Serial 1173; the original is available (37A-D3).

Select Committee on a Military and Post Road From New York to Washington

Authorized Jan. 12, 1863, to consider the expediency of such a road "in order to facilitate the transportation of the mails, and arms, troops,

and munitions of war"; appointed Jan. 13, to consist of Reuben E. Fenton
(N. Y.), William Kellogg (Ill.), William H. Wadsworth (Ky.), Aaron A.
Sargent (Calif.), and James E. English (Conn.).

There are no papers of the committee as such. Its report was printed
as H. Rept. 63, 37 Cong., 3 sess., Serial 1173; the original is available
(37A-D3).

Select Committee to Investigate Charges Against the Commissioner of Patents

Authorized and appointed Jan. 30, 1863, to inquire into charges contained in a "pamphlet entitled 'An Exposition of D. P. Holloway's Management of the Affairs of the Patent Office, ' purporting to be signed by R.
Betts." The committee consisted of William P. Sheffield (R. I.), John H.
Rice (Maine), Warren P. Noble (Ohio), Edwin H. Webster (Md.), and Rowland E. Trowbridge (Mich.).

There are no records of the committee as such. Its report, to which
is appended the testimony taken, was printed as H. Rept. 48, 37 Cong., 3
sess., Serial 1173; the original is available (37A-D3).

Other Committees

There are papers (37A-G21. 6) referred to the Select Committee on the
Celebration of Washington's Birthday (appointed Feb. 10, 1862), but no
papers of two other House select committees of the 37th Congress--those on
Reduction of Government Expenditures (appointed July 16, 1861) and to Investigate Charges of Corruption Published in the New York Tribune (appointed July 2, 1862).

38TH CONGRESS

Select Committee to Consider a Bill to Establish a Bureau of Emancipation

Authorized Dec. 14, 1863; appointed Dec. 16, to consist of Thomas D.
Eliot (Mass.), William D. Kelley (Pa.), Anthony L. Knapp (Ill.), Godlove S.
Orth (Ind.), Sempronius H. Boyd (Mo.), Martin Kalbfleisch (N. Y.), Amasa
Cobb (Wis.), Lucien Anderson (Ky.), and George Middleton (N. J.). The
committee's minority report (H. Rept. 2, 38 Cong., 1 sess., Serial 1206)
is of special interest.

Records. --Committee papers (38A-E23. 2) and those referred to the
committee (38A-G25. 1).

Select Committee on the Pacific Railroad

Authorized Dec. 14, 1863, as a committee to which was referred a bill
(H. R. 5) "to aid in the construction of a railroad and telegraph line to the
Pacific Coast by the northern route." By resolution of Dec. 15, 1863, all
documents and resolutions in relation to Pacific railroads were to be re-
ferred to "a special committee of thirteen, " presumably this committee;
it was appointed Dec. 16, to consist of Thaddeus Stevens (Pa.), A. Carter
Wilder (Kans.), John B. Steele (N. Y.), Hiram Price (Iowa), Cornelius
Cole (Calif.), Warren P. Noble (Ohio), Ignatius Donnelly (Minn.), John R.
McBride (Oreg.), William G. Steele (N. J.), Joseph W. McClurg (Mo.),

Oakes Ames (Mass.), George H. Yeaman (Ky.), and Lorenzo D. M. Sweat (Maine). (Similar committees had existed in earlier Congresses, including the 36th, for which records are available, and the 37th.)

Records.--Papers referred to the committee (38A-G25.4).

Select Committee on the Rebellious States

Authorized Dec. 15, 1863, as a committee to which was referred the part of the President's message of Dec. 8 that related to the "duty of the United States to guarantee a republican form of government to the States in which the governments recognized by the United States have been abrogated or overthrown." The committee was appointed Dec. 16, 1863, to consist of Henry Winter Davis (Md.), George S. Boutwell (Mass.), James C. Allen (Ill.), James M. Ashley (Ohio), Reuben E. Fenton (N. Y.), William S. Holman (Ind.), Nathaniel B. Smithers (Del.), Henry T. Blow (Mo.), and James E. English (Conn.). H. R. 244 was reported by the committee on Feb. 15, 1864.

Records.--Committee papers (38A-E23.6) and those referred to the committee (38A-G25.6).

Select Committee on Foreign Immigration

Authorized Dec. 15, 1863, as a committee to which was referred the part of the President's message to Congress of Dec. 8 that concerned immigration; appointed Dec. 16, to consist of Elihu B. Washburne (Ill.), Josiah B. Grinnell (Iowa), John Law (Ind.), John D. Baldwin (Mass.), and James S. Rollins (Mo.). The Presidential message had urged establishing a system to encourage immigration. The committee's report was printed as H. Rept. 56, 38 Cong., 1 sess., Serial 1206.

Records.--Committee papers (38A-E23.3) and those referred to the committee (38A-G25.3).

Select Committee on a Railroad From New York to Washington

Authorized Jan. 6, 1864, "With authority to examine into the expediency of the establishment of a new route for postal and other purposes between New York and Washington"; appointed Jan. 7, to consist of Augustus Brandegee (Conn.), John B. Alley (Mass.), Samuel J. Randall (Pa.), John F. Farnsworth (Ill.), Daniel W. Voorhees (Ind.), James Brooks (N. Y.), Edwin H. Webster (Md.), James A. Garfield (Ohio), and Ithamar C. Sloan (Wis.).

Records.--Committee papers (38A-E23.5) and those referred to committee (38A-G25.5).

Select Committee on a Western National Armory

Authorized Feb. 1, 1864, "to inquire into the expediency and propriety of establishing a national armory at some point west of the Alleghany mountains"; appointed Feb. 2, to consist of Francis W. Kellogg (Mich.), James K. Moorhead (Pa.), John O'Neill (Ohio), Isaac N. Arnold (Ill.), Henry L. Dawes (Mass.), James F. McDowell (Ind.), William H. Randall (Ky.), Benjamin F. Loan (Mo.), and Charles A. Eldridge (Wis.).

Records.--Papers referred to the committee (38A-G25.2).

Select Committee to Investigate the Charge Against F. P. Blair, Jr.

Authorized and appointed Mar. 23, 1864, to investigate a charge made by Joseph W. McClurg (Mo.) against Francis P. Blair, Jr. (Mo.), "of violating the laws in the matter of an alleged liquor speculation, and to inquire into the genuineness or falsity of the alleged order for the purchase of liquor, bearing date June 3, 1863." (On the date in question Blair was a major general on duty near Vicksburg.) The committee consisted of William Higby (Calif.), Brutus J. Clay (Ky.), and John V. L. Pruyn (N. Y.).

There are no records of the committee as such. Its report, with the testimony heard, was printed as H. Rept. 61, 38 Cong., 1 sess., Serial 1206; the original is available (38A-D1).

Select Committee on Defenses of the Northeastern Frontier

Resolutions of the legislature of Maine, approved Mar. 25, 1864, asking the Federal Government to provide proper defenses for the northeastern frontier of that State, were referred with related memorials to a select committee authorized Apr. 25, 1864, and appointed the next day. The committee consisted of John H. Rice (Maine), John B. Alley (Mass.), Samuel S. Cox (Ohio), James T. Hale (Pa.), James W. Patterson (N. H.), William Radford (N. Y.), and John F. Driggs (Mich.). Its work called for "inquiry into systems of military defence, the value of railways as a means of attack and defence in time of war, and a careful consideration of the force of national obligation and of public faith growing out of the complex relations of federal and State governments under our national constitution." Its report (H. Rept. 119, 38 Cong., 1 sess., Serial 1207) accompanied H. R. 541.

Records.--Committee papers (38A-E23. 4).

Select Committee to Investigate Charges Against the Treasury Department

Under House resolution of Apr. 30, 1864, a committee was appointed on the same day to investigate and report upon the allegations made by Representatives Francis P. Blair, Jr. (Mo.) and James Brooks (N. Y.) and "any other allegations which have been or may be made affecting the integrity of the administration in the Treasury Department." The committee consisted of James A. Garfield (Ohio), James F. Wilson (Iowa), James Brooks (N. Y.), Henry Winter Davis (Md.), John T. Stuart (Ill.), Reuben E. Fenton (N. Y.), John L. Dawson (Pa.), Thomas A. Jenckes (R. I.), and William G. Steele (N. J.). It met intermittently from May 3 to June 29, 1864, and inquired into "the printing of the national securities in the Treasury Department, and the alleged immoralities of persons employed therein." Its report (H. Rept. 140, 38 Cong., 1 sess., Serial 1207) examines not only the organization and operations of the First Division of the Currency Bureau but the history of the printing of public money from the time when the Government first undertook to issue currency. The report also throws light on the investigative activities of Col. Lafayette C. Baker, Provost Marshal of the War Department, while he was detailed to the Secretary of the Treasury and during the deliberations of this committee. The committee's journal and the verbatim testimony are printed with its report.

There are no records of the committee as such, but its original report is available (38A-D1).

Select Committee on Invalid Pensions

Authorized Dec. 15, 1864, "to investigate all the facts and circumstances relating to the practical working of our pension laws as a system
of permanent relief to military or naval invalids; to inquire into the actual
and present condition of such invalids, and to report what measures, relating to their future disposition, will best secure to such of them as are
able to labor a life support, independent of a government pension." The
committee was appointed Dec. 20, 1864, to consist of John A. Griswold
(N. Y.), Kellian V. Whaley (W. Va.), Sidney Perham (Maine), William B.
Washburn (Mass.), William H. Miller (Pa.), John H. Hubbard (Conn.), and
Lewis W. Ross (Ill.).

There are no papers of the committee as such. Its report was printed
as H. Rept. 28, 38 Cong., 2 sess., Serial 1235; the original is available
(38A-D2).

Select Committee on Charges Against Lucien Anderson

Authorized Jan. 18, 1865, to investigate charges of "corruption, brib-
ery, and malfeasance" made against Representative Anderson (Ky.) by
Brig. Gen. Speed S. Fry and Col. John Mason Brown in Sept. 1864; ap-
pointed Jan. 19. As finally composed the committee consisted of Green
Clay Smith (Ky.), Glenni W. Scofield (Pa.), John T. Stuart (Ill.), John H.
Hubbard (Conn.), and James S. Rollins (Mo.).

There are no papers of the committee as such. Its report was printed
as H. Rept. 29, 38 Cong., 2 sess., Serial 1235; the original is available
(38A-D2).

Select Committee on Assault by A. P. Field on Hon. W. D. Kelley

Authorized Jan. 23, 1865, to inquire into an assault by Field (a claimant for a seat in the House from Louisiana) on Representative Kelley (Pa.),
occurring on Jan. 20. The committee was appointed Jan. 24, 1865, to consist of Fernando C. Beaman (Mich.), Edward H. Rollins (N. H.), James C.
Robinson (Ill.), John D. Baldwin (Mass.), and Dwight Townsend (N. Y.).

There are no papers of the committee as such. Its report, with the
testimony, was printed as H. Rept. 10, 38 Cong., 2 sess., Serial 1235;
the original is available (38A-D2).

Select Committee to Investigate Charges Against the Commissioner of Patents

Authorized Feb. 8, 1865, to investigate "charges of gross fraud and
corruption in office . . . against the Commissioner of Patents [D. P. Hol-
loway] and placed on the desks of the members of this house, and signed
by a gentleman who offers to prove the same"; appointed Feb. 10, 1865, to
consist of William Higby (Calif.), Augustus Frank (N. Y.), James H.
Cravens (Ind.), Sydenham E. Ancona (Pa.), and Jesse O. Norton (Ill.).
This committee's report was printed as H. Rept. 26, 38 Cong., 2 sess.,
Serial 1235.

Records.--Committee papers (38A-E23. 1).

Other Committees

Some House select committees of the 38th Congress do not appear to have reported or otherwise to have been active. These were the committees on a National Bankrupt Law (appointed Dec. 23, 1863); on the Purchase of Congressional Annals and Debates (appointed Mar. 14, 1864); and on Condition of the Indian Tribes (appointed Jan. 18, 1865). There are no committee papers as such of the Select Committee on the Chemist of the Department of Agriculture (appointed Jan. 20, 1864), but the original of its report (H. Rept. 35, 38 Cong., 1 sess., Serial 1206) is available (38A-D1). The same is true of the Select Committee on Allowing Heads of Departments Seats on the Floor (appointed Feb. 9, 1864) the original of whose report (H. Rept. 43, 38 Cong., 1 sess., Serial 1206) is available (38A-D1).

39TH CONGRESS

Select Committee on Freedmen

Authorized Dec. 6, 1865, as a committee to which was referred the part of the President's message of Dec. 4 that concerned the condition of freedmen; appointed Dec. 11, to consist of Thomas D. Eliot (Mass.), William D. Kelley (Pa.), Godlove S. Orth (Ind.), John A. Bingham (Ohio), Nelson Taylor (N. Y.), Benjamin F. Loan (Mo.), Josiah B. Grinnell (Iowa), Halbert E. Paine (Wis.), and Samuel S. Marshall (Ill.). This committee was later directed to inquire into the political and civil rights of freedmen, the desirability of an appropriation for needy whites and freedmen, and labor contracts between freedmen and their former masters in South Carolina. On Dec. 10, 1866, after the authorization of a standing Committee on Freedmen's Affairs, Dec. 4, the members of this committee were reappointed to the new standing committee.

The records of this select committee were inherited by the standing committee replacing it and are so described above.

Select Committee on the War Debts of the Loyal States

Authorized Dec. 11, 1865, as a committee to which was referred a bill (H. R. 5) "to reimburse the loyal States for advances made and debts contracted in support of the war for the preservation of the Union"; appointed Dec. 14, to consist of James G. Blaine (Maine), Samuel Hooper (Mass.), Benjamin F. Loan (Mo.), Benjamin M. Boyer (Pa.), William A. Darling (N. Y.), Tobias A. Plants (Ohio), and William A. Newell (N. J.). Isaac R. Hawkins (Tenn.) was appointed on Dec. 10, 1866.

There are no manuscript records of the committee. Its report was printed as H. Rept. 16, 39 Cong., 1 sess., Serial 1272.

Select Committee to Investigate Charges Against the Provost Marshal General's Bureau

Authorized Apr. 30, 1866, "to investigate the statements and charges made by Hon. Roscoe Conkling, in his place, last week, against Provost Marshal General Fry and his bureau; whether any frauds have been perpetrated in his office in connexion with the recruiting service; also to inquire into the statements made by General Fry in his communication to

Hon. Mr. Blaine, read in the House this day"; appointed May 1, 1866, to consist of Samuel Shellabarger (Ohio), Benjamin M. Boyer (Pa.), Burton C. Cook (Ill.), and Samuel L. Warner (Conn.).

There are no manuscript records of the committee. Its journal and the testimony taken are appended to its printed report (H. Rept. 93, 39 Cong., 1 sess., Serial 1272).

Select Committee to Investigate the Memphis Riots and Massacres

Authorized May 14, 1866, to investigate the riots in Memphis, which began on May 1, "and particularly to inquire into the origin, progress, and termination of the riotous proceedings, the names of the parties engaged in it, the acts of atrocity perpetrated, the number of killed and wounded, the amount and character of the property destroyed." Appointed May 14-15, 1866, to consist of Elihu B. Washburne (Ill.), John M. Broomall (Pa.), and George S. Shanklin (Ky.). The committee reached Memphis on May 22 and immediately proceeded with its investigations, which involved examining 170 witnesses.

Two other groups investigated this affair. One, a commission instituted by Maj. Gen. George Stoneman, commanding the Department of the Tennessee, had nearly completed its labors when the House committee arrived in Memphis. The other was instituted by Bvt. Maj. Gen. Clinton B. Fisk, Assistant Commissioner of the Freedmen's Bureau for the States of Kentucky and Tennessee. The testimony of witnesses before these commissions, "except where the same witnesses were examined by the committee, was verified as being such testimony, made a part of the record," and submitted with the report of the House committee.

There are no records of the committee as such. Its journal, the testimony, and various exhibits are appended to its printed report (H. Rept. 101, 39 Cong., 1 sess., Serial 1274); the original (incomplete) is available (39A-E1). The document depicts "the state of things" in Memphis at the time and certain conditions during and following the war, including particularly Negro-white relationships and the work of the Freedmen's Bureau.

Select Committee to Investigate the Assault by the Hon. Lovell H. Rousseau Upon the Hon. J. B. Grinnell

Authorized and appointed June 15, 1866, to investigate the assault on June 14 by Lovell H. Rousseau (Ky.) on Josiah B. Grinnell (Iowa), both Members of the House. The committee consisted of Rufus P. Spalding (Ohio), Nathaniel P. Banks (Mass.), John Hogan (Mo.), Henry J. Raymond (N. Y.), and Martin Russell Thayer (Pa.). To the committee's report (H. Rept. 90, 39 Cong., 1 sess., Serial 1272) is appended testimony on political attitudes in Kentucky during and after the war.

There are no papers of the committee as such, but its original report is available (39A-E1).

Select Committee to Investigate the Affairs of Southern Railroads

Authorized Dec. 4, 1866, "to examine into and report . . . the past and present relations existing between the federal government and the railroads in the States lately in rebellion," the amount of money spent by United States authorities during their operation of the roads, the amount of money owed by each of the railroad companies to the Government, "and all other facts that may be deemed of importance . . . also . . . what . . . would be the proper course to be taken by the government in regard to such railroads or railroad companies. " This committee, appointed on Dec. 10, 1866, consisted originally of Horace Maynard (Tenn.), Joseph W. McClurg (Mo.), Ulysses Mercur (Pa.), Henry D. Washburn (Ind.), and John W. Chanler (N. Y.). Philetus Sawyer (Wis.) was appointed later. It met from Dec. 13, 1866, until Mar. 2, 1867, took "a considerable amount of testimony, oral and documentary," but reached no conclusions. It was reappointed in the 40th Congress, on Mar. 27, 1867, with the same duties and powers, and on July 12, 1867, was instructed "to inquire into the expediency of reporting a bill declaring forfeited to the United States all lands granted by Congress, in the year 1856, to Mississippi, Alabama, Florida, Louisiana, and Arkansas, to aid in the construction of railroads. "

The committee's journal and the testimony it heard were printed in H Rept. 34, 39 Cong., 2 sess., Serial 1306 and H. Repts. 3 and 15, 40 Cong., 2 sess., Serial 1357. The first report (1, 055 p.) pertains primarily to Federal military use of Southern railroads during the war. It includes appended annual reports of some of the principal railroad companies for the war period; the testimony, among others, of Phil H. Sheridan, E. R. S. Canby, M. C. Meigs, and Edwin M. Stanton; and much information concerning the U. S. Military Railroads operating under General McCallum. The second report (130 p.) contains testimony taken from Oct. 18 to Dec. 10, 1867, relating primarily to both Union and Confederate use of the railroads during the war and to their wartime internal management. The third (53 p.) presents the committee's conclusions.

There are no records of the committee as such, but its original reports are available (39A-E2, 40A-E2).

Select Committee on the Murder of Union Soldiers in South Carolina

Authorized Dec. 6, 1866, to investigate the circumstances attending the murder of "three soldiers of the army of the United States . . . in October, 1865, in South Carolina, under circumstances of peculiar cruelty" and to determine "by whose procurement and action . . . reprieve, transfer, and discharge [of those condemned by a military commission for the murder] were made"; appointed Dec. 10, 1866, to consist of Frederick A. Pike (Maine), John F. Farnsworth (Ill.), and Edmund Cooper (Tenn.). This committee was directed subsequently to investigate and report on "the confinement in jail at Walterboro', South Carolina, of Henry Miller, under sentence of death, for the alleged crime of desertion from the rebel army and acting as a spy for General Sherman during the late war, and on pretence of highway robbery"; "the murder of Edward M. Knowles, first lieutenant, company K, 42d Indiana regiment, at Augusta, Georgia, in December, 1864, while a prisoner of war"; the murders of "a United States soldier named Crego, " at Nashville, Tenn., in Dec. 1866, of "Frank Erickson, a Union soldier," at Summerville, Tenn., in the same month, and of "Captain Montgomery . . . by confederate soldiers under the command of George W. Chilton, now seeking admission as a member of this house";and the "alleged punishment by publicly whipping citizens of the United States in North Carolina, and particularly at Raleigh and vicinity, and the burning alive of citizens in South Carolina while confined or imprisoned in jail. " The majority and minority reports, with the

testimony taken, were printed as H. Rept. 23, 39 Cong., 2 sess., Serial 1305.
   Records. --Committee papers (39A-F28. 2).

Select Committee on the New Orleans Riots

Authorized Dec. 6, 1866, to go to New Orleans and investigate "all
matters connected with the recent bloody riots in that city, which took place
the last of July and first of August, 1866"; appointed Dec. 10-18, to consist of Thomas D. Eliot (Mass.), Samuel Shellabarger (Ohio), and Benjamin M. Boyer (Pa.). On Dec. 17, 1866, this committee was directed to
investigate also the "alleged frauds in the New Orleans custom-house, and
the appointment of rebels therein. "
   There are no records of the committee as such. Its journal (Dec. 11,
1866- Feb. 2, 1867) and testimony taken are appended to its printed reports
(H. Rept. 16, 39 Cong., 2 sess., Serial 1304, and H. Rept. 25, 39 Cong.,
2 sess., Serial 1305), the originals of which are available (39A-E2). In
addition, H. Ex. Doc. 68, 39 Cong., 2 sess., Serial 1292, contains copies,
submitted by the Adjutant General's Office (Jan. 14, 1867), "of all reports
and testimony of military commissions and other papers relating to the
riot, " as well as the proceedings and report of an Army board convened to
investigate the matter; the original of the last is available (39A-G2). Both
reports, although dealing essentially with the postwar situation, throw light
on wartime conditions and events (for instance, the use of the city's fire
bells for signaling during the war).

Select Committee on Alleged Private Meetings of Members of the House
With a View to a Corrupt Bargain With the President

Authorized and appointed on Feb. 16, 1867, to inquire whether any
Members of the House had met privately with others "with a view to a
corrupt bargain, " in case the report of the Committee on the Judiciary,
then considering the impeachment of President Johnson, should present a
report unfavorable to the President. The committee consisted of John
Wentworth (Ill.), Adam J. Glossbrenner (Pa.), and Henry Van Aernam
(N. Y.).
   Records. --Committee papers (39A-F28. 1).

40TH CONGRESS

Select Committee on the Assassination of President Lincoln

Authorized and appointed July 8, 1867, by a House resolution the pre-
amble of which asserted that "no investigation of all the facts and circumstances connected with the assassination of the late lamented President. . .
has been had by competent authority, tending to show who were the persons
engaged in the conspiracy to do the act, its inducement, its objects, its
instruments, and the means of its accomplishment. " The committee's
members were Benjamin F. Butler (Mass.), Samuel Shellabarger (Ohio),
George W. Julian (Ind.), Hamilton Ward (N. Y.), and Samuel J. Randall
(Pa.).
   The committee made no report. There are no records of the committee
as such, but the Butler papers in the Library of Congress contain items relating to its work.

Select Committee on the Treatment of Prisoners of War and Union Citizens

Authorized July 10, 1867, to investigate "the treatment of prisoners of war and Union citizens held by the confederate authorities during the recent rebellion"; appointed July 11, to consist of John P. C. Shanks (Ind.), William A. Pile (Mo.), Abner C. Harding (Ill.), Aaron F. Stevens (N. H.), and William Mungen (Ohio). In its Report on the Treatment of Prisoners of War, by the Rebel Authorities, During the War of the Rebellion (H. Rept. 45, 40 Cong., 3 sess., Serial 1391) the committee covered only the "first part of the subject assigned," informing the House that it could not "make full report touching the treatment of Union citizens so held." "Impressed with the magnitude and importance" of its work, the committee considered that it had "endeavored . . . to give the House and the country a faithful and true official history of the wrongs and sufferings endured by the national soldiers and loyal citizens at the hands of the confederate authorities."

The field of inquiry was so extensive, "necessarily embracing nearly every State of the Union," that different members of the committee were assigned to collect and arrange preliminary information from different areas of the country. The first formal personal testimony was taken in Boston from 92 witnesses, Oct. 16-Nov. 2, 1867; later, 22 witnesses were examined at Washington and 25 at St. Louis. These, the committee held, "were selected from different sections of the country, from every arm of the military service, and from almost every grade in these various branches." Their testimony covered prison life; treatment of prisoners by Confederate officers and men; the food and shelter provided; "their treatment when sick; the barbarous methods resorted to in order to induce them to enlist in the rebel army, and in fact everything necessary to make up a complete history of the whole scope of life and suffering in southern prisons."

The committee had access to the records of the Wirz trial, the captured Confederate records, and the official documents of the War Department. Excerpts from these, a special report from the War Department, the testimony taken, and statements sent in response to a circular issued by the committee are printed with its report. These papers include a "Consolidated Statement of the Number of Federal Soldiers in Service, Died, Captured, Paroled, Exchanged, Died in Rebel Prisons, Escaped, Enlisted in Confederate Service, &c., and the number of Confederate Soldiers Captured, Paroled, Exchanged, Died, Escaped, Enlisted in the United States Service, &c., during the Rebellion of 1861-65. as shown by the records of the Adjutant General's Office"; also a "Detailed Statement of the Number of Confederate Prisoners of War Captured by the Federal Forces, Paroled, Exchanged, Released on taking Oath of Allegiance, Escaped from Federal Authorities, Enlisted in the United States Service, and the Number Unaccounted for during the Rebellion of 1861-65, as shown by Records of Confederate Prisoners of War filed in the Adjutant General's Office."

There are no records of the committee as such. The original of its report (incomplete) is available (40A-E3).

Select Committee on Soldiers' and Sailors' Bounties

Authorized and appointed July 18, 1867, to consult the Paymaster General and the Second Auditor of the Treasury on transferring all claims arising under the bounty bill of July 1866 from the Paymaster General to the Second Auditor, "and how far the use of the muster rolls of the army in the Adjutant General's office can be made available in facilitating the adjustment of said bounties." The committee was composed of Henry D. Washburn (Ind.), Halbert E. Paine (Wis.), and James Lawrence Getz (Pa.). On July 19, 1867, it was authorized to inquire into the cause of delay in paying bounties. Its report was printed as H. Rept. 5, 40 Cong., 2 sess., Serial 1357.

Records.--Committee papers (40A-F28.3).

Select Commitee on Reconstruction

Appointed Dec. 10, 1867, as a House select committee after the termination of the Joint Committee on Reconstruction of the 39th Congress; composed originally of Thaddeus Stevens (Pa.), George S. Boutwell (Mass.), John A. Bingham (Ohio), John F. Farnsworth (Ill.), Calvin T. Hulburd (N. Y.), Fernando C. Beaman (Mich.). Halbert E. Paine (Wis.), James Brooks (N. Y.), and James B. Beck (Ky.). On Dec. 7, 1868, the committee was directed to "examine into the condition of public affairs" in Virginia, Mississippi, Texas, and Georgia; on Dec. 14, 1868, to investigate the "Ku-Klux outrages . . . practiced upon peaceable and law-abiding citizens of the United States in the State of Tennessee and elsewhere"; and on Jan. 28, 1869, to make an inquiry concerning the representation of Georgia in the House under the Reconstruction Act of Mar. 2, 1867 (14 Stat. 428).

Reports of the committee were printed as H. Repts. 10 and 21, 40 Cong., 2 sess., Serial 1357; H. Rept. 74, 40 Cong., 2 sess., Serial 1358; H. Rept. 108, 41 Cong., 2 sess., Serial 1438; and H. Rept. 37, 41 Cong., 3 sess., Serial 1464. For the committee's hearings see H. Misc. Doc. 52 and 53, 40 Cong., 3 sess., Serial 1385.

Records. 40th Cong.--Applications for the removal of legal or political disabilities imposed by the Fourteenth Amendment (40A-H21.1 to 40A-H21.22); papers pertaining to impeachment of the President (40A-H21.24), the proposed partition of Texas (40A-H21.25), reconstruction in Virginia (40A-H21.26), starvation in South Carolina (40A-H21.27), and various problems of reconstruction (40A-H21.28). 41st Cong.--Committee papers (41A-F28.2); petitions, memorials, etc., on the removal of legal and political disabilities (41A-H18.1) and other subjects (41A-H18.2). There are also a docket and 4 index volumes covering both the 40th Congress and the 41st (40A-F28.4).

Select Committee on the Impeachment of the President

Under House resolutions of Feb. 24, 1868, introduced by Thaddeus Stevens, two select committees were appointed: (1) a committee to inform the Senate that the House would, in due time, "exhibit particular articles of impeachment" against President Johnson and "make good the same" and to "demand that the Senate take order for the appearance of said Andrew Johnson to answer to said impeachment"; and (2) a committee to prepare and report the articles of impeachment. To the former were appointed Thaddeus Stevens (Pa.) and John A. Bingham (Ohio). To the latter were appointed George S. Boutwell (Mass.), Thaddeus Stevens (Pa.), John A. Bingham (Ohio), James F. Wilson (Iowa), John A. Logan (Ill.), George W. Julian (Ind.), and Hamilton Ward (N. Y.).

Records.--Papers referred to the latter committee (40A-H20. 1).

Select Committee on Alleged Corruption in the Impeachment Trial

By a House resolution of May 16, 1868, the managers of the impeachment of President Johnson were converted into a committee "to investigate whether improper or corrupt influences have been used to influence the determination of the Senate upon the articles of impeachment exhibited by the House of Representatives against the President of the United States." The managers to conduct the impeachment were Thaddeus Stevens (Pa.), John A. Bingham (Ohio), George S. Boutwell (Mass.), James F. Wilson (Iowa), Benjamin F. Butler (Mass.), Thomas Williams (Pa.), and John A. Logan (Ill.).

There are no papers of the committee as such. Its report was printed as H. Rept. 75, 40 Cong., 2 sess., Serial 1358. See also H. Rept. 44, 40 Cong., 2 sess., Serial 1357.

44TH CONGRESS

Select Committee to Investigate the Affairs of the Freedman's Savings and Trust Co.

Authorized Jan. 5, 1876, "to ascertain . . . the causes of failure, the parties responsible therefor, the nature, character, and value of all collateral and other securities"; appointed Jan. 10, to consist of Beverly B. Douglas (Va.), Taul Bradford (Ala.), William S. Stenger (Pa.), Haywood Y. Riddle (Tenn.), Charles E. Hooker (Miss.), Archibald M. Bliss (N. Y.), Charles B. Farwell (Ill.), Rufus S. Frost (Mass.), and Joseph H. Rainey (S. C.). The committee's report (H. Rept. 502, 44 Cong., 1 sess., Serial 1710) is introduced by a history of the bank, which was chartered by an act of Mar. 3, 1865 (13 Stat. 510), and prints the testimony taken.

Records. 44th Cong.--Docket (44A-F39. 8).

46TH-48TH CONGRESSES

Select Committee on the Payment of Pensions, Bounty, and Back Pay

Authorized Jan. 12, 1880, "to examine and inquire into the method and manner of payment of pensions, arrears of pensions, bounty, and back pay, and to ascertain whether any irregularities exist in the payment of the same"; appointed Jan. 23, 1880, and reappointed in the 47th and 48th Congresses.

Records. 46th Cong.--Minutes (46A-F41. 2); committee papers (46A-F41. 1); referred papers (46A-H28. 1). 47th Cong.--Committee papers (47A-F33. 1); referred papers concerning bounty payment to Union veterans of the Civil War (47A-H25. 1), legislation to increase pensions of veteran amputees (47A-H25. 2), pensions for Union soldiers who had been confined in Confederate prisons (47A-H25. 3), repeal of the limitations clause of the Arrears of Pension Act (47A-H25. 4), and other subjects (47A-H25. 5). 48th Cong.--Committee papers (48A-F43. 1); referred papers concerning compensation of Civil War veterans for loss of income resulting from wartime

inflation (48A-H34. 1), equalization of bounties (48A-H34. 2), land grants for
Union veterans (48A-H34. 3), legislation for the benefit of Union veterans
who had been prisoners of war (48A-H34. 4), pensions for all honorably discharged Union veterans (48A-H34. 5), pensions for disabled veterans (48A-
H34. 6), recommendations for passage of bills affecting veterans' welfare
(48A-H34. 7), revision of pension rates for commissioned officers of volunteers (48A-H34. 8), widows' pensions (48A-H34. 9), and other matters (48A-
H34. 10).

III.   THE JUDICIARY

The judicial power of the United States was vested by Article III of the Constitution in a Supreme Court and such inferior courts as Congress might establish.   The jurisdiction of the Federal courts was declared to extend to all cases in law and equity arising under the Constitution, the laws of the United States, and treaties; to cases affecting ambassadors, other public ministers, and consuls; to admiralty and maritime cases; and to suits involving the United States, between two or more States, between a State and citizens of another State, between citizens of different States, between citizens of the same State claiming lands under grants of different States, and between a State or its citizens and foreign nations, citizens, or subjects.   In cases affecting ambassadors, other public ministers, and consuls and in those to which a State was a party the Supreme Court was to have original jurisdiction.   The provisions of the Constitution regarding the judiciary were implemented by the Judiciary Act of Sept. 24, 1789 (1 Stat. 73), which established the Supreme Court, circuit courts, and district courts.   These courts and the Federal courts established in the Territories by later acts of Congress are discussed below.   In most of the Southern States Federal courts did not function during the Civil War; for these States the Confederate court records are discussed in the accompanying Guide to the Archives of the Government of the Confederate States of America.   Federal courts that functioned during part of the Civil War period in some Southern States--Arkansas, Florida, Louisiana, and Virginia--and courts in the border States--Kentucky, Missouri, and Tennessee--are, however, discussed below.

SUPREME COURT OF THE UNITED STATES

Besides providing original jurisdiction to the Supreme Court in some of the cases mentioned above, the Constitution in Article VI declared the Constitution, the laws of the United States, and the treaties to be the "supreme Law of the Land."   The power of judicial review that the Supreme Court came to exercise in determining the constitutionality of State and lower Federal court decisions and of Federal and State statutes made the Court a body of great importance in the Government.

At the time of Lincoln's inauguration the authorized membership of the Supreme Court was a Chief Justice and eight Associate Justices (act of Mar. 3, 1837; 5 Stat. 176).   There were then two vacancies caused by the deaths of Peter V. Daniel and John McLean, and on Apr. 15, 1861, John A. Campbell resigned to join the Confederates.   In 1862 Lincoln appointed three Republicans--Noah H. Swayne, Samuel F. Miller, and David Davis--as

79

Associate Justices, and in the following year he designated Stephen J. Field, a Democrat friendly to the Union, to fill the ninth associate justice-ship, created by an act of Mar. 3, 1863 (12 Stat. 794). After the death of Chief Justice Roger B. Taney in Dec. 1864, Lincoln appointed Salmon P. Chase, who had been Secretary of the Treasury, as Chief Justice. When Associate Justice John Catron died in the spring of 1865, Lincoln's ap-pointees became a majority of the court, and the vacancy was not filled.

During the Civil War the Supreme Court met on the first Monday in December and continued in session until the following March or April. In the other months of the year the justices sat on the circuit courts to which they were assigned, usually in the circuits where they resided.

The staff of the Supreme Court consisted of a Reporter, a Clerk, a Deputy Clerk, a Marshal, and a crier. Benjamin C. Howard, who had been Reporter since 1843, resigned on Sept. 13, 1861; Jeremiah S. Black, formerly chief judge of the supreme court of Pennsylvania and Attorney General under Buchanan, was appointed Reporter in December 1861. When Black resigned in Mar. 1864 to practice law, he was succeeded by another Pennsylvania law-yer, John W. Wallace, who some years before had been reporter of the U. S. Circuit Court for the Third Circuit. Wallace continued as Reporter until 1876. In the lucrative post of Clerk, William T. Carroll served from 1827 until his death on July 13, 1863. He was succeeded by Daniel W. Middleton, who had been the deputy clerk. The Clerk was responsible for preparing the records of the Court. The Marshal of the District of Colum-bia, a position to which President Lincoln appointed Ward H. Lamon on July 26, 1861, had the additional duty of serving, executing, and process-ing the orders and decrees of the Supreme Court. The crier performed the minor functions of proclaiming the orders of the Court and announcing that it was in session or that it had adjourned.

At the outbreak of the Civil War, with Congress not in session, the protection of the Nation had to be undertaken by the Executive. To preserve the Union, the President or the heads of departments acting on his authority adopted various measures the constitutionality of which became a subject of controversy and sometimes of judicial determination. A blockade of the Southern coast was proclaimed; the enlargement of the Army and Navy be-yond their legal limits was authorized; the writ of habeas corpus was sus-pended; military arrest and military trial, censorship, and military sup-pression of newspapers were instituted; and "disloyal" newspapers were excluded from the mails. Congress later passed acts of doubtful consti-tutionality, including those relating to confiscation, suspension of the writ of habeas corpus, the income tax, conscription, paper money, the test oath, and the partition of Virginia.

Most of the constitutional issues raised by wartime acts of the Execu-tive and Congress were not determined by the Supreme Court during the war. Because the complexion of the Court was uncertain, the administra-tion did not press cases upon the Court; and the Court itself sought to avoid making decisions on the constitutional aspects of cases in order not to har-ass the administration. But the Court did consider a number of war-related cases. In Ex parte Gordon--involving Nathaniel Gordon, who had been found guilty of engaging in the African slave trade and had been condemned to death by the U. S. Circuit Court for the Southern District of New York-- the Supreme Court declined on Feb. 17, 1862, to review the case, since it had been considered by a court of competent jurisdiction. In the important prize cases decided on Mar. 10, 1862, the Court sustained the legality of the President's proclamation of blockade and other executive acts. In two cases in the December Term 1863--the legal tender case (Roosevelt v. Meyer) and a habeas corpus case (Ex parte Vallandigham)--the Court avoided the determination of constitutionality by declaring it had no jurisdiction. Two cases in the following term--The Schooner Andromeda and Mrs. Alexander's Cotton--involved enemy property. Some cases decided early in 1865 concerned the end of the blockade, and in other prize cases the Court established the doctrine of "continuous voyage" and ulterior destination. In the same session several decisions on slavers (Kate, Sarah, Weathergage, and Reindeer), against which libels of forfeiture had been filed in the District Court for the Southern District of New York, were upheld.

Most of the business of the Supreme Court during the war was routine. Many of the cases heard involved titles to mining claims and to lands in California that had been acquired under Spanish and Mexican grants. Other cases concerned such matters as arbitration, bank collections, bankruptcy, bridges, collision at sea, contracts and charters, corporate problems, estates, ferry rights, import duties, the jurisdiction of the Court, mortgages, partnerships, patent rights, the right of appeal, ships' cargo, State laws, tariff taxes imposed by States and cities, and usury. Much of the litigation was of the petty sort that the Court later refused to review.

For years after 1865 the Supreme Court rendered decisions related to the war. These concerned military tribunals, provisional courts, the status of the Confederate States and their legislation, the effect of pardon and amnesty upon the rights of claimants for property seized during the war, the power of judges to interfere by habeas corpus with military custody, the rights of citizens not in military service, rights of officers and soldiers in enemy territory, the duration of the war, debts to an enemy, reimbursement to States for funds spent for equipping troops, contracts, and trading with or for the enemy. Other decisions related to acts of Congress, including confiscation, abandoned and captured property, the test oath, income tax, direct tax, license tax, and paper money (legal tender cases). Cases also arose from the civil rights acts adopted after the war and from the Civil War amendments to the Constitution. The determination of these constitutional questions enhanced the power of the Federal Government and established precedents for Federal action in later national emergencies.

In Dec. 1866 the Supreme Court again began to hear cases appealed from Federal courts and State supreme courts in the Southern States. Cases from those States, which had been docketed in the December terms of 1859 and 1860, had been continued from term to term during the war and were finally decided from 1866 to 1868.

Chief Justices during the war period, with dates of appointment:

> Roger B. Taney, Mar. 15, 1836.
> Salmon P. Chase, Dec. 6, 1864.

Associate Justices:

> James M. Wayne, Jan. 9, 1835.
> John Catron, Mar. 8, 1837.
> Robert C. Grier, Aug. 4, 1846.
> Nathan Clifford, Jan. 12, 1858.
> Noah H. Swayne, Jan. 24, 1862.
> Samuel F. Miller, July 16, 1862.
> David Davis, Dec. 8, 1862.
> Stephen J. Field, Mar. 10, 1863.

Hampton L. Carson, The History of the Supreme Court of the United States . . . (Philadelphia, 1902. 2 vols.); Felix Frankfurter and James M. Landis, The Business of the Supreme Court; a Study in the Federal Judicial System (New York, 1928); James G. Randall, Constitutional Problems Under Lincoln (Urbana, Ill., 1951); David M. Silver, Lincoln's Supreme Court (Urbana, Ill., 1956); Charles Warren, The Supreme Court in United States History (Boston, 1926. 2 vols.). See also Dorothy L. (Campbell) Tompkins, comp., The Supreme Court of the United States; a Bibliography (Berkeley, Calif., 1959).

Record Group 267. --Most of the records of the Supreme Court consist of case files and related records. The extensive series of appellate case files, 1792-1909, comprise principally transcripts of cases appealed from U. S. circuit and district courts and from supreme courts of States and Territories. For the December Term 1860 through the December Term 1864 there are 623 cases in 92 boxes. Besides transcripts the case files contain other documents concerning Court proceedings, including charts, maps, drawings, other exhibits, correspondence, and judgments. The transcripts comprise a variety of legal documents developing the facts in the case and the action of the lower courts; in some kinds of cases, such as prize cases, the variety is greater than in others. A chronological record of cases filed is in dockets, which show the title of each case, the court from which it was appealed, the documents filed and the date of filing, and the disposition of the case. More useful in finding any particular case is a card index to appellate cases, arranged alphabetically by names of parties, which gives the number under which each case is filed. There were only 33 original jurisdiction case files for the years 1860-64; and some of these, including Ex parte Vallandigham, are apparently missing. These cases are entered in the front of the rough dockets; the documents include complaints, answers, replications, affidavits, subpenas, orders, judgments, and some correspondence. The case files constitute an important source not only for constitutional history but also for social, economic, local, and maritime history and for biography.

The covers on the transcripts in the appellate case files show Court actions, and the related documents are in the same files. One file of manuscript and printed opinions, both containing revisions, is arranged by case number. Engrossed copies are bound by terms in volumes, which contain indexes of the names of parties. These files contain numerous opinions that do not appear in the published reports. Opinions in original jurisdiction cases are in a separate file. With the transcripts, however, are copies of mandates or prescripts to lower courts communicating the judgment of the Supreme Court in order that appropriate execution or proceedings could be taken. Mandates missing from this series can sometimes be found in a file of duplicate mandates. The case correspondence on appellate cases, 1793-1910, contains letters received, telegrams, drafts of letters sent, orders, decrees, and judgments. Arranged by appellate case number, this correspondence documents the handling of the cases by the Court. The small amount of correspondence in original jurisdiction cases, 1855-1909, contains only a few papers for the war period.

A chronological record of the proceedings of the Court is in minute books. The engrossed minutes contain data relating not only to cases but also to appointments of Court personnel, including their commissions, oaths of office, and bonds; attendance of Justices; orders for the admissions of attorneys to the bar of the Supreme Court; addresses by Attorneys General introducing their successors; commissions of Attorneys General; memorial proceedings for deceased Justices; the swearing in of Justices; resignations; and the forming of rules for the Court. Occasional pieces of correspondence, such as Taney's letter to the Secretary of the Treasury, Feb. 16, 1863, protesting against the income tax on the salaries of judges of Federal courts, are also entered in the minutes.

Admissions of attorneys to practice before the bar of the Court can be ascertained from several records. Attorney rolls, 1790-1909, contain in chronological order the signatures of attorneys admitted. Several alphabetical lists in volumes give the dates of admission of attorneys and their places of residence. An alphabetical card index supplies the same information. The published United States Reports list the names of attorneys admitted at each session of the Court.

Various records maintained by the Clerk of the Court give information on other aspects of its management. A file of letters received, 1806-87, contains letters from attorneys, the Assistant Attorney General, solicitors of the executive departments, railroads, banks, publishers of law journals, clerks of State courts, and others, forwarding transcripts of records of lower courts and fee bonds, requesting information on the outcome of cases and copies of pertinent documents, recommending appointments, or enclosing drafts in payment of court costs. Litigants submitted fee bonds of $200 as guarantee for the payment of costs of suits. An account of actual fees charged by the Clerk for individual cases is in the fee books, 1818-1909. Copies of bills on printed forms, issued to law firms for the costs of suits, are also available for 1803-77. Other small files include administrative orders of the Court and oaths of loyalty taken, 1864-66, by members of the bar.

Records available on microfilm: minutes, 1790-1950 (M 215); dockets, 1791-1950 (M 216); attorney rolls, 1790-1951 (M 217).

James R. Browning and Bess Glenn, "The Supreme Court Collection at the National Archives," American Journal of Legal History, 4: 241-256 (July 1960). After 1817 the Supreme Court employed reporters to prepare reports upon cases decided by the Court, for publication under contracts with private publishers. These reports provided lawyers and the Justices themselves with an ever-increasing store of precedents upon which to draw in handling new cases. The full title of the official edition of Supreme Court reports is Reports of Cases Argued and Adjudged in the Supreme Court of the United States [December Term 1860- December Term 1865](Washington, W. H. & O. H. Morrison, 1861-67; vols. 65-70 U. S. Rep.). The first 90 volumes of the reports are usually cited by the names of the reporters instead of as "U. S. Rep." The reports contain summaries of the facts in the cases and opinions and judgments of the Justices. Black used the summary prepared by the Justice as well as the text of the Justice's opinion. Wallace prepared his own summaries of the facts or used those of the Justices if they preferred him to do so. Not all cases decided by the Court were reported; both Black and Wallace omitted many cases for which there were opinions (131 U. S. Rep., appendix, xvii). A few additional cases of the Civil War period appear in 131, 154 U. S. Rep., appendixes. Changes were made in some of the

opinions reported by Wallace, presumably with the approval of the
Justices who authored them. The
exhaustion of the supply of the Reports and the need for a complete
and uniform edition resulted in the
publication by the Lawyers' Cooperative Publishing Co. of an unofficial reprint entitled United States
Supreme Court Reports; Cases Argued and Decided in the Supreme
Court of the United States (Newark
and Rochester, N. Y., 1882-date).
Printed in uniform type in compact
double-column pages, this "Lawyers'
Edition"--cited as U. S. Rep. (L.
Ed.)--contains all the cases in the
official edition from 1790, including
those in 131 and 154 U.S. Rep. appendixes; it also contains annotations, tables of references to cases
in later volumes of the series and
in circuit and district court reports,
and an index to the tables. In connection with the reports see George
E. Wire, "Index to Memoirs, Orders
and Rules of Court, Admissions to
the Bar, and Other Interesting Material Found in United States Supreme Court Reports, Volumes One
to Two Hundred and Ninety-one, Inclusive," Law Library Journal,

28:27-39 (Jan. 1935).

Because law reports are published in chronological order, law
publishing companies have devised
digests to serve as indexes. The
thoroughness and completeness of
these digests make legal literature
the best indexed of all professional
literature. The digests serve as
subject indexes to the reported
cases and contain tables of cases,
defendant-plaintiff tables, word and
phrase indexes, cases listed by popular name, descriptive-word indexes,
indexes to annotations, and tables of
statutes by popular name. The principal digests for Supreme Court reports are the following: United States
Supreme Court Digest 1754 to Date
(St. Paul, Minn., West Publishing
Co., 1943-date); and Digest of United
States Supreme Court Reports (Rochester, N. Y., Lawyers' Cooperative
Publishing Co., 1948-date). Volume
14 of the latter digest contains the
following useful tables: "Table of
Laws Cited and Construed" and Ta-
bles of Cases Affirmed, Reversed,
Reheard, etc., in the Supreme Court."
The American Digest and the Federal
Digest, cited below, also cover the
Supreme Court reports.

Records in Other Custody. -- The Supreme Court has retained printed
records and briefs of its cases. Printing of the records in the case files
began in 1832 in small editions, primarily for the use of the Court and the
lawyers, but some copies have been distributed to libraries of law schools
and bar associations. The set in the Supreme Court library is arranged by
term and docket number. In the three other libraries (the Law Library of
Congress, the Library of the Association of the Bar of the City of New York,
and the Philadelphia Bar Association Library) that have printed records and
briefs from the beginning, they are arranged by U. S. citation. For the 6
volumes (65-70 U. S. Rep.) covering the Civil War period there are 42 volumes of records and briefs. The complete set numbers hundreds of volumes, and those for later years are also available in other libraries. The
Law Library of Congress lends volumes of which it has second copies.

H. C. Hallam, Jr., and Edward
G. Hudon, "United States Supreme
Court Records and Briefs; a Union
List, With a Note on Their Distri-
bution and Microfilming," Law
Library Journal, 40:82-82 (May
1947).

Collections of papers of the Chief Justices and some Associate Justices have been preserved. The principal groups of Taney papers are in the Maryland Historical Society, the Library of Congress, and the Taney House in Frederick, Md.; other papers are in the Historical Society of Pennsylvania, the North Carolina Department of Archives and History, the William L. Clements Library, and Dickinson College. The Chase papers are chiefly in the Historical Society of Pennsylvania and the Library of Congress, but scattered correspondence is in many other places. The manuscripts of Nathan Clifford are in the Maine Historical Society. The papers of Stephen J. Field are in the University of California and the Oregon Historical Society. The Library of Congress has the main group of papers of John McLean. Willard L. King of Chicago has made a collection of microfilm copies of the papers of David Davis from family and other sources in the course of preparing a biography. A box of legal documents of Noah H. Swayne is in the Ohio Historical Society. Some papers of Samuel Nelson are in the New York State Historical Association and among the Clifford papers in Maine.

U. S. DISTRICT AND CIRCUIT COURTS

Under the article of the Constitution granting it authority to establish inferior courts, Congress by the Judiciary Act of 1789 divided the country into 13 judicial districts and 3 judicial circuits. The district and circuit courts are discussed together in this section because (1) the powers of district and circuit courts in some cases coincided, (2) in some of the western States during the Civil War the district court judges were empowered to hold circuit courts without the presence of a Supreme Court justice, and (3) when the old circuit courts were finally abolished in 1912 their records and business were transferred to the district courts.

In 1789 each of the original colonies participating in the Revolution (except Rhode Island and North Carolina, which had not yet ratified the Constitution) was set up as a district, for which the President was to appoint a single judge. Maine, then part of Massachusetts, and Kentucky, then part of Virginia, were made separate judicial districts. Appeals could be taken from decisions of the district courts to the circuit courts.

In later years, as Territories became States, Congress created new judicial districts and divided some of the more populous States into two districts. (The courts in the Territories were also established by Congress later and during the Territorial period were Federal courts.)

The district courts handled principally criminal, admiralty, and bankruptcy cases and suits brought by the United States. These courts, as well as the circuit courts, had original jurisdiction in cases involving crimes and offenses against the laws of the United States, cases in which aliens sued for torts in violation of international law or of treaties, and suits at common law in which the United States or its officers were involved and in which the amount exceeded $100. Cases arising under an act of Mar. 3, 1845 (5 Stat. 732), to prevent "frauds on the revenues of the Post Office Department" and violations of the franking privilege, could be prosecuted before circuit, district, and Territorial courts. The same courts could determine violations of the act to provide a national currency (June 3, 1864, 13 Stat. 116). Both district and circuit courts could determine the extradition of alleged criminals, and they and the State courts were empowered to naturalize aliens.

The district courts had original cognizance in admiralty and maritime cases, including seizures under U. S. customs, navigation, or trade acts; and in suits against consuls and vice consuls. Admiralty jurisdiction was interpreted by the Supreme Court to extend not only over the high seas but also over such interior waters as navigable lakes, rivers, and canals. Besides the registry, licensing, regulation, inspection, navigation, and seizure and forfeiture of vessels and cargo, American admiralty law is concerned with prizes, ransom, military salvage, titles to vessels, actions to recover ships, and maritime contracts and torts.

Congress enlarged the jurisdiction of the district courts by various acts. The limited criminal jurisdiction conferred by the Judiciary Act of 1789 was extended by an act of Aug. 23, 1842 (5 Stat. 517), to all crimes and offenses against the United States not punishable by death.

The district courts exercised a limited equity jurisdiction also. To protect the personal liberty of citizens of the United States, the Constitution prohibits the suspension of the writ of habeas corpus except in cases of rebellion or invasion. Accordingly the Judiciary Act of 1789 gave to all U. S. courts the power to issue writs of habeas corpus. The President, however, suspended the writ in 1861; and Congress by an act of Mar. 3, 1863 (12 Stat. 755), authorized him to suspend it when necessary for the public safety.

In addition to normal peacetime litigation, the district courts soon after the outbreak of the Civil War were flooded with other kinds of cases. Under their admiralty powers these courts determined the legality of the seizure of vessels and cargoes by the U. S. Navy. Many prize cases were adjudicated by district courts at New York, Boston, Philadelphia, Providence, Baltimore, Washington, Key West, New Orleans, and Springfield, Ill. Under an act to define and punish conspiracy (July 31, 1861; 12 Stat. 284) and an act to suppress insurrection, punish treason and rebellion, and confiscate the property of Confederates (July 17, 1862; 12 Stat. 589), indictments for treason were brought in many districts. The law authorized the seizure of property of Confederate Government officials and certain other classes of "rebels." The forfeiture of property was made a judicial process enforceable through U. S. district, circuit, and Territorial courts, under the direction of the Attorney General and district attorneys. Confiscation suits were necessarily limited to areas where Federal courts were in operation, and the actual property confiscated was chiefly in the North. Even there, although many cases were instituted, not much property was confiscated; for most cases were dismissed, appealed, adjusted, or decided in favor of the owner. In 1861 began a vigorous campaign to prosecute in the district courts persons engaged in the slave trade. Under the provisions of the act for collecting direct taxes in insurrectionary districts (June 7, 1862, 12 Stat. 424, sec. 8), appeals for the redemption of lands sold for payment of the taxes (discussed elsewhere in this Guide under Department of the Treasury) could be made to the district courts. These courts also were given jurisdiction (act of Mar. 2, 1863, 12 Stat. 698) of cases against persons in the military and naval service who attempted to defraud the Government by presenting fictitious claims. Cases involving loyalty oaths occurred during and after the war. By an act of Feb. 13, 1862 (12 Stat. 339), persons conveying spirituous liquor to Indians on reservations were made liable to prosecution in district courts and to punishment by fine and imprisonment.

The district courts, of course, needed other officials besides the judges. The President was empowered by the Judiciary Act of 1789 to appoint district attorneys and marshals, the former to act as prosecuting counsel for the Government and the latter to function as administrative officers of the courts. Later on, the courts were also provided with U. S. commissioners, who issued warrants for the arrest of persons charged with offenses against Federal law; determined whether they should be imprisoned or admitted to bail; enforced decisions of foreign consuls and vice consuls in controversies involving vessels of their respective nations; issued warrants for the arrest of fugitives from foreign justice and of deserting seamen; and took stipulations in admiralty suits. The clerks of the courts, appointed by the judges, did the paperwork and kept the records. District attorneys, marshals, and clerks were compensated by fees, which were regulated by act of Congress (Aug. 16, 1856; 11 Stat. 49). The judges approved the accounts of those officials in the States and the Territories before their transmission to the Secretary of the Interior. All court officials were required to take the loyalty oath prescribed by an act of July 2, 1862 (12 Stat. 502). Another act required the oath of allegiance from men summoned to serve as jurors, veniremen, or talesmen (June 17, 1862; 12 Stat. 430). This requirement automatically disqualified those who had fought for the Confederacy or had given aid to the "rebellion."

As the States in the South seceded from the Union the judges of the U. S. district courts there resigned their commissions or became inactive. District judges of the Confederacy took their places and sometimes even continued to use the same record books. (The judge of the Southern District of Florida remained loyal to the United States.) When areas of the South were taken by Union forces, the President appointed new judges; and before the end of hostilities Federal courts were thus reestablished in the Northern District of Florida, the Eastern District of Louisiana, the Eastern District of Virginia, the District of Arkansas, and the districts in Tennessee.

President Johnson's proclamations, May-July 1865, for the restoration of State governments in the South directed the resumption of sessions of the U. S. courts. It was difficult, however, to find persons who could take the test oath required by the act of July 2, 1862; consequently the appointment of judges and other court officials was delayed. Lawyers likewise were prohibited from practicing before any Federal courts unless they subscribed to the same oath (act of Jan. 24, 1865; 13 Stat. 424). In Texas the antebellum judges, having had no Confederate service, were able to reopen the courts after obtaining other court personnel. Judges were appointed in North Carolina and Georgia in 1865 and in South Carolina and Mississippi in the spring of 1866.

The types of records developed by the Federal courts were early standardized and were similar to those used by the courts of the English seaboard colonies, which in turn had been based on English models. The most important records for the history of the courts are the minutes, which present a record of their activities and give information on sessions, judges, judgments and orders, findings and verdicts of juries, sentences, agreements for the settlement of cases, names of attorneys admitted to practice, names of grand and petit jurors, appointments of court officials, orders for the naturalization of aliens, approval of administrative accounts, and rules of practice. The diverse papers relating to individual cases are usually filed in several types of case files according to area of jurisdiction such as law, equity, chancery, criminal, habeas corpus, prize, admiralty, and bankruptcy. In courts with only a small amount of business, however, the case papers are often in single consolidated files. The dockets contain a record of papers filed and of proceedings regarding cases. Entries in the dockets are chronological by session of the court, but alphabetical indexes in the docket volumes make them indispensable finding aids. The clerks of some courts prepared "final records" or "complete records" containing copies of case papers; these are sometimes the most complete records of cases remaining.

Records relating to prize cases are accompanied by materials that yield information regarding Confederate activities. Documents captured aboard blockade runners include not only lists, logs, registers, ledgers, cargo manifests, etc., relating to the vessels themselves but also personal papers of passengers that throw light on conditions in the South or on the activities of Confederate officials.

The Judiciary Act of 1789 had constituted the 13 judicial districts as three judicial circuits--eastern, middle, and southern. (Maine and Kentucky were not included in the circuits, but the district courts for those districts were given circuit court jurisdiction except in appeals and writs of error.) At first the circuit court sat semiannually in each district and was presided over by two Justices of the Supreme Court and the district judge; an amendment of 1793 (1 Stat. 333), however, provided that only one Supreme Court Justice and the district judge might hold circuit court.

An act of Apr. 29, 1802 (2 Stat. 157), set up six circuits and provided that the judges for each circuit court should be the Supreme Court Justice residing in the circuit and the district judge; the Chief Justice of the United States was assigned to the Fifth Circuit. In 1807 (2 Stat. 420) the States of Kentucky, Tennessee, and Ohio were set up as the Seventh Circuit, for which another Associate Justice had to be added to the Supreme Court.

Because some remote judicial districts could not be provided with circuit courts, circuit court powers were conferred on their district courts. Thus at the start such provision was made for Maine and Kentucky, and the same provision was made for States subsequently admitted to the Union (except North Carolina, Rhode Island, and Vermont, over which adjacent circuit courts could easily extend jurisdiction) and for new districts formed out of existing judicial districts, such as the Northern District of New York and the Western District of Pennsylvania. Appeals could be taken from the district courts of Maine and Western Pennsylvania to adjoining circuit courts, but appeal from the Kentucky District was direct to the Supreme Court. The conferral of circuit court powers on the district courts established farther west was usually by reference to the Kentucky act or in the language of that act; hence most appeals from district courts acting as circuit courts were taken direct to the Supreme Court.

Better provision was made for the judicial needs of the West by an act of Mar. 3, 1837 (5 Stat. 176), which repealed parts of previous acts vesting circuit court powers in district courts, established nine judicial circuits, and increased the membership of the Supreme Court to nine. The composition of the circuits was slightly modified by an act of Aug. 16, 1842 (5 Stat. 507). The pattern established by this act and still unchanged at the outbreak of the Civil War included nine circuits, as follows:

First: Maine, New Hampshire, Massachusetts, Rhode Island.
Second: Vermont, Connecticut, New York (Southern and Northern
          Districts).
Third: New Jersey, Pennsylvania (Eastern and Western Districts).

Fourth: Maryland, Delaware, Virginia (Eastern and Western
            Districts).
Fifth: Alabama, Louisiana.
Sixth: North Carolina, South Carolina, Georgia.
Seventh: Ohio, Indiana, Illinois, Michigan.
Eighth: Kentucky, Tennessee (Eastern and Western Districts),
            Missouri.
Ninth: Mississippi, Arkansas.

States admitted to the Union after 1842 were not added to the judicial circuits immediately. By 1860 Texas, Florida, Wisconsin, Iowa, Minnesota, Kansas, California, and Oregon had entered the Union but had not been assigned to circuits. In his annual message of Dec. 3, 1861, President Lincoln declared that the country had outgrown its judicial system and recommended that all the States be accommodated with circuit courts or else that these courts be abolished and the judicial functions be performed by the district courts and the Supreme Court. He believed that adding enough Supreme Court Justices to take care of the new circuit courts would make the Supreme Court too large; and he suggested that Supreme Court Justices serve in some of the circuits and that new circuit judges be provided for the rest, or else that new circuit judges be provided for all the circuits. An act of July 15, 1862 (12 Stat. 576), provided for the reorganization of the judicial circuits; the first three circuits remained as before, and the others were composed as follows:

Fourth: Maryland, Delaware, Virginia, North Carolina.
Fifth: South Carolina, Georgia, Alabama, Mississippi, Florida.
Sixth: Louisiana, Texas, Arkansas, Kentucky, Tennessee.
Seventh: Ohio, Indiana.
Eighth: Michigan, Wisconsin, Illinois.
Ninth: Missouri, Iowa, Kansas, Minnesota.

The Supreme Court was to continue to allot Justices to the circuits; no special circuit judges were provided.

Some modifications of and additions to the circuits were made shortly. To satisfy the States concerned, the Seventh and Eighth Circuits were changed by an act of Jan. 28, 1863 (12 Stat. 637), the Seventh to consist of Ohio and Michigan, and the Eighth to consist of Illinois, Indiana, and Wisconsin. By an act of Feb. 9, 1863 (12 Stat. 648), Wisconsin was transferred to the Ninth Circuit. A Tenth Circuit, to consist of California and Oregon, was created by an act of Mar. 3, 1863 (12 Stat. 794); and the newly created State of Nevada was added to this circuit by an act of Feb. 27, 1865 (13 Stat. 440).

During the war, in those Southern States where Federal authority had been reestablished, circuit courts were held by the judges of the district courts. But Chief Justice Chase, whose circuit included Virginia, and Associate Justice James M. Wayne, who was assigned to the Fifth Circuit, did not participate in the sittings of the circuit courts. They considered it improper to preside over courts in the South while martial law prevailed and while the writ of habeas corpus was still suspended. Not until after President Johnson issued his proclamations of Apr. 2 and Aug. 20, 1866, declaring the insurrection at an end, did the Justices of the Supreme Court again begin to hold circuit courts in the South. Chief Justice Chase presided over the circuit court at Raleigh, N. C., in June 1867.

During the Civil War the circuit courts had both original and appellate jurisdiction. They had original cognizance of all civil suits at common law or in equity if the amount in dispute exceeded $500, if the United States was a plaintiff or an alien was a party, or if the suit was between citizens of two different States. The circuit courts shared with the district courts jurisdiction over crimes and offenses punishable by Federal law, cases brought by aliens for violations of the law of nations or of treaties of the United States, and suits at common law where the United States was the plaintiff. Most of the criminal cases eventually were tried in the circuit courts, and they likewise tried the mass of civil litigation between private individuals and corporations handled by the Federal courts. The circuit courts had appellate jurisdiction over the district courts in civil cases involving over $50 and in admiralty and maritime cases involving over $300. Before the act of Mar. 3, 1863 (12 Stat. 759), which provided for direct appeal to the Supreme Court in prize cases involving over $2,000, appeals in these cases were made from the district to the circuit courts. Jurisdiction over other matters was conferred on the circuit courts by special acts of Congress. Suits brought in a State court against civil or military officials of the United States for their actions under authority of the President or of acts of Congress could be removed for trial to the U. S. circuit court for the district (act of Mar. 3, 1863; 12 Stat. 756).

The circuit courts continued in existence for many years after the Civil War. A revision of the circuits by an act of July 23, 1866 (14 Stat. 209), abolished the Tenth Circuit and reduced the number again to nine. After resident circuit judges were provided for each of the circuits by an act of Apr. 10, 1869 (16 Stat. 44), the Justices of the Supreme Court no longer sat on the circuit courts. In 1891 appellate jurisdiction was transferred from the circuit courts to the new circuit courts of appeal.

In the discussion below, the district and circuit courts are listed under the States in alphabetical order, since each State comprised one or more judicial districts and in turn was part of a judicial circuit. Among the records of most district and circuit courts are records of bankruptcy under the act of 1867; these include many bankruptcy cases that grew directly out of the war. Because practically all the courts have such records, however, they are not mentioned specifically for every court.

Erastus C. Benedict, The American Admiralty; Its Jurisdiction and Practice, With Practical Forms and Directions (New York, 1870); Alfred Conkling, The Admiralty Jurisdiction; Laws and Practice of the Courts of the United States . . . (Albany, 1857. 2 vols.), and A Treatise on the Organization, Jurisdiction, and Practice of the Courts of the United States . . . (Albany, 1870); Homer S. Cummings and Carl McFarland, Federal Justice; Chapters in the History of Justice and the Federal Executive (New York, 1937); Luella C. Gettys, The Law of Citizenship in the United States (Chicago, 1934); Harold M. Hyman, To Try Men's Souls; Loyalty Tests in American History (Berkeley, Calif., 1959); Roscoe Pound, Organization of Courts (Boston, 1940); Edward McCrady, "Appendix; Inquiry Into the Subject of the Territorial Limits and Jurisdiction of the Circuit and District Courts of the United States Divided Into Districts," in Robert W. Hughes, comp., Report of Cases Decided in the Circuit and District Courts of the United States for the Fourth Circuit, 3:665-690 (Washington, 1877-83. 5 vols.);

William M. Robinson, Jr., Justice in Grey; a History of the Judicial System of the Confederate States of America (Cambridge, Mass., 1941); William A. Russ, Jr., "The Lawyer's Test Oath During Reconstruction," Mississippi Law Journal, 10:154-167 (Feb. 1938).

Before 1880 haphazard reports on decisions of district and circuit courts were published in unofficial compilations, legal periodicals, newspapers, and treatises. To search through these diverse sources was a problem for attorneys. The success of the Federal Reporter, a systematic compilation of reports on Federal court decisions (initiated by the West Publishing Co. of St. Paul, Minn., in 1880), caused that company to undertake the collection of reports for decisions made before 1880. Several years later, 18,000 cases were reported in The Federal Cases; Comprising Cases Argued and Determined in the Circuit and District Courts of the United States From the Earliest Times to the Beginning of the Federal Reporter [1789-1880] (St. Paul, 1894-97. 30 vols.). In this work the reports are arranged alphabetically by name of plaintiff and are numbered consecutively. Several thousand new cases not generally available in a library of Federal cases are included, but the compilation can still be supplemented from other published sources and court records. Because of its comparative completeness, uniformity, and accuracy, however, Federal Cases is the standard compilation. An appendix (vol. 30) contains cases omitted in the earlier volumes, including some for 1861-65; and a digest volume contains a table of citations and an alphabetical table of cases. The table of citations is valuable for historical as well as legal research, for it lists cases reported in other compilations for

circuit and district courts, in periodicals, and in special compilations. Federal Cases (vol. 1) also contains lists and biographical sketches of judges of the courts.

Another collection of cases, Federal Decisions; Cases Argued and Determined in the Supreme, Circuit, and District Courts of the United States, Comprising the Opinions of Those Courts From the Time of Their Organization to the Present Date, Together With Extracts From the Opinions of the Court of Claims and the Attorneys General, and the Opinions of General Importance of the Territorial Courts, annotated by William G. Meyer (St. Louis, Mo., Gilbert Book Co., 1884-89. 30 vols.), may be useful because of its different arrangement. Federal Decisions presents cases alphabetically by subject matter from the regular series of reports, periodicals, and State reports. Important decisions are reported in full; but most cases concerning slavery and the embargo are digested, and many prize cases are omitted altogether.

The legal bibliographies cited in this Guide in the section on the Supreme Court contain lists of special compilations of reports for circuit and district courts. Those that cover the Civil War period are cited below in the sections on the individual courts.

Lawyers' aids can also be historians' aids. Digests and tables of citations facilitate using the compilations of cases. Those pertaining to Federal cases are Federal Digest, 1754 to Date, Covering Supreme Court of the United States, United States Court of Appeals for the District of Columbia, United States Circuit Courts of Appeals, United States Court of Customs and Patent Appeals, District Courts of the United States, United States Court of Claims, as Well as All Other Federal Courts From the Earliest Times to Date

(St. Paul, West Publishing Co.,
1940-date); and American Digest;
Century Edition of the American
Digest; a Complete Digest of All
Reported American Cases From
the Earliest Times [1658] to 1896
(St. Paul, West Publishing Co.,
1897-1904. 50 vols.), which covers
State as well as Federal courts.

Special compilations contain
decisions made chiefly by the lower
Federal courts. One such compilation is Helen T. Catterall, ed.,
Judicial Cases Concerning American
Slavery and the Negro (Washington,
1926-37. 5 vols.). Culled from volumes of judicial reports as well as
publications of States and historical
societies, these cases illustrate the
complications arising in American
life from the institution of slavery;
and some of them show the local effects of the war, of the Emancipation Proclamation, and of the Thirteenth Amendment.

A statement of money received
by the U. S. Treasury on account
of property seized, condemned, and
confiscated under the act of July 17,
1862, contains a list of the titles of
cases arranged according to Federal
judicial districts (S. Ex. Doc. 58,
40 Cong., 2 sess., Serial 1317).

During the Civil War the Federal
courts did not exercise exclusive
jurisdiction over admiralty matters.
State courts also handled admiralty
cases until decisions of the Supreme
Court in 1866 (The Moses Taylor,
and The Hine v. Trevor, 4 Wall.
411, 555) held that the grant of admiralty jurisdiction to the district
courts by the Judiciary Act of 1789
was exclusive. Reports on some
admiralty cases before 1866, therefore, are in the reports of State
courts, for which data can be found
in the legal bibliographies.

Descriptions of records of the
Federal courts are in the Survey of
Federal Archives, Inventory of Fed-
eral Archives in the States, Series
II, the Federal Courts. These were
published for all the States except
Idaho, New Jersey, South Carolina,
West Virginia, and Wyoming. For
these States serial reports embodying information about the court records are in the Records of the Work
Projects Administration (Record
Group 69) in the National Archives.
Since the preparation of the Survey's
inventories, however, quantities of
court records have been transferred
to the Federal Records Centers.
Records of other courts are in the
National Archives. Only part of the
records in the National Archives and
none of those in the Records Centers
have been inventoried.

Reports of circuit court decisions
appear in published compilations for
some of the circuits existing at the
time of the Civil War. These collections, however, were selective; and
some of them deliberately omitted
cases relating to the war as being
no longer of current interest. The
compilations available include: William H. Clifford, comp., Reports of
Cases Determined in the Circuit
Court of the United States for the
First Circuit, From April Term,
1858 [to May Term, 1878] (Boston,
1869-80. 4 vols.); Samuel Blatchford, comp., Reports of Cases Argued and Determined in the Circuit
Court of the United States for the
Second Circuit [1845-87] (New York,
1852-88. 24 vols.); John W. Wallace,
comp., Cases in the Circuit Court of
the United States for the Third Circuit [1842-62] (Philadelphia, 1849-
71. 3 vols.); Robert Hughes, comp.,
Reports of Cases Decided in the Circuit Courts of the United States for
the Fourth Circuit; Most of Them
Since Chief Justice Waite Came
Upon the Bench; and of Selected
Cases in Admiralty and Bankruptcy
Decided in the District Courts of
That Circuit [1792-1883] (Washington,
1877-83. 5 vols.); Bradley T. Johnson, comp., Reports of Cases Decided by Chief Justice Chase in the
Circuit Court of the United States for

the Fourth Circuit During the Years 1865 to 1869, Both Inclusive, in the Districts of Maryland, Virginia, North Carolina, and South Carolina (New York, 1876); William S. Flippin, Reports of Cases Argued and Determined in the Circuit and District Courts of the United States for the Sixth Judicial Circuit [1859-81] (Chicago, 1881-82. 2 vols.); Josiah H. Bissell, comp., Cases Argued and Determined in the Circuit and District Courts of the United States, for the Seventh Judicial Circuit [1851-83] (Chicago, 1873-83. 11 vols.); James M. Woolworth, comp., Cases Determined in the United States Circuit Courts for the Eighth Circuit by the Hon. Samuel F. Miller, L. L. D., One of the Associate Justices of the Supreme Court [1863-69] (Chicago, 1870). The reports on circuit court decisions from the foregoing compilations and other sources were republished in Federal Cases and Federal Decisions, already described.

For other information on the Federal courts and their personnel see, in this Guide, the sections on the General Records of the Department of State, the "judiciary accounts" in the section on the Department of the Interior, the Attorney General's papers in the General Records of the Department of Justice, and records relating to confiscation cases in the section on the Department of the Treasury. The section on the Department of the Navy contains information and a bibliography regarding vessels taken as prizes and tried by district courts. For other related records, see Congress.

Arkansas

The act admitting Arkansas to the Union (June 15, 1836, 5 Stat. 51) set it up as a single judicial district and directed the court to hold sessions at Little Rock in April and November. The western counties of the State were assigned to the Western District by an act of Mar. 3, 1851 (9 Stat. 594). The court for that district met at Van Buren, and that for the Eastern District continued to meet at Little Rock. Arkansas seceded from the Union in May 1861; and Daniel Ringo, who was then filling both Federal judgeships in the State, resigned his commission. Union forces got control of the part of Arkansas north of the Arkansas River by midsummer of 1863, and on Sept. 10 they captured Little Rock. A restored State government, organized by Unionists, began to operate in the occupied part of Arkansas in the spring of 1864. On May 2, 1864, President Lincoln nominated Henry C. Caldwell, a lawyer who was colonel of the 3d Iowa Cavalry, as district judge in Arkansas. Cases handled by Judge Caldwell included confiscation proceedings against the property of Confederates, suits arising under the direct tax law of 1861, treason cases, slave contracts, and contracts based on Confederate monetary values. He began sitting as a circuit court judge in 1865, and among the criminal cases he handled were three against former Confederates for treason.

Record Group 21. -- The extant records of the U. S. district courts for both districts of Arkansas, dating from 1865, are in the Federal Records Center at Fort Worth, Tex. Those for the Eastern District include equity cases from 1865, and criminal cases from 1866.

Records of the U. S. Circuit Court for the Eastern District of Arkansas, also in the center at Fort Worth, include a rule docket, 1865-92; criminal cases, 1866-1956; chancery cases, 1865-1936; and law cases, 1865-1936.

California

Soon after its admission as a State, California was divided at the 37th parallel (act of Sept. 28, 1850; 9 Stat. 521) into two judicial districts. The seat of the Northern District came to be at San Francisco and that of the Southern District at Los Angeles. These district courts at first had circuit court powers in civil and criminal matters, but when a circuit court for California was provided (act of Mar. 2, 1855; 10 Stat. 631) and a special circuit judge was appointed, such powers were revoked. The district courts continued, however, to have authority (sec. 9 of an act of Mar. 3, 1851; 9 Stat. 632) to review land cases on appeal from decisions of the board of land commissioners. The Southern District was abolished by an act of July 27, 1866 (14 Stat. 300), and the records of both the district and circuit courts were transferred to San Francisco.

The district courts in California were vested by the act of 1850 with concurrent jurisdiction and powers then exercised in civil cases by circuit courts of the United States. After the erection of California into a separate circuit (act of Mar. 2, 1855; 10 Stat. 631), Matthew H. McAllister was appointed circuit court judge and presided over the sessions of the court at San Francisco. California was joined with Oregon to form the Tenth Judicial Circuit by an act of Mar. 3, 1863 (12 Stat. 794).

George Cosgrave, Early California Justice; the History of the United States District Court for the Southern District of California, 1849-1944, ed. by Roy V. Sowers (San Francisco, 1948).

Records in Other Custody. --Records of the U. S. District Courts for both districts of California, in the custody of the court at San Francisco, date chiefly from 1851. They include minutes; judgments and decrees; common law, equity, civil, criminal, land, and admiralty cases; related registers; commissioners' records; naturalization records; court exhibits; court opinions; oaths of office; and correspondence. Some 6, 000 cubic feet of records of the court, 1851-1950, were scheduled for transfer to the Federal Records Center at South San Francisco in the spring of 1961. Records available on microfilm in the National Archives include court minutes, 1851-1949, judgments and decrees, 1850-1950, and a sales book, 1851-1917.

The records of the U. S. circuit court, 1855-1911, were transferred to the district court at San Francisco in 1912 and are still in its possession. The case files are interfiled with those of the district court. Other records include minutes; judgment records; registers of decrees, equity decrees, and admiralty decrees; common rule books; and naturalization records. A microfilm of these records, except those for naturalization, is in the National Archives.

Connecticut

The U. S. District Court for the District of Connecticut, established by the Judiciary Act of 1789, met alternately at New Haven and Hartford. Connecticut was assigned to the Second Judicial Circuit in 1802 and remained in that circuit thereafter. The circuit court also met at New Haven and Hartford.

Record Group 21. -- The records of the district court were held for many years in the Court and Custom House at New Haven, but most of them are now in the Federal Records Center at Dorchester, Mass. They include case files, dockets, minutes, and naturalization records. Records of the circuit court, in the same center, include minutes, case files, dockets, equity orders, and final records.

Delaware

The U. S. District Court for the District of Delaware, established by the Judiciary Act of 1789, met at Wilmington during the Civil War. There likewise were held the sessions of the circuit court, which since 1802 had been in the Fourth Circuit.

Record Group 21.--Records of the district court in the Federal Records Center at Philadelphia include equity case files, 1843-1950; law case files, 1824-1942; admiralty cases, 1834-1952; criminal cases, 1829-1949; and naturalization records, 1840-1910. The case files of the circuit court are interfiled with those of the district court. Separate naturalization records of the circuit court, 1845-1902, are also in the center.

District of Columbia

A judicial system was provided for the District of Columbia by an act of Feb. 27, 1801 (2 Stat. 103). A circuit court was established, and appointments of a marshal, an attorney, and justices of the peace were authorized. The chief judge of the District of Columbia was empowered (act of Apr. 29, 1802; 2 Stat. 166) to hold a district court of the United States twice a year in the District of Columbia. The district court was to "have and exercise within the said district the same powers and jurisdiction" given to other U. S. district courts. The appointment of a judge to hold sessions of a criminal court was authorized by an act of July 7, 1838 (5 Stat. 306). The criminal court tried cases of crime committed within the District and had the jurisdiction both of a State court or local tribunal and of a U. S. circuit court.

The circuit court, established in 1801, was composed of three judges appointed by the President and had all the powers vested in circuit courts of the United States. It exercised civil jurisdiction in both law and equity and had criminal jurisdiction until the creation of a separate criminal court in 1838. It had appellate jurisdiction over judgments of the district court, the criminal court, the orphans' court, and justices of the peace. Appeals could be made to the circuit court from decisions of the Commissioner of Patents in patent cases (acts of Mar. 3, 1839, Aug. 30, 1852; 5 Stat. 354, 10 Stat. 75). Jurisdiction over applications for divorce was granted to the circuit court by an act of June 19, 1860 (12 Stat. 59). Writs of mandamus issued by this court frequently involved important principles and considerable sums of money and often concerned the legality of actions of the Federal executive departments. An act of Apr. 16, 1862 (12 Stat. 376), abolishing slavery in the District of Columbia required slaveowners to file with the clerk of the circuit court schedules of slaves manumitted and empowered the clerk to issue certificates to persons freed. Slaves whose owners failed to file schedules could submit to the court their claims for freedom (act of July 12, 1862; 12 Stat. 538).

The courts of the District of Columbia were reorganized by an act of Mar. 3, 1863 (12 Stat. 762), which abolished the old circuit, district, and criminal courts and established a supreme court of the District of Columbia, with general jurisdiction in law and equity. The act authorized the President to appoint four justices and designate one as chief justice. The supreme court had the powers and jurisdiction formerly exercised by the circuit court. Any one of the justices could (1) hold a District Court of the United States for the District of Columbia, with the powers and jurisdiction of other U. S. district courts; (2) hold a criminal court for the trial of offenses within the District; and (3) hold a special term of the supreme court to decide cases at law and in equity. Aggrieved parties might appeal from special terms of the supreme court to its general terms, which were held by three justices. Final judgments, orders, or decrees could be taken upon writ of error or appeal to the Supreme Court of the United States. Appeals could be made from the judgments of justices of the peace in the District of Columbia to the supreme court of the District. Justices of the peace could be removed at a general term of that court.

Because of its location in the Nation's capital, the supreme court of the District of Columbia tried many civil and criminal cases of national rather than local interest. These included suits against executive officers of the Federal Government, cases involving title to the public domain throughout the country, cases concerning disbursements of appropriations by Congress, and cases arising under other acts of Congress. Criminal cases related to the Civil War concerned enticing soldiers to desert, aiding and abetting rebellion, and treason. Property confiscation cases were also tried. Slavery was not abolished in Maryland until Oct. 1864; consequently the supreme court of the District of Columbia handled a number of fugitive slave cases. Vessels captured by the Potomac Flotilla and other Union ships were brought before the court for condemnation under the prize laws.

Job Barnard, "Early Days of the Supreme Court of the District of Columbia," Columbia Historical Society, Records, 22:1-35 (1919); Frederick L. Siddons, "The Supreme Court of the District of Columbia," National University Law Review, 7:1-13 (Jan. 1927); Lawrence F. Schmeckebier, The District of Columbia; Its Government and Administration (Baltimore, 1928); John C. Proctor, ed., Washington Past and Present; a History (New York, 1930. 5 vols.).

Record Group 21. --Records of the District of Columbia courts are in the National Archives. The minutes of the district court, 1802-63, relate largely during the war period to proceedings in prize and confiscation cases but also contain orders for the naturalization of aliens (with information about the aliens themselves), bonds, oaths of office, appointments, letters, libels, and orders of the court. The case files of the district court, 1863-1929, consist chiefly (for the war period) of papers concerning prize and confiscation cases but include some cases involving violations of the revenue laws and admiralty cases involving damages, wages, and collisions. Earlier papers are in an admiralty case file, 1839-63, for which a docket book covers 1857-63. The only finding aid to the later case files is the indexes to dockets, 1863-1921, which are typewritten lists of the names of plaintiffs and defendants arranged in rough alphabetical order. The dockets have been retained by the court. A small file of copyright papers, 1856-63, consists of pamphlets, songs, title pages of books and pamphlets, and titles and legends for Civil War photographs taken by Mathew B. Brady and others. The records of the criminal court, 1838-63, include minutes, case papers, dockets, appearances, and recognizances. Criminal case files nos. 4731, 5920, and 6594 concern John H. Surratt; habeas corpus case no. 46 concerns Mary Surratt; and district court case no. 191 relates to a suit brought by Admiral Farragut for bounty payment to the officers and sailors of his fleet for destroying the Confederate fleet at New Orleans in 1862.

The kinds of records developed by the supreme court grew out of its powers and jurisdiction. The minutes of its general terms, 1863-1903, contain for the war period a record of proceedings in cases handled by the court sitting in general term; commissions of judges; oaths of officers; minutes of justices' meetings; appointments of commissioners, committees, notaries, and constables; judgments on appeals in law, equity, and criminal cases; orders; petitions of members of the bar; entries relating to the admission of attorneys, memorial services for judges and officials, and adoption of rules; and hearings on the removal of justices of the peace. For law cases there are case files, 1863-1934, and related minute books, dockets, judgments, an index to judgments of the general term, and an index to ejectment suits. Equity case files, 1863-1905, are accompanied by minute books, dockets, an equity index, and order books. With the criminal case files, 1863-1934, are minute books and dockets. Habeas corpus case files and dockets, 1863-1933, and an appeal docket, 1863-95, are available. Other records include mechanics' liens, 1863-1934; the clerk's docket of jail commitments, 1864-65; bonds and other papers concerning the appointment of notaries public, 1860-93; and naturalization records, 1863-1909.

The old circuit court records are a part of the records received by the National Archives from the U. S. district court. The minutes, 1801-63, contain entries on the admission of attorneys, announcements of the deaths of judges and attorneys, appointments of constables and notaries public, calendars of cases, commitments of fugitive slaves, naturalization proceedings, records of jury panels and discharge of jurymen, proceedings in cases, resignations of constables, and rules of practice. Case papers, 1802-63, are filed chronologically according to type of documents. Dockets contain sections for trials, appearances, "judicials," appeals, and recognizances; under these, cases are entered numerically. For chancery cases there is a separate file of papers and related records. Smaller files are available for habeas corpus cases, 1820-63; fugitive slave cases, 1861-63; and divorce cases, 1860-63. Manumission and emancipation papers, 1857-63, relate to voluntary manumissions, emancipation under the act of Apr. 16, 1862, and claims for emancipation filed by slaves whose masters had failed to file schedules under that act. Naturalization records, 1802-1910, were also maintained by the circuit court; an alphabetical card index to these has been prepared by the National Archives.

Justices of the peace were required by an act of Mar. 1, 1823 (3 Stat. 743), to keep records of their proceedings and upon leaving office to deliver them to the clerk of the circuit court. A small group of such dockets among the court records includes one for John D. Clark of Washington, June 1861-Jan. 1864, and one for Robert White of Georgetown, June 1850-July 1871. These yield some information about life in the capital during the war.

John A. Hayward and George C. Hazleton, comps., Reports of   Cases, Civil and Criminal, Argued and Adjudged in the Circuit Court of the District of Columbia From March Term, 1840, to Jan. Term, 1863 (Washington, 1892-95. 2 vols.); District of Columbia Digest, 1658 to Date; A Complete Digest of the District of Columbia Reports, Including Decisions of the Circuit Court, the Early Maryland Cases, as Well as Decisions of the United States Supreme Court in Cases Appealed From the District of Columbia Courts . . . (Washington, St. Paul, 1936-date); Franklin H. Mackey, comp., Reports of Cases Argued and Adjudged in the Supreme Court of the District of Columbia, Sitting in General Term, From Its Organization in 1863 to November 19, 1868 (Washington, 1889). Patent cases tried in the District, 1859-63, appear in Federal Cases. A transcript, "Trial of John H. Surratt . . . ," is in The Reporter, 3:57-405, 4:1-552 (June 17-Sept. 24, 1867). See also National Archives, Office of Civil Archives, Preliminary Inventory [NC-2] of the Records of the United States District Court for the District of Columbia, comp. by Janet Weinert (Washington,1962).

Florida

When Florida was admitted as a State in 1845 it was set up as a single judicial district (act of Mar. 3, 1845; 5 Stat. 788). An act of Feb. 23, 1847 (9 Stat. 131), however, divided the State into Northern and Southern Districts at a line drawn east and west from the northern point of Charlotte Harbor. The principal seats of the courts were St. Augustine and Key West. The act of 1847 authorized the judge of the district court at Key West to license salvage vessels and their masters. When Confederate forces early in 1861 occupied northeastern Florida, the district court at St. Augustine ceased operations. In southern Florida, where Federal troops held Fort Taylor at Key West and Fort Jefferson on Dry Tortugas, the district court at Key West continued to function. It became an important prize court, handling cases involving 299 vessels. After Union forces reoccupied Fernandina and St. Augustine in Mar. 1862, a judge was appointed; he reopened the U. S. District Court for the Northern District of Florida at St. Augustine in Oct. 1864. This court also handled many prizes, brought in by the blockading squadron. The judge of the district court at Key West, remaining loyal to the Union, apparently held circuit court.

Record Group 21. --Records of both Florida district courts have been transferred to the Federal Records Center at East Point, Ga. Admiralty records for the Southern District include case files, 1864-1908; minutes, 1862-85; a docket, 1861-97; record books, 1847-1912; order books, 1862-1913; a derelict docket, 1861-1927, pertaining to salvaged vessels; a wrecking license register, 1862-1917; a day book, 1861-89, showing fees and expenditures; and ledgers, 1861-65. Records of the Northern District include criminal case files, dockets, naturalization records, and jury papers.

Records in Other Custody. --Naturalization records for the Southern District are held by the district court at Miami.

Illinois

The U. S. District Court for the District of Illinois was established by an act of Mar. 3, 1819 (3 Stat. 502). The court met at Vandalia from 1819 until its transfer to Springfield in 1839. The State was divided by an act of Feb. 13, 1855 (10 Stat. 606), into a Northern District at Chicago and a

Southern District at Springfield, and the circuit court also met in those
cities. At this time the records of the old District of Illinois, 1819-55,
and the records of the circuit court to 1855 were transferred to Chicago.
In the Chicago fire of 1871 these records and those of the Northern District, 1855-71, were destroyed.

Record Group 21. -- The records of the Southern District for the years
after 1855 are in the Federal Records Center at Chicago. They include
civil, criminal, law, and admiralty case files and dockets. The court at
Springfield tried some prize cases, of which records are available.

Records of the circuit court for the Southern District of Illinois (Springfield) are also in the center at Chicago. The papers (1855-1911) relating
to cases--law, chancery, equity, and criminal--are in one consolidated
file in numerical order. There are also minutes, dockets, judgments and
executions, a complete record in chancery, a complete law record, and
indexes.

Indiana

Soon after Indiana became a State an act of Mar. 3, 1817 (3 Stat. 390),
established it as a judicial district. The district court moved with the
capital to Indianapolis in 1825. A few confiscation cases were tried before
the Indianapolis district court during the Civil War, and the circuit court at
the same place handled the trial of the Hilligos brothers for the murder of
a draft officer.

Record Group 21. -- The records of the district court at Indianapolis
are in the Federal Records Center at Chicago. They include law cases;
dockets; a chancery record, complete record, and criminal record; order
books; an admiralty journal; and record of Government cases. Records of
the circuit court for Indiana, also in the center at Chicago, include case
files, 1837-1912, chancery record books, common law record books, appearance dockets, and judgment dockets.

Iowa

The act admitting the State of Iowa (Mar. 3, 1845; 5 Stat. 789) set it up
as a single Federal judicial district. The District of Iowa was divided by
an act of Feb. 26, 1853 (10 Stat. 171), into Northern, Central, and Southern
Divisions, with seats at Dubuque, Iowa City, and Burlington, respectively.
An act of Mar. 3, 1859 (11 Stat. 437), established a Northern Division
at Dubuque, a Southern Division at Keokuk, and a Western Division at Des
Moines. Traffic on the Mississippi River gave rise to many admiralty cases
that were tried by the Iowa district court. The district court exercised circuit court jurisdiction before 1862; in that year the district was provided
with a circuit court assigned to the Ninth Judicial Circuit.

Record Group 21. -- Some district court records for Iowa are in the
Federal Records Center at Kansas City, Mo. The records from Des Moines
include equity, law, and criminal files, 1842-1933. Criminal case files
from Dubuque cover 1863-1947. Bankruptcy records, 1867-83, from Dubuque are in the National Archives.

Records in Other Custody. -- Other records of the District of Iowa were
found by the Survey of Federal Archives. The clerk at Dubuque had minutes, 1850-1932; civil dockets, 1859-1931; bar dockets, 1857-83; fee books,
1860-95; a record of marshal's receipts, 1850-70; correspondence and

reports, 1850-64; and praecipes, subpenas, and certificates of discharge of witnesses. A deputy clerk at Fort Dodge had equity cases, 1858-94, and criminal cases, 1856-96. The records at Keokuk included law and equity cases, court calendars, jury records, case records, journals, miscellaneous orders, attorneys' applications for admission to the bar, grand jury reports, oaths of office, bonds, and correspondence, dating chiefly from 1849, and an admiralty record, 1859-77. Records at Des Moines included a minute book of the Western Division, 1858-64, appearance dockets, judgment dockets, fee books, a court calendar, and criminal and civil dockets, 1849-1907.

The Survey of Federal Archives found records of the old circuit court in the custody of the clerk of the U. S. district court at Des Moines. Circuit court records described in the Survey's inventory include law cases, 1860-1909; dockets recording law, equity, and criminal cases; law and equity calendars, 1863-97; equity cases, 1862-1909; and a judgment index. Other dockets among the records of the district court were also used to record circuit court cases.

Kansas

When Kansas was admitted as a State on Jan. 29, 1861 (12 Stat. 128), it was established as a single judicial district. The district court met initially at Topeka, but in later years it sat also at Leavenworth, Fort Scott, Wichita, and Salina. The business of the court at Topeka during the Civil War included confiscation cases and indictments for treason, conspiracy, and mutiny. The district court exercised circuit court jurisdiction in civil cases. The act of July 15, 1862, however, provided for Kansas a circuit court in the Ninth Judicial Circuit.

Record Group 21. -- Some records of the district court at Topeka are in the Federal Records Center at Kansas City, Mo. These include criminal case files, 1861-1932, containing indictments for the war period; law case files, 1861-1932, containing confiscation cases; the chancery final record, 1861-62; the criminal final record, 1861-86; the final record of confiscation cases, 1863-80; and other final record books, 1857-62. Case files of the circuit court, 1861-1912, are also in the center at Kansas City.

Records in Other Custody. -- The dockets and indexes to the records of both district and circuit courts have been retained by the district court at Topeka.

Kentucky

The district court provided for Kentucky by the Judiciary Act of 1789 met for many years at Frankfort. An act of June 15, 1860 (12 Stat. 36), prescribed additional terms at Louisville, Covington, and Paducah. Kentucky sought to remain neutral during the secession crisis in 1861, but after its invasion by both Confederate and Union forces it became a battleground. Kentuckians fought on both sides during the Civil War. Thomas B. Monroe, Sr., judge of the district court, resigned early in Oct. 1861 and joined the Confederacy. Bland Ballard was immediately appointed as his successor; and, since the Union Army controlled most of the State, the Federal courts continued to sit. At the Nov. 1861 term of the district court at Frankfort indictments for treason were brought against 32 prominent Kentuckians who had gone over to the Confederacy, including John C. Breckinridge, former

Vice President. A conviction for treason was found against Thomas C.
Shacklett in the district court at Louisville in 1863. Associate Justice
Catron presided over the circuit court in Kentucky in the spring of 1861,
but sessions in later years appear to have been held by Judge Ballard of
the district court.

Record Group 21. --In the Federal Records Center at Chicago are a
consolidated file of civil, law, equity, and criminal cases for the district
court at Frankfort; and, for the court at Louisville, equity cases, dockets,
order books, and some volumes of the complete record. Circuit court records from Louisville in the center at Chicago include order books, 1860-
1909; the complete record, 1860-1911; dockets, 1861-1911; and minutes,
1863-1911. From Covington there are criminal case files, 1860-1911.

Records in Other Custody. --Some book records were retained by the
courts. The records at Frankfort include an index to cases, the final record, an order book, executions, a general cross-index to suits, ignored
indictments in criminal cases, papers relating to cases dismissed by U. S.
commissioners, a roll of attorneys, and correspondence. Among the records at Covington are a final record and an execution docket. Records at
Louisville include clerk's fiscal records, minutes, court calendars, rules
of practice, final records, criminal cases, a criminal docket, and bonds
required from citizens during the Civil War to insure good behavior. At
Paducah are minutes, order books, bankruptcy records, and a roll of attorneys. The inventory published by the Survey of Federal Archives describes other records of the circuit courts at Louisville and Covington and
records of the courts at Frankfort and Paducah. The dates given for some
of the series include the Civil War period.

Louisiana

The Territorial courts of Louisiana were succeeded by a U. S. district
court upon the admission of Louisiana as a State (act of Apr. 8, 1812; 2
Stat. 703). The State was subdivided into Eastern and Western Districts in
1823; these were consolidated in 1845 but reconstituted in 1849. The court
in the Western District met in annual sessions at Opelousas, Alexandria,
Shreveport, and Monroe; and the court in the Eastern District held sessions
at New Orleans. The district courts ceased to function early in 1861 after
the secession of Louisiana.

The capture of New Orleans in May 1862 by Federal forces was promptly
followed by the establishment of a military government under Gen. B. F.
Butler. He set up a provost court presided over by Maj. J. M. Bell, who
tried both civilians and military personnel, chiefly for criminal offenses.
Bell was succeeded in Dec. 1862 by Judge Charles A. Peabody, and the
latter was followed in June 1863 by Augustus De Berkeley Hughes. The provost court also tried persons charged with violating General Butler's orders
and regulations, administered oaths of allegiance, handled applications for
the emancipation of slaves, and tried other types of cases. This court was
abolished on Aug. 31, 1863, by an order of the Provost Marshal General,
Department of the Gulf.

During 1862 it became evident that provision must be made for the administration of justice in areas under Federal control outside of New Orleans and for the adjudication of claims by foreign residents of that city for
damages and injuries suffered at the hands of U. S. forces. President
Lincoln, therefore, by Executive order of Oct. 20, 1862, erected the U. S.

Provisional Court for the State of Louisiana, with the powers and jurisdiction of both a district and a circuit court. Charles A. Peabody was appointed judge and empowered to select a prosecuting attorney, a marshal, and a clerk. The judge and his staff arrived at New Orleans in Dec. 1862 and the opening of the court was proclaimed on the 29th. Judge Peabody declined to handle prize cases and was reluctant to accept confiscation cases. In view of Peabody's attitude Rear Admiral Farragut, commanding the West Gulf Blockading Squadron, urged the Secretary of the Navy to recommend the establishment of a prize court at New Orleans. Consequently the U. S. District Court for the Eastern District of Louisiana was reopened at New Orleans in 1863, and prize and confiscation cases were transferred to it. An act of July 28, 1866 (14 Stat. 344), required the transfer to this court of "all suits, causes, prosecutions, and proceedings in the United States provisional court for the State of Louisiana, with the records thereof." Louisiana was attached in 1862 to the Sixth Judicial Circuit, and the judge of the district court reopened the circuit court at New Orleans on June 24, 1863.

Charles A. Peabody, "United States Provisional Court for the State of Louisiana, 1862-1865," American Historical Association, Annual Report, 1892, p. 197-210;

Elizabeth J. Doyle, "New Orleans Courts Under Military Occupation, 1861-1865," Mid-America, 42:185-192 (July 1960).

Record Group 21.--Records of the courts that functioned in New Orleans during the war are in the Federal Records Center at New Orleans. Records of the district court include minutes from June 1863, case files, and a fee book, 1863-65. For the provisional court there are case files, Dec. 30, 1862-1865. The provost court recorded its early proceedings, May 4-Oct. 1862, in a minute book of the discontinued district court (see also Record Group 110, below). Bankruptcy records, 1867-94, for the Eastern District of Louisiana are in the National Archives. Records of the circuit court for the Eastern District of Louisiana, also in the center at New Orleans, include minutes, case files, and dockets.

Record Group 110.--The proceedings of the provost court, Oct. 1862-Aug. 1863, are recorded in a volume labeled "Opinions, U. S. Circuit Court" [June 1855-June 1858], among the records of the Provost Marshal General's Bureau in the National Archives.

Records in Other Custody.--The inventory published by the Survey of Federal Archives describes other circuit court records then in the custody of the clerk of the district court at New Orleans. Some of these records that apparently relate to the Civil War period include judgment dockets; civil witness books; chancery order books; fiscal records; attorneys' oaths of allegiance, 1863-64; and exhibits.

Maine

Though still a part of Massachusetts, Maine was set up as a separate Federal judicial district by the Judiciary Act of 1789. The court met for many years at Portland. Because Maine is a seaboard State, part of the business handled by the court has been admiralty cases. The State of Maine had been assigned since its creation in 1820 to the First Judicial Circuit.

Record Group 21. --Case files, 1790-1937, minute books, dockets, and naturalization records are in the Federal Records Center at Dorchester, Mass. Bankruptcy records, 1867-98, are in the National Archives. Case files, 1820-1911, and minutes of the circuit court are also in the center at Dorchester.

U. S. District Court, Maine, Reports of Cases Argued and Determined in the District Court of the	United States, for the District of Maine, 1822 -1866 (Boston, 1856-74. 3 vols.).

Records in Other Custody. --The Survey of Federal Archives found other records of the circuit court in the custody of the clerk of the district court at Portland. Records relating to the war period include dockets, an order book in equity, naturalization records, and appointment records.

Maryland

The U. S. District Court for the District of Maryland opened at Baltimore in 1790 and has continued to hold terms in that city, where after 1837 the circuit court also met.

Chief Justice Taney, sitting on circuit in 1861, issued a writ of habeas corpus directing the deliverance to the court of John Merryman, a secessionist imprisoned by the military authorities. The writ was ignored and Taney wrote an opinion on the illegality of Lincoln's suspension of the writ. Sixty treason cases, including that of Merryman, were docketed in the circuit court at Baltimore in 1861. At the Nov. 1861 term of the court Taney, sitting with Judge William F. Giles, continued the cases; and he did not attend later sessions of the court because he did not want the cases brought to trial. The indictments were dropped after the war. Chief Justice Chase sat on the circuit court at Baltimore at the April and November terms of 1865.

W. Calvin Chesnut, "History of the Federal Courts in Maryland," Maryland State Bar Association,	Reports, 41:63-89; Carl B. Swisher, Roger B. Taney (New York, 1935).

Record Group 21. --Records of the court in the Federal Records Center at Alexandria, Va., include equity case files, 1802-61; criminal case files, 1789-1879; civil case files, 1802-61; law case files, 1789-1879; admiralty case files, 1790-1877; and recognizances, 1832-89. Records of the circuit court in the same center include criminal case files, 1789-1878; equity case files, 1802-1912; and civil case files, 1803-80.

Records in Other Custody. --Other district court records, listed in the Survey of Federal Archives inventory, are presumably still held by the court at Baltimore. These include minutes, an index of judgments, petitions related to the libeling of ships and goods, protests of nonpayment of bills, surety undertakings, subpena dockets, and a record of executions of judgments. Records of the marshal include letters sent, account books, and correspondence. Habeas corpus papers include those relating to Ex parte Merryman, referred to above. A prize-case docket contains the record of proceedings in condemnation of vessels and cargoes during the Civil War, and a file of prize cases contains papers on the vessels libeled. Records of the circuit court found by the Survey of Federal Archives in the custody of

the district court included minutes and an index of judgments, record of
judgments, roll of attorneys, and an order book in chancery.

Massachusetts

Massachusetts exclusive of the District of Maine was constituted a Federal judicial district by the Judiciary Act of 1789. The State has remained
a single district with the principal seat at Boston. The court at that place
handled numerous prize cases during the Civil War. The circuit court, assigned to the First Judicial Circuit, also met at Boston.

Record Group 21. -- The Federal Records Center at Dorchester, Mass.,
has many records of the U. S. district court at Boston. They include equity,
law, civil, criminal, and admiralty case files, 1789-1917; dockets; final
records; indexes; miscellaneous records, 1850-1920; primary declarations;
and petitions for naturalization. Bankruptcy records, 1867-78, are in the
National Archives. The records of the circuit court are also in the center
at Dorchester. Case files of all types are in a consolidated file, 1790-1911.
Other records include minutes, 1790-1906; final records, 1790-1911; rules,
1849-64, 1894-1911; naturalization records, 1845-1911; and orders and receipts, 1832-1911.

Francis E. Parker and John Lathrop, comps., Decisions of Hon. Peleg Sprague in Maritime, Admiralty, and Prize Causes in the District Court for Massachusetts, From 1861 to . . . 1864 (Philadelphia, 1861; Boston, 1868. 2 vols.).

Michigan

The new State of Michigan was designated by an act of July 1, 1836 (5
Stat. 61), as the District of Michigan, with one judge to hold two sessions
annually of the district court at Detroit. The State was divided by an act of
Feb. 24, 1863 (12 Stat. 660), into the Eastern District, with the seat at
Detroit, and the Western District, with the seat at Grand Rapids. The cir-
cuit courts met at the same places.

Record Group 21. -- Some records of both districts are in the Federal
Records Center at Chicago. Those for the Eastern District include law
cases, 1837-1939; criminal cases, 1816-1936; and equity cases, 1840-1943.
For the Western District there are law and equity cases dating from 1864.
Records of the circuit court for the Eastern District of Michigan in the Cen-
ter at Chicago include law cases, 1837-1911, and equity cases, 1838-1911.

Records in Other Custody. -- The courts have retained the dockets, indexes, and other book records relating to the above case files; also, according to the Survey of Federal Archives inventory, admiralty cases and naturalization records. The district court at Detroit retained the dockets and
indexes to the circuit court records of the Eastern District of Michigan.
The Survey of Federal Archives also found at Detroit criminal case files,
1816-1912, and a calendar, 1837-78, of that circuit court. Other circuit
court records found by the Survey at Grand Rapids included a journal, 1863-
1918; rule book, 1863-1917; index to civil docket, 1863-68; chancery order
book, 1863-1925; and chancery index, 1863-1917. The different types of
case files were interfiled with the case files of the district court, and the
same dockets were used by both courts.

Minnesota

Minnesota was admitted as a State by an act of May 11, 1858 (11 Stat. 285), and a section in that act regarding the judiciary constituted the State as the District of Minnesota. The judge was directed by an act of Mar. 3, 1859 (11 Stat. 402), to hold a fall session of the court at St. Paul and a summer session at Preston. The seat of the summer session was transferred in 1861 from Preston to Mankato and in 1866 to Winona. Circuit court jurisdiction was conferred upon the district court for Minnesota upon its creation in 1858. The District of Minnesota was provided with a circuit court, in the Ninth Circuit, by the act of July 15, 1862. The court met at St. Paul twice annually.

Record Group 21. --Most of the records of the District court at St. Paul have been transferred to the Federal Records Center at Kansas City, Mo. These records comprise case files and related book records and include an admiralty record book, 1864-65; a chancery record book, 1861-1911; criminal record books, 1860-91;an execution docket, 1862-83; a complete record-book, 1863-66; minutes, 1862-1911; a chancery complete record book, 1861-62; and common rules and orders, 1858-1919.

The records of the circuit court, in the center at Kansas City, include minutes, 1862-1911; criminal case files, 1862-1900; chancery case files, 1862-1913; law case files, 1862-1914; equity case files, 1862-1914; an admiralty complete record book, 1864-65; chancery complete record books, 1861-1911; chancery common rule and order books, 1862-1911; criminal complete record books, 1860-91; an execution docket, 1862-83; law complete record books, 1862-66; and miscellaneous record books, 1862-1911.

Records in Other Custody. -- An admiralty docket, 1859-64, is in the U. S. district court at St. Paul, but the case files to which it relates are missing.

Missouri

After the admission of Missouri as a State in 1821, an act of Mar. 16, 1822 (3 Stat. 653), set it up as the District of Missouri. When the State was divided (act of Mar. 3, 1857; 11 Stat. 197) into Eastern and Western Districts, the seat of the former was at St. Louis and of the latter at Jefferson City. At the outbreak of the Civil War the Southern sympathizers in Missouri, led by the Governor, controlled the State government; but it was ousted from the capital by Federal forces. An application by the legislature (which had reassembled at Neosho) for admission to the Confederacy was accepted in Nov. 1861. Confederate control was never established in the State, however, and the Federal courts continued to meet within the military lines of the Union. The Federal authorities moved against Southern sympathizers by bringing indictments for treason, conspiracy, mutiny, and enticing soldiers to desert. Under the confiscation laws efforts were made through the courts to seize real estate, personal possessions, and cargoes belonging to Confederates.

Record Group 21. --Most of the old records of the U. S. District Court for the Eastern District of Missouri are in the Federal Records Center at Kansas City, Mo. They include case files; law, equity, and criminal records; final records; a record of loyalty oaths; a general index; executions; and naturalization records. Confiscation and revenue cases date from 1863.

The records of the circuit court for the Eastern District of Missouri, in the same center, include law and equity case files, 1824-1912, which contain also some criminal cases through 1865; and criminal case files, 1864-96. In addition there are complete and final records (criminal, law, and equity), 1839-90; an equity case record, 1839-1933; a law case record, 1838-1920; a criminal case record, 1864-96; a general index to direct cases, 1838-1923; an abstract of judgments, 1839-1910; and executions, 1839-95.

Records in Other Custody. --A far less extensive body of records for the Western District is still in the possession of the court at Jefferson City. It includes criminal case files, record books, and a roll of attorneys. The dockets of the court for the Eastern District have been retained by the court at St. Louis.

Nevada

A U. S. district court for the District of Nevada, authorized by an act of Feb. 27, 1865 (13 Stat. 440), held its first session at Carson City in Oct. 1865.

Records in Other Custody. --The Survey of Federal Archives found records of the district court for Nevada in the custody of the clerk of that court at Carson City. Records dating from 1865 include criminal cases, criminal final records, an index to equity cases, an equity journal and minutes, judgment dockets, law and equity minutes, and clerk's fiscal records and oaths of office taken by Federal officials.

New Hampshire

The State of New Hampshire was established as a judicial district by the Judiciary Act of 1789. The court met for years at Exeter and Portsmouth. The seat at Exeter was transferred to Concord in 1881.

Records in Other Custody. --Records held by the district court at Concord, as listed by the Survey of Federal Archives, include files of criminal and civil cases, admiralty cases, and equity cases. The records of the circuit court are presumably in the custody of the district court at Concord, N. H., and they may have been consolidated with the records of that court.

New Jersey

The district court established in New Jersey by the Judiciary Act of 1789 was to meet alternately at New Brunswick and Burlington. An act of June 4, 1844 (5 Stat. 660), provided that the sessions were to be held at Trenton only. New Jersey was assigned to the Middle Circuit by the Judiciary Act of 1789, with Trenton designated as the seat of the court. The District of New Jersey became part of the Third Circuit in 1802 and continued thereafter in that circuit.

Record Group 21. --The National Archives has bankruptcy records, 1867-78; and (on microfilm) minutes, 1789-1950, and civil dockets, 1863-1923. Naturalization petitions, 1838-1906, and some admiralty case files are in the Federal Records Center at New York. Records of the circuit court include minutes (microfilm), 1790-1911, and dockets (microfilm), 1862-1911.

Records in Other Custody. --The court at Trenton has retained the original minutes, 1789-1879; case files, 1863-1912; an index of indictments, 1849-71; and admiralty cases before 1863. The court also has (on microfilm) criminal case files, 1849-1914; admiralty case files, 1863-1944; minutes, 1789-1950; civil dockets, 1863-1911; and admiralty dockets. Records of the circuit court, in the custody of the district court at Trenton, include minutes, 1790-1881; an execution docket, 1829-69; and microfilm of the case files, 1819-1911, and related dockets, 1862-1911.

New York

The State of New York was constituted a judicial district by the Judiciary Act of 1789. The New York District was subdivided by an act of Apr. 9, 1814 (3 Stat. 120), into a Southern District with sessions at New York City and a Northern District with sessions at Utica, Salem, and Canandaigua. An act of Feb. 25, 1865 (13 Stat. 438), divided the Southern District into Eastern and Southern Districts, with seats at Brooklyn and New York City respectively. The court in the Southern District of New York was primarily concerned during the 19th century with admiralty and maritime matters, minor criminal prosecutions, and bankruptcy proceedings. During the war this court handled more prize cases than any other court in the country, and it formulated procedures followed by other prize courts. Assigned since 1802 to the Second Judicial Circuit, there had been since 1837 circuit courts in both of the judicial districts of New York. The circuit court in the Southern District handled important civil cases, some criminal cases, prize cases, and the case of the Confederate privateer Savannah.

Record Group 21. -- The records of the U. S. District Court for the Southern District of New York, in the National Archives, are extensive and varied. The minutes, 1789-1913, and judges' opinions, 1846-1917, relate to all types of proceedings. Admiralty records include case files, 1790-1912; dockets, 1828-1907; logs of ships involved in cases, 1839-1920; a docket for cases appealed to the U. S. circuit court, 1839-83; stipulations for libelants' costs, 1817-1902; stipulations for claimants' or respondents' costs, 1817-1904; bonds filed by claimants, 1854-1909; and libels for seamen's wages and related papers, 1830-73. Records of prize cases of the Civil War period include case files, logs of prize vessels, a prize commissioners' register, a cargo book, a cashbook, a ledger, a record of the disposition of prize vessels, and correspondence. Law records include case files, 1795-1906; dockets, 1844-1906; rule books, 1800-1878; judgment records, 1795-1911; praecipes, 1839-68; writs of capias, 1792-1867; a process register, 1839-67; an execution register, 1797-1870; and a bail register, 1797-1867. Records relating to internal revenue matters include petitions for the remission of fines, penalties, and forfeitures and related papers, 1796-1897; warrants of remission issued by the Secretary of the Treasury, 1790-1876; and complaints and other papers relating to "frauds committed on the revenue," 1863-73. The small quantity of habeas corpus case files, 1852-83, indicates that few applications for the writ were filed. Criminal case files and dockets cover 1845-68. U. S. commissioners' records include dockets, 1845-1910; minutes of testimony, 1855-1914; cost books, 1836-66, containing a record of fees and costs incurred by commissioners; a bail register, 1855-68; and affidavits, orders, depositions, and related papers, 1831-78.

The records of the circuit court for the Southern District of New York are with the records of the district court for that district in the National Archives. General records include minutes, 1790-1875, and recognizances, 1797-1912. Appellate jurisdiction records include case files, 1793-1911, and dockets, 1845-1912. More numerous are the records relating to the original jurisdiction of the court; law case files, 1790-1912; dockets, 1846-1912; judgment records, 1799-1911; judgment dockets, 1795-1911; praecipes, 1856-75; writs of capias, 1792-1877; bail certificates, 1791-1863; and a bail register, 1813-72. Records relating to customs and internal revenue include case files in suits brought by the United States, 1847-75, and related dockets; and case files in suits against collectors of customs, 1833-1903. There are also equity case files, 1792-1911, and related dockets; habeas corpus case files, 1828-1914; and criminal case files, 1790-1912. Records of the circuit court for the Northern District of New York are in the Federal Records Center at New York City. They include minutes, 1857-70; law case files; equity case files; dockets, 1846-95; rule books, 1812-68; and a calendar, 1853-66.

U. S. National Archives, Preliminary Inventory [No. 116] of the Records of the United States District Court for the Southern District of New York, comp. by Henry T. Ulasek and Marion Johnson (Washington, 1959); Madeline R. Robinton, An Introduction to the Papers of the New York Prize Court, 1861-1865 (New York, 1945); Samuel Blatchford, comp., Reports of Cases in Prize Argued and Determined in the Circuit and District Courts of the United States for the Southern District of New York, 1861-65 (Washington, 1866); Reports of Cases Argued and Determined in the Circuit Court of the United States for the Second Circuit, 1845-1887 (New York, 1852-88. 24 vols.).

Ohio

When Ohio was admitted as a State it was set up as a judicial district (act of Feb. 19, 1803; 2 Stat. 201). After meeting at Chillicothe for some years, the district court was removed in 1820 to Columbus and in 1842 to Cincinnati. The Ohio District was divided by an act of Feb. 10, 1855 (10 Stat. 604), into a Northern District (Cleveland) and a Southern District (Cincinnati). The court at Cincinnati tried many admiralty cases arising from commerce and traffic on the Ohio River. During the Civil War it handled confiscation cases also. When Ohio was divided into two districts the circuit court for the Southern District was directed to sit at Cincinnati and that for the Northern District at Cleveland. The litigation in the court in the Southern District on civil matters involved damage, trespass, assumpsit, and chancery cases; and on criminal matters involved chiefly counterfeiting and mail theft cases.

Record Group 21. --Records of the district court for the Southern District (Cincinnati) in the Federal Records Center at Chicago include admiralty records, 1852-1906; order books, 1802-63; and dockets, 1808-1930. Records of the district court for the Northern District (Cleveland), in the same center, include criminal records, 1863-1917; admiralty records, 1855-1904; civil and criminal case files, 1853-1911; and naturalization records, 1855-1902.

In the center at Chicago also are records of the circuit courts in Ohio. Records for the Southern District include the complete record, 1808-92; law records, 1863-1919; the chancery record, 1828-1919; an appeal record, 1858-93; an order book, 1802-63; dockets, 1808-1930; and an admiralty appeal record, 1858-93. The case files were combined with those of the district court. Records for the Northern District include a chancery record,

1855-1912, and law record, 1855-1906.

Records in Other Custody. --Records retained by the district court at Cincinnati include case files, journals, patent infringement cases, a roll of attorneys, and witness books. The book records retained by the court at Cleveland, dating mostly from 1855, include journals, dockets, a general index to cases, chancery order books, admiralty records, criminal records, a U. S. commissioner's docket, naturalization records, a roll of attorneys, fee books, witness and jury dockets, and official bonds. Other records of the circuit court for the Northern District of Ohio, found by the Survey of Federal Archives in the custody of the clerk of the district court at Cleveland, include law and equity cases, 1855-1913, and journals, 1855-1911.

Lewis H. Bond, comp., Reports of Cases Decided in the Circuit and District Courts Within the Southern District of Ohio [1856-71](Cleveland, 1872. 2 vols.).

Oregon

When Oregon became a State, its Territorial courts were replaced by a U. S. district court under an act of Mar. 3, 1859 (11 Stat. 437). The court held sessions at Salem until its seat was changed by an act of Feb. 19, 1864 (13 Stat. 5), to Portland. Upon its establishment in 1859 the district court was given circuit court powers. The district was joined with California by an act of Mar. 3, 1863 (12 Stat. 794), to form the Tenth Circuit; and the circuit court was directed to meet at Portland.

Record Group 21. --Records of the U. S. district court for Oregon are in the Federal Records Center at Seattle, Wash. They include case files, journals, dockets, oaths of court officers, and applications for admission to the bar. Records of the circuit court for Oregon are also in the center at Seattle. Covering part of the war period are minutes, 1863-1911, and case files.

Matthew P. Deady, comp., Reports of Cases Determined in the Circuit and District Courts of the United States of Oregon and California, 1859-1869 (San Francisco, 1872).

Records in Other Custody. --The court at Portland has retained some records, including bonds of marshals and clerks and naturalization records from 1859.

Pennsylvania

The State of Pennsylvania constituted one of the original 13 judicial districts created by the Judiciary Act of 1789. The State was divided by an act of Apr. 20, 1818 (3 Stat. 462), into Eastern and Western Districts, with seats at Philadelphia and Pittsburgh respectively. Trials of Southern privateers occurred at Philadelphia in 1861, and the court there subsequently handled many prize cases resulting from captures by the U. S. Navy. Circuit courts also held sessions at Philadelphia and Pittsburgh.

Record Group 21. --Records of the U. S. District Court for the Eastern District of Pennsylvania for the years before 1912 are in the National Archives. The minutes of the court date from May 1790. Admiralty records include case files, 1789-1911; dockets, 1802-1910; stipulations for libelants' costs, 1849-1913; stipulations for claimants' or respondents' costs, 1849-1907; bonds for costs on appeal, 1851-1912; bills of court costs, 1846-73; records of writs of survey issued, 1789-1878; and orders for writs of survey, 1856-61. Special files for prize cases tried during the Civil War include case files, dockets, fire insurance policies on prize vessels and their cargoes, docket of costs, and miscellaneous prize papers. Bankruptcy records under the act of 1867 include case files, 1867-78, dockets, indexes, bonds of assignees, and a record of bankruptcy costs. Law case files and related dockets are available for 1789-1911. Records relating to forfeitures in customs, internal revenue, and other cases include case files, 1789-1910, containing informations, libels, defendants' pleas, counterclaims, depositions, proclamations, recognizances, writs of attachment, decrees of condemnation, writs of sale, orders for the distribution of proceeds, orders for surveys, orders for payments, and related motions, orders, and papers. The cases are concerned with the slave trade, prizes of war, smuggling, false invoices, irregularities in handling goods, noncompliance with inspection laws, violations of acts of Congress, assault and battery on the high seas, giving assistance to the rebellion, and insurrection. Related records include information dockets, 1808-1907; statements of facts in forfeiture cases appealed to the Secretary of the Treasury, 1792-1918; and warrants for the remission of forfeitures, 1831-92. The equity case file, 1843-1911, is docketed in the law case file docket. Criminal case files cover 1791-1813 and 1832-1911; and there are related dockets, 1791-1911; a record of criminal cases, 1860-71; and recognizances of bail, 1850-63. Habeas corpus case files, 1791-1915, are docketed in the criminal case file dockets and the U. S. commissioner's criminal return docket, 1864-1915.

Extensive case files and some other records of the U. S. District Court for the Western District of Pennsylvania (Pittsburgh) are in the Federal Records Center at Philadelphia. These records include minute books, 1818-1938; law and equity cases, 1815-1938; criminal cases, 1848-1938; admiralty cases, 1846-1938; judgment dockets, 1817-1942; and cash books, 1810-1949.

Voluminous records of the circuit court for the Eastern District of Pennsylvania are in the National Archives. They include minutes, 1792-1911, and bonds, 1841-1905. Law case files, 1790-1911, are accompanied by dockets; praecipes, 1792-1880; and writs, 1790-1880. More extensive are the equity case files, 1790-1911, with dockets. There are also small files of habeas corpus cases, 1848-62; criminal cases, 1791-1883; indictments, 1861-65, against Confederate privateers for treason and piracy; pardon papers issued in criminal cases; correspondence; appointment papers; and loyalty oaths of attorneys, 1865-67.

National Archives, Preliminary Inventory [No. 124] of the Records of the United States District Court for the Eastern District of Pennsylvania, comp. by Marion M. Johnson, Mary Jo Grotenrath, and Henry T. Ulasek (Washington, 1960); Theodore McFadden, comp. and ed., Cadwalader's Cases; Being Decisions of the Hon. John Cadwalader, Judge of the District Court of the United States for the Eastern District of Pennsylvania, Between the Years 1858 and 1879; Comprising Some Ruling Opinions on Questions of Prize and Belligerency Arising During the Civil War, Together With Decisions in Admiralty, in Equity and at Common Law (Philadelphia, 1907. 2 vols.); Boyd Crumrine, ed.,

Pittsburgh Reports; Containing Cases Decided by the Federal and State, Courts of Pennsylvania, Chiefly at the City of Pittsburgh [1853-73], Originally Published in the Pittsburgh Legal Journal (Philadelphia, 1872-73. 3 vols.); D. F. Murphy, The Jeff Davis Piracy Cases; Full Report of the Trial of William Smith for Piracy . . . (Philadelphia, 1861).

Records in Other Custody. --Dockets for the district court case files and other records have been retained by the district court at Pittsburgh.

Rhode Island

The provisions of the Judiciary Act of 1789 were extended to Rhode Island by an act of June 23, 1790 (1 Stat. 128). The District of Rhode Island has always been coextensive with the limits of the State, and until 1912 the court met alternately at Newport and Providence. Sessions of the circuit court also were held at those places.

Record Group 21. --Most of the records of the district court for Rhode Island are in the Federal Records Center at Dorchester, Mass. Because the court's business was not extensive, case files of all types were kept in one consolidated file from 1791 to the 1880's. Other records include minutes, 1790-1920; dockets, 1790-1920; final records, 1791-1924; a record of bills of cost, 1852-75; executions returnable, 1790-1887; and transcriptions of assignments of copyrights, 1842-65. Records relating to bankruptcy under the act of 1867 are in the National Archives. Records of the circuit court, in the center at Dorchester, include minute books, 1790-1912; consolidated case files, 1791-1911; dockets, 1791-1911; final records in law actions, 1790-1909; an index to final records, 1790-1890; an order book, 1849-62; and naturalization records, 1802-1906.

Records in Other Custody. --The district court has retained at Providence its naturalization records.

Tennessee

The State of Tennessee was established as a Federal judicial district by an act of Jan. 31, 1797 (1 Stat. 496), and sessions of the district court were held alternately in the early years at Knoxville and Nashville. By an act of Feb. 24, 1807 (2 Stat. 421), Tennessee was divided into a District of East Tennesee (Knoxville) and a District of West Tennessee (Nashville). An act of June 18, 1838 (5 Stat. 249), directed the holding of a district court also at Jackson in western Tennessee. Several counties were separated from the District of West Tennessee by an act of June 18, 1839 (5 Stat. 313), to form the Middle District, for which the court was to be held at Nashville. The seat of the District of West Tennessee was transferred by an act of July 11, 1862 (12 Stat. 537), from Jackson to Huntington and by an act of Jan. 26, 1864 (13 Stat. 2), from Huntington to Memphis.

Union forces invaded Tennessee early in 1862 and captured Forts Henry and Donelson and the city of Nashville, forcing the Confederate State government to flee. West Tennessee was occupied in June 1862 and put under martial law. A civil commission was formed at Memphis in Apr. 1863 to handle complaints and suits of loyal citizens concerned with debts, contracts, frauds, and the recovery of property. Federal Judge West H. Humphreys had refused to hold court in Tennessee in 1861 and had accepted an appointment as district judge under the Confederacy. Connally F. Trigg

was appointed to the Federal judgeship in 1862 and held court that year at
Nashville, but the opening of other courts had to await the pacification of
the State. He finally held court at Memphis, Mar. 1864, and at Knoxville,
May 1864. The business of these courts included prosecutions for treason,
internal revenue suits, and seizures of property under the confiscation acts.

Associate Justice Catron presided over the U. S. circuit court at Nashville in the spring of 1861 and again Apr.-July 1862. At the latter session
indictments for treason were brought against Gov. Isham G. Harris, Brig.
Gens. Gideon J. Pillow and Samuel R. Anderson, and 40 other Confederates. But they were out of reach of the court, and no trials occurred. Illness kept Justice Catron from circuit duty and from attendance on the
Supreme Court during 1864-65. But he returned to Nashville and held a
term of the circuit court in the spring of 1865 not long before his death.
District Judge Connally F. Trigg opened the U. S. circuit courts at Memphis and Knoxville in the spring of 1864.

Record Group 21.--Records of all the district courts in Tennessee are
in the Federal Records Center at East Point, Ga. Those for East Tennessee include civil, law, equity, and criminal case files; execution, appearance and judgment, and rule dockets; minute books; a roll of attorneys; an
order book; and a fee book. Records for the Western District, from 1864,
include about the same series; and records of the civil commission at Memphis include minutes, dockets, and a final record, 1863-64. Records of the
Nashville court include case files, enrolling dockets, rule dockets, judgment dockets, minute books, and amnesty oaths taken during 1865-67. Records of the circuit courts for Tennessee are also in the center at East Point.
For the court at Nashville there are minutes, case files, and dockets; and
amnesty oaths, 1865-67. Starting in 1864, the records of the Knoxville
court and Memphis circuit courts include minutes, case files, and dockets.

Vermont

The State of Vermont was made a Federal judicial district by an act of
Mar. 2, 1791 (1 Stat. 197), with the district court to hold terms alternately
at Rutland and Windsor. The circuit court for Vermont had been in the Second Circuit since 1802.

Record Group 21.--Records of the district court for Vermont were
transferred in 1959 to the Federal Records Center at Dorchester, Mass.
They include a case file, 1792-1888, and civil dockets, 1801-1906. Records of the circuit court, in the same center, include case files and dockets.

Virginia

The U. S. District Court for the District of Virginia, established by the
Judiciary Act of 1789, met alternately at Richmond and Williamsburg. The
part of the State including most of what became West Virginia, west of the
summit of the mountains, was designated as the Western District of Virginia
by an act of Feb. 4, 1819 (3 Stat. 478). Within this new district sessions
were to be held at Clarksburg, Lewisburg, and Wythe Courthouse (Wythe-
ville). The Western District was extended eastward by an act of May 26,
1824 (4 Stat. 48), in general to include northwestern Virginia as far as the
Blue Ridge Mountains; and the court was also to meet at Staunton. A term
of the court in the Western District was also ordered in 1842 for Wheeling,
and Charleston replaced Lewisburg. The judges of both districts of Virginia

resigned in 1861 to become judges for the same districts under the Confederate Government. On Mar. 27, 1863, John C. Underwood was appointed district judge for the Eastern District of Virginia; and a year later he opened his court at Alexandria, which had become the seat of the "loyal government" of Virginia under Gov. Francis H. Pierpont. The Western District of Virginia was abolished by an act of June 11, 1864 (13 Stat. 124), which created the District of West Virginia; and the Eastern District thereupon became the District of Virginia.

The district court at Alexandria prosecuted confiscation cases against citizens of Alexandria, Fairfax, and Loudoun Counties who were adherents of the Confederacy; and after the opening of the district court at Richmond on July 19, 1865, confiscation suits were also brought against citizens of that city and Henrico County. Norfolk had been occupied by Federal forces on May 10, 1862, and in 1863 a district court was opened there to handle confiscation cases. The confiscation cases were suspended in Sept. 1865 and were eventually dismissed. Thirty-four indictments for treason were brought against prominent Confederates in the district court at Richmond after the war.

After being put in the Fourth Circuit (act of Aug. 16, 1842; 5 Stat. 507), Virginia remained in that circuit. The sessions of the circuit court at Richmond were suspended in 1861. An act of Feb. 25, 1865 (13 Stat. 440), directed the circuit court to hold sessions at Norfolk. It met there in May 1866 but adjourned to Richmond pursuant to an act of May 22, 1866 (15 Stat. 51). A hearing on an indictment for treason against Jefferson Davis was held by the circuit court at Richmond in Dec. 1868, but Chief Justice Chase and Judge John C. Underwood could not agree and sent a certificate of division to the Supreme Court. As the Government did not want the case tried by the Supreme Court, a nolle prosequi was entered in the circuit court and the case was dismissed by the Supreme Court.

Roy F. Nichols, "United States   American Historical Review, 31:266-
vs. Jefferson Davis 1865-1869,"   284 (Jan. 1926).

Record Group 21. --Records of the reinstituted Federal courts at Alexandria, Norfolk, and Richmond, 1863-65 (in the National Archives), relate to confiscation and treason prosecutions. They include a confiscation docket for libels filed at Alexandria from Sept. 9, 1864, to July 25, 1865, and a "complete final record" (actually incomplete) for the cases at Alexandria. The final record in confiscation cases, July 1, 1863-Feb. 8, 1864, contains the texts of documents such as libels of information, orders from the district attorney to the marshal for the seizure of property, notices of trial, judge's orders for trial, proceedings of the court, and decrees of condemnation, concerning which entries appear in the docket. A file of confiscation cases tried at Alexandria, 1863-65, contains libels of information; notices of seizure, libel, time, and place of trial; orders of seizure; and orders for process. In the National Archives also is a confiscation docket of the Richmond court, July 19-Sept. 9, 1865, containing entries for 436 cases.

Most of the records of the circuit court for the Eastern District of Virginia in the National Archives date from 1866, though a few antedate the war. A minute book, May 7, 1866-May 9, 1868, relates to both civil and criminal cases and contains entries regarding indictments for treason against some ex-Confederates. Papers relating to treason cases are in the criminal case files. There are also law case files, 1866-1911; equity case files, 1866-78; a law rule book, 1866-1902; and a chancery rule book, 1866-1901.

Records in Other Custody. --Other records are still retained by the courts. Records of the Alexandria district court, now in the custody of the court at Richmond, include a confiscation docket, Aug. 1863-Aug. 1864; confiscation order books, July 1863-May 1866; a confiscation judgment docket, Oct. 1863-May 1866; and an office docket, 1863-65. Records of the Norfolk district court, now at Richmond, include a confiscation docket, Nov. 1864-May 1865, and a confiscation judgment docket. In the court at Norfolk are orders of seizure under the confiscation act; amnesty oaths, June 25-Oct. 26, 1865; and certificates for amnesty oaths, Jan.-Dec. 1865. This court handled a wide range of business, and in its custody also are law order books for criminal and civil cases from Nov. 1863, admiralty order books from July 1864, and a judge's docket from Aug. 1864. In the district court at Richmond is a file of its confiscation cases, similar in content to the Alexandria file, together with confiscation dockets. A small file of indictments for treason contains information about a number of prominent Virginians. Other records are in the Virginia State Library at Richmond.

West Virginia

The northwestern counties of Virginia remained loyal to the Union, and the Federal courts there continued to meet. After secession, the people of the region set up a reorganized government for the State of Virginia, and in May 1862 they adopted a constitution for a new State. President Lincoln on Dec. 31, 1862, approved an act of Congress (12 Stat. 633) providing for the admission of the State of West Virginia when its constitution should provide for the gradual emancipation of slaves. This change was made, and on June 20, 1863, West Virginia was admitted to the Union. Later in that year the "panhandle" counties of Jefferson and Berkeley were added to the State. In the meantime John J. Jackson had been appointed, on Aug. 3, 1861, as district judge for the Western District of Virginia, and the U. S. district court had met in the western part of the district. By an act of June 11, 1864 (13 Stat. 124), the jurisdiction of the Western District of Virginia was made coextensive with the limits of the State of West Virginia, which was designated as the judicial District of West Virginia. Hundreds of indictments for treason were filed against Confederate sympathizers in West Virginia in 1862, but these were nolle prossed in the fall of 1865 after the accused had given loyalty bonds. The act of 1864 contains no specific mention of circuit court jurisdiction, but circuit court powers had been vested in the district court for the Western District of Virginia by an act of Feb. 4, 1819 (3 Stat. 479), and under that authority the district court for the District of West Virginia may have exercised circuit court jurisdiction after 1864. An act of July 23, 1866 (14 Stat. 209), assigned West Virginia to the Fourth Circuit.

Records in Other Custody. --Records retained by the court at Wheeling include a minute book and docket, 1843-62; a criminal docket book, 1843-62; admiralty cases, 1855-94; dockets, 1862-1911; indictments, 1863-1936; an order book, 1843-69; loyalty bonds, 1862-65; and naturalization records, 1856-66. A trial docket and minute book, 1843-73, and a fee book of the court at Charleston are now in the West Virginia University Library. The court at Clarksburg has order books that appear to cover the Civil War period.

Wisconsin

The Territorial courts of Wisconsin were succeeded by a U. S. district court under an act of May 29, 1848 (9 Stat. 234). The court was to be held once a year at Madison and at Milwaukee but was to be open at all times to hear and decide cases of admiralty and maritime jurisdiction that could be handled without a jury. Under authority of an act of Aug. 6, 1846 (9 Stat. 57), the district court for the new State of Wisconsin exercised circuit court jurisdiction. In the reorganization of 1862 a circuit court for Wisconsin was established and put in the Eighth Circuit, but it was transferred by an act of Feb. 9, 1863 (12 Stat. 648), to the Ninth Circuit.

Record Group 21. -- Many records of the district court at Milwaukee are in the Federal Records Center at Chicago. They include law cases, 1862-1908; admiralty cases, 1853-1907; criminal cases, 1849-1929; chancery cases, 1849-1908; appearance dockets, 1849-62; and records of confiscation cases under the act of 1862. Records of the circuit court at the center at Chicago include case files; law, chancery, and execution dockets; and judgment records.

Records in Other Custody. -- The court at Milwaukee has retained its civil and criminal dockets and indexes, from 1849, and its naturalization records. The inventory published by the Survey of Federal Archives in 1939 lists some records of the district court at Madison: a judgment record, 1852-1918; a final equity and law record, 1862-73; a final chancery record, 1850-75; and a naturalization docket, 1855-84.

TERRITORIAL COURTS

Migration into the West in the decade before the Civil War and the discovery of new mining areas in remote sections of the huge Territories that then covered the Rocky Mountain region necessitated measures for the government of the settlements. Proposals were made in Congress for the division of the Territories, but legislation was not possible until the departure of the Southerners, who opposed it over the issue of slavery. Meanwhile, mining districts were organized all over the West and continued to be organized even after the creation of new Territories. Miners from California who went to the new mining camps in what are now the States of Colorado, Nevada, Idaho, Arizona, Montana, and Washington were influential in having mining laws like California's adopted for the government of the camps. Though primarily designed to safeguard claims to mines, these mining laws also provided for local government and the administration of justice. Thus developed an American common law of mines, which came to be recognized by legislation of Territories and States and by decisions of the courts. From the time of the discovery of gold in California Congress had followed a hands-off policy in regard to mining operations; but finally, when there were 1,150 mining camps in operation in the West, it gave recognition to the mining laws by an act of July 26, 1866 (14 Stat. 251), which also provided for the miners' acquisition of title to public mineral lands. Miners' courts continued to operate, in the new Territories organized in the West, during the Civil War, and in cooperation with vigilance committees they strove to suppress lawlessness. Responsible to general meetings of miners and staffed with judges, sheriffs, collectors, and surveyors, the miners' courts were the most effective of the local courts. When the mining camps developed into permanent settlements, the miners' courts gave way to the regular systems of local government provided for by the Territorial and State legislatures.

Hubert H. Bancroft, Popular Tribunals (San Francisco, 1887. 2 vols.); Jim Dan Hill, "The Early Mining Camp in American Life," Pacific Historical Review, 1:295-311 (1932); Curtis H. Lindley, A Treatise on the American Law Relating to Mines and Mineral Lands Within the Public Land States and Territories and Governing the Acquisition and Enjoyment of Mining Rights in Lands of the Public Domain (San Francisco, 1914. 3 vols.); Charles H. Shinn, Mining Camps; a Study in American Frontier Government (New York, 1885). A number of local mining laws and regulations of the Civil War period are printed in Clarence King, ed., The United States Mining Laws and Regulations Thereunder, and State and Territorial Mining Laws, to Which Are Appended Local Mining Rules and Regulations (H. Misc. Doc. 42, pt. 14, 47 Cong., 2 sess., Serial 2144; Washington, 1885).

The judicial systems of the Territories at the time of the Civil War were provided for by the acts of Congress establishing the Territorial governments. For each Territory the organic act vested judicial power in a supreme court, district courts, probate courts, and justices of the peace. The three justices for each Territory, appointed by the President for 4-year terms, sat together as the supreme court; and each judge presided over a district court. The supreme and district courts had jurisdiction over cases arising under United States or Territorial law, and they had chancery as well as common law jurisdiction. Acts of the Territorial legislatures prescribed more specifically the jurisdiction of the district courts in civil and criminal cases. Naturalization oaths could be taken before the Territorial courts. Writs of error, bills of exception, and appeals were allowed from district courts to the Territorial supreme court; and writs of error and appeals could be taken from that court to the Supreme Court of the United States. District attorneys and marshals of Territories were appointed by the President with the approval of the Senate, and court clerks were appointed by the judges. The duties of clerks and the types of records they were to keep were prescribed by Territorial laws.

The boundaries of the judicial districts and the assignment of judges to them were determined by the Territorial legislatures. An act of Congress of Aug. 16, 1856 (11 Stat. 49), authorized the justices of the Territorial supreme courts to decide the times and places for holding court in their respective districts and to limit the length of terms. Courts were to be held at no more than three places in any one Territory. This restriction imposed a burden of difficult travel upon litigants, and the law was modified by an act of June 14, 1858 (11 Stat. 366), which authorized the judges of the Territorial district courts to hold court within their respective districts in counties where courts had been established by the Territories and to try all cases except those in which the United States was a party. The expenses of such courts, however, were to be paid by the Territories or the counties. To the extensive jurisdictions of the district judges this act, when implemented by the Territories, added extensive itineraries.

Some legislation of the Civil War period was enforceable in the Territorial courts. Suits for the condemnation of confiscated property and prosecutions for treason were handled by those courts. Contracts made by emigrants could be enforced in Territorial courts (act of July 4, 1864; 13 Stat. 386).

Judges of probate courts were either elected or appointed by the Governors of the Territories. These courts were concerned with the probating of wills, the administration of estates, and the guardianship of minors and others; and they had original jurisdiction in civil, criminal, and chancery cases. In addition to their judicial duties, probate judges usually became involved in the administration of county affairs and the maintenance of the peace. Justices of the peace, in accordance with an act of June 15, 1844 (5 Stat. 671), were to be elected by the people. They had jurisdiction in civil cases involving small amounts of money and over petty criminal offenses and breaches of the peace.

The Territorial supreme courts did not handle much business in their early period, for appeals to them involved expenses in travel and other costs. Since the trial judge (district court judge) was included in the membership of the supreme court, suitors were reluctant to appeal; they believed that the trial judge could win over one of the other judges to his opinion. Furthermore the district courts had broad jurisdiction. These considerations explain the relatively few published Territorial supreme court reports for the Civil War period.

In accordance with established practice, when Territories became States the Territorial court records were transferred to State courts. The records of the Territorial supreme courts were usually delivered to the State supreme courts, and the records of the district and probate courts to the local courts of the State (superior, district, or county courts). Records relating to Federal cases pending in the Territorial courts, however, were transferred to the U. S. district courts in the newly established States.

Francis N. Thorpe, ed. , The Federal and State Constitutions, Colonial Charters, and Other Organic Laws of the States, Territories, and Colonies, Now or Heretofore Forming the United States of America (H. Doc. 357, 59 Cong. , 2 sess. , Serials 5190-5194; Washington, 1909. 7 vols.); Charles Kettleborough, ed. , The State Constitutions and the Federal Constitution and Organic Laws of the Territories and Other Colonial Dependencies of the United States of America (Indianapolis, 1918). Both the Historical Records Survey and the Survey of Federal Archives covered the records of the courts, depending on where they were found, but neither survey completed its task. The titles of inventories published are in U. S. Works Projects Administration, Bibliography of Research Projects Reports; Check List of Historical Records Survey Publications, comp. by Sargent B. Child and Dorothy P. Holmes (Washington, 1943); this also contains a list of depositories of unpublished Historical Records Survey material.

Information regarding Territorial supreme court records that have been microfilmed is in U. S. Library of Congress, Photoduplication Service, A Guide to the Microfilm Collection of Early State Records (Washington, 1950). The published reports of the State supreme courts, which are cited below under the appropriate Territories, contain other data pertaining to the courts, including lists of names of judges of Territorial supreme courts and lists of names of attorneys admitted to practice. Digests of supreme court reports sometimes contain the same information. Lists of the Territorial judges are in Clarence E. Carter, ed. , The Territorial Papers of the United States, Volume I, General (Washington, 1934), and are usually included in the works on the Western States by Hubert H. Bancroft.

Arizona Territory

Arizona, then the western part of the Territory of New Mexico, was occupied by Confederate forces from Texas during the early part of the war. The area was declared to be a territory under Confederate protection on Aug. 1, 1861, and civil courts were established. But an invasion by Union forces from California in May 1862 forced the withdrawal of the Confederate troops and of Southern sympathizers who were developing mines. The commander of the Union forces, Col. James H. Carleton, proclaimed a military government over the area on June 8, 1862, and replaced the civil courts by military commissions. In 1863 the part of the Territory of New Mexico west of the 32d degree of longitude was set up as the Territory of Arizona by an act of Feb. 24 (12 Stat. 664). This act vested the judicial power in a supreme court of three judges and inferior courts to be constituted by the legislative council. By a proclamation of Apr. 9, 1864, the Governor divided the Territory into three judicial districts, assigned judges to them, and ordered sessions of the court in the first district at Tucson, the second at La Paz, and the third at Prescott. The Territorial legislature met late in 1864 and adopted the Howell code, which provided that Pima County should constitute the first judicial district, Yuma and Mohave Counties the second, and Yavapai County the third. With the growth of population and the formation of new counties the composition of judicial districts and the terms of court were often changed.

Historical Records Survey, Ari-   Territory of Arizona, 1864-1912
zona, The District Courts of the   (Phoenix, Ariz., 1941).

Records in Other Custody. --When Arizona became a State in 1912 the records of its Territorial courts were disposed of in accordance with provisions of its constitution. The records of the Territorial supreme court passed into the possession of the State supreme court, and those of the district and probate courts were transferred to the superior courts, which took over the jurisdiction of the inferior Territorial courts except for Federal matters.

The records of the first judicial district of the Territory of Arizona are in the custody of the clerk of the superior court of Pima County at Tucson. A case file of civil actions starts in 1864; and there is an index to this file for cases 1-486 for the years 1864-74. There is a similar numerical file for criminal cases. Naturalization records include declarations of intent to become citizens; each gives the name of the declarant, the declaration, the renunciation of allegiance to the former sovereign, the date, and the signatures of the declarant and the clerk of the court. An index in a separate volume facilitates name searches in the declarations. The volume of declarations also contains oaths of allegiance to the U. S. Government taken by officials of the district and records of appointments of officials.

In the same custody are the records of the Territorial probate court for the first judicial district. Dating likewise from 1864, these records include case files and minutes of proceedings in probate cases. A volume, May 17, 1864-Mar. 21, 1866, contains the proceedings of the probate court in the administration of local affairs, probate minutes, wills admitted to probate, letters of administration and bonds, criminal complaints and bonds, notices of court terms, and documents recorded by the clerk, including field notes of surveys, mining claims, mining water rights, deeds to mines and other realty, realty mortgages, livestock brands, and marriage certificates.

Colorado Territory

The Territory of Colorado was formed from the territories of Nebraska, Utah, and New Mexico, and from what remained of the Kansas Territory after the State of Kansas had been admitted to the Union, by an act of Feb. 28, 1861 (12 Stat. 172). The act provided for the usual Territorial judicial system and for the division of the Territory by its legislature into three judicial districts. Gov. William Gilpin in July 1861 appointed the judges to their districts and announced a term of the supreme court to meet in Denver in Sept. 1861. The new Territorial legislature met in Denver in the same month, adopted civil and criminal codes, and divided the Territory into counties and judicial districts. The first judicial district comprised the region east of the Rocky Mountains, with its seat at Denver; the second, the northwest corner of the Territory, with its seat at Central City; and the third, the southwestern part of the Territory, with its seat at Pueblo. The legality of the miners' courts in the mining districts was recognized, their decisions were confirmed, and provision was made for the transfer of cases from them to the regular Territorial courts.

Record Group 21.--Although Colorado's State constitution provided for the transfer of the records of the Territorial district courts to the State's district courts, the records of the first judicial district (Denver) passed into the custody of the U. S. District Court for the District of Colorado at Denver. Now in the Federal Records Center at Denver, they comprise civil and criminal case files, 1861-76, dockets, and minutes of proceedings. The dockets also cover naturalization cases. In the same depository are criminal case files for the second and third judicial districts, unaccompanied by dockets or indexes. The civil case files for the second judicial district are missing.

Offenses entered in the dockets include theft of horses, mules, oxen, cattle, and gold dust; assault with intent to kill; murder; robbery of the mail; selling or giving liquor to the Indians; failure to pay taxes; timber cutting; and perjury or subornation of perjury in fraudulent homestead filings. The records also document indictments for treason brought by the Government and suits involving the confiscation of property under Civil War legislation. Civil suits cover types of litigation common to all the western Territories. These include suits for personal injuries in stagecoach accidents and for the loss of merchandise being freighted across the plains; suits for debt, bigamy, divorce, desertion, nonsupport, infidelity, and cruelty; and suits relating to wagon roads. Stagecoach and freight lines were so constantly involved in lawsuits that the court records constitute a good source for their history. Suits concerning the ownership of mining properties were also numerous.

Records in Other Custody.--Records of the Territorial supreme court were transferred, in accordance with the terms of the Colorado constitution of 1876, to the supreme court of the State. Files of civil cases tried before the Arapahoe County Court in the Territorial period, 1862-76, and of probate cases in the same county, 1864-76, are in the Municipal Building at Denver.

The records of the mining districts, which include records of miners' courts extending into the Territorial period, are in the offices of the county clerks (Thomas M. Marshall, "The Miners' Laws of Colorado," American Historical Review, 25:426-439, Apr. 1920).

See also Thomas M. Marshall, ed.,
Early Records of Gilpin County,
Colorado, 1859-1861 (Boulder,
Colo., 1920); King, ed., U. S.
Mining Laws, p. 346-494. Reports
on supreme court cases dating
from the January Term of 1864 are
in Moses Hallett, comp., Reports
of Cases at Law and in Chancery
Determined in the Supreme Court of
Colorado Territory (Denver, 1872).

Dakota Territory

The part of Nebraska Territory north of the 43d parallel and the region
west of Minnesota was organized as Dakota Territory by an act of Mar. 2,
1861 (12 Stat. 239). The three judicial districts authorized by that act
were established by proclamation of the Governor, July 30, 1861, and
judges were assigned to hold court at Vermillion, Yankton, and Bon Homme,
for the first, second, and third districts, respectively. A Territorial act
of Jan. 9, 1863, named the counties composing each district, designated the
places mentioned above as the seats, and ordered terms twice yearly. Other
acts concerned civil and criminal procedure and defined the jurisdiction of
the courts and of justices of the peace and the duties of juries. In 1889
Congress divided the Territory into the States of North and South Dakota.

Record Group 21.--Some of the records of the district courts of Dakota
Territory formerly in the U. S. district court at Sioux Falls, S. Dak., have
been transferred to the Federal Records Center at Kansas City, Mo. Records of the first judicial district (Vermillion) include criminal and law case
files, 1863-77, and a journal and record book, 1861-77. The records for the
second judicial district (Yankton) relate largely to the years after the Civil
War but include a journal and record book, 1861-73, and a court calendar,
1864-77.

Records in Other Custody.--Other records of the district courts were
found by the Survey of Federal Archives. Some case files (apparently of the
second judicial district, 1861-89) were held by the U. S. district court, at
Sioux Falls, S. Dak. In the same court were naturalization lists and memoranda of fees and expenses. Other materials--in the county courthouse at
Yankton--included naturalization records, 1858-89, a trial docket, 1864-
71, journals, 1861-86, a U. S. marshal's ledger, 1862-71, and letter books
containing copies of letters sent by the U. S. commissioner to offices in
Washington.

Idaho Territory

This Territory was created by an act of Mar. 3, 1863 (12 Stat. 808),
from part of Washington Territory. At first Idaho Territory was composed
approximately of what became Idaho, Montana, and Wyoming; but it was reduced to about the present limits of the State of Idaho in 1864, when the Territory of Montana was formed and when what was to become the Territory of
Wyoming was transferred to Dakota Territory. The judicial system provided for in sec. 9 of the organic act was organized by the Territorial government in 1863. At the first term of the court for the second judicial district (Boise County) in Feb. 1864, indictments were entered for murder,
manslaughter, assault, robbery, grand larceny, perjury, obtaining money
under false pretenses, and minor offenses. The first term of the Territorial supreme court was held at Boise in Jan. 1866.

Records in Other Custody.--The records of the district courts were

transferred, as provided by the State constitution, to the district courts of
the counties, and the records of the probate courts to the county probate
courts. These records for Nez Perce County are described in the inventory published by the Historical Records Survey. The district court records for that county include a court calendar of civil and criminal cases set
for hearing; a register showing the status of the cases in court; a voluminous case file for both types of cases; a cash and fee book; and a record of
judgments issued by the court in civil cases, indexed alphabetically by
name. The beginning date of the case file is given as 1862 and that of the
other records as 1864. The probate court records for the same county
concern proceedings in the settlement of estates; letters testamentary; letters of administration; records on guardianship, adoptions, and dependent
children; and various orders and decrees. There are also a probate fee
book, a cash book, and a record of wills.

Montana Territory

The mining camps east of the Bitter Root Range in Idaho Territory were
included by an act of May 26, 1864 (13 Stat. 85), in Montana Territory.
Under this act the first legislature, 1864-65, passed laws establishing judicial districts and counties, adopted a code of law, and defined the functions
of the courts, including probate courts. The judges of the district courts
arrived in the fall of 1864 and undertook the organization of the courts.
Under Territorial law the probate judges were elected in each county. Much
of the courts' business involved criminal cases, and in attempting to cope
with criminals the courts had to compete with vigilantes. The first term
of the Territorial supreme court was held at Virginia City in May 1865.
For several years the supreme court rarely delivered opinions in writing;
usually it simply issued orders to affirm or reverse the lower court.

Records in Other Custody. --When Montana became a State in 1889 the
records of the district and probate courts were transferred to the State
district courts. The records for the Territorial district court at Virginia
City (Madison County) include civil and criminal case files and a journal of
court proceedings that shows the actions taken on the cases. For some
years a consolidated record was kept of judgments and decrees, judgment
docket, executions, bonds, letters, wills, and probate actions. An alphabetical name index to this record also covers civil, criminal, and probate
cases, which are arranged numerically. Naturalization records do not
begin until 1865.

Nebraska Territory

That part of the Indian country west of Missouri, Iowa, and Minnesota
Territory was constituted by act of May 30, 1854 (10 Stat. 277), as Kansas
and Nebraska Territories. Kansas became a State on Jan. 29, 1861, but
Nebraska Territory, with reduced limits after the creation of Colorado and
Dakota Territories, continued until Feb. 9, 1867. Toward the end of 1854
the Governor by proclamation established judicial districts in Nebraska
Territory; justices were appointed to them; the judges of probate were designated. On Mar. 16, 1855, the Territorial legislature outlined the judicial
districts, assigned judges to them, and defined their jurisdiction. The
court for the first district met in Omaha, for the second in Nebraska City
and Falls City, and for the third in Dakota City.

Record Group 21. --The records of the courts of Nebraska Territory have been transferred to the Federal Records Center at Kansas City, Mo., from the U. S. district court at Omaha, Nebr. The records of the Territorial supreme court are incomplete: dockets, journals, other book records, and case files for 1864-67 are missing. Some case files, 1859-63, are available. A file of general records, 1855-62, consists of appointment papers of court personnel, motions to admit attorneys, and court orders and rules. For the first judicial district there are an incomplete file of case papers, 1856-66; a docket, 1859-66; a journal, 1859-66; the complete and final record, 1859-67; the application of John Bowden for a writ of habeas corpus; and general records containing appointment papers, attachments for contempt of court, minutes of bar meetings, orders, and resolutions of the grand jury. More complete are the case files, 1855-66, of the second judicial district, for which there are also a docket, 1862-66; the complete and final record, 1862-66; and general records containing appointment papers, attendance records, grand jury subpenas and related papers, and warrants. The single extant record of the third judicial district is the complete and final record, 1861-67.

James M. Woolworth, Reports   dates for the cases, but some of
of Cases in the Supreme Court of   them were apparently decided in the
Nebraska (Chicago, 1871), gives no   1860's.

Records in Other Custody. --In the Nebraska State Historical Society among the archives of the State is a minute book, June 1858-June 1867, of the Nebraska Territorial supreme court. A microfilm copy of this is in the Library of Congress.

Nevada Territory

Nevada Territory was created from the western part of Utah Territory, which in 1854 had established Carson County as the seat of its third judicial district. Neither the district court nor the probate judge had much business, however, until mining in the area developed during 1858-59. To provide a government for the mining camps, Nevada Territory was created by an act of Mar. 2, 1861 (12 Stat. 209). The government of the Territory was organized at Carson City in July, and on July 17 the Governor issued a proclamation establishing the supreme, district, and probate courts and justices of the peace. The Territory was divided into three judicial districts and judges were assigned to them. Many suits to determine the ownership of mining claims, for which there was a fierce scramble on the rich Comstock lode, and many criminal cases were handled by the Territorial courts.

Nevada Territory was short-lived. Congress adopted the enabling act of Mar. 21, 1864 (13 Stat. 30), and the President by proclamation of Oct. 31, 1864, admitted the State of Nevada.

Records in Other Custody. --The records of Territorial district courts passed into the possession of the district courts set up by the State constitution. The records for Douglas County, beginning early in the Civil War period, include a calendar, a minute book, a register of actions, case papers, a judgment docket, jury lists, venires and trial and grand jury reports, and naturalization records. Similar records are available for Washoe County at Reno and probably for other counties. The probate court records also were transferred to the State district courts. The records of the Territorial supreme court were taken over by the State supreme court.

New Mexico Territory

A provisional civil court, which functioned in New Mexico during the period of military government, 1846-51, was succeeded in 1851 by a regular Territorial system of courts provided by an act of Sept. 9, 1850 (9 Stat. 449). The judges held court in the counties in their districts and traveled regular circuits. A Confederate invasion of 1862 resulted in a temporary occupation of Santa Fe and Albuquerque, giving Southern sympathizers an opportunity to show their colors. After Union reoccupation, martial law in the Territory kept the operation of the courts at a minimum. Indictments for treason were brought against citizens of the Territory in all the judicial districts; but the accused, some of whom were prominent citizens, were never brought to trial. Prosecutions for the confiscation of the property of Confederates were more successful.

Arie W. Poldervaart, Black-Robed Justice; a History of the Administration of Justice in New Mexico From the American Occupation in 1846 Until Statehood in 1912 (Albuquerque, 1948); Aurora Hunt, Kirby Benedict, Frontier Federal Judge; an Account of Legal and Judicial Development in the Southwest, 1853-1874 (Glendale, Calif., 1961); Edward D. Tittmann, "The Last Legal Frontier" and "The Exploitation of Treason," New Mexico Historical Review, 2:219-227, 4:128-145 (July 1927, Apr. 1929).

Records in Other Custody. --When New Mexico was admitted as a State in 1912 and constituted as the judicial District of New Mexico, the records of the Territorial district courts that related to Federal cases and proceedings were transferred to the clerk of the U. S. district court at Santa Fe. That office still has custody of records of the seven Territorial judicial districts that existed in 1912. The records include criminal, civil, and miscellaneous case records of trials, 1852-1912; and case dockets, judgment dockets, miscellaneous dockets, minute books of court proceedings, registers of actions filed, naturalization records and declarations, registers of attorneys admitted to practice, analysis report registers, and cash dockets of expenses. Similar records are in the custody of the district courts of the counties in which the Federal justices tried cases arising under Territorial laws according to an act of June 14, 1858 (11 Stat. 366).

The records of the Territorial supreme court were transferred to the supreme court of New Mexico. They include case files, a supreme court record, and opinions. Though these records date from 1852, they are meager during the early years, as in some terms the number of cases handled was very small.

A microfilm of the supreme court record or docket, Jan. 1852–Jan. 1867, is in the collection of early State records in the Library of Congress.

Utah Territory

The Mormons who settled in the Great Salt Lake Valley in 1847 managed their own affairs for several years. The general assembly of the State of Deseret, which they organized in 1849, provided for a judicial system consisting of county courts and a supreme court. Congress by act of Sept. 9, 1850 (9 Stat. 453), created the Territory of Utah; and Brigham Young, the leader of the Mormons, was appointed Governor. On Aug. 8, 1851, he issued a proclamation dividing the Territory into three judicial districts, assigning justices to them, and designating the times and places for holding the district courts.

Records in Other Custody. --When Utah became a State in 1896, the records of the Territorial district and probate courts were transferred to the State district courts. The records of the district court for the County of Utah include for the Territorial period minute books, an appearance docket, exhibits in criminal and civil cases , naturalization records, and a probate record, docket, and cost book. The Historical Records Survey inventories show that there are district or probate court records for Box Elder, Morgan, Sanpete, Tooele, Wasatch, and Weber Counties; presumably there are also records for other counties. Some records of the Weber County court and other materials relating to Utah courts are in the Bancroft Library of the University of California at Berkeley. Records of the Territorial supreme court, in the custody of the supreme court of Utah, include no material for the Civil War period.

Washington Territory

The organic act of Washington Territory, Mar. 2, 1853 (10 Stat. 175), authorized its judicial system. In the same year the President appointed judges, and early in 1854 the district courts were opened in districts set up by the Governor. The Territorial legislature passed acts in 1854 concerning the composition of the judicial districts and the jurisdiction of the district and probate courts and of the justices of the peace. The appointment of a wreckmaster, to assume charge of marine wrecks, anticipated the filing of admiralty cases. The district judges met at Olympia in Dec. 1854 in the first session of the Territorial supreme court.

Arthur S. Beardsley and Donald A. McDonald, "The Courts and Early Bar of Washington Territory," Washington Law Review and State Bar Journal, 17:57-82 (Apr. 1943).

Records in Other Custody. --The Washington State constitution of Aug. 22, 1889, provided for the transfer of the records of the Territorial district courts and probate courts to the superior courts in the counties and the records of the Territorial supreme court to the State supreme court. The clerk of the superior court of Cowlitz County has probate records for the Territorial period and a journal of the district court of Pacific County, 1858-75. The court clerk in King County has journals and execution dockets of the district court, 1854-89, and probate records. The court records of Clark County were destroyed. Inquiries directed to the clerks of the superior courts of other counties would undoubtedly uncover other collections of court records. The records of the Territorial supreme court in the custody of the State supreme court include case files, a journal, and opinions, orders, and decrees. Rarities among Territorial judicial records are the justice of the peace dockets for Chehalis precinct, 1859-72, and Boisfort precinct, 1857-68 and 1872-79, both in Lewis County.

Washington (Terr.) Supreme Court, Reports of Cases Determined in the Supreme Court of the Territory of Washington From 1854 to 1879, comp. by John B. Allen (Olympia, 1879), contains cases for

the December Terms of 1861 and   an appendix to Washington (Terr.),
1862. The opinions of the supreme   Journal of the Council, 1864-65.
court, 1854-64, are published in

U. S. COURT OF CLAIMS

Throughout the war the military and naval forces of the United States, wherever they operated, seized and used private property of all kinds. Army detachments or foraging parties scoured the country for provisions, fodder, horses, mules, and wood--especially rail fences, a convenient source of firewood for campfires. Receipts for such property were sometimes given so that owners could claim remuneration. Churches, hospitals, schools, colleges, museums, saloons, and private dwellings were occupied and used for headquarters, offices, hospitals, quarters, and warehouses. It mattered not to the Army who the owner was--a loyal citizen, a southern Unionist, a Confederate, or a foreigner. Property was appropriated not only in occupied areas of the South and in the border States, where Federal armies took the offensive, but also in such States as Maryland and Pennsylvania, where Confederate invasions brought in large Union forces. The U. S. Government had no legal obligation to pay for the large amount of Confederate property seized or destroyed in the South, but it did have an obligation under international law to reimburse foreigners for seized property or bodily injury. The claims of foreigners were adjudicated chiefly by international commissions, whose activities and records are described elsewhere in this Guide.

The huge number of other claims against the Government resulting from war necessitated a better means for their adjudication. The Court of Claims, established by an act of Feb. 24, 1855 (10 Stat. 612), was merely a factfinding body that investigated claims and sent reports to Congress for its action. Because the court had no authority to issue enforceable judgments it had not greatly relieved Congress of the heavy burden of claims. Moreoever, since at the beginning of the Civil War two of the three judges were holdovers from the Buchanan administration and since business was to be heavier, the Lincoln administration desired to enlarge the court. In his first annual message, Dec. 3, 1861, Lincoln recommended that the Court of Claims be given authority to make final judgments, subject to appeal on questions of law to the Supreme Court. An act of Mar. 3, 1863 (12 Stat. 765), conferred this authority, provided for two additional judges, authorized them to appoint commissioners, and stipulated that the court was to hold one annual session beginning on the first Monday in October. The act extended jurisdiction of the court to cover "private claims against the Government, founded upon any law of Congress, or upon any regulations of an executive department, or upon any contract" with the Government. The earlier act of 1855, which that of 1863 amended, had authorized the hearing of any claims referred to the court by either House of Congress. In addition the new act gave the court "jurisdiction of all set-offs, counterclaims for damages, whether liquidated or unliquidated, or other demands whatsoever, on the part of the Government" against claimants. Judgments of the court were to be final except for cases involving over $3,000, which either party might appeal to the Supreme Court.

The jurisdiction of the Court of Claims over war claims was modified, extended, or restricted by subsequent legislation. An act of Mar. 3, 1863 (approved Mar. 12; 12 Stat. 820), gave the court jurisdiction over claims of owners of captured and abandoned property that had been collected and disposed of by agents of the Treasury Department. This act pertained to such commodities as cotton, rice, sugar, and tobacco, but not to armaments, munitions, ships, steamboats and other craft, furniture, forage, and military supplies. Claimants under the act were required to show proof of ownership and of loyalty to the United States during the war. Under this act the court between 1864 and 1883 considered 1,578 claims for $77,785,962 and awarded $9,833,423 (18 Ct. Cl. 703-704). An act of July 4, 1864 (13 Stat. 381), provided that the jurisdiction of the court was not to extend to any claim against the United States resulting from "the destruction or appropriation of, or damage to, property by the army or navy" during the war. Soon afterwards the court decided that it was estopped by this act from determining some cases then pending (Corbett's Case, Oct. 1864, 1 Ct. Cl. 139). The act of July 4, 1864, was amended by an act of Feb. 21, 1867 (14 Stat. 397), which declared that it "shall not be construed to authorize the settlement of any claim for supplies or stores taken or furnished for the use of, or used by, the armies of the United States, nor for the occupation of, or injury to, real estate, nor for the consumption, appropriation, or destruction of, or damage to, personal property, by the military authorities or troops of the United States, where such claim originated during the war for the suppression of the southern rebellion, in a State, or part of a State, declared in insurrection by the proclamation of the President of the United States, dated July first [1862]."

The claims of disloyalists originating before Apr. 13, 1861, were barred from payment by an act of Mar. 2, 1867 (14 Stat. 571). An act of June 25, 1868 (15 Stat. 75), provided that the United States might appeal to the Supreme Court adverse judgments of the Court of Claims. Sec. 7 of this act authorized the executive departments to send to the court claims made upon them which involved "disputed facts or controverted questions of law" if the amount involved exceeded $3,000 or if the decision would affect a class of cases or establish a precedent. Aliens who were citizens of nations that accorded reciprocal privileges to citizens of the United States were allowed to file claims in the court under an act of July 27, 1868 (15 Stat. 243).

The act of July 4, 1864, cited above, required the Quartermaster General and the Commissary General to examine claims of loyal citizens of States outside the Confederacy and, if convinced that the claims were just and the claimants loyal, to report them to the Third Auditor of the Treasury for settlement. The terms of this act excluded claims of loyalists in the seceded States. They might, of course, present their claims to Congress; but, since Representatives from the Southern States were admitted only gradually during 1866-70, very few such claims were submitted. Favorable legislation on these claims came finally with an act of Mar. 3, 1871 (16 Stat. 524), under which loyalists in the seceded States might present their claims to the Southern Claims Commission. When this commission was terminated in 1880, there were still many unsatisfied claimants who turned to Congress for relief.

Agitation for further consideration of claims resulted in the adoption of the Bowman Act, Mar. 3, 1883 (22 Stat. 485). By this legislation either House of Congress or any executive department might refer claims to the Court of Claims for investigation of the facts through judicial procedure and for report of its findings to Congress or the department. Actually, under the terms of this law and of other limiting legislation, only claims that had previously been presented to some officer or tribunal could be received.

A modification of the Bowman Act was effected by the Tucker Act, Mar. 3, 1887 (24 Stat. 505), which permitted the referral to the court of any bill providing for the payment of a claim except a pension bill. Under the terms of this act many new claims came before the court, among them petitions of churches and schools.

The court continued to consider cases under all these acts until their repeal by sec. 145 of the Judicial Code of Mar. 3, 1911 (36 Stat. 1137); but under sec. 151 of the code some other claims were heard until an act of Mar. 3, 1915 (38 Stat. 996), deprived the court of all jurisdiction over Southern war claims.

Although the Court of Claims sits in Washington, its jurisdiction has always been nationwide. In the early days proposals for giving the district courts jurisdiction over claims against the Government were made, but these were rejected in favor of a central court at the National Capital with a bench specializing in the law of claims and with the necessary papers available in the Government files. According to a decision of the Supreme Court in 1867 (United States v. Alire, 6 Wall. 573), judgments can be given only for money. Appropriations are made by Congress in gross sums to satisfy the judgments of the Court of Claims. Since cases are decided on written documentary evidence and oral evidence is not heard by the court, the files are usually voluminous.

A direct tax of $20,000,000 for war revenue was apportioned among the insurrectionary States as well as the loyal ones by sec. 8 of an act of Aug. 5, 1861 (12 Stat. 294). Measures for collecting this tax in the South were prescribed by an act of June 7, 1862 (12 Stat. 422), under which lands of defaulting owners were seized and sold in a number of Southern States. Sales of land under the authority of that act continued until 1866. The constitutionality and inequities of the law were attacked after the war, and efforts to obtain redress finally resulted in an act of Mar. 2, 1891 (26 Stat. 822), for reimbursing to the States the amounts collected under the direct tax act. Cases of individual restitution authorized by the act were handled by the Court of Claims.

An act of July 27, 1861 (12 Stat. 276), directed the Secretary of the Treasury to indemnify States for expenses incurred in raising, equipping, paying, and transporting troops for the Union Army. Years after the war several States brought suit in the Court of Claims for reimbursement. Many drafted men from Kentucky who had paid commutation or furnished substitutes but who still had been drafted sued for the refunding of money paid by them (act of Feb. 28, 1867, Mar. 1, 1869; 14 Stat. 417, 15 Stat. 282).

No general law has given the Court of Claims jurisdiction over claims by Indian tribes against the Government. But many acts have been passed giving the court special jurisdiction in such suits as those relating to claims of loyal Indians, claims of freedmen among Indian tribes, the enrollment of Indians, compensation for lands taken from them, failure by the Government to afford protection to them, and the restoration of annuities to the Sioux. Further particulars on the relation of most of these claims to the Civil War are in the section of this Guide on the Office of Indian Affairs. An act of Mar. 3, 1891 (26 Stat. 851), vested in the Court of Claims jurisdiction over claims for depredations by Indians on the property of citizens of the United States. Within the 3 years stipulated by the act 10,841 claims were presented to the court. Some of these were for depredations in the early years of the 19th century, but most arose from Indian hostilities in the years following 1860 and from Indian attacks on miners, ranches, stagecoaches, and trains.

Among the kinds of claims considered by the Court of Claims are many relating to the Civil War. The Army and Navy cases include claims for bounty for destroying armed vessels, bounty for military service, arrears of widows' pensions, pay of officers' servants, transportation after discharge, reimbursement for dismissal of officers, and loss of horses in service. Captured property cases arising from the war include claims for captured and destroyed property, for the occupancy and use of property, and for rents of abandoned property; claims by aliens who were alleged to have given aid and comfort to rebellion; claims for mules captured in transitu; and many claims relating to Confederate cotton. Cases arising from contracts with the Government concern Army transportation (including horses, mules, wagons, and gunboats), General Frémont's contracts, muskets and other arms, provisions, supplies, wood, and construction. Many of the cases referred by Congress to the court originated during the war and concerned stores, supplies, cotton, and wood taken by United States forces, occupation of and damage to buildings, infringement of patents, reimbursement for losses sustained from false imprisonment, and payment for the use of machines. Real property cases, in which compensation was claimed for rent and damage to buildings, involved many structures in the South and in Washington, D. C. Shipping cases included the capture of vessels, salvage, charters, detention of ships under neutrality laws, seizure of steamboats and other vessels, loss of vessels, and damage to or collision and destruction of vessels in military service. Disbursing officers' cases relate to claims for funds lost without negligence on the part of the officers.

As the above discussion indicates, the Court of Claims records afford valuable data on many subjects. They give much information on the conduct of Unionists in the South during the war, the operations of the Army and the Navy in the South, and their administrative and procurement practices. Indian cases document relations with the tribes and conditions on the frontier that was subject to Indian depredations. Cases involving captured Confederate property throw light on slavery and plantation economy during the war.

The act establishing the Court of Claims authorized the President to appoint three judges and a solicitor to represent the Government before the court. Soon afterwards (Aug. 6, 1856; 11 Stat. 30) the President was authorized to appoint an assistant solicitor, and the solicitor was permitted to employ a deputy. The office of solicitor was abolished by an act of June 25, 1868 (15 Stat. 75), which transferred its functions to the Attorney General.

Judges of the Court of Claims during the war period:
George P. Scarburgh, May 8, 1855.
Edward G. Loring, May 6, 1858.
James Hughes, Jan. 20, 1860.
Joseph Casey, May 23, 1861.
David Wilmot, Mar. 7, 1863.
Ebenezer Peck, Mar. 10, 1863.
Charles C. Nott, Feb. 22, 1865.

Stanton J. Peelle, "History and Jurisdiction of the United States Court of Claims," Columbia Historical Society, Records, 19:1-21 (1916); William A. Richardson, History, Jurisdiction, and Practice of the Court of Claims (United States) (Washington, 1885); Frank W.

Klingberg, The Southern Claims
Commission (Berkeley and Los
Angeles, 1955); Randall, Consti-
tutional Problems Under Lincoln;
U. S. Congress, House Committee
on War Claims, "The Law of Claims

Against Governments, Including the
Mode of Adjusting Them and the Procedure Adopted in Their Investigation," (H. Rept. 134, 43 Cong. , 2
sess. , Serial 1658; Washington,
1875).

Record Group 123. -- The Court of Claims records in the National Archives consist chiefly of several large series of case files. The largest
of these and the most significant for the Civil War period is the general-
jurisdiction case files, 1855-1939. These files comprise petitions stating
the claimants' cases, answers, and other pleadings; motions, briefs, powers of attorney, depositions, affidavits, interrogatories, transcripts of
testimony, orders, findings of facts, and conclusions of law; opinions of the
Court of Claims, petitions for certiorari, orders, mandates, and opinions
of the Supreme Court; and counterclaims filed by the Government. Evidentiary materials filed by claimants and the Government include correspondence, contracts, construction permits, patents, blueprints, drawings,
charts, wills and testaments, titles to real estate, certificates, indictments, vouchers, invoices, and publications. These cases cover claims
in which suits were brought directly in the court for violation of contracts,
violation of Indian treaties, infringement of patents, unlawful imprisonment, and loss of funds by disbursing officers; tax claims; and claims for
pay of Army, Navy, and civilian employees of the Government. Other
cases relating to the Civil War in these files concern property abandoned
and captured during the war and seizures of property after the war.
   Congressional-jurisdiction case files, 1884-1943, contain papers about
claims referred to the court by Congress for investigation and report.
These include petitions and memorials; copies of congressional bills and
resolutions; orders to and reports of commissioners; answers, motions,
briefs, depositions, and affidavits; interrogatories and orders; findings on
loyalty; and findings of fact and opinions of the court. Evidentiary materials, many of them derived from Government records, include correspondence, contracts, muster rolls, certificates of burial, oaths of allegiance,
inventories of captured subsistence stores, detailed statements of military
service, proceedings of courts-martial, and documents from captured Confederate archives. Oversize materials such as maps, blueprints, drawings, record books, statements, and other exhibits are in a separate file.
   Far less numerous are the departmental-jurisdiction case files, 1883-
1943, relating to claims referred by the departments under the Bowman
and Tucker Acts. For cases founded upon the Constitution or statutes the
court could render judgments; for other cases it reported findings of fact
and conclusions of law. The files contain letters from the departments referring claims to the court; orders referring cases to claims commissioners and reports of the commissioners; petitions, answers, other pleadings,
motions, briefs, depositions, and interrogatories; orders remanding cases
for argument; and findings of fact and opinions of the court. Evidentiary
materials furnished by the departments relate to transports, mail routes,
sales of property, money advanced as bounty to U. S. recruits, and the
numbers of recruits mustered and delivered by the States.
   Claims for Indian depredations had to be submitted to the Court of
Claims within 3 years of the passage of the act of Mar. 3, 1891, but consideration of the claims went on through 1920. The adjudication of the

claims produced an extensive file, arranged by case number, 1-10842.
The records, like the other case files, consist of documents presenting
the facts in the cases; evidentiary materials, furnished chiefly by the Office of Indian Affairs; and the findings of the court. A list of the names of
tribes involved is in the inventory cited below, and their names are indexed
in the reports of the court cited elsewhere.

National Archives, Preliminary
Inventory [No. 58] of the Records of
the United States Court of Claims,
comp. by Gaiselle Kerner (Washington, 1953).

Printed materials on the decisions of the Court of Claims include
the reports regularly submitted to
Congress, 1855-63, and printed in
the congressional series; a list of
these reports is in Hicks, Materials
of Legal Research (3d ed.), p. 487,
and in U. S. Superintendent of Documents, Tables of and Annotated Index to Congressional Series, p. 253.

Compilations of the reports in
bound volumes are in law libraries.
The reports contain much documentation on individual cases, including
petitions, opinions of the Attorney
General, claimants' briefs or arguments, opinions, bills for the relief
of claimants, and documentary evidence. A statement of judgments
of the Court of Claims, 1863-67, is
in H. Misc. Doc. 50, 40 Cong., 1
sess., Serial 1312. Sec. 9 of an act
of June 25, 1868 (15 Stat. 77), requiring the submission by the court
of annual statements of judgments,
resulted in a long series of such
statements that were published as
congressional documents. Beginning in 1891 there are also lists of
judgments on Indian depredation
claims. Lists of dismissed cases
are also in the congressional series.
For congressional cases see also
U. S. Congress, House, Digest of
Claims Referred by Congress to the
Court of Claims From the 48th to the
51st Congress, Both Inclusive, for
a Finding of Facts Under the Provisions of the Act Approved March
3, 1883, Known as the Bowman Act,
comp. by J. B. Holloway (Wash-

ington, 1891); U. S. Court of
Claims, Reports of the Court of
Claims, in Congressional Cases, to
the Sixty-Second Congress, Third
Session, and Sixty-Third Congress,
First Session (Washington, 1913; in
Serials 6366, 6504, 6535, 6536,
6548); and U. S. Court of Claims,
Congressional Claims; Motion to
Dismiss for Want of Jurisdiction
Under Act of March 4, 1915, Sec. 5
(the Crawford Amendment); Schedule
of Congressional Claims Attached
Thereto, December Term, 1914
(Washington, 1915). The last title
contains a list of 2,254 claims, with
docket numbers, names of claim-
ants, names of attorneys, and in-
formation on the nature of the claims.
Other special lists that were com-
piled for the Senate Committee on
Claims include List of War Claims,
Including a Few Exceptional Cases
of Claims for Churches; Also List of
Other Claims to Which Objections
Appear, Such as Laches, No Proof
of Loyalty, Insufficient Evidence as
to Facts, Evidence of Payment, and
Statutory Bars, With a Statement of
Each Case . . . (Washington, 1912),
Churches and Institutions of Learning Destroyed by United States Military Forces During the Civil War, but
Not as an Act of Military Necessity,
the Materials Having Been Appro-
priated and Used (Washington, 1912),
and List of War Claims Confined
Entirely to Claims for Use and Occupation or Rent of Church Buildings,
College Buildings, and Other Public
Buildings by the Military Forces of
the United States During the War,
Coupled in Some Cases With a Claim
for Damages Done to the Building
During the Occupancy, With a Statement of Each Case . . . (Washington,

1912). A list of Indian tribal claims, 1881-1946, is in H. Rept. 2503, 82 Cong., 2 sess., Serial 11528 (Washington, 1953). Available for research use at the National Archives is a typewritten compilation entitled "U. S. General Accounting Office, Claims Division, Indian Tribal Claims Section, Indian Tribal Cases Decided in the Court of Claims of the United States Briefed and Compiled to June 30, 1947," comp. and ed. by Edgar B. Smith.

The publication of a regular series of reports on the decisions of the Court of Claims resulted from an act of Congress (Mar. 17, 1866; 14 Stat. 9) requiring the court to transmit copies of decisions to the heads of departments and other interested officials. The reports are in U. S. Court of Claims, Cases Decided in the Court of Claims of the United States . . . With Abstract of Decisions of the Supreme Court in Court of Claims Cases [1863/65-date] (Washington, 1867-date). 25 Ct. Cl. xxxi-cclxiii contains an al-phabetical list of cases, an analytical table of cases, a list of Supreme Court decisions, and a list of opinions arranged alphabetically by name of judge. In the same volume (p. vii-xx) is a roll of attorneys admitted to practice before the Court of Claims, 1855-90. Another alphabetical list of cases is in 40 Ct. Cl. cli-ccxlii; this is followed by an alphabetical list of Supreme Court decisions from 2 Wall. to 198 U. S. Rep. in cases appealed from the Court of Claims. Indexes of cases by claimant's name are in 89, 99, 110, 120, and 130 Ct. Cl.

The most comprehensive digest is the United States Court of Claims Digest, 1855 to Date; Covering Court of Claims Reports and Appealed Cases Decided in Supreme Court of the United States (St. Paul, Minn., West Publishing Co., 1950-59. 9 vols.). The Federal Digest and the American Digest also cover reports of the Court of Claims.

Records in Other Custody. --Extensive runs of book and other records have been retained by the Court of Claims. The journal from 1855 contains a daily record of proceedings with the names of judges present; information on cases argued; admissions of attorneys; lists of cases reported to Congress or continued; a record of court orders, judgments, appointments, commissions, and oaths of office; announcements and memorial proceedings; lists of commissioners; and rules of practice. Besides dockets for different kinds of cases, there is a card index, 1855-date, arranged alphabetically by name of claimant. An index to Indian depredation cases has sections for both claimants and Indian tribes against which suits were brought. There are also a register of attorneys admitted to practice, 1855-1918, and a card roster of attorneys, 1855-date. A card roster of court personnel, 1855-date, brings together information from scattered sources. The rules of practice adopted by the court on May 8, 1863, required claimants to have petitions setting forth their claims printed for presentation to the court and also required the printing of testimony and briefs. These printed records of claims date from the October Term 1863 and consist of hundreds of bound volumes.

IV. THE PRESIDENCY

A few records that were accumulated in the White House and used by successive Presidents are now in the National Archives. Most Presidents, however, regarding such records as their personal papers, have carried them off in accordance with the precedent established by George Washington and followed by his successors. Many of these papers, after years in possession of the President's families, have eventually been acquired by' libraries and historical societies.

Record Group 130. --Four volumes pertain to the Civil War. A register of nominations sent by the President to the Senate lists the department or office to which the nomination belonged, the name of the man nominated, the State of his residence, the date of his nomination, the office to which he was nominated and its locality, whether the nomination was confirmed or rejected, the date of confirmation or rejection, the date of commission, and remarks. Similar information appears in a register of nominations to diplomatic and military posts. A register of Army court-martial cases, Jan. 1863-Apr. 1865, contains data under the following headings: charge, plea, sentence, recommendation of the commanding general, report of the Judge Advocate General, action of the President, and date. Another register, of acts and resolutions of Congress, gives titles, dates of approval, and bill numbers.

Letters from the President and Executive orders signed by him are in the files of most of the departments and agencies, which also contain letters received by them bearing endorsements by the President. Statutes, Executive orders, and proclamations signed by the President are in the general records of the U. S. Government, once maintained by the Department of State. Applications, recommendations, petitions, acceptances, and resignations addressed to the President are in the general records of the State Department and in the Attorney General's papers. Original messages of the President are in records of the House of Representatives and the Senate, and among Senate records are letters of nomination for appointment signed by the President.

Surveys have been made in the National Archives for materials relating to Presidents Lincoln and Johnson. During 1948-49 a search for Lincoln letters, telegrams, and other documents was made by Helen D. Bullock for the Abraham Lincoln Association of Springfield, Ill. A card catalog embodying her findings is in the National Archives. Ten years later a search for Andrew Johnson's papers was made by F. Helen Beach for the editor of the Papers of Andrew Johnson. The President's messages (without accompanying documents) are pub-

lished in James D. Richardson, ed. ,   1897 (H. Misc. Doc. 210, 53 Cong. ,
A Compilation of the Messages and   2 sess. , Serial 3265; Washington,
Papers of the Presidents, 1789-   1896-99. 10 vols.).

Records in Other Custody. --As has been noted, it was long-established
practice for Presidents to take their papers with them when they left office.
This practice was followed by James Buchanan, by Abraham Lincoln's administrator, and by Andrew Johnson. No guide to Government records relating to the Civil War would be complete without some discussion of them
and their publication.

Buford Rowland, "The Papers   Archivist, 13:195-211 (July 1950).
of the Presidents," American

Abraham Lincoln Papers

Soon after Lincoln's death his papers were shipped by Judge David
Davis, administrator of his estate, to Davis' home in Bloomington, Ill. ;
later they were deposited in a bank vault there. In 1874 Robert Todd
Lincoln lent the papers to John G. Nicolay and John Hay for use in their
biography of Lincoln and their collection of his writings. About 30 years
later the papers were returned to Robert Lincoln in Chicago. After his
retirement the younger Lincoln removed to Washington in 1912 and took
the papers with him. After working on them for some years he deposited
them in 1919 in the Library of Congress, and he gave them to the Library
in 1923. Before being opened to the public in 1947, the Robert Todd Lincoln collection of Lincoln papers was arranged chronologically, restored,
bound, cataloged, indexed, and microfilmed. The 169 volumes for the
period of Lincoln's Presidency contain many letters from Cabinet members, generals, and Members of Congress; applications for office make
up about half of the collection. Apart from this collection, the Library
of Congress has a considerable quantity of other Lincoln manuscripts from
diverse sources and still more in the Herndon-Weik collection and the
John G. Nicolay papers.

Helen D. Bullock, "The Robert   1947, May 1950); Emanuel Hertz,
Todd Lincoln Collection of the Pa-   The Jesse W. Weik Collection of
pers of Abraham Lincoln" and "The   Lincoln Documents and Manuscripts
Papers of John G. Nicolay, Lin-   (n. p. , n. d.); David C. Mearns, The
coln's Secretary, " Library of Con-   Lincoln Papers; the Story of the Col-
gress, Quarterly Journal of Cur-   lection, With Selections to July 4,
rent Acquisitions, 5:3-8, 7:3-8 (Nov. 1861 (Garden City, N. Y. ,1948. 2 vols.).

Other important groups of Lincoln papers are in the Chicago Historical
Society, the William Rainey Harper Memorial Library of the University of
Chicago, the Illinois State Historical Library, the Brown University Library,
the Henry E. Huntington Library, the Houghton Library of Harvard Univer-
sity, and the New York Public Library. Besides original manuscripts, the
Illinois State Historical Library at Springfield has a microfilm of the Robert
Todd Lincoln collection and the photostats collected by the Abraham Lincoln
Association for the compilation of Lincoln's writings edited by Roy P. Basler.
The library keeps up the catalog prepared by the association and collects

newly discovered Lincoln documents for publication in a supplementary volume. The Nicolay and Hay papers in the same library contain telegrams from State Governors giving the official returns in the presidential election of 1864, each bearing the name of the State in Lincoln's hand. Brown University has 485 telegrams written by Lincoln, 1862-65. The papers of John Hay, Lincoln's secretary and biographer, are in the Illinois State Historical Library. The papers of Edward D. Neill, one of the President's private secretaries during 1864-65, in the Minnesota Historical Society, contain some communications addressed to Lincoln.

Descriptions of Lincoln collections are in a series of articles in the Abraham Lincoln Quarterly, Mar. 1940-Mar. 1943; Albert H. Griffith, "Lincoln Literature, Lincoln Collections, and Lincoln Collectors," Wisconsin Magazine of History, 15: 148-167 (Dec. 1931); Harry E. Pratt, "Lincolniana in the Illinois State Historical Library, " Illinois State Historical Society, Journal, 46:373-400 (Winter 1953); and Carl Sandburg, Lincoln Collector; the Story of Oliver R. Barrett's Great Private Collection (New York, 1949.) All earlier compilations of Lincoln writings have been superseded by The Collected Works of Abraham Lincoln, edited by Roy P. Basler, Marion Dolores Pratt, and Lloyd A. Dunlap and published by the Rutgers University Press in 9 volumes in 1953. This carefully edited collection contains 6, 870 items, more than three times the number in the second edition of the Complete Works of Abraham Lincoln by Nicolay and Hay. The Basler work includes all known Lincoln writings except routine endorsements and certain types of documents of which the record copies are in the National Archives. In volume 8, p. 430-591, is a valuable chronological list of writings of which no text has been found, forgeries, spurious or dubious items attributed to Lincoln, and routine endorsements. Letters received by Lincoln, which are often of great importance, remain largely in manuscript; some are printed, however, in the works by Mearns and Sandburg cited above. The letters received are included in the catalog in the Illinois State Historical Library and in the Library of Congress, Index to the Abraham Lincoln Papers (Presidents' Papers Index Series; Washington, 1960).

James Buchanan Papers

Buchanan not only kept the letters he received but also made memoranda of important conversations and transactions. After he retired from office he obtained from his correspondents copies of his own letters of which he had kept no copies. His papers were lent to George Ticknor Curtis in 1880 for use in writing a biography, and later they were given to the Historical Society of Pennsylvania in Philadelphia. The collection includes both official and private correspondence. Other collections of Buchanan letters are in the Dickinson College Library, Franklin and Marshall College Library, Lancaster County Historical Society, Library of Congress, New-York Historical Society, Pennsylvania Historical and Museum Commission, Pierpont Morgan Library, Princeton University Library, and Rutherford B. Hayes Library. The Library of Congress also has Buchanan's letters to his niece, Harriet Lane Johnston, who served as his hostess in the White House, and letters to many other persons whose papers are in the Library.

During the Civil War Buchanan wrote a legalistic defense of his administration, which was published in New York and London in 1865 as Mr. Buchanan's Administration on the Eve of the Rebellion. Selections from his papers, including correspondence, messages, and memoranda, Jan.-Mar. 1861, are published in George T. Curtis, Life of James Buchanan, 2:433-499 (New York, 1883. 2 vols.); and in John Bassett More, ed., The Works of James Buchanan, Comprising His Speeches, State Papers, and Private Correspondence, 11:93-156 (Philadelphia, 1908-11. 12 vols.). Mr. Buchanan's Administration is reprinted, ibid., vol. 12. See also The Messages of President Buchanan, With an Appendix Containing Sundry Letters From Members of His Cabinet at the Close of His Presidential Term, comp. by J. Buchanan Henry (New York, 1888).

Andrew Johnson Papers

The Library of Congress has acquired papers of Andrew Johnson in several accessions by purchase, gift, or exchange from his descendants or others. These acquisitions consist largely of original manuscripts but include some photostats. Though the collection is most important for the period of Johnson's Presidency, it also contains documents relating to his military governorship of Tennessee and to earlier years. Included are letters sent, letters received, and related indexes; messages and other communications to Congress; applications for and appointments to office and related lists; proclamations; a list of acts and resolutions of Congress; endorsements by the President on documents referred to the departments; a record of court-martial cases referred to the President and his action on them; alphabetical lists of the names of persons to whom amnesty was granted; a scrapbook of newspaper clippings; and other miscellaneous printed materials. A detailed description of the collection is in the microfilm prepared by the Library of Congress. Other Johnson letters are in the Duke University Library, Rutherford B. Hayes Library, Tennessee Historical Society, and Tennessee State Library. Reproductions of Johnson papers have been assembled by Prof. LeRoy P. Graf of the University of Tennessee for the published edition of Johnson's papers.

Russell M. Smith, "The Andrew Johnson Papers," Library of Congress, Quarterly Journal of Current Acquisitions, 17:13-16 (Nov. 1959).

Hannibal Hamlin Papers

The papers of Hannibal Hamlin, Vice President from 1861 to 1865, are in the Maine State Library. They include many letters to Hamlin in his official capacity as President of the Senate; letters from heads of departments, other officials, and the President; communications regarding appointments and campaign matters; and letters of congratulation. There are few outgoing letters in this collection. The Illinois Historical Survey of the University of Illinois has photostats of letters written by Hamlin to his wife from Washington, 1860-63 and 1865.

Maine, University, Department of History and Government, A Reference List of Manuscripts Relating to the History of Maine, comp. under the direction of Elizabeth Ring, pt. 2, p. 164-166 (Orono, 1938-41. 3 pts.).

John C. Breckinridge Papers

John C. Breckinridge, Vice President from 1857 to 1861, became a brigadier general in the Confederate States Army in Nov. 1861, a major general in 1862, and Secretary of War of the Confederacy in Feb. 1865. After the war he returned to Lexington, Ky., and lived in a friend's house, where he stored his uniforms, personal mementos, and papers. When the house was destroyed by fire, the papers of Breckinridge for the period of his Vice Presidency and the Civil War were burned. Hence the gap for the years 1857-62 in the collection of his papers in the Library of Congress. Some other Breckinridge papers are in the Chicago Historical Society.

V. DEPARTMENT OF STATE

The Department of State during the Civil War had its usual responsibilities for the conduct of foreign relations of the United States and for certain domestic matters. The Secretary of State directed the activities of United States ministers and consuls stationed abroad, commissioned them, negotiated with representatives of foreign states resident in the United States, issued exequaturs to foreign consuls, and provided representation for the United States at international congresses and expositions. The Department published the laws of the United States, issued pardons and passports, and supervised Territorial affairs and immigration. It preserved, besides the strictly departmental records, the original statutes, treaties, Executive orders and proclamations, the records of the Continental Congress and the Congress of the Confederation, and records of U. S. participation in international claims commissions.

The Department had only a small staff to carry on its work. William H. Seward was appointed Secretary of State on Mar. 5, 1861, and on the same date his son Frederick W. Seward became Assistant Secretary of State. The latter position had been authorized by an act of Mar. 3, 1853 (10 Stat. 212), its incumbent to perform duties prescribed by the Secretary. William H. Trescot, who had been Assistant Secretary since June 1860, had resigned in December 1860 after the secession of his native State, South Carolina. William Hunter was continued as chief clerk, a position he had held for years. He supervised the operations of the Department, and after the assault on the Sewards, in April 1865, he was for a time Acting Secretary of State. Seward appointed John A. Jones as Superintendent of Statistics on Mar. 7, 1861, and designated George E. Baker as disbursing clerk on Apr. 1, 1861. Other employees of the Department in 1861 included 21 clerks, 2 messengers, and 4 watchmen. The loyalty purge resulted in several new appointments, but in 1865 there were only 23 clerks. One of these was a translator; others did various kinds of paperwork.

Few changes in organization occurred during the war. The compilation and publication of the biennial register of Government employees was transferred by an act of Feb. 20, 1861 (12 Stat. 141), to the Department of the Interior. A clerk, Erastus D. Webster, was employed during 1861 to handle correspondence relating to political prisoners and "rebels." John Brown was appointed Commissioner of Immigration on July 4, 1864.

Successive Secretaries of State during the war period:

Jeremiah S. Black, Dec. 17, 1860.
William H. Seward, Mar. 4, 1861.

Gaillard Hunt, The Department of State of the United States; Its History and Functions (New Haven, 1914); Graham H. Stuart, The Department of State; a History of Its Organization, Procedure, and Personnel (New York, 1949); U. S. Department of State, Inventory of Archives in the Bureau of Indexes and Archives (Washington, 1897); Claude H. Van Tyne and Waldo G. Leland, Guide to the Archives of the Government of the United States in Washington, p. 2-56 (Washington, 1907).

Record Group 59. --For many years before the State Department records were transferred to the National Archives, they had been kept in the various archives offices of the Department and consequently had long been dissociated from the bureaus which created them.   The Bureau of Indexes and Archives (1873-1926), the Bureau of Rolls and Library (1874-1921), and the Archives Section of the Division of Publications (1926-38) bound the records and arranged them in the series in which they have continued to be maintained by the National Archives, as described below.

Records in Other Custody. --The papers of Jeremiah S. Black are in the Library of Congress.   For his short tenure as Secretary of State, the collection includes a few papers relating to official business, among them applications and recommendations for appointments in the consular service and in the Department, memoranda, drafts, and correspondence.

The papers of William Henry Seward were bequeathed by his grandson to the University of Rochester Library.   This large collection covers Seward's public and private career and includes letters from men prominent in public life, drafts of his diplomatic despatches, speeches, and State Department vouchers and receipts.   The letters received by Seward from President Lincoln, however, were retained by the family, were subsequently sold to the Fred L. Emerson Foundation, and are now in the Seward home and museum at Auburn, N. Y.   Many letters from Seward to Lincoln are in the Robert Todd Lincoln collection of Lincoln papers in the Library of Congress.   Papers of Frederick W. Seward, 1861-63, are in the New York Historical Society.

Margaret Butterfield, "The William Henry Seward Papers," University of Rochester Library Bulletin, 7:7-11 (Autumn 1951).

DEPARTMENTAL RECORDS

As noted above, the strictly departmental records of the State Department were brought together in one very large record group and cannot now be described according to bureau provenance.   Instead they are described below under headings denoting the departmental functions they document.

Diplomatic Correspondence

Record Group 59. --The diplomatic correspondence constitutes one of the largest bodies of records of the Department of State and consists of several series.   The instructions are copies of communications to U. S. diplomatic representatives abroad and pertain to many aspects of foreign relations.   Arranged chronologically by country or groups of countries, the volumes for the Civil War period contain registers that facilitate finding instructions sent to particular ministers.   For instructions to the U. S. Minister in Great Britain, 1861-62, there is a special index. Despatches are reports to the Department from diplomatic representatives abroad, with voluminous enclosures such as copies of notes to and replies from foreign governments and other manuscript and printed material. Both the despatches and the relevant registers, which are in separate volumes, are arranged chronologically by country or area. Like the instructions to ministers, the despatches cover a wide range of subjects, including treaty negotiations, claims, the protection of American citizens, deaths of American citizens, ceremonial matters, internal political and other affairs and economic conditions in the foreign countries, the colonization of American Negroes, the administration of legations and consulates, and messages of sympathy and condolence on Lincoln's death.

The Department also corresponded with missions of foreign nations in Washington. Notes to foreign missions (available also on microfilm, M 99) consist of copies of communications to those missions, bound in volumes chronologically by country. The corresponding series, notes from foreign missions, is similarly bound. The subject matter of these series, much expanded by matters connected with the war, is varied in character. Correspondence with the British Legation concerned the capture of blockade runners and the seizure of suspected vessels; improper treatment of seized vessels; Confederate cruisers in British colonial ports and the denial of courtesies to Federal cruisers in those ports; the escape of Confederate ships from British ports; complaints from British ships of surveillance by American ships; requests from prisoners to be released from the oath of allegiance and the breaking of the oath by other prisoners upon being released; claims by seamen for exemption because they were British subjects; claims of shipowners for damages; intercepted despatches; customs regulations, decisions, and duties; claims of foreign subjects for release from the military forces; arrests of spies; shipments of munitions under fraudulent labels; and the transmission of treasonable documents under fictitious labels. As with most records of the Department, registers and indexes are available. For countries that did not maintain diplomatic representatives in the United States, there is a small quantity of correspondence separately bound.

Another form of diplomatic correspondence, much less voluminous, is that between the heads of governments. Such ceremonial letters are written in connection with the accrediting or recall of diplomatic representatives, the announcement of important events concerning the families of heads of states, or notification of changes in government. Some material of this character is in the regular correspondence files, but most of it is in special files. Communications to foreign sovereigns and states consist of letters regarding the recall of ministers, replies to ceremonial letters, condolences, and other matters of ceremony. Letters from foreign sovereigns and states ("ceremonial letters") are announcements and acknowledgments connected with extraordinary occasions and are sometimes elaborately prepared, wrapped, or boxed. Credences are copies of letters of credence, commission, full powers, and recall of American diplomatic representatives and acknowledgments of similar communications from foreign governments.

The diplomatic correspondence of the Civil War period is much more voluminous with some countries, such as Great Britain and France, which became more nearly involved in the American conflict, than it is with others.

The efforts of Confederate agents in Great Britain and France to procure
the construction of warships for the Confederate Navy resulted in a campaign on the part of the American ministers in those countries to block
those efforts. Charles Francis Adams, the U. S. Minister in Great Britain, in conjunction with the consuls at Liverpool and London, hired detectives and spies to watch dockyards, gun factories, and armories in order
to uncover Confederate activities and to get evidence for presentation to
the British Foreign Office. The despatches from Great Britain and France
document these countermeasures against the Confederates, as well as protests made concerning accommodations afforded to Confederate cruisers at
the ports of those countries; and they report on visits by U. S. naval officers and their occasional disregard of international courtesies, the propa-
ganda of the Confederates, and their procurement of war materials. Other
facets of U. S. foreign relations--such as foreign attitudes toward the
blockade of the Confederate coast, the Trent affair, and the demands by
Adams upon the British Government for payment for damages done to
U. S. merchant ships by Confederate cruisers let loose upon the seas by
the negligence of the British--evoked diplomatic correspondence. The
entry of Confederate vessels into South American ports, especially those
of Brazil, also became the subject of diplomatic correspondence. A series of volumes concerning "guano islands" in which American citizens
were interested contains some correspondence of the war period.

Much of the material mentioned above is available on microfilm. Among
the more important microfilm publications for Civil War study are the diplomatic instructions (M 77), which contain also instructions to special
missions, discussed below; the diplomatic despatches from most of the
European nations, including France (M 34), the German States (M 44),
Great Britain (M 30), and the Italian States (M 90); and diplomatic despatches from Latin America, including Brazil (M 121), Central America
(M 219), Chile (M 10), and Mexico (M 97).

Van Tyne and Leland, Guide, p.
7-20, contains an analysis of the diplomatic archives by country. More
extended description for the countries concerned is in the Guide to
Materials on Latin America in the
National Archives, comp. by John P.
Harrison (Washington, 1961). Much
diplomatic correspondence published during the Civil War is listed
in Adelaide R. Hasse, Index to
United States Documents Relating to
Foreign Affairs, 1828-1861 (Car-
negie Institution of Washington, Publication No. 185, pts. 1-3. Washington, 1914-21), and in Benjamin
Perley Poore, A Descriptive Catalogue of the Government Publications
of the United States, September 5,
1774-March 4, 1881 (S. Misc. Doc.
67, 48 Cong. , 2 sess. , Serial 2268.
Washington, 1885). The Department
of State began in 1862 to issue annual
compilations of diplomatic correspondence to accompany the President's annual messages to Congress.
Entitled Papers Relating to Foreign
Affairs (continued to the present
time and now entitled Foreign Relations; Diplomatic Papers of the
United States), the diplomatic correspondence for the years indicated
is also published in the following congressional documents:

1861.	S. Ex. Doc. 1, 37 Cong. ,	2 sess. ,	Serial 1117.
1861-62.	H. Ex. Doc. 1, 37 Cong. ,	3 sess. ,	Serial 1156.
1862-63.	H. Ex. Doc. 1, 38 Cong. ,	1 sess. ,	Serials 1180-1181.
1863-64.	H. Ex. Doc. 1, 38 Cong. ,	2 sess. ,	Serials 1216-1219.
1864-65.	H. Ex. Doc. 1, 39 Cong. ,	1 sess. ,	Serials 1244-1247.
1865-66.	H. Ex. Doc. 1, 39 Cong. ,	2 sess. ,	Serials 1281-1283.

Leo F. Stock, ed., United States Ministers to the Papal States; Instructions and Despatches, 1848-1868 (American Catholic Historical Association, Documents, vol. 1. Washington, 1933), contains correspondence on the apprehension of John H. Surratt, suspected of implication in the assassination of President Lincoln. Correspondence on Surratt is also in H. Ex. Docs. 9 and 25, 39 Cong., 2 sess., Serials 1288, 1289; and H. Rept. 33, 39 Cong., 2 sess., Serial 1305. Correspondence on the capture of British vessels carrying contraband of war for the Confederate States is in S. Ex. Doc. 27, 37 Cong., 3 sess., Serial 1149. Archival, manuscript, and published sources and secondary works are described in Samuel F. Bemis and Grace C. Griffin, Guide to the Diplomatic History of the United States, 1775-1921 (Washington, 1935). John Bigelow, U. S. Consul General in Paris and Minister to France, published much pertinent correspondence in vols. 1-3 of his Retrospections of an Active Life (New York, 1909-13. 5 vols.). Microfilms of correspondence in the records of the British and French Foreign Offices are in the Library of Congress. Special compilations of correspondence include "Insurgent Privateers in Foreign Ports," Apr. 28, 1862, H. Ex. Doc. 104, 37 Cong., 2 sess., Serial 1136. Extensive ones on conditions in Mexico include the following:

H. Ex. Doc. 100, 37 Cong., 2 sess., Serial 1136.
H. Ex. Doc. 23, 37 Cong., 3 sess., Serial 1161.
H. Ex. Doc. 54, 37 Cong., 3 sess., Serial 1162.
S. Ex. Doc. 11, 38 Cong., 1 sess., Serial 1209.
S. Ex. Docs. 5, 6, 8, 93, 39 Cong., 1 sess., Serials 1237, 1263.
H. Ex. Doc. 76, 39 Cong., 2 sess., Serial 1294.

Correspondence With Special Agents

Special Agents were sent abroad during the Civil War on a variety of missions. Prominent men such as Archbishop John J. Hughes, Bishop Charles P. McIlvaine, Thurlow Weed, and William M. Evarts visited Europe and through contacts with government officials and others sought to influence public opinion in favor of the Union. Evarts and William Whiting were employed as counsel to prepare evidence on the fitting out of vessels in England and France for the Confederate Navy. The espionage assignments of Henry S. Sanford, William M. Walker, and B. W. Sanders in Europe were to obtain information regarding the activities of Confederate agents. Sanford was also instructed to offer General Garibaldi a commission as major general in the U. S. Army. William S. Thayer, the American consul general in Egypt, was instructed in 1861 to have an agent (Ayoub Bey Trabulsi) obtain information at Mediterranean seaports of Turkey that might be helpful in preventing depredations on American commerce by Confederate vessels and information on the cultivation of cotton in Egypt. Thayer was directed in 1862 to accompany the Pasha of Egypt to London and to obtain information from him and from manufacturers there on the cultivation of cotton in Egypt and India. Isaac F. Redfield was sent abroad in 1866 as counsel for the United States for recovering property from persons acting under the authority of Confederate agents. The mission of George H. Sharpe in Europe in 1867 was to identify U. S. citizens concerned with the assassination of President Lincoln and the attempted assassination of Secretary Seward. Alexander H. Schultz was sent to Europe in 1864 to inspect certain consulates.

Other agents were sent to places in the Western Hemisphere. George Ashmun went early in the war to Canada to inform the officials there of the situation in the United States and to prevent the fitting out of vessels as Confederate privateers. The United States did not then exchange diplomatic representatives with Canada; Ashmun was not recognized and was soon recalled. To help prevent the violation of the Canadian frontier by Confederate sympathizers, Preston King was sent in 1863, with the approval of the British Minister to the United States, to confer with Canadian officials. Lemuel D. Evans was assigned in 1861 to watch the interests of the United States on the Mexican border, and in 1862 Robert W. Shufeldt was sent as an observer to Mexico. To reach an understanding on U. S. rights to transport troops across the Isthmus of Panama, Daniel E. Sickles was dispatched to Panama and Colombia in 1865. After the capture of New Orleans in 1862 Cuthbert Bullitt sought information there about the quantity of cotton ready for market and the attitude of the planters regarding its sale and exportation, and Reverdy Johnson investigated complaints from foreign consuls regarding the actions of Maj. Gen. Benjamin F. Butler. An unofficial agent of Secretary Seward in the South was his friend Samuel Ward, who accompanied William Howard Russell, the noted English correspondent, on a tour of the South in 1861 and who reported on conditions there in letters (signed with the pseudonym of Carlos Lopez) to Seward and to George E. Baker, disbursing agent of the Department of State.

Rena M. Andrews, Archbishop Hughes and the Civil War (Chicago, 1935); Chester L. Barrows, William M. Evarts (Chapel Hill, N. C., 1941); Brainerd Dyer, The Public Career of William M. Evarts (Berkeley, 1919); Harriet A. Weed, ed., The Life of Thurlow Weed, Including His Autobiography and a Memoir (Boston, New York, 1884. 2 vols.); Henry M. Wriston, Executive Agents in American Foreign Relations (Baltimore, 1929); Harriet C. Owsley, "Henry Shelton Sanford and Federal Surveillance Abroad, 1861-1865," Mississippi Valley Historical Review, 48:211-228 (Sept. 1961).

Record Group 59. --The principal records relating to special agents are the instructions to special missions and the despatches from special agents. Copies of the instructions are sometimes bound with the despatches, which often are accompanied by enclosures and exhibits. Lists of agents, arranged in different ways, are also available. Most of the documentation concerning special agents, however, is in the regular diplomatic and consular correspondence, the letters sent, and the miscellaneous letters.

Exact citations to all the documents, an alphabetical list of agents, and a brief description of their missions are in National Archives, List of Documents Relating to Special Agents of the Department of State, 1789-1906, comp. by Natalia Summers (Special List No. 7. Washington, 1951). A report by Reverdy Johnson concerning complaints by foreign consuls in New Orleans against General Butler is in S. Ex. Doc. 16, 37 Cong., 3 sess., Serial 1149.

Records in Other Custody. --The agents who went on unofficial missions wrote personal letters regarding their activities, and some of these are in collections of private papers. Selected papers of Seward and Weed in the University of Rochester Library, of Archbishop Hughes in the Archives of the Archdiocese of New York, and of Bishop McIlvaine in Kenyon College Library, Gambier, Ohio, have been published on 17 microcards (616 pages) as Mission Abroad, 1861-1862; a Selection of Letters From Archbishop Hughes, Bishop McIlvaine, W. H. Seward, and Thurlow Weed (Rochester, N. Y., University of Rochester Press, Micro-Publication Service, c.'1954). Eleven letters written by Weed from London and Paris to Lincoln or Seward are in the Lincoln papers in the Library of Congress, and the same collection contains two letters from Bishop McIlvaine.

Many letters from Weed appear in Frederick W. Seward, Seward at Washington, as Senator and Secretary of State (New York, 1891. 2 vols.). See also Glyndon G. Van Deusen, "The Thurlow Weed Collection, " University of Rochester Library Bulletin, 1:21-25 (Feb. 1946); and Tennessee State Library and Archives, Manuscript Section,

Register [of] Henry Shelton Sanford Papers, General Sanford Memorial Library, Sanford, Florida, comp. by Harriet C. Owsley (Nashville, 1960). Concerning the letters from Ward among the Seward papers, see Margaret Butterfield, "Samuel Ward, A lias Carlos Lopez, " University of Rochester Library Bulletin, 12:23-33 (Winter 1957).

Consular Correspondence

Record Group 59.--The main series of consular correspondence are similar to the several series of diplomatic correspondence and are similarly arranged. Instructions to consuls contain most of the communications and lists of enclosures from the Department to consular officers. Forms were used to acknowledge despatches received from consuls and to send routine instructions. Separate series are devoted to consular oaths of office, bonds, and exequaturs; to notices of confirmation of appointments; and to the delivery of Government property to newly appointed consuls. The instructions and most of the other series are indexed in one series of index volumes.

The principal file of incoming communications consists of the consular despatches, arranged chronologically by post and registered. Both the instructions and despatches concern the consular functions described below, under Foreign Service posts. Bound with the despatches are quarterly returns of the arrival and departure of vessels, and statements of fees received. In this series also are some messages of condolence and sympathy on the death of President Lincoln (others, from nations rather than cities, are in the diplomatic despatches). Especially useful for tracing the activities of Confederate agents and blockade runners are the consular despatches from Bristol, Liverpool, and London, England; Bordeaux, France; Halifax, Montreal, and Quebec, Canada; Nassau, New Providence, Bahama Islands; Hamilton, Bermuda; Havana, Cuba; Matamoros, Tampico, and Vera Cruz, Mexico; Belize, British Honduras; and Puerto Rico. Consuls were much more numerous than ministers, from whom they were often far removed; and their despatches should not be overlooked for reports on political affairs.

Consular despatches for the Civil War period from 28 ports or localities are available on microfilm, but of the consulates mentioned above only despatches from Puerto Rico (M 76) and Vera Cruz (M 183) have been microfilmed. Other consular despatches that contain some pertinent materials are those from Acapulco (M 143), Callao (M 135), Ciudad Juárez (Paso del Norte) (M 184), Honolulu (M 144), Mazatlán (M 159), Monterrey (M 165), Panama (M 139), Sydney (M 173), and Valparaiso (M 146).

The Department published some consular despatches and reports in the Commercial Relations series beginning in 1855, discussed below. Correspondence of 1861-65 and some of 1866 relating to the arrest of John H. Surratt is in Leo F. Stock, ed., Consular Relations Between the United States and the Papal States; Instructions and Despatches, 2:203-307 (Washington, 1945).

The Department also sent notes to consular representatives of foreign countries in the United States and received notes from them. Notes to foreign consuls concern the protection of foreigners in the United States, their discharge from the U. S. Army, requests for certificates of death and other papers, extradition proceedings, the violation of neutrality laws, and other matters.

Miscellaneous Correspondence

Record Group 59. --Correspondence other than diplomatic and consular is largely in the "domestic letters" (outgoing) and the "miscellaneous letters" (incoming). This correspondence, chiefly about internal affairs, contains letters to and from officials of the Government in Washington and elsewhere, Territorial and State officials, and private individuals. The domestic letters (available on microfilm, 1784-1906, as M 40) include letters to the Secretary of the Navy about the movement of vessels carrying munitions to the Confederacy, the arrest of disloyal citizens, blockade runners, and Confederate cruisers; to department heads about Territorial affairs; to Territorial officials about appointments and commissions, the publication of Federal statutes, and Territorial acts; to the Secretary of War about Confederate agents and passes for the agents of foreign governments; to the Secretary of the Treasury about the free entry of goods for diplomatic representatives and the transmission of bonds; to the Fifth Auditor of the Treasury about the compensation of consuls and their accounts; to the Register of the Treasury about American vessels wrecked on foreign shores; to dispatch agents about the forwarding of departmental mail; to the Solicitor of the Treasury about criminal offenses committed by American seamen; to the Attorney General about political prisoners and the issuance of pardons; to U. S. attorneys about papers seized from prize vessels and the trial of prize cases; to the Post Office Department about the interception of letters of suspected persons; to U. S. marshals, transmitting Presidential pardons; to Congress about various matters; to newspapers about the publication of the laws; and to individuals about the protection of American commerce, the issuance of passports, claims against foreign governments, claims for damages suffered from attacks by Confederate cruisers, and the stations of consuls. The same subjects are also covered by the miscellaneous letters received (the register of which has been microfilmed as M 17). The miscellaneous letters also include letters from the Secretary of War regarding the release of prisoners from parole and the discharge of foreigners from the Army, and condolences and expressions of sympathy on the death of Lincoln. Communications on other war-related subjects are likely to be found in these files--for instance, letters concerning the procurement of niter from Europe, an activity that more directly involved the War Department. Important documentation on the restoration of State governments in the South during 1865 is also in these files. Both domestic and miscellaneous letters are indexed, and there is a special index for claims.

Besides the foregoing voluminous correspondence files, there are smaller special files of correspondence and reports. In some report books are letters to the President and committees of Congress on matters concerning the Department, such as appropriations, the publication of the laws, and Territorial affairs. Circulars issued by the Department to officials under its supervision are in a special series that contains not only departmental issuances but also those of other departments affecting the duties of State Department officials. Some of the letters from publishers and others regarding the publication of the laws are in a separate file; others are in the miscellaneous letters received. The reports of bureau officers include reports and memoranda to the Secretary of State on claims, treaties, questions of international law, U. S. legislation, the organization of the Department, and other matters affecting the foreign relations of the United States. Consular bonds were transmitted to the Department of the Treasury by form letters, which were separately bound. Lists of publishers of the laws were maintained.

Appointment Records

In 1789 the Secretary of State had been given the duty of making out, recording, and affixing the seal of the United States to all civil commissions issued to officers appointed by the President. This function of the Department led to its becoming the custodian not only of commissions but also of other records relating to the appointment of civil officials.

In accordance with an agreement reached in the Cabinet in Apr. 1861, Secretary Seward required all personnel of the Department to renew their oaths of allegiance to the Government. Not long after this was done, they were all required by an act of Aug. 6, 1861 (12 Stat. 326), to take an oath affirming future loyalty to the Constitution and the Government and swearing fidelity notwithstanding any State legislation. Communications went out from the Department in the same month to Territorial, diplomatic, and consular officers directing that the oath be administered to all persons in the employ of the Government. An investigation of the loyalty of employees, conducted by Secretary Seward, resulted in the discharge of many men for disloyalty and the suspension of others pending the completion of investigations.

Harold M. Hyman, Era of the Oath; Northern Loyalty Tests During the Civil War and Reconstruction (Philadelphia, 1954). Information about employees discharged for disloyalty from the State Department and other departments is in H. Rept. 16, 37 Cong., 2 sess., Serial 1144.

Record Group 59. --The most important file of appointment records consists of applications from men seeking office and of recommendations from others on their behalf. These papers are filed alphabetically by name of applicant under each Presidential administration; but those for the Civil War are in one file for 1861-69, with no break between the Johnson and Lincoln administrations. The communications are addressed to the President, the Secretary of State, the heads of other departments and agencies, Representatives, and Senators; and they are often accompanied by covering letters and endorsements, with comments by the persons to whom the letters were written. The Department did not usually reply to applications and recommendations, but the action taken on appointments can be found in other records. Copies of commissions were usually kept in volumes containing forms filled in with the requisite information. The letters in which the original commissions were sent to the appointees were copied in the volumes of domestic letters. Acceptances from appointees are in a file with orders from executive departments requesting the issuance of commissions. Attested copies of Senate resolutions confirming or rejecting Presidential nominations are arranged in a chronological series. The resolutions are printed in the Executive Journal of the Senate and are indexed in these volumes both by name of nominee and by class of appointment. A small file of declinations and resignations is also available. Oaths of office are arranged chronologically, and there is an index for those of employees of the Department of State.

By the time of the Civil War different kinds of commissions were kept in separate volumes. Those for the more important officers, such as heads of departments and other officials in Washington and Governors and secretaries of Territories, were recorded in "Temporary Presidential Commissions" and "Miscellaneous Presidential Permanent and Temporary Commissions." Separate volumes were maintained for attorneys, deputy postmasters, judges, justices of the peace of the District of Columbia, marshals, employees of the Department of State, diplomatic officials, and consular officials. Numerous lists facilitate finding the names of incumbents of particular positions or, when the names are available, ascertaining what positions were held. Most useful for the latter purpose is an alphabetical card record of appointments, 1789-1933.

Information on the appointment and service of personnel can be found in several registers. A register of officers of the Department of State and the Foreign Service, 1774-1882, is arranged by office and alphabetically by country but is not indexed. A register of consular officers of the United States, 1775-1893, is arranged alphabetically by name of post and thereunder chronologically.

Pardon Records

From 1789 to about 1853 the Secretary of State shared with the Attorney General responsibility for recommending to the President pardons for offenses against the laws of the United States and the District of Columbia. By about 1853, however, the handling of investigations and correspondence connected with the petitions for pardon was assigned to the Attorney General. The Department of State continued to issue and record warrants of pardons and commutations of sentence until by Executive order of June 16, 1893, that function was also transferred to the Department of Justice.

Record Group 59. -- Pardons issued by the President for war-related offenses before July 14, 1865, were copied in volumes containing printed forms, in which were also recorded pardons of criminals convicted by

Federal courts. Requisitions for the pardon of criminals were received
from the Attorney General, by whom the petitions for pardon were received and filed. Upon receipt of the requisition the Department of State
prepared the warrant and sent it to the President for signature, after which
it was countersigned by the Secretary of State and the great seal was affixed. The pardons are recorded in chronological order, and there is a
name index alphabetized by the first letter only of the surname.
     For a description of related records see the section on the Pardon Clerk
under the Attorney General's Office elsewhere in this Guide.

Passport Records

     The Secretary of State was authorized by sec. 23 of an act of Aug. 18,
1856 (11 Stat. 60), to grant and issue passports and to cause them to be
granted, issued, and verified in foreign countries by U. S. diplomatic or
consular officers. The denial of passports was used during the war to prevent citizens with treasonable designs from leaving the country. By regulations adopted on Aug. 19, 1861, persons were prohibited from going
abroad without passports and from landing in the United States without passports signed by a U. S. minister or consul. To expedite departure from
New York the dispatch agent of the Department of State at that port was authorized to issue passports. By an act of Aug. 6, 1861 (12 Stat. 326), loyalty oaths were required of all applicants for passports. In the United
States collectors of customs and notaries were empowered to administer
the oaths. A circular issued by Secretary Seward on Nov. 12, 1861, announced that no person, whether citizen or foreigner, would be allowed to
pass the lines of the U. S. Army in any direction without a passport signed
by the Secretary. In an effort to control traffic on the northern border,
passports were required in 1864 for persons going to Canada.

U. S. Department of State, The   lations Governing Its Issuance by
American Passport; Its History and   the Department of State (Washington,
a Digest of Laws, Rulings and Regu- 1898); Hyman, Era of the Oath.

     Record Group 59. -- Passport applications constitute the largest file
among the passport records. Filed chronologically by date of application,
the papers contain, besides the application, documents proving the citizenship of the applicant, including affidavits by friends and relatives; letters
of introduction and commendation; birth, baptismal, and marriage certificates; naturalization certificates; seamen's certificates; oaths of allegiance;
and physical descriptions. Applications received in New York, Aug. 24,
1861-Feb. 24, 1862, and in Boston Jan. 1-Feb. 19, 1862, are in separate
files; and there is an index and register for the former. Some of the information in the applications was entered in registers, which also show whether
or not the passport was issued. The index is alphabetized only by the first
letter of the surname. More useful than the registers in finding information
on applicants is an alphabetical card index compiled from the registers. A
file of requisitions for special passports, which were issued to U. S. diplomatic and consular personnel, foreign diplomatic personnel, and some
American citizens, includes some requisitions for the war period. The special passports issued were copied on forms contained in volumes. Some
certificates of naturalization are in a separate file. Certificates of citizen-

ship executed on printed forms before notaries in Boston, with physical descriptions and oaths of allegiance, cover 1860-61.

Extradition Papers

Extradition was provided for by treaties between the United States and other countries and was further controlled by an act of Aug. 12, 1848 (9 Stat. 302). The Department of State, to which the function of extraditing fugitives had been assigned before the war, attempted to obtain from Canada and Great Britain the extradition of Confederates who, posing as passengers, captured American vessels at sea or on Lake Erie, and of a band of soldiers who attacked St. Albans, Vt. Usually, however, such attempts were unsuccessful because the persons involved were held to have belligerent status.

John Bassett Moore, A Treatise on Extradition and Interstate Rendition (Boston, 1891. 2 vols.); U. S. Department of State, Report on Extradition, With Returns of All Cases From August 9, 1842, to January 1, 1890 and an Index, comp. by John Bassett Moore (Washington, 1890); L. N. Benjamin, comp. , The St. Albans Raid; or, Investigation Into the Charges Against Lieut. Bennett H. Young and Command, for Their Acts at St. Albans, Vt. , on the 19th October, 1864, Being a Complete and Authentic Report of All the Proceedings on the Demand of the United States for Their Extradition, Under the Ashburton Treaty (Montreal, 1865).

Record Group 59. --A file of extradition case papers contains documents grouped by cases arranged in chronological order. The case files concern both American citizens and citizens of foreign countries and include applications for extradition, copies of court proceedings, and requests for the issuance of warrants of surrender. These warrants, which were signed by the Secretary of State, required the delivery of fugitives by U. S. marshals or other public officers to the authorized representatives of foreign governments. An index to the cases is arranged alphabetically by country and thereunder chronologically. Copies of the texts of warrants of arrest and warrants of surrender are in a volume for 1843-68. The mandate or warrant of arrest is an order by the President to judges of Federal or State courts to consider the evidence of the alleged crime and, if the evidence is found sufficient to sustain the charge, to certify this to the Secretary of State in order that he may issue a warrant of surrender. The case papers appear to be incomplete, for there are documents in the volume of warrants that do not appear in those papers. An index (by country and subject) to extradition cases before 1877 briefs correspondence relating to extradition cases in the various series of diplomatic correspondence, miscellaneous letters received, and domestic letters. A few other warrants of arrest and of extradition are in the pardon books, described above.

Exequaturs and Related Records

Consuls newly appointed by foreign countries to serve in designated places in the United States presented their commissions to the Department of State and on this evidence were given exequaturs signed by the President and the Secretary of State and bearing the seal of the United States.

Record Group 59. --Copies of exequaturs are in bound volumes containing printed forms on which the name, country, and post of each consul is entered. The data in the exequaturs are duplicated in an index, arranged alphabetically by country and thereunder by date of exequatur. The commissions of consuls are copied in volumes entitled "Commissions of Foreign Consuls, " in the foreign languages and also (after Sept. 24, 1863) in English in a separate set of volumes.

John Bassett Moore, A Digest of International Law, 5:12-15 (Washington, 1906. 8 vols.). Correspondence concerning exequaturs is in notes from and to foreign consuls, described above.

Territorial Papers

Affairs of the Territories, which the Department of State had administered since the formation of the Government, continued under its jurisdiction until 1873. The Department was primarily concerned with appointments and other personnel matters, the publication of U. S. statutes in the Territories, the printing of Territorial laws, and the preservation of records.

Clarence E. Carter, "Apprenticeship for American Statehood, " Department of State, Bulletin, 12: 1109-1114 (June 17, 1945); Earl S. Pomeroy, The Territories and the United States, 1861-1890; Studies in Colonial Administration (Philadelphia, 1947); Vincent G. Tegeder, "Lincoln and the Territorial Patronage; the Ascendancy of the Radicals in the West," Mississippi Valley Historical Review, 35:77-90 (June 1948).

Record Group 59. --Much of the documentation on the Territories has been brought together in manuscript volumes designated as Territorial Papers. These contain letters from Governors and secretaries of Territories to the Secretary of State and the President; reports; and journals of executive proceedings, which vary a good deal in content and often include local correspondence, commissions, Territorial acts, and lists of acts. Territories in existence during the Civil War for which there are documents in this series include Arizona, Colorado, Dakota, Idaho, Montana, Nebraska, Nevada, New Mexico, Utah, and Washington.

Papers for the following Territories are available on microfilm: Colorado (M 3), Dakota (M 309), Nebraska (M 228), Nevada (M 13), Utah (M 12), and Washington (M 26). Van Tyne and Leland, Guide, p. 35-47; David W. Parker, Calendar of Papers in Washington Archives Relating to the Territories of the United States (to 1873) (Washington, 1911); Clarence E. Carter, "The Territorial Papers of the United States, " American Archivist, 8:122-135 (Apr. 1945). Other records relating to the Territories are among the records of the Departments of War and Treasury, the Attorney General, the Senate, the House of Representatives, the General Land Office, the Office of Indian Affairs, and the Bureau of Mines. The Department of State did not systematically file all records relating to Territories in its Territorial papers, and much similar material is in the miscellaneous and domestic letters and in the appointment papers.

STATE DEPARTMENT

Disbursement Records

From 1834 to 1870 a disbursing agent handled the accounts and disbursements of the State Department.

George E. Baker served as disbursing agent from Apr. 1, 1861.

Record Group 59. --The disbursing agent's correspondence was kept in a few series of records. Press copy books, 1832-1916 (1861-66, 6 vols.), contain copies of outgoing letters, addressed to diplomatic and consular officers, ambassadors, and ministers in Washington, officials of the Treasury Department and other departments, dispatch agents, newspaper publishers, and private individuals and firms. These letters discuss accounts, checks, funds, appropriations, the purchase of supplies, the publication of proposals, publishing the laws, appointments, discharges, payments, the admission of goods for foreign legations, medals, and salary payments. The more voluminous letters received, 1825-1908 (1861-65, 14 vols.) concern the same subjects as the letters sent. A chronological register of letters received, 1829-71 (7 vols.), is useful in finding communications from specific individuals. A separate index to the registers by the first letter of personal names is available, 1824-66 (4 vols.). Letters received from the Fifth Auditor and the First Comptroller were bound separately in chronological order, 1829-Dec. 1862 (14 vols.).

Accounting records in different forms provide information on the expenditures of the Department. Besides appropriation ledgers, 1835-1910 (13 vols.), showing expenditures under appropriation titles, there are general and special ledgers, and ledgers for contingencies, the Northeast Executive Building, and miscellaneous expenses, 1857-67 (1 vol.). The last-named ledgers include expenditures for foreign missions and foreign intercourse, postage and office rent of consuls, publishing laws, bringing home criminals, and preserving archives, and other office expenses. Drafts of appropriations for the Department of State include estimates for 1861 only. In a daybook of miscellaneous expenses, 1852-67 (1 vol.), are records of the Department's expenditures for salaries, supplies, equipment, services, and miscellaneous items. Cashbooks, 1785-1925, with gaps (1861-65,1 vol.), contain a record of cash on hand or on deposit with the Treasurer of the United States. Separate records were kept of newspaper subscriptions and expenses for an extra clerk, of accounts for stationery, copper-plate printing, books and maps, and miscellaneous expenses; of payments to publishers of laws; and of expenses for the upkeep and maintenance of the Northeast Executive Building. A series of requisitions on the Treasurer for the issuance of warrants for the payment of obligations of the Department and the Foreign Service, 1818-71 (28 vols.), is indexed alphabetically by name. Monthly payrolls, 1855-1903 (11 vols.), showing the salary payments made to regular employees and extra clerks are useful for information on personnel changes, particularly in view of the scarcity of other records relating to personnel.

Concerning expenditures relating to the Foreign Service there are still other records. Ledgers for the contingent expenses of foreign intercourse cover expenses for couriers, the publication of death notices, telegrams, salaries of dispatch agents and consuls, travel, the reception of foreign dignitaries, postage of foreign missions, funeral expenses of consuls, the care of archives, and treaty cases. These ledgers were discontinued in 1861, but a register of consular accounts for contingent expenses was begun in that year. There are also daybooks for the contingent expenses of foreign intercourse. A special record book was kept for postage and miscellaneous contingent expenses of consuls; another for office rent; and a daybook for flags, arms, postage, etc. Letters of credit to London bankers gave notification that certain Foreign Service officers had been appointed and that they were authorized to draw for salary and contingent expenses.

Yearly statements of the contingent expenditures of the Department during the Civil War are in the following congressional documents:

1861. H. Ex. Doc. 39, 37 Cong., 2 sess., Serial 1129.
1862. H. Ex. Doc. 42, 37 Cong., 3 sess., Serial 1161.
1863. H. Ex. Doc. 23, 38 Cong., 1 sess., Serial 1187.
1864. H. Ex. Doc. 36, 38 Cong., 2 sess., Serial 1223.
1865. H. Ex. Doc. 32, 39 Cong., 1 sess., Serial 1255.

Lists of consular officers and reports of fees received by consuls, arranged alphabetically by place of consulate, are in the following documents:

1861-62. S. Ex. Doc. 2, 38 Cong., 1 sess., Serial 1176.
1863-64. S. Ex. Doc. 32, 38 Cong., 2 sess., Serial 1209.
1865. S. Ex. Doc. 63, 39 Cong., 1 sess., Serial 1238.

A statement of the money spent for salaries, blank books, office rent, and the preservation of archives of U. S. consulates in Europe, July 1, 1862, to June 30, 1866, is in S. Ex. Doc. 35, 39 Cong., 2 sess., Serial 1277.

Immigration Records

Though the Department of State, pursuant to sec. 5 of an act of Mar. 2, 1819 (3 Stat. 489), had submitted to Congress since 1820 annual compilations of statistics on immigrants arriving in the United States, no official in the Department was specially charged with the administration of immigration until an act of July 4, 1864 (13 Stat. 386), provided for the appointment of a Commissioner of Immigration. There had been a marked decline in the number of immigrants entering the country during 1861 and 1862, owing to the outbreak of the war and resultant unsettled economic conditions, but soon labor was needed in many fields to replace men in the armed services. To encourage immigration and protect immigrants from abuses by transportation companies and their agents, the Commissioner of Immigration was appointed. Under the act of 1864 a Superintendent of Immigration in New York was appointed to look after the interests of immigrants arriving in that port, the main immigrant port of entry. The Office of Commissioner of Immigration was abolished in 1868, and in 1874 the function of compiling immigration statistics was transferred to the Department of the Treasury. Successive Commissioners of Immigration during the war period:

John Brown, July 4, 1864.
Horace N. Congar, Nov. 28, 1864.

Darrell H. Smith and H. Guy Herring, The Bureau of Immigration; Its History, Activities, and Organization (Baltimore, 1924). The following documents contain information on the origin and early history of the Office of the Commissioner of Immigration: S. Rept. 15, 38 Cong., 1 sess., Serial 1178; H. Ex. Doc. 56, 38 Cong., 1 sess., Serial 1206; and H. Ex. Doc. 66, 39 Cong., 1 sess., Serial 1256.

Record Group 59. --Three volumes constitute the records of the Commissioner of Immigration. A volume of copies of letters sent, Aug. 1864-Oct. 1867, contains letters to other Government departments and to the Superintendent of Immigration at New York regarding the regulation of immigration, the duties of the Superintendent, and other matters. Another volume contains a name and subject index to these letters. A third volume is a register of letters received, with synopses of them; the letters themselves have not been found.

Other correspondence concerning immigration is in the miscellaneous letters received, the domestic letters, and the consular despatches of the Department of State. The annual reports on immigration, arranged by customs district, give statistics on the number of passengers arriving in the United States and contain data as to occupation, sex, age, country of origin, and country of intended residence. These reports are published in the following congressional documents:

1861. H. Ex. Doc. 111, 37 Cong., 2 sess., Serial 1137.
1862. H. Ex. Doc. 67, 37 Cong., 3 sess., Serial 1163.
1863. H. Ex. Doc. 53, 38 Cong., 1 sess., Serial 1189.
1864. H. Ex. Doc. 76, 38 Cong., 2 sess., Serial 1229.
1865. H. Ex. Doc. 66, 39 Cong., 1 sess., Serial 1256.

Consular Trade Reports

The task of gathering statistics and preparing an annual report to Congress on the commerce and commercial regulations of foreign nations was assigned by an act of Aug. 16, 1842 (5 Stat. 507), to the Department of State. A clerk did this work for some years, but an act of Aug. 18, 1856 (11 Stat. 139), provided for the appointment of a Superintendent of Statistics. From reports received from U. S. consular and diplomatic agents, his office compiled annual reports on the Commercial Relations of the United States, which were published in the congressional document series in 1842, 1843, 1844, and annually after 1855 until 1903, when the function was transferred to the Bureau of Foreign and Domestic Commerce.

Superintendents of Statistics during the war years:

Hugh C. McLaughlin, July 1, 1858.
John A. Jones, Mar. 7, 1861.

Lawrence F. Schmeckebier and Gustavus A. Weber, The Bureau of Foreign and Domestic Commerce; Its History, Activities, and Organization (Baltimore, 1924).

Record Group 59. --The only record is a register of consular trade reports received, Dec. 1856-Dec. 1864 (1 vol.), in which the reports are entered chronologically under the initial letter of the name of consular post. The reports themselves are bound with other communications in the consular and diplomatic despatches. They constitute a useful source for the history of U. S. foreign commerce during the war.

The texts of many consular trade reports made during the war and abstracts from others are published in the Commercial Relations of the United States (compiled for years ending on Sept. 30) in the following congressional documents:

1861. H. Ex. Doc. 45, 37 Cong., 2 sess., Serial 1130.
1862. H. Ex. Doc. 63, 37 Cong., 3 sess., Serial 1169.
1863. H. Ex. Doc. 41, 38 Cong., 1 sess., Serial 1190.
1864. H. Ex. Doc. 60, 38 Cong., 2 sess., Serial 1227.
1865. H. Ex. Doc. 56, 39 Cong., 1 sess., Serial 1260.
1866. H. Ex. Doc. 81, 39 Cong., 2 sess., Serial 1295.

"Civil War Papers"

The Department of State had certain special functions related to the war besides those already discussed. These wartime activities accrued to the Department because of their relation to its other work and because Secretary Seward was a strong executive, eager to assume new responsibilities. Some of these duties were later transferred to other departments to which they more logically belonged, but at the outbreak of war the Government had to act speedily to insure its preservation. For a while before Feb. 25, 1862, for instance, the Secretary of State censored telegraph messages sent from Washington. Rather arbitrarily, some records of such unusual activities of the State Department have been grouped in a special series known as Civil War papers.

Political Prisoner Records

On the outbreak of war the Government had to take extraordinary measures for its protection and preservation. Soon after the President suspended the writ of habeas corpus on Apr. 27, 1861, police officials and other prominent men in Baltimore, where the passage of troops from the North had been impeded, were arrested and confined in a U. S. fort. By early summer of 1861 it had become fixed policy to hold under military arrest political spies, Confederate sympathizers, and officials whose acts and statements were inimical to the Government. In Sept. 1861 several members of the Maryland legislature were seized to prevent the passage of an act of secession. Nearly a thousand persons suspected of actual or potential treason or disloyalty were arrested by order of the Secretary of State or of military authorities and confined in military prisons in the East. These political prisoners were held without trial and were released only on order of Secretary Seward after being examined under his direction and taking an oath of allegiance. Most of the prisoners were still in confinement when President Lincoln by an order of Feb. 14, 1862, transferred jurisdiction over them to Secretary of War Stanton. In the same month Stanton established a commission to pass on the release of the prisoners. Secretary Seward in 1861 appointed special agents who were stationed at several points on the northern border to detect and arrest Confederate agents attempting to enter United States territory. Besides these agents, the consul at Quebec and agents at Halifax, St. John's, and other Canadian seaports engaged in ferreting out Confederate plotters. A counterspy, Lafayette C. Baker, was employed in the summer of 1861.

Lafayette C. Baker, History of the United States Secret Service (Philadelphia, 1867); Frederic Bancroft, The Life of William H. Seward, 2:254-280 (New York, London, 1900. 2 vols.); John A. Marshall, American Bastile; a History of the Illegal Arrests and Imprisonment of American Citizens During the Late Civil War (Philadelphia, 1869); George F. Milton, Lincoln and the Fifth Column (New York, 1942); James G. Randall, Constitutional Problems Under Lincoln (Urbana, Ill., 1951).

Record Group 59. --Concerning political or state prisoners there are a number of State Department records. These include a correspondence file containing communications with prisoners, petitions, histories of cases, and related papers, arranged alphabetically by name of prisoner; outgoing letters, copied in a volume that also contains intercepted messages; and a file of letters, to 1863, from Col. Martin Burke, who commanded the prisons at Forts Lafayette and Hamilton. Useful in tracing individual cases are a register of letters received and sent regarding persons arrested for treason, records of arrests for treason and disloyalty, a list of "treason papers," and a list of disloyal persons in Alexandria, Va. Other records include letters seized at the time of the arrest of William W. Glenn, the editor of the Baltimore Exchange; and letters of Rose O'Neill Greenhow, Confederate spy, and Henry M. Warfield, member of the Maryland legislature. An exhibit in a case of suspected disloyalty consists of the minutes of a committee for the relief of needy persons in Alexandria.

Two volumes of "secret correspondence," Apr. 1861-Feb. 1863, contain outgoing letters regarding political prisoners, the employment of agents and detectives, the surveillance of suspected persons, the dismissal of consuls and other persons disloyal to the United States, the acceptance of companies of soldiers from the Territories, and the seizure of vessels.

Some records of the Commission for State Prisoners are also among this collection, having been transferred at some time from the custody of the commissioners or of the War Department. A letters-sent book contains letters, Feb. 17-May 21, 1862, signed by the commissioners, Maj. Gen. John A. Dix and Edwards Pierrepont, and their secretary, Erastus D. Webster, and also by the Secretary of War Stanton, the Adjutant General Lorenzo Thomas, and Assistant Secretary of War P. H. Watson. There is also incomplete copy of the proceedings of the commissioners for Feb.27-May 9, 1862, in their examination of prisoners.

Much of the correspondence on political prisoners and memoranda from the record book entitled "Arrests for Disloyalty" is printed, together with records of the War Department and of the Attorney General, in U. S. War Department, The War of the Rebellion; a Compilation of the Official Records of the Union and Confederate Armies, ser. 2, vol. 2 (Washington, 1897).

Pardon and Amnesty Records

By acts of July 31, 1861, and July 17, 1862 (12 Stat. 284, 589), Congress fixed penalties for "conspiracy" and "rebellion," but sec. 13 of the latter act also authorized the President to extend pardon and amnesty

to persons who had participated in the rebellion. The policy of granting
amnesty to prisoners of war was begun on a limited scale in the fall of 1861,
but commanders in the field were not generally authorized to grant amnesty
to persons taking the oath of allegiance until after an agreement was reached
with the Confederate Government on July 22, 1862, for the exchange of prisoners. On Feb. 14, 1862, Lincoln directed Secretary Stanton to release
all political prisoners and other persons held in military custody if they
gave parole not to render aid or comfort to the enemies of the United States.
Those who kept parole were later to be granted amnesty. In the border
States and in areas of the Confederacy conquered by the Federal Army, amnesty was granted to prisoners of war, recruits who had fought with the
Confederate Army, and civilians who had aided the Confederate occupation.
President Lincoln's proclamation of Dec. 8, 1863 (13 Stat. 737), offered
full pardon to persons who had taken part in the rebellion (except for six
classes of persons) upon their taking and adhering to an oath of allegiance.
The same proclamation provided that only persons who had taken the oath
and had not violated it could take part in reestablishing a State government.
Oaths were administered by military governors, military commanders of
departments, and men designated by them.

Amnesty and reconstruction were coupled by President Johnson in proclamations issued on May 29, 1865. The amnesty proclamation (13 Stat.
758) granted amnesty and pardon, with restoration of civil rights, to persons who had participated in the rebellion except for 14 classes; and persons belonging to those classes might make special application to the President. By obtaining pardon civil rights were recovered, further confiscation
of property was prevented, and voting rights were reestablished. Pardons
were freely granted by President Johnson during 1865 and were even granted,
before the end of that year, to Cabinet officers of the Confederacy. Only a
few prominent Confederate leaders remained unpardoned by the fall of 1867.

Jonathan Truman Dorris, Pardon and Amnesty Under Lincoln and
Johnson; the Restoration of the Confederates to Their Rights and Privileges, 1861-1898 (Chapel Hill, N. C.,
1953).

Record Group 59. --The Department of State kept the amnesty oaths
taken under Presidential proclamations. The principal file consists of individual amnesty oaths, 1864-66, arranged alphabetically by State and thereunder alphabetically by the first two letters of the surname; it contains also
acceptances of the President's warrants of pardons and military paroles. A
small supplementary file, alphabetical by name, contains other individual
oaths, with no indication of their geographical origin. Oaths administered by
field officers in Louisiana, Little Rock, Ark., and Missouri, 1863-65 (9
vols.), are on sheets with the oath printed at the top, followed by signatures
of persons subscribing to it. A somewhat larger file of oaths on rolls is arranged alphabetically by State and thereunder numerically. A register of
oaths taken under Lincoln's proclamation of Dec. 8, 1863, and the supplementary proclamation of Mar. 26, 1864 (13 Stat. 741), fills 4 volumes.
This register contains 22,659 names and addresses of oath takers through
May 1865 (Dorris, Pardon and Amnesty, p. 71). A list or index of the far
more numerous amnesty oaths taken under Johnson's proclamation of
May 29, 1865, fills 12 volumes.

Other registers, lists, and indexes are finding aids for the oaths of
particular individuals. There are registers of oaths administered at

Summerville, S. C., 1865; Missouri, no date; and Upson County, Ga., Aug. - Oct. 1865. Lists are available for Apalachicola, Fla., no date; " mouth of the White River, " 1865; "deserters from the Army of the Confederacy, " 1863-64; Huntsville, Ark., 1865; and Little Rock, Ark., 1863-65.

Pardons issued from 1865 to Aug. 1867 under the proclamation of May 29, 1865, were recorded chronologically in 25 separate indexed volumes, for which there is also an alphabetical name index (2 vols.). There are also requisitions for amnesty pardons from the President and the Attorney General (2 ft.); a register of pardons sent to the Attorney General, 1865; a record of the disposition of pardons, 1865-68; a list of persons accepting amnesty pardons, 1865-Dec. 1868; a list of pardons sent to the Governors of States; receipts for pardons; and a list of pardons returned to the President.

Petitions for pardons from persons included in the excepted classes (with supporting papers) are in the records of the Adjutant General's Office (Record Group 94). Other pardon records are in the records of the Pardon Clerk (Record Group 204), and in the applications in the files of the House Select Committee on Reconstruction (in Record Group 233).

Records of the Restoration of State Governments

Both Lincoln and Johnson tried by executive action to restore loyal governments in the South. Lincoln attempted to reestablish Federal authority in Tennessee, Louisiana, and Arkansas, after parts of those States were occupied by Union forces, by appointing military governors. Lincoln's amnesty proclamation of Dec. 8, 1863, provided that when a tenth of the number who had voted in the Presidential election of 1860 should establish a loyal government, it would be recognized. Under this plan, governments were set up in Tennessee, Louisiana, and Arkansas; but Congress refused to admit the Congressmen elected and thereby withheld recognition. When West Virginia became a State the "loyal government of Virginia" that had been functioning in that area moved to Alexandria and was recognized by both Lincoln and Johnson as the government of Virginia. After the war and during the 1865 recess of Congress Johnson, who considered that Tennessee, Louisiana, Arkansas, and Virginia were already "reconstructed," issued between May 29 and July 13, a series of proclamations designating provisional governors of the other seven former Confederate States and instructing them to organize constitutional conventions. By the end of 1865 new State governments had been elected in the South, but when Congress met in Dec. 1865 it again refused to admit Congressmen from the Southern States and it took steps to reconstruct the South on its own terms.

Record Group 59. --Historically associated with the admission of new States into the Union, the State Department participated in the postwar restoration of State governments in the South. Records of this activity include a file of correspondence between the Secretary of State and the provisional governors, which contains also manuscript and printed copies of constitutions, ordinances, resolutions, messages, addresses, proclamations, and other documents; a separate volume of documents concerning the provisional government of Florida; and some papers on the reorganization of Arkansas during 1864.

The correspondence and other documents of 1865 mentioned above were transmitted to the Senate by the President on Mar. 6, 1866, and were printed as S. Ex. Doc. 26, 39 Cong., 1 sess., Serial 1237.

Many letters written by Secretary Seward to the Governors of the States in 1865 are in the domestic letters, indexed under the names of the States (not the Governors). A few letters to the Governors of Tennessee, Louisiana, and Virginia, 1862-64, are in earlier volumes of this series.

Alabama Claims Papers

These records of claims against Great Britain for the Civil War depredations of Confederate cruisers built in England were once a part of the "Civil War papers" in Record Group 59 but were transferred to the postwar Courts of Commissioners of Alabama Claims (see below). After use by these courts they were returned to the State Department with the court records and are now a part of Record Group 76. The claims and the circumstances giving rise to them are therefore described below under the Courts of Commissioners for Alabama Claims.

Record Group 59. --Some records relating to the claims, though not the claims papers themselves, are in this record group. They consist chiefly of correspondence of the State Department with U. S. Minister Charles Francis Adams in London and are in the series of diplomatic instructions and diplomatic despatches.

Other Records

Record Group 59. --As a result of its wartime activities the Department accumulated other small lots of papers. A file of letters, 1861-62, contains requests from persons in the North for passes to various points in the South. Wives wanted to rejoin their families; children wanted to rejoin their parents; and other persons wanted to see their relatives. Southerners caught in the North wanted to visit the South to collect debts or to protect their pecuniary interests. Passes seem to have been granted only rarely; such endorsements on letters as "inexpedient," "refused," or "prohibited" indicate that most requests were denied. The many refusals may explain why the file ends in 1862. The letters received in 1862 are briefly registered in a book. Lincoln issued some passes throughout the war; the texts of many of them are published in Basler's edition of his works.

Parts at least of other items in the Civil War papers are undoubtedly related to communications in the regular correspondence series of the Department. Minutes of the board of a military organization in New Orleans, apparently composed of British residents of that city, indicate that it engaged in target practice and social functions. Intercepted letters often were grounds for the arrest of suspected persons; such letters in the files were written by Confederate officials, agents, other Southern sympathizers, and residents of the South; and with them are clippings from Southern newspapers. A small batch of drafts of outgoing letters includes letters to Army officers introducing men offering their services to the Army and letters of congratulation and thanks. Transcripts of letters of the Secretary of the Navy concern the establishment of the blockade of the Southern coast. Other records include a bounty roll recording payments to members of Co. B, 41st Regiment, New York City; a few papers concerning the Confederate seizure of the Willet S. Robbins and the Alice Gibson; some bonds (unarranged) posted by men liable to be drafted into the military service; enclosures to diplomatic despatches from London consisting of three resolutions from antislavery societies and an address from the British and Foreign Anti-Slavery Society; manuscript and printed material on the operations of the C. S. S. Alabama; and a memorandum of Mar. 22, 1861, on the possible withdrawal of the garrison from Fort Sumter.

Another significant original document is the declaration, June 13, 1861, of the people of the northwestern counties of Virginia represented in a convention at Wheeling, contesting the legality of Virginia's secession. The text of this document, without the names of its signers, appears in S. Misc. Doc. 99, 37 Cong., 2 sess., Serial 1124, and in Virgil A. Lewis, How West Virginia Was Made . . ., p. 86-87 (Charleston, W. Va., 1909).

The poor response to the call for volunteers for the Army led to the adoption of limited conscription in Aug. 1862 and the passage of a draft act on Mar. 3, 1863 (12 Stat. 731). Under the terms of this act the President on May 8, 1863, issued a proclamation (13 Stat. 732) announcing that aliens who had declared their intention to become citizens and who were in the United States 65 days after that date would not be allowed to avoid the draft on the plea of alienage. The State Department became involved in the release from military service of aliens who were drafted from 1862 onward. The records of this activity include an alphabetical case file containing draft notices, depositions of aliens regarding their foreign citizenship, and correspondence. Other correspondence of the Secretary of State regarding the release of aliens is in separate letter books (indexed) and in files of loose papers. An alphabetical list of draft cases shows the States and counties from which the aliens were drafted.

FOREIGN SERVICE POST RECORDS

The United States maintained Foreign Service posts throughout the world at the time of the Civil War. These posts included legations, consulates general, consulates, vice-consulates, consular agencies, and commercial agencies. The legations, in some 27 of the principal countries of the world, were in the charge of ministers; no ambassadors were appointed by the United States until 1893. The consuls general were authorized to communicate with the heads of governments in the countries to which they were appointed, and they supervised and gave advice to U. S. consular officers within their districts. The consuls general, consuls, and commercial agents were divided into three classes according to the provisions of an act of Aug. 18, 1856 (11 Stat. 52), which designated the places to which the several classes were to be appointed. Commercial agents were appointed by the Department of State and sent abroad to promote U. S. commercial interests. They were not necessarily recognized by the governments of the countries where they resided; sometimes their appointments were secret. Consular agents served under full consular officers at ports or inland towns different from those at which their principals resided.

Consular officers were appointed to reside in foreign countries, especially at seaports. The chief duties of consuls were to look after the interests of American commerce and seamen; to receive from masters of vessels registers, sea letters, and passports; to recover deserters; to collect and remit the assets of deceased American citizens; to exercise toward their countrymen the role of judges, arbiters, and peacemakers; to serve as registers of marriages, births, and deaths and as notaries issuing passports; and to promote emigration to the United States.

During the Civil War the consuls also engaged in other activities

important to the Union military effort.   The consular offices became centers of an espionage network composed of numerous detectives and spies,
who kept watch on Confederate agents and collected evidence of their operations.   This system was most highly developed in Great Britain, but consuls in France, Canada, the West Indies, and other areas also reported on
the activities of Confederate agents.   These reports became the basis of instructions to other consuls to attempt to thwart Confederate designs.   Some
of the reports sent by consuls to the State Department were channeled to
other departments of the Government, particularly to the Navy Department.
Consuls also reported on blockade runners and on the shipment of munitions
that appeared to be destined for the Confederacy.   Regarding these matters,
the consuls at ports in the West Indies were under instruction to notify the
commanders of blockading squadrons, who might try to capture the suspected vessels.   The main business of consulates at some European ports,
such as Bremen, Hamburg, and Scandinavian ports, was to promote emigration to the United States.

An act of Aug. 2, 1861 (12 Stat. 285), authorized the President to appoint consuls at other ports where it seemed advisable.   Experience had
indicated that the Government was best served by salaried consuls prohibited from engaging in trade.   The State Department, therefore, to improve
the possibilities of getting intelligence of the operations of Confederate
cruisers, appointed new consuls with fixed compensation, or changed the
pay of other consuls to fixed compensation, at the principal ports in the
West Indies, four ports in Mexico, two in Central America, three in Brazil, and one in Venezuela.   For the protection of U. S. commerce in the
Mediterranean, salaried consuls were appointed at Algiers, Barcelona,
Valencia, Lisbon, Malta, three important ports in Italy, three in France,
one on the Black Sea, and two in Turkey.   To protect commerce elsewhere
two appointments were made on the northern coast of Spain, one in Norway,
two in Sweden, and three in Chinese and other eastern waters. Arms and
munitions for the South were being sent from ports in England to other British ports, where they were transshipped in small vessels, to run the blockade. To disrupt this traffic, salaried consuls were appointed at Bristol,
England; Cardiff, Wales; St. John's, Newfoundland; and Prince Edward
Island in Canada. The salary of a vacant consulship at Gaboon, Africa, was
raised in an effort to get a consul who would help protect commerce and suppress the slave trade.   Actually only 7 new consulates were created: at Cardiff, Wales; Lisbon, Portugal; Otranto and Taranto, Italy; Scio, Turkey;
St. Marc, Haiti; and Quebec, Canada.

Nels M. Hokanson, Swedish Immigrants in Lincoln's Time (New
York, London, 1942); Chester L.
Jones, The Consular Service of the
United States; Its History and Activities (Philadelphia, 1906); Halvdan
Koht, "When America Called for
Immigrants, " Norwegian-American
Studies and Records, 14:159-183
(1944); Graham H. Stuart, American Diplomatic and Consular Practice (New York, London, 1936); and
the following issuances of the U. S.

Department of State: Regulations
Prescribed by the President for Consular Officers of the United States
(Washington, 1856), Regulations Prescribed by the President in Regard to
the Appointment, Compensation, and
Duties of Consular Clerks (Washington, 1864); The United States Consul's
Manual; a Practical Guide for Consular Officers, and Also for Merchants, Shipowners, and Masters of
American Vessels in All Their Consular Transactions (Washington, 1863);

The Foreign Service of the United States; Origins, Development, and Functions, by William Barnes and John Heath Morgan (Washington, 1961); and Register of the Department of State, in Four Parts; Corrected to March 1, 1874 (Washington, 1874). The last publication is a historical register with dates of appointment of diplomatic agents of the United States and also contains lists of heads of foreign missions in the United States, a list of treaties and conventions, and an index. Lists of the diplomatic, consular, and other U. S. officials in foreign countries are also in the Official Register, 1861-65. A List of Diplomatic and Consular Officers of the United States in Foreign Countries; Also List of Foreign Ministers, Their Secretaries and Attachés, Credited to the Government of the United States was first issued by the Department of State in 1856; issues appeared also in 1857, 1859, and 1865. A list of consulates, sent by the Secretary of State to the Senate, with a letter of Jan. 8, 1862, regarding the establishment of new consulates, is in S. Ex. Doc. 12, 37 Cong., 2 sess., Serial 1121. Other lists of consular officers dated Dec. 9, 1863, and Dec. 31, 1864, are in H. Ex. Doc. 10, 38 Cong., 1 sess., Serial 1187; and S. Ex. Doc. 32, 38 Cong., 2 sess., Serial 1209. Recommendations of the Secretary of State in 1864 for further changes in consulates, for increased salaries, and for authority to appoint "consular pupils" are in H. Misc. Doc. 77, 38 Cong., 1 sess., Serial 1200. Augustus E. Ingram, "When Was This Consulate First Opened?" American Foreign Service Journal, 17:522-526 (Sept. 1940), describes an alphabetical card index in the Department of State that gives the dates of establishment of consulates and diplomatic posts.

With certain nations whose laws, customs, and social systems differed greatly from those of Western nations, the United States before the Civil War (like other nations of the West) had concluded treaties and conventions providing extraterritorial jurisdiction for its ministers and consuls. By acts of Congress of Aug. 11, 1848, and June 22, 1860 (9 Stat. 276; 12 Stat. 72), giving effect to the treaties, representatives of the United States were to adjudicate disputes between American nationals and try civil and criminal cases in which American nationals were defendants. A circular of the Secretary of State, Sept. 1, 1860, transmitting a copy of the act of June 22, 1860, with directions to execute it and to prepare the prescribed forms and regulations and the required returns to the Department, was addressed to ministers and consuls in China, Japan, Siam, Persia, Turkey, Tripoli, Tunis, Morocco, and Muscat.

Green H. Hackworth, Digest of International Law, 2:493-621 (Washington, 1940-44. 8 vols.); Frank B. Hinckley, American Consular Jurisdiction in the Orient (Washington, 1906); Moore, Digest of International Law, 2:593-755. The regulations prepared for the U. S. consular courts in Turkey are published in S. Ex. Doc. 25, 37 Cong., 3 sess., Serial 1149, p. 3-17.

Record Group 84. --The records of Foreign Service posts are useful for information on many subjects. They show the part played by the posts in diplomatic negotiations, supply data on the administration of the posts and their personnel, and give much information on political and economic conditions in the foreign countries. The records of consular offices are important for the history of American trade, shipping, and individual ships and their officers and crews. American ships continued in both the whaling and guano trades during the Civil War; these activities can be traced in the records of posts in the Pacific Ocean area. Visits by Confederate cruisers and their depredations on American ships were regularly reported to the Department of State, and pertinent documentary evidence was obtained and filed. From consuls in England came reports of the construction of Confederate vessels, the shipment of munitions, and the departure of blockade runners.

Meredith B. Colket, Jr., "The Preservation of Consular and Diplomatic Post Records of the United States," American Archivist, 6:193-205 (Oct. 1943); John P. Harrison, "The Archives of United States Diplomatic and Consular Posts in Latin America," Hispanic American Historical Review, 33:168-183 (Feb. 1953), which has been incorporated in the Guide to Materials on Latin America in the National Archives (Washington, 1961); Carl L. Lokke, "France in the National Archives," Institut français de Washington, Bulletin, n. s., No. 5-6, p. 16-27 (Dec. 1957); Hunter Miller, "Transfer to the Department of State of the Older Archives of Certain American Embassies, Legations, and Consulates," American Historical Review, 39:184-185 (Oct. 1933); National Archives, List of Foreign Service Post Records in the National Archives, comp. by Mark G. Eckhoff and Alexander P. Mavro (Special List No. 9. Washington, 1958); National Archives, Preliminary Inventory [No. 60] of the Records of Selected Foreign Service Posts, comp. by Alexander P. Mavro (Washington, 1953). Records of the Fifth Auditor of the Treasury on the accounts of the diplomatic service are described below under the Department of the Treasury.

Records of diplomatic posts consist of instructions from the Department and copies or duplicates of despatches to it; notes from the governments of the countries where the posts were located and copies of notes to them; copies of instructions and despatches to subordinate consulates, and despatches and reports from them; records of passports issued; correspondence with individuals, business firms, and organizations; records of births, marriages, and deaths of American citizens; records regarding the disposal of property, the settlement of estates, and the protection of American citizens; declarations of citizenship; journals and memoranda; financial records and property inventories of the posts; and registers and indexes of the various series of correspondence. The correspondence with the Department in the post records is duplicated in the Department's files, which are easier to use. But enclosures in the instructions from the Department are more easily available in the post records than in the Department's files, where they are scattered in the various series of outgoing correspondence. Other correspondence is available only in the post records, except when copies were transmitted to the Department with despatches.

The records of consular posts consist of instructions from the Department and from the supervising consular office, and copies of despatches and reports to them; correspondence with individuals, business firms, and organizations; records of fees received for notarial, shipping, and miscellaneous services; records of passports issued; records of births, marriages, and deaths of American citizens; records regarding the disposal of property, the settlement of estates, and the protection of American citizens; certifications of merchandise shipped from or received in the district; journals and memoranda; financial records and property inventories of the posts; and various registers and indexes. For seaport consulates there are also records of the arrival and departure of American vessels and descriptions of their cargoes, ships' daily journals, registers of seamen, records of services performed for American ships and seamen, marine protests, and other maritime documents. For posts in the countries where ministers and consuls exercised judicial authority there are court records. Occasional private papers among the records include personal journals, ships' logs, and muster rolls. Parts of the records of some posts have been destroyed by fire, earthquake, volcanic eruptions, and revolutionary activities. The places affected by such catastrophes include Belize, Chihuahua, Ciudad Juárez, Colón, Durango, Guayaquil, Managua, St. Pierre (Martinique), and Valparaiso.

CLAIMS COMMISSION AND COURT RECORDS

As a result of European emigration, which had been running strong for years, there were in the South in 1861 many foreigners who became victims of military operations. Among the 233,650 persons of foreign birth in the South in 1860 English, Irish, Scotch, Welsh, French, and Germans predominated. In smaller numbers there were also Italians, Scandinavians, Poles, Spaniards, and Mexicans. Some of these foreigners suffered loss of property including even vessels, personal injury, or imprisonment at the hands of U. S. military, naval, and civil authorities. The victims made application to the representatives of their countries in the United States for the procurement of compensation.

During and after the Civil War the representatives of foreign countries presented to the U. S. Government claims of their subjects resident in the United States for wartime damages. Such claims were presented particularly on behalf of citizens of Great Britain, France, Germany, and Italy.

The historic method of adjudicating such claims had been through diplomatic channels or through joint commissions consisting of representatives of the United States, of the foreign nation involved, and of neutral nations. Such commissions were eventually provided for by conventions signed with Great Britain and France. As the number of Italian claims was small, no claims convention was negotiated, and the claims were settled over a period of years through ordinary diplomatic channels. Documentation regarding these claims is in the diplomatic correspondence described above and in claims files of the War Department. A similar procedure was evidently followed in regard to the claims of German subjects. As shown by the investigation made by Sister Mary Philip Trauth and presented in the work cited below, the research involved in tracing the settlement of Italian and German claims is necessarily prolonged, since the pertinent documents are scattered among many volumes in the diplomatic correspondence. Proposals put forth over a period of years for the establishment of a special court to handle these claims were never embodied in legislation.

Edwin M. Borchard, "International Responsibility of the State for Injuries Sustained by Aliens During Civil War, " American Political Science Association, Proceedings, 10:117-124 (1913-14); Ella Lonn, Foreigners in the Confederacy (Chapel Hill, N. C. , 1940); Mary Philip Trauth, Italo-American Diplomatic Relations, 1861-1882; the Mission of

George Perkins Marsh, First American Minister to the Kingdom of Italy (Washington,1958); U. S. Congress, House Committee on War Claims, The Law of Claims Against Governments, Including the Mode of Adjusting Them and the Procedure Adopted in Their Investigation (H. Rept. 134, 43 Cong., 2 sess., Serial 1658. Washington, 1875).

Depredations on American merchant ships during the Civil War by Confederate cruisers constructed in England and allowed to depart over the protests of the American Minister resulted in claims for losses and damages against the British Government. Because most of the losses were inflicted by the C. S. S. Alabama, these claims became known as the Alabama claims. That vessel and others were not only built in England but also equipped at sea with armament supplied from England, largely manned by British seamen, and later fueled and provisioned in British colonial ports. The Alabama, the Florida, and the Shenandoah preyed on Union shipping in the North and South Atlantic, the Gulf of Mexico, and the Caribbean, and on whaling vessels in the Pacific from 1862 to 1865. Other Confederate vessels, such as the Georgiana, the Georgia, and the Rappahannock, were also obtained from England, but only the Georgia became a raider for a short time. Since the ships and cargoes captured by these cruisers could not be taken through the Northern blockade of the Confederate coast or to neutral ports, most of them were burned at sea after being pillaged of materials useful to their attackers. Other vessels with too many passengers to be taken off or with neutral cargoes were allowed to proceed upon giving bond payable to the Confederacy 6 months after the end of the war. In all 260 merchant ships carrying cargo worth $20,000,000 were destroyed by Confederate raiders. Since marine insurance did not usually provide full coverage and since it was carried chiefly by American underwriters, much of the loss was merely transferred from the owner to the insurer. Sharp increases in insurance premiums caused American merchants to turn to neutral bottoms and caused shipowners to sell their vessels at sacrifice prices to foreign citizens, chiefly British. As a result, besides the 110,000 tons that were burned, 800,000 tons were transferred to foreign ownership. This loss of over 1,000 vessels reduced the American merchant fleet by more than half the tonnage of 1860. Yet, though American shipping suffered serious damage, the foreign commerce of the North prospered during the Civil War.

Word of attacks by Confederate cruisers reached the State Department from all over the world. The masters, other officers, and crews of American ships were put ashore at many ports by the Confederate vessels or by other vessels to which they had been transferred by the raiders. The master of a sunken ship usually appeared before the U. S. consul at the foreign port and executed a master's or marine protest, in which he stated the circumstances of the attack. These and other documents the consuls forwarded to the Department of State. Other masters of ships who found their way to U. S. ports prepared depositions before notaries public. These were sent to the Department by shipowners who submitted claims for the destruction of their vessels and by masters who had lost professional instruments and personal effects. As the Secretary of State received reports of the destruction of American ships, he directed the American Minister in Great Britain, Charles Francis Adams, to present the claims to the British Government, with copies of documentary evidence that the Department provided. A proposal for arbitration of the claims, submitted by Adams in Oct. 1863, was rejected; but correspondence and negotiation on the claims continued.

The claims papers accumulated by the Department of State became so voluminous that during 1865-66 E. Peshine Smith, an attorney, was engaged to examine and abstract them. On July 27, 1866, he was given the position of Examiner of Claims, authorized by an act of July 25 (14 Stat. 226). An abstract of claims arising from attacks by the Alabama, the Shenandoah, the Florida, and the Georgia, presumably prepared by Smith, was forwarded by Secretary Seward to Charles Francis Adams on Aug. 27, 1866 (Foreign Relations, 1866, pt. 1, p. 177-203). In accordance with an act of July 20, 1868 (15 Stat. 96), the office of Examiner of Claims was abolished on June 30, 1869. Smith was appointed as a State Department clerk on the following day and probably continued his work on claims. He was again appointed. Examiner of Claims on June 7, 1870, after the office was reestablished by a joint resolution of May 27, 1870 (16 Stat. 378); but an act of June 22, 1870 (16 Stat. 162), provided for the transfer of the office to the newly created Department of Justice. More claims were filed after the ratification of the Treaty of Washington, and the receipt of these was followed by the preparation in 1871 and 1872 of enlarged lists of claims.

On Oct. 28, 1865, the State Department issued a circular telling claimants how claims were to be submitted. A sworn statement or memorial was required, setting forth minutely and particularly the facts and circumstances and requesting the interposition of the U. S. Government with the foreign government concerned. In claims for loss of a ship or cargo certified copies of the ship's registry, with originals or certified copies of clearances, cargo manifests, and other papers carried on the ship's last voyage, had to be submitted. Other documents required when appropriate were insurance policies and naturalization papers.

Efforts to find a means to settle the claims and other controversial matters were continued. Conventions agreed upon between the two governments in 1868 and 1869 were not approved by the Senate. After informal discussions between Secretary of State Hamilton Fish and Sir John Rose, it was agreed by an exchange of notes that a joint commission should meet in Washington to negotiate a treaty for the adjustment of outstanding issues. Soon afterwards Secretary of State Hamilton Fish, Robert C. Schenck, Samuel Nelson, Ebenezer Hoar, and George H. Williams were appointed as the American commissioners. The Joint High Commission met on Feb. 27, 1871, and its deliberations resulted in the signing of the Treaty of Washington on May 8, 1871 (17 Stat. 863; Malloy, Treaties, 1:700-722), which provided for the arbitration of the Alabama claims, the adjudication by a mixed commission of the claims of citizens of the two countries for damages and injuries suffered during the war, and the settlement of other matters.

The tribunal of arbitration met at Geneva, Switzerland, during 1871-1872. The arbitrator for the United States was Charles Francis Adams, for Great Britain Sir Alexander Cockburn, and the three neutral arbitrators were Justice Jacques Staempfli of Switzerland, Marcos Antonio D'Araujo of Brazil (Viscount d'Itajubá), and Count Frederic Sclopis of Italy. The American agent was J. C. Bancroft Davis, who was assisted as counsel by Caleb Cushing, William M. Evarts, and Morrison R. Waite. Lord Tenterden was the British Agent and the counsel were Sir Roundell Palmer, Mountague Bernard, and Arthur Cohen. The award made by the tribunal on Sept. 14, 1872, held Great Britain responsible for the destruction caused by the Alabama and her tender Tuscaloosa; by the Florida and her tenders Clarence, Tacony, and Archer; and by the Shenandoah after her departure from

Melbourne, Australia, where she enlisted men for her crew, on Feb. 18, 1865. But in connection with the Georgia, Sumter, Nashville, Tallahassee, and Chickamauga, it was decided that Great Britain had not failed in her responsibilities as a neutral and was therefore not responsible for the destruction they caused. Claims for Destruction by certain other vessels, including the Sallie, Jefferson Davis, Music, Boston, and V. H. Joy, were not considered because of lack of evidence. A total of $15,500,000 in gold was awarded to the United States as indemnity.

Robert A. Albion and Jennie B. Pope, Sea Lanes in Wartime; the American Experience, 1775-1942 (New York, 1942); Samuel F. Bemis, A Diplomatic History of the United States (New York, 1936); George W. Dalzell, The Flight From the Flag; the Continuing Effect of the Civil War Upon the American Carrying Trade (Chapel Hill, N. C., 1940); R. I. Lovell, "The Case for the Alabama, "Queen's Quarterly, 42:515-522 (Winter 1935-36); Moore, History and Digest of International Arbitrations, 1:495-682; Goldwin A. Smith, The Treaty of Washington, 1871; a Study in Imperial History (Ithaca, N. Y., 1941); U. S. Department of State, Correspondence Concerning Claims Against Great Britain, Transmitted . . . in Answer to the Resolutions of December 4 and 10, 1867, and of May 27, 1868 (Washington, 1869-71. 7 vols.); U. S. Department of State, Papers Relating to the Treaty of Washington, also published as S. Ex. Doc. 11, 40 Cong., 1 sess., Serials 1394-1398 (Washington, 1872-74. 6 vols.); National Archives, Preliminary Inventory [No. 135] of Records Relating to Civil War Claims-- United States and Great Britain, comp. by George S. Ulibarri and Daniel T. Goggin (Washington, 1962).

Record Group 76.--The Alabama claims papers consist of documents relating to the claims of American citizens for damages sustained by them as owners, freighters, or insurers of American ships; or as owners, shippers, or insurers of the cargoes of such vessels; or as charter parties for the service of such ships. Besides claims of owners or insurers for the loss of the ships or their cargoes, the file includes papers relating to the claims of masters for the loss of instruments, charts, and personal effects, for salary during periods of unemployment, for subsistence, and for passage home; of seamen for most of the same expenses; and of passengers for personal effects, stores, expenses, and household furniture. The documentation of claims includes statements or memorials, marine protests, registers of ownership, cargo manifests, crew lists, agreements between masters and seamen, letters of administration, statements of damages, certificates of the value of vessels, statements of insurance companies on their payment of insurance, demands for indemnification, copies of insurance policies, assignment of claims, letters of attorney, depositions, affidavits, shipping articles, clearances, and correspondence.

Since they contain lists of the papers for individual claims, the following volumes serve as inventories of the Alabama claims papers: U. S. Department of State, Revised List of Claims Filed With the Department of State, Growing Out of the Acts Committed by the Several Vessels, Which Have Given Rise to the Claims Generically Known as The Alabama Claims (Washington, 1872); and an earlier list published in 1871, both separately and as vol. 7 of U. S. Department of State, Correspondence Concerning Claims Against Great Britain. The replies of the

Department of State to communications from claimants are in its domestic letters; other material on
claims for Confederate depredations
may be found in the consular correspondence and in the records of some
foreign service posts.

The Treaty of Washington stipulated that each party should prepare
written or printed copies of the case or brief and counter case with their
supporting documents, and an argument for delivery to each of the arbitrators of the Geneva Tribunal and to the agent of the other party.   The arbitrators were also to keep a record of their proceedings and duplicate copies
of the award were to be made.   The cases, counter cases, and arguments
were printed and submitted by the agents of the United States and Great
Britain to the arbitrators at the appointed times.   Copies of the printed
documents presented by the American agent and most of those presented
by the British agent are in the National Archives.   The documents were
reprinted by the Department of State in Papers Relating to the Treaty of
Washington (Washington, 1872-74.   6 vols.; also published as part 2 of
Foreign Relations for 1872).   Besides the cases, counter-cases, and arguments, this compilation contains instructions to the U. S. agent and counsel, correspondence, supplemental arguments, the report of the U. S.
agent, the proceedings of the arbitrators, the report of the U. S. counsel,
opinons of the arbitrators, and the decision and award of the arbitrators.
The materials in the National Archives include an index prepared by the
U. S. agent entitled Alphabetical List of the Documents and Correspondence
Submitted with the Cases and Counter Cases of the United States and of
Great Britain to the Tribunal of Arbitration at Geneva.
The volumes of evidence submitted to the tribunal by the U. S. agent
along with his case consisted of the 7 volumes of Correspondence Concerning Claims Against Great Britain which had previously been published by
the Department of State in 1869-1871, and the lists of claims published in
1871 and 1872, previously cited.   A set of these volumes in the Department
of State library has the title "Evidence of the United States" and is numbered consecutively with the case.   The volumes of evidence contain many
documents of the war period derived from the records of the Department of
State and of other executive departments relating to the construction and
operations of the Confederate cruisers.   The U. S. Government also published the case of Great Britain in 1872 separately and as H. Ex. Doc.282,
42 Cong. , 2 sess. , Serials 1517-1519.   These volumes contain correspondence of British officials of the war period relating to the Confederate cruisers.   The counter case of Great Britain containing additional documents is
in H. Ex. Doc. 324, 42 Cong. , 2 sess. , Serial 1521.

The titles of the numerous documentary publications resulting from
the Geneva Tribunal are in Bemis
and Griffin, Guide to the Diplomatic
History of the U. S. , p. 405-409,
and in the catalog of the Library of
Congress (available in book form in
large libraries). The decision and
award is also in Malloy, Treaties,
1:717-722, in Caleb Cushing, The
Treaty of Washington; Its Negotiation, Execution and the Discussions
Relating Thereto (New York, 1873), p.
275-280, and in Thomas W. Balch,
The Alabama Arbitration (Philadelphia, 1900), p. 131-141. The original
award is in the file of exchange treaties in the National Archives (Record
Group 11). Cushing states (p. 126)
that a third signed copy of the award
and the archives of the tribunal were
placed in the records of the Council

of State of the Canton of Geneva, and Bemis and Griffin (p. 412) also use the word "archives", but they probably mean the printed records referred to above.

Mixed Commission on British and American Claims

By articles 12-17 of the Treaty of Washington the United States and Great Britain agreed that all claims on the part of corporations, companies, or private individuals of the two nations arising out of acts against persons or property during the period Apr. 13, 1861, to Apr. 9, 1865, that were not claims referred to in article 1 (Alabama claims), should be referred to a Mixed Claims Commission. The commissioners appointed were Russell Gurney for Great Britain; James Somerville Frazer for the United States; and Count Louis Corti, the Italian Minister to the United States, chosen by both countries. At the Commission's first meeting, Sept. 26, 1871, Corti was selected to preside; Robert Safford Hale was received as agent and counsel of the United States; James Mandeville Carlisle was received as counsel of Great Britain, and Henry Howard as agent of Great Britain. Thomas C. Cox, appointed secretary of the Commission on Sept. 27, had charge of the records, concerning which rules were prescribed by the Commission. It met in Washington until May 10, 1873, and then after a recess held the rest of its sessions, from June 10 to Sept. 25, at Newport, R. I.

Adjudicating the claims involved extensive investigation and resulted in considerable documentation. British citizens presented 478 claims for sums totaling with interest about $96,000,000. Of the 19 American claims, amounting to less than $1,000,000 exclusive of interest, 12 grew out of the raid on St. Albans, Vt., made by Confederates who came across the border from Canada. Others resulted from the detention at Calcutta of American vessels laden with saltpeter and from a raid by Confederate soldiers upon the American steamers Philo Vance and Island Queen on Lake Erie. Documentary evidence regarding the claims was sought by the U. S. agent from the archives of all the departments of the Federal Government and from records of the Confederate Government that were in Federal possession. Testimony was taken in writing all over the United States and in many different parts of the world by special counsel sent out from Washington or by local counsel under the instruction of the U. S. agent. Aid was also obtained from Thomas H. Dudley, who had been U. S. consul at Liverpool, and Joseph Nunn, vice consul general at London. The cases of American citizens against Great Britain were handled by private counsel with the general aid and supervision of the U. S. agent. The resulting disposition of the British claims was as follows: 30 dismissed as not within the jurisdiction of the Commission; 258 disallowed as unwarranted; 8 withdrawn by the British agent; 1 dismissed but later refiled; and 181 allowed, for $1,929,819. All the American claims were dismissed.

Mixed Commission on British and American Claims Under Article XII of the Treaty of Washington, 1871, Report of Robert S. Hale, Esq., Agent Counsel of the United States Before the Commission on Claims of Citizens of the United States Against Great Britain, and of Subjects of Her Britannic Majesty Against the United States . . . (Washington, 1874), also published in Foreign Relations of the Unites States, 1873, pt. 2, vol. 3; Moore, History and Digest of International Arbitrations, 1:683-702.

Record Group 76. --The records of the Commission and its staff were, upon its termination, deposited in the Department of State. A journal recording the proceedings of the Commission contains information on its organization, the adoption and amendment of rules, proceedings on individual claims, and opinions and decisions of the Commission. The docket of British claims contains abstracts of actions regarding the claims of British citizens against the United States, recorded by claim number. The numbers were evidently assigned as the claims were presented, and entries were made for the proceedings, motions, orders, etc. , under each claim in chronological order. A file of original proofs, filed by claim number, contains the documents collected for each claim; these consist of evidence supplied by Government departments, memorials of claimants setting forth their claims, testimony, depositions, and exhibits of both the Government and the claimant, drafts of arguments, briefs, demurrers of the United States, notices, motions, correspondence, and indentures. A similar file of original proofs for American claims against the British Government is much less voluminous. Much of the material in these files was printed for the Commission's use. One set of 35 volumes contains memorials, demurrers, briefs, and decisions; rejoinders of defense; and surrejoinders of claimants. Another set of 39 volumes labeled "Testimony" contains depositions, cross-examinations by counsel, exhibits, and proofs for claimants. Since the volumes average 800 pages each, the 74 volumes in these two series total 59, 200 printed pages, largely of documentary material relating to events of the Civil War. A copy of a list of judgments and decisions, prepared for the Secretary of State and giving data for each claim, is also available. Registers of both the British and the American claims present chronological records of the actions taken. Awards contain brief statements of what was decided and the amount of the award, sometimes only the amount of the award and in other cases only the statement that the claim was disallowed. Some memoranda received by the U. S. agent from the Department of State contain abstracts of correspondence of that Department for 1862-68 relating to claims. Copies of correspondence furnished to the agent were incorporated into the file of original proofs. Several small files of correspondence concern chiefly the procurement of evidence and testimony. Some notices on printed forms sent to the U. S. agent by the secretary of the Commission pertain to case actions taken by the Commission. Files of receipted bills, telegrams, and shorthand notes of the "stenographic clerk" complete the inventory of the records.

The evidence of the period of the Civil War and the testimony relating to that decade, which are in the files of original proofs of claims and in the printed sets, constitute an extensive and varied documentation. Since the claims by British subjects against the United States originated largely in occupied territory in the South and off its shores, the material is useful for the history of the Confederacy and of the occupying Federal forces. The documents are a source for local history, economic conditions, military government, commerce, and military and naval operations of both the North and the South. Biographical and genealogical data can be found in memorials submitted by claimants, and personal data are also in the testimony furnished by Southerners as well as British claimants. Some of the latter had long been residents of the South, and the documents they submitted contain information on their occupations and place of residence.

The extensive printed series of memorials and testimony are also in the Library of Congress, from which they can be borrowed on interlibrary loan. They are cataloged under the same authorship as Hale's report cited above. This report contains a "Schedule of Claims Presented to the Commission by Claimants Against the Respective Governments, With Indexes to Same," which with its alphabetical index to personal names and ship names is a useful finding aid for the files of original proofs and the printed compilations of documents based upon those files. A return of claims of British subjects against the U. S. Government, compiled by the British Government from its records, is printed in Foreign Relations of the United States, 1864, pt. 1, p. 736-763, and contains data about claims that were later referred to the Mixed Commission. Since these lists contain both names of the claimants and data about the places at which the incidents connected with the claims occurred, they can be used to identify files that researchers may want to use.

Court of Commissioners of Alabama Claims (1)

To distribute the award made by the Geneva Tribunal as indemnity for damages by Confederate cruisers, Congress by an act of June 23, 1874 (18 Stat. 245), established the Court of Commissioners of Alabama Claims. The President on June 24, 1874, nominated as judges Hezekiah G. Wells of Michigan, Martin Ryerson of New Jersey, Kenneth Rayner of Mississippi, William A. Porter of Pennsylvania, and Caleb Baldwin of Iowa, with John Davis of Massachusetts as clerk; and the nominations were confirmed by the Senate. The judges met in Washington on July 22 and proceeded to organize the court. John A. J. Creswell appeared on that day as the U. S. counsel. After adopting rules on July 24, the court adjourned to allow the claimants time to prepare their cases for trial. The court reconvened in Oct. 1874 and continued in existence until Dec. 29, 1876. It processed in all 2,068 claims aggregating $14,500,000 and made awards of $9,316,120.

The act establishing the court limited its jurisdiction to claims directly resulting from damage caused by the Confederate cruisers Alabama and Florida and their tenders, and by the Shenandoah after her departure from Melbourne, Australia. Some of the claimants were residents of Southern ports, for commerce was permitted with such ports after their occupation by Federal forces. Records relating to these claims were transferred from the Department of State to the court in Oct. 1874 (see the Alabama claims papers described above). The U. S. counsel was represented in many cities by assistant counsel, who examined witnesses for the Government and cross-examined witnesses for claimants. Upon the termination of its sessions the records of the court were deposited in the Department of State.

Nearly all the claims were for the loss of property destroyed by the insurgent cruisers. Types of claims not allowed are described in the reports of the clerk, John Davis, cited below. In most cases the court, working under pressure, simply entered judgment for a certain amount without giving reasons for its decision. Davis gives for some cases what in his opinion were the rulings of the court upon questions of law.

Moore, History and Digest of International Arbitrations, 5:4639-4685. A report of the clerk of the court dated Nov. 1, 1875, is in Foreign Relations, 1875, 1:xxxi-xxxv. Another of Davis' reports, dated Jan. 5, 1877, some opinions of the court, its rules, and legislation relating to the court are printed in S. Ex. Doc. 21, 44 Cong., 2 sess., Serial 1719.

Record Group 76. --The rules of the court and the law establishing it required the filing of papers relating to claims and the keeping of a record of proceedings. The journal of the court contains copies of the judges' commissions; information on the court's organization, its adoption and revision of rules, and its admission of attorneys; and proceedings in cases, including awards and occasional opinions. Papers and evidence relating to claims, filed by claim number, include petitions of claimants setting forth the circumstances of the claims, amendments to the petitions, demurrers of U. S. counsel, letters from claimants' counsel, testimony of claimants and witnesses, exhibits presented by claimants, certificates of the clerk of the court, correspondence of the Civil War period concerning the presentation of claims, charters, ships' registration papers, printed congressional documents showing the previous presentation of the claims to Congress, and certified manifests of cargo. Most of the foregoing documents were printed and bound together with attorneys' briefs and arguments; one set was arranged by claim number and another set of the same printed documents was arranged alphabetically by name of the ship destroyed. The actions on individual claims are entered in docket books, arranged by claim number. In the indexes to these books the names are entered by the first letter of the surname only. A register of claims is similarly arranged. Some special indexes by the names of vessels show those destroyed by particular Confederate cruisers. There are also a record of claims arising from the destruction of particular vessels, useful in connection with the second compilation of printed documents mentioned above, and separate files of the opinions and memoranda of the court and bulletins of awards announced.

Correspondence, maintained in separate series of letters sent and letters received, relates chiefly to supplying information, appointing attorneys and commissioners, procuring evidence, and making staff appointments and salary payments. Other records include attorneys' certificates of admission to the bar; estimates by experts of the value of vessels; and bills, requisitions, and vouchers relating to contingent expenses.

Among the records of the court the claims file is the most important for the history of the Civil War. The documents in this file, some of which are dated during the war years, contain information on the operations of Confederate cruisers and on U. S. merchant ships and their personnel, cargoes, and equipment. Petitions by claimants contain biographical and genealogical data in addition to the facts regarding the claim.

U. S. Court of Commissioners of Alabama Claims, Index to Claimants before the Court of Commissioners of Alabama Claims (Washington, 1877), contains alphabetical lists of claimants and of ships and is useful as an index to the claims files. The printed records of the court are in the Library of Congress and in the Department of State Library. Records of the Fifth Auditor of the Treasury on the payment of claims allowed by the court are described below under the Department of the Treasury.

Court of Commissioners of Alabama Claims (2)

After the first Court of Commissioners of Alabama Claims completed its work, other claimants sought from Congress legislation to make payments to them from the undisbursed balance of the fund received from Great Britain under the Geneva award. The first court had been limited in its jurisdiction to claims resulting from losses caused by the "inculpated cruisers"--the Confederate vessels for whose depredations Great Britain had

been held responsible by the Geneva Tribunal. In addition there were claimants for damages by the "exculpated cruisers"--those for whose depredations Great Britain had not been held responsible. Other claimants wanted
reimbursement for premiums paid on war risk insurance, as did insurers
who had taken risks on property destroyed by "inculpated cruisers. " An
act approved June 5, 1882 (22 Stat. 98), provided for adjudicating two classes
of these claims. One class was claims for the payment of premiums for war
risks to corporations, agents, or individuals. The other class was claims
resulting from damages to vessels and cargoes by Confederate cruisers
even if the loss or damage occurred within 4 miles of shore. Though claims
that had been proved by the first court under the act of 1874 were excluded,
this provision admitted a large number of claims--not only more claims for
damages by the Alabama, Florida, and Shenandoah, but also claims for damages by other Confederate cruisers.

The three justices appointed by the President met in Washington on July
13, 1882, to organize the court. The presiding justice was Hezekiah G.
Wells of Michigan, who had served as presiding judge of the first court; the
other judges were James Harlan of Iowa and Asa French of Massachusetts.
When Wells resigned on Nov. 10, 1884, he was succeeded by Harlan and
Andrew S. Draper of New York was made a judge. John A. J. Creswell
was again appointed as U. S. counsel, and Daniel W. Fessenden of Maine
became clerk. The staff of the court also included assistant counsel, a
disbursing clerk, assistant clerks, and examiners. Three revenue-marine
officers were assigned to the court by the Secretary of the Treasury to fix
values on vessels, cargoes, and freight destroyed. At first authorized for
2 years, the life of the court was extended to Dec. 31, 1885; and the clerk
was employed for another 6 months to wind up its business.

A total of 5,751 claims were filed amounting to $28,000,000. Of the
1,602 claims for damages by cruisers, there were 994 judgments for the
claimants, 378 judgments for the United States, and 230 claims dismissed;
the amount awarded, including interest, was $3,346,016. Of the 4,149 claims
for reimbursement of war risk insurance premiums, there were 3,622 judgments for the claimants, 260 judgments for the United States, and 267 claims
dismissed; the amount awarded, including interest, was $16,312,944. Judg-
ments for the damage by cruisers were paid in full, but the available funds
permitted a payment of only 54 percent on the war risk insurance claims allowed.

To facilitate the work of the court, the Department of State in Oct. 1882
transferred to it the records of the first court and other claims that had been
filed in the Department. These records, accompanied by those that the second court created, were returned to the State Department when the court was
terminated.

Moore, History and Digest of   4664; H. Rept. 945, 49 Cong., 1
International Arbitrations, 5:4657-   sess., Serial 2437.

Record Group 76. --The records of the second Court of Commissioners
of Alabama Claims are similar to those of the first court but are more extensive because of the larger number of claims. Proceedings of the court
are recorded in its journal, and drafts of the proceedings form a separate
file. A numerically arranged claims file includes petitions and amended
petitions from claimants, schedules of insurance premiums paid, depositions, powers of attorney, stock certificates, clerk's certificates, briefs
for claimants, correspondence, appointments of commissioners to take

testimony, certificates of citizenship, cross-examination of witnesses, motions, and rules. Docket books, in which actions relating to the claims were entered by claim number, facilitated their orderly handling and control. At considerable cost some of the documents in the claims were printed for the use of the court, attorneys, and others, in an edition of only 65 copies. This set of 58 volumes (labeled "Petitions") contains not only petitions presented by the claimants but also exhibits, such as proofs of naturalization, schedules of insurance premiums paid, powers of attorney, and lists of personal effects lost.

Other evidence presented to the court is in different files. Volumes of "Claimant's Exhibits" are arranged by claim number; for a particular claim there may be one or several books. Submitted by business firms and insurance companies, these volumes were too bulky and irregular to file in the claims file. They comprise account books, cashbooks, daybooks, invoices of cargo, journals, ledgers, and letter books. Many cover periods before and after the war and therefore contain much more information than that concerning the claims in question; they constitute a significant sample of business records of the period. No list of the volumes is available, but the list of claims cited below gives the names of firms for which there are presumably records. A file of sea letters or ships' papers for whaling vessels, 1862-65, signed by President Lincoln and Secretary of State Seward, includes (for some vessels) ship registers, oaths of allegiance of masters, depositions, and crew lists. Concerning the C. S. S. Florida and other Confederate cruisers there is a small miscellaneous group of depositions and other papers. Records kept aboard the cruisers (some of which are in this record group) are discussed in the section on the Confederate Navy in the Guide to the Archives of the Government of the Confederate States of America.

Lists of the court's awards as recorded in the journal are in lists of judgments and decisions (separate lists for insurance and damage claims), which were prepared for submission to the Secretary of State. Besides giving information like that in the docket books, these lists give the names and addresses of attorneys in the various cases. A file of the bulletins that periodically announced the awards of the court is also available.

A register of U. S. commissioners, appointed to take testimony, is in two parts, one by name of commissioner and the other by his residence. Letters sent by the clerk fill 8 press copy books, and acknowledgments of the receipt of documents 4 more. There are also letters received, a few applications for office, corrections on lists, papers received too late for filing, printing estimates, petitions withheld from docket, powers of attorney, and estimates of the value of vessels captured by Confederate cruisers and their cargoes. The financial aspect of the court's activities can be traced in the disbursing clerk's account book, vouchers, and accounts.

The following work pertains both to the claims file and to the printed records: U. S. Court of Commissioners of Alabama Claims, Alphabetical Index to Claimants Before the Court of Commissioners of Alabama Claims (Washington, 1884). The court also published small compilations of opinions, rules, orders, circulars, and official communications, which embody material in its manuscript files. The printed records of the court are available in the Library of Congress and the Boston Public Library. Records of the Fifth Auditor of the Treasury on payment of claims allowed by the court are described below under the Department of the Treasury.

French and American Claims Commission

French subjects preferred a considerable number of claims against the United States for loss and injury at the hands of the Union Army and Navy, 1861-66. Most of these claims arose in Louisiana and were presented to the French consul in New Orleans, sent by him to the French Legation at Washington, and submitted by the Legation to the U. S. Government. During military operations and the occupation of the South, the armed forces of the United States destroyed or seized houses, markets, offices, boats, farm animals, cotton, agricultural produce, rosin, lumber, rum, and other merchandise and personal property; and in doing so they sometimes injured or imprisoned individuals. Property belonging to French subjects was seized both on land and sea.

Claims of American citizens against France resulted from seizures by French military forces during the French intervention in Mexico, 1861-67, of American vessels at sea en route to Mexican ports, of American goods on those vessels, and of property of American residents in Mexico. These American residents reported their injuries to U. S. consuls, who transmitted the information to the Department of State.

From the time of the war onward, the American and French Governments exchanged diplomatic correspondence on the means of settling these claims. Not long after French forces retired from Mexico the rule of Napoleon III in France was eclipsed by the Franco-Prussian War. During that conflict and during the reign of the Commune in Paris in the early months of 1871 American residents in France, particularly in Paris, suffered injuries for which they presented claims to the United States. These claims also were involved in the negotiations between the two governments that finally culminated in the Claims Convention of Jan. 15, 1880 (Malloy, Treaties, 1:535-539). This agreement provided for the establishment of a joint commission to adjudicate all the pending claims. An act of Congress, June 16, 1880 (21 Stat. 296), authorized the President to appoint a U. S. Commissioner and an agent, authorized the former to participate in drafting rules and regulations for the conduct of the Commission's business, provided funds, and stipulated that the records produced by the Commission or duplicates of them should be deposited in the Department of State.

The Commission met in Washington on Nov. 5, 1880, and continued to meet until Mar. 31, 1884. The French Commissioner was Louis de Geofroy, the French Minister to the United States; the American Commissioner was Asa Owen Aldis; and the neutral Commissioner was the Baron de Arinos, Brazilian Minister to the United States, who was named by the Emperor of Brazil. At the request of the other commissioners, the Baron de Arinos acted as presiding officer. Washington F. Peddrick, who had been appointed secretary of the Commission by the President, was designated by the Secretary of State as disbursing agent on behalf of the United States. Arthur Lanen appeared as agent for French claims. At the second meeting of the Commission, Nov. 23, George S. Boutwell was recognized as agent and counsel of the United States, and Charles Adolphe de Chambrun as counsel on the part of France. The French also engaged a secretary, an acting appointment being given first to M. de Geofroy. Rules for the preparation and submission of evidence, the taking of testimony (to be procured in both the United States and France), and the keeping of records were adopted on Nov. 23, 1880. W. O. Dénègre, retired lawyer who had had long experience in Louisiana, was employed by the United States as an agent in that State to examine witnesses, investigate claims, and search for and prepare evidence.

The Commission handled more than 700 claims. Those of citizens of France against the United States totaled 726 with a monetary value of $17, 581, 000, which with interest rose to $35, 000, 000. Nineteen claims for an aggregate sum of $2, 427, 544 were filed by citizens of the United States against France. By oral testimony and by documentary evidence from the files of the War, State, Navy, and Treasury Departments and especially from the "Rebel Archives" in the War Department, the American counsel was able to defeat many fraudulent claims and to reduce greatly the sums involved in other claims. The claims of 33 persons who had become American citizens were rejected by the Commission for lack of jurisdiction on the ground that the convention covered only the claims of French citizens. According to the final award the United States paid France $625, 566. 35 in full satisfaction of all claims, and France paid the United States 13, 659 francs 14 centimes for claims arising during the French intervention in Mexico, the Franco-Prussian war, and the Insurrection of the Commune.

Moore, History and Digest of International Arbitrations, 2:1133-1184; French and American Claims Commission, The Final Report of the Agent and Counsel of the United States, With Treaties and Schedule of Claims (Washington, 1884), also published with exhibits A to I in H. Ex. Doc. 235, 48 Cong. , 2 sess. , p. 40-229, Serial 2305; The French and American Claims Commission, 1880-1884; Minutes of the Proceedings of the Commission (Washington, 1880-84).

Record Group 76. --The Commission accumulated a variety of records. The manuscript journal of proceedings (printed as Minutes of the Proceedings of the Commission) gives information on the adoption and revision of rules, the procedure of the Commission, orders and actions in individual cases, opinions, dissenting opinions, decisions, and awards. Individual case files, which make up most of the Commission's records, contain memorials that set forth in prescribed form the facts relative to the claim, amendments to memorials, correspondence, documents from the files of departments and offices of both the U. S. and the French Governments, depositions for the claimant or for the Government, appointments of commissioners to take testimony, notices relative to the taking of depositions, office files of claimants, birth certificates, powers of attorney, opinions, orders, decisions, and awards. Most of the foregoing documents were included with briefs and arguments of counsel in records of cases, of which 50 copies were printed. The printed material amounting to 60, 000 pages is included in the case files; there is also a box of unfiled case papers. Docket books record chronologically actions on individual claims and are provided with an alphabetical index. An incomplete register of claims, notices of the taking of depositions, and a record of awards are in separate volumes. Other records include correspondence, lists of claims, and a record of disbursements.

The claims of French subjects against the United States document the treatment of civilians in the South, and especially in Louisiana, by Union military forces; give much information on military operations, military government, and economic conditions; and contain personal data on claimants and witnesses. The claims of American citizens against France give useful information on the activities of Americans in Mexico and adjacent U. S. territory, on French military and naval operations, on the cotton trade through Matamoras, and on the claimants themselves.

Sets of the printed Records of Claims (78 vols.) are in the Library of Congress and the library of the Department of State; no set was transferred with the records to the National Archives. Volumes 1-73 contain French claims against the United States, and volumes 74-78 contain American claims against France. An indexed List of Claims, also printed, serves as an index to individual claims files. "A Report From Secretary of State Concerning the Transactions of French and American Claims Commission, "

(H. Ex. Doc. 235, 48 Cong. , 2 sess. , Serial 2305), contains the final report of the United States agent, which was also published separately, and considerable correspondence relating to the Commission. Nearly 2,000 pages of accounts and vouchers of the disbursing agent are printed in H. Ex. Doc. 248, 48 Cong. , 2 sess. , Serial 2306. The Commission's rules were separately published. Correspondence on claims antedating the formation of the Commission is in the diplomatic and other correspondence series of the Department of State.

Other Claims Commissions

Several conventions were signed during the war or soon afterwards for the settlement of claims that antedated the war, including some that arose during the wars of independence in the Spanish colonies. Under conventions with Ecuador, Peru, and Colombia awards were made by mixed commissions. A claim put forward by Peru for compensation for the loss of the Alleghanian and its cargo of guano in Chesapeake Bay as a result of a Confederate naval attack was dismissed for lack of jurisdiction. A convention with Great Britain of 1863 provided for the determination of compensation due the Hudson's Bay Company and the Puget Sound Agricultural Company, two British organizations which had operated in the Oregon country before the boundary settlement of 1846, for damages suffered since that settlement and for the transfer of their property and rights to the United States. Though most of the claims handled by the United States and Mexican Claims Commission provided for by the Convention of 1868 had arisen before the Civil War, some were related to American military operations at the mouth of the Rio Grande, the northern bank of which was occupied by U. S. forces late in 1863, and in the upper Rio Grande area, where Union and Confederate Armies fought for control.

Mary A. Gray, "Settlement of the Claims in Washington of the Hudson's Bay Company and the Puget Sound Agricultural Company," Washington Historical Quarterly, 21:95-102 (Apr. 1930); Ralph R. Martig, "Hudson's Bay Company Claims, 1846-69," Oregon Historical Quarterly, 36:60-70 (Mar. 1935); Moore, History and Digest of International Arbitrations, vols. 1 and 2; Louis C. Nolan, "The Relations of the United States and Peru With Respect to Claims, 1822-1870," Hispanic American Historical Review, 17:30-66 (Feb. 1937); E. Taylor Parks, Colombia and the United States, 1765-1934 (Durham, N. C., 1935).

Record Group 76. --Records of these commissions, deposited in the Department of State upon the conclusion of their work, are similar in character and organization. They include individual claims files, dockets, lists of claims, journals of proceedings, opinions and awards, briefs and arguments, reports of the commissioners, and correspondence. In content these records are like those of the British and American and the French and American

Claims Commissions described above and of the Indian Claims Commissions described under the Department of the Interior, below.

British and American Joint Commission for the final Settlement of the Claims of the Hudson's Bay and Puget's Sound Agricultural Companies, [Papers] (Washington, Montreal, 1865-69. 14 vols. in 13); United States and Mexican Claims Commission, "Claims on the Part of citizens of the United States and Mexico Under the Convention of July 4, 1868, Between the United States and Mexico" (S. Ex. Doc. 31, 44 Cong., 2 sess., Serial 1720. Washington, 1877), including reports of the U. S. agent, Nov. 23, 1876, and Jan. 29, 1877, and schedules of claims; United States and Mexican Claims Commission, Report to the Secretary of State by J. Hubley Ashton, Esq., Agent of the United States Before the United States and Mexican Claims Commission, October 28, 1874 (Washington, 1874); "Report of the Commissioners in Relation to Claims of Peruvian citizens," Nov. 27, 1863, H. Ex. Doc. 18, 38 Cong., 1 sess., Serial 1187.

Mixed Courts of Justice (Slave Trade)

A treaty between the United States and Great Britain of June 7, 1862 (12 Stat. 1225; Malloy, Treaties, 1:674-687), provided that U. S. and British naval vessels might search merchant vessels of either country within 200 miles of the coast of Africa and south of the 32d parallel of north latitude and within 30 leagues of the coast of Cuba, if such vessels were suspected of engaging in the slave trade. Ships that were detained for trial might be taken to New York, Cape Town, or Sierra Leone, where Mixed Courts of Justice were to be established to try such cases. An additional article to the treaty, adopted on Feb. 17, 1863, extended the right of search to waters within 30 leagues of the islands of Madagascar, Puerto Rico, and Santo Domingo. An act of Congress of July 11, 1862 (12 Stat. 531), authorized the President to appoint U. S. judges and arbitrators for these courts. The regulations for the courts, which were appended to the treaty, required the designation for each court of a secretary or registrar to keep a register of the court's acts.

The appointment of judges and arbitrators during 1862 and 1863 was followed by the organization of the courts. Truman Smith became judge of the New York court, and Cephas Brainerd the arbitrator. Alonzo Stephan, the initial appointee as judge of the court at Cape Town having declined, Benjamin Pringle was appointed on Feb. 19, 1863, and William L. Avery was made arbitrator of that court. The judge of the court at Freetown, Sierra Leone, was Charles V. Dyer (1863-66), and later George W. Palmer. The first arbitrator of that court, Timothy R. Hibbard, was succeeded in 1866 by F. A. Whittlesey. A convention signed by the United States and Great Britain on June 3, 1870 (16 Stat. 777-781; Malloy, Treaties, 1:693-697), provided that the courts should cease their activities on the date of the exchange of ratifications of the convention (Sept. 16). Instructions sent by the Secretary of State to the judges of the courts on Sept. 16, 1870, directed that unless there was unfinished business before them they should close and that an inventory of papers and other property belonging to the Government should be sent to the Department.

A. Taylor Milne, "The Lyons-Seward Treaty of 1862, "American Historical Review, 38:511-525 (Apr. 1933). There was once a parcel of papers of the courts among the records of the Department of State (Moore, Digest of International Law, 2:947; Van Tyne and Leland, Guide, p. 31), but these papers were not among the records transferred to the National Archives. Correspondence to and from the judges and arbitrators and copies of their commissions are in the General Records of the Department of State (Record Group 59). Some of this correspondence reports the movements of Confederate naval vessels. Other correspondence and accounts are in the records of the Office of the Secretary of the Interior (Record Group 48). Records of the courts are in the British Public Record Office, London, England.

VI. DEPARTMENT OF THE TREASURY

The Civil War records of the Department of the Treasury document functions that even before the war required an elaborate field organization. The Department had been established by an act of Sept. 2, 1789 (1 Stat. 65), and even before 1861 its increasingly complicated financial structure and the assignment to it of some nonfiscal functions had resulted in the Department's including many bureaus and offices that eventually were to be transferred elsewhere--notably to the Department of Commerce and the General Accounting Office.

As the Civil War opened the Treasury Department's organization, besides the Office of the Secretary, comprised the Offices of the First and Second Comptrollers, the Treasurer of the United States, the Register, and the Solicitor; the separate offices of the six Auditors designated numerically except for the Auditor for the Post Office Department; the Office of the Commissioner of Customs; and the Bureau of Construction. The U. S. Mint at Philadelphia, the branch mints, and the assay offices operated as a part of the Department; so did the Customs Service, the U. S. Coast Survey, the Office of the Superintendent of Weights and Measures, the Steamboat-Inspection Service, the Light-House Service, the Revenue-Cutter Service, and the Marine Hospital Service. All these offices and services continued through the Civil War--some with functions curtailed or redirected to the war situation, others with greatly increased responsibilities.

On June 30, 1861, as the Secretary of the Treasury observed in his 1864 report, the national debt was "comparatively so inconsiderable as hardly to deserve the name." The opening of the war, however, created an entirely new situation in Government finance, and the Treasury Department necessarily entered new fields of fiscal activity. Within the 4 years from 1861 to 1865 the national debt increased more than 2 1/2 billion dollars, a new national currency system was created, and new sources of revenue were tapped. Besides enlarging its existing offices the Department created new offices for its new responsibilities. These included significantly the Office of Internal Revenue (1862) and the Office of the Comptroller of the Currency (1863). The former controlled the work of the several direct tax commissions in the Southern States; and the latter (known also as the National Currency Bureau) supervised the so-called First Division (or Engraving or Printing Bureau), established in 1862. Still another function was added with the establishment of the Secret Service Division (1865) as a part of the Office of the Solicitor of the Treasury. Details of these new activities and of the records resulting from them are given under the appropriate headings, below.

With all its new and expanded activities, the Department soon filled the Treasury Extension and rented buildings in the neighborhood besides. In the Register's Office, for instance, the "extraordinary increase in the national expenditures" had its effects. "The large loans, represented by treasury notes, coupon bonds, and registered stock, which have been made since the month of March last," wrote the Register in his annual report for 1861, ". . . have had a similar effect upon the business of the loan office." Expansion was general; increases in the work of the offices of the Auditors and the Comptrollers were as great as the added duties of the Register's Office. In the office of the Second Auditor the war period resulted in the "great embarrassment" of insufficient room for the files and an increased clerical force. The Office of the Fourth Auditor during fiscal year 1865 received 66,822 letters, over a third more than in fiscal 1864. In several Treasury bureaus or offices the employment of many "female clerks" helped to relieve administrative pressures.

The work of the Commissioner of Customs was expanded when he was put in charge of accounts of captured and abandoned property. He also kept the accounts of commercial intercourse with the States and parts of States declared to be in insurrection; and he had general charge of all matters pertaining to captured and abandoned property. These functions--discussed in the detailed descriptions below--grew more complex and demanding with the establishment, beginning in 1862, of nine special agencies to restrict commercial intercourse and (later) to control abandoned, captured, and confiscable property.

Printed as congressional documents, the wartime fiscal year reports of the Secretary of the Treasury on The State of the Finances were as follows:

1860. S. [i. e. H.] Ex. Doc. [2], 36 Cong. , 2 sess. , Serial 1093.
1861. S. Ex. Doc. 2, 37 Cong. , 2 sess. , Serial 1121.
1862. S. Ex. Doc. 1, 37 Cong. , 3 sess. , Serial 1149.
1863. H. Ex. Doc. 3, 38 Cong. , 1 sess. , Serial 1186.
1864. H. Ex. Doc. 3, 38 Cong. , 2 sess. , Serial 1222.
1865. H. Ex. Doc. 3, 39 Cong. , 1 sess. , Serial 1254.
1866. H. Ex. Doc. 4, 39 Cong. , 2 sess. , Serial 1287.

The reports of heads of the Department's offices, bureaus, etc. , are appended to these reports. A plan for the reorganization of the Treasury Department at the end of the war was presented by the U. S. Revenue Commission (H. Ex. Doc. 34, 39 Cong. , 1 sess. , Serial 1255). See also the Secretary's report of July 4, 1861, S. Ex. Doc. 2, 37 Cong. , 1 sess. , Serial 1112.

OFFICE OF THE SECRETARY OF THE TREASURY

On Dec. 6, 1860, Secretary of the Treasury Howell Cobb, in a letter to the people of Georgia, advocated immediate secession, and he was the first Southern member of President Buchanan's Cabinet to resign. In his place Buchanan appointed Philip F. Thomas of Maryland, but Thomas resigned within a month because of his Southern sympathies. It thus fell to John A. Dix, who became Secretary of the Treasury on Jan. 15, 1861, to maintain the nation's financial stability in the last months of the Buchanan administration. Salmon P. Chase, Lincoln's appointee, was Secretary of the Treasury during much of the war.

George Harrington served as the only Assistant Secretary until, 4 days after the passage of an act of Mar. 14, 1864 (13 Stat. 22), Maunsell B. Field was appointed as another Assistant Secretary. Still a third was added when William E. Chandler was so appointed on Jan. 5, 1865.

It is not proposed to give to this Guide a history of Government fiscal operations under the successive Secretaries of the Treasury, their Assistant Secretaries, and their corps of assistants (among whom may be named especially Register L. E. Chittenden, Treasurer F. E. Spinner, Second Comptroller J. M. Brodhead, and Second Auditor E. B. French). They did their work so as to assure victory and economic stability in the end. The records they left behind, however--except for the few that are in print-- have been little used for historical research. Hence the attention to detail here in the descriptions of the functions and records of the Secretary's Office and other offices of the Department. The increasing administrative responsibilities of the Office of the Secretary during and immediately after the Civil War resulted in the gradual development of the Office into an organization of many small divisions and units, increasing as new functions were assumed. In 1863, for example, apparently only one division, the Loan and Treasury Note Branch, was operating as a functional unit in the Office, but by 1865 this had apparently been divided into a Loan Branch and a Note and Redemption Division and an Internal Revenue Branch had been added. Although this handful of administrative units may not indicate the scope of activities within the immediate purview of the Secretary's Office, the records created in the Office most assuredly do. They include not only the highest-level letters and reports on the collection of the revenue, the supervision of expenditures, and the management of the public debt and the national currency, but also--often as separate "units" or series--records relating to all matters of Treasury Department concern during the war.

Successive Secretaries of the Treasury during the Civil War period:

> Philip F. Thomas, Dec. 12, 1860.
> John A. Dix, Jan. 15, 1861.
> Salmon P. Chase, Mar. 7, 1861.
> William P. Fessenden, July 5, 1864.
> Hugh McCulloch, Mar. 9, 1865.

Annual reports of the Secretary of the Treasury on The State of the Finances, cited above; Morgan Dix, comp., Memoirs of John Adams Dix (New York, 1883. 2 vols.); Diary and Correspondence of Salmon P. Chase, American Historical Association, Annual Report, 1902, vol. 2 (Washington, 1903); Francis Fessenden, Life and Public Services of William Pitt Fessenden (Boston and New York, 1907. 2 vols.).

Record Group 56. --Most series of Secretary's correspondence lack subject indexes, but chronological registers of correspondence, including abstracts of letters, are available for the Civil War period. The extensive and varied letters received by the Secretary came to him from Congress, the President, and other executive departments, from within the Department of the Treasury, and from the general public. The letters from Congress during the war are in separate subseries, beginning earlier, of letters from individual Representatives and committees of the House and of letters from the Senate. More important in documenting the adoption and changes of official policies are the letters received from executive officers (the President and the Cabinet). Besides communications from the departmental secretaries (State, War, Navy, and Interior) there are series of those received by the Secretary of the Treasury during the war from the Postmaster General and city postmasters; from the Attorney General and the Federal judiciary in the States and Territories; from the General Land Office and receivers of public moneys; from other Interior agencies on Indian, patent, census, and pension matters; from the Court of Claims; and from the Smithsonian Institution. Other incoming wartime or war-related correspondence, organized by subject, concerns internal revenue informer cases, 1865-71; internal revenue and navigation, from 1860; and national banks. There are also miscellaneous letters received, mainly from the general public; many of these throw light on such wartime matters as blockade running, seizures, and frauds.

In separate subseries of incoming correspondence are letters received during the war from the following Treasury offices or agencies: the Assistant Secretaries of the Treasury; the Treasurer of the United States; the Register; the First and Second Comptrollers; the Solicitor; the Commissioner of the Currency, from 1863; the Commissioner of Customs; the six Auditors; the First Division (that is, the Bureau of Engraving or Printing), from 1862; the Construction Branch (later the Office of the Supervising Architect); the Assistant Treasurers at Boston, Denver, New Orleans, New York, Philadelphia, San Francisco, and St. Louis; the U. S. depositaries at Baltimore, Chicago, Cincinnati, Detroit, Louisville, and Pittsburgh, with special reports of funds on hand; and the collectors of customs (available as National Archives Microfilm Publication 174, in many rolls for the Civil War period).

Letters sent to Lincoln by the Secretary of the Treasury are on p. 461-533 of a volume of fair copies of letters to the President, Apr. 9, 1833-Mar. 19, 1866; among these are letters sent by Chase dealing with the collection of duties and enforcement of revenue laws in Southern ports, the restriction of trade between Illinois and Missouri, and the Fort Pillow massacre. There are also series of fair copies of the Secretary's letters to the executive departments, Members of Congress and congressional committees, Federal courts, and private individuals. The Secretary's wartime letters to collectors of customs are in many volumes organized separately for the collectors at the principal ports of Baltimore, Boston, New Orleans, New York, and Philadelphia; the collectors at Pacific ports (available in part as National Archives Microfilm Publication 176); and the collectors at small ports. Moreover, there are copies of letters to or concerning collectors and assessors of internal revenue, State officers, and banks, 1862-78 (37 vols.); appraisers and surveyors, 1845-78 (14 vols.); depositaries, 1863-67 (2 vols.); subtreasuries, 1840-78; and marine hospitals, 1833-78 (17 vols.). In other letter books are copies of letters sent during the war relating to the Steamboat-Inspection Service, Indians, public lands, "awards and decisions," and foreign matters; and telegrams sent are in a 6-volume series, 1850-74. Also, letters sent (and those received) by the Secretary concerning restricted commercial intercourse with and in the States declared to be in insurrection should be especially noted.

There are many series of personnel registers, correspondence, oaths, and commissions that offer possibilities for studying the effects of the war on Treasury Department personnel management--resignations, dismissals, employment of "females," and postwar readjustments. Personnel records of those holding Treasury offices during the war are in an alphabetically arranged series, 1789-1945, which contains oaths of loyalty and some correspondence. These may be supplemented by the records of Treasury Department commissions, particularly the volume for the period June 5, 1858-Mar. 2, 1867 (containing chiefly commissions of collectors of customs, surveyors of customs, and appraisers of merchandise), and an order book, Mar. 4, 1861-Mar. 29, 1873, which contains a copy of Lincoln's commission to Chase as Secretary of the Treasury. (The order book contains also orders issued by the Secretary and the Assistant Secretaries for the internal government of the Department, including, for instance, one on participation of Department personnel in the Lincoln funeral procession.) There are also a register of depositaries, 1863-69; a file of resignations received from customs and mint personnel, assistant treasurers, and special agents, 1834-73; and other registers of Treasury Department employees, their oaths, appointments, and commissions.

Among miscellaneous records of the Secretary's Office that cover the war period are manuscript and printed copies of Treasury Department circulars and a digest of the Secretary's decisions and instructions, 1833-63, compiled 1861-64 from his correspondence with collectors of customs.

Among postwar records in this record group are those pertaining principally to claims brought against the Government for property captured, confiscated, or illegally seized during the war. These include correspondence and other records of or relating to the nine Special Agencies established to control commercial intercourse and captured, abandoned, and confiscable property (see the separate description of these under Special Agencies, below); correspondence of the Division of Captured and Abandoned Property and successor divisions, 1864-1906; and miscellaneous records relating to all types of captured and abandoned property, 1863-75. Among these records are papers relating to cotton claims arising under sec. 5 of an act of May 18, 1872 (17 Stat. 134), authorizing and directing the Secretary of the Treasury to pay lawful owners or their legal representatives for cotton seized after June 30, 1865, by Government agents acting unlawfully and in violation of their instructions. In attempting to prove that their cotton was seized unlawfully many claimants gave personal data such as their age, residence, marital status, occupation, and other circumstances of their lives during the war. Relating generally to all these claims is an index (ca. 100,000 cards), prepared not only from these records but from those of the Special Agencies, Court of Claims records, and the Secretary's wartime correspondence regarding restricted commercial intercourse with and in the States declared to be in insurrection. Also of interest are records concerning alleged corrupt practices of Attorney Galen Green in his handling of certain Tennessee Civil War claims, 1882-83.

Some Civil War records originally a part of the Secretary's files were transferred to other offices when the function to which they relate obtained bureau status within the Treasury Department or was transferred to another executive department. For information about these records see Office of the Register, Office of the Supervising Architect, U. S. Coast Survey, Steamboat-Inspection Service, Light-House Board, U. S. Revenue-Cutter Service, and Marine Hospital Service, below. The records of the Secretary's Office relating to the supervision of coinage, to 1873, are now a part of Record Group 104 (Records of the Bureau of the Mint).

Records in Other Custody. --Howell Cobb papers are at both Duke University and the University of Georgia. Salmon P. Chase papers are in the Historical Society of Pennsylvania and the Library of Congress. Papers of William Pitt Fessenden and Hugh McCulloch are in the Library of Congress, and other McCulloch papers are at the University of Indiana. All these papers should be consulted, since they are believed to contain some official records. See especially a letter book of Fessenden in the Library of Congress covering the time of his service as Secretary.

OFFICE OF THE FIRST COMPTROLLER

The act establishing the Department of the Treasury in 1789 provided for a Comptroller to superintend the adjustment and preservation of the public accounts. After the authorization of four additional auditors and an additional comptroller by an act of Mar. 3, 1817 (3 Stat. 366), the Comptroller became known as the First Comptroller and had the duty of examining accounts settled by the First and Fifth Auditors and of certifying the balances to the Register of the Treasury. He was also instructed to superintend the recovery of debts due the United States and to direct suits and legal proceedings.

When the Civil War began, the following accounts of the First and Fifth Auditors and the Commissioner of the General Land Office were being certified by the First Comptroller to the Register: judiciary accounts (expenses of courts and court personnel); salaries (for judges, other court personnel, and employees in the executive branch); diplomatic and consular accounts; accounts of receipts and disbursements for public lands and surveying; accounts relating to the public debt, public printing, and the U. S. Mint and its branches; expenditures for the Territories; and miscellaneous accounts, including those for public buildings, the insane asylum, the penitentiary, and suppression of the slave trade. By fiscal year 1865 the First Comptroller was handling in addition Patent Office and internal revenue accounts. Successive First Comptrollers during the Civil War:

Elisha Whittlesey, 1861.
William Hemphill Jones (acting), 1863.
R. W. Tayler, 1865.

Civil War annual reports of the   those of the Secretary of the Treas-
First Comptroller, appended to   ury on The State of the Finances.

Record Group 217. --Letters received in the First Comptroller's office during the Civil War are in several general series, 1795-1870 (71 vols.), and in supplementary series of diplomatic and consular letters, 1861-91 (55 vols.), and Territorial letters, 1835-91 (21 vols.). There is a register of letters received, 1850-1915 (40 vols.). Letters sent (fair copies) are in miscellaneous letter books, 1802-66 (89 vols.), and in other books of letters pertaining to the internal revenue, 1864-66, land offices, 1829-64 (15 vols.), and Territorial subjects, 1854-80 (10 vols.). Press copies of letters sent pertaining to the internal revenue, 1862-70, are also available.

The appropriation ledgers of or pertaining to the Civil War period are in the following series: agriculture, customs, diplomatic, diplomatic and civil, internal revenue, judiciary, Navy, pension, public debt, Treasury and Interior, and War; these series begin in 1837, except for War, which begins in 1853. There is an internal revenue tax journal, 1862-67.

The pertinent series of registers are as follows: Registers of accounts-- First Auditor, 1861-94 (22 vols.), and 1830-76, with gaps (14 vols.), with a separate index, and Fifth Auditor, 1863-76 (2 vols.), with a separate index; and Registers of claims--under revenue laws, 1857-69, and under laws providing bounty for capturing slavers, 1855-65.

OFFICE OF THE SECOND COMPTROLLER

The additional comptroller authorized for the Treasury Department by the act of Mar. 3, 1817, cited above, was designated as the Second Comptroller and was instructed to examine the accounts settled by the Second, Third, and Fourth Auditors and to certify the balances to the Secretary of the Department in which the expenditures were incurred. In 1861 these accounts were being certified to the Register of the Treasury, and at that time they included "those connected with and embracing expenditures by the pay department of the army, the Indian bureau, the recruiting branch of the service, the medical and hospital and ordnance departments, reported by the Second Auditor; those belonging to the quartermaster's subsistence, and engineer departments, and of the Pension bureau, reported by the Third Auditor; and those of pursers or paymasters in the navy and in the marine corps, and of navy agents and navy pension agents, reported by the Fourth Auditor . . ."

About 1864 the Office prepared a new edition of its Digest of Decisions, adding its numerous decisions from 1852. The Second Comptroller in his fiscal year 1865 report called attention to two decisions he considered important because of the many claims affected--that in regard to the pay allowed officers for their servants and that on the question of bounties claimed by deserters.

J. Madison Cutts, appointed Second Comptroller in 1861, was succeeded in 1863 by J. M. Brodhead.

Civil War annual reports of the Second Comptroller, appended to those of the Secretary of the Treasury on The State of the Finances.

Record Group 217.--Letters received are in a general series, 1811-94 (174 vols.), and in a special series of letters from delinquent officers, 1865-70 (11 vols.). Although there seem to be no copies of letters sent during the Civil War period, the postwar letters sent, dating from the late 1870's, often throw light on claims and other war-related concerns of the Second Comptroller. Reports received from the Second, Third, and Fourth Auditors, during and after the war, are in several series of report books. The Third Auditor's reports contain the settlement data for Southern claims allowed by the Commissioners of Claims, 1871-78; comparable data after 1878 are in the registers of claims, 1878-94 (36 vols.). Other pertinent records include prize lists, 1863-65 (16 vols.).

OFFICE OF THE COMMISSIONER OF CUSTOMS

This Office did not administer the Customs Service--a function of the immediate Office of the Secretary of the Treasury until 1927--but it had

comptroller responsibilities vested originally in the Office of the First
Comptroller. It existed from its creation by an act of Mar. 3, 1849
(9 Stat. 396), until its discontinuance by an act of July 31, 1894 (28 Stat.
205).

The Commissioner examined and revised as necessary the statements
of customs accounts submitted to him by the First Auditor and he certified
them to the Register, but his statutory responsibilities did not involve the
interpretation of laws relating to duties and entries. To his Office was assigned also, in 1863, the duty of "the keeping of the accounts, giving the
necessary instructions, and furnishing proper forms to collectors, special
agents, &c. , in relation to coastwise and internal commerce, and the supervision of abandoned or captured property in insurrectionary States. "
The Commissioner was thus brought into direct relationship with the nine
Special Agencies (see below). The Division of Restricted Commercial Intercourse and Captured and Abandoned Property, established within his
Office to handle this work, was transferred after the war to the Office of
the Secretary, where its functions were to continue until 1906.

The "duty of devising and putting into operation some system" to combat "the great and rapidly increasing evil of smuggling" was a matter the
Commissioner took in hand "notwithstanding the task is one of no ordinary
magnitude and difficulty. Our very extended frontier line, separating us
from the British provinces, together with our long line of sea-coast, with
its innumerable bays and inlets, which afford such secure retreats for very
small craft, present strong temptations to the depraved and avaricious
smuggler to carry on his illegal and demoralizing avocation. "

T. Feran, Acting Commissioner of Customs in 1861, was replaced by
N. Sargent as Commissioner in 1862.

Civil War annual reports of the   nances; Laurence F. Schmecke-
Commissioner of Customs, appended   bier, The Customs Service . . .
to those of the Secretary of the   (Baltimore, 1924).
Treasury on The State of the Fi-

Record Group 217. --In this record group are practically all extant records of the Commissioner of Customs except those directly related to and
intermingled with the records of the Special Agencies and those relating to
commercial intercourse and abandoned or captured property that were inherited and continued by the Office of the Secretary. The letters received
(ca. 30 vols. for the war period) are in series beginning before and ending
after the war, from the customs districts, the Secretary of the Treasury,
and other officials of the Department; and there are copies of miscellaneous
letters sent (3 vols. , Oct. 1860-Dec. 1865) covering the war. This correspondence , although it relates chiefly to customs accounts, contains information about events and transactions in the Customs Service that are of
considerable interest in relation to the war. There are separate series of
letters sent relating to smuggling, 1865-69 (2 vols.), and captured property,
1868-75. Report books covering the war period pertain to customs collections; excess of deposits and debentures, from 1862; legal advice; and
steamboats, to 1861. There are also registers of special accounts, 1857-65;
of miscellaneous accounts, 1853-94; of accounts involving arrivals of vessels with deceased persons aboard; of accounts pertaining to internal and
coastwise intercourse, 1862-64; of accounts for steamboat fees, from 1864;
and of collectors' construction accounts.

OFFICE OF THE REGISTER

The act establishing the Treasury Department in 1789 provided for a Register of the Treasury "to keep all accounts of the receipts and expenditures of the public money, and of all debts due to or from the United States; to receive from the Comptroller the accounts which shall have been finally adjusted, and to preserve such accounts with their vouchers and certificates; to record all warrants for the receipt or payment of moneys at the Treasury, certify the same thereon, and to transmit to the Secretary of the Treasury, copies of the certificates of balances of accounts adjusted. " An act of Feb. 20, 1863 (12 Stat. 656), authorized an Assistant Register.

In 1862 the Office of the Register comprised three divisions--Loans, Receipts and Expenditures, and Commerce and Navigation. The Loans Division transacted business pertaining to the public debt. It was the transfer office for registered and coupon bonds, and it received daily the certificates of stock for transfer and made out, recorded, and issued new certificates. The Loans Division also recorded and issued most of the evidence of assignable indebtedness against the United States. It prepared schedules of the semiannual interest on registered bonds, with estimates of the interest falling due on coupon bonds, and it received and preserved interest coupons when paid.

The Division of Receipts and Expenditures was the "counting-house" of the Treasury. This Division kept the accounts with all agents and disbursing or receiving officers and separate accounts for all appropriations; signed and recorded warrants for receipts in and disbursements from the Treasury; and entered all accounts connected with the Treasury. Accounts showing a balance against the United States were usually copied; and the copies, properly certified, were transmitted by this Division to the Office of the Secretary of the Treasury, where warrants were made for their payment. Most disbursing officers made quarterly settlements; others made monthly settlements; and some of the assistant treasurers settled accounts daily. As a basis for settlements the Division of Receipts and Expenditures furnished certificates to the proper Auditors showing the balances upon the last settlements and the advances since then. The Division received from the executive departments their estimates of appropriations, to be "digested, condensed, and put into proper form" for submission by the Secretary of the Treasury to Congress. The Division also prepared and published annually a volume to show in detail the receipts and expenditures of the Government: receipts from all sources (except the Post Office Department) and the districts in which they were collected, with the names of the officers collecting them; and the aggregates of expenditures under each appropriation, with the names of the officers or persons making the disbursements.

During the Civil War estimates of appropriations, by fiscal year, were published in various ways--privately, by the Government Printing Office, or as congressional documents; estimates for additional appropriations for a given fiscal year are included in the volume of estimates for the succeeding year. The estimates printed as congressional documents were as follows:

1861.	H. Ex. Doc. 1, 36 Cong. , 1 sess. , Serial 1043.
1862.	H. Ex. Doc. 1, 36 Cong. , 2 sess. , Serial 1092.
1862-63.	H. Ex. Doc. 1, 37 Cong. , 2 sess. , Serial 1127.
1864-65.	H. Ex. Doc. 2, 38 Cong. , 1 sess. , Serial 1186.
1865-66.	H. Ex. Doc. 2, 38 Cong. , 2 sess. , Serial 1222.
1866-67.	H. Ex. Doc. 3, 39 Cong. , 1 sess. , Serial 1254.

The fiscal year statements of Government receipts and expenditures for the war period printed as congressional documents were as follows:

1861. H. Ex. Doc. 36, 37 Cong., 2 sess., Serial 1129.
1862. H. Ex. Doc. 8, 38 Cong., 1 sess., Serial 1187.
1863. H. Ex. Doc. 84, 38 Cong., 1 sess., Serial 1195.
1864. H. Ex. Doc. 73, 38 Cong., 2 sess., Serial 1229.
1865. H. Ex. Doc. 12, 39 Cong., 2 sess., Serial 1288.
1866. H. Ex. Doc. 315, 40 Cong., 2 sess., Serial 1346.

Since 1789 the administration of the laws imposing a duty on the tonnage of vessels and providing for the registering and clearing of vessels and the regulation of the coastwise trade had been under the control of the Secretary of the Treasury, with enforcement the responsibility of customs officials. Supervision of these matters--concerning marine documents and navigation and tonnage statistics--had been turned over to the Register of the Treasury in 1793 and was to remain a function of his Office until 1866. The third division of the Register's Office in the 1862 organization--the Division of Commerce and Navigation--received from collection districts and other sources returns and statements showing the value and descriptions of articles imported and exported, whether in American or foreign vessels; the rate and amount of duties; and the sources and destinations of imports and exports. The Division corrected these returns, entered them, and compiled them for an annual report; compiled statements for Congress and other agencies; made estimates and statements for new tariffs; prepared forms for returns of imports and exports, duties, and tonnage from the collection districts; compiled the statements and tables for the annual report of the Secretary of the Treasury on The State of the Finances; and handled correspondence relating to these matters. It also kept books on the importation and exportation of foreign merchandise. A separate unit was responsible for keeping the tonnage accounts received from the collection districts.

The Register's fiscal year reports of the Commerce and Navigation of the United States for the war period are available as unnumbered documents in the congressional serials as follows:

1861. Serial 1140 (printed 1862).
1862. Serial 1170 (printed 1864).
1863. Serial 1197 (printed 1865).
1864. Serial 1231 (printed 1865).
1865. Serial 1268 (printed 1866).

The Civil War loans and Treasury note issues led to the organization, about June 30, 1864, of a Notes and Coupon Division, with an initial complement of 10 clerks, increased to 85 soon after the war ended. A residuum of the old Loan Division appears to have continued, for a time at least, to prepare schedules of interest payable on registered stock; but the new Division facilitated a task to which the Register from 1863 had given "first attention"--that of "preparation and placing in the hands of parties scattered over all that part of the country under the national control of . . . millions of dollars in securities, the greater part of which pass like bank notes without endorsement, without the loss of a single dollar to the government or to the subscribers, with all the incidental labor connected with the subject."

The Civil War records of the Register no longer exist intact. They have been transferred, along with the functions they concern, to many successive agencies, so that they are now divided among Record Groups 39 (Bureau of Accounts--Treasury), 217 (General Accounting Office), 53 (Bureau of the Public Debt), and 41 (Bureau of Marine Inspection and Navigation). The Register's extant records relating to the Civil War in these record groups are described below in that order.

L. E. Chittenden, appointed Register of the Treasury in 1861, was succeeded on Aug. 10, 1864, by S. B. Colby.

Civil War annual reports of the Register, appended to those of the Secretary of the Treasury on The State of the Finances; published compilations of appropriations estimates and of receipts and expenditures as cited above; Rafael A. Bayley, The National Loans of the United States (2d ed. , Washington, 1882); William F. De Knight, History of the Currency of the Country and of the Loans of the United States (Washington, 1900).

Record Group 39. -- The records described here, although preponderantly of the Register's office, include some records of the offices of the several Auditors and possibly some records of the First and Second Comptrollers. In general they constitute the pertinent parts of the extant original records of the receipts and expenditures of public funds since the beginning of the Government. For the Civil War period, or related to the war, these records (now part of the records of the Bureau of Accounts, Treasury Department) include appropriation warrants, registers of other types of warrants, ledgers, and journals; these are useful for studies of Federal fiscal management in the war period.

Besides the records mentioned above, all of which span the Civil War period, there are in this record group the following account books: national bank weekly accounts, Nov. 1863-June 1869 (12 vols.); depositaries' weekly accounts, 1863-67 (19 vols.); Treasury daily statements, 1863-68 (15 vols.); and statements of U. S. stock redemption, Dec. 1853-Dec. 1861. There are also a few volumes relating to captured and abandoned property.

Record Group 217. --Among the records of the General Accounting Office are papers tentatively identified as original records of either the Secretary or the Register of the Treasury (for the Civil War period, probably of the latter). These, in series chiefly beginning before and ending after the war, include ledgers (general Treasury, miscellaneous Treasury, customs, customs auxiliary, customs emolument, diplomatic, Interior, Interior civil, Judiciary emolument, and Army auxiliary) and registers of warrants (customs, expenditures, internal revenue, quarterly salaries, and individual War).

Record Group 53. --Since loans floated before the Civil War accounted for much of the work of the Register's Office during the war, the records of these earlier loans are important to an understanding of wartime finances. They include accounts relating to the Spanish indemnity of 1836, the loan of 1842, the Mexican indemnity of 1846, the loan of 1847, the bounty land scrip of 1847, the loan of 1848, the Texas indemnity of 1850, the loan of 1858, and the loan of 1860. After the establishment of the Division of Loans within the Secretary's office in 1868, the Register was relieved of activities pertaining to the public debt. The Civil War loans and Treasury note issues were authorized, however, during the period when he functioned as the bookkeeper of the Government; and it is appropriate, therefore, to mention here the records of these loans. Collectively these records are of direct interest in studies of wartime finances, but the individual transactions they record are not of great research value. They relate to the loans of Feb. 1861, July and Aug. 1861, 1862, 1863, Mar. 1864 ("Ten-Forties"), Mar. 1864 ("Five-Twenties"), June 1864, and 1865; Treasury note issues of Mar. and July 1861; the Oregon war debt loan authorized by an act of Mar. 2, 1861 (12 Stat. 198); the railroad loans of 1862; and the consols of 1865, 1867, and 1868.

Miscellaneous other records include a few papers about lost, stolen, or destroyed certificates of indebtedness, ca. 1863, the counterfeiting of Treasury notes, 1862, legal tender notes, 1862-95, and the case of Adams Express Co. vs. Abram Kannes in regard to "Seven-Thirties," 1865; and a book of stock exchange quotations, 1863. There are also a letter addressed to the President about small currency stamps, endorsed by Lincoln, Aug. 15, 1862, and a volume of letters sent by Secretary Chase concerning loans.

National Archives, Preliminary Inventory [No. 52] of the "Old Loans" Records of the Bureau of the Public Debt, comp. by Philip D. Lagerquist, Archie L. Abney, and Lyle J. Holverstott (Washington, 1953).

Record Group 41. --The records of the Register that are primarily marine documents and related records were transferred to the Bureau of Marine Inspection and Navigation. Records especially significant for the Civil War are certificates of enrollment, certificates of registry, and license certificates. Related records kept at customhouses during the Civil War--also now in this record group--are described under the Customs Service.

The Register's copies of certificates of enrollment, or "enrollments"--entitling vessels of 20 tons or more to engage in the coasting trade--identify vessels by class, name, dimensions, tonnage, master, owner, and home port. Although partly charred they are available for the Civil War period for many major and minor ports (except for ports controlled by the Confederacy).

The Register's copies of certificates of registry--necessary for vessels engaged in foreign trade--similarly identify vessels by class, name, dimensions, tonnage, master, owner, and home port. Although partly charred these too are available for the Civil War period for many ports (again, except for ports controlled by the Confederacy).

Certificates of license, or "licenses"--entitling vessels of 5 to 20 tons to engage in the coasting trade, whaling, or the cod or mackerel fishery--similarly identify vessels by class, name, dimensions, place and date of construction, master, owner, and home port. The Register's files of licenses for the Civil War period are very scanty.

There are also a record of ship registers, 1815-1912, and of enrollments, 1815-1911, for ports of the United States, in many volumes arranged by ports; a record of American and foreign tonnage entered and cleared in American ports, July 1, 1852-June 30, 1862 (2 vols.); and a list of foreign-built vessels admitted to American registry, 1853-1913 (included in a 1-vol. record of foreign vessels so admitted). The Register's record of U. S. vessels built, which fills several volumes, shows only the number built at particular ports. Other data consolidated by the Register from reports of customs collectors relate to tonnage in each customs district, to 1867; and to vessels lost at sea, condemned, sold to foreigners, captured, commissioned as privateers, or newly built, to 1866--but the names of ships do not appear in these statistical records.

OFFICE OF THE TREASURER OF THE UNITED STATES

The act of 1789 establishing the Department of the Treasury provided for a Treasurer, whose duty it was "to receive and keep the monies of the United States, and to disburse the same." The Office of the Treasurer was and is essentially the banking facility for the Federal Government, and during the Civil War period the Treasurer and the assistant treasurers received money due from any and all sources. Payments were made by the Treasurer upon warrants issued by the Secretary of the Treasury, countersigned by the First Comptroller, and recorded by the Register. The Treasurer was also the fiscal agent for the United States in paying the interest on the public debt, in issuing and redeeming U. S. notes, and in redeeming the circulating notes of national banks. Appropriations for the Post Office Department were disbursed by the Treasurer upon warrants of the Postmaster General, registered and countersigned by the Auditor for the Post Office Department (Sixth Auditor).

The Treasurer's quarterly accounts were rendered to the First Comptroller and, when settled, to the Secretary of the Treasury. At the end of every fiscal year the Treasurer, each assistant treasurer, each depositary, and the cashier of each national bank designated as a depositary, reported to the Secretary of the Treasury the condition of every standing account. The number of open accounts in the Washington office in fiscal year 1864 was 482, against 368 in 1863 and 232 in 1861--an increase of over 100 percent in 2 years. In fiscal year 1862, in addition to the existing "transfer account" with the assistant treasurer at New York, similar accounts were opened with the assistant treasurers at Boston and Philadelphia.

The Treasurer's receipts on account of the War Department in fiscal year 1865 consisted mainly of refunds to the Treasury by Army disbursing officers and the proceeds of confiscation; those on account of the Navy Department were similar refunds and the proceeds from captures.

The work of the Treasurer and the assistant treasurers was further increased by the many depositories designated under an act of Feb. 25, 1863 (12 Stat. 665), "to provide a national currency," although these depositories were "of great help" to the Treasurer's Office "in the collection of the internal revenue tax, and in the procuring of subscriptions to and the placing of the various government loans."

The Treasurer considered his Office to be understaffed as its work increased under wartime pressures. "But for the employment of females," he reported in 1864, "whose compensation is low, and in most cases too low, it would have been impossible to have carried on the business of the office with the compensation allowed." In the following year the Office received and answered--"most of them, it is true, by the filling up of printed circulars"--105,064 "official letters."

F. E. Spinner, who succeeded William C. Price as Treasurer of the United States on Mar. 16, 1861, served until June 1875.

Civil War annual reports of the of the Treasury on The State of
Treasurer of the United States, the Finances.
appended to those of the Secretary

Record Group 50. --The Treasurer's permanent accounting records of
the Civil War period comprise general ledgers; journals and ledgers of
receipts and disbursements, from 1862; warrants and registers of warrants; registers of drafts and checks; national bank stock registers, from
1864; and statements of quarterly accounts. These, no less than the Treasurer's correspondence, constitute a largely unexploited but potentially rich
source of information on the nation's economic structure, its banking and
other financial institutions, and the Government's financial transactions
during the war. There are letter books containing copies of letters to
Treasury and other Federal officials and to national banks, with some related registers and indexes. The Treasurer's records relate closely to
those of the Register.

OFFICE OF THE FIRST AUDITOR

The act establishing the Treasury Department in 1789 provided for an
auditor (later known as the First Auditor). The First Auditor reported his
disbursements for the fiscal year ending June 30, 1861, under 18 heads,
including (besides the disbursements mentioned above), those for the judiciary; Treasury Department; lighthouses, lifesaving stations, marine
hospitals, and steamboat inspectors; and public buildings, the penitentiary,
and the insane asylum. By fiscal year 1864 the First Auditor reported disbursements under 20 more heads, including such new expenses as those
for timber agents, California land claims, the Superintendent of Public
Printing, the Commissioner of Agriculture, and the Capitol extension and
dome.
     D. W. Mahon, acting First Auditor in 1861, was succeeded in 1862 by
First Auditor T. L. Smith.

Civil War annual reports of of the Secretary of the Treasury on
the First Auditor, appended to those The State of the Finances.

Record Group 217. --The record of letters and accounts received is in a
series of registers, 1853-94 (34 vols.); copies of letters sent on general
subjects are in a series extending to 1887 (53 vols.); and copies of letters
sent on customs matters are in a series extending also to 1887 (31 vols.),
with some duplicate press copies. There are marine hospital, lighthouse,
and judicial reports, 1853-88 (ca. 100 vols.), and many registers of audit
and other registers pertaining to general Treasury, congressional, customs,
internal revenue, Mint and Territorial, judicial (salary), steamboat inspectors', and miscellaneous accounts, usually spanning the Civil War period;
also registers of bonds (general, customs, and internal revenue collectors').
Other records include abstracts of payments to assistant marshals for taking
the census, 1860-61.

OFFICE OF THE SECOND AUDITOR

The Second Auditor was authorized by an act of Mar. 3, 1817 (3 Stat. 366). During the Civil War he received and adjusted accounts relating to the pay, clothing, and recruiting of the Army and to armories, arsenals, ordnance, and the Indian Office; he reported the balances to the Second Comptroller for decision. The work of examining the rolls and reporting to the Pension Office on applications for pensions also devolved upon the Office of the Second Auditor, who in the first year of the war had to hire at least 50 additional clerks. The business of the Second Auditor's Office involved close liaison not only with the Second Comptroller but also the Commissioner of Pensions, the Surgeon General, the Paymaster General, the Chief of Ordnance, and the Commissioner of Indian Affairs.

By the end of the war the claims on account of soldiers who had died in service were being rapidly settled, but many more claims were being received from soldiers who had been mustered out. "Thousands of such are received every month that are groundless, yet they must be briefed, filed and examined as well as those of a meritorious character." At the same time several clerks were spending all their time in settling paymasters' accounts so that prompt payment could be made to soldiers who had been confined in Confederate prisons.

E. B. French was Second Auditor during the Civil War.

Civil War annual reports of the   of the Secretary of the Treasury on
Second Auditor, appended to those   The State of the Finances.

Record Group 217. --In 1889 the Second Auditor received by transfer many records from the Office of the Paymaster General of the War Department. Insofar as these have been identified as Paymaster General's records of the Civil War period or as relating to the war, they are described under the War Department, although they now constitute a part of Record Group 217. The Second Auditor's Civil War correspondence is in a general register of letters received, 1839-99, with gaps (65 vols.), and in series of copies of letters sent on general subjects, 1817-86 (70 vols.), on claims (including medical claims), 1861-85 (9 vols.), and on recruiting, 1864-75 (3 vols.). There is a general index to War Department appropriation ledgers, 1817-80 (1 vol.), and there are ledgers for paymasters' accounts (beginning in 1864) and a local bounty ledger, 1865. The journals relating to the Civil War period comprise the general journal, 1851-68 (7 vols., nos. 14-20); the paymasters' journal (beginning in 1864); and the claims journal, 1867-71 (1 vol.).

Registers

Registers of accounts: Miscellaneous settlements, 1862-1900 (16 vols.); paymasters, from 1860. Bounty registers: certificates--to colored soldiers, 1867-70 (10 vols.); certificates--local bounty, 1866-79; certificates issued--colored cavalry and miscellaneous, 1867-70. Treasurer's certificates: Auditor's (Treasurer) certificates paid, Paymaster General, 1865-85 (37 vols.). Claims registers: general--Civil War and after, 1860-1900 (121 vols.); recruiting, ca. 1860-85. Registers of payments: Army, 1862-75; militia and colored troops, 1863-67 (2 vols., nos. 1 and 3);

volunteers, 1861-65 (2 vols.);   Eastern Veterans Reserve Corps and colored, 1862-65; officers, 1861-69 (12 vols.); and Hawkins Taylor Commission, 1861-71. There is also an index to registers of Civil War payments, n. d.

OFFICE OF THE THIRD AUDITOR

The act of Mar. 3, 1817, cited above, replaced the Accountant of the Department of War by the Third Auditor and the Second Comptroller of the Treasury. During the Civil War the Third Auditor received and adjusted accounts for subsistence of the Army, fortifications, the Military Academy, military roads, and the Quartermaster's Department, as well as claims for military pensions and for horses and other property lost in military service; and he reported the balances to the Second Comptroller.

A Collection Division prepared transcripts for suit and superintended the collection of balances due from former disbursing officers. Other work of the Third Auditor's Office during the Civil War was organized, though not necessarily in divisions of these names, under these headings: repayments; Quartermaster's Division; commissaries' accounts; pension agents' accounts; engineer accounts; State claims under an act of July 27, 1861 (12 Stat. 276); miscellaneous claims; Oregon War claims under an act of Mar. 2, 1861 (12 Stat. 198); horse claims; steamboat claims; and claims for loss or destruction of railroad engines and cars.

At the end of the war the Third Auditor recommended that the examination and settlement of claims be transferred to an independent "Bureau of Claims. " In fiscal year 1865 alone the Third Auditor had handled nearly 7, 000 cases, involving more than $8, 000, 000; these were concerned with "almost every question of statute and common law, including marine and insurance decisions. "

Aside from the work of the Claims Division, the Third Auditor was all but overwhelmed by the settlement of accounts in the quartermasters', commissaries', pensions, and State war claims divisions. These accounts in 1865 consisted of "cart-loads of vouchers--every one of which and each item of which . . . [had] to be carefully examined with reference to contracts, laws and regulations; the calculations all revised; suspensions and disallowances carefully noted and entered up, and full statements prepared for the action of the Comptroller. " (Some old claims for losses during the Mexican War still remained unadjusted at the outbreak of the Civil War; but, because almost all claimants lived in the "so-called seceded States, " it had been decided "to let them rest at present, giving a preference to claims arising out of recent losses. ")

Successive Third Auditors during the Civil War period:

R. J. Atkinson, 1861.
Elijah Sells, 1864.
John Wilson, 1865.

Civil War annual reports of   those of the Secretary of the Treas-
the Third Auditor, appended to   ury on The State of the Finances.

Record Group 217. --The extant records of or pertaining to the Civil War period consist of correspondence, records of accounts, and claims files.

Correspondence

Copies of many letters sent are in the general letter books, 1817-73 and 1886-96 (198 vols.); these, for the Civil War as for other periods, pertain to the settlement of claims, pension and quartermaster accounts, and the military service of officers and soldiers, including service in the Western Gunboat Flotilla. (There is a 1-vol. chronological index to the general letters sent to 1867.) Special series of copies of letters sent, supplementing the general letter books, include congressional and executive letters, 1832-64 (16 vols.), pertaining to claims, pensions, pay, accounts, etc.; letters to pension agents, 1868-1900 (143 vols.); many volumes of "horse claims" letters, particularly for the period 1862-75, with related letters awarding the claims, 1865-66 (10 vols.); Oregon and Washington Indian war claim letters, 1861-71 (6 vols.); letters concerning State claims for reimbursement for military services and supplies furnished, primarily during the Civil War, 1861-95 (22 vols.); and letters to the Quartermaster General and War Department fiscal agents concerning accounts and returns for property and services, 1855-69 and 1871-88 (34 vols.). Letters received comprise a general claims file from Apr. 1864; and there are letters and affidavits of soldiers' nonindebtedness, ca. 1863-65 (4 1/2 ft.).

Records of Accounts

Ledgers include the miscellaneous ledger, 1817-96; the appropriation ledger, 1829-94; a commissary and pension ledger, opened in July 1865, continuing accounts previously recorded in the miscellaneous ledger; and an assistant commissary ledger to June 1865. The miscellaneous journal, 1817-95, also spans the Civil War period; and a commissary and pension journal, opened in July 1865, corresponds to the ledger opened at the same time.

Pertinent registers of accounts, all for the Quartermaster Department, are: money accounts, in 4 series (ca. 25 vols. related to the war period); personal charges--money, ca. 1861-98 (2 vols.); transportation of volunteers, 1861-64; transportation of colored troops, 1863-64; and property, 1861-62.

The following accounts pertain to claims of Union prisoners of war held in Confederate prisons: a consolidated index of claims for both the Civil and the Spanish-American Wars, 1866-1902 (3 vols.); a register of claims for commutation of rations to prisoners of war held in the Confederate States, 1866-98 (29 vols.); an alphabetical register of commutation of rations of prisoners of war, 1861-76, compiled by the Commissary of Subsistence, ca. 1882; and a record of accounts for commutation of rations to prisoners of war, 1864-71 (3 vols.).

Records of settlements of Civil War transactions comprise the miscellaneous series, 1817-78 (12 vols., including all accounts settled by the Third Auditor before June 1865 except horse claims); supplementary records of miscellaneous settlements, 1817-78 (12 vols.); miscellaneous claims settlements, 1878-94 (5 vols.); a record of internal revenue transfer settlements showing taxes withheld from pay to the military, compiled in 1866 (3 vols.); subsistence and pension settlements, 1865-78 (2 vols.); pension accounts settlements, 1878-96 (3 vols.); settlement of pension agents' accounts, ca. 1861-1911 (3 vols.), with a register of accounts of pension agents, 1861-84 and 1886-90 (1 vol.), and an index volume, 1861-1901; Army pension settlements, ca. 1864-94 (4 vols.); engineer disbursing officers' accounts settlements, 1855-85 (2 vols.); settlement of horse claims accounts, 1866-78 (1 vol.); subsistence settlements, 1841-85 (13 vols.), in roughly alphabetical arrangement; and a general record of all accounts settled, 1857-94 (15 vols.).

Among other records pertaining to pensions are a register of pension agents' accounts, 1839-68; a register of claimants and deceased pensioners, ca. 1882-89; and reports of the Commissioner of Pensions and other records pertaining to the issuance of artificial limbs, 1870-76 (6 vols.).

There are also records of accounts pertaining to Army subsistence, 1865-78 (456 ft.), which, although postwar, are of interest because they include the settled accounts of officers assigned to the Bureau of Refugees, Freedmen, and Abandoned Lands; settled accounts for subsistence and small pension settlements, 1865-78 (450 ft.), which include accounts for commutation of rations while soldiers were prisoners of war and abstracts of expenditures made for the Bureau of Refugees, Freedmen, and Abandoned Lands; and abstracts of expenditures on account of the Quartermaster's Department, 1861-68 (36 ft.), with related indexes (3 vols.).

Of exceptional interest, because of the lack of detailed records elsewhere, are the rolls and papers relating to the accounts of the Western Gunboat Flotilla (or "Fleet"), 1861-62 (12 ft.). This Flotilla, until its transfer to the Navy Department, was under the control of the Quartermaster General of the War Department. The records consist of muster, pay, and receipt rolls; ledgers for officers and for men; officers' and men's receipt books; returns of provisions and of undrawn rations; stewards' returns; registers of allotments; cash books; journals; checkbooks; and miscellaneous other papers relating to the gunboats Benton, Cairo, Clara Dolsen, Connestoga, Eastport, Emerald, Essex, General Bragg, Great Western, Judge Torrence, Lexington, Louisville, Mound City, Nebraska, Pittsburg, St. Louis, and Tyler.

Claims Records

Both the index to miscellaneous claims, 1847-97 (10 vols.), and the registers of miscellaneous claims, 1847-1910 (52 vols., incomplete), contain references to Southern Claims Commission cases (see below); and the first volume of the former (1847-68) has a special index to claimants of the reward for the capture of Jefferson Davis. There is also an index to fraudulent claims investigated by E. J. Allen and H. S. Olcott for the War Department, referred to the Third Auditor, Oct. 20, 1863 (1 vol.), ca. Feb. 1862-Oct. 20, 1863. Still more records on horse claims include an index to such claims, 1861-95 (2 vols.); dockets, 1861-95 (12 vols.); an index to awards for horse claims, 1861-65 (2 vols.); and another index to such claims, in two parts, one for the Mexican War and the other for all other wars, 1837-92 (1 vol.).

Certain special claims files, however, are among the most valuable for Civil War research. These are:

(1) State claims records, 1861-1900 (102 ft.), filed under an act of July 27, 1861 (12 Stat. 276), and supplementary acts and relating to reimbursing the States for expenditures for the "Common Defense--War of the Rebellion, 1861-65," consisting chiefly of documents submitted in evidence

of expenditures such as payrolls, muster-in and muster-out rolls, and Civil War bonds, notes, coupons, and bounty bonds and certificates issued by States.

(2) Steamboat claims records, comprising accounts for steamboat and related property claims, 1863-88 (3 ft.); a register of awards, 1863-88; a combined register of awards and claims audited and transmitted to the Second Comptroller for revision, 1863-82; and copies of letters sent to claimants and their representatives regarding claims for lost steamboats and cargo, 1863-71 (4 in.).

(3) Dakota Indian War (1862) claims, 1862-78 (1 1/2 ft.).

(4) Minnesota Sioux Indian War claims, 1862-63 (1 ft.).

(5) Southern Claims Commission (i. e., Commissioners of Claims) case files of allowed claims, ca. 1871-90 (98 ft.), each typically consisting of a petition or application of the claimant, a transcript of testimony of the claimant and the witnesses, often some correspondence (or powers of attorney, wills, vouchers, and other supporting papers), the summary report of the Commissioners to Congress, and a record of the settlement. (The case files of disallowed claims are in the records of Congress and are described elsewhere in this Guide. The series of Third Auditor's letters sent relating to claims, mentioned above, contains information relating to these claims and to the work of the Commission; and the Third Auditor's indexes and registers of the miscellaneous claims provide much information about the settlement of the allowed Southern claims.)

National Archives, unpublished   General Accounting Office, comp.
Preliminary Inventory of the Rec-   by Albert U. Blair.
ords of the Third Auditor in the

OFFICE OF THE FOURTH AUDITOR

The Fourth Auditor was authorized by the act of March 3, 1817, cited above. During the Civil War he adjusted all accounts of the Navy Department, including Navy pensions, and reported the balances to the Second Comptroller. In the last year of the war his business more than doubled. Among the duties of the Office that involved "complicated and laborious calculations" were the preparation of reports giving admission to the Naval Asylum, bounty land cases, and pension cases, "the names of the persons making the applications being scattered through rolls of many years." The preparation of prize lists was another laborious activity. In his fiscal year 1863 report, commenting on the increase "in a ratio constantly augmenting," of the work of his Office, the Fourth Auditor gave the following comparisons: At the beginning of the Lincoln administration there were about 100 disbursing officers in the Navy; in 1863 there were 487. National vessels afloat in 1861 numbered 42; in 1863, over 500, with more soon to be launched. Requisitions for drafts for the naval service and for the pension service in 1861 totaled 780, amounting to $11,856,201.98; in 1863 they numbered 2,170, amounting to $63,553,426.74. In 1861 the number of letters received was 10,955; in 1863 it was 48,227.

The Fourth Auditor transmitted to the Second Comptroller, for his revision and approval, accounts "comprising every species of naval expenditure, from the rations of a marine and the prize money of a sailor, to the pay of an Admiral and the cost of a monitor." Two important divisions of the Office settled accounts of Navy agents and paymasters. (The statement of differences of <u>one</u> such account alone, the Fourth Auditor reported, filled "a book of 147 pages of foolscap paper.") The Allotment Division received and registered allotments by which a sailor made "provision out of his wages for his family, dependents, and creditors." In addition, the "captures and brilliant exploits of our gallant navy . . ." made "the division of prize money . . . one of vast importance and of vast extent."

On Sept. 1, 1863, the Fourth Auditor issued a new digest of "Rules in Regard to the Transactions of Business at the Office of the Fourth Auditor of the Treasury." With the end of the war, his Office had still more work in answering appeals for information about missing men who had been in the naval service.

Hobart Berrian, appointed Fourth Auditor in 1861, was succeeded by Stephen J. W. Tabor on June 1, 1863.

Civil War annual reports of the   of the Secretary of the Treasury on
Fourth Auditor, appended to those   <u>The State of the Finances.</u>

Record Group 217. --In 1866, when the letter books of his Office had become too numerous for ready reference, the Fourth Auditor instituted a "new system of indexing." At that time there were on hand in his Office 949 bound volumes of letters containing correspondence in unbroken series from Sept. 17, 1798, as follows: letters received, from 1798 (672 vols.); general correspondence, letters sent, from Sept. 17, 1798 (121 vols.); paymasters' correspondence, letters sent, from Jan. 1, 1835, the date of the separation from the general correspondence (59 vols.); executive correspondence, letters sent, from Apr. 28, 1820, the date when this series was established (11 vols.); Navy agents' correspondence, letters sent, from Oct. 1862, the date of establishing this series (7 vols.); "key books," including letters sent and received after Jan. 1, 1834 (48 vols.); and reported accounts, from July 1, 1834 (31 vols.). Most of this correspondence is extant. Letters received are in a general series and in supplementary series of letters from the Secretary of the Navy, the Navy bureaus, the Commissioner of Pensions, the Postmaster General, the Secretary of the Treasury, the Second Comptroller, and other Treasury Department officials. There is a 2-part register of correspondence received, the second part of which (78 vols., incomplete) opens on Sept. 1. 1861, and closes in 1898. The copies of letters sent are in a general series and in supplementary series of letters to officials of the executive agencies, Navy agents, and Navy paymasters. There are an index to the general outgoing letter books, 1859-64 (2 vols.); general registers of letters sent, from 1861; and an index to letters sent to paymasters, 1860-67 (2 vols.).

The Fourth Auditor's general accounts, covering in whole or in part the Civil War period, include the appropriation ledger; the general ledger, which includes the accounts of paymasters and of other disbursing officers, with an index; the general journal, with a cross-index; the naval officers' ledger; the Auditor's certificates of settled accounts; and a register of miscellaneous accounts received for settlement. The accounts proper are in two main series. One, a numerical series 1817-97 (114 ft.), contains accounts and claims of Navy agents, paymasters, and recruiting officers, Navy and privateer pension agents, and paymasters and quartermasters of the Marine Corps; as well as accounts and claims of naval and marine officers and men and of private citizens. Many of these claims include as vouchers such personal records as copies of birth and marriage certificates, wills, and pension certificates. The other main series, ca. 1798-1913 (1,644 ft.), arranged alphabetically, consists of accounts that were originally a part of the numerical series. There is also a record of Freedmen's Bureau accounts, 1867-82 (1 vol.), showing payments made by the Navy Department for money due colored sailors.

Records of claims accounts comprise the Fourth Auditor's certificates of settled claims, 1831-82 (49 vols.); a register of settlements for deceased officers and men, 1864-98 (3 vols.); a register of claims, 1863-95 (21 vols.), relating to those in the abovementioned numerical and alphabetical series of accounts; registers of indemnity claims settled, 1864-99 (2 vols.), disallowed claims, 1847-98 (1 vol.), and claims returned for perfection, 1866-80 (1 vol.); and certificates of settlement of claims on Marine Corps accounts, 1855-69 (2 vols.).

The accounts of paymasters and other disbursing officers are covered by several volumes of indexes and by registers of paymasters and vessels, paymasters' accounts received, and advances to officers; and there is an index to Navy agents' accounts. There is also a paymasters' bond book, 1861-97. For the Civil War period there are quarterly abstracts of receipts and expenditures of Navy agents and paymasters at Baltimore, Boston, New York, Norfolk, Philadelphia, Portsmouth, San Francisco, and Washington.

The Navy pension accounts arising from the Civil War are in the journal, 1849-69 (1 vol.), and ledger, 1849-96 (3 vols.). There are also reconciling statements of pension agents' accounts, 1855-82 (3 vols.); certificates of settled pension accounts, 1844-70 (2 vols.); a 1-vol. index to pension agents' accounts, many of which are in the abovementioned numerical or alphabetical series of accounts; a register of pensioners and agents by State, 1859-68 (1 vol.); a record of beneficiaries of the U. S. Naval Asylum, 1856-78 (1 vol.); and monthly abstracts of pension payments, 1864-83 (9 vols.).

Bounty and prize accounts comprise a register, 1865-1902 (4 vols.), of bounty and transfer bounty claims (the latter due to Navy claimants for service in the Army); a register relating to installments paid on Civil War bounty, 1866-98 (1 vol.); the Fourth Auditor's certificates of examination and adjustment of prize claims, 1863-84 (75 vols.); a register of prize accounts, ca. 1815-98 (15 vols.); a Civil War prize list, compiled ca. 1865 (4 vols.); and a register of suspended Civil War prize claims, 1888-97 (1 vol.).

Among pay and personnel records are registers of allotments, which until the end of the Civil War were maintained separately for officers and men; registers of officers, showing appointments, promotions, etc. , from 1861; and the "service records" of enlisted men, 1837-92 (9 vols.), showing dates of enlistment and separation and periods of service on particular vessels.

Among other records is a 1-volume history of "Civil War Boats,"compiled ca. 1865, indexed by names of vessels.

National Archives, unpublished   ment--The United States General
Preliminary Inventory of the Records Accounting Office, comp. by
of the Auditor for the Navy Depart-   William H. Hernandez, Jr.

OFFICE OF THE FIFTH AUDITOR

The Fifth Auditor was authorized by the act of Mar. 3, 1817, cited above. During the Civil War he adjusted accounts for diplomatic and other activities under the State Department and reported the balances to the First Comptroller. In fiscal year 1863 his Office had the new and onerous duty of auditing the accounts of the newly appointed assessors and collectors of internal revenue. His annual reports for the war period show (1) the expenses of all diplomatic missions abroad, (2) salaries paid to and fees received from consular officers, (3) amounts expended in arresting seamen charged with crime in foreign countries, and (4) amounts disbursed by consular officers for the relief of destitute seamen.

In 1861 the Fifth Auditor exposed the "considerable peculation," dating from 1858, of the American consul at Liverpool, who "found a kindred and congenial association in the ranks of the rebel conspiracy." In the same year the Auditor recommended the appointment of a consul general for the islands and coast of the Pacific, to stop "the wholesale robbery practiced under cover of our humane provisions for sick and destitute seamen"; and in 1862 he concerned himself with losses in the payment of consular salaries "in consequence of the derangement of our currency and the extravagant rates of foreign exchange."

John C. Underwood, appointed Fifth Auditor in 1861, was succeeded in 1863 by Charles M. Walker.

Civil War annual reports of the Fifth Auditor, appended to those of the Secretary of the Treasury on The State of the Finances.

Record Group 217. -- Letters sent during the Civil War are in a series of fair copies, 1817-69 (26 vols.); they include letters relating to collectors' and assessors' accounts after 1863. There are also press copies of letters sent from 1844 to 1900 (370 vols.). Other general records include certifications to the First Comptroller of Department of State accounts, 1817-95 (47 vols.), with reports or certifications dealing with internal revenue from Dec. 1, 1862 (vol. 30). The semiannual emolument returns of marshals, attorneys, and clerks of the Federal District Courts also cover the war period. Reports on the settlement of wartime accounts of disbursing clerks of certain executive departments (and the Office of Internal Revenue after 1863) are in a series, 1860-94 (9 vols.); and there are registers of accounts received, reports on accounts for salaries of consular officials and on accounts from masters or owners of vessels or their agents for passage of destitute American seamen, registers of expenditures for relief of such seamen, and registers of miscellaneous consular accounts adjusted-- all in series spanning the war period. There are also registers of salaries paid to and fees received by consular officials, 1862-81 (3 vols.). Both the series of letters sent and the accounts registers yield important information about the cessation and resumption of Treasury Department activities in the South.

Besides the records mentioned above relating to the internal revenue there are reports of accounts from collectors, from 1864; reports of amounts awarded by the Commissioner of Internal Revenue as drawbacks, from 1863; reports of accounts for salaries and contingent expenses of assessors, from 1863; several registers of collectors' internal revenue accounts; registers of collectors' reports of expenses in collecting internal revenue, from 1863; and correspondence concerning special allowances for revenue officials, from 1863.

A series pertaining to the <u>Alabama</u> claims, 1876-77 and 1884-95 (24 vols.), consists in part (vols. 1-3) of reports of accounts received in the Department of State arising from judgments of the Court of Commissioners of Alabama Claims under an act of June 23, 1874 (18 Stat. 245), and in part (vols. 4-24) of reports of accounts submitted and paid under acts of June 5, 1882, and June 3, 1884 (22 Stat. 98, 23 Stat. 33).

National Archives, unpublished Preliminary Inventory of the Rec- ords of the Fifth Auditor of the Treasury, comp. by Joyce B. Davis.

OFFICE OF THE AUDITOR OF THE TREASURY FOR THE POST OFFICE DEPARTMENT (SIXTH AUDITOR)

The Auditor of the Treasury for the Post Office Department, or, as he came to be called, the Sixth Auditor, was authorized by sec. 8 of an act of July 2, 1836 (5 Stat. 81). During the Civil War he adjusted all accounts of the Post Office Department, and his decisions were final if not appealed to the First Comptroller within a year. He superintended the collection of debts due the Post Office Department and of penalties imposed on postmasters and mail contractors; he directed civil and criminal suits, legal proceedings, and other legal measures to enforce payment of amounts due the Post Office Department; he instructed attorneys, marshals, and clerks on these matters; and he received from the U. S. courts returns of the status and progress of such suits and legal proceedings. He had charge of all land and other property assigned to the United States in payment of debts due the Post Office Department, and he regularly received reports on changes of postmasters.

In the first year of the war the Sixth Auditor investigated the loyalty of mail contractors and others in the service of the Post Office Department; and he made "vigorous" efforts to collect amounts due from "late postmasters," including those of the seceded States. He declared that his "extensive and diversified labors" embraced "the functions of an auditor, comptroller, register, and solicitor." Notwithstanding "the widespread pecuniary embarrassment occasioned by the existing unhappy rebellion," his efforts to collect the scattered revenues of the Post Office Department were by 1862 "crowned with unusual success."

In the last year of the war the Sixth Auditor's Office included a Money Order Division, a Pay Division, and a Collecting Division, besides the Examiner's Division, the work of which had decreased after a radical change in the method of settling the quarterly accounts of postmasters, made under sec. 15 of an act of July 1, 1864 (13 Stat. 339).

Successive Sixth Auditors during the Civil War:

G. Adams, 1861
Elijah Sells, 1864 (also Third Auditor).
J. M. McGrew (acting), 1865.

Civil War annual reports of the Sixth Auditor, appended to those of the Secretary of the Treasury on The State of the Finances.

Record Group 217. -- The only extant records of the Sixth Auditor for
the Civil War period appear to be a series of registers of postmaster accounts, from Oct. 1862, in the Federal Records Center at Alexandria, Va.

OFFICE OF THE SOLICITOR OF THE TREASURY

An act of May 29, 1830 (4 Stat. 414), provided for the appointment of
a Solicitor of the Treasury to take charge of the legal activities of the Department. His primary function was to recover debts due the United
States, a responsibility that had been vested successively in the Comptroller of the Treasury, the First Comptroller of the Treasury, and the Treasury Agent. During the Civil War the Solicitor superintended all civil suits
for the recovery of debts due the United States except those arising in the
Post Office Department; he instructed the U. S. attorneys, marshals, and
clerks of court in all matters relating to these suits and their results; and
he received returns covering each term of the U. S. courts, showing the
progress and condition of the suits. The Solicitor was responsible also for
the custody and disposal of property, including real estate, acquired in
satisfaction of judgments or assigned to the United States in payment of
debts (except property assigned for debts to the Post Office Department).
Although control of property was transferred to the Commissioner of Internal Revenue by sec. 2 of an act of Mar. 2, 1867 (14 Stat. 471), the Solicitor during the war had power to sell and dispose of such property for
the benefit of the Government.

As of 1861 the suits filed in the several judicial districts by the Solicitor were chiefly (1) those on Treasury transcripts of official settlements
of the accounts of defaulting public officers, contractors, and others, as
adjusted by Treasury accounting officers; (2) those for the recovery of
fines, penalties, and forfeitures for violations of the revenue laws; and
(3) those on warehouse transportation bonds for duties on goods imported.
Other judicial suits coming under the supervision of the Office as the war
progressed included prize cases, libels, and suits under wartime acts of
1861 and 1862 (12 Stat. 255, 319, 404, 589); suits for fines, penalties, and
forfeitures under the new internal revenue laws; and miscellaneous suits
in which the Government was interested.

Beside supervising suits in which the United States was a party or had
an interest, the Solicitor was given two other important duties during the
war. (1) An act of Mar. 3, 1863 (12 Stat. 737), provided that under the direction of the Secretary of the Treasury he should take cognizance of
"frauds upon the revenue" and should supervise measures to prevent and
detect them. By the same act the Secretary of the Treasury was authorized
to appoint three revenue agents to aid in the prevention, detection, and
punishment of such frauds. Two agents so authorized were appointed in
1863 and were put under the Solicitor's direction, one to reside in New York
City and to work in that and other domestic ports, and the other to be employed in Europe. The latter began his duties in Paris in August 1863. (2)
Beginning in 1863, the Solicitor's office was made responsible also for detecting and bringing to trial counterfeiters of Treasury notes and other
U. S. securities and coin (see Secret Service Division, below).

In 1863 the Solicitor, when asked by the Navy Department to investigate
alleged frauds in the sale of the prize steamer Anne at New York, instituted a general inquiry into "irregularities in the custody and disposition

of prize property, and the proceeds thereof" in New York City. His elaborate report to the Secretary of the Navy, with evidence and exhibits, Aug. 5, 1863, was printed (595 p.) as H. Ex. Doc. 74, 38 Cong., 1 sess., Serial 1194.

Transfer of the Solicitor's Office to the Department of Justice in 1870 brought it under the Attorney General's supervision.

Edward Jordan, appointed Mar. 28, 1861, served as Solicitor of the Treasury during the war.

Civil War annual reports of the Solicitor of the Treasury, appended to those of the Secretary of the Treasury on The State of the Finances.

Record Group 206. --Except for most of the records concerning land acquired by the United States in payment of debt (see Record Group 121, below) and for records concerning counterfeiting (see Secret Service Division, below), the Civil War records of the Solicitor's Office are concentrated in this record group. Unbound letters received during the war (ca. 10 ft.) are in several series extending beyond 1865 and generally covered by registers. Letters from U. S. attorneys, clerks of court, and marshals (with gaps for the Federal Districts in the Confederacy) pertain generally to the status of suits. Letters from the Secretary of the Treasury concern such matters as the postponement of suits, the defense of suits against collectors of customs, the prosecution of suits under the revenue laws, the sale of condemned goods, site titles (for instance, of lighthouses), the release of seized steamers, the collection of evidence, the remission of forfeitures, claims for refund of customs duties, and the need for the Solicitor's opinions on many subjects. There are letters from the U. S. Treasurer and the Assistant Treasurers, letters from the First Comptroller of the Treasury concerning transcripts of accounts adjusted, the transmittal of papers about miscellaneous suits, and similar matters; letters from the Second Comptroller transmitting supplementary statements of accounts and other papers relating to suits and accounts; letters from the Comptroller of the Currency, dating from 1863, concerning such matters as taxes imposed on national banks, action to be taken against banks, violations of the National Bank Act, and receivership of banks; and letters from the Commissioner of Customs concerning bond surveyors, suits against collectors of customs, reports on customs bonds delivered, and similar matters. Other letters originated with the six Auditors of the Treasury Department; the Commissioner of Internal Revenue, from 1862, concerning deposits of fines collected, delays in suits, opinions of cases, official bonds, etc.; revenue agents, from 1862, concerning "frauds upon the revenue"; the Light-House Board, from 1862; the Director of the Mint; the Register of the Treasury; the Supervising Architect of the Treasury; the Commissioner of Indian Affairs, the Commissioner of Patents, the Commissioner of the General Land Office, and other Interior Department officials; the Navy Department; the Post Office Department; and the Secret Service Division, from 1863, relating to the suppression of counterfeiting and including a report by W. P. Wood of his operations against counterfeiting before his appointment to head the Division in July 1865. A file of miscellaneous letters received, 1821-95, is arranged alphabetically by writer's name and thereunder chronologically.

Among the reports received are those of clerks of Federal courts on proceedings in cases involving the United States and on judgments and decrees entered in district courts, 1857-80 (15 vols.); similar reports of U. S. attorneys; and fiscal reports of U. S. attorneys of the Southern District of New York, 1865-70 (3 vols.), on prize and confiscation cases, customhouse bond suits, internal revenue cases, suits against collectors of customs, seizure cases, and suits against the United States.

Rough drafts of letters sent are in a single series, 1820-81. For the Civil War period these relate to specific cases and are addressed chiefly to U. S. attorneys, clerks of court, and marshals, but some letters are addressed to the Secretary of the Treasury, other Government officials, and private individuals. There are also fair copies of letters sent on "debts and suits, " July 1860-Dec. 1865 (7 vols.). The Solicitor's reports on customs suits date from 1864.

Covering the war period are separate registers of confiscation suits; suits brought on customhouse bonds; suits brought for fines, penalties, and forfeitures; suits under the internal revenue law; suits against agents and officers of the Government; prize suits; suits on Treasury transcript; and miscellaneous other suits. There are also dockets of accounts transmitted for suit.

Copies of the wartime opinions of the Solicitor are in a volume for June 1861-Dec. 1864 and in the first of a 3-volume series combining opinions of the Attorney General, the Solicitor of the Treasury, and district attorneys.

Record Group 121. --The records of the Solicitor of the Treasury for the Civil War period that are now part of the records of the Public Buildings Service chiefly concern land acquired by the United States in payment of debt. Volume 3 of a 4-volume series of warranty deeds to land conveyed by the United States covers 1847-1903 and consists of copies of the original deeds; volume 4 of the same series consists of copies of deeds (postwar) to property sold under an act of Mar. 3, 1863 (12 Stat. 740), empowering the Solicitor, with the approval of the Secretary of the Treasury, to sell land acquired by judicial process in payment of debts; there is an incomplete deed-holder index and a place-name index to these volumes. There are also fair copies of warranty deeds to land acquired by the United States, 1843-78 (1 vol.), duplicating in part a series of record copies of deeds and accompanying papers relating to land so acquired; a volume listing lands belonging to the Government, with information on their disposition, 1822-79; and letters received by the Solicitor from attorneys and special agents, 1855-66 (8 in.).

National Archives, Preliminary   Lane Van Neste and Virgil E. Baugh
Inventory [No. 110] of the Public   (Washington, 1958).
Buildings Service, comp. by W.

Secret Service Division

The Secret Service Division, although not created until July 1865, originated under an appropriation act of June 23, 1860 (12 Stat. 102), which granted $10,000 (to be expended under the direction of the Secretary of the Treasury) for detecting and bringing to trial counterfeiters of coin. An act of July 11, 1862 (12 Stat. 533), included counterfeiters of Treasury notes, bonds, or other U. S. securities. An Acting Agent for the U. S.

Treasury in Detecting Frauds of Government Securities supervised the operations of agents under this appropriation, but in Dec. 1863 Secretary Chase put all measures to prevent and punish counterfeiting under the supervision of the Solicitor of the Treasury and directed detectives and others employed against counterfeiting to report to the Solicitor and receive their instructions from him. Counterfeiting greatly increased, however, after the passage of the National Bank Act of 1863 and the issuance of notes and bonds by chartered banks. Congress therefore by an act of July 2, 1864 (13 Stat. 351), appropriated $100,000 for expenses in detecting counterfeiters and bringing them to trial. After Secretary McCulloch on July 5, 1865, designated William P. Wood, then Superintendent of the Old Capitol Prison, as "chief of the detective force to act under the directions of the Solicitor of the Treasury, in detecting and bringing to punishment persons engaged in counterfeiting," the Secret Service Division was established within the Office of the Solicitor. The twofold "mode of operation adopted," as explained by the Solicitor in a circular of 1865 to U. S. district attorneys, marshals, and clerks of court, was "first, by the offer of rewards for services or information tending to the suppression of counterfeiting; and, second, by direct efforts to collect information, and make seizures and arrests."

When the Office of the Solicitor was transferred to the Department of Justice in 1870 the Secret Service remained in the Treasury Department.

Record Group 87. --The correspondence of the early years of the Secret Service is apparently not extant, but there are registers of letters received, sent, and referred. So-called "registers of reports," Dec. 1864-Feb. 1871 (13 vols. on microfilm), are actually transcripts or abstracts of agents' monthly reports describing arrests made by them, their other activities, and property confiscated--all relating to the detection of counterfeiting. Copies of a few letters to and from the Solicitor are in the volumes of abstracts. The early part of a series, 1863-1906 (40 vols.), of "Description and Information of Criminals" pertains to the Civil War period; for this there is an incomplete index, 1863-99 (3 vols.), and a related register of counterfeiters, 1863-73 (1 vol.). There are also a few fiscal records dating from 1865 and a volume (labeled "Receipt Book") listing "members of old force retained" and "new operatives employed" in 1869.

National Archives, Preliminary   comp. by Lyle J. Holverstott
Inventory [No. 16] of the Records   (Washington, 1949).
of the United States Secret Service,

OFFICE OF INTERNAL REVENUE

The Office of Internal Revenue was created by an act of July 1, 1862 (12 Stat. 432), which charged the Commissioner, under the direction of the Secretary of the Treasury, "with preparing all the instructions, regulations, directions, forms, blanks, stamps, and licenses, and distributing the same, or any part thereof, and all other matters pertaining to the assessment and collection of the duties, stamp duties, licenses, and taxes which may be necessary to carry this act into effect." The sweeping revenue act taxed incomes, estates, public utilities, occupations, liquors, tobacco, and other commodities, as well as banks, insurance companies, and advertisements. It imposed stamp taxes on certain commercial papers, medicines, perfumes, cosmetics, and playing cards. An act of June 30,

1864 (13 Stat. 223), changed many tax rates and imposed additional taxes but had no significant effect on administrative requirements.

George S. Boutwell became the first Commissioner of Internal Revenue on July 17, 1862, and by Jan. 1863 the States that had not seceded had been divided into 183 collection districts corresponding in number and generally in area to their congressional districts. At this time the personnel employed in assessing and collecting the revenue totaled 3,882, including those in the Commissioner's office and the collectors, deputy collectors, assessors, and assistant assessors in the field. The offices of assessors and assistant assessors were abolished by an act of Dec. 24, 1872 (17 Stat. 401), but during the Civil War the district assessors stood at the center of the internal revenue system. The position of Deputy Commissioner of Internal Revenue was created by sec. 19 of an act of Mar. 3, 1863 (12 Stat. 725), which also (sec. 20) authorized the Secretary of the Treasury to appoint three revenue agents "to aid in the prevention, detection, and punishment of frauds upon the revenue."

Commissioner Joseph J. Lewis, in his 1863 report, asserted that the war had increased the funds needed by the Government so suddenly that, in contrast to the gradual growth of systems of taxation in other countries, it had become necessary to create and organize "with unprecedented rapidity" a new system of revenue and that "many of the particular provisions of the law must, for the present, be regarded as experiments, and their administration may be expected to point the way to gradual improvements." The administration of the existing laws, he believed, afforded "valuable data for an inquiry into the sources from which any further increases of revenue must be derived."

The act of July 1, 1862, required that separate accounts be kept at the Treasury of all receipts from internal duties in each State, Territory, and collection district, and that separate accounts be kept of the amount of each kind of duty or tax collected. Furthermore, the supervision of the assessment and collection of the direct tax imposed by sec. 8 of an act of Aug. 5, 1861 (12 Stat. 294), became a major responsibility of the Commissioner (see below).

In 1864 the Commissioner's Office apparently included a deputy commissioner, a cashier of internal revenue, a chief clerk, and a number of divisions having charge of (1) general correspondence, (2) correspondence on manufactures, (3) claims for drawbacks, (4) "detective operations," and (5) claims for abatement of taxes erroneously assessed. In 1866 the report of the U. S. Revenue Commission (H. Ex. Doc. 34, 39 Cong., 1 sess., Serial 1255) described the Office as "at present receiving more money every quarter than the whole annual revenue of the government prior to 1860."

Successive Commissioners of Internal Revenue during the period of the Civil War:

> George S. Boutwell, July 17, 1862.
> Joseph J. Lewis, Mar. 18, 1863.
> William Orton, ca. July 1, 1865.
> E. A. Rollins, ca. Nov. 1, 1865.

Annual reports of the Commissioner of Internal Revenue, 1862-70, appended to those of the Secretary of the Treasury on The State of the Finances; Laws and Resolutions Relating to the Direct and

Excise Taxes (H. Misc. Doc. 26, 37 Cong., 3 sess., Serial 1171); George S. Boutwell, A Manual of the Direct and Excise Tax System of the United States . . . (Boston, 1863); Laurence F. Schmeckebier and Francis X. A. Eble, The Bureau of Internal Revenue; Its History, Activities, and Organization (Baltimore, 1923).

Record Group 58.--Copies of telegrams sent and press copies of letters sent from 1862, in series extending into the 1900's; assessment lists, 1862-65 (ca. 500 ft.), showing, for the loyal States, data on the direct tax, the income tax, and excise taxes; and a record of income tax withheld from Federal salary payments, 1862-65 (1 vol.). Also instructions from President Lincoln, 1863-65, concerning the resumption of internal revenue collections in areas of the Confederacy and recommendations for appointments; and original executive orders from 1862, signed by the President, relating to the organization and operation of the Office of Internal Revenue.

Records of the district offices of internal revenue include the following: assessment lists, 1862-65 (5 ft.), of the Camden, N. J., office (Federal Records Center, Philadelphia); assessment lists and related tax records, 1862-73 (15 ft.), of the Buffalo, N. Y., office (Federal Records Center, New York City); and assessment lists, 1863-65 (2 vols.), of the Denver, Colo., office (Federal Records Center, Denver).

The Index to Record Books Containing the Letters Written in the Office of the Commissioner of Internal Revenue Since Its Organization in 1862 (Washington, 1882) classifies the letter books of the Civil War period.

Direct Tax Commissions

Sec. 8 of an act of Aug. 5, 1861 (12 Stat. 294), apportioned an annual direct tax of $20,000,000 among all the States and Territories and the District of Columbia. Only one such annual payment was required, however; acts of July 1, 1862, and June 30, 1864 (12 Stat. 489, 13 Stat. 304), suspended further collections. Under the provision that each State or Territory and the District of Columbia might pay its own quota, all of them formally assumed obligation to pay the tax except Delaware, the Territory of Colorado, and the 11 States of the Confederacy. (Provision was made eventually for collections in Delaware and Colorado by internal revenue officers.)

Special procedures were necessary, of course, to collect this tax in the seceded States, and an act of June 7, 1862 (12 Stat. 422), provided for the "Collection of direct Taxes in Insurrectionary Districts within the United States" when the provisions of the act of Aug. 5, 1861, could not be "peaceably executed." The President was empowered, with the advice and consent of the Senate, to appoint a board of three tax commissioners "for each of said States in which such insurrection exists." No appointment of the "Commissioner of Taxes," authorized by the act of Aug. 5, 1861, had been made; but after most of the loyal States had assumed their apportionment of the $20,000,000 tax the collection of the tax in the "insurrectionary districts" was assigned to the Office of Internal Revenue, to which the boards of tax commissioners authorized by the act of June 7, 1862, were made responsible. Under the 1862 act every parcel of land was valued and taxed in proportion to the amount of tax to be paid by each State. If the owner did not pay the tax plus a 50 percent penalty within 60 days, the land would be advertised for sale; and within another 60-day period the owner could pay the tax, penalty, costs of advertisement, and 10 percent interest on the tax. Otherwise the land would be sold or leased to the highest bidder. The land could be redeemed, however, by the original owner within 60 days after the sale, if he paid the tax, penalty, 15 percent interest, and the expenses of the sale and the subsequent proceedings. The boards of direct tax commissioners completed the assessment rolls in several of the Southern States and collected some of the taxes in all the States except Alabama. In Virginia, South Carolina, Florida, Arkansas, and Tennessee lands were sold for the nonpayment of taxes charged against them.

Later legislation affecting the work of the boards and the Office or Bureau of Internal Revenue included an act of Feb. 6, 1863 (12 Stat. 640), amending the 1862 act with respect to the requirements for the redemption of property sold for default of taxes; an act of Mar. 3, 1865, creating the Bureau of Refugees, Freedmen, and Abandoned Lands (13 Stat. 507), sec. 4 of which provided that loyal male refugees or freedmen might purchase abandoned tracts of land; an act of July 16, 1866 (14 Stat. 175),confirming the sales made to "heads of families of the African race" of land in St. Helena's Parish, S. C. ; and an act of Mar. 2, 1891 (26 Stat. 822), providing for paying to the original owners any surplus proceeds of the land sold for direct taxes and for refunding to members of the armed forces any amounts they had paid toward the purchase of land the title to which had reverted to the United States because of failure to complete payment.

"It is evident, " the Commissioner of Internal Revenue wrote prophetically in his 1865 annual report, "that when the duties of the Commissioners under the present laws shall be completed, the burdens imposed . . . will have fallen unequally upon the people of the districts lately in insurrection. Some will have paid little . . . while others will have lost their entire estates. " The statutory remedy in default of payment of taxes was the sale at public auction of the lands taxed, but on May 17, 1865, after the end of hostilities, the Commissioner of Internal Revenue directed the several boards of commissioners "to suspend all sales of lands for taxes in districts before that time in insurrection until otherwise ordered. " Collections, however, continued (in some States with greater success than before) until, under sec. 14 of an act of July 28, 1866 (14 Stat. 331), Secretary McCulloch ordered their discontinuance and the dissolution of the commissions (except those in Florida and South Carolina) at the following dates: Alabama, Sept. 30, 1866; North Carolina, Dec. 1, 1866; Georgia and Louisiana, Dec. 15, 1866; Mississippi, Dec. 31, 1866; Texas, Feb. 28, 1867; Arkansas, Mar. 5, 1867; and Virginia and Tennessee, Apr. 30, 1867.

The commission for Florida was dissolved on Apr. 15, 1867, but the South Carolina Commission was continued, to perform duties imposed by secs. 7, 8, and 10 of an act of July 16, 1866 (14 Stat. 175), and to collect deferred payments for lands that had been bid in by the United States at tax sales and had afterwards been sold on 3 years' time to members of the Army and the Navy. In 1870 this commission was discontinued, and its functions were transferred to the collector of internal revenue at Charleston.

Record Groups 58, 217. --Both the records of the State commissions (see below) and those originating in the Treasury Department should be consulted. The latter include letters received and sent by the First Comptroller and letters sent and reports received by the Fifth Auditor (Record Group 217), as well as the letters sent by the Commissioner of Internal Revenue (Record Group 58). A direct tax ledger book, 1874-93 (Record Group 217), is an account of receipts and expenditures showing the amount refunded to each State in accordance with the act of Mar. 2, 1891, cited above. There are also (all in Record Group 58) the following registers: of tax sale certificates for land sold for direct tax in Tennessee, South Carolina, Florida, and Virginia, 1863-ca. 1878; of applications to redeem property and make final payments, 1872-ca. 1874 (2 vols.); of certificates of release 1873-79, under sec. 2 of an act of June 8, 1872 (17 Stat. 331); of sales made in Beaufort County, S. C., in Dec. 1875 and Jan. 1876, and in Memphis, Tenn., in May 1878, under the same act; of claims for refunding taxes and penalties illegally collected in South Carolina, Arkansas, and Louisiana, 1886-91; of claims for return of purchase money to purchasers of land sold for direct tax in Tennessee, Florida, Virginia, and Arkansas, 1871-88; of revenue derived from direct tax levied in each county of Virginia, North Carolina, Georgia, Alabama, Texas, Tennessee, Arkansas, and South Carolina; of lands subject to direct taxation at Fernandina, Fla. ; of Virginia applications for redemption, 1874; and of Texas and South Carolina claims for refunding interests and costs, 1871-72 (2 vols.). There are also in Record Group 58 a "History of Proceedings of Direct Tax Commissioners in Virginia" and a record of Virginia applications for redemption, 1874.

State Direct Tax Commissions

The records maintained by the State commissions were notably the assessment lists and the direct tax receipt books. The assessment lists (Record Group 217), arranged by State and county, consist of about 1, 100 volumes, 1865-66, for all States except Florida. The information they usually contain includes a description of the land, the number of acres and lots, valuation, tax, penalty, and owner's name, but there are some variations. The direct tax receipt books (also Record Group 217), arranged by State, district, and county, consist of about 470 volumes, 1865-66, for all States except Alabama, Florida, Louisiana, and Tennessee; they show the names of the owners and the amounts paid. There are also bundles of miscellaneous records of or relating to the several commissions, 1866-74 (Record Group 217), in which Alabama and Texas are not represented. These bundles comprise cash accounts, statements of receipts and disbursements, schedules of certificates of deposits, vouchers, commissioners' reports, Fifth Auditor's reports, and accounts and vouchers for refunding taxes. Other records, which constitute for the most part the operating records of the several commissions, are described below, State by State; these are divided between Record Group 217 and Record Group 58 as indicated.

Alabama (established ca. Aug. 1865 with the appointment of Commissioners E. S. Hamil and Robert T. Smith; dissolved Sept. 30, 1866). No separable records except the assessment lists described above.

Arkansas (established Dec. 29, 1864 , with the appointment of Commissioners Enoch H. Vance, Huling Cowperthwait, and Charles E. Stoddard; dissolved Mar. 5, 1867). Record Group 217.--Diary of Charles E. Stoddard, Dec. 12, 1864-Feb. 7, 1865; and the following records, all 1855-56 : cash receipt books, itemizing money received from landowners (5 vols.); a receipt book covering payments for services rendered the commission; a register of taxes paid within 60 days (4 vols.); and account books (2 vols.). Also the assessment lists and direct tax receipt books described above.

Florida (established Sept. 15, 1862, with the appointment of Commissioners Lyman D. Stickney, John S. Sammiss, and Harrison Reed; discontinued Apr.15, 1867). Record Group 217.--Letter book containing copies of letters of the commissioners, the Secretaries of the Treasury and of War, the Commissioner of Internal Revenue, and other officials, 1862-67; a volume containing abstracts of money received in St. Augustine and Fernandina for land and lots sold, 1863-67, and another volume listing land sold in Fernandina, 1865-66; register of taxes paid within 60 days and of land sold, 1863-65; register of taxes paid within 60 days and within 120 days, 1863-65; register of lots bid in at direct tax sales, 1863-65 (2 vols.); tax sale certificates, 1863-65; register of redemptions of land within 60 days after sale, 1865-66; and a list of lands belonging to the Florida Railroad Co. , with applications to redeem these lands, 1862-66. Also the assessment lists described above.

Georgia (established ca. Aug. 1, 1865, with the appointment of Commissioners T. P. Robb, Samuel A. Pancoast, and John C. Bates; dissolved Dec. 15, 1866). Record Group 217. --Receipt account books, 1865-66 (2 vols.). Also assessment lists and the direct tax receipt books described above.

Louisiana (established ca. Nov. 1864 with the appointment of Commissioners E. M. Randall, George W. Ames, and D. Urban; dissolved Dec. 15, 1866). Record Group 217. --Register of taxes paid within 60 days (6 vols.). Also the assessment lists described above.

Mississippi (established Mar. 13, 1866, with the appointment of Commissioner A. B. Alderson; dissolved Dec. 31, 1866). No records except the assessment lists and the direct tax receipt books described above.

North Carolina (established ca. Nov. 1864 with the appointment of Commissioners Hiram Potter and E. H. Sears; dissolved Dec. 1, 1866). No records except the assessment lists and the direct tax receipt books described above.

South Carolina (established in Oct. 1862 with the appointment of Commissioners W. E. Wording, W. Henry Brisbane, and A. D. Smith; D. N. Cooley, Willis Drummond, and J. D. Martyn appointed later; dissolved Oct. 28, 1870). Record Group 217. --Contracts for lease of land in the Parish of St. Helena, district of Beaufort, 1863-72; register of taxes paid within 60 days, 1862; abstract of redemptions in Beaufort district, 1863-66 (2 p. of 1 vol.); certificates for land bid in by the United States and later sold by the commissioners to "heads of families of the African race, " 1863-65 (1 vol.); ledger and journal of the collector of internal revenue, Charleston, to whom the Commission's functions were transferred, 1871-76 (2 vols.); also the assessment lists and the direct tax receipt books described above. Record Group 58. --Minutes, 1862-70 (1 vol.); correspondence, comprising a general file, 1862-ca. 1893 (3 ft.), press copies of letters sent, 1863-67 (1 vol.), papers relating to school farm lands, 1866-99 (2 vols. and unbound papers), correspondence relating to leases, 1866-ca. 1898 (5 in.), and letters received from the Office of the Commissioner of Internal Revenue, 1870-76 (5 vols.); land certificates, 1863-86 (2 ft.); applications to purchase land by preemption, filed in response to a circular issued by Gen. Rufus Saxton to freedmen of South Carolina, authorizing them to locate on land set aside for them, 1864 (10 in.); other applications, 1872-ca. 1899 (4 ft.), to redeem real estate sold for direct tax, to redeem and make final payments, and for refund of surplus proceeds of real estate sold for direct tax; papers relating to claims, 1891-92 (9 in.), filed in the U. S. Court of Claims by owners or their heirs under sec. 4 of an act of Mar. 2, 1891 (26 Stat. 823), for surplus proceeds of land sold for direct tax, and relating to Army, Navy, or Marine claims, 1899 (5 in.), under the same act; registers of claims for refunding interest, 1886-92, and of claims for surplus proceeds from direct tax sales in the Parishes of St. Helena and St. Luke, 1891-98; ledger of receipts and expenditures, 1862-70; cash book, 1862-72; memoranda of expenses, 1869-76 (1 vol.); copies of reports of receipts and expenditures, 1863-70 (5 in.); and manuscript and printed maps of the Parishes of St. Helena and St. Luke, with related documents including annotated plans of Beaufort and Port Royal.

Tennessee (established ca. Nov. 7, 1863, with the appointment of Commissioners Delano Smith, Elisha P. Ferry, and John B. Rodgers; A. A. Kyle appointed later; dissolved Apr. 30, 1867). Record Group 217. --Registers of taxes paid within 60 days, 1865, of taxes paid within 120 days, 1865-66 (7 vols.), and of sales of land in Shelby County; also the assessment lists described above. Record Group 58. --Cash book, 1865-67.

Texas (established in Oct. 1865 with the appointment of Commissioners Robert K. Smith, Andrew J. Coleman, and A. H. Latimer; dissolved Feb. 28, 1867). Record Group 217. --Register of taxes paid within 120 days, 1865-66; also the assessment lists and the direct tax receipt books described above. Record Group 58. --Journal, 1865-66.

Virginia (established Mar. 7, 1863, with the appointment of Commissioners Gillet F. Watson, William J. Boreman, and John Hauxhurst; A. Lawrence Foster appointed later; dissolved Apr. 30, 1867). Record Group 217. --Redemption books for Alexandria County, 1863-66 (2 vols.); also the assessment lists and the direct tax receipt books described above.

National Archives, Preliminary Inventory [No. 14] of the Records of the United States Direct Tax Commission for the District of South Carolina, comp. by Jane Greene (Washington, 1948), and unpublished Preliminary Inventory of the Records of the United States Direct Tax Commissions of the Southern States, 1862-1893, comp. by Donald R. Gruver.

Commission for the Revision of the Revenue System

An act of Mar. 3, 1865 (13 Stat. 487), authorized the Secretary of the Treasury to appoint a commission of three to investigate the revenue system and recommend "the sources from which such revenue should be drawn, and the best and most efficient mode of raising the same. " The Commission was organized in June 1865 by the appointment of David A. Wells of New York, Stephen Colwell of Pennsylvania, and Samuel Snowden Hayes of Illinois. It took up specifically for investigation sources of revenue "which our own experience and the experience of other countries have indicated as likely to be most productive under taxation, and most capable of sustaining its burdens. "

Neither the Commission's records nor its original report (printed as H. Ex. Doc. 34, 39 Cong. , 1 sess. , Serial 1255) appears to be extant. The printed report is of special interest because of its findings on cotton production and marketing and the manufacture of cotton products--aspects of the subject "Cotton as a Source of National Revenue." The work of the Commission was continued by David A. Wells as Special Commissioner of Revenue in 1866.

OFFICE OF THE COMPTROLLER OF THE CURRENCY
(NATIONAL CURRENCY BUREAU)

The Office of the Comptroller of the Currency, known also as the National Currency Bureau, was created by an act of Feb. 25, 1863 (12 Stat. 665), to provide "a national currency secured by United States bonds." Hugh McCulloch, the first Comptroller of the Currency, had been president of the State Bank of Indiana. On June 30, 1863, the First National Bank of Philadelphia was chartered under the act, and by November 134 national banks had been organized. The Comptroller wrote in his 1863 report that the national currency system contemplated "the organization of national banks, which, by becoming its financial agents . . . [might] aid the government in the safekeeping and transmission of its revenues, and the transaction of its business," and that through the national banks "a safe and uniform circulation . . . [might] be furnished to the people." The war would not be " an unmixed evil financially" if it resulted in the establishment of a banking system that, "without an interference with the rights of the States, and without detriment to their solvent institutions," would provide a bank note circulation "as solvent as the nation itself, and uniform in value."

The repealing and reestablishing act of June 3, 1864 (13 Stat. 99)--often called the 1864 National Bank Act--preserved the continuity of the Office of the Comptroller of the Currency by confirming appointments already made. The Comptroller was to perform his duties under the general direction of the Secretary of the Treasury. The relationship of these duties to those of the "Engraving Unit," which came to be known as the First Division of the National Currency Bureau, is discussed below.

McCulloch gave particular attention to the too-rapid increase of national banks, the suspension of specie payments, currency expansion, and price inflation. "It is of the greatest importance," he observed in his 1864 report, "that the national currency system should be independent of politics and freed from political influences. To effect this, and to facilitate the business of the banks with the Comptroller . . . the bureau should be made an independent department, and removed from Washington to Philadelphia or New York."

Although the recommended removal did not materialize, the National Currency Bureau prospered, and by Mar. 8, 1865, when McCulloch resigned to become Secretary of the Treasury, most of the State banks had given way to the national banking associations. This shift facilitated financial settlements at the end of the war.

Hugh McCulloch, Comptroller of the Currency from Mar. 9, 1863, was succeeded on Mar. 21, 1865, by Freeman Clarke.

Annual reports of the Comptroller of the Currency, 1863-67, appended to those of the Secretary of the Treasury on The State of the Finances; John Gilbert Heinberg, The Office of the Comptroller of the Currency; Its History, Activities, and Organization (Baltimore, 1926); A. M. Davis, Origin of National Banking System (S. Doc. 582, 61 Cong., 2 sess., Serial 5634; Washington, 1910).

Record Group 101. --The records of the National Currency Bureau for the Civil War period were largely inherited and augmented by the various divisions of the Bureau of the Comptroller of the Currency in its postwar reorganizations. The relatively few Civil War records expanded into series that continued, in some cases, into the present century. Those that became eventually records of the Division of Reports include the reports of national bank examiners, from 1863, with related correspondence, and some miscellaneous correspondence of the Comptroller of the Currency. These records are of value for research in economic reconstruction and the restoration of Treasury Department control over the national banking system in the South.

The records that eventually went to the Organization Division of the Bureau of the Comptroller of the Currency include copies of reports on the organization of national banks, from 1865; organization files (arranged by bank charter number) relating to national banks no longer in existence, from 1863; and opinions of the Solicitor of the Treasury (with some opinions of the Attorney General) relating to banks and banking, 1865-93.

The records that went to the Division of Insolvent National Banks of the Bureau of the Comptroller of the Currency include general correspondence of the Comptroller on the administration of receiverships, from 1865, consisting for the immediate postwar period almost exclusively of letters sent by receivers to the Comptroller; and receivership records sent to the Comptroller by receivers, from 1865.

Also eventually a part of the records of the Division of Insolvent National Banks were the records of the Comptroller of the Currency pertaining to the liquidation of the Freedman's Savings and Trust Co. This company was chartered by an act of Mar. 3, 1865 (13 Stat. 510), for the benefit of freed slaves; and soon after its establishment the military savings banks at Beaufort, S. C., and Norfolk, Va., were transferred to it. By 1870 the company had 33 branch offices, including one in New York City. The company failed in 1874; and under sec. 7 of an act of June 20 of that year (18 Stat. 132), the trustees were authorized to select, with the approval of the Secretary of the Treasury, three commissioners "to take charge of all the property and effects" of the bank and act as receivers, reporting to the Secretary. An act of Feb. 21, 1881 (21 Stat. 377), authorized the Secretary of the Treasury to appoint the Comptroller of the Currency to administer the affairs of the company. The Comptroller then began to liquidate the affairs of the company, and reports on it were submitted to Congress until 1920. Among the resulting records are letters received by the commissioners and by the Comptroller of the Currency as an ex officio commissioner, 1870-1914 (27 ft.); press copies of letters sent by them, 1874-1913 (34 vols.); minutes and journals, 1865-74 (7 vols.); printed annual reports, 1881-1919; signature books, constituting registered signatures and personal identification data of depositors; a dividend payment record, 1882-89 (16 vols.); and an index to deposit ledgers (including index to depositors of the Norfolk, Va., Savings Bank).

This record group includes also records of the issuance of national banknotes, which began under the acts of Feb. 25, 1863, and June 3, 1864, already cited. There are ledgers of circulation accounts of national banks, from 1863; ledgers of national banknotes received for issuance to national banks, from 1863; and registers of Treasury numbers on national bank currency, 1864.

National Archives, unpublished Preliminary Checklist of Records of the Organization Division of the Bureau of the Comptroller of the Currency, 1863-1944, comp. by Lyle J. Holverstott; unpublished Preliminary Checklist of the Records of the Division of Reports of the Bureau of the Comptroller of the Currency, 1863-1935, comp. by Maxcy R. Dickson and J. Eric Maddox; Preliminary Checklist of Records of the Division of Insolvent National Banks of the Bureau of the Comptroller of the Currency, 1865-1945, comp. by Lyle J. Holverstott, Maxcy R. Dickson, and J. Eric Maddox (Washington, 1946).

First Division (Engraving or Printing Bureau)

This division of the Office of the Comptroller of the Currency "had its origin in an attempt to trim and separate treasury notes by machinery"-- work done by hand until the summer of 1862. An act of Feb. 25, 1862 (12 Stat. 346), authorized the engraving of signatures on Treasury notes and the imprinting of the Treasury Department seal on the notes after they had been delivered by the engravers. Trimming and separation of the notes by machinery was commenced, and an act of July 11, 1862 (12 Stat. 532), authorizing an additional issue of national currency, empowered the Secretary of the Treasury to have the notes or any part of them engraved and printed at the Treasury, to purchase machinery and materials, and to employ necessary personnel. In August 1862 was begun the work of affixing the seal, trimming, and separating, and of procuring and keeping the plates and special dies for the printing. The newly created Office of the Comptroller of the Currency apparently directed the engraving functions that had already begun and the printing functions that began with the printing of fractional currency under an act of Mar. 3, 1863 (12 Stat. 711).

The designation of the engraving or printing unit as First Division, National Currency Bureau, came into official use by 1864, although reports of House committees refer to the office also as the Printing Bureau. With the unit's rapid growth its direction by the Comptroller of the Currency seems to have become more and more nominal. Comptroller of the Currency McCulloch, testifying on May 11, 1864, before the House Select Committee to Investigate Charges Against the Treasury Department (H. Rept. 140, 38 Cong., 1 sess., Serial 1207), was asked to state his "views of the Printing Bureau, or the printing of the currency at the Treasury Department." He replied that he had "not given special attention" to this and that he had "never regarded that department as having any legal connection" with his. Evidence of the First Division's relative independence is seen also in the correspondence between the Division Chief and the Comptroller of the Currency.

By Feb. 1, 1865, the First Division had 31 subdivisions employing 527 operatives engaged in "engraving, printing, and preparing for issue the various securities and currency authorized by Congress, and such checks, drafts, and other forms as are required by the Treasurer and assistant treasurers of the United States, and the designated depositaries; in printing the circulars, blank forms, envelopes, and other letter-press printing required by this department, as well as some incidental work for other departments; in ruling and preparing for binding such forms and tables as are directed; in stereotyping and electrotyping such work as is necessary, and in making and repairing the machinery used in the building."

Spencer M. Clark was Chief of the First Division, National Currency Bureau, during the Civil War.

Record Group 318. --The wartime records of the First Division, although small in quantity, show the details of both its printing and its engraving functions. Correspondence and orders received, 1864-65 (ca. 6 in.), include orders for notes, bonds, and coupons; orders for printing (usually of commissions and other "blanks" for Government agencies); and letters from the American Bank Note Co. Copies of letters sent, Apr. 26, 1862-Dec. 9, 1863, and Apr. 28, 1864-Aug. 3, 1866 (vols. 1-2 and 4-7; vol. 3 missing), contain orders to place advertisements in newspapers, specifications for the design and printing of notes, and other correspondence with or concerning the several note companies of the period (American Bank Note Co. of New York, Continental Bank Note Co. of New York, and Union Bank Note Co. of Newark, N. J.).

OFFICE OF THE SUPERVISING ARCHITECT

The prewar Bureau of Construction of the Treasury Department was superseded in 1862 by the Office of the Supervising Architect. The new Office was known also during the war as the Construction Bureau or Branch, but these names eventually fell into disuse. Although it had the functions of a bureau, the Office was technically a unit in the Office of the Secretary of the Treasury.

Supervision of the Government's building activities outside the District of Columbia had been assigned to the Construction Branch in 1853, and as head of the new branch "a scientific and practical engineer" was detailed from the Army. General regulations affecting this work (published in the Secretary's 1853 report on The State of the Finances) stipulated that the duties would comprise: "the selection and purchase of sites for all buildings under the Treasury Department; the procuring of cession of jurisdiction to the United States by the States in which the sites may be situated; the making of plans and estimates for custom-houses, mints, and marine hospitals; the general superintendence of their construction; and the collection, arrangement, and preservation of all reports, memoirs, estimates, plans, and models relating to all buildings in charge of the Treasury Department. "

After 1861 the Engineer in Charge was replaced by a Supervising Architect. As the Secretary of the Treasury explained to the House Ways and Means Committee in 1864 (H. Misc. Doc. 37, 38 Cong. , 1 sess. , Serial 1200), he had abolished the office of the "engineer" because he had "found no authority of law" for it; and in point of fact the first law referring specifically to the "construction branch" was a deficiency appropriations act of Mar. 14, 1864 (13 Stat. 27). (The act authorized the employment of clerks in the branch "only during the rebellion and for one year after its close," but continuing annual appropriations extended the life of the branch.)

The immediate effect of secession was the stoppage of work on the public buildings in the seceded States and a ban on deliveries of materials for such work. Furthermore, no new buildings appear to have been begun during the war, although work on the Treasury Extension was resumed in February of 1862. Through 1865 the chief work of the Office was supervising repairs and alterations of existing public buildings.

Officers in charge of this Office during the Civil War period:

S. M. Clark, Acting Engineer in Charge, Bureau of Construction, 1860.
Isaiah Rogers, Supervising Architect, July 28, 1862.
A. B. Mullett, Supervising Architect, Sept. 30, 1865.

Civil War annual reports of the Engineer in Charge, Bureau of Construction (1861), and of the Supervising Architect (1862-65), appended to those of the Secretary of the Treasury on The State of the Finances; R. H. Thayer, History, Organization, and Functions of the Office of the Supervising Architect . . . (Washington, 1886); Darrell Hevenor Smith, The Office of the Supervising Architect of the Treasury . . . (Baltimore, 1923).

Record Group 121. --The wartime general correspondence of the Office comprises fair copies of letters sent by the Secretary of the Treasury, Mar. 1851-Feb. 1863 (13 vols.), concerning the acquisition of building sites and the construction, repair, and maintenance of public buildings, with some duplicate press copies (12 vols.) and a partial register (1 vol.) of the letters concerning customhouses and other buildings; fair copies of letters sent by the Engineer in Charge and the Supervising Architect, Sept. 1852-Aug. 1862 (4 vols.), concerning the selection and acquisition of building sites and the construction and repair of buildings (also with some duplicate press copies and partial registers extending beyond the Civil War period); fair copies (May 1855-Feb. 1863) and press copies (May 1856-Mar. 1863) of letters sent concerning the Treasury Extension (4 vols.); and one long series of letters received, 1843-1910, arranged alphabetically by name of city or other geographic location, concerning site acquisition or building construction, leasing, alteration, maintenance, or repair, with registers, 1857-1901. There are some original building plans, architects' sketches, and construction specifications, dating from 1840, and some glass plate negatives, dating from 1857, of Federal buildings and other structures in Washington and other cities; for the negatives there are numerical, subject, and place indexes prepared in the 1930's by the Works Progress Administration. The fragmentary fiscal records that span the Civil War period consist of combined appropriation ledgers and daybooks, 1816-1906 (3 vols.), concerning funds for site purchase and the construction of public buildings; and accounting ledgers and journals, 1855-71 (6 vols.), related to the Treasury Extension. A register of leases, bonds, contracts, and agreements, ca. 1846-89, contains chronological entries under each of those headings, related generally to sites and construction.

National Archives, Preliminary Inventory [No. 110] of the Records of the Public Buildings Service, comp. by W. Lane Van Neste and Virgil E. Baugh (Washington, 1958).

U. S. MINT AND BRANCH MINTS

The Mint of the United States was founded in Philadelphia in 1792. During the Civil War--and until the creation of the Bureau of the Mint in 1873--the branch mints and the assay office at New York were supervised by the Director of the Mint. At the war's outbreak three branch mints, established by Congress in 1835 (4 Stat. 774; 5 Stat. 147, 602), were in Confederate territory--at New Orleans, La., Charlotte, N. C., and Dahlonega, Ga. A fourth branch, authorized in 1852 (10 Stat. 11), was at San Francisco. The mint at Philadelphia and the branch mint at New Orleans had been made public depositories or subtreasuries by an act of Aug. 6, 1846 (9 Stat. 59). During the war Congress authorized branch mints at Denver (12 Stat. 382) and Carson City, Nev. (12 Stat. 770), but the Carson City mint did not open until 1870.

The Director of the Mint at Philadelphia received no reports from the branch mints at New Orleans, Dahlonega, and Charlotte after Jan. 31, Feb. 28, and Mar. 31, 1861, respectively; but the coinage for the fiscal year ending June 30, 1861, was greater than that of any former year. The branches at Dahlonega and Charlotte--both seized by Southern forces--were not reopened after the war, and the branch at New Orleans was not reopened until 1879, for reasons given by the Director of the Mint in his 1862 report:

Although New Orleans is now, and has been for some months, in the possession of the Union forces, yet the operations at the branch mint in that city have not been resumed, nor is it expedient or necessary that they should be. After the suppression of the rebellion, and the pacification of the country, the branch located there might again be successfully and usefully operated; till then it should remain closed. No consideration, of public or private interest, would . . . justify the reopening of the branches at Dahlonega or Charlotte. They ought not to have been established; and, having been the source of useless expenditure, they should not . . . be again employed for minting purposes.

When, on Feb. 18, 1861, the Director of the U. S. Mint was informed that the required weekly returns were not being submitted by the New Orleans Branch Mint, he became concerned about the legality of the New Orleans coinage, since it could not be subjected to the required tests. He took the position that coins struck in New Orleans after Jan. 31, 1861, would be illegal; but since these coins could not be distinguished from the ones coined in January, all the New Orleans coinage of the year 1861, he believed, should be discredited by the Government. At this time the coins stamped at New Orleans were designated by the letter O on the reverse of each piece; S designated San Francisco; D, Dahlonega; and C, Charlotte. The coinage of the mint at Philadelphia was known by the absence of any mint mark. Coinage dies were prepared at the Philadelphia Mint for the use of the branches.

In 1864 substitution of a bronze alloy for the nickel mixture previously used for minor coinage was highly successful, and the demand for 1- and 2-cent pieces was "unprecedented." In fiscal year 1864 "some interesting experiments were made with aluminum as an alloy for coins; not with a view to displace the bronze coinage, but to propose a system of tokens for five and ten cents." The motto "In God We Trust" was first put on U. S. coins during the war.

James Pollock, former Governor of Pennsylvania, was Director of the Mint from 1861 to 1866.

Civil War annual reports of the Director of the Mint, appended to those of the Secretary of the Treasury on The State of the Finances; Jesse P. Watson, The Bureau of the Mint . . . (Baltimore, 1926).

Record Group 104. --The subjects of particular interest in the extant records are the loss of the branch mints at Dahlonega, Charlotte, and New Orleans; the low minor-coin production during the war due to the lack of silver; the production of military medals; and the taking of loyalty oaths in 1861 by U. S. Mint employees. These matters are documented in the general correspondence of the U. S. Mint at Philadelphia, now in a chronological series combining letters received and copies of those sent, 1792-1899, covered partly by registers. The Civil War correspondence of the U. S. Mint with branch mints and assay offices (letters received and drafts or press copies of replies) includes that with officials of the Denver Branch Mint (from 1862); the New York Assay Office (to 1864); and the San Francisco Branch Mint. There is some correspondence (to 1864) concerning the establishment of a branch mint at Carson City, Nev. Also spanning the Civil War period are copies of letters sent by the Treasurer of the Mint; some records concerning assays of coins, of metals destined for coinage, and of ore samples deposited; records relating to the maintenance of the bullion fund (copper, gold, and silver) and to gold and silver deposits and purchases; records of the manufacture of coins and of related coinage activities (including a register of coins received for exchange at the Mint, 1861-64, from banks, firms, or individuals); and records of the weighing of copper and silver. Although the statutory authority for making medals dates from 1873, there is a medal fund account book, 1861-68. Chronological statistics on U. S. coinage, 1794-1888, are in a 1-volume history. Other records of the war period include weekly accounts of the amount and value of silver and gold used at the Mint; the Director's orders; visitors' registers; the Treasurer's auditing books, from 1864; registers of warrants for ordinary expenses and for the payment of deposits; a record of the sale of "sweeps" (i. e., metal sweepings) at the San Francisco Branch Mint, 1857-65; financial statements of the treasurers of branch mints in account with the Director of the Philadelphia Mint, 1855-72 (3 vols.), in which are some certificates of deposit, 1860-65; and an order book, 1853-81, relating to materials or supplies for the Mint furnished by private firms or persons. Among personnel and related records are a register of employees, 1849-84, and an appointment register, 1865.

Among records of the Branch Mint at Charlotte, N. C., are the following series that begin as Federal records but continue from Apr. 1861 as Confederate records: a register of gold bullion received and coins paid, to May 1861; a journal of bullion deposits, to Oct. 1861; a gold bullion weigh book, to May 1861; a journal and ledger of ordinary accounts, to Mar. 1862; and a daybook, to Mar. 1862.

Records of the Denver Branch Mint (in the Federal Records Center at Denver) include copies of letters sent by its superintendent, Dec. 1862-July 1874 (2 vols.), among which are a report of the robbery of the mint in 1863 and an appeal to the Territorial Governor for ammunition to supplement the mint arsenal in the event of any Indian attack "instigated by Rebel sympathizers." Other extant wartime records of the Denver Mint are depositors' signatures and references, ledger and journal of bullion deposits, daybooks, registers of warrants for payment of deposits, and the assayer's register of gold and silver bullion--all from 1863.

The San Francisco Branch Mint's Civil War records (in the Federal Records Center at San Francisco) relate chiefly to deliveries, deposits, and assays of gold and silver bullion; there are also copies of correspondence with the Director of the Mint at Philadelphia, a visitors' register, and some accounting records.

The records of the U. S. Mint and the branch mints should be used in relation to those of the Secretary of the Treasury on mint matters, to 1873. The latter, also in this record group, include correspondence about the motto "In God We Trust."

National Archives, Preliminary Inventory [No. 40] of the Records of the United States Mint at Philadelphia,   comp. by Lyle J. Holverstott and Jean McNiece (Washington, 1952).

CUSTOMS SERVICE

The Customs Service, created by an act of July 31, 1789 (1 Stat. 29), became part of the Department of the Treasury when the Department was established a few weeks later. The organic act specified the customs districts and ports of entry and provided for the appointment of customs officers and the collection of duties. Collectors of customs were made responsible for administering the regulations governing the registry and clearing of vessels (act of Sept. 1, 1789; 1 Stat. 55); for collecting, from ships arriving from foreign ports, hospital dues for the relief of sick and disabled seamen (act of July 16, 1798; 1 Stat. 605); for receiving crew lists from masters of vessels bound for foreign ports (act of Feb. 28, 1803; 2 Stat. 203); for receiving passenger manifests from the masters of vessels arriving from foreign ports (act of Mar. 2, 1819; 3 Stat. 488); for collecting statistics of exports, imports, and tonnage (act of Feb. 10, 1820; 3 Stat. 543); for recording all papers affecting titles to vessels (act of July 29, 1850; 9 Stat. 440); and for participating in the selection of local steamboat inspectors and enforcing safety regulations for arriving or departing steamers (act of Aug. 30, 1852; 10 Stat. 61).

These, at the beginning of the Civil War, were the manifold responsibilities of the Customs Service. Each customs district was provided with a collector and a surveyor; in some districts there was a naval officer also; and in a few there were more than one surveyor. Although the statutory responsibilities of the Service were not appreciably affected by the war, there were indirect effects resulting from the new internal revenue laws. The report of the House Committee on Expenditures of its investigation of frauds alleged in connection with the New York Customhouse (H. Rept. 30, 39 Cong., 2 sess., Serial 1305) throws considerable light on the operations, responsibilities, and prerogatives of collectors of customs during the war. In the New York Customhouse the activities of the "seizure bureau" had been greatly enlarged and stimulated by an act of Mar. 3, 1863 ("to prevent and punish frauds upon the revenue, and to provide for the more certain collection of claims . . . "). In 1864 (see H. Rept. 111, 38 Cong., 1 sess., Serial 1206) the duties of the New York Customhouse were distributed among 10 divisions.

The secession of Southern States in 1860 and 1861 was accompanied by the seizure of many customhouses, and even before the outbreak of hostilities secession affected U. S. commerce. The seizure of the customhouse at New Orleans, for instance, prevented the delivery of imported goods consigned to Louisville, Ky., a port of delivery with entry at New Orleans. The 20 interior ports of delivery above New Orleans, in fact, included not only Louisville but Memphis, Tenn.; Cincinnati, Ohio; Evansville, Ind.; St. Louis, Mo.; Wheeling, Va.; Pittsburgh, Pa.; and Cairo and Alton, Ill. During the war almost all the customhouses in the South ceased to operate for the United States, and many became agencies of the Confederacy. Even in ports taken over and operated by U. S. forces the customhouses were often employed for other purposes; the New Orleans Customhouse, after being used as a Confederate factory for gun carriages, was used by U. S. military authorities as a prison.

The Confederate operation of U. S. customhouses resulted, of course, in the creation of Confederate rather than U. S. records, and these, if extant, are described in the accompanying Guide to the Archives of the Government of the Confederate States of America. Among the first Southern ports to be reopened for U. S. customs after the war were Apalachicola, Charleston, Galveston, Mobile, New Bern, Norfolk, Pensacola, Plymouth, Richmond, Savannah, and Wilmington.

Civil War annual reports of the Secretary of the Treasury on The State of the Finances, cited above; Laurence F. Schmeckebier, The Customs Service . . . (Baltimore, 1924); William H. Futrell, The History of American Customs Jurisprudence (New York, 1941).

Record Groups 36, 41. --The Office of the Secretary of the Treasury administered the Customs Service until the establishment of the Bureau of Customs in 1927; soon after the Civil War a Division of Customs was created in the Secretary's Office. The functions of the Office relating to customs had no connection with those of the Commissioner of Customs, who from 1849 to 1894 performed the duties of a comptroller--see the separate discussion of the Commissioner's Office. The Civil War records of the Secretary's Office relating to the Customs Service are mentioned under the Office of the Secretary. Those kept at customhouses by collectors and other officials during the Civil War, described here, are generally extant, but the original records of each customhouse are now divided between Record Group 36 (Records of the Bureau of Customs) and Record Group 41 (Records of the Bureau of Marine Inspection and Navigation). This division is indicated below.

In Record Group 36 are Civil War crew lists and shipping articles; passenger lists of vessels entering U. S. ports; records of the entrance and clearance of vessels; daybooks, waste books, cash books, blotters, abstracts of moneys received, and quarterly returns; impost books; cargo manifests; records relating to revenue cutters, marine hospitals, lighthouses, and internal revenue or direct taxation; and correspondence of collectors with persons and officials outside the Customs Service or the Treasury Department. These records for the Civil War period document the importation, exportation, and appraisal of merchandise; the activity of revenue cutters assigned to ports; and their maintenance of the blockade and protection of the "cotton fleet." A sampling, not necessarily indicative, shows the availability of the following: Baltimore, Md., Customhouse--Revenue-Cutter Service shipping articles, 1863-64; list of permits granted for shipment of powder, shot, guns, etc., to Southern States, 1865-66. Georgetown, D. C., Customhouse--authorizations to clear merchandise being shipped by sutlers, 1862-65, with a few bonds given as surety against transfer or sale to insurgents, and records pertaining to the revenue steamers Tiger and Northerner, stationed on the Potomac, 1862-65. New York Customhouse--letters from the Secretary of the Treasury to George Denison, naval officer at the port, June 1861-Aug. 1865; other letters to Denison, 1861-65, concerning "contraband of war," seizures of merchandise on ships bound for Nassau and Havana, and investigations of these seizures; letters to the collector concerning appointments or containing criticism of employees, with several endorsements by Horace Greeley, 1861-62; letters from customs officers in Baltimore, Md., and Charleston, S. C., to the special deputy naval officer at New York, seeking information on seizures, etc., 1863-70; other letters from foreign firms and individuals abroad dealing with invoices, bills of lading, and accounts, 1855-67; the diary of S. H. Browne, Nov. 1863, written aboard the blockade runner C. S. S. Dee, Nassau, Bahama Islands, to Wilmington, N. C., and return; and a few inbound and outbound ship manifests, with shippers' oaths, 1861-65, that the cargo was not "to be used to give aid or comfort for the enemy."

In Record Group 41 are records relating to the licensing, enrolling, and registering of vessels, including bills of sale, mortgages, leases, and other conveyances; oaths and bonds of masters and owners; and other documentation and ownership records, but excluding licenses for vessels over 20 tons. Here also are records relating to the building, inspection, and admeasurement of vessels. The terms employed in these records are defined in the entry on the Office of the Register of the Treasury, above. The documentation for merchant vessels of the United States for 1860-66 approximates 100,000 papers (ca. 50 ft.). Among them are documents for about 500 steamers that went into or out of U. S. Navy and Army service during the period, about 100 Confederate steamers captured or destroyed while in the Confederate Navy or merchant sevice, and about 100 British or Confederate steamers captured as prizes and later registered as U. S. vessels (among them the Ella Worley, the Ella, and the Annie). There are also records showing the ownership before and after the war of many vessels chartered by the Army during the period.

Other customhouse records of the Civil War period are in several Federal Records Centers. The Dorchester, Mass., Center has some records of collectors at Boston, Fall River, and New Bedford, Mass.; Portland, Maine; Hartford, New Haven, and New London, Conn.; and Newport and Providence, R. I. The Center in Philadelphia has some records of the Philadelphia collector. The Center in New York has some records not only of the collector at New York but also of collectors at Buffalo and many northeastern ports; these are of particular interest because they include correspondence on smuggling from Paris, confiscation of mail from the Confederacy, requests for permits to trade with Southern ports, Copperhead activity in the New York Customhouse, and the protection of that customhouse during the draft riots. Still other records of collectors for the Civil War period are in the Federal Records Centers at East Point, Ga., Chicago, San Francisco, and Seattle. The records of the collector at Olympia, in the Seattle Center, relate among other matters to the withdrawal of the revenue cutter Shubrick, the arrival of the bark Torrent (which carried the famed Mercer girls to the Northwest), and the reservation and sale of town sites on public lands under the law of 1863.

National Archives, unpublished Preliminary Inventory of the Records of the Bureau of Marine Inspection and Navigation, comp. by Forrest R. Holdcamper.

MARINE HOSPITAL SERVICE

This Service, which in 1902 was to become the Public Health and Marine Hospital Service and in 1912 the Public Health Service, originated under an act of July 16, 1798 (1 Stat. 605), to provide temporary relief and maintenance of sick and disabled seamen in hospitals already established or to be acquired. A tax on seamen--paid by masters of all merchant ships arriving from foreign ports to the collectors of customs at the ports of arrival and by the masters of coastal vessels--was collected almost continuously from 1798 to 1870 and was supplemented by appropriations from other Government funds. Until the creation of a central administrative agency for the Marine Hospital Service by an act of June 29, 1870 (16 Stat. 169), directors of the marine hospitals established at various ports--usually ex officio the collectors of customs--rendered quarterly accounts direct to the Secretary of the Treasury.

In 1861 there were 24 U. S. Marine hospitals: along the Atlantic and Gulf coasts at Portland, Chelsea, Norfolk, Ocracoke, Wilmington, Charleston, Key West, St. Marks, and Mobile; on the Pacific coast at San Francisco; on the Mississippi River at Natchez, Napoleon, St. Louis, Burlington, and Galena; on the Ohio River at Paducah, Evansville, Louisville, Cincinnati, and Pittsburgh; and along the northern lakes at Chicago, Detroit, Cleveland, and Burlington. Concerning the marine hospitals at the outbreak of the Civil War, Secretary Chase wrote in his report of 1861:

> The number has been increased far beyond necessity or utility, and to the serious prejudice of the fund for sick and disabled seamen . . . At present, indeed, some of these hospitals are made available for the benefit of the troops, but this use must necessarily be partial and temporary. Of these, therefore, as well as those not thus used, the Secretary recommends that those least advantageously situated and employed be disposed of . . . and that no new structures be undertaken except in cases of the clearest expediency or necessity.

As a result of this recommendation an act of Mar. 1, 1862 (12 Stat. 348), authorized the Secretary to rent marine hospitals to municipal authorities and to contract with hospitals for the medical treatment of seamen. In point of fact the "mode of accommodation" used during the war varied: it included care in private hospitals, private homes, city hospitals, and infirmaries, and even "city counsel" care.

Statements of expenditures and receipts of the marine hospital fund, by fiscal year, appended to the Civil War annual reports of the Secretary of the Treasury on The State of the Finances; Laurence F. Schmeckebier, The Public Health Service . . . (Baltimore, 1923).

Record Group 90.--Now part of the records of the Public Health Service, the Civil War records of the Marine Hospital Service consist chiefly of letters and reports received by the Secretary of the Treasury, 1861-67 (11 vols.), from collectors or surveyors of customs and others concerning the hospitalization and care of individual sick and disabled seamen, the provision of funds and supplies, the staffing of marine hospitals, and similar matters. Included is some correspondence on the seizure of marine hospitals by the Confederacy and on the military and other use made of marine hospitals during the war (particularly for the care of wounded and sick soldiers and for emergency hospitalization after battles); offers or requests to lease for local purposes the less used marine hospitals; reports by boards of visitors and other inspectors on conditions at hospitals; and contracts and bids for the private care of seamen. This correspondence includes occasional copies of letters sent by the Secretary; from 1865 it is arranged by State of origin or destination. (The main file of letters on marine hospitals sent by the Secretary is in Record Group 56--see Office of the Secretary.)

There is also a "Statement of the Marine Hospital Fund," 1861-64 (3 vols.), showing expenditures and supplying sketchy statistical information on the number of patients and deaths.

Few hospital registers and related records for the Civil War period are extant, but the Federal Records Center in New York City has those kept by the Seamen's Rest and Retreat, Staten Island, 1843-88, including the minutes of its board of trustees, 1863-77.

National Archives, unpublished   ords of the Public Health Service,
Preliminary Checklist of the Rec-   comp. by Leo Pascal.

U. S. REVENUE-CUTTER SERVICE

The seagoing military service established by an act of Aug. 4, 1790 (1 Stat. 145), which authorized the construction and equipment of cutters to enforce the collection of customs and tonnage duties, was the nucleus of the U. S. Coast Guard. This service was under the administrative control of the Treasury Department. With no official name for the cutter force the semi-official terms Revenue Service and Revenue-Marine became popular, but Congress referred to the "United States revenue cutter service" in an act of Feb. 4, 1863 (12 Stat. 639). From 10 to 20 cutters at a time were in commission during the Revenue-Marine's first half-century; the service was expanded beginning in 1840; but after the Mexican War it gradually dwindled. The Revenue-Marine thus was unprepared for war in 1861, and it was further weakened at the outbreak of hostilities by the loss of some ships turned over by their commanders to Confederate or Southern State authorities. Its operations, however, were greatly expanded by the war. The President ordered many of its cutters to cooperate with the Navy, and those so assigned helped to seize Confederate shipping and ports, to maintain the blockade, to protect Union shipping, and to increase the Navy's support of Army operations.

The protection of the revenue became more important than ever with the higher tariffs of 1861, 1862, and 1864. From 1862 onward the Service aided also in preventing illegal immigration--specifically the importation of coolie labor, forbidden by an act of Feb. 19, 1862 (12 Stat. 340). In short, as Evans emphasizes in his "definitive history," no attempt was made to transform the Revenue-Marine into a "little navy," for "the vessels acquired by the Treasury were needed first and foremost for marine safety and law enforcement under war-time pressure." Despite the Navy's priority for the ships, the Revenue-Marine managed to acquire some of the additional tonnage it needed by purchase from private owners. One such acquisition was the Naugatuck (known as the Ironsides and as the E. A. Stevens), which had been designed by its owner to demonstrate the theories of the Stevens Battery. The cutter fleet was augmented also by the Treasury's own building program.

Cutters that participated in the war or in single episodes of extraordinary interest included the Miami, in which President Lincoln, Secretary Stanton, Secretary Chase, and General Viele made a secret reconnaissance down the Potomac in May 1862; the Naugatuck, which participated in the engagement against Sewell's Point; and the Harriet Lane, in the Navy's service from before the fall of Sumter until her capture at Galveston in 1863.

Stephen H. Evans, The United   bibliography in H. Doc. 670, 62 Cong.,
States Coast Guard, 1790-1915; a   2 sess., Serial 6298.
Definitive History (Annapolis, 1949);

Record Group 26. --Now part of the records of the United States Coast Guard, the Civil War records of the supervision of the Revenue-Marine or

Revenue-Cutter Service were originally records of the Office of the Secretary of the Treasury. The letters received comprise those from collectors of customs, 1861-65 (25 vols.); miscellaneous letters, 1861-64 (7 vols.); and letters from officers of revenue-cutters, 1861-65 (18 vols.)--all in registered series beginning before and ending after the war. Fair copies of the Secretary's letters sent on "Revenue-Marine and Boats," 1861-65, are in volumes 18-27 of that series, and there are 14 volumes of press copies of letters sent during the war. This correspondence relates chiefly to the operation of vessels active during the war and includes particulars on the surrender of vessels to the Confederacy by their officers who were Southern sympathizers, the construction of new vessels, and the transfer of private vessels from civilian to military use. Application files and registers cover the Civil War service of 85 officers of the Service and show the earlier Federal employment of Confederate officers; there are also 2 volumes of official copies of officers' commissions for the war period.

The series of logs or abstracts or transcripts of logs of Coast Guard vessels includes many logs of vessels in the Revenue-Marine or Revenue-Cutter Service during the Civil War. The logbook entries include data on the weather, crew, and significant activities of the cutter. The log of the Cutter Miami, Apr.-May 1862, records trips by President Lincoln with his family or members of his Cabinet and a trip to Fortress Monroe to protect the landing of troops there; and the logs of other cutters presumably contain useful information about tne war. The series includes the last logs kept in Federal service by several vessels that joined the Confederacy. Vessels whose available logs cover all or part of the war period are the following: Aaron Brown, Agassiz, Antietam, Ashuelot, Bronx (formerly Addison F. Andrews), Crawford, Cruiser, Cuyahoga (formerly Santa Anna), E. A. Stevens (named Naugatuck for 6 months in 1863), Flora (later Nemaha), George M. Bibb, Hercules, Isaac Toucey, Jacob Thompson, James Campbell, James C. Dobbin, Jefferson Davis, Jeremiah S. Black, Joe Miller, Joseph Lane (formerly Campbell), Kewanee, Mahoning (later Levi Woodbury), Miami (formerly Lady le Marchant), Morris, Naugatuck, Nemaha (formerly Flora), Northerner, Pawtuxet, Philip Allen, Reliance, Shubrick, Tiger, Varina, Wayanda, William H. Seward, and William L. Marcy. Muster rolls are available for many of these and other Revenue-Cutter Service vessels operating during the Civil War; these are monthly lists of officers and other personnel assigned to cutters, showing dates of enlistments and leave, discharges or desertions, and ranks and ratings.

National Archives, Preliminary Checklist of the Records of the United States Coast Guard, 1915-1941, comp. by Hope Frances Kane (Washington, 1945), and List of Logs of United States Coast Guard Vessels in the National Archives, 1790-1941, comp. by Thornton W. Mitchell and Arthur Dyer (processed by the U. S. Coast Guard; Washington, 1944).

STEAMBOAT-INSPECTION SERVICE

Although the Steamboat-Inspection Service was not put definitely under the control of the Secretary of the Treasury until 1871, the "Steamboat Act" of Aug. 30, 1852 (10 Stat. 61), had given the Secretary some indirect supervision over the work of the Service. Under sec. 18 of this act, which superseded earlier laws for safeguarding the lives of passengers and crews on steamboats and other vessels, 9 (later 11) supervising inspectors were appointed by the President with the advice and consent of the Senate. These inspectors acted in a dual capacity. As a board they established regulations for the uniform administration of the inspection laws and defined the territory to be supervised by each inspection. As an individual each inspector in his own district supervised the work of local inspectors, helped in the actual work of inspection, reported cases of neglect or inefficiency to the Secretary of the Treasury, and furnished the Secretary with technical information. Under sec. 9 of the act local inspectors-usually one for hulls and one for boilers--were chosen (subject to the approval of the Secretary of the Treasury) by a commission consisting of the district collector of customs, the supervising steamboat inspector, and the judge of the U. S. district court. Local inspectors also had twofold responsibilities: as a board they licensed and classified engineers and pilots of passenger-carrying steamers and investigated accidents, and as individuals they inspected hulls, boilers, and equipment.

Besides approving the appointment of local inspectors, the Secretary of the Treasury, under the 1852 act, received reports of the Board of Supervising Inspectors, checked on the operations of the inspection laws, and made appropriate recommendations to Congress. He was represented at the annual meetings of the Board by a personal agent. During the Civil War such meetings were held at Philadelphia, Boston, New York, and St. Louis; and the reports of the Board president, sent soon after each meeting to the Secretary of the Treasury, show that despite "the great disturbing element which results from the war, in the use of steamers as transports by the government to carry troops," both inspectors and steamboat owners seemed "ready in their compliance with the provisions of the law." The war affected the Steamboat-Inspection Service also because parts of some of its supervising districts were occasionally or continually under Confederate jurisdiction.

Investigation of wartime steamboat disasters not only detected violations of safety regulations but helped improve safety standards. Among such disasters were the loss of the Nevada, Feb. 7, 1862, bound from Sacramento to San Francisco; of the Golden Gate, July 27, 1862, with 138 passengers and a crew of 37 en route from San Francisco to Panama; and of the Pocohontas in a gale at Cape Hatteras Inlet, Jan. 18, 1862, while en route to North Carolina carrying horses for the Burnside Expedition. Other disasters included the collision of the George Peabody and the West Point on the Potomac River near Ragged Point, Aug. 13, 1862; the sinking of the Acacia in the Mississippi, Aug. 20, 1862, en route from Memphis, Tenn., to Helena, Ark. ; the destruction by fire, at the wharf at St. Louis, of the H. D. Bacon, the T. L. McGill, the Wm. H. Russell, the A. McDowell, and the Estella, Oct. 27, 1862; the explosion of the boiler of the J. H. Dickey on the Illinois shore of the Mississippi, Nov. 5, 1862, with a loss of 14 lives; and the burning of the Ruth, Aug. 4, 1863, 6 miles below Cairo, with a loss of 30 lives and a quantity of U. S. notes--an affair investigated by a War Department commission discussed elsewhere in this Guide.

John Shallcross, president of the Board of Supervising Inspectors of Steamboats in 1861, was succeeded in 1864 by P. B. Stillman.

Civil War reports of the Board of Supervising Inspectors of Steamboats, appended to the annual reports of the Secretary of the Treasury on The State of the Finances; Lloyd M. Short, Steamboat-Inspection Service . . . (New York and London, 1922).

Record Group 41. --Now among the records of the Commerce Department's Bureau of Marine Inspection and Navigation, the extant Civil War records of the Steamboat-Inspection Service consist of files of both the Office of the Secretary of the Treasury and some of the supervising districts. The former include copies of letters sent by the Secretary to supervising and local inspectors (and to collectors of customs acting as inspectors) dealing with inspections of vessels, accounts, complaints, rules and regulations, and appointments; and some letters and reports received by him, chiefly on personnel matters, steamboat disasters, and inspections. Covering the Civil War also are an index to the Board's proceedings as printed during the war; samples of the forms employed in licensing and certifying vessels; and copies of commissions for local inspectors of hulls and boilers.

Most of the records of supervisory inspectors' offices, 1852-1911, have been lost or destroyed. For the Civil War period only those of the Sixth District, at Louisville, Ky. (including affidavits of loyalty and oaths of allegiance for officers of steam vessels, 1862-65), are available. The extant Civil War records of local inspectors or boards (chiefly copies of certificates of inspection of vessels, applications for license as pilot or engineer-- some with oaths of allegiance--and reports of casualties and violations) originated at Burlington, Vt. , Fairfield and New London, Conn. , New York City, Philadelphia, Baltimore, Cleveland, and Detroit.

National Archives, unpublished   of the Bureau of Marine Inspection and
Preliminary Inventory of the Records   Navigation, comp. by F. R. Holdcamper.

U. S. COAST SURVEY

After a suspension of some 20 years the systematic survey of the U. S. coasts, authorized by an act of Feb. 10, 1807 (2 Stat. 413), was resumed under an act of July 10, 1832 (4 Stat. 570), which revived the earlier act. From this time until 1903, except for 1834-36, the Survey operated under the Treasury Department. In 1836 its name was changed from Survey of the Coast to Coast Survey, and in 1878 to Coast and Geodetic Survey.

Alexander D. Bache had succeeded Ferdinand R. Hassler as Superintendent of the Coast Survey in 1843. Carrying out a plan drawn up by a board established by an act of Mar. 3, 1843 (5 Stat. 640), Bache had divided the coasts in "sections" and had established many field parties to work simultaneously under a master plan and uniform standards. As regent of the Smithsonian Institution, president of the American Association for the Advancement of Science, and first president of the National Academy of Sciences, Bache could cooperate effectively with the American scientific community of the time. His contacts with the Army and the Navy were close and continuous: he served on a Navy commission to consider the location of a navy yard in New England and on the Navy's Commission on Conference, and he kept abreast of the surveys of the Army's Corps of Engineers. During the Confederate penetration of Pennsylvania he was chief engineer with State military and civil authorities in planning and providing the defenses of Philadelphia.

In 1861 surveys of the coast were in progress in every seaboard State and Territory, either in the field, afloat, or in the Washington office, "pressing forward to completion, according to a determined plan which would have finished it on the Atlantic and Gulf coast in some eight years. " Despite the Confederate seizure of two Survey vessels in Charleston harbor and the necessity for assistants to abandon their work on occasion, there was little significant property loss. During the war, however, the usual field operations were necessarily restricted. In the South they were carried on only when practicable, usually in association with naval operations. Surveys ordered during the war for defense purposes--for instance, those carried on in the vicinity of Washington--were often combined with the Survey's work. Because Army and Navy officers assigned to the Survey returned to service--some to Confederate service--operations from 1861 were generally carried out by civilians.

The danger of Confederate attack on some northern cities, particularly Washington, led the Survey to concentrate work on the waters and land around Washington, Baltimore, St. Louis, Philadelphia, and a few New England cities. It made detailed surveys along the Delaware, Potomac, Rappahannock, James, Tennessee, and Mississippi Rivers; and it mapped the Eastern Shore of Maryland and Virginia and an area near Manassas, Va. Water approaches to New England ports were surveyed as far north as Portland, Maine; the effective range of artillery near Washington and New York was determined; and geodetic data were provided for many military posts. Survey units were active in many field campaigns, and Coast Survey steamers (including the Corwin, the Bibb, and the Vixen), when not actually employed for Survey purposes, were used by the Navy. The Survey aided DuPont's assault on forts guarding Port Royal, S. C., by sounding and buoy-laying; facilitated Farragut's penetration of the lower Mississippi River; and examined Charleston Bar in preparation for an attack in that area; and Survey ships and men were used in the Union blockade of the southeast coast. During the sieges of Vicksburg and Port Hudson the Survey gave direct assistance in the Mississippi and Yazoo Rivers; Sherman had several Survey employees with him on his march to the sea; and Survey personnel aided the attack on Fort Fisher, near Wilmington, N. C. One of the most active Coast Survey topographers served with the Direct Tax Commission for Florida, at its request, and while there supervised the erection of more earthworks at Jacksonville.

The unprecedented demand for maps and charts strained to the utmost the Survey's resources. It had issued fewer than 10,000 charts annually before the war, but it produced 44,000 in 1862 and 66,000 in 1863.

Because the Washington office of the Coast Survey was regarded as another "party," it--like the field parties--was directed by an Assistant in Charge, who during Bache's absence acted as Superintendent. When Maj. W. H. Palmer died in June 1862, J. E. Hilgard succeeded him as Assistant in Charge. His office included Computing, Hydrographic, Tidal, Drawing, Engraving, Lithographing, Photograph and Electrotype, and Miscellaneous Divisions. Some of the wartime work of these divisions may be noted briefly. The Computing Division (under Charles A. Schott) had the continuing task of investigating and discussing the "secular change of the magnetic density (horizontal and total) on the Atlantic, Gulf, and Pacific Coasts of the United States." The Hydrographic Division (under C. P. Patterson, a former naval officer, who was to become Superintendent in 1874) examined and verified original hydrographic work, furnished sailing directions, compiled hydrographic sketches, and made projections for hydrographic parties. The Tidal Division (under L. F. Pourtales) prepared tide tables from data supplied by permanent stations. The Drawing Division (successively under Lt. Thomas Wilson, Henry L. Whiting, Capt. Thomas J. Lee, A. M. Harrison, and-- from 1864--J. E. Hilgard, the Assistant in Charge) prepared the maps and

charts, after compiling the topographic and hydrographic data for them.
As an example of its special activities, it produced hastily by photography
a "military map of the ground of occupation and advance of the Army of the
Potomac," which it furnished "in much less time than could have been done
by any other process." The Engraving Division (successively under Lt. J. R.
Smead and Edward Wharton) engraved the finished maps and charts and
added to them, as needed, "sailing directions, soundings, title letterings
and sand outlines." It was successful in engraving on copper from reductions by photography "with as much facility as from hand reductions." The
Lithographing Division (successively under W. L. Nicolson, F. A. P.
Barnard, and W. W. Cooper) was organized in May 1861 to help the Engraving Division supply charts to the Navy more rapidly and to print "a set
of descriptive memoirs and sailing directions for the coast, for the use of
naval and military commanders." The Photograph and Electrotype Division
(under George Mathiot) reduced the original sheets of the Survey by photography, made electrotypes of the engraved plates, and extended "the application of photography in the copying of drawings of important tables, letters
and maps not produced in the office." The Miscellaneous Division (headed
successively by Lt. N. H. McLean, R. D. Cutts, Edward Goodfellow, W. L.
Nicolson, and F. A. P. Barnard) consisted of a printing office, a map room,
and a distributing office for maps and reports.

Bache remained the nominal head of the Coast Survey after a stroke in
1864 until his death in 1867.

The annual reports of the Super-   war period were published as con-
intendent of the Coast Survey for the   gressional documents as follows:

1861. H. Ex. Doc. 70, 37 Cong. , 2 sess. , Serial 1134.
1862. H. Ex. Doc. 22, 37 Cong. , 3 sess. , Serial 1165.
1863. H. Ex. Doc. 11, 38 Cong. , 1 sess. , Serial 1188.
1864. H. Ex. Doc. [15], 38 Cong. , 2 sess. , Serial 1224.
1865. H. Ex. Doc. 75, 39 Cong. , 1 sess. , Serial 1264.

Almost as valuable for historical   also U. S. Department of Commerce,
purposes are the Superintendent's   The Coast and Geodetic Survey; 150
wartime estimates of appropria-   Years of History (Washington,1957);
tions (see especially those in Serials   and Gustavus A. Weber, The Coast and
1127, 1186, 1222, and 1254). See   Geodetic Survey... (Baltimore, 1923).

Record Group 23. --The records of the Superintendent's immediate office are fairly complete for the Bache period. His general correspondence,
1844-65 (305 vols.), comprises letters received and copies of those sent,
as well as other papers, on internal administrative matters and field activities; included is his private correspondence (19 vols.), containing considerable information on the ante bellum American scientific community. (Most
of the 1864 and all of the 1865 records actually consist of the correspondence
of J. E. Hilgard, Assistant in Charge, acting for Bache. For a checklist of
the titles of the Bache correspondence volumes, see the National Archives
inventory cited below.) There are also a correspondence register, 1860-67;
a volume of "statistics," with other useful information, 1857-63; records of
Bache's service on a commission to consider the location of a navy yard at
League Island in the Delaware River, New London (Conn.), or Narragansett
Bay, 1862-63 (1 vol.); records relating to the defenses of Philadelphia,

1863-64 (2 vols.); and correspondence about the improvement of Boston Harbor and a proposed Cape Cod ship canal, 1859-61 (1 vol.). Reflecting Bache's work as a member of the Commission on Conference are the 1861 "Notes on the Coast of the United States" (7 vols.), prepared for the confidential use of the Navy, and (in vol. 3 of a subseries of reports, papers, and memoranda of the Superintendent, ca. 1859-98) copies of reports made in 1861 by the same Commission to the Secretary of the Navy on naval operations against the Confederacy. Some letters to Bache are in a volume of correspondence, 1863-75, with Harry Mitchell, specialist in the effects of tides and currents on the shoreline and in the erection of structures to modify these effects.

Closely related to the records of the immediate Office of the Superintendent are those of the Assistant in Charge of the Washington office. For the Civil War period these include letters received, press copies of letters sent to the Superintendent, and fair copies of letters sent that relate to the organization and procedures of the Washington office. There are miscellaneous indexes to this correspondence and 4 volumes of "occupations" (service histories) of Survey employees, 1844-1902, with gaps.

With the incoming letters of Disbursing Agent Samuel Hein are 2 documents relating to the Coast Survey's Civil War service and 2 registers, 1843-64 and 1843-81, of "authorities" for procurement, personnel actions, and the maintenance and repair of Survey buildings and vessels. Other records of the period kept by the disbursing agent include a volume showing deductions for "Tax on Salaries," 1862-64 and 1868.

The Hydrographic Division's wartime records consist of letters received, 1863-65, from Survey personnel (including those from Bache in 1863); a register of the receipt of logbooks from field parties; and abstract vouchers of the monthly expenses of hydrographic parties, 1860-64--mainly for pay and subsistence of the crews of the Arago, the Bailey, the Bibb, the Corwin, and the Vixen.

The Computing Division is represented in the war period by some "Reports, Base-Bars," 1844-98 (2 vols.), prepared or received by Division Chief C. A. Schott; geodetic reports; and some articles on geodesy, most of them by Schott, reprinted from appendixes to the annual reports of the Survey.

Although the Engraving, Lithographing, Drawing, and Photograph and Electrotype Divisions are not represented by distinct series of records for the Civil War period, their work is indicated in a record of labor costs for engraved plates, 1855-98 (which incidentally provides a history of the various editions of maps printed from the plates), and in a record of costs for preparing and altering plates from which charts were printed, 1844-1904.

Most of the scientific records of the Survey during the Civil War are in the collection assembled by the Survey's Library and Archives, which has served as a central filing point for such records since 1844. They include chiefly observations made by Survey field parties, classified according to the type of observation or computation involved, in separate "series" beginning before, continuing during, and ending long after the war. The following Library and Archives registers are also available: "personal accounts," 1850-1906 (5 vols.), which are registers of scientific records received; section registers, ca. 1844-87 (10 vols.), recording the receipt of geodetic, magnetic, astronomic, and gravity observations and computations; a register of hydrographic records received, 1834-98; registers of the receipt of observations of tides, 1832-98 (2 vols.); a register of the receipt of topographic sheets from field parties, 1834-1900; and a register of the receipt of hydrographic charts prepared by field parties, 1836-1901.

The logbooks of Survey vessels during the Civil War are in an extensive series, 1846-1947, arranged alphabetically by name of vessel; these logs supplement records of scientific observations. Other field records include those of a hydrographic party attached to the Mississippi Squadron; among these are letters describing some military and naval operations.

There are also cartographic records, from 1851, including nautical and outline charts, some showing primary triangulations, from the Survey's annual reports; and published and annotated nautical charts, from 1839, of the shorelines and coastal areas of the United States, showing such details as soundings, topography of shorelines, lifebuoys, lighthouses, and break-waters and giving sailing directions.

Civil War records of the Office of the Secretary of the Treasury pertaining to the Coast Survey are also in the record group, presumably transferred to the Coast and Geodetic Survey in 1903 when the agency was assigned to the newly extablished Department of Commerce and Labor. There are a volume of letters received, 1861-64, which contains letters to Secretary Chase from Superintendent Bache as president of the National Academy of Sciences; copies of letters sent, 1834-73 (5 vols.), which, during Bache's tenure, contain occasional references to his diverse official and private activities, including his service on the Light-House Board; and a few letters and other papers, dating from 1860.

National Archives, Preliminary   the Coast and Geodetic Survey, comp.
Inventory [No. 105] of the Records of   by Nathan Reingold (Washington, 1958).

OFFICE OF THE SUPERINTENDENT OF WEIGHTS AND MEASURES

During the period of the Civil War (and until the establishment of the National Bureau of Standards in 1901) the Superintendent of the Coast Survey served also as Superintendent of Weights and Measures. This office had originated at about the time the Survey of the Coast was revived in 1832, when the necessity for obtaining accurate meteorological instruments for survey work became apparent. The Office of Weights and Measures became the custodian of all the standards of weights and measures adopted by the Treasury Department except the troy pound at the U. S. Mint at Philadelphia. During the war it served not only the Coast Survey but also the Customs Service and other branches of the Government.

Gustavus A. Weber, The Bureau   and Organization (Baltimore, 1925).
of Standards; Its History, Activities

Record Group 167. --Among the records of the National Bureau of Standards are records of the former Office of Standard Weights and Measures, 1830-1901. Those of the Office of the Superintendent of Weights and Measures for the Civil War period include quarterly reports of accounts current, abstracts, and vouchers, 1845-66; the Superintendent's correspondence; computations of length, weight, density, and the like; and relevant observations and notes. (Because the executive head of this Office was also head of the Coast Survey, the records of the Survey contain much material relating to the Office; see U. S. Coast Survey, above.)

Also in this record group are papers of Jonathan Homer Lane, a principal examiner in the Patent Office and an assistant to Benjamin Peirce in the Office of Weights and Measures. His records include a research paper entitled "The Abolition Excitement," prepared in 1843 at Phillips Exeter Academy; letters, 1859, dealing with the dismissal of Whigs--including Lane--during the Buchanan administration; several documents, 1855-61, relating to a "visual telegraph" that Lane believed would be useful in war; and scientific notes concerning breech-loading cannon and the trajectory of projectiles, 1862-63.

LIGHT-HOUSE BOARD

An act of Aug. 31, 1852 (10 Stat. 119), created a Light-House Board, to be appointed by the President and attached to the Office of the Secretary of the Treasury. The Board comprised two officers of the Navy, two engineer officers of the Army, two civilian scientists, and another Navy officer and another Army engineer officer to serve as secretaries. The original Board--composed of the six members of a board of inquiry that had recently investigated the lighthouse service--concentrated on eliminating the administrative and scientific defects it had uncovered; and in the immediate prewar period it scientifically classified aids to navigation, perfected appliances, sought the latest equipment, and achieved adequate local supervision by dividing the coasts into districts and providing each district with an inspector (appointed from the Navy) and an engineer (appointed from the Army). The inspectors supervised the operation of the lighthouse service, and the engineers attended to construction and maintenance. The Board existed until an act of 1910 created the Bureau of Lighthouses in the Department of Commerce.

On Oct. 22, 1860, there were 425 lighthouses and lighted beacons on the coast and in the harbors of the United States and 47 "light-vessels" in operation. The Board believed that the lighthouse establishment had "about reached its maximum under our present limits, and that very few additional lights, no more perhaps than it may be found proper from time to time to discontinue, need to be added to meet all the just and reasonable wants of navigation." The 12 Light-House Districts through which control was administered during the Civil War were the following:

First: from the northern boundary of the United States to Hampton Harbor, N. H.

Second: from Hampton Harbor, N. H., to Gooseberry Inlet (or Point), Mass.

Third: from Gooseberry Inlet, Mass., to Squam Inlet, N. J., including the coasts of Long Island, Long Island Sound, the Hudson River, and Lake Champlain.

Fourth: from Squam Inlet, N. J., to Metomkin Inlet, Va., including Delaware Bay and its tributaries.

Fifth: from Metomkin Inlet, Va., to New River Inlet, N. C., including Chesapeake Bay and the sounds of North Carolina. (Most of the southern part of this District was controlled by the Confederacy, 1861-65. Immediately after the war an engineer was sent to "the waters of North Carolina" to reestablish such lights as might be necessary.)

Sixth: from New River Inlet, N. C., to Mosquito Inlet, Fla. (after 1862 to the lighthouse at Cape Canaveral). (Slow recovery of territory by U. S. forces impeded the Board's operations in this district, although an engineer examined the lighthouses there in 1863.)

Seventh: from Mosquito Inlet to Egmont Key, Fla.; after 1863 from St. Augustine to Egmont Key. (The lights in this district were kept in operation during the war.)

Eighth: from Sea Horse Key, Fla. (in 1864 from Egmont Key), to the western extremity of Lake Pontchartrain, La. (See note in the next paragraph.)

Ninth: from the passes of the Mississippi River to the Rio Grande. (The Eighth and Ninth Districts received during the war the special attention of the Board, and at the end of hostilities no effort was spared to reestablish the lights and other aids to navigation that had been discontinued by the Confederacy.)

Tenth: the coasts of Lakes Ontario and Erie and the St. Lawrence, Niagara, and Detroit Rivers.

Eleventh: the coasts of Lakes St. Clair, Huron, Superior, and Michigan, including Green Bay.

Twelfth: the entire Pacific coast of the United States.

With the outbreak of the war the service was affected chiefly by the seizure or destruction of its installations in the South. As the Light-House Board reported in 1861,

The extinguishment of lights from light-houses, removal of light-vessels, and the destruction or removal of all the other aids to navigation existing from the northern boundary of Virginia to the Rio Grande, excepting those on the peninsula of Florida (Jupiter Inlet to Dry Tortugas,) was continued until about the 24th of April, when the whole was accomplished. In a few instances the persons seizing the property claimed to do so by authority, and gave receipts for it; in others, the United States agents charged with its custody connived at the seizures, and in some instances the property was burned in mere wantonness.

From July 1861 the Board was without the services of an engineer secretary, and from June 7, 1862, without those of a naval secretary, since it was "difficult, if not impossible, to withhold from the more exciting and imposing scenes of the camp or the ship young officers eligible and qualified for the useful but less brilliant duties of the desk." In 1863 a committee of two was formed to obtain information to justify the Board's request "for such additional specific appropriations as the daily increasing and important commerce of the northwest calls for"; its report is appended to that of the Board for fiscal year 1863.

When the war ended the Board instructed the acting lighthouse engineers in the Southern districts to inquire about and if possible recover lighthouse property--the "illumination apparatus" and other material scattered during hostilities. Of the 164 lights discontinued in the Confederacy, 94 were rebuilt or repaired and relighted by 1866.

Adm. William B. Shubrick, elected the first chairman of the Light-House Board in 1852, served with minor interruptions for 19 years.

Civil War annual reports of the Light-House Board appended to those of the Secretary of the Treasury on The State of the Finances; D. P. Heap, Ancient and Modern Light-Houses (Boston, 1889); George Weiss, The Lighthouse Service . . . (Baltimore, 1926).

Record Group 26. --Some of the records of the Light-House Board were destroyed by the fire in the old Commerce Department Building in 1921; and Heap, writing in 1889, mentioned that the Board had "had to move four times since its organization in 1852, each time with damage and loss to its archives." Many of the surviving records are so badly damaged by fire and water that they can be used only under exceptional circumstances or after they have been repaired. The extant records, however, not only substantially document the wartime activities of the service but reveal the extent of damage to or discontinuance of the Southern lighthouses. The minutes of Board meetings, 1852-87 (11 vols.), are available. Many letters received during the war are in series of "official letters" from other Government agencies and foreign governments, 1833-1900 (67 vols.), on general matters; "department" letters to both the Board and the Secretary of the Treasury, 1861-1900 (45 vols.), on personnel details, bids, and appropriations; and "miscellaneous" letters from shippers, manufacturers, and others, 1833-1900 (42 vols.), concerning chiefly technical details of construction and navigation aids. There are also "lighthouse letters," 1860-64 (2 vols.), that apparently were originally part of the files of the Office of the Secretary of the Treasury; these contain notices of the capture of stations by Confederate forces, reports of raids and depredations, requests for guards, and requests from the Army and Navy for additional services. There is a subject index, on slips, to the incoming correspondence, 1852-1900.

Fair copies of letters sent during the war are in several series. These include letters signed by the Secretary of the Treasury, 1851-93 (12 vols.), on matters of policy; and the following letters sent by the Board: to the Secretary, 1852-94 (12 vols.); to Members of Congress, 1852-90 (3 vols.); to superintendents of lights, 1853-90 (10 vols.), concerning almost exclusively fiscal matters and equipment; to superintendents of lights and district inspectors and engineers, 1852-96 (2 vols.), on operational and personnel matters; to the Corps of Engineers, 1852-73 (1 vol.); to collectors of customs, the First Auditor of the Treasury, and other agency heads, 1859-88 (10 vols.); and to private individuals, factories, and firms, 1852-95 (20 vols.). There are also press copies of some of these.

The Light-House Districts, listed above, are represented by separate series of letters received from district inspectors or engineers during the war except for the Fourth, Sixth, Eighth, Ninth, and Tenth Districts. There are registers of letters received from the First and Seventh Districts. Fair copies of wartime letters sent to district inspectors or engineers are in separate series for all except the First and Fifth Districts. For the Third Lighthouse District the records kept in the district office also are extant.

Correspondence relating to the personnel of the service, 1821-1902 (12 ft.), includes nominations of lighthouse keepers and their assistants and records of appointment, promotion, transfer, and termination of service. There are also letters sent about appointments of keepers, 1861-66 (2 vols.),

Miscellaneous files now in this record group include some letters from engineer officers concerning lighthouse construction, ca. 1849-ca. 1876, and the title papers of vessels under the control of the Light-House Board, 1853-95. In more general series maintained or continued by the U. S. Coast Guard are papers relating to lighthouse sites; drawings, paintings, and photographs of lighthouses and lanterns; and "lighthouse scrapbooks"--all containing material of Civil War interest.

SPECIAL AGENCIES OF THE TREASURY DEPARTMENT

An act of July 13, 1861 (12 Stat. 257), prohibited commercial intercourse between people in areas "in a state of insurrection" and citizens of the rest of the Union and provided that merchandise being transported for commercial purposes from or to the Confederacy should be forfeited to the United States. The President, however, might "license and permit commercial intercourse . . . in such articles, and for such time, and by such persons, as he, in his discretion, may think most conducive to the public interest." The Secretary of the Treasury was authorized to appoint the officers necessary to enforce this law at places where there were no customs officers. The basic law was amended by acts of May 20, 1862 (12 Stat. 404), and July 2, 1864 (13 Stat. 375). The latter act permitted the President to license only the commerce necessary to supply the needs of loyal citizens in the occupied parts of the South and the traffic necessary for them to "bring or send to market" goods that they or their employees had produced.

Because the Secretary of the Treasury was given control over commercial intercourse, Treasury special agents became responsible for supervising trade and commerce in areas of the Confederacy occupied by the U. S. Army. They also, under acts of July 17, 1862, and Mar. 3, 1863 (12 Stat. 589, 820), and July 2, 1864 (cited above), were responsible for receiving and collecting abandoned, captured, and confiscable property. As Supervising Special Agent Benjamin Flanders reported from New Orleans in 1863, his duties were threefold--the "supervision or management of Internal trade"; the "collection, care and disposal of abandoned or Captured Property"; and "general Supervision of the Officers and interests of the Treasury Department in this District." Before the end of Mar. 1863 both War and Navy Department orders directed that captured and abandoned property be turned over to the Treasury agents.

The Special Agency system at first was somewhat haphazard; agents were appointed but no definite areas were assigned to them. Later five separate agencies were created, each assigned to a specific geographical jurisdiction; and by Treasury regulations of July 29, 1864 (approved by the President on July 30), a complete reorganization took place. Under these regulations a General Agent to supervise all agencies was appointed, and the existing agencies were redefined to form seven agencies. Ten months later, by the Treasury Department's amended general regulations of Apr. 25, 1865, the Eighth and Ninth Special Agencies were added. On June 13, 1865, the President lifted restrictions on commerce east of the Mississippi River, and on June 27 the Secretary of the Treasury curtailed the enforcement of regulations on captured and abandoned property. By this time the Special Agencies' functions concerning "refugees and freedmen" and abandoned lands had passed to the War Department's Bureau of Refugees, Freedmen, and Abandoned Lands. The responsibilities for abandoned lands had been manifest, but another significant function of the Special Agencies (formalized in the Treasury regulations approved by the President on July 30, 1864) had been that of "providing for the employment and general welfare of all persons within the lines of national military occupation . . . formerly held as slaves, who are or shall become free." Under superintendents of freedmen, the Treasury Department had established "freedmen's home colonies" for temporary shelter and care, and the superintendents had kept records of the freedmen in such colonies.

The Treasury regulations of July 29, 1864, explicitly ordered the Special

Agencies to maintain other records, and the records kept attest to the general observance of these orders. Local special agents were to keep records of permits, certificates, and bonds. Assistant special agents were to keep "a record of all their official transactions"--including authorizations to sell or transport goods; inspections, appointments, and seizures made by them; bonds required for shipment; and fees received. And, at the top level, the Supervising Special Agents were to keep "a record of all their official transactions, showing fully the name and location of each local special agent and agency aid appointed by them, and the compensation of each; of conferences with generals commanding departments, and designations of military lines . . . of all authorities given for supply stores, stating the date, name of trader, and amount of goods authorized; of the inspection of supply stores, and the results; of all authorities given for the transportation of products, to whom given, and the locality from which and to which transportation is permitted; . . . of all appointments of agency aids upon cars, vessels and boats; of all seizures and detentions of vessels or vehicles departing or attempting to depart after clearance has been refused; of all securities required and received of owners or holders of goods in danger of being transported to insurgents, and of their action if security was not given. "

For "abandoned, captured, and confiscable" personal and real property, equally detailed records were to be kept. Moreover, books of account were required to show "products or moneys" received. If a Federal court was in operation, copies of the records of confiscable lands and other property had to be sent to the appropriate U. S. district attorney that he might institute proceedings for confiscation.

The Commissioner of Customs, responsible for keeping accounts of captured and abandoned property and of commercial intercourse with States and parts of States declared "in insurrection," had some supervision over the Special Agencies. The postwar Division of Restricted Commercial Intercourse and Captured and Abandoned Property--a part of the Commissioner's Office--had duties that required extensive use of the agencies' records. These responsibilities and the resulting records of the Office of the Commissioner of Customs are described above, but it should be noted that papers that apparently belong in the files of either the Commissioner or the Secretary of the Treasury are among the agencies' records. Most of the records of the Special Agencies pertaining to the care of freedmen were taken over and continued by the Assistant Commissioners of the Bureau of Refugees, Freedmen, and Abandoned Lands; these are described under the War Department, in the section on that Bureau. The remaining--and more voluminous--records, described agency by agency below, are in amount about equally divided between those pertaining to restricted commercial intercourse and those pertaining to captured, abandoned, and confiscable property. Besides the agency records there are, in Record Group 56, records belonging to the General Agent, who supervised the nine agencies, containing at least some letters received by him.

In Record Group 56 are the manuscript general regulations prescribed by Secretary of the Treasury Fessenden on July 29, 1864, and approved by President Lincoln on July 30, 1864; related handwritten instructions signed by the Secretary of the Navy, the Secretary of War, and the Quartermaster General; and other printed and manuscript regulations. The entire set of regulations, as finally approved, together with pertinent acts of Congress and Presidential proclamations, is included in

the 1864 report of the Secretary of   Finances (H. Ex. Doc. 3, 38 Cong.,
the Treasury on The State of the   2 sess., Serial 1222).

First Special Agency (Valley of the Mississippi)

The First Special Agency was created Sept. 11, 1863, to comprise "the district of the United States west of the Alleghany Mountains, known as the Valley of the Mississippi and extending southward, so as to include so much of the States of Alabama, Mississippi, Arkansas, and Louisiana as is or may be occupied by national forces operating from the North." With the reorganization of July 1864 much of the area of the First Special Agency was allocated to the new Second Special Agency, and the Supervising Special Agent of the First Special Agency, William P. Mellen, officially became General Agent, supervising all the agencies. Under this new arrangement the First Special Agency had jurisdiction over the trans-Allegheny region as far as the mouth of the Tennessee River (Paducah, Ky.) and southward to include parts of Alabama, Georgia, North Carolina, and Virginia that were or might be occupied by Union forces. In Aug. 1865 the boundaries were formally extended in Georgia and Alabama to take in about two-thirds of each State. Successively serving as Supervising Special Agent after Mellen were B. R. Bonner, T. C. Callicot, James R. Dillin, and H. M. Bulkley.

Record Group 56.--Since the First and Second Special Agencies were at one time united, complete segregation of the records of each has not been possible. The records that can be identified as belonging to the First Special Agency, ca. 1863-65 (about 115 vols. and many unbound papers), comprise correspondence of the Supervising Special Agent; personnel records; records relating to the Franklin, Tenn., district, the Huntsville (Athens, Ala.) district, areas in Georgia, and the Knoxville and Nashville districts; records relating to general trade and specifically to trade and supply stores, to cotton, and to captured, abandoned, or confiscated property; records concerning customhouses or surveyors of customs; and miscellaneous records. Many applications of soldiers to establish trade or supply stores include copies of their discharge certificates. Among the records relating to cotton is a "Full story of cotton seizures, purchases and shipments," 1863-65 (3 vols.).

Second Special Agency (Tennessee, Arkansas, Mississippi, Louisiana)

The territory of the Second Special Agency--the Mississippi Valley west of the mouth of the Tennessee River, including western Tennessee, Arkansas, and the parts of Mississippi and Louisiana occupied by U. S. forces operating from the north--was set off from the First Special Agency in the reorganization of 1864. W. W. Orme and David G. Barnitz served successively as Supervising Special Agent.

Record Group 56.--Since the Second Special Agency was at one time united with the First, complete segregation of the records of each has not been possible. The records that can be identified as belonging to the Second Special Agency, ca. 1863-65 (about 160 vols. and several ft.), comprise general records and records of the Cairo, Helena, Little Rock, Memphis, Natchez, St. Louis, Skipwith, and Vicksburg districts. The general records include the Supervising Special Agent's correspondence, personnel records, some letters throwing light on economic and political conditions,

and records relating to cotton and trade and to captured or abandoned property. Among the district records are reports of the passage of goods
through picket lines (Memphis); letters received concerning the leased or
captured plantations and freedmen employed on them (Natchez); and correspondence of the assistant special agent (Vicksburg) about the opening up of
the Mississippi River trade and conditions in Vicksburg. (The Little Rock
district's bonds of applicants to establish trade stores illustrate the precise
information often found; on the printed forms the words "supply store" are
crossed out and words such as dental office, photographic gallery, bakery, etc.,
are written in. In another district permits were granted "to make and repair clothing," "to make and repair Harness and Saddlery," to operate
"Eating Houses" and "Billiard Rooms, " and "to repair Boots and Shoes.")
The many permits and other papers required for supplies taken into Natchez indicate the rigid control exercised.

Record Group 105. --Some records of the Vicksburg district of the Sec-
ond Special Agency (ca. 15 vols.) are among the records of the Bureau of
Refugees, Freedmen, and Abandoned Lands, which succeeded to certain
functions of the Treasury agents. These records are described under War
Department--Bureau of Refugees, Freedmen, and Abandoned Lands--
Assistant Commissioner for Mississippi.

Third Special Agency
(Louisiana, Mississippi, Texas, Arkansas, Alabama, Florida)

Benjamin F. Flanders became Supervising Special Agent at New Orleans
on May 16, 1863, with jurisdiction over Louisiana, Mississippi, and Texas.
Under Treasury regulations approved by the President on Sept. 11, 1863,
his area was designated as the Fifth Special Agency, to comprise Texas and
the areas in Louisiana, Arkansas, Alabama, and Mississippi occupied by
U. S. forces operating from the south. On June 3, 1864, Flanders was assigned control of the west coast of Florida and Key West, but under the reorganization of July 1864 his area became the Third Special Agency and no
longer included Arkansas, Texas, and the port of Key West. On Apr. 25,
1865, the boundaries of the agency were "modified so that it comprises so
much of the States of Louisiana and Mississippi as lies south of Grand Gulf,
and including that place."

Record Group 56. --The close relationship of Flanders with George S.
Denison (a friend of Secretary Chase and a special agent and acting collector of customs at New Orleans), the extension of Flanders' authority at
times over parts of Florida and Texas, and particularly his dealings with
military officials in regard to freedmen before the establishment of the Bureau of Refugees, Freedmen, and Abandoned Lands give peculiar value to
some records of his agency. The records, ca. 1863-65 (about 132 vols.
and many unbound papers), are organized by subject--New Orleans shipping, trade in prohibited articles, trade and supply stores, purchase and
transport of family and plantation supplies, marketing of plantation products, cotton (chiefly records of the agency's Captured Cotton Bureau), plantation property (chiefly records of the agency's Plantation Bureau), and
other real and personal property. There also are general correspondence
files, personnel and payroll records, and records relating to the general
work of the agency (such as journals, ledgers, cash books, accounts current, and monthly statistical returns of agency business). Among the incoming letters are some endorsed by N. P. Banks, E. R. S. Canby, S. A.

Hurlbut, and other military officers, and letters from George S. Denison; the outgoing letters include copies of letters to Chase, Fessenden, McCulloch, Banks, Canby, and Denison. There are also correspondence and other papers of G. W. Brackenridge, including his report of a trip to Mexico, Mar. 11-Apr. 20, 1864, and his conversations with Mexican Government officials. Included in the records about supply stores are some soldiers' discharge papers.

Fourth Special Agency (Texas)

Before a separate agency for Texas was set up under the reorganization of July 1864, the State was part of the Third and later of the Fifth Special Agency. But no agents appear to have been appointed expressly for the Fourth Special Agency until the surrender of Confederate General Kirby-Smith; instead, agents appointed for Texas by B. F. Flanders, Supervising Special Agent of the Third Special Agency, reported to him at New Orleans. The best known of these agents were G. W. Brackenridge and H. C. Warmoth, some of whose records are among those of the Third Special Agency. On July 28, 1865, Secretary McCulloch appointed O. N. Cutler, then purchasing agent at New Orleans, as Special Agent to collect captured and surrendered cotton in Texas and in Louisiana west of the Mississippi. But Flanders' agents continued to operate in Texas, and McCulloch decided to divide the Fourth Special Agency into two divisions under O. H. Burbridge and Cutler. Neither of these agents, however, ever left for Texas. The situation was somewhat clarified on Oct. 3, 1865, when Cutler resigned, Burbridge apparently was transferred to the Third Special Agency, and George S. Denison was appointed Supervising Special Agent for the entire Fourth Special Agency. Less than 3 months later, however, Denison, discouraged by the state of affairs, resigned; and on Dec. 26 George W. Dent was appointed his successor.

Record Group 56.--Correspondence and other papers of Supervising Special Agent Cutler, June-Nov. 1865 (6 in.); a little correspondence of the assistant special agents; press copies (some illegible) of letters sent by Denison and his successor George W. Dent, Oct. 1865-Apr. 1866; a few letters received and other papers of Denison and Dent, 1865-66; and accounts, permits to ship, and property lists relating chiefly to cotton, 1865-66 (6 vols. and a few unbound papers).

Other Denison material is among the records of the Third Special Agency, of which he was an agent before going to Texas. Letters of Denison to Secretary Chase, May 1862-Mar. 1865, are printed in the Diary and Correspondence of Salmon P. Chase (American Historical Association, Annual Report, 1902, 2:297-458); the originals of these are in the Salmon P. Chase papers at the Library of Congress. Also at the Library, in the George S. Denison papers, are family letters written by Denison from Texas and Louisiana.

Fifth Special Agency (South Carolina, Georgia, Florida)

In Dec. 1861 Secretary Chase sent Edward L. Pierce to visit the captured Sea Islands off the coast of South Carolina and report on the conditions of the Negroes there; and on Feb. 19, 1862, he appointed Pierce a special agent of the Treasury Department to superintend "the culture of

plantations and the employment of laborers thereon." Pierce's activities
were reduced by the transfer of such affairs from the Treasury to the War
Department on July 1, 1862. On May 1, 1863, however, a full-fledged
Treasury agency was established in the parts of South Carolina, Georgia,
and Florida occupied by U. S. troops operating from the south.

Pierce was appointed Supervising Special Agent, and about June 1863
the region he administered became the Fourth Special Agency, comprising
the States of South Carolina, Georgia, and Florida. Albert C. Browne
succeeded Pierce as Supervising Special Agent of the then Fourth Special
Agency on Sept. 23, 1863, and under the reorganization of July 1864 much
of what had constituted the Fourth Special Agency became the Fifth--"the
south and east part of Florida, including Key West," South Carolina, and
the part of Georgia occupied by U. S. forces operating from the south.
(The western part of Florida was put under the Third Special Agency and
later was absorbed by the Ninth. The part of Georgia occupied by U. S.
forces operating from the north was put under the First Special Agency.)
The boundaries of the Fifth Special Agency were considerably modified by
amended general regulations of Apr. 25, 1865, creating the Eighth Special
Agency, consisting of South Carolina and "so much of the State of Georgia
as lies in and east of the valley of the Ogeechee river, including the city of
Savannah. "

Record Group 56. --The records, 1863-66 (ca. 37 vols. and many unbound papers), comprise general correspondence, regulations, accounts,
and reports; records of shipping and property registration; records relating to the Sea Islands area of South Carolina; and a very few records relating to Florida. The Sea Islands records--pertaining to Beaufort, Hilton
Head, etc. --are among the most important of this agency. They consist of
a sales book of captured, confiscated, or abandoned property; schedules of
appraised captured or abandoned property; papers relating to the establishment of trade and to supply stores; and papers relating to incoming and outgoing shipments and to supplies for families and plantations. Still more
important is the "Port Royal Correspondence"--original letters to Secretary
Chase, 1861-62 (1 vol.), from officials concerned with Port Royal after its
capture in Nov. 1861, particularly the military authorities, the collector of
customs at New York, Lt. Col. William H. Reynolds (detailed from the War
Department to handle cotton captured at Port Royal and other Southern ports),
and E. L. Pierce. The correspondence gives details about the establishment of Federal authority in this important coastal region and the exploitation of the famous "Sea Island cotton" and describes the earliest means
adopted to care for and educate the freedmen. Also among the records of
this agency are those of or relating to Gazaway Bugg Lamar, an important
Confederate financier, president of the Bank Convention of the Confederate
States and an active blockade runner. The Lamar records include personal
letter books, 1861-65 (4 vols.); the "Lamar Cotton Books, " 1862-64 (2 vols.);
stock books of the Southern Steamship Co. of Alabama and Georgia and of the
Exporting and Importing Co. of Georgia, 1863 (2 vols.); newspaper clippings,
1865; and a record of shipping marks of seized cotton at Thomasville, Ga.

Sixth Special Agency (North Carolina)

North Carolina, within the jurisdiction of the original Third Special
Agency from Sept. 11, 1863, was constituted as the Sixth Special Agency
under the reorganization of July 1864, "excepting so much thereof as lies

north of Albemarle sound and east of Chowan river." David Heaton, who
had headed the old Third Agency, continued as Supervising Special Agent of
the Sixth.

Record Group 56. --The records, ca. 1863-65 (17 vols. and many unbound papers), comprise Heaton's correspondence and reports; accounts
and reports of local special agents; applications to set up trade and supply
stores; applications to import or export and to ship products locally; a record of cotton and miscellaneous property received and shipped; Heaton's
account with C. B. Dibble & Co., New York City; records of leases of abandoned plantations and other property; records of vessel arrivals and departures, coastwise inbound manifests, cargo manifests, and internal revenue
tax collections at Wilmington, N. C.; and records of the sale or other disposition of captured and abandoned property. Heaton's scanty correspondence includes the original of a letter to Maj. Gen. B. F. Butler, June 23,
1864; a copy of a letter to Lt. Gen. U. S. Grant, Apr. 24, 1865; and two
printed letters, May 24, 1864, to Chase, and Feb. 11, 1865, to Fessenden,
concerning the work of the agency.

Record Group 105. --A record of leases at Wilmington, N. C., Mar. 21-
July 13, 1865, is among the records of the Assistant Commissioner for
North Carolina of the Bureau of Refugees, Freedmen, and Abandoned Lands;
see under War Department.

Seventh Special Agency (Virginia, North Carolina)

Under Treasury regulations of July 29, 1864, the Seventh Special Agency
comprised "that section of country lying east of the Alleghany mountains,
and extending southwardly to include so much of the State of North Carolina
as lies north of Albemarle sound and east of Chowan river." Most of this
area had been under the jurisdiction of the old Second Special Agency, created Sept. 11, 1863. Hanson A. Riley, who had headed that agency, became
Supervising Special Agent of the Seventh; he was later to become Solicitor
of the Treasury.

Record Group 56. --The records of the old Second Special Agency and the
successor Seventh Special Agency, ca. 1863-65 (75 vols. and many unbound
papers), were and are kept together. They are of particular interest because they relate to agency jurisdiction over an area largely under U. S.
military control. The Supervising Special Agent had his office in Washington,
D. C., and was in direct contact with the Treasury Department. His records consist of letters received and sent, with registers; some miscellaneous papers (including returns for taxes on salaries paid); and reports received of customs transactions.

Among this agency's records are those of local and assistant special
agents at Norfolk (concerning captured or seized and abandoned property,
collection of rents, and trade stores); at Hagerstown, Md., and Harper's
Ferry (especially interesting because of the military activity in this area
and relating primarily to the capture and seizure of property); and at Alexandria, Va. (concerning captured and abandoned property, "traders" in the
city, and the restoration of personal property). Comprehensive records apparently maintained by agency headquarters chiefly concern internal and
coastwise commerce and include reports from customs officers and agents
and authorizations to trade and to open trade stores. There are also many
account books.

Records of liaison with the military include a few papers, Sept. 21,

1863-Feb. 18, 1864, and a bound volume, Sept. 21, 1863-Aug. 6, 1864, recording conferences with military commanders (Brig. Gen. B. F. Kelley,
Maj. Gen. George G. Meade, Maj. Gen. George S. Shipley, and others); inventories of captured and abandoned property in the hands of or turned over
by the military (several vols.); and military permits, 1863-65, to transport
food and other goods through the lines, with registers.

Eighth Special Agency (South Carolina, Georgia)

By the Treasury Department's amended general regulations of Apr. 25,
1865, two more Special Agencies were established. One of these, the Eighth,
comprised South Carolina and "so much of the State of Georgia as lies in and
east of the valley of the Ogeechee river including the city of Savannah." T. C.
Callicot, who had been Supervising Special Agent of the First Special Agency,
was transferred to head the Eighth.

Record Group 56. --The relatively few records of this agency contain several items of interest: some copies of Confederate papers made by or for the
agency; a record of "cotton shipped A. 1. ," Nov. 20, 1861-Feb. 7, 1865,
certified by a former officer of the Confederate customhouse at Charleston
on Jan. 10, 1866; estimates of disbursements and monthly accounts current, 1865-66; a cotton registration book, Mar.-May 1865; and records
of leases for houses and tenements at Charleston, June-July 1865.

Ninth Special Agency (Florida, Alabama)

By the Treasury Department's amended general regulations of Apr. 25,
1865, the new Ninth Special Agency included the "west part of Florida and
so much of the State of Alabama as lies south of the Alabama and Mississippi Railroad." The Alabama area was slightly curtailed in Aug. 1865 to
the part of the State south of Sumter, Marengo, Dallas, Lowndes, and Russell Counties. T. C. A. Dexter was appointed Supervising Special Agent in
Apr. 1865; he resigned in October and was succeeded by J. M. Tomeny.
(Dexter was later arrested and charged with fraud during his term of office.)

Record Group 56.--The records, ca. 1865-66 (38 vols. and a few un-
bound papers), consist of general correspondence; records of the Pensacola,
Apalachicola, and Mobile offices; and records relating to cotton transactions.
Incoming letters, addressed chiefly to Dexter, include letters from Secretary McCulloch, Assistant Secretary Hartley, and Commissioner of Customs
Sargent. (A volume of Tomeny's letters sent, begun in the Second Special
Agency and continued in the Ninth, is with the records of the former agency,
Memphis office .) Records concerning cotton relate to seizures, steamer
shipments, collections, and deliveries; there are a "cotton book" in which
appears (p. 172) a general summary of cotton received by Tomeny, Nov. 1,
1865-Mar. 31, 1866, and its disposition; and a "cotton register," June 2-
Sept. 30, 1865 (3 vols.).

U. S. PURCHASING AGENTS

Sec. 8 of an act of July 2, 1864 (13 Stat. 377), provided for the appointment by the Secretary of the Treasury of agents authorized "to purchase for
the United States any products of states declared in insurrection," paying no
more than three-quarters of their market value and drawing only on the funds
received from the sale of captured or abandoned property.

Secretary McCulloch discontinued the work of these agents east of the Mississippi as of June 13, 1865, and west of the Mississippi as of June 24, "returning to sellers all property or money received or collected since those dates." After the suspension of purchases, the agents' duties were confined to the securing of property, chiefly cotton, captured by Federal military forces.

Records of two of the purchasing agents (at New Orleans and Memphis) are sufficiently extensive to warrant separate entries, below. There is, in addition, an order book of the purchasing agent at Nashville.

U. S. Purchasing Agent at New Orleans

On Oct. 1, 1864, O. N. Cutler was appointed U. S. Purchasing Agent at New Orleans. He bought cotton almost exclusively, and he also arranged for its sale. Much of the cotton was consigned for sale to the collector of customs at New York, who also acted as cotton agent, and some was resold to those from whom it had been purchased. Cutler's activities ended about July 1, 1865.

Record Group 56. --Records of products (chiefly cotton) purchased, received, and sold, 1864-65 (5 vols. and unbound papers).

U. S. Purchasing Agent at Memphis

From Oct. 5, 1864, to about June 24, 1865, George H. Ellery was U. S. Purchasing Agent at Memphis. His office was known informally as the U. S. Cotton Agency.

Record Group 56. --Records of the purchase, sale, and shipment of cotton, 1864-65 (18 vols. and unbound papers); telegrams from New York giving daily cotton quotations, Jan. 28-June 23, 1865; and a "daily record," Dec. 1864-May 1865, giving both New York and St. Louis quotations.

VII. WAR DEPARTMENT

When Fort Sumter was attacked the entire military force at the disposal of the Government amounted to 16,006 Regulars, stationed principally in the West to hold the Indians in check. The call for 75,000 volunteers for 3 months' service, in Apr. 1861, was favorably received. Under an act of July 22, 1861 (12 Stat. 268), the States were asked to furnish 500,000 volunteers to serve not more than 3 years; and by an act of July 29, 1861 (12 Stat. 279), the addition of 25,000 men to the Regular Army was authorized. Recruiting for the Regular Army, however, was ineffectual because young men preferred the volunteer service; and in consequence 153 companies of the authorized Regular Army were still unorganized on May 31, 1865. By mid-July of that year, however, with the reduction of the volunteer force, the ranks of these regular companies were filled.

The aggregate of the quotas charged against the several States, under all calls made by the President from Apr. 15, 1861, to Apr. 14, 1865, when drafting and recruiting ceased, was 2,759,049; and the aggregate credited on the several calls and inducted into the service of the United States (in the Army, Navy, and Marine Corps) was 2,656,553. This number did not include the "emergency men" called into service during the summer of 1863 by the States of New York, New Jersey, and Pennsylvania, or those furnished by the States of Ohio, Indiana, and Illinois during the "Morgan raid"--amounting in all to more than 120,000 men, who served for periods of some 2 or 3 weeks. Furthermore, it was the rule of the Department "to take into account the whole number of men mustered, without regard to the fact that the same persons may have been previously discharged, after having been accepted and credited on previous calls."

The withdrawal of Southerners or Southern sympathizers tended at once to weaken the Army and the War Department. The 313 officers who resigned from the service constituted nearly a third of all those in the Army. Among them were Adj. Gen. Samuel Cooper, who resigned on Mar. 7, 1861, and Q. M. Gen. Joseph E. Johnston, who resigned on Apr. 22. Many employees on the regular staff of the Secretary's office and the bureaus also resigned. (See S. Ex. Doc. 7, 38 Cong., 1 sess., Serial 1176, for a list of officers of the Regular Army who left the service between Dec. 1, 1860, and Dec. 1, 1863, indicating which of them did so "to engage in the rebellion against the government of the United States.") The effects of the war were felt initially by the Quartermaster General's, Ordnance, Commissary, Medical, and Adjutant General's bureaus. As Meneely observed in The War Department, 1861:

The Quartermaster Office was extremely hard pressed by the demands made upon it by the army for quartermasters and assistants. Many of its trained personnel had already been transferred to field work, weakening the bureau's administrative service, and further requests were constantly being made. Inexperienced officers who had to learn their business as they went along were a source of much embarrassment. So overwhelmed was the office that Meigs was often obliged to hire assistants even though he was without legal authority to do so.

The clamor for commissions and rank and the intervention not only of the President but of the Secretaries of State and the Treasury in the War Department's affairs added to the initial confusion.

Besides the immediate office of the Secretary of War, the 1861 War Department comprised eight bureaus headed by career officers, some of whom had served in the Army since the War of 1812. These were the Adjutant General's Office, the Paymaster General's Office, the Surgeon General's Office, the Office of the Commissary General of Subsistence, the Quartermaster General's Office, the Engineer Bureau, the Bureau of Topographical Engineers, and the Ordnance Office. Except for the Bureau of Topographical Engineers these offices were to continue essentially unchanged, although greatly expanded, during and after the Civil War; and to them were to be added the Judge Advocate General's Office (1862), which became the Bureau of Military Justice in 1864, the Cavalry Bureau (1863), the Provost Marshal General's Bureau (1863), the Office of the Chief Signal Officer (1863), the Office of the Inspector General (1863), and the Bureau of Refugees, Freedmen, and Abandoned Lands (1865). The Bureau of Topographical Engineers was to be united in 1863 with the Engineer Bureau. Four other offices (some directed from outside of Washington) of status almost equal to that of the bureaus were to come into being: the Office of the Commissary General of Prisoners (1861), the Office of the Commissioner for Exchange of Prisoners (1862), the Office of the Director and General Manager of Military Railroads of the United States (1862), and the U. S. Military Telegraphs (1861). The War Department Telegraph Office (1861) was to operate virtually as a subdivision of the immediate office of the Secretary of War. In the postwar period the War Records Office(1874) and the Record and Pension Office (1889) were to be created to deal with matters of Civil War concern. The changing functions, organizational structures, and interrelationships of these many offices are described below.

Distinct from the bureau organizations of the War Department proper was the Headquarters of the Army, which soon moved from New York City to Washington. Responsibility for the administrative and operational direction of the forces in the field was vested in the headquarters of the several military divisions, to each of which were subordinated a number of military departments, with changing geographical boundaries and one or more armies (sometimes corresponding to and serving as departments). To the armies were assigned, as appropriate, the regiments of the Regular Army and the volunteer regiments. The regiments were grouped in part within the 25 numbered corps (several of which, although different, were identified successively by the same numeric designation) and in part as the Cavalry Corps, the Invalid Corps (which became the Veteran Reserve Corps), and the Corps d'Afrique (which became the U. S. Colored Troops). The field organization also comprised a few military governorships and separate districts during the war, five reconstruction districts after the end of hostilities, and--at a lower level--the regional headquarters of the Bureau of

Freedmen, Refugees, and Abandoned Lands. There were, moreover, the fixed posts, camps, and stations, and the related prison camps; quartermaster installations, including the several depots; the armories and arsenals of the Ordnance Department; and the field offices of the Engineer Department. This Guide attempts to account for the extant records of the major headquarters and of other significant activities within the elaborate field organization.

Equal to, if not surpassing, the administrative demands imposed during the Civil War upon the War Department were those arising from its postwar responsibilities. Its new responsibility for the administration of the laws relating to refugees, freedmen, and abandoned lands, was carried out simultaneously with its activities in disbanding the volunteer forces; collecting arms, ordnance, and military stores scattered over the theater of war; selling or otherwise disposing of unserviceable material; storing--in arsenals, magazines, and depots--materials fit for further use; settling and adjusting war claims; and recruiting and organizing the Regular Army. The Department's operations during the first year of peace included also completing the seaboard defenses and providing them with armaments; planning and carrying on harbor and river improvements; establishing posts and garrisons on the frontier and in the Indian country; and testing the various improvements of breech-loading small arms.

The annual reports, by fiscal year, of the Secretary of War appeared in the following congressional documents:

1861. S. Ex. Doc. 1, 37 Cong., 2 sess., Serial 1118.
1862. H. Ex. Doc. 1, pt. 4, 37 Cong., 3 sess., Serial 1159.
1863. H. Ex. Doc. 1, 38 Cong., 1 sess., Serial 1184.
1864. (submitted Mar. 1, 1865). H. Ex. Doc. 83, 38 Cong., 2 sess., Serial 1230.
1865. H. Ex. Doc. 1, 39 Cong., 1 sess., Serial 1249.
1866. H. Ex. Doc. 1, 39 Cong., 2 sess., Serial 1285.

Fred Albert Shannon, The Organization and Administration of the Union Army, 1861-1865 (Cleveland, 1928. 2 vols.); Theo. F. Rodenbough and William L. Haskin, eds., The Army of the United States . . . (New York, 1896); Raphael P. Thian, comp., Legislative History of the General Staff of the Army of the United States . . . 1775 to 1901 (Washington, 1901); Frederick Phisterer, Statistical Record of the Armies of the United States (New York, 1884); Francis B. Heitman, Historical Register and Dictionary of the United States Army . . . (Washington, 1903. 2 vols.); Col. H. L. Scott, Military Dictionary . . . Relating to Land Forces (New York, 1861); A. Howard Meneely, The War Department, 1861: a Study in Mobilization and Administration (New York, 1928); Bvt. Maj. Gen. Emory Upton, The Military Policy of the United States (Washington, 1904); [Office of the Secretary of War], List of the Records and Files of the War Department . . . (Washington, 1890).

OFFICE OF THE SECRETARY OF WAR

President Buchanan's refusal to order Maj. Robert Anderson, who had occupied Fort Sumter, back to Fort Moultrie resulted in the resignation of Secretary of War John Buchanan Floyd on Dec. 29, 1860, and the appoint-

ment of Joseph Holt as Secretary ad interim until his appointment as Secretary of War on Jan. 18, 1861. Floyd, who was to be a conspicuous general officer of the Confederate Army until his death in 1863, had been
involved, in his last year of office as Secretary of War, in other controversies, including those concerning the appointment of a Quartermaster
General and the sending of arms to the Southern States in excess of their
requirements.

Joseph Holt had served in the Buchanan administration first as Commissioner of Patents and then, from Mar. 1859, as Postmaster General.
His conscientious Unionism led him to establish several commissions to
investigate war contracts; and on Sept. 3, 1862, he was to be appointed as
the first Judge Advocate General of the Army, to head eventually the Bureau of Military Justice. Simon Cameron became Secretary of War on
Mar. 5, 1861; he had been a candidate for the presidential nomination at
the Republican national convention of 1860; and he resigned his seat in the
Senate to accept the Cabinet office, tendered by President Lincoln with
misgivings. The embarrassments to which the administration was subjected
as the result of Cameron's actions in departmental administration, however, led to his removal from the Washington scene by appointment as
Minister to Russia.

Cameron's successor, Edwin McMasters Stanton, took formal charge
of the War Department on Jan. 20, 1862. Stanton's great success as
counsel for the U. S. Government in the California land cases of 1858 had
led to his appointment as Attorney General on Dec. 20, 1860, but he had
returned to private life with the inauguration of Lincoln. As Secretary of
War he was and remains one of the most controversial political figures of
the Civil War period, and his conception of his responsibilities and prerogatives considerably influenced the making of major decisions and the settlement of military and nonmilitary issues. A natural consequence of having
no General in Chief, as Upton observes, was the rise of a council composed
of the chiefs of the War Department bureaus, invited by Stanton to daily conferences. (Extracts of the proceedings of some of these meetings appear in
Gorham's biography of Stanton, cited below.) The Secretary's close relations with the Joint Committee of Congress on the Conduct of the War affected his standing with President Johnson, and on Aug. 12, 1867, Johnson
suspended Stanton and named Ulysses S. Grant as Secretary of War ad interim. (When the Senate declined to concur in this suspension, the President, on Feb. 21, 1868, formally directed Stanton's removal from office
and named Adj. Gen. Lorenzo Thomas as Secretary of War ad interim.
Stanton, however, refused to relinquish his office until, after the Johnson
impeachment failed, he resigned on May 26, 1868.)

Of the several Assistant or Second Assistant Secretaries of War, listed
below, Charles A. Dana, whose nomination as Second Assistant Secretary
under an act of Jan. 19, 1864 (13 Stat. 1), was confirmed on Jan. 26, engaged in activities of special interest. He had served earlier on the commission to examine claims at Cairo, Ill., and in Mar. 1863 had been
appointed special commissioner of the War Department to investigate and
report upon conditions in the Western armies. (For Dana's printed reports
in the latter capacity, see Official Records . . . Armies, ser. 1, vol. 24,
pt. 1, p. 63-117.) In his Recollections Dana describes his duties at the
War Department as the making of contracts for supplies of all kinds and
the examination of accounts before payments could be made. "Not a little
of my time at the department was taken up with people who had missions

of some kind within the lines of the army. " He was detached to the Army of the Potomac for a while; and later he spent much time investigating charges against defaulting contractors and dishonest agents and ordering arrests of persons suspected of disloyalty to the Government. At about the time of Lincoln's assassination it was his duty to receive the reports of the officers of the "secret service" in every part of the country. Assistant Secretary John Tucker had served earlier (from May 1861) as General Transportation Agent of the War Department.

Successive Secretaries of War during the Civil War period:
    John Buchanan Floyd, Mar. 6, 1857.
    Joseph Holt, Jan. 18, 1861 (ad interim, Dec. 31, 1860).
    Simon Cameron, Mar. 5, 1861.
    Edwin McMasters Stanton, Jan. 15, 1862.
Assistant or Second Assistant Secretaries of War:
    Thomas A. Scott, Aug. 3, 1861.
    Peter H. Watson, Jan. 24, 1862.
    John Tucker, Jan. 29, 1862.
    Christopher P. Wolcott, June 12, 1862.
    Charles A. Dana, Jan. 28, 1864.

Annual reports of the three wartime Secretaries cited above; The War of the Rebellion: A Compilation of the Official Records of the Union and Confederate Armies (Washington, 1880-1901. Serials 1-111 and 114-130); George C. Gorham, The Life and Public Services of Edwin M. Stanton (Boston and New York, 1899. 2 vols.); Diary of Gideon Welles, Boston and New York, 1911. 3 vols.); Charles A. Dana, Recollections of the Civil War: With the Leaders at Washington and in the Field in the Sixties (New York, 1898).

Record Group 107. --All the records of the Secretary's Office pertinent to the Civil War fall within the period when the incoming correspondence of the War Department was registered in large record books and the letters sent were copied in similar volumes. Copies of letters sent appear chronologically in the series of 151 "Military Books," 1800-1870. Each such volume contains an index principally by name of addressee; and from Apr. 1, 1862, to May 12, 1865, the correspondence was so great that two sets of volumes, labeled A and B, were kept concurrently. Interfiled with this series and a part of it are separate volumes of "Military Books, Executive, " which contain copies of letters sent to the President, other departments, and bureaus of the War Department, Feb. 1, 1864-Dec. 31, 1870; but copies of earlier letters sent to the President (through 1863) are in separate volumes. Copies of letters sent, orders, and telegrams (the last with index) relating to the recruiting and organization of volunteer State troops, 1862-65 (4 vols.), are in separate series, as are orders and endorsements, 1846-70, relating to letters referred to War Department bureaus (26 vols.).

Letters received are in a single series, 1801-89, arranged, in accordance with symbols assigned in the registers of letters received, by initial letter of surname of writer or office and thereunder by number. Grouped separately for each year, 1862-70, are letters from the President, War Department bureaus, and other executive departments. Not necessarily representative but suggestive of the nature of some other special subject groups within (or perhaps strays from) the main document file are the "unentered papers, 1861" on the organizing of Northern units; applications for appointment as brigade surgeon, 1861; miscellaneous papers relating to prisoners of war, 1864-65; and correspondence regarding aliens, 1863-65. A few papers relating to the Old Capitol Prison, 1862-65, consist of lists of "spies, " prisoners of war, and "releases. "

Besides the main series of registers of letters received, 1800-1889 (227 vols., of which nos. 175-224 cover 1861-65), the following special registers and indexes are useful: the so-called "Irregular Books, " 1861-65 (5 vols.), abstracting letters received relating to the recruiting, drafting, and raising of troops, among other subjects; the so-called "E. B. Books, " 1862-70 (22 vols.), abstracting letters received from the President, bureaus of the War Department, and other executive departments; and an isolated register (presumably, in part at least, of papers and letters filed in the Adjutant General's Office) concerning chiefly prisoners, deserters, discharges, and appointments requiring presidential action, July 1, 1865-Mar. 13, 1866. There are also name and subject indexes to letters received, 1861-89 (33 vols.).

There is a special file of papers in the case of Annie E. Jones, who was arrested for activities as a spy during the Civil War.

Other record books of interest and value are those containing an "index of telegrams seized at the several telegraph offices herein named, by the order of the Secretary of War, April 1861"; copies of "letters of certain persons hostile to the United States seized by order of the Secretary of War, November 25, 1864-May 3, 1865"; statements of legal actions undertaken by the Solicitor of the War Department and of the history and records of that office, Nov. 1862-Feb. 1864; copies of presidential orders and recommendations relating to prisoners, deserters, discharges, and appointments, July 1865-Mar. 1866; and statements pertaining to statistical returns of troops, Mar. 1863. There are records of passes, etc., granted by the Secretary of War, 1863-66, permitting travel in military zones (6 vols.); and 4 books containing stubs of passes admitting persons to the area of the Army of the Potomac, Mar. 2-21, 1863.

Drafts of the Secretary's orders, although incomplete, are available for the period Jan.-Sept. 1862 (1 vol.).

Among the series of personnel records pertinent to Civil War research, all of which span or extend beyond the war period, are incomplete lists of personnel of the War Department and its bureaus; of these a volume, 1875-81, listing the employees responsible for the compilation of the Official Records . . . Armies may be of special interest. Letters of application for positions in the War Department (including reports of examining boards for clerkships, 1863-66), with related registers, are also available.

The secretary's fiscal records, maintained by the Chief Disbursing Clerk of the War Department, consist principally of abstracts of contingent expenses of agents, bureaus, and offices of the War Department (11 vols., 1836-86), with indexes; miscellaneous account books; receipts books for salaries paid to clerks of the Secretary's office, 1853-64 (3 vols.); and the Secretary's articles of agreement with contractors. Other financial records are in Record Group 203, as described below.

National Archives, Preliminary Checklist of the Records of the Office of the Secretary of War, 1800-1942, comp. by Lucille H. Pendell (1945). Available on microfilm: letters of the Secretary to the President, 1800-1863 (M 127), and reports to Congress, 1803-70 (M 220).

Record Group 203. -- The Secretary's financial records that were inherited by the Office of the Chief of Finance include, for the Civil War
period, copies of his letters to the Secretary of the Treasury relating to
estimates, expenditures, and the issuance of warrants for the War Department (in a 4-vol. series extending to 1867); registers of letters received,
1863-70 (3 vols.), concerning fiscal matters; registers of Treasury Department appropriation warrants for the War Department (in 6 vols. extending to 1913); registers of requisitions for funds on the Second Auditor
(in 39 vols. extending to 1894) and on the Third Auditor (in 44 vols. extending to 1894); an index to the registers of requisitions, 1860-65 (1 vol.);
registers of war credit requisitions for funds (in 14 vols. extending to
1898); and ledgers of accounts under appropriations (in 48 vols. extending
to 1940).

There is also a register of requisitions for funds, 1868-1906, authorized by an act of July 27, 1868 (15 Stat. 402), that provided for the distribution of the reward offered by the President for the capture of Jefferson
Davis.

Records in Other Custody. -- Meneely, in The War Department, 1861,
wrote that his efforts to find the Simon Cameron papers had been unsuccessful and that probably none of them, except the comparatively small
group in the Pennsylvania Historical Society, were in existence. Recently,
however, a previously unknown collection of Cameron's papers, 1853-65,
found in the Historical Society of Dauphin County, has been microfilmed by
the Pennsylvania Historical and Museum Commission at Harrisburg. The
Edwin M. Stanton papers in the Library of Congress include copies of letters sent, Mar. 1863-June 1865 (5 vols.); telegrams sent to and received
from Charles A. Dana, 1864-65 (2 vols.); and a volume of orders, letters,
decisions, and memoranda, Jan.-Oct. 1862. Unbound Stanton papers in the
Library include 40 letters from President Lincoln; President Johnson's
letter of Feb. 21, 1868, dismissing Stanton from the Cabinet; and letters
from many other public figures of the period.

War Department Telegraph Office

Although a distinct administrative unit, the War Department Telegraph
Office, established early in 1861, operated essentially within the purview
of the Secretary himself. As recalled by David Homer Bates, who in his
genial reminiscences, Lincoln in the Telegraph Office (New York, 1907),
styled himself "Manager of the War Department Telegraph Office, and
Cipher-Operator, 1861-1866," the office "was first located in Chief Clerk
Sanderson's room adjoining that of the Secretary of War, on the second
floor of the building in the southeast corner"; it was shifted to other locations in May and in October; and a "final change was made soon after the
Monitor-Merrimac fight in March, 1862, when Secretary of War Stanton
directed the office to be located in the old library room." Other quotations from Bates throw considerable light on the work of the office:

The War Department telegraph office was the scene of many vitally
important conferences between Lincoln and members of his cabinet,
leading generals, congressmen and others, who soon learned that
when the President was not at the White House he could most likely
be found in the telegraph office. . . .

All military telegraph despatches from or to Washington of necessity passed through the War Department office. The operators were fully occupied in the work of transmitting and receiving these messages over the wires, and the cipher-operators in translating the more important ones into and out of cipher. There was no time to spare for the task of filing them away in an orderly, careful manner, but the Government was fortunate in having the right man for such an important duty, and historians of the Civil War for all time have cause to be grateful to Major Albert E. H. Johnson for his preliminary work toward the great array of volumes of the "Official Records" published by authority of Congress, which contains thousands of military telegrams all carefully filed by him. . . .

During the entire war, the files of the War Department telegraph office were punctuated with short, pithy despatches from Lincoln. For instance, on May 24, 1862, he sent ten or twelve to various generals; on May 25, as many more; and from one to a dozen on nearly every succeeding day for months. It is also worthy of remark that Lincoln's numerous telegrams . . . were almost without exception in his own handwriting, his copy being remarkably neat and legible, with seldom an erasure or correction.

Record Group 107. -- The files of telegrams comprise those received and sent by the President, the Secretary of War, the General of the Army, the Adjutant General, the Provost Marshal General, and the commanders of divisions, departments, and armies. The arrangement in volumes is generally chronological; most volumes contain name indexes. These are grouped as follows:

Telegrams sent. These include telegrams sent by President Lincoln, Mar. 10, 1864-Apr. 12, 1865 (1 vol.), and President Johnson, Apr. 16, 1865-Jan. 15, 1868 (1 vol.). There are also volumes of telegrams sent by the Secretary of War, Apr. 27, 1861-July 30, 1881 (44 vols.); Maj. Gen. Henry W. Halleck (originals), July 29, 1862-Apr. 19, 1865 (8 vols.); Maj. Gen. Henry W. Halleck (copies), July 29, 1862-Apr. 26, 1865 (6 vols.); Gen. Ulysses S. Grant, Mar. 23, 1864-Feb. 25, 1869 (5 vols.); Maj. Gen. Ambrose E. Burnside, Nov. 9, 1862-Jan. 26, 1863 (1 vol.); Maj. Gen. Joseph Hooker, Jan. 27-June 28, 1863 (1 vol.); Maj. Gen. George G. Meade, June 28, 1863-Apr. 18, 1865 (2 vols.); Maj. Gen. George B. McClellan, Jan. 1-Nov. 12, 1862 (10 vols.); General McClellan and staff, Mar. 1-Sept. 16, 1862 (1 vol.); Maj. Gen. John Pope, July 2, 1862-June 19, 1865 (2 vols.); Provost Marshal General James B. Fry, Mar. 23, 1863-May 28, 1868 (11 vols.), also Fry's telegrams concerning enrollment, Aug. 4, 1864-May 28, 1866 (1 vol.); and Judge Advocate Levi C. Turner, Aug. 9, 1862-Sept. 3, 1864 (1 vol.). There are also telegrams sent, Apr. 5-Nov. 7, 1862, that originated with the Army of the Potomac (8 vols.), and those of the General of the Army and the Adjutant General, Jan. 26, 1866-May 31, 1882 (25 vols.).

Telegrams received. These include telegrams received by the President, Mar. 17, 1863-Feb. 22, 1868 (6 vols.); the Secretary of War, Apr. 6, 1861-May 7, 1870 (51 vols.); Maj. Gen. Henry W. Halleck, July 19, 1862-May 3, 1865 (23 vols.); Gen. Ulysses S. Grant, Mar. 22, 1864-Feb. 27, 1869 (5 vols.); the War Department from General Grant, Mar. 10, 1864-Feb. 2, 1865 (2 vols.); General Grant from the War Department, Mar. 10, 1864-Nov. 16, 1868 (1 vol.); Maj. Gen. Ambrose E. Burnside, Nov. 9, 1862-Jan. 24, 1863 (1 vol.); Maj. Gen. Joseph Hooker, Jan. 29-

June 28, 1863 (1 vol.); Maj. Gen. George G. Meade, June 28, 1863-Mar.
28, 1865 (1 vol.); Maj. Gen. George B. McClellan, June 27-Nov. 5, 1862
(1 vol.); Maj. Gen. John Pope, July 15, 1862-Aug. 4, 1865 (1 vol.); and
Provost Marshal General James B. Fry, Apr. 2, 1863-May 28, 1868 (19
vols.), also telegrams to Fry concerning enrollment, Dec. 19, 1863-May
22, 1866 (4 vols.). There are also press copies of telegrams received by
the President, Nov. 15, 1862-Mar. 4, 1869 (9 vols.), and Mar. 11, 1864-
July 31, 1867 (2 vols.); by the Secretary of War, Oct. 31, 1861-Sept. 20,
1875 (34 vols.), and Apr. 1, 1869-Feb. 16, 1876 (12 vols.); by General
Halleck, July 30, 1862-Apr. 20, 1865 (8 vols.); by General Grant, May 24,
1867-Aug. 6, 1868 (1 vol.); and by the General in Chief (W. T. Sherman),
Aug. 6, 1868-Oct. 8, 1869 (1 vol.).

Other telegrams sent and received. These comprise 2 volumes of telegrams sent and received by the Office of the Secretary of War and the War
Department in 1861; telegrams sent from New Orleans, Nov. 12, 1864-
June 14, 1869 (1 vol.); and press copies of "official telegrams received at,
sent from, and passing through Fortress Monroe, Va.," Apr. 14-July 1,
1862.

Many telegrams were selected
from these records for publication
in Official Records of the Union and
Confederate Armies. Those sent and
received by Halleck were published
by the War Department Printing Office in 1877 in 5 volumes of telegrams
received and 4 of telegrams sent.

ADJUTANT GENERAL'S OFFICE

An act of Mar. 3, 1813 (2 Stat. 819), established an Adjutant General's
Department and an Inspector General's Department under one head, but separate heads for the two departments were provided by an act of Mar. 2, 1821
(3 Stat. 615). The strength of the Adjutant General's Department, established at 20 by an act of Aug. 3, 1861 (12 Stat. 287), remained constant
during the Civil War, although grade promotions were authorized by an act
of July 17, 1862 (12 Stat. 597). Neither the authorized strength--neces-
sarily supplemented by Volunteer officers--nor the grades fully satisfied
the Adjutant General. "According to the regulations of our Army," he informed the House Committee on Military Affairs on Apr. 29, 1862, "and to
the theory and customs of our service, the assistant adjutant general of
every army, army corps, division and brigade, is, by the very nature of
his office, chief of the staff on which he serves." With respect to the work
of his own office at the end of the first year of war the Adjutant General, in
his fiscal year 1862 report, wrote as follows:

> So much is the business pertaining to the Adjutant General's bureau
> made up of details that it is not easy to define what are its prominent
> branches. It is the source from which the regulations, orders, and
> much of the military correspondence of the Secretary of War and gen-
> eral-in-chief of the army issue. It is the place of deposit of the purely
> military records: such as muster-rolls, which contain the history of
> every soldier of the army; returns, which show the actual condition of
> each army corps, division, brigade and regiment, from month to month;
> files of enlistments and certificates of discharge of enlisted men. Here
> are made out the commissions of all military officers appointed by the
> President of the United States; and all commissions as well as resigna-

tions and casualties affecting such officers are here recorded. The
annual Army Register, containing the military history of all officers so
commissioned, is also made up, printed, and distributed under supervision of this bureau. From here the various books of instruction, so
liberally furnished by the government to its troops, and all blanks used
by the army, except in the disbursing departments of the staff, are
distributed . The forms of the several blanks are also contrived, and
the printing of them is supervised here. The recruiting service for
the regular army, and the muster in and out of the volunteer regiments,
with the several details of organization, drawing of requisitions for
funds, and auditing accounts for expenditures in both services, are
here regulated and supervised. From this summary it is to be inferred
that constant reference must be made to this bureau for information on
points of military law; for interpretation of regulations, and the custom
of service; for reports to enable the treasury and pension bureaus to
settle claims in behalf of officers and enlisted men; for replies to relatives of soldiers residing in all parts of the civilized world; for reports
on which to decide claims to commissions and pay on irregular musters;
for examination of proceedings of boards, and reports involving the discharge, and restoration of volunteer officers; for reports on administration and discipline for the Secretary of War and general-in-chief; and
for statements of the strength and stations of the several armies.

By May 1, 1863, when the recruiting service was turned over to the
newly created Provost Marshal General's Bureau, the Adjutant General had
recruited about two-thirds of the whole number of Civil War volunteers. He
continued to have charge of the organization of volunteer troops, established
and managed general depots for them, cared for recruits (including those
enlisted by the Provost Marshal General), supervised their organization
into regiments and companies intended for new commands, and controlled
their movements as replacements.

The Adjutant General's responsibilities for recruiting for the Regular
Army also continued during the war. By 1864 the management of all the
recruiting service for the Regular Army had been put under the immediate
superintendence of Brig. Gen. Philip St. George Cooke, who established
his headquarters at New York City. Cooke was assisted by the commanding
officers of the several regiments, who acted as superintendents. Principal
depots for the general service were maintained at Fort Columbus, New
York Harbor (for infantry), and at Carlisle, Pa. (for the mounted service).
Subdepots, which also were the headquarters of the regiments, were main-
tained at Fort Trumbull, Conn. (3d Art. and 14th Inf.), Fort Richmond,
New York Harbor (5th Art.), Newport Barracks, Ky. (2d Inf.), Fort Wood,
New York Harbor (6th Inf.), Fort Columbus, New York Harbor (8th Inf.),
Fort Independence, Boston Harbor (11th Inf.), Fort Hamilton, New York
Harbor (12th Inf.), Newport Barracks, Ky. (13th Inf.), Fort Adams, R. I.
(15th Inf.), Fort Ontario, N. Y. (16th Inf.), Fort Preble, Maine (17th Inf.),
Camp Thomas, Ohio(18th Inf.), and Fort Wayne, Mich. (19th Inf.). Although
with the termination of hostilities the regiments of the Regular Army were reduced to mere skeleton organizations, the recruiting service was again progressing favorably by October 1865, when the two principal depots for the
general recruiting service were still at Fort Columbus and Carlisle Barracks.

A resolution of Congress, May 19, 1864 (13 Stat. 406), provided for the
printing, in chronological order, of official reports of the operations of the

armies of the United States. In the same year the Adjutant General's Office began to copy the reports dating from Dec. 1, 1860, and officers of the Army from whom such reports were due were called upon to forward them. This compilation, the Adjutant General reported in 1864, "when properly arranged and indexed as required by the resolution, will be of great historical value, and should not be hurried to completion until it can be properly done. " In the last year of the war and just after its conclusion the office expended "much attention and labor" upon the "preparation of the documents relating to the rebellion" required to be printed by this resolution. In point of fact, however, the project was abandoned, although it was later revived under the program of the War Records Office for the publication of the Official Records. The enormous task of compiling, for printing, the register of volunteer officers called for by a resolution approved June 30, 1864 (13 Stat. 412), was, however, completed.

In his role of archivist for the Army the Adjutant General began to acquire custody, as the war ended, of the records of discontinued military commands. The organization and servicing of these, in addition to his own records and those of certain War Department bureaus whose records were inherited with their functions, came to constitute a major function of his office. By 1866 a total of 3,353 "boxes" containing the records of 2,165 organizations had "been received, carefully examined, and arranged for easy reference. " At this time and for some years afterward the individual military records of Civil War soldiers were kept in the Office of the Adjutant General, although their medical records were kept in the Surgeon General's Office. The work of arranging these papers for the purpose of record and pensions was so great that the two offices ultimately accumulated a backlog of thousands of cases. The establishment of the separate division of the War Department known as the Record and Pension Office as a solution to this problem is discussed elsewhere in the Guide.

The formal units of the Adjutant General's Office existing during the war included the Volunteer Service Division and the Recruiting, Enlisted, Commission, Colored Troops, and Drafted Division, Branches, or Bureaus, as they were variously called. The Enrollment and Disbursing Branches were added in 1866, to continue certain functions of the inactivated Office of the Provost Marshal General, and the Freedmen's Branch was created in 1872 to carry on unfinished business of the discontinued Bureau of Refugees, Freedmen, and Abandoned Lands. The details of the functions of these several units are given below.

Col. (later Brig. Gen.) Lorenzo Thomas, who succeeded Col. Samuel Cooper on Mar. 7, 1861, served as Adjutant General until Feb. 22, 1869. During much of the year 1863 Thomas was employed under special directions from the Secretary of War "in a responsible sphere of duties in the southwest"--the organization of Negro regiments in the Mississippi Valley. In Thomas' absence Col. Edward D. Townsend was in charge of the Washington office.

Annual reports of the Adjutant General, 1861-68, appended to those of the Secretary of War; Maj. Livingston Watrous, A Brief History of the Adjutant General's Department From June 16th, 1775, to December 31st, 1925 (Governors Island, N. Y. , 1927); War Department General Orders, Special Orders, and Circulars, 1861-70; National Archives, Preliminary Inventory [No. 17] of the Records of the Adjutant General's Office, comp. by Lucille H. Pendell and Elizabeth Bethel (Washington, 1949).

Record Group 94. -- The single registry of records maintained by the Adjutant General's Office before the Civil War was progressively split during the war into a number of different registries. Insofar as they can be identified with the several divisions existing during and after the Civil War, the records of the Adjutant General's Office are described under these divisions, discussed later in this chapter. The records mentioned immediately below are general records that because of their comprehensive nature cannot be so identified. These consist of the general correspondence and related records; the special collections relating to the Civil War; the files of orders; muster rolls, returns, and station books; and miscellaneous other records.

General Correspondence and Related Records

Copies of letters sent span the period of the war in a series extending from 1800 to 1889 (95 vols., including index vols.), as do copies of endorsements, 1850-89 (52 vols.), and of reports to the Secretary of War, 1825-70 (8 vols.). (The "rules for keeping books" at the Headquarters of the Army and in the Adjutant General's Office, explained in detail in William P. Craighill, The Army Officer's Pocket Companion, published in New York in 1862, offer an excellent contemporary description of the manner of maintaining and indexing the records.) There are also copies of letters and telegrams (1 vol.) sent by Adjutant General Thomas, chiefly to the Secretary of War and to general officers, while Thomas was on duty in the field in 1863; manuscript copies of telegrams (2 vols.) sent from the Adjutant General's Office, 1864-66, with additional press copies; and copies of endorsements, 1864-67, pertaining to status changes of individual officers (7 vols.).

Letters received are in one series, 1805-89 (620 ft.), arranged chronologically by year, then alphabetically by name of writer, then numerically to correspond to the letters-received registers; the latter, 1814-89 (133 vols.), record many communications received that are no longer to be found. There is a separate subject index (1 vol.) to the letters received from 1861 to 1870. Within the series of letters received numerous consolidations of related material were developed, including papers concerning individual officers of the Regular Army except officers who joined the Confederate Army. There is, however, a small consolidation of papers concerning Robert E. Lee.

The materials separated from the main "documents" or letters received file, because of their bulk or special character, were relegated to 235 "trunks." These materials are still arranged according to their original "trunk" numbers, among which the following numbers are especially important:

1. Report of the Commission "to examine and report upon the plan of the present forts, and sufficiency of the present system of defenses for the City [of Washington]," Dec. 24, 1862.

3. Reports of special commissions appointed in June 1865 to investigate the inventories of the quartermaster depots at New York, Philadelphia, Cincinnati, St. Louis, and Louisville.

4. The report of Bvt. Brig. Gen. Daniel C. McCallum, Director and General Manager, Military Railroads United States, 1861-66; papers concerning an arrest for distributing fraudulent poll books among Pennsylvania soldiers; papers concerning the Memphis riots of 1866; proceedings, other

records, and final report (Jan. 15, 1866) of the special commission convened at Boston and Washington to investigate and report facts concerning certain Germans who were brought from Prussia under alleged contracts with Julian Allen and M. D. Ross of Boston and who were enlisted in the U. S. service as substitutes or otherwise in Massachusetts in 1864.

5. Various oaths of allegiance, particularly those administered in western Virginia, 1861-62.

10. Consolidated file of papers concerning the adjudication of claims for the rewards offered for the apprehension of Jefferson Davis and of the "assassins" of Abraham Lincoln. (For printed reports concerning the pursuit and capture of Davis, see Official Records . . . Armies, ser. 1, vol. 49, pt. 1, p. 515-557.)

30. Papers concerning the review of the court-martial of Fitz-John Porter, including the report of the board, Mar. 19, 1879.

31. Preliminary and final reports, proceedings, and other records (including testimony taken) of the American Freedmen's Inquiry Commission.

32. Papers concerning the health and treatment of Jefferson Davis as a prisoner at Fort Monroe, Va., including reports (printed in Official Records . . . Armies, ser. 2, vol. 8, passim) on the state of his health.

36. Papers concerning the British-American Claims Commission, containing claims of British citizens residing in the United States who suffered property and other losses in war areas.

86. Manuscript copy of the proceedings of the general court-martial of Brig. Gen. William A. Hammond, Surgeon General, used presumably in the review of this case.

A "general information index," 1794-1918 (18 ft.), which records difficult searches by War Department clerks, contains the names of U. S. officers who made reports on their Civil War service during and after the war. A small but useful series (4 ft.) brought together for reference by Department clerks consists of 288 numbered "envelopes" of original documents dating from the early 1800's; among these the following numbers relate to the war:

3. Documents concerning the raising of Civil War troops in New England and adjacent States.

8, 9, 28. Records concerning the Bureau of Refugees, Freedmen, and Abandoned Lands, including proceedings of the court of inquiry investigating charges against Brig. Gen. Oliver O. Howard.

23. Testimony of Union soldiers concerning "outrages" committed by the citizens of Winchester, Va., May 23, 1862.

24. Papers concerning the trial of the "Chicago Conspirators" to free Confederate prisoners of war, Apr. 1865.

29-31 and 33-35. Presidential proclamations, 1863-65.

32. Papers concerning hospitality given Confederate cruisers in foreign ports and the reopening of Southern ports.

40. Papers concerning the U. S. Christian Commission.

41. Papers concerning the Provost Marshal General's Office.

43. Papers concerning citizens of Virginia imprisoned at Camp Chase, Columbus, Ohio.

60. Memorandum on Regular Army units in the first Battle of Bull Run.

65. List of monies taken from banks and banking institutions in New Orleans, Aug. 17, 1863.

68. News clippings concerning John Wilkes Booth.

84. Papers concerning the explosion of ordnance stores at City Point, Va., on Aug. 9, 1864.

90-A and 90-B. Reports and plans concerning cemeteries for the Union dead.

95. Papers concerning the refunding of commutation money.

103. Statistics of Union Army deaths.

104. Data concerning officers of the U. S. Regular Army who joined the Confederate Army or who left the service either by resignation or desertion.

108. History of Camp Douglas, Ill. (with anecdotes about Confederate prisoners by the Rev. E. B. Tuttle, post chaplain), 1865.

116. Documents concerning the organization of the Executive Mansion staff and the War Department, 1861-65.

132. Papers concerning military operations against Richmond and other papers relating to troop composition, casualties, and operations in the several military departments.

143. Report of deaths occurring among the "three-months volunteer organizations," 1861.

146. Papers concerning Arkansas, including the Army of Arkansas.

149. Papers concerning the Army of the Ohio.

150. List of officers of the Army of the Potomac.

151. List of officers of the Army of the Tennessee.

152. Statement of the Army corps that existed during the Civil War.

162. Papers concerning the board to examine Dr. Solomon Andrew's "aerial machine," 1864.

163. Statement by the Bureau of Pensions, Mar. 20, 1916, on the ages of men who enlisted in the Union Army during the Civil War.

166. Opinions of the Solicitor of the War Department, May 1864, concerning the liability to draft, exemption of drafted men, furnishing of substitutes, exemption of a member of the Society of Friends, status of a slave if drafted, etc.

169. Reference cards on Andersonville Prison.

171. Papers concerning the "Andrews raid."

175. Papers concerning transportation methods, 1861-65.

176. Army War College Study No. 13, pt. 3, "The War of the Rebellion."

180. Articles of agreement between Maj. C. C. Sibley, U. S. A., and Col. Earl Van Dorn, C. S. A., relative to U. S. Army officers and men who might become prisoners of war, Apr. 25, 1861.

186. Reports concerning the Atlanta campaign.

188. Descriptions of Bacon Race Church (a Confederate fortified encampment) and Camp Barclay, D. C. (a Pennsylvania volunteer cavalry encampment), 1861-62.

189. Papers concerning the Baltimore riot of Apr. 18, 1861.

192. Description of Camp Barry, D. C., and a history of "Barry's Farm."

194. Papers concerning the defining of Civil War battles.

195. Badge of United Confederate Veterans, a drawing with explanation.

196. Papers concerning the marking of battlefields.

201. Description of Battery Benson, Md., one of the Defenses of Washington.

204B. Memorandum on the capture and burning of Roswell Factory, which manufactured cloth for the Confederate Army.

206-208. Papers concerning bounty, bounty jumpers, and bounty claims.

215. Report giving the names and ranks of officers on the staff of Gen. Ambrose E. Burnside after ca. 1862.

219. Original journal of the march of the Northwestern Indian Expedition ι from Fort Tully, Dakota Territory, to the Yellowstone River and back to "the Sioux City," 1864.

223. Photostatic copies of reports, with maps, of the 20th Army Corps' campaign from Atlanta to Savannah.

233. Papers concerning Civil War locomotives.

243. Many papers about Confederate prisoners of the Union, prisoner exchange, the numbers of Union and Confederate prisoners who died in prison, and prison administration.

244. Papers concerning the battle of Vicksburg and Vicksburg National Park.

250. Maps, particularly of areas of Virginia, bearing on the war.

252. Compilation of orders and circulars pertaining to the Invalid Corps.

269. Papers concerning Civil War hospitals and surgeons.

274. Papers concerning the Battle of Chickamauga.

Among other records of considerable significance to Civil War research that cannot be attributed to any particular division of the Adjutant General's Office, a "special file," 1790-1946 (6 ft.), includes many items of interest. In this file, which is not confined to the Civil War, are a holographic letter, marked "private," dated Oxford, Miss., Dec. 14, 1862, from Lt. Gen. U. S. Grant to Maj. Gen. H. W. Halleck, containing observations pertaining to officers on his staff; five holographic letters, Gen. R. E. Lee to Lt. Gen. Grant, Apr. 7-9, 1865, before the surrender at Appomattox; an official copy of the report by Assistant Surgeon J. J. Woodward of the autopsy of President Abraham Lincoln, dated Apt. 15, 1865; the report of Assistant Surgeon Charles A. Leale, U. S. Vols., on the assassination and death of Lincoln; the diary of Brig. Gen. Wm. Preston, C. S. A., containing a memorandum account of the death of Gen. Albert Sidney Johnston, at the Battle of Shiloh, Tenn., April 1862; the parole of honor signed by Gen. R. E. Lee, C. S. A., and members of his staff at Appomattox Court House, Va., Apr. 9, 1865; and--significantly, because it illustrates the occasional "special filing" of documents of historic value--the holographic letter of Lt. Gen. U. S. Grant to Maj. Gen. H. W. Halleck, May 10, 1864, containing the expression "propose to fight it out on this line if it takes all summer."

Special Civil War Collection

Apart from the principal document files many series and isolated pieces relating directly to the Civil War are in the records of the Adjutant General's Office. These include, notably, the series of "Generals' Papers and Books" (51 ft.), containing papers collected not only from War Department sources but from the families of Civil War generals for use in the compilation of the Official Records of the Union and Confederate Armies. For the Civil War period the series contains papers in varying quantities of the following general officers: Alexander Asboth, 1862-63; John G. Barnard, 1861-65; Don Carlos Buell, 1861-63, 1865; Ambrose Everett Burnside, 1854-65; Samuel Wylie Crawford, 1861-62; Quincy Adams Gillmore, 1863-

65; Henry Wager Halleck, 1862-69; Joseph Hooker, 1863-64; Stephen
Augustus Hurlbut, 1861; William Scott Ketchum, 1863-66; Irvin McDowell,
1862; Wesley Merritt, 1863-65; Ormsby McKnight Mitchel, 1861-62; William Tecumseh Sherman, 1862-65; George Henry Thomas, 1862-65; Daniel
Ullmann, 1862-65; and Lewis Wallace, 1863.

The generals' personal reports of their service during the war are
available in a series of responses (14 vols.) to requests of the Adjutant
General, in 1864 and again in 1872, for brief summaries of battles in which
they had participated; and there is a volume containing printed copies of
the reports of various commanders of military operations in 1863. Other
comprehensive information is available in typewritten sketches (nos. 1-88,
covering the period 1861-62) of the principal military commands in the
Union and Confederate armies; a "statistical book" showing numbers of
Union troops furnished by the States; a "battle book" listing battles in which
volunteer organizations participated; a "Chronological List of Battles, Engagements, etc., in Which Troops of the Regular Army Have Participated";
and an "Index of Battle Engagements During the Civil War" (2 vols.).
Civil War staff officers' papers (20 ft.) consist of reports by and concerning officers serving on the staffs of armies, divisions, departments, corps,
and brigades.

Materials on specialized subjects of Civil War interest include a volume concerning the confinement at the Dry Tortugas (Fla.) Prison of deserters who had been condemned to death by courts-martial but whose
sentences had not been reviewed by the President; records relating to Army
bands (5 in.); records relating to pilots, the "Balloon and Construction
Corps," and sutlers (5 in.); papers relating to Indian prisoners held at military posts in the West, 1861-65 (5 in.); 2 "horse books," 1862-64, relating
to the furnishing of horses and horse equipment for the Army, claims for
horses lost, etc.; correspondence, 1861-64 (5 in.), concerning the appointment of staff officers from private life by Maj. Gen. John C. Frémont,
commanding the Western Department; and a register of captured flags,
1861-65.

Other records of value for Civil War research include a digest of the
decisions of the Second Comptroller of the Treasury, Mar. 1817-Sept.
1894 (and of the Comptroller, Oct. 1894-Dec. 1905), affecting the War
Department; the accounts current, dating from 1863, of the several assistant adjutants general in military divisions, departments, etc.; registers
of clerks employed in the bureaus of the Adjutant General's Office; a record of authorizations, from 1862, of admissions of insane soldiers to the
Government Hospital for the Insane (now St. Elizabeths) and a register,
with a separate index, of insane soldiers, 1853-1919; and records, 1864-83
(ca. 3 ft.), of the administration of the "Provost Fund," which consisted of
unexpended balances in the custody of provost marshals at the close of the
Civil War (including money belonging to deserters and to Confederate prisoners of war and any other small miscellaneous amounts coming in any unusual way into the custody of military authorities).

Orders

The Adjutant General's collection of the orders of the War Department
and of military commands is the most complete in existence. Dating from
1797, it comprehends both manuscript and printed general, special, and
other orders of the War Department; of armies, brigades, divisions, and

corps; and of military divisions, departments, districts, and posts. Two lists of the contents of the collection and a card index to sources of issuance facilitate its use. There is also a register of distribution of War Department general orders, 1863-68.

As defined by the revised regulations of 1861, general orders of armies, divisions, brigades, and regiments were intended to announce the time and place of issues and payments; hours for rollcalls and duties; the number and kind of orderlies and the time when they should be relieved; police regulations and the prohibitions required by circumstances and localities; returns to be made and the forms for them; laws and regulations for the Army; promotions and appointments; eulogies or censures of corps or individuals; "and generally, whatever it may be important to make known to the whole command." Special orders were those that did not concern the troops generally and did not need to be published to the whole command; for instance, those relating to the march of some particular corps, the establishment of some post, the detaching of individuals, and the granting of requests.

Until May 1, 1864, the proceedings of general courts-martial were published in War Department (AGO) general orders; but from that date the orders publishing such proceedings were numbered in a distinct series and were not generally distributed to the Army.

Muster Rolls

The muster rolls of Regular Army organizations for the Civil War period are in a single series extending from 1821 to 1912, arranged by arm of service, then numerically by regiment, then alphabetically by company, troop, or unit. The rolls of volunteer organizations are arranged by State and then in the same way as the Regular Army rolls; this series, embracing chiefly the Mexican and Civil Wars but including Indian wars, was used in the preparation of index-record cards by the Record and Pension Office.

Muster rolls, or lists of all men actually present on parade or otherwise accounted for, were prepared by the Army until 1918 on days of muster or review of troops under arms in order to take account of their numbers, inspect their arms and accouterments, and examine their condition. The several types of muster rolls include descriptive rolls, muster-in and muster-out rolls (for volunteer units only), and the regular muster-for-pay rolls. By 1861 the face of the muster roll had columns for numbers, names, ranks, enlistment records, dates last paid, bounties (paid and due), names of those present, and remarks. The reverse showed a recapitulation, alterations, books and blanks on hand, a record of events, and a space to denote the number of recruits required, number wounded in action, and number of horses on hand. The great influx of volunteers during the Civil War required expansion of the muster roll to include travel to the rendezvous. Later the face of the roll carried the numbers, names, ranks joined for service and enrolled at general rendezvous, when and where mustered into service, dates last paid, men present, and remarks, with the usual categories on the reverse. The muster-in rolls showed the age, birthplace, occupation, and personal description of each man. Each corps was given a commissary of musters (with two enlisted clerks) to exercise general supervision over the muster-in and muster-out of troops. To each division was assigned an assistant commissary of musters. These commissaries coordinated all muster rolls and sent them to the Adjutant General. By War Department General Order 94, May 15, 1865, a chief mustering officer was assigned at each State rendezvous to take charge of mustering out and to see that regimental records and colors were preserved.

AGO Circular 60, Aug. 1, 1864, required all commanders of colored troops enlisted before Jan. 1, 1864, to ascertain (and enter on muster rolls for pay purposes) which of the soldiers had been freemen on or before Apr. 19, 1861. Such muster rolls constituted authority for the Pay Department to pay these soldiers (from the time of their entry into service to Jan. 1, 1864) the difference between the pay they had received and the full pay allowed by law in the same period to white soldiers.

Returns, Station Books, and Related Records

The monthly or other periodic returns required during the Civil War by Army regulations from the commanders of departments, divisions, posts, brigades, regiments, etc., reveal the location and strength of units and the names of commissioned officers and their whereabouts. The returns of individual regiments of volunteers, on which index-record cards were prepared, are filed with the muster rolls, but those of Regular Army organizations for the Civil War period are in a single series, 1800-1916, arranged by arm of service, then by regiment. Other returns of the period include those of the geographical divisions, departments, and districts; and, separately maintained, those of the Headquarters of the Army, the Adjutant General's Department, the Topographical Engineers, the Corps of Engineers, the Medical Department, the Ordnance Department, the Quartermaster's Department, the Pay Department, and the Subsistence Department. The returns of the many forts and other military posts, camps, and stations, which are arranged alphabetically by post name in one series, ca. 1800-1916, are essentially complete for the Civil War except for periods when certain posts were occupied by Confederate forces. There is a card index to the post returns for the Civil War period, as well as to a separate series of Army corps returns. Compilations of the Adjutant General's Office based on the returns received consist of a volume of the consolidated returns of the Army, 1863-64; memoranda of returns received, 1861-1917 (15 vols.); the station book of troops, 1861-66 (44 vols.), showing organization, place, and State in which both Regular and volunteer troops were stationed at the end of each month, and the command to which they were assigned; station books of officers and organizations of the Regular Army, 1861-1915 (186 vols.), in subseries for the Civil War period relating to infantry, cavalry and artillery, general and staff officers, and Signal Corps and hospital chaplains, often giving biographical data such as occupation and place and date of marriage; and the yearly station books of volunteer officers, 1861-1915 (35 vols.), in subseries for the Civil War period relating to generals, general and staff officers, Signal Corps and hospital chaplains, and the Veteran Reserve Corps. There are also a volume of the post office addresses of former general and volunteer staff officers, dating from 1862, and "Retained Copies of Reports," 1861-65 (2 vols.), containing miscellaneous compilations relating to the strength and equipment of the Army and including such details as the strength of Union and Confederate forces in certain battles, the distribution and average yearly strength of the Army for different periods, and the number of guns in General Grant's army before Richmond and Petersburg, Mar. 31, 1865.

Other Records Relating to the Regular Army

The records described below were created within the Adjutant General's Office; the regimental and company records kept by organizations in the field are described elsewhere. Abstracts of soldier's records in the Regular Army form an unbroken sequence, 1798-1914, in large volumes using a 2-page spread for each enlistment; one page summarizes the items on the enlistment paper, and the other continues the record of the soldier's career. The file of enlistment papers, extending from 1798 to 1894, is itself incomplete, as are files of "personal papers of enlisted men, 1861-65," certificates of disability, and "final statements" (relating to death and interment of soldiers and the disposition of their effects). There are also, for the Regular Army, reports of physical examinations of candidates for admission to the U. S. Military Academy, dating from 1861 (these may be records of the Surgeon General rather than the Adjutant General); registers of discharges of invalids, 1862-63 (14 vols.); and a register of transfers from the Invalid Corps (Veteran Reserve Corps) after restoration to health.

Other Records Relating to Volunteer Organizations

These are records created within the Adjutant General's Office; the regimental and company records kept by volunteer organizations in the field are described separately. These AGO records include histories of various organizations to Mar. 31, 1863 (81 vols.), submitted in response to Ordnance Circular 13, Mar. 18, 1863; registers of deceased soldiers, 1861-64 (11 vols.); registers, 1861-66, of discharges of volunteer officers (5 vols.; one vol. missing) and discharges of volunteers for disability (incomplete in 3 vols.); and a volume pertaining to the organization and command of Civil War Army corps, giving the names of commanders chronologically, together with newspaper clippings relating to corps history.

Volunteer Service Division

This Division, organized in Oct. 1861, handled the authorization, recruiting, service, and discharge of volunteer troops as organizations, including the officer personnel of such organizations. In July 1879 the Freedmen's Branch, which had been organized to dispose of the unfinished business of the Bureau of Refugees, Freedmen, and Abandoned Lands, was consolidated with the Colored Troops Division; and in 1888 that Division was in turn consolidated with the Volunteer Service Division. This Division was one of several transferred to the Record and Pension Office in 1889.

Record Group 94. -- The correspondence consists of copies of letters sent, 1861-89 (64 vols.); copies of endorsements, 1861-70 (18 vols.); and letters received, 1861-89 (640 ft.). The letters and endorsements sent are indexed (65 and 15 vols.); and the letters received are registered in 71 volumes and indexed in 28. This correspondence was with Members of Congress, Governors of States, State adjutants general, chiefs of bureaus of the War Department, and others; it relates to the functions of the Division stated above. There is also a register of actions of military commissions in cases involving officers of volunteers and an index to officers' files in this Division and the Enlisted Branch.

Recruiting Division

The Recruiting Division was organized on July 1, 1862, and was put in charge of all recruitment for the Army. It was abolished in 1882, when its duties were taken over by the Enlisted Branch.

Record Group 94. --Copies of letters sent and endorsements, dating from 1862, continue series previously established in the Adjutant General's Office; these are indexed from 1863. The letters received also date from 1862 and are registered and indexed. Besides this general correspondence, which is concerned with all aspects of recruiting, the following separate series are pertinent to the Civil War: telegrams received by Maj. Thomas M. Vincent, Assistant Adjutant General, 1863-65, from officers reporting on the recruiting and mustering out of troops (5 vols.); proceedings of boards of inspection appointed to examine recruits reported unfit for military service, 1861-66 (1 ft.); reports by State adjutants general on troops furnished, 1862-64 (2 vols.); a register of "Passes Given to Agents of Various States and Townships to Recruit in Rebel States," 1864; other registers of reports received from and contracts made by recruiting officers; and a volume of statements of disbursements made by recruiting officers on account of the Volunteer Recruiting Service, 1861-66.

Enlisted Branch

This branch, created in Dec. 1862, had charge of the business of the Adjutant General's Office concerning recruitment, discharge, transfer, furlough, and other actions relating to enlisted men for both the regular and volunteer forces. Its functions concerning volunteers were transferred to the Record and Pension Office in 1889, and those relating to the Regular Army were absorbed by the Principal Record Division of the Adjutant General's Office in 1890.

Record Group 94. --Copies of letters sent, 1863-89 (154 vols.), usually in response to inquiries relating to recruitment, discharge, furlough, etc., of enlisted men of the Regular Army and volunteer forces, with indexes (19 vols.); letters received, 1862-89 (1,433 ft.), on subjects comparable to those of the letters sent, with registers (393 vols.) and indexes (31 vols.); an index to special orders relating to enlisted men, 1864-65; and an index to information relating to general prisoners and deserters, 1865-72. In addition, the so-called Addison files, taken over from the Chief Clerk of the Adjutant General's Office by the Enlisted Branch, contain similar materials for the Civil War period through 1862 and include an index to letters received relating to soldiers, 1861-62 (1 vol.).

Commission Branch

This Branch, organized on Jan. 1, 1863, was one of several new branches created within the Adjutant General's Office in that year. By the end of the war its functions included the preparation, issuance, and accurate registry of all letters of appointment and commissions to officers appointed by the President; the regulating of officer promotion and succession; the preparation of promotion orders; the issuance of ordnance sergeants', hospital stewards', and sutlers' warrants; and the solution of questions of rank and pay as well as questions of organization of the Army under various acts of Congress. The Branch also prepared the **Army Register**.

<u>Record Group 94.</u> -- The several series of letters and endorsements sent relating to officer appointments, pay, promotions, etc., include records inherited by the Commission Branch upon its organization and thus span the war period; the letters received date from 1863 and are registered and indexed for the war period. Copies of letters of appointment from the Secretary of War informing officers of their appointment by the President, 1829-95, include the war period in 16 volumes (3 ft.), as do Army promotion letters, 1829-77, in 4 volumes (1 ft.). Numerous registers, for the most part begun before the Civil War and continued afterward, are available separately for Army commissions (containing copies of executed commissions issued by the President); brevet commissions (containing such copies as well as notations justifying the commissions, as for gallant service); appointments in the Invalid Corps or the Veteran Reserve Corps, 1863-65; appointments in the U. S. Colored Troops, 1863-66; and appointments of quartermasters, 1864-65. "Senate rolls" (original resolutions confirming nominations for Army appointments and promotions) and related registers, also spanning the war period, are available. There are also some fully executed Army commissions, signed by the President but never delivered to the designated recipients. Several volumes of copies of letters of appointment for limited service, as provided by acts of Congress, pertain respectively to general officers for "Additional Force," 1861-62; provost marshals, 1863; surgeons for the Board of Enrollment, 1863; commissioners for the Board of Enrollment, 1863; officers for the Veteran Reserve Corps, 1864-65; officers for U. S. Colored Troops, 1863; and officers for the Invalid Corps, 1863-64. Among many other special registers are those of Army commissions in Hancock's First Army Corps, 1864-65; of noncommissioned officers (from 1862); of officers dismissed; of post traders; of paymasters (from 1864); and of commissioned line officers of the Army. The personal reports of retired officers, beginning in 1864, indicate their whereabouts, changes in address, and other matters relating to their recall to service. There are also manuscript lists, kept current to show dates of commissions, resignations, dismissals, and deaths; these supplement the <u>Official Army Register of the Volunteer Force of the United States Army for the Years 1861, '62, '63, '64, '65</u> (8 vols. Washington, 1865-67), prepared by the Adjutant General's Office and published by order of the Secretary of War in compliance with a joint resolution of Congress of Mar. 2, 1865 (13 Stat. 570).

Bureau For Colored Troops

Immediately after the issuance of the Emancipation Proclamation, diligent efforts were begun to raise colored troops. As a preparatory measure AGO Special Order 97, Mar. 1, 1863, established a board, to convene immediately in Washington, "to examine and report upon a system of Tactics for Colored Troops" that had been prepared by Brig. Gen. Silas Casey. The Adjutant General, Lorenzo Thomas, was sent to the Mississippi Valley to organize the recruiting system there; and AGO General Order 143, May 22, 1863, established in the Adjutant General's Office a bureau "for the record of all matters relating to the organization of colored troops." Under departmental authority, before the establishment of the Bureau, colored regiments had been raised in Massachusetts, North Carolina, South Carolina, and Kansas and in the Department of the Gulf and the Valley of the Mississippi. Those organized in the Department of the Gulf under General

Banks had been designated as the Corps d'Afrique; and, as mentioned above, those in the Mississippi Valley were being organized under the personal direction of the Adjutant General. Under these circumstances the new Bureau turned its attention to the middle and eastern States. On June 17, 1863, a recruiting commissioner for U. S. Colored Troops (Maj. George L. Stearns) was appointed, with headquarters at Philadelphia, where a citizens' committee was already engaged in raising colored troops. (Stearns had the later title of "commissioner for the organization of colored troops in Middle and East Tennessee," and in this capacity he was replaced on Feb. 9, 1864, by Capt. R. D. Mussey.) By Oct. 1863 a number of recruiting stations for colored troops had been established also in Maryland. The Governors of other States were authorized to raise colored regiments.

With standardization of recruiting measures the designation U. S. Colored Troops gradually replaced more colorful or fanciful titles such as Corps d'Afrique and Zouaves d'Afrique. Examining boards for prospective officers (usually white) in the colored service were in session from time to time at Washington, Cincinnati, St. Louis, New Orleans, Davenport (Iowa), and Richmond (from Apr. 1865).

On July 15, 1865, the date on which the last organization of colored troops was mustered in, the maximum number in service at any one time during the war was reached. They were distributed as follows:

120 infantry regiments	98,938
12 heavy artillery regiments	15,662
10 heavy artillery batteries	1,311
7 cavalry regiments	7,245
Total	123,156

The entire number of colored troops commissioned and enlisted during the war, as computed in 1865, was 186,097; the loss during the war from all causes except muster-out was 68,178.

After the war the Bureau became known as the Colored Troops Division, and in 1879 it inherited the remaining business of the Freedmen's Branch (see below). It was consolidated with the Volunteer Service Division in 1888 and was transferred with that Division to the Record and Pension Division of the War Department on July 16, 1889.

Col. Charles W. Foster, appointed ca. May 22, 1863, served during the war as Chief of the Bureau for Colored Troops.

Civil War annual reports of the Chief of the Bureau for Colored Troops, appended to those of the Adjutant General; Dudley Taylor Cornish, The Sable Arm; Negro Troops in the Union Army, 1861-1865 (New York, 1956).

Record Group 94. --Records of the Bureau include copies of letters sent, Dec. 1863-Mar. 1888, to Members of Congress, State Governors, Army officers, recruiting agents, and others, pertaining to the recruitment, organization, and service of colored units and their officers (22 vols., with 22 vols. of name indexes); copies of letters sent and endorsements and memoranda relating to recruiting, 1864-68 (8 vols., indexed in 2 vols.); other endorsements and memoranda, 1864-78 (14 vols., with 10 vols. of name indexes); a main series of letters received, 1863-88 and later

(135 ft.), and a special series relating to recruiting, 1863-68 (12 ft., with 58 vols. of indexes or registers); and letters received by Adjutant General Thomas relating to colored troops, 1863-65 (1 ft., with a register and a name index). Records concerning officers of U. S. Colored Troops, 1863- 68 (8 ft.), include applications for appointment, registers and rosters, a register of resignations, an index to an appointment book not extant, a few fully executed commissions (signed by the President) that were never de- livered, and the proceedings of the Cincinnati and St. Louis examining boards, as well as lists of applicants passed by those boards and boards at Davenport, New Orleans, Washington, and Richmond. (Notifications and other letters concerning applicants are in the series of letters sent and re- ceived.) Other records include descriptive lists of colored volunteers, 1864 (54 vols.), enlisted under General Order 135, Department of the Mis- souri, Nov. 14, 1863; colored troops registers, 1869 (2 vols.), showing whether "slave or free on or before April 19, 1861"; and a record of regi- ments of U. S. Colored Troops, 1863-65 (1 vol.). There are also a useful index, 1863-65 (2 vols.), to War Department Special Orders concerning colored troops and a compilation, "The Negro in the Military Service of the United States" (8 vols., 2 1/2 ft.), containing copies of official records, State papers, etc., relating to the military status and service of Negroes from the colonial period through the Civil War, prepared in 1888 in the Colored Troops Division.

The records of the several Slave Claims Commissions, whose work was generally overseen by the Bureau for Colored Troops, are described under Miscellaneous War Department Commissions.

Records in Other Custody. -- The papers of George L. Stearns, recruit- ing commissioner, in the Stearns collection in the Kansas State Historical Society cover the Civil War period.

Drafted Bureau

The Drafted Bureau was added to the organization of the Adjutant Gen- eral's Office in 1863 to regulate the distribution of drafted men to regi- ments after they had been delivered at the principal rendezvous by provost marshals. Besides its primary responsibility for the establishment and maintenance of draft rendezvous and for related funds and property, this Bureau had charge of all business relating to court-martial cases after they had been reported upon by the Bureau of Military Justice, and it had supervision over military prisoners. Its functions were taken over on Mar. 1, 1866, by the General Courts Martial Division, which became the Fund Branch in 1871.

Record Group 94. --Copies of letters sent, July 1863-Dec. 1866 (3 vols.), chiefly to officers in charge of draft rendezvous, relating to drafted forces and to civil and military prisoners, with index (2 vols.); endorse- ments and memoranda on correspondence received, 1863-66 (2 vols.), with index (incomplete in 1 vol.); letters received, 1863-66 (1 1/2 ft.), from of- ficers in charge of draft rendezvous, with registers (5 vols., incomplete) and indexes (3 vols., incomplete); and consolidated trimonthly reports re- ceived from draft rendezvous, July 1863-July 1865 (4 in.).

Enrollment Branch

In anticipation of the discontinuance of the Office of the Provost Marshal General on Aug. 28, 1866, the business of that Office was trans-

ferred (by AGO General Order 66, Aug. 20, 1866) to the Adjutant General's
Office, where the residual work was taken over by the newly created Enrollment Branch and the Disbursing Branch. The former was charged initially with answering calls for information from the Second Auditor of the
Treasury, the Pension Office, the Paymaster General, and State and local
authorities, and with miscellaneous business. In addition, it commenced
the work of consolidating and transferring the names of all men drafted into
the service of the United States during the war into books especially prepared and arranged by States and districts. This branch (known also as the
Enrollment Division) continued to function until it was transferred to the
Record and Pension Division (later Office) of the War Department in July
1889. As the Enrollment Division of that Office it continued to maintain
custody of, and to furnish information from, "the general records of the
late Provost-Marshal-General's Bureau and its various branches, including those of the superintendents of the volunteer recruiting service, and the
chief mustering and disbursing officers and acting assistant provost-
marshals-general of States. "

Record Group 94. --Certain records created by the Enrollment Branch
are intermingled with or continue records of the Office of the Provost
Marshal General. Those of the Branch allocated to Record Group 94 include only the registers of letters received, 1867-68 (2 vols.), indexes to
these registers, 1866-68 and later (5 vols.), and indexes to letters sent
and endorsements, of indeterminate date (5 vols.).

Disbursing Branch

In anticipation of the discontinuance of the Office of the Provost Marshal
General on Aug. 28, 1866, the business of that Office was transferred (by
AGO General Order 66, Aug. 20, 1866) to the Adjutant General's Office,
where the residual work was taken over by the newly created Enrollment
Branch (see above) and the Disbursing Branch. The latter was responsible
for all disbursements from the fund for "collecting, drilling, and organizing
volunteers" and the "enrollment and draft fund, " as well as for business
relating to all accounts and claims connected with the raising of troops during the war. The Disbursing Branch (later Division) became the Bounty and
Claims Division in 1884 and was transferred to the Record and Pension Division (later Office) of the War Department in July 1889. As a division of
the same name in that Office it continued to maintain, and furnish information from, the disbursement records of the Office of the Provost Marshal
General and of the Bureau of Freedmen, Refugees, and Abandoned Lands.
It also kept the records of the various Slave Claims Commissions (see
under Miscellaneous War Department Commissions)..

Record Group 94. --Certain records created by the Disbursing Branch
and its successor are intermingled with or continue records of the Office
of the Provost Marshal General. The incomplete records allocated to Record Group 94 comprise press copies of letters sent, 1867-75 (40 vols.), in
part illegible; telegrams received and copies of letters sent relating chiefly
to the mustering and pay of volunteer troops and the payment of bounty to
them, 1862-78 (125 vols.); a register of letters received (1866 only); an
undated list of "minority cases" (minors who refunded bounty money); and
the account books of disbursing officers, with related records, 1862-66
(57 vols.), concerning pay, bounty, claimants, and claims, including
claims transferred to the Second Auditor of the Treasury.

Freedmen's Branch

Upon discontinuance of the Bureau of Refugees, Freedmen, and Abandoned Lands (see later in this section), on June 30, 1872, the Bureau's unfinished business was turned over to the Adjutant General's Office and vested in the Freedmen's Branch, created to carry it on. It consisted essentially of receiving, passing upon, and paying claims of colored soldiers and sailors or their heirs for bounty, pension, arrears of pay, commutation of rations, and prize money. An act of Dec. 15, 1877 (20 Stat. 11), provided that, if the work was not finished before Jan. 1, 1879, the Freedmen's Branch would be closed and all its papers would be turned over to the Paymaster General. The Freedmen's Branch was finally closed on June 30, 1879.

Record Group 94. -- The records of the Freedmen's Branch pertain almost exclusively to its functions as stated above. They include copies or rough drafts of letters sent, 1872-79 (23 vols.), with indexes (18 vols.); and letters received, 1872-79 (30 ft.), with registers (11 vols.). There are also employee records; reports, including a report (1 vol.) by the officer in charge giving background data on the organization of the Branch, 1872-73; papers relating to the financial and other affairs of the Bureau of Refugees, Freedmen, and Abandoned Lands and to the Howard Court of Inquiry, 1872-74 (9 in.); and bounty registers, 1874-78 (3 vols. and 3 index vols.). The records of field disbursing offices operating under the Freedmen's Branch consist of series, separate for each office, of letters sent, letters received, registers of letters received, and registers of claims; these date for various periods within the years 1872-78 for the following offices: Charleston and Columbia, S. C.; Fort Johnston, N. C.; Fort Monroe, Va., Fort Leavenworth, Kans. (no letters received); Louisville, Ky.; Memphis, Tenn.; Nashville, Tenn.; Natchez, New Orleans, and Vicksburg; New Bern, N. C. (no letters received); New Orleans, La.; Savannah and Charleston (no letters sent or received); St. Louis, Mo. (no letters sent); and Vicksburg, Miss. About 40 volumes of Freedmen's Branch records that were in existence as late as 1906 are now missing; but the more important series are virtually intact.

Archive Office

By AGO General Order 60, Apr. 7, 1865, the War Department directed commanders in the field to send captured Confederate records to Washington; and by General Order 127, July 21, 1865, it ordered "That a Bureau be organized in the Adjutant General's Office for the collection, safekeeping, and publication of the Rebel Archives that have come into possession of this Government." The latter order appointed Francis Lieber as Chief of the new Bureau and directed the Quartermaster General to "furnish suitable apartments and buildings for the collation and custody of the archives mentioned." Establishment of the Bureau had been suggested to Secretary Stanton by Professor Lieber as a measure to provide for the preservation, arrangement, and classification of the captured records. Because of the wording of the order the unit became generally known as the Bureau of Rebel Archives; but by the Adjutant General's regulations of Aug. 23, 1865, its official title was given as Archive Office of the War Department, and publication was dropped from its specified functions. The Archive Office, however, furnished assistance to the War Records Office of the War Department when the publication project was revived in 1874.

In 1878 Marcus J. Wright, formerly of the Confederate Army, was appointed agent of the War Department to obtain the gift or loan of Confederate records from private persons and historical societies; and systematic efforts were made to supplement the fragmentary collection then in the War Department. The purchase of two groups of papers and the acquisition of other material by gift or loan increased the size of the collection.

In 1881 the Archive Office became the Archive Branch of the Record Division in the Office of the Secretary of War. The details of the program of the Archive Office in its systematic collecting of Confederate records are given in the accompanying Guide to the Archives of the Government of the Confederate States of America.

Carl L. Lokke, "The Captured Confederate Records Under Francis Lieber," American Archivist, 9:277-319 (Oct. 1946).

Record Group 109. --As distinguished from the records of the Confederacy, which it administered as an archival agency, the records of the Archive Office itself consist chiefly of correspondence, reports, and lists of the records received. Press copies of letters sent, 1865-80 (3 vols.), relate chiefly to administrative matters, to collecting Confederate records, and to furnishing information from them (e. g., after 1870, to the Commissioners of Claims). The abstracts, 1892-94, of answers to inquiries (3 vols. and 2 index vols.) facilitate use of the letters both sent and received. The letters received, 1865-81, measure 1 foot; there is a related register and a volume of copies of endorsements on the letters.

Among reports are the draft of Francis Lieber's report (Jan. 18, 1866) to the Secretary of War on the nature of the records then in the Archive Office and the reports of Marcus J. Wright. Records throwing light on the methods and procedures of the Office include the relevant orders and regulations, 1865-81 (3 in.); a collection of copies of letters from other files bearing upon the work of the Office, 1865-80 (1 in.); and a clerk's time book, 1891-94. Informational materials accumulated by the Office include newspaper clippings, 1874-94 (2 vols.), many of which concern the Confederate records; a small collection (3 in.) of Confederate military operational maps; an index to local Confederate military organizations; and an "Index to Field Returns, Morning Reports, Organizations, etc., C. S. Army, 1861-65." The control records of the Office include notably the catalogs (17 vols.) of Confederate military records received by Marcus J. Wright, 1878-1900, and the schedule (2 vols.) of papers referring to the exchange and treatment of prisoners in Southern prisons. There is also a list of the Confederate pay, quartermaster, ordnance, medical, and recruiting accounts received by the Archive Office in 1865 (1 vol.).

National Archives, Preliminary Inventory [No. 101] of the War Department Collection of Confederate Records, comp. by Elizabeth Bethel (Washington, 1957), p. 304-307; War Record Publication Office, Catalogue of Written and Printed Battle Reports on File in the Archive Office, War Department (Washington, 1878).

ENGINEER DEPARTMENT

In time of peace engineering responsibilities had been divided between the Corps of Engineers and the Corps of Topographical Engineers; the former had charge of permanent defense works and of certain other public construction, and the latter surveyed the lakes, explored the West, and marked State and international boundaries. Soon after the outbreak of the Civil War, however, it became evident that responsibilities for engineer duties with armies in the field could not be divided between two organizations.

Engineer Bureau

The Corps of Engineers originated in an act of Mar. 16, 1802 (2 Stat. 137). It was responsible for planning, constructing, and repairing all fortifications and other defense works and for planning and constructing such civil works of the Government as might be assigned. Its additional wartime duties, as prescribed by regulations applicable at the outbreak of the Civil War, were to present plans for the attack and defense of military works; to lay out and construct field defenses, redoubts, entrenchments, roads, military bridges, etc.; to form a part of the vanguard to remove obstructions; and, in retreat, as a part of the rearguard, to erect obstacles and to destroy roads, bridges, etc., in order to retard an enemy's pursuit.

On the outbreak of war the Engineer Bureau called to Washington the available officers of engineers for assignment to combat duty. Thus most such officers were withdrawn from the construction of fortifications of the seacoast and northern frontier; and the Engineer Bureau recognized at the outset that their places on construction could be filled only from civil life--"that is, by thus using the services of ex-officers of engineers, and by recalling other valuable assistants who have heretofore aided our labors." Topographical surveys for the armies in the field covered the country traversed and the particular sites occupied. The Engineer Bureau itself did the work of engraving, lithographing, photographing, and issuing sheets for officers in the field and various branches of the service. From field "reconnaissances" of enemy positions detailed maps of scenes of operations were prepared and "multiplied by photography" for distribution throughout the Army.

With the merging of the Corps of Topographical Engineers into the Engineers Corps in accordance with an act of March 3, 1863 (12 Stat. 743), the work of the discontinued Topographical Bureau was assumed by the Engineer Bureau. An act of Aug. 3, 1861 (12 Stat. 287), had provided for the addition of six officers to each of the two corps and three additional companies of engineer soldiers to the Corps of Engineers; and an act of Aug. 6, 1861 (12 Stat. 317), had added a company to the Corps of Topographical Engineers and further increased the officer complement by six for each of the two corps. (One company of engineer soldiers, created at the outbreak of the Mexican War, was still in service at the outbreak of the Civil War.)

Important to the work of the Engineer Bureau during the war were the many engineer boards established to undertake special inquiries or inspections. Information about some but not necessarily all of these is available chiefly in the correspondence files of the Engineer Bureau, described below. Such boards were created to examine and report on the defenses of Washington (AGO S. O. 497, Nov. 9, 1863); to examine and report on "Timby's revolving iron towers" for harbor defense (AGO S. O. 388, Dec. 10, 1862); to examine and report on the means to defend the Potomac Aqueduct, as connected with the defenses of Washington (AGO

S. O. 388, Aug. 29, 1863); to examine and report on "Mr. A. C. Currier's Shot Proof Dome" (AGO S. O. 264, June 15, 1863); to examine projects for further defenses of San Francisco Harbor (AGO S. O. 365, Aug. 17, 1863); to examine "Dr. Solomon Andrews' 'Aerial Machine'" (AGO S. O. 119, Mar. 16, 1864); "to devise such modification to our system of Sea Coast Fortifications, as may be deemed necessary in view of the increased calibre and range of modern artillery, and the additional power of armored vessels of war, to contend against land defences" (AGO S. O. 41, Jan. 27, 1864); and to inspect the forts in Maryland, northeast Virginia, and the District of Columbia (AGO S. O. 533, Oct. 9, 1865).

Boards on which both the Engineer and Ordnance Departments were represented had the following duties: (1) to regulate and fix the number and caliber of the cannon at permanent fortifications, also the number and kind of guns for field batteries (AGO S. O. 314, Nov. 26, 1861); (2) to examine and report upon "Wappich's improvements in gun-carriages" and "improved method in loading heavy shots" (AGO S. O. 71, Feb. 13, 1865, and AGO S. O. 160, Apr. 5, 1865); and (3) to examine into and report on J. W. Reid's plan "for revetting fortifications with cast-iron, bullet-proof curtains for embrasure port holes" (AGO S. O. 189, Apr. 25, 1863).

A board of engineer and quartermaster officers was appointed (AGO S. O. 35, Jan. 22, 1863) to consider and report upon improvements in pontoons and their transportation "as presented by Mr. Francis." This board was reconvened (by AGO S. O. 130, Mar. 20, 1863) to consider and report upon "Mr. Sartain's pontoon bridge" and to examine "any other pontoon bridge equipage that may be referred to it by the Corps of Engineers."

The Chief Engineer continued through the Civil War as the Inspector of the U. S. Military Academy; the functions and records of this office are treated separately below. He served also as a member of the Light-House Board, which is discussed under Department of the Treasury elsewhere in this Guide.

Successive Chief Engineers during the war period:

Col. (later Maj. Gen.) Joseph G. Totten, in office when the war began.
Brig. Gen. Richard Delafield, Apr. 22, 1864.

Reports of the Chief Engineer, 1861-65, appended to those of the Secretary of War; W. Stull Holt, The Office of the Chief of Engineers of the Army . . . (Baltimore, 1923); Col. Henry L. Abbot, "The Corps of Engineers, " in Theo. F. Rodenbough and William L. Haskin, eds., The Army of the United States (New York, 1896); F. Stansbury Haydon, Aeronautics in the Union and Confederate Armies . . . (Baltimore, 1941).

Record Group 77. -- The Engineer Bureau's records relating to the Civil War include notable cartographic and pictorial materials, described below. Its textual records consist chiefly of correspondence. Most of the letters sent are in a 25-volume series beginning in 1812 (vols. 20-25); there are subject indexes to volumes 18-22 (1853-64). Copies of letters to engineer officers are in a 40-volume series beginning in 1812 (vols. 32-39); and subject indexes to these cover the Civil War period. Copies of communications to the Secretary of War and Congress are in a series beginning in 1836 (vols. 10-12); these also are indexed for the Civil War period. There are also a record of papers referred, 1839-70 (9 vols.), to other bureaus or offices, and an index to letters sent, 1812-67, relating to the acquisition and reservation of public lands, principally for fortifications. Copies of the annual reports submitted by the Chief Engineer to the Secretary of War are available in 4 volumes, 1842-67. The series of letters received extends from 1838 to 1866; within this the Secretary of War's letters, 1852-66, are filed separately. Registers of letters received cover the war period, but the indexes begin in 1864. A card index (9 ft.), covering records from 1789 to 1889, is alphabetical by significant topics, projects, localities, and individuals mentioned in several correspondence series, including that of the Topographical Bureau (see below).

Regulatory issuances or directives especially applicable to the Corps of Engineers and the Corps of Topographical Engineers during the Civil War include a volume of circulars and office memoranda on office procedures, 1861-71; duplicate volumes entitled "Orders of the Engineer Department during the Rebellion," 1861-65; and a record of orders received and transmitted, 1863-69. Orderly books, 1811-74 (4 vols.), contain copies of Engineer Department orders and War Department orders affecting the Engineer Department; and there are general orders and circulars of Headquarters, Corps of Engineers, largely in manuscript, 1838-65.

Several series of copies of letters sent and received involving claims for wartime losses and damage are among the records of the postwar Second and Fourth Divisions of the Office of the Chief of Engineers. Related to these, in part, are registers of claims, showing disposition, 1860-70 (3 vols.), and a "Claims Index--Memoranda of Special Cases, 1862-94" (1 vol.). Among other indexes to claims papers are those relating to "non-payment rolls" of men employed in Virginia and North Carolina during the war and of contrabands who worked on Fort Pickering, Memphis, Tenn., 1862-63; the rolls referred to by the latter index are among the claims papers. There is also correspondence about claims arising from the Engineer Department's cutting of timber around fortifications around Washington, 1862-65. A pamphlet containing memoranda of the procedure to be followed in the examination of the engineer records for Civil War claims cases is also in the records.

A chronologically arranged file, 1834-66 (3 ft.), contains contracts and related proposals for supplies, equipment, and services for the Engineer Department, as well as lists of contracts made. Fiscal records consist of ledgers of disbursements (vols. 3-4 of a 25-volume series); requisitions for funds, to 1863; payrolls for work at Fort Jefferson, Fla., 1860-62, and for work on the fortifications of the Army of the Potomac, 1862-63, the former with "slave rolls"; and payrolls of the Pioneer Brigade, Army of the Cumberland, at Fort Jefferson, Dec. 1862-Feb. 1863.

Personnel records consist of monthly returns of the 1st "Battalion of Engineers" from Dec. 1861; monthly returns of officers; and a record of officers of the Engineer Corps, 1857-70 (vol. 1 of 4 vols.). There is also a "List of Commanders of Corps, Divisions, Brigades, and Regiments, composing the Armies of the Potomac and James from May 1, 1864, to May 1, 1865; also, of the Army of the Potomac, during portions of 1862 and 1863, embracing the battles of Antietam, Fredericksburg, Chancellorsville, Gettysburg, and Mine Run," compiled from the returns in the Office of the Adjutant General.

(The records of territorial and army commands and of the 25 corps, described below, should be used to supplement the records of the Engineer Bureau in the study of engineer operations in the field and especially under combat conditions. These field records are in Record Group 98 with the exceptions indicated.)

For the immediate postwar period an index to reports of Boards of Engineers on Seacoast Defenses, 1865-71(1 vol.), may be noted.

Copies of official letters and reports sent by Joseph G. Totten during his military career as cadet at the U. S. Military Academy and officer and Chief of the Corps of Engineers, and the letters received by him from Col. Sylvanus Thayer, are preserved in a series, 1803-64 (10 vols.), together with a related group of unbound letters received. Also in this record group are the official papers of Col. John N. Macomb, 1857-77 (1 ft.), documenting his service under the Topographical Bureau as chief engineer of the Department of New Mexico, as a combat engineer during the Civil War, and as officer in charge of postwar river improvements in Wisconsin and Illinois.

Papers concerning land acquisition by the Engineer Bureau and the Topographical Bureau were brought together in 1867; these eventually composed a file arranged by State or Territory, containing papers dating from 1794. Since the lands involved include both those acquired from private owners and public lands reserved for military purpose, they may prove useful in research in the Civil War period.

Cartographic Records

In the extensive collection of maps dated from the late 18th century to 1935 and organized by the Office of the Chief of Engineers are many maps relating to the Civil War. The records are found in three distinct files: (1) the "Headquarters Map File," (2) the "Fortifications File," and (3) the general or published cartographic records file.

The "Headquarters Map File" includes manuscript and annotated maps, plats, sketches, profiles, and diagrams of the Civil War period, arranged largely by State or group of States in series designated by letters and thereunder by map number. A card catalog, prepared by the Office of the Chief of Engineers, is arranged geographically. The records include a few State and county maps that were copied or acquired from various sources at the beginning of the war and were annotated with the latest information available; maps of military departments and other large areas (compiled by the Bureau of Topographical Engineers for military purposes) showing rivers, streams, roads, railroads, cities, towns, villages, churches, and sometimes mills, factories, and other buildings; maps and sketches, prepared from reconnaissances and surveys in the field in anticipation of maneuvers or attacks, showing the terrain and topographic features in detail, the defenses of towns and cities and other strategic points, and all roads in the vicinity; maps, diagrams, and sketches of battlefields during or immediately after the action; sketches showing daily routes of march of the different Army corps in some of the campaigns; general campaign maps compiled from the sketches; and battlefield maps, compiled from topographic surveys made after the war, showing the positions of troops of the opposing armies and lines of works in the adjacent country. There are a few maps prepared to facilitate investigation of the conduct of military operations in certain campaigns and battles. The file also contains several maps that can be identified as captured Confederate maps made during the war and many that were probably captured and used to obtain information about the country and in the compilation of other military maps. A portfolio of copies of Confederate maps is also included.

The "Fortifications File" consists of manuscript and annotated maps, plans, and drawings relating to permanent and temporary fortifications. Records of the Civil War period pertaining to fortifications include plans for the expansion of the facilities of forts already established and maps and plans of temporary forts and batteries erected for the defense of major cities and coastal areas by the Union forces. There are also a few captured plans of Confederate forts and maps and plans of former Confederate defenses made by the Union forces at the time of capture and after occupation. The records are arranged numerically by assigned drawer and sheet number. A typescript list describes the records by name of fortification or by subject entry.

The general or published cartographic records file includes maps of several Civil War military departments, maps compiled for military purposes covering large areas of some of the States (particularly Virginia and Tennessee), and a few military maps of smaller areas. Most of the maps are rather general, as are those of the military departments described above as part of the "Headquarters Map File." The smaller area maps usually show more detail and sometimes include names of residents. There are also a few maps pertaining to the defenses of cities, a few campaign maps, and many maps of battlefields. Most of the battlefield maps show the positions of the Union and Confederate forces in color, the physical features of the field as nearly as possible as at the time of battle, wooded and open areas, and farms and houses with family name of residents. The manuscript compilations for many of the maps are in the "Headquarters Map File." Many of the battlefield maps were published in 1867, some appeared in the 1870's, and a few were issued in revised editions at later dates. The published maps are arranged chronologically by date of publication or by date of information if the date of publication is not given.

Many Federal maps are noted in Richard W. Stephenson, comp., Civil War Maps; an Annotated List of Maps and Atlases in Map Collections of the Library of Congress (Washington, 1961).

Photographic Records

The Civil War photographs in this record group are among those segregated from the "Headquarters Map File" and the "Fortifications File" described above. They include scenes of Fort Morgan, Ala. , 1864 (40 prints); Fort Williams near Fort Hudson, La. , 1863 (32 stereographs); Jefferson Barracks, Mo. , 1865 (a colored lithograph); Quartermaster Department and Engineer Corps transport ships and quarters in Georgia and Tennessee, 1863-64 (37 prints); water and railway routes in and near Chattanooga, Tenn. , 1864 (9 prints); the defenses of Knoxville, Tenn. , 1864 (4 rolled prints); Harper's Ferry, W. Va. , and Berlin, Md. , 1862-64 (8 prints); Harper's Ferry, 1862 (2 prints); forts and installations in Washington, D. C. , Petersburg, Va. , and Atlanta, Ga. , 1863-64 (7 prints); and Confederate artillery and artillerymen at Pensacola, Fla. , ca. 1863 (2 prints). Other photographs are interspersed in the textual records, and engineers' activities are shown in photographs allocated to other record groups.

Herman Haupt, Photographs, Illustrative of Operations in Construction and Transportation (Boston, 1863). The National Archives has assembled copies of the 81 photographs described in this publication and bound them with a copy of the narrative.

Topographical Bureau

The Topographical Bureau in the War Department was constituted by the Department's General Order 26, June 22, 1831, and the Bureau existed separately until, by the act of Mar. 3, 1863, cited above, the Corps of Topographical Engineers was merged with the Corps of Engineers. The duties of the Corps of Topographical Engineers related generally to mapping and topographical surveys. Specifically, they consisted of surveys for the defense of the frontiers, surveys of sites for fortifications, reconnaissance of the country through which troops were to pass or operate, the examination of routes of communication by land or by water (both for supplies and for military movements), the construction of military roads, and the construction of civil works as assigned. The outbreak of hostilities affected the work of the Topographical Bureau immediately. Its scientific explorations and surveys had been largely dependent on the availability of military officers, and many of these were recalled to their regiments for active service. Capt. George G. Meade (Brigadier General of Volunteers) continued as Superintendent of the Survey of the Northern and Northwestern Lakes until Aug. 31, 1861, when he was relieved. The survey of the delta of the Mississippi and the removal of obstructions from the river's mouth were interrupted, and the latter work was suspended formally on Mar. 7, 1861. The Survey of the Northern and Northwestern Lakes continued, however, and by 1864 was reported to have developed harbors "where, by the construction of suitable gun batteries, the large commercial marine of the lakes would find protection against a hostile fleet. "

On Apr. 5, 1861, the Office of Exploration and Surveys, which Maj. Andrew A. Humphreys had directed under the immediate supervision of the Secretary of War, was put under the Chief of the Corps of Topographical Engineers. The work then in progress involved the completion of the road from Fort Benton to Fort Walla-Walla and the preparation of final reports of the exploration of the San Juan River, of the artesian well expedition, and of recent explorations in Nebraska. (About 2 ft. of the records of the Office of Exploration and Surveys, 1857-63, in Record Group 77, for the most part antedate the Civil War; but Humphreys' "miscellaneous war records, " 1861-65, are a part of the records of the War Records Office in Record Group 94.)

Successive Chief Topographical Engineers:
   Col. John J. Abert, in office when the war began.
   Col. Stephen H. Long, Sept. 9, 1861.

Annual reports of the Chief Topo- pended to those of the Secretary of graphical Engineer, 1861-62, ap- War; other references cited above.

Record Group 77. --Some of the records of the Topographical Bureau were continued by the Engineer Bureau. A 31-volume series contains (in vols. 22-29) copies of letters sent by the Topographical Bureau, from 1861 to Apr. 4, 1863, and thereafter by the Chief Engineer; these are indexed. Copies of letters sent to the Secretary of War on topographical matters are in a separate series, 1843-67 (10 vols.). Letters received by the Topographical Bureau to Apr. 1863, and thereafter those received by the Chief Engineer relating to topographical matters, 1832-65 (88 ft.), are registered for the entire period and indexed for May 1, 1864-Nov. 22, 1865. There is, however, a small file of unregistered reports, 1836-64, pertaining to river

and harbor improvements. Also preserved separately are monthly returns
of topographical engineers to 1863 and copies of contracts for the survey
and improvement of rivers and harbors to 1863.

Records available on micro-   Engineer Bureau on topographical
film: copies of letters sent by the   matters, 1829-70 (M 66).
Topographical Bureau and by the

Record Group 27. --The meteorological reports of the Survey of the
Northern and Northwestern Lakes, 1859-76 (13 ft.), submitted to the Topographical Bureau and later to the Engineer Bureau, were transferred to the
Signal Office at an undetermined date. These are now a part of the records of the Weather Bureau.

National Archives, List of Cli-   Archives, comp. by Lewis J. Darter,
matological Records in the National   Jr. (Washington, 1942).

District Engineer Offices

Record Group 77. --Of the few extant records of district engineer offices, those of the Baltimore district appear to be the most useful for Civil
War research. They comprise records relating to the construction of Fort
Carroll, Md., including a letter book, 1852-66; time rolls of men employed,
1863-65; a register of materials, including lumber and carpenter tools,
1852-65; and various time books and payrolls, ca. 1856-67; also payrolls
for Murray Hill Battery and for construction of the magazine at Fort
McHenry, 1861-68; payrolls for Fort Federal Hill and Fort Marshall, 1861-
64; a letter book concerning material furnished by Fort Carroll for work at
Fort McHenry, 1863-65; and an account book of materials received for Fort
McHenry, 1865. A few records of the Washington, D. C., and Charleston,
S. C., districts also span the period of the war.

Defenses of Washington

Immediately after the bombardment of Fort Sumter improvised defenses
of Washington were begun by obstructing bridges and roads; but the commanding position of Arlington Heights made occupation of the opposite shore
of the Potomac indispensable. Alexandria as well as Arlington Heights had
to be included in this occupation, which was effected when three columns
crossed the Potomac on the night of May 23, 1861. After the Union disaster
at Bull Run in July 1861 earthworks were hastily thrown up on the hills en-
circling Washington. The complete system of defense, however, resulted
from the work of a commission appointed by the Secretary of War, Oct. 25,
1862, "to examine and report upon the plan of the present forts and sufficiency of the present system of defenses for the city." This commission
is discussed under Miscellaneous War Department Commissions elsewhere
in this Guide.
The defense strategy for Washington was to occupy with field forts
commanding points within cannon range of each other, so that cannon fire
could sweep all approaches to the city. Upon their completion these defenses were considered to be among the most powerful and elaborate ever
devised for a city. Although begun under circumstances that precluded
any thoroughly organized system of labor, a permanent organization was

achieved after the diastrous Virginia campaigns of the spring and summer
of 1862 and was maintained until the close of the war. The works were
divided into the defenses north and the defenses south of the Potomac, each
immediately supervised by a civil engineer. The organization of each of
these two "departments" included a draftsman to prepare plans and maps,
an assistant engineer to help in laying out the work and to make field surveys, a clerk, two or more superintendents, and a fluctuating labor force.
Details of troops were used in the construction whenever practicable.

The Defenses took possession of sites for its several works "with
little or no reference to the rights of the owners or the occupants of the
lands--the stern law of 'military necessity' and the magnitude of the public
interests involved in the security of the nation's capital being paramount to
every other consideration." No compensation for damage or occupation of
lands was made or promised, but the release of lands after the war accounts for many of the records kept.

At the termination of the war in April, 1865 [Bvt. Maj. Gen. John
G. Barnard stated in his report], the "defenses of Washington" consisted
of 68 inclosed forts and batteries, having an aggregate perimeter of
22, 800 yards, (13 miles,) and emplacements for 1, 120 guns, 807 of
which and 98 mortars were actually mounted; of 93 unarmed batteries for
field-guns, having 401 emplacements; and of 35, 711 yards (20 miles) of
rifle-trenches, and 3 block-houses. Thirty-two miles of military roads,
besides the existing roads of the District and the avenues of Washington,
served as the means of communication from the interior to the defensive
lines, and from point to point thereof. The entire circuit, including the
distance across the Potomac from Fort Greble to Fort Lyon, (four
miles,) was, as has already been stated, thirty-seven miles.

Bvt. Maj. Gen. J. G. Barnard,   No. 20. Washington, 1871); Stanley
A Report on the Defenses of Wash-   W. McClure, The Defenses of Washington to the Chief of Engineers,   ington, 1861-1865 (Washington, U. S.
U. S. Army (Professional Papers of   Department of the Interior, 1957).
the Corps of Engineers U. S. Army,

Record Group 77. -- The records include copies of letters sent by Gen.
John G. Barnard, Chief Engineer, Army of the Potomac, superintending
construction of the defenses, Apr. 1-June 24, 1862 (1 vol.); copies of
letters sent by the Chief Engineer, Defenses of Washington, 1862-66 (2
vols.); two registers of letters received, Dec. 1861-Dec. 1862 and Sept.
1862-June 1865, which record letters that have not been found; copies of
endorsements on letters referred to the headquarters, Sept. 1862-Dec.
1865 (1 vol.); and headquarters special orders, Aug. 1862-July 1865 (1
vol.). Records of the construction of entrenchments or fortifications include papers, 1865, relating to the Government's release of lands taken
during the war for the Defenses of Washington and a survey of timber and
wood taken, 1863 (1 ft.); several volumes of requisitions, orders, and accounts for supplies purchased or services procured (including articles
purchased for the Washington Aqueduct and the Capitol extension); and time
books showing work done on the entrenchments at Chain Bridge, Camp
Bunker Hill, Camp Woodbury, Camp Cedar Hill, Fort Ethan Allan, Fort
Marcy, Rozier's Bluff, and south of the Potomac. There are also a volume of notes by General Barnard, 1863-64, regarding armaments of forts,

etc.; and inspection reports, plans, and descriptions pertaining to the armament of forts and batteries of the Defenses of Washington.

Records in Other Custody. -- The Manuscript Division, Library of Congress, has a letter-press book containing copies of letters written by members of the staff of the Office of [the Chief of?] Engineers regarding the defense of Washington south of the Potomac, May 9, 1862-June 6, 1865.

Inspector of the U. S. Military Academy

From 1812 until 1866 the Chief Engineer was responsible for supervising the U. S. Military Academy at West Point, N. Y. At first he himself was Superintendent of the Academy, but from 1817 he detailed engineer officers for that post and he became Inspector of the Academy, with the duty of reporting to the Secretary of War on its internal administration. When he was relieved of this duty by AGO General Order 54, July 30, 1866, he was directed to "turn over all the books, records, and papers relating to the Academy to the Adjutant General of the Army." The several series of records thus transferred all terminate ca. 1866, although after that date other records were maintained by the Adjutant General.

The Academy was seriously affected by the Civil War. Many cadets from the seceding States withdrew, and many of the younger officers who had been employed as assistant professors were called to service in the field. The 1863 Board of Visitors (of which "R. W. Emerson, Massachusetts" was a member) reported that 19 graduates of the Academy from the "free States" had resigned from the Army between Nov. 1860 and Jan. 1, 1862, and that 178 "slave State graduates" had resigned in the same period. On the other hand, 133 graduates "from slave States" and 623 from "free States" had "maintained their loyalty."

Record Group 94. -- The records of the Chief Engineer relating to the Academy, up to 1866, are valuable for any investigation concerning cadets who later served on either side in the Civil War; and the wartime administration of the Academy is probably also a subject insufficiently exploited. The correspondence consists of copies of letters sent to the Academy Superintendent, Members of Congress, other Government officials, cadets, and others concerning Academy administration, the conduct and work of the cadets, appointments, etc., 1812-67 (25 vols.); letters from the Engineer Department to the Secretary of War, endorsed and apparently returned, 1824-66 (1 ft.); and letters, reports, returns, and other papers received, concerning Academy conditions and events, the course of study, Academy buildings, the conduct and standing of cadets, and related matters, 1819-66 (24 ft.). "Abstracts of Letter Books" (3 vols.) contain abstracts of annual reports and of acts of Congress relating to the Academy, copies and extracts of Academy orders, and copies of letters and reports from the Chief Engineer to the Secretary of War and the congressional committees on military affairs. There is also a volume of orders issued by the Engineer Department and the Inspector of the Academy, 1814-67. The annual reports of the Board of Visitors, 1826-66 (15 in.), and papers relating to appointments on the Board, 1823-66 (2 ft.), are especially significant; the former were printed as appendixes to the annual reports of the Chief Engineer. Records relating to the standing of cadets consist of merit rolls, 1818-66 (9 in.); monthly class reports and conduct rolls, 1831-66 (15 in.); and reports of the Academic Board and medical boards on the examination of candidates for admission, 1816-65 (9 in.). Application papers of cadets,

1814-66 (37 ft.), with an index, contain congressional nominations and in some cases much information on family backgrounds. There are registers of cadet applicants, 1819-67 (38 vols.), with an index; and registers of applications for appointment-at-large, 1860-67 (3 vols.).

Records available on microfilm: letters sent, 1812-67 (25 vols.), "Abstracts of Letter Books," 1836- 64, and records of orders, 1814-67 (M 91).

Record Group 77.--Records of the Chief Engineer pertaining to the Military Academy that could not be separated for transfer to the Adjutant General, such as those in general letter books or registers, are in this record group. There is a separate index to letters received concerning the Academy, 1845-67. Copies of the wartime annual reports of the Board of Visitors are in a 4-volume series, 1842-67, of copies of the Chief Engineer's reports to the Secretary of War; 4 orderly books, 1811-74, contain among other orders those of the Academy; and there is a list of officers and cadets of the Academy, 1862.

A commission authorized by sec. 8 of an act of June 21, 1860 (12 Stat. 68), examined "into the organization, system of discipline, and course of instruction of the . . . Academy . . . to ascertain what modification, or changes, if any, are desirable in order that the academy shall best accomplish the objects of its establishment." It was composed of Senator Jefferson Davis, commission president, Representatives Henry Winter Davis and John Cochrane, and Maj. Robert Anderson, Capt. A. A. Humphreys, and Lt. J. C. Ives of the U. S. Army. Its report (Dec. 13, 1860) was printed as S. Misc. Doc. 3, 36 Cong., 2 sess., Serial 1089; the original of this and the letters received by the commission from Capt. E. O. C. Ord, Adj. Gen. S. Cooper, Capt. George G. Meade, and Bvt. Col. Robert E. Lee (among many others whose views were requested) are in the files of the Senate (Record Group 46) under 36A-G9.

OFFICE OF THE CHIEF OF ORDNANCE AND THE ORDNANCE DEPARTMENT

By an act of Apr. 5, 1832 (4 Stat. 502), a separate appropriation for the "ordnance service" restored it to the status it had before being "merged in the artillery" by an act of Mar. 2, 1821 (3 Stat. 615). Not until the passage of an act of Aug. 3, 1861 (12 Stat. 287), however, was its commanding officer given the title "chief of ordnance." When the Civil War began, the Ordnance Department had charge of the arsenals and armories and was responsible for furnishing all ordnance and ordnance stores to the military service. The act of Aug. 3, 1861, and one of Mar. 3, 1863 (12 Stat. 743), authorized increases in officer strength.

Although by 1863 the Ordnance Department had manufactured or bought what it regarded as "an immense quantity of supplies," it deplored the necessity of "relying too much on private parties, no matter how large their resources, for the principal munitions of war"; and it took measures to enlarge several of the principal arsenals--Watertown, Watervliet, Allegheny, St. Louis, Washington, and Benicia, Calif. The Department intended "to procure, if possible, in this country every article required, whether in the crude or manufactured state, and, with the exception of such articles as sulphur and saltpetre, there is no reason to doubt that this plan can be fully carried out; thus securing to our own people the bene-fit of our large expenditures, and rendering us independent of foreign nations." As regards small arms, the Ordnance Department by 1863 con-sidered the United States to be "perfectly independent of foreign aid":

> The wisdom of the measures adopted by the War Department in September, 1862, for the purpose of procuring a supply of iron suitable for the manufacture of muskets and other firearms, the product of our own manufactories, . . . has been fully demonstrated. Iron of a quality fully equal to the celebrated irons manufactured in England and Norway is now produced in ample quantity to meet all our present wants, and the product can be increased to any desirable extent, thus relieving us entirely from our former dependence on European producers for this indispensable article.

The manufacturing capacity of the arsenals was increased steadily un-til May 1865, when the immediate demand for munitions of war ceased. The manufacture and purchase of ordnance supplies were then reduced, and provisions were made for storing the vast quantities that had been issued to the Army or captured from Confederate forces.

Throughout the war the Ordnance Department felt seriously the lack of a greater number of Regular Army officers, "educated for and experienced in their peculiar duties"; and the Chief of Ordnance in his annual report for the last year of the war wrote that the necessity to employ acting Ordnance Department officers "caused much embarrassment and confusion, and was detrimental to the public service and interest."

The enlargement of the Ordnance Department in 1861 and again in 1863 brought increased responsibility to the Office of the Chief of Ordnance. In 1863 this Office consisted of the following Divisions: Executive, Archives, Book and Blank, Contract, Cash, Construction and Model, Property Re-turns, Requisition and Supply, Records, and Statistical. An Inspection Division, which existed for a short time, was merged in Sept. 1864 with the Construction Division to form the Construction and Inspection Division. At the close of the war the number of divisions was reduced to four; in 1869 they comprised Divisions for the Archives; Construction; Property; and Ac-counts, Claims, and Statistics.

Successive Chiefs of Ordnance in the war period:
Brig. Gen. James W. Ripley, Aug. 3, 1861.
Brig. Gen. George D. Ramsey, Sept. 15, 1863.
Brig. Gen. Alexander B. Dyer, Sept. 12, 1864.

Annual reports of the Chief of Ordnance, 1861-65, appended to those of the Secretary of War; The Ordnance Manual for the Use of the Officers of the United States Army (Philadelphia, 1862); Proceedings of a Court of Inquiry Convened at Washington, D. C., November 9, 1868 . . . To Examine Into the Ac-cusations Against Brig. and Bvt. Major General A. B. Dyer, Chief of Ordnance (Washington, 1869).

Record Group 156. -- The records of the Office of the Chief of Ordnance as now constituted are more intelligibly described by the functions with which they deal than by their divisional provenance. Supplementing the general records of letters and endorsements sent, 1812-89 (115 vols.), are separately kept copies of those sent to the Secretary of War for the same period (27 vols.); to Ordnance Department officers, 1839-89 (81 vols.); and to national armories, Sept. 1860-Sept. 1861 (1 vol., including telegrams). There are a separate index to letters and endorsements sent to the Secretary of War, 1860-70, and a comprehensive index to all the above series except the communications to national armories.

The main file of letters and other communications received during the Civil War is arranged chronologically by year, then alphabetically by initial letter of surname or office of writer, then numerically to correspond to entries in registers of letters received. There are also separate registers of letters received by the Inspection Division, Sept. 1861-Dec. 1870 (2 vols.); the Construction Division, July 1863-Nov. 1870 (2 vols.); and the Returns Division, Dec. 1865-Nov. 1869 (1 vol.); but the documents to which these refer have not been found. Another separate series of registers, 1812-70 (3 vols.), incompletely indexed, contains abstracts of communications about inventions and of proposals received for improvements in ordnance; and a subseries of the "special file," also 1812-70, relates to inventions in general. (The collection of approximately 92 ft. of records on many subjects, 1812-1912, gathered together by the Ordnance Department in its "special file," is particularly rich in materials pertaining to the Civil War. It is more fully described below.)

Among records created for administrative use are orders and regulations governing office procedures, 1822-71 (1 vol.); a register of military organizations in the service of the United States, 1861-64; a register of the receipt of company histories from volunteer and regular troops and other units, 1864; and a register of books and pamphlets procured for the library of the Office of the Chief of Ordnance, 1863-65.

A Collection of Annual Reports and Other Important Papers, Relating to the Ordnance Department..., prepared under the direction of Brig. Gen. Stephen V. Benét (Washington, 1878-90. 4 vols.), includes, for the Civil War period, significant amounts of papers reproduced from the records of the Office of the Chief of Ordnance and printed under these heads: cannon, carriages, etc.; Ordnance Department; arsenals and armories; small arms; ammunition, powder, etc.; accoutrements and equipments; Harper's Ferry property; contracts; militia; enlisted men; hours of labor; transportation; and patents, royalties, etc.

Records of Procurement, Issuance, Property Accountability, Testing, and Experimentation

These records document the principal function of the Ordnance Department to furnish all "ordnance and ordnance stores" for the military service. The term, as defined in the 1861 Revised Army Regulations, comprehended "all cannon and artillery carriages and equipments; all apparatus and machines for the service and manoeuvres of artillery; all small arms and accoutrements and horse equipments; all ammunition; all tools and materials for the ordnance service; and horse medicines, materials for shoeing, and all horse equipments whatever for the light artillery."

Records of procurement consist primarily of book records containing copies of contracts and related "statements of contracts" recording fulfilment; copies of letters sent relating to orders and contracts; registers of contracts and orders; the ledger of receipts on orders and contracts; registers of manufacturers' and suppliers' proposals and offers; and the register of field requisitions for ordnance stores. In addition, for the Civil War period, the procurement function is documented in statements of purchase, 1861-62 (2 vols.); a record of purchase, 1861-67 (1 vol.), of cannon, projectiles, and small arms (prepared in response to a House resolution of Mar. 15, 1867); statements of purchases, 1861-67, under contracts in excess of $1,000 (1 vol.); statements of open-market purchases, 1861-67, in excess of $1,000 (1 vol.); certificates of inspection and receipt, 1864-65 (4 vols.); and registers of orders for supplies and equipment and of inspection after fabrication, 1864-65 (2 vols.). Press copies of confidential letters sent, 1863-66 (1 vol.), some of which are in cipher, relate to such matters as the manufacturing capacity of mills, the expansion of manufacturing facilities, and policies on granting contracts.

Records of the issuance of arms and other ordnance equipment to the militia of States and Territories are in several volumes of a series spanning the Civil War period. Other records of issuance include registers of guns and carriages, from 1861, and 4 volumes of registers, 1862-73, showing the number of cannon and carriages required for and supplied to forts from 1862 and to batteries from 1864. Registers of the sale of ordnance stores begin in 1864.

The pertinent records of ordnance accountability include records of the receipt and examination of registers of property returns, 1861-66, and several series of summary statements of ordnance and ordnance stores on hand at forts, armories, arsenals, depots, permanent batteries, and garrisons, and in the hands of artillery, cavalry, and infantry regiments at different dates during the war. A "Register of Inventories of Ordnance Stores Under [AGO] General Orders No. 167, Oct. 24, 1862," consolidates inventories submitted by the commanding officers of detachments, companies, regiments, and posts. There are also control registers of the resignation of officers accountable for ordnance and ordnance stores, Nov. 1864-Apr. 1865 (2 vols.), used in accountability clearance. (Registers of letters of resignation, 1864-67 and 1869-70, are in a separate series.)

Researchers interested in tests of and experiments with ordnance and ordnance stores should examine first the reports of experiments, 1826-71 (23 vols.), some of which are illustrated, and the related registers of correspondence and reports, 1812-70 (3 vols.); these concern cannon, artillery carriages and implements, small arms, ammunition, etc. Two other registers relate to Rodman guns fabricated between 1860 and 1869; and there are abstracts of officers' reports, 1863-64 (2 vols.), on the merits and faults of small arms, accouterment, and horse equipment. The inspection reports themselves are fragmentary, but there are registers of those received, 1861-75 (3 vols.). Related subseries in the "special file" consist of the records of the Commission on Ordnance Claims and Contracts, 1861-62 (for details see Miscellaneous War Department Commissions elsewhere in this Guide), correspondence with Norman Wiard and other papers relating to the Wiard gun, 1861-64; reports of inspections of powder manufactured at private powder works, 1861-70, and of ordnance and ordnance equipment manufactured privately and at arsenals, 1862-70; records, 1862-64 and 1874-75, relating to Robert Tillson, a manufacturer of horse equipment during the war who subsequently alleged breach of contract; company and other reports of damaged arms, 1864-70; and correspondence regarding the inventions of Clifford Arrick, 1864-68. The "special file" contains also material relating to trials and experiments, 1818-70, including papers of or concerning boards of officers appointed to conduct tests and examinations, 1827-69.

(The records or reports of many Ordnance Department boards are in the files of the Adjutant General, Record Group 94. Such special boards during the Civil War included those established to examine at Washington arsenal "a primer which will be presented for trial"; "to consider and report upon the policy of arming New Madrid with heavy ordnance, and whether field artillery will not be sufficient for the defense of that place"; to design wrought iron carriages for siege and field guns and to consider whether changes were necessary in the wooden gun carriages then being built; and to examine, test, and recommend for adoption a suitable breech-loader for muskets and carbines and a repeater or magazine carbine. Another board was appointed to revise the system of blank forms of accounts and returns prescribed for the Ordnance Department. Boards on which both the Ordnance and Engineer Departments were represented are noted in the section on the Engineer Department in this Guide.)

Other records of the Office of the Chief of Ordnance that relate specifically to arsenals and armories consist of statements of ordnance stores manufactured at the principal arsenals from 1861; statements of the motive power, machines, and manufacturing capacity of arsenals on Jan. 1, 1864; a journal of accounts paid, 1861; and a "statement of fabrications," Apr. 15, 1861-June 30, 1867, prepared for the congressional Joint Select Committee on Ordnance. The records created at arsenals and armories, a part of this record group, are described separately, below.

Fiscal Records

Detailed statements of estimates of Ordnance Department appropriations for the Civil War period are in a series running from 1816 to 1904 (8 vols.). Also of value to research in Department finances of the period are the following series, all dating from 1861 or early in the war and continuing beyond its end: ledgers of appropriations; journals of accounts examined and sent to the Second Auditor of the Treasury for settlement; registers of "refundments" to appropriations in the settlement of accounts; registers of requisitions for remittances; registers of office expenditures; and the monthly ("post") accounts of Ordnance Department officers at arsenals, armories, and other posts and stations. Series begun later include "requisition blotters" from 1863 and registers of cash accounts and estimates from 1864. There are also weekly statements of obligations incurred, Jan. 1862-Sept. 1863 (1 vol.).

Registers of claims presented for payment to the Office of the Chief of Ordnance, 1862-93 (6 vols.), and a separate register of rejected claims, 1866-84, show the kind of services rendered or supplies furnished and by whom, the amount of money involved, and the final action on the claims. There is also a record of claims presented to the Commission on War Claims at St. Louis--the Davis-Holt-Campbell Commission (see Miscellaneous War Department Commissions, elsewhere in this Guide).

Records Relating to Personnel

Records of appointments, assignments, and transfers are in the series of "military histories of ordnance officers," 1815-1922 (8 vols.), referred

to contemporaneously as the état de service; and comparable records for
enlisted men are in registers of enlistments and discharges, 1829-70
(2 vols.). The monthly returns of the Ordnance Department also cover the
period of the war. Personnel records, 1864-65, in the "special file," discussed above, include applications of officers for appointment in the Ordnance Department and applications for clerkships.

National Archives, unpublished "Preliminary Inventory of the Records of the Office of the Chief of Ordnance," comp. by Roger Ashland, Elizabeth Bethel, Mabel E. Deutrich, George O'Keefe, and Myra Trever.

The Ordnance Board

A Board of this name met from time to time before and during the
Civil War to consider and report on matters of interest to the Ordnance
Department. The Board constituted by AGO Special Order 410, Sept. 12,
1863, was directed "to meet at such times and places, and to examine and
report upon such matters, as the Chief of Ordnance, with the approval of
the Secretary of War, may direct."

Ordnance Board, Proceedings . . . at Its Session on the 24th, 25th, and 26th Sept., 1863 . . . (Washington, 1864). The Board was the subject of certain investigations of the Joint Select Committee on Ordnance (see S. Rept. 173, 40 Cong., 2 sess., Serial 1320).

Record Group 156. --A volume of the Board's proceedings covers the
periods Oct. 1859-Sept. 1863 and Jan.-Feb. 1868.

Boards of Examination for Ordnance Officers

Record Group 156. --Five volumes, 1863-67, contain the following
papers: copies of AGO general and special orders convening boards of
Ordnance Department officers to examine officers for promotions and
commissions; reports of proceedings and recommendations; copies of letters and endorsements sent; background sketches of officers examined;
written answers to examination questions; and records of ratings.

Inspectors of Ordnance

Under the Act of May 14, 1812 (2 Stat. 732), that established the Ordnance Department, it was the duty of the head of the Department to direct
the inspection and proving of ordnance, cannon balls, shells, shot, and
powder procured for the Army. To inspect and test the articles contracted
for, officers and other employees of the Department were assigned to
foundries and factories having contracts with the Department.

Inspector of Cannon and Projectiles, New York, N. Y.

Record Group 156. --Register of letters received, Mar.-Oct. 1865.

Inspector of Artillery

In Aug. 1862 an officer of artillery was ordered to report to the Chief
of Ordnance as Inspector of Artillery. This position appears to have been
terminated in Aug. 1866, when the same officer was appointed as a member of a board to inspect arms, ammunition, and military stores at U. S.
forts and arsenals and to make recommendations for their disposition.

Record Group 156. --Copies of letters sent by Headquarters, Inspector
of Artillery, U. S. Army, 1862-Jan. 1867 (1 vol.), relating to armament
for batteries, the assignment of recruits, and other personnel actions; synopses of letters received and copies of endorsements sent, Nov. 1862-1865
(1 vol.); register of and index to letters received, Aug. 1861-Aug. 1865;
and a record of battery stations, showing assignment of Ordnance Department officers, acting officers, and sergeants, 1861-64 (1 vol.).

Arsenals, Armories, and Ordnance Depots

The records described below are primarily those kept at the several
arsenals and armories in existence during the Civil War, as distinguished
from records of the Office of the Chief of Ordnance relating to or received
from such establishments. In the case of arsenals or armories whose
Civil War records have not been preserved or cannot be identified, the records of the Office of the Chief of Ordnance may be used for information on
their operations; these include the arsenals at Apalachicola (Fla.),
Charleston (S. C.), Columbus (Ohio), Detroit, Fayetteville (N. C.), Fort
Union (N. Mex.), Harper's Ferry, Indianapolis, Little Rock, Pikesville
(Md.), Rome (N. Y.), St. Louis, and Vancouver (Wash.).

The 1861 Revised Army Regulations required field officers of the Ordnance Department to keep the following records: a company return book,
consisting of retained duplicates, bound together; a monthly return book,
containing other monthly returns and statements; an account book, containing copies of the quarterly accounts current and their endorsed statements, of abstracts of money disbursed, and of estimates for funds; a
letter book of copies of letters sent; files of letters received; files of orders
received; an annual inventory book, made "by binding together the retained
inventories"; and, at manufacturing armories and arsenals, such other
books as were necessary to show the details of operations. Armories,
arsenals, ordnance agencies, and depots were required to keep special
books, corresponding to the various abstracts entered on the quarterly return, for "stores received from the Army," "received from contractors,"
and "received from sundry persons"; and for "fabrications," "repairs,"
"purchases," and "stores taken up." Special books were also to be kept
for "issues to the Regular Army," "issues to the Volunteers and Militia,"
"issues to forts and permanent batteries," "issues to officers for their
personal use," "issues to sundry persons," and "condemned stores."
Similar but less extensive records were required at all other posts (such
as forts, permanent batteries, and barracks) and in the field where officers had stores in charge (as did the acting Ordnance Department officers of brigades, divisions, or Army corps). But regimental and company
officers transacting business connected with ordnance stores could so com-
press their records that in "an ordinary pocket memorandum book" could be
kept "all data required by a company officer to make out returns of Ordnance stores for a year."

Allegheny Arsenal (Pittsburgh, Pa.)

Established 1814.

Record Group 156. --Of the records series for this arsenal, those covering the Civil War period include letters and other communications received and copies of those sent, with registers of the latter; copies of the
quartermaster's letters sent; post orders; the monthly returns of an ordnance company stationed at the arsenal; individual enlistment papers;
monthly returns of hired men; payrolls; contracts, deeds, and reports of
survey; and estimates of funds required. There are also for the war period
memoranda of telegrams and orders for stores (1 vol.) and a record of ordnance received from contractors (1 vol.).

Augusta Arsenal (Augusta, Ga.)

Established 1817; seized by Georgia State troops ca. Jan. 24, 1861.

Record Group 156. --Of about 120 feet of records, dating from about
1825, those for the Civil War period include only an account book, 1864.
(For records of the Augusta Arsenal under the C. S. A., see the accompanying Guide to the Archives of the Government of the Confederate States
of America.)

Baton Rouge Arsenal (La.)

The barracks and arsenal were occupied almost continuously from 1810
until Jan. 10, 1861, when the post surrendered to Louisiana State troops.
The arsenal was reoccupied by U. S. forces, ca. May 9, 1862.

There appear to be no extant records of this arsenal.

Benicia Arsenal (Calif.)

Established as an ordnance depot Aug. 25, 1851, near Benicia, Calif.;
designated as the principal depot for ordnance and ordnance stores for the
Division of the Pacific, Nov. 8, 1851; converted to an "arsenal of construction," Apr. 1852. This arsenal was important to the entire west coast.

Record Group 156. --Records of this arsenal, 1849-1937 (50 ft.), include
for the war period copies of letters sent, 1851-68; an index to letters sent,
1808-1907; instructions for making ordnance returns, 1865; and a muster
roll, 1861.

Champlain Arsenal (Vergennes, Vt.)

Established 1826; discontinued 1855; reestablished 1861.

Record Group 156. --Records for the war period include only monthly
returns.

Fortress Monroe Arsenal (Old Point Comfort, Va.)

Established 1824.

Record Group 156. --Of the records of this arsenal, 1824-1901 (ca.
40 ft.), those relating to the Civil War include copies of letters sent (with
a separate series of letters, telegrams, and endorsements sent to the
Chief of Ordnance, July 1864-June 1865, and another of press copies of

telegrams sent, Apr. -Nov. 1864); letters received, with a separate series of those from the Chief of Ordnance; returns of the ordnance company stationed at the arsenal; returns of hired men (from 1864); and lists of ordnance and ordnance stores received and issued (to 1862).

Frankford Arsenal (Bridesburg, Pa.)

Established 1816.

Record Group 156. --The arsenal's records, 1816-1943 (ca. 1,500 ft.), include for the Civil War period copies of letters and telegrams sent (with separate series of those sent to the Chief of Ordnance, those sent relating to ordnance and ordnance stores, and those sent to quartermasters, all from 1862); and letters and telegrams received, with a register from 1864 and with a separate series of those from the Chief of Ordnance. There are also copies of letters and telegrams sent regarding powder inspection and storage, Nov. 1863-Oct. 1866; copies of the military storekeeper's letters sent, Nov. 1862-Dec. 1867; 4 volumes containing historical information on the fabrication of ordnance at the West Point, South Boston, Fort Pitt, and Scott foundries, dating generally from 1865; guard reports, Apr. -Dec. 1863; and returns of hired men, 1864-67.

Harper's Ferry Arsenal (Va.)

Established 1794; destroyed Apr. 18, 1861, to prevent its falling into the hands of the Confederates; lands etc. sold Nov. 30, 1867.

No records of the arsenal appear to be extant.

Kennebec Arsenal (Augusta, Maine)

Established 1827.

Record Group 156. --Of the records of the arsenal, 1831-1901 (ca. 30 ft.), those for the Civil War period include copies of letters, telegrams, and endorsements sent; letters received; letters sent and received by the commissary of subsistence; letters sent and received by the arsenal quartermaster; orders and circulars; morning reports of the ordnance company at the arsenal; muster rolls and payrolls of the ordnance detachment; monthly post returns; work returns; and returns of ordnance and ordnance stores.

Louisville Ordnance Depot (Ky.)

A temporary depot existing for a few years during the Civil War.

Record Group 156. --Press copies of letters sent, 1863 (2 vols.); letters received from the Chief of Ordnance, 1863 (1 vol.); letters and orders received from military commands, 1861-63 (1 vol.); telegrams received, 1863 (1 vol.); and monthly payrolls, 1863 (1 in.).

Mount Vernon Arsenal (Ala.)

Established 1829; taken by Alabama State troops Jan. 4, 1861; reestablished in 1865.

Record Group 98. --Records of the arsenal, 1865-94 (11 ft.), include for the Civil War decade copies of letters sent, registers of letters received, endorsements, and orders, all dating from 1865.

Nashville Ordnance Depot (Tenn.)

A temporary depot established during the Civil War; discontinued soon after Dec. 1865.
Record Group 156. --Copies of letters sent, 1862-64 (1 vol.).

New York Arsenal (Governor's Island, N. Y.)

The ordnance depot established on Governor's Island in New York Harbor became the New York Arsenal in 1835.
Record Group 156. --"Inspection letter book," June 1861-Aug. 1862, containing copies of letters and telegrams sent regarding the inspection of ordnance received on contract, rejection of ordnance, and nonfulfillment of contracts; also copies of letters from the Watervliet Arsenal.

Rock Island Arsenal (Ill.)

Established 1863.
Record Group 156. --Morning reports, July 1862-Nov. 1865; descriptive books, 1865-68; and reports of stores issued to, received from, and purchased by the Army, from 1862.

San Antonio Arsenal (Tex.)

Established 1855; taken by Texas State troops Feb. 16, 1861; reestablished 1865.
Record Group 156. --A volume of copies of letters and endorsements sent dates from Nov. 1865.

Springfield Armory (Mass.)

Established 1794. After the armory at Harper's Ferry was destroyed to prevent its use by Confederates, the Government had to rely on the single armory at Springfield and on private establishments for its supply of arms. Felicia Johnson Deyrup in Arms Makers of the Connecticut Valley . . . (Smith College Studies in History, 33. Northampton, 1948) states that the Springfield Armory's records are "the most important source of information on small arms manufacture in the Connecticut Valley."
Record Group 156. --Records of the armory, 1794-1920 (ca. 190 ft.), include the following series pertinent to the Civil War: copies of letters and endorsements sent; letters and endorsements received from the Chief of Ordnance, with registers from 1864, and those received from other sources; correspondence of the military storekeeper and paymaster; some orders, including general orders; report to the commanding officer on tests of ordnance; payrolls of civilian employees; and contracts, including those with James S. Howard & Co., James Boyd & Sons, Warren H. Wilkinson, Emerson Gaylord, Joseph Davy & Co., Bemis & Call, and James M. Frazee & Co. Correspondence with Samuel Colt's company is included.

Washington Arsenal (D. C.)

Established 1816. Among wartime activities at this arsenal was the convening of a board to examine "such fire-arms as may be presented"

(AGO S. O. 311, Nov. 21, 1861) and of another board (AGO S. O. 210,
June 17, 1864) "to investigate the cause of an explosion which occurred
to-day at that place. "

Record Group 98. --Only a morning report file (July 1864) represents
the Civil War period in the 3 feet of records of the arsenal in this record
group.

Record Group 156. --There is a volume of photographs of guns and
gun carriages at the arsenal, ca. 1866.

Watertown Arsenal (Mass.)

Established 1816.

Record Group 156. --Records of the arsenal (over 250 ft.) include for
the Civil War period only a court-martial record book, 1862-71; employees'
time books; returns of hired men; and a file containing historical data,
1816-1908.

Watervliet Arsenal (West Troy, N. Y.)

Established 1814.

Record Group 156. --Records of the arsenal (about 390 ft.) include for
the Civil War period copies of letters, telegrams, and endorsements sent,
with a register from Jan. 1864; registers of letters and telegrams received (but the communications registered are missing for the period);
copies of letters sent by the ordnance storekeeper and paymaster; post
orders (from 1864); a powder account book, 1860-61; summary statements
of work completed; a record of metal tests of 15-in. shells, 1865-67; guard
reports (from 1865); morning reports; muster rolls and payrolls (from
1862); monthly returns of the ordnance company stationed at the arsenal
(from 1863); descriptive books (from 1865); and employees' payrolls. See
also New York Arsenal, above.

QUARTERMASTER GENERAL'S OFFICE AND
QUARTERMASTER'S DEPARTMENT

A Quartermaster's Department, headed by the Quartermaster General,
was established for the Army by an act of Mar. 28, 1812 (2 Stat. 696),
which also provided for a Commissary General of Purchases. By this act
the Quartermaster General was put in charge of purchasing "military
stores, camp equipage and other articles" for the troops and of providing
transportation for the Army. The Commissary General of Purchases was
to procure for the Army "all arms, military stores, clothing, and . . .
articles of supply. " The Office of the Commissary General of Purchases
was abolished in 1842, and its functions and records were transferred to
the Office of the Quartermaster General. From then until World War I the
Quartermaster's Department, later the Quartermaster Corps, was the
Army supply agency for almost all commodities and services except food.
During the Civil War there emerged a well defined pattern of headquarters
organization, which remained basically unchanged until about 1912.

Quartermaster General Joseph E. Johnston, who served later in the
Confederate Army, resigned on Apr. 22, 1861; and on June 13 Brig. Gen.
Montgomery C. Meigs succeeded him. (Under orders of Secretary of War
Holt, Meigs had resumed charge of constructing the "Capitol Extension"--

the new dome-- and the Post Office Building on Feb. 27, 1861, and of
building the Washington Aqueduct on Feb. 22.) By June 30, military operations had resulted in a 20-fold increase of business in the Quartermaster General's Office; and, although several extra and temporary clerks had
been hired, the staff was obviously inadequate for the required examination
and "analyzation" of accounts of field quartermasters. By Nov. 1862 the
work of the Office was so far in arrears that Meigs urged the appointment
of 120 additional clerks "to examine in a reasonable time the mass of accounts and returns which have accumulated during the past year, and to
keep up the correspondence necessary to settle the accounts promptly hereafter, and compel Officers to make their returns regularly and correctly."
By the end of 1863 the diversified functions of the Quartermaster's Department were stated in the Quartermaster General's report for that year as
follows:

> It is the duty of this department to provide quarters, hospitals, and
> transportation for the army, and prisoners of war, and transportation
> for all military stores, provisions, camp and garrison equipage, ord-
> nance and ordnance stores; to direct the survey and superintend the
> opening and repairing of roads, and the construction and repairs of
> bridges which may be necessary to the movements of any part of the
> army, or as communications between the posts on the frontier and
> between those posts and the interior; to provide good and sufficient
> storehouses for all military supplies; to provide materials and direct
> and superintend the constructing and repairing of quarters, barracks,
> hospitals, storehouses, stables, and other necessary buildings for the
> accommodation of the army and the security of public property; to pur-
> chase all fuel, forage, straw, and stationery required for the army,
> and have them transported to the posts where they may be wanted, and
> issued to those entitled to them; to purchase all horses, oxen, mules,
> and harness, and all wagons, carts, boats, and other vessels, with
> their equipments, for the transportation of the army and for garrison
> purposes; to have the custody of the same, and be responsible for their
> proper use; to purchase all cavalry and artillery horses; to construct,
> repair, and maintain all telegraph lines necessary for military pur-
> poses, and to provide for the maintenance of the steam-ram fleet on
> the western rivers.

By 1864 the Office in Washington handled two general classes of ac-
counts--those for the receipt, transfer, and expenditure of money; and
those for the receipt, transfer, and issue of property. The former were
sent by accountable officers direct to the Third Auditor of the Treasury.
This official, after a preliminary examination, transmitted them to the
Quartermaster General for "administrative examination," and later received them again for final examination and settlement. Property accounts
were sent direct by accountable officer to the Quartermaster General, in
whose office they were examined and by whom they were transmitted to the
proper Treasury official (either the Second Auditor or the Third Auditor)
for final examination and settlement.
   Although recognizing, as a "measure of justice and protection, both to
the government and to the officers," that the examinations of accounts
should be prompt, the Quartermaster General had to report (1864) that
"the increasing business of this department, from the increase of the army

and the growth of the operations attending the supply and transportation of
the troops in this gigantic war," had "continued to outrun the means provided by law." A general realignment of work was effected, however, under an act of July 4, 1864 (13 Stat. 394), which divided the functions of the
Office among nine divisions. During and for some time after the Civil War
these divisions were designated numerically, as in the act cited above
(First Division, Second Division, etc.), but they were known also by
names indicating their general functions--relating respectively to the supply
of public animals, clothing and equipment, ocean and lake transportation,
rail and river transportation, regular supplies, barracks and quarters,
military trains and incidental allowances, inspections, and the keeping of
records and correspondence. Their functions are described below.

Another act of July 4, 1864 (13 Stat. 381), removed from the Court of
Claims jurisdiction over "any claim against the United States growing out
of the destruction or appropriation of, or damage to, property by the army
or navy, or any part of the army or navy, engaged in the suppression of the
rebellion, from the commencement to the close thereof." Such claims if
made by "loyal citizens in States not in rebellion," were to be presented to
the Quartermaster General or the Commissary General of Subsistence, as
appropriate. The regulations governing the submission of claims to both
the Quartermaster General and the Commissary General of Subsistence
were published in QMG General Order 35, Aug. 29, 1864. Investigation
and adjudication of these "Fourth of July claims," as they soon were called,
continued long after the war to constitute an important responsibility of the
Quartermaster General. In the present century a new class of Civil War
claims--the so-called Confederate horse claims--were handled in the
Quartermaster General's Office. These arose under an act of Feb. 27,
1902 (32 Stat. 43), which authorized the payment of former officers and
enlisted men of the Confederate Army for horses, sidearms, and baggage
taken from them by Federal troops in violation of the terms of surrender.
The time for filing these claims was extended for 12 months after passage
of an act of May 30, 1908 (35 Stat. 499).

The Quartermaster's Department made use of many boards to undertake
special inquiries or inspections. Information about some but not necessarily all of these is available chiefly in the consolidated correspondence
file described below. Such boards were created to examine and report on
"the merits of certain military hats to be submitted for inspection by C. L.
Pascal of Philadelphia" (AGO S. O. 308, Nov. 18, 1861); to consider "what
changes or additions should be made to the uniform clothing of the Army"
(AGO S. O. 31, Feb. 11, 1862); to examine and report on "the merits of the
Cavalry Raiding Equipments, invented by Lt. -Col. Walter King" (AGO S. O.
3, Jan. 4, 1865); and to examine and report on "Wood's Patent Knapsack,
Haversack, and Canteen" (AGO S. O. 22, Jan. 14, 1865) and on "Weston's
Shoulder Brace" (AGO S. O. 62, Feb. 8, 1865). A board of engineer and
quartermaster officers to consider and report on "pontoon bridge equipage"
is discussed under the Engineer Department. Boards for the examination
of the qualifications of officers of the Quartermaster Department were established by AGO S. O. 317, Sept. 23, 1864, at New Orleans (for the district comprising the Departments of Arkansas and the Gulf), City Point, Va.
(for the district comprising the Armies operating against Richmond, including the Department of Virginia and North Carolina), Atlanta, Ga. (for the
district comprising the Departments of the Tennessee, the Cumberland, and
the Ohio), and St. Louis, Mo. (for the district comprising the Departments

of Missouri, Kansas, and the Northwest, and the Northern Department).
The work of these examining boards is documented principally in the files
of the Eighth Division of the Quartermaster General's Office, described
below.

The Quartermaster General helped to establish the U. S. Military
Railroads and the U. S. Military Telegraphs, and these agencies were
staffed or directed largely by quartermaster personnel. He also was
chiefly responsible for bringing about the creation of the Office of the
Commissary General of Prisoners. These new War Department bureaus
were, however, independent of the Quartermaster General's Office during
the war, and they are discussed in separate sections of this Guide. Another
new agency, the Cavalry Bureau, closely related to the Quartermaster
General's Office, is also separately treated.

Brig. Gen. (later Maj. Gen.) Montgomery C. Meigs served as Quarter-
master General from June 13, 1861. Maj. Ebenezer S. Sibley was Acting
Quartermaster General from Apr. 22, 1861, when Brig. Gen. Joseph E.
Johnston resigned, until Meigs' appointment; and Col. Charles Thomas
was Acting Quartermaster General from Aug. 1863 to Jan. 9, 1864, when
Meigs was on inspection duty in the field.

Annual reports of the Quarter-
master General, 1861-65 and later,
appended to those of the Secretary
of War; H. A. Royce, A Sketch of the
Organization of the Quartermaster's
Department from 1774 to 1876
(Washington, 1876); Russell F.
Weigley, Quartermaster General of
the Union Army; a Biography of M. C.
Meigs (New York, 1959); Sherrod E.
East, "Montgomery C. Meigs and the
Quartermaster Department," Military
Affairs, 25:183-196 (Winter 1961-62).
The Quartermaster General published
in 1887 (copyright 1888) Flags of the
Army of the United States Carried
During the War of the Rebellion,
1861-1865, To Designate the Head-
quarters of the Different Armies,
Army Corps, Divisions and Brigades.
Other publications are noted below.

Record Group 92. --As noted in the National Archives Guide (1948), the
records of the Office of the Quartermaster General "have been subject to
many unrecorded transmutations during a long and complex history of moving, reorganization, and refiling." This is especially true of the records
of the Civil War period, even though in 1864 the Office had been reorganized
into nine divisions with well defined prerogatives and responsibilities, as
noted above. The records belonging to the wartime divisions, insofar as
they can be so identified, are described in the separate entries below.
Other files--of the Quartermaster General's Office as a whole or of divisions established after the war--consist essentially of correspondence,
claims records, and a good deal of miscellany.

There are many volumes of fair copies of miscellaneous letters sent,
in several series spanning the Civil War, as well as copies of endorsements and memoranda. These are elaborately indexed or abstracted.
There are also many volumes of press copies of letters sent by the Quartermaster General to the Secretary of War, the Adjutant General, and the
heads of other departments and bureaus. These also are abstracted or indexed.

In its consolidated correspondence file, 1794-1915, the Quartermaster
General's Office brought together in one alphabetic arrangement, by personal name or subject, papers drawn from many records series, including

some records of agencies whose functions the Office had inherited. This important file, which fills more than 1,000 boxes, is indispensable to Civil War research. Its vast subject scope and 120-year time span make it formidable. A random sampling of subjects on which Civil War records can be found, however, shows the following: Andersonville, Ga.; cotton (captured, claims, etc.); freedmen; horses; hospitals; Indians; Navy; pensions; pricelists; rebels (officers, property, prisons, etc.); rent; riots; roads; Sanitary Commission; sutlers; tents; transportation; Union prisoners; uniforms; and unknown soldiers. The consolidated correspondence file contains also records pertaining to many forts and other installations having quartermaster activities and to vessels, buildings, and other structures for which the Department was responsible.

The claims files stem principally from the Quartermaster General's responsibility for the so-called "Fourth of July claims," discussed above. Claims considered under the act of July 4, 1864, are recorded in a document file, which is controlled by indexes of claims considered, approved, or rejected. There are voluminous case files related to these and other Civil War claims, arranged by name of claimant, 1861-89; papers and an index concerning Confederate horse claims (ca. 10 ft.); 12 printed and manuscript volumes relating to claims in various Southern States; and some records of railroad claims. The considerable correspondence relating to claims is recorded in several series of letter books or in registers of letters received. The claims filed under the act of July 4, 1864, can be used effectively to explore personal attitudes during the war because a prerequisite for payment of claims was the establishment of the claimants' loyalty. Many claims are supported by documentary evidence of supplies or services furnished.

For detailed information about the claims documentation see Wiley Britton, The Aftermath of the Civil War; Based on Investigation of War Claims (Kansas City, 1924). In the records of the Third Auditor of the Treasury (Record Group 217) is a transcript of the proceedings, 1867-69 (1 vol.), of the Steedman Commission made by the Commissary General of Subsistence from the original records on file at that time in the Quartermaster General's Office. The commission convened at Jasper, Marion County, Tenn., pursuant to Departmental Order No. 329 (special field order, Dec. 8, 1863), to adjust the claims of citizens of Marion County against the U. S. Government for damages to their property. At the end of the proceedings are an index of orders governing the commission and an alphabetical index by name of claimant.

Among miscellaneous records of the Office are "depot notes and telegrams," 1861-75 (8 vols.); records relating to Andersonville and Libby Prisons (12 vols.); papers and correspondence relating to sutlers; some sketches covering the Civil War history of forts and other permanent posts; a list of Civil War vessels and pilots, compiled 1900-1903 (possibly related to records of the Third and Fourth Divisions); records relating to U. S. flags and Army uniforms; and many photographs of persons, equipment, and installations. There are also files of reports by the Quartermaster General to the Secretary of War and of printed orders, circulars, and manuals of the Quartermaster's Department; some "Quartermaster Decisions," 1842-70 (10 vols.); and another volume of decisions and circulars, 1865.

First Division (Supply of Public Animals)

This Division had charge of the purchase, procurement, and disposition of horses and mules for cavalry, artillery, and wagon and ambulance trains, and for any other military purpose. The Chief Quartermaster of Cavalry (from Dec. 27, 1863), became Chief of this Division on its organization in August 1864. Toward the end of the war the Division had charge of the sale of surplus public animals, and at the same time it began to handle "Fourth of July claims" for animals taken for public use.

The several officers in charge of purchasing depots of the Cavalry Bureau and the First Division bought 193,388 cavalry horses, Jan. 1, 1864-May 9, 1865; and 20,714 artillery horses and 45,921 mules, Sept. 1, 1864-May 9, 1865. (The First Division had no records of the number of animals purchased by the Cavalry Bureau before Sept. 1, 1864.)

Brig. Gen. James A. Ekin was Chief of the First Division from Aug. 2, 1864.

Record Group 92. -- The consolidated correspondence file and the other series of letters sent and received, described above, contain records of or pertaining to the First Division. Besides these there are an index of letters sent pertaining to the supply of public animals, 1865-69 (2 vols.), and a series of letter books, 1867-68 (36 vols.), concerning claims. Records directly related to those of this Division are described under the Cavalry Bureau.

Second Division (Clothing and Equipage)

This Division handled the purchase, procurement, issue, and disposition of cloth and clothing, knapsacks, camp and garrison equipment, and all soldier equipment provided by the Quartermaster's Department. It also examined and analyzed property accounts of officers' returns for clothing and camp and garrison equipment.

Clothing and most of the camp and garrison equipment of the Army were procured by contract, by purchase, and by manufacture at the principal quartermaster depots. The outbreak of war found the Quartermaster's Department prepared only to supply the existing Army--a paper force of about 13,000 men, with actual strength seldom more than 10,000. Many militia regiments called into Union service were clothed and equipped by State authorities. When authorized by the War Department, the Quartermaster's Department might reimburse a State for such expenditures; in other cases the Treasury Department made reimbursement under special acts of Congress. By the beginning of the second year of the war, however, the manufacture and purchase of Army clothing and equipment were brought under control.

Col. Alex. J. Perry was Chief of the Second Division during the Civil War.

Record Group 92. -- The records of the Division for the war period include materials inherited upon its activation. There are separate series of copies of letters sent relating to clothing and equipment for Regulars, 1861-65 (26 vols.), clothing and equipment for volunteers, 1861-65 (36 vols.), and clothing in general, 1827-70 (34 vols.); there is an index to letters sent relating to clothing and equipment, 1862-66 (5 vols.). There are both a register and a subject index of letters received in the Division, 1864-66; some of these letters are in the consolidated correspondence file

described above. Antedating this Division but relating to its functions is
a volume of abstracts of contracts, 1861-63, for items such as "bed
sacks," greatcoats, ponchos, and whips. Volumes 13-16, 1859-67, of
registers of contracts--a series extending to 1912--relate in part to items
furnished by this Division and in part to those furnished by the Fifth Division. There are also some quartermaster depot reports, 1862-66 (2 vols.),
on camp and garrison clothing and equipment.

Third Division (Ocean and Lake Transportation)

This Division had charge of the purchase, charter, "hire," and maintenance of vessels used in transporting troops, prisoners of war, and their
supplies, "on the ocean, and the bays and sounds connected therewith, and
upon the northern and northwestern lakes, including all vessels propelled
by steam or otherwise, owned or employed by the War Department, excepting river steam vessels and barges upon the western rivers."

Quartermaster operations required the employment of a large fleet of
ocean steamers and sailing vessels. To prevent abuse in the chartering of
vessels to the Government each charter gave the United States the right,
under certain conditions, to purchase the chartered vessel. By 1864 the
Quartermaster's Department owned 39 ocean steamers, 45 river and bay
steamers, 20 steam tugboats, 2 barks, 2 brigs, 21 schooners, and 29
barges. Besides these, the coastal fleet of chartered vessels aggregated
158,694 tons. After the surrender of the Confederates in the Atlantic seaboard States, the vessels belonging to the Government were sold and the
chartered vessels were discharged. In his 1865 report the officer who directed the work of this Division noted that at the outbreak of war the Union
had been unprepared except for

an ample supply of ships and steamers, the importance of which was
very great in a country like ours, penetrated in every direction by
navigable rivers, and indented on the coast by deep and sheltered harbors.

Nothing contributed more to the success of our cause than this,
enabling us, with the assistance of the navy, to concentrate rapidly
and secretly large bodies of troops upon the weak points of the enemy,
and in this way New Orleans, Hilton Head, Fort Fisher, City Point,
Mobile, and the great Mississippi Valley were cleared of the rebels . . .

In the first rush of troops to the war . . . many unsuitable vessels
were employed by the service and paid at high prices. This was rem-
edied as soon as possible by the Quartermaster General, and a scale
of prices fixed per ton . . . and stringent orders issued that no vessel
should be sent with troops to sea unless she had been properly constructed for such purpose.

Beginning on Apr. 1, 1865, a log of "movements and transactions" had
to be kept aboard each vessel used by the Quartermaster's Department in
ocean and lake transportation. At the end of a voyage the log was sent to
the Quartermaster General's Office.

Col. George D. Wise was Chief of the Third Division during the Civil
War.

Record Group 92. -- There are press copies of letters sent, 1863-67
(25 vols.), with an index, Nov. 27, 1865-Sept. 25, 1867 (1 vol.). Fair

copies of letters sent, 1863-67 (14 vols.), pertaining to "Water Transportation" relate both to this Division and the Fourth (Rail and River Transportation), as do 8 volumes of "charter books," 1863-67 (actually registers of letters received). Still other materials that relate to both the Third and Fourth Divisions include a register of vessels chartered at Philadelphia, 1862-65 (2 vols.); several other registers of vessels chartered; an index of steamers owned and chartered by the Government, undated but probably of the Civil War period; records of arrival and departure of quartermaster-chartered vessels at various ports, 1864-66 (ca. 10 ft.); and the journals or logs of many quartermaster-chartered or Government-owned vessels for the Civil War period. The consolidated correspondence file described above contains other records of this Division.

A "List of Ocean and Lake Vessels Chartered, Hired, or Otherwise Employed . . . " during the war (227 p.), giving the number lost and the compensation paid for the losses, compiled in the Quartermaster General's Office, 1868, was printed as H. Ex. Doc. 337, 40 Cong., 2 sess., Serial 1346.

Fourth Division (Rail and River Transportation)

In 1863 Col. Lewis B. Parsons was made Superintendent of Transportation of Supplies by Water on the Western Rivers and all "accounts for charters of steamers on the western rivers" were ordered sent to his office at St. Louis for examination and settlement. Uniform rates for transportation of troops and freight were established, "and all the resources of the immense steamboat interest of the west were brought to contribute to the regular, prompt, and abundant supply of the armies operating on the Mississippi and its tributaries." Parsons continued and enlarged these functions when he became Chief of the Fourth Division, which had charge of the purchase, charter, "hire," and maintenance of all transportation for the Army "and its supplies by land and upon the western rivers, (other than transportation by animal power in the field, and at camps, garrisons, posts, depots, and stations,) including all railroad and telegraph lines operated by the United States for military purposes, and of all steam rams and gunboats owned or employed by the War Department upon the western rivers."

The Division, thus responsible for general management of rail and river transportation, concerned itself primarily with installing a uniform system of procuring transportation to replace the previous practice of allowing each quartermaster to act independently, "some being good and others notoriously defective, in furnishing no proper checks and resulting in irregularity, confusion and much loss to the government." By arranging to have transportation accounts regularly audited in the Fourth Division, the Division Chief brought up the arrears of complex unadjusted accounts for millions of dollars. An agreement made early in the war with a convention of railroad companies continued in force despite wartime inflation.

The Quartermaster General reported (1865) that the activity of the Department's "transportation branch" had never been greater than after hostilities had ceased--"its duty embracing the transportation to their homes of the greater part of an army of a million men, the collection and transportation to depots, for storage or for sale," of surplus animals and stores. Beginning Mar. 1, 1865, a log or "daily journal" had to be kept, for later transmittal to the Fourth Division, by "boats belonging to Government, or

being under charter, impressment, or otherwise in Government service
on the Mississippi river and its tributaries. "

Col. Lewis B. Parsons, who had been put in charge of the western
river transportation in 1863, was made Chief of the Fourth Division upon
its organization.

Record Group 92. -- There are press copies of letters sent, 1865-68
(15 vols.), with an index (5 vols.). The letters received, 1865-70, are
registered (10 vols.), but many of them are in the consolidated correspondence file described above. A volume of information concerning vessels engaged in the Mexican War and on "western rivers" during the Civil War
may be a record of this Division. Of unusual importance is a compilation
of quartermaster instructions, decisions, and orders pertaining to river
and rail transportation during the Civil War (4 vols.). Some of the claims
handled by the Division in the postwar period are documented by press
copies of claim letters sent, 1870 (ca. 50 vols.), and a register of claims,
1871-91 (19 vols.); but the quartermaster claim files described above
should be consulted. Other records closely related to the work of the Division, some of which may have been its own files, are discussed under U.S.
Military Railroads and U. S. Military Telegraphs.

Fifth Division (Regular Supplies)

This Division procured, issued, and disposed of forage, straw, and
stationery for the Army and maintained monthly records of quantities delivered under contract. Daily reports were required from the principal
supply depots and weekly reports from all others. This reporting system,
although not adopted until the last year of the war, and the establishment
of purchasing and contracting depots at strategic points prevented competition by the many purchasing offices seeking supplies in the same market.

This Division also examined claims for fuel, forage, and other supplies
arbitrarily taken by the military and not accounted for or imperfectly reported. These claims if found valid were referred to the Third Auditor of
the Treasury for settlement.

Col. S. L. Brown was Chief of the Fifth Division from Sept. 7, 1864.

Record Group 92. --Records of the Division include fair copies of letters sent, 1865-68 (15 vols.); press copies of letters sent relating to
claims, 1867 (ca. 40 vols.); an index of letters sent, 1864-67 (3 vols.);
registers of letters received, 1865-68 (3 vols.); a record of issues to the
militia, 1864-65 (12 vols.); and many miscellaneous records concerning
horses, mules, forage, and other property. Letters received by the Division are in the consolidated correspondence file of the Quartermaster
General's Office, described above.

Sixth Division (Barracks and Quarters)

This Division had charge of the erection, procurement, maintenance,
and disposition of all barracks, hospital buildings, storehouses, stables,
bridges (other than railroad bridges), wharves, and other structures built
in whole or in part of lumber, and of all lumber, nails, and hardware for
building purposes. It also administered the rental and commutation of
quarters for officers and the rental of quarters for troops and of grounds
for cantonments or other military purposes. In addition it repaired and
maintained buildings and grounds used for military purposes except those

under the charge of other bureaus of the War Department, and it provided for extra pay to soldiers employed in erecting barracks or other fatigue duty. Also it purchased and supplied heating and cooking stoves for barracks, quarters, hospitals, offices, and storehouses.

In the last year of the war the most costly structures built by the Quartermaster's Department were hospitals. At the close of hostilities construction ceased, and the Division increased its work in considering claims and questions arising from the occupation of grounds and buildings by the military.

The Division also received the reports of interments registered during the war--"white and black, loyal and disloyal"--and had charge of national cemeteries and the burial of deceased soldiers "and others dying in the service of the United States in hospitals in and about Washington. " (The officer in charge of this work reported that he had "succeeded in preparing a mortuary record for future reference giving a succinct history of the deceased, every page of which has been compared with the records of hospitals, and up to the present date believed to be the most reliable register of the dead extant. ")

Col. James J. Dana was Chief of the Sixth Division during the Civil War.

Record Group 92. --Few records documenting the original functions of this Division appear to be extant, and most of these are in the consolidated correspondence file described above. Two files of leases, 1864-90, contain some information on the war; and there is a volume relating in part to buildings used by the Army in Charleston, S. C. , and Memphis, Tenn. , Nov. 21, 1862-June 16, 1865.

The Division's "cemeterial" function, however, resulted in the beginning of voluminous and complex quartermaster records series that were continued and augmented after the war. These records, although by no means all created by the Sixth Division, are described collectively here. There are several series of copies of letters sent, ca. 1861-88 (ca. 65 vols.); these are separately but incompletely indexed (ca. 21 vols.). Two series of letters received from 1863 (ca. 50 ft.) are arranged respectively by name of writer and name of cemetery; these are separately but incompletely indexed (ca. 44 vols.). The more than 200 burial registers of national and post cemeteries chiefly concern the interment of Civil War soldiers or veterans. There are also records concerning the burial of soldiers of the U. S. Colored Troops; reports of inspection and other records about superintendents of national cemeteries; cemeterial record cards; records of cemetery expenditures; records pertaining to approach roadways to national cemeteries; and many maps, sketches, and photographs.

Records relating specifically to the interment of Union soldiers include two series, 1861-79 (15 ft.), arranged respectively by name of military organization and name of State or cemetery.

Records concerning the burial of Confederates include a correspondence file (5 ft.) and a "geographic" file (6 ft.); lists of the Confederate dead, showing place of burial; press copies of letters sent, 1909-12 (6 vols.), by the Commission for Marking the Graves of Confederate Dead; copies of contracts for such marking; and miscellaneous other records.

Roll of Honor: Names of Soldiers Who Died in Defense of the American Union, Interred in the National and Other Cemeteries . . . (Washington, 1865-71. 27 vols.); Alphabetical Index to Places of Interment (Washington, 1868).

Seventh Division (Military Trains and Incidental Allowances)

This Division procured, issued, and disposed of wagons, ambulances, traveling forges, and harness, except those furnished by the Ordnance Department; hardware except as otherwise provided; and fuel for officers and enlisted men and for camps, garrisons, hospitals, posts, storehouses, offices, public transports, steam rams, and Army gunboats. It had charge of all animal transport and of the construction and repair of roads other than railroads. It also paid wagon and forage masters and clerks to officers of the Department; the expenses of courts-martial, military commissions, and courts of inquiry; and mileage allowances to officers. It purchased supplies for prisoners of war (and for refugees on the direction of the Secretary of War); portable heating and cooking stoves; and stationery, blanks, and blank books for the Department. It had charge of printing its own and the departmental orders and reports and of "the proper and authorized expenses for the movements and operations of an army not expressly assigned to any other division or department."

By June 1864 the Army trains had become highly efficient. The organization and size of the trains of an active army, as perfected by 4 years of experience in the field, were set forth in Special Order 44, Headquarters Armies of the U. S., City Point, Va., June 28, 1864. The troops operating in the great western plains and the mountain regions of New Mexico, Colorado, Utah, and Idaho were supplied principally by trains from the quartermaster depots, to which supplies were conveyed by contract.

Col. Benjamin C. Card was Chief of the Seventh Division during the Civil War and also headed the Ninth Division.

Record Group 92. --Extant records of this Division are in the consolidated correspondence files described above.

Eighth Division (Inspections)

This Division had charge of all inspections of the Quartermaster's Department and all reports made by inspecting officers. It analyzed and preserved the reports and, through the Quartermaster General, sent to the chiefs of the proper divisions the parts of the reports that concerned them. The officers assigned to inspection duty were empowered "not only to report and to point out any errors or abuses which they . . . [might] discover in the practical operations of the Quartermaster's Department, but to give . . . the orders . . . immediately necessary to correct and to prevent a continuance of such abuses or errors."

In his annual report for the fiscal year 1865, the Quartermaster General characterized the work of this Division as follows:

> The Eighth Division is the division of inspection. Its duties are delicate and difficult. It receives, registers, analyzes, and prepares for action of the Quartermaster General all reports of the regular inspectors, or of officers acting as inspectors under orders of the Quartermaster's department, and all reports of inspection of that department by the inspectors general of the army which may be referred to this office for action.
>
> It keeps the roster of the officers of the Quartermaster's department, and keeps a careful and minute record of the service of all officers as reported to this office. It also prepares and records the

general and special orders of the department, and its nominations for assignments to duty.

From his appointment in Aug. 1864 to Oct. 10, 1865, the Division's Chief, himself engaged in inspection duty, transmitted to the Quartermaster General 49 separate reports of inspection and investigation made in the North, the East, and the States of Kansas and Missouri. At the same time (up to June 30, 1865), the Division received from officers of the Quartermaster's Department 216 inspection reports and 579 related communications. The Division Chief believed that investigations involving the conduct of officers had been thorough and efficient, although mistakes had been made "by a want of shrewdness and propriety of action." The entries in the inspection books were "in fact briefs of the original papers, and not merely skeletons. Every name of a person, however insignificant, occurring in these papers is alphabetically entered, so that one name being recollected, all the facts pertaining to the transaction can be at once ascertained."

The Eighth Division also received, entered, and acted upon reports of Army boards of survey; and it received and compiled the annual reports of quartermaster officers. It routed quartermaster official bonds to the Secretary of War for approval and transmittal to the Second Comptroller. It also supervised the work of the different boards to examine qualifications of officers of the Quartermaster Department.

Col. George B. Rutherford was Chief of the Eighth Division from Aug. 24, 1864.

Record Group 92. --Records documenting the Division's inspection function include a record of inspections, 1864-67 (2 vols.); reports of inspection and boards of survey, 1864-67 (3 vols.), with indexes (2 vols.); and the inspection reports of Bvt. Brig. Gen. James F. Russling, 1866-67 (1 vol.), which give detailed information about western posts. For other records of inspection the consolidated correspondence file described above should be consulted.

The Division's correspondence comprises copies of letters sent, 1865-69 (8 vols.), indexed in 3 volumes; and letters received, 1864-67 (5 ft.), with registers (2 vols.) and indexes (10 vols.). The annual reports of quartermaster officers to the Quartermaster General, 1862-78 (5 vols. and 15 ft.), are supplemented by "personal narrative reports," 1864-68 (11 vols.), and abstracts of reports, 1862-64 (2 vols.). These reports were required to show:

The stations, marches, and duties of the officer during the year, or for such time as he served in the Quartermaster's Department. To be given in the form of a personal narrative report, stating at what places and with what commands the officer served, the dates of changes of stations, the marches and journeys, battles, sieges, and skirmishes in which he has borne a part; whether any property under his charge has been lost, destroyed, or captured by the enemy, and its value; what rebel property captured by our armies has fallen into his hands; what was its value, and what disposition has been made of it.

The annual reports included also statements on clothing and camp and garrison equipment, public moneys, amounts paid for railroad or other land transportation, the number of miles and location of railroads constructed, the number of miles and location of telegraph lines constructed, and the number of vessels chartered or employed.

Records of appointments and assignments include those relating to acting assistant quartermasters from 1863 (13 vols.) and to volunteer officers, 1861-65 (6 vols.). There are also lists of quartermaster clerks, superintendents, wagon masters, printers, etc., as of Sept. 30, 1865; lists of civilian clerks and messengers in the Quartermaster General's Office, 1861-70; and a volume relating to the battalion of clerks of the Quartermaster General's Office, Cos. A-C, 1864.

Ninth Division (Records and Correspondence)

This Division was legally responsible for all correspondence, returns, reports, and records received and kept in the Office of the Quartermaster General and for their referral to other divisions of the Office and to government departments. In point of fact, however, its principal duty was to examine the accounts of disbursing officers and officers responsible for public property, except for the accounts examined in the Second Division (Clothing and Equipage). During the 4-year period July 1, 1861-June 30, 1865, the Division received 176, 402 accounts and examined and sent to the Treasury 63, 259. "These are not single vouchers," the Quartermaster General reported in 1865, "but accounts, many of which contain hundreds, and some of them thousands, of single vouchers. They represent the expenditure of over one thousand millions of dollars in money, and the use and application of the property purchased therewith."

Col. Benjamin C. Card was Chief of the Ninth Division during the Civil War. He also headed the Seventh Division.

Record Group 92. --Extant records of this Division, except those incorporated in the consolidated correspondence file described above, consist principally of officers' money accounts from 1864.

Western Gunboat Fleet

In 1861 and 1862 the Quartermaster's Department built a fleet of ironclad gunboats and one of steam rams, which were officered and manned by the Navy and War Departments "conjointly." These fleets were of great help in military operations along the Mississippi River and its tributaries. The gunboat fleet was transferred from the War Department to the Navy Department under an act of July 16, 1862 (12 Stat. 587); the fleet of steam rams, however, continued under the War Department. (AGO General Order 150, Oct. 1, 1862, ordered the Chief Quartermaster of the gunboat fleet, Capt. G. D. Wise, to "settle up all indebtedness of the fleet to the 1st of October, make the usual returns and . . . close his accounts, and report by letter to the Quartermaster General.") In ordering the transfer Secretary of War Stanton noted that the "brilliant and important services of the gun-boats at Fort Henry, Fort Donelson, Columbus, Island No. 10, Pittsburg Landing, Memphis, Vicksburg, Natchez, Baton Rouge, and generally in independent action or in cooperation with the Army on the Western rivers, will constitute one of the brightest pages in the history of the war."

Captain Wise, in his final report of Sept. 14, 1863 (printed as part of the Quartermaster General's report for 1865), confirmed that the "flotilla was under the command of naval officers, and subject to naval rules; while at the same time its whole organization was a part of the army, and its expenditures paid from that department. " Final transfer was not made until Sept. 30, 1862.

Warren D. Crandall and Isaac D. Newell, History of the Ram Fleet and the Mississippi Marine Brigade in the War for the Union on the Mississippi and Its Tributaries; the Story of the Ellets and Their Men (St. Louis, 1907); report of the Chief Quartermaster, Western Gunboat Fleet, cited above.

Record Group 217. -- Records of and relating to the Western Gunboat Fleet (or "Flotilla") that were forwarded to the Third Auditor of the Treasury are described under Treasury Department.

Record Group 92. -- A volume entitled "Vessels of Mississippi Marine Brigade and Ram Fleet, " 1862-64, is available. Other related records are principally in the consolidated and other correspondence files of the Quartermaster General's Office.

Quartermaster Depots and the Field Organization

The Quartermaster General considered the field organization of his Department to be "simple and efficient. " Each corps, brigade, or regimental quartermaster took orders and instructions both from the commander of the troops to which he was attached and from his immediate superior in the Quartermaster's Department. Officers were assigned also as chief quartermasters of military departments or of principal depots. These officers, under the direction of the Quartermaster General's Office, contracted for and purchased supplies and provided for their inspection, storage, safekeeping, and transportation from the principal depots in the loyal States to subordinate or advanced depots established on the border or in areas won from the Confederacy. In addition to the principal depots at New York, Philadelphia, Cincinnati, and St. Louis, other depots for manufacture and purchase were established during the war at Quincy, Ill. , Steubenville, Ohio, and Milwaukee, Wis. At important army posts, garrisoned by troops, regimental quartermasters attached to the garrisons usually acted as post quartermasters.

Record Group 92. -- The considerable quantity of field records of the Quartermaster's Department include records of all command levels for the Civil War period. Many of these relate to supply problems during war and reconstruction. Especially significant are the records of the principal quartermaster depots at Philadelphia (Schuylkill Arsenal) and Cincinnati. The relatively complete records kept at Philadelphia include letters sent and received, inspection books, and records of purchases. (Other records of quartermaster installations or of quartermaster officers serving in the field during the Civil War are in Record Group 98, Records of the United States Army Commands.)

OFFICE OF THE PAYMASTER GENERAL

An act of May 8, 1792 (1 Stat. 279), provided for a "paymaster to reside near the head-quarters of the troops of the United States"; and an act of Apr. 24, 1816 (3 Stat. 297), established a Pay Department headed by a Paymaster General. During the Civil War the Paymaster General, under the direction of the Secretary of War, was responsible for the administration of the Pay Department in all its details. The subordinate paymasters, whose exclusive duty was the disbursement of public money, were subject to orders only of the Secretary of War, the Paymaster General, and the senior officers of their own geographical departments. They were, however, subject to arrest by the senior officer of the command to which they might be assigned. Any such arrest had to be reported immediately to the Paymaster General so that he might bring the case before the Secretary of War.

The Pay Department was the only one within the military establishment that needed no law for its expansion during the Civil War; sec. 25 of an act of July 5, 1838 (5 Stat. 259), had authorized the President, whenever volunteers or militia should be called into the service of the United States, to appoint additional paymasters to serve as long as needed to pay the new troops. The number of such additional paymasters in the service in 1864 was 319; they had been appointed on recommendations of examining boards at Washington, Cincinnati, Louisville, and St. Louis.

The Paymaster General established pay districts that generally corresponded in number and geographical limits to the military departments. In each pay district a corps of paymasters was constituted and was made responsible to a selected officer. This single officer received all the funds required for the payments, distributed them to his subordinate paymasters, directed and arranged the payments to the troops, and superintended the performance of all the duties required of the Pay Department.

In allusion to the "onerous" duties of the Department, the Paymaster General in his fiscal year 1864 report emphasized the immense labor involved in disbursing, necessarily at stated periods and in small sums, the "large annual sum" of $350,000,000. In his report on the last year of the war, when praising the members of his immediate staff, he described their wartime work as follows:

With payments simultaneously progressing at sixty different points, widely separated, with the necessity of keeping each one supplied with funds from day to day, and a necessity also that each should have no more than required for immediate disbursement--drawing from the treasury at the rate of $20,000,000 per week, and compelled to make close estimate and careful watch of its daily distribution, so that the demand at each given point should be surely supplied, and yet no more than supplied; telegrams and letters continually pouring in, noting the movement and destination of troops, and repeating these notices to the proper points of rendezvous; applications and appeals constantly arriving, requiring immediate answers; new questions arising and referred to this office for instructions etc.--kept our thoughts, our pens, our press, and the telegraph in constant requisition by day and by night.

The maximum number of paymasters employed at any one time during the war was 447. Total disbursements during the war were over $1,100,000,000. Within the three months of June, July, and August of 1865 the Pay Department made final payment of approximately $270,000,000 to some 800,000 men--a task of which the Paymaster General wrote in his report:

When the manner of these payments is observed, with a knowledge of the particularity required in each case, the accounts varying in amounts, each to be separately computed in its several items of pay, clothing, bounty, &c., with such stoppages as may be chargeable deducted, the final amount stated and the signature of each officer and man to be appended in duplicate to the receipt rolls, a just appreciation may be formed of the stupendous labor involved. No similar work of like magnitude, regarding its immensity both as to men and money, and the small limit of time in which it has been performed, has, it is believed, any parallel in the history of armies.

The rapid disbandment of volunteer regiments at the close of the war threw upon the Pay Department a great accumulation of "referred claims" transmitted for adjustment of payment. These had arisen chiefly from the inability of muster-out officers to compile a complete history of the pay, clothing, bounty, etc., because of the large numbers of enlisted men. In such cases no final settlement was possible at the time of discharge. The Division of Referred Claims, established in the summer of 1865, comprised a group of 12 paymasters and 64 clerks operating under a chief supervising paymaster. Each claim sent to the Division required search in previous payrolls on file in the Paymaster General's Office and in the Office of the Second Auditor of the Treasury Department, besides referral to the Adjutant General's Office. From 1866 the Office was responsible for the examination of accounts to establish eligibility of former soldiers to receive additional bounty authorized by an act of July 28, 1866 (14 Stat. 322). Actually, however, "in consequence of the pressure upon the treasury, (Second Auditor,) and . . . of what was considered to be the greater facilities of the pay department," the Paymaster General's Office had paid most of the bounties accruing during the war except those due to deceased officers and men. In 1866 a board of officers prepared rules for bounty payments, to include those for colored soldiers (see Claim Division, under Bureau of Refugees, Freedmen, and Abandoned Lands, below).

Paymasters General during the war:
  Col. Benjamin F. Larned, in office when the war began.
  Maj. Cary H. Fry (acting), July 15, 1862.
  Col. Timothy P. Andrews, Dec. 11, 1862.
  Col. Benjamin W. Brice, Nov. 29, 1864.

Civil War annual reports of the   H. Rept. 5, 40 Cong., 2 sess.,
Paymaster General, appended to   Serial 1357; H. Rept. 33, 40 Cong.,
those of the Secretary of War;   3 sess., Serial 1388.

Record Group 99.--The letters sent by the Paymaster General during the Civil War are in a series of volumes of miscellaneous letters sent, 1808-89, for which a volume of "Digests of Important Letters," 1808-71, constitutes a partial but important finding aid. Letters received, 1861-65, are abstracted in registers and are indexed; these constitute parts of a series, 1799-1870, alphabetically arranged by name of writer, then by year. There are also registers of and indexes to letters "Received From Departments" (that is, other bureaus of the Government), 1862-65 (4 vols.), and copies of endorsements made on letters received, 1860-69 (4 vols.). Four other volumes, 1865-66, register "Letters Received Claims." Decisions, opinions, etc., recorded in the correspondence are indexed, 1808-93 (7 vols.), and are digested on record cards, 1808-1912 (3 ft.). Wartime or war-related fiscal records consist of general ledgers,

1864-77, for pay of the Army, pay of officers, pay of volunteers, pay of officers at the U. S. Military Academy, and payment of bounties; registers of requests for funds (part of 12 vols., 1854-1912); records of receipts and expenditures (part of 12 vols., 1838-71); a register of paymasters' accounts rendered and transmitted to the Treasury Department's Second Auditor, 1863-73; registers of payments to officers (part of 125 vols., 1826-1913, with name index), to troops (part of 14 vols., 1841-1913), to discharged soldiers (part of 40 vols., 1839-1916), to hospital nurses and stewards (3 vols., 1859-80), to enlisted men on Treasury certificates (1 vol., 1862-94), to sergeants and post noncommissioned staffs (part of 13 vols., 1861-1915), and to various detachments of artillery, infantry, etc. (part of 7 vols., 1849-73); paymasters' accounts of drafts, 1865 (1 vol.); and a record of soldiers' deposits, 1865-68 (1 vol.).

Personnel records include personal histories of paymasters, 1848-89 and 1863-67 (2 vols.), and of additional paymasters (part of 7 vols., 1861-1910); registers of paymasters, 1815-68 and 1861-64 (2 vols.); board proceedings for the examination of officers for the Pay Department, 1864-67 (1 1/2 ft.); personal reports of paymaster clerks, 1864-65; and lists of civilian employees of the Office (part of 9 vols., 1861-1911).

National Archives, Preliminary Inventory [No. 9] of the Records of the Office of the Paymaster General, comp. by Roland C. McConnell (Washington, 1948).

Record Group 92. --After the Office of the Paymaster General was abolished and its responsibility for paying the troops was transferred to the Office of the Quartermaster General in 1912, the latter office removed many documents from the Paymaster General's general correspondence files for interfiling with Quartermaster General's records in a consolidated subject file. Insofar as they relate to the Civil War these are described in this Guide under Office of the Quartermaster General.

Record Group 217. --The records of the Second Auditor of the Treasury Department include the following original records of the Paymaster General, which were transferred to the Second Auditor's Office in 1889: registers and abstracts, in several series and consisting of many volumes, of payments to soldiers, 1863-66; registers of auditor's certificates paid, 1865-85 (42 vols.); and a few series of war-related claims registers.

SURGEON GENERAL'S OFFICE AND THE MEDICAL DEPARTMENT

An act of Apr. 4, 1818 (3 Stat. 426), gave to the Medical Department for the first time a permanent chief with the title of Surgeon General and an act of Mar. 2, 1821 (3 Stat. 616), prescribed its peacetime organization. The Department was variously named, both before and during the Civil War. An act of June 21, 1860 (12 Stat. 67), referred to the "medical corps"; one of Aug. 3, 1861 (12 Stat. 288), to the "medical staff"; and one of Apr. 16, 1862 (12 Stat. 378), to the "Medical Department" in its title and the "medical corps" in its text. An act of Dec. 27, 1862 (12 Stat. 633), speaks of the "medical inspector's department" as a part of the "medical corps." Early in 1861 the medical staff of the Army comprised the Surgeon General, 30 surgeons, and 83 assistant surgeons; but when war began, 3 surgeons and 21 assistant surgeons resigned and 3 other assistant surgeons were dismissed for disloyalty.

During the war several acts of Congress--those of Aug. 3, 1861, and
Apr. 16 and Dec. 27, 1862, cited above--increased the organization of the
regular medical staff to comprise a Surgeon General, an Assistant Surgeon
General, a Medical Inspector General of Hospitals, 16 medical inspectors,
and 170 surgeons and assistant surgeons. (Many Regular Army officers
became medical directors of corps and armies, and others served as medical inspectors or medical purveyors or were assigned to field or hospital
service.)

In addition, between Apr. 1861 and the end of the war 547 surgeons and
assistant surgeons of volunteers were appointed, 2,109 volunteer regimental surgeons and 3,882 volunteer regimental assistant surgeons were
mustered into service, and 75 acting staff surgeons and 5,532 acting assistant surgeons were employed. The act of Aug. 3, 1861, already cited, provided also for a Corps of Medical Cadets, who served as dressers at
general hospitals and ambulance attendants in the field; and an act of May
20, 1862 (12 Stat. 403), provided for not more than six storekeepers.

The beginning of the war found the medical establishment essentially
unchanged since the end of the War with Mexico. After 50 years of service,
the ailing Surgeon General, Thomas Lawson, died on May 15, 1861, at
Norfolk, Va. He was succeeded by Surg. Gen. Clement A. Finley, who
retired on Apr. 14, 1862, after service dating from 1818. In this first
year of war there was no ambulance service or other efficient method of
transporting the wounded; and between the first aid stations at the front and
the base hospitals far in the rear "there was nothing."

Asst. Surg. William A. Hammond, though junior to many other officers
of the Medical Department, was appointed Surgeon General on Apr. 25,
1862. Although he met some resistance to reforms in the Department, his
own energy was to bring about a relatively efficient medical organization.
The reorganization authorized by the act of Apr. 16, 1862, had been the result of recommendations made at the request of Maj. Gen. George B.
McClellan. Throughout the war the innovations of the U. S. Sanitary Commission influenced medical policy, as when its furnishing hospital railway
cars in 1862 paved the way for the Government's providing regular hospital
trains. Equally influential were the innovations of the Medical Director of
the Army of the Potomac, Jonathan Letterman, as in the case of his system
of evacuation (which afterward was extended to all of the armies), his medical supply plan, and his field hospital plan. The system of organization
that finally evolved made the medical director of each army or geographical
department responsible for medical operations in the command to which he
was assigned.

In May 1864 the Office of the Assistant Surgeon General, with Col.
Robert C. Wood in charge, was established at Louisville, Ky., to expedite
the shipment of medical supplies "to points developed by emergencies," to
insure "the proper distribution and presence of medical officers and their
assistants where their services were most required, and to provide com-
fortable, abundant, and available hospital accommodation for the sick and
wounded of the Armies of the West and Southwest." Under the direction of
the Surgeon General, the Assistant Surgeon General had immediate control
of medical affairs in the Department of the Northwest, the Northern Department, the Departments of Kansas and Missouri, and the Departments composing the Division of the Mississippi.

The Medical Inspector General supervised the sanitary condition of the
Army, whether in transports, quarters, or camps; the hygiene, police,

discipline, and efficiency of field and general hospitals; and the assignment of duties to medical inspectors. The status of women nurses employed under the supervision of Dorothea Dix was clarified by the rules published in AGO General Order 351, Oct. 29, 1863, requiring that surgeons apply through medical directors to Miss Dix or her agents for the assignment of nurses and that she or her agents provide those appointed with "certificates of approval." While on duty in general hospitals these nurses were "under the exclusive control of the senior medical officer."

Administrative policies affecting the Medical Department, continually controversial in the early stages of the war, were settled for the most part before its end. The control of military hospitals, for example, was placed definitely under medical officers in Dec. 1864, to meet objections to their supervision by line officers; and in Feb. 1865 the Medical Department was given exclusive control of hospital transports and boats. Except for these modifications the express exclusion of medical officers from command, by sec. 8 of an act of Feb. 11, 1847 (9 Stat. 125), was the rule during the Civil War.

Late in the summer of 1863 sanitary conditions in the Departments of the South and the Gulf appeared to require special attention, and Surgeon General Hammond was directed to visit Hilton Head, Charleston Harbor, Key West, and New Orleans, making his headquarters in New Orleans and reporting to the Secretary of War every 10 days. Ostensibly to let him give his full attention to this work, Medical Inspector Gen. Joseph K. Barnes was, by AGO Special Order 396, Sept. 3, 1863, "empowered to take charge of the Bureau of the Medical Department of the Army, and to perform the duties of Surgeon General during the absence of that officer." Hammond had aroused hostility in the War Department, however; and on Aug. 18, 1864, after a court-martial, he was dismissed from the service on charges of disorder and negligence in the purchase of inferior blankets, medicines, and medical stores. His sentence was later annulled, and he has since been recognized as a conscientious Surgeon General, who greatly and favorably influenced the development of the Medical Department during and after the war. Barnes succeeded Hammond as Surgeon General and continued the improvements initiated by his predecessor. He obtained for the Medical Department exclusive control of general hospitals, hospital ships, and hospital camps; saw to the development of the Army Medical Museum and the Library of the Surgeon General's Office; and supervised the compilation of the Medical and Surgical History of the War of the Rebellion.

The intention to prepare this history for publication had been announced to the medical staff on June 9, 1862, in a circular from the Surgeon General's Office, and by the end of that year the Office had collected and was systematically arranging a "large number of memoires and reports of great interest to medical science, and military surgery especially." In 1863 the office published a Consolidated Statement of Gunshot Wounds, by Surg. J. H. Brinton and a Report of Sickness and Mortality of the Army, by Asst. Surg. J. J. Woodward; but the projected scope of the "history" led to revision of recording and reporting methods. A medical board had been convened in July 1862 to revise forms employed in the returns of sick and wounded; and in Nov. 1863 the medical directors of armies in the field were required to forward direct to the Surgeon General, after every engagement, duplicates of their reports to their several commanding generals of the killed and wounded. The medical directors were required, moreover, to take steps to collate and prepare for transmission to the Surgeon General's Office "all obtainable statistics and data in connection with past and future operations . . . which may be essential or useful in the accurate compilation of the Medical and Surgical History of the War." In Jan. 1864 the "Register of Sick and Wounded" in use in general hospitals was replaced by two registers, one of the sick and wounded and another of surgical operations; and in Feb. 1864 separate reports were required for sick and wounded prisoners of war and for white and colored troops "in order to obtain with greater facility the sickness and mortality rates of each." Further efforts to perfect the returns included the adoption, in Mar. 1864, of a classified return of wounds and injuries received in action, a report of wounded, and a report of surgical operations. In Feb. 1865 the medical directors of armies in the field and of detached commands were instructed to transmit to the Surgeon General's Office "all reports in their possession from the Recorders of Divisions or other Field Hospitals" as well as "all reports of individual cases of gunshot injury" previous to the new system of registration of wounds. Finally, on Apr. 6, 1866, the medical directors were required to transfer to the Surgeon General's Office "all Registers of Hospitals, Consolidated Registers of Soldiers treated, and all information in their possession pertaining to the Sick, Wounded, Discharged, and Dead during the War."

At the close of the war a valuable store of information was added in the form of parts of the Confederate hospital records. The uses to which all the sources of available data were put in the compilation of the "history" are explained in the prefatory remarks to the "medical" and "surgical" volumes of part 1 of that work (see bibliographical note, below).

The collection and forwarding of medical specimens, as directed by the Surgeon General's circular of May 21, 1862, necessitated the establishment of an Army medical museum; at the end of 1863 this contained over 3,000 specimens and assumed a value and importance that justified "recommendation of a small annual appropriation." The exhibits, which included valuable specimens of morbid anatomy, surgical and medical, and projectiles and foreign bodies removed from wounds, became the nucleus of the collections of the present Army Medical Museum, the first Catalogue of which (960 p.) was issued in 1866.

At the end of 1865 the alphabetical register of the dead had not been completed, but the records of the Medical Department contained 30,000 special reports "of the more important forms of surgical injuries, of disease, and of operations." These, with statistical data and the pathological collection of 7,630 specimens, constituted a "mass of valuable information" that was being rapidly arranged and tabulated.

In this connection [the Surgeon General wrote in his 1865 annual report] and as illustrating more in detail the importance of this work, the army medical museum assumes the highest value. By its array of indisputable facts, supported and enriched by full reports, it supplies instruction otherwise unattainable, and preserves for future application the dearly-bought experience of four years of war. Apart from its great usefulness, it is also an honorable record of the skill and services of those medical officers whose contributions constitute its value, and whose incentive to these self-imposed labors has been the desire to elevate their profession.

In the latter part of 1865 the Surgeon General's Office supervised the public auction of the vast amount of medicines and hospital supplies that became surplus through the reduction of the Army. The business of the Office was increased also by the immediate need to examine and settle the accounts of staff and regimental medical officers mustered out of service and to answer applications from the Pension Office for "official evidence of cause of death." These applications in the fiscal year 1865 averaged 1,550 a month.

Under Army regulations the Secretary of War appointed from time to time during the war boards of not fewer than three medical officers each to examine applicants for appointment as assistant surgeon and to examine assistant surgeons for promotion. These boards were required to "scrutinize rigidly the moral habits, professional acquirements, and physical qualifications of the candidates." They also examined candidates for appointment as medical cadets. Boards of this type were in session at various times during the war at Washington, New York, Hilton Head (S. C.), New Orleans, Memphis, Little Rock (Ark.), Cincinnati, Boston, Philadelphia, and St. Louis.

In U. S. general hospitals throughout the country, hospital examining boards inspected and reported on employees, and on patients to determine their ability to rejoin their regiments. In 1863 two boards (at Annapolis and Cincinnati) were formed to reduce the serious absence of officers from duty. All officers who had left their commands because of ill health were ordered to appear, as soon as they were able to travel, before one of these boards. Upon completion of its examination the board in each case recommended the officer for light duty, for further leave of absence, or for medical treatment, in accordance with his condition. If found fit for duty, the officer concerned was ordered forthwith to his regiment. The reports of these boards served to guide the Adjutant General in making details; and when used in connection with regimental reports they constituted a complete system of accountability for absence from duty.

Medical boards were appointed also to examine convalescents, under special instructions of the Provost Marshal General, and to determine their eligibility for admission into the Invalid Corps, later the Veteran Reserve Corps. Boards were established also to examine into the physical qualifications of members of the graduating classes at West Point. Still other medical boards were appointed to revise the regulations for the Medical Department, to determine the character and causes of typhoid fever, to recommend what general rules should determine the degree of physical disability that should disqualify a man for the Invalid Corps, and to prescribe rules governing boards of enrollment in deciding who should be exempt from draft as physically or mentally unfit for the service. Of special importance to the Medical Department was the board (appointed by AGO S. O. 260, Aug. 5, 1864) to examine thoroughly the management and military control of U. S. general hospitals; it was composed of Maj. Gen. E. A. Hitchcock, Brig. Gen. W. S. Ketchum, Brig. Gen. Richard Delafield, and 1st Lt. A. W. Kroutinger.

Successive Surgeons General during the war period:
Col. Thomas Lawson, in office when the war began.
Col. Clement A. Finley, May 15, 1861.
Brig. Gen. William A. Hammond, Apr. 25, 1862.
Brig. Gen. Joseph K. Barnes, Aug. 22, 1864.

Annual reports of the Surgeon General, 1861-66, appended to those of the Secretary of War; Harvey E. Brown, The Medical Department of the United States Army From 1775 to 1873 (Washington, 1873); Maj. Charles Smart, "The Medical Department," in Theo. F. Rodenbough and William L. Haskin, eds., The Army of the United States (New York, 1896); P. M. Ashburn, A History of the Medical Department of the United States Army (Cambridge, 1929); James A. Tobey, The Medical Department of the Army; Its History, Activities, and Organization (Baltimore, 1927); Alex H. Meneely, The War Department, 1861; a Study in Mobilization and Administration (New York, 1928).

See also The Medical and Surgical History of the War of the Rebellion (1861-1865), prepared under the direction of the Surgeon General (Washington, 1870-88. 3 parts of 2 vols. each). The Medical Volume of part 1 (prepared by J. J. Woodward), comprises "a series of statistical tables presenting a summary view of the facts embodied in the monthly reports made to the Surgeon General with regard to the Sickness of the Army, the Deaths, and the Discharges from service on surgeon's certificate of disability"; that of part 2 (prepared also by Woodward) treats of "the Alvine Fluxes"; and that of part 3 (prepared by Charles Smart) consists of an analysis of the medical statistics of the war, a description of the general hospitals, and chapters on fevers, other miasmal diseases, scurvy, diseases attributed to non-miasmal exposures, and certain other (including locally endemic) diseases. The Surgical Volume of part 1 (prepared by George A. Otis) contains a chronological summary of engagements and battles (with remarks and references of medical significance) and describes wounds and injuries of the head, face, neck, spine, and chest; that of part 2 (also prepared by Otis) describes wounds and injuries of the abdomen, pelvis, back, and upper extremities; and that of part 3 (prepared by George A. Otis and D. L. Huntington) treats wounds and injuries of the lower extremities, miscellaneous injuries, wounds and complications, anesthetics, the medical staff and materia chirurgica, and the transportation of the wounded. Valuable in the use of these volumes is the Surgeon General's Circular 6, Report on the Extent and Nature of the Materials Available for the Preparation of the Medical and Surgical History of the Rebellion (166 p.).

General Records

Record Group 112. -- The records of the Surgeon General's Office most important to research on the Civil War are now chiefly in Record Group 94, and there are other wartime records of the Office in Record Groups 15 and 27 (see below). In Record Group 112, however, are most of the correspondence, some personnel records, the fiscal and property records, and a few records pertaining to hospitals; these are described here. Also in Record Group 112 are the records of Army medical boards appointed during the war (and earlier and later) to examine applicants for appointment as assistant surgeons and to examine assistant surgeons for promotion. These comprise ca. 10 vols. of proceedings, correspondence, lists of candidates, and merit rolls of boards convened during the war in Washington, New York City, Philadelphia, Cincinnati, and Beaufort, S. C., as well as papers received or created in the Surgeon General's Office relating to the work of the boards.

Copies of letters (and endorsements) sent are in a general series, 1818-89 (90 vols., with index), and in the following additional series for the war period: letters to the Secretary of War, 1837-66 (6 vols. and 5 index vols.); letters to officials of War Department bureaus, 1862-89 (25 vols. and 31 index vols.); and "military letters" to Medical Department officers, 1862-72 (18 vols.). Other volumes contain copies of reports on administrative matters made to the Secretary of War and of endorsements relating to supplies and accounts (from 1864) and the mustering out of troops (from Mar. 1865).

Letters received during the war are in a series extending from 1818 to 1889 (530 ft.), arranged alphabetically by writers' surnames and thereunder by year; there are registers (63 vols.) and indexes (40 vols.) of letters received, 1822-89. Other records include a volume of copies of letters received from the Secretary of War, the Adjutant General, and other War Department officials, Oct. 1860-Mar. 1861, and a register of requests received for discharges and transfers, 1864-65.

Among personnel records in this record group are registers of Regular and volunteer medical officers and hospital stewards; a station book showing service of medical officers at particular posts, 1857-91; a set of pamphlets (one for each corps) listing medical officers serving with the 25 Civil War Army Corps; service data and an index relating to wartime contract surgeons; a register of medical officers serving with Regular Army regiments, 1861-76; a "Necrology of Medical Officers," 1861-96; service data on medical cadets, 1862-65 (4 in.); and registers of arrivals in the Surgeon General's Office of volunteer medical officers, 1862-67, and of Regular Army medical officers, 1862-89.

Among records of medical supplies and property those of Civil War interest include abstracts of the property returns of medical officers in the field, 1858-66 (1 vol.), and schedules of medical and hospital property returns examined and sent to the Second Auditor, 1863-67 (2 vols.). Wartime fiscal records include records of requisitions for funds; many volumes of disbursing officers' accounts, daybooks, ledgers, abstracts of disbursements, and related books; records of the settlement of medical officers', surgeons', and contract surgeons' accounts; and a few records of claims for payment of medical services and supplies.

Practically all records of the Surgeon General's Office relating to Civil War hospitals are in Record Group 94 (see below), but in Record Group 112 there are several volumes giving names, locations, dates of opening and closing, and other details of general and other Army hospitals of the war period. Also available are monthly reports of sick and wounded, from 1861.

Most records of the Surgeon General's Office concerning the issuance of artificial limbs, trusses, and other prosthetic appliances are now in Record Group 15 (see below).

In Record Group 109 (War Department Collection of Confederate Records) is a register, 1862-65 (5 vols.), apparently compiled by the Surgeon General's Office, of the deaths of Confederates in Union prisons.

Meteorological records of the Civil War period, originally belonging to the Surgeon General's Office, are now in Record Group 27 (see below).

Records Transferred to the Record and Pension Office

Record Group 94. -- The Civil War records of the Surgeon General's Office allocated to this group comprise those transferred, principally for

purposes of "carding, " to the Record and Pension Office. Although not
created by that Office, they remained associated with the carded medical
records for use by the Adjutant General's Office in preparing official certifications of military service. Such of these records as relate to military
service, with the exception of duplicates, were carded. They consist of
administrative records, medical and surgical reports, records of casualties, and hospital records.

The records of the administration of the medical service, particularly
with respect to the personnel employed, comprise several series of
monthly and miscellaneous returns of medical officers, maintained for the
most part separately by military departments and Civil War armies and
Army corps (ca. 30 ft.); station cards, station books, service record
cards, correspondence, orders, property account records, and assignment records of surgeons, assistant surgeons, and acting assistant surgeons, 1861-65 and later (ca. 4 ft.); contract books and pay accounts of
contract surgeons, 1861-65 and later (ca. 3 ft.); card records of draft
surgeons, 1861-65 (3 in.); returns of, and other papers relating to, hospital stewards (over 5 ft.); monthly returns of contract nurses in hospitals,
including hospitals afloat, 1861-65 (10 ft.), and a register of colored contract nurses during the war; correspondence concerning the appointment,
discharge, and Civil War service of medical cadets (4 ft.); and monthly
reports of medical officers at recruiting stations, from 1864. There are
also a 1-volume list of medical officers serving at permanent posts, 1860-
93; several registers of other medical personnel; a 1-volume record of
medical officers serving with the artillery, 1861-65; a volume of "Accounts
of Physicians Serving With Freedmen, Refugees, etc., Who Have Been
Paid From the Medical and Hospital Appropriation, " 1862-64; and a record
of payment for medical services, 1863-64 (2 vols.). Other war-related
records created for administrative or informational purposes include reports of chaplains stationed at hospitals (3 1/2 ft.); reports on searches
for information on contract surgeons (6 in.); a volume including a record
of inquiries for pension purposes, 1865-68, and a list of applicants for
artificial limbs, Aug. 1870; a chronological list of battles with data on the
disposition of the wounded (2 vols.); an "Alphabetical Index to Casualties,
Battles, Skirmishes, Naval Engagements, Railroad Accidents, Explosions,
Indian Fights, etc. , " 1861-81 (1 vol.); and a volume containing organizational data on armies and Army corps compiled from published and unpublished sources. The "personal papers" of medical officers and physicians
(360 ft.), alphabetically arranged by name, include papers of the Civil
War period.

The Civil War medical and surgical records proper consist principally
of File A and bound manuscripts (16 ft.), comprising surgeons' reports on
medical matters, surgical cases in hospitals, casualties, the organization
and duties of the medical departments of various commands, and medical
and surgical work in various campaigns; File B, extending into the 1870's
(1 ft.), containing reports on methods of treatment and transportation of the
wounded, and on wagons, litters, ambulances, trusses, and other medical
apparatus and inventions; File D, extending into the 1880's, containing reports on medical and surgical cases (22 ft.); File F, 1861-89 (2 ft.), including lists of casualties in various engagements and correspondence with
Confederate authorities concerning the wounded; and the "SSD File" (about
1 ft.), including correspondence concerning applications for artificial limbs,
the transfer of wounded soldiers from one hospital to another, and medical

reports on individual cases. Also available are papers, 1861-65, of John H. Brinton, surgeon of volunteers (10 vols.); and some special reports, extending into the 1880's (2 ft.), on diseases, wounds, deaths, medical equipment, and medical inventions.

Records of Civil War deaths and other casualties consist of the following: registers of deaths, volunteers (63 vols.); a register of deaths, U. S. Colored Troops; regimental casualty lists (17 ft.); army corps, army, and departmental casualty lists (19 ft.); casualty lists of commissioned officers; a list of casualties during the Shenandoah Campaign (1 vol.); and a list of deaths in the U. S. Naval Service. There are indexes to the above casualty lists (10 ft.); indexes to casualties reported by surgeons (13 vols.); a regimental index to casualties at Antietam, Fredericksburg, Chancellorsville, Gettysburg, and "Wilderness to Cold Harbor"; a chronological index to the casualty lists; and certain casualty sheets of wounded that appear to relate to a hospital register of the New England Soldiers Relief Association.

The field records of hospitals, 1821-1912, include, for the Civil War period, subseries of the following headings: States and Territories; Army Corps; Departments; and U. S. Army Regimental. The first (arranged alphabetically by State or Territory) includes, under H, "Hospitals Afloat." The army corps books (76 ft.) are devoted exclusively to the 25 Civil War corps; the regimental books include hospital records for the Regular Army and the U. S. Colored Troops. Various lists facilitate the finding and use of these volumes, which consist in general of registers of sick and wounded, order and letter books, clothing and descriptive books, account books, rosters, and prescription and case books. These are the original records of military hospitals of all classes. Army regulations of 1863 required the senior medical officer of each hospital, post, regiment, or detachment to keep and deliver to his successor "a register of patients (Form 9); a prescription book (Form 10); a diet book (Form 10); a case book; a meteorological register (Form 11); copies of his requisitions, annual returns, and quarterly reports of sick and wounded; and an order and letter book, in which will be transcribed all orders and letters relating to his duties." Other records of or pertaining to hospitals include a "Record of General Hospitals," 1862-66 (1 vol.); a register of surgical operations at the Christian Street General Hospital, Philadelphia; fragmentary papers (3 in.) concerning hospital trains and steamers; some of the so-called "B Books" or registers of patients in hospitals (indexed); hospital registers of deaths, 1860-89 (18 vols.), and of discharges, 1861-68 (8 vols.); a record of transfers from one hospital to another, 1861-65 (4 vols.); and other hospital records in the series of so-called "E Books" and "F Books." Useful as finding aids for these records are an index to Civil War hospitals, an "Index to Army Corps Organization--Hospitals--Civil War Period," and an index to organizations by State with reference to hospital records available. There are also a list of post and general hospitals having no records on file and a list of Civil War organizations of which there were (ca. 1883) no treatment records on file.

National Archives, Preliminary Inventory [No. 17] of the Records of the Adjutant General's Office, comp. by Lucille H. Pendell and Elizabeth Bethel, p. 107-132 (Washington, 1949).

Records Transferred to the Veterans Administration

Record Group 15. -- From 1862 until 1930 the Surgeon General's Office adjudicated claims for artificial limbs and appliances for veterans (except World War I veterans) and for all retired personnel of the Regular Army. Although only the current case files were transferred by the Surgeon General's Office to the Veterans Administration in 1930, the then inactive files (which include most of the materials of Civil War interest) are now also part of the records of the Veterans Administration. In this record group the records pertaining to the furnishing of prosthetic devices to Civil War veterans are included in more general series. The artificial limb case files, 1861-1930 (200 ft.), are arranged alphabetically by name of veteran regardless of war; each case usually contains, in support of the veteran's application, a pension certification, a transcript of medical and hospital records, depositions of the veteran's officers or comrades, and related papers. Registers and indexes related to the case files include the general registers of approved claims, 1870-1911 (2 ft.); a general index to claims, 1870-85 (3 vols.); and a register of soldiers supplied with artificial legs at Chicago, Mar. 1863-Nov. 1864 (this includes copies of the "Instructions to Soldiers Entitled to the Patent Wilcox Leg" and gives for each case a complete history of the veteran's service and disability). Records concerning the procurement of artificial limbs include a volume recording orders issued in the Northern Department and the Departments of Ohio and the Lakes, 1862-70; and procurement orders issued at New York, 1862-70 (2 vols.).

Records relating to the issuing of trusses include registers of trusses issued, 1872-95 (4 vols.), and 1882-1923 (3 vols.); an account book, 1872-75, itemizing expenditures for truss issuance; and copies of correspondence with veterans, examining surgeons, and manufacturers of trusses, 1875-84 (1 vol.). These records in general reveal the kinds of ruptures and the kinds of trusses specified and issued to applicants.

National Archives, unpublished Preliminary Checklist of Records of the Veterans Administration Pertaining to the Issuance of Artificial Limbs, Trusses, and Other Prosthetic Appliances, 1862-1935, comp. by Evangeline Thurber.

Meteorological Records

Record Group 27. -- Meteorological registers maintained by regimental surgeons or post physicians from 1819, together with other meteorological records of the Surgeon General's Office, have become a part of the records of the Weather Bureau. For the Civil War period they often contain illuminating data; there are, for example, a volume kept by the post physician containing weather data for Fort Sumter, Dec. 1860-Apr. 1861, and additional volumes kept by the Charleston Board of Health (with entries for April 12, 1861). The registers in principal use during the Civil War are small volumes labeled "U. S. A. Hospital Department Meteorological Register." A completed register contains observations for about 6 years and gives thermometer, hygrometer, wind, weather, and precipitation readings.

National Archives, List of Climatological Records in the National Archives (Special List No. 1. Wash-ington, 1942), comp. by Lewis J. Darter, Jr.

OFFICE OF THE COMMISSARY GENERAL OF SUBSISTENCE

The Subsistence Department during the Civil War continued --under acts of Apr. 14, 1818 (3 Stat. 426), and Mar. 2, 1821 (3 Stat. 615)--to be responsible for purchasing and issuing all subsistence for the Army. The Department was responsible also for the subsistence of all prisoners of war and political prisoners, of a great many contrabands, and of suffering Union families in invaded areas of the Confederacy.

During the summer of 1861 the Commissary General of Subsistence was occupied in supplying the large army collected at Washington and with overseeing procurement of subsistence stores for the Department of the West, the troops at Cairo and in its vicinity, the Department of Western Virginia, and the troops in Kentucky. At the outbreak of war the Subsistence Department had only 12 officers of all grades; but an act of Aug. 3, 1861 (12 Stat. 287), added 12 commissaries, and one of Feb. 9, 1863 (12 Stat. 648), added 5, bringing the total to 29 officers of all grades. These were supplemented by many more commissaries of volunteer troops, so that on Apr. 30, 1865, there were in service in the Subsistence Department 29 officers of the permanent establishment and 535 commissaries of volunteers, a total of 564. By AGO Special Order 366, Oct. 26, 1864, eight boards for the examination of "officers of the Commissary Department" were established.

Under an act of July 4, 1864 (13 Stat. 381), loyal citizens of States "not in rebellion" submitted to the Commissary General of Subsistence claims for subsistence they had furnished the Army, with proofs. The Commissary General then examined the claims and, if payment was recommended, reported them to the Third Auditor. The Department's disbursements from July 1, 1861, to June 30, 1865, amounted to $361, 786, 991. 83. The excess supply of subsistence stores on hand at the close of the war was reduced by sale.

Successive Commissaries General of Subsistence during the war:
Col. George Gibson, in office from Apr. 18, 1818.
Col. Joseph P. Taylor, Sept. 29, 1861.
Brig. Gen. Amos B. Eaton, June 29, 1864.

Annual Reports of the Commissary General of Subsistence, 1862-65, appended to those of the Secretary of War; John W. Barriger, Legislative History of the Subsistence Department of the United States Army From June 16, 1775, to August 15, 1876 (2d ed. ; Washington, 1877); [War Department], Regulations for the Subsistence Department of the Army of the United States (Washington, 1863).

Record Group 192. --The correspondence of the Commissary General of Subsistence for the war period is in a series of copies of letters sent, 1818-89 (132 vols.); in a separate series of letters sent to the Secretary of War, 1840-89 (10 vols.); and in a series of letters received, 1828-87 (500 ft.). There is an index to the letters sent to the Secretary of War, 1854-66; and the letters received are abstracted in registers. This correspondence relates in general to administrative matters; to money accounts and officers' returns of subsistence property and stores; to claims for the commutation of rations; to proposals and contracts to furnish, and purchases of, subsistence supplies and services; and to personnel matters. A special file of letters received, 1865-70 (48 ft.), of which there are abstracts in registers

(8 vols.), relates in part to claims for subsistence furnished by loyal citizens (claims under the act of July 4, 1864; see above), and to claims of former prisoners of war for the commutation of rations. The letters referred to the Commissary General by other Government agencies, 1862-67 (26 ft.), are in a separate series; these are controlled by registers and (from 1865) by indexes. The postwar correspondence includes letter press copies (1 vol.) of endorsements, 1890-94, to inquiries from the Second Auditor of the Treasury for information about the cost of rations during the Civil War at various camps, posts, and stations.

The "provision books," which cover the entire period of the war, show the amounts of provisions on hand at stated periods at particular posts or in the charge of accountable officers; there are indexes to these affecting volunteer subsistence officers, 1861-67 (4 vols.). Of economic interest are statements, 1861-87 (6 vols.), of the cost of the ration, as reported monthly by subsistence officers; and 2 "quotation books," 1865--compendiums showing the daily changes in price quotations for specific subsistence commodities at different purchasing depots.

Fiscal records of the war period comprise estimates of appropriations, "blotters" (daily record) of money transactions with commissaries and contractors, records of expenditures, copies of requests made to the Secretary of War (for funds to be placed to the credit of officers and for money to be paid from the Treasury in settlement of claims), and registers of accounts and returns received from subsistence officers. In 2 "stoppage books" are recorded paymasters' reports of stoppages of payments to commissioned officers for subsistence stores, 1861-70.

Records concerning contracts include copies of contracts (incomplete, 10 ft.) let by the Office of the Commissary General of Subsistence during the war for fresh beef, beef cattle, rations, and other subsistence; registers of bids accepted, 1863-71 (3 vols.); registers of contracts for complete rations, 1863-95 (2 vols.), with a name index for 1863-71; and registers of beef and fresh meat contracts, 1820-94 (4 vols.).

Personnel records include a register of appointments, assignments, transfers, and duties of Regular Army commissaries of subsistence, 1853-94; records of examinations for appointment to commissary offices, 1854-65 (13 vols.); reports of the proceedings of the board that examined the qualifications of commissary officers, 1864-65 (1 ft.); papers relating to the issuance of commissions, 1862-65 (1 ft.); "carded" personnel records of volunteer commissary officers, 1861-65 (2 ft.); a register of commissary officers of volunteer troops, 1861-65; monthly lists of officers on duty in the Subsistence Department submitted by Army departments, posts, and stations, 1863-67 (2 ft.). Other personnel records may be in Record Group 92 (see below).

National Archives, Preliminary Checklist of the Records of the Office of the Commissary General of Subsistence, comp. by Roland C. McConnell (Washington, 1946).

Record Group 92. -- After the abolition of the Office of the Commisary General of Subsistence in 1912 and the transfer of its responsibility for subsistence to the Office of the Quartermaster General, the latter Office removed many documents from the Commissary General's general correspondence files for interfiling with Quartermaster General's records in its consolidated subject file. The materials belonging to the Commissary

General's Office for the Civil War period that are now in this file are believed to be extensive, but they must be sought by subject.

Record Group 217. -- The records of the Commissary General of Subsistence pertaining to claims, with the exceptions noted above, were transferred to the Auditor for the War Department (Third Auditor) in the Department of the Treasury in Apr. 1907 in order to facilitate the settlement of claims growing out of the Civil War. They were transferred to the General Accounting Office in 1921 and are now considered part of this record group. Among them are a 1-volume index to special and confidential letters received in the Claims Branch of the Subsistence Bureau, ca. 1873-95; a register of claims received by the Bureau for subsistence furnished the U. S. Army and for commutation of rations, 1863-77 (8 vols.), with additional entries made in the office of the Third Auditor; and a register of claims, 1864-77 (21 vols.), under the act of July 4, 1864, with information on the loyalty of claimants.

U. S. MILITARY TELEGRAPHS

On Apr. 27, 1861, Col. Thomas A. Scott was "appointed to take charge of the railways and telegraphs between Washington City and Annapolis"; and on May 23, 1861, he was "appointed to take charge of all Government railways and telegraphs or those appropriated for Government use" (see also U. S. Military Railroads). On Nov. 25, 1861, Capt. Anson Stager was "assigned to duty as general manager of the Government telegraph lines"; and on Dec. 1, 1861, the Secretary of War reported to the President the establishment of a "telegraphic bureau. "

An act of Jan. 31, 1862 (12 Stat. 334), authorized the President to take possession of railroad and telegraph lines if in his judgment the public safety so required. Under this act, all telegraphic lines were taken over on Feb. 26, 1862. Edward S. Sanford, president of the American Telegraph Co., was made "military supervisor of telegraphic messages throughout the United States"; and Stager was made "military superintendent of all telegraphic lines and offices in the United States. " This "possession and control" was "not intended to interfere in any respect with the ordinary affairs of the companies or with private business. " By AGO General Order 38, Apr. 8, 1862, commanding officers were required on the requisition of Stager (then Colonel), or of his assistants, to detail troops as necessary for the construction, repair, and protection of military telegraph lines.

In Sept. 1862 Stager officially transferred to the assistant superintendents, U. S. Military Telegraphs, in the several military departments "the military telegraph lines and property . . . of which they were previously in nominal charge. " Until Apr. 1863 Stager's headquarters were in Washington; after that, in Ohio. "It is my duty as commanding officer of the Military Telegraph Department, " he wrote in his annual report for 1863, "to exercise a general supervision of all its lines, to give such orders and directions to the subordinate officers in this branch of the public service as may . . . be necessary . . . , and to supervise the purchase of all the material which the wants or exigencies of the various departments may demand. " The public, he believed, had "but a faint conception of the magnitude of the uses of the army telegraph. " From a "close estimate" it appeared that in fiscal year 1863 at least 1, 200, 000 telegrams were sent and received over the military lines. Reporting from Cleveland on fiscal year 1864 operations, Stager estimated that a monthly average of 1, 000 men had "been

engaged in the military telegraph service within the several departments"
and that 600,000 more telegrams had been transmitted than during the previous fiscal year.

The importance of the U. S. Military Telegraphs lies partly in the fact
that before the Civil War there never had been in the United States "a use
of the telegraph as an agency for disseminating intelligence upon the battlefield; connecting the different armies, much less placing the Commander in
Chief of the Army himself, at Washington, in touch with all of the commanding generals of the Army, as this agency enabled President Lincoln to
do." The Senate Committee on Pensions in its report on "Relief of Telegraph Operators Who Served in the War of the Rebellion," Aug. 7, 1904
(S. Doc. 251, 58 Cong., 2 sess., Serial 4592), found it "surprising that so
important an arm of the service during that war should have been organized
on a civil basis and its members only regarded as employees of the Quartermaster's Department." As Col. William B. Wilson testified before the
committee, "No solemn act of Congress authorized its formation; no dig-
nified Presidential paper proclaimed its advent, nor did any formal 'general
order' define its status. It took its place as a right, moved with the rapidity of thought and the silence of night." Soon after the war the telegraph
equipment was sold or otherwise disposed of and the employees were discharged, "only a few confidential operators being still retained for cipher
correspondence with commanders of important districts." During the war
about 15,000 miles of military telegraph lines had been constructed and
operated and the military telegraph "corps" had consisted of some 1,200
operators.

Annual report of Col. Anson Stager, Chief, U. S. Military Tele-graphs, fiscal year 1865, and the wartime annual reports of the Quar-termaster General, appended to those of the Secretary of War; S.	Doc. 251, 58 Cong., 2 sess., Serial 4592, which contains a "Compilation of Documents" concerning military telegraph operations during the Civil War as published in the Official Rec-ords . . . Armies.

Record Group 92. -- The administrative records of the U. S. Military
Telegraphs do not appear to be extant. There are, however, an alphabetically arranged set of cards showing the service histories of employees of
the telegraph lines, 1861-65, and some certificates of service prepared
pursuant to S. Rept. 1927, 58 Cong., 2 sess., Serial 4575, "Relief of Telegraph Operators Who Served in the War of the Rebellion." There is some
reason to believe that the agency was linked administratively with the War
Department Telegraph Office and thus was subject to the direct control of
Secretary of War Stanton or Assistant Secretary of War Thomas A. Scott.
The records of the Secretary and those of the Adjutant General and the
Quartermaster General contain materials relating to the agency and its
operations. As explained elsewhere in this Guide, the Chief Signal Officer
was unable during the war to get control of the telegraph system; his files,
however, should be examined for records concerning the relationship of
signal and telegraphic operations.

U. S. MILITARY RAILROADS

Early in the Civil War the problems of railroad and telegraphic communications were so closely related that on May 23, 1861, Col. Thomas A.

Scott was given "charge of all Government railways and telegraphs or those appropriated for Government use" (see U. S. Military Telegraphs). When Scott became Assistant Secretary of War his assistant, Capt. R. N. Moreley, was given the management of the military railroads and, to facilitate his work, was made a disbursing officer of the Quartermaster General's Office. Moreley reported to the Secretary that the business in the first 6 months of the war was "to repair and reconstruct what the enemy have destroyed--at times and places difficult to procure material and under circumstances unfavorable to an economical expenditure," but that activities were confined largely to Washington, Annapolis, Alexandria, and Fortress Monroe.

An act of Jan. 31, 1862 (12 Stat. 334), authorized the President to take possession of telegraph and railroad lines in the United States "when in his judgment the public safety may require it" and "to place under military control all the officers, agents, and employés belonging to the telegraph and railroad lines thus taken . . . so that they shall be considered as a post road and a part of the military establishment." The act gave to the Secretary of War and his agents immediate control and supervision of "the transportation of troops, munitions of war, equipments, military property and stores, throughout the United States." Secretary Stanton, in appointing Col. Daniel C. McCallum "military director and superintendent of railroads in the United States" on Feb. 11, 1862, authorized him "to enter upon, take possession of, hold and use all railroads, engines, cars, locomotives, equipments, appendages, and appurtenances, that may be required for the transport of troops, arms, ammunition, and military supplies of the United States, and to do and perform all acts and things that may be necessary and proper to be done for the safe and speedy transport aforesaid." McCallum characterized his organization as "a great construction and transportation machine, for carrying out the objects of the commanding generals," to be managed "solely with a view to efficacy in that direction."

When the director assumed his duties, the 7-mile road from Washington to Alexandria was the only railroad in Government hands. The ultimate extent of the jurisdiction of the U. S. Military Railroads is indicated by the fact that at different times during the war 17 railroads were used as military lines in Virginia, Maryland, and Pennsylvania; 19 in Tennessee, Georgia, Mississippi, and Arkansas; and 4 in North Carolina.

On Sept. 16, 1862, Brig. Gen. Hermann Haupt pointed out in a letter to Major General Halleck that "the Department of Military Railroads, excepting perhaps for the immediate vicinity of the capital, is without a head," and that the department should be reorganized to "procure information, put it in shape to be readily accessible, secure system and uniformity in administration, correct abuses, and promote efficiency." Haupt's office in the War Department at this time was known as the Office of Construction and Transportation of U. S. Military Railroads. The field organization was improved when Secretary of War Stanton, on Oct. 19, 1863, by special order issued at Louisville, Ky., appointed John B. Anderson "General Manager of all Railways in the possession of the Government, or that may from time to time be taken possession of by military authority, in the Departments of the Cumberland, the Ohio, and the Tennessee." Officers, agents, and employees of the railways were put under Anderson's "general direction and control, subject to the approval of the Quartermaster General."

In Dec. 1863, however, McCallum himself examined the condition of the railroad lines that supplied the armies then encamped near Chattanooga,

Tenn.; and on Feb. 4, 1864, General Grant appointed him general manager of all railways in possession of the Government in the departments named above and the Department of Arkansas, which together constituted the Military Division of the Mississippi. In that division McCallum reorganized the administration of the U. S. Military Railroads into two distinct departments, a "transportation department" and a "construction corps." The transportation department included divisions or subdepartments responsible for (1) managing the movement of trains; (2) maintaining road and structures--keeping the roadway, bridges, buildings, and other structures in repair, building new structures, and rebuilding old ones when necessary; and (3) maintaining rolling stock--keeping in order the locomotives and cars and managing the shops where such work was done. In the Division of the Mississippi the transportation department at its maximum strength employed about 12, 000 men.

As the war went on, both Union and the Confederate forces came to understand better the nature, capacity, and value of railroads; and the Federal Government made extraordinary preparations to counter the destruction of track and bridges by the enemy. The small construction corps, about 300 men in 1863, was the beginning of an organization that afterwards numbered in the East and West nearly 10, 000. In each department of railroad construction and repair skilled workmen were grouped in divisions, gangs, and squads and were supplied with abundant materials, tools, mechanical appliances, and transportation.

With few exceptions the military railroads were operated under orders issued by the Secretary of War or by army commanders; and it became the duty of the Director and General Manager to make the military railroad organization "sufficiently comprehensive to permit the extension of the system indefinitely." After the war, however, by Executive order of Aug. 8, 1865, the railroads were returned to their former owners.

Col. (later Bvt. Brig. Gen.) Daniel C. McCallum served as Director and (later) General Manager, U. S. Military Railroads, from Feb. 11,1862.

United States Military Railroads; Report of Bvt. Brig. Gen. D. C. McCallum, Director and General Manager, From 1861 to 1866 (H. Ex. Doc. 1, 39 Cong., 1 sess., Serial 1251); U. S. War Department, Military Railroads 1861-1867 (undated compilation of general orders, instructions, and reports); R. E. Riegel, "Federal Operation of the Southern Railroads During the Civil War," Mississippi Valley Historical Review, 9: 126-138 (Sept. 1922); H. Ex. Doc. 155, 39 Cong., 1 sess., Serial 1267; H. Repts. 3 and 15, 40 Cong., 2 sess., Serial 1357. Names of railroads taken over by the Government are given in McCallum's report.

Record Group 92. --After the war the records of the U. S. Military Railroads were transferred to the Quartermaster General's Office and were to some extent intermingled with the records of that Office. The extant identifiable records, however (more than 100 ft.), afford fairly complete documentation of Federal control of railroads during the Civil War. They are, moreover, important for the history of railroad companies used as military lines, especially those in the South. The books of letters sent from headquarters, the incoming correspondence (or "document files"), and the volumes of compilations of reports received from the field cover the entire period of the agency's existence, and all are registered or indexed. Records of the field organization and those of the headquarters office relating to the field are in general arranged by location of railroads and include daily work reports, freight books, engine ledgers, labor and material accounts, and much miscellaneous material. There is also a register of letters received concerning the indebtedness of Southern railroads and some records that may belong or relate to the Fourth Division (Rail and River Transportation) of the Quartermaster General's Office. Other records of the Quartermaster General's Office, particularly the consolidated correspondence file, should be searched for additional materials.

OFFICE OF THE COMMISSARY GENERAL OF PRISONERS

Neither the Federal Government nor the Confederacy was at first prepared to handle large numbers of prisoners of war, nor was there much past experience with the problem. Little was done on the Union side to regularize prisoner-of-war control until Oct. 7, 1861, when Lt. Col. (later Bvt. Brig. Gen.) William Hoffman was detailed for duty as Commissary General of Prisoners under the supervision of the Quartermaster General. (Measures taken by the C. S. A. to handle prisoners of war are discussed in the Guide to the Archives of the Government of the Confederate States of America.)

In recommending, on July 12, 1861, the appointment of a "commissary of prisoners," Quartermaster General Montgomery C. Meigs had referred to the previous existence of such an office, when the Government had the care of prisoners of war, kept "the muster list of prisoners," negotiated "exchanges according to the cartel," and sent "funds to the commissary of the enemy for use of our friends in their power." On Oct. 26 Meigs ordered Hoffman to establish headquarters in New York City and a depot for prisoners of war on Johnson's Island in Sandusky Bay. Earlier, prisoners had been confined principally in the coastal fortifications at New York and elsewhere. On Apr. 18, 1862, Hoffman's office was transferred from New York to Detroit, and on Oct. 7, 1862, to Washington.

On June 17, 1862, by AGO General Order 67, Hoffman was made "subject only to the orders of the War Department"--and thus relieved of the necessity to report to the Quartermaster General--and became entirely responsible for the "supervision of prisoners of war sent by generals commanding in the field to posts or camps prepared for their reception." (On Mar. 19 Hoffman had complained to the Quartermaster General that his office was "not known to the generals, and any information I have about movements of prisoners I pick up from the newspapers and other chance sources.") All matters relating to prisoners of war were now to "pass through him," and his general duties, as later clarified by changes in the 1861 Army Regulations, were to be those of an inspector. He regulated the issuance of clothing to prisoners, granted paroles for medical reasons, and controlled the use of funds from ration savings at prison hospitals and stations; and he was required to keep a "full record of all prisoners."

Although he received and maintained full records of the prisoners confined in Union prisons, including records of parole made in effecting exchanges of prisoners, the negotiations between representatives of Union and Confederate authorities on prisoner-of-war exchange were conducted, on the part of the Union, under the immediate supervision of the Secretary of War (see Commissioner for Exchange of Prisoners, below). The Commissary General of Prisoners had direct charge, however, of U. S. officers and men on parole from Confederate imprisonment and of correspondence relating to them. The reception, care, and ultimate disposition of paroled Union prisoners were carried out at camps especially set up for these purposes; a revealing report of inspection, describing perhaps typical conditions in these camps as well as the records they kept, is printed in Official Records . . . Armies, ser. 2, vol. 5, p. 328-337. Under a basic circular of the Commissary General of Prisoners, July 7, 1862, Confederate prisoners in each camp were divided into companies; and registration, accounting, and reporting were systematized. Rolls accompanying arriving prisoners were required to be carefully checked; if there were no rolls, they were to be "immediately made out containing all the information required as correct as can be from the statements of the prisoners themselves."

On Nov. 11, 1864, by AGO General Order 280, the functions of the Office were divided. Brig. Gen. H. W. Wessells was assigned "to duty at Washington as Inspector and Commissary-General of Prisoners for the section of the country east of the Mississippi River"; and Hoffman, thus relieved, was assigned "as Inspector and Commissary-General of Prisoners for the region west of the Mississippi." Direction of the Office of Commissary General of Prisoners at Washington was, however, restored to Hoffman on Feb. 1, 1865, by AGO Special Order 51. Except for this short period when responsibility for the work was divided geographically, Hoffman served as Commissary General of Prisoners until his relief by Maj. Gen. E. A. Hitchcock on Nov. 3, 1865. Hitchcock, who previously had been Commissioner for Exchange of Prisoners, remained in charge until Aug. 19, 1867, when the Office was discontinued and its records were transferred to the Prisoner of War Division of the Adjutant General's Office.

Confederates still imprisoned at the end of the war were released by stages. Early in May 1865 prisoners below the rank of colonel who had been willing to take the oath of allegiance before the fall of Richmond were released on parole. On June 6, 1865, a release order (AGO G. O. 108) provided for the discharge of all enlisted men of the Confederate Army and petty officers and seamen of the Confederate Navy upon their taking the oath of allegiance; and for the discharge of all Confederate officers, of the rank of captain or lower in the Army or below the rank of lieutenant in the Navy, provided they were not graduates of the U. S. Military or Naval Academies and provided they took the oath of allegiance. As many as possible were to be discharged daily, and the Quartermaster General was to furnish transportation either by rail or by steamboat to the point nearest the prisoners' homes. In July 1865 the President ordered the release of all prisoners of war except those captured with Jefferson Davis. By Oct. 20, 1865, of more than 96,000 prisoners of war captured and confined by the Union Army, only 6 remained.

In the year following the war the staff of the Office was reduced by about a third. In this immediate postwar period two divisions conducted and recorded the correspondence. A third division handled cases involving Federal prisoners of the Confederacy and was expected to furnish on request "the complete record of each soldier from the time of his capture until his exchange and return to duty with his company." A fourth division maintained and completed the records pertaining to Confederate prisoners of the United States and made numerous reports from them. It compiled, in 1865-66, a "complete index of all monthly returns, post returns, and

inspection reports received from the several prisons and hospitals during
the rebellion. " And a fifth division had charge of claims for commutation
of rations due Federal prisoners of the Confederacy. Statistics of the Office show that during the war the United States Government exchanged and
paroled 329, 963 "Rebels" and the Confederacy exchanged and paroled
152, 015 "Federals. "

Successive Commissaries General of Prisoners:

> Bvt. Brig. Gen. William Hoffman, Oct. 7, 1861.
> Maj. Gen. Ethan A. Hitchcock, Nov. 3, 1865.

Annual reports of the Commissary General of Prisoners, appended to those of the Secretary of
War; Official Records . . . Armies,
ser. 2, vols. 1-8, passim; Lt. Col.
George G. Lewis and Capt. John

Mewha, History of Prisoner of War
Utilization by the United States
Army, 1776-1945 (Department of
the Army, Pamphlet 20-213. Washington, 1955).

Record Group 249. -- This record group contains all the extant records
of the Commissary General of Prisoners except those pertaining to Confederate prisoners, which are in Record Group 109 (see below). The general correspondence comprises fair copies of letters sent, 1862-67 (13
vols.), with press copies of some (ca. 55 vols.); letters received, 1862-
67, arranged chronologically by year and thereunder alphabetically by
name of sender (ca. 60 ft.); and telegrams received, 1862-65 (ca. 2 ft.).
There are also fair copies of endorsements and memoranda sent and various indexes and registers of letters and telegrams.

Records pertaining primarily to Union prisoners--covering both the
circumstances of their imprisonment by Confederates and their exchange,
parole, and processing by Federal authorities--include compiled data on
U. S. troops captured by the enemy, 1862-65 (3 vols.); "Records of Exchanged Federal Prisoners of War U. S. A. ," 1862-65 (ca. 34 vols.); a
record of deaths of Union prisoners of war in Southern prisons and hospitals, 1862-65 (2 vols.), and in parole camps, 1862-65 (3 vols.); a register of Union prisoners who died at Andersonville, Ga. , Richmond, Va. ,
and other Southern prisons, 1861-65 (4 vols.); an additional Andersonville
death register (1 vol.) and original burial lists at Andersonville; and many
other registers of Union prisoners in Southern camps, usually postwar
copies or compilations made in the Adjutant General's office. There are
also detailed records, 1862-65 (ca. 60 ft.), of the arrival and disposition
of exchanged or paroled Union prisoners at Alexandria, Va.; Annapolis,
Md. ; Benton Barracks, Mo. ; Camp Chase, Ohio; City Point, Va. ; College
Green Barracks, Md. ; Cox's Wharf, Va. ; Fort Delaware, Del. ; Jacksonville, Fla. ; Fort Jefferson, Fla. ; Johnson's Island, Ohio; Northeast Ferry,
N. C. ; and Camp Parole, Md.

Other records include miscellaneous rolls of Union prisoners of the
Confederacy, 1861-65 (ca. 3 ft.); a letter book of Headquarters, Paroled
Prisoners, 1862-63; and an index to miscellaneous records of prisoners of
war, apparently compiled in the Adjutant General's Office in 1867 (13
vols.). In several volumes are recorded rolls received of both military
and political prisoners and other information about political prisoners.

Record Group 109. -- Most of the records of the Commissary General of
Prisoners pertaining to Confederate prisoners were transferred to the
War Department Collection of Confederate Records because of their close

relationship to other records in that collection. Among the more important of these is a general file, 1861-65 (227 ft.), arranged by prison or
station at which prisoners were confined, which contains a great variety of
prisoner lists, accounts, inspection reports, orders, and correspondence.
Other records, apparently compiled or kept in the Office of the Commissary
General of Prisoners, include registers of prisoners, 1863-65 (4 vols.);
death registers, 1862-65 (5 vols.); registers of prisoners' applications for
release, 1864-65 (2 vols.); a register of prisoners and deserters released
on taking the oath of allegiance to the United States, 1863-65 (2 vols.); a
register of prisoners of war whose release was ordered, 1865 (1 vol.); a
record of unclaimed money belonging to Confederate prisoners, 1865-66
(1 vol.); a record of the effects of deceased Confederate prisoners, 1862-
65 (1 vol.); papers relating to Confederates in Union hospitals, 1861-65
(8 ft.); tabulations of data on Confederates confined in Union prisons, undated (6 in.); and parole rolls, 1862-65 (21 ft.).

Also in this record group are related records that appear to have been
kept originally in the several military departments of the U. S. Army.
These include rolls of civilians taken prisoner by the Eighth Army Corps,
1864-65 (2 ft.); lists of civilians (mainly in Missouri, Kentucky, and the
Department of the Pacific) taking the oath of allegiance or giving bond,
1862-64 (3 in.); registers of prisoners at the military hospital at Covington, Ky., 1862 (part of 1 vol.), in the Department of the Cumberland,
1862-65 (3 vols.), in the custody of the provost marshal, Memphis, Tenn.,
1863-65 (4 vols.), in the Department of the Missouri (officers), 1862 (1
vol.), and in the Army and Department of the Ohio, 1864 (1 vol.); and registers of paroles and oaths at Richmond, Va., 1865 (3 vols.), at Bowling
Green, Va., 1865 (1 vol.), in West Tennessee, 1865 (1 vol.), in the Division of West Mississippi, 1865 (4 vols.), and in the Department of the
Gulf, with entries chiefly for men who surrendered at Citronelle, Ala.,
on May 4, 1865 (26 vols.).

Military Prisons for Confederate Prisoners of War

Some Army posts in existence when the Civil War began served principally or partly as military prisons for Confederate prisoners of war and
for political or state prisoners. Other prisons were established as new
posts. The principal Federal military prisons were operated at the following places:

Alton, Ill.	Little Rock, Ark.	New Orleans, La.
Camp Butler, Ill.	Point Lookout, Md.	Fort Pickens, Fla.
Camp Chase, Ohio	Louisville, Ky.	Rock Island, Ill.
Fort Columbus, N. Y.	Fort McHenry, Md.	St. Louis, Mo.
Fort Delaware, Del.	McLean Barracks, Ohio	Ship Island, Miss.
Camp Douglas, Ill.	Memphis, Tenn.	Fort Warren, Mass.
Elmira, N. Y.	Fort Mifflin, Pa.	Washington, D. C.
Johnson's Island, Ohio	Camp Morton, Ind.	Wheeling, W. Va.
Fort Lafayette, N. Y.	Nashville, Tenn.	Fort Wood, N. Y.

The Allegheny City Penitentiary, Pa., and the Ohio Penitentiary were
also important places of confinement, and many prisoners of war were
held in other civil prisons or in the custody of provost marshals. For
information particularly about political and state prisoners see Office of
the Provost Marshal, below.

Record Groups 98, 109, and 156.--Many records of local prison administrations became part of the War Department Collection of Confederate Records (Record Group 109), although they are U. S.--not C. S. A.--records; but other prison records are in Record Group 98 (U. S. Army Commands). For at least one military prison (Rock Island) there are records in Record Group 156 (Office of the Chief of Ordnance). All these are records kept at Federal prisons as distinguished from reports and other papers sent by them to the War Department. They are as follows:

Alton, Ill. Records, 1862-65 (2 ft.), in Record Group 109 comprise letters received and copies of letters sent; registers and rolls of military prisoners; registers of civilian prisoners; descriptive lists of civilian, Confederate, and Federal prisoners released; rolls of prisoners received, discharged, released, transferred, paroled, and escaped; morning reports; guard and policing reports; a mess book; receipts for articles delivered; a record of money sent to prisoners; and a ledger of prisoners' accounts.

Camp Butler, Ill. In Record Group 109 are registers and a descriptive roll of Confederate prisoners, 1862-63 (6 in.).

Camp Chase, Ohio. In Record Group 109 are records pertaining primarily to Confederate prisoners, 1862-65 (3 ft.), comprising registers and descriptive lists of prisoners; burial registers; lists of prisoners paroled, transferred, died, or released; mess books; statistical and mess reports, accounts ledgers, and a record of money received from prisoners; a record of receipt of articles delivered to prisoners; and stubs of prisoners' receipts. For records relating particularly to state and political prisoners at Camp Chase, see Office of the Provost Marshal.

Cincinnati, Ohio. In Record Group 98 is a list of prisoners at McLean Barracks, 1863-64, with related records. In Record Group 109 are other records (8 in.) of McLean Barracks, comprising registers of Confederate prisoners, including civil prisoners, 1863-65, and order books, 1863-65.

Fort Columbus, N. Y. In Record Group 109 is a register of Confederate prisoners, Mar.-Sept. 1862.

Fort Delaware, Del. In Record Group 109 are records pertaining to Confederate prisoners, 1863-65 (6 1/2 ft.), comprising registers of prisoners, registers of Confederate officers in the prison hospitals, hospital records, a death register, morning reports of prisoners, records of articles received for and delivered to prisoners, receipts for money sent by the Adams Express Co., and ledgers and other accounts.

Camp Dennison, Ohio. An undated register of Confederate prisoners at this camp is filed with the records of Gratiot Street Prison, St. Louis, in Record Group 109.

Camp Douglas, Ill. In Record Group 98 are morning reports of prisoners of war confined at the camp, 1864-65 (2 in.). Record Group 109 includes other Camp Douglas records pertaining to Confederate prisoners, 1862-65 (3 1/2 ft.): registers of prisoners; a record of deaths; a record of sentenced prisoners; morning reports of prisoners; records of checks and packages received for prisoners; ledgers of prisoners' accounts; a "memorandum book," with a list of doctors who were prisoners of war and practiced at the camp; a "miscellaneous record book," with a list of articles stolen from prisoners; and an index to letters sent.

Elmira, N. Y. In Record Group 109 are registers (including death registers), morning reports, records of accounts, and other records pertaining to Confederate prisoners, 1864-65 (2 ft.).

Hart's Island, N. Y. In Record Group 109 are general orders, special orders, and registers pertaining to Confederate prisoners, 1865 (9 in.).

Hilton Head, S. C. In Record Group 109 are receipts for letters containing money sent to Confederate prisoners at this post, 1864-65 (1/2 in.).

Johnson's Island, Ohio. In Record Group 98 are a few letters received, 1864. In Record Group 109 are the main records pertaining to Confederate prisoners, 1862-65 (1 1/2 ft.). These comprise copies of letters sent; registers (including a death register); a record of prisoners received, released, and transferred; a register of amnesty rolls; stubs of prisoners' receipts for money; and a record of the examination of express packages received for prisoners.

Knoxville, Tenn. In Record Group 109 are registers of Confederate prisoners, 1863-65 (5 in.).

Fort Lafayette, N. Y. In Record Group 109 are registers of Confederate prisoners (some of which are filed with the records of Fort McHenry, Md.; and of Gratiot Street Prison, St. Louis, Mo.) and accounts of money and prisoners' effects, 1861-65 (2 in.).

Little Rock, Ark. In Record Group 109 are registers of Confederate prisoners, including political prisoners, 1863-65 (5 in.).

Louisville, Ky. In Record Group 109 are records relating to Confederate prisoners, including political prisoners, 1862-65 (2 ft.), comprising registers and rolls of Confederate deserters received at the prison.

Fort McHenry, Md. In Record Group 98 are some returns of prisoners, 1864-65. Records in Record Group 109 (11 in.) comprise registers of prisoners, 1861-65, and a ledger of prisoners' accounts.

Camp Morton, Ind. In Record Group 109 are registers and lists of Confederate prisoners, a descriptive book of prisoners released, a death register, morning reports, a ledger of accounts, a record of receipts for cash, and a cash book, 1862-65 (ca. 2 ft.).

New Orleans, La. In Record Group 109 are registers of Confederate prisoners (with special registers of officers) and a hospital register, 1863-65 (9 in.).

Newport News, Va. In Record Group 109 are a register of prisoners, ledgers of prisoners' accounts, and a petty cash book, 1865 (8 in.).

Fort Pickens, Fla. In Record Group 109 is a register of prisoners, 1862 (part of a volume containing entries for several prisons and filed with the records of Gratiot Street Prison, St. Louis, Mo.).

Point Lookout, Md. Records relating to Confederate prisoners in Record Group 109, 1863-65 (5 ft.), comprise copies of letters sent, registers of prisoners transferred to and received from Hammond General Hospital; records of prisoners enlisting in the U. S. Army or Navy, released for labor on public works, taking the oath of allegiance, and paroled or released after taking the oath; records of clothing issued and packages delivered to prisoners; invoices of money letters and registered letters received for prisoners; and lists and invoices of money and valuables received from and returned to prisoners (a volume with one such list also contains a list of vessels boarded and searched at Point Lookout).

Raleigh, N. C. A record of Confederate prisoners, 1865-66, is in Record Group 98.

Rock Island, Ill. In Record Group 109 is a register of Confederate prisoners, with related "memorandum and blotter," and an index volume, 1863 (1 ft.). In Record Group 156 is a record of prisoners, 1863-65 (1 vol.), and a register of Confederate dead at Rock Island, compiled in 1912 by the War Department's Commission for Marking Graves of Confederate Dead.

St. Louis, Mo. Registers of Confederate prisoners received in the Gratiot Street and Myrtle Street prisons, 1862-65 (5 in.), are in Record Group 109.

Ship Island, Miss. In Record Group 109 are registers of Confederate prisoners (including a burial register), morning reports, and prisoners' receipts for packages, 1864-65 (5 in.).

Fort Warren, Mass. Records relating to Confederate prisoners, 1861-65 (10 in.), in Record Group 109 include copies of letters sent, registers and lists of prisoners received, prisoners' accounts, and cash books.

Washington, D. C. (Old Capitol Prison). In Record Group 109 are a register of prisoners, 1863-65, and a record of visitors' passes, 1864-65. For records relating particularly to state and political prisoners in Old Capitol Prison, see Office of the Provost Marshal.

OFFICE OF THE COMMISSIONER FOR EXCHANGE OF PRISONERS

On July 12, 1862, the President, through the Secretary of War, authorized Maj. Gen. John A. Dix at Fortress Monroe "to negotiate a general exchange of prisoners with the enemy." The ensuing cartel, signed by General Dix for the Federal Government and by Maj. Gen. D. H. Hill for the Confederate States of America, was announced in AGO General Order 142, Sept. 25, 1862. The articles of this agreement stipulated a detailed scale of equivalents as the basis for exchanges--"man for man and officer for officer," but a commanding general or admiral, for instance, was the equivalent of 60 privates or common seamen. The cartel also dealt with the problem of civilian prisoners and the actual mechanics of parole and exchange, and it prohibited further military service of released prisoners of war. The negotiators did not anticipate that large numbers of prisoners of war would be held either in the Confederacy or in the North, and they made no provision for the uniform treatment of captured soldiers.

AGO General Order 187, Nov. 15, 1862, detailed Maj. Gen. Ethan A. Hitchcock as Commissioner for the Exchange of Prisoners. Until early in 1863 the system of exchange agreed upon in the cartel apparently was respected by both sides, but the unwillingness of the Confederacy to exchange "man for man" and to agree to the exchange of colored troops or their white officers led to its breakdown.

Late in 1864 Secretary Stanton designated Maj. Gen. Benjamin F. Butler at Fortress Monroe to negotiate for and effect prisoner exchanges; and Commissioner Hitchcock for a time, as he reported to Stanton, "had very little to do in the matter of exchanges." Butler, indeed, conducted his work in this field under the title "Commissioner of Exchange," and Stanton authorized other commanders "to open communications with the enemy, and to effect exchanges whenever they could be made on equal terms."

Maj. Gen. Ethan A. Hitchcock served as Commissioner for the Exchange of Prisoners from Nov. 15, 1862, to Nov. 3, 1865, when he succeeded Bvt. Brig. Gen. William Hoffman as Commissary General of Prisoners.

See especially Official Records . . . Armies, ser. 2, passim. The report of Commissioner Hitchcock dated Nov. 30, 1863, is appended to that of the Secretary of War for that year. In his general report for the fiscal year 1865, also appended to that of the Secretary, Hitchcock traced the history of the exchange and appended its documentation. Correspondence "between the authorities of the United States and the rebel authorities on the exchange of prisoners, and the different propositions connected with that subject," Jan. 1863-Jan. 1864, is printed in S. Ex. Doc. 17, 38 Cong., 1 sess., Serial 1176. Correspondence extending "over a period of time from June, 1862," copies of which were furnished to the House of Representatives by the Adjutant General in response to House Resolution of Dec. 21, 1864, pertaining to the exchange of prisoners, is printed in H. Ex. Doc. 32, 38 Cong., 2 sess., Serial 1223.

Record Group 249. -- The correspondence of the Commissioner for Exchange of Prisoners, 1862-65 (3 ft.), appears to be virtually intact, but it should be used in relation to letters received from the Commissioner that are in the files of the Secretary of War, the Adjutant General, and the Commissary General of Prisoners. Commissioner Hitchcock's own correspondence, unbound and arranged alphabetically by name of correspondent or by subject, comprises both letters received and copies or drafts of those sent. The "correspondence relating to the business of exchanges" includes letters from Robert Ould, the Confederate "Agent of Exchange"; broadsides of posted prison rules, filed under "Johnson's Island"; and many other items of interest.

Records in Other Custody. -- There are sizable amounts of Hitchcock papers in the Library of Congress, the Missouri Historical Society, and the Thomas Gilcrease Institute of American History and Art at Tulsa, Okla. These may contain some papers of or relating to Hitchcock's office as Commissioner for Exchange of Prisoners.

BUREAU OF MILITARY JUSTICE

When the Civil War began, the staff administration of military justice was too limited to meet the new demands arising from extensive military operations. An act of Mar. 2, 1849 (9 Stat. 351), had authorized the appointment of a Judge Advocate of the Army; but one Judge Advocate was wholly inadequate to administer military justice. Accordingly, an act of July 17, 1862 (12 Stat. 598), authorized the appointment of a Judge Advocate General and several subordinate judge advocates, one for each army in the field. The latter comprised the commissioned judge advocates, of whom 39 were appointed before the war ended. In practice, however, the Secretary of War, the commanders of departments or corps, or others authorized to convene general courts-martial habitually designated, in each order detailing a court, a particular officer to act as judge advocate in the case. In his testimony before the House select committee that investigated charges against Provost Marshal General Fry (H. Rept. 93, 39 Cong., 1 sess., Serial 1272), Secretary of War Stanton estimated that of the many cases on record at that time in the Bureau of Military Justice "perhaps not one-twentieth" had been prosecuted by commissioned judge advocates.

Under the act of July 17, 1862, the Judge Advocate General received from the Adjutant General for review the records of courts-martial; and an act of June 20, 1864 (13 Stat. 145), made him the head of the Bureau of Military Justice, whose duties and functions were defined more particularly by AGO General Order 270, Oct. 11, 1864, to receive, revise, report on, and record the proceedings of courts-martial, military commissions, and courts of inquiry of the armies of the United States.

According to his own record, the "business despatched" in the Bureau of Military Justice by the Judge Advocate General, ca. Sept. 1862-Nov. 1865, was as follows:

67,844 general courts-martial and military commissions reviewed.

17,953 reports made "as to the regularity of proceedings on applications for restoration to the service, the pardon of offenders, the remission or commutation of sentences, and upon miscellaneous questions referred to this office, " including "letters of instructions upon military law and practice to judge advocates, reviewing officers, and others. "

Bvt. Maj. John F. Lee, in office as Judge Advocate of the Army when the war began, was succeeded on Sept. 3, 1862, by Col. (later Brig. Gen.) Joseph Holt, who had the title Judge Advocate General.

Annual Reports of the Judge Advocate General, 1863-65, appended to those of the Secretary of War; Brig. Gen. George B. Davis, A Treatise on Military Law of the United States . . . (New York, 1912); S. V. Benêt, A Treatise on Military Law and the Practice of Courts-Martial (New York, 1862), which shows forms of court-martial orders and the mode of recording the proceedings.

Record Group 153. --Records of the Bureau of Military Justice (later the Office of the Judge Advocate General) concerning the administration of justice during the Civil War consist of correspondence files, some records of investigation, and formal records of courts and military commissions. Copies of letters sent are in a series, 1842-89 (57 vols.), incompletely indexed in a 1-volume subject index and 3 volumes of name indexes. As described by Acting Judge Advocate Gen. G. Norman Lieber in an 1889 report these letters contain "a transcript of all reports upon the proceedings of general courts-martial, military commissions, and courts of inquiry; upon application of military prisoners for pardon or mitigation of sentence; upon the legal sufficiency of charges and specifications submitted to the office for examination; upon the legal formality and sufficiency of bonds and contracts given, made, or accepted by the military authorities . . . and also copies of opinions furnished upon the miscellaneous and varied questions of law from time to time submitted to the office, and also forms of deeds, licenses, and other legal instruments prepared in the office. "

The letters received are part of a chronologically arranged series, 1854-94; these are abstracted in a number of registers. There is also a separate compilation of copies of opinions and decisions of the Attorney General, 1821-70 (5 vols.), concerning the administration of military justice and the legal actions of the War Department.

Records of investigations pertinent to the Civil War include testimony, reports, and correspondence regarding the investigation (by the Provost Marshal, Department of the Missouri) of the activities of the Order of American Knights of the Golden Circle, 1864 (1 ft.); and copies of letters sent by Maj. L. C. Turner to the Secretary of War and others concerning alleged Confederate sympathizers, with related correspondence of the Judge Advocate General, 1864-70 (3 vols.). There are also records (supplementary to the military commission case papers, MM 3951) assembled

in preparing the case against the Lincoln "assassins," arranged by surname of the accused, Apr. 1865 (2 ft.), many of which are abstracted in a
1-volume register; and a register of letters received, Apr.-Aug. 1865,
by Col. H. L. Burnett, his endorsement book, Apr.-June 1865, and his letters sent, Apr.-July 1865 (1 vol.), all relating to the assassination suspects.

The proceedings in extenso of courts and military commissions are
discussed below.

National Archives, **Preliminary**   (War), 1808-1942, comp. by George
Checklist of the Records of the Of-   J. Stansfield (Washington, 1945).
fice of the Judge Advocate General

Military Commissions, Courts of Inquiry, and General Courts-Martial

The significance to research of the records of the military courts of
the Civil War period is best understood when the cases with which they
were concerned are sampled. The information given here may be helpful
in suggesting the extent and character of these records. Until May 1, 1864,
the proceedings of general courts-martial were published in War Department (AGO) general orders; thereafter such proceedings were numbered in
a separate series of orders. Proceedings of trial by court-martial published as congressional documents include those of the trial of Maj. Gen.
Fitz John Porter, Nov. 1862-Jan. 1863 (H. Ex. Doc. 71, 37 Cong., 3
sess., Serial 1163; see also Official Records . . . Armies, ser. 1, vol.
12, pt. 2, p. 505-536 and supplement); and of the trial of Maj. David H.
Hastings, Jan. 1864 (H. Ex. Doc. 54, 38 Cong., 2 sess., Serial 1229).
The more detailed discussion, below, of military commissions and courts
of inquiry is followed by a summary description of the single series which
contains the records of the three types of Civil War military courts.

The practice, dating from 1847, of using military commissions as authorized tribunals in time of war was renewed and firmly established during
the Civil War. The Judge Advocate General in his report for the year 1865
evaluated such commissions as "indispensable for the punishment of public
crimes in regions where other courts had ceased to exist, and in cases of
which the local criminal courts could not legally take cognizance, or which,
by reason of intrinsic defects of machinery, they were incompetent to pass
upon." The notable examples of trials by military commission are those
of Clement L. Vallandigham in Ohio; of Lambdin P. Milligan and his associates in Indiana; of the assassins of Abraham Lincoln and their accom-
plices; and of Henry Wirz, the commander of the Confederate prison at
Andersonville, Ga. These commissions often acted essentially as courts
of inquiry, as in the controversial cases of Maj. Gen. Don Carlos Buell,
when a military commission appointed Nov. 20, 1862, investigated and reported on the operations under his command (see bibliographical note,
below); of Cols. Thomas H. Ford and Dixon S. Miles for the evacuation
of Maryland Heights and the surrender of Harper's Ferry (see Official Records . . . Armies, ser. 1, vol. 19, pt. 1, p. 549-803); and of "the late
Colonel J. M. Chivington," whose activities "in his recent campaign against
the Indians [the 'Sand Creek massacre'], in . . . 1864" were investigated
by a military commission in 1865 (see S. Ex. Doc. 26, 39 Cong., 2 sess.,
Serial 1277). Among other important military commissions were those
trying John H. Gee, "late keeper of the rebel military prison at Salisbury,

N. C. "; James W. Duncan, "late of the C. S. Army," for violations of the laws of war at Andersonville, Ga.; G. St. Leger Grenfelt and others for "conspiring . . . to release the rebel prisoners of war . . . at Camp Douglas, near Chicago"; and Robert C. Kennedy on charges of "irregular and unlawful warfare" in attempting to burn and destroy New York City. Other cases tried by military commissions involved such offenses as un- authorized trading or commercial intercourse with the enemy; unauthorized correspondence with the enemy; blockade-running; carrying mail across the lines; drawing a bill of exchange upon an enemy, or upon a party in a north- ern city by an enemy; dealing in, negotiating, or "uttering" Confederate securities or money; manufacturing arms, etc., for the enemy; furnishing the enemy contraband of war or dealing in contraband in violation of mili- tary orders; publicly expressing hostility to the U. S. Government or sym- pathy with the enemy; coming within the lines of the Army without authority; violating a flag of truce; violating an oath of allegiance or an amnesty oath; violating parole by a prisoner of war; aiding prisoners of war to escape; unwarranted treatment of Federal prisoners of war; burning, destroying, or obstructing railroads, bridges, steamboats, etc., used in military op- erations; cutting telegraph wires between military posts; recruiting for the enemy within the Federal lines; engaging in guerila warfare; helping Fed- eral soldiers to desert; resisting or obstructing an enrollment or draft; impeding enlistments; violating orders against selling liquor to soldiers or other orders in a district under military government; attempting without success to aid the enemy by transporting contraband to him; and conspiracy by two or more to violate the laws of war by destroying life or property in aid of the enemy. A military commission established in Washington in 1863 sat indefinitely to investigate and determine the disposition of cases of al- leged desertion, prolonged absence without leave, and breach of arrest.

The military commission "for the trial of David E. Herold, George A. Atzerodt, Lewis Payne, Michael O'Laughlin, Edward Spangler, Sam- uel Arnold, Mary E. Surratt, Sam- uel A. Mudd, and such other pris- oners as may be brought before it, implicated in the murder of the late President, Abraham Lincoln, and the attempted assassination of the Honorable William H. Seward, Sec- retary of State, and in an alleged conspiracy to assassinate other of- ficers of the Federal Government, at Washington City, and their aiders and abettors," was appointed by AGO S. O. 211, May 6, 1865, to meet on May 8, 1865, or soon thereafter. Detailed for the com- mission were Maj. Gen. David Hunter, Maj. Gen. Lewis Wallace, Bvt. Maj. Gen. August V. Kautz, Brig. Gen. Albion P. Howe, Brig. Gen. Robert S. Foster, Bvt. Brig.

Gen. Cyrus B. Comstock, Brig. Gen. T. M. Harris, Bvt. Col. Hor- ace Porter, Lt. Col. David R. Clen- denin, and Brig. Gen. Joseph Holt (Judge Advocate and Recorder). By S. O. 216, May 9, 1865, General Comstock and Colonel Porter were relieved by Bvt. Brig. Gen. James A. Ekin and Bvt. Col. C. H. Tomp- kins. Although never officially pub- lished, four versions of the trial of the "conspirators" were issued in book form shortly after the commis- sion had completed its labors: by Barclay and Co. of Philadelphia; by T. P. Peterson and Bros., also of Philadelphia; by Benjamin Perley Poore; and by Benn Pitman. Pitman, recorder to the military commission in the case, had the approval of its members to compile for publication "an authentic record of the trial . . . such record to include the testimony, documents introduced in evidence, discussion of points of law raised during the trial, the addresses of the counsel for the accused, the reply of the Special Judge Advocate, and the findings and sentences"; and, by authority of the Secretary of War, Judge Advocate General Holt approved the project on June 30, 1865. The work was published the same year by Moore, Wilstach, & Baldwin of Cincinnati and New York. A facsimile edition of Pitman's compilation is currently available with an introduction by Philip Van Doren Stern (New York, 1954).

Congressional documents constituting primary sources for the study of the Lincoln assassination plot are the following: H. Ex. Doc. 90, 39 Cong., 1 sess., Serial 1263, letter from the Secretary of War concerning awards for the capture of Booth and others; H. Rept. 99, 39 Cong., 1 sess., Serial 1272, "Reward for the Capture of Booth"; H. Ex. Doc. 9, 39 Cong., 2 sess., Serial 1288, report of the Secretary of State on the discovery and arrest of John H. Surratt; H. Rept. 104, 39 Cong., 1 sess., Serial 1272, "Assassination of Lincoln"; H. Ex. Doc. 25, 39 Cong., 2 sess., Serial 1289, report of the Secretary of State, with the papers, on the discovery and arrest of John H. Surratt; H. Rept. 33, 39 Cong., 2 sess., Serial 1305, the discovery and arrest of Surratt; H. Ex. Doc. 68, 40 Cong., 2 sess., Serial 1332, report of George H. Sharpe on the assassination of Lincoln; H. Rept. 7, 40 Cong., 1 sess., Serial 1314, impeachment investigation, including testimony of E. M. Stanton before the House Judiciary Committee in 1867; H. Ex. Doc. 36, 40 Cong., 2 sess., Serial 1330, letter from the Secretary of War Ad Interim on the claim of H. B. Sainte-Marie for compensation for information leading to the arrest of John H. Surratt; and H. Rept. 743, 43

Cong., 1 sess., Serial 1626, report on the "petition of Richard H. Garrett for compensation for barn and other property burned at Caroline County, Virginia, in capturing J. Wilkes Booth and D. C. Harold."

The record of the trial by military commission of Henry Wirz, as compiled in the office of the Adjutant General in 1866, was published as H. Ex. Doc. 23, 40 Cong., 2 sess., Serial 1331; one of the chief values of this compilation is its index, which refers not only to the printed page numbers but also to the page numbers of the manuscript record, in considerable detail by subjects and names of witnesses. The record of the trial (Jan.-Feb. 1865) of G. St. Leger Grenfelt et al. before a military commission at Cincinnati was printed as H. Ex. Doc. 50, 39 Cong., 2 sess., Serial 1290. In this affair, known as the Chicago conspiracy, the accused were charged with conspiracy, in violation of the laws of war, "to release the rebel prisoners of war confined . . . at Camp Douglas, near Chicago," and "to lay waste and destroy the city of Chicago." The record throws light on the Order of American Knights, the Sons of Liberty, and the Society of the Illini. For record of the trial of Clement L. Vallandigham on the charge of "publicly expressing . . . sympathy for those in arms against the Government . . . ," see Official Records . . . Armies, ser. 2, vol. 5, p. 633-646.

Pitman also published records of the trials of H. H. Dodd et al., "in permanent and respectable book shape," under the title The Trials for Treason at Indianapolis Disclosing the Plans for Establishing a North-Western Confederacy . . . (Cincinnati, Moore, Wilstach, & Baldwin, 1865). A later edition of this work, apparently from the same plates, was published in 1892 by the News Publishing Co., Salem, Ind.

After the discovery, in 1872,

that the proceedings of the 1862-63 military commission in the case of Maj. Gen. Don Carlos Buell had been lost or misplaced, Pitman prepared for the War Department a new transcription from "the phonographic notes" taken by him as the reporter; for the circumstances of this arrangement and for the text of the proceedings so transcribed, see Official Records . . . Armies, ser. 1, vol. 16, pt. 1, p. 5-726. See also James B. Fry, Operations of the Army Under Buell from June 10th to October 30th, 1862, and the "Buell Commission," p. 107-109 (New York, 1884).

To facilitate research in the records of Civil War courts of inquiry appointed by the War Department, an alphabetized and relatively complete list of such courts follows. Field commands ordered many other inquiries.

Allegheny Arsenal Court of Inquiry

Appointed by AGO S. O. 288, Oct. 10, 1862, to investigate an explosion at Allegheny Arsenal, Pittsburgh, and to examine into the conduct of the commandant, Col. John Symington.

Alton Military Prison Court of Inquiry

Required by AGO S. O. 207, Aug. 26, 1862, to assemble at Alton, Ill., on Sept. 3, "to inquire into the circumstances of the escape of thirty-six prisoners of war from the military prison at Alton, on or about the 25th of July, 1862." The court's proceedings were printed in Official Records . . . Armies, ser. 2, vol. 4, p. 486-489.

Camp Chase Court of Inquiry

Appointed by AGO S. O. 330, Oct. 3, 1864, to convene at Camp Chase, Columbus, Ohio, on Oct. 6 or soon thereafter, "to examine into the circumstances connected with the escape of certain rebel Prisoners of War from Camp Chase, on or about the 30th of May, 1864."

Cotton, etc., Transactions Court of Inquiry

Organized under AGO S. O. 88, Feb. 23, 1863, to inquire about the participation by officers in "traffic in cotton or other produce on the Mississippi river or its tributaries." The court was required initially to meet and organize "with all convenient dispatch" at Cairo, but AGO S. O. 96, Feb. 28, 1863, changed its location to St. Louis. Its records are in Record Group 159 (Office of the Inspector General) rather than in the main series of Judge Advocate General's case files.

Crittenden-McCook Court of Inquiry

Convened by AGO G. O. 322, Sept. 28, 1863, "to inquire and report upon the conduct of Major Generals [Alexander McD.] McCook and [Thomas L.] Crittenden, in the battles of the 19th and 20th inst."--that is, Chickamauga. AGO Special Order 13, Jan. 9, 1864, extended the investigation to include Maj. Gen. James S. Negley; the records of all three cases were published in <u>Official Records</u> . . . <u>Armies</u>, ser. 1, vol. 30, pt. 1, p. 930-1053.

Downing-Todd Court of Inquiry

Appointed by AGO S. O. 88, Feb. 23, 1864, to assemble at Wheeling, W. Va., on Mar. 7, 1864, or as soon thereafter as practicable, for the purpose of "examining into the nature of alleged fraudulent transactions of Captain W. R. Downing, Assistant Quartermaster of Volunteers, John Todd, and other persons, named in the statement of Captain James, Assistant Quartermaster of Volunteers."

Duane-Michler Court of Inquiry

Appointed by AGO S. O. 288, June 30, 1863, "to investigate the facts and circumstances connected with the capture and paroling" of Maj. James C. Duane, Corps of Engineers, and Capt. Nathaniel Michler, Corps of Engineers, "on the 28th instant, in Maryland."

Dyer Court of Inquiry

This court convened in Washington on Nov. 9, 1868, in compliance with AGO S. O. 217, Sept. 10, 1868, "to examine into the nature of the transactions of Brigadier and Brevet Major General A. B. Dyer, Chief of Ordnance, and of the accusations against that officer contained in the Report of the Select Committee on Ordnance of the Senate and House of Representatives, submitted to the Senate on the 17th of July 1868." The inquiry pertained to General Dyer's conduct in reference to an 1864 contract with Dickson & Zane for providing 20,000 "Amsterdam projectiles." The court was dissolved by AGO G. O. 51, May 15, 1869, which contains a résumé of its deliberations and opinion. See <u>Proceedings of a Court of Inquiry Convened at Washington, D. C., November 9, 1868 . . . to Examine Into the Accusations Against Brig. and Bvt. Major General A. B. Dyer, Chief of Ordnance</u> (Washington, 1869).

Gillingham Court of Inquiry

Appointed by AGO S. O. 380, Aug. 25, 1863, "to investigate the circumstances attending the capture, by the enemy, of about 100 Government horses from Captain Edward E. Gillingham, 13th New York Cavalry, near Annandale, Virginia, on the 24th instant."

Howard Court of Inquiry

Under a joint resolution of Congress, Feb. 13, 1874 (18 Stat. 285), a court of inquiry was convened (AGO S. O. 35, Feb. 16, 1874; amended by AGO S. O. 51, Mar. 9, 1874) in Washington on Mar. 3, 1874, "to fully investigate all the charges against Brigadier General O. O. Howard,"-- charges of mismanagement of the Disbursing Branch of the Bureau of Refugees, Freedmen, and Abandoned Lands, and confusion and imperfection in the Bureau's records. The court met from Mar. 3 to May 9, 1874, and conducted investigations that resulted in General Howard's acquittal. Its opinion was published in AGO G. O. 75, July 3, 1874. (Testimony, exhibits,

and the argument of the judge advocate are in Record Group 94 rather than
in the main series of case records.)

McDowell Court of Inquiry

Appointed by AGO S. O. 350, Nov. 17, 1862, at the request of Maj.
Gen. Irvin McDowell, to examine accusations made against him and to
report an opinion in the case. The court, "having completed its investigations, and reported that, in its opinion, the interests of the public service
do not require any further investigation into the conduct of Major General
McDowell," was dissolved by AGO S. O. 88, Feb. 23, 1863. For printed
proceedings, see Official Records . . . Armies, ser. 1, vol. 12, pt. 1,
p. 36-332.

McFarland Court of Inquiry

Appointed by AGO S. O. 378, Aug. 24, 1863, "to investigate the circumstances attending the loss, by theft, of a large sum of public money
in the hands of Major [Henry] McFarland, Pay Department." Dissolved by
AGO S. O. 421, Sept. 19, 1863.

McKay Court of Inquiry

Appointed by AGO S. O. 532, Dec. 1, 1863, to meet in the "Camp of the
2d Army Corps," Army of the Potomac, on Dec. 10, or soon thereafter, to
investigate the murder of Capt. Thomas McKay, "late of the 20th Regt.
Mass. Volunteers."

Martindale Court of Inquiry

Appointed by AGO S. O. 280, Oct. 6, 1862, to investigate charges
against Brig. Gen. John H. Martindale.

Petersburg Court of Inquiry

Appointed by AGO S. O. 258, Aug. 3, 1864, to convene "in front of
Petersburg" on Aug. 5 or soon thereafter "to examine and report upon the
facts and circumstances attending the unsuccessful assault on the enemy's
position, on the 30th of July, 1864."

Porter Court of Inquiry

Appointed by AGO S. O. 222, Sept. 5, 1862, to meet in Washington on
Sept. 6 or soon thereafter, "to investigate the facts and circumstances
connected with the alleged neglect of duty of Major General Fitz John
Porter in not marching and engaging the enemy between the 27th and 30th
of August; also those connected with the delay of Major General Franklin
in moving his corps to reinforce Gen. Pope's army between the 26th and
31st of August; and also those connected with the conduct of Brig. General
Charles Griffin on the 29th and 30th of August and especially of language
used by him disrespectful of his superior officers." The Porter case was
reopened in 1878, when the War Department appointed a board to reinvesti-
gate the affair.

Ruth Court of Inquiry

On Aug. 4, 1863, the steamer Ruth, with a party of paymasters aboard and about $2, 600, 000 in U. S. notes to pay the army of General Grant, was destroyed by fire on the Mississippi River, below Cairo. All money on board was burned. A court of inquiry, instituted by AGO S. O. 408, Sept. 11, 1863, convened in St. Louis on Sept. 21. Its opinion, published in AGO G. O. 344, Oct. 19, 1863, was that the steamer was fired by an incendiary, not "for the particular purpose--although that may have been an additional object--of destroying the public funds on board, but in conformity with what appears to be a plan of the rebels for the destruction of the water transportation in the Valley of the Mississippi, and thus crippling the movements of our armies. "

Springfield Armory Fire Court of Inquiry

Appointed by AGO S. O. 240, July 18, 1864, to investigate and report on the fire of July 2, 1864.

Warren Court of Inquiry

Appointed by AGO S. O. 287, June 29, 1863, to meet at Fort Leavenworth, Kans. , "to investigate the facts and circumstances connected with the official conduct of Captain George F. Warren, Assistant Quartermaster of Volunteers, while on duty with the Army of the Frontier. "

West Point Courts of Inquiry

A court of inquiry was appointed by AGO S. O. 342, Nov. 12, 1862, to inquire into reported misconduct of certain cadets at West Point. A later court was appointed by AGO S. O. 438, Sept. 30, 1863, to investigate accusations against other cadets.

Winchester-Martinsburg Evacuation Court of Inquiry

Appointed by AGO S. O. 346, Aug. 4, 1863, "to investigate the facts and circumstances connected with the recent evacuation of Winchester by the command of Maj. Gen. R. H. Milroy, U. S. Volunteers, and the evacuation of Martinsburg by the command of Brigadier General D. Tyler, U. S. Volunteers. " The court was instructed to "report whether the orders of the General-in-Chief in regard to the evacuation of Winchester were complied with; and, if not, by whom they were disobeyed, " and "whether the retreat of the command was properly conducted and the public property suitably cared for; and, if not, what officer or officers were in fault. " Similarly, with respect to the retreat from Martinsburg, the court was to report whether it was "properly conducted and the public property suitably cared for; and, if not, what officer or officers were in fault. " AGO S. O. 394, Sept. 2, 1863, modified its purpose, with respect to Winchester, to "inquire into and report the facts and circumstances in regard to the evacuation of Winchester. " For printed proceedings, see Official Records . . . Armies, ser. 1, vol. 27, pt. 2, p. 88-169.

Record Group 153. -- The case files of military commissions, courts of inquiry, and general courts-martial of the Civil War period are in a series, 1809-94, arranged alphabetically by key letters arbitrarily assigned to cases and numerically thereunder. This series contains records of most of the abovementioned courts of inquiry and military commissions; these records include documents concerning the organization and personnel of courts, statements of charges and specifications, the pleas and arraignments of defendants, exhibits, proceedings, statements of findings and sentences, reports of reviewing authorities, statements of action by the Secretary of War and the President, and related correspondence and other papers. Finding aids for Civil War cases consist of a register, 1811-90 (15 vols.); summaries of cases in the letters-sent books; and the compiled opinions and decisions of the Attorney-General, 1821-70. Certain case files, 1861-65 (ca. 4 ft.), lost during the Civil War and recovered by the Judge Advocate General in 1890 and 1891, are grouped separately although recorded in the registers.

Records in Other Custody. -- The Joseph Holt collection in the Library of Congress contains papers relating to the prosecution of the conspirators in the Lincoln assassination and letters exchanged between Holt and James Speed, Attorney General in Johnson's Cabinet, concerning the petition to commute Mary Surratt's death sentence to life imprisonment. Also in the Library are the "military diaries" of Gen. August Valentine Kautz, which cover his service as a member of the military commission in the Lincoln assassination case. Some exhibits in that case were transferred by the War Department to the Lincoln Museum. The Museum also has the diary, Apr. 14-21, 1865, of John Wilkes Booth, once in the possession of the War Department but not exhibited at the trial. (Testimony concerning Booth's diary and the fate of his letter to the National Intelligencer is in H. Rept. 7, 40 Cong., 1 sess., Serial 1314.)

Office of the Assistant Judge Advocate General, Louisville

The Office of the Assistant Judge Advocate General at Louisville, Ky., was established by AGO General Order 230, July 16, 1864, which directed the forwarding to him (instead of to the Judge Advocate General) of all records of courts-martial and military commissions within the Military Departments of the Ohio, the Tennessee, the Cumberland, the Missouri, Arkansas, and Kansas. The Assistant Judge Advocate General was enjoined to call for records of courts and commissions not received by him "in due season"; to examine them; to return for correction such as were incomplete; and to give immediate notice of serious defects to the proper commander, so that sentences might not be illegally executed. He was required to forward all complete records to the Judge Advocate General but was not to make reports on them unless so instructed by the Judge Advocate General. The Office was discontinued by AGO General Order 1, Jan. 5, 1867, which directed that the records previously sent to Louisville be sent direct to the Judge Advocate General at Washington.

Col. (later Bvt. Brig. Gen.) William M. Dunn was Assistant Judge Advocate General, July 16, 1864-Jan. 5, 1867.

Record Group 153. -- Registers of court-martial case files received by Colonel Dunn, 1864-67 (6 vols.), with an incomplete index, 1865-67 (5 vols.); and an endorsement book, 1864-66.

OFFICE OF THE JUDGE ADVOCATE

AGO General Order 95, Aug. 5, 1862, appointed Maj. Levi C. Turner "associate judge-advocate for the army around Washington" and ordered "all cases of state prisoners and also cases of military arrests in the District of Columbia and the adjacent counties of Virginia . . . specially assigned to him for investigation and determination." Three days later the Secretary of War ordered that "all U. S. marshals and superintendents or chiefs of police of any town, city, or district . . . arrest and imprison any person or persons who may be engaged, by act, speech, or writing, in discouraging volunteer enlistments, or in any way giving aid and comfort to the enemy, or in any other disloyal practice against the United States." Arrests were to be reported immediately to Judge Advocate Turner "in order that such persons may be tried before a military commission."

Turner's activities thus brought him into direct contact with Federal and local law-enforcement officers throughout the United States and made him an important instrument in bringing to justice those accused of treasonable or subversive activities. He issued instructions on the investigation of state prisoners held in Federal prisons (for instance, on Aug. 23, 1862, to Reuben Hitchcock, special commissioner to investigate the cases of state prisoners held at Camp Chase); or he himself conducted such examinations.

Turner's office, which should not be confused with the Office of the Judge Advocate General (a later name of the Bureau of Military Justice), apparently continued until shortly before his death in 1867.

Record Group 94. -- The records of Judge Advocate Turner are part of the Turner-Baker papers, brought together after the war by the Bureau of Military Justice (see Office of the Provost Marshal, below). This arrangement work began in 1869; the arrangement of Turner's papers was completed in 1871 and of Baker's in 1873. The papers remained in the Bureau of Military Justice (later the Office of the Judge Advocate General) until they were turned over to the Record and Pension Office in 1894.

The Bureau of Military Justice carefully and quite properly kept Turner's papers separated from Baker's. Turner's reports and his letters and other papers received, 1862-66, with notes and endorsements thereon, are principally in a numerical case file, 1-4119 (ca. 50 ft.), for which there is an alphabetical name and subject index (1 vol.) compiled in the Bureau of Military Justice. The same volume indexes the Baker papers. The separate but smaller series of documents received by Baker, 1861-65 (4 ft.), is also arranged numerically, 1-B to 845-B. Unbound papers (preponderantly Turner's) outside these principal series include lists of prisoners at Camp Chase, Fort McHenry, and other prisons, and of prisoners released at Camp Chase; records of releases from Johnson's Island, Alton (Ill.), Fort Delaware, and Camp Chase; some statements of prisoners; applications for passes to travel and to visit prisoners; orders of Judge Advocate Turner for prisoners and witnesses to be sent before courts-martial or military commissions; papers of or relating to the Board of Police Commissioners; rough drafts of Judge Advocate Turner's letters and endorsements, 1862-66; "Flag of Truce" boat papers ("Lists of applicants to come North, and go South" and "Lists of persons going up and coming down James River"); oaths of allegiance (chiefly of Virginians); a list of men arrested en route to Canada to evade the draft; lists of deserters; receipts for prisoners; and bonds and certificates of exemption and bonds for "holding to

military service. " Book records comprise, besides records of or relating
to prisons (see below), a record of political prisoners detained throughout
the North, 1862-64; an index of secret service payments by the War Department disbursing clerk, 1861-70; a record of secret service fund receipts and disbursements; ledgers apparently of the Trader's Bank,
Nashville (3 vols.); and Judge Advocate Turner's letter book.

The collection includes also prison registers, commitment and release
records, prisoners' statements, and records of visitors (19 vols. in all),
of or pertaining to Old Capitol, Carroll, Forrest Hall, and other prisons.

Much of Turner's correspondence is printed in Official Records
. . . Armies, ser. 2, vols. 2-8, and ser. 3, vols. 2, 3, and 5, passim.

OFFICE OF THE PROVOST MARSHAL

On Sept. 12, 1862, Secretary of War Stanton appointed Lafayette C.
Baker "special provost-marshal for the War Department . . . to exercise
the powers and do and perform the functions pertaining to that office during
the pleasure of the President. " Previously Baker had been employed in
"detective" or "secret" services for the Commanding General of the Army,
Winfield Scott, and for Secretary of State Seward. Baker, who in his
memoirs styled himself "Chief, National Detective Police, " considered that
his "bureau" had a continuous life despite the transfer of his activities from
one department of Government to another. Work for the War Department
involved him in cases of disloyalty, treason, vandalism, and conspiracy and
in espionage on behalf of the Government. He was prominent in the apprehension of John Wilkes Booth and the other "conspirators" in the Lincoln
assassination, and he had a hand in the imprisonment of Jefferson Davis and
the trial of Henry Wirz. For the Treasury Department he investigated its
First Division (Engraving and Printing Bureau).

On June 29, 1863, Baker was appointed Colonel of the First Regiment,
District of Columbia Cavalry. According to his own account the "importance of the bureau, and its rapidly accumulating business, rendered a
military force, exclusively under my control, a necessity. "

Baker was "relieved from duty as Provost Marshal of the War Department" on Nov. 7, 1863, but he continued his activities as a special agent.
After the draft call of Dec. 19, 1864, he investigated, at the request of
Provost Marshal General Fry, frauds in the recruiting service, not only
in the draft and volunteer recruitment for the Army, but also in the recruiting service of the Regular Army and in Navy recruitment.

Baker's office should not be confused with the Provost Marshal General's Bureau, created in 1863. His official connection with the War Department ended when he was honorably mustered out on Jan. 15, 1866. He
died 2 years later. He was and remains a controversial figure.

Record Group 94. --After the Civil War the Bureau of Military Justice
was given "the duty of systematically arranging and indexing, for purposes
of ready reference, the important state papers belonging to the offices of the
late Colonel L. C. Turner, judge advocate, and Brigadier General L. C.
Baker, provost marshal. " From this assignment resulted the collection
now known as the Turner-Baker papers, which is described under the Office of the Judge Advocate, above.

Much of Baker's correspondence is printed in his History of the United States Secret Service (Philadelphia, 1867), and in Official Records . . . Armies, ser. 1, vols. 19, 21, 25, 29, 41, and 46-48; ser. 2, vols. 1, 2, 4, 6, and 8; and ser. 3, vols. 2-5, passim. See also the report of the House Select Committee to Investigate Charges Against the Treasury Department (H. Rept. 140, 38 Cong., 1 sess., Serial 1207). Related records are in Record Group 110.

CAVALRY BUREAU

AGO General Order 236, July 28, 1863, announced the establishment in the War Department of the Cavalry Bureau, to have charge of the organization and equipment of the Army's cavalry forces and to provide for their mounts and remounts. Reports of inspection, assigned to promote the efficiency of the cavalry service, were to be forwarded from the field to the head of the Cavalry Bureau at the end of each month and were to cover the following points: "what service the troops inspected have done since last inspected; how many miles their horses have traveled within the month; what character of service has been required of them, and under what circumstances it has been rendered; what appears to have been the care taken of them, as regards treatment, shoeing, &c., &c.; what has been the quantity and character of the rations of forage issued to them; if there have been any deficiency of forage, and who is responsible therefor, &c., &c.; and . . . any other information . . . which it may be advisable should come to the notice of the Bureau."

Veterinary surgeons of cavalry were selected by the Chief of the Cavalry Bureau but appointed by the Secretary of War; the appointment records were kept in the Adjutant General's Office.

Early in Aug. 1863 it was decided that the Quartermaster General should continue to furnish the army with horses "until the chief of cavalry should notify him that the Cavalry Bureau was able and ready to take this duty upon itself." It was decided also to construct a cavalry depot "capable of accommodating from ten to twelve thousand horses, sick and well," at Giesboro Point, on the Potomac near Washington. A similar depot at St. Louis and temporary accommodations for horses at either Louisville, Ky., or Columbus, Ohio, were planned. More than 16,000 unserviceable horses were on hand near Washington in 1863; it was believed that most of these, with proper care and treatment, could again become fit for service. The cavalry depots would, it was hoped, minimize future losses of horses such as those sustained after the battle of Gettysburg. AGO General Order 119, Mar. 24, 1864, appointed a board to inspect the mounted troops and as a further measure a cavalry officer was especially assigned (AGO S. O. 133, Mar. 31, 1864) to proceed from point to point to "examine into the use of government horses, which are suitable for cavalry purposes, by persons not authorized by regulations and orders so to use them," reporting the results of each examination to the Bureau Chief.

By AGO General Order 162, Apr. 14, 1864, the Cavalry Bureau was put under the command of the Chief of the Army Staff. Thereafter the organization, equipment, and inspection of cavalry were to be carried out by a specially assigned cavalry officer, and the purchase and inspection of horses and their subsistence and transportation by a specially assigned officer of the Quartermaster's Department. The Bureau was abolished by AGO General Order 83, Oct. 4, 1866.

The successive chiefs of the Cavalry Bureau were Maj. Gen. George Stoneman, Brig. Gen. James H. Wilson, and Lt. Col. James A. Ekin.

Wartime annual reports of the Chief of Cavalry, appended to those of the Secretary of War; Theo. F. Rodenbough and William L. Haskin, eds. , The Army of the United States . . . (New York, 1896).

Record Group 92. --Some of the Cavalry Bureau's records were transferred to the Quartermaster General's Office and intermingled with the records of that Office. These records include fair copies of letters sent and abstracts of letters received, 1863-66 (2 vols.); compiled reports of "persons and articles employed and hired" at Washington in Oct. -Nov. 1863 and at Giesboro Point in 1864 (1 vol.); an invoice book kept at Giesboro Point, July 1864-Aug. 1866; and morning reports of Bureau employees. Other records, which may belong to the First Division of the Quartermaster General's Office, include a volume entitled "General Halleck Book No. 1," containing transcriptions of the Bureau's correspondence with Halleck as Chief of Staff, 1864; an "Officer's Book," of transcriptions of Bureau correspondence, 1864-67; a "Quartermaster's Book," of copies of Bureau correspondence with assistant quartermasters in the field, Apr. -June 1864; and a letter book of Col. James A. Ekin, containing copies of letters received concerning Cavalry Bureau property accounts, 1864-67.

Record Group 98. --The Cavalry Bureau's records in this record group include a small amount of loose papers (letters received) and the following "book" records: copies of letters sent, 1863-66 (2 vols.); copies of endorsements and memoranda sent, 1863-66 (3 vols.); a "telegram book," 1864-65; several registers and indexes of letters received, 1863-66; and some letter books of the special inspectors of cavalry in the Departments of the Ohio and of Arkansas. There are also volumes of general and special orders, inspection records, strength and muster records, and workmen's accounts; and a register of applications for appointment of veterinary surgeons.

PROVOST MARSHAL GENERAL'S BUREAU

AGO General Order 140, Sept. 24, 1862, announced the newly created post of Provost Marshal General of the War Department; and a similar order of Oct. 1, 1862, announced the appointment of Simeon Draper of New York to the position and enjoined that he be "respected accordingly." With headquarters at Washington, the Provost Marshal General had immediate supervision, control, and management of a corps of special provost marshals. These arrangements were superseded by an act of Congress, Mar. 3, 1863 (12 Stat. 731), which created the Provost Marshal General's Bureau and provided for a provost marshal and a board on enrollment in each congressional district. Pursuant to the act, AGO General Order 67, Mar. 17, 1863, detailed Col. James B. Fry "Provost Marshal General of the United States"; and AGO General Order 111, May 1, 1863, put under his "special charge and direction" all enlistments of volunteers.

The more important duties of the Bureau were the arrest of deserters, the enrollment of men for the draft, and the enlistment of volunteers. Through the Bureau the Federal Government took direct control of much business previously handled by the States. The provost marshals of the several congressional districts, aided by a commissioner and a surgeon in each, became in effect recruiting officers; and they were made responsible to acting provost marshals general appointed in the several loyal States. "This system," Provost Marshal General Fry stated in his final report, ". . . met the wants of the service; recruits were rapidly obtained by voluntary enlistment or draft, and such strict regard was paid to their physical fitness, before accepting them, as to greatly reduce the enormous loss on account of discharges for physical disability, which had prevailed during the first two years of the war."

Under the direction of the Bureau all men liable to conscription were enrolled; a more economical method of recruiting was devised and put in operation; desertion was deterred; and the quotas of men furnished by various parts of the country were equalized. The Bureau compiled detailed records on the physical condition of more than a million of the men examined during its existence and compiled statistics (from the official muster rolls and monthly returns) of all casualties in the entire military forces of the Nation during the war. The Provost Marshal General believed that the "extension of the Bureau over the country brought together the Government and the people by closer ties, nurtured that mutual confidence and reliance through which the civil war was conducted to a successful termination, and developed a consciousness of national strength." Recruiting for the Regular Army remained a function of the Adjutant General during the war.

A Joint Resolution of Congress of Feb. 24, 1864 (13 Stat. 402), directed the Provost Marshal General to enlist men desiring to enter the naval service of the United States, but an act of June 3, 1864 (13 Stat. 119), repealed this resolution. Thereafter the Bureau was required merely to credit on the quotas assigned for draft the enlistments reported by the Navy Department. Because recruitment for the Army and the Navy was conducted according to entirely different rules and the War and Navy Departments had divided responsibility for credits allowed on the draft for naval enlistments, some fraud and abuse in filling quotas occurred, especially during the last year of the war.

The Bureau was at first composed of seven branches responsible for (1) general and miscellaneous business; (2) enrollment and draft; (3) deserters--their arrest, return, descriptive lists, etc.; (4) medical affairs and statistics; (5) the Invalid (later Veteran Reserve) Corps; (6) disbursements and accounts under the enrollment act; and (7) disbursements and accounts under an appropriation for collecting, organizing, and drilling volunteers. These branches eventually became known by the names given in the separate entries below. The acting assistant provost marshals general in the States and the provost marshals' districts and boards of enrollment are also separately discussed below.

At the end of the war, as quickly as "the exigencies of the service" allowed, the Provost Marshal General reduced his force. By Nov. 1865 the surgeons and commissioners of boards of enrollment in all the districts had been discharged, the districts had been consolidated, and only 33 provost marshals remained in service. In accordance with an act of July 28, 1866 (14 Stat. 337), AGO General Order 66, Aug. 20, 1866 (effective Aug. 28), discontinued the "Bureau and Office of the Provost Marshal General of the United States" and transferred to the Adjutant General's Office "all business relating in any way to the Provost Marshal General's Bureau, or the raising of troops, with all the accounts and claims connected therewith, or whatever character or date, or whensoever incurred." This business the Adjutant General divided between newly established Enrollment and Disbursing Branches, the work and records of which are described in this Guide under the Office of the Adjutant General. The Bureau's Medical Branch, however, was transferred to the Office of the Surgeon General to assure compliance with the act of July 28, 1866, with regard to publishing the Bureau's medical statistics.

Col. (later Brig. Gen.) James B. Fry was Provost Marshal General from Mar. 17, 1863, until the office was discontinued in 1866.

The "Final Report Made to the Secretary of War, by the Provost Marshal General . . ." Mar. 17, 1866, is printed as a part of H. Ex. Doc. 1, 39 Cong., 1 sess., Serials 1251 and 1252; it covers the entire history of the Bureau.

Record Group 110. --"The records will be voluminous," Provost Marshal General Fry anticipated on Apr. 2, 1863, "and I don't think there is room enough at my disposal in the War Department." The extant records in this record group approximate 1,600 feet. Since the functions of the Provost Marshal General stemmed from those that before and during the first year of the war were responsibilities of the Adjutant General, many records series begin in the Adjutant General's Office, continue for the period 1863-66 in the Provost Marshal General's Bureau, and are again continued in the Adjutant General's Office. The records of the Bureau that can be identified as belonging to its several branches are described under those branches, below. Fair copies of letters sent are in a main series of several volumes for each year, well indexed; and the principal file of letters received, 1863-66 (ca. 30 ft.), on matters of concern to the Bureau as a whole (as distinguished from letters filed in the several branches) is alphabetically arranged by name of correspondent and thereunder chronologically. The letters received are abstracted in many registers arranged by year and thereunder alphabetically by name of correspondent; there are several volumes for each year. Other records apparently not belonging to branches include "roughs" of letters sent, applications for membership on boards of enrollment, papers pertaining to fraud cases, and historical reports submitted by provost marshals. Associated with these records are correspondence and accounts concerning "scouts, guides, spies, and detectives."

Enrollment Branch

Organized about June 1, 1863, the Enrollment Branch superintended the operations of local boards of enrollment. The Adjutant General's Office had kept accounts, with States only, on volunteers called for and recruited, but the Enrollment Branch opened accounts with each enrollment district of the loyal States. On July 1, 1864, the system of accounts was changed by requiring mustering officers to report enlistments and musters, monthly and quarterly, to the acting assistant provost marshal general of the State to which recruits were to be credited. The Branch also received and kept the enrollment sheets of the loyal States, consisting of the original enrollment (May-June 1863) with corrections and revisions (1863-65). A board to examine and correct the quotas of the States and districts under the call for volunteers of Dec. 19, 1864, was appointed by the President on Feb. 6, 1865, to consist of Attorney General James Speed, Brig. Gen. Richard Delafield, and Col. C. W. Foster. Its report was published in AGO General Order 22, Feb. 17, 1865, and its "calculations of the quota of each and every district endorsed by us as correct" were filed with the Provost Marshal General.

Successive Chiefs of the Enrollment Branch:
> Capt. Henry E. Maynadier, June 1, 1863.
> Capt. (later Maj.) T. A. Dodge, May 20, 1864.
> Capt. (later Maj.) George E. Scott, Dec. 5, 1864.

Record Group 110. --The Chief of the Branch in his final report described the "full set of record books" kept by the Branch as consisting of "letters received," "letters sent," "indorsements and memoranda," "quotas and credits by States," and "quotas and credits by districts." The "average of about five hundred communications" received and answered monthly, he said, concerned chiefly "questions of enrolment, disputed credits, requests for certificates of credit to obtain local bounty, and applications for return of commutation money." There are several volumes of fair copies of letters sent, 1863-66, continued in the Adjutant General's Office. A considerable quantity of letters received, 1863-66, is arranged alphabetically by name of correspondent. There are indexes and abstracts of this correspondence. The records of persons enrolled in the draft and the consolidated lists (Classes 1, 2, and 3) are organized as essentially one series of several hundred volumes, arranged by State and thereunder by congressional district.

Deserters Branch

This Branch was organized on Apr. 8, 1863, after the issuance of AGO General Order 72 of Mar. 24, requiring commanders of regiments, independent battalions, companies, and batteries (and certain other officers) to report monthly to the Provost Marshal General the names of deserters from their commands during the previous month or of deserters not previously reported. The Deserters Branch was established to receive the required reports and handle all official correspondence relating to deserters. After two years of experience, the Branch adopted the following operational system: Reports received were "briefed" and "districted," that is, marginally annotated to show the district in which each deserter was likely to be found. Copies of descriptive lists of deserters were made out and forwarded to district provost marshals, and a consolidated copy of all descriptive lists was sent to the acting assistant provost marshal general in each State. Finally, the returns were filed in a systematic arrangement of States and regiments. This work was "necessarily large"; and at the "season of hardest labor" (the winter of 1864-65, when reports of desertion averaged about 6,000 a month and arrests of deserters 4,000) it required a chief clerk, 8 or 9 other clerks for special duties, and some 15 copyists.

The officer in charge of the Deserters Branch also controlled the "blank department," which received from the public printer, maintained accountability of, and filled provost marshals' requisitions for, the blank forms used in headquarters and in the district offices.

Successive Chiefs of the Deserters Branch:
> Maj. Chauncey McKeever, Apr. 8, 1863.
> Capt. W. R. Pease, Oct. 1, 1863.
> Capt. Henry Stone, Nov. 23, 1863.
> Capt. W. R. Pease, Feb. 9, 1864.
> Capt. George E. Scott, May 2, 1864.
> Maj. T. A. Dodge, Dec. 5, 1864.

Record Group 110. --Fair copies of letters sent, 1863-66, are in several volumes; and letters received, 1863-66 (several ft.) are arranged alphabetically by name of correspondent; this correspondence is abstracted or indexed. Other records include compilations concerning deserters reported and arrested, records of descriptive lists of deserters sent to district provost marshals, and a great quantity of original reports of desertion.

Medical Branch

The Medical Branch was organized on Jan. 11, 1864, to instruct surgeons of boards of enrollment and to promote uniform understanding of the prescribed medical regulations. The Branch was responsible for preparing and forwarding to the boards the medical record books and other forms used to report on the examination of recruits, substitutes, and drafted or enrolled men. It also detailed medical officers as inspectors of boards of enrollment, and it received, examined, and tabulated monthly medical reports giving particulars of the findings of physical examinations. The Provost Marshal General believed that these records, constituting a complete history of the medical examination of 1,014,776 men, afforded "the means of examining into complaints as to improper action in holding to service or enlisting men physically unfit, with an intelligent understanding of the facts in the case, " and insured "a radical discovery and exposure of attempts at fraudulent enlistment. " He averred also that the medical statistics compiled by the Branch were "greater in extent, and believed to contain, in a minute and available form, more valuable information than this, or perhaps any other, country has hitherto possessed. "

Bvt. Col. B. H. Baxter served as chief medical officer from Jan. 11, 1864.

Record Group 110. --In his final report, Colonel Baxter discussed the importance and extent of the records in his Branch in the following terms:

The final reports of surgeons of boards of enrolment give the medical results of the examination of 605,045 drafted men . . ., exhibiting the distinct diseases for which these men were found unfit for military service . . . .

There are also, in addition to the above records . . ., monthly medical reports, . . . including name, age, nativity, occupation, height, chest measurement at inspiration and expiration, complexion, color of eyes and hair, white or colored, married or single, physique, and result of examination of 508,735 . . . men, and the reports of boards of examination, showing the disabilities for which enlisted men were recommended for transfer to the Veterans Reserve Corps.

In addition to the statistical records . . ., able and valuable reports have been received from surgeons of boards of enrolment . . . .

These reports cover two thousand pages in manuscript . . ., and the important information and useful suggestions contained therein are of great interest and value. . . .

Colonel Baxter related his records to those of the Surgeon General's Office and those of the Pension Bureau as follows:

In the medical branch . . . are filed medical records relating to the physical aptitude of this nation for military service.

The important and highly interesting medical records, showing in what way the soldier has been disabled, are on file in the Surgeon General's office, and when published will doubtless present to the world highly scientific medical results never before equalled in reference to the hygiene of armies.

The Pension Bureau contains the records of those who, having been discharged from service on account of wounds or diseases, return to civil life.

Among the extant records in this record group are quarterly reports from States or military departments of men discharged for disability, 1862-66 (ca. 10 ft.), and monthly reports from districts of surgeons' examinations, 1864-66 (ca. 10 ft.). The records of greatest medical significance were presumably taken over by the Surgeon General's Office.

Statistics, Medical and Anthropological of the Provost-Marshal-General's Bureau, Derived From Records of the Examination for Military Service in the Armies of United States During the Late War of the Rebellion, of Over a Million Recruits, Drafted Men, Substitutes, and Enrolled Men, comp. by J. H. Baxter (Washington, 1875. 2 vols.).

Veteran Reserve Corps Branch

The organization of an Invalid Corps was authorized by AGO General Order 105, Apr. 28, 1863, to consist of companies and, if desirable, of battalions. The companies were to be made up of (1) officers and enlisted men of commands then in the field who because of wounds or service-connected disease were unfit for field service but were capable of effective garrison or other light duty; (2) officers and enlisted men still in service and on the rolls who were absent from duty in hospitals or convalescent camps or who were otherwise under the control of medical officers; and (3) officers and enlisted men who had been honorably discharged because of wounds or disease and who wanted to reenter the service. The Provost Marshal General was responsible for executing this order; the troops organized under it were to be under the control of his Bureau; and a new branch was set up to handle the work. Transfers to the corps were announced in the General Orders of the War Department until May 1, 1864, when a new series of orders "Announcing Transfers to the Veteran Reserve and Signal Corps" was begun. The Invalid Corps was renamed "Veteran Reserve Corps" by AGO General Order 111, Mar. 18, 1864, apparently because of the effects upon morale of the confusion of the initial letters "IC" with the same letters when used by inspectors to mark condemned property (that is, "Inspected--Condemned").

Record Group 110. -- The letters received, chiefly applications for assignment to the Invalid (later the Veteran Reserve) Corps, 1863-65 (ca. 14 ft.), are arranged alphabetically by name of correspondent. There are also volumes of abstracts of the letters received, of fair copies of letters sent, and of fair copies of endorsements and memoranda sent; and an order book.

Disbursing Branch

This Branch, which apparently came into existence with the establishment of the Provost Marshal General's Bureau, examined and paid all accounts pertaining to the Bureau. Until July 1, 1864, the Branch accounted centrally for Bureau funds deposited throughout the country with the several Assistant Treasurers of the United States. After that date each division of the Branch paid all classes of accounts incurred within the purview of its responsibility, as follows: First Division--payment of the salaries of all employees in the districts of the Eastern States; Second Division--the same for the Western States; Third Division--travel pay of discharged drafted men, and payment for postage, telegrams, advertising, subsistence and lodging, and expenses incurred in the arrest or pursuit of deserters; Fourth Division--purchases of Bureau public property and payment for rent and transportation.

The extensive work of the Branch is shown by the fact that from May 1863 to Jan. 1866 it received 69,267 letters, sent 20,659, made 20,929 endorsements, examined and paid 105,398 accounts, and drew 155,127 checks.

Maj. H. R. Rathbone was chief of the Disbursing Branch.

Record Group 110. --Letters sent by the Branch, 1863-66, are in several volumes of a general series and in many volumes kept separately for the divisions of the Branch. Letters received, 1863-67 (ca. 50 ft.), are arranged by year and thereunder alphabetically by name of correspondent; most of these came from district provost marshals. The letters received are elaborately abstracted in many volumes. Reports from district provost marshals of "persons and articles hired," 1863-65 (ca. 30 ft.), are arranged by State and thereunder by congressional district. Other Branch records include summary statements of "draft and substitute funds," 1863-65 (1 ft.); summary statements of the bounty fund, 1862-66 (2 ft.); and records of "bounty and premium paid," 1862-65 (ca. 50 ft.). The accounts kept by the four divisions are also available under the general title "enrollment and draft accounts."

Volunteer Recruiting Branch

The Adjutant General was authorized to disburse an appropriation for collecting, drilling, and organizing volunteers but no separate branch appears to have been established to manage the disbursement until May 1862. When the Provost Marshal General's Bureau was established the disbursement function was assigned to the Bureau's Volunteer Recruiting Branch.

Successive Chiefs of the Volunteer Recruiting Branch:

    Lt. Col. W. A. Nichols, ca. May 1862.
    Maj. O. D. Greene, May 1, 1863.
    Bvt. Brig. Gen. Chauncey McKeever, Aug. 26, 1863.

The historical report, Volunteer Recruiting Branch (Document No. 10), appended to the Provost Marshal General's final report, cited above, contains a table showing the amount of each different bounty, the authority under which it was paid, the class to whom it was paid, and the dates between which it was available.

Record Group 110. -- The work of the Branch is indicated in the books and other records it kept. Requisitions for funds were recorded in a "Register of Requisitions, Volunteer Service." Accounts were opened with each disbursing officer to whose credit funds had been placed, and the accounts were recorded in a book entitled "Volunteer Disbursing Service Monthly Statements." Separate books were opened to keep the record of certain expenses incurred in enrolling and drafting 300,000 militia for 9 months' service under the President's order of Aug. 4, 1862, but these were found to be impracticable and unnecessary and were abandoned. The Branch also kept a record of contracts approved for subsisting and lodging recruits, rent of recruiting offices, etc. It received from mustering and disbursement officers weekly reports of public funds on hand and monthly reports of "persons and articles hired and employed." A "Register of Requisitions for Bounties" and a book, "Monthly Statement--Pay of Bounty to Regulars and Volunteers on Enlistment," were maintained until June 1, 1865, when the payment of bounties ceased. The extant records include many books of accounts of these types.

There are also copies of letters sent by the Branch, in several volumes of fair copies, and separate fair copies of endorsements sent. There are letters received, 1862-67 and later (ca. 12 ft.), pertaining to "collecting, drilling and organizing volunteers"; for these there are both registers (11 vols.) and indexes (11 vols.).

Offices of Acting Assistant Provost Marshals General

After the President asked for volunteers and called up the State militia, certain factions began to discourage enlistments in their opposition to the war and the draft. To restrain them provost marshals were appointed in some of the States upon nomination of their Governors, to act under the Governors' directions. Ultimately the Army officer designated in a State as acting assistant provost marshal general supervised the provost marshals for the congressional districts in the State. The acting assistant provost marshal general also inspected the work of boards of enrollment in his State, maintained liaison with State civil officers, and saw to it that the provost marshals under his control used all possible means to arrest deserters. The office of the Acting Assistant Provost Marshal General, Illinois, whose report the Provost Marshal General appended to his own final report as typifying the work of offices at that level, had an organization comprising "departments" of general and miscellaneous business, accounts, deserters, quotas and credits, returns and reports, and the Veteran Reserve Corps; and a medical branch.

Record Group 110. --Some records are available for most, if not all, of the State offices of acting assistant provost marshals general; for the more heavily populated States these records are comparatively voluminous. In a few cases an acting assistant provost marshal general had responsibility for more than one State. The several hundred volumes and a large quantity of unbound records are dispersed in a large series containing also the records of the district provost marshals, which follow those of the acting assistant within the file for each State.

Provost Marshals' Districts and Boards of Enrollment

The act of Mar. 3, 1863, required that, for greater efficiency in assembling and organizing recruits and in arresting deserters and spies, the

United States be divided into districts corresponding to the congressional districts of the States. The District of Columbia also constituted a provost marshal's district, and each Territory constituted one or more as the President directed. The President appointed for each district a provost marshal, who was required to arrest deserters; to detect, seize, and confine spies; and to call together, preside over, record the proceedings of, and announce and enforce the orders and decisions of the board of enrollment for his district.

The board of enrollment was responsible for registering the men in its district. Usually subdistrict enrolling officers registered all men between the prescribed ages, and the board consolidated their lists by entering names alphabetically upon sheets ruled and printed for the purpose. As ex officio president of the board and keeper of its records, the district provost marshal identified himself with the board in most aspects of his work.

Record Group 110. -- The final report of the provost marshal for the Fourth Congressional District, Maryland (printed as Document No. 12 of the Provost Marshal General's final report) described the records of his office as follows: (1) Record of deserters arrested, a book in which were entered descriptions of all apprehended deserters with "the histories of the arrests and disposition made of the men." (2) Record of drafted men, a book in which "an exact and complete roll of persons drawn in the draft" was entered. (3) Record of public property seized, a book recording all public property seized from unauthorized persons and turned in to the Quartermaster's Department. (4) Record of the enrollment, consolidated on enrollment lists, by subdistricts alphabetically arranged, and "bound in volumes of suitable size for convenient reference." (5) Record of the proceedings of the board of enrollment. (6) Record of letters sent, "kept in accordance with instructions for officers of the Adjutant General's Department." (7) Record of letters received, made "in accordance with the mode adopted by the Adjutant General's Office." (8) Record of indorsements. (9) Record of telegrams, a book in which "all telegrams received were recorded, and numbered in the order of their dates." (10) Record of special orders. (11) Record of the medical examination of volunteers, enrolled men, drafted men, and substitutes, kept by the surgeon of the board.

Most of the offices of district provost marshals and their boards of enrollment appear to be represented in the extant records. The character of these records conforms closely to the typical description given above. There are more than a thousand of these volumes, arranged by State and thereunder by congressional district. They show, as few other War Department records do, local situations and conditions, since they record facts not only about the draft but also about local machinery instituted to handle it. The draft books consist of enrollment lists, descriptive lists of drafted men called into service, and lists of persons exempted from the draft.

OFFICE OF THE CHIEF SIGNAL OFFICER AND THE SIGNAL CORPS

An act of June 21, 1860 (12 Stat. 66), provided for the addition to the staff of the Army of "one signal officer" to have charge of "all signal duty, and of all books, papers, and apparatus connected therewith." This position was filled on June 27, 1860, by Maj. Albert J. Myer, whose active interest in sign language had led to the development, in 1856, of a system of visual signaling. Two weeks after his appointment Major Myer was ordered to the Department of New Mexico to participate in Lt. Col. E. R. S. Canby's expedition against the Navahos. "In the beginning," Glassford wrote in his history of the Signal Corps, "the corps was enfolded in the enthusiasm and determination of Myer. In fact there was no corps, but there was Myer. A chief without a corps, it was his consuming ambition to surround himself with a staff of trained assistants; he succeeded in his ambition in 1863."

In May 1861 Myer was recalled from the West to establish a signal system for the Army. Although he was assigned to General McClellan's staff in Aug. 1861 and eventually became Chief Signal Officer, Army of the Potomac, he retained his position as Signal Officer of the Army, a title changed to Chief Signal Officer by sec. 17 of an act of Mar. 3, 1863 (12 Stat. 753). For a time the corps had no distinct organization; it was made up of officers detailed from other branches of service. The 1863 act, however, provided that the Chief Signal Officer would direct a corps consisting of "one lieutenant-colonel; two majors, who shall be inspectors; and for each army corps or military department . . . one captain and as many lieutenants, not exceeding eight, as the President may deem necessary." In support of the bill (H. R. 352) for organizing the Signal Corps, the Senate Committee on Military Affairs and the Militia on Feb. 9, 1863 (S. Rept. 82, 37 Cong., 3 sess., Serial 1151), had pointed out that the "rebel congress" by two acts had "organized the signal service of the regular army" and that to "compete with this" the United States had no legally authorized force; that the private soldiers who had served under the Signal Officer for a year and a half had not had open to them "even the grade of corporal"; and that the officers were shut out from "legitimate and just promotion." In reporting to the Senate committee, Maj. Gen. Henry W. Halleck, although he had "never used the signal corps in the field" and had "never seen the operation of the system," relied on the judgment "of the officers who have employed signal officers in the field" to "respectfully recommend an increase in the corps." The provisional establishment of the corps was made permanent after the war by sec. 22 of an act of July 28, 1866 (14 Stat. 335).

The previous development of four independent bodies of signal officers serving with armies in the northeast, southeast, southwest, and northwest theaters of conflict presented the problem of achieving uniform signal efficiency and of embodying these four distinct organizations into a single corps. Because of its uncertain future the Signal Corps in its formative period was staffed largely with subalterns of volunteer regiments detached for this special service, but the unwisdom of detailing officers for signal duty soon became apparent.

To free himself from the routine of the Signal Camp of Instruction (organized at Georgetown to train assistants; see below) Myer opened an office on or about Nov. 5, 1861, in Washington. The office became permanent on Mar. 16, 1862, when Lt. Samuel T. Cushing was ordered to "assume temporary charge of the office" with responsibilities for the "procuring and furnishing of signal supplies for the Army of the United States, and . . . the preservation of the records of the Corps." The Chief Signal Officer himself regarded the date of the appointment of civilian clerks to replace soldiers (Apr. 1, 1863) as that on which the Office became a permanent organization as "an office for records; for the issuing of orders; a purchasing and disbursing office; an office for the issuing of supplies to officers, and for the auditing of their accounts; the headquarters of the Corps; and, virtually, a bureau office." Under the act of Mar. 3, 1863, cited above, a board of officers headed by the Chief Signal Officer examined officers then on signal duty in the Army of the Potomac, the Middle Department, and the Departments of Washington and Virginia. The board examined also candidates for commission in the Signal Corps, the enlisted men of the signal parties on duty in Washington, and other candidates for enlistment in or transfer to the corps. Auxiliary boards examined signal personnel or candidates elsewhere, and provision was made for a review board to oversee the work of the auxiliary boards.

The organic act of 1860 had explicitly authorized the Signal Officer to have charge of all signal duty and all "apparatus connected therewith," but a conflict over the control of telegraph communication developed between Myer and the Superintendent of the U. S. Military Telegraphs (see above), to which had been assigned responsibility for military telegraph service before Myer returned from the West. Although he failed to get control of the electric telegraph system, the Signal Officer succeeded temporarily in obtaining signal telegraph trains for a portable system of telegraphy. Colonel Myer's later attempt, in the fall of 1863, to secure some control over the "electric telegraphs" resulted in the removal of the portable system from the jurisdiction of the Signal Corps, the transfer of the telegraph trains to the U. S. Military Telegraphs, and Myer's relief as Chief Signal Officer of the Army. His successor, Lt. Col. William J. L. Nicodemus, the acting chief, was dismissed by AGO General Order 304, Dec. 26, 1864, because he had published the annual report of the Signal Corps "without the knowledge or sanction of the Secretary of War." The dismissal order was rescinded, however, and Nicodemus was restored to his former rank on Mar. 31, 1865. Col. Benjamin F. Fisher, appointed Chief Signal Officer on Dec. 3, 1864, was in turn succeeded by Colonel Myer, who was restored to the office on July 28, 1866. (From May 1864 to the end of the war Myer had been signal officer of the Division of West Mississippi.)

At the end of the war the Chief Signal Officer noted that his Office was threefold in character. It was, first, the headquarters of the Signal Corps, where the records were collected, completed, and filed, and where the "advisory superintendence and control" of the special duties of the corps were exercised. Second, it constituted a purchasing and disbursing office, from which supplies of signal stores and equipment were issued. Third, it was an office for the examining of signal accounts and the returns of signal stores.

Successive heads of the Signal Corps during the Civil War period:

Maj. (later Col.) Albert J. Myer, June 27, 1860.

Lt. Col. William J. L. Nicodemus (acting), ca. Nov. 15, 1863.

Col. Benjamin J. Fisher, ca. Dec. 3, 1864.

Col. Albert J. Myer, July 28, 1866.

Annual reports of the Chief Signal Officer, 1861-65, were published in Official Records . . . Armies as follows: ser. 3, vol. 1, p. 694-697 (1861); ser. 3, vol. 2, p. 754-760 (1862); ser. 3, vol. 3, p. 948-961 (1863); ser. 3, vol. 4, p. 818-841 (1864); and ser. 3, vol. 5, p. 152-156 (1865). The 1863 and 1865 reports were also printed in H. Ex. Doc. 1, 38 Cong., 1 sess., Serial 1184, p. 167-177; and H. Ex. Doc. 1 (pt. 2), 39 Cong., 1 sess., Serial 1250, p. 999-1002. The reports were also separately published, as in the case of the 1864 report. In 1864 Myer published A Manual of Signals for the Use of Signal Officers in the Field. The Signal Office published in 1891 a Preliminary List of Officers and Enlisted Men Who Served on Signal Duty During the War of the Rebellion, 1861 to 1866.

Record Group 111. -- The general correspondence of the Office consists of copies of letters sent, July 1860-Dec. 1869 (8 vols., nos. 1-8, and loose papers); and letters and telegrams received, 1861-69 (13 ft.), for which there are registers (7 vols., nos. 9-15). Other series include a small file of letters received, 1862-65, commending the Signal Corps; copies of indorsements sent on letters received, 1863-70 (5 vols., nos. 16-20); and copies of letters sent relating to supplies, Jan.-July 1862 (1 vol., no. 83). There is a useful volume of synopses of letters sent and received, 1861-69, compiled after 1875, pertaining to such matters as the organization and staffing of the Signal Corps, signal equipment, and the use of signals in the Navaho expedition. Record copies of orders and circulars issued, Aug. 1861-Dec. 1869 (initially from the Signal Camp of Instruction at Georgetown) are in 4 volumes (nos. 21-24).

Copies and drafts of annual reports of the Chief Signal Officer, with enclosures, are available for 1862-63. Of equal importance are the reports received from officers of the Signal Corps, 1860-66 (2 ft.), on their operations during the Navaho expedition in the Department of New Mexico, 1860-61, and on their Civil War operations in departments and armies, relatively complete for 1861-63 but fragmentary for 1864-66. There are also copies of operational reports of the corps (5 vols., nos. 26-30) during both the Navaho expedition and the Civil War. Reports of Signal Corps officers' inspections of divisions, departments, districts, and a few stations cover the period Sept. 1863-May 1866 (2 ft.).

Letters sent by the Assistant Superintendent of the Signal Corps Recruiting Service, 1864-65, are in 1 volume (no. 31). Other records relating to the personnel of the corps include a volume (no. 25) of synopses of the military histories of officers, 1860-67; reports of boards of examiners at the Signal Camp of Instruction and at headquarters of departments, recommending individuals for transfer to the Signal Corps, 1861-64 (7 in.); a descriptive book (no. 150A), 1861-65, pertaining to both officers and enlisted men of the corps; another volume (no. 80) containing, in part, a list of signal officers, 1861-62, and a list of signal personnel captured by the enemy between 1863 and 1865; records of courts-martial at the Signal Camp of Instruction and in the Middle Military Department, 1862-65 (1 in.); a volume (no. 76) recording enlistments in the Signal Corps, 1863-64; and annual and quarterly returns of "alterations" and casualties in the Signal Corps, including returns of deceased soldiers of signal detachments, 1863-66 (3 in.). Unbound records include miscellaneous papers, 1862-65 (2 ft.), pertaining chiefly to the constitution, proceedings, and dissolution of boards of examination but including the morning reports of the signal detachment at New Orleans, Dec. 1862-Sept. 1865 (6 in.). (Records of signal detachments, however, are normally associated with those of the military departments in which they served. For example, Lt. Paul Brodie's message book, which records the signals of the detachment posted on the roof of the Winder Building on the night of Apr. 14, 1865, is among the records of the Department of Washington.)

Besides other miscellaneous papers, 1860-69 (2 ft.), relating primarily to signal operations and to personnel matters, the records include copies of messages exchanged between signal stations in the Army of the Potomac and military departments, Jan. 1862-May 1863 and 1864 (3 vols., nos. 41, 42, and 44); also a volume (no. 73) of orders, letters, lists of signal codes, and other papers kept by Capt. Charles L. Davis, Oct. 1861-July 1863, in part during his service as Chief Signal Officer, Department of Virginia. Finally, there are some private letters, 1864-65, apparently intercepted and examined for possible hidden messages in code or cipher or for information on conditions behind the Confederate lines.

National Archives, unpublished Preliminary Inventory of the Records of the Office of the Chief Signal Officer, comp. by Mabel E. Deutrich. See also Deutrich, "Wigwags About Lincoln's Death," Signal, 11:6 (Feb. 1957).

Brady Collection of Civil War Photographs

Most of this collection of photographs, made by or under the direction of Mathew B. Brady, was purchased from him in 1875 under an act of Mar. 3 (18 Stat. 391), which appropriated $25,000 to "enable the Secretary of War to acquire a full and perfect title to the 'Brady collection of photographs of the war,' and to secure by purchase the remainder now in the possession of the artist." Brady was one of the foremost photographers of his time. With official permission, he and his assistants accompanied the armies during the Civil War to photograph battle and camp scenes, and they produced a remarkable pictorial record. The collection purchased from Brady comprises approximately 6,000 collodion (glass-plate) photographic negatives, 1861-74, in a numerical arrangement. Added to the collection as a photographic index are mounted photographic prints made from, but not corresponding in dimensions to, the collodion negatives and arranged alphabetically by surname of subject or geographical location; another set of the mounted photographic prints is arranged numerically. There are also film negatives of the mounted photographs; negative images on microfilm (made at the National Archives); and approximately 900 film positives. The collection now includes also contact photographic prints corresponding to the collodion negatives, made in 1946-52 to check on deterioration.

Supplementing the collection purchased from Brady are approximately 100 other Brady collodion negatives, of which there are also contact photographs, mounted photographs, and film negatives.

Use of the Brady collection is facilitated by two lists, both prepared in the Office of the Chief Signal Officer; one is a caption list (133 p.) and the other (24 p.) shows the names of Union and Confederate officers whose photographs are in the collection. There is also a numerical list (518 p.), prepared in the National Archives, of all the glass-plate negatives in the collection.

The Brady-Handy collection in the Library of Congress is described in the Library's Quarterly Journal of Current Acquisitions, 13:3 (May 1956); see also Hirst D. Milhollen and Donald H. Mugridge, Civil War Photographs, 1861-1865; a Catalog of Copy Negatives Made From Orig-

inals Selected From the Mathew B. Brady Collection in the Prints and Photographs Division of the Library of Congress (Washington, 1961). Many Brady photographs are reproduced in Roy Meredith, Mr. Lincoln's Camera Man (New York, 1946). See also the article on Brady in the Dictionary of American Biography; the booklet published by him in 1870, Brady's National Photographic Collection of War Views and Portraits of Representative Men; and Josephine Cobb, "Mathew B. Brady's Photographic Gallery in Washington," in Records of the Columbia Historical Society of Washington, D. C., 1953-1956, p. 28-69 (Washington, 1959).

Other Photographic or Pictorial Materials

Besides the Brady collection there are other Signal Corps collections of photographic or pictorial materials relating to the Civil War. One of these consists of approximately 2,300 film negatives of photographs, paintings, sketches, and drawings, 1861-74, in a numerical arrangement. There are mounted photographic prints corresponding to these; and the collection includes approximately 30 collodion negatives of photographs showing U. S. and Confederate fortifications in Atlanta, 1864. There are also, in a separate series, about 150 film negatives made from photographs of Quartermaster Corps transports in 1864, with mounted prints of these.

The comprehensive "Collection of Signal Corps Official Photographs," assembled between 1917 and 1938, contains approximately 110,000 glass-plate negatives and film negatives illustrating events in American military history from 1750 to 1938; there are mounted photographic prints corresponding to these negatives. Parallel or related developments on the American frontier and with respect to the American Indian during the period of the Civil War are depicted in several series of photographs of American frontier forts, U. S. Army units during the Indian wars, American Indians and Indian life, and Indian fighters--all dating from 1860.

Also on deposit is a print of "Screen Magazine No. 552," on Mathew Brady--a motion picture film, with sound track (2 reels, 35 mm.), produced by the Army Signal Corps in 1957.

Several unpublished lists or card indexes, prepared in the National Archives, facilitate the use of these collections. They include lists of Civil War views from sources other than Brady, of photographs showing ships in the Civil War period, of photographs of gunboats and transports in the Quartermaster's Department during the Civil War and beyond to 1872, and of railroad views in the Civil War period; and a card index of photographs of notables in the Civil War period. Finding aids prepared in the War Department include an Army War College list of Civil War views from sources other than Brady and the List of Photographs and Photographic Negatives Relating to the War for the Union, Now in the War Department Library . . . (Washington, 1897).

Records in Other Custody. -- The Albert J. Myer papers in the U. S. Army Signal Corps Museum at Fort Monmouth, N. J., contain, among other records that may be official in character, two Civil War message books of original manuscript messages kept by Lt. A. W. Bartlett; papers relating to Myer's New York Harbor tests, which resulted in the decision of the U. S. Army Signal Board (of which Col. Robert E. Lee was chairman) to adopt Myer's system for the Army; and records pertaining to the organizing of the Signal Corps in 1863.

Signal Camp of Instruction

On orders of Aug. 29, 1861, from Maj. Albert J. Myer (then with General McClellan at the headquarters of the newly formed Army of the Potomac) to Lt. Samuel T. Cushing, to "put the signal party in Camp of Instruction at Red Hill, Georgetown, tomorrow," the establishment of the Signal Camp of Instruction was announced by its General Order 1 on Aug. 31. The camp continued operations until Mar. 1862, when the Army of the Potomac took the field. It was discontinued on May 8, 1862, but was later reestablished as a school for officers and men and as a rendezvous for members of the Signal Corps when their duties required their presence in Washington. The headquarters of the Signal Corps was located for some time at the camp.

J. Willard Brown, The Signal Corps, U. S. A., in the War of the Rebellion (Boston, 1896); Lt. W. A. Glassford, "The Signal Corps," in Theo. F. Rodenbough and William L. Haskin, eds., The Army of the United States . . . (New York, 1896).

Record Group 111. --Copies of letters sent, Sept. 1863-Feb. 1865 (2 vols., nos. 100 and 57, the latter containing also copies of letters sent by the Chief Signal Officer, Department of Washington, Mar.-Aug. 1865); copies of indorsements sent, May 1864-Feb. 1865 (1 vol., no. 63--of special interest because it has indorsements sent by the Chief Signal Officer, Department of Washington, Mar.-Aug. 1865); orders and circulars received and issued, and letters received, Nov. 1862-Feb. 1865 (2 ft.); general and special orders issued, Mar. 1863-Feb. 1865 (1 vol., no. 64); daily and a few weekly morning reports, Apr. 1-May 5, 1862, and a few daily reports for Mar. 1862; a volume (no. 96) containing lists of enlisted men assigned to the camp, with personal data; and a fragmentary series of the proceedings of, and papers relating to, courts-martial at the camp.

National Archives, unpublished Preliminary Inventory of the Records of the Office of the Chief Signal Officer, comp. by Mabel E. Deutrich.

OFFICE OF THE INSPECTOR GENERAL

The Office of the Inspector General, abolished by an act of Aug. 23, 1842 (5 Stat. 512), was revived by an act of Jan. 12, 1846 (9 Stat. 2). At the outbreak of the Civil War two inspectors general were serving in the Army. An act of Aug. 3, 1861 (12 Stat. 287), provided for five assistant inspectors general with the rank of major; and one of Aug. 6, 1861 (12 Stat. 318), provided for two more inspectors general with the rank of colonel. By sec. 10 of an act of July 17, 1862 (12 Stat. 599), one assistant inspector general was authorized for each Army corps.

The number of inspectors general (those with the rank of colonel) remained at four throughout the war. In 1863 the Adjutant General directed the inspector general on permanent station in Washington to receive monthly reports from all inspectors; and in 1864 the office thus established became responsible for receiving all inspection reports that previously had been submitted to the Commanding General or to the Adjutant General. When not assigned to the armies in the field the inspectors general were under the orders of the Secretary of War. The organization of inspectors within an army command depended largely on the system devised by the assigned inspector general; there were, for instance, about 75 inspectors in the Army of the Potomac responsible to Inspector General Edmund Schriver, whose plan "required every brigade, every division, and every army corps to have an inspector."

The "ordinary duties of inspection," defined after the war (AGO G. O. 5, Jan. 22, 1866), were essentially to ascertain "the condition as to efficiency, discipline, supplies, etc., of bodies of troops, and the resources,

geographical features, lines of communications and supply, the military
wants, etc. , of any section of the country; the military status in any field
of operations; the condition and supply of military materials of various
classes; the condition of the administrative or disbursing departments of
the service; the efficiency and conduct of military commanders and agents;
the cause of failure or delay in movements or operations; of losses by accidents, disasters, etc. , and in general, all matters pertaining to the
military art or having interest in a military point of view. "

An act of Mar. 19, 1862 (12 Stat. 371), required that the inspectors
general of the Army should institute a board of officers to prepare a list
or schedule of articles that might be sold by sutlers to the officers and
soldiers of the volunteer service; and AGO S. O. 172, July 26, 1862, formally appointed Cols. Randolph B. Marcy, Delos B. Sacket, and Henry
Van Rensselaer as such a board. Another board on which an inspector
general served was that appointed by AGO Special Order 275, Oct. 10,
1861, "to examine into the merits of Professor Horsford's patent self-
raising bread preparation. "

Col. Sylvester Churchill, who had been Senior Inspector General from
June 25, 1841, retired Sept. 25, 1861, and on Aug. 9, 1861, Col. Randolph
B. Marcy became Senior Inspector General.

Maj. J. P. Sanger, "The In-   the United States (New York, 1896);
spector General's Department, "   Civil War annual reports of the
in Theo. F. Rodenbough and Wil-   Secretary of War, passim.
liam L. Haskin, eds. , The Army of

Record Group 159. -- The records most significant for Civil War research are the inspection reports, which in accordance with the Army regulations of 1861 were required to show the discipline and training of the
troops and the condition of their arms and clothing; the state of kitchens,
messes, barracks, guardhouses, and other post buildings; the management
of funds and care of records; the ability of line and staff officers; and the
conduct of courts-martial. These reports are filed in the series of letters
received from 1863 but are registered and extracted in separate volumes
from 1864. Besides a general index to and registers of letters received,
from 1863, there are 2 volumes of indexes to the 1864-65 extracts of inspection reports. The correspondence comprises also copies of letters
sent, 1863-89 (5 vols. and a 1-vol. index), and an endorsement book,
1863-67. Among miscellaneous records are the proceedings and reports
of the court of inquiry on the sale of cotton and other produce at St. Louis,
Mo. , 1863, with an index (see note on this court under Bureau of Military
Justice); papers concerning an inspection of the Louisville, Ky. , Quartermaster Depot in July 1865; memoranda of inspections by Gen. Edmund
Schriver, 1864; notes on inspections of forts and troops around Washington,
1864; and papers concerning a controversy about Cowles & Co.

National Archives, Preliminary   1939, comp. by Richard W. Giroux
Checklist of the Records of the Of-   (Washington, 1946).
fice of the Inspector General, 1814-

BUREAU OF REFUGEES, FREEDMEN, AND ABANDONED LANDS

An act of Mar. 3, 1865 (13 Stat. 507), established in the War Department "to continue during the present war of rebellion, and for one year thereafter" a Bureau of Refugees, Freedmen, and Abandoned Lands for the "supervision and management of all abandoned lands, and the control of all subjects relating to refugees and freedmen from rebel states, or from any district of country within the territory embraced in the operations of the army." The act provided that the President should appoint a Commissioner to head the Bureau and an Assistant Commissioner for each State declared to be in insurrection. The Commissioner was given "authority to set apart, for the use of loyal refugees and freedmen, such tracts of land within the insurrectionary states as shall have been abandoned, or to which the United States shall have acquired title by confiscation or sale, or otherwise." The new Bureau may be said to have been inaugurated on the morning of May 12, 1865, when, as Oliver Otis Howard wrote in his Autobiography, Secretary of War Stanton "sent for the papers." These, when the clerk in charge brought them--in a "large, oblong bushel basket heaped with letters and documents"--Stanton extended to Howard "with a smile and said 'Here, General, here's your Bureau.'" A formal War Department order appointing Howard Commissioner was issued the next day.

Before the Bureau was established, the military commanders, special agents of the Treasury Department, and various benevolent societies had dealt with the matters with which it was to be concerned. They had attempted to regulate the sale, leasing, and cultivation of abandoned lands; to oversee the employment of Negroes; to distribute rations, medicines, and supplies to the needy; to transport freedmen, refugees, and teachers; to provide for freedmen's education; to promote justice; and to help freedmen in filing claims against the Government. The work had been hindered, however, by lack of systematic and centralized administration. No such hindrance was to impede the work of the new Bureau, which Paul S. Peirce's study (1904) found to be "in the broadest sense of the term . . . a political organization, unique and gigantic," eventually "a full-fledged government, exercising throughout the unreconstructed South, legislative, executive and judicial authority, and in all, supported by the military forces of the United States." Its first objective, according to Secretary Stanton, in his annual report for 1865, was "to supply the immediate necessities of those whose condition was changed by hostilities, . . . either escaping or escaped from slavery to obtain freedom, or . . . driven from their homes by the pressure of war, or the despotism of the rebellion. Its aid was designed for the needy of both races, white and black, and to administer as well aid from the government and from charitable individuals and associations."

General Howard initially organized the Freedmen's Bureau (as it came to be known) in four divisions: "one of lands, embracing abandoned, confiscated, and those acquired by sale or otherwise; one of records, embracing official acts of the Commissioner, touching labor, schools, quartermaster and commissary supplies; another of financial affairs; and the fourth the medical department." Later, apparently growing out of the Records Division (actually the office of the Bureau's adjutant general), the Bureau had an Education Division, a Chief Quartermaster's Office, and an Archive Division. Eventually a Claim Division was established, responsible for certain functions of the Land Division, and there appears to have

been a separate office for the assistant inspector general. The details of
the organization and responsibilities of these Divisions are given below.

The Bureau operated in all the former Confederate States and in Delaware, Kentucky, Maryland, Missouri, West Virginia, and the District of
Columbia. Assistant Commissioners, in charge of defined geographical
areas, exercised all of the functions of the Bureau under the direction of
the Washington headquarters. Most of the Assistant Commissioners were
officers detailed from the Army, and the jurisdiction of each usually corresponded with that of a military division or department and embraced a
single State. By 1866, whenever practicable, military commanders in the
States were being appointed Assistant Commissioners. Although the State
organizations were supposed to include at least a medical officer, a finance
officer, an inspector, two or more district superintendents, an officer in
charge of schools, and enough local agents to provide adequate Bureau
representation, actual practice varied from State to State. Unfortunately
the use of soldiers and officers borrowed from the nearest military organizations confused administration and (at least in the public eye) identified the Bureau with the occupying armies.

The Freedmen's Bureau undertook many tasks in addition to its major
functions of administering relief and supervising labor. Commissioner
Howard felt that the most urgent need of the freedmen was education, and
from the first he devoted more attention to this than to any other branch of
his work. Other tasks included finding missing persons and officiating at
the marriage of Negroes. (The Bureau's Circular 5 of May 30, 1865, provided for the designation of officers to keep a record of marriages in
"places where the local statutes make no provisions for the marriages of
persons of color." When no clergyman could "conveniently be reached,"
commissioned officers of the Freedmen's Bureau were authorized to perform the ceremony. "The registry books will be so arranged that marriages shall be recorded in alphabetical order of the surname of bridegrooms.
This will make reference to the books easy.")

The 1866 investigation by Gen. James B. Steedman and Gen. Joseph S.
Fullerton of the Bureau's operations in Virginia and North Carolina resulted
in widely publicized disclosures of maladministration that tended to shake
public confidence (see H. Ex. Doc. 120, 39 Cong., 1 sess., Serial 1263).
President Johnson had expressed his opposition to an extension of the Bureau's responsibilities on Feb. 19, 1866, when he vetoed a bill to amend the
act establishing the Bureau. An act of July 16, 1866 (14 Stat. 173), nevertheless, continued the Bureau for 2 more years, and sec. 2 extended its
supervision and care to "all loyal refugees and freedmen . . . to enable
them as speedily as practicable to become self-supporting citizens of the
United States, and to aid them in making the freedom conferred by proclamation of the commander-in-chief, by emancipation under the laws of
States, and by constitutional amendment, available to them and beneficial
to the republic." An act of July 6, 1868 (15 Stat. 83), extended the life of
the Bureau for yet another year, but the Secretary of War was required to
discontinue the Bureau's operation in any State "fully restored in its constitutional relations with the government of the United States," including
representation in Congress, unless, in his opinion, further continuance
of the Bureau in such a State was necessary. In no event, however, was the
educational work of the Bureau to be affected until a State had made suitable
provision for the education of the children of its freedmen.

An act of July 25, 1868 (15 Stat. 193), required the Commissioner to discontinue Bureau activities in the several States by the end of the year, except for functions pertaining to education and the payment of "moneys due the soldiers, sailors, marines, or their heirs." Orders went out promptly for the settlement of outstanding accounts, the sale of public property no longer needed, the restoration of abandoned lands to their owners, and the relinquishment to civil magistrates and other civil officials of full responsiblity for the welfare of freedmen. The freedmen's hospitals at New Orleans, Vicksburg, Louisville, Richmond, and Washington could not be closed at once without exposing many helpless patients to great distress. Since local authorities were not available to take charge of these hospitals, the Commissioner, with the approval of the Secretary of War, determined to continue them until an appeal could be made to Congress for further action. The continuance of the hospitals at Richmond, Vicksburg, and Washington was authorized by an act of Apr. 7, 1869 (16 Stat. 8).

As the result of a resolution offered in the House of Representatives by Fernando Wood of New York in 1870, the operations of the Freedmen's Bureau were investigated by the Committee on Education and Labor; and the brief report of the majority (H. Rept. 121, 41 Cong., 2 sess., Serial 1438) exonerated General Howard of charges of "malversation and dereliction of duty." The Bureau's operations as it neared its end were restricted to the care of the hospital in the District of Columbia; the collection and payment of bounties and other money due colored soldiers, sailors, and marines; such supervision of the educational work as could be given; and such other aid as could be rendered by counsel alone. The collection and payment of bounties, however, took up the time of nearly all the agents and clerks remaining on duty.

The Sundry Civil Appropriations Act of June 10, 1872 (17 Stat. 366), provided for the discontinuance of the Bureau from and after June 30 of that year; consequently the Bureau's unfinished business (except that relating to the Freedmen's Hospital and Asylum at Washington) was turned over to the Adjutant General's Office on July 1. Asst. Adj. Gen. Thomas McC. Vincent, to whom the Adjutant General assigned "immediate supervision and charge of the duties lately devolving" on the Freedmen's Bureau, reported that the Bureau's records were confused and incomplete when removed from Howard University. General Howard, however, maintained not only that the records had been well kept but that any seeming deficiency in them could be explained by (a) the Bureau's inability, through lack of sufficient funds, to index, brief, and put in final arrangement the accounts and reports of the various divisions and districts; (b) carelessness in transferring the records; and (c) the unfamiliarity of the new force with them. Some of the records of the Bureau were found afterward in the Washington office of the Baltimore and Ohio Railroad, where they had remained in boxes for over 18 months.

Further disclosures, after the Bureau's demise, of discrepancies in its accounts, particularly of the Claim Division, were investigated by a War Department court of inquiry convened under a joint resolution of Feb. 13, 1874 (18 Stat. 285), presided over by General Sherman; but the court was as strong in its approval of General Howard's administration as the House Committee on Education and Labor had been in 1870.

National Archives, Preliminary Checklist of the Records of the Bureau of Refugees, Freedmen, and Abandoned Lands, 1865-1872, comp.

by Elizabeth Bethel, Sara Dunlap, and Lucille Pendell (Washington, 1946); Oliver Otis Howard, Autobiography (New York, 1907); Paul Skeels Peirce, The Freedmen's Bureau; a Chapter in the History of Reconstruction (State University of Iowa, Studies in Sociology, Economics, Politics, and History, vol. 3, no. 1. Iowa City, 1904); Henderson H. Donald, The Negro Freedman (New York, 1952); George R. Bentley, A History of the Freedmen's Bureau (Philadelphia, 1955); War Department, Judge Advocate General's Department, Proceedings, Findings and Opinion of Court of Inquiry . . . in the Case of Oliver Otis Howard (Washington, 1874). Compilations of orders issued by and reports received from assistant commissioners appear in S. Ex. Doc. 27, 39 Cong., 1 sess., Serial 1238; S. Ex. Doc. 6, 39 Cong., 2 sess., Serial 1276; H. Ex. Doc. 70, 39 Cong., 1 sess., Serial 1256; and H. Ex. Doc. 329, 40 Cong., 2 sess., Serial 1346. The report of the Committee on Freedmen's Affairs, Mar. 10, 1868 (H. Rept. 30, 40 Cong., 2 sess., Serial 1357), reviews the work of the Bureau. Annual reports of the Commissioner were printed as follows:

1865. H. Ex. Doc. 11, 39 Cong., 1 sess., Serial 1255.
1866. H. Ex. Doc. 1, 39 Cong., 2 sess., Serial 1285.
1867. H. Ex. Doc. 1, 40 Cong., 2 sess., Serial 1324.
1868. H. Ex. Doc. 1, 40 Cong., 3 sess., Serial 1367.
1869. H. Ex. Doc. 1, 41 Cong., 2 sess., Serial 1412.
1870. H. Ex. Doc. 1, 41 Cong., 3 sess., Serial 1446.
1871. H. Ex. Doc. 1, 42 Cong., 2 sess., Serial 1502.

Records Division

This Division, headed by the adjutant general of the Bureau, was one of the four established at first by Commissioner Howard. Since it recorded "official acts of the Commissioner, touching labor, schools, quartermaster and commissary supplies," its records cover the whole range of Bureau activities.

Record Group 105. --The main file of Bureau correspondence includes copies of many letters sent over Howard's signature; letters, reports, and other papers received by him; and correspondence of the adjutant general and other Bureau officials. Much of this correspondence, which relates to all aspects of Bureau functions, is addressed to or received from the Secretary of War, other War Department officials, the Assistant Commissioners in the several States in which the Bureau operated, State Governors, and various societies interested in freedmen. There are copies of letters sent, May 1865-June 1872 (7 vols., with 5 vols. of indexes and 6 vols. of press copies); a volume of press copies of letters sent relating to claims for bounties and pensions, July-Sept. 1868; copies of letters authorizing school building expenditures, Sept. 1869-June 1870 (2 vols.); rough drafts of letters sent from the Commissioner's office, 1867-70 (5 in.); copies of endorsements, May 1865-Jan. 1871 (6 vols.), with indexes (6 vols.); and letters received, May 1865-May 1872 (ca. 10 ft.), with registers (18 vols.) and indexes (18 vols.). Other records of relatively high importance are the weekly, monthly, and annual reports of the Assistant Commissioners, 1865-70 (4 ft.), some of them abstracted (4 vols.); station books showing assignments of officers and civilians, 1866-72 (7 vols.); lists of civilian appointments, 1866-72 (2 vols., with partial index); copies of letters of appointment

and of revocation of appointment, Oct. 1867-June 1872 (10 vols.); and copies of circulars and circular letters of instruction, issued usually by order
of Commissioner Howard, May 1865-July 1869 (1 vol.). There are also a
file of papers relating to the Bureau's operations, 1865-68 (5 in.), received
from the Executive Mansion in 1874; some letters, 1867-68 (5 in.), received
by T. D. Eliot, chairman of the House Committee on Freedmen's Affairs,
urging continuance of the Bureau; lists of destitute persons in South Carolina,
1866 (5 in.), and articles of agreement with the planters of that State, 1867
(5 in.); and papers relating to the claim of Maj. George J. Alden, 1865-70
(5 in.), concerning property leased to him in Florida. Still other records
include reports on rations issued by the Assistant Commissioners, 1865-
69 (20 in.); weekly inspection reports of buildings occupied by the Commissioner and by Howard University, 1869-70 (5 in.); and a file of letters and
affidavits concerning criminal offenses against freedmen in Texas, 1868
(5 in.).

Records in Other Custody. --The Oliver Otis Howard papers in the Bow-
doin College Library, Brunswick, Maine, include letters received during
Howard's term as Commissioner of the Freedmen's Bureau, 1866-72 (47
vols.). Other Howard papers are at Howard University, Washington, D. C. ,
and Lincoln Memorial University, Harrowgate, Tenn.

Land Division

The act establishing the Freedmen's Bureau charged it with the supervision and management of all abandoned lands--that is, lands taken by the
Government while their lawful owners were voluntarily absent bearing arms
or otherwise aiding or encouraging the Confederacy. Most such property
was held by Treasury agents, and they, in compliance with the Secretary of
the Treasury's circular of June 27, 1865 (prompted by Executive order of
June 2, 1865), turned their holdings over to the Bureau. Other agencies of
the Government did the same. The control of abandoned lands and of those
confiscated or otherwise acquired was made the responsibility of the Land
Division.

The initial policy was to restore lands only to those former owners "who
could show constant loyalty, past as well as present." President Johnson,
however, insisted that a person pardoned was entitled to immediate restoration of his land (unless it had been sold under confiscation decree). The Bureau thereupon issued Circular 15, Sept. 12, 1865, which promulgated the first
definite rules on property restoration. The restoration of abandoned property
greatly disappointed the freedmen who had expected gifts of land from the
Government. By Oct. 1868 nearly all the abandoned lands had been restored
to their owners.

Successive heads of the Land Division:

Maj. William Fowler, 1865.

Maj. Gen. Albion P. Howe, 1867.

Record Group 105. --The surviving records of the Land Division, 1865-
70 (less than 8 ft.), comprise copies of letters sent and endorsements; office memoranda; the Division's special orders and circulars; letters received,
registered and indexed; a list of confiscated property (1 vol.); registers
of abandoned lands and confiscated property (9 vols.); applications and orders
for property restoration; and monthly and yearly reports from Assistant Commissioners listing abandoned and confiscated lands in their custody. Each
entry in the property registers shows name of owner; description, location,

and value of property; date of abandonment, seizure, or confiscation; and by whom and when restored; and sometimes gives additional remarks.

Claim Division

In Mar. 1866 the officer heading the Land Division began to act without charge as claim agent for colored soldiers and to prepare for settlement their bounty and other claims. This activity, soon formalized as the Claim Division, arose from the constant complaints to agents and officers of the Bureau by discharged colored soldiers who had been defrauded of the amounts due them or had been induced to believe that bounties and arrears of pay were due them when such was not the case. Many discharged soldiers were idly waiting in cities for action on their claims, and the expense of feeding and lodging them fell on the Government. The Commissioner had reason to believe that brokers charged exorbitant fees when they actually made collections and sometimes retained the entire amount collected. The Claim Division was organized, therefore, to prevent such frauds on colored soldiers and to help those who were destitute in obtaining money that otherwise might be lost to them. Officers and field agents of the Bureau were directed to receive all claims presented by colored soldiers and sailors and their families for arrears of pay, bounty, pensions, and prize money and to forward them to the office in Washington for settlement. The Claim Division was responsible also for the examination of Treasury certificates and checks issued in settlement of colored soldiers' claims; under a joint resolution of Congress of Apr. 10, 1869 (16 Stat. 55), these were made payable to the soldiers themselves, the Commissioner, or some other public official, and payments to claim agents or persons holding soldiers' powers of attorney were forbidden. From 1870 the Commissary General of Subsistence referred to the Claim Division, for necessary evidence, the claims of colored soldiers for commutation of rations while prisoners of war; and the Pension Office sent communications and checks to colored pensioners through the Division.

Record Group 105.--Records of assistance to discharged colored soldiers and sailors and their families, in the collection of amounts due them, 1866-72 (ca. 38 ft.), consist principally of copies of letters sent (with indexes), copies of endorsements, and letters received (with indexes and registers) by the Certificate, Complaints, and Prosecution Branches of the Claim Division. Certificate Branch records include also a register of claimants and registers of certificates received from attorneys acting on behalf of claimants. Records of the Prosecution Branch, which are very important for establishing the facts of military service of many individual colored soldiers and sailors during the Civil War, include such items as long lists of names of persons entitled to bounty (in the registers of letters received); pension claims and pension record books; pay and bounty claims; and claims for prize money, commutation of rations, and substitute money.

Medical Division

Although the act establishing the Freedmen's Bureau made no provision for medical or hospital service, the Medical Division was soon set up in the Bureau. Its first duty was to meet the needs of persons in actual physical distress, by detailing surgeons in the several States and furnishing medical supplies. In the summer of 1865 the surgeons were instructed to relieve the Medical Department of the Army of the care of sick refugees and freedmen, to aid the Assistant Commissioners in establishing new hospitals, and to minister to the sick. They were assisted by a staff of physicians and medical attendants. Many of the hospitals previously established by the Army, the Sanitary Commissions, and freedmen's aid societies were continued and enlarged, as were the asylums and "colonies" or infirmaries; a few hospitals were replaced by dispensaries or other less expensive establishments. The maximum number of hospitals was reached in Sept. 1867, with a capacity of 5,292 beds. Peirce estimated that nearly a million persons were given medical aid by the Bureau during its existence, at a total cost to the Government of approximately $2,000,000.

Successive chief medical officers of the Bureau:

C. W. Horner, 1865.

L. A. Edwards, 1866.

R. Reyburn, 1869.

Record Group 105. --The extant correspondence of the Medical Division in this record group consists of copies of letters sent by the Chief Medical Officer, 1867-70 (1 vol.); copies of his endorsements, 1865-71 (3 vols.); and letters received from the chief medical officers serving under the Assistant Commissioners in the several States, 1866-70 (10 in.). There are an index to the letters sent and a partial register of those received. A volume listing names and addresses of Bureau surgeons is not dated.

Record Group 94. --Bureau medical records that were mingled with those of the Surgeon General and eventually became part of the files of the Record and Pension Office by association with the carded records (see the section on that Office) include monthly returns of commissioned medical officers and physicians employed under contract, 1865-69 (6 in.); contracts with female employees at hospitals, 1865-69 (3 in.), and with service personnel such as ambulance drivers and druggists, 1865-70 (3 in.); reports on such service personnel, 1868-71 (1 1/2 ft.); and reports and receipt rolls of Medical Department personnel hired in North Carolina, 1866-68 (3 in.).

Education Division

The Bureau's educational work was under the general direction of Capt. S. L. Taggart, and each Assistant Commissioner appointed a superintendent of education for his State.

Record Group 105. --The Division's records include copies of letters sent, 1866-68, by the Inspector of Schools and Finance and the Office of the General Superintendent of Schools (2 vols.), with a name index; press copies of letters sent by the Office of the General Superintendent of Schools, 1866-71 (7 vols.); copies of endorsements on letters received, June 1867-Sept. 1870 (1 vol. , indexed); and copies of letters of appointment to the Division, Aug. 1869-Nov. 1870 (1 vol.). Letters received by the General Superintendent of Education, 1866-70 (20 in.), include those from societies and individuals interested in the education of freedmen and from State Superintendents of education; these are registered (3 vols.) and indexed (4 vols.). Other important records are reports of State superintendents of education, 1865-70 (4 ft.), abstracted in part; schedules of schools and rental accounts received from secretaries of private freedmen's aid societies, 1868-70 (5 in.); abstracts of monthly statistical reports of State superintendents of education, Oct. 1866-June 1870 (1 vol.); lists of teachers employed by such organizations as the Friends Freedmen Association of Philadelphia, the American Missionary Society, and Presbyterian Committee on Home

Missions (1 vol.); and materials pertaining to the histories of societies interested in freedmen.

Office of the Chief Disbursing Officer

When the Bureau was established the Chief Disbursing Officer was put in charge of finances drawn from miscellaneous sources, since it was thought that abandoned and confiscated Confederate property would provide sufficient revenue for the Bureau's support. Eventually, however, the Disbursing Officer handled the following funds:

Refugees' and freedmen's fund: the money derived from miscellaneous sources from which the current expenses of the Freedmen's Bureau were paid until July 1, 1866, consisting of the surplus of the War Department's "Department of Negro Affairs" and receipts from the sale of crops grown on abandoned lands, the rental of real estate, the sale of Confederate property, transportation and supplies, the school tax, and various other sources.

"Retained" or "irregular" bounty fund: a fund created by the retention of a part of the money sent by some of the States to officers serving in the South to buy substitutes among the colored people and thus fill up the States' quotas under the draft. This fund, by President Johnson's order of June 2, 1865, was turned over to the disbursing officers of the Bureau of Refugees, Freedmen, and Abandoned Lands; and an act of Mar. 2, 1867 (14 Stat. 545), designated the Commissioner of the Bureau as trustee of the fund and authorized him to invest it in U. S. bonds for the sole benefit of the soldiers themselves "or their legal representatives." This money was not considered public funds but was held in trust by the United States for the holders of certificates of deposit. The Bureau's agents were active in discovering rightful claimants and expediting payments.

Destitute relief fund: an appropriation, by a joint resolution of Congress, Apr. 17, 1866 (14 Stat. 353), of $25,000 for "the temporary relief of the destitute population of the District of Columbia," and other appropriations, 1867 and 1868 (15 Stat. 20, 41).

Appropriation fund: a part of the Army appropriation, necessary after June 30, 1866, because of insufficient revenue from abandoned lands and other captured property.

School fund: a fund created under sec. 12 of an act of July 16, 1886 (14 Stat. 176), which empowered the Commissioner "to seize, hold, use, lease, or sell" real properties "formerly held under color of title by the late so-called confederate states . . . and to use the same or appropriate the proceeds derived therefrom to the education of the freed people."

Pay, bounty, and prize money fund: a fund created by a joint resolution of Congress, Mar. 29, 1867 (15 Stat. 26), requiring that payments in settlement of claims for pay, bounty, prize money, or other moneys due to colored soldiers, sailors, or marines be made to the Commissioner of the Freedmen's Bureau, whose agents would then locate and pay the rightful claimants.

Besides disbursing payments from these funds, the Chief Disbursing Officer managed the procurement and distribution of commissary supplies.

Successive holders of this office:

Lt. Col. (later Brig. Gen.) George W. Balloch.

Maj. J. M. Brown.

Record Group 105.--The general files of the Chief Disbursing Officer comprise copies of miscellaneous letters sent, Apr. 1867-Dec. 1872 (9 vols.), with indexes (8 vols.); miscellaneous letters received, 1865-72

(39 vols.), with indexes and registers (8 vols.); copies of letters sent relating to estimates of funds needed by field offices, Aug. 1866-Apr. 1867 (1 vol.); daily statements of funds, Oct. 1871-June 1872 (1 vol.); and letters received from the Chief Quartermaster authorizing payment of claims against the Quartermaster's Department, 1866-71 (1 ft.). The records pertaining specifically to the different funds handled consist of the journal, June 1865-Jan. 1872, and accounts current, Oct. 1865-Sept. 1870, of the "refugees and freedmen fund"; accounts current of the "school fund"; ledger of the "appropriation fund," July 1866-Mar. 1872; and, with respect to bounties, registers of payments, Apr. 1867-June 1872, indexed, registers of vouchers, 1867-72, consolidated reports on unpaid claims, 1869-71, and copies of letters sent, Apr. 1867-70 (10 vols., with indexes by personal name). Other financial records include the disbursing officers' accounts current and disbursement ledgers, 1866-71; monthly reports of rents received on abandoned property held by the Bureau, 1865-68; reports of expenditures by disbursing officers, 1865-Feb. 1866; and miscellaneous other records, including contraband fund accounts. There is a small file of inventories of the effects of deceased colored citizens and soldiers who were employed by the Bureau at the time of their death.

Office of the Chief Quartermaster

Although not provided for in the initial organization of the Washington office of the Bureau, the appointment of an officer to direct the distribution of quartermaster's supplies soon became necessary. The transportation of refugees and freedmen to places where work had been found for them also became an important function of this Office.

Record Group 105. --The letters sent by the Chief Quartermaster, Oct. 1866-June 1872 (7 vols. of copies and 15 of press copies), are addressed principally to officials in the various Assistant Commissioners' headquarters and to societies interested in freedmen; these are indexed (7 vols.). Other correspondence consists of letters received, 1866-69 and 1871-72 (2 ft., registered in 3 vols. and indexed in 5); and letters referred to the Chief Quartermaster by endorsement, Sept. 1866-Jan. 1871 (2 1/2 ft., registered in 3 vols. and indexed in 7). The Chief Quartermaster's records also include registers, Nov. 1866-Apr. 1871, of transportation accounts with railroad and steamship companies (3 vols.); a register, Dec. 1868-May 1871, of passenger and freight transaction claims; records of expenditures for rent, repair, and construction of schoolhouses, 1867-70 (1 vol.); rosters of Bureau officers, 1865-71 (5 vols.), with indexes (2 vols.); station books showing assignments of officers and civilians, 1868 (3 vols.); special orders received from the Commissioner, Sept. 1869-Apr. 1871; and copies of special orders issued by the Chief Quartermaster, Oct. 1866-Dec. 1870.

Office of the Assistant Inspector General

Special Order 36 of the Bureau of Refugees, Freedmen, and Abandoned Lands assigned to an Assistant Inspector General the distribution of supplies to destitute persons in the South.

Record Group 105.--The records preserved separately by this Office, all pertaining to its supply functions, include press copies of letters sent, Mar. 1867-Aug. 1868 (1 vol.); copies of letters transmitting returns to the Third Auditor of the Treasury, Mar. 1867-Apr. 1868 (10 in.); letters received, 1867-68 (5 in.), with a register; and copies of congressional resolutions and War Department orders concerning the relief of the destitute, with associated correspondence, 1867 (1 vol.).

Archive Division

This Division received and stored the records of the Bureau offices as they were closed, especially the field records maintained by the headquarters of the Assistant Commissioners and their subordinate district and subdistrict headquarters.

Record Group 105. --Press copies of letters sent by the Division, July-Dec. 1869 (1 vol.); copies of endorsements for the same period (1 vol.); a register of letters received, Jan. 1869-Oct. 1870; and a list (2 vols.) of the book records of some of the Bureau's divisions.

Assistant Commissioners' Headquarters

The defined geographical areas administered under the direction of the Bureau by Assistant Commissioners are discussed below, and the important facts about the offices and records of the Assistant Commissioners are given. The following quotation from the report of Maj. Gen. Thomas J. Wood, Assistant Commissioner for Mississippi, Oct. 30, 1866, reflects an ideal conception of the functions of the Bureau's field organization:

> The duties performed by officers are . . . to keep themselves well informed on the following points, viz: 1st, number of freedmen under charge; 2d, condition and manner in which they are being treated and paid; 3d, kind of contracts, and whether the freedmen understand the force of their obligations; 4th, whether any sick, old, or infirm are suffering from want of clothing, food, or medical attendance, and to have them in such cases transferred to the regular bureau hospitals for care and treatment; 5th, how many schools are in session and how many have been opened, what their condition is, and what can be done for their improvement; 6th, disposition of the white people to the black; 7th, the manner in which the State laws affecting the freedmen are administered.
> Officers are . . . directed to put themselves in communication with prominent citizens of either color, and with the State and other officials resident within their districts. They must obtain the confidence of both white and colored citizens, that the white citizens may know that the bureau officer is to labor faithfully to instil into the colored man's mind the necessity of obeying the laws, and to seek to improve himself by education and by faithful and honest labor; that the interests of all classes are coincident; that the colored citizen has a friend and counsellor in the bureau officer, anxious to secure all to him which will add to his comfort and happiness, and to secure to him through the courts all his rights of person and property as a citizen.

Alabama

On July 26, 1865, Brig. Gen. Wager Swayne became Assistant Commissioner for Alabama, with headquarters at Montgomery. On Aug. 30 the State was divided into five districts with headquarters at Mobile, Selma,

Montgomery, Troy, and Demopolis. Centers of Bureau operations were
later established also at Huntsville, Greenville, Tuscaloosa, and Talla-
dega. Since Alabama, occupied by Union forces relatively late in the war,
had no lands classified as abandoned, the Bureau there was supported at
first by the sale and rental of property formerly belonging to the Confederate government. General Swayne had to rely almost entirely on the
military and State authorities for officers to act as agents and for necessary
supplies. The judges of the State were Bureau agents appointed for the administration of justice, and the State legislature created the Office of Commissioner for the Destitute to assist in distributing provisions. The organization of the Bureau, at first purely experimental, took shape by Nov. 1865.
It consisted mainly of officers stationed wherever they could be obtained by
detail to advise and protect the freedmen and to do for the extremely poor
whatever resources would permit. The number of such officers was unfortunately few and was constantly reduced by the removal and muster-out of
their regiments. Their principal care was the charge of labor contracts.
Great numbers of these were examined, explained to the freedmen, and,
if fair and mutually acceptable, approved.

  With respect to educational work in Alabama, the Assistant Commissioner quoted in his 1867 report the evaluation of a "distinguished officer"
of the Third Military District that "the marvelous progress made by the
freed people in education and knowledge finds no parallel in history."

  Successive Assistant Commissioners:

  Brig. Gen. (later Maj. Gen.) Wager Swayne, July 26, 1865.
  Bvt. Brig. Gen. Julius Hayden, Jan. 14, 1868.
  Bvt. Brig. Gen. Oliver L. Shepherd, Mar. 31, 1868.
  Bvt. Maj. Gen. Thomas H. Ruger, Aug. 13, 1868.
  Bvt. Lt. Col. Edwin Beecher, Aug. 18, 1868.

  Record Group 105. --The extant records of this headquarters (ca. 30 ft.)
consist chiefly of book records (ca. 200 vols.) of the Assistant Commissioner's office, the inspector general and disbursing officer, the chief medical officer, the chief quartermaster, the superintendent of education, and
the district and subdistrict offices, 1865-72. These book records (listed in
1 vol.) include registers of letters received, letters-sent books, endorsements, orders and circulars, claims records, employment registers, contracts, freedmen's court records, hospital records, and registers of complaints. For the Assistant Commissioner there are also files of letters and
telegrams received, circulars and circular letters, and reports. Unbound
records of the superintendent of education consist of letters received, teachers' school reports, other reports, and miscellaneous papers. Unbound
records of the chief quartermaster comprise letters received and reports
of "persons and article hired." Among other unbound records are applications and certificates for relief, land reports, test oaths, rosters of justices of the peace, and various narrative and statistical reports. Unbound
records of the districts and subdistricts include labor contracts and reports
on them, articles of agreement, and reports of cases tried.

Arkansas

  See Missouri and Arkansas, below.

District of Columbia

Although the act creating the Bureau made no reference to the District of Columbia, General Howard immediately called to Washington Col. John Eaton, Jr., from the Mississippi Valley, where he had been superintending freedmen, and put him in charge of Bureau activities in Washington and the District. By the end of 1865 a general school system had been established and hospitals were in operation at Washington, Alexandria, and Freedmen's Village. Five "intelligence offices"--employment offices for freedmen--were in operation. Eaton's jurisdiction included at first the District of Columbia; the Maryland counties of Prince Georges, St. Marys, Charles, Calvert, and part of Anne Arundel; and the Virginia counties of Alexandria, Fairfax, and Loudoun. (On Aug. 16, 1866, Loudoun County was detached from this district.) A competent officer was put in charge of each county, and there were also a local superintendent for the cities of Washington and Georgetown, an officer at Freedmen's Village and in charge of the farm at Arlington, Va., and an officer for the three counties of Virginia, with headquarters at Alexandria. When Bvt. Maj. Gen. J. M. Schofield was given command of the First Military District, he was made Assistant Commissioner for the entire State of Virginia. The counties of Alexandria and Fairfax were detached in Mar. 1867, therefore, from the supervision of the Assistant Commissioner for the District of Columbia, who at the same time was assigned charge of freedmen's affairs in West Virginia also.

Since no freedmen's or provost courts operated in Maryland and the District of Columbia, a solicitor to work in freedmen's interests was appointed early in 1866. Also appointed was a superintendent of marriages, with whom all agents of the Bureau, the preachers of colored churches, and other volunteer workers were required to cooperate in behalf of the freedmen.

To combat abuses of the apprentice system in Maryland, Henry Stockbridge of Baltimore was appointed, Apr. 2, 1867, as the Bureau's special agent. In the field of education, although the Bureau did not conduct schools or pay teachers' salaries in Washington and vicinity, it provided most of the buildings for schools, and it sponsored Howard University, chartered by an act of Mar. 2, 1867 (14 Stat. 438). On Aug. 15, 1868, the Bureau's affairs in Maryland and Delaware were assigned to the Assistant Commissioner for the District of Columbia. The settlement of the claims of the many colored soldiers recruited in those States resulted in an extensive workload.

Successive Assistant Commissioners:

Bvt. Brig. Gen. John Eaton, Jr., May 1865.
Bvt. Brig. Gen. Joseph S. Fullerton, Dec. 4, 1865.
Bvt. Brig. Gen. Charles H. Howard, Feb. 7, 1866.

Record Group 105.--The extant records (ca. 29 ft.) consist chiefly of book records (ca. 100 vols.) of the Assistant Commissioner, the superintendent of education, the inspector general, the quartermaster and disbursing officer, the local superintendent, the first subdistrict, Freedmen's Village, and the employment agents, 1865-70. These book records (listed in 1 vol.) include registers of letters received, letters-sent books, endorsements, orders and circulars, marriage records, station books of officers and civilians, registers of applicants for servants, and reports concerning land, rations, clothing, and the erection of schoolhouses. Other (unbound) records of the Assistant Commissioner include letters received, and those of the superintendent of education comprise letters received, school reports, deeds to school buildings, and miscellaneous related papers.   There are also reports on abandoned or confiscated lands, occupation of "tenements" under Bureau charge, and the issuance of rations, clothing, and medicine.   Letters received by the quartermaster and disbursing officer and related contracts and proposals concern the requisitioning, transportation, furnishing, and "funding" of supplies.   Records of the employment of freedmen and care of the destitute are in files of the local superintendent, who had charge of such matters.   Other records pertain to Freedmen's Village at Arlington Heights; sick and wounded refugees and freedmen at Freedmen's Hospital; the Industrial School and home schools for freed children; the Commission for the Relief of Destitute Colored Persons in the District of Columbia; and the receipt and disbursement of funds.   "Descriptive lists of freed people for whom transportation is requested by employment agents" (15 in.) show the personal characteristics of freedmen, names of former owners, and former residences.

Florida

Jurisdiction over freedmen's affairs in Florida appears for a time to have been vested in the office of the Assistant Commissioner at Beaufort, S. C.; but on Sept. 19, 1865, Bvt. Col. Thomas W. Osborn was designated as Assistant Commissioner for Florida, with headquarters at Tallahassee. The system of "freedmen's affairs" inaugurated in eastern Florida during the war had brought freed people within the Union lines and, long before the end of hostilities, had established educational and agricultural facilities for them.   Each subdistrict, composed of several counties, was under the supervision of an Army officer, with a civil agent to attend to detailed business under his general direction.   The agents were either judges, justices of the peace, ex-officers of volunteers, or citizens of character and influence who were willing to do the work.   The State courts were given jurisdiction over all freedmen's cases that could properly be brought before them, but the agents watched the cases to ensure impartial justice. For matters especially subject to the decision of the Bureau (such as the division of crops, the stipulations and fulfilment of contracts, and the sequestration of property of refugees) its agents established boards of arbitration, which settled disputes without recourse to the courts.
Successive Assistant Commissioners:
Bvt. Col. Thomas W. Osborn, Sept. 19, 1865.
Bvt. Maj. Gen. John G. Foster, June 1, 1866.
Col. John T. Sprague, Dec. 5, 1866.
Bvt. Brig. Gen. George W. Gile, Nov. 1, 1868.
Record Group 105.--The extant records (ca. 8 ft.) consist chiefly of book records (ca. 25 vols.) of the Assistant Commissioner, the superintendent of education, the surgeon in chief, and the district offices, 1865-72.   These book records include registers of letters received, letters-sent books, endorsements, orders and circulars, books showing rations issued, and bounty registers; they are indexed (1 vol.).   Unbound records of the Assistant Commissioner include letters and special orders received, oaths of office, copies of his land reports, reports of boards of officers to establish rents, and annual and monthly operations reports of subordinate officials.   There are also letters received by the superintendent of education and school reports; reports of agents describing homesteads on which

freedmen were settled; letters received by the chief disbursing officer; and ration applications.

Other records relating to the operations of the Bureau in Florida are among those of the Assistant Commissioner for South Carolina.

Georgia

Administration of Bureau affairs in this State was for a time vested in the office of the Assistant Commissioner at Beaufort, S. C. On Sept. 22, 1865, however, Brig. Gen. Davis Tillson assumed his duties as Assistant Commissioner for Georgia, with headquarters at Augusta.

Because it was impossible to get enough Army officers to staff the Bureau in Georgia, 244 civil agents were appointed on the recommendation of members of the State Convention. These agents were to serve without salary but were authorized to retain their fees from employers and freedmen for witnessing and approving contracts. When it became apparent that the powers so delegated had been abused, this system was discontinued and only salaried agents were employed for Bureau duty. The fee system, although practiced in some other States under Bureau control, had a prejudicial influence upon neighboring States where it was not used, and it came to be regarded with suspicion by the freed people. At the time of the change to salaried agents in Georgia (Feb. 1867), the supervision of civilian agents remote from the central office was strengthened by the organization of 11 districts, each including a number of contiguous counties; and a better system was adopted for transacting current business and transmitting reports.

The administration of justice through the Bureau's courts in Georgia and by provost courts and military commissions was a continuing problem for both the Assistant Commissioner and the commander of the military department encompassing the State.

Successive Assistant Commissioners:

Brig. Gen. Davis Tillson, Sept. 22, 1865.
Col. Caleb C. Sibley, Jan. 14, 1867.
Bvt. Brig. Gen. John R. Lewis, Oct. 16, 1868.

Record Group 105. --The extant records (ca. 50 ft.) consist chiefly of book records (ca. 400 vols.) of the Assistant Commissioner, the superintendent of education, the surgeon in chief, the chief quartermaster and disbursing officer, and the district and subdistrict offices, 1865-72. These book records include registers of letters received, letters-sent books, endorsements, orders and circulars, station books of officers and rosters of civil agents, accounting records, hospital records, registers of contracts, registers of complaints, records of bounty claimants, and records of trials and freedmen's courts; they are indexed (1 vol.). Unbound records of the Assistant Commissioner include letters, telegrams, and orders and circulars received; appointment papers and oaths; and reports on operations and other matters, including murders and assaults. There are also letters received by the superintendent of education, reports from teachers, and other school reports; letters received by the chief quartermaster and disbursing officer; and records of the surgeon in chief, comprising letters received, contracts, returns of sick and wounded refugees and freedmen, returns of medical officers, and reports on medical attendants. There are also unbound records of districts and subdistricts (ca. 7 ft.).

Other records of the operations of the Bureau in Georgia are among those of the Assistant Commissioner for South Carolina.

Kentucky

Although Kentucky had not been one of the Confederate States, Commissioner Howard appointed an Assistant Commissioner for that State. Until June 13, 1866, when Bvt. Maj. Gen. Jeff C. Davis assumed charge as Assistant Commissioner, the State was administered jointly with Tennessee under Maj. Gen. C. B. Fisk, with Bvt. Brig. Gen. John Ely in immediate charge of Kentucky. When Kentucky was given its own Assistant Commissioner, district headquarters were established at Lexington, Louisville, Paducah, and Bowling Green. The agents in the central district, which had no chief superintendent, reported direct to the Assistant Commissioner.

In 1867 Commissioner Howard wrote: "The peculiar political condition of the State, its relations to the general government, its legislative enactments, and judicial decrees, have rendered the administration of bureau affairs perplexing, and the necessity of protection for freed people painfully apparent." It was hoped that the Bureau could be virtually discontinued in Kentucky in Feb. 1868, but the social and economic problems resulting from the war influenced Howard to continue the Bureau's activities in Kentucky until 1872.

Successive Assistant Commissioners:

Bvt. Maj. Gen. Jeff C. Davis, June 13, 1866.
Bvt. Brig. Gen. Sidney Burbank, Feb. 18, 1867.
Bvt. Maj. Gen. Benjamin P. Runkle, Jan. 7, 1869.

Record Group 105. --The extant records (ca. 27 ft.) consist chiefly of book records (ca. 190 vols.) of the Assistant Commissioner, the superintendent of education, the disbursing officer, the agent for payment of bounties, the chief medical officer, and the district and subdistrict offices, 1866-72. These include registers of letters received, letters-sent books, endorsements, orders and circulars, inspection reports, bounty records, marriage records, records of complaints and trials, and records of contracts; they are indexed (1 vol.). Unbound records of the Assistant Commissioner include his letters received, which after 1868 related chiefly to his functions as disbursing officer and chief superintendent of schools; monthly statistical reports received from districts; and reports received or rendered on land, relief, and other matters. There are also teachers' school reports and related papers; the chief medical officer's letters received, the returns of medical attendants and medical officers, and the returns of sick and wounded; a file of labor contracts; personnel rosters and reports of "persons and articles hired"; and loyalty oaths executed as prerequisite to employment by the United States. There are also district and subdistrict records (about 4 ft.), unbound.

Other records of the operations of the Bureau in Kentucky are among those of the Assistant Commissioner for Tennessee.

Kentucky and Tennessee

The Assistant Commissioner for these States entered upon his duties on June 26, 1865, with headquarters at Nashville, Tenn. His jurisdiction appears to have included for a time the northern part of Alabama. The headquarters staff included an assistant adjutant general, an assistant quartermaster, a medical director, a district inspector, a solicitor of freedmen's courts, and a superintendent of schools. Although the area administered was divided originally into districts, these were abolished on Oct. 30, 1865;

thereafter the county agents reported direct to the Assistant Commissioner. Work on behalf of the freedmen in Tennessee, although not without its problems, progressed far more smoothly than in Kentucky, where opposition was stronger.

The two States continued to be administered jointly until June 13, 1866. Records of the joint administration are found chiefly among those of the Assistant Commissioner for the State of Tennessee.

The Assistant Commissioner for Kentucky and Tennessee was Brig. Gen. Clinton B. Fisk, June 26, 1865-June 12, 1866.

Louisiana

The appointment of Chaplain Thomas W. Conway as Assistant Commissioner for Louisiana was announced on June 13, 1865, and the organization of headquarters at New Orleans was announced on July 14. On Aug. 9, 1865, Louisiana was divided into districts corresponding to its parishes. Later, a district might include one to three parishes; and still later (1868) there were eight districts averaging six parishes each.

To each parish was assigned an agent, or assistant superintendent, who was if possible an officer of the Army. Civilians who had acted as resident agents were gradually relieved of their duties. In no other State were there so many difficult questions with reference to labor, the status of the freedmen, and the power of military authorities. Assistant Commissioner Absalom Baird's rules governing labor contracts, one of which provided that all members of a family should contract to work together, were among the most comprehensive of such regulations.

Much abandoned property was held during the year 1865, but it was restored as rapidly as claimants could present proper proofs of ownership and loyalty. During 1865 this property, which included both large plantations and city land and buildings, furnished all the funds necessary for the Bureau's work. Nearly all the property, however, was restored to its former owners by Jan. 1, 1866. The school system was especially well developed.

Bureau courts were abolished in Louisiana as soon as the legislature provided for the protection of the freedmen, with the understanding that Bureau officers should retain the right to appear in the courts in defense of freedmen. In cases of manifest injustice by the civil authorities the Assistant Commissioner retained the right to interpose and if necessary to organize a court made up of officers and citizens for the trial of offenders.

Successive Assistant Commissioners:

Chaplain Thomas W. Conway, June 13, 1865.
Bvt. Brig. Gen. Joseph S. Fullerton, Oct. 16, 1865.
Bvt. Maj. Gen. Absalom Baird, Oct. 1865.
Maj. Gen. Philip H. Sheridan, ca. Oct. 1866.
Bvt. Maj. Gen. Joseph A. Mower, Nov. 27, 1866.
Lt. Col. William H. Wood, Dec. 4, 1867.
Bvt. Maj. Gen. Robert C. Buchanan, Jan. 2, 1868.
Bvt. Maj. Gen. Edward Hatch, Aug. 24, 1868.

Record Group 105. --The extant records (ca. 70 ft.) consist chiefly of book records (ca. 540 vols.) of the Assistant Commissioner, the board of education and general superintendent of schools, the quartermaster, the agent for the payment of bounties, the assistant commissary of subsistence, the land department, the chief medical officer, the superintendent of Negro labor, the plantation department, the provost marshal general, freedmen's home colonies, and district offices.   These book records (listed in 1 vol.) include registers of letters received, letters-sent books, endorsements, orders and circulars, rosters of employees, bounty records, contract records, employment registers, tax books, registers of colored persons, records of laborers conscripted, trial dockets of freedmen's courts, records of complaints, journals of business, marriage records, and hospital records, 1864-72 (a few antedating the establishment of the Bureau).   Unbound records of the Assistant Commissioner include letters, orders and circulars, and reports received; the last consist of statistical and other routine reports received from districts, reports on plantations by inspectors of freedmen, and reports of district operations.   Unbound records relating to education include the correspondence of the board of education for freedmen and the general superintendent of schools, school reports, and reports of "tuition tickets" sold.   Unbound medical records include the chief medical officer's letters received, papers relating to Freedmen's Hospital at New Orleans, the returns of medical officers, hospital morning reports, weekly reports of cholera cases, and the chief medical officer's contracts.   There are also lists of orphans at the Freedmen's Hospital Orphan Asylum.   Still other unbound records include letters received and other papers of the assistant commissary of subsistence, laborers' payrolls and labor contracts, a file of papers in the case of T. H. Hannon (a Bureau official of Carroll Parish tried for embezzlement), and records of districts and subdistricts (7 ft.).

Maryland

The Assistant Commissioner for the District of Columbia was responsible for the Bureau's operations in Maryland until the appointment of an Assistant Commissioner for that State in Mar. 1866.   The counties of Montgomery, Prince Georges, Charles, Calvert, and St. Marys, however, remained under the jurisdiction of the Assistant Commissioner for the District of Columbia.   In June 1866 six counties of Virginia and two of West Virginia were added to the jurisdiction of the Assistant Commissioner for Maryland; but on Sept. 1, 1866, the Virginia and West Virginia counties were transferred to the jurisdiction of the Assistant Commissioner for Virginia.   Unlike the practice in other States, field operations in Maryland were handled not by local officers but by inspectors and agents sent out by the Assistant Commissioner.

Like the Assistant Commissioner for the District of Columbia, the Assistant Commissioner for Maryland had to cope with frequent complaints about the illegal apprenticing of colored children, particularly in the lower counties of the State, a practice that, he reported, "but for the righteous decision of the Chief Justice of the United States, recently announced . . . might have reached alarming proportions."

In 1867 the Assistant Commissioner for Maryland was made reponsible for protecting freedmen and supervising freedmen's schools in Delaware. When Brig. Gen. Horace Brooks was relieved on Aug. 15, 1868, operations in Maryland and Delaware--by that time reduced to educational work and the settlement of soldiers' claims--were assigned to the Assistant Commissioner for the District of Columbia and West Virginia.

Successive Assistant Commissioners:
Bvt. Maj. Gen. George J. Stannard, Mar. 30, 1866.
Lt. Col. Robert Chandler, July 1, 1866.
Maj. Gen. Francis Fessenden, July 20, 1866.

Bvt. Maj. Gen. Edgar M. Gregory, Sept. 1, 1866.
Brig. Gen. Horace Brooks, Feb. 1, 1868.

Record Group 105.--The extant records (ca. 12 ft.) consist chiefly of book records (ca. 55 vols.) of Commissioner Howard, the Assistant Commissioner for Maryland, the claim division, the complaint division, the chief quartermaster, the special agent and disbursing officer, and the district offices, 1866-72. These book records (listed in 1 vol.) include registers of letters received, letters-sent books, endorsements, orders, records of apprentices, pay and bounty records, account books, pension books, and a register of complaints. Unbound records (some of which were continued by the Assistant Commissioner for the District of Columbia or by the Office of the Commissioner after the closing of the Maryland office) include letters, reports, and orders and circulars received by the Assistant Commissioner; retained copies of his reports; letters of complaints; claims, including pay-and-bounty and pension claims; the disbursing officer's letters received; oaths of office and other personnel records; and letters and other papers received by the subassistant commissioners at Baltimore and Annapolis. A separate series of the complaint division's letters received relates in part to the apprenticing of colored children.

Other records concerning the operations of the Bureau in Maryland are among those of the Assistant Commissioner for the District of Columbia.

Mississippi

Early in 1863 Col. John Eaton, Jr., was assigned to duty as superintendent of freedmen in the Mississippi Valley; he continued in this post until May 1865, when the Bureau of Refugees, Freedmen, and Abandoned Lands was organized and the States of Mississippi, Tennessee, Missouri, and Arkansas were organized under separate Bureau headquarters. The Assistant Commissioner for Mississippi assumed his duties on June 20, 1865. Headquarters were established at Vicksburg, and on July 24 northern, southern, and western district superintendencies were established. At a later date 8 districts were established, and in 1867 Mississippi was divided into 24 subdistricts. The Bureau's responsibilities in the State are described in the quotation from Maj. Gen. Thomas J. Wood, above (p. 364).

The "experiment" of uniting the offices of Assistant Commissioner and military commander was first made in Mississippi.

Successive Assistant Commissioners:
Col. Samuel Thomas, June 20, 1865.
Bvt. Maj. Gen. Thomas J. Wood, May 1, 1866.
Bvt. Maj. Gen. Alvan C. Gillem, Jan. 24, 1867.

Record Group 105. --The extant records (ca. 40 ft.) consist chiefly of book records (ca. 330 vols.) of the Assistant Commissioner, the superintendent of education, the chief medical officer, the quartermaster and disbursing officer, and the districts and subdistricts, 1864-72. These book records include registers of letters received, letters-sent books, endorsements, orders and circulars, marriage records, station books and rosters, rental books, records of freedmen's courts, hospital records, bounty records, and various other registers (of complaints and of plantations, abandoned houses, and abandoned property); these records are indexed (1 vol.). Unbound records of the Assistant Commissioner comprise incoming letters, orders and circulars, rosters, and operations and other reports, including a file of complaints and reports of outrages. Unbound medical records consist of the chief surgeon's letters received, muster rolls and payrolls of the hospital corps, contracts with employees, returns of sick and wounded, statements of hospital funds, accounts for the treatment of marines at the U. S. Army post hospital, reports of medical attendants, and the personal reports of medical officers. Still other unbound records are labor contracts, school reports, papers relating to the settlement of freedmen's accounts with planters, amnesty oaths, reports of "persons and articles hired" at Vicksburg, reports of issuance of relief supplies, and records (4 ft.) of districts and subdistricts.

Among the records of this headquarters are records of the special agent of the Treasury at Vicksburg (under the Second Special Agency), 1863-65 (2 ft.), pertaining to abandoned and confiscable lands, houses, and tenements; leased plantations; rentals; and assignment of buildings to individuals. (Other records of the Second Special Agency are described under the Department of the Treasury.)

Missouri and Arkansas

The Assistant Commissioner for these States assumed his duties on June 10, 1865, with headquarters at St. Louis and jurisdiction extending to Indian Territory. On July 10 district superintendencies were established in Arkansas at Little Rock, Pine Bluff, Helena, Arkadelphia, Camden, Washington, Monticello, and Paraclifta. On July 21 district superintendencies were established for Missouri at St. Louis, Cape Giradeau, Pilot Knob, Springfield, Cassville, and Rolla, and also at Fort Leavenworth, Kans. When Missouri abolished slavery and enacted laws to protect the rights of freedmen, the operations of the Bureau were withdrawn from that State.

In Arkansas the relief of general destitution and hunger was a major part of the Bureau's work. The homesteading program there was relatively unsuccessful. In Feb. 1867, because of difficulty and delay in communication, the Arkansas districts were abolished, and each officer who had been on duty as superintendent or general superintendent was put in charge of a county or several counties as agent.

Successive Assistant Commissioners:
      Brig. Gen. John W. Sprague, June 10, 1865.
      Brig. Gen. Edward O. C. Ord, Oct. 26, 1866.
      Brig. Gen. Charles H. Smith, Apr. 2, 1867.

Record Group 105.--The extant records of this headquarters (ca. 37 ft.) consist chiefly of book records (ca. 200 vols.) of the Assistant Commissioner, the superintendent of education, the disbursing officer, and the district and subdistrict offices, 1865-72. These book records include registers of letters received, letters-sent books, endorsement books, orders and circulars, station books of officers, registers of claims, bounty registers, marriage records, contracts, registers of complaints, employment registers, and hospital registers; there are two lists (separate for Arkansas and Missouri) of these volumes, which include also the book records of the predecessor General Superintendent of Freedmen (1864-65). Among unbound records are letters and operations reports received by the Assistant Commissioner; letters and teachers' reports received by the superintendent of education and his monthly reports; labor contracts and freedmen's accounts; the chief disbursing officer's letters received concerning claims and other financial matters; oaths of office; papers relating to the revocation of appointments; and records of ration and clothing requirements. Other reports relate to children apprenticed and to land matters.

<u>North Carolina</u>

The Assistant Commissioner for this State arrived at Raleigh on June 22, 1865, and on July 1 he entered on duty. Eastern, central, and western district superintendencies were created on July 15, with headquarters at New Bern, Raleigh, and Greensboro; superintendents were required to divide their districts into a convenient number of subdistricts. On Aug. 18 a southern district was set up with headquarters at Wilmington. In 1867 there were 10 subdistricts, but on Mar. 1, 1868, the State was divided into the 4 districts of Goldsboro, Raleigh, Wilmington, and Morganton, and these in turn were divided into sections averaging 3 counties each.

Little abandoned property was held in North Carolina, the greater part having been restored to its former owners before July 1865. Until July 1, 1866, the expenses of the Bureau were defrayed from a special freedmen's fund, previously created in the State. In 1866 the jurisdiction of the Assistant Commissioner over cases of violence and outrage was gradually transferred to the civil courts, which became willing to receive the testimony of witnesses without distinction of color.

In 1867 liberal donations from Northern philanthropists enabled the Bureau to relieve previously unaided cases of destitution in the State. These included, besides freedmen, "poor white people, women and children, whose husbands, fathers, or brothers were killed or crippled during the rebellion." The Bureau aided these destitute persons as far as possible. The early schools for freedmen in North Carolina were "exceedingly prosperous."

When the civil government of the State became fully established on July 1, 1868, the authority given Bureau officers to adjudicate civil suits was discontinued; but these agents still acted as counsellors and advisers of freedmen.

Successive Assistant Commissioners:

 Col. E. Whittlesey, June 22, 1865.
 Bvt. Maj. Gen. Thomas H. Ruger, May 16, 1866.
 Bvt. Maj. Gen. John C. Robinson, June 20, 1866.
 Col. James V. Bomford, Dec. 1, 1866.
 Bvt. Maj. Gen. Nelson A. Miles, Apr. 6, 1867.
 Jacob F. Chur, Oct. 15, 1868.

<u>Record Group 105.</u> -- The extant records (ca. 40 ft.) of this headquarters consist chiefly of book records (ca. 270 vols.) of the Assistant Commissioner, the superintendent of education, the inspector, the chief quartermaster and disbursing officer, and the district and subdistrict offices, 1865-72. These book records (listed in 1 vol.) include registers of letters received, letters-sent books, endorsement books, orders and circulars, school reports, registers of complaints, registers of outrages, hospital record books, and financial records. Unbound records of the Assistant Commissioner consist of letters, telegrams, orders and circulars, and miscellaneous reports received; the last include reports on lands, sanitation, freedmen's camps, rations issued, cases tried, indentured persons, destitute persons, and the issuance of relief supplies. Other unbound records are letters received in the inspector's office, letters received by the superintendent of education and miscellaneous other school papers, and records (10 ft.) of districts and subdistricts.

South Carolina

Bvt. Maj. Gen. Rufus Saxton, who had been responsible for freedmen's affairs in the Sea Islands and some coastal counties of South Carolina, became Assistant Commissioner in this State on June 10, 1865, with headquarters at Beaufort. For a time his jurisdiction extended over Florida and Georgia, despite the existence of a separate Georgia headquarters at Augusta. In South Carolina, district headquarters were established originally at Anderson, Beaufort, Charleston, Colleton, Columbia, Georgetown, Orangeburg, Chesterfield, Darlington, Kershaw, Marlboro, and Richland; but by 1868 only six districts were needed.

Brig. Gen. Robert K. Scott, who succeeded Saxton, reported that upon beginning his duties he found no records of any sort, his "predecessor" having taken them, "as he said to enable him to make up his report." According to Scott's report of Nov. 1, 1866, "Everything was in confusion, all the abandoned property in the State, including houses and plantations seized by the agents of the United States treasury had recently been turned over to the bureau," upon which "devolved the delicate and arduous duty of determining the validity of claims for the restoration of this property to the original owners." He "found the freed people in a most wretched condition" from want of food and clothing. Camps and hospitals were established, and many people were gathered together and fed and clothed by the Bureau.

The Assistant Commissioner had also to explain to freedmen the impossibility of their retention of the Sea Islands, which had been turned over to them by military authority. This task was the more difficult, General Scott wrote, "from their having occupied the islands under such positive assurance from men whose high official position would seem to justify the claimant in resisting any encroachments upon his supposed privileges." With respect to these claims, sec. 9 of an act of July 16, 1866 (14 Stat. 175), authorized the Assistant Commissioners for South Carolina and Georgia "to give each person having a valid claim a warrant upon the direct tax commissioners for South Carolina for twenty acres of land."

After the discontinuance of Bureau courts in the State, jurisdiction over most cases in which colored persons were parties was transferred to a military provost court.

By 1867 the Bureau's educational work in the State was being conducted with marked success. The duties of Bureau agents in ensuring justice for freedmen continued through 1868.

Successive Assistant Commissioners:

Bvt. Maj. Gen. Rufus Saxton, June 10, 1865.
Brig. Gen. Robert K. Scott, Jan. 20, 1866.
Bvt. Col. John R. Edie, July 31, 1868.

Record Group 105. --The extant records (ca. 48 ft.) consist chiefly of book records (ca. 280 vols.) of the Assistant Commissioner, the superintendent of education, the inspector, the provision and claim division, the assistant commissary of subsistence, the chief medical officer, and the districts and subdistricts, 1865-72. These book records include registers of letters received, letters-sent books, endorsements, orders and circulars, property and land records, claims and bounty records, accounting records, contracts, records of freedmen's courts and complaints, hospital records, records of rations issued, and records relating to supplies, crops, and provisions; they are indexed (1 vol.). Unbound records of the Assistant Commissioner include letters received and reports received or rendered on operations, abandoned or confiscated lands, contracts, outrages, education, and the issuance of rations, clothing, and medicine to freedmen. Unbound records of the superintendent of education include letters received and teachers' and other school reports; and those of the chief medical officer include letters received, returns of sick and wounded freedmen, morning reports of "Old Folks Home," and personal and other reports of medical officers. Other unbound records include letters received and miscellaneous records of the assistant commissary of subsistence; the claims division's letters received; records relating to the inspector's office; the provost marshal's records of cases tried; letters, including applications, received by the provision bureau; and additional records of districts and subdistricts (11 ft.), consisting of correspondence, orders and circulars, reports of murders and outrages, reports of operations, quartermaster papers, provost court papers, rosters and records of indentures, labor contracts, amnesty oaths, records relating to the restoration of property, and hospital and school records.

Some of these records are closely related to those of the Direct Tax Commissioners for South Carolina, described under Department of the Treasury.

Tennessee

Until June 13, 1866, Tennessee was administered by the Assistant Commissioner for Tennessee and Kentucky. Tennessee was organized into three districts: Middle Tennessee, the agents in which reported direct to the Assistant Commissioner at Nashville; West Tennessee, comprising all counties west of the Tennessee River, under a chief superintendent, with headquarters at Memphis; and East Tennessee, comprising the counties east of the Cumberland mountains, also under a chief superintendent, with headquarters at Chattanooga.

Difficulties of administration led to a thorough reorganization in January 1867. Many agents were discharged and others were appointed, the fee system was abolished, and the agents were thereafter paid regular salaries. In 1868 the State was divided into the districts of Nashville, Pulaski, Chattanooga, Knoxville, and Memphis.

Successive Assistant Commissioners:

Bvt. Maj. Gen. Clinton B. Fisk, June 13, 1866.
Bvt. Brig. Gen. John R. Lewis, Sept. 1, 1866.
Bvt. Maj. Gen. William P. Carlin, Jan. 18, 1867.
James Thompson, Oct. 31, 1868.

Record Group 105. --The extant records (ca. 47 ft.) consist chiefly of book records (ca. 220 vols.) of the Assistant Commissioner, the superintendent of education, the chief quartermaster and disbursing officer, the general claim agents, and the districts and subdistricts, 1865-72. These book records include registers of letters received, letters-sent books, endorsements, orders and circulars, marriage records, bounty and claim records, contracts, registers of complaints, and records of freedmen's courts; there is an index of these (1 vol.). The Assistant Commissioner's unbound records include letters and orders and circulars received; appointment papers and oaths of office; reports received or rendered on operations, inspections, and other matters, including outrages and riots; and lists of land and property taken over as abandoned or confiscable and applications and petitions for property restoration. Unbound records of the superintendent of education include letters received, teachers' and other school reports, and deeds to schoolhouses; and those of the general claims agent consist of letters received concerning pension, bounty, and arrears of pay. Other unbound records include letters received by the disbursing office, leases for abandoned property, records of the indenture of apprentices, labor contracts, and plantation owners' agreements with the special agent of the Treasury Department. There are also unbound records of districts and subdistricts (7 1/2 ft.).

Texas

The appointment of Brig. Gen. Edgar M. Gregory as Assistant Commissioner for the State of Texas was announced on Sept. 19, 1865, and headquarters were established at Galveston on Sept. 21. On Dec. 5, 1865, offices of subassistant commissioners were announced, with headquarters at Marshall, Houston, Victoria, Austin, Brenham, Columbus, Hempstead, Anderson, Courtney, Woodville, Millican, and Leona. The organization of the Bureau was not extensive in Texas, owing to the State's size, scattered population, and lack of railroads. The Army occupied a few of the largest cities but could give no protection to officers in the interior. Military commanders cooperated with the Assistant Commissioner and aided him in carrying out his orders.

Since Texas was occupied by Union forces rather late in the war and had no "abandoned lands," the Bureau in the State was supported at first by the sale and rental of former Confederate government property.

In order to consolidate military and Bureau jurisdiction, the responsibility for freedmen's affairs in Texas was assigned to the military commander, Bvt. Maj. Gen. Charles Griffin, on Jan. 24, 1867. On relieving Gen. Joseph B. Kiddoo as Assistant Commissioner, General Griffin found 14 officers and 15 civilians on duty as subassistant commissioners. Except for one man, these were stationed in the southern part of the State and in no case farther than 180 miles from the Gulf of Mexico. Because all the troops except those on or near the Indian and Mexican frontiers were stationed near the coast and because agents of the Bureau were almost powerless unless military forces were nearby, scarcely a third of the State and only half the population were reached by the Bureau. Reports of outrages, robbery, and murder in remote parts of the State were received frequently. As soon as the troops could be properly distributed, the State was divided into subdistricts, and all post commanders were directed to report to General Griffin as subassistant commissioners of the subdistricts in which their respective posts were located. By May 31, 1867, there were 57 subdistricts, in the charge of 69 agents, 38 of whom were officers, so stationed as to extend protection to the most distant areas of the State.

In Feb. 1868 agents were directed to turn over to the local authorities all civil and criminal cases that involved freedmen, except cases concerned with labor contracts. Criminal cases were necessarily transferred, as the Bureau had no means of administering punishment. Yet a careful scrutiny was maintained over court decisions and, if petty and inadequate fines were imposed, offenders were rearrested and proper penalties were inflicted.

The plan of school organization was to have each subassistant commissioner act as superintendent of education for his district; he was ordered to visit monthly every school for freedmen, whether public or private, and by all proper means to obtain donations of land for schools, the title to be vested in colored trustees. On land so obtained, buildings were erected, with the local agent making contracts (subject to approval by the Assistant Commissioner) for the completion or repair of buildings and for their equipment. Officers were required to visit and encourage private, night, and Sunday schools. If possible, the officers were to help such schools become self-sustaining; and they were authorized to rent buildings for the use of private schools if necessary. The effect of this arrangement after 4 months was to increase attendance by about 5,000 pupils.

The assignment of Bvt. Maj. Gen. Joseph J. Reynolds as Assistant Commissioner for Texas united this command with that of the Fifth Military District.

Successive Assistant Commissioners:

Bvt. Brig. Gen. Edgar M. Gregory, Sept. 19, 1865.
Bvt. Maj. Gen. Joseph B. Kiddoo, Apr. 2, 1866.
Bvt. Maj. Gen. Charles Griffin, Jan. 24, 1867.
Bvt. Maj. Gen. Joseph J. Reynolds, Sept. 21, 1867.
Maj. Gen. Edward R. S. Canby, Jan. 18, 1869.
Bvt. Maj. Gen. Joseph J. Reynolds, Apr. 8, 1869.

Record Group 105. -- The extant records (ca. 22 ft.) consist chiefly of book records (ca. 170 vols.) of the Assistant Commissioner, the superintendent of education, the quartermaster and disbursing officer, and the districts, 1865-72. These book records (listed in 1 vol.) include registers of letters received, letters-sent books, endorsements, orders and circulars, records of criminal offenses, records of schools and teachers, registers of contracts and complaints, and accounting records. Unbound records of the Assistant Commissioner include letters received; rosters; and reports pertaining to lands, murders and other outrages, "persons and articles hired, " and the issuance of relief supplies to freedmen. Unbound records of the superintendent of education consist of letters received, contracts for repair and construction of schools, reports on school buildings owned by the Bureau and other parties, correspondence relating to appointment of teachers, and teachers' and other school reports. There are also unbound letters (3 in.) received by the quartermaster and disbursing officer and unbound records (1 ft.) of districts.

Virginia

The Assistant Commissioner for Virginia took up his work on June 15, 1865, at Richmond. At first the counties of Alexandria, Fairfax, and Loudoun were under the jurisdiction of the Assistant Commissioner for the District of Columbia. In June 1866 six Virginia counties were transferred to the jurisdiction of the Assistant Commissioner for Maryland; but on Sept. 1, 1866, these counties and the West Virginia counties in which the Bureau operated were assigned to the Assistant Commissioner for Virginia. In Mar. 1867, Alexandria and Fairfax Counties were transferred to the Assistant Commissioner for Virginia, and the West Virginia counties were transferred from him to the Assistant Commissioner for the District of Columbia.

The State of Virginia was organized at first in eight districts, each of which had subdistricts corresponding to county boundaries, except that two or more counties in the same subdistrict, with a colored population of less than 5,000 each, might when practicable be united. Some colored soldiers' wives and families, left behind when the troops were transported from

City Point to Texas, were sent to Texas at public expense; and a "colony of upwards of a hundred signifying its wish to go to Liberia, through a colored agent, was transported from Lynchburg to Baltimore, where the colonization Society took complete charge. " Eventually, jurisdiction of the Virginia headquarters was extended over West Virginia, which, because of its few freedmen, required little attention.

The Bureau's jurisdiction over freedmen's cases was transferred to the State courts as quickly as assurance could be obtained that such a transfer would not be abused. From districts where civil authorities had been given full power to try and punish freedmen for crimes, however, came frequent complaints of manifest injustice by judicial officers and of abuse of authority by executive officers of the State government. The Assistant Commissioner considered the provisions on the statute books to be "still partial, and in the hands of prejudiced magistrates too often used for the oppression of the colored man. "

Since most abandoned property in Virginia was quickly restored, little was held by the Assistant Commissioner.

Successive Assistant Commissioners:
> Col. Orlando Brown, June 15, 1865.
> Maj. Gen. Alfred H. Terry, May 1866.
> Bvt. Maj. Gen. John M. Schofield, Aug. 15, 1866.
> Bvt. Brig. Gen. Orlando Brown, Mar. 20, 1867.

Record Group 105. --The extant records (ca. 65 ft.) consist chiefly of book records (ca. 500 vols.) of the Assistant Commissioner, the superintendent of education, the chief quartermaster and financial agent (disbursing officer), and the district and subdistrict offices, 1865-72. These book records (listed in 1 vol.) include registers of letters received, letters-sent books, endorsements, orders and circulars, station books, school reports, registers of complaints, freedmen's court records, census records, contract registers, and marriage registers. Unbound records of the Assistant Commissioner include letters, orders and circulars, and operations reports received. Among unbound records relating to property are applications for its restoration, land reports, reports relating to taxation, and reports of a board of officers for the establishment of rents. Other unbound reports relate particularly to destitute or indigent freedmen, the labor supply, the administration of justice, outrages and abuses, and freedmen's courts (including some court proceedings). Unbound records of the superintendent of education consist of letters received, school reports, and records of inspection of schools. Muster rolls of enlisted men on detached duty with the Assistant Commissioner are with these records.

Other records relating to the operations of the Bureau in Virginia are among those of the Assistant Commissioners for the District of Columbia and for Maryland.

WAR RECORDS OFFICE

The agency commonly known as the War Records Office produced the monumental work The War of the Rebellion; a Compilation of the Official Records of the Union and Confederate Armies. Douglas Southall Freeman wrote in The South to Posterity that the compilation "amazed the south" by its "impartiality. " "If it be true, " Freeman adds, "that the War between the States is now, with a few regrettable omissions, the most thoroughly studied military conflict of modern times, the reason is the availability of the Official Records. " This project of selection and publication had been inaugurated in 1864, carried on with indifferent success until 1866, and then permitted to languish until 1874. In that year a fund was provided by an act of June 23 (18 Stat. 222), for its continuance under the control of the Secretary of War, and a special clerical force was set up to carry on the work. This force at first was nominally under the direction of the Chief Clerk of the War Department, but the Adjutant General exercised a good deal of control over it, since he had charge of the records upon which much of the compilation was based. On May 3, 1875, and again on July 25, 1876, attempts were made to reorganize the work by placing it under specific civilian clerks who were to act as "superintendents. " Since these men, however, were expected to supervise the compilation in addition to their regular duties and without extra pay, the results were superficial and unsatisfactory. During this period the group working on the project apparently had no consistent title, although it is referred to at least once in correspondence as the "Rebellion Records Division. " The last of the civilian "superintendents" resigned on Dec. 8, 1877.

On Dec. 14, 1877, Capt. Robert N. Scott was detailed to take charge of the editing and compilation, and he established a definite organization directly responsible to the Secretary of War. This was called at first the Publication Office, War Records, but was later and more generally known as the War Records Office.

In 1880 some attempt was made to centralize control of the original records being used in the compilation, but it does not appear that the War Department's Archive Office, which had custody of the Confederate records, was ever actually transferred to or merged with the War Records Office. The latter continued under a single head until, by an act of Mar. 2, 1889 (25 Stat. 970), the work came to "be conducted, under the Secretary of War, by a board of three persons, " an Army officer and two civilians. The board was dissolved, however, in 1898; by an act of Feb. 24, 1899 (30 Stat. 871), the War Records Office was merged in the Record and Pension Office, effective July 1 of that year. It continued thereafter as the Publication Branch.

Although the last volume of the Official Records was published in 1901, the Publication Branch existed for several years afterward. Its interest, however, was not confined to its former work, and the use of the office mark of the War Records Office appears to have been discontinued after 1903.

The War of the Rebellion; a Compilation of the Official Records of the Union and Confederate Armies (Washington, 1881-1901. 130 "serials" comprising 70 vols., general index, and atlas); reports of the volumes published, in the annual reports of the Secretary of War, 1877-1902 (referred to by different headings and after 1899 printed with the report of the Record and Pension Office). The published Official Records (available also on microfilm as National Archives Microcopy 262) are organized in series as follows: I. "Formal reports, both Union and Confederate, of the first seizures of United States property in the Southern States, and of all military operations in the field, with the correspondence, orders and returns relating specifically thereto. " II. "Correspondence, orders, reports and returns, Union and Confederate, relating to Prisoners of War and (so far as the military authorities were concerned) to State or political prisoners. " III. "Correspondence, orders, reports and returns of the Union authorities (embracing their correspondence with the Confederate officials) not relating specially to the subjects of the first and second series. It embraces the annual and special reports of the Secretary of War, of the General-in-Chief and of the chiefs of the several staff corps and departments; the calls for troops and the correspondence between the National and the several State authorities." IV. "Correspondence, orders, reports and returns of the Confederate authorities, similar to that indicated for the Union officials, as of the third series, but excluding the correspondence between the Union and Confederate authorities given in that series." See also Dallas D. Irvine, "The Genesis of the Official Records," Mississippi Valley Historical Review, 24:221-229 (Sept. 1937).

Record Group 94. --Systematic filing and indexing of correspondence of the War Records Office did not begin until the reorganization of the agency in 1877, although some letter books were kept earlier. Thereafter, several improvements in recordkeeping were made, such as the inauguration of a subject card index in 1894 (now missing except for letters A-Ch and R-Sn) and the separation, about 1882, of the papers pertaining to the sale and distribution of the Official Records from those pertaining to its preparation and publication. These files as finally organized consist primarily of manuscript copies of letters sent, 1875-82 (2 vols.), with additional press copies, 1878-94 (17 vols.); and letters received, 1877-94 (5 ft.). This correspondence was with officials, including former officials, of the Federal Government and of State governments, the Southern Historical Society, and private individuals; it relates to the assembling and selection of documents for publication. There is a separate series of press copies of letters sent, 1892-95, regarding the Atlas to Accompany the Official Records of the Union and Confederate Armies; and an indexed file of general correspondence, 1894-1903 (1 1/2 ft.), which after 1899 concerns the correction of errors in the published volumes of Official Records and the preparation of the general index. Also in separate series are letters received from Union officers, 1875-77 (3 in.), in reply to War Department requests for reports missing from the files.

As distinguished from records created by the War Records Office, there are also in the Office's files documents that originated elsewhere in the War Department. Some of these were borrowed for the publication and not returned; others were sent to the Office for its retention. (There is a 2-volume index of letters received by the Secretary of War, 1862-65, that were forwarded to the Office.) The Confederate records were made available to the War Records Office by the Archive Office and were all returned; but many of the other borrowed documents were retained and some were intermingled with documents contributed from private sources. These retained records include the "Union battle reports," 1861-65 (50 ft.), consisting of both those published in the Official Records and those not; selections from the original records of most of the 25 Army corps, 1861-65 (6 ft.); selections from the original records of many geographical military commands, 1861-65 (31 ft.); and "miscellaneous war records," 1861-65 (2 ft.), containing papers relating to the command of Brig. Gen. Andrew A. Humphreys. Also among the records are photographic prints and photolithographs of military installations in Georgia, South Carolina, Tennessee, and Virginia, annotated for publication in the Atlas; manuscript maps from which plates were prepared for the Atlas; and related materials.

Records of the distribution and sale of the Official Records comprise a register of letters received, 1893-94; a register and papers relating to distribution of the published volumes, 1895-97; papers relating to distribution to Members of the 56th and 57th Congresses, 1903-4 (3 in.); reports on or letters about official transactions concerning sales and distribution; and card records of remittances received, 1895-98 (3 in.). Earlier records of the distribution, commenced in 1882, were kept by the War Department Library but do not appear to be extant.

The extant administrative records of the War Records Office comprise attendance records of employees, 1883-90; payrolls, 1887-94; and account books.

National Archives, Preliminary   comp. by Lucille H. Pendell and
Inventory [No. 17] of the Records   Elizabeth Bethel, p. 132-138 (Wash-
of the Adjutant General's Office,   ington, 1949).

RECORD AND PENSION OFFICE

By orders of the Secretary of War of July 3 and 16, 1889, the divisions of the Adjutant General's Office that kept the muster rolls and other military records of volunteers were consolidated with the Record and Pension Division of the Surgeon General's Office. Since 1886 this Division, under Capt. and Asst. Surg. Fred C. Ainsworth, had been using a new "index-record card system" to solve the problem presented by the dilapidation of Civil War medical records through use in adjudicating claims and to speed up such work. The hospital records transcribed on index-record cards consisted of "more than twenty thousand registers, each pertaining to some particular hospital or command, and all of them together containing more than ten million separate and distinct entries." Because each card to which information was transcribed not merely indexed a certain record but was itself a reproduction of at least part of the record, the term index-record card was aptly chosen. The new office organized under Ainsworth in 1899 was the Record and Pension Division of the Office of the Secretary of War. Its work embraced "subjects of every conceivable nature relating to the service of organizations, officers, and enlisted men, including inquiries for information from records dating from the earliest history of the Government," and its operations in the first year required 75 rooms on 4 floors of the State, War, and Navy Building.

In 1890, after the carding of the medical records was virtually completed, the application of the same system to other military records was begun. Histories of volunteers were compiled from company muster rolls (normally made out ever 2 months), company and regimental monthly returns, company morning report books, company and regimental descriptive books, and other records. Since the rolls and returns were frail and torn after 25 years of constant use, measures to prevent their further deterioration were imperative. "From a purely business standpoint," Ainsworth wrote in his fiscal year 1890 report, ". . . and aside from all sentimental considerations, these records are simply invaluable, and the child is not yet born who will live to see the day when reference to them will no longer be necessary." The "only feasible method" for preservation and ready use, he believed, was to copy each entry on every record on a separate slip or card, then to arrange these cards by regiment, next by individual name, and finally in chronological order. All the cards relating to a soldier would thus fall together and would show his history from "muster in" to termination of service.

This activity was established permanently as the Record and Pension Office of the War Department by an act of May 9, 1892 (27 Stat. 27). The Office was organized in two distinct branches. One of these, concerned with current business, had 12 divisions; the other, the "Tenth Street Branch," in the old Ford's Theater, had 4 divisions and was concerned with reproducing the records of volunteer troops by the index-record card system. The "Ford's Theater disaster" of June 9, 1893 (the collapse of parts of the floors of the second and third stories, resulting in 22 deaths), interrupted the carding; and in 1894 the 16 divisions of the Office were reduced to 7, including the restored "Tenth Street Branch" and the "Seventeenth Street Branch," for repairing and consolidating records.

An order of the Secretary of War, May 15, 1894, transferred to the Record and Pension Office the general returns of the Army relating wholly or in part to the volunteer forces; records relating to the appointment, commissioning, and personnel of general and staff officers of these forces; and "all records, files, books, manuscripts, orders, returns, or correspondence in any Bureau that pertain exclusively or principally to the volunteer forces of any war or the officers and enlisted men thereof." Upon receipt of these records steps were taken to apply to them the index-record card system adopted for the other records of the volunteer forces. The same order transferred the "Confederate archives," which were eventually to be carded also.

The work of the Office continued as one of the functions of the Military Secretary's Office, which was established by an act of Apr. 23, 1904 (33 Stat. 262), to consolidate the Adjutant General's Office with the Record and Pension Office. A previous requirement, by an act of Feb. 25, 1903 (32 Stat. 884), for compiling a complete roster of the officers and enlisted men of the Union and Confederate armies intensified the effort to complete the index-record cards for Confederate military service. To supplement the information in muster rolls and other records of Confederate troops and in Federal records of Confederate prisoners of war, arrangements were made with the Governors of former Confederate States to borrow any records of Confederate troops that were in State custody. Historical societies and other custodians were similarly requested to lend appropriate records.

Not pertinent to the purpose of this Guide are the circumstances and effects of the transfer to the Record and Pension Office, from elsewhere in the War Department and from other executive departments, of records of wars before the Civil War and those of the Spanish-American War.

Annual reports of the Division, the Office, the Military Secretary, and the Adjutant General, to 1912, appended to those of the Secretary of War, especially those for fiscal years 1892 (H. Ex. Doc. 1, pt. 2, 52 Cong., 2 sess., Serial 3077) and 1905 (H. Doc. 2, 58 Cong., 3 sess., Serial 4781); Siert F. Riepma, "A Soldier-Archivist and His Records; Major General Fred C. Ainsworth," American Archivist, 4:178-187 (July 1941); Mabel E. Deutrich, Struggle for Supremacy; the Career of General Ainsworth (Washington, Public Affairs Press, 1962).

Record Group 94. --The principal series of carded Union records--pertaining to individual members of Civil War volunteer organizations (13,268 ft.)--contains information copies from such original records as muster

rolls, returns, descriptive books, and morning reports. The arrangement by State, then by arm of service, then numerically by regiment, and
then alphabetically by soldier's name, permits the inclusion within each
regimental file of a pertinent "record of events." Use of this series is
facilitated by a general index, also on cards (1,027 ft.), arranged by State
and thereunder by soldier's name, with separate groups of cards for the
following miscellaneous volunteer organizations: U. S. Sharp Shooters;
Signal Corps; U. S. Volunteers; Confederate prisoners of war who enlisted
in the U. S. service; Capt. Turner's Company of Volunteer Prisoners;
Veteran Reserve Corps; Brigade Bands; Departmental Corps; Indian Home
Guards; enlisted men of the U. S. Army transferred to the Mississippi
Flotilla, Feb. 1862; Pioneer Brigades (Army of the Cumberland); Varner's
Battalion of Infantry; and U. S. Colored Troops.

Carded medical records for enlisted and noncommissioned men of the
Regular Army are in a series beginning in 1821 and ending in 1884 (318
ft.); and those for members of volunteer organizations are in a single series
(1,431 ft.) covering both the Mexican and Civil Wars; these show the treatment of men in hospitals and their disposition after hospitalization. Other
series of carded medical records pertain to members of the Marine Corps
treated in Army hospitals, 1821-84 (3 in.); the Gunboat and Naval Service,
1861-65 (2 ft.); the Pioneer Corps, 1861-65 (6 in.); and hospital stewards,
noncommissioned officers, and musicians, 1821-84 (4 1/2 ft.). There are
also carded records relating to Civil War staff officers (35 ft.) and carded
service records of hospital attendants, matrons, and nurses, 1861-65
(36 ft.).

Related records of the Record and Pension Office, useful in supplementing or substantiating the information carded, include an extensive "document
file" of correspondence concerning the military service of volunteer soldiers,
with abstracts on record cards and a card index; a record (1 vol.) of books
transferred from the Adjutant General's Office to the Record and Pension
Office in June 1894; an index to correspondence relating to the correction of
rolls and other records; and lists of the records of military organizations
carded, including organizations of the Confederate Army. "Ainsworth's
Bible," a scrapbook containing general information on the history of the
Record and Pension Office, is file 2,637,718 in the "document file" of the
Adjutant General's Office, 1890-1917.

National Archives, Preliminary   comp. by Lucille H. Pendell and
Inventory [No. 17] of the Records   Elizabeth Bethel, p. 97-128 (Wash-
of the Adjutant General's Office,   ington, 1949).

Record Group 109. -- Although allocated to this record group because of
their relationship to the War Department Collection of Confederate Records,
the carded records showing the military, naval, and marine service of Confederate officers, noncommissioned officers, and enlisted men are also
postwar creations of the Record and Pension Office. They are mentioned
here, therefore, although they are described in the accompanying Guide to
the Archives of the Government of the Confederate States of America.

MISCELLANEOUS WAR DEPARTMENT COMMISSIONS

Besides the military commissions that acted as courts (see discussion
of these under Bureau of Military Justice, above), many special commis-

sions of the War Department were appointed during the Civil War to examine claims, to conduct investigations ordered by Congress, and to make inquiries. The work and records of the more important of these commissions are described below. In general the commissions are discussed in the order of the dates of their establishment.

Commission on War Claims at St. Louis

This commission was established by direction of the President and by order of the Secretary of War, Oct. 25, 1861, to investigate and settle claims arising from mismanagement and fraud in the Department of the West. The commission consisted of David Davis, Joseph Holt, and Hugh Campbell. It convened on Nov. 6, 1861, at St. Louis. Through the English- and German-language newspapers of St. Louis public notice was given of the organization of the commission and of the requirements for the presentation of claims, and all claims filed on or before Jan. 10, 1862, were considered.

Some 1,200 witnesses testified, and claims for more than $8,000,000 were presented. First examined were those for money borrowed or seized from banks. "Naturally enough," the commission reported, "in a city under martial law, these advances have assumed the courteous designation of 'loans, ' though the testimony makes it manifest that . . . they were anything but voluntary." Other classes of claims included those for making or providing tents, those for horses and mules, those connected with steamboats, those pertaining to railroad transportation, those for Army clothing and equipment, and those involving construction of barracks. In adjudicating claims for Army clothing the commission often found it necessary to obtain possession of "such of the books and papers of the parties relating to these transactions as were within . . . reach." On Jan. 9, 1862, the commission began to send to the Secretary of War vouchers for payment. These deliveries were continued regularly as its decisions were pronounced.

The commission's report of Mar. 10, 1862, to the Secretary of War, was printed as H. Ex. Doc. 94, 37 Cong., 2 sess., Serial 1135. Although this was devoted principally to "an exposure of the abuses which characterized the late administration of this department," under Frémont, it bore "testimony to the integrity which has generally been displayed by merchants, mechanics, and manufacturers when permitted to deal directly with the government."

Record Group 217. --The commission's records, which passed to the custody of the Third Auditor of the Treasury Department, consist principally of the claims files proper (10 ft.). These contain duplicates of claims under $1,000 allowed in full; duplicates of claims under $1,000 allowed in part; duplicates of claims over $1,000 allowed in full and allowed in part; claims withdrawn and rejected; and letters and telegrams received and copies of letters, telegrams, and circulars sent. There are also a volume of abstracts of claims approved for payment, Jan. 1, 1862-Mar. 31, 1863; a "receipt register" (2 vols.) of claims paid in full; a "receipt register" of claims dismissed; and transcripts of hearings, Aug. 31, 1861-Mar. 10, 1862 (8 vols. and additional papers).

Record Group 156. --A record of "Volunteer Organizations Who Furnished Their Horse Equipments, 1861 to 1865, and Memoranda of Claims for Ordnance and Ordnance Stores Against Military Department of the West Prior to October 14, 1861," constitutes in part a record of such claims presented by individuals and commercial firms to the commission.

Commission to Visit Union Prisoners

Bishop Edward R. Ames of the Methodist Episcopal Church and Hamilton Fish of New York were appointed on Jan. 25, 1862, "to visit the prisoners belonging to the Army of the United States now in captivity at Richmond, in Virginia, and elsewhere, and under such regulations as may be prescribed by the authorities having custody of such prisoners relieve their necessities and provide for their comfort at the expense of the United States." The commission was also to "make or procure a list of all the prisoners so held in captivity" but was not to "seek, obtain or report information or have communication on any subject not immediately relating to its humane and Christian object." The Secretary of War of the Confederate States appointed James A. Seddon and Charles M. Conrad to confer with Ames and Fish, but Secretary Benjamin's instructions to the Confederate commissioners required them to negotiate matters beyond the concern of the U. S. commissioners. The latter had "no authority to act in behalf of this [U. S.] Government in regard to the exchange of prisoners or any other purpose than the simple one of providing for the comfort of prisoners, if allowed to do so." That purpose having failed, Secretary Stanton directed Ames and Fish on Feb. 11, 1862, to return to Washington.

Although there are no manuscript records of the commission, its report to the Secretary, Feb. 14, 1862, was printed in Official Records . . . Armies, ser. 2, vol. 3, p. 261.

Commissions to Investigate Political Imprisonment

An act of Mar. 3, 1863 (12 Stat. 755), "relating to Habeas Corpus, and regulating Judicial Proceedings in Certain Cases," required that persons held under military authority as state or political prisoners, or otherwise than as prisoners of war, be released from custody in the lack of proper proceedings. On Mar. 23, 1863, the Judge Advocate General was designated to execute the provisions of the act. This official, as required, furnished the appropriate judges of the U. S. circuit and district courts with prisoner lists; these were compiled from rolls of prisoners confined at St. Louis, Alton, Louisville, Sandusky, Wheeling, Camp Chase, Fort Lafayette, Fort McHenry, and Fort Delaware and in the Old Capitol Prison at Washington.

On Feb. 27, 1862, Secretary Stanton had appointed Maj. Gen. John A. Dix and Edwards Pierrepont of New York as a "special commission of two persons, one of military rank and the other in civil life, . . . to examine the cases of state prisoners remaining in the military custody of the United States, and to determine whether, in view of the public safety and the existing rebellion, they should be discharged, or remain in military custody, or be remitted to the civil tribunal for trial." Thus, before the passage of the act of Mar. 3, 1863, cited above, measures had been taken by the Secretary to examine and resolve these cases. He continued the same course in regard to persons arrested by State authorities or military commanders without his own authority or that of the President or the Secretary of State. Reuben Hitchcock (replaced in Nov. 1862 by Samuel Galloway) investigated cases at Camp Chase; another commission (Benjamin S. Cowan, Roswell Marsh, and Samuel W. Bostwick) was organized to examine political or state prisoners in St. Louis, Alton, Chicago, "or any other camp, military prison, or post in the department of the Missouri" where such prisoners were confined under

U. S. authority; and still another (John C. King and Hugh L. Bond) was appointed on Jan. 9, 1864, for the examination of prisoners confined at Fort Delaware or elsewhere in the Middle Department. In the Eastern Department General Dix was directed "to investigate the cases of persons arrested and detained in Fort Lafayette and other military prisons . . . which have been used, by direction of the President, for the custody of persons seized by naval officers while engaged in blockade running or illicit trade, and which class of prisoners is not specified in the act of Congress of March 3, 1863." For detailed information, see Official Records . . . Armies, ser. 2, passim.

Record Group 59. --Some records of the Commission for State Prisoners (the Dix-Pierrepont commission) and related records formerly kept in the War Department are now a part of the "Civil War papers" in the general records of the State Department. These are described under the Department of State, above.

In Record Group 94, papers of the Office of the Judge Advocate (Turner), described elsewhere in this Guide, are directly related to the work of the several commissions mentioned above.

Records in Other Custody. --In the Manuscript Division of the Library of Congress is a volume of letter press copies of reports written at Camp Chase, Ohio, by Commissioners Reuben Hitchcock and Samuel Galloway, Sept. 1, 1862-June 10, 1863, pertaining to criminal and court-martial proceedings.

Commission on Ordnance Claims and Contracts

The shortage of ordnance in the early months of the war forced the War Department to abandon its policy of procurement from domestic manufacturers and to resort to purchase abroad. "The vast demands suddenly springing up, without any immediate increase of the supply, led to speculations and exorbitant prices," the Secretary of War later reported. On Mar. 13, 1862, Secretary Stanton appointed Joseph Holt and Robert Dale Owen as a special commission to audit and adjust all ordnance contracts, orders, and claims. The commission's decision was to be "final and conclusive" for the War Department "on all questions touching the validity, execution, and sums due or to become due" on such contracts and "upon all other questions arising between contractors and the government." The commission met in Washington, beginning on Mar. 17, 1862, and immediately invited persons interested in the cases referred to it "to appear and offer such suggestions and proofs as they might deem advisable in support of their respective claims." The 104 cases involved claims amounting to $50,000,000. The commission disposed of all the cases by investigating and preparing a special report on each and adjourned on July 16, 1862. The final report of the commission, July 1, 1862 (S. Ex. Doc. 71, 37 Cong., 2 sess., Serial 1123; also Official Records . . . Armies, ser. 3, vol. 2, p. 188-195), reflected its considered judgment:

It may be stated, generally, that we have found the system, under which have been issued the numerous orders or contracts for ordnance and ordnance stores that have been referred to us, strongly marked with improvidence. The amount of these orders or contracts has been ascertained to be largely in excess of the public wants, and the prices fixed by many of them beyond necessity or reason.

The unexampled demand for arms consequent upon the sudden breaking out of the present gigantic rebellion, and the extraordinary circumstances under which the government arsenals were drained of their best weapons before a blow was struck, afford some explanation of the excess of price referred to; yet, it must be confessed, not by any means a full and satisfactory one. It is to be traced, in a large degree, to a neglect of those common precautions which prudent men of business exercise in the conduct of their business affairs; some of which, too, had been specially provided for and required by acts of Congress.

Record Group 156. --Now a part of the "special file" of the Office of the Chief of Ordnance, the commission's records consist of its docket, an apparently fragmentary copy of its proceedings, and its decisions.

Cairo Claims Commission

In June 1862, at the instance of the House Select Committee on Government Contracts, Secretary Stanton appointed George S. Boutwell, Stephen T. Logan, and Charles A. Dana as a commission to examine a mass of claims at Cairo the payment on which had been suspended by the Quartermaster General "on a suspicion of their being tainted by the fraudulent practices of public officers." Thomas Means was appointed solicitor for the Government. The commission was organized at Cairo on June 18, but 2 days later Judge Logan resigned because of illness and Shelby M. Cullom was appointed in his place. Because the Quartermaster's Department at Cairo had been organized hastily and the demands on it had increased rapidly, its accounts were in great confusion. The commission therefore decided to make a full investigation of all disbursements; it examined 1,696 claims, amounting to $599,219.36; and it approved claims amounting to $451,105.80. Most of those rejected were for losses suffered in the active operations of the Army. "Many claims of this description were also presented by men whose loyalty to the Government was impeached by credible witnesses." A few claims were rejected because of fraud.

The commission finished its work at Cairo on July 31, 1862. Dana went at once to Washington with the report and put it in the hands of the Secretary on Aug. 5. "It was never printed," Dana wrote later, "and the manuscript is still in the files of the War Department."

Charles A. Dana, Recollections   1898); H. Rept. 2, 37 Cong., 2 sess., of the Civil War . . . (New York,   Serials 1142-1143.

No records of the commission have been found. Related records, including some of the enclosures to Dana's report and the report of the solicitor, are in the consolidated correspondence file of the Office of the Quartermaster General, some filed under "Cairo" and some under "Lumber Frauds."

Commission on Washington Defenses

The military threat to Washington revealed the inadequacy of its defenses, and on Oct. 25, 1862, by War Department Special Order 312, Secretary Stanton appointed a commission "to examine and report upon the plan of the present forts and sufficiency of the present system of defenses for the city." The commission consisted of Bvt. Brig. Gen. Joseph G. Totten, Chief Engineer; Brig. Gen. Montgomery C. Meigs, Quartermaster General; Brig. Gen. William F. Barry, Chief of Artillery; Brig. Gen. John G. Barnard, Chief Engineer, Defenses of Washington; and Brig. Gen. George W. Cullum, Chief of Staff to the General in Chief. It investigated for 2 months the defense system for the city.

Although the whereabouts of other records of this commission are not known, its original report is in a special file (trunk 1) maintained by the Adjutant General (Record Group 94). This report was printed in Official Records . . . Armies, ser. 1, vol. 21, p. 903-916, and was quoted at length in Bvt. Maj. Gen. J. G. Barnard, A Report on the Defenses of Washington to the Chief of Engineers, U. S. Army (Professional Papers of the Corps of Engineers U. S. Army, No. 20. Washington, 1871). For related records see the Defenses of Washington, under the Engineer Department, above.

Commission on Claims of Officers and Men, Western Department

An act of Mar. 25, 1862 (12 Stat. 374), authorized "pay and bounty as in cases of regular enlistment" for officers and men "whether mustered into actual service or not, where their services were accepted and actually employed by the generals who have been in command of the department of the West, or the department of the Missouri." Under joint resolutions of July 12, 1862, and Feb. 16, 1863 (12 Stat. 623, 824), payments were suspended and President Lincoln on Mar. 16, 1863, appointed three commissioners (Hawkins Taylor, Charles T. Sherman, and Francis T. Russell) to examine and report on claims arising under the provisions of the act. The commission held its sessions in St. Louis and James Fletcher served as its principal secretary. The scope of the commission's inquiry and the nature of its records are clarified by the following passage from its "Instructions to Claimants":

It is desirable that a short and comprehensive statement should accompany the papers of each claimant, whether an individual claim or company claim, showing the date, locality, authority, and immediate causes for the organization or services, the county or counties in which the services were rendered, the nature and extent of such services, and the date and place when discharged, and such other facts and circumstances that may throw light upon his or their claim or claims.

Company rolls should in all cases, when obtainable, be filed as the evidence of claim; and when so filed, they must be made out in the same manner and with as full detail as rolls made out for drawing pay under the army regulations, and must be accompanied by evidence of the authority for the organization of the company, and for the calling of the same into active service, or the acceptance of said service by the commanding officer.

Claims for services by 274 companies were submitted, of which 247 were allowed. Of 374 individual claims submitted, 97 were allowed.

Report of Commission on   souri, Sept. 1863 (H. Ex. Doc. 14,
Claims in the Department of Mis-   38 Cong. , 1 sess. , Serial 1187).

Record Group 94. --Register (docket) of claims allowed (2 vols.), with
an index (2 vols.), 1863. The register is cross-referenced to the Adjutant
General's document files (also in this record group) relating to the individuals concerned.

American Freedmen's Inquiry Commission

Because of the "great and constantly increasing" numbers of Negroes
coming under the care of the War Department, Secretary Stanton appointed
Robert Dale Owen, James McKaye, and Samuel G. Howe, on Mar. 16,
1863, as "commissioners to investigate the condition of the colored population emancipated by acts of Congress and the President's proclamation of
January 1, 1863, and to report what measures will best contribute to their
protection and improvement, so that they may defend and support themselves; and also, how they can be most usefully employed in the service of
the Government for the suppression of the rebellion. " On June 2, 1863,
Capt. George W. Nichols was assigned to aid in the investigation.

The commission's preliminary report to the Secretary of War, June
30, 1863 (S. Ex. Doc. 53, 38 Cong. , 1 sess. , Serial 1176; also Official
Records . . . Armies, ser. 3, vol. 3, p. 430 ff.), discusses "Negroes as
Refugees, " "Negroes as Military Laborers, " "Negroes as Soldiers, "
"Character of Organization Proposed, " "Details of Organization Proposed, "
and "General Results. " The final report of May 15, 1864 (congressional
document cited above; also Official Records . . . Armies, ser. 3, vol. 4,
p. 289 ff.), reviews the history of slavery and discusses emancipation and
"The Future in the United States of the African Race. " "There is involved, " the commission reported, ". . . the great question whether, in
the course of human events, with or without the aid of precautionary measures, it be likely that the two races hitherto the dominant and subordinate
shall be able, when both shall be free, persistently to endure side by side,
and to live together in one common country harmoniously and with mutual
advantage. "

Record Group 94. --The commission's records are in a special file
(trunk 31) of the Adjutant General's Office. They consist chiefly of the
testimony taken and are grouped geographically as follows: (1) District
of Columbia; (2) Fortress Monroe, Norfolk, and Portsmouth; (3) Department of the South; (4) North Carolina; (5) New Orleans and the Mississippi;
(6) Department of the Tennessee; (7) Kentucky, Tennessee, and Missouri;
(8) Arkansas and Indian Territory; (9) Haiti and the South; (10) Canadian
testimony; (11) Louisiana testimony. An index to the records shows the
names of witnesses. Included also in the special file is a copy of the commission's preliminary report of June 30, 1863, submitted as a printed
pamphlet to the Secretary of War, and the original manuscript of its final
report of May 15, 1864, the printed versions of which are cited above. In
addition, there are supplemental reports (not printed as public documents)
by Howe ("The Self-Freedmen of Canada West, " dated May 14, 1864), and
McKaye ("The Emancipated Slave Face to Face With His Old Master, Valley of the Lower Mississippi, " dated May 14, 1864). (A manuscript copy
of the commission's final report and of the supplemental reports are in the
records of the Senate, Record Group 46, under 38A-G3.) The records in-

clude also a file of extracts relating to slavery, made by the commission from Debates on the Adoption of the Federal Constitution.

Records in Other Custody. --About 50 letters addressed to the American Freedmen's Inquiry Commission are in the Manuscript Division, Library of Congress.

Commission on Enrollment and Quotas of New York City and State

By order of Secretary Stanton this commission was appointed on Dec. 5, 1863, "to revise the enrollment and quotas of the city and State of New York, and report whether there be any, and what, errors or irregularities therein, and what corrections, if any, should be made." The commission consisted of William F. Allen (N. Y.), Gen. John Love (Ind.), and Chauncey Smith (Mass.). To test the regularity and correctness of the New York enrollment, the commission made comparisons with other States.

Although there appear to be no manuscript records of the commission its report of Feb. 16, 1864, was printed in Official Records . . . Armies, ser. 3, vol. 4, p. 102 ff.

Slave Claims Commissions

Sec. 24 of an act of Feb. 24, 1864 (15 Stat. 11), provided for the enrollment for the draft of "all able-bodied male colored persons, between the ages of twenty and forty-five years, resident in the United States"; the freeing of drafted slaves and the payment of bounties to their former masters, if loyal; and, furthermore, the appointment by the Secretary of War of "a commission in each of the slave States represented in Congress, charged to award to each loyal person to whom a colored volunteer may owe service a just compensation, not exceeding three hundred dollars, for each such colored volunteer, payable out of the fund derived from commutations, and every such colored volunteer on being mustered into the service shall be free." The work of these commissions was generally supervised by the Bureau for Colored Troops of the Adjutant General's Office. The Bureau's disbursing officer had direct responsibility for disbursements on behalf of the commission for Maryland. A joint resolution of Congress of Mar. 30, 1867 (15 Stat. 29), suspended "all further proceedings" under sec. 24 of the 1864 act and under sec. 2 of an act of July 28, 1866 (14 Stat. 321), and directed the Secretary of War to dissolve the commissions.

Record Group 94. --The extant records of the slave claims commissions consist principally of registers kept by the commissions of Delaware, Kentucky, Maryland, Missouri, Tennessee, and West Virginia, 1864-66 (14 vols.). Related records, maintained by the Bureau for Colored Troops or elsewhere in the Adjutant General's Office, include disbursement vouchers, 1864-66 (3 vols.), with a possibly related register, 1863-64; and a register of claims for Kentucky, Maryland, and Tennessee, 1864-67.

Commission on Colored Refugees

By Secretary Stanton's order of June 2, 1864, Samuel W. Bostwick and Thomas Hood were appointed commissioners to investigate and report upon the condition and treatment of colored refugees at Nashville, Tenn., and at Louisville and Camp Nelson, Ky.

Although there appear to be no separate records of this commission the records of the Secretary of War (Record Group 107) and of the Adjutant General (Record Group 94) probably contain related materials. The commissioners' report of Dec. 28, 1864 (printed as S. Ex. Doc. 28, 38 Cong., 2 sess., Serial 1209), described conditions at Nashville, Clarksville, and Gallatin, Tenn., and Huntsville, Ala. Camp Nelson had been abandoned, but the commission nevertheless reported on the condition of refugees in Kentucky.

Commission on Corrupt Practices in the South

This commission was created by Presidential order of Dec. 10, 1864, to investigate and report upon the corrupt practices of civil and military administrators in certain sections of the South. Maj. Gen. William F. Smith and Henry Stanberry of Ohio were appointed members, but after Stanberry declined the position it was vacant until James T. Brady of New York was appointed in Apr. 1865. In the meantime investigations proceeded under the direction of General Smith. Later Lt. Col. Nicolas Bowen, Judge Advocate, was also appointed to the commission. Among the matters investigated were the government of the city of New Orleans, the conduct of the special agents of the Treasury there, and trade permits issued by the New Orleans Customhouse; also cotton transactions along the Mississippi River and in Texas, the management of abandoned property, freedmen's affairs, and provost marshals' courts.

The final report of the commission was submitted to the Secretary of War on Sept. 23, 1865. On May 2, 1866, President Johnson, in reply to a resolution of the House of Representatives, transmitted a report from Secretary Stanton indicating that it was "not deemed compatible with the public interests to communicate to the House the report made by General Smith and the Hon. James T. Brady of their investigations at New Orleans, La."

Record Group 94.--Testimony of witnesses, exhibits, reports, and related papers, 1864-65 (12 ft.); and the manuscript final report, Sept. 23, 1865, signed by Smith, Brady, and Bowen.

Commissions to Inspect Quartermaster Depots

In compliance with a congressional resolution of Mar. 3, 1865, Secretary Stanton appointed a number of special commissions to inspect the inventories on hand at the quartermaster depots at New York, Philadelphia, Cincinnati, St. Louis, and Louisville.

There appear to be no extant records of these commissions, but the originals of their reports to the Secretary are in a special file (trunk 4) maintained by the Adjutant General (Record Group 94).

Commission on Enlistment of Germans as Substitutes

This commission (consisting of Bvt. Maj. Gen. Robert C. Buchanan, Bvt. Maj. Gen. Gershom Mott, and Bvt. Maj. Gen. Seth Williams) was appointed by AGO Special Order 610, Nov. 22, 1865, as amended by Special Order 625, Dec. 1, 1865, to "investigate and report the facts in relation to the enlistment of certain Germans into the United States service as substitutes, or otherwise, in the State of Massachusetts, in the year 1864, brought from Prussia under alleged contracts with Julian Allen and M. D. Ross, of Boston." The commission was to meet in Boston and Washington, notify the Prussian Minister in Washington, the Governor of Massachusetts, and the Provost Marshal General of the time and place of its meetings, "and hear and report such proofs and their conclusions on the evidence as may be brought before them within a reasonable time, either by the authorities of the State of Massachusetts, the Provost Marshal of the United States, or by or on behalf of the Prussian Legation."

Record Group 94.--The proceedings, other records, and final report of this commission are in trunk 4 of a special file maintained by the Adjutant General.

Commission on Rewards for Apprehension of Lincoln Assassins and Others

So many conflicting claims were filed for the rewards offered "for the apprehension of the murderers of the late President Abraham Lincoln" and for the apprehension of Jefferson Davis and others that an AGO general order on the subject (No. 164, Nov. 24, 1865) was issued. The order announced that all persons claiming such rewards should file their claims and proofs with the Adjutant General "for final adjudication by the special commission appointed to award and determine upon the validity of such claims, before the first day of January next," and that thereafter no claims would be accepted. These instructions related to rewards for the apprehension of John Wilkes Booth, Lewis Payne, G. A. Atzerodt, and David E. Herold, as well as Jefferson Davis; the order revoked rewards previously offered for the arrest of Jacob Thompson, Beverly Tucker, George N. Sanders, William G. Cleary, and John H. Surratt. The commission consisted of Asst. Adj. Gen. Edward D. Townsend and Judge Advocate General Joseph Holt. Its findings (Jan. 13, 1866) were sent to the Speaker of the House by Secretary of War Stanton on Apr. 18, 1866, and were printed as H. Ex. Doc. 90, 39 Cong., 1 sess., Serial 1263.

Record Group 94.--The commission's records appear to have been consolidated with other papers relating to these claims in trunk 10 of a special file maintained by the Adjutant General.

Commissions on State Expenditures for the War

Under an act of July 27, 1861 (12 Stat. 276), and supplementary acts separate groups of commissioners were appointed in the postwar period to verify the expenditures by the various States in enrolling, equipping, subsisting, transporting, and paying State forces called into service after Jan. 1, 1862. Appointments of these commissions were usually announced in AGO general orders. When possible a nearby depot quartermaster was directed to provide for a commission "a suitable apartment" and other administrative support, and in each case the commissioners were required to send the Secretary of the Treasury a report of the balance due the State, together with "all the testimony taken."

There appear to be no separate records of these commissions, but the State claims records of the Third Auditor of the Treasury Department (Record Group 217) comprise in large part their documented reports; these are described elsewhere in this Guide. Records of the Secretary of War (Record Group 107) and of the Adjutant General (Record Group 94) should also be consulted.

Canby Claims Commission

This postwar commission handled claims--largely growing out of the Civil War--not falling under the jurisdiction of any War Department bureau. Col. DeWitt Clinton was recorder.

Record Group 107. --There are letters and papers relating to various claims, 1866-68 (6 in.), received by the commission's recorder; and 18 bound volumes, 1866-88, consisting of indexes, registers of letters received, and reports.

HEADQUARTERS OF THE ARMY

The 1857, 1861, and 1863 editions of Army Regulations omitted entirely the provisions in earlier regulations (especially detailed in regulations of 1841) defining the authority and duties of the Commander of the Army. The 1841 regulations had put the "military establishment . . . under the orders of the Major General commanding in chief in all that regards its discipline and military control." The omission of such a provision from the 1857 regulations did not, however, in the opinion of Maj. Gen. Winfield Scott, take from his office "in any degree . . . any power, authority, honor, or command, conferred upon that high office by law." Congress had first provided for a lieutenant general to command the Army in an act of May 28, 1798 (1 Stat. 558), and under sec. 9 of an act of Mar. 3, 1799 (1 Stat. 752), the Commander of the Army was commissioned "General of the Armies of the United States." Upon his return from Mexico, where he commanded only one of the armies of the United States, Scott was first assigned to command the Eastern Division; but under War Department General Order 27, May 10, 1849, he resumed command of the Army.

Headquarters of the Army, composed of the Commanding General and his staff, had had no fixed location, and at the outbreak of the Civil War it was in New York City. Scott went immediately to Washington and established Headquarters there. This location was confirmed by AGO General Order 94, Nov. 1, 1861, announcing Maj. Gen. George B. McClellan's assumption of command of the Army. On July 23, 1862, Maj. Gen. Henry W. Halleck succeeded McClellan; and when Lt. Gen. Ulysses S. Grant in turn succeeded Halleck (AGO General Order 98, Mar. 12, 1864), Headquarters was to be both "in Washington and also with Lieutenant-General Grant in the field."

As he wrote later to Grant, McClellan, when called to the command in 1861, "dispensed with the machinery of a separate office" by merging "all the routine service and records of the command-in-chief with those of the adjutant-general's office." Scott, in contrast, in both his New York and Washington offices, had had "his own adjutant-general and entirely distinct records; the adjutant-general of the United States Army being then simply the adjutant-general of the Secretary of War." General McClellan recalled, "I kept nothing for myself but the original rough drafts." No written reports "were retained in my office, which was, after all, simply a place for the transaction of business, and not a place of record." Although McClellan's successors in the office of Commanding General did not adhere entirely to his views, their methods of administration resulted in a close relationship between their records and those of the Secretary of War and the Adjutant General.

Successive Commanding Generals of the Army during the Civil War:
Maj. Gen. (Bvt. Lt. Gen.) Winfield Scott, July 5, 1841.
Maj. Gen. George B. McClellan, Nov. 1, 1861.
Maj. Gen. Henry W. Halleck, July 23, 1862.
Lt. Gen. (later Gen.) U. S. Grant, Mar. 12, 1864.

Wartime reports of the Commanding General of the Army, appended to those of the Secretary of War; Memoirs of Lieut. -General Scott, LL. D., Written by Himself (New York, 1864. 2 vols.); McClellan's Own Story (New York, 1887);

Telegrams Sent by Major Gen. H. W. Halleck, While General-in-Chief and Chief of Staff (Washington, 1877. 4 vols.); Personal Memoirs of U. S. Grant (New York, 1885-86. 2 vols.).

Record Group 108. -- There are several volumes of fair copies of letters sent, 1849-68, by the Commanding General to the Secretary of War, Members of Congress, chiefs of War Department bureaus (especially the Adjutant General), staff and line officers, other Government officials, and private citizens. These letters relate to operations, discipline, instruction, troop movements, inspections, arms and equipment, regulations, general Army administration, and other matters. Press copies of letters sent, July 1862- Apr. 1865, are also available; and both fair and press copies include, for Mar. 1864- Apr. 1865, copies of letters sent by Maj. Gen. Henry W. Halleck as Chief of Staff. There are also press copies of "reports and important letters" sent, Nov. 1862-Oct. 1865, and Oct. 1864- Apr. 1865 (2 vols.), principally to the Secretary of War and general officers (again, beginning in Mar. 1864, from Halleck as Chief of Staff). A volume of press copies of letters sent, June 1864- Apr. 1865, by Robert N. Scott, aide-de-camp and Assistant-Adjutant General at Headquarters, contains extracts from inspection reports referred to commanders. Some of the letters-sent volumes are indexed by names or subject, and there are also separate index volumes. Copies of endorsements on letters and other documents received are in several volumes.

The letters received by the Commanding General during the Civil War are arranged as follows: for 1861, by initial letter of writer's surname, then numerically; for 1862, numerically in two subseries under initial letter of writer's surname; for 1863, in two subseries, numerically and numerically under initial letter of writer's surname, respectively; and for 1864-65, in two subseries for each year, numerically under initial letter of writer's surname, for (1) documents received by the office of Maj. Gen. Halleck as Chief of Staff and (2) other documents received at Headquarters. The general registers of letters received, of which 5 volumes cover the war period, are similarly arranged. Other registers include those of letters received from officers, 1865-69 (5 vols.), and received from and returned to War Department officials, 1862-65 (6 vols.). Aside from the main series of letters sent and received are small files of correspondence pertaining to the Signal Corps, Nov. -Dec. 1863; and to the Texas frontier, civil rights in Florida, and the New Orleans riot, all 1866.

There are separate files of telegrams. Fair copies of those sent cover the period Sept. 1862- Aug. 1863, and there are other copies (including drafts and some related correspondence) for Dec. 1860-Nov. 1861 and Aug. -Dec. 1863. There are also originals of telegrams sent, principally by Major General Halleck, Apr. -July 1862 (6 vols.). Telegrams received

comprise those received by Brig. Gen. Lorenzo Thomas, Adjutant General,
Jan. 1862-May 1863 (5 vols.), relating to troop movements, personnel,and
administration; those received by Headquarters of the Army, 1861-62 and
1864-69 (11 vols. and unbound papers), relating to operations, administration, and policy; and those received in cipher and decoded, 1862-65 (19
vols.), addressed to the President, the Secretary of War, the Chief of
Staff, and others. There are also press copies of telegrams received at
different periods between 1862 and 1867 (4 vols.) by Headquarters Army of
the Potomac and by the War Department for Headquarters of the Army.

The general and special orders among the records of Headquarters of
the Army are fragmentary and the searcher should use instead the complete series of these in the records of the Adjutant General.

Among other records are reports of inspections of field headquarters
and installations, 1861 and 1864-66; lists of officers recommended for
brevet, 1862-68; some abstracts, 1865 and 1867, of papers relating to the
movement of Confederate troops to Mexico and to Texas-Mexico frontier
clashes; a record of action on applications by commissioned officers for
leave, resignation, or discharge, 1863-65 (2 vols.); correspondence and
other papers, Sept. 1864 (1 vol., press copies), of special agent R. C.
Hutchinson concerning the arrest of John C. Burnet, assistant at Natchez
in the Treasury Department's First Special Agency; and a few requisitions,
receipts, and accounts.

Some miscellaneous papers in this record group include a few semiof-
ficial or private papers of Capt. Henry W. Bowers, 1862-63, 1865; Col.
Theodore S. Bowers, 1863-65, 1866; Col. Cyrus B. Comstock, 1864; and
Capt. William A. Cameron, 1864-65. There are also the originals of 15
letters, 1862-67, sent by Secretary of the Navy Gideon Welles to the House
and Senate Naval Affairs Committees and the President Pro Tem of the
Senate.

National Archives, Preliminary   "Index to Records of the Command-
Checklist of the Records of the   ing General of the U. S. Army,
Headquarters of the Army, 1825-   1775-1903," compiled by the Adju-
1903, comp. by Jerome Thomases   tant General's Office--for the book
(Washington, 1946). An unpublished   records only--is available.

Records in Other Custody.--The principal collections of the papers of
George B. McClellan and Ulysses S. Grant are in the Library of Congress.
The Library has also some Winfield Scott papers and many Henry W. Hal-
leck items, including about 200 telegrams. Other papers of these four
Civil War Commanding Generals are widely scattered in other important
depositories in the United States.

TERRITORIAL COMMANDS AND ARMIES

In the decade after the War with Mexico the division of the United States
into geographical areas to facilitate military command and operations had
been satisfactorily adjusted for peacetime purposes. The beginning of hostilities in the Civil War, however, and the subsequent diversion of forces
from one part of the country to another during the war and increasingly
complex command relationships in the field required frequent boundary
changes for the military geographical divisions. The works of Thian, Dyer,
and Phisterer, cited below, and the wartime general and special orders of

the Adjutant General must be used in tracing these changes and in identifying the names of the commanders as of given periods.   Military divisions were the principal territorial commands; each division was divided into two or more departments; and the departments as a rule were subdivided into districts.   Troop or organizational commands at their highest level were divided into armies, but army commands frequently coincided with departmental commands.   A thorough understanding of the command structure is essential, therefore, for effective research in the extant records of the very many separate headquarters and organizations.   Moreover--just as in using Official Records . . . Armies, "It is necessary . . . in order to find in the index references to the operations of a particular brigade or higher organization, to first ascertain the name of the commanding officer of the organization for the period in question"--a knowledge of the succession of individual command enables the researcher to move from the records of one command to another when his interest is in military biography. The military career of Maj. Gen. Benjamin F. Butler, for instance, is documented in large part by the extant records of the Department of Annapolis, the Department of Virginia, the Department of the Gulf, and the Department of Virginia and North Carolina--the Civil War commands he successively held.   Burnside, Sheridan, Ord, Banks, Canby, Dix, Wool-- these and almost all other general officers were moved frequently from one command to another and left behind them as records of their former headquarters many of their letters received, the copies of those sent by them or by their orders, and other papers.

Military divisions existing at one time or another during the Civil War were as follows:

Middle Military Division   Military Division of the Potomac
Military Division of the James   Military Division of the Southwest
Military Division of the Mississippi Military Division of West Missis-
Military Division of the Missouri   sippi

At the end of the war the United States was divided (by AGO G. O. 118, June 27, 1865) into the five following military divisions:

Military Division of the Atlantic   Military Division of the Pacific
Military Division of the Gulf   Military Division of the Tennessee
Military Division of the Mississippi

Geographical departments existing at one time or another during the war had the following names:

Department of Annapolis   Department of the Mississippi
Department of Arkansas   Department of the Missouri
Department of the Cumberland   Department of the Monongahela
Department of the East   Mountain Department
Department of Florida   Department of New England
Department of the Gulf   Department of New Mexico
Department of Kansas   Department of New York
Department of Kentucky   Department of North Carolina
Department of Key West   Department of Northeastern Virginia
Department of Maryland   Northern Department
Middle Department   Department of the Northwest

Department of the Ohio

Department of the Pacific

Department of Pennsylvania

Department of the Potomac

Department of the Rappahannock

Department of the Shenandoah

Department of the South

Department of the Susquehanna

Department of the Tennessee

Department of Texas

Department of Utah

Department of Virginia

Department of Virginia and North Carolina

Department of Washington

Department of the West

Department of West Virginia

Western Department

Department of Western Virginia

In the immediate postwar period many of the departments listed above were still in existence and the following additional ones were established:

Department of Alabama

Department of California

Department of the Carolinas

Department of the Columbia

Department of Georgia

Department of the Lakes

Department of Louisiana

Department of the Platte

Department of South Carolina

Armies existing at one time or another during the war were known by the following names:

Army of Arkansas

Army of the Cumberland

Army of Georgia

Army of the Gulf

Army of the James

Army of Kentucky

Army of the Middle Military Division

Army of the Mississippi

Army of the Ohio

Army of the Potomac

Army of the Shenandoah

Army of the Tennessee

Army of Virginia

Army of West Virginia

Record Group 98. -- Most of the records of the military divisions, departments, and armies existing during the Civil War are in one large collection assembled by the Adjutant General's Office. These are the records kept by the commands as distinguished from related records (such as reports received from them) kept in many offices of the War Department, especially in the Adjutant General's Office, and described elsewhere in this Guide. They consist of considerable quantities of bound volumes of correspondence and "document files" of unbound correspondence and other papers. For many commands--because they were already in existence when the war began or because they continued after the war (often renamed)--the several series significant for Civil War research begin before and end after the war; and postwar or wartime redefinitions or redesignations of commands had the result of bringing forward under their later names the records of some of the Civil War commands. More important to an understanding of this collection, however, is the fact that the many organizational changes often caused intermingling of the records of two or more commands. The records of the Department of the Tennessee, for instance, are in part inseparable or indistinguishable from those of some other commands, notably the Army of the Tennessee, the Military Division of the Tennessee, and the Department of the Cumberland.

The reports and correspondence relating to Civil War battles, cam-

paigns, skirmishes, and incidents that were printed in Official Records
. . . Armies were reproduced in large part from these command records;
the researcher whose interest is principally in materials relating to such
military operations, therefore, will find his needs essentially satisfied in
Official Records, although he may wish to compare the printed versions
with the original documents. The more or less intact records of these
commands, however, afford an opportunity for investigating aspects of
administration and logistics not adequately covered in Official Records.
There are master lists or indexes of the commands represented, book
indexes of the contents of the records of most commands, and, finally, the
indexes that themselves are inseparable parts of the records--such as registers of letters and telegrams received and sent.

The researcher may expect to find in these records, for any particular
command, the files of the staff officers assigned to headquarters, of the
boards and commissions appointed, and of the divisions, brigades, districts, and subdistricts operating within the command. The staff at an
army headquarters was usually a reflection of the bureau organization of
the War Department itself. The staff of the Army of the Potomac, for instance, consisted in 1862 of a chief engineer, a topographical engineer, a
medical director, a chief quartermaster, a commissary of subsistence, a
chief of ordnance, a provost marshal, a judge advocate, a superintendent
of telegraphic operations, a chief signal officer, and (for guard and police
duty) a commandant of general headquarters. The Civil War records of the
Department of the Gulf--and this example is not intended to suggest that
these records are of greater importance than those of other departments--
include the records of the judge advocate, the inspector general, the commissary of musters, the chief of artillery, the chief of engineers, the chief
signal officer, the provost marshal general, the board of appointments, the
board of improper enlistments, the board of prison inspectors, the general
recruiting service, the sequestration commission, the prisoners commission, the commissary of prisoners, the agent of prisoner exchange, the
military agent, and the board of enrollment. The records of the Department of the Gulf comprise also the files of the provost court, the river
police, the provost sheriff, the police jail and other prisons, the Defenses
of New Orleans, and the recruiting depot.

The records of the Department of the Tennessee (mentioned above as in
part intermingled with the records of the Army of the Tennessee and other
commands) may be described in some detail to suggest the general character
of the records of the military divisions, departments, and armies. The
commanding general's records comprise copies of letters sent, Oct. 1862-
Oct. 1863 and Mar. 1864-Mar. 1867 (including copies of letters exchanged
by General Grant and Confederate General Pemberton on the surrender of
Vicksburg to Union forces); letters received, with registers and endorsements, Oct. 1862-Mar. 1867; copies of telegrams sent, July 1863-Dec. 1864
and July 1865-June 1866; telegrams received, 1862-64 and June-Dec. 1865;
and various orders, registers (of leaves, furloughs, resignations, discharges, and transportation orders), rosters, and reports. Records of the
chief commissary of musters consist of copies of letters sent, Jan.-July
1865; letters received, Jan.-July 1865; endorsements on letters received,
Oct. 1864-July 1865; and a register (1 vol.) of officers and men mustered
into the Army of the Tennessee, Dec. 1864-July 1865. The inspector general's records include copies of letters sent, May 1863-Dec. 1866, with
gaps; inspection reports, 1865-67; a register of letters received, June 1863-

Dec. 1866, with gaps; and endorsements on letters received, July 1865-
Feb. 1866, and Aug.-Dec. 1866. Other records include oaths of allegiance
to the Union and bonds to be forfeited if the signer should aid the Confederacy, 1861-65 (maintained by the provost marshal); correspondence of
the blanks and records office, 1865-67; correspondence of the judge advocate's office, 1865-66; and a series of miscellaneous letters and reports
received, 1862-67, at the several headquarters of the Department of the
Tennessee, the Military Division of the Tennessee, the Department of the
Cumberland, the District of East Tennessee, the District of Middle Tennessee, and the District of West Tennessee.

"Special Index for the Principal Armies, Army Corps, Military Divisions and Departments," in Official Records . . . Armies: General Index . . . (Serial 130), p. xliii-xlvii; Raphael P. Thian, Notes Illustrating the Military Geography of the United States (Washington, 1881); Frederick Phisterer, Statistical Record of the Armies of the United States (New York, 1884); Frederick H. Dyer, A Compendium of the War of the Rebellion (New York, 1959. 3 vols.); Francis B. Heitman, Historical Register and Dictionary of the United States Army . . . (Washington, 1903. 2 vols.); Adjutant General's Office, General and Special Orders, 1860-65.

Record Group 94.--Not all documents printed in Official Records were
restored to the files from which they had been removed. The miscellaneous
records of military commands withdrawn for the use of the War Records
Office and not returned include some of the Middle Military Division, the
Military Division of the Mississippi, the Military Division of West Mississippi, the Department of Arkansas, the Department of the Gulf, the Department of Kansas, the Middle Department, the Department of the Mississippi,
the Department of the Missouri, the Department of New Mexico, the Department of the Northwest, the Department of Ohio, the Department and
Army of the Tennessee, the Department of Virginia and North Carolina, the
Department of Washington, the Department and Army of West Virginia, the
Army of Georgia, the Army of Kentucky, and the Army of the Potomac.

ARMY CORPS

By sec. 9 of an act of July 17, 1862 (12 Stat. 598), Congress authorized
President Lincoln "to establish and organize army corps at his discretion,"
and eventually 25 corps were in service during the Civil War. Sources of
information for the histories of the First to the Twenty-fifth Army Corps
of the Civil War period are in general the same as the sources, cited above,
for information on the territorial commands. Actually, however, more than
25 organizations are involved, for reactivations of corps under numerical
designations borne previously by discontinued or reassigned corps amounted
to the creation of entirely new organizations. Each corps operated within
one of the armies or a geographical department. The observations in the
discussion of territorial commands and armies, above, with respect to the
advantage to effective research of a good deal of knowledge about command
structure and assignment changes, are equally applicable in using the corps
records. As in the case of the territorial commands and armies, again,
corps documents of campaign significance were extensively printed in
Official Records . . . Armies, but the great mass of corps records, partic-

ularly relating to administrative and logistical matters, was not published.

Record Groups 94, 98. --The records of the corps themselves, described below, are best understood when used in conjunction with records relating to the corps in the records of the Adjutant General's Office (Record Group 94). The Adjutant General's document files of correspondence received and letter books of outgoing correspondence are especially valuable for research in matters of corps administration. The series of "Historical and Statistical Records of the Principal Military Commands in the Union and Confederate Armies"--prepared after the war--contains some information on corps tactical formations; and a 1-volume record of "Organization and Commands of Army Corps" gives the names of commanders, arranged chronologically by period of service under corps, and contains newspaper clippings (1892-93) relating to the histories of some of the corps. (Many other records relating to the 25 corps are noted elsewhere in this Guide, but some of these may be mentioned briefly here. In Record Group 77 there is a list, compiled in the Engineer Bureau, of commanders of corps and other elements of the Armies of the Potomac and the James. Records of the Surgeon General's Office in Record Group 112 include pamphlets listing medical officers serving with the 25 corps. The printed general, special, and other orders of these corps are most readily available in the Adjutant General's collection of orders, dating from 1797, in Record Group 94.)

The records of the First to the Twenty-fifth Army Corps and those of the geographical departments are not entirely distinguishable because in certain instances the command of a corps was identical with that of a department. The records of each corps consist of the files of correspondence, orders, circulars, and other papers kept at corps headquarters and of similar division and brigade records. The division and brigade records are often imperfect, incomplete, or missing for some periods owing to the fact that the troops assigned were scattered in the various districts, subdistricts, and posts of the geographical area within which the corps operated. The researcher wishing to examine the records of any corps will do well to examine first the book index (compiled in the Adjutant General's Office) of the records of that corps. Each such index is prefaced by a list of successive commanders, a general statement about the corps records, and the facts about its history that are important to an understanding of its records. In each index the list of the records of the corps headquarters (general correspondence, orders, and records of the corps staff) is followed by lists of division and brigade records and, if applicable, of detachment, expedition, and post records.

The extant records of 17 of the corps are divided between Record Groups 94 and 98; those of 6 of the corps appear to be entirely in Record Group 98, intact as corps records; and those of 2 of the corps are intermingled with the records of other commands in Record Group 98.

The table on the next page shows the quantity of corps records in Record Group 98, states whether a book index of the records is available, notes the existence of other corps records in Record Group 94, and explains why the records of 2 of the 25 corps are not in the main corps collection.

Record Group 98

Corps	Index vols.	Registry vols.	Document boxes	See notes
1	2	20	13	*
2	1	108	53	*
3	1	48	19	*
4	1	43	13	*
5	1	78	13	*
6	1	101	17	
7	none	none	none	**
8	1	174	59	
9	1	79	10	*
10	1	38	7	*
11	1	28	6	
12	1	29	4	
13	1	48	8	*
14	1	63	4	*
15	1	66	14	*
16	1	99	22	*
17	1	52	9	*
18	1	7	2	*
19	1	25	3	
20	1	50	19	*
21	1	11	3	*
22	none	none	none	***
23	1	28	6	*
24	1	51	14	*
25	none	56	20	
Total	23 vols.	1,302 vols.	338 boxes	

*In Record Group 94 are reports, letters, telegrams, returns, orders, and circulars of these corps. Some of these documents are originals taken from the corps records and others are copies.

**Although not in the main corps collection, the records of the Seventh Army Corps, which was constituted from troops of the Department of Arkansas, are elsewhere in Record Group 98. The records of the corps (as well as the records of the Arkansas Expedition and the Army of Arkansas) are in part inseparable from the records of the Department of Arkansas.

***Although not in the main corps collection, the records of the Twenty-second Army Corps, which was constituted from troops of the Department of Washington, are elsewhere in Record Group 98. In large part the corps records are inseparable from the records of the Department.

As in the case of the territorial commands and armies the corps records in themselves must be distinguished by the researcher from the records relating to the corps that are in the files of superior commands and of the bureaus of the War Department. Since the document files kept by the

Second Corps (see table above) are among the largest, the subjects to
which they pertain may be mentioned to suggest the kinds of materials the
searcher is likely to encounter. Aside from the usual circulars, orders,
passes, and certificates, these Second Corps documents pertain to matters such as recruiting, deserters and stragglers, burials, prisoners,
sutlers, the Pioneer Corps, loss and capture of arms and colors, "citizen"
teamsters and other employees, the Ambulance Corps, and "organization,
reorganization & consolidation."

REGULAR ARMY REGIMENTS

At the outbreak of the Civil War the Regular Army consisted of the 1st,
2d, 3d, and 4th regiments of artillery, formed under an act of Mar. 2,
1821 (3 Stat. 615), the 1st and 2d regiments of dragoons, organized under
acts of May 23, 1836 (5 Stat. 33), and Apr. 4, 1844 (5 Stat. 654); the regiment of mounted riflemen organized under an act of May 19, 1846 (9 Stat.
13); the 1st and 2d regiments of cavalry, organized under sec. 8 of an act
of Mar. 3, 1855 (10 Stat. 639); the 1st to the 7th regiments of infantry,
organized under an act of Mar. 3, 1815 (3 Stat. 224), and the act of Mar.
2, 1821, cited above; the 8th regiment of infantry, organized under an act
of July 5, 1838 (5 Stat. 256); and the 9th and 10th regiments of infantry,
organized under sec. 8 of the act of Mar. 3, 1855, cited above. This
Army establishment was increased in the first year of the war by the formation of the 5th regiment of artillery under an act of July 12, 1861 (12
Stat. 269); the organization of 6 cavalry regiments, under an act of Aug. 3,
1861 (12 Stat. 289), by redesignating regiments of dragoons, riflemen, and
cavalry previously authorized and by consolidating them into the Cavalry
Corps; and the organization of the 11th to the 19th regiments of infantry
under an act of July 29, 1861 (12 Stat. 279). Each artillery regiment consisted usually of 8 or 12 batteries; each cavalry regiment consisted of 3
battalions (each battalion with 2 squadrons and each squadron with 2 companies); and each infantry regiment consisted of 2 or more battalions, with
8 companies to the battalion.

Record Group 98. --The regimental records in this record group are
those actually kept by organizations in the field, and are to be distinguished
from those relating to regiments kept in the Adjutant General's Office and
elsewhere in the War Department and described accordingly in this Guide.
The Revised United States Army Regulations of 1861, issued in 1863, defined the books for each regiment to be the regimental order book, to contain regimental orders, with an index; the letter book, to contain the
correspondence of the commanding officer on regimental subjects, with an
index; an "index of letters required to be kept on file"; and the descriptive
book, to contain a "list of the officers of the regiment, with their rank, and
dates of appointment, and promotions; transfers, leaves of absence, and
places and dates of birth; . . . [and] the names of all enlisted soldiers,
entered according to priority of enlistments, giving their description, the
dates and periods of their enlistment; and, under the head of remarks, the
cause of discharge, character, death, desertion, transfer, actions in which
engaged, &c.; in short, every thing relating to their military history."
Each company kept a descriptive book, a clothing book, an order book, and
a morning report book. "One page of the [company] descriptive book will
be appropriated to the list of officers; two to the non-commissioned officers;

two to the register of men transferred; four to register of men discharged; two to register of deaths; four to register of deserters--the rest to the company descriptive list."

For the Civil War period these regimental records are in series of "record books," ca. 1858-70, and series of "document files" of correspondence and other papers, 1860-1900. They consist essentially of materials of the character required by the regulations summarized above. A list of regimental books, arranged by organization and giving brief descriptive titles, dates, and volume numbers, is available.

VOLUNTEER REGIMENTS

Official Army registers of the volunteer forces for the period of the Civil War were published by order of the Secretary of War, in compliance with a joint resolution of the Senate and the House of Representatives, Mar. 2, 1865 (13 Stat. 570). These give names of regiments, short historical accounts of their organization, names of officers, and lists of casualties. Vols. 1-7 are arranged by State. Vol. 8 contains sections on the Territories, Veteran Reserve Corps, U. S. Veteran Volunteers (First Army Corps), U. S. Volunteers, and U. S. Colored Troops. There is an index to battles and names in each volume.

Official Army Register of the Volunteer Force of the United States Army for the Years 1861, '62, '63, '64, '65 (Washington, 1865-67. 8 vols.). Manuscript lists supplementing the registers are in the files of the Commission Branch, Adjutant General's Office, as noted under that Office.

Record Group 94. -- The records of the volunteer regiments consist of "book records" (ca. 1,600 ft.)--regimental descriptive books, letter books, order books, and clothing books; company descriptive books and order books; and regimental consolidated morning report books and company morning report books. For many regiments not all of these kinds of books will be found; but some of them are available for most regiments. In the case of a few regiments all of the "book records" are bound in one volume. The typical contents of the various "books" are as follows:

Regimental descriptive book: Rosters of commissioned officers for different dates; lists of commissioned officers by rank, with remarks; lists of noncommissioned staff officers; list of promoted officers showing rank and date of promotion; list of officers transferred from and to the regiment showing rank and date of transfer; list of officers resigned showing rank and date of resignation; lists of deaths of officers showing rank and date of death; and alphabetical list of enlisted men and noncommissioned officers, with personal data and remarks.

Regimental letter book: Index of letters sent (alphabetical by addressee); copies of letters sent, arranged chronologically; letters received, arranged alphabetically and chronologically; and endorsements (sometimes entered in a separate volume called the endorsement book).

Regimental order book: General orders, special orders, and court-martial orders, sometimes including circulars and requisitions for men for sentry and other duty.

Clothing book: Clothing accounts with noncommissioned officers and enlisted men, giving only the date of issue, value, and when the account was settled. (These books are no longer extant except when bound with other records.)

Company descriptive book: Lists of commissioned officers, noncommissioned officers, enlisted men, men transferred, and men discharged; registers of deaths with date, place, and cause; registers of deserters; descriptive roll of company, giving personal data.

Regimental consolidated morning report book: A strength report made daily on a standard form and entered chronologically, showing the disposition and condition of the regiment and usually its location. Strength given by company.

Company morning report book: Strength report made on a form allowing space for each day, giving the same information as the regimental morning report book.

Company order book: Chronologically arranged copies of all company orders.

The overall organization of these records is alphabetical by State or Territory, thereunder by branch of service (cavalry, heavy and light artillery, and infantry), then numerical by regiment or battery. The following States or Territories are represented: Alabama, Arkansas, California, Colorado Territory, Connecticut, Delaware, District of Columbia, Florida, Illinois, Indiana, Iowa, Kansas, Kentucky, Louisiana, Maine, Maryland, Massachusetts, Michigan, Minnesota, Mississippi, Missouri, Nebraska Territory, Nevada, New Hampshire, New Jersey, New Mexico Territory, New York, North Carolina, Ohio, Oregon, Pennsylvania, Rhode Island, Tennessee, Vermont, Virginia, Washington Territory, West Virginia, and Wisconsin. The records include also those of organizational elements of U. S. Colored Troops, U. S. Sharpshooters, U. S. Volunteers, U. S. Veteran Volunteers, and Veteran Reserve Corps.

FORTS, CAMPS, AND OTHER ARMY POSTS

Records of some U. S. Army posts existing during the Civil War are treated summarily in this section. These are records actually kept at forts and other "fixed" stations and are to be distinguished from related records kept by the Adjutant General's Office and other War Department bureaus. Records created by Army posts incidental to their serving as temporary military prisons for Confederate prisoners of war and records of military prisons themselves are discussed elsewhere, under the Office of the Commissary General of Prisoners. Also excluded from treatment here are ordnance arsenals and armories (see the Office of the Chief of Ordnance) and quartermaster depots (see the Office of the Quartermaster General).

At each post the commanding officer was required to see that the following books were kept: a morning report book, a guard report book, an order book, and a letter book. Copies of the monthly post returns were required to be filed and kept; the original post returns were forwarded periodically to the Adjutant General. For 38 of the Army posts in existence during the Civil War decade, there are no post records. Only 36 posts have copies of letters sent and only 10 have letters received. Records of many posts are fragmentary. Some posts, in Southern areas, were surrendered to the Confederacy early in the war and were not reactivated after the war. Frontier posts during the war were especially subject to Indian attack or harassment, and for some of them there are few or no records.

Other posts were inactive during the war; still others may have kept records that were lost either in shipment to Washington or by some other hazard.

In the discussion below a few of the U. S. Army posts with extant records for the Civil War decade (or some part of it) are listed in alphabetical order. The reader should note that this is not a "sampling" of post records. The posts listed are those with the more nearly complete or the more significant records for the Civil War period. At the end of the list is an entry for the U. S. Soldiers' Home.

Fort Abercrombie, N. Dak.

The first United States military post in North Dakota; established as a camp on Aug. 28, 1857. When the Civil War broke out all regular troops were recalled from this fort, and in July 1861 it was garrisoned by volunteer organizations from Minnesota. From this fort and from Fort Wadsworth just south of it went the expeditions against the Dakota Indian tribes led by Gen. Henry Hastings Sibley in 1863 and Gen. Alfred Sully in 1864. Capt. James L. Fisk's expeditions of 1862 and 1863, which escorted trains of miners and settlers to the Montana and Idaho goldfields, passed through this fort.

Record Group 98. -- Fragmentary records (7 ft.), 1860-77.

Posts at Alexandria, Va.

At the outbreak of the war Alexandria was taken and fortified because of its nearness to Arlington Heights, its command of the navigation of the Potomac, and its connection with the railroad system of the South. Fort Ellsworth was soon built, and about Sept. 1, 1861, Forts Worth, Reynolds, and Ward were commenced. Somewhat later Forts Barnard and Lyon were begun. In 1862 Forts Weed, Farnsworth, O'Rourke, Willard, and Williams were constructed. Between Fort Ward and Fort Worth an almost unbroken line of trenches, supported by powerful batteries, covered the line of defense; this was continued to Fort or Battery Baresche, near Fort Reynolds. Early in 1863 a barbette battery of 6 guns, Battery Rogers, was built on Jones' Point. The fortifications were held by Union troops until the end of hostilities, when they were gradually dismantled and abandoned.

Record Group 98. -- Several items, 1863-69 (4 in.), including reports of the strength of different units and of convalscents, deserters, invalids, etc., in the area, 1864; and daily work reports and freight records of a quartermaster depot at Alexandria, 1863-65.

Fort Craig, N. Mex.

Established Mar. 31, 1854; abandoned Sept. 1884.

Record Group 98. -- Records, 1852-85 (15 ft.), include copies of letters sent; guard reports, from 1862; and provost marshal's records, from 1863.

Posts at Hilton Head, S. C.

On Nov. 7, 1861, Fort Walker, a Confederate fort on Hilton Head Island, was captured by U. S. forces. The fort was renamed Fort Welles, and a strong earthwork built behind it was named Fort Howell. Hilton Head became the headquarters of the Department of the South in Apr. 1862. In Sept. 1864 the entrenchments were known as Fort Sherman. In Apr. 1866 the post of Hilton Head was established, and on Jan. 14, 1868, it was abandoned.

Record Group 98. --Records (6 in.) comprise copies of letters sent by the post quartermaster, 1865-66, and the post engineer officer, 1861-63; and miscellaneous papers, 1862-64.

Post at Huntsville, Ala.

Established Jan. 1864 by the 17th Iowa Volunteer Infantry.

Record Group 98. --Records of the original and successor posts, 1863-74 (2 ft.), include letters received, from 1864; a register of letters received, from 1865; copies of letters sent, from 1865; morning reports of sick and wounded, from 1864; and a list of hospital attendants, 1864-65.

Fort Independence, Mass.

This fort, on Castle Island in Boston Harbor, was named Fort Independence in Aug. 1799. It was abandoned in 1833, regarrisoned and again abandoned in 1836, again regarrisoned in 1851, and finally abandoned in 1879.

Record Group 98. --A fragmentary file (4 in.) includes copies of post surgeon's letters sent, 1858-61 (also letters sent from Fort Jefferson, Fla., 1861-65); a prescription and diet book, 1857-61 (with similar records for Fort Jefferson, 1861-66); and miscellaneous reports, 1866-67.

Fort Jefferson, Fla.

The fortification on Garden Key, construction of which was begun in 1846, became Fort Jefferson in 1850; it was garrisoned by U. S. troops throughout the Civil War. Dr. Samuel A. Mudd, convicted of conspiracy in the Lincoln assassination, was imprisoned at the fort, 1865-69. The fort was abandoned on Jan. 11, 1874, although later regarrisoned.

Record Group 98. --Records (33 ft.); those of Civil War interest include copies of letters sent, 1866-70; endorsements, 1868-73; registers of letters received, 1846-62; a document file, 1844-98; orders and circulars, 1866-72; morning reports of sick and wounded, 1862-63, 1865; morning reports, 1866-73; records relating to the construction of the post (chiefly progress reports), 1847-72; employees' time books, 1846-65; and miscellaneous material, 1847-97. The records were indexed in a WPA project in 1935. A letter book kept originally by Army Surgeon Adam N. McLaren, who was transferred from Fort Independence, Mass., to Fort Jefferson in Jan. 1861, is filed with the records of Fort Independence (see above); this book was used from 1862 to 1865 by other surgeons at Fort Jefferson to record their letters sent. Also with the Fort Independence records is a prescription and diet book, containing Fort Jefferson entries for 1861-66.

Fort Kearny, Nebr.

Established as Fort Childs about Apr. 1848 near Grand Island; renamed Fort Kearny Jan. 31, 1849; discontinued 1871.

Record Group 98.--Records (3 ft.) include copies of letters sent, 1861-65; registers of letters received, 1865-66; endorsements, 1865-71; orders, 1852-71; morning reports, 1861-62; and guard reports, 1863-66.

Fort Klamath, Oreg.

Established Sept. 5, 1863, to protect the emigrant route and settlers in Klamath Valley, when Col. C. S. Drew arrived from Camp Baker with Co. C, 1st Oreg. Cavalry. The fort was occupied by volunteer troops until July 8, 1867, and was abandoned in 1890.

Record Group 98.--Records, 1862-90 (12 ft.), include copies of letters sent, from 1862; and a document file, from 1863.

Fort Laramie, Wyo.

Established June 26, 1849, in what in 1868 was to become Wyoming Territory; abandoned 1890.

Record Group 98.--Records, 1849-90 (26 ft.), include for the Civil War period copies of letters sent, a document file, and orders.

Fort Leavenworth, Kans.

Established in May 1827; thereafter continuously occupied. During the Civil War the post was twice threatened by Confederates and was a major base of operations in the West. An ordnance arsenal was located at the fort, 1860-74, and one of the several schools of artillery practice operated there, ca. Jan. 1860-Jan. 5, 1861.

Record Group 98.--Records, 1844-1941 (461 ft.),. include copies of letters sent, 1861-62 and 1865; registers of letters received, from 1864; a document file; orders, including those of the Artillery School of Practice, 1860-61, and of U. S. Forces at Independence (Mo.), 1862-66; a post journal of events, 1864; a report on citizen prisoners, 1863-64; muster rolls, from 1862; post and regimental returns; post surgeon's copies of letters sent, from 1865; and descriptive books of casuals, from 1864.

Fort Monroe, Va.

The present fort, begun after the War of 1812 as Fortress Monroe, was renamed Fort Monroe in 1832. A major center for military operations during the Civil War, it served as headquarters for the Peninsular Campaign of 1862 and for several waterborne expeditions.

Record Group 98.--Records, 1817-1940, include a few concerning the war. These comprise copies of letters and telegrams sent, 1865; "official telegrams received at, sent from and passing through Fortress Monroe," 1862-65; endorsements, 1861-64; orders and circulars; descriptive lists, 1862-65; and, in the records of the Artillery School of Practice, court-martial records from 1864.

Post at Raleigh, N. C.

Although Raleigh was occupied by Federal forces during the closing days of the war, a post there does not seem to have been formally established until Apr. 1866.

Record Group 98.--Records, generally postwar (4 ft.), include a record of prisoners, 1865-66, and (in a volume of resignations and commissions, 1835-36, a State record) oaths of allegiance, 1865.

Camp San Juan Island, Wash.

Established as Camp Pickett in July 1859 by Capt. George E. Pickett and his Co. D, 9th U. S. Infantry; name later changed to San Juan and still later to Fred Steele. In 1868 the post was renamed Camp San Juan Island.

Record Group 98.--Records (2 ft.), include copies of letters sent, 1859-74; letters received, 1859-65; and orders, 1859-74 (including those of Fort Townsend).

Post and District of Savannah, Ga.

This post, sometimes known as Oglethorpe Barracks, was seized by Georgia State troops on Jan. 26, 1861. Savannah and the post were captured by Federal forces in Dec. 1864. The post was abandoned on Apr. 23, 1879.

Record Group 98.--Post records (2 ft.) include copies of letters sent, 1866-70, and of endorsements, 1867-79; orders, 1868-79; a station book, 1865; and record of prisoners, 1866. Here also are records of the Military District of Savannah, consisting of copies of letters sent, 1865, and of endorsements, 1865-66.

Fort Snelling, Minn.

Established Aug. 24, 1819; abandoned Sept. 14, 1946.

Record Group 98.--Records, 1862-1924 (71 ft.), include copies of letters sent, from 1863; orders and circulars, from 1862; rosters; morning reports, 1865; copies of letters and endorsements sent by the post surgeon, from 1864; a medical history of the post, 1865-1905; hospital morning reports, 1863-64; sick reports, from 1864; and prescription books, from 1865.

Fort Stanton, N. Mex.

Established May 4, 1855. On Aug. 2, 1861, because of the Confederate invasion of New Mexico, Fort Stanton was abandoned by Federal troops. It was occupied by Confederates for a short time, abandoned in Sept. 1861, reoccupied by Federal troops on Apr. 8, 1863, and finally abandoned on Aug. 17, 1896.

Record Group 98.--Records, 1859 and 1863-96 (18 ft.), include, for the Civil War period, copies of letters sent, letters received, proceedings of the council of administration, and orders.

Fort Stockton, Tex.

Established Mar. 23, 1859, as Camp Stockton; renamed Fort Stockton May 23, 1860; reoccupied July 7, 1867, under the jurisdiction of the Fifth Military District (see Military Government, below).

Record Group 98.--Records, 1867-86 (6 ft.), include copies of letters sent, endorsements, and letters received (with registers) during the period of the Fifth Military District.

Fort Union, N. Mex.

Established at Mora July 26, 1851. Fort Union, headquarters of the 1st N. Mex. Volunteers, was the scene of the Civil War activities of Col. Christopher (Kit) Carson. The fort was abandoned on May 15, 1891.

Record Group 98.--Records, 1852-91 (18 ft.), include, for the Civil War period, copies of letters sent; letters received; endorsements, 1865-73; registers of letters received, 1865-67; orders, 1858-62 and 1864-72; and records of the post council of administration, July 1861-June 1863.

Fort Vancouver, Wash.

Columbia Barracks, established by the 1st U. S. Artillery in 1849, was renamed Fort Vancouver in 1853. There was an arsenal at the fort from 1859 to 1881. In 1879 the fort was renamed Vancouver Barracks; it was inactivated in 1946.

Record Group 98.--Records, 1850-1921 (45 ft.), include, for the Civil War period, copies of letters sent, with indexes; a decimal correspondence file (a postwar rearrangement); orders and circulars; records of the post council of administration; a register of sick and wounded, to 1863; and morning reports of sick and wounded.

Post at Vicksburg, Miss.

When Vicksburg surrendered to Federal forces on July 4, 1863, it was garrisoned by elements of the 62d Ill. Infantry, 2d Miss. Infantry, and 12th La. Infantry, under the command of Brig. Gen. John E. Smith. The post was abandoned in May 1870 although it was later reestablished.

Record Group 98.--Records, (1 1/2 ft.), include reports of the Vicksburg Marine (later Freedmen's) Hospital, 1863-68.

U. S. Soldiers' Home

An act of Mar. 3, 1851 (9 Stat. 595), established a Military Asylum for former soldiers of the Army; and an act of Mar. 3, 1859 (11 Stat. 434), changed the name of the institution to Soldiers' Home. From 1859, and continuing through the Civil War period, the Board of Commissioners was composed of the Commissary General of Subsistence, the Surgeon General, and the Adjutant General. President Lincoln occupied the Riggs house on the Home grounds from about midsummer to early November of the years 1862, 1863, and 1864.

Col. Paul R. Goode, The United States Soldiers' Home; a History of Its First Hundred Years (Richmond, 1957). At the time of Col. Goode's research the records at the Home covering the Civil War period included letter books containing transcripts of letters sent by the Secretary of the Board of Commissioners, order books, morning reports, a register of checks signed by the secretary-treasurer, a register of letters received by the secretary of the Board of Commissioners, and records of the proceedings of the board.

Record Group 231.--The records of the Home for the Civil War period include morning reports and registers of inmates.

Records in Other Custody. --Among records still kept at the Home are
those of the Board of Commissioners, intact from the board's first session
in 1851. The files of the board's proceedings may throw light on events and
activities at the Home during the Civil War, when it was used as a summer
White House. Other important records retained at the Home include its
principal financial records since 1851 and case histories of patients. See
also the bibliographical note, above.

MILITARY GOVERNMENT

Military government was instituted during the Civil War in occupied
areas of the South whenever local conditions appeared to require it. Since
U. S. Army experience in military government was limited (the notable experience having been in Mexico under Gen. Winfield Scott), principles and
policies for military government had been only imperfectly formulated.
The special situation in Tennessee resulted in the appointment of Andrew
Johnson as military governor of the State on March 3, 1862. His government and that of Maj. Gen. Benjamin F. Butler, who established military
government in New Orleans on May 1, 1862, are particularly inviting subjects for research, since they afford so great an opportunity for comparison
and contrast. The records pertinent to such research, however, are elu-
sive; and the researcher must rely principally on the records of the military
divisions and departments (discussed above) that included the States of
Tennessee and Louisiana within their boundaries. The same is true for
other military governments set up by Union forces during the war--
especially in Arkansas, Texas, Georgia, and Virginia.

The establishment of military government in the Southern States as a
feature of the system imposed under the Reconstruction Acts was due primarily to the fact that the introduction of Negro suffrage was thought to be
possible only through a show of strength. In May and June of 1865 President Johnson had appointed Provisional Governors for the Southern States
and had ordered the enforcement of Federal laws in those States. These
measures were intended to have the result, when a State's constitution
should have been amended, of restoring the State "to its constitutional relations to the Federal Government"; but Congress, by an act of Mar. 2,
1867 (14 Stat. 428), divided the 10 Southern States into 5 military districts,
each to be commanded by an officer not below the rank of brigadier general.
Under the act the primary duties of these commanders were "to protect all
persons in their rights of person and property, to suppress insurrection,
disorder, and violence, and to punish, or cause to be punished, all dis-
turbers of the public peace and criminals." Their duties in the reorganization of the State governments, as set forth in an act of Mar. 23, 1867 (15
Stat. 2), were extended to include the registration of qualified voters who
had taken the oath of allegiance to the United States, the supervision of the
election of delegates to State constitutional conventions, and the transmittal
to the President of certified copies of the constitutions adopted.

Under the act of Mar. 2, 1867, Virginia was to constitute the First
District; North Carolina and South Carolina the Second District; Georgia,
Alabama, and Florida the Third District; Mississippi and Arkansas the
Fourth District; and Louisiana and Texas the Fifth District. AGO General
Order 10, Mar. 11, 1867, in conformity with the act, assigned commanders
and announced locations of the several headquarters. The powers of these
commanders were both civil and military; and the civil powers exercised

were usually referred to as "military government." So far as their military duties were concerned, district commanders were subordinate to the General of the Army and the Secretary of War just as were department commanders. In their civil capacity, however, district commanders were entirely independent of both the General of the Army and the Secretary, except in matters of removal, appointment, and detail. An act of July 19, 1867 (12 Stat. 14), defined the powers of the district commander to suspend or remove from office persons occupying positions in the civil government of the State concerned; the provisional governments established by President Johnson were thus made subject to the military commanders. A joint resolution of Feb. 18, 1869 (15 Stat. 344), provided for the removal from office of persons holding civil offices in the "provisional governments" of Virginia, Texas, and Mississippi who could not take the oath of allegiance and directed the district commanders to fill the resulting vacancies by the appointment of persons who could take the oath. As the historian Dunning observed:

Military government in the South, 1867-70, was merely incidental to reconstruction proper. The maintenance of order was but a negative function of the district commander under the Reconstruction Acts; his positive and most characteristic duty was that of creating in each state subject to him a political people. Having given to such a people a definite existence, he was furthermore to communicate to it the initial impulse toward the organization of a government for itself, and then to retire into the background, maintaining an attitude of benevolent support until Congress should decree that the new structure could stand alone.

Annual reports of the commanders of the five districts are appended to those of the Secretary of War for 1867 (40 Cong., 2 sess., H. Ex. Doc. 1, Serial 1324), 1868 (40 Cong., 3 sess., H. Ex. Doc. 1, Serial 1367), and 1869 (41 Cong., 3 sess., H. Ex. Doc. 1, Serial 1446). For selected instructions, orders, and correspondence pertaining to the five districts up to July 1867, see 40 Cong., 1 sess., H. Ex. Doc. 20, Serial 1311. A compilation of general and special orders issued by district commanders to February 1868 was printed as H. Ex. Doc. 342, 40 Cong., 2 sess., Serial 1346. See also William Archibald Dunning, Essays on the Civil War and Reconstruction and Related Topics (New York, 1931), and John W. Burgess, Reconstruction and the Constitution (New York, 1907).

The records of the five military districts are discussed below. They are closely related to the records of territorial commands (military divisions and departments) of the same period and of the Bureau of Refugees, Freedmen, and Abandoned Lands.

First Military District (Virginia)

By General Order 1, Mar. 13, 1867, Bvt. Maj. Gen. J. M. Schofield, in announcing his assumption of command of this district, ordered all officers under the then existing provisional government of Virginia to "continue to perform the duties of their respective offices, according to law, unless otherwise hereafter ordered in individual cases, until their successors shall be duly elected and qualified." The staff officers then on duty at

Headquarters Department of the Potomac were assigned to corresponding
duties at Headquarters First Military District. In order to give "adequate
protection to all persons in their rights of person and property, in cases
where the civil authorities may fail, from whatever cause, to give such
protection, and to insure the prompt suppression of insurrection, disorder,
and violence," military commissioners were appointed with jurisdiction
over the subdistricts of Richmond, Fort Monroe, Petersburg, Lynchburg,
Winchester, Alexandria, and Fredericksburg.

Under General Schofield's administration the military government exercised the power conferred on it by Congress "only so far as might be
necessary to accomplish the purposes for which that power was conferred."
Although the civil government was "interfered with only when it was believed to be necessary," Schofield did not hesitate "to exercise any of the
functions of local government when the necessity for such exercise was
believed to exist."

In 1868, among the more important questions considered by Maj. Gen.
George Stoneman, Schofield's successor, were the Methodist Church con-
test, commonly known as the Baltimore Conference question; the removal
of Randolph Macon College from Boydton to Ashland; the payment of the
State's semiannual interest; the payment of the small note issue by the
city of Richmond; the collection of the amounts owed to the State by railroad companies; the appointment of State proxies and directors; the apportionment of taxes; the extension of the "stay law"; and the Presidential
election. In Maj. Gen. E. R. S. Canby's administration the making of
appointments to fill civil vacancies in accordance with a joint resolution
of Congress of Feb. 18, 1869 (15 Stat. 344), constituted one of the most
important duties.

AGO General Order 14, Mar. 12, 1867, annexed the counties of Alexandria and Fairfax to the First Military District. The district was attached
to the Military Division of the Atlantic by AGO General Order 18, Mar. 16,
1869. It ceased to exist when Virginia complied with the Reconstruction
Acts; and AGO General Order 11, Jan. 29, 1870, constituted that State and
the States of Maryland, West Virginia, and North Carolina as the Department of Virginia.

Successive commanders of the First Military District:

Bvt. Maj. Gen. John McAllister Schofield, Mar. 11, 1867.
Bvt. Maj. Gen. George Stoneman, June 1, 1868.
Bvt. Maj. Gen. Alexander S. Webb, Apr. 2, 1869.
Brig. and Bvt. Maj. Gen. Edward R. S. Canby, Apr. 20, 1869.

Record Group 98. -- The records of the First Military District, 1867-69
(ca. 150 ft.), the subjects of which are suggested by the discussion above,
consist of letters received and copies of letters sent, orders, rosters, reports of inspection and other reports, special files on civil affairs and on
military commissions, and registration records. The records of subdistricts and posts are included.

Second Military District (North Carolina and South Carolina)

Maj. Gen. Daniel E. Sickles assumed command of this district on Mar.
21, 1867. The military subdistricts of North and South Carolina were discontinued in Apr. 1867, and the territory embraced in the command was
divided into posts. This organization was found to facilitate the transaction
of business and the prompt administration of justice. Post commanders

were immediately responsible for seeing that people within their jurisdiction obeyed all existing laws and orders.

To bring about more efficient administration of justice and to give greater security to life and property, the sheriffs and other officers of municipal organizations within the district were put under the immediate control of a military officer--the provost marshal general. Sheriffs, chiefs of police, city marshals, chiefs of detectives, and town marshals in North and South Carolina were ordered to report to him.

The civil affairs bureau of the district headquarters, which originally dealt only with matters relating to registration under the Reconstruction Acts, was given widely increased duties after July 1867, including those pertaining to civil administration and the administration of civil and criminal justice.

In its final year the district headquarters was concerned primarily with the modification of the jury system in the two States, the enforcement of laws protecting persons and property, and matters pertaining to registration and election. The military government interfered with the local courts only in the exceptional cases growing out of the war; these generally were (1) actions or prosecutions for actions committed during hostilities and alleged to have been committed under orders or authority of either belligerent; (2) cases where the local courts attempted to validate the unexecuted judgments of Confederate courts rendered during the war; and (3) cases where the local courts denied the right of appeal or removal to the U. S. courts.

This district ceased to exist when North and South Carolina complied with the Reconstruction Acts; and by AGO General Order 55, July 28, 1868, the two States (with Georgia, Alabama, and Florida) were constituted as the Department of the South.

Successive commanders of the Second Military District:

> Maj. Gen. Daniel E. Sickles, Mar. 21, 1867.

> Bvt. Maj. Gen. Edward R. S. Canby, Aug. 26, 1867.

Record Group 98. --The records of the Second Military District, 1867-68 (ca. 100 ft.), the subjects of which are suggested by the discussion above, consist of letters received and copies of those sent, orders, and inspection and other reports. The files of the provost marshal general, the judge advocate, and the civil affairs bureau are distinguishable. There are also records relating to local posts, including loyalty oaths and reports of crimes and outrages.

Third Military District (Georgia, Alabama, and Florida)

General Pope assumed command of this district at Montgomery, Ala., on Apr. 1, 1867. According to his first report (Oct. 1, 1867), lacking information as to the extent of his powers, he understood the Reconstruction Acts to have established "a military government over these States, supervisory in its character, and to which the provisional State governments were made, in almost all respects, subordinate." For the "protection of person and property" and for the preservation of "peace and good order," he believed that the military government had final responsibility but that as far as possible the civil and criminal administration should be left in the hands of the provisional State governments, subject, however, to military review and revision if necessary. Subdistricts were established for the three States, that of Florida incorporating the existing district of Key West.

The condition of affairs early in 1868, when General Meade took command, was as follows: in Georgia a convention elected under the Reconstruction Acts was in session at Atlanta but was hampered by lack of funds; in Alabama a convention had met, framed a constitution, nominated State officers, and adjourned; in Florida members of a convention had been elected, but this body was not to meet until Jan. 20. The financial difficulties of the Georgia Convention received the special attention of the commander, as did the effects of the "Relief Laws" passed by the conventions of Alabama and Georgia, intended to relieve debtors from the immediate pressure of their creditors. As in all the districts, the commander of the Third Military District was under great pressure to remove incumbents from office.

This district ceased to exist when Georgia, Alabama, and Florida complied with the Reconstruction Acts; and AGO General Order 55, July 28, 1868, constituted the three States (with North and South Carolina) as the Department of the South. The following passage from General Meade's final report as Third Military District Commander reveals both the nature of his responsibilities and the problems he encountered:

> The inauguration of civil government was to me, personally, a source of great relief, charged as I had been with almost unlimited powers. Notwithstanding the utmost effort on my part . . . I found myself the subject of virulent abuse, my motives impugned, and every imaginable mode of attack resorted to that malice and partisan malignity could devise. Determined from the first to ignore all partisan considerations, . . . I encountered . . . the animosity of both sides, without having the benefit of the sympathy of either.

Two years later, conditions in Georgia necessitated its again being made a military district (by AGO G. O. 1, Jan. 4, 1870). This status continued until Georgia complied with the Reconstruction Acts and ratified the 14th and 15th Amendments to the Constitution. Then (by AGO G. O. 104, Aug. 3, 1870) the State again became a part of the Department of the South. Brig. Gen. Alfred H. Terry, Commander of the Georgia Military District during this period, directly exercised his powers through the civil authorities of the State in the following matters: an investigation into the eligibility, under the Reconstruction Acts, of certain men to seats in the legislature of Georgia and the exclusion of some of them; the removal from office of two county officers, and the appointment of others to fill their places; and the arrest of a few persons on the charge of murder, attempt to murder, or complicity in murder.

Successive commanders of the Third Military District:

Bvt. Maj. Gen. John Pope, Apr. 1, 1867.
Bvt. Brig. Gen. Caleb C. Sibley, Jan. 1, 1868.
Maj. Gen. George G. Meade, Jan. 6, 1868.
Bvt. Maj. Gen. Alfred H. Terry (Military District of Georgia),
    Jan. 4, 1870.

Record Group 98. --The records of the Third Military District, 1867-68 (ca. 55 ft.), the subjects of which are suggested by the discussion above, consist of correspondence, orders, rosters, and inspection and other reports. The records about civil affairs are separate and include election returns. Records of the Military District of Georgia, 1870-71, are in separate series.

Fourth Military District (Mississippi and Arkansas)

Bvt. Maj. Gen. E. O. C. Ord assumed command of this district on Mar. 26, 1867. On Apr. 6 he created two subdistricts, that of Mississippi (headquarters at Vicksburg) and that of Arkansas (headquarters at Little Rock). The operation of the civil laws was not "interfered with when those laws were administered equally towards all classes, except to remove from the civil courts cases of crimes charged against persons who for having opposed the rebellion had reason to fear prejudice against them; also cases where freedmen were maltreated or defrauded, and the courts were practically closed against them, and of cases of horse-stealing and violations of the acts of Congress." For all such cases military commissions were organized. The officers of the provisional State governments were not removed unless it became necessary.

So many complaints from merchants, planters, and freedmen were filed with the arbitration boards established in 1867 by General Ord, with the offices of agents of the Freedmen's Bureau, and with the State civil courts that in 1868 General Gillem devoted much attention to these problems. In protecting the rights of person and property, however, he did not interfere with local tribunals "except in rare instances, where, from excitement or prejudice, engendered either by political feeling or local animosities," he was convinced that justice would not be done.

When Arkansas complied with the Reconstruction Acts, that State (with Louisiana) was constituted as the Department of Louisiana (AGO G. O. 55, July 28, 1868). The Fourth Military District then consisted only of the State of Mississippi; and by AGO General Order 18, Mar. 16, 1869, it was included in the Military Division of the South.

Bvt. Maj. Gen. Adelbert Ames, who took command of the Fourth Military District on Mar. 17, 1869, was both commander of the district (by then only the State of Mississippi) and Provisional Governor of the State. Since the latter post demanded his presence at the State capital, he transferred the district headquarters from Vicksburg to Jackson on Mar. 30, 1869. His policy was to use the troops, except for their ordinary post duty, only for "expeditions into the country for the purpose of arresting lawless characters who had been guilty of murder or other serious offenses," to ensure "the safety of . . . persons and the quiet of communities." When Mississippi complied with the Reconstruction Acts, it was attached to the Department of the Cumberland, and the district ceased to exist (AGO G. O. 25, Feb. 26, 1870).

Successive commanders of the Fourth Military District:

Bvt. Maj. Gen. Edward O. C. Ord, Mar. 11, 1867.
Bvt. Maj. Gen. Irvin McDowell, Dec. 28, 1867.
Bvt. Maj. Gen. Alvan Gillem, June 30, 1868.
Bvt. Maj. Gen. Adelbert Ames, Mar. 17, 1869.

Record Group 98. --The records of the Fourth Military District, 1867-70 (ca. 120 ft.), the subjects of which are suggested by the discussion above, consist of correspondence, circulars, orders, and inspection and other reports. The correspondence about civil affairs is separate, as are the records of the subdistricts and posts.

Fifth Military District (Louisiana and Texas)

Maj. Gen. P. H. Sheridan assumed command of this district on Mar. 19, 1867. He reported on Nov. 21, 1867, that he had found, "upon a close

examination of the existing civil governments of those two States, that
nearly every civil functionary, from the governor down, . . . had been
elected on confederate grounds." In consequence, he adopted the "one
sensible course to pursue," the removal of "every civil officer who did
not faithfully execute the law, or who put any impediment in the way of its
execution."

The problems of the district commander, especially in Texas, were
aggravated during 1868 by the Ku Klux Klan, which, according to Bvt.
Maj. Gen. J. J. Reynolds, purposed "to disarm, rob, and in many cases
murder Union men and negroes, and as occasion may offer, murder
United States officers and soldiers; also to intimidate everyone who knows
anything of the organization but who will not join it." By Oct. 1869 the
commander noted that juries seemed more willing to find accused persons
guilty of murder and other high crimes. By then the ordinary civil machinery of the State was in operation, aided when necessary and practicable
by the military. The authorization of voluntary county organizations of
citizens to combat an increasing number of Indian raids was cordially approved by the people in some Texas counties.

When Louisiana complied with the Reconstruction Acts, that State
(with Arkansas) was constituted as the Department of Louisiana (AGO G. O.
55, July 28, 1868), and the Fifth Military District then consisted only of
Texas. When that State also complied with the Reconstruction Acts, it was
constituted as a separate military department, part of the Military Division
of the South (AGO G. O. 35, Mar. 31, 1870).

Successive commanders of the Fifth Military District:

Maj. Gen. Philip H. Sheridan, Mar. 19, 1867.
Bvt. Maj. Gen. Charles Griffin, Sept. 6, 1867.
Bvt. Maj. Gen. Joseph A. Mower, Sept. 16, 1867.
Maj. Gen. Winfield S. Hancock, Nov. 29, 1867.
Bvt. Maj. Gen. Joseph J. Reynolds, Mar. 18, 1868.
Bvt. Maj. Gen. Robert C. Buchanan, Mar. 25, 1868.
Bvt. Maj. Gen. Joseph J. Reynolds, July 28, 1868.
Bvt. Maj. Gen. Edward R. S. Canby, Nov. 4, 1868.
Bvt. Maj. Gen. Joseph J. Reynolds, Mar. 5, 1869.

Record Group 98. -- The records of the Fifth Military District, 1867-70
(ca. 80 ft.), the subjects of which are suggested by the discussion above,
consist of general files of correspondence, orders, and reports; the files
of the judge advocate, the inspector general, the commissary of musters,
the chief engineer, and the civil affairs officer; and the records of subordinate posts. Most of the materials pertaining to Texas are in separate
series.

VIII. OFFICE OF THE ATTORNEY GENERAL

The appointment of "a meet person, learned in the law" as Attorney General was authorized by sec. 35 of the Judiciary Act of Sept. 24, 1789 (1 Stat. 93). His duties were to prosecute and conduct all U. S. suits in the Supreme Court and to give advice and opinions on questions of law to the President and heads of departments. The Attorney General did not become a Cabinet member until the Department of Justice was established by an act of June 22, 1870 (16 Stat. 162). For many years he had only a small staff; that authorized by an act of Mar. 3, 1859 (11 Stat. 420), consisted of an assistant "learned in the law" and five clerks.

The Attorney General during most of the Civil War was Edward Bates. A lawyer of St. Louis, who had been attorney general of Missouri and a candidate for the Republican presidential nomination in 1860, he was appointed on Mar. 4, 1861, and took the oath of office two days later. He resigned in Nov. 1864, after his influence in the administration had waned. Joseph Holt declined the post, preferring to remain Judge Advocate General of the Army; and on Dec. 1, 1864, the appointment went to James Speed, a lawyer of Kentucky who had served in the State senate from 1861 to 1863. Titian J. Coffey, of Indiana, Pa., who had studied law in Bates' office in St. Louis and had helped to organize the Republican Party in Pennsylvania, succeeded Alfred B. McCalmont as Assistant Attorney General on Apr. 4, 1861. He resigned in Apr. 1864 to take a position under contract with the Attorney General as U. S. counsel in prize cases pending in the Supreme Court. He was succeeded on May 11, 1864, by J. Hubley Ashton, who had been assistant U. S. district attorney for eastern Pennsylvania. Bates, Coffey, four clerks, and a messenger took the oath of office on Apr. 22, 1861. In May 1861 Coffey asked for a clerk to help him handle the California land claims, and one was appointed. Of the other clerks, one was chief clerk; another, messenger and confidential agent for the Attorney General; another, opinion clerk; and the fourth, pardon clerk. Many lawyers were employed as special counsel during the war to assist the Attorney General, especially in California land cases before the Supreme Court of the United States.

Legislation before and during the Civil War enlarged the duties of the Attorney General. By 1861 he counseled treaty commissioners, advised the Solicitor of the Treasury, made recommendations on applications for pardons, passed on the title to lands bought by the Government, acted for the Government in the defense and settlement of private land claims, and adjudicated claims under treaties with foreign nations. In regard to the judiciary he received applications for appointments, transmitted commissions, and administered leaves of absence. War brought him responsibility for proceedings under an act of Aug. 6, 1861 (12 Stat. 319), which authorized

the seizure of property used or about to be used for insurrectionary purposes and under acts of July 31, 1861 (12 Stat. 284), and July 17, 1862
(12 Stat. 589), providing for the punishment of treason and conspiracy and
for the confiscation of property of "rebels." Sec. 4 of a later act (June 15,
1864; 13 Stat. 129) assigned to the Attorney General the task of determining
questions of law respecting the pay of colored soldiers. Besides preparing
California land cases for argument before the Supreme Court of the United
States, the Assistant Attorney General wrote opinions and acted as Attorney
General in his chief's absence. An act of Aug. 2, 1861 (12 Stat. 285),
charged the Attorney General with the general superintendence of district
attorneys and marshals and required them to submit to him reports of their
proceedings.

Successive Attorneys General during the war period:

Edwin M. Stanton, Dec. 20, 1860.
Edward Bates, Mar. 4, 1861.
James Speed, Dec. 1, 1864.

The Diary of Edward Bates, 1859-1866, ed. by Howard K. Beale, American Historical Association, Annual Report, 1930, vol. 4 (Washington, 1933); Homer Cummings and Carl McFarland, Federal Justice; Chapters in the History of Justice and the Federal Executive (New York, 1937); Arthur J. Dodge, "Origin and Development of the Office of the Attorney General" (H. Doc. 510, 70 Cong., 2 sess., Serial 9035. Washington, 1929); Albert G. Langeluttig, The Department of Justice of the United States (Baltimore, 1927); Floyd A. McNeil, "Lincoln's Attor-ney General, Edward Bates, " in Iowa, University, Abstracts in History, From Dissertations for the Degree of Doctor of Philosophy, 2:148-158 (Iowa City, 1934); William M. Robinson, Jr. , Justice in Grey; a History of the Judicial System of the Confederate States of America (Cambridge, Mass. , 1941). "Counsel Employed by the Attorney General, " Mar. 3, 1868 (H. Ex. Doc. 198, 40 Cong. , 2 sess. , Serial 1341), gives the names and fees paid to lawyers as special counsel to assist the Attorney General and district attorneys, 1861-67.

Record Group 60.--The General Records of the Department of Justice contain most of the records created by the Attorney General's Office during the Civil War. These are discussed immediately below by type. Thereafter the pardon and claims records, in other record groups, are discussed.

Outgoing letters of the Attorney General, 1818-90, copied in letter books, are addressed to the President and heads of Government agencies; officers and Members of Congress; Governors of States; judges, district attorneys, marshals, and clerks of court (including those in the Territories); and others. These letters concern appointments to and removal from office, commissions and bonds, leaves of absence, resignations, opinions, pardons, land claims, prosecutions under legislation relating to confiscation and treason, the com-pensation of attorneys employed to assist the district attorneys, the seizure of telegrams passing between the North and the South, the release of vessels captured by blockading squadrons, the bailing of prisoners, trials of crews of Confederate privateers, and political prisoners.

Letters received make up most of a series known as the Attorney Gen-eral's Papers, 1790-1870. They consist of letters received by the President and referred to the Attorney General and letters from heads of departments and other executive agencies, Congress, the Supreme Court, and the Court of Claims. There are a few letters from Presidents Lincoln and Johnson, and some referred letters bearing Presidential endorsements. Letters from judges, district attorneys, marshals, clerks of court, and State officials are arranged by State or Territory. Communications from private citizens form a smaller segment of the file. The letters referred by the President's office, which originated in both States and Territories, are resignations, acceptances, recommendations and testimonials for appointments, representations regarding proposed legislation, and letters and petitions regarding Territorial problems. There are letters, reports, and other papers pertaining to California land claims. Still other materials consist of drafts and copies of letters sent and of opinions; accounting records such as invoices, receipts, orders for payment, statements, and requests for warrants; contracts for the employment of special attorneys and legal counsel; oaths of office; and administrative orders. Some of these papers relate to the regular business of the Attorney General's Office, such as the prosecution of land cases, the rendering of opinions, judicial affairs, claims, Territorial affairs, and pardons. Others concern legal problems incidental to the war, such as those concerning the suspension of the writ of habeas corpus, military arrest, political prisoners, commerce with the South, trials of crews of Confederate privateers, the slave trade, loyalty oaths, confiscation cases, treason cases, Copperheads, the blockade, fugitive slaves, freedmen, the administration of the draft law, prize cases involving vessels captured attempting to run the blockade, the prosecution of Jefferson Davis, and pardons of ex-Confederates. A register of letters received is of some aid to the researcher.

The legal opinions rendered during the war by the Attorney General to the President and heads of departments are recorded in parts of two volumes. The Government's greatly expanded activities, its adoption of measures of questionable legality, and the enactment of much new legislation resulted in requests for opinions on many diverse subjects. Numerous routine opinions were submitted on such matters as accounts, appointments, claims, contracts, compensation, the duties of Government officials, fees, and pay. Opinions arising from wartime activities concerned the arrest of paroled "rebels," bounties to troops, captures of steamers, the distribution of prize money, the pardoning and other powers of the President, passports, the suspension of the writ of habeas corpus, volunteer naval forces, captured property, running the blockade from ports of the United States, the retirement of naval officers, and the admission of West Virginia. An act of Mar. 3, 1865 (13 Stat. 514), authorized the Attorney General to employ an editor to prepare for publication the opinions issued after Mar. 1857 and to make a contract with a publisher. The opinions thus issued constitute a contribution to American law and are useful also for historical research.

The Attorney General had been required by a joint resolution of Sept. 11, 1841 (5 Stat. 468), to examine and report on the validity of U. S. title to land for armories, arsenals, forts or fortifications, navy yards, customhouses, lighthouses, and other public buildings. Thenceforth no public money was paid for land until the Attorney General had issued a favorable opinion as to the title. The title opinions, far fewer than the opinions on questions of law, were entered in a separate volume; only a few of them were published.

Department of Justice, Official Opinions of the Attorneys General of the United States . . . [1791-date] (Washington, 1852-date).

Volumes 10 and 11, Jan. 1861-Dec. 1865, edited by J. Hubley Ashton, comprise 940 pages. This compilation does not include all the opinions in the manuscript volumes. Letters requesting opinions and occasional related documents are in the Attorney General's Papers. A useful companion volume to the published opinions is U. S. Department of Justice, Digest of the Official Opinions of the Attorneys-General of the United States, . . . 1789 to 1881 (Washington, 1885).

Since 1853 the Attorney General's Office had handled correspondence on the appointment of Federal judicial and legal officers: judges of the district courts, district attorneys, marshals, wardens and trustees of penal institutions, justices of the peace and notaries in the District of Columbia, and judges of special courts. There are separate files containing applications and recommendations for appointment to positions in the judicial districts, 1853-1903; the Attorney General's Office, 1850-1913; the Supreme Court, 1853-93; the Territories, 1857-97; and the Court of Claims, 1855-1901. Some of these letters were addressed to the Attorney General; others were sent to the President, heads of Government departments, Members of Congress, and other officials and were referred by them to the Attorney General. A few documents contain endorsements by the President, but most are merely referred by his secretary. The appointment records, arranged by State or Territory, also include testimonials, protests against appointments, resolutions, requests for removals, resignations, declinations, acceptances, and complaints against officeholders. Besides biographical data, issues of newspapers, and photographs, these records contain valuable information on conditions in the Territories and on military government in many areas.

The appointments actually made may be found in other records: a register of appointments as district and Territorial judges, 1857-70; lists of judges, attorneys, marshals, and clerks of courts, 1862-86; a record of appointment of attorneys, 1857-70; and a list of judges appointed in the States, Territories, and the District of Columbia, 1857-75. An order book contains information on the employment of personnel in the Attorney General's Office and other data on office organization and operations. A register of nominations, 1864-1905, contains the names of men nominated as judges, district attorneys, marshals, justices of the peace, and members of the "levy court" in the District of Columbia and gives information on commissions issued. (Record copies of commissions for judicial appointments are in the General Records of the Department of State, Record Group 59. The appointment files for the Territories of Oregon and Washington are available on microfilm, M 198 and 224, and the accompanying pamphlets contain indexes to the names of applicants in those files.)

One of the clerks in the Attorney General's Office was concerned with disbursements, but the only extant record is a daybook beginning in Mar. 1864. It contains a record of disbursements for salaries, contingent expenses, books, legal assistance and other expenses in the adjudication of California land claims, and the payment of special counsel. (Judiciary accounts were supervised during the war by the Secretary of the Interior; see elsewhere in this Guide.)

Records in Other Custody. --A large collection of papers of Edward Bates, in the Missouri Historical Society at St. Louis, contains about 60 letters relating to his official duties as Attorney General during the war. The original of his diary, the printed version of which has been cited, is in the Manuscript Division of the Library of Congress.

PARDON CLERK

About 1853 the Attorney General had taken over from the Secretary of State the function of handling petitions for pardon and making recommendations on them to the President, who under the Constitution has the sole authority to pardon offenses against the laws of the United States. The addition of this and other duties in the Office of the Attorney General resulted in the hiring of three temporary clerks and in the authorization by sec. 6 of an act of Aug. 4, 1854 (10 Stat. 572), of four permanent clerks one of whom undoubtedly did the paperwork on pardon cases. The position of pardon clerk was filled during the Civil War successively by John M. Cooper, Edmund C. Stedman, and Matthew F. Pleasants, but the earliest specific mention of this position was in an act of Mar. 3, 1865 (13 Stat. 516). Pleasants continued to fill the post, examining and arranging petitions and other documents relating to pardons for the consideration of the Attorney General. So many pardon applications were filed during 1865 that another regular clerk and two temporary ones were assigned to assist. Years later, by an act of Mar. 3, 1891 (26 Stat. 946), an "attorney in charge of pardons" was authorized, and the Civil War pardon records were transferred to him.

Record Group 204. --Petitions or applications made by prisoners or by others on their behalf, with related documents, were accumulated in pardon case files, 1853-1946. The investigation of a case resulted in the gathering of letters of recommendation; character affidavits; correspondence; reports of district attorneys, trial judges, wardens, prison physicians, and Government agencies regarding the facts of the case and the conduct of the prisoner; the Attorney General's recommendation and report to the President; and the receipt for the warrant if issued. The files are arranged numerically in labeled jackets. Docket books, 1853-1923, in which cases are entered chronologically by date of petition and which are indexed by the name of the petitioner, give information on the history of each case. The docket books and related case files are indexed on cards (1853-89) arranged alphabetically by name of applicant. Lists of applications received, cases referred to district attorneys, applications refused, and pardons granted, for 1861-65, break down the chronological record of cases in the docket books and are useful for a study of the administration of the cases. Copies of requisitions for pardon warrants, 1861-81 (8 vols.), sent to the Secretary of State by the Attorney General contain the texts of pardon statements, which are duplicated in the pardon warrants issued by the Secretary. Since the alphabetical name indexes for the volumes of requisitions for 1861-71 (3 vols.) give the judicial districts, it is possible to ascertain illegal activities by locality. The last 5 volumes of requisitions contain alphabetical name indexes.

The pardon records concern many crimes against the United States, including arson, counterfeiting, detaining and robbing the mail, embezzlement, engaging in the slave trade and service on board a slaver, failure to deposit public monies, forging applications for pensions and other claims, insulting an officer, keeping a bawdy house, manslaughter, murder, obstructing execution of process, perjury, persuading a witness not to testify, riot, smuggling, and violating the internal revenue law. More directly war-related cases covered by the pardon records include mutiny, bearing arms against the United States, aiding "rebels," conspiracy against the Government, treason, enticing and aiding soldiers to desert, desertion, harboring deserters, opening recruiting stations for enlisting soldiers to fight against the United

States, complicity in the attack on troops in Baltimore in Apr. 1861, and violation of the rules and customs of war. In the files are papers relating to many prominent Confederate officials and officers and to such notorious persons as Dr. Samuel A. Mudd.

National Archives, Preliminary   comp. by Gaiselle Kerner (Washing-
Inventory [No. 87] of the Records of   ton, 1955).
the Office of the Pardon Attorney,

Record Group 94. --President Johnson's proclamation of May 29, 1865 (13 Stat. 758), granting amnesty and pardon to persons who had participated in the rebellion, required special applications for pardon from 14 excepted classes of persons, such as officers of the Confederate Government, U. S. judges who had resigned to aid the rebellion, the higher Confederate military or naval officers, former U. S. Army or Navy officers who had resigned to evade duty, Southern officers who had been educated at the U. S. Military or Naval Academy, Governors of Southern States, persons with property valued at more than $20,000, and persons who had violated the oath of amnesty taken under the proclamation of Dec. 8, 1863. Upon recommendation from the Attorney General, the President issued a warrant for a pardon; and, after the pardon had been filled out and signed by the Secretary of State and the President, it was forwarded to the Governor of the State concerned for transmittal to the petitioner.

Applications submitted by persons in the excepted classes were filed by the pardon clerk in a separate file of amnesty papers and have been so maintained. The file includes also oaths of allegiance, recommendations and petitions for executive clemency, affidavits, reports of boards of investigation, correspondence, and acknowledgments of pardon warrants. The applications, received through the Governors of the Southern States or through officers in charge of military departments in the South, bear their endorsements. Some case files include originals or copies of documents relating to the applicants, such as appointments from the Confederate Government. The applications contain much personal information about the writers and their activities during the war; in the case of high ranking officers and officials the files are often of considerable interest. With the amnesty papers are lists compiled for use in handling the applications, such as lists of members of the Confederate Congress, Confederate Army and Navy officers, and prominent Confederate officials. Included also are a petition to the President for general amnesty, July 21, 1868, several petitions to the President for amnesty for Jefferson Davis, and some protests against pardoning him. The amnesty papers are arranged alphabetically by name under the various States. In 1894 these papers were transferred from the Department of Justice to the Record and Pension Office of the War Department.

Jonathan T. Dorris, "Pardon Seekers and Brokers; a Sequel of Appomattox," Journal of Southern History, 1:276-292 (Aug. 1935). Related records are in the General Records of the Department of State (Record Group 59). A list of the names of persons of the 13th excepted class pardoned under the proclamation of May 29, 1865 (owners of taxable property worth over $20,000), arranged alphabetically by State, is printed in H. Ex. Doc. 99, 39 Cong., 1 sess., Serial 1263. Other lists of names of those pardoned after Apr. 15, 1865, including high officers and officials and other adherents of the Confederacy, are in H. Ex. Doc. 31, 39 Cong. , 2 sess. , Serial 1289; H. Ex. Doc. 116, 39 Cong. , 2 sess., Serial 1293; and H. Ex. Doc. 32, 40 Cong. , 1 sess. , Serial 1311. The lists in these documents can be used as an index to the amnesty papers.

ASSISTANT ATTORNEY GENERAL FOR CLAIMS CASES

Under an act of June 25, 1868 (15 Stat. 75), the Attorney General on July 1 took over the prosecution of suits on behalf of the Government in the U. S. Court of Claims. For 2 or 3 years the Assistant Attorney General in charge of Court of Claims cases appears to have been quartered with the court, but after the Department of Justice was created he and his several clerks had offices in that Department. Claims relating to the Civil War continued to be filed long after the war had ended. In 1891 another Assistant Attorney General was appointed to take charge of Indian depredation cases. In 1934 the function of defending claims against the Government was assigned to the Claims Division of the Justice Department, and in 1937 the Court of Claims Section was created in that Division. Some years later this section became part of the Civil Division, which handled the civil litigation of the Government.

Record Group 205. --Although most of the records of the Court of Claims Section accumulated after the Civil War, many relate to claims that arose during the war. A volume of miscellaneous letters received, 1860-83, contains letters addressed to the Solicitor of the Court of Claims, the Attorney General, and the Assistant Attorney General about the gathering of evidence on claims. A file of letters received, 1888-1914, contains letters on the same subject and letters relating to different kinds of claims and to administrative matters. Outgoing letters on the above subjects are available in fair copies, 1872-1914, and in press copies, 1868-1912. In separate volumes are letters sent, 1906-7, asking information on claims of volunteer officers for extra pay and allowances for service as officers of the U. S. Army during the Civil War. A volume of reports from special attorneys in the field, 1899-1905, relates largely to Civil War claims that involved a determination of the claimants' loyalty. Incomplete but useful finding aids are lists of different types of cases, 1880-1915; an index to cases decided, 1883-1920; and a judgment index, 1885-1917.

The Assistant Attorney General kept case files, dockets, and other records about different types of cases. The case files are not nearly so complete, especially for the early years, as those maintained by the Court of Claims, but they contain the same kinds of documents; and the dockets duplicate the information in the dockets maintained by the Court of Claims. (These are discussed in this Guide under the Court of Claims.) General-jurisdiction case records include case files, 1855-1945; dockets, 1855-1914; docket cards, 1903-38; dockets for cases relating to officers' pay and allowances, 1903-15; letters sent by Robert S. Hale, Special Counsel of the Treasury Department for the defense of suits in the Court of Claims, 1868-70; letters sent on cotton cases, 1870-75; and dockets for cotton cases, 1868-90. Congressional-jurisdiction case records include case files, 1884-1944; remanded case files, 1891; dockets, 1884-1914; a judgment docket, 1885-94; an index to claimants, 1891-1903; a record of cases, 1884-1912; a general docket for remanded cases, 1886-91; and a record of remanded cases, 1891. Departmental-jurisdiction case records include case files, 1883-1943; a docket, 1883-1913; docket cards, 1883-1941; and a record of cases, 1883-1911. Indian-depredation case records include case files, 1891-94; dockets, 1891-1917; judgment dockets, 1892-1921; a card index to Indian tribes, 1891-94; an index to claimants and tribes, 1891-94; letters sent, 1891-1913, and letters received, 1891-1915.

COMMISSIONER TO REVISE AND CODIFY THE LAWS OF THE DISTRICT OF COLUMBIA

Under the authority of an act of May 20, 1862 (12 Stat. 403), the President nominated Richard S. Coxe, John A. Wells, and Philip R. Fendall as commissioners to codify the laws of the District of Columbia, but Congress adjourned without confirming the appointments. In the following year under sec. 17 of an act of Mar. 3, 1863 (12 Stat. 765), the President nominated as commissioner Return J. Meigs, then clerk of the supreme court of the District of Columbia. He was confirmed on Mar. 14, 1863, but he appears to have declined the appointment. On June 20 the Attorney General sent a commission to Richard S. Coxe, a lawyer of Washington, D. C.; Coxe accepted and immediately entered upon the duties of the 6-month appointment. The only result of his efforts, however, was a report to the Congress, Dec. 1863, in which he reviewed the history of previous attempts to codify the laws and recommended a procedure for codification if Congress should provide adequate time and funds for this work. Congress, however, took no further action.

Although no records of the commissioner have been found, his report, mentioned above, is printed as H. Misc. Doc. 18, 38 Cong., 1 sess., Serial 1199. The Code of the District of Columbia (to March 4, 1929) . . . (Washington, 1930. 2 vols.) contains a historical account and bibliography relating to the codes of laws of the District of Columbia.

U. S. ATTORNEYS AND MARSHALS

District attorneys and marshals were appointed by the President in each judicial district under the Judiciary Act of 1789. As new Territories were created, judges, district attorneys, and marshals were appointed for them. At first the district attorneys were not under the authority of the Attorney General; they performed services for other departments of the Government and corresponded direct with them. An act of Aug. 2, 1861 (12 Stat. 285), gave the Attorney General nominal superintendence of attorneys and marshals; but, since they continued to report to the Solicitor of the Treasury and to receive directions from the heads of departments, this law had little effect. A similar stipulation in sec. 16 of an act of June 22, 1870 (16 Stat. 164), was more effective, since by sec. 3 of the same act the law officers of the other executive departments were transferred to the newly created Department of Justice.

The district attorneys prosecuted persons for crimes and offenses under U. S. laws and acted in civil suits that concerned the United States. A description of the wide variety of offenses prosecuted is given above in the section on pardon records. Pursuant to a joint resolution of Sept. 11, 1841 (5 Stat. 468), district attorneys were required on request of the Attorney General, "to furnish . . . assistance or information . . . in relation to the titles of public property" within their districts. During the war the district attorneys became involved in prosecutions for treason and conspiracy, the confiscation of property of "rebels," trials of Southern privateers, and suits against vessels seized in attempting to run the blockade of the Southern coast. So heavy was this business in some ports that under the act of Aug. 2, 1861, cited above, special counsel was employed to assist district attorneys in the Southern District of New York, the Eastern District of Pennsylvania, the Southern District of Ohio, and the Eastern District of Missouri.

Marshals were the administrative officers of the district courts. They executed warrants and judgments of the courts; provided courtrooms, offices, supplies, and conveniences for judges; and had custody of Federal prisoners. They attended to the sale of prize vessels and cargoes and kept financial records of the transactions. They also disbursed the salaries and expenses of attorneys, marshals, and district courts, and they supervised the taking of the decennial censuses. By direction of President Lincoln, July 31, 1861, marshals in the vicinity of forts that held political prisoners were to supply lodging and subsistence for such prisoners. The marshals aided the Secretary of the Interior in enforcing the laws against the African slave trade under special appropriations made for that purpose. Compensation for such work by marshals and district attorneys was provided by sec. 3 of an act of Mar. 14, 1862, and by a joint resolution of Mar. 3, 1863 (12 Stat. 368, 829).

The names of the district attorneys and marshals serving in each judicial district are in the Official Register. Since the Federal courts in the Confederate states were closed from Nov. 1860 to 1865 or 1866, except in the Southern District of Florida (Key West), the Attorney General had fewer district attorneys to deal with than before the war. All the marshals in the Southern States transferred their allegiance to their States. As parts of the Confederacy were conquered by the North, Federal courts were reestablished, new attorneys and marshals were appointed, and the functions of the Attorney General's Office were resumed.

Record Group 118. --Records of district attorneys and marshals have been very imperfectly preserved. For many of the districts in existence during the Civil War there are no extant records; for others there are only fragments. Descriptions of the records in existence in the 1930's are in the Inventory of Federal Archives in the States; Series V, the Department of Justice, compiled and published by the Survey of Federal Archives. Since that time, however, some of the records have been transferred to the National Archives or to Federal Records Centers. In the National Archives are, for the District Attorney of the Eastern District of Missouri (St. Louis), letters-sent books, part of 1861 and Nov. 1863-Mar. 1866; for the Eastern District of Virginia (Richmond), a book of seizure orders issued by the District Attorney, June 15-Sept. 15, 1865, under the confiscation act of July 17, 1862; and for the Southern District of New York (New York City), a few case files for customs cases. The Survey of Federal Archives inventory for Massachusetts contains an entry for correspondence of the district attorney relating in part to prizes taken by the Navy during the Civil War and other entries for docket books for prize cases and commissioners' cases. Other inventories list some records for district attorneys at San Francisco, Indianapolis, Omaha, Carson City, New York City, Cleveland, and Providence. These records usually consist of dockets and other records concerning cases. The inventories also list marshals' records for San Francisco, Grand Rapids, St. Paul, Omaha, New York City, Cleveland, Portland (Oreg.), Philadelphia, Pittsburgh, and Milwaukee. The marshals' records usually consist of account books, dockets, and records of processes served.

Much information concerning the activities of district attorneys and marshals is in other record groups, especially Records of the Attorney General (Record Group 60), the Naval Records Collection of the Office of Naval Records and Library (Record Group 45), Records of the Solicitor of the Treasury (Record Group 206), Records of District Courts (Record Group 21), and correspondence files of the executive departments. The attorneys' and marshals' commissions are in the General Records of the Department of State (Record Group 59). Correspondence of the Marshal for the Southern District of New York with the Secretary of the Interior concerning the slave vessel Augusta and other documents relating to the case are published in S. Ex. Doc. 40, 37 Cong., 2 sess., Serial 1122. Lists of vessels seized and men arrested under charge of engaging in the slave trade, May 1, 1852-May 1, 1862, are in S. Ex. Doc. 53, 37 Cong., 2 sess., Serial 1122.

IX. POST OFFICE DEPARTMENT

The Office of the Postmaster General was created by an act of Sept. 22, 1789 (1 Stat. 70), which provided that the existing regulations governing the postal establishment should be continued. An act of Feb. 20, 1792 (1 Stat. 232), provided in detail for a Post Office Department, and subsequent legislation enlarged its duties. Two Assistant Postmasters General were authorized by an act of Mar. 3, 1825 (4 Stat. 102); and an act of July 2, 1836 (5 Stat. 84), authorized a third. In 1830 the Postmaster General became a regular member of the President's Cabinet.

By the closing months of the Buchanan Administration the Post Office Department, in addition to the immediate Office of the Postmaster General, comprised the Appointment Office, the Contract Office, and the Finance Office, headed respectively by the First, Second, and Third Assistant Postmasters General; and the Inspection Office, under the Chief Clerk of the Department. The Dead Letter Office operated as a part of the Finance Office. The departmental organization was to continue essentially unchanged during the Civil War, although the adding of new or greater responsibilities (such as those pertaining to the handling of dead letters, the new money order system, and the railway mail service) was to affect the internal organization of the several offices. The functions of the Inspection Office were transferred to the Contract Office in 1864.

It has been said that the Civil War is represented in the records of the Post Office Department chiefly by a gap for the Confederacy. Although the Department's policy of retaining records in summary form and disposing of detailed records regarding individual post offices--a policy adopted under an act of 1881 (21 Stat. 412) and later provisions for the disposition of useless papers--may hamper a search for minute details of postal service during the Civil War, it cannot fail to intensify the use of the records that do survive.

OFFICE OF THE POSTMASTER GENERAL

Joseph Holt, who had become Postmaster General in 1859 after serving as Commissioner of Patents, was appointed Secretary of War on Jan. 18, 1861. Horatio King, his successor as Postmaster General, had served Holt as First Assistant, but in the few weeks that remained of the Buchanan Administration King could hardly begin to cope with the disruption of postal service in the South as additional States seceded. It remained for President Lincoln's appointee, Montgomery Blair, to apply an act of Feb. 28, 1861 (12 Stat. 177), which authorized the Postmaster General to discontinue postal service on routes where the service could not "be safely continued, or the post office revenues collected, or the postal laws maintained." On May 27, 1861, Blair directed discontinuance of the service "in the so-called seceded States, except in Western Virginia," and later he suspended service in "West and Middle Tennessee." The wartime published Lists of U. S. post offices continued, however, to show Southern post offices (with the names of postmasters omitted). The Postmaster General, however, wrote in his 1861 annual report:

> It was not deemed advisable to fill orders [for stamps] from post-masters in States which claim to have "seceded", without first ascertaining their disposition to hold themselves personally responsible for such amounts as might be sent them. With this in view, a circular was prepared, about twelve hundred copies of which were addressed to different postmasters upon the receipt of their orders. Nine hundred replies were received, all but twenty of which avowed the personal responsibility of the writers for all revenues accruing at their respective offices, and their regret at the action of their State authorities. Stamps were accordingly sent them until June 1, [1861,] when it appeared that the postal service could no longer be safely continued.

Stamps and stamped envelopes remaining unaccounted for in the hands of postmasters in the seceded States on Oct. 1, 1861, were valued at $207,000; and 8,535 post offices in those States made no returns to the U. S. Post Office Department for the third quarter of 1861. In order to prevent the fraudulent use of stamps unaccounted for, the Department in Aug. 1861 changed the design and distributed new stamps and envelopes; old stamps were withdrawn and destroyed. By an act of July 11, 1862 (12 Stat. 530), the time fixed for the limitation of suits against the sureties of postmasters by the act of Mar. 3, 1825, cited above, was made inapplicable in the States declared to be in insurrection.

The "extraordinary condition of the country and the exigencies of the service in certain States" made it necessary to increase the number of special agents from 16 to 20 during the first year of the war. These agents were "the eyes and hands of the department, to detect and arrest violators of the law, and to render the mails a safe and rapid means of communication." Although the duties of route agents were different, they were always of "greater importance and more onerous" than was "commonly apprehended," and required the same "qualities of character." The Department was called upon also to act on the question of excluding from the mails various "disloyal" newspapers and other publications. Although it "could not and would not interfere with the freedom [of the press] secured by law . . . it could and did obstruct the dissemination of that license which was without the pale of the Constitution and law. The mails established by the United States government could not, upon any known principle of law or public right, be used for its destruction."

Military operations brought the necessity of delivering unprecedented quantities of mail to the troops and of receiving from them their letters home. Shortage of mailpouches and locks in 1862 led to the recovery of those accumulated in some post offices; in the Chicago office several hundred had piled up--some packages of letters still in them indicated "great neglect originally." Many local post offices, such as the one at Cairo, Ill., were confronted with appalling congestion of mail due to a heavy concentration of troops in the vicinity. An act of July 22, 1861, as amended (12 Stat. 270, 332), authorized the transmission of the "unpaid" letters of soldiers, sailors, and marines; and beginning about July 1, 1864, postage stamps were regularly supplied to the Armies of the Potomac and the Cumberland by special agents of the Department stationed at City Point and Chattanooga. The heavy military mail influenced the inauguration of the railway postal service, aggravated the problem of dead letters, and brought about the creation of the money order system--all discussed in some detail below. The public and official concern for the welfare of Union soldiers and sailors was to find expression toward the end of the war in an act of Mar. 3, 1865 (13 Stat. 507), prohibiting for the first time the sending of obscene publications by mail.

Throughout the war the Post Office Department continued to give attention to postal reform. The Postmaster General in his 1862 annual report acknowledged the active cooperation he had received in all efforts for improvement, from the "present intelligent and efficient postmasters at Philadelphia, New York, and Boston, as well as the aid derived from the investigations and representations of Mr. Pliny Miles and the Hon. John Hutchins." A representative of the Department attended the International Postal Conference that met in Paris on May 11, 1863, under the presidency of the Director General of Posts of France, M. Vidal. The Postmaster General adopted the rules agreed on by the conference as a basis for the treaties "hereafter to be made under the direction of this department." In 1864 correspondence was begun with several of the postal departments represented at the Paris conference for the negotiation or revision of postal conventions.

The resumption of U. S. postal service in the Southern States preoccupied the Post Office Department in 1865 and 1866, and by Nov. 1 of the latter year 3,234 of the 8,839 post offices in the South had been reopened. The details of this work, as given by Postmaster General Dennison in his 1865 annual report, are of interest:

> The closing of the war brought with it the necessity of restoring the postal service in the southern States. No time was lost in offering to the citizens of those States all those facilities which they were in condition to accept. Special agents were appointed to assist in the work of restoration. The provisional governors were notified of the readiness of the department to appoint postmasters upon their recommendation. They were also advised of its desire to put the mail on all the railroads within their respective States as soon as informed by them that the roads were ready to carry them, and the companies proper parties to intrust with their transportation. . . .

> Although the service has been restored in each of the southern States, it is not so general as the department has desired and the wants of the citizens require, because of the difficulty of procuring contractors and postmasters who can take the oaths prescribed by the acts of July 2, 1862, and March 3, 1863, requiring uniform loyalty to the government during the rebellion as the condition of holding office and for the conveying of the mails.

The Postmasters General during the Civil War period:
    Joseph Holt, Mar. 14, 1859.
    Horatio King, Feb. 12, 1861.
    Montgomery Blair, Mar. 5, 1861.
    William Dennison, Sept. 24, 1864.

Post Office Department, The Postal Laws and Regulations, Published by Authority of the Postmaster General, comp. by Joseph A. Ware (Washington, 1866)--more useful than the 1859 compilation because it contains Civil War legislation affecting the postal service; List of Post Offices in the United States . . . (Washington, 1859) and subsequent issues of 1862, 1865, and 1867 under similar titles; D. D. T. Leech, The Post Office Department of the United States of America. . . (Washington, 1879).

The fiscal year reports of the Postmaster General for the war period were published as Congressional documents as follows:

1861. S. Ex. Doc. 1, vol. 3, 37 Cong., 2 sess., Serial 1119.
1862. H. Ex. Doc. 1, vol. 4, 37 Cong., 3 sess., Serial 1159.
1863. H. Ex. Doc. 1, vol. 5, 38 Cong., 1 sess., Serial 1184.
1864. H. Ex. Doc. 1, vol. 5, 38 Cong., 2 sess., Serial 1220.
1865. H. Ex. Doc. 1, vol. 6, 39 Cong., 1 sess., Serial 1254.
1866. H. Ex. Doc. 1, vol. 4, 39 Cong., 2 sess., Serial 1286.

Record Group 28.--Copies of letters sent by the Postmaster General pertinent to the Civil War are in three letter books: no. 5, J. Holt--H. King, Mar. 18, 1859-Mar. 6, 1861, which contains letters concerning the accounts of postmasters in the seceded States; no. 6, M. Blair, Mar. 7, 1861-Sept. 27, 1864, in which are many letters concerning the inauguration of the railway postal service; and no. 7, W. Dennison, Oct. 1, 1864-July 6, 1866, which contains letters on the reestablishment of postal service in the Southern States. (Van Tyne and Leland in 1907 noted that these letter books "contain letters relating to the movement in the South against abolitionist documents; inquiries directed by the department to southern postmasters regarding their intentions; non-delivery of Fort Sumter mail at Charleston; letters regarding continuance of franking privileges to southern members of Congress; removals of postmasters on account of disunion sentiments; refusals to support the Constitution of the United States; instructions to postmasters at offices seized by the Confederacy; service in loyal parts of Virginia; mail service to forts, etc.") Most other important postal matters of the period are also discussed in these letters, among which are those addressed to the President and Members of Congress. In the extensive series of "orders" or "journals," dating from 1835, volumes 47-55 (Sept. 21, 1860-Apr. 24, 1865) and volume 56, "Compensation of Postmasters" (Oct. 1, 1864-Dec. 26, 1866), should be consulted. These copies of the Postmaster General's orders relate to such matters as the establishment, discontinuance, and reestablishment of post offices; changes in the names and sites of post offices; appointments of postmasters; and violations of postal laws and regulations. The orders appear to cover adequately, for the war period, the discontinuance and later resumption of postal service in the Southern States, the appointment of special postal agents, route advertisements, and the exclusion of "disloyal" newspapers from the mails. There is a scrapbook of circulars, notices, etc., 1823-71, containing, among other items of research value, news clippings about the distribution of anti-slavery publications.

National Archives, Preliminary Inventory [no. 99] of the Records of the Office of the Postmaster General, comp. by Arthur Hecht (Washington, 1957).

Records in Other Custody. --The papers of Horatio King and of Montgomery Blair in the Library of Congress should be consulted.

Money Order Office

Although the Money Order Office was to be transferred in 1892 to the jurisdiction of the First Assistant Postmaster General, and thence in 1905 to that of the Third Assistant Postmaster General, it was first established within the Office of the Postmaster General. The need to provide soldiers and others with a way to send small amounts of money by mail led Postmaster General Blair to advance a plan to furnish money orders for a small fee, and an act of May 17, 1864 (13 Stat. 76), authorized the Postmaster General to establish "under such rules and regulations as he may find expedient and necessary, a uniform money-order system at all post-offices which he may deem suitable therefor." By Dec. 1 of that year a superintendent and an assistant had been appointed, 141 post offices had been designated as money order offices, and the system had begun to operate. The procedures followed--see especially Ch. XLIV of the 1866 Postal Laws and Regulations-- were developed carefully and comparisons were made with similar systems elsewhere; for instance, two special agents were sent to Canada in 1864 to investigate the postal money order business there. "The tendency of the system," the Postmaster General observed in his 1864 annual report, was "to exclude money from the mails, the presence of which in letters is a frequent cause of the loss of correspondence, even when the latter does not contain money."

From the establishment of the money order system on Nov. 1, 1864, to the end of the fiscal year (June 30, 1864), the orders issued amounted to $1,360,122.52. The law had fixed a limit of $30 on money orders although in exceptional cases more than one order might be procured. This limitation seemed at the time reasonable, since the average amount in "money letters" received at the Dead Letter Office in fiscal year 1862 was $4.53, and in 1863 and 1864 was $4.20. The proponents of the new system reasoned that by excluding money from the mails the ordinary correspondence, which usually suffered also in any rifling of the mails, would be more secure.

C. F. Macdonald was Superintendent of the Money Order Office during the war period and for some years thereafter.

There are no extant records of the Money Order Office before 1868, but the Postmaster General's letter books and orders of the Civil War period give some information on the money order system.

APPOINTMENT OFFICE

An Assistant Postmaster General was appointed under the Continental Congress, and his position was continued in the postal establishment under the Constitution. With the authorization of a Second Assistant his title became the First Assistant Postmaster General, and during the Civil War his office was known as the Appointment Office. This Office supervised the appointment and regulation of all postmasters and the establishment and discontinuance of post offices. Military operations considerably influenced the policies and work of the office. Early in 1862, for instance, First Assistant Postmaster General Kasson, in view of "the advance of the army into Tennessee," wrote the Department's special agent at Fort Donelson that the mail service should "keep pace, to a reasonable extent," with the Army's movements, "in order to afford the facilities necessary to its efficiency, as well as to the communications between it and the Headquarters at Washington and elsewhere."

This Office also distributed stationery and office supplies to post offices; supervised the pay of clerks and the granting of extra allowances to postmasters; appointed and paid special, route, local, and "blank" agents, as well as baggage masters in charge of mails; and handled the foreign correspondence of the Post Office Department, including that related to foreign mail transportation. This Office had the primary responsibility for the Department's role in negotiating and concluding postal treaties or conventions.

John A. Kasson, appointed First Assistant Postmaster General in 1861, was succeeded in 1863 by Alexander W. Randall, who became Postmaster General in 1866.

Record Group 28. --The records of appointments of postmasters during the Civil War are in a series of 105 volumes, 1789-1930. These show the names of postmasters and dates of their appointment; the dates of discontinuance, reestablishment, and changes in names of post offices; and, occasionally, changes in their location. Arrangement of entries within a State or Territory is roughly alphabetical by county and thereunder by post office. (For the Southern post offices of the war period there are normally no entries except dates of reestablishment.) To these appointment records there is an index, alphabetical by name of post office, 1855-69 (2 vols.).

There is also a card file, 1863-99, pertaining to carriers separated from the postal service. No other Civil War records of the First Assistant Postmaster General are extant except for the record copies of the modified or concluded postal conventions (with Belgium, Bremen, Guatemala, Hamburg, Italy, and the United Kingdom of Great Britain and Ireland), which are now a part of the records of the Second Assistant Postmaster General.

National Archives, Preliminary Inventory [no. 36] of the Records of the First Assistant Postmaster General, 1789-1942, comp. by Frank J. Nivert and Arthur Hecht (Washington, 1951).

CONTRACT OFFICE

The Second Assistant Postmaster General, authorized by an act of Apr. 30, 1810 (2 Stat. 593), headed the Contract Office, which during the Civil War conducted mail "lettings" and contracted for inland mail transportation. It supervised and regulated mail contractors and the routes of mail transit, including distributing offices, and it decided on the increase or diminution of service on mail routes. The duties of the Office included rerouting the overland mail service to avoid interruption by Indians; making contracts with railroad companies; establishing sea routes for the conveyance of mail between ports in the United States; providing alternate routes when the usual overland routes ran through areas occupied by Confederate forces; and making postal arrangements for the armies. The Contract Office reported weekly to the Sixth Auditor of the Treasury all contracts executed and all orders affecting accounts for mail transportation; prepared statistics on the mail service and the reports of mail contracts or "lettings"; and reported also new service originated, curtailments ordered, and additional allowances granted. Postmasters at the ends of routes received from this Office the statements of mail arrangements prescribed for their routes.

Before 1864 mail was sorted at the large post offices, and only mail intended for delivery at local points on railroad lines was sorted in railroad cars; but by that year the Railway Post Office Service--established in 1862 to facilitate the distribution of overland mail on the route from Hannibal to St. Joseph, Mo. --had been extended to the eastern seaboard. In the same year there was established the Office of the Superintendent of Railway Mail Service, which was to become a part of the Office of the Second Assistant Postmaster General about 1873. The Railway Mail Service, as recalled by D. D. T. Leech of the Post Office Department, made it possible to give "an expedition to the mails equal to that to passengers, by sorting and distributing them while on their passage, instead of sending them to the large terminal post offices for that purpose, where they suffered a delay of from 12 to 24 hours."

George W. McLellan was appointed Second Assistant Postmaster General in 1861 and served until 1869.

Record Group 28. --The registers for "star" route contracts of the Civil War period are in one series, 1814-1930. (The "star" route service derived its name from the practice of marking with stars or asterisks the advertisements of contracts requiring only "due celerity, certainty, and security," so as to distinguish them from contracts requiring a set schedule or other specific performance terms.) For making contracts to carry the mails over the established "post roads" the Union was divided into four contract "sections"; a "letting" for one of these sections occurred every year, and contracts were made at such "lettings" for 4 consecutive years, beginning July 1. These "sections" and their current contract terms were in 1862 as follows:

1. Maine, New Hampshire, Vermont, Massachusetts, Rhode Island, Connecticut, and New York: current term to end June 30, 1865.

2. New Jersey, Pennsylvania, Delaware, Maryland, and Ohio: current term to end June 30, 1864.

3. Virginia, North Carolina, South Carolina, Georgia, and Florida: current term to end June 30, 1863.

4. Michigan, Indiana, Illinois, Wisconsin, Iowa, Missouri, Kentucky, Tennessee, Alabama, Mississippi, Arkansas, Louisiana, Texas, California, Minnesota, Oregon, New Mexico, Utah, Washington, Nebraska, and Kansas: current term to end June 30, 1866.

"Post roads" included roads declared to be such by acts of Congress, all waters on which steamboats regularly passed from port to port, the navigable canals of the several States when used for carrying mail, all railroads in the United States, "roads on which the Postmaster General causes the mail to be carried from the nearest post offices on legally declared post roads, to court-houses not otherwise provided with the mail, " all roads to special offices, and the post roads established by the Postmaster General under an act of Mar. 3, 1851 (9 Stat. 637).

The contract registers are arranged chronologically by contract term. Those for the following 4-year terms (several vols. for each term) cover the period of interest to this Guide: 1857-61, 1858-62, 1859-63, 1860-64, 1861-65, 1862-66, 1863-67, 1864-68, and 1865-69. For each contract is given such information as the mail-route number, terminals of the route and the intervening post office stops, distances between post offices on the route, time schedule, and the facts of contract award; and there are in each volume copies of the advertisements inviting proposals for carrying the mail in the State or States concerned. (Since the Civil War period saw the inauguration and highest development of the Pony Express, contract 12578 with the Overland Mail Co. , to "run a Pony Express" from Jan. 1861 to June 1864, may be noted.) The extensive indexes to these registers (also chronological by contract term and thereunder by State) often include additional information such as the discontinuance of the United States post offices in the Southern States after secession and the reopening of these offices after the war. There is also an index of "star" route mail contractors, 1833-77 (36 vols.).

Other extant Civil War records of the Contract Office are fragmentary. They include copies of "Telegraphic Dispatches Sent" (2 vols. ; 1852-Nov. 1861, Mar. 1861-July 1873); a register of special routes and local agents and clerks, 1853-61 (marked 1858), showing discontinuances in the South in 1861, and a continuation volume (marked 1860) for the war period containing a register of special agents (for example, "New York to Southern Forts and Blockading Squadrons--Steamer 'McClellan'"); and a roster of railway postal clerks from 1861.

National Archives, Preliminary Inventory [no. 82] of the Records of the Bureau of the Second Assistant Postmaster General, 1814-1946, comp. by Arthur Hecht (Washington, 1955).

Inspection Office

Early in the war the Chief Clerk of the Post Office Department headed an Inspection Office, with functions that had been variously assigned in the prewar period; but on Mar. 3, 1864, the Postmaster General ordered the Inspection Office "dispensed with," and transferred to the Contract Office "the duties of supervision and inspection of mail service of all kinds. " The duties were explicitly stated as follows:

examining registers of the departures and arrival of the mails, report of mail failures, noting the delinquencies of Contractors, Agents, and Messengers, preparing cases thereon for the action of the Postmaster General, conducting correspondence in relation to complaints against Contractors, Couriers, Agents and Messengers and receiving and examining certificates of the service of route agents and baggage Masters in charge of mails, and making the necessary report to the Auditor for their payment.

This assignment of duties to the Contract Office also includes furnishing blanks for mail registers and report of mail failures; providing and sending out Mail bags, Locks, and Keys, and doing all other things which may be necessary to secure a faithful and exact performance of mail service; and in like manner the supervision of Special Agents and others engaged in the arrangement of mail service, the detection of Mail depredators, or violations of law by private expresses, or by the forging or illegal use of postage stamps, are transferred to and placed in charge of the Contract Office.

William A. Bryan, as Chief Clerk, headed the Inspection Office until its transfer to the Contract Office.

Record Group 28.--Few records of this office for the Civil War period exist. There is, however, a register, dating from Aug. 1864, of arrests for offenses against the postal laws.

FINANCE OFFICE

The office of the Third Assistant Postmaster General, authorized by an act of July 2, 1836 (5 Stat. 84), was known during the Civil War as the Finance Office. This Office supervised any financial business of the Department that was not legally a duty of the Sixth Auditor of the Treasury. The work included handling accounts with the depositories of the Department, issuing warrants and drafts in payment of balances reported by the Sixth Auditor to be due to mail contractors and other persons, supervising the accounts of officers under order to deposit their quarterly balances at designated points, and superintending the rendition by postmasters of their quarterly returns. The Finance Office had charge of the Dead Letter Office, of the issuing of postage stamps and stamped envelopes for the prepayment of postage, and of the related accounts. To this Office postmasters directed their quarterly returns of postage, postmasters at draft offices their quarterly reports of net proceeds, and postmasters at depositing offices their certificates of deposit. The Finance Office received also the weekly and monthly returns of the depositories of the Department and all applications and receipts for postage stamps and stamped envelopes.

Departmental finances were affected considerably by the war. Estimates of total expenditures for 1863 were actually less, however, than those for immediately previous years because only partial estimates were made for the cost of postal service in States where it had been suspended. It was assumed that restoration of service in those States would take place gradually, and that in the process many expensive mail routes, from which little revenue had been derived, might be curtailed or discontinued. Estimates for "blanks" and wrapping paper remained constant, for in case of the resumption of the postal service in the States of the Confederacy a large quantity of these and other supplies would be required. There could be no diminution in the estimates of the costs of mail bags, locks, and keys; expenditures for these were actually greater than before.

Alexander N. Zevely was appointed Third Assistant Postmaster General in 1859 and served until 1869.

Record Group 28. --Except for fragmentary records of the Disbursing Clerk, almost no records of the Finance Office for the Civil War period are extant; there is but a single volume of letters received from postmasters in May 1861, chiefly routine requests for stamps. The Disbursing Clerk's records consist of a daybook of disbursements, 1861-65, which also includes a record of appointments and removals of clerks; a record of salary payments, 1851-62; a payroll record for engineers, watchmen, and laborers, Apr. 1859-Sept. 1865; a ledger of abstracts of salaries and departmental appropriations, 1855-92; a record of appropriations for blank books, binding, stationery, etc., 1859-78 (1 vol); a daybook of contingent expenses, 1862-65; and a letter press volume of outgoing correspondence, Aug. 1862-Oct. 1872.

National Archives, Preliminary Inventory [no. 114] of the Records of the Bureaus of the Third and Fourth Assistant Postmasters General, the Bureau of Accounts, and the Bureau of the Chief Inspector of the Post Office Department, comp. by Arthur Hecht, Fred W. Warriner, Jr., and Charlotte M. Ashby (Washington, 1959).

Dead Letter Office

Although the money order system inaugurated in 1864 solved, if belatedly, some dead letter problems, many still remained. As the result of the suspension of mail from the loyal States to States of the Confederacy, the accumulation of undeliverable mail in the Dead Letter Office was considerable. An act of Jan. 21, 1862 (12 Stat. 332), authorized the return to the writers, whenever their names could be ascertained, of all dead letters "except those containing circulars and other worthless matter." Army officers receiving private letters "for transmittal through the lines of the U. S. troops to persons living in the enemy's country" were instructed, on Jan. 29, 1862, to send them to the Dead Letter Office except when "addressed to officers and men detained as prisoners by the insurgents." The statistics of the Office's operation for the period Nov. 1, 1861-Nov. 1, 1862, were discussed by the Postmaster General in his 1862 annual report as follows:

46, 697 letters written in the loyal States and directed to States under insurrectionary control. These, when susceptible of restoration, were stamped "mails suspended," and returned to the writers.

3, 198 letters from sections of the country subject to rebel control, and addressed to persons in the loyal States. Greater portion of such letters were forwarded to their destination.

13, 463 foreign letters, directed to localities in this country with which postal communication is discontinued. Letters of this class were stamped "mails suspended," and returned to the countries where they originated.

There was continued, progressive increase in the dead letters received in the remaining 3 years of the war. An analysis in 1863 showed that most of the letters contained daguerreotypes or card photographs (many sent by soldiers and their correspondents):

The whole number of such dead letters exceeds by 85% the amount thereof received in the preceding year. It will be observed, that while there has been a very considerable increase in the quantity of dead letters containing money and of those covering daguerreotypes and miscellaneous articles, the number of such as contain deeds, bills of exchange, drafts, etc. , has sensibly diminished. The increase of the two former classes is doubtless owing in a great degree, to the fact that the mails are very generally used by the large number of persons in the military service of the United States, and by their numerous correspondents, for the transmission of money, photographs, and similar articles of value, while, on the other hand, they have less occasion to forward by mail deeds, drafts, or negotiable paper, than other classes of the community. The nature of the military service and the many accidents to which soldiers are liable necessitates frequent changes of locality, which retard or prevent the delivery of their letters, and many of these are, in consequence, sent to the dead-letter office. Upwards of 5, 000 money letters, being nearly one-fourth of the whole of that class of letters received during the year, were addressed to soldiers.

In the next fiscal year (1864) the dead letters returned to senders included

11, 116 letters and packages containing muster rolls, descriptive lists, and soldiers' discharge papers--returned to the Adjutant General's, the Quartermaster General's, and other public offices; and even in the first fiscal year after the war (1866) 8, 918 dead letters enclosing soldiers' discharges and other military papers were returned.

There are no records of the Dead Letter Office for the period of the Civil War. The Postmaster General's letter books and orders may be consulted on policies affecting the Office. During the war the Dead Letter Office employed the first women appointed to departmental positions.

X. DEPARTMENT OF THE NAVY

In 1861 the naval establishment of the United States consisted of the same elements that it had comprised since its creation in 1798: the Navy Department, naval vessels, shore establishments, and the Marine Corps.

The Navy Department administered both the Navy and the shore stations. It consisted of the Office of the Secretary of the Navy; the headquarters of the Marine Corps; and the Bureaus of Yards and Docks, of Construction, Equipment, and Repairs, of Provisions and Clothing, of Ordnance and Hydrography, and of Medicine and Surgery. On the recommendation of Secretary of the Navy Gideon Welles these Bureaus, which had been created by an act of Aug. 31, 1842 (5 Stat. 579), were reorganized by an act of July 5, 1862 (12 Stat. 510). According to that act the duties of the Bureau of Construction, Equipment, and Repairs were divided among three new Bureaus: Equipment and Recruiting, Construction and Repair, and Steam Engineering. Those of the Bureau of Ordnance and Hydrography were divided between two new Bureaus: Ordnance and Navigation. At this time responsibility for enlisted personnel was transferred from the Office of the Secretary to the Bureau of Equipment and Recruiting. In the opinion of Secretary Welles the new organization brought about a better distribution of the Department's work and simplified and facilitated its business.

Early in 1861 most of the vessels of the Navy were serving on distant stations. The squadrons to which they were attached were the following: the East India, Brazil, Pacific, Mediterranean, and African Squadrons and the Home Squadron. The vessels in the last-named Squadron were in the Gulf of Mexico. The rest of the Navy's 90 vessels were used as storeships for squadron supply or as receiving ships for new personnel; one was on special service in Japan; and others were laid up at navy yards. Secretary Welles recalled many of the vessels from foreign stations and began to increase the Navy by preparing for sea duty those that had been dismantled at navy yards, by purchasing others from private owners, and by contracting for the construction of still others. By 1865 the Navy had a total of 670 vessels.

Two branches of the Treasury Department, the Revenue-Cutter Service and the Coast Survey, cooperated with the Navy during the Civil War. Under the orders of the President some revenue cutters were transferred to the Navy and served in the blockade off the Atlantic coast, on Chesapeake Bay, and on the Potomac River. Other cutters cruised along the coast to help protect American shipping. The Coast Survey made many surveys connected with naval expeditions during the war and furnished the Navy with hydrographic sheets and war maps. Some correspondence on these services is in the records of the Secretary of the Navy, but most of the documentation on the operations of the Revenue-Cutter Service and the Coast Survey during the war is in their own records and those of the Treasury Department.

Robert W. Daly, "Pay and Prize Money in the Old Navy, 1776-1899," U. S. Naval Institute, Proceedings, 74:967-971 (Aug. 1948), hereafter cited as U. S. Nav. Inst., Proceedings; Charles H. Davis, Life of Charles Henry Davis, Rear Admiral, 1807-1877 (Boston, New York, 1899); Charles O. Paullin, "A Half Century of Naval Administration in America, 1861-1911," U. S. Nav. Inst., Proceedings, 38:1306-1336; 39:165-195, 735-760 (Dec. 1912, Mar., June, 1913); Madeline R. Robinton, An Introduction to the Papers of the New York Prize Court, 1861-1865 (New York, 1945); "Naval Force of the United States--Where Ships Are Now Stationed, etc.," Feb. 21, 1861, H. Rept. 87, 36 Cong., 2 sess., Serial 1105; U. S. Navy Department, Official Records of the Union and Confederate Navies in the War of the Rebellion (Washington, 1894-1927. 31 vols.), hereafter cited as Official Records . . . Navies; U. S. Navy Department, Register of the Commissioned, Warrant, and Volunteer Officers of the Navy of the United States, Including Officers of the Marine Corps and Others (Washington, 1861-65), hereafter cited as Navy Register; "Report of the Secretary of the Navy, July 4, 1861," printed in S. Ex. Doc. 1, 37 Cong., 1 sess., Serial 1112 (p. 85-111); U. S. Navy Department, Report of the Secretary of the Navy, 1861-65 (Washington, 1861-65); Howard K. Beale and Alan W. Brownsword, eds., Diary of Gideon Welles, Secretary of the Navy Under Lincoln and Johnson (New York, 1960. 3 vols.); Richard S. West, Gideon Welles, Lincoln's Navy Department (Indianapolis, New York, 1943); and his Mr. Lincoln's Navy (New York, 1957).

OFFICE OF THE SECRETARY OF THE NAVY

When Gideon Welles was appointed as Secretary, Mar. 5, 1861, the Office of the Secretary of the Navy consisted of a chief clerk, a register and disbursing clerk, nine clerks who prepared and recorded correspondence, a warrant clerk, and two messengers. Charles W. Welsh, who had served in the previous administration, was replaced on Mar. 14 as chief clerk by Hobart Berrian, who served until May 5. Gustavus V. Fox, a former naval officer who had come to Washington to offer his services, replaced Berrian on May 9. On Aug. 31, 1861, a month after Fox had become Assistant Secretary, William Faxon was appointed as chief clerk, and he continued in that capacity throughout the war. He was responsible for administration of records, correspondence, and personnel of the Secretary's Office and for management of the finances of the Navy Department.

To implement the more aggressive policy of Lincoln's administration toward the South, Secretary Welles had to strengthen the Navy immediately. To accomplish this and to manage the affairs of the Department in a time of crisis, when the loyalties of naval officers were uncertain, he found it desirable to obtain more assistance. In Mar. 1861 he ordered Commodore Silas H. Stringham to report to his office to assist in the detailing of officers. When war came in the following month, Stringham was detached, and an Office of Detail was created under Comdrs. Charles H. Davis and Maxwell Woodhull. Besides assigning officers to duty, this Office handled the appointment and instruction of volunteer officers, the purchasing of ships, and related matters.

Successive Secretaries of the Navy during the war period:
Isaac Toucey, Mar. 6, 1857.
Gideon Welles, Mar. 5, 1861.
Record Group 45. -- The records of the Secretary's Office relating to the Civil War are in the Naval Records Collection of the Office of Naval Records and Library (Record Group 45), except where otherwise indicated. In order to bring related series of records together they are described below by type.

Correspondence

The correspondence of the Secretary's Office is general in subject matter in that it relates to most or all of the functions performed by that Office or even by the Navy Department, for the Secretary was often involved in matters handled by the bureaus. Most of the volumes relating to the Civil War are parts of longer series begun long before the war and continued after it. The letters sent are broken down by various classes of correspondents. A series of "Letters to Officers of Ships of War," 1798-1886 (available on microfilm as M 149), contains letters not only to officers in command of ships but also to other officers, commanders of flotillas and squadrons, commandants of Navy Yards, the Superintendent of the Naval Academy, and the Superintendent of the Naval Observatory, and even to midshipmen, paymasters, and engineers. The letters addressed to naval officers became so voluminous that in Sept. 1861 a new series, "Letters to Flag Officers," was begun; this contains letters to officers in charge of squadrons, flotillas, or single vessels. As these two series include orders and instructions on the operations of the vessels composing the blockading squadrons and of other naval vessels, they are of great importance for the Civil War. Letters to the Commandant and other officers of the Marine Corps are in another series of letter books, 1804-86 (Record Group 80). A series of "General Letter Books," 1798-1886, contains letters of appointment, instructions, and miscellaneous communications on diverse matters to other persons, including civilian agents of the Navy Department, contractors, Members of Congress, the Superintendent of the Coast Survey, Governors of States, Federal and local officials, bureaus of the War Department, and private individuals. Other series of letters-sent books include letters to Congress, 1798-1886 (chiefly to presiding officers and chairmen of committees); to commandants of Navy Yards and navy agents, 1808-65; to the President; to Cabinet officers and other agency heads, 1821-86; and to the Chiefs of Bureaus of the Navy Department, 1842-86; there is also a series of confidential letters, 1843-79. The foregoing series constitute a full record of the outgoing communications of the Secretary of the Navy, but investigators interested in specific subjects or areas of naval activity will have to spend much time paging through all the pertinent volumes, for the indexes at the front of the volumes and the separate "Key to Office Letters" are useful primarily for the names of correspondents.

Letters received by the Secretary of the Navy comprise a number of series corresponding to the letters-sent files. The most important series relating to naval operations is the 102-volume "Squadron Letters," 1841-86 (available on microfilm as M 89). These are arranged by squadron in several subseries, so that an investigator interested in a particular squadron will find the letters segregated. The subseries are listed in Appendix B of the National Archives' preliminary checklist for Record Group 45 and in the

List of National Archives Microfilm Publications. Other letters concerning naval actions are in the "Captains' Letters" (available as M 125), but this series was discontinued from Dec. 1861 to Jan. 1866. Still other reports on naval actions are in the "Commanders' Letters," 1804-86 (M 147), and the "Officers' Letters," 1802-86 (M 148), though most of the communications in these series concern only the writers. Communications from both regular and volunteer officers are in the "Officers' Letters." A special series was set up in Jan. 1862. This came to be called "Admirals', Commodores', and Captains' Letters," 1862-65; for the first 6 months, however, the letters in the volumes are largely from captains since the other grades were not created until an act of July 16, 1862 (12 Stat. 583). Continued only until Dec. 1865, this series concerns chiefly routine matters of personnel and the repair of ships. Information on the Marine Corps during the Civil War is in a series of letters received from the Commandant and officers of the corps, 1828-86 (Record Group 80).

Other records pertain largely to the industrial and business activities of the naval establishment. A voluminous series of letters from commandants of navy yards and shore stations, 1848-86, concerns chiefly the movement and repair of ships; the appointment, detachment, and leave of naval and Marine Corps personnel; and the employment of laborers. Far less numerous are letters from navy agents and naval storekeepers, 1843-65, dealing with supplies and accounts. Letters from the President and the executive departments, 1837-86, and from the chiefs of the bureaus of the Navy Department, 1842-85, are in separate series. More varied in content are miscellaneous letters received, 1801-84 (136 vols. for 1861-65). These include letters from shipbuilders, business firms, Congressmen, former naval personnel, relatives of naval personnel inquiring about the fate of their kinsmen, agents and boards of the Navy Department, Presidential secretaries, State and Federal officials, naval officers asking leave, and imprisoned Confederate officers asking exchange; there are also intercepted letters of "rebels," and telegrams from the U. S. Military Telegraphs and from other sources. Besides the indexes at the front of the volume there is a separate index to letters received.

Directives

An act of July 14, 1862 (12 Stat. 565), provided that orders, regulations, and instructions issued by the Secretary of the Navy were to be recognized as regulations of the Navy Department, subject to alterations made by him and approved by the President. During the war the Secretary issued many directives, on many different subjects. General orders went out as they had in the past in an unnumbered series, but in Jan. 1863 the first numbered series was instituted. Printed regulations were issued separately during the war on such subjects as pay, pensions, prize money, sea service, and the Navy uniform. A codification of previous issuances, Regulations of the Navy Department, was published in 1863; and a new edition appeared in 1865. The general orders of the 1863 series and circulars of the war period were published by the Navy Department in 1887. Orders, circulars, and instructions form part of series covering longer periods of time in Record Group 45 (in volumes and in subject file IG) and in Record Group 80. These are largely printed, and their circulation resulted in their preservation elsewhere, as among the papers of naval officers, described below under Squadrons and Flotillas.

Personnel Records

Personnel records concern the appointment, employment, resignation, and retirement of officers and civilian personnel. Resignations of officers because of their Southern sympathies began to be received in the Navy Department in Nov. 1860 after Lincoln's election, and by the middle of 1861 a total of 259 officers had resigned or been dismissed. By Dec. 1, 1863, a total of 422 officers of the line had resigned. Lists of names of officers who resigned (which serve as an index to the volumes of resignations) are in the Navy Register, 1861, p. 93; 1863, p. 108-112; and 1864, p. 112, 191-195. Lists of names of officers dismissed between Jan. 1861 and Dec. 1863 appear ibid., 1863, p. 112-115; 1864, p. 113-114, 197-198; and in the report of the Secretary of the Navy for 1861. The Navy Registers also contain information about officers on active duty. The loss of so many experienced officers necessitated the recall of retired officers and the appointment of volunteer officers from the merchant marine. During 1861-65 some 7,500 volunteers were commissioned as line officers, engineers, paymasters, and surgeons. Chaplains continued in service but were not increased in number. Some increase occurred in the clerical staff of the Navy Department. An oath of allegiance was required of persons serving in the civil, military, and naval departments of the Government, by an act of July 2, 1862 (12 Stat. 502), which prescribed the form to be used.

Letters and other documents relating to officer personnel, which in later practice were brought together in individual service records, were bound during the war in chronological or alphabetical order. These bound volumes include resignations, unaccepted resignations endorsed as "dismissed," letters or "acceptances" from regular and volunteer officers acknowledging the receipt of commissions and warrants and enclosing oaths of allegiance in separate series (those from Marine Corps in Record Group 80), copies of warrants issued to naval engineers, oaths of allegiance from officers, letters of appointment and orders to volunteer officers, correspondence on appointments of volunteer officers, orders to volunteer officers of the Mississippi River Squadron, orders and letters to acting master's mates and mates, and letters of resignation from volunteer officers dated in May 1865.

Research concerning officers can be further pursued in several other types of records. Lists of officers serving on ships and with squadrons are bound in volumes by ship names; an alphabetical index to personal names facilitates their use. There are registers for applications for appointments as surgeon's mates, assistant surgeons, pay officers, chaplains, engineer officers, volunteer officers, master's mates, acting masters, and ensigns; and registers of requests for reinstatement. Other registers give information (with some biographical data) on the service of engineer officers, captains' clerks, paymaster's clerks, and pay stewards; men appointed on recommendation of Members of Congress; and available officers. The service records of volunteer officers can be found in still other registers. Applications for orders, orders issued, acknowledgments of orders, and orders and detachments issued to the Mississippi Squadron are registered; there is also a register of commissions and warrants issued to officials of the Navy Department, chiefly Chiefs of Bureaus (Record Group 80). A few muster rolls and payrolls of vessels and shore stations are in Record Group 45 (item 90 and appendix C, item 92), but most rolls are in Record Group 24, Records of the Bureau of Naval Personnel. For brief

periods of the war there are lists of military and civilian personnel at the
navy yards of Boston, New York, Pensacola, Philadelphia, Portsmouth,
and Washington.

Legal Records

The legal and regulatory functions of the Office of the Secretary of the
Navy produced records relating to contracts, claims, prize vessels and
their cargoes, prisoners, courts-martial, courts of inquiry, and investigations. Under sec. 9 of the Judiciary Act (1 Stat. 77), cases of vessels captured while attempting to run the blockade were taken to U. S. district
courts for adjudication. The net proceeds from 1,151 vessels captured,
condemned as prizes, and sold from May 1861 through Apr. 1865 amounted
to $20,501,527, which was distributed among the officers and crews of the
capturing vessels. Prize lists of the names of such officers and crews
were sent to the Navy Department and, after the decrees were received
from the courts, were forwarded to the Fourth Auditor of the Treasury,
who made the payments. Lists of the names of the vessels captured and of
the captors are in Report of the Secretary of the Navy, 1865, p. 457-535,
and in H. Ex. Doc. 279, 40 Cong., 2 sess., p. 2-33; Serial 1343. Confederates captured aboard vessels or ashore by the U. S. Navy were taken
to Fort Lafayette, N. Y., or other military prisons, but persons who could
prove foreign nationality were released.

Among the legal records the principal series relating to prize cases
consists of case files or dossiers for particular claims; these contain letters from naval officers; U. S. attorneys and marshals; the Second Comptroller, the Fourth Auditor, and the Solicitor of the Treasury; the Solicitor
of the Navy; and private claimants, informers, and others. Some case
files include prize lists, inventories of prizes, libels of information, records of proceedings of courts and boards, copies of correspondence, and
other documents. Other records relating to prizes include registers, lists
of vessels, and indexes of prizes, prize lists, registers of prisoners captured on blockade runners, court decrees concerning the distribution of
prize money, and summaries of district court proceedings in prize cases.
Still other records in this group include files of correspondence with consuls relative to blockade runners and Confederate cruisers and correspondence on Confederate prisoners of war and on investigations of frauds in
naval procurement. A volume of contracts for the manufacture of machinery for vessels covers only Aug. -Dec. 1862. Though many other documents on the above topics are in other correspondence series, these special
files constitute an important segment of the documentation.

Fiscal Records

Accounting records were kept throughout the Navy Department, but final
responsibility for fiscal matters rested in the Office of the Secretary of the
Navy, which had correspondence on this subject with Congress, the President, the Secretary of the Treasury, and the Treasurer of the United States.
A disbursing clerk and a warrant clerk functioned in the Office during the
war. Under an act of Mar. 3, 1817 (3 Stat. 366), navy accounts were
transmitted to the Fourth Auditor of the Treasury; and this official, after
examining and certifying them, forwarded them to the Second Comptroller
for payment. The adjusted accounts were kept thereafter by the Fourth

Auditor and are described under the Department of the Treasury.

The extant fiscal records in the Navy Department are fragmentary.
Volumes of letters received from the Fourth Auditor and the Second Comptroller, 1847-84, contain form letters communicating the status of the accounts of paymasters, pursers, and navy agents; acknowledgments of the
receipt of bonds from these officers and of documents; notices of death of
naval personnel; contracts; and letters concerning the settlement of accounts, payments to prize commissioners, complaints about prize money,
claims for lost property and arrears of pay, recovery of prize money erroneously paid, submission of returns by pay officers, and the administration of fiscal matters. Bills approved by the Secretary of the Navy for
services, supplies, and equipment cover 1853-95 (Record Group 80).

Other Records

Reports from a Board of Naval Examiners, Jan.-July 1862, relate to
inventions and other scientific projects referred to it by the Secretary of
the Navy for examination. The retained records of this board are discussed
below, under Boards and Commissions. Replies by the Secretary to persons
who submitted inventions, etc., are copied in the "General Letter Books."
The work of the board was continued during 1863-65 by another body called
the Permanent Commission, whose reports fill a thick volume. Correspondence between the Secretary of the Navy and the Secretary of the Treasury and other correspondence concerning the employment and supply of
revenue cutters serving under the Navy, which was copied from various
records of the Secretary's Office, make up another volume.

Records in Other Custody. --Secretary Welles accumulated a valuable
body of papers while in office and took them with him on his departure.
His son, Edgar T. Welles, appears to have lent part of the papers--12
letter books, 1862-69--to the Office of Naval Records and Library for use
in its publication program. The Welles papers were eventually given to the
Library of Congress. The collection includes letter books, diaries, narratives supplementary to the diaries, scrapbooks of newspaper clippings for
the period when Welles was Secretary of the Navy, and many letters from
naval officers, which afford interesting information on the war. Other collections of Welles papers are in the New York Public Library, the Illinois
State Historical Library (a small group of letters concerning Lincoln's
selection of his Cabinet officers), and the University of California Library
at Los Angeles (letters addressed to Welles in 1861 concerning appointments in the Navy Department and in the Naval Academy).

Handbook of Manuscripts in the   A. Howard Meneely, ed., "Three
Library of Congress, p. 520 (Wash-   Manuscripts of Gideon Welles,"
ington, 1919); New York Public   American Historical Review, 31:484-
Library Bulletin, 29:209 (Apr. 1925);   494 (Apr. 1926).

Photographs accumulated by the Navy Department over the years are
now in the Navy Pictorial Archives in the Naval History Division of the
Department. Though some of the photographs are contemporary, most of
them are copies of photographs by Brady and other photographers and
photographs of paintings, models, and monuments. The collection includes
pictures of naval actions, ships, officers, and navy yards. The pictures of
ships show scenes aboard as well as the ships themselves. The pictures of

naval heroes of the Civil War include Confederate as well as Union officers, and there are a few pictures of naval officers' wives. The pictures of navy yards are of indoor as well as outdoor scenes. The portrait collection includes oil paintings of Isaac Toucey by G. B. Matthews and of Gideon Welles by Matthew Wilson.

Office of the Assistant Secretary of the Navy

The creation of the Office of the Assistant Secretary of the Navy was recommended by Secretary Welles in his report to Congress of July 4, 1861. He considered an Assistant Secretary necessary to relieve him of much detailed work. He was authorized to make the appointment by an act of July 31, 1861 (12 Stat. 282), and on that date he appointed Gustavus V. Fox, who served as Assistant Secretary until 1868. With 18 years experience as a naval officer, Fox was eminently qualified to assist Welles in regard to professional matters. He came to play an important role in directing the naval war and in managing Navy Department affairs, especially negotiations with contractors and legal matters.

Apparently Fox kept no separate files except for such papers as he considered personal. There are, however, many letters addressed to Fox in the regular letters-received files of the Secretary's Office, described above. These are particularly numerous in the "Miscellaneous Letters," indicating that Fox was responsible for handling part of this correspondence--that with contractors working for the Navy Department, for instance. Since he acted as Secretary in Welles' absence, some of the letters were probably addressed to Fox at such times.

Richard S. West, Jr., "(Private and Confidential) My Dear Fox--." U. S. Nav. Inst., Proceedings, 63:694-98 (May 1937).

Records in Other Custody. --Fox carried off from the Navy Department a quantity of his papers, which were eventually given to the Naval History Society and are now deposited with its collection in the New-York Historical Society. Selections from the papers, principally correspondence with admirals commanding blockading squadrons, were published under the editorship of Robert M. Thompson and Richard Wainwright as Confidential Correspondence of Gustavus Vasa Fox, Assistant Secretary of the Navy, 1861-1865 (New York, 1918-19. 2 vols.). These volumes are important for research on naval operations; most of the letters are as much concerned with official matters as are in the letters in the Secretary's Office.

Office of the Solicitor and Naval Judge Advocate General

Early in 1864 the discovery of frauds in connection with naval contracts resulted in the employment of a counsel by the Navy Department. Before this Secretary Welles had attended to the legal business of the Department, had delegated it to the Assistant Secretary, or had obtained legal advice from other officials within the Government, including the Attorney General. To find and investigate evidence of fraud against the Navy Department, Col. Lafayette C. Baker was detached for a short period by the War Department; he was succeeded by Col. H. S. Olcott, who was designated as a "special commissioner" (detective) by Secretary Welles on Feb. 16, 1864. A month later the need for an attorney to scrutinize evidence and act as judge advocate in general court-martial cases against persons accused of fraud led to the engagement of Nathaniel Wilson as counsel. H. H. Goodman was also employed as a special counsel and judge advocate in fraud cases during 1864-65. To investigate and prepare for trial cases of theft at the Philadelphia Navy Yard, William E. Chandler, an attorney of Concord, N. H., was employed in 1864.

The development and magnitude of this legal business were called to the attention of the chairmen of the House and Senate Committees on Naval Affairs by Secretary Welles in letters of Feb. 10 and Feb. 20, 1865. He pointed out that the suits involved large sums of money and much detailed work, that many general court-martial cases required scrutiny and careful preparation, that the forms and execution of contracts needed care and attention, that frauds and abuses by contractors and employees necessitated investigation and prosecution, and that miscellaneous legal questions were innumerable. With these letters he supplied a draft of an act authorizing the President to appoint a Solicitor and Naval Judge Advocate General. Under an act of Mar. 2, 1865 (13 Stat. 468), the appointment was given to Chandler. He resigned on June 17, 1865, to become Assistant Secretary of the Treasury and was succeeded in July 1865 by John A. Bolles of Massachusetts. A circular of Mar. 14, 1877, designated a Naval Solicitor and Judge Advocate, whose title was changed by another circular of July 2, 1878, to Acting Judge Advocate. Finally an act of June 8, 1880 (21 Stat. 164), authorized the President to appoint an officer of the Navy or the Marine Corps to serve for a term of 4 years as Judge Advocate General in the Navy Department.

After the establishment of the Office of the Judge Advocate General the Secretary of the Navy issued a circular, June 28, 1880, directing that matters involving questions of law were to be referred to the Judge Advocate General and that records of all general and summary courts-martial, courts of inquiry, and naval examining and retiring boards were to be filed in the new Office. Some transfers of records apparently occurred, but such records are now divided between Record Group 125, Records of the Office of the Judge Advocate General, and Record Group 45, Naval Records Collection of the Office of Naval Records and Library.

Henry P. Beers, "Historical Sketch of the Office of the Judge Advocate General," U. S. Nav. Inst., Proceedings, 67:670-674 (May 1941); "Report of the Secretary of the Navy, Communicating . . . Information in Relation to the Printing of the Argument of the Judge Advocate in the Trial of Franklin W. Smith, and in Relation to the Employment of Agents or Detectives by the Navy Department," Feb. 28, 1865, S. Ex. Doc. 30, 38 Cong., 2 sess., Serial 1209; [Report of the Senate Select Committee on Contracts for Naval Supplies, June 29, 1864], S. Rept. 99, 38 Cong., 1 sess., Serial 1178.

Record Groups 45, 125. --The correspondence of the solicitors and others who investigated frauds during 1864-65 is in several series of records. Letters received from Olcott, Wilson, Goodman, and Chandler, Feb.-Dec. 1864, are separately bound in 4 volumes. Letters sent by Chandler as special counsel, Dec. 1864-Apr. 1865, are in one press copy book. Letters sent by Chandler as Solicitor and Naval Judge Advocate General and by his successor, Bolles, are in a volume of fair copies, Mar. 1865-Jan. 1866. Other letters of the Solicitor of the Navy are in some miscellaneous case files relating to prize cases, claims, complaints, charges, and courts of inquiry, which span the war period but are indexed only from 1863.

Throughout the Civil War the Secretary of the Navy sent questions on legal matters to the Attorney General. The replies he received are in a series of "Opinions of the Attorneys General."

Numerous letters to the Solicitors and others mentioned above are in the general letter books in the Records of the Office of the Secretary of the Navy (Record Group 45), and letters received from them are in the miscellaneous letters received in the same group. The general court-martial cases of Scofield & Co. (no. 4072) and Smith Brothers (Franklin W. Smith and Benjamin G. Smith) contain further correspondence (Record Group 125). For both the administrative and legal aspects the documentation appears to be complete.

Also in Record Group 125 are a few other series of records covering longer periods of time containing some material relative to the Civil War. Nearly half a foot of papers is in a file of the proceedings of investigators and boards of investigation regarding charges against civilian employees of navy yards. A volume of miscellaneous papers relating to naval discipline, including arrests, courts-martial, desertions, dismissals, and suspensions, contains a few documents concerning the attack of the U. S. S. Essex on the C. S. A. ram Arkansas. A file of personnel reports from commanding officers of naval vessels and shore stations contains material on the punishment of enlisted men and their conduct, lists of prisoners in naval prisons and prison ships, lists of officers, and reports of the proficiency of officers.

Office of the Commissioner of the Naval Code

Under a joint resolution of Congress of Mar. 3, 1863 (12 Stat. 825), Charles B. Sedgwick, former U. S. Representative from New York, was appointed on Mar. 28, 1863, to revise and codify the naval laws of the United States.

On Mar. 1, 1864, Sedgwick transmitted to the Speaker of the House the text of the code of naval laws, and both his letter and the code are printed in H. Ex. Doc. 47, 38 Cong., 1 sess., Serial 1189. No records of the Commissioner have been found. The letter of appointment and his acceptance are among the records of the Office of the Secretary of the Navy (Record Group 45).

Office of Naval Records and Library

The Office of Naval Records and Library developed from two elements of the Navy Department. The library of the Department was placed under the Office of Naval Intelligence when that Office was established in the Bureau of Navigation by General Order 292, Mar. 23, 1882. Shortly afterwards Prof. James R. Soley was put in charge of the library. An act of July 7, 1884 (23 Stat. 185), provided a small staff for "collecting, compiling and arranging the naval records of the war of the rebellion." This function was entrusted to Soley, thus bringing under one director the Departmental Library and the Naval War Records Office. By an order of Oct. 19, 1889, the Office of the Library and Naval War Records was transferred to the Office of the Secretary of the Navy. An appropriation act of Mar. 4, 1915 (38 Stat. 1025), consolidated the allowances for the two offices into a single sum for the Office of Naval Records and Library.

The Office was transferred by order of the Secretary, July 1, 1919, to the Office of Naval Intelligence, which in May 1915 had become a part of the Office of the Chief of Naval Operations. The Office of Naval Records and Library is now part of the Naval History Division, which developed during World War II.

In assembling Civil War documents for publication the Office of Naval Records and Library drew upon various sources. About 1889 it received the records of the Office of the Secretary of the Navy; these included the "Squadron Letters," other letters received from officers, and letters to officers. All the pertinent series in these records were searched page by page, and copies were made for the compilation. The documents copied were stamped in red, "C. N. W. R."; those not copied were marked with a zero. Documents copied but not published evidently found their way into the area and subject files set up by the Office. The records of bureaus were drawn upon in a similar manner. War charts of waters off the Southern States were collected, and a list of them was published in 1889.

Examination of the records of the Secretary's Office revealed that, though the reports from the commanders of squadrons and vessels were present, the correspondence between them and their subordinates was frequently missing. The Office of Naval Records and Library therefore began an extensive and long-continued program for finding and acquiring the private papers of officers of both Union and Confederate Navies. Requests for funds were eventually successful, and an agent was employed to assist the Director in the necessary inquiries and travel. Through such effort the Office received gifts of important lots of papers and was allowed to make copies from others. The Office usually left intact log books and bound letter books containing copies of outgoing communications. The letters received by naval officers, however, were "archived" or placed in area and subject files, which are described below.

After years of preparation, volume 1 of the Official Records of the Union and Confederate Navies in the War of the Rebellion appeared in 1894, and volume 30, the last, in 1922. An index volume was published in 1927. Most of the documents printed are in series 1 (27 vols.), which concerns the operations of Union and Confederate naval vessels on the Atlantic and Gulf coasts and inland waters and the operations of cruisers on the high seas. Volume 1 of series 2 contains statistical data on both U. S. and C. S. A. Navies, letters of marque and reprisal issued by the Confederacy, a list of muster rolls of the Confederate Navy, and a long document relative to a Confederate congressional investigation of the Navy Department; volume 2, correspondence of the Confederate Navy Department, 1861-65; volume 3, proclamations by President Davis and Confederate diplomatic correspondence. Insofar as the conduct of naval operations was concerned, the first series embraces only a selection of the available correspondence. For detailed studies of many aspects of the naval history of the Civil War the original records are indispensable.

Record Group 45. -- The Office of Naval Records and Library received as gifts the papers of many officers who served during the Civil War and copied letters relating to the war from other collections lent to it. Since these copies and the original letters received were usually distributed in the area file and the subject file, it is not possible to give complete descriptions of the individual collections of papers. By tracing an officer's service during the war through personnel records in the Secretary's Office and biographical directories such as Hamersley and the Navy Registers, it would be possible to find the papers of an individual in the files mentioned above. The following list contains the names of officers and others whose records are deposited in or lent to the Office of Naval Records and Library:

Adams, Henry A.	Gardner, J. W.	Perkins, George H.
Alden, James	Glisson, O. S.	Porter, David D.
Ammen, Daniel	Goldsborough, H. A.	Preble, George H.
Arnold, H. N. T.	Goldsborough, John R.	Price, Cicero
Bailey, Theodorus	Goldsborough, Louis M.	Prichett, J. M.
Baird, G. W.	Green, J. F.	Radford, William
Balch, G. B.	Greer, J. A.	Ransom, George M.
Bartlett, J. R.	Haggerty, F. S.	Reynolds, William
Beardslee, L. A.	Harwood, Andrew A.	Rhind, A. C.
Beaumont, John C.	Hooker, Edward	Rockwell, Charles H.
Bell, Henry H.	Howell, J. C.	Rodgers, C. R. P.
Bishop, Joshua	Hull, Joseph B.	Rodgers, John
Blake, H. C.	Jenkins, Thornton A.	Rodgers, George W.
Boutelle, C. O.	Johnston, John V.	Roe, F. A.
Braine, D. L.	Kilgore, W. F.	Rowan, Stephen C.
Breese, K. Randolph	Lardner, J. L.	Rutherford, W. H.
Browne, William R.	Latch, Edward B.	Sands, B. F.
Bunce, F. M.	Lee, Samuel P.	Sartori, L. C.
Chase, W.	LeRoy, William E.	Shober, J. F.
Clitz, John M. B.	Low, William W.	Shock, William H.
Colhoun, E. R.	Luce, Stephen B.	Shufeldt, Robert W.
Colvocoresses, G. M.	McCann, W. P.	Simpson, Edward
Cooke, A. P.	McCauley, Edward Y.	Sims, C. S.
Corbin, Thomas G.	Mackay, George	Slattery, D. P.
Craven, T. A. M.	McKean, William W.	Smith, Melancton
Craven, T. T.	Mackie, J. F.	Somers, Rudolph S.
Crosby, Pierce	Macomb, William H.	Steedman, Charles
Dahlgren, John A.	Mahan, Alfred T.	Stevens, Thomas H.
Davenport, Henry K.	Marchand, John B.	Stevenson, J. H.
Davis, Charles H.	Marston, John	Street, William T.
DeKrafft, James C. P.	Megler, J. G.	Stribling, C. K.
Doss, Sylvester	Mervine, William	Taylor, William R.
Downes, John	Morgan, G. W.	Trenchard, Stephen D.
Drayton, Percival	Morton, G.	Van Dyke, B. G.
DuPont, Samuel F.	Mullany, J. R. M.	Walke, Henry
Dyer, N. M.	Newman, W. B.	Watmough, Penrod G.
Eagle, Henry	Nourse, J. E.	Welch, Will I.
Ealer, H. A.	Palmer, James C.	Welles, Gideon
Eastman, T. H.	Parker, J.	Wilkes, Charles
Ellet, Col. A. W.	Parrott, E. G.	Wilson, T. D.
Farragut, David G.	Parsons, L. B.	Winslow, John A.
Flusser, C. W.	Patterson, Thomas H.	Wise, Henry A.
Foote, Andrew H.	Paulding, L.	Woodhull, Maxwell
Frailey, J. M.	Pearson, George F.	Worden, John L.
Gansevoort, Guert	Pendergrast, Garrett J.	Yost, G. R.

An "area-chronologic file" was set up to take care of part of the records accumulated by the Office of Naval Records and Library. By 1920, when the Office had completed the preparation of copy for its publication on the

Civil War, it had acquired and stored (in cupboards in the attic of the State, War, and Navy Building) a considerable collection of old naval records. Although a large part of this material consisted of bound records of the Secretary's Office, there was much other material in boxes and bundles. The condition of these records was brought forcefully to the attention of the head of the Office when in 1923 they had to be moved to the Navy Department Building on Constitution Avenue. The collection was regarded as poorly arranged and of so diverse a character--including as it did the papers of many naval officers--as to be difficult to use for answering inquiries.

It was decided, therefore, to "archive" the loose papers according to the system already adopted for the records of World War I by the Historical Section, with which the Office of Naval Records and Library had become associated in 1919. The system involved "archiving" the records according to geographical areas and chronologically thereunder, and it was modeled after the system adopted by the British historical section during World War I. Capt. Dudley W. Knox had originally used the system in London in 1919, while he was in charge of the Historical Section of Headquarters U. S. Naval Forces Operating in European Waters, for records relating to the operations of those forces. After he became head of the Office of Naval Records and Library and of the Historical Section in the Navy Department in 1921, he initiated the "archiving" of the records of the Department for the war period according to the same system. He did this after study of the matter and consultation with eminent "archivists" in Washington, including Gaillard Hunt, former Chief of the Division of Manuscripts of the Library of Congress. It was believed that the area-chronologic file was the best arrangement to enable the Historical Section to accomplish its assigned task of preparing a compilation of naval records for World War I and that such a file would also facilitate the research necessary to answer routine inquiries received by the Department. Consequently the mass of what was regarded as "heterogenous" records underwent for several years after 1923 an "archiving" process according to which individual groups of papers were broken down and filed in the area-chronologic file.

Other materials were also added to the area-chronologic file and to the built-up subject file. These include papers removed from the records of the Office of Detail, the Bureau of Navigation, and other bureaus; and other papers from private sources that continued to come into the Office of Naval Records and Library. The research potential of the files was enhanced by the addition of photographs, drawings, maps, broadsides, clippings from newspapers, published articles, copies of documents in print, and cross-reference sheets. An examination sometimes discloses the source of particular documents, but in other cases the source is no longer identifiable. The material in these files relates to both the Union and the Confederate Navies.

The area file, 1798-1910, contains documents relating to all parts of the world. The oceans and their tributary seas and rivers are divided into geographical areas, to which are assigned documents concerning operations by U. S. naval vessels. Part of this file (38 boxes or parts of boxes in 12 ft.) relates to the Civil War. In the files for the different areas are records relating to the squadrons' operations. The file for area 7 (North Atlantic Ocean) contains material on the North Atlantic Blockading Squadron, but since Cape Lookout rather than the southern boundary of North Carolina is the southern line of the area, other material for the same squadron is in the

file for area 8, which also contains papers concerning the South Atlantic
Blockading Squadron. For the period of the Civil War there are two subdivisions of area 8: area 5, the Mississippi River and all its tributaries;
and area 6, the Gulf of Mexico, limited on the southeast by a line from
Key West due south to Cuba and a line from Cape San Antonio, Cuba, to the
northeast extremity of the Yucatan Peninsula. Key West itself was in
area 6. The file for area 6, therefore, comprises papers relating to the
Gulf Blockading Squadron and to the successor East and West Gulf Blockading Squadrons. The eastern part of the North Atlantic Ocean and all the
South Atlantic Ocean, including the waters off the coast of South America,
make up area 4, in which are documents relating to the operations of Union
and Confederate cruisers and of the Union Mediterranean and African
Squadrons. A small quantity of papers concerning the Pacific Squadron is
in the file for area 9, and just a few papers concerning the East Indian
Squadron are in the area 10 file. Area 11 pertains to the Navy Department,
other executive departments, and the White House.

The area file constitutes an important body of records for the operations of the squadrons on the Southern coast and inland waters of the United
States. Some of the papers in the area file are the actual records of officers who commanded squadrons and of others who captained vessels making
up the squadrons. Not all the letters are from naval officers; in the area
4 file, for instance, are communications from William H. Aspinwall and
John Murray Forbes, confidential agents of Secretary Welles in London and
in Paris in 1863.

Because some of the records accumulated by the Office of Naval Records and Library could not be fitted into the area file, the subject file was
set up to accommodate them. For this file an alphabetic classification
scheme (in which certain letters were not used) has for its main divisions
the following subjects:

A. Naval Ships: Design, Construction, etc.
B. Ordnance
D. Communication
E. Engineering
H. Battles and Casualties to Ships
I. Instructions
K. Nautical Technology and Science
M. Medical
N. Personnel
O. Operations of Naval Ships and Fleet Units
P. Bases, Naval
R. Prisoners and Prisons
S. Merchant Ships and Commerce
V. Governmental Relationships--Domestic and Foreign
X. Supplies (including Finance)
Y. Pensions and Pensioners
Z. History

A more complete breakdown of the subject file is in a manual available
at the National Archives. The whole file covers the years 1775 to 1910 and
comprises 814 boxes (271 ft.). Records relating to both the Union and the
Confederate Navies in the Civil War are in many of these boxes, and to estimate their quantity is impracticable. Much of the material concerns logis-

tics. The file classifications containing the most material are those relating to ships and personnel. The largest subdivision, ZB, containing papers relating to naval officers, has been retained by a section of the Division of Naval History quartered in the National Archives Building.

A collection of journals, logs, and diaries acquired from naval officers includes a number of items relating to the Civil War. These are available for the following officers: John C. Beaumont, Henry H. Bell, Richard G. Davenport, Isaac DeGraff, George F. Emmons, David G. Farragut, J. C. Gregg, Charles H. Guider, Edward B. Latch, William W. Low, William M. C. Philbrick, George M. Ransom, George C. Remey, and Stephen D. Trenchard. William B. Cushing presented a volume of reminiscences. There are other items for the following ships: Augusta, Colorado, Cowslip, Genesee, Ino, Lancaster, Lexington, Matagorda, Metacomet, Mississippi, Monitor, Rachel Seaman, Santee, and Tioga. Most of these items relate to squadrons, but since a single ship was at times assigned to different squadrons, it was difficult to put them with any squadron.

Several other series contain a few pertinent items. There are, for instance, a log of the merchant ship Tacony, Oct. 1862-June 1863; account books for brief periods for the Brooklyn and the Metacomet; a signal log for the New Hampshire; and watch, quarter, and station bills for the Canandaigua, Constellation, Miami, Pittsburg, Susquehanna, and Wabash. Two British vessels, the Sophia and the Pevensey, are represented by logs. Other miscellaneous records are indexes to official bonds executed by Navy agents, pursers, naval storekeepers, and paymasters; and a book containing regulations on pay, retirement, sea service, prize money, and pensions.

Several catalogs, indexes, and registers prepared by the Office of Naval Records and Library facilitate the use of some of the records. A card catalog of titles and dates of volumes and binders in the Naval Records Collection has both chronological and subject divisions. Some registers of vessels of the U. S. and Confederate States Navies during the Civil War give information and the sources for it. A card index to general courts-martial, 1861-67, continues one for earlier years in the records of the Secretary's Office. An incomplete index to prizes partially covers the years 1861-68. Several registers of papers received from naval officers are also incomplete.

BUREAU OF CONSTRUCTION, EQUIPMENT, AND REPAIRS

As noted earlier, the Bureau of Construction, Equipment, and Repairs, which at the beginning of the war had charge of building, equipping, and repairing all naval vessels, was abolished by an act of July 5, 1862; and its duties were distributed among the Bureau of Construction and Repair, the Bureau of Steam Engineering, and the Bureau of Equipment and Recruiting.

The Chief of the Bureau, Nov. 18, 1853-July 23, 1862, was Capt. John Lenthall.

Record Group 19. --Most of the records of the Bureau of Construction, Equipment, and Repairs were transferred to the three successor bureaus in 1862, and information concerning them is given under the entries for those bureaus, below. A few small volumes containing records of the Bureau, however, are in this record group. These include a volume of letters from the Boston Navy Yard, Sept.-Dec. 1861; and contracts and specifications for screw gunboat machinery, July 1861, for screw sloop machinery, Sept.-Dec. 1861, and for steam machinery, 1853-May 1862. Invoices of stores shipped to foreign ports extend to 1862. For the sloop Narragansett there is a record of the receipt and issuance of stores, 1859-62. A record of the cost of building and repairing vessels contains data, by bureaus and ships, for 1826-62. A letter to President Lincoln, 1861, offering to sell information about vessels under construction at Toulon, France, is accompanied by a statement of the strength of the French fleet in 1858. A letter from Dr. Benjamin Vallentin, Mar. 16, 1862, describes a plan to capture or destroy the Confederate ironclad Virginia (the Merrimac).

BUREAU OF CONSTRUCTION AND REPAIR

Under the act of July 5, 1862, the Bureau of Construction and Repair took over from the former Bureau of Construction, Equipment, and Repairs the design, construction, and repair of the hulls of naval vessels and of equipment and apparatus. It was also responsible for lumber, plates, and tools used in building vessels. It had charge of vessels not in commission, vessels under repair, and the mooring and docking of vessels.

The principal agent of the Bureau at shore establishments was the naval constructor, who had charge of the construction and repair of all vessels and superintended the workmen employed in such work at navy yards. Other naval constructors helped superintend construction at private shipyards, but inspectors stationed at the yards supervised the actual building.

The use of private shipyards was necessary during the war because the navy yards could not build vessels fast enough, and moreover they were fully occupied for many months in equipping and preparing all available vessels. Between 1861 and 1866, 55 steam vessels were built at the navy yards; 124 were constructed under contract by private firms; 323 steamers were purchased or captured; and a few steam vessels were transferred from other executive departments. The Civil War Navy also included 112 sailing vessels, whose day of usefulness was passing. Under orders issued in May 1861 the construction of eight screw sloops was begun at navy yards at Portsmouth, Boston, New York, and Philadelphia. (The navy yard at Brooklyn, N. Y., is referred to in records as either the Brooklyn or the New York Navy Yard, and these terms are used interchangeably in the rest of this section.) Contracts were made in 1861 to build 23 gunboats, light-draft but heavily armed, for use in the blockade. Twelve double-bowed, paddle-wheeled steamers for shallow inland waters were also contracted for in 1862. Several river gunboats, built by James B. Eads at St. Louis for the War Department, were transferred to the Navy Department late in 1862. In the following year 20 light-draft, single-turreted monitors designed for use on shallow rivers and other inland waters were contracted for, but when completed they had such structural defects that they were useless. The construction of several large wooden frigates and sloops of war was begun in 1863.

The era of the Civil War introduced into the American Navy the ironclad war vessel. The favorable report on the construction of ironclads, submitted by a board of officers headed by Commodore Joseph Smith on Sept. 16, 1861 (see Board on Ironclad Vessels, below), was quickly followed by contracts for building the Galena, the New Ironsides, and the Monitor. The success of the Monitor on Mar. 9, 1862, against the Confederate armored vessel Virginia (Merrimac), led to a contract in the same month with its builder, John Ericsson, for six improved monitors. In the summer of 1863 contracts were made for seven iron double-bowed ships. Toward the end of 1863 the Navy Department decided upon the construction (at navy yards with plate obtained by contract) of four armored, double-turreted monitors of 5,600 tons, but these battleships were never completed.

The superintendence of the construction of the first ironclads was entrusted by the Department to Joseph Smith. It would normally have been the responsibility of John Lenthall, Chief of the Bureau of Construction, Equipment, and Repairs; but Lenthall--who had been chiefly responsible for the design of the outstanding wooden frigates, such as the Merrimac-- did not look with favor upon ironclads. In 1862 Smith became Chief of the Bureau of Yards and Docks, and this explains why the records of that Bureau contain some papers relating to ironclads (see below).

The Chief of the Bureau from July 23, 1862, to 1871, was Capt. John Lenthall.

James P. Baxter, 3d., The Introduction of the Ironclad Warship (Cambridge, Mass., 1933); Frank M. Bennett, The Steam Navy of the United States (Pittsburgh, 1896); Report of the Secretary of the Navy, 1861-65.

Record Group 19. --Many records of the Bureau of Construction and Repair are now part of the records of the Bureau of Ships. The outgoing letters are separately bound according to class of correspondent and include letters to the Secretary of the Navy concerning vessels in service, construction and repairs to vessels, timber and other materials for vessels, personnel, funds for the Bureau, and other matters. Letters to officers concern the construction and repair of vessels, requisitions for funds, materials, payrolls, etc.; and they include for July 1861-Nov. 1863 many letters to Rear Adm. Francis H. Gregory, the General Superintendent of Ironclads at New York City. Letters sent to Gregory from Nov. 1863 are in a separate volume. A series of miscellaneous letters sent includes letters to newspapers, the Fourth Auditor of the Treasury, and other individuals, firms, and contractors on the following topics: advertisements for proposals to supply timber and other materials and to construct or repair vessels, contracts for repairs or construction, payments for advertisements, and the performance of contracts. Letters received from these correspondents touch on the same subjects. Those from Gregory and his successor, Commodore Cadwalader Ringgold, contain many enclosures consisting of correspondence and reports of engineers and inspectors under their jurisdiction, reports of boards appointed to make surveys of vessels or to submit recommendations on the claims of contractors for extra costs incurred in building vessels, and other reports on the construction, purchase, and alteration of gunboats under contract.

Incoming papers include letters received and reports. Most of the letters received are in a single series, Jan. 1862-Dec. 1867; they include letters from private concerns, shipbuilders, private individuals, the Fourth Auditor of the Treasury, and others. The letters concern bids, awards, the execution of construction contracts, payments for wages and materials, inventions, the sale of vessels by the Government, and advertisements. Beginning in Jan. 1864, letters and telegrams from contractors were separately bound. There are smaller runs of letters received from the Secretary of the Navy, from officers, and from the commandant of the Philadelphia Navy Yard. Reports of local inspectors of ironclads contain data on progress in the construction of vessels.

Other correspondence of the Bureau, including both original papers and copies derived from its files, are in the subject file of the Office of Naval Records and Library, discussed above. (The "archiving" procedure explains the disappearance from the Bureau files of some of the correspondence and other records listed in the first volume, p. 6 and 7, of Robert W. Neeser's Statistical and Chronological History of the United States Navy, 1775-1907, published in 2 volumes, New York, 1909.)

Information on naval vessels is available in several other files. Some reports on ships under construction or repair include an alphabetical list of surveys and reports for the Civil War period. There are records about the acquisition of ships and others about their disposal. Reports of boards of survey present data on the condition of ships and their equipment. A compilation by a naval constructor at the Philadelphia Navy Yard contains instructions and specifications for the building of ships. With proposals and other papers, 1861-62, relating to ironclad gunboats are documents concerning a board appointed by Secretary Welles in 1862 to examine and report upon the proposals. Other records include contracts for the construction of naval vessels, 1861-64, bound alphabetically by name of vessel; a small compilation containing data on the raising of sunken vessels, which gives leads useful in searching other records; a small volume of miscellaneous material concerning war vessels, 1863-65; some separately filed reports on the performance and condition of vessels, beginning in 1864; and monthly reports on work done on naval vessels at the Mare Island Navy Yard, 1862-65.

Other records concern materials, supplies, and stores. Contracts for materials and machinery for vessels and hardware are accompanied by specifications and certifications of sureties. Data regarding the articles on hand at navy yards and stations, the quantity issued, and their value can be found in returns of stores. The use of stores by ships is exemplified by a record of the receipt and issuance of stores by the Ino, 1861-62. For the North Atlantic Blockading Squadron there are a ledger of supplies, 1864-65, and a record of supplies received at the Norfolk Navy Yard, 1864-65.

The fiscal operations of the Bureau are documented in several series, some of which are voluminous. Statements of the transfer of the value of services and supplies for work at navy yards to the accounts of other bureaus and statements of the transfer of funds appropriated are chronologically arranged. A record of the cost of acquiring, repairing, and equipping ships covers ships purchased and ships built under contract and gives information on the disposition of ships. Another record shows the amount of funds and the value of stores received and expended at navy yards. A record of payments on contracts for ships, 1861-64, is conveniently arranged by name of ship. In another volume is a record of accounts approved for payment to contractors who constructed or repaired vessels, for advertisements asking bids, and for other purposes, 1864-68. Statements of payments made to contractors, of current contracts, and of outstanding vouchers are filed together by name of navy yard from which they were received. There is also a record of requisitions for funds drawn on the Secretary of the Navy in favor of naval agents and paymasters.

A few records of the Bureau relate to its personnel. The proceedings of boards to examine applicants for appointment as assistant naval constructors, Apr.-May 1862, contain the examination questions, the applicants' answers, and the boards' recommendations. Another file includes letters of application and recommendations for appointments as assistant naval constructors from 1865 onward.   A series of reports lists occupations at certain navy yards; another shows the number of employees on the payroll chargeable to the bureau.

Another series of records includes the following miscellaneous items: invoices and bills of lading, showing stores shipped; lists of newspapers authorized to publish advertisements; newspaper clippings of proposals and advertisements of sales; and proposals of 1862 to build a wharf at Port Royal, S. C.

Ship plans for the Civil War period are in a numerically arranged file, 1794-1910. The file comprises chiefly plans of U. S. naval vessels accumulated by offices and bureaus of the Navy Department, but it also contains plans of foreign naval vessels, a few Confederate vessels, U. S. navy yards, and ships' facilities at foreign ports. Card indexes, arranged alphabetically by name of ship or by class of ship or in other ways, facilitate the use of the plan file. A miscellaneous file contains still other plans, 1863-1919.

National Archives, Preliminary Inventory [No. 133] of the Records of the Bureau of Ships, comp. by Elizabeth Bethel, Ellmore A. Champie, Mabel E. Deutrich, Robert W. Krauskopf, and Mark N. Schatz (Washington, 1961).

Photographs assembled by the Bureau of Ships and its predecessors include some materials relating to the Civil War--pictures of ships, scenes on ships, battles, individual officers, groups of officers, and shore establishments. These are largely copies of artists' drawings, sketches, and paintings rather than contemporary photographs. In some cases, however, they are postwar photographs of vessels and persons who served in the war. A small quantity of other pictorial material on the Navy is in the Mathew B. Brady collection in the Records of the Office of the Chief Signal Officer (Record Group 111) and in the Records of the War Department General Staff (Record Group 165).

BUREAU OF EQUIPMENT AND RECRUITING

The Bureau of Equipment and Recruiting was one of the new bureaus established by the naval reorganization act of July 5, 1862. In accordance with that act, the Secretary of the Navy directed, on Oct. 8, 1862, the transfer of "all matters pertaining to fuel, hemp, rigging and sails, anchors and cables, furniture, cooking utensils, stores in master's, boatswain's and sailmaker's departments, together with towage, pilotage, recruiting and transportation of men, with the materials, labour and bills of expenses, connected therewith hitherto under the Bureau of Construction." On Nov. 7 of the same year the Secretary of the Navy issued a detailed directive to the Bureau, setting forth "the varied duties connected with recruiting for the Navy."

To perform its duties the Bureau was given charge of all ropewalks and shops manufacturing anchors, cables, rigging, and other equipment. Inspectors of equipment were stationed at shipyards to see that specifications were met. The equipping and supplying of ships at navy yards was carried on under the direction of equipment officers. Articles supplied to vessels passed into the charge of the vessels' equipment officers, who were required to maintain records of them and to submit returns to the Bureau.

Recruiting was carried on at naval rendezvous and on receiving ships and other naval vessels. After their acceptance recruits were trained on board ships.

The administration of enlisted men and of recruiting and apprentice training was transferred to the Bureau of Navigation in 1889, and the Bureau of Equipment and Recruiting was thereafter known as the Bureau of Equipment. In 1910 the Bureau was abolished and its functions were transferred to the other bureaus of the Navy Department.

Successive Chiefs of the Bureau during the war period:

Rear Adm. Andrew H. Foote, Aug. 1862.

Comdr. Albert N. Smith, June 1863.

Record Group 24. --The 1889 transfer from the Bureau of Equipment and Recruiting of personnel duties, including the supervision of enlisted personnel, recruits, and naval apprentices, was accompanied by the transfer of correspondence volumes dating from 1862. This correspondence is now part of the records of the Bureau of Naval Personnel. Letters sent, bound chronologically according to class of correspondent, include letters to the Secretary of the Navy, to officers, to commandants of navy yards and stations, to the commandant at Mound City, to commanders of squadrons and naval forces on station, to the Superintendent of the Naval Academy, to Navy agents and pay officers, and to the Fourth Auditor; there are also letters sent concerning recruiting and miscellaneous letters sent. The letters received include letters from the Secretary of the Navy, from officers, from commandants of navy yards, from Navy agents and pay officers, from the Fourth Auditor and the Second Comptroller, from the Fourth Auditor concerning bounty payments for service in the Civil War, and from miscellaneous correspondents. Registers index both the letters sent and the letters received. There is also a volume of letters received by the commanding officer of the U. S. naval rendezvous in New York, Aug. 1863-Apr. 1865.

Other correspondence volumes, relating to coal, coal agents, hemp, china, glass and plated ware, or addressed to or received from naval storekeepers, purchasing agents, and purchasing paymasters, which were probably transferred to the Bureau of Supplies and Accounts, are now missing. (See the list in Neeser, Statistical and Chronological History, 1:9).

Records relating to enlisted personnel are also now in this record group. Series of records that are helpful in tracing the service of enlisted men are weekly returns of enlistments at naval rendezvous, 1855-91, and on board receiving ships, 1855-1902, keys to enlistment returns (an index to the preceding series), 1846-1902, muster rolls, and logbooks. These and other personnel records were indexed on cards; a copy of the index, on microfilm, is in the National Archives. This index actually abstracts information from the records and presents it in chronological order. Correspondence concerning enlisted men who applied for pensions, filed claims, asked for discharge documents or service records, etc., is in jackets filed alphabetically by name. This conveniently arranged file, 1842-85, contains many jackets for men with Civil War service. There are also extensive lists of recruits who enlisted as substitutes and volunteers, Feb. 1864-June 1865, and returns for similar recruits enlisted at Boston, June-Dec. 1864. Shipping articles set forth the conditions of enlistment and contain signatures of sureties for bounties paid and wages advanced and signatures of witnesses and parents of minors. Besides noting the conduct and proficiency of enlisted personnel, conduct books contain information on the enlistment, physical description, and personal history of each man; but since they are arranged alphabetically by name of vessel they are difficult to use. Discharge papers date from Jan. 1, 1864 (the earlier ones, for which there is an index, are missing), and contain copies of discharges, discharge certificates, descriptive lists of men, and correspondence. Discharge orders dating from Feb. 4, 1864, contain the names of men to be discharged. The types of personnel employed on receiving ships can be ascertained from the index to personnel on the Ohio, 1861-65, and from a register of personnel received on board ships at Baltimore. Other pertinent records include continuous service certificates, correspondence relating to medals of honor, 1863-65, and returns of deserters.

Concerning naval apprentices, there are registers, a muster roll, returns, a general record of apprentices on the Sabine, correspondence and reports on training aboard that ship, shipping articles, and parents' consent to enlistment; most of these records date from July 1864.

National Archives, Preliminary   comp. by Virgil E. Baugh (Wash-
Inventory [No. 123] of the Records   ington, 1960).
of the Bureau of Naval Personnel,

BUREAU OF MEDICINE AND SURGERY

The Bureau of Medicine and Surgery was established by an act of Aug. 31, 1842 (5 Stat. 579). Its duties included administering naval hospitals, dispensaries, and laboratories; and furnishing medicines, medical supplies, stationery, blank books, forms, and instruments. It also controlled the preparation, inspection, storage, and transportation of these materials; and it gave medical examinations to candidates for enlistment and to naval personnel.

During the war the naval hospitals had to be enlarged and increased in number to care for the sick and injured of the Navy. While the hospital at Boston was being extended the adjacent marine hospital was used for Navy personnel. In Philadelphia a hospital was set up in the Naval Asylum. Extra space was found in a temporary building and in a marine barracks at New York, where an addition to the naval hospital was undertaken. In Washington the Government Hospital for the Insane (St. Elizabeths Hospital) provided quarters for a naval hospital throughout the war. Reoccupied on Sept. 1, 1862, the hospital at Norfolk was soon filled with sailors from the North Atlantic Blockading Squadron. Other hospitals had to be provided for men of the blockading squadrons; so temporary ones were set up at Beaufort, New Bern, and Port Royal. A temporary structure at Pensacola, where Confederates had completely destroyed the hospital, was built to serve the West Gulf Blockading Squadron; and the Treasury Department made the marine hospital at Key West available for the East Gulf Blockading Squadron. For personnel manning the vessels that operated on the lower Mississippi River and its tributaries, a hospital was opened at New Orleans, Dec. 1863. The sick and wounded of the Mississippi River Squadron were cared for in hospitals at Mound City, Ill., first in an Army hospital and later in one procured by the Navy. The Mound City hospital was moved in 1863 to a more central location at Memphis, Tenn. A hospital ship, the Red Rover, a former Confederate vessel refitted at St. Louis, plied the waters of the Mississippi. At Mare Island, Calif., there was a hospital for men of the Pacific Squadron.

Many medical officers were employed by the Navy during the war. Fleet surgeons and assistant surgeons served with the blockading squadrons, though there were none on some of the smaller vessels. Others served at navy yards and on receiving ships. Medical officers were also assigned to naval examining and retiring boards. At New York a surgeon had charge of the laboratory that provided medical kits for naval vessels.

Successive Chiefs of the Bureau during the war period:

Surgeon William Whelan, Oct. 1, 1853.
Surgeon Phineas J. Horwitz, June 12, 1865.

The wartime reports of the Bureau were published each year with the Secretary of the Navy's annual Reports.

Record Group 52. --The correspondence files of the Bureau, 1861-65, are part of a series of bound volumes, 1842-86. Both letters sent and letters received are arranged chronologically and include correspondence of medical officers, ashore and afloat, with officials of the Navy Department, Navy agents, naval storekeepers, and others. The letters relate to all the business of the Bureau, including the procurement and distribution of medical stores and equipment for ships, dispensaries, and hospitals; medical surveys; pensions; the appointment of medical officers, surgeon's stewards, apothecaries, and civil employees; admissions to the Government Hospital for the Insane; and the preparation and submission of periodic and special reports. Each volume is indexed by name, and there is a partial register for the letters received.

Several extensive series of records prepared in the field and sent to the Bureau for review and filing contain information on the medical history of naval personnel. Medical journals of shore stations and of ships contain information on sick and injured personnel (including the diagnosis and treatment of each case) and statistics. Abstracts of patients received from other naval shore establishments list the names of persons admitted to the sick list, with the nature of each man's disease or injury. A file of "hospital tickets" and case papers contains letters to hospitals requesting the admission of patients and papers concerning the treatment and disposition of the cases. Since the foregoing records are arranged by station or other establishment, it is easier to find records concerning individuals if their stations are known. The stations can be ascertained from some of the records described in the paragraph below.

Compilations of medical certificates and casualty lists provide further information on individuals. In one extensive series are certificates of medical examinations of naval and marine corps men, and in supplementary series are certificates of death, disability, pension, and medical survey examination. An alphabetical index helps in finding certificates for individuals, and the information on the certificates is useful in searching in the records described in the paragraph above. For physical examinations by medical examiners at naval and marine recruiting stations and other centers, there is a separate series of certificates. Volumes of death lists include one for 1858-65, arranged by name of the deceased. Of two volumes of casualty lists, one, Apr. 1861-July 1865, is arranged chronologically but has a name index; and another, Apr. 1862-July 1870, is arranged alphabetically by name.

Some personnel records give information on the naval service of surgeons and other medical personnel. The names of officers who served on ships and at stations are in a list of medical officers, arranged alphabetically by name

of ship or station. Copies of orders and of requests for assignment are
in chronologically arranged volumes; these are indexed by personal name
and thus permit tracing the officers' successive assignments. Brief
statements of the service of naval officers are in a volume covering 1842-
73. Concerning acting medical officers there is a special compilation of
statements of service, 1860-70. Articles of agreement and oaths of allegiance executed by surgeon's stewards, apothecaries, and nurses com-
pose a series begun in 1861, when the enlistment of such personnel was
sharply increased.

A historical data file compiled by the Administrative History Section
during World War II and consisting largely of typed or photostat extracts
from printed materials relating to the history of naval medicine, longhand
notes on data sheets, and departmental and other publications, contains
some folders relating to the Civil War.

Registers of patients that give the nature of disease or injury, personal
information, and the disposition of the case are available for hospitals at
the Naval Academy, the naval base at Key West, and the navy yards at
New York, Norfolk, Philadelphia, Portsmouth, and Washington.

National Archives, Preliminary
Inventory [No. 6] of the Records of
the Bureau of Medicine and Surgery,
comp. by Kenneth F. Bartlett
(Washington, 1948). A logbook of
the Red Rover, Dec. 1862-Jan.
1865, is in the records of the Bureau of Navigation. Carded medical
records of Navy and Marine Corps
personnel are in the records of the
Adjutant General's Office (Record
Group 94).

BUREAU OF NAVIGATION

The Bureau of Navigation was established by the naval reorganization
act of July 5, 1862, as the scientific bureau of the Navy Department. To it
were transferred from the old Bureau of Ordnance and Hydrography supervision of the Naval Observatory and Hydrographical Office, the Nautical
Almanac Office, and the U. S. Naval Academy. Another training function,
that of administering the naval apprentice system, was assigned to the Bureau on the revival of the system in 1864. Throughout the Civil War duties
connected with officer personnel were handled by the Office of Detail (discussed below), and after 1862 enlisted personnel were under the supervision
of the Bureau of Equipment and Recruiting (see above).

Navigation officers at navy yards acted as agents of the Bureau and had
charge of the storage and issuance of instruments, apparatus, charts, nautical books, signal books, logbooks, library books, and other supplies. The
Bureau was organized by James M. Gilliss, Superintendent of the Naval
Observatory and Hydrographical Office. The name of the Bureau of Navigation was changed in 1942 to Bureau of Naval Personnel.

Successive Chiefs of the Bureau during the war period:
Lt. Comdr. James M. Gilliss (acting), July 1862.
Rear Adm. Charles H. Davis, Nov. 1862.
Capt. Percival Drayton, Apr. 28, 1865.
Rear Adm. David Dixon Porter, Aug. 8, 1865.
Capt. Thornton A. Jenkins, Aug. 24, 1865.

Henry P. Beers, "The Bureau
of Navigation, 1862-1942," American Archivist, 6:212-252 (Oct.
1943).

Record Group 24. -- The Bureau of Navigation adopted for its correspondence files the system then used in other parts of the Navy Department. Outgoing letters were copied into bound letter books, and separate
series of these were kept for different types of correspondents. The letters sent thus were divided into letters to the Secretary of the Navy and
Navy Bureaus; to officers on ships; to officers commanding navy yards
and stations; to navigation officers; to Navy agents, pay officers, and
storekeepers; to officers of the engineer corps; to the Nautical Almanac
Office; to the Naval Observatory; to and concerning the Naval Academy;
letters sent concerning appointments as acting engineers; letters sent concerning naval apprentices; miscellaneous letters sent; and personal letters
of the Chief of the Bureau. Most of the foregoing series begin in late July
or early Aug. 1862. There are corresponding series of letters received.
A single set of registers serves as an index to both letters sent and letters
received. Correspondence relating to the administration of the Naval Academy is in the regular files of the Bureau. Segregated files consist of correspondence on applicants for admission to the Academy, beginning in 1862,
and correspondence on applicants for appointments as naval cadets at
large, beginning in June 1863.

As a result of the transfer of the Office of Detail to the supervision of
the Chief of the Bureau of Navigation on Apr. 28, 1865, that official began
signing routine orders to naval officers. Civil War and earlier records
transferred at that time remained in the custody of the Bureau, since it
acquired control of the personnel of the Navy. Records relating to officers
for the Civil War period include commissions and warrants; abstracts of
service records; Senate confirmations of appointments; certifications of
age; proceedings and reports of examining boards for appointments and
promotions in the Engineer Corps; letters sent transmitting appointments,
accepting resignations, and embodying orders; testimonial letters concerning engineers; registers of officers of the Engineer Corps; reports from
ships and stations on the conduct and efficiency of line and staff officers;
reports on officers under instruction and for arrest on the U. S. S. Savannah, New York Navy Yard, Jan. 1863-Sept. 1864; and ship books containing
complements and rosters of officers on vessels. There is also a chronological file of papers in jackets relating chiefly to naval cadets who failed
in examinations, resigned, or were dismissed; the index to this file was
retained by the Bureau. (Other records pertaining to officers are in the records of the Office of the Secretary of the Navy in Record Group 45 and in the
records of the Office of the Judge Advocate General, Record Group 125.)

An act of Aug. 14, 1888 (25 Stat. 442), authorized the issuance of certificates of discharge to certain enlisted men of the Navy and Marine Corps
who had been charged with desertion during the Civil War. Applications for
relief were to be filed within 5 years from the date of the act. An act of
Apr. 14, 1890 (26 Stat. 55), authorized the issuance of certificates of discharge or orders or acceptance of resignation to persons who had enlisted
under assumed names in the Army and the Navy during the Civil War and
who had been honorably discharged. These laws resulted in applications
for certificates of discharge, to which there is an index, 1890-94. Records
were also kept of the certificates of discharge issued under each act.

Muster rolls are a primary source of information about personnel; they
contain entries concerning the receipt, transfer, and discharge, desertion,
or death of crew members of ships or personnel of stations. Those for the
period of the war are arranged alphabetically in a series, 1860-79. The

rolls are missing or incomplete for some vessels, as it was not always possible to send them in regularly. A special file of muster rolls for May-July 1861 and Apr., May, and Oct. 1863 consists of rolls sent in by ships when they captured prize vessels; these rolls were to be used in the distribution of prizes. (Related records in the area file in Record Group 45 include a register of pilots who served with squadrons, a special register for the Mississippi River Squadron, and correspondence and orders; a list of vessels, with information on their acquisition, launching, commissioning, and disposal; and muster rolls.)

U. S. Navy Department, Bureau of Naval Personnel, Medal of Honor, 1861-1949, the Navy (Washington, 1949). Other records relating to enlisted men and apprentices are described above under the section on the Bureau of Equipment and Recruiting.

The logs of naval vessels and stations--chronological records of occurrences--are of value not only for the vessels and stations concerned and actions in which they took part but also for information on the service of officers and men. The logs are frequently searched for evidence regarding claims, pensions, and other benefits. They are usually of less value for naval actions and expeditions than the more detailed reports submitted by the officers, but they should not be neglected. Logs for vessels of the Civil War period form part of a large series, 1801-1946. Specifically the logs, some of which are on printed forms, supply information on the vessel's speed, course, and direction; the force of the wind; weather, temperature, and barometer readings; the sighting of ships (sometimes with their names and nationality); the handling of the vessel; and incidents at ports visited. The logs also record the receipt and issuance of supplies. Manuscript finding aids include an alphabetical card index and an alphabetical list of logs for the war period.

U. S. Navy Department, Office of Naval Records and Library, List of Log Books of U. S. Vessels 1861-1865 on File in the Navy Department (Office Memorandum No. 5; Washington, 1898). Neeser's Statistical and Chronological History gives (1:76-248) references to logbooks containing entries about naval actions and (2:318-458) references to logbooks containing entries about captures of prize vessels.

Office of Detail

The Office of Detail, established in 1861 in the Secretary's Office, was assigned to the Bureau of Navigation on Apr. 28, 1865. The detailing of officers, previously done by the Office of Detail, was thereafter done by the Chief of the Bureau. The Office of Detail was abolished, though the Bureau continued its functions, pursuant to General Order 372, June 25, 1889.

Record Group 24. --Records of the Office of Detail among the records of the Bureau date from early May 1865 and contain material relating to demobilization activities. Earlier records of the Office of Detail, accumulated while it was attached to the Secretary's Office, were maintained by the Secretary's Office and were retained there in 1865. Except for some miscellaneous letters sent, the records of the Office of Detail consist of letters received, bound according to class of correspondent; from rear admirals, commodores, captains, and commanders; from officers commanding fleets and squadrons; from lieutenant commanders and other officers; from navy yards; and from miscellaneous correspondents. There is also a register of letters received.

U. S. Naval Observatory and Hydrographical Office

This office originated in 1830 as the Depot of Charts and Instruments and was attached from 1842 to 1862 to the Bureau of Ordnance and Hydrography; under the reorganization of 1862 it became a branch of the Bureau of Navigation. During the Civil War the Office functioned largely as a service agency for the purchase and care of charts and navigational instruments and for their distribution to the greatly expanded force of naval vessels. Its scientific work was perforce curtailed: the collection of meteorological data from merchant vessels was suspended, but astronomical observations were continued and data were prepared for publication. Comdr. Matthew Fontaine Maury resigned on Apr. 20, 1861, to join the Confederacy.

Successive heads of the Office during the war period:
> Comdr. Matthew F. Maury, Dec. 14, 1854.
> Comdr. James M. Gilliss, Apr. 23, 1861.
> Rear Adm. Charles H. Davis, Apr. 28, 1865.

Gustavus A. Weber, The Hydrographic Office; Its History, Activities and Organization (Baltimore, 1926).

Record Group 37.--Records of the Hydrographic Office contain several series of letters sent that were taken over in 1862 from the Bureau of Ordnance and Hydrography; these include letters to the Secretary of the Navy and to bureau heads, to the Depot of Charts and Instruments, to commandants of navy yards and port captains, to Navy agents, to assistant inspectors of ordnance, to officers, and to miscellaneous correspondents. Most of these series extend to Feb. or Mar. 1863. Several binders contain letters received from Navy agents, the Nautical Almanac Office, and assistant inspectors of ordnance; these files end in Aug. 1862 and are registered.

Maps of the war period among the records of the Hydrographic Office include a map of the naval depot at Mound City, produced by a Coast Survey party under F. H. Gerdes, who was attached to the Mississippi Squadron, 1863-64; a map of the Memphis Navy Yard; one of Carondelet City, prepared for the Western Navy Yard Commission; and one of the proposed site for a navy yard near Pittsburgh. (Related Civil War cartographic records include, in Record Group 38, maps of the approaches to Vicksburg and the Confederate defenses, maps of the Ohio River between Mound City and Cairo prepared by the party commanded by Gerdes, and sketches of the harbors of Charleston and Port Royal. Similar materials are in Record Group 23 and Record Group 77.)

Record Group 45.--Letters received from the Secretary of the Navy, the Naval Academy, and miscellaneous sources, 1861-62 (the end of a series for Aug. 1842-July 1862), relating to hydrography, are in the Naval Records Collection of the Office of Naval Records and Library. A volume of abstracts of bills approved under appropriations for the Naval Observatory, the Nautical Almanac Office, and the Hydrographical Office includes a bit of material for 1861-62.

Record Group 78. --The records of the Naval Observatory contain a series of letters sent, 1842-62, the last two volumes of which record letters of 1861-62. Outgoing letters, 1862-65, are copied in other volumes according to class of correspondent; they include letters to the Secretary of the Navy, to Navy officers, and to miscellaneous correspondents. Indexes are in the volumes up to Sept. 1865 and thereafter in separate registers. The letters received are arranged chronologically. As indicated by the description of its wartime functions, the correspondence of the Naval Observatory and Hydrographical Office is chiefly routine.

National Archives, Preliminary Checklist of the Records of the Naval Observatory, 1840-1929, comp. by Kenneth F. Bartlett and James R. Masterson (May 1946), and Preliminary Inventory [No. 39] of the Records of the Hydrographic Office, comp. by Walter W. Weinstein (Washington, 1952).

Records in Other Custody. --The Naval Historical Foundation collection in the Manuscript Division of the Library of Congress contains letters sent, 1833-85 (covering only Apr. 4-Sept. 15, 1865, in the war period).

Nautical Almanac Office

This Office was established in July 1849 to undertake the preparation of the American Ephemeris and Nautical Almanac. Until 1866 it was in Cambridge, Mass., for access to Harvard University's scientific and library facilities. The Office reported directly to the Secretary of the Navy until 1859, when it was put under the Bureau of Ordnance and Hydrography. It was assigned to the Bureau of Navigation in 1862 and remained there for almost three decades. In 1889 it was transferred to the Bureau of Equipment, and in 1894 to the Naval Observatory. During the Civil War the Office continued to publish the Almanac.

Successive Superintendents of the Office during the war period:
Comdr. Charles H. Davis, Nov. 23, 1859.
Prof. Joseph Winlock, Sept. 18, 1861.

Record Group 78. --Letters received are available from Sept. 1864 and letters sent from Nov. 1864.

Records in Other Custody. --Other records of the Nautical Almanac Office, in the Naval Historical Foundation collection in the Library of Congress, include press copies of letters sent to the Chief of the Bureau of Navigation, Jan. 1863-Oct. 1869 (1 vol.); and letters received, 1849-84, including several boxes for the war period about the work and administration of the Office, its publications, accounts, personnel, and appropriations.

U. S. Naval Academy

The Naval Academy was opened as a school for midshipmen at Fort Severn, Annapolis, Md., in Oct. 1845. After the Civil War began and Federal troops arrived at Annapolis, the school was transferred to Newport, R. I., in May 1861 and occupied quarters provided by the War Department at Fort Adams. As these proved unsuitable, another move was made on Oct. 1, into the Atlantic House, a large hotel rented by the Government. The fourth class of the Academy was quartered on the U. S. S.

Constitution at moorings on Goat Island, and that vessel and the frigate Santee served as school ships. From 1850 to the departmental reorganization of July 1862, the Academy was under the Bureau of Ordnance and Hydrography; thereafter it was under the Bureau of Navigation.

Successive Superintendents of the Academy during the war period:

Capt. George S. Blake, Sept. 15, 1857.

Rear Adm. David D. Porter, Sept. 9, 1865.

James R. Soley, Historical Sketch of the United States Naval Academy (Washington, 1876).

Record Group 181. --General and other correspondence; orders concerning the administration of the Academy; proceedings of the academic board; proceedings of boards of examiners, including results of examinations of midshipmen for promotion; journal of the board of visitors, recording the academic standing of classes, discipline, and general management of the Academy; reports on the standing of midshipmen in courses of instruction; reports on the conduct of midshipmen, with a record of offenses; a roll book of midshipmen; a register of candidates for admission; and accounts.

Records in Other Custody. --The journal of the officer of the day, 1845-1955, is in the Naval Academy Library.

Chaplain Corps

The Chaplain Corps did not become the Chaplains' Division until 1917. During the Civil War the corps was small, with an authorized strength of only 24. Besides conducting religious services, visiting the sick, and instructing sailors in religion, the chaplains were in charge of the schooling of boys enlisted in the Navy.

Clifford M. Drury, The History of the Chaplain Corps, United States Navy (Washington, 1949-50. 2 vols.); U. S. Navy Department, Bureau of Naval Personnel, Chaplains' Division, United States Navy Chaplains, 1778-1945; Biographical and Service-Record Sketches of 3,353 Chaplains, Including 2 Who Served in the Continental Navy, comp. under the direction of Capt. Clifford M. Drury (Washington, 1948).

Record Group 45. --Chaplains were regarded as staff officers of the Navy, and correspondence and other records relating to them for the period of the Civil War are in the regular files of the Office of the Secretary of the Navy.

Record Group 24. --In preparing the publications cited above the Chaplains' Division built up or acquired several files of material relating to chaplains in the Navy. One of these is a file of biographical and service information and other data concerning chaplains; another is a file of pictorial materials.

BUREAU OF ORDNANCE

The Bureau of Ordnance and Hydrography was established in 1842 with cognizance over magazines; the manufacture, issue, and use of ordnance and ammunition; and the mounting of ordnance on board ships. The hydrographic functions then given to the Bureau were transferred by the naval reorganization act of 1862 to the Bureau of Navigation, and the name of the Bureau was changed to Bureau of Ordnance.

Under the wartime necessity to supply ordnance for a greatly enlarged navy and to counter innovations by the Confederate Navy, the work of the Bureau was greatly expanded. Advances in naval ordnance included the improvement of armor; the rifling of gun barrels; and experimentation on and development of mines, explosive shells, spar torpedoes, armor plate, and big guns. Ordnance materials were manufactured at the navy yards at Portsmouth, Boston, New York, Philadelphia, and Washington. Beside the ordnance depots at these yards, others were maintained at Fort Norfolk, Baltimore, Mound City, Mare Island, Port Royal, Key West, Pensacola, and New Orleans. Ordnance officers at those establishments had charge of the manufacture and storage of ordnance and the supplying of vessels. The Government owned no gun factories, and the only private ones prepared to make heavy guns were the South Boston, Fort Pitt, and West Point Foundries. Contracts for manufacturing guns of different caliber were made with the following firms: Builders' Foundry, Z. Chafee, Providence, R. I.; Fort Pitt Foundry, Knap Rudd & Co., Pittsburgh, Pa.; Portland Co., J. Sparrow, Portland, Maine; Scott Foundry, Seyfert McManus & Co., Reading, Pa.; South Boston Foundry, Cyrus Alger & Co., Boston; West Point Foundry, R. P. Parrott, Cold Spring, N. Y.; and Hinckley Williams & Co., Boston.

The work carried on at the foundries was supervised by naval inspectors of ordnance. Powder was obtained from plants operated by the E. I. Dupont de Nemours & Co., Wilmington, Del.; Oriental Powder Co., South Windham, Maine; Union Powder Works, Dover, N. H.; Hazard Powder Co., New York City and Hazardville, Conn.; Schaghticoke Powder Co., Schaghticoke, N. Y.; and American Powder Co., Boston. Niter was procured from the New Haven Chemical Works. Projectiles, including shot, shell, shrapnel, grape, and canister, were made at both navy yards and private plants.

Successive Chiefs of the Bureau during the war period:
> Capt. George A. Magruder, Sept. 24, 1860.
> Commodore Andrew A. Harwood, Apr. 24, 1861.
> Rear Adm. John A. Dahlgren, July 23, 1862.
> Capt. Henry A. Wise, June 25, 1863.

Report of the Secretary of the   U. S. Navy Inst., Proceedings,
Navy, 1861-65; Navy Register,   75:213-24 (Feb. 1949).
1861-65; "The Bureau of Ordnance,"

Record Group 74.--The Bureau's correspondence, 1842-84, was kept in volumes according to class of correspondent. Letters sent were copied in letter books for the following classes: letters to the Secretary of the Navy and heads of bureaus, naval officers, navy yards and stations, inspectors of ordnance and factory officials, and miscellaneous correspondents. Press copies of letters sent are in one chronological arrangement in a large series, 1861-1911. A press copy book of letters sent by Capt. H. A. Wise, 1863, includes many personal letters. Letters received are from the same correspondents, and some contain reports of tests, drawings, and pictures. Some miscellaneous letters received, 1842-84, include letters from private individuals, firms, and other correspondents and concern ordnance supplies, procurement, shipments, and payments. The work done by the foundries mentioned above can be traced in these files.

Many records document the technical work of the Bureau. There is correspondence (usually in one or a few volumes) relating to gun manufacture, the Wiard semisteel gun, the Ames wrought-iron gun, the Murphy iron wheel for gun carriages, 11-inch guns, 15-inch guns, 12-inch rifled guns, the Puritan gun carriage, and miscellaneous ordnance. Volumes of reports record the proof of 13-inch guns and concern also gun exercises and target practice. Because the proper maintenance, distribution, and improvement of guns required the keeping of detailed records, there are records of the armament of naval vessels, registers of naval guns, reports on the service of guns on ships, and reports from navy yards on the disposition of guns. For the New York Navy Yard there are lists of captured, condemned, and unserviceable guns. The submission of many inventions entailed much work for the Bureau and the Washington Navy Yard, where they were examined. Their handling and disposition can be traced in volumes of letters and reports, accounts approved for payment, and annual estimates of funds.

There are also plans, drawings, and sketches of guns, machinery, ordnance parts, and ordnance plants; maps showing sources of supply; and photographs. Some "guns afloat record cards," for guns purchased or manufactured by the Navy Department and later scrapped or expended, contain data on the number of rounds fired, the ships on which the guns were mounted, and their disposition. (This file can be used to find information about guns now set up in parks, on courthouse lawns, and in public buildings throughout the country.)

Other records, chiefly financial, include a record of the deliveries of ordnance, accounts approved for payment, annual estimate of funds, and contract ledgers.

For two ordnance boards there are small quantities of records. Those for a board appointed in 1863 to determine the suitability of rifled guns for the Navy include proceedings, a report on the manufacture and tests of Parrott guns, and related papers. For a board appointed in Jan. 1865 to investigate the testing and adoption of the Parrott 100-pound rifled guns, there is a report including correspondence, sketches, and diagrams.

Some separately filed records contain pertinent items. These include correspondence and reports of Rear Adm. John A. Dahlgren, Jan. 1860-July 1862; 4 volumes of correspondence relating to niter and 5 relating to powder; confidential letters received by Comdr. R. B. Hitchcock, inspector of ordnance, Washington, D. C., 1861; letters received relating to Diller's powder, 1862-73; correspondence on the establishment of a niter magazine at Boston, 1863-65; letters received from the Mississippi Squadron relating to armament, 1863-65; correspondence relating to the powder boat Louisiana, which participated in the attack on Fort Fisher, N. C., 1864-65; correspondence relating to the powder boats employed in the attacks on Forts Caswell and Fisher, 1864-65; and letters received relating to torpedoes used by the Union and Confederate Navies, 1863-67.

National Archives Preliminary Inventory [No. 33] of the Records of the Bureau of Ordnance, comp.   by William F. Shonkwiler (Washington, 1951).

Record Group 45.--The Naval Records Collection of the Office of Naval Records and Library includes outgoing letters of Capt. H. A. Wise in 5 volumes, Jan. 1862-Apr. 1868. Regarding the Wills and Gowen submarine armor, there is a volume of statements and testimonials from Thomas F. Wills, 1862.

Records in Other Custody.--Papers of Captain Wise, 1861-68, are in the New-York Historical Society.

Naval Ammunition Depot, Fort Mifflin, Pa.

The first land for this depot, on an island in the Delaware River near League Island, within the limits of the city of Philadelphia, was acquired in 1855 by transfer from the War Department.

Record Group 74.--Surviving records of the depot consist of receipts and correspondence, June-Aug. 1863, and a requisition and order book, Feb. 1863-June 1865.

Naval Ordnance Depot, New Orleans, La.

This depot was established after the capture of New Orleans in 1862 as a depot for the West Gulf Blockading Squadron.

Record Group 45.--A press copy book of letters sent, in which not all the letters are now legible, contains letters of the depot, Oct. 1863-Dec. 1865.

BUREAU OF PROVISIONS AND CLOTHING

The Bureau of Provisions and Clothing, established in 1842, retained its name under the reorganization of 1862. It supplied the Navy with provisions, clothing, small stores, water, and contingent stores and kept accounts of them. Its representatives were paymasters aboard ships and Navy agents ashore who acted as purchasing officers and inspectors of provisions.

Paymaster Horatio Bridge was Chief of the Bureau, 1854-69.

"The Bureau of Supplies and ceedings, 75:343-354 (Mar. 1949).
Accounts," U. S. Nav. Inst., Pro-

Records of this Bureau for the period of the Civil War are not extant. Thousands of pieces of correspondence, however, between the Bureau Chief, Horatio Bridge, and Secretary of the Navy Welles and heads of bureaus and offices of the Navy Department are in their records. Other letters are in the files of the shore establishments of the period. Still other documents relating to the operations of the Bureau are in the records of the Fourth Auditor of the Treasury Department (Record Group 217).

BUREAU OF STEAM ENGINEERING

Under the naval reorganization act of 1862 the Bureau of Steam Engineering took over from the old Bureau of Construction, Equipment, and Repairs the designing, building, fitting out, repairing, and engineering of steam machinery used in naval vessels, of steam pumps, and of steam heaters. Because the Navy Department after the outbreak of the Civil War adopted the policy of building only steam vessels, the Bureau's work in designing steam machinery and preparing drawings and specifications was greatly expanded. Most of the engines were built at private plants, under the Bureau's supervision. The shops at navy yards were almost exclusively engaged at first with repairs to steam machinery, but by 1864 they also built steam machinery. During the war the Bureau tested and experimented with various types of engines, valve gears, screw propellers, and boilers. It tested the burning properties of coal from different mines and made experiments with petroleum. Engineer officers, who served at navy yards and at private shipyards as inspectors of machinery and who had charge of the engine rooms aboard ships, were required to submit periodic reports.

In 1920 the name of the Bureau was shortened to Bureau of Engineering, and in 1940 it was consolidated with the Bureau of Construction and Repair to form the Bureau of Ships.

Commodore Benjamin F. Isherwood was Chief of the Bureau, 1862-69.

Bennett, Steam Navy of the United States; Report of the Secretary of the Navy, 1861-65.

Record Group 19. --The correspondence of the Bureau is bound in volumes according to class of correspondent. Most of the volumes begin in July 1862; correspondence for 1861 and the first half of 1862 relating to steam machinery was transferred to the Bureau of Construction and Repair. The outgoing letters include letters to the Secretary of the Navy; to chiefs of bureaus; to engineers at navy yards and on ships concerning contracts, tests, specifications, and requisitions; to naval officers commanding squadrons, ships, and navy yards and to naval storekeepers concerning the construction and repair of steam machinery, procurement of materials, and changes in specifications and designs; to Navy agents, paymasters, and pay inspectors concerning requisitions for funds, procurement of materials, purchases, payments, and prices; to contractors (shipbuilders, foundries, and iron works) concerning contracts for engines, boilers, and steam machinery, specifications, and the procurement of materials; and to the commandant of the Norfolk Navy Yard. Incoming letters, which treat the same subjects and personnel matters, are from officers, superintending engineers, and contractors. There are also reports on the progress of work on steam machinery from inspectors of machinery for ironclad steamers; these were transmitted through the General Inspector of Ironclads at New York.

Other records of the Bureau for the Civil War period are not extensive. Surveys of the condition of machinery and reports on the performance of engines in wharf trials originated with engineer officers at navy yards and shipyards and in the office of the General Superintendent of Ironclads. Several items relating to supplies include lists of engineer stores on board vessels, 1861-64; bills for steam machinery and equipment and extra work done by contractors, 1863-66; monthly statements of contracts for supplies made by the Navy agent at the Portsmouth Navy Yard, 1862-65; and invoices of stores shipped by the naval storekeeper at Boston, 1863-64. Other items include releases from inventors and patent holders, giving the Navy Department free use of patents for steam machinery and accessories; specifications for a steam sloop of war designed and proposed by Alban C. Stimers; and a record of examinations taken by applicants for appointment as chief or as assistant engineer.

A file of plans contains tracings, drawings, blueprints, and vandykes of hulls, engines, boilers, auxiliary machinery, and equipment of naval vessels. Some of the plans are those taken over from the Bureau of Construction, Equipment, and Repairs; but most of the plans date from 1861.

Steam logs, kept by engineer officers on ships and submitted daily to the commanding officers, record hourly data on the speed of the vessel, direction and force of the wind, course of the vessel, performance of engines, amount of fuel used, temperature in engineroom and on deck, and amount of concentration of water in the boiler; daily figures on fuel consumed and knots run; latitude and longitude; and remarks on the condition of the sea and any unusual occurrences. Lists of the logs are available. (A useful tool is the chronological list of steam vessels in an appendix in Bennett's Steam Navy.)

Record Group 45. -- A register of acting assistant engineers, May 1861-July 1865, is in this record group.

BUREAU OF YARDS AND DOCKS

This Bureau was established in 1842 as the Bureau of Navy Yards and Docks, a designation shortened in 1862 to Bureau of Yards and Docks. Since its creation the Bureau has been responsible for the design, construction, and maintenance of buildings, utilities, harbor structures, service structures, and storage facilities at navy yards and stations. During the Civil War, navy yards were in operation at Portsmouth (Kittery, Maine), Boston (Charlestown), New York (Brooklyn), Philadelphia, Norfolk (Gosport), Washington, Pensacola (Warrington), and San Francisco (Mare Island). Navy yards and naval stations are discussed in greater detail at the end of this section. Civil engineers were stationed at most of the yards.

Rear Adm. Joseph Smith was the Chief of the Bureau, 1846-69.

Record Group 45. -- Records of the Bureau in this record group comprise copies of correspondence concerning ironclads, in subject file AD (the originals of these are described under Record Group 71, below) and some payrolls of navy yards.

Record Group 71. -- The records of the Bureau date from 1842 or even earlier and for most of the 19th century are in bound volumes. The largest series comprise letters sent and letters received, separately bound by class of correspondent. The letters sent are to commandants of yards and stations, to civil engineers, to Navy agents and paymasters, to the Secretary of the Navy and heads of bureaus, and to miscellaneous correspondents, including contractors and others. Letters received are in separate volumes--from commandants, from governors of the Naval Asylum, from other persons at the Naval Asylum, from Navy agents and paymasters, from officers, from the Secretary of the Navy and bureaus, and from miscellaneous writers. Separate registers are available for letters sent and letters received. A series of circulars to commandants includes a small quantity for 1861-65.

The correspondence for 1861-63 includes letters to and from C. S. Bushnell, John Ericsson, Merrick and Son, A. C. Stimers, and C. W. Whitney, relating to the construction of the first American ironclads.

Several other types of records, small in quantity, cover the period of the Civil War. Those relating to personnel include monthly reports of officers and others at stations, Jan. 1861-Dec. 1864; semiannual returns of

apprentices employed at navy yards; payrolls for yards at Mound City,
1862-65, New Orleans, 1861-65, New York, 1861-65, Pensacola, 1861-65,
Philadelphia, 1861-65, Port Royal, 1864-65, Portsmouth, 1861-65, and
Washington, 1861-65; and schedules of hours and wages for various occupations at navy yards, Oct. 1864-Dec. 1865. Contracts and bonds, with
specifications and plans, fill several volumes. There are also ledgers
showing payments made on contracts, including a small volume on contracts for ironclads, 1861-64. A record of bids received includes one list
of bids on Mississippi River gunboats, 1862. Bundles of bids accepted and
rejected by the Philadelphia Navy Yard, 1861-64, are samples of such documents. Other financial records include a file of Navy agents' exhibits and
vouchers, with supporting documents, showing payments made under appropriations. Inventories of stores are available for most of the yards.
The Bureau's annual reports of expenditures and estimates, 1861-65, fill
more than 3 volumes. Besides annual reports of the Chief of the Bureau,
in narrative form, and annual reports from civil engineers, with statistics,
these volumes contain many drawings and blueprints; and they constitute a
good starting point for tracing the history of yards and stations. Further
information on these establishments is in some monthly reports of expenditures on improvements and in a series of ledgers recording expenditures
for buildings, improvements, repairs, and equipment. Buildings and works
at yards are depicted in a large series of plans, drawings, and blueprints;
a list of plans fills several volumes. (Another file of plans is in the Federal Records Center at Alexandria, Va.) An extensive pictorial file, relating principally to construction at navy yards and other shore establishments, contains some pictures of buildings, dwellings, gatehouses, and
marine railways in existence at the yards during the war.

Records relating to the Naval Asylum at Philadelphia include muster
rolls of pensioners and inmates; a register of inmates; quarterly reports
of the receipt and issuance of clothing, tobacco, and pocket money; weekly
reports on subsistence; a manuscript history with a collection of notes
compiled in 1877-78 by Edward Hooker; and a journal.

Still other records include plans and specifications for an armored
steam corvette submitted by John W. Nystrom of Philadelphia in 1861;
journals of daily events at yards, including the yard at New York, Jan. -
Dec. 1863 (2 vols.), and the yard at Norfolk, Sept. 1862-Nov. 1863
(1 vol.); a copy of John Ericsson's specification for a floating battery,
1862; a muster roll of "contrabands" at Port Royal, 1863; and a manuscript history of the Gosport (Va.) Navy Yard. One pertinent item in a
small collection of records of naval site boards is the journal of the board
appointed in 1862 to select a site for a navy yard at League Island, New
London, or Narragansett Bay (see Naval Boards and Commissions, below).

National Archives, **Preliminary**   comp. by Richard G. Wood (Wash-
Inventory [No. 10] of the Records   ington, 1948).
of the Bureau of Yards and Docks,

Naval Home

Opened in 1833 at Philadelphia as an asylum for disabled officers, seamen, and marines, the Naval Home was under the commandant of the
Philadelphia Navy Yard until 1838, when it became an independent agency.
It was under the jurisdiction of the Bureau of Yards and Docks from 1849 to
1898 and then was transferred to the Bureau of Navigation.

Albert Gleaves, "The U. S.
Naval Home, Philadelphia," U. S.
Nav. Inst., Proceedings, 57:473-
476 (Apr. 1931).

Record Group 24. --A long run of letters sent by the Naval Home to the
Navy Department and other correspondents is incomplete for the war period; it covers only Mar. 1861-Oct. 1862. Information on the weather,
occurrences, personnel actions, the receipt of supplies and provisions,
and chapel services is entered in a logbook.

U. S. MARINE CORPS

The Marine Corps was established by an act of Congress of July 11,
1798 (1 Stat. 594). Besides providing for raising and organizing "a corps
of marines," this act authorized the Commandant of the corps to appoint
an Adjutant, a Paymaster, and a Quartermaster. The corps was at first
subject to the regulations of both the Army and the Navy, but an act of
June 30, 1834 (4 Stat. 712), put it under the laws and regulations of the
Navy. A depot of supplies was established at Philadelphia about 1857. The
corps lost about half its officers by resignation and dismissal during the
months before the Civil War. Early in Lincoln's administration steps were
taken to replace them and to build up the enlisted strength of the corps, but
at no time during the war did its numbers exceed 3,900. In 1861 Marine
detachments garrisoned military posts threatened by Confederates, including Fort Washington on the Potomac, Fort McHenry at Baltimore, and Fort
Pickens near Pensacola. Marine guards were continued at the navy yards,
and late in 1862 guard detachments were also supplied for new stations at
Mare Island in San Francisco Bay and at Cairo, Ill., the base of the flotilla
on the Mississippi River. A detachment was also assigned to the navy yard
at Pensacola after its recapture. Other detachments served aboard ships
of the blockading squadrons and on receiving ships.
Successive Commandants of the Marine Corps during the war period:
Col. John Harris, Jan. 7, 1859.
Col. Jacob Zeilin, June 9, 1864.

Clyde H. Metcalf, A History
of the United States Marine Corps
(New York, 1939); Navy Register,
1861-65.

Record Group 127. --Records of the Commandant's Office consist
mainly of correspondence. Letters sent relate to assignments, discharges,
desertions, orders, courts-martial, policy decisions, movements of
Marine detachments, and the administration of the corps. Name and subject indexes to the letters sent are in separate volumes. Letters received
are part of a file for 1816-1903, arranged chronologically under the first
letter of the subject or name of correspondent. In a separate series are
incoming and outgoing orders concerning matters of discipline, general
orders, promotion orders, orders from the Secretary of the Navy, some
detail-to-duty orders, and copies of court-martial proceedings.
Records concerning personnel are among the records of the Marine
Corps Adjutant and Inspector. Two parts of a file of letters received cover
the Civil War; one is arranged alphabetically within each year, and the other
is a chronological file. Information on the duty of officers, noncommissioned officers, and privates is in a chronological file of muster rolls,
indexed by ship or station. For 1865 only there are reports on the monthly

detail of officers. Detailed information regarding enlisted personnel, including vital statistics and physical descriptions, is in some compiled records called "size rolls." Still more information for enlisted men is in a voluminous file of service records, containing forms and correspondence relating to enlistment, medical records, and termination of service. Parts of single volumes covering longer periods of time contain registers of desertions and discharges, rosters of officers, and statistical returns of Marine Corps personnel on ships and stations.

The extant records of the Quartermaster, who was concerned with the procurement and distribution of supplies, the construction of buildings, matters of transportation, etc., are incomplete. Fair copies of outgoing letters extend only to Jan. 8, 1863; but letters sent, 1863-65, are available in press copy books. An incomplete file of letters received, 1823-1906, includes some letters of the Civil War period.

In this century the Historical Section of Marine Corps Headquarters built up a file of material of especial historical interest, which is composed of official letters and reports removed or copied from the regular files. The order of Sept. 8, 1919, establishing the Section directed the collection of material for a history of the corps, and the records were eventually used by Col. C. H. Metcalf for his book cited above. As the file is chronologically arranged, the records for the Civil War (1 ft.) are segregable. The file is covered in part by a subject card index. In a file of casualty cards, 1798-1941, there is for the Civil War a separate drawer containing two sets of cards, one in chronological and the other in alphabetical order. For marine barracks at Boston, Philadelphia, and Washington there are files of letters, muster rolls, and officer-of-the-day reports and morning reports, which were retained as samples of such records.

The only extant records of the Depot of Supplies at Philadelphia appear to be officer-of-the-day reports, 1859-1911.

National Archives, Preliminary   1944, comp. by Fred G. Halley
Checklist of the Records of the   [Sept. 1946].
United States Marine Corps, 1798-

NAVAL BOARDS AND COMMISSIONS

During the Civil War various naval boards and commissions were set up for special tasks. Some were established by Secretary Welles to execute acts of Congress, others to help him in performing the duties of the Navy Department. To carry out their functions, these boards had to keep journals or records of proceedings and collect information and evidence. Records of some of the boards and commissions are extant, but those of others have disappeared.

Naval and Marine Corps Examining Boards

An act of July 16, 1862 (12 Stat. 583), divided the active list of line officers of the Navy into nine grades--rear admirals, commodores, captains, commanders, lieutenant commanders, lieutenants, masters, ensigns, and midshipmen. Previously there had been only three grades of commissioned officers--captains, commanders, and lieutenants. The act also required the Secretary of the Navy to appoint a board of not fewer than three officers to scrutinize the list of line officers and report in writing on those considered worthy of promotion. The board was appointed on July 22 and met under the chairmanship of Capt. William B. Shubrick from July 24 to Aug. 6. Since Secretary Welles himself selected the officers for appointment as rear admirals, the task of the board was to pass on subordinate grades.

An act of Apr. 21, 1864 (13 Stat. 53), required all officers below the rank of commodore to take mental and physical examinations before boards of three officers to determine their professional qualifications. These acts of 1862 and 1864 inaugurated a permanent series of naval examining boards for the promotion of officers.

Record Group 45. --The letters of appointment, record of proceedings, daily reports of the board containing the names of officers recommended for promotion (with certificates for individual officers), and original letters from the Secretary of the Navy are in subject file NI of this record group. All this material except the certificates is printed in H. Ex. Doc. 56, 38 Cong., 1 sess., Serial 1189; and in S. Ex. Doc. 23, 38 Cong., 1 sess., Serial 1176.

Record Group 125. --Records of proceedings for individual officers are filed alphabetically in a file running from 1861 to 1903. The records contain various documents relating to the professional experience and physical fitness of officers. Included are copies of orders, testimony of candidates and witnesses, copies of correspondence, and the findings of the board.

Naval Retiring Board

An act of Congress of Aug. 3, 1861 (12 Stat. 289), provided that commanding officers of the Army, Navy, and Marine Corps who had served 40 years might be retired at their request and that other officers who were incapable of performing their duties must be retired. A Naval Retiring Board under the presidency of Capt. Hiram Paulding was ordered on Sept. 16, 1861, and it convened at the Brooklyn Navy Yard soon afterwards. Paulding was shortly succeeded by Commodore George W. Storer. The board soon had to act under a new law--an act of Dec. 21, 1861 (12 Stat. 329)--providing that officers whose names had been in the Navy Register for 45 years or who had reached the age of 62 must be retired from active service. The President, however, was authorized to assign officers so retired to shore duty and to detail others from the retired list for command of squadrons or ships when the good of the service required.

Record Group 45. --A few records in subject file NI include letters from Secretary Welles to the President, Nov. 23, 1860-Nov. 20, 1863, transmitting records of proceedings in regard to individual officers, with recommendations; bills for accommodations at the Pierrepont House, Jan. - Aug. 1862; bills for the legal services of Philip Hamilton, Dec. 1861-Mar. 1864; bills for office supplies; and receipts for disbursements.

Record Group 125. --"Records of Proceedings" of Naval and Marine Retiring Boards are in chronological order in bound volumes. Those for naval officers for the period 1861-65 are in 10 volumes; those for marine officers are separately bound until 1871, after which they are interfiled with those for naval officers. The marine boards' records are similar in content to those of the naval examining boards.

General Courts-Martial and Courts of Inquiry

General courts-martial and courts of inquiry have been used for the trial and punishment of naval personnel from the earliest days of the Navy. Provisions concerning the courts and their practices are in acts of Congress and in Navy Regulations. Ordinarily, courts of inquiry were merely fact-finding bodies, but their findings could be used by courts-martial (act of July 17, 1862; 12 Stat. 605, art. 23).

Record Group 45. --Records of proceedings of general courts-martial and courts of inquiry during the Civil War are part of a long series, 1799-1867. They are arranged by case number in approximately chronological order, and for 1861-65 they number 78 volumes. Registers and a card index compiled by the Office of Naval Records and Library for 1861-67 facilitate finding the records for individual officers. Each case file normally contains the original precept appointing the board; copies of the charges and specifications of charges; minutes of the board, including a verbatim transcript of testimony; the plea of the defendant; copies of correspondence introduced as part of the testimony; the findings of the court; the sentence if the defendant was found guilty; endorsement of the Secretary of the Navy and sometimes of the President; and exhibits. These records are useful not only for biographical information on individuals but also for naval history in general. Court of inquiry cases dated before Apr. 1864 are bound with the general court-martial cases, but later cases are separately bound.

Requests for, general orders relating to, and charges, specifications and findings in particular cases are in Official Records . . . Navies. The proceedings in the court-martial of Commodore Charles Wilkes, which resulted in his suspension for 3 years, are in H. Ex. Doc. 102, 38 Cong., 1 sess., Serial 1195; and the record of the court of inquiry in his case is in H. Ex. Doc. 103, 38 Cong., 1 sess., Serial 1195.

Summary Courts-Martial

These courts were authorized by secs. 4-11 of an act of Mar. 2, 1855 (10 Stat. 627), for the trial of petty officers and persons of lower rating for offenses that warranted greater punishment than commanders of ships and yards were authorized to inflict but that were not serious enough to require general courts-martial.

Record Group 125. --The proceedings of summary courts-martial were required by law to be transmitted to the Navy Department. But it has long been the practice to destroy these records, since the findings are recorded in personnel files. For the Civil War period, as for earlier and later years, such records are no longer extant. There is, however, for the whole war period an index which gives some information on the individuals concerned.

Board for Purchase of Vessels

Under instructions of the Secretary of the Navy, July 15, 1861, a board composed of Samuel M. Pook (a naval constructor) and an engineer and an ordnance officer assigned by the Brooklyn Navy Yard was instructed to examine vessels offered to the Navy, to determine their fitness and adaptability for naval use. The board was assisted and accompanied in its inspections by George D. Morgan, a New York businessman who was appointed purchasing agent. Vessels of various types--including barques, steamers of light draft, ferryboats, and fast side-wheel steamers--were to be selected. Pook was authorized to contract for alterations in order to fit the vessels for naval service.

"Letter of the Secretary of the Navy . . . Relative to the Employment of George D. Morgan, of New York, to Purchase Vessels for the Government," Jan. 15, 1862, printed in S. Ex. Doc. 15, 37 Cong., 2 sess., Serial 1121; "Report of the Committee on Naval Affairs . . . Relative to the Employment of George D. Morgan. . . to Purchase Vessels for the Government . . . ;" Jan. 17, 1862, S. Rept. 9, 37 Cong., 2 sess., Serial 1125; Richard S. West, Jr., "The Morgan Purchases," U. S. Nav. Inst., Proceedings, 66:73-77 (Jan. 1940).

The activities of the board are documented in Record Group 45 in many letters written (separately) by Pook and Morgan to Secretary Welles. These are in the volumes of miscellaneous letters received for the second half of 1861. In the same volume is a brief report by Morgan, Nov. 29, 1861, which is printed (with a list of vessels purchased or chartered) in Report of the Secretary of the Navy, 1861, p. 138-139, and in S. Ex. Doc. 15, 37 Cong., 2 sess., Serial 1121, p. 20-21. Letters to Pook and Morgan, including their original instructions, are in the general letter books. Reports by officers detailed by the commandant of the Brooklyn Navy Yard to examine the armament and machinery of vessels are in the "Commandants' Letters." Subject file AY contains letters from Morgan, bills of sale, certificates of ownership, and correspondence on the purchase of individual ships. No separate records of the board have been found.

Board of Naval Examiners

During 1861 the Navy Department was flooded with so many proposals, plans, and suggestions about ships, their armament, apparatus, etc., that toward the end of that year a board was appointed to consider them. By an instruction of Dec. 27, Commodore William B. Shubrick, Capt. Charles Wilkes, and Naval Constructor Samuel M. Pook were designated to examine and report upon inventions and scientific projects referred to them by the Secretary. The board functioned until July 1862, leaving its task unfinished on the detachment of its members. It was succeeded after a lapse of time by the Permanent Commission.

Record Group 45.--The records of the board include a volume of letters and drawings, Mar. 1861-July 1862, which were referred to it; and a volume of minutes, Jan.-July 1862. (Other correspondence about inventions is in the records of the naval bureaus. The original reports made by the board to the Secretary of the Navy are described above, under the Office of the Secretary of the Navy, and below, under the Permanent Commission.)

Board on Ironclad Vessels

Acting on a recommendation of Secretary Welles, Congress on Aug. 3, 1861 (12 Stat. 286), authorized him to appoint a board of three officers to investigate plans and specifications for the construction or completion of iron- or steel-clad war vessels and appropriated $1,500,000 for their construction if the board's report should be favorable. Accordingly an advertisement was issued for offers, and on Aug. 8 the Secretary appointed a board consisting of Commodore Joseph Smith, Commodore Hiram Paulding, and Comdr. Charles H. Davis. On Sept. 16 the Board recommended the construction of three ironclads, later named the Monitor, Galena, and New Ironsides. In Dec. 1861 Secretary Welles requested a large appropriation for other ironclads, and an act of Feb. 13, 1862 (12 Stat. 338), provided $10,000,000 for 20 more such vessels.

The documents referred to above are printed in Report of the Secretary of the Navy in Relation to Armored Vessels (Washington, 1864), printed also as H. Ex. Doc. 69, 38 Cong., 1 sess., Serial 1193. The report of Sept. 16 is also printed in Report of the Secretary of the Navy, 1861, p. 152-156, in S. Ex. Doc. 86, 40 Cong., 2 sess., p. 3-6, Serial 1317; and in Bennett, Steam Navy of the United States, 1:264-272. The manuscript report is in the records of the Secretary of the Navy, Bureau Letters, 1862 (not 1861), vol. 3, no. 90. The Secretary's report of 1864 contains many documents concerning the ironclads in action during the war. A secondary account based on Navy Department records is in Baxter, Introduction of the Ironclad Warship, p. 238 ff. No records of the board itself have been found.

Board to Examine the Stevens Battery (1)

In accordance with a suggestion of Secretary Welles, Congress on July 24, 1861 (12 Stat. 328), authorized him to appoint a board to examine the Stevens battery at Hoboken, N. J. A contract for this ironclad steam vessel had been negotiated by the Navy Department with Robert L. Stevens in 1843, but the battery was still incomplete. The board was to determine the cost of completing it, the length of time necessary, and the expediency of doing it; and Commodore Silas H. Stringham was so instructed on Oct. 11. The board assembled at the Brooklyn Navy Yard on Nov. 1 under the presidency of Stringham, with the following other members: Commodore William Inman, Capt. Thomas A. Dornin, Chief Engineer Alban C. Stimers, and Joseph Henry, Secretary of the Smithsonian Institution. The naval members of the board reported on Dec. 24 against the completion of the battery, but Henry in a minority report favored its completion.

An entry recording the receipt of the report on Dec. 27 appears in the Secretary's records in the "Key to Letters Received," but neither the report nor any records of the board itself have been found. The report is printed in H. Ex. Doc. 23, 37 Cong., 2 sess., Serial 1127.

Board to Examine the Stevens Battery (2)

After Congress on Apr. 17, 1862 (12 Stat. 380, sec. 2), provided $783,294 to complete the Stevens battery, Secretary Welles on Apr. 19 appointed Capt. Charles H. Davis as president of another board to re-examine the battery and to report whether its completion would produce for the public service an efficient steam battery. The other members of this board were Lt. Col. Richard Delafield, U. S. A.; Prof. Alexander D. Bache, Superintendent of the Coast Survey; Samuel M. Pook, naval con-

structor; Samuel V. Merrick of Philadelphia; and Moses Taylor of New˚
York. The board met on Apr. 23 and a week later reported against the
completion of the vessel on Stevens' plans but held that it might be made
satisfactory by modifications. Secretary Welles considered the report
vague and inconclusive, and on May 5 he requested the members of the
board to state individually the modifications required to make the battery
effective. After receiving these reports, however, Welles wrote to the
Speaker of the House, on May 28, 1862 (H. Ex. Doc. 121, 37 Cong., 2
sess., Serial 1137), that since Congress had stipulated that the battery be
completed according to Stevens' plans, he did not recommend its completion. A joint resolution of July 17, 1862 (12 Stat. 628), relinquished all
"right, title, and interest" of the United States in the battery to Stevens'
heirs.

No records of the board have been found, although the report of May 1,
1862, and the individual reports of that month made to the Secretary of the
Navy are all registered in the "Key to Letters Received."

Board to Select Site for a Navy Yard

Secretary Welles recommended to Congress in March and again in
June 1862 the establishment of a navy yard at which iron vessels of war
could be built, and the city of Philadelphia offered a site on League Island,
near the confluence of the Delaware and Schuylkill Rivers. An act of July
15, 1862 (12 Stat. 575), authorized the Secretary to accept the island if the
title was perfect to the low water mark and if a board of officers by a survey approved its acquisition. Sec. 2 of this act required the board to examine also the harbor of New London, Conn., and the waters of Narragansett Bay as possible sites. Secretary Welles on Aug. 12 appointed a board
with Rear Adm. Silas H. Stringham as president, Commodore William H.
Gardner, Commodore G. J. Van Brunt, Capt. John Marston, Prof. A. D.
Bache, and W. P. S. Sanger, a civil engineer. After convening at New
London on Aug. 26, the board devoted nearly 2 months to the survey of that
and the other two harbors. A report signed by Stringham, Gardner, Van
Brunt, and Sanger, Oct. 24, 1862, recommended New London over the
other places. A minority report of the same date by Marston and Bache
favored League Island. Secretary Welles in his annual report of Dec. 1,
1862, and again on Jan. 22, 1863 (H. Ex. Doc. 45, 37 Cong., 3 sess.,
Serial 1161), recommended the acceptance of League Island; and it was
acquired in 1868.

Record Group 45. --The original manuscript reports of the board and
other papers, including some relating to Narragansett Bay; extracts from
a report of Apr. 17, 1820, on sites for naval depots; and some printed material are in subject file PS of this record group. (The reports and related
documents are printed in S. Ex. Doc. 9, 37 Cong., 3 sess., Serial 1149.)
A number of letters from Stringham to Secretary Welles dated Aug.-Oct.
1862 are in "Admirals', Commodores', and Captains' Letters."

Record Group 71. --The journal of the board is among the records of the
Bureau of Yards and Docks.

Commission of Conference

A board of officers was formed in June 1861 to plan naval operations
against the Southern coast, where bases would be needed, to devise meth-

ods for making the blockade more effective, and to collect necessary information. The commission met from June to Sept. 1861 under the chairmanship of Capt. Samuel F. DuPont; the other members were Capt. Charles H. Davis, U. S. N.; Maj. John G. Barnard, U. S. A.; and Alexander D. Bache, Superintendent of the Coast Survey. Serving as a board of strategy, the commission prepared several important confidential reports concerning both the Atlantic and the Gulf coasts of the Confederacy. These were used in planning expeditions against Hatteras Inlet and Port Royal.

Record Group 45. -- Incomplete records of the commission are in subject file ON. These include a penciled journal of proceedings, June 25-July 26, 1861; a report, July 13, on Bull's Bay, St. Helena Sound, and Port Royal; penciled drafts of reports, July 16, July 26, Aug. 9, Sept. 3, and Sept. 19 (all of which are printed in Official Records . . . Navies, ser. 1, vols. 12 and 16); a draft of a supplementary memoir, Sept. 2, on the coast of North Carolina; a report of Sept. 5 on placing obstructions at the mouth of the Savannah River (marked "withdrawn"); a draft of a report on Beaufort Harbor and the capture of Fort Macon; and a list of charts and maps. In Official Records . . . Navies (ser. 1, vol. 12, p. 195-198) is a report of July 5, 1861, which is not among the records of the commission.

Commission to Select a Site for a Navy Yard on Western Waters

Secretary Welles under an act of June 30, 1864 (13 Stat. 323), appointed a commission to choose a site for a navy yard on the Mississippi River or one of its tributaries. The commission was composed of Rear Adm. Charles H. Davis, Lt. Col. A. H. Bowman, and George W. Blunt, a civilian. It met at St. Louis on Nov. 21, 1864, and thereafter spent several weeks inspecting points on the Mississippi and Ohio Rivers, including St. Louis, Carondelet, Evans Landing, Mound City, Fort Massac, Memphis, Cairo, Louisville, Cincinnati, New Albany, and Pittsburgh. In its report of Feb. 4, 1865, the commission recommended Carondelet as the site of a navy yard for construction and the continuance of Mound City as a station for equipment, stores, and repairs. This report was printed as S. Ex. Doc. 19, 38 Cong. , 2 sess. , Serial 1209; the original manuscript is in the Records of the United States Senate (Record Group 46).

Record Group 45. -- The records of the commission are in subject file PS. These records consist of a draft of the commission's report, a list of ironclads built or repaired on western rivers, a record of the commission's itinerary, an estimate of expenses, a table of distances on western rivers, a list of maps accompanying the report, original letters from residents of river towns recommending them as sites for the navy yards, and reports by officers on proposed sites.

Permanent Commission

This body was formed by a precept of Feb. 11, 1863, to carry on the work of examining inventions, plans, devices, etc. , submitted to the Navy Department. A predecessor group, the Board of Naval Examiners, had been disbanded before completing its task. The original members of the commission were Commodore Charles H. Davis; Joseph Henry, Secretary of the Smithsonian Institution; and Alexander D. Bache, Superintendent of the Coast Survey. The commission was organized on Feb. 20 under Davis' chairmanship and continued to meet throughout the war.

Nathan Reingold, "Science in the Civil War; the Permanent Commission of the Navy Department," Isis, 49:307-318 (Sept. 1958).

Record Group 45. --The commission's records include letters referred, reports on the projects referred, minutes, and letters received from the Secretary of the Navy and from associates who advised the commission. (A volume containing the original reports of the commission is in the records of the Office of the Secretary of the Navy; see above.)

Boards on Claims

Civil War contracts for war vessels gave rise to contractors' claims for additional compensation for alterations and extra work, delays allegedly caused by the Government, and increased costs of labor and materials when the time for completing contracts had been extended. These claims by contractors led to the organization, between 1863 and 1870, of six boards of naval officers having widely divergent instructions but all passing in one way or another on all or part of these claims.

The first board, known as the Board of Aug. 1863, was appointed on June 25, 1863, to examine and report on the claims of two companies for extra work and extra expense on several vessels. It made its report on Aug. 29 and transacted no further business.

On Oct. 7, 1863, the Chief of the Bureau of Construction and Repair reported to Secretary Welles on the confused condition of accounts of vessels under construction and asked that a board be appointed to examine the extent of the Government's liability in each case. Accordingly, on Oct. 16 the Secretary appointed Adm. Francis H. Gregory president of a board, known as the Gregory Board, to examine and report upon the cost of the changes made since the contracts had been awarded in the vessels of the monitor class then under construction for the Navy Department. This board met irregularly from Oct. 26, 1863, until Jan. 1865, when it took up the various contractors' accounts and prepared them for settlement. The contractors submitted their claims directly to the board without the intervention of the Navy Department. The board recommended the amounts to be paid, and the Bureau of Construction and Repair paid these amounts.

After the death of Admiral Gregory, Oct. 4, 1866, his senior assistant, Commodore Cadwalader Ringgold, assumed Gregory's duties as General Superintendent of Ironclads and as president of the board. The board continued to pass on the bills of contractors and to submit recommendations to the Navy Department until Nov. 1, 1866, when the Office of the General Superintendent of Ironclads was closed. Coincident with the closing of that Office, Commodore Ringgold was appointed president of a board to pass on a number of accounts of contractors. The two continuous boards over which Commodore Ringgold presided were considered as one board and known as the Ringgold Board. It considered some claims received directly from the contractors and others referred to it by the Navy Department. Its procedure was similar to that of the Gregory Board. The Ringgold Board submitted a complete report of its work on May 4, 1867.

On Mar. 9, 1865, the Senate passed a resolution to inquire into and determine how much the vessels of war and steam machinery contracted for by the Navy Department in 1862 and 1863 had cost the contractors over and above the contract price and allowances for extra work. Only vessels that had given satisfaction to the Department, however, were to be considered.

To carry out the inquiry Secretary Welles on May 25, 1865, appointed Commodore Thomas O. Selfridge president of a board known as the Selfridge Board, which met at the New York Navy Yard on July 5 and adjourned on Dec. 23, 1865. This board, furnished with a list of vessels that had given satisfaction to the Navy Department, received claims from contractors directly. Its report stated the excess of cost to contractors but did not determine how far the Government was responsible for any increased cost over and above the contract price and allowance for extra work.

By an act of Congress of Mar. 2, 1867 (14 Stat. 424), Secretary Welles was directed to investigate the claims of all contractors for building vessels of war and their steam machinery under contracts made after May 1, 1861, and before Jan. 1, 1864. The Secretary was to "ascertain the additional cost which was necessarily incurred by each contractor in the completion of his work by reason of any changes or alterations in the plans and specifications required, and delays in the prosecution of the work occasioned by the government, which were not provided for in the original contract." He was directed to report to Congress a tabular statement of each case, giving the name of the contractor, a description of the work, the contract price, the total increased cost of the work over the contract price, and the amount of the cost that was due to alterations or delay by the Government. On July 6, 1867, Commodore J. B. Marchand was appointed president of a board known as the Marchand Board, to gather the required information. This board met in Washington, D. C., from July 8 to Oct. 16, 1867, when it was dissolved; but it was reconvened on Nov. 26, 1867, to consider two more claims and was finally dissolved on that date. The board submitted a tabular statement of the results of its investigations, which Secretary Welles transmitted to Congress on Dec. 4, 1867.

The last claims board, known as the Boggs Board, was established by order of the Secretary of the Navy, Aug. 6, 1869, to examine the claims of two companies for expenses over the contracts to construct several harbor and river monitors. Commodore Charles S. Boggs was president of this board, which met on Aug. 17 and adjourned on Aug. 20, 1869. The board was reconvened in Nov. 1869 to consider another claim, but it was finally dissolved on Nov. 19, 1869. It recommended payment of the first two claims.

As a result of the reports and recommendations of all these boards the Navy Department paid a number of claims, some in the amounts recommended by the boards and others in part; and Congress by special acts and in appropriation acts provided for direct payment of other claims and referred still others to the U. S. Court of Claims for judgment and payment of the amounts found due. Some of these claims were not settled until years after the war.

Record Group 19. --(1) Papers relating to accounts and supplies contain wage and price data compiled from Senate reports and 20th-century reports of the Department of Labor, navy yard payrolls, and contractors' books; correspondence of 1907 regarding prices in the 1860's; diagrams and graphs concerning wages and prices; memoranda of prices consisting of documents of the Civil War period and compilations of later dates; compilations of data regarding payments in connection with changes in specifications and extra work; letters forwarding approved bills; and proposals and advertisements for the construction of vessels and for materials and supplies. These are arranged by envelope number (1-10, 42, 43, 117-118A, 601-602, 604-614 and 620).

(2) Papers relating to war vessels, consisting of correspondence between superintending constructors, inspectors, contractors, and the Navy Department at the time of construction of the vessels; compilations of data regarding costs; analyses of the claimants' evidence before boards of naval officers; and, in Court of Claims cases, bound volumes containing "correct copies" of letters, progress reports, bills, contracts, specifications, blueprints, and financial statements forwarded in response to the call of the Department of Justice. These are arranged in numbered envelopes by name of vessel (except for a few papers filed under the heading "Miscellaneous Vessels"), the class of vessel (such as light-draft monitors), or the name of the contractor (envelope nos. 21, 23, 31, 33, 35-36, 72-103, 123-541, and 703-812). Filed separately are 14 volumes of "correct copies" of documents submitted in Court of Claims cases, most of which bear envelope numbers but which are not arranged numerically.

(3) Papers relating to boards of naval officers, consisting of calculations regarding expenditures and costs submitted to or compiled by the Ringgold Board; papers relating to the establishment and organization of the Gregory and Selfridge Boards, with some related correspondence; proceedings of the Marchand Board; and a report of the Boggs Board containing information regarding its establishment, membership, and awards made. These are arranged by name of board in numbered envelopes (52-60).

(4) Papers relating to Admiral Gregory's Office of General Superintendent of Ironclads, consisting of orders to principal inspectors, correspondence with local inspectors, reports of expenditures and other accounting records, correspondence and estimates concerning the pay of employees, and correspondence concerning the administration of the office. These are arranged in numbered envelopes (105-116).

(5) Miscellaneous records, consisting of correspondence regarding devices for removing harbor obstructions, ideas for new devices, and patents; orders and correspondence regarding the assignment of inspecting engineers; records of the Port Royal, S. C., Working Party (evidently a force engaged in repairing and refitting naval vessels), consisting of letters and reports regarding costs, employees, and repairs and other needs of naval vessels; tables relating to ironclads; charters; "unsorted" and "unidentified" papers; and papers relating to a few Court of Claims cases. These are arranged in numbered envelopes (615-701), except for the Court of Claims papers, which are filed by case number.

Besides the foregoing files there are some other materials. In the early 1890's, when cases involving certain Civil War vessels were tried by the U. S. Court of Claims, several boards, each consisting of two naval officers, were appointed to aid the Department of Justice in preparing the defense. The boards made reports including correspondence, instructions to the former boards, and the results of inquiries relating to the following vessels: Ashuelot, Manayunk, Naubuc, Nauset, Squando, and Wassuc. A small lot of miscellaneous records includes the proceedings of the Marchand Board and proceedings in the U. S. Court of Claims regarding the Secor and Co. claims. Many printed volumes relating to Court of Claims cases involving naval vessels, most of which developed from Civil War contracts, embody Navy Department documentation on the construction of the vessels, as well as petitions, depositions, and evidence of the claimants, evidence and depositions for the defendant, histories of the cases, and findings of facts.

Record Group 45.--Other records of claims boards are in subject file

AC in this record group. Boxes 23 and 24 of file AC contain the report and related papers of the Selfridge Board. The proceedings of that board are printed in S. Ex. Doc. 18, 39 Cong., 1 sess., Serial 1237; and its report and proceedings are in S. Rept. 1942, 57 Cong., 1 sess., 25-28, Serial 4264, which also contains some information on the Marchand Board. Some copies of official documents relating to light-draft monitors, made for the Marchand Board, are in subject file AC, boxes 20-22. (The Government attorney and the naval constructor who reinvestigated cases originally considered by the Marchand Board discovered the records of that board in June 1909 in the home of Marchand's daughters in Annapolis, Md. Arrangements were made for their transfer to the Navy Department, as they were official records; and they were placed in the custody of the Bureau of Construction and Repair.) The proceedings of the Marchand Board were printed in S. Ex. Doc. 3, 40 Cong., 2 sess., Serial 1316.

OFFICE OF THE GENERAL SUPERINTENDENT OF IRONCLADS

This Office was established in New York City by an order of the Secretary of the Navy of July 10, 1861, under the direction of Capt. (later Rear Adm.) Francis H. Gregory, to superintend the construction and equipping of gunboats being built under contract. At that time principal inspectors who were to report to Gregory were designated for Massachusetts and Maine; Connecticut and New York; Philadelphia; Wilmington, Del.; and Baltimore. Under them were local inspectors at individual shipyards. Gregory was notified on May 10, 1862, that Chief Engineer Alban C. Stimers was to have charge of the ironclad monitors being built on the plans of John Ericsson and of the Whitney steamer. Subsequently Stimers and Assistant Secretary Fox had charge of the construction of light-draft monitors. By instruction of Sept. 12, 1862, Gregory was given supervision of all wooden and iron vessels (and machinery for them) being constructed for the Navy by contract outside of navy yards on the Atlantic coast. He was to receive instructions relating to this assignment from the Bureau of Construction and Repair and the Bureau of Steam Engineering and was to report to them. Later in the same month ironclad steamers being built at Pittsburgh and Cincinnati under the supervision of Chief Engineer James W. King were put under Gregory's superintendence. Stimers became General Inspector of Ironclads under Gregory and held the position until its abolition on June 14, 1864. Some inspection duties were assigned to Chief Engineer W. W. W. Wood in Oct. 1862. The Navy Department thus developed at New York an agency to superintend the construction of ironclads. The staff included engineers and draftsmen who prepared drawings for the vessels. Commodore Cadwalader Ringgold became an assistant to Gregory in 1864 and upon Gregory's death (Oct. 4, 1866) succeeded him as Superintendent. The Office was occupied during 1865-66 in completing the construction of vessels that had been contracted for and in settling claims of contractors. A letter from Secretary Welles to Ringgold, Oct. 25, 1866, indicates that the Office was to be discontinued on Nov. 1.

Record Group 19. -- Most of the records of the General Superintendent of Ironclads consist of correspondence with the Navy Department, inspectors, other naval officers, contractors, and others regarding the construction of ironclads and steam machinery, alterations, administrative matters, payments to contractors, inspections, and trials of completed vessels. Besides the letters there is a small file of telegrams, Dec.-Mar. 1866. Financial records include registers of payments on contracts, 1861-63, account books of inspectors' pay and expenses and of office and other supplies, and a record of bills paid for extra work and repairs on vessels. In a thin volume are a list of vessels purchased for Farragut's squadron, 1864, and other lists of vessels. A list of officers reporting for duty covers July 1863 to Oct. 1866. Records of the General Inspector of Ironclads include press copies of letters sent to the General Superintendent, the Navy Department, commandants of navy yards, contractors, local inspectors and engineers, and others; and, in separate volumes, letters received from the same correspondents. Some of the outgoing letters relate to light-draft monitors and harbor and river monitors. There is also a file of letters sent to the General Superintendent, transmitting reports of local inspectors of vessels and steam machinery. Separately bound are a small lot of letters received from Snowden and Mason, of Pittsburgh, concerning the <u>Manayunk</u> and the <u>Umpqua</u>. Estimates for office supplies and the pay of personnel, a time record of employees, a record of drawings of monitors sent to contractors, requisitions for office supplies, and a list of equipment for light-draft monitors make up the rest of the General Inspector's records.

Much of the foregoing material is duplicated in the records of the Bureaus of Construction and Repair and Steam Engineering, in which are the original letters and reports from the General Superintendent and copies of letters sent to him. Other letters from Gregory, Stimers, and Wood are in subject file AC, boxes 20-22, Naval Records Collection of the Office of Naval Records and Library (Record Group 45); some of these are copies and others were apparently removed from the files of those officers. Still other letters from these men are in the correspondence volumes of the Office of the Secretary of the Navy.

The foregoing items are only a part of the records accumulated by the General Superintendent of Ironclads and his associate, the General Inspector. Many other items are listed in Neeser's <u>Statistical and Chronological History</u>. 1:7. Some of these items as well as some that are records of the Bureau of Construction and Repair have been distributed in the subject file (and probably in the area file) by the Office of Naval Records and Library. Neeser's list provides leads for searches in those files. Some of the records ascribed by Neeser to the Office of the General Superintendent of Ironclads, such as the extensive series of progress reports on the construction of vessels and machinery, are actually records of the Bureau of Construction and Repair. The breaking up of these files makes more difficult the task of investigating the operations of the General Superintendent.

OFFICE OF THE SUPERINTENDENT OF IRONCLAD GUNBOATS

In May 1862 Capt. Joseph B. Hull was ordered to St. Louis to superintend the construction of gunboats (at that city and at Pittsburgh, Cincinnati, and Mound City) for the Mississippi River Squadron. A naval constructor was associated with Hull at St. Louis, and inspectors were stationed at the river ports where the vessels were built. Hull was ordered on Sept. 1, 1864, to transfer his office to Pittsburgh, where two steamers still to be completed were under construction. He remained at Pittsburgh until his detachment from duty there early in November.

Record Group 45. --Some of Captain Hull's correspondence accumulated at St. Louis,Jan. 1863-July 1864, is in subject file AC in this record group. Among the papers are letters from the naval constructor, inspectors, contractors, the Secretary of the Navy, and the Chiefs of the Bureaus of Construction and Repair and Steam Engineering; reports from inspectors; copies of contracts; and some copies of outgoing letters. Hull's letters sent, June 15, 1862-Sept. 12, 1864, are in 2 volumes. Many letters from and to Hull are in the correspondence volumes of the Bureau of Construction and Repair, the Bureau of Steam Engineering, and the Office of the Secretary of the Navy.

SQUADRONS AND FLOTILLAS

A blockade of the coast of the Southern States from Virginia to Texas was proclaimed by President Lincoln on Apr. 19 and 27, 1861 (12 Stat. 1258, 1259). Enforcement of the blockade became the principal task of the Union Navy during the war. For some months the blockade was not very effective; but it improved as more ships became available and were assigned to the blockading squadrons. By cutting the South off from overseas sources of munitions, other supplies, and naval vessels, the blockade contributed greatly to the decline of its military strength and its ultimate defeat. Vessels on the blockade exercised the right under international law of stopping and searching neutral ships to ascertain their destinations and inspect their cargoes. The cases of ships captured as blockade runners, as carriers of contraband of war, or as vessels that were enemy property were taken to prize courts for adjudication.

The blockading of 3,549 miles of Confederate coast--from Alexandria, Va., to the Rio Grande--was undertaken by the Union Navy soon after the blockade was proclaimed. A patrol was begun on the Potomac River in Apr. 1861 to intercept Confederate trade and communications and to protect Union traffic on the river. The Potomac Flotilla, active throughout the war, cooperated at times with the Army. The Atlantic Coast from Virginia to Cape Florida was at first assigned to the Atlantic Blockading Squadron. After the number of vessels on this coast was increased, the original squadron was divided, Sept. 23, 1861, into the North Atlantic and the South Atlantic Blockading Squadrons, with the line between them the boundary between North and South Carolina. The Gulf Coast Squadron, formed in June 1861, covered at first the whole coast from Cape Florida to the Rio Grande, but it too was divided when additional vessels became available. On Feb. 21, 1862, the East Gulf and the West Gulf Blockading Squadrons were established, with the dividing point at Pensacola. A flotilla of small vessels cooperated with and protected the Army on the James and York Rivers during July and Aug. 1862. A naval force convoyed the army of Major General Butler up the James River in May 1864, and thereafter a flotilla was maintained on that river to immobilize Confederate naval vessels on its upper waters. A flotilla formed on the St. Johns River in Florida early in 1864 continued to operate on its waters. A flying squadron was organized in Sept. 1862 to search out Confederate cruisers preying upon American commerce in the West Indies and to seize blockade runners operating out of the Bahamas. The West India Squadron also escorted vessels carrying gold from the Isthmus of Panama to New York when danger appeared to threaten. In the summer of 1861 the Union Navy established a flotilla that developed into the Mississippi River Squadron. The Squadron aided the Army in reducing fortified places and opening the river, and then it maintained a constant patrol to keep it open. The Ohio, Tennessee, and Cumberland Rivers were also patrolled. A mortar flotilla on the Mississippi River aided in attacks on towns held by the Confederates.

Foreign squadrons were maintained, though with fewer ships, during the Civil War. Besides considerations of general policy there was the added necessity to cope with the wide-ranging attacks by Confederate cruisers on American vessels. To pursue and capture or destroy those cruisers, the Union Navy also dispatched cruisers on the high seas, particularly the eastern Atlantic and the South Atlantic. Single vessels were at first maintained on the African, Brazil, East India, and Mediterranean stations. (The assignment of the African Squadron was the suppression of the slave trade.) Several vessels attached to the Pacific Squadron protected American vessels sailing between California and the Isthmus of Panama, sometimes forming actual convoys. The whaling fleet in the Bering Sea, which was largely destroyed by the Confederate cruiser Shenandoah in 1865, was beyond the surveillance of the Squadron.

The blockading squadrons, which early in 1865 comprised 472 vessels with 2,455 guns, were quickly reduced after the cessation of hostilities. Orders went out on May 1 for a one-half reduction in the squadrons, and by early summer only 30 steamers remained on the blockade. The squadrons on the Atlantic and Gulf coasts were consolidated into the Atlantic Squadron and the Gulf Squadron. The Potomac Flotilla was disbanded on July 31, and the Mississippi Squadron on Aug. 14. Naval vessels and personnel released from blockading duty were assigned to reestablished and enlarged foreign squadrons.

Certain publications are very helpful in searching the records of the Navy Department for information relative to the squadrons, the vessels that composed them, and the officers and crews who manned the vessels. The Navy Registers contain data regarding both the ships and personnel of the squadrons (1863, p. 178-209; 1864, p. 208-242; 1865, p. 236-280). The Registers for 1861-65 contain alphabetical lists of vessels of the Navy with data on their stations or condition. Lists of vessels in the squadrons at different times and other special lists are in Official Records . . . Navies, which also contains (ser. 2, vol. 1, p. 27-246) historical information and statistical data concerning individual ships. A brief history of the operations of the squadrons in Lewis R. Hamersly, The Records of Living Officers of the U. S. Navy and Marine Corps . . . , p. 257-312

(Philadelphia, 1870), is followed by a list of the officers and vessels engaged in the most important naval battles of the war (p. 313-343). A chronology of ship engagements, with much information, including references to manuscript and printed sources, is in Neeser's Statistical and Chronological History, 2:76-248. Useful but incomplete is Bradley S. Osbon, Hand Book of the United States Navy; Being a Compilation of All the Principal Events in the History of Every Vessel in the United States Navy, From April, 1861, to May, 1864 (New York, 1864). In U. S. Navy Department, Annual Report, 1861-65, are 2,270 pages of reports from officers and other documents, many of which were subsequently reprinted in the Official Records . . . Navies. Lists of vessels built and purchased for the Navy are printed in H. Ex. Doc. 280, 40 Cong., 2 sess., Serial 1343, p. 6-25, 26-33. See also U. S. Navy Department,

Office of Naval War Records, List of U. S. Naval Vessels, 1861-1865, Including the Ellet Ram Fleet and Mississippi Marine Brigade; Appendix, List of U. S. Coast Survey Vessels, 1861-1865 (Office Memorandum No. 4, Washington, 1891); Marcus W. Price, "Ships That Tested the Blockade of the Carolina Ports, 1851-1865," "Ships That Tested the Blockade of the Gulf Ports, 1861-1865," and "Ships That Tested the Blockade of the Georgia and East Florida Ports, 1861-1865," American Neptune, 8:196-241, 11:262-290, 15:97-132 (July 1948, Oct. 1951, Apr. 1955); U. S. Navy Department, Office of the Chief of Naval Operations, Naval History Division, Dictionary of American Naval Fighting Ships (Washington. 1959-   ).

Record Group 45. --Correspondence and other records relating to squadron operations are in an extensive group of letter books of naval officers. More than half of these (249 vols., ca. 30 ft.) relate to the Civil War, and most of the records can be easily identified with particular squadrons and are separately described below. These letter books are especially valuable for squadron history because they contain the letters to the Navy Department that in the Department's files are scattered in many different volumes of numerous series. The squadron files also contain correspondence, such as that with subordinate officers, local officials, officers at shore stations, and Confederate officers, which is not in the files of the Secretary's Office or of the bureaus.

The commanding officers of squadrons, some of whom had held their posts for long periods of time, were allowed by the Navy Department at the end of the war to retain their correspondence files. The Secretary of the Navy could have issued an order requiring their transmittal to the Department but seems not to have done so. Consequently such squadron records as the Office of Naval War Records later received came to it from the hands of the officers who had taken the trouble to retain the records. (For a chronological list of the letter books, see the National Archives preliminary checklist for Record Group 45, p. 133-139.) Other records retained by the commanding officers after the Civil War have, however, been deposited by them in private libraries or in Federal agencies other than the National Archives. Such records are listed below under the appropriate squadrons as records in other custody. Information about them has been derived from the list of publications that follows.

Information about records in other custody relating to the squadrons is largely derived from the following guides, which are grouped together here to save space: Philip M. Hamer, ed., Guide to Archives and Manuscripts in the United States (New Haven, Yale University Press, 1961); Henry E. Huntington Library, Huntington Library Collections, comp. by George Sherburn and others, Huntington Library Bulletin, no. 1: 33-106 (May 1931); Handbook of Manuscripts in the Library of Congress, and List of Manuscript Collections in the Library of Congress to July, 1931, comp. by Curtis W. Garrison (Washington, 1932; reprinted from the American Historical Association, Annual Report, 1930, p. 123-249); U. S. Naval Academy Museum, Catalogue of the Christian A. Zabriskie Manuscript Collection (Annapolis, 1956), and Catalogue of Manuscripts (Annapolis, 1957); U. S. Navy Department, Office of the Chief of Naval Operations, Naval History Division, Brief Guide

to U. S. Naval History Sources   (Washington, July 23, 1957).
in the Washington, D. C. Area

North Atlantic Blockading Squadron

Record Group 45. -- Letters sent by Rear Adm. Louis M. Goldsborough
(Flagship Minnesota), Sept. 1861-Sept. 1862; correspondence of Acting
Rear Adm. David D. Porter (Flagship Malvern), Sept. 1864-May 1865;
letters sent by Acting Rear Adm. William Radford (Flagship Malvern),
Apr.-Oct. 1865; correspondence of Commodore William Radford, commanding the New Ironsides, Dumbarton, and Phlox, Aug. 1864-Apr. 1865;
orders received and issued by the Squadron, Nov. 1861-Apr. 1865; letters
received by Comdr. Henry K. Davenport, commanding the Hetzel, Dec.
1861-June 1864; registers of letters received by Davenport from Acting
Rear Adm. Samuel P. Lee, Mar. 1863-May 1864; letters sent by Capt.
Guert Gansevoort, commanding the Roanoke, Jan.-Sept. 1864; letters sent
by Lt. Comdr. Penrod G. Watmough, commanding the Kansas, Dec. 1863-
Feb. 1865; correspondence of Comdr. John C. Beaumont, commanding the
Mackinaw, Apr.-Nov. 1864; registers of the batteries of vessels, volunteer officers, ships and officers, appointments and promotions, and vessels examined and passed off Fortress Monroe.
    Records in Other Custody. -- An extensive collection of Rear Adm. Louis
Goldsborough's papers is in the Manuscript Division of the Library of Congress, and others are in the New York Public Library and Duke University
Library. Voluminous papers of Rear Adm. Samuel P. Lee, who commanded the Squadron from Sept. 1862 to Oct. 1864, are in the Naval Historical Foundation collection in the Manuscript Division, Library of
Congress; and more of his papers are in Princeton University Library.

South Atlantic Blockading Squadron

Record Group 45. -- Letters sent by Lt. Penrod G. Watmough, commanding the Curlew, Potomska, and Memphis, Jan. 1861-Oct. 1862;
correspondence of Comdr. Daniel Ammen, commanding the Seneca,
Sebago, and Patapsco, Oct. 1861-June 6, 1863, and June 1864; correspondence of Capt. George F. Emmons, commanding the Hatteras, R. R. Cuyler,
and Brooklyn, Oct. 1861-Sept. 1863, and journal of the blockading of Ber-
wick Bay, S. C., by the Hatteras, July-Nov. 1862; letters sent by Capt.
C. R. P. Rodgers, commanding the Wabash, Nov. 1861-May 1863; letters
sent by Comdr. Thomas H. Patterson, commanding the Chocura and the
James Adger, Mar. 1862-Oct. 1864, May-June 1865; letters sent by
Comdr. John Rodgers, Jan.-June 1863; letters sent by Comdr. William
Reynolds, commanding the Vermont, Nov. 1862-Nov. 1864; correspondence
of Comdr. John C. Beaumont, commanding the Sebago and the Nantucket,
Dec. 1862-Sept. 1863; correspondence of Comdr. Daniel Ammen, com-
manding the Mohican, Oct. 1864-Mar. 1865; letters sent by Comdr. William Reynolds, commanding the New Hampshire, Dec. 1864-July 1865;
Rear Adm. Samuel F. DuPont's general orders, Oct. 1861-July 1863.
    Records in Other Custody. -- The papers of Rear Adm. Samuel F.
DuPont, who commanded the Squadron from Sept. 1861 to July 1863, are
in the Eleutherian Mills Historical Library, Greenville, Del. (The publication Official Dispatches and Letters of Rear Admiral DuPont, U. S.

Navy, 1846-48, 1861-63, Wilmington, Del. , 1883, contains nearly 500 pages of letters for the above period. A selection of DuPont's letters for the years 1861-65 is being edited by Rear Adm. , Ret. , John D. Hayes.) DuPont was succeeded by Rear Adm. John A. Dahlgren, who remained in command until July 12, 1865. His papers in the Library of Congress and the New York Public Library cover the Civil War period. Capt. John L. Worden, commander of the Monitor during its engagement with the Merrimac on Mar. 9, 1862, commanded the Montauk, 1862-63. Collections of his papers are in the Lincoln Museum, Lincoln Memorial University, Harrogate, Tenn. , and in the Naval Historical Foundation collection at the Library of Congress. Correspondence of Comdr. Thomas Patterson, 1862-65, is in the Division of Naval History, Navy Department. Lt. Comdr. Stephen B. Luce commanded the Nantucket and the Macedonian, 1863-65; and letters and orders are in his papers in the Naval Historical Foundation manuscripts.

Gulf Blockading Squadron

Record Group 45. -- Letters sent by Rear Adm. William Mervine, Feb. - Sept. 1861; letters sent by Capt. Henry Eagle, commanding the Santee, June 1861-Mar. 1862; letters sent by Flag Officer William W. McKean, Flagship Niagara, Nov. 1861-June 1862.

Records in Other Custody. -- The papers of Surgeon Gustavus R. B. Horner in the Naval Historical Foundation collection in the Manuscript Division, Library of Congress, contain some material for this Squadron for 1861-62.

East Gulf Blockading Squadron

Record Group 45. -- Correspondence of Acting Rear Adm. Theodorus Bailey (Flagships St. Lawrence, Magnolia, San Jacinto, and Dale), Dec. 1862-Aug. 1864; letters sent by Acting Master William R. Browne, commanding the Restless, Jan. -July 1864; letters sent by Acting Vol. Lt. Charles H. Rockwell, commanding the Gem of the Sea, Jan. -Sept. 1864; consular letters to Rear Adm. C. K. Stribling, Oct. 1864-June 1865; orders and circulars received and issued, Jan. 1863-June 1865; orders issued by Rockwell, commanding the Hendrick Hudson, Nov. 1864-July 1865; log of the general headquarters of the Squadron, Key West, July 1863-July 1864.

Records in Other Custody. -- Comdr. Robert W. Shufeldt captained the Proteus in this Squadron, 1863-65. Part of the period is covered by his letters and all of it by an order book in the Naval Historical Foundation collection in the Manuscript Division, Library of Congress.

West Gulf Blockading Squadron

Record Group 45. -- Correspondence of Rear Adm. David G. Farragut (Flagships Hartford and Tennessee), Sept. 1861-Dec. 1864; correspondence of Commodore Henry H. Bell, commanding the Brooklyn and the Pensacola, July 1862-July 1864; correspondence of Comdr. William H. Macomb, commanding the Genesee and the Shamrock, July 1862-Mar. 1865; correspondence of Fleet Surgeon James C. Palmer, Aug. 1863-Oct. 1865; correspondence of Capt. George F. Emmons, commanding the Lackawanna, Oct. 1864-Feb. 1865; detachment orders issued by Rear Admiral Farragut, June-Nov. 1864.

Records in Other Custody. --Other correspondence of both Farragut and Bell is in the U. S. Naval Academy Museum, Annapolis, Md. The correspondence, 1862-65, of Capt. Thornton A. Jenkins, Fleet Captain under Farragut in 1863, is in the Division of Naval History, Navy Department.

Mississippi River Squadron

Record Group 45. --Letters sent by Comdr. John Rodgers, Aug. 1861-Sept. 1861; letters sent by Flag Officer Andrew H. Foote, Sept. 10, 1861-Feb. 1862; letters sent by Acting Rear Adm. Charles H. Davis (Flagships Benton and Eastport), Dec. 1861-Oct. 1862; correspondence of Rear Adm. David D. Porter, Oct. 1862-Oct. 1864; letters sent by Acting Rear Adm. Samuel P. Lee (Flagships Black Hawk and Tempest), Oct. 1864-Aug. 1865; letters received by Lt. Joshua Bishop, commanding the General Bragg, July 1861-Feb. 1864; correspondence of Comdr. Henry Walke, commanding the Taylor, Carondelet, and Lafayette, Aug. 1861-Aug. 1863; letters sent by Comdr. Edward Y. McCauley, Apr.-June 1865; orders issued by Lt. Comdr. K. Randolph Breese, commanding the Black Hawk, Apr. 1863-Sept. 1864; orders received by Lt. Joshua Bishop, June 1861-Sept. 1863; registers of officers, Aug. 1861-July 1865; register of leaves of absence, Oct. 1864-July 1865. (The records of Elisha W. Dunn, paymaster of the Squadron, were destroyed when the wharf boat on which he had his office burned on the night of June 1, 1864; see S. Rept. 35, 39 Cong., 1 sess., Serial 1240.)

Records in Other Custody. --Papers of Comdr. Rodgers, May-Sept. 1861, are in the Naval Historical Foundation collection in the Library of Congress. The papers of Rear Adm. Andrew H. Foote, who commanded the Squadron, Aug. 1861-May 1862, are in the Library of Congress; they include correspondence and journals for the Civil War. (Many of Foote's papers are printed in James M. Hoppin, Life of Andrew Foote, Rear-Admiral United States Navy, published in New York in 1874.) Other correspondence of Rear Adm. David D. Porter, commander of the Squadron from Oct. 1862 to the summer of 1864, is in the Library of Congress, the Henry E. Huntington Library at San Marino, Calif., the United States Naval Academy Museum, and the New-York Historical Society. The collection in the Huntington Library contains hundreds of documents relating to operations on the lower Mississippi River. Rear Adm. Samuel P. Lee assumed command on the Mississippi River on Nov. 1, 1864; most of his files are in the Naval Historical Foundation collection at the Library of Congress and in Princeton University Library. Records of Capt. Henry Walke, in command of the Taylor, Carondelet, and Lafayette, 1861-63, include letters, orders, reports, surgeon's reports, and reports of prisoners; these are in the Division of Naval History. Lt. Comdr. Thomas O. Selfridge while attached to the Squadron, 1862-64, kept a letter book, which is in the Naval Historical Foundation collection. The correspondence of Fleet Surgeon Ninian Pinkney, 1863-65, is in the same collection.

Several other records of the Mississippi River Squadron were recently in the possession of Robert R. Lasher, Jr., of New Paltz, N. Y., in 1942. They included records of the Chillicothe, 1863-65, a smaller quantity of papers of the Ozark, and a few miscellaneous papers of the Osage.

Robert R. Lasher, A Cata-
logue of Some Mississippi Squadron
Papers, Collection of George P.
Lord, Lt., U. S. N., Act. Vol.,
comp. by Lawrence H. van den
Berg, Jr., and Arnold R. Verduin
[n. p., 1942?].

Potomac River Flotilla

Record Group 45. -- Letters sent and received, July 1862- Dec. 1863;
orders issued and received, Feb. 1862- June 1865; correspondence of
Acting Master William T. Street, commanding the Primrose and the
Fuchsia, Mar. 1863- Aug. 1865.

James River Flotilla

Record Group 45. -- Letters sent by Comdr. John Rodgers, commanding
the Galena, Apr.- Nov. 1862; letters sent by Capt. Maxwell Woodhull, commanding the Cimerone, July- Sept. 1862; correspondence of Comdr. George
W. Rodgers, commanding the Tioga, July- Aug. 1862.

Pacific Squadron

Record Group 45. --Correspondence of Capt. Cicero Price, commanding
the Jamestown, Sept. 1862- Sept. 1865; letters sent by Comdr. Henry K.
Davenport, commanding the Lancaster, Sept. 1864- Apr. 1866; letters received by Lt. Comdr. Joshua Bishop, Aug. 1864- Aug. 1866.
Records in Other Custody. --The papers of Rear Adm. David McDougal
in the U. S. Naval Academy Museum include some letters concerning the
Wyoming in the Pacific Squadron, 1863- 64.

NAVY YARDS AND NAVAL STATIONS

The shore establishments of the Navy were of course expanded during
the Civil War. In 1861 there were navy yards at Portsmouth, Boston,
New York, Philadelphia, Norfolk, Washington, Pensacola, and San Francisco. Hospitals were connected with the yards at Boston, New York,
Norfolk, and Pensacola and with the Naval Asylum at Philadelphia. The
personnel at the yards included the commandant (who was a captain too
old for sea service), a commander, lieutenants, surgeon, paymaster,
chaplain, boatswain, carpenter, sailmaker, Navy agent, naval storekeeper,
naval constructor, civil engineer, clerk, and the Marine Corps guard. The
commandants received instructions from bureau chiefs as well as from the
Secretary of the Navy, for the bureaus had cognizance of work carried on
at the yards. Employees at the yards increased from 3,844 in 1861 to
16,880 in 1865.
Other shore establishments were set up on the coast of the Confederacy
early in the war to serve as headquarters for the squadrons and as shelters
for naval vessels in stormy weather. Key West, held by Federal forces
throughout the war, was designated in Dec. 1861 as headquarters of the
East Gulf Blockading Squadron and was used as a rendezvous and supply
station for vessels sailing to and from the Gulf of Mexico. In the same
month Ship Island, Miss., which had been evacuated by Confederates, was
made headquarters of the West Gulf Blockading Squadron. This headquarters was removed in the summer of 1862 to Pensacola. Port Royal, S. C.,

after its capture in Nov. 1861, became the base of the South Atlantic Blockading Squadron. Beaufort, N. C., was designated in July 1864 as headquarters of the North Atlantic Blockading Squadron. A naval station was
set up at New Orleans after the capture of that city in Apr. 1862, to serve
the West Gulf Blockading Squadron.

The Mississippi River Squadron used a number of river ports as repair
and supply depots. A floating navy yard was maintained at Cairo, Ill.,
where a wharf boat was used as a shelter for supplies, materials, and tools
and as headquarters of the Squadron, and barges were used as shops. After
2 years at Cairo the establishment was moved in May 1864 to Mound City,
and soon afterwards the burning of the wharf boat necessitated the building
of storage sheds and shops on shore. The commission to choose a site for
a navy yard on the Mississippi River recommended in Feb. 1865 the adoption of Mound City, and that place was used thereafter for a number of
years. In Memphis, where from 1844 to 1854 there had been a navy yard
used primarily as a ropewalk, a naval station was set up in June 1862 for
the Mississippi Squadron. The abandonment of this station was ordered on
July 1, 1865.

All these new stations on the Atlantic and Gulf coasts of the Confederacy
and on the Mississippi River were regarded during the Civil War as temporary establishments and were not listed in the Navy Registers. The
stations were subordinate to the squadrons they served; consequently there
was little communication between them and the Navy Department. Records
of the permanent navy yards and stations (except Sacketts Harbor, N. Y.,
inoperative during the Civil War) are discussed separately below.

Gerald M. Capers, Jr., The
Biography of a River Town; Memphis, Its Heroic Age (Chapel Hill,
N. C., 1939); Charles O. Paullin,
"Early Naval Administration under
the Constitution," and "A Half Cen-
tury of Naval Administration in
America, 1861-1911," U. S. Nav.
Inst. Proceedings, 32:1001-1030,
39:156-195 (Sept. 1906, Mar.
1913); Fletcher Pratt, Civil War
on Western Waters (New York,
1956); U. S. Bureau of Yards and
Docks, Federal Owned Real Estate
Under the Control of the Navy Department (Washington, 1937); "Letter of the Secretary of the Navy,
Communicating the Report of the
Commission . . . 'to Select the
Most Approved Site for a Navy Yard
or Naval Station on the Mississippi
River or Upon one of Its Tributaries,' and Recommending an Appropriation to Cover the Expenses of
Said Commission," S. Ex. Doc. 19,
38 Cong., 2 sess., Serial 1209;
U. S. Navy Department, Instructions for Navy Yards (Washington,
1859).

Record Group 45. --Most of the documentation relating to the naval
establishments on the coasts of the Confederacy and on the Mississippi
River is in the squadron records described above. Further documentation
can undoubtedly be uncovered among the records of the Navy Department,
but much of it is scattered in numerous series and would be hard to find.
For all navy yards and stations there is much material in the records of the
Office of the Secretary of the Navy and the bureaus, for they were all concerned with activities at the navy yards. The Naval Records Collection of
the Office of Naval Records and Library contains for the Mound City Naval
Station letters sent by the commandant to the Navy Department and other
correspondents, July-Oct. 1864, Dec. 1864-Dec. 1865 (4 press copy

books), and letters received, July 1864-Dec. 1865 (5 vols.). Among the
letter books in the same collection is one for the New Orleans Naval Station containing letters, June-Sept. 1865, sent by Comdr. John Downes.

Baltimore Naval Station

In the early part of the war a carpenter and an engineer at Baltimore
attended to the repairs of vessels of the North Atlantic Blockading Squadron.
Capt. Thomas Dornin was appointed to command of a naval station at Baltimore in May 1862 and was given charge not only of the repair of naval vessels there but also of the receiving ship and the recruiting rendezvous.
He served as commandant from May 1862 to Dec. 1865.

Record Group 45. -- The only extant record of the station itself is a volume of orders issued by the commandant, Jan. 1863-Mar. 1864. Documentation relating to the station, however, is in this record group among
the records of the Secretary's Office. For example, the file of letters
received from commandants contains letters from the commandant at
Baltimore, 1862-65 (4 vols.), and letters to him are in Letters to Officers,
Ships of War (vols. 67-79). (Other records relating to the station are
among records of the bureaus.)

Boston (Charlestown) Navy Yard

The Boston Navy Yard was established in 1800 at Charlestown, Mass.,
at the confluence of the Charles and Mystic Rivers. The yard came to be
used for building, repairing, and outfitting naval vessels and for the manufacture of chain, rope, and other naval supplies. During the war the yard
was enlarged in land, buildings, equipment, and personnel. Among the
vessels outfitted there were some captured Confederate ships.

Successive commandants of the Boston Navy Yard:

> Capt. William L. Hunson, Apr. 30, 1859.
> Commodore John B. Montgomery, June 3, 1862.
> Rear Adm. Silas H. Stringham, Dec. 15, 1863.

Record Groups 45, 181. --Records of the commandant's office include
correspondence with the Secretary of the Navy and bureaus of the Navy
Department; and letters received from the Secretary of the Navy, Oct.
1861-May 1863, Nov. 1863-Dec. 1864. Other correspondence comprises
miscellaneous letters received (letters from contractors and merchants,
naval personnel's requests for leave or transfer, applications for positions, surveys and estimates for repairs, letters from State officials,
and reports and drawings);letters from commandants of other yards and
from commanders of ships about supplying, repairing, and equipping vessels, recruiting activities, and personnel transfers; correspondence with
officers attached to the yard and commanding departments of it; and correspondence with surgeons. Other records covering the period of the war in
whole or in part include Navy Department orders and circulars, reports of
surveys of property and personnel, lists of officers on duty at the yard and
on vessels attached to it; lists of crews of vessels; indentures of apprentices,
semiannual records of apprentices, and records of examinations of applicants;
requests for leave; deeds; and monthly reports on labor costs, materials expended, and cash balances. For the engineer's department there are correspondence, annual reports, and schedules of materials required. A quantity
of muster rolls and payroll ledgers, watch logs, and correspondence of this

yardare in the Federal Records Center, New York City.   A three-volume
manuscript history of the Boston Navy Yard(1875), by Commodore George H.
Preble (microfilmed by the National Archives as M 118) is in Record Group 45.
For records of the marine barracks see the section on the U. S. Marine Corps.

National Archives, Preliminary
Checklist of Records of the Boston
Navy Yard, 1811-1942, comp. by
Richard G. Wood (1946); U. S.
Survey of Federal Archives, Inven-
tory of Federal Archives in the
States, Series VII, The Department
of the Navy, No. 20, Massachusetts
(Boston, 1937).

New York (Brooklyn) Navy Yard

In New York, where in 1796 a shipyard had been rented for building the
frigate President, a site for a navy yard was purchased in 1801 on Wall-
about Bay, Brooklyn.   During the Civil War this yard, with the largest
work force of all the navy yards, built 14 large vessels and altered and
fitted out over 400 merchant ships for Navy use.   Employment increased
from 1,650 men in 1861 to 5,000 in 1865.
    Successive commandants of the New York Navy Yard:
        Capt. Samuel L. Breese, Nov. 1, 1858.
        Rear Adm. Hiram Paulding, Oct. 25, 1861.
        Rear Adm. Charles H. Bell, May 1, 1865.
    Record Groups 45, 181. --Records of the office of the commandant in-
clude correspondence with the Navy Department, with naval officers at the
yard and aboard ships, with the receiving ships North Carolina and Vermont, and with the naval rendezvous at the yard.   An order book of the
naval storekeeper contains abstracts of receipts or requisitions for supplies, Mar.-Oct. 1863.   Other records of the New York Navy Yard, including muster rolls and payroll ledgers, watch logs, and correspondence,
are in the Federal Records Center, New York City.

U. S. Survey of Federal Ar-
chives, Inventory of Federal Ar-
chives in the States, Series VII,
The Department of the Navy, No. 31,
New York (New York, 1940); James
H. West, A Short History of the New
York Navy Yard ([New York], 1941.
Processed).

Norfolk (Gosport) Navy Yard

Established in 1800, this yard was known for many years as the Gosport
Navy Yard, but after Gosport became part of Portsmouth (Va.) it was designated as the Norfolk Navy Yard to distinguish it from the existing Portsmouth Navy Yard (see below).   In the face of imminent Confederate attack,
the Union naval force at the yard destroyed property and withdrew on the
night of Apr. 20, 1861.   On May 10, 1862, when Norfolk surrendered to the
Union Army, the Confederates set the navy yard afire and evacuated it.   It
was used thereafter by the Union Navy as a naval depot and repair station.
    Successive commandants of this navy yard:
        Commodore Charles S. McCauley, Aug. 1, 1860.
        Capt. John W. Livingston, May 20, 1862.
        Capt. John M. Berrien, Nov. 16, 1864.
        Commodore Robert B. Hitchcock, Oct. 31, 1865.

Richmond C. Holcomb, A Century With the Norfolk Navy Hospital 1830-1930 (Portsmouth, Va., 1930); Edward P. Lull, History of the United States Navy Yard at Gosport, Virginia (Washington, 1874); A. C. Cunningham, "The Development of the Norfolk Navy Yard," U. S. Nav. Inst., Proceedings, 36:221-237 (Mar. 1910); report on the surrender and destruction of the navy yards at Pensacola and Norfolk, Apr. 18, 1862, printed in S. Rept. 37, 37 Cong., 2 sess., Serial 1125.

Record Group 181. --Records of the Norfolk Navy Yard were destroyed in the fires of 1861 and 1862. Records for 1862-65 also seem to have disappeared; records of this yard in this record group begin in 1866. Recourse must be had therefore to the correspondence of the commandants and other records transmitted to the Navy Department, which are among the records of the Office of the Secretary of the Navy and of the bureaus.

Pensacola Navy Yard

This yard was established in 1826, largely on public land on Pensacola Bay, as a repair and supply base for vessels of the West India Squadron. The yard was surrendered to the State of Florida on Jan. 12, 1861; its personnel was removed under a flag of truce by the U. S. S. Supply the next day. The Confederates set fire to the yard and evacuated it on May 9, 1862. Early in the following summer it became a depot for the West Gulf Blockading Squadron.

Successive commandants of this navy yard:
Capt. James Armstrong, Oct. 30, 1860.
Commodore William Smith, Dec. 29, 1862.
Comdr. James F. Armstrong, Oct. 6, 1864.

Record Group 45. --There are no Civil War records of this yard before 1862. Letters sent by the commandant to the Secretary of the Navy, the bureaus, the commander of the West Gulf Blockading Squadron, and others begin in Dec. 1862, and the corresponding file of letters received starts in Jan. 1863. A record of the assignment and detachment of personnel begins in Dec. 1862. Logbooks in which are recorded the arrivals and departures of vessels and personnel, unusual occurrences, and information regarding the employment of seamen and laborers begin in Jan. 1865. A journal of daily activities also contains a register of deaths.

Philadelphia Navy Yard

A site in the Southwark district of Philadelphia, previously rented by the Navy Department, was bought for this yard early in 1801 under authority of an act of Feb. 25, 1799 (1 Stat. 622). The construction of buildings was immediately undertaken; and improvements--including a marine barracks, a "ship-house," and a drydock--were made in subsequent years.

Successive commandants of this navy yard:
Rear Adm. Samuel F. DuPont, Dec. 1860.
Commodore James L. Lardner, June 1861.
Commodore Thomas Turner, Sept. 1861.
Commodore Garrett J. Pendergrast, Oct. 1861.
Commodore Cornelius K. Stribling, Nov. 1862.
Commodore Joseph B. Hull, Nov. 1864.

Record Groups 45, 181. --Records of the commandant's office include correspondence with the Secretary of the Navy, bureaus of the Navy Department, naval officers, and others; and a register of orders issued to officers for duty at the yard or detachment from it. There is also a volume of letters sent by Henry Etting, paymaster on the receiving ship Princeton, Sept. 1862-Jan. 1864. A daily record of work on vessels and other records relating to shipyard operations are in the Federal Records Center, New York City.

U. S. Survey of Federal Archives, Inventory of Federal Archives in the States, Series VII, The Department of the Navy, No. 37, Pennsylvania (Philadelphia, 1940).

Portsmouth Navy Yard

The Portsmouth Navy Yard, established in Jan. 1801 on Dennett's Island in the Piscataqua River south of Kittery, Maine, was fortified after the outbreak of the Civil War, and a recruiting rendezvous was opened there. During the war the yard was used for the construction and repair of wooden ships.

Successive commandants of this navy yard:
Capt. George F. Pearson, Oct. 1, 1860.
Commodore Theodorus Bailey, Sept. 30, 1864.

George H. Preble, History of the United States Navy-Yard, Ports- mouth, N. H. (Washington, 1892).

Record Group 181. --Records of the commandant's office include correspondence with the Secretary of the Navy and bureaus, miscellaneous correspondence, orders and registers of orders issued to personnel of the yard, circulars, and a register of the employment and discharge of civilian employees. Records of the industrial department include a record of muster and payrolls, muster books, correspondence, reports of work completed, foreman's orders, time books of hours worked, accounts of materials used on vessels, records of cost of labor on vessels, accounts of work done by painters, a list of articles required by the joiner shop, a requisition book of the caulker's department, bills issued to commanders of vessels for labor and materials used in their repair, shop time books of employees' hours, the master carpenter's stock journal, a daily stock book of consumption of lumber, daily reports of material used by smiths, requisitions from the mast maker, a record of costs of labor and material used on ships, and inspector's reports of articles received. Morning reports and reports of the sergeant of the guard and the officer of the day show the distribution and duty of the Marine Guard and record incidents occurring in the different watches. For the naval hospital the only file is correspondence concerning the award of contracts, appointments, allowances, requisitions for medicines and supplies, patients, shipment of medicines, and general activities.

U. S. Survey of Federal Archives, Inventory of Federal Archives in the States, Series VII, The Department of the Navy, No. 18, Maine (Rockland, Maine, 1940).

San Francisco (Mare Island) Navy Yard

This yard, 20 miles north of San Francisco, was established in Sept. 1854 as a base for the Pacific Squadron. A detachment of Marines arrived at the yard in December 1862.

Successive commandants of the yard:

> Capt. Robert B. Cunningham, July 16, 1858.
> Capt. David McDougal, Mar. 13, 1861.
> Capt. William H. Gardner, June 4, 1861.
> Capt. Thomas O. Selfridge, May 27, 1862.
> Capt. David McDougal, Oct. 17, 1864.

Record Group 181.--Some correspondence of the commandant with the Secretary of the Navy and the bureaus is available, but not all the series are complete for the war period and there are no letters received from the Bureau of Ordnance. A file of letters from the commandant to the successive officers commanding the Marine guard begins in July 1863. Logbooks containing a daily record of activities are available for Feb. 1861-Aug. 1862.

Washington Navy Yard

In 1799 a site for this yard was acquired in the District of Columbia (on the Anacostia River, an eastern branch of the Potomac), and early in 1800 a superintendent was appointed. Although the yard declined in importance toward the middle of the 19th century as a yard for the building and repair of naval vessels, it developed a specialization in ordnance work under the supervision of Lt. John A. Dahlgren. At the outbreak of the Civil War the commandant and nearly all the other officers at the yard resigned to join the Confederacy. During the war the yard repaired vessels, conducted an ordnance laboratory, and served as a base for the Potomac Flotilla.

Successive commandants of this navy yard:

> Capt. Franklin Buchanan, May 26, 1859.
> Comdr. John A. Dahlgren, Apr. 22, 1861.
> Commodore Andrew A. Harwood, July 22, 1862.
> Commodore John B. Montgomery, Dec. 31, 1863.

Henry B. Hibben, "Navy Yard, Washington; History From Organization 1799 to Present Date," S. Ex. Doc. 22, 51 Cong., 1 sess., Serial 2682; Taylor Peck, Round-Shot to Rockets; a History of the Washington Navy Yard and the U. S. Naval Gun Factory (Annapolis, 1949).

Record Groups 45, 181.--The few volumes of records of the Washington Navy Yard in Record Group 45 consist of letters sent to the Secretary of the Navy, Jan. 1858-June 1868; miscellaneous letters sent, July 1864-June 1869; letters received from the Secretary of the Navy, Nov. 1861-June 1866; telegrams sent, Nov. 1862-Oct. 1863; telegrams received, Nov. 1862-Sept. 1863; orders issued, Nov. 1860-Feb. 1865; and a record of work performed, June 1861-Aug. 1872. Record Group 181 contains correspondence and other records of the yard.

Records in Other Custody.--A daybook, 1861-68, showing articles ordered and supplied, is in the New York Public Library.

XI. DEPARTMENT OF THE INTERIOR

The Department of the Interior was established by an act of Mar. 3, 1849 (9 Stat. 395), which brought together unrelated functions pertaining to the internal affairs of the country that up to then had been charged to other departments of the Government. The President was authorized to appoint a Secretary of the Interior, who was to supervise the Patent Office, the General Land Office, the Office of the Commissioner of Indian Affairs, the Office of the Commissioner of Pensions, the Office of the Commissioner of Public Buildings, the Census Office, the Board of Inspectors and the warden of the U. S. Penitentiary for the District of Columbia, the accounts of marshals, clerks, and other officers of courts of the United States, and the agents of lead and other mines of the United States and their accounts.

The assignment of other activities to the Department in later years considerably enlarged its operations. The Secretary of the Interior conducted correspondence with the Governors of States and U. S. boundary commissioners regarding the survey of boundaries between States and Territories of the United States. Though the supervision of Territories was not transferred from the Department of State until 1873, the Secretary of the Interior for years before that date had supervised the expenditure of funds for Territorial libraries and for public buildings in the Territories. An act of Feb. 5, 1859 (11 Stat. 379), made him responsible for receiving, arranging, safekeeping, and distributing public documents and for keeping copyrighted materials and a record regarding them. The 1860 census was conducted under the control of the Secretary of the Interior. From the Department of State there was transferred (act of Feb. 20, 1861; 12 Stat. 141) the work of compiling the Official Register. The Superintendent of Public Printing, who was appointed in 1861 to head the Government Printing Office, reported to the Secretary of the Interior. The Secretary also supervised the Government Hospital for the Insane (St. Elizabeths Hospital), the Columbia Institution for the Deaf and Dumb (Gallaudet College), and the care of transient patients in District of Columbia hospitals.

Still other functions came to be performed by the Department during the war. The President assigned to it responsibility for suppressing the African slave trade and for colonizing free Negroes in Africa and elsewhere. An act of Feb. 13, 1862 (12 Stat. 338), gave to the Secretary of the Interior the task of procuring and distributing cottonseed and tobacco seed. Agents appointed by the Secretary obtained these seeds in occupied areas of the South and distributed them in those other areas where they could be used. Early in 1863 a Returns Office was set up in the Secretary's Office for filing contracts made by the Government. In 1862 the enactment by Congress of legislation for land grants to Pacific railroads required still other duties.

The places of confinement of persons convicted by Federal courts were to
be designated by the Secretary of the Interior (act of May 12, 1864; 13 Stat.
74). The places of confinement of juvenile offenders convicted in any U. S.
court were also to be designated by the Secretary (act of Mar. 3, 1865; 13
Stat. 538).

The Secretary of the Interior had supervision of Federal interests in
the District of Columbia. During the war the District consisted of the cities
of Washington and Georgetown and Washington County (the area within the
District outside of those municipalities). The city of Washington was governed by a mayor and city council under a charter granted by Congress,
which had exclusive legislative control over the District. The population
expanded greatly during the early part of the war, and large military forces
were soon encamped in and around the city. Negroes from the South who
had sought refuge in Washington became dependent upon public support, as
did many others who were attracted to the city. Congress had provided for
many different kinds of services and improvements in the District, including accommodations for courts, a penitentiary and a jail, an auxiliary police force under the control of the mayor, public squares and other open
spaces, streets and avenues, street lights, shade trees, sewers and drains,
an infirmary, firehouses, an armory, and bridges across the Potomac and
Anacostia Rivers. The jurisdiction of the Secretary of the Interior was
limited during the war to work on public lands and on streets that had been
in whole or in part improved by the Government. The Secretary was also
responsible for preventing improper appropriation and use of public streets
and lands.

Wartime conditions resulted in legislation by which new duties regarding
District matters were designated for the Secretary. The Metropolitan Police,
organized under an act of Aug. 6, 1861 (12 Stat. 323), reported annually in
writing to the Secretary. The extension of the Capitol and the control of the
Potomac River waterworks were transferred from the War Department to
the Interior Department in 1862. The supervision of the "Long Bridge" over
the Potomac River, however, was shifted to the War Department in 1863.
The act to incorporate the Washington and Georgetown Railroad Co. , May
17, 1862 (12 Stat. 388), stipulated that the Secretary of the Interior should
determine its route between the Washington Navy Yard and Georgetown. He
was also required by a joint resolution of Mar. 3, 1863 (13 Stat. 827), to
approve the location of a telegraph line to be constructed in the District by
the Independent Line of Telegraph, a New York corporation. The Secretary
was to approve the installations of the Union Gas-Light Co. before it could
sell gas (act of Apr. 8, 1864; 13 Stat. 43). The jail, formerly under the
control of the marshal of the District, was by an act of Feb. 29, 1864 (13
Stat. 12), placed under a warden to be appointed by the President and to report to the Secretary of the Interior.

Besides his administrative functions the Secretary of the Interior had
judicial duties. Cases were referred to him from the Pension Office, the
General Land Office, and the Office of the Commissioner of Indian Affairs.
This business included private land claims and relations with the Indians
as well as pension cases and bounty land claims. During the war attorneys
were employed by the Department in Washington and elsewhere for legal
purposes (S. Ex. Doc. 24, 38 Cong. , 2 sess. , Serial 1209).

OFFICE OF THE SECRETARY OF THE INTERIOR

In 1861 the Secretary of the Interior headed an immediate staff consisting of a chief clerk, 3 disbursing clerks, 9 other clerks, 3 messengers, 12 watchmen, and 3 laborers. Also subordinate to him was a clerk in charge of the distribution of congressional documents, under whom there were an assistant, a messenger, a packer, and two laborers. There were also a clerk and two assistants concerned with correspondence regarding the suppression of the African slave trade. Moses Kelly, the chief clerk continued from the previous administration, was replaced late in 1861 by Watton J. Smith. W. W. Lester was acting chief clerk from Jan. 10 to Mar. 4, 1861, while Kelly was Acting Secretary. Smith's resignation took effect on May 2, 1863, and he was succeeded on the next day by Hallet Kilbourne, who was transferred from the Census Office. Kilbourne resigned on Feb. 15, 1865, and was succeeded by George C. Whiting as acting chief clerk. Until the appointment of the Assistant Secretary, the chief clerk had general charge and supervision of the business of the Department under the direction of the Secretary and acted as Secretary in the latter's absence.

Specialization of functions had developed among the clerks in the Office of the Secretary from its early days. By 1852 different clerks were assigned to correspondence relating to judicial expenditures, land matters, pensions, bounty lands, applications, and miscellaneous matters. There were also a bookkeeper and assistant to the disbursing agent, a recording clerk, an endorsing and registering clerk, and a copyist (S. Ex. Doc. 128, 32 Cong., 1 sess., Serial 627). Other clerks were added as new functions were acquired; in June 1865 a clerk for public works was employed. Some of these clerkships developed after the war, as the work of the Office of the Secretary expanded, into divisions, which took charge of the records that the clerks had accumulated. The divisions of the Secretary's Office eventually performed much work that logically belonged to the bureaus and offices of the Department, and in 1907 the divisions were abolished and their functions were distributed among the Department's bureaus and offices. At that time the old division files were closed, and a modern system of filing and indexing was instituted.

To relieve the Secretary of some of his onerous duties, recommendations that had been made before the war for the appointment of an Assistant Secretary of the Interior were renewed in 1861 by Acting Secretary Kelly and Secretary Smith. On July 8, 1861, Smith stated that the current business of the Department prevented him from giving adequate attention to the legal cases presented for his consideration and requested authority for the appointment of an assistant qualified in the law. Such authority was provided by an act of Mar. 14, 1862 (12 Stat. 369); and John P. Usher, an attorney of Indiana, was appointed Assistant Secretary of the Interior on Mar. 22, 1862. He served until he became Secretary; and he was succeeded on Jan. 29, 1863, by William T. Otto, who continued as Assistant Secretary until 1871.

Because of many postwar changes in the organization of the Office of the Secretary the records of the Civil War period and later records relating to the war are described below by the principal functions or subjects to which they pertain rather than by the divisions that created or maintained them.

Successive Secretaries of the Interior during the war period:

Jacob Thompson, Mar. 6, 1857.
Moses Kelly (acting), Jan. 10, 1861.

Caleb B. Smith, Mar. 5, 1861.
John P. Usher, Jan. 6, 1863.
James Harlan, May 16, 1865.

Wilhelmus B. Bryan, A History of the National Capital From Its Foundation Through the Period of the Adoption of the Organic Act (New York, 1916. 2 vols.); Allen C. Clark, "Richard Wallach and the Times of His Mayoralty," Columbia Historical Society, Records, 21: 195-245 (1918); Edward M. Douglas, Boundaries, Areas, Geographic Centers and Altitudes of the United States and the Several States (U. S. Department of the Interior, Geological Survey Bulletin. Washington, 1932); Henry B. Learned, "The Establishment of the Secretaryship of the Interior," American Historical Review, 16: 751-773 (July 1911); Earl S. Pomeroy, The Territories of the United States (Philadelphia, 1947); John Claggett Proctor, ed., Washington Past and Present; a History (New York, 1930); Elmo R. Richardson and Alan W. Farley, John Palmer Usher; Lincoln's Secretary of the Interior (Lawrence, Kans., 1960); Laurence F. Schmeckebier, The District of Columbia; Its Government and Administration (Baltimore, 1928); Emmett Womack, History and Business Methods of the Department of the Interior (Washington, 1897).

Annual reports for the Department, 1861-66, under the title of Report of the Secretary of the Interior (Washington, 1861-66), were published as the following congressional documents:

1861. S. Ex. Doc. 1, 37 Cong., 2 sess., Serial 1117.
1862. S. Ex. Doc. 1, 37 Cong., 3 sess., Serial 1157.
1863. S. Ex. Doc. 1, 38 Cong., 1 sess., Serial 1182.
1864. S. Ex. Doc. 1, 38 Cong., 2 sess., Serial 1220.
1865. S. Ex. Doc. 1, 39 Cong., 1 sess., Serial 1248.
1866. S. Ex. Doc. 1, 39 Cong., 2 sess., Serial 1248.

Miscellaneous Records

Record Group 48. --Functions not performed by other units of the Office of the Secretary came to be assigned to the Patents and Miscellaneous Division, which acquired the records relating to these functions. This Division was also known at different times as the Miscellaneous Division and as the Pensions and Miscellaneous Division.

Most of the outgoing letters of the Civil War period are in a series of so-called "miscellaneous" letter books. These contain copies of letters, telegrams, and circulars addressed to officials of the Department, heads of the other departments, Congressmen, committees of Congress, the President, district attorneys, marshals, presidential secretaries, Territorial Governors, and other individuals. The letters concern appointments, the census, claims, colonization of Negroes, District of Columbia affairs, procurement and distribution of cottonseed, jails, Pacific railroads, the U. S. Penitentiary for the District of Columbia, the maintenance of prisoners in the penitentiary at Albany, N. Y., public buildings and public works, the telegraph in the District of Columbia, the medical care of transient paupers, Territorial affairs, wagon roads, and arrangements for the care of criminals under the act of May 12, 1864 (already cited). Separate series of letters were also maintained for District of Columbia affairs; public buildings and grounds; the jail and charitable institutions in the District of Columbia; the Capitol extension, the new dome, and other construction projects in and around the Capitol; Patent Office affairs; the Government Hospital for the Insane; the Columbia Institution for the Deaf and Dumb and the Maryland Institution for the Instruction of the Blind; the Washington Aqueduct; and financial matters. Most of these separate series are also available in letter press copies, and among these are also a volume of correspondence of the Secretary concerning policy decisions and copies of official and private correspondence of Assistant Secretary Otto, 1863-69. Indexes in the letter books and some special index volumes help in finding the letters to any particular individual.

The extensive files of letters received during the war constitute a number of series. In these, under various arrangements, are correspondence with the congressional printer; Senate and House resolutions calling for information, with copies of replies thereto; requests from the President for reports on proposed legislation and copies of replies to him; papers about the Executive Mansion; letters from the Secretary of State regarding patents and pensions, the extradition of alien fugitive criminals, and requests from foreign nations for information; letters from the heads of other departments and agencies; letters on the Navy Pension Fund; letters from the General Land Office and the Office of Indian Affairs; correspondence and other papers relating to the Patent Office, its agricultural unit, and the maintenance of the Patent Office Building; and letters from Territorial officials. They relate also to the Capitol and other public buildings; District of Columbia affairs (including correspondence from Edward C. Carrington about compensation for services rendered in confiscation cases); the Metropolitan Police; the care of transients; roads and bridges, public buildings, hospitals, water and gas supplies, and the jail; management of and admissions to Government-supported hospitals in the District of Columbia; clerical personnel of the Department, stationery bids, and buildings rented by the Government; and census affairs. Besides a general register of the letters received, by name of correspondent, there are special registers for the Capitol extension, Patent Office affairs, and financial matters.

The relatively few other records contain little for the war period. Opinions of the Attorney General cover questions concerning employees and pension and patent cases. Briefs of land cases relate to instructions to surveyors general, patents for land, claims, preemption entries, lawsuits, donations, and town commons. On printed forms are orders for the admission of patients to the Government Hospital for the Insane and of students to the Columbia Institution for the Deaf and Dumb. There is also a file of requisitions for funds from the Commissioner of Public Buildings and the disbursing agent of the Executive Mansion.

Some of the foregoing records contain little material relating to the Civil War, but others are important for a study of the operations of both the Government and institutions of the District of Columbia greatly affected by the war. Many of these records are the sole primary sources for the history of the District of Columbia because records of the District Government before 1871 have largely disappeared.

The letters received in the Secretary's Office from the Territories of Colorado, Dakota, Idaho, and Washington comprise only a few pieces, relating to the shipment of books and to public buildings. Records available on microfilm: letters received and executive proceedings and official correspondence for Idaho Territory (M 191), and letters received for Washington Territory (M 189).

Record Group 77. --Copies of letters sent by the Secretary or the Assistant Secretary, July 1862-May 1867 (1 vol.), relate to the Washington Aqueduct. This letter book presumably passed to the Chief of Engineers in 1867, when the superintendence of the aqueduct was transferred to him from the Interior Department.

Record Group 109.--In the War Department Collection of Confederate Records are 2 press copy books of letters sent by Jacob Thompson, 1857-60, chiefly concerning U. S. political conditions and appointments in the Department of the Interior.

Records in Other Custody.--The papers of some of the Secretaries of the Interior are still extant. The papers of Caleb B. Smith in the Library of Congress antedate the Civil War. Of some 250 papers of John P. Usher in the Kansas State Historical Society for the period of his secretaryship, few relate to his official duties. Another collection of Usher's papers, about twice as large and containing some material on his Government service, is in the possession of Alan W. Farley, a lawyer of Kansas City, Kans., who with Elmo Richardson has used them for a biography of Usher. Harlan's papers were lent by his daughter, Mrs. Robert Todd Lincoln, to Johnson Brigham for use in a biography published in 1913. The papers were returned to Mrs. Lincoln and have since disappeared. A small group of Harlan's papers is in the State Historical Society of Iowa. A collection of painted portraits of the Secretaries of the Interior, in the Interior Department, includes likenesses of those who served during the war.

Personnel Records

Record Group 48. --Correspondence and other records relating to wartime Interior appointments were accumulated by the Office of the Secretary. Letter books contain copies of outgoing letters on appointments made by the Secretary and by the President to positions in the Department in Washington and to field positions such as surveyors general, registers and receivers, pension agents, and Indian agents; and letters on appointments made by the heads of the Department's bureaus and offices. Other outgoing letters concern promotions, transfers, dismissals, and resignations. In the same volumes are communications from the appointment clerk to the disbursing clerk regarding personnel changes. Applications and recommendations for appointments form an extensive file containing individuals' "jackets," arranged by chronological period and thereunder by departmental office and type of position and locality. These papers, which include many signed testimonials, relate to positions in the Department and in the field filled by the President and to less important clerical positions filled by the Secretary. Many of the communications are addressed to the President and bear his endorsements or those of his secretary. These files also contain charges and complaints against officials, protests against their removal, acknowledgments of the receipt of commissions and oaths of office, recommendations for reappointments, and Senate confirmations of appointments. Many of the documents pertain to appointments in the Territories. (Some applicants who failed to obtain appointments were allowed to withdraw their papers.) Registers of applications for appointment provide brief information giving the names of applicants, their States of residence, the positions sought, and sometimes remarks regarding the referral or withdrawal of the papers. These registers also cover applications for promotions and resignations. The appointment papers are useful not only for Civil War biographical data but also for the wartime administrative history of the Department

and its field agencies, local history, research in Territorial affairs, and
the study of local and national politics of the 1860's.

Other incoming communications regarding personnel were maintained
in other files. One file contains charges against persons under consideration for appointment and against persons already in office. A file of "miscellaneous" letters received (registered only for 1863-64) relates to employees in general; correspondence concerning claims for debt against
employees, investigations of personnel, and political charges against employees is likewise segregated; and other small files contain communications from the General Land Office, relating to changes in the locations
of land offices and other matters, and notices from President Johnson in
1865 regarding Cabinet meetings.

Other volumes supply data on the appointments actually made. (Copies
of letters of the President nominating persons for specific positions are in
the Executive Journal of the Senate.) Presidential letters of appointment
for temporary positions and for appointees who were later confirmed by
the Senate are in volumes containing printed forms filled out with information as to name, position, and date. These volumes are indexed by name,
but a consolidated card index, prepared by the National Archives, is more
useful than the volume indexes.

Some lists and registers of personnel are useful for determining the
names of wartime departmental clerks, Indian agents, registers and receivers of land offices, surveyors, and surveyors general. The Secretary's
orders, circulars, and general instructions and Executive orders relating
to the Department, which were copied from the letters sent books and other
sources, provide a useful compilation on personnel and administrative matters.

Pension Records

Record Group 48. --Though during and after the Civil War the routine
business of handling pensions was the function of the Pension Office, the
involvement of the Secretary of the Interior in appeals and other matters
resulted in an accumulation of records in his Office. Outgoing letters relating to pension matters were copied into a separate set of volumes containing letters to the Commissioner of Pensions, pension agents, the President, the Secretary of the Treasury, the Secretary of the Navy, Congress,
district attorneys, and other individuals. Some letters embody decisions
on pension claims; other letters concern pension agents, bounty land warrants, requests for information about pensioners and for pension papers,
the amendment of pension laws, and information regarding pensions. The
volumes are indexed by name of correspondent and pension claimant and
can be used for investigating pensioners and the administration of the pension system generally. The Secretary's decisions on pension appeals are
also indexed in a volume labeled "Pension Appeals, Abstract of Decisions."
A file of papers on pension appeals contains original reports from the Commissioner of Pensions (setting forth the reasons for the denial of pensions),
memoranda, correspondence, and reports of medical referees. Arranged
alphabetically by name of claimant, this file contains information concerning the war service of claimants, resultant disabilities, steps taken to obtain pensions by servicemen or their widows, and the final disposition of
the cases. Other files of incoming communications concern criminal proceedings against attorneys practicing before the Pension Office and their

disbarment, suspension, or restoration; fee appeals; and pension frauds. There are letters from the Secretary of State; and there is other correspondence about the restoration of pensions to Southerners. A "Register of Letters Received, Pensions" shows that letters were received from the heads of departments, the Attorney General, auditors, the President, the Clerk of the House of Representatives, the Second Comptroller, and private citizens about pensions, bounty land claims, appointments, pension agents, accounts, deposits of funds, appeals on denial of pensions, and pension laws. Many of these letters were referred to the Commissioner of Pensions for his action. Available also is a digest of decisions of the Secretary on legal problems connected with pension and bounty land claims.

Records Relating to Suppression of the Slave Trade and to the Colonization of Negroes

The Lincoln administration quickly adopted measures for strict enforcement of laws prohibiting the slave trade. The Department of the Interior was already involved in the suppression of the trade through its supervision of the accounts of judicial officers. On May 2, 1861, by Presidential order the Department was charged with the execution of the slave trade laws, a function which earlier had been chiefly a responsibility of the Department of the Navy. Adequate appropriations were obtained and instructions were given to U. S. marshals to apprehend persons and vessels engaged in the slave trade. George C. Whiting was soon assigned to handle the necessary correspondence, and with the help of some other clerks he continued to be in charge of it throughout the war. John Seys, U. S. Agent for Liberated Africans at Monrovia, Liberia, was transferred to the Interior Department from the jurisdiction of the Department of the Navy. Seys, a Methodist missionary, continued to have charge of repatriated Negroes sent to Liberia by the American Colonization Society under contracts with the U. S. Government, made pursuant to an act of June 16, 1860 (12 Stat. 40). (In 1864 the agency in Liberia was discontinued as no longer necessary.) The Secretary of the Interior became responsible in 1862 for paying the salaries of the U. S. judges and arbitrators of the Mixed Courts of Justice established at New York, Cape Town, and Sierra Leone (see under the Department of State, above).

During the war the U. S. Government itself attempted to engage in colonization activities. An act of Apr. 16, 1862 (12 Stat. 365), providing for the emancipation of slaves in the District of Columbia, appropriated funds for the emigration of free Negroes of the District to Haiti or Liberia. A further appropriation to colonize slaves emancipated in the District of Columbia was made on July 16, 1862 (12 Stat. 582). These funds were also to be applied toward the colonization of slaves freed by the confiscation act of July 17, 1862 (12 Stat. 591), which granted freedom to escaped or captured slaves of persons "in rebellion" and which authorized the President to arrange with governments having possessions in the West Indies or other tropical regions to receive from the United States Negroes seized from slavers. Contracts were made by the Government with owners of concessions in the countries concerned for the colonization of Negroes in Chiriqui, Colombia (i. e. , Panama), in 1862 and on Île à Vache, Haiti, in 1863. The former contract was canceled, however, because of objections by diplomatic representatives of the Central American nations. Some colonists were actually sent to Île à Vache, but the experiment was unsuccessful.

On Aug. 4, 1862, President Lincoln appointed the Rev. James Mitchell to
assist the Secretary of the Interior with the emigration of Negroes, and
Mitchell continued in the post until June 30, 1864. Senator Samuel C. Pomeroy was designated as agent of the Government for the proposed colony in
Chiriqui. After news of unsatisfactory conditions at Île à Vache reached
the Department, D. C. Donnohue was sent to Haiti in Oct. 1863 to examine
and report on those conditions.

Frederick Bancroft, The Col-
onization of the American Negroes,
1801 to 1865 (Norman, Okla., 1957);
Willis D. Boyd, "The Île à Vache
Colonization Venture, 1862-1864,"
Americas, 16:45-62 (July 1959);
William DuBois, The Suppression
of the African Slave-Trade to the
United States, 1638-1870 (Cam-
bridge, 1896); Walter L. Fleming,
"Deportation and Colonization; an
Attempted Solution of the Race
Problem," Studies in Southern His-
tory and Politics; Inscribed to Wil-
liam Archibald Dunning, p. 3-30
(New York, 1914); Rayford W. Logan,
The Diplomatic Relations of the
United States with Haiti, 1776-1891
(Chapel Hill, N. C., 1941); Page
Milburn, "The Emancipation of Slaves
in the District of Columbia," Colum-
bia Historical Society, Records, 16:96-
119 (1913); Ludwell Lee Montague,
Haiti and the United States, 1714-1938
(Durham, N. C., 1940); James A.
Padgett, "Ministers to Liberia and
Their Diplomacy," Journal of Negro
History, 22:50-92 (Jan. 1937); Paul J.
Scheips, "Lincoln and the Chiriqui
Colonization Project," Journal of Ne-
gro History, 37:418-453 (Oct. 1952);
Ernest J. Yancy, Historical Lights
of Liberia's Yesterday and Today
(New York, 1954).

Record Group 48.--The Interior Department's records relating to the
suppression of the slave trade and the colonization of Negroes cover the
years 1854 to 1879, but most of them relate to the period 1861-72. A letter book contains copies of letters sent by the Secretary of the Interior,
George Whiting as acting chief clerk, and other Department officials to
U. S. marshals, district attorneys, heads of departments, the President,
Members of Congress, the First Comptroller of the Treasury, the First
Auditor of the Treasury, the U. S. Agent for Liberated Africans at Monrovia, the judges and arbitrators of the Mixed Courts of Justice, the American Colonization Society, S. C. Pomeroy, James Mitchell, and D. C.
Donnohue; the letters relate both to the suppression of the slave trade and to
the colonization of Negroes. Press copies of outgoing letters include some
letters that are not in the book of fair copies. Communications received
from the abovenamed correspondents, as well as contracts, agreements,
accounts, requisitions, and reports, provide extensive documentation of
these wartime activities of the Government and of President Lincoln's
interest in the colonization of Negroes. The incoming documents are
entered in a register covering 1858-72. All the records of the Office
on the suppression of the slave trade are available on microfilm
(M 160).

Paul Lewinson, comp., A Guide
to Documents in the National Archives for Negro Studies (American
Council of Learned Societies, Committee on Negro Studies, Publication
No. 1. Washington, Mar. 1947);
Roland C. McConnell, "Importance
of Records in the National Archives
on the History of the Negro," Journal
of Negro History, 34:135-142 (Apr.
1949); U. S. Library of Congress,
Division of Manuscripts, Handbook

of Manuscripts, p. 374. Other pertinent material is in records of the
U. S. district courts (Record Group
21); logs and letter books of the African Squadron in the Naval Records
Collection of the Office of Naval Records and Library (Record Group 45);
records of the U. S. Senate (Record
Group 46); diplomatic and consular
correspondence, especially with
U. S. representatives in Great Britain, Liberia, Haiti, Cuba, Colombia,
and the Central American countries
(Record Group 59); records of the
Department of Justice (Record Group
60); and the records of U. S. district
attorneys and marshals (Record
Group 118). The consular letters
from Monrovia in Record Group 59
include a few letters from John Seys
as U. S. Agent for Liberated Africans. See also the section below on
records relating to judiciary accounts. Some of the correspondence,
contracts, and accounts from the

records of the Office of the Secretary of the Interior and from other
record groups mentioned above are
published in H. Ex. Doc. 12, 37 Cong.,
2 sess., Serial 1127; H. Ex. Doc. 41,
36 Cong., 2 sess., Serial 1097; S. Ex.
Doc. 40, 37 Cong., 2 sess., Serial
1122; S. Ex. Doc. 55, 39 Cong., 1
sess., Serial 1238; H. Ex. Docs. 222
and 227, 41 Cong., 2 sess., Serial
1425; and H. Ex. Doc. 46, 47 Cong.,
1 sess., Serial 2027. Reports from
John Seys, 1860-61, are in H. Ex.
Doc. 28, 37 Cong., 3 sess., Serial
1161. A number of letters from Seys
to the American Colonization Society
were published in its magazine The
African Repository, vols. 37-39 (1861-
63). A large collection of records of
the American Colonization Society
and papers of Ambrose W. Thompson,
president of the Chiriqui Improvement
Co. on whose lands the Government
sought to colonize Negroes, are in
the Library of Congress.

Financial Records

Record Group 48.-- Correspondence and other wartime records of the
Secretary of the Interior relating to disbursements were kept by the disbursing clerk. Letters were sent by the Secretary to a number of correspondents, including the Secretary of the Treasury about requisitions and
statements of funds needed; the Treasurer of the United States about pension funds, the deposit of drafts, and amounts of funds required; the First
Auditor of the Treasury transmitting accounts for adjustment; the Attorney
General requesting opinions; Congress transmitting estimates of funds required and answering requests for additional information; commissioners
and superintendents of the Department concerning estimates, appropriation
warrants, and the collection of internal revenue; the First Comptroller of
the Treasury returning lists of balances; pension agents about the deposit
of funds; surveyors general and superintendents of Indian affairs on remittances; and other individuals on pension payments and the payment of drafts.
The letters received during the war are missing, but a register gives the
names and addresses of the correspondents, the dates and purport of the
communications, and their disposition; these letters pertained to requisitions for funds, accounts current, acknowledgments, lists of balances,
payment of accounts, estimates, and pensions.

To enable the Department properly to disburse funds appropriated by
Congress, various records were kept by the disbursing clerk. Appropriation warrants issued by the Treasury Department supply information on the
amounts of the appropriations and the specific titles under which they were
to be credited in ledgers. Appropriation ledgers, which were kept in two
series--for civil expenditures and for Indian and pension expenditures--

enabled the Department to determine the source of funds and the balance on hand and to prevent undue accumulation of public funds in the hands of disbursing agents. A subject index to the ledgers and a consolidated index prepared by the National Archives are finding aids for specific wartime expenditures or those of the postwar period related to the war. Additional information as to the purposes for which money was spent can sometimes be found in the record of refundments made to the Government and the record of contingent accounts. A separate record was kept of cash payments for construction and other activities connected with public buildings and institutions. Payrolls record payments for personal services, showing names, positions, time, salary, and signatures. Quarterly accounts current, rendered by the disbursing clerk to the Treasury Department, show receipts and disbursements balanced. An act of July 1, 1862 (12 Stat. 432), levied a tax of 3 percent on salaries of Federal employees in excess of $600 per year. A record of the funds withheld under this act was maintained. A record of expenditures connected with President Lincoln's funeral shows also expenses for nursing care for Mrs. Lincoln.

The amounts of funds provided by Congress under various wartime appropriations and the amounts expended thereunder or carried to the surplus fund by the Department can be found in the following congressional documents: S. Ex. Doc. 13, 37 Cong., 2 sess., Serial 1121; H. Ex. Doc. 20, 37 Cong., 3 sess., Serial 1159; S. Doc. 22, 38 Cong., 1 sess., Serial 1176; and H. Ex. Doc. 23, 38 Cong., 2 sess., Serial 1223. Statements of the contingent expenses are in H. Ex. Doc. 12, 37 Cong., 2 sess., Serial 1127; H. Ex. Doc. 34, 38 Cong., 1 sess., Serial 1189. Disbursements of Indian superintendents and agents for 1860-61 are shown in S. Ex. Doc. 31, 37 Cong., 2 sess., and for 1861-62 in S. Ex. Doc. 39, 37 Cong., 3 sess., Serial 1149.

Records Relating to Indian Affairs

During the Civil War, as before and later, the Secretary of the Interior had extensive responsibility for Indian affairs. He considered and approved claims, conveyances of land, and contracts; conducted correspondence on Indian affairs with the heads of the executive departments; and granted authority to the Commissioner of Indian Affairs to expend funds for the relief of Indians, considered suggestions from him, and issued instructions and decisions to him on many different matters. He attended to negotiations with Indian tribes, transmitted Indian treaties to the President for submission to the Senate, and arranged to carry out treaty provisions. He managed Indian trust funds, which accumulated from the Government's payments promised to the Indians for lands or other valuable considerations conveyed by treaty and from payments made by private parties to Federal officers for the lease or purchase of Indian lands or for other benefits derived from lands. The funds so accumulated for many tribes were invested by the Department in Federal, State, city, or railroad bonds, the interest on which was collected when due. The proceeds were used for the benefit of the tribes, for the education of Indian children, and for the care of Indian orphans. Late in 1860 the funds amounted to $3,396,241.82. The stock certificates and coupons and a small amount of specie were kept at first by a clerk in the Office of the Secretary, but on July 10, 1861, the custody of the stock and the function of collecting interest due were transferred to the Commissioner of Indian Affairs. Despite the actual transfer of the stock, however, the Secretary continued to be concerned with the trust funds.

Though the Indian Territory Division was established long after the war, its involvement with matters relating to the citizenship of the freedmen in the Five Civilized Tribes and with the dissolution of those tribes produced records relating to the war period. The Division became concerned with the administration of the various acts of Congress, 1898-1906, requiring the preparation by the Dawes Commission of census rolls of the Five Civilized Tribes and the allotment of lands among their members.

Felix S. Cohen, Handbook of Federal Indian Law, With Reference Tables and Index (Washington, 1945); Laurence F. Schmeckebier, The Office of Indian Affairs; Its History, Activities and Organization (Baltimore, 1927).

Record Group 48. --The records of the Secretary's Office relating to Indian affairs for the Civil War period are part of the records of the Indian Division, which was in operation by 1870. These records should be differentiated from the more voluminous records of the Commissioner of Indian Affairs and the field agencies, described elsewhere. After the abolition of the Indian Division in 1907, the records described below were cared for in the Secretary's Office until 1920; they were then transferred to the Office of Indian Affairs, from which they were received by the National Archives.

The correspondence files contain considerable material on the conduct of Indian affairs during the war. The letters sent, copied in two letter books, are to the Commissioner of Indian Affairs, the Secretary of War, the Secretary of the Treasury, the President, the Commissioner of the General Land Office, the Paymaster General, the Attorney General, Members of Congress, and other persons. They relate to claims of Indians under treaties, claims of citizens for damages inflicted by Indians, relations between Army officers and Indians, the survey and conveyance of Indian lands, the protection of the Indians by the Army and the furnishing of arms to the Indians, the sale of the property of Indian agencies, the establishment of reserves for mail stations and of postal communication with Indian agencies and military posts, the payment by the Indians of debts due, and requests for legal opinions. An index volume extends only to 1862.

Letters sent concerning Indian trust funds are recorded in a separate series of letter books, of which a single volume covers 1857-66. The letters are from the Secretary of the Interior to presidents and cashiers of banks, the Secretary of the Treasury, the Assistant U. S. Treasurer at New York, district attorneys, treasurers of railroad companies, the Commissioner of Indian Affairs, the President, the Secretary of War, the Register of the Treasury, Congress, and State treasurers, auditors, agents, and Governors. These letters are concerned with the management of the Indian trust funds and the collection of interest on the stocks in which the funds were invested. Because some of the funds were invested in bonds of Southern States, the interest on which became uncollectible, income from the funds dropped during the war.

Letters received include notably those to the Secretary from the Commissioner of Indian Affairs. Other series are in boxes labeled as follows: Executive (President), Dept. War, Treas. Dept. , Dept. State, Office Attorney General, General Land Office, and Miscellaneous. The executive correspondence consists largely of communications addressed to the President and referred by his secretaries to the Secretary of the Interior and of Presidential orders. Especially pertinent to the Civil War are the letters from the War Department, which concern the furnishing of subsistence, escorts, and quarters to Indian agents, the attitude of Indians, military and Indian reservations, the recall of permits to trade and the protection of Indian traders, negotiations with Indians by Army officers and treaties concluded by them, the arming of Indians, the use of annuities to subsist prisoners, the formation of Indian regiments of home guards, relief for Indians, and the subsistence of Indian prisoners. Letters from U. S. marshals, Congressmen, military officers, superintendents of Indian affairs, Indian agents, Indian chiefs, the Commissioner of the General Land Office, Governors of States and State judges, and private individuals are filed in a series of "Miscellaneous" papers. The subject matter of these letters and those from the Commissioner of Indian Affairs, previously mentioned, concerns authorizations and powers of attorney; recommendations for appointments, acceptances of appointment, and applications for reappointment; appeals from decisions of the Commissioner of Indian Affairs; claims for pay; schools and Indian goods; complaints against Indian agents; contracts for articles to be furnished to Indian agencies; bids on Indian land; the removal of Indians; charges against traders; settlement on Indian reservations; the protection of commerce on the plains; annuities; and most other matters already mentioned. A general register and special registers of letters relating to Indian trust funds, letters from the Commissioner of Indian Affairs, and Indian treaties should be used in connection with the correspondence, for much of it was referred to the Commissioner of Indian Affairs or elsewhere. Other correspondence concerns the Indian trust funds and the activities of the commissioners who were appointed in 1863 to collect evidence and report upon the damages to property during the Sioux uprising in Minnesota in 1862.

Concerning Indian trust funds and claims there are a few other wartime records. These include a list of bonds and stock certificates held in trust for the Indian tribes, dated 1861; a statement of interest on nonpaying stocks belonging to loyal Indian tribes, including interest up to July 1863; and a record of purchases of war bonds with Indian trust funds, Aug. 1861-May 1863. Other files relating to the funds are available for certain Indian tribes, Indiana State bonds, and Kansas State bonds; there are also a record of other State bonds bought for the trust funds, memoranda relating to State and private bonds, letters of transmittal of certificates of deposit and coupon drafts, and recapitulations of trust fund accounts. A register of Indian depredation claims covers some depredations in Nebraska, 1864-65, and California, 1862. Claims for Sioux depredations, 1863-68, and claims of individuals against Indians or for services rendered to Indians are also documented.

Records relating to freedmen among the Five Civilized Tribes are in correspondence and census rolls. The correspondence runs for over 30 years from the early 1870's and is arranged by tribe except for one part that is general in content. In the census rolls are separate listings for the freedmen of the different tribes and for their children. These census rolls are printed in U. S. Commission to the Five Civilized Tribes, The Final Rolls of Citizens and Freedmen of the Five Civilized Tribes in Indian Territory ([Washington], n. d.).

Records Relating to Wagon Roads

The building of wagon roads in the West had been in the charge of the Secretary of the Interior from 1857 to 1860. The Pacific Wagon Road Office was established in the Department of the Interior in Mar. 1857 under ▸the superintendence of Albert H. Campbell, who in 1861 became chief of the Topographic Bureau of the C. S. A. War Department. The U. S. Government's building of wagon roads was suspended during the war except for some roadbuilding by the Army. Emigrants continued to move into the Northwest, however, under military escort, and the flow of settlers and gold seekers increased after the war. To connect the Middle West with the western Territories to which the emigrants were moving, Congress by an act of Mar. 3, 1865 (13 Stat. 516), provided for the construction of roads in the Territories of Idaho, Montana, Dakota, and Nebraska. Temporary charge of the records, the examination of accounts, and the superintendence of building were given to an Interior Department clerk, Henry Beard, on Apr. 27, 1865.

At the end of May 1865, when Lt. Col. James H. Simpson was detailed as an engineer to the Interior Department to assist with railroad work, he was also given the superintendence of wagon roads. He remained as engineer in charge until 1867.

W. Turrentine Jackson, Wagon   Trans-Mississippi West, 1846-1869
Roads West; a Study of Federal Road   (Berkeley and Los Angeles, 1952).
Surveys and Construction in the

Record Group 48. --Although the records of the Secretary of the Interior relating to wagon roads cover 1857 to 1887, there are gaps in most of the series from 1861 to 1865, the years when roadbuilding was suspended. Upon resumption of construction in 1865, the letters were recorded in the volume that had been used for letters of 1857-61. Signed by the Secretary and after Aug. 24, 1865, by Simpson or the Secretary, the letters were sent chiefly to superintendents and disbursing agents, appointing them to positions, giving instructions, or acknowledging bonds and oaths of office. There are also copies of letters to Territorial delegates regarding the appointment of superintendents, to the Secretary of the Treasury asking for funds, and to the Secretary of War asking for firearms for the road parties. Press copies of letters sent are also available. The incoming letters for specific roads are filed together and include letters from Territorial delegates; letters from superintendents accepting appointments, transmitting bonds and oaths of office and accounts, requesting funds, and reporting upon the survey and construction of roads and bridges; and letters of recommendation for the employment of engineers and surveyors. The communications are entered in a register by the first letter of the surname of the writers. Records relating to wagon roads are available on microfilm (M 95).

Records Relating to Lands and Railroads

In the management of the public lands the Secretary of the Interior had broad responsibilities. He was concerned with obtaining appropriations; with setting aside reservations for lighthouses, military posts, and other public purposes; and with allotting public land for schools and universities. The Secretary also considered many other matters submitted to him by the Commissioner of the General Land Office; these concerned bounty land

locations, preemptions, land warrants, private land claims, improvements
on lands ceded by the Indians, surveys, and claims of land officers. When
the Government began to make land grants to States to aid in the construction of railroads, in 1850, the correspondence on this subject was recorded
or filed with the other correspondence on land matters. Surveys for Pacific
railroads were made in the 1850's, but it was not until after Representatives
of the Southern States withdrew from Congress that the first Pacific Railroad Act was passed, July 1, 1862 (12 Stat. 490). Construction was actually begun during the war by the Union Pacific and the Central Pacific Railroads on the eastern and western sections, respectively, of a single transcontinental railroad. In connection with this line and later with other lines
for which land grants were made by Congress, the Secretary of the Interior
acquired the duties of communicating with the railroads regarding their acceptance of the conditions of the acts of Congress, the appointment by the
President of the Government directors on the boards of the railroads, the
appointment of commissioners to inspect the railroads upon their completion, the approval of routes, the determination of the gage of railroad
tracks, and the withdrawal of lands from sale and their granting to the railroads.

Until after the war the Secretary handled land and railroad matters with
only such clerical assistance as he needed. At his request, however, the
War Department on May 31, 1865, detailed an engineer officer, Lt. Col.
James H. Simpson, to assist with the railroad and wagon road work. A Pacific Railroad Division was set up in May 1867, and in 1870 a Lands and
Railroad Division was established. This division was abolished in 1907,
and its functions were transferred to the General Land Office and the Reclamation Service.

John Debo Galloway, The First
Transcontinental Railroad; Central
Pacific, Union Pacific (New York,
1950); Lewis H. Haney, A Congres-
sional History of Railways in the
United States, 1850-1887 (Madison,
Wis., 1910); Oscar Lewis, The Big
Four; the Story of Huntington, Stan-
ford, Hopkins, and Crocker, and of
the Building of the Central Pacific
(New York, 1938); Nelson Trottman,
History of the Union Pacific; a Fi-
nancial and Economic Survey (New
York, 1923).

Record Group 48. --Correspondence and other records of the Lands and
Railroad Division relate to the war period. Most of the outgoing letters are
to the Commissioner of the General Land Office, and in addition to the matters mentioned above they also concern mail route preemptions, instructions
on surveys and other matters, estimates for appropriations, surveys of
boundaries between Territories and States, and accounts for newspaper advertising. There are also letters to the executive departments, the President, committees of Congress, the First Comptroller, the Solicitor of the
Treasury, the Commissioner of Indian Affairs, and others on various matters connected with public lands. The press copy books from which these
letter books were copied are also available. Letters sent concerning boundaries were kept in a separate series (which terminates, however, on May
15, 1861). A new book opened on Oct. 29, 1862, for outgoing letters pertaining to the Pacific railroad, contains letters to presidents of railroad
companies, railroad construction companies, the President, the Commissioner of Public Lands, Governors of States, Lt. Col. J. H. Simpson, and
others. This book also contains letters sent by Simpson beginning on Aug.
29, 1865.

Letters received include letters and opinions from the Attorney General; letters from the Office of Indian Affairs, the General Land Office, the Secretary of State, the Treasury Department, the War Department, and the Secretary of the Navy; House resolutions and letters; and Senate resolutions. In an alphabetical file are letters from individuals, including Congressmen, Government officials (filed by name), land officers, and Territorial officials; the letters relate to military land patents, appointments, surveys, preemption claims, and requests for information. Letters received relating to land-grant railroads are filed chronologically under each railroad (Central Pacific, Union Pacific, etc.) and include letters from presidents of railroads relating to the gage of railroad tracks, recommendations from Congressmen and others for prospective appointees as Government directors and commissioners of railroads, applications for appointment as commissioners, applications for employment on the construction of railroads, applications for changes in route, maps of railroad locations, reports of Government directors relating to routes, acceptances and declinations of appointments as directors and commissioners, orders from the President regarding appointments as directors and commissioners, acceptances by the railroad of the legislative conditions of the land grant, reports on the construction of the railroad, and letters from Lt. Col. J. H. Simpson. Reports of the commissioners to the President upon their examinations of completed sections of the railroads, with recommendations of the Secretary of the Interior and the endorsements of the President, supply considerable detail about the condition of the railroads and constitute an important source for the history of their construction. The other records mentioned above are also useful for railroad history and are valuable from the Governmental administrative viewpoint. Registers help in finding letters from different classes of correspondents.

Several other records also cover the war period. An "Appeal Docket, Judiciary Business, " 1861-63, relates to land cases; pension cases; and cases concerning the accounts of U. S. marshals, clerks of U. S. courts, attorneys, Territorial secretaries, and Indian agents. A file of annual and semiannual reports from railroads (printed and manuscript) begins in 1862 and supplies a variety of information on organization, ownership, property, and finances. Some repayment case registers contain data about the repayment of purchase money for lands sold to individuals.

A quantity of letters and other documents relating to the Pacific railroad, 1863-65, was included by Simpson in his report to the Secretary of the Interior, Nov. 23, 1865, H. Ex. Doc.1, 39 Cong. , 1 sess. , p. 871-992, Serial 1248. President Lincoln was much interested in the building of the Pacific railroad; a number of his Presidential papers relating to the Union Pacific Railroad, from the files of the Secretary of the Interior, are published in John M. Starr, Jr. , Lincoln and the Railroads; a Biographical Study (New York, 1927).

Records Relating to War Contracts

In procuring supplies, arms, horses, equipment, and vessels for prosecuting the war, hasty action by the War and Navy Departments in 1861 permitted dishonest contractors and Government agents to perpetrate graft and fraud. The rules and regulations provided by law to protect the Government's interest were in large part suspended in order to hasten the purchasing process. After word of these practices reached Congress an act of June 2, 1862

(12 Stat. 411), to prevent and punish fraud by officers entrusted with making Government contracts, required the Secretaries of War, Navy, and Interior to have all contracts put in writing and signed by the contracting parties, and to file copies of them with the Returns Office, to be established in the Department of the Interior under a clerk appointed by the Secretary. The clerk was to keep an index book of contracts, which was to be open to public inspection. On July 17, 1862, however, the operation of this act was suspended until Jan. 1863 (12 Stat. 600). The Secretary of the Interior on Mar. 24, 1863, appointed Philip Williams clerk in charge of the Returns Office, and he continued in the position throughout the war. The Office and its records (with the exception of a few postwar records now in Record Group 48) were transferred in 1929 to the General Accounting Office.

Alexander H. Meneely, The War Department, 1861; a Study in Mobilization and Administration (New York, 1928). H. Rept. 2, 37 Cong., 2 sess., Serial 1143 (pts. 1 and 2), contains testimony collected by the House Select Committee on Government Contracts and its journal.

The contract file kept by the Returns Office was disposed of during the 1940's under the regular procedure for the disposal of Government records. The original contracts are now in the National Archives among the records of the General Accounting Office (Record Group 217). Files of contracts are in the records of some subdivisions of the executive departments. A list of contracts made by the War Department during 1861 is in H. Ex. Doc. 101, 37 Cong., 2 sess., Serial 1126; and a list of Quartermaster Department contracts, Dec. 1863-Feb. 1865, is in H. Ex. Doc. 84, 38 Cong., 2 sess., Serial 1230.

Records Relating to Distribution of Public Documents

A joint resolution of Jan. 28, 1857 (11 Stat. 253), provided that copies of journals and other documents of Congress that had been deposited with the Library of Congress and the Secretary of State for distribution should thereafter be deposited with the Secretary of the Interior for distribution to colleges, public libraries, athenaeums, literary and scientific institutions, and boards of trade or public associations. An act of Feb. 5, 1859 (11 Stat. 379), charged the Secretary of the Interior with receiving, arranging, safekeeping, and distributing not only documents of Congress but also books printed or purchased for the executive branch or any of its departments. Such publications as were then held by Congress or the departments were to be transferred to the Secretary of the Interior, who was to keep a register showing the quantity and kind of publications received and their distribution. A clerk who was put in charge of the work was designated in the Official Register as Superintendent of Congressional Documents and Journals, but his status was not official until an act of Mar. 3, 1869 (15 Stat. 292), provided that the Secretary of the Interior should appoint a Superintendent of Public Documents to perform the duties prescribed by the act of 1859. This position in the Interior Department was abolished by secs. 61 and 64 of an act of Jan. 12, 1895 (28 Stat. 610, 611), which authorized the Public Printer (head of the Government Printing Office) to appoint a Superintendent of Documents.

Successive Superintendents of Public Documents during the war period:
John H. Wheeler, Oct. 20, 1857.
James Wilson, Mar. 16, 1861.
John H. Dillon, Mar. 1, 1863.

The register mentioned above and the correspondence were kept by the Document Room, as the document distribution office was referred to (S. Rept. 507, 50 Cong., 1 sess., p. 54, Serial 2521); but these records were apparently disposed of either before or after the transfer of the function to the Government Printing Office. Information regarding appointments as Superintendent can be found in the records of the Appointments Division, Office of the Secretary of the Interior (Record Group 48).

Records Relating to Judiciary Accounts

An act of Mar. 3, 1849 (9 Stat. 395, Sec. 4), transferred from the Secretary of the Treasury to the Secretary of the Interior supervision over the accounts of district attorneys, marshals, clerks, and other officers of U. S. courts. These officials were compensated for their services and reimbursed for costs by a fee system according to regulations prescribed by acts of Feb. 26, 1853, and Aug. 16, 1856 (10 Stat. 161; 11 Stat. 49). They were required to submit semiannual returns of their emoluments and to pay into the Treasury the excess above certain maximums. By direction of the President, Nov. 1, 1861, the expenses of arresting, holding, and subsisting political prisoners seized by order of the Secretary of State or the Secretary of War were to be paid from the judiciary fund; and the Secretary of the Interior thereupon applied to these expenditures the rules governing the adjustment of marshals' accounts. When the Department of Justice was established in 1870, supervision over the judiciary accounts was transferred, along with the pertinent records, from the Secretary of the Interior to the Attorney General.

Record Group 60.--Correspondence makes up most of the records relating to the administration of the judiciary fund and the supervision of judicial accounts by the Secretary of the Interior in the 1860's. The outgoing letters ("Letter Books, Judiciary No. --, Department of the Interior") are addressed to marshals, district attorneys, clerks, judges, the President, heads of departments, officials of the Treasury Department, and others. They concern the routine expenses of district and circuit courts (such as those for the rental and furnishing of buildings or offices, the care and conveyance of prisoners, the employment of deputies and substitute counsel, and the payment of witness fees and salaries of court officials), requisitions for funds, and acknowledgments of emolument returns. This material pertains to U. S. courts in the Territories as well as those in the States. For the period of the war there is correspondence on the suppression of the slave trade, the return to Africa of Negroes taken from slavers, and the prevention of counterfeiting.

The letters received, arranged chronologically by judicial district, contain much material on wartime activities. Letters from marshals concern blockade runners held as prisoners, prize cases, claims for professional services in prize cases, the storage and disposition of confiscated vessels and cargoes, and expenditures for police protection of public property during the draft riots in New York City. Other letters pertain to legal suits or contain protests regarding the conduct of marshals and other officers. (These letters supply information supplementary to that in the Attorney General's papers, described elsewhere in this Guide.) A register of letters received contains a chronological record of incoming letters classified in separate volumes for "executive" (i. e., departments and agencies), Congress, "miscellaneous," States, and Territories.

The Secretary of the Interior's supervision of judicial accounts resulted also in the accumulation of a few other wartime records. A requisition book contains a record, by judicial district, of requisitions for funds received from marshals and of the amounts remitted to them. Emolument returns-- compiled from statements of fees and emolument returns received from marshals, district attorneys, and clerks --show for each judicial district in the States and Territories the gross receipts, the amount of office expenses deducted therefrom, and the net receipts. Another volume supplies data relative to courtroom rent and furniture, and still another contains abstracts of opinions and decisions on judiciary accounts.

GENERAL LAND OFFICE

By cession from some of the original States and by acquisition from foreign nations the Federal Government before the Civil War had become the owner of a vast public domain--the region from the Appalachians to the Mississippi, the Florida Peninsula and the Gulf of Mexico coast, the Trans-Mississippi West, and finally the Southwest. In the early years of the United States the public land had been disposed of by the Offices of the Secretary of the Treasury and the Register of the Treasury. The General Land Office had been established in the Department of the Treasury by an act of Apr. 25, 1812 (2 Stat. 716), and in 1849 had been transferred to the Department of the Interior. In 1946 its functions were made part of the duties of the Bureau of Land Management in the Department.

During the Civil War years public land was disposed of in several ways provided for by acts of Congress. It was sold to individuals at private sales and auctions for a minimum of $1.25 an acre, though at the public sales for which proclamations were issued by the President it went to the highest bidders. The Government was more interested in having the land settled and developed than in getting revenue from its sale, and the constant trend had been toward liberalization of the terms on which land could be acquired. The Preemption Act of Sept. 4, 1841 (5 Stat. 453), allowed settlement on public land prior to survey and gave squatters the right to acquire the land they had improved. The Graduation Act of Aug. 4, 1854 (10 Stat. 574), sought to dispose of land that had been on the market for a long time by offering it at low rates--"graduated" from 12 1/2¢ to $1 per acre. This act, however, was repealed by one of June 2, 1862 (12 Stat. 413). Land bounties were still available to veterans under several acts of Congress, and veterans could dispose of their land scrip for cash. Mineral lands were reserved from sale and leased to operators before 1846, but an enactment of that year made them available for sale at higher prices. Settlers in Oregon became eligible for donations of public land under the Donation Act of Sept. 27, 1850 (9 Stat. 496), which was extended by legislation in 1854 to settlers in Washington and New Mexico.

Large quantities of land were granted to States and Territories for a variety of purposes. It had long been a practice to make grants for the benefit of common schools and for the establishment of "seminaries of learning" or State universities. Other grants were made with authority to sell the land to defray the cost of erecting public buildings. Upon their admission to the Union, the States of Kansas (1861) and Nebraska (1864) were given grants of salt-spring lands. Grants for wagon roads were resumed in 1863 when lands were given to Michigan and Wisconsin to aid in the construction of a military wagon road from Fort Wilkins on Copper Harbor, Mich., to Fort Howard on

Green Bay, Wis. The first grants of lands for penitentiaries were made in the enabling acts of 1864 for Nevada and Nebraska. To aid in building a canal from Lake Superior to Portage Lake across the northern tip of the Northern Peninsula of Michigan, 400,000 acres of land were granted to that State in 1865-66. Grants of swamp and overflowed lands were made to several States under acts of 1849 and 1850 to enable them to reclaim those lands. During the war grants of land were still being certified to States under acts of the 1850's to aid in the construction of railroads, and legislation was passed for additional grants. Towns located on surveyed public land were allowed to acquire their sites at the minimum price and dispose of them in lots under State or Territorial legislation (act of May 23, 1844; 5 Stat. 657). Mail contractors on routes west of the Mississippi River were allowed preemption rights up to 640 acres on land occupied as mail stations (act of Mar. 3, 1855; 10 Stat. 684). But this act was modified by one of June 21, 1860 (12 Stat. 70), which reserved land for use as mail stations only while it was so used and provided for its sale when the stations were abandoned.

During the war the Republican-controlled Congress adopted other measures that in previous years had been opposed by Southern Members. Under the Homestead Act of May 20, 1862 (12 Stat. 392), a settler could obtain up to 160 acres of land without payment except for a small filing fee, on condition that he occupied and cultivated the land for 5 years. A later act of Mar. 21, 1864 (13 Stat. 35), required of soldiers only a single year's residence. After the Pacific Railroad Act of July 1, 1862 (12 Stat. 490), authorized huge grants of land to corporations to aid in the construction of railroads, the General Land Office became responsible for the withdrawal of such lands from public sale. The passage of the Agricultural College Act (the Morrill Act) of July 2, 1862 (12 Stat. 503), culminated a long agitation for granting land to aid in founding agricultural and mechanical colleges. Not only States with public lands benefited from this act, but also Eastern States with no public lands were allowed to apply for land scrip, to be located on the public lands elsewhere. An act of Mar 3, 1863 (12 Stat. 754), authorized the President to reserve townsites in strategic locations and directed the Secretary of the Interior to have them surveyed into lots and sold. The mining boom in the Rocky Mountains during the war resulted in the enactment of a more favorable townsites act on July 1, 1864 (13 Stat. 343). This act repealed the act of May 3, 1844, enlarged the preemption allowed to municipalities from 320 to 640 acres, authorized the survey and sale of lots, and allowed preemptions to actual settlers on lots. The States "in rebellion," where in 1861 there were nearly 48,000,000 acres of public land, were denied the benefits of the land bounties provided by Congress during the war. Proposals for the confiscation of land in the South that were presented to Congress were not enacted, however, and in 1866 the Homestead Act was extended to that region. An act of June 21, 1866 (14 Stat. 66), limited the disposal of land in the South to entries under the Homestead Act and restricted the entries to 80 acres each. By an act of July 23, 1866 (14 Stat. 208), the time allowed to States to accept land grants under the Agricultural College Act was extended to July 23, 1869; and the time within which the States must establish their colleges was extended to 5 years from the date of their filing acceptance of land grants.

Under all this legislation and other enactments the General Land Office at the time of the Civil War had many duties. It directed the survey of public lands by the surveyors general and the subsequent sale of land by the local land offices. It attempted to protect timber on public lands, and it supervised withdrawals of public land for use as military posts, Indian reservations, and lighthouse sites. The Secretary of the Interior transferred from his immediate office in 1861 to the Commissioner of the General Land Office the supervision of the running and marking of boundaries between Territories of the United States and States; and in 1864 (act of Apr. 8; 13 Stat. 39) the Office became responsible for surveying Indian reservations. The Office also handled the repayments that sometimes had to be made to individuals who had purchased land, and it issued patents for public lands disposed of.

To execute acts of Congress regarding the public lands the Commissioner had to issue many rules and regulations for the guidance of surveyors general, their deputies, and registers and receivers who were in charge of the land offices. A troublesome and laborious task was that of settling private land claims originating in grants made by Spain and Mexico in the region of the Southwest acquired by treaty from Mexico. With so many different enactments controlling the disposal of lands, it was inevitable that disputes should arise over claims to land; and the adjustment of these legal questions was a heavy burden for the General Land Office. Decisions of the Commissioner in regard to suspended preemption land claims were subject to the approval of the Board of Equitable Adjudication, consisting of the Secretary of the Interior, the Attorney General, and the Commissioner of the General Land Office (act of Aug. 3, 1846; 9 Stat. 51). The cartographic operations of the Office included the preparation not only of plats, but also of State maps, maps of the United States, and special maps.

Wartime brought some special regulations. Early in the war it was provided that preemption entries of men who entered military service would be held in abeyance until their return and that in case of death the claims would be confirmed to their heirs or legal representatives. By direction of the Secretary of the Interior, the Commissioner of the General Land Office instructed registers and receivers on Jan. 6, 1862, to require persons claiming preemptions or donations of land to take the oath of allegiance before receiving certificates and evidence of the claims. Surveyors general were instructed by the same circular to require deputy surveyors to take the oath.

A divisional organization initiated in the General Land Office in 1836 continued without much change until a few years after the Civil War. But there were in subsequent years so many changes of function from one division to another that it is not possible in a brief description to take up the records according to the divisional organization. Instead, they are described below by type of record of the function they document. It should be noted that records described just below are those of the General Land Office in Washington; field records of surveyors general and district land offices are discussed later in this section.

Successive Commissioners of the General Land Office during the war:
Joseph S. Wilson, Feb. 23, 1860.
James M. Edmunds, Mar. 19, 1861.

Milton Conover, The General Land Office; Its History, Activities and Organization (Baltimore, 1923); Thomas Donaldson, The Public Domain; Its History, With Statistics (H. Misc. Doc. 45, pt. 4, 47 Cong., 2 sess., Serial 2158, Washington, 1884); Paul W. Gates, "The Homestead Act in an Incongruous Land System," American Historical Review, 41:652-681 (July 1936); Benjamin H. Hibbard, A History of

Public Land Policies (New York, 1939); Lucile Kane, "Federal Protection of Public Timber in the Upper Great Lakes States," Agricultural History, 23:135-139 (Apr. 1949); Matthias N. Orfield, Federal Land Grants to the States, With Special Reference to Minnesota (Minneapolis, 1915); Roy M. Robbins, Our Landed Heritage; the Public Domain, 1776-1936 (Princeton, N. J., 1942); U. S. Department of Agriculture, Land; the Yearbook of Agriculture 1958 (Washington [1959]); U. S. General Land Office, "Report of the Commissioner of the General Land Office," 1861-1866, in U. S. Department of the Interior, Annual Report of the Secretary of the Interior (Washington, 1862-67); Francis H. White, "The Administration of the General Land Office" (Ph. D. dissertation, Harvard University, n. p., n. d.; photostat in National Archives Library).

Correspondence and General Files

Record Group 49. --The outgoing letters for the war period are recorded in chronological order in letter books. There are separate volumes of letters to surveyors general, registers and receivers, the executive departments, and the First Comptroller of the Treasury, relating not only to the survey and disposal of land but also to administrative and personnel matters. Other volumes contain letters on administrative matters, abandoned military reservations, agricultural college land scrip, Indian lands, military bounty land warrants and scrip, mineral entries and claims, preemption matters, private land claims, railroad grants, repayments to purchasers of land, school selections, State selections, swamp and overflowed lands, and timber trespassing. Some miscellaneous letters sent (available on microfilm, M 25) include letters to Members of Congress, recorders of land titles, Governors, and other State officials, attorneys, agents, and private individuals relating to land sales and other matters. Most of the volumes of letters are indexed, and for some classes of correspondents there are special index volumes.

Unlike the letters sent, which were copied into separate volumes by clerks and maintained by different divisions of the Office, most of the letters received were kept in one large chronological file. This series contains letters from registers and receivers, Government departments and officers, lawyers, agents, business firms, State officials, foreign governments, and private individuals. These letters relate to land entries, claims, patents, copies of records, appeals, charges, protests, payment of fees, deeds, accounts, legislation, surveys of Indian reservations, township plats, military warrants and locations, caveats, donation land claims, maps, charts, diagrams, appointments and dismissals of agents and officers, confirmation and rejections of claims, and other matters concerning the administration of the public domain. In a separate file, arranged by States and Territories, are letters from surveyors general relating to the survey of the public land. Letters received from registers and receivers and other correspondents relating to surveys and surveying matters are in another file. The use of these large files is facilitated by several registers--of letters received from land registers and receivers, from surveyors general, from Members of Congress, from the Pension Office, and other correspondents, relating to Indian lands, preemption claims, private land claims, Virginia military warrants and scrip, and miscellaneous subjects.

Other Washington office records (beyond those discussed at length below) consist of series covering long periods of time. A file of Executive

orders concerns lighthouse sites and military and naval reservations and
other public land matters. Presidential proclamations--issued to announce
public land sales, postpone sales, open and close land offices, and remove
land areas from sale--are available in both original and record copy form.
Few orders and proclamations were issued during the war, but the files include many for wartime military sites. Bylaws for mining districts
in Colorado, 1860-64, are in one volume. Some special files concern Indians, Indian allotments, and treaty and trust lands. Orders to publishers
of newspapers, 1860-65, fill another volume. Lists are available of Agricultural College Act selections, railroad land grant selections and adjust-
ments, wagon road selections, and Des Moines River lands and their purchasers. Lists of U. S. land patents for entries in Southern States issued
during the war but held for later dispatch to the registers are indexed by
land office. Records relating to the valuation of Sioux Indian lands, 1864-
66, are in 2 volumes. On hand also are many worn-out tract books, of
which transcripts are now in the Bureau of Land Management. Records
relating to surveys include surveying contracts, bonds, and related papers.
A collection of painted portraits of Commissioners of the General Land Office includes likenesses of both Wilson and Edmunds.

The records of most discontinued land offices have been turned over to
the appropriate States (and are discussed below), but some not wanted by
the States are in the National Archives. These include a large collection of
tract books for land offices in Alabama, Arkansas, Kansas, Mississippi,
Missouri, New Mexico, and Oklahoma. There are also other records for
some district land offices, including a register of cash certificates for
Springfield, Ill. ; a record of homestead locations for Indianapolis, Ind. ;
and records of homestead applications, cash sales, or locations for Council
Bluffs, Fort Dodge, Kanesville, and Sioux City, Iowa.

Military Reservation Files

Many military posts, arsenals, navy yards, and naval stations used
during the Civil War had been established on public land, by Executive order or act of Congress. When such reservations were ordered, the General Land Office notified the district land offices of the withdrawal of the
reserved land from entry and, if the land was unsurveyed, directed that
surveys be closed at the boundaries of the reservations. When the reservations were no longer needed, they were restored to the public domain by
act of Congress or Executive order and again put under the General Land
Office for survey and disposal. Such restorations were made by separate
acts of Congress until a general act of July 5, 1884 (23 Stat. 103), provided
for the disposal of abandoned and surplus military reservations. The abandoned reservations disposed of in the years soon after the Civil War included some that had been in Federal possession during the war and others
that had been taken over by the Confederacy in 1861.

Information on military reservations can be found in various publications. The dates of Executive
orders for Army reservations are
in Clifford L. Lord, ed. , Presidential Executive Orders, 2:443-
447, 532-542, and for Navy reservations ibid. , 448-450, 593-596, and
in Historical Records Survey, New
Jersey, List and Index of Presidential
Executive Orders, p. 320-353, 361-
381 (Army) and p. 387 (Navy). The
publication of the U. S. Judge Advocate General's Department entitled

United States Military Reservations, National Cemeteries, and Military Parks; Title, Jurisdiction, etc. , p. 476-490 (Washington, 1916), contains a list of military reservations turned over by the War Department to the Interior Department, or otherwise disposed of, 1850-1915, as well as data about individual reservations. Other lists are in Donaldson, The Public Domain, p. 250-254, 748, 1258-1259. Relinquishments under the general act of 1884 are listed in S. Ex. Doc. 73, 51 Cong., 1 sess., p. 2-4, Serial 2686.

Record Group 49.--The abandoned military reservation files consist of dossiers relating to particular reservations, with no systematic arrangement. The dossiers usually contain Executive orders; correspondence between the Secretary of the Interior and the Secretaries of War and the Navy; correspondence between the General Land Office and its divisions; land title papers; and plats, maps, blueprints, and tracings showing the extent and boundaries of reservations and the improvements, buildings, and facilities on them. In turning over reservations for disposal, the War Department transferred also the pertinent title papers, correspondence, and other documents; consequently the file contains full information on the creation, restoration, appraisal, and disposal of reservations. It is an important file for the history of forts, though not for any military engagements of which they may have been the scene. A register facilitates finding reservations within particular States and briefs individual documents. The files cover military reservations acquired by purchase from private owners as well as those created from the public lands.

National Archives, Index to General Land Office Abandoned Military Reservations Files, 1822-1937, comp. by Arthur Hecht and Lester W. Smith ([Washington] 1945). Related records are available in the National Archives. Outgoing letters about the reservations are in the correspondence and general files of the Land Office, discussed above. In the general records of the Department of the Interior (Record Group 48) are correspondence relating to the appointment of appraisers of abandoned military reservations and their oaths of office and commissions. Maps and documents concerning the construction of some of the forts are in the records of the Office of the Chief of Engineers (Record Group 77). Military reservation files of Adjutant General's Office and the Judge Advocate General's Office are in Record Groups 94 and 153, respectively. Records of the Office of the Quartermaster General (Record Group 92) also contain materials relating to military reservations. Information about reservations that have become national parks and monuments is in the records of the National Park Service (Record Group 79).

Nonmilitary Reservation File

Reservations were also set aside from the public land for the use of Indian tribes and as lighthouse sites. Before the Civil War the Indian title to most of the land east of the Mississippi River (except for a few reservations) had been extinguished by treaties, and most of the Indians had been removed to reservations west of the river. The policy of purchasing the rights to lands claimed by the Indians and of concentrating the tribes on small reservations was continued during the war. The lands were held by the tribes as a whole; allotments in severalty were made only by treaty or act of Congress until the adoption of an allotment act of Feb. 8, 1887 (24

Stat. 388). Through the years the reservations were reduced by additional purchases by the Government, and the General Land Office surveyed and sold this "excess" land.

Cessions of Indian lands in the various States can be traced in Charles C. Royce, "Indian Land Cessions in the United States, " U. S. Bureau of American Ethnology, Eighteenth Annual Report, 1896-97, pt. 2, p. 521-997 (Washington, 1899). This publication also contains a chronological schedule of treaties and acts of Congress authorizing allotments in severalty among Indians. See also Donaldson, Public Domain, p. 728-739 for a schedule of Indian reservations, arranged alphabetically by State or Territory and showing the authority (treaty, Executive order, or act of Congress) for their establishment; and other lists in Lord, ed. , Presidential Executive Orders, 2:266- 267, 426-427, and Historical Records Survey, New Jersey, List and Index of Presidential Executive Orders, p. 302-353. These two compilations also supply data on the establishment of lighthouse reservations.

Record Group 49. --In content the nonmilitary reservation file is similar to the abandoned military reservation file. There are separate registers of documents for Indian reservations and lighthouse reservations and an alphabetical card index to the nonmilitary reservations.

Land-Entry Papers and Related Files

The documents executed by entrymen, registers, and receivers and sent to the General Land Office as evidence of the issuance of land patents constitute an extensive series of case files. These include cash and pre-emption entries made under the general land laws, entries under the Graduation Act and the Homestead Act, townsite dockets, private land claim dockets, lieu selection dockets, mineral cases, and entries under the military land bounty acts antedating the Civil War. Townsite entries were made during the war in a number of trans-Mississippi States and Territories (see the list in Donaldson, Public Domain, p. 300-305). At the opening of the Civil War there were still private land claims to be settled in Louisiana, Missouri, Florida, New Mexico, Arizona, Colorado, and California.

No military land bounty was enacted for soldiers or veterans of the Civil War. Such legislation was proposed in Congress during the war, but the homestead policy prevailed. Men in the military service (if their families or family members were living on lands to be entered under the Homestead Act) were allowed to make affidavits before their commanding officers instead of at district land offices (act of Mar. 21, 1864; 13 Stat. 35). An act of July 15, 1870 (16 Stat. 320), extended the privilege of entering 160 acres (instead of the 80 acres allowed by the Homestead Act) on alternate sections within railroad grants to persons who had been in military service for 90 days. Many veterans took advantage of the shortened residence period allowed by an act of Apr. 2, 1872 (17 Stat. 49), which provided that the time spent in military service could be deducted from the 5-year period required by the Homestead Act but required a minimum of 1 year's residence. Men discharged because of wounds received or disability incurred in line of duty might apply the full terms of their enlistments on the residence requirement of the Homestead Act. The act of 1872 also allowed veterans who had previously entered for less than 160 acres to enter for more land up to a total of 160 acres and extended the allowed benefits to widows and orphan children of those entitled to homesteads. Certificates for soldiers' additional homestead rights were declared to be assignable by an act of Aug. 18, 1894 (28 Stat. 397).

Record Group 49. -- The contents of land-entry case files vary according to the type of entry. Cash entries, containing applications, receipts, and final certificates, are the simplest. Homestead, soldiers' additional homestead, and mineral entry case files contain applications, proofs, affidavits, public notices, and final certificates or certificates of entry. If entries were contested the documentation was increased by testimony, briefs, arguments, notices of appeal, declaratory statements, and opinions. The arrangement of the many series varies greatly and can be ascertained from the finding aid cited below. There is no overall index to the land-entry papers, but there are abstracts of registers' entries, which are of some assistance, and there are a number of special indexes. When the legal description of the land in question is known, the case file can be found through the use of the transcripts of tract books in the Bureau of Land Management, Department of the Interior. The land-entry papers, like other case files, are valuable for local wartime history and for information on individuals. Records available on microfilm: abstracts of donation land claims in Oregon (M 145) and in Washington (M 203).

National Archives, Preliminary   by Harry P. Yoshpe and Philip P.
Inventory of the Land-Entry Papers   Brower (Washington, 1949).
of the General Land Office, comp.

The military bounty land warrant records consist of case files and related materials. The dossiers include warrants (on the backs of which assignments are often recorded in longhand), applications for locations, identification papers, certifications of locations, copies of wills and records on the appointment of administrators, certificates of courts as to heirs, assignments on printed forms, patents, and correspondence. The cover of each case file bears identifying information and data as to the action taken. Abstracts in volumes assist in finding the papers for individuals in the dossiers, which are arranged by the act of Congress under which warrants were issued and thereunder according to the acreage involved and the warrant number. Registers are available for warrants issued under the various acts, and there are also dockets relating to suspended or canceled warrants. Under the various acts there are also volumes containing records of monthly returns of locations made in the land offices.

Various records, 1864-1904, relate to soldiers' additional homestead entries. Most of these are abstracts or dockets of applications and entries, which are either arranged alphabetically or indexed alphabetically, giving the name of soldier and information on his original entry and additional entry, the location, a statement of his military service, and the Government action taken. The foregoing volumes serve as indexes to the documents relating to the entries in the land-entry papers.

The land scrip records include the original warrants that were exchanged for scrip, applications for scrip, stubs of scrip certificates, record copies of scrip issued in exchange for military warrants, agricultural college scrip, surveyors' general scrip, and various indexes and lists.

Records relating to private land claims consist of case files and other materials. These case files, known as private land claim papers or dockets, form a segment of the land-entry papers. The papers consist of notices and evidence of claims, survey notes, plats, affidavits, deeds, abstracts of title, testimony, transcripts of court proceedings, copies of court decisions, appeals, correspondence, and other records. The papers are arranged alphabetically by State and thereunder by case file numbers, with indexes and dockets for some of the States. For California the National Archives also has the original land grant papers assembled by the Board of Land Commissioners, and for Arizona those assembled by the surveyor general. Concerning claims and pueblos in New Mexico there are some miscellaneous documents.

Supreme Court records (Record Group 267) and Justice Department records (Record Group 60) contain materials relating to land cases in California.

Records in Other Custody. --Other records relating to private land claims are in many repositories. The land offices of the Bureau of Land Management at Santa Fe, N. Mex. , and Phoenix, Ariz. , have important records, including in the former place the records of the surveyor general and those of the court of private land claims. Records relating to California land cases are among the records of the U. S. district courts at San Francisco and Los Angeles. The principal records concerning private land claims in Louisiana, Missouri, and Florida are in the possession of those States.

The Spanish land grant records of New Mexico are calendared in Ralph E. Twitchell, The Spanish Archives of New Mexico, vol. I (Cedar Rapids, Iowa, 1914). Concerning those of California, see "Land Grant Records That Survived a Great Fire, " Historical Society of Southern California, Quarterly, 26:38-44 (Mar. 1944). The New Mexico land grant records are available on microfilm in the National Archives, the University of New Mexico Library, the Bancroft Library of the University of California, and the Henry E. Huntington Library; see Albert J. Diaz, comp. , A Guide to the Microfilm of the Papers Relating to New Mexico Land Grants (Albuquerque, 1958). The Arizona Department of Library and Archives at Phoenix has a microfilm of the land grant records in the National Archives.

Cartographic Records

Record Group 49. --The mapping activities of the General Land Office and of the offices of surveyors general resulted in cartographic records, many of which have been transferred to the National Archives. Record sets of the published Land Office maps of the United States, States, and Territories exhibit a wealth of information regarding the survey and disposal of public lands, the lines of military and Indian reservations, and boundaries. The "Old Map File" of the Office's Division of Surveys contains chiefly maps prepared by deputy surveyors, showing the progress of surveys, land grants to railroads, boundaries, private land claims, homesteads, Indian reservations, military reservations, mineral lands, mining districts, mining claims, roads, and railroads. A collection of township plats covers the States of Alabama, Illinois, Indiana, Iowa, Kansas, Mississippi,

Missouri, Ohio, Oklahoma, Oregon, Washington, and Wisconsin. Other township plats--for Arkansas, California, Colorado, Idaho, Montana, New Mexico, Oregon, South Dakota, Utah, and Wyoming--show mining claims and mines; and still other township plats show Oregon donation claims and Indian lands. There are also plats of townsites and other sites; and plats for private land claims in Arizona, California, Colorado, Florida, and New Mexico and a few plats for private land claims in Louisiana, Illinois, and Missouri. Survey plats showing surveys and resurveys of base lines and meridians and exterior boundaries of townships are available for most public land States. Another series contains maps and plats relating to surveys of National, State, and Territorial boundaries. Other maps and diagrams show the rights of way through public lands of railroads, canals, and military and wagon roads; and the limits of land grants to railroads. Field notes are available for some of the surveys upon which the foregoing maps were based.

Records of Surveyors General

A system of surveys with rectangular townships 6 miles square and sections of 640 acres was adopted by the land ordinance of 1785 and an act of May 18, 1796 (1 Stat. 464). This act also provided for the appointment of a Surveyor General, who was to contract with professional surveyors and recommend their commissioning as deputy surveyors. As new territories were formed, other surveyors general were appointed; the Official Register of Sept. 30, 1861, lists them for Illinois and Missouri, Iowa and Wisconsin, Minnesota, California, New Mexico, Dakota, Colorado, Nevada, Oregon, Kansas and Nebraska, Washington, and Utah. In 1862 the Territories of Utah and Colorado were joined in a single surveying district and the Territories of Colorado and Nevada in another district (act of May 30; 12 Stat. 409).

Surveying was continued during the war, though the Government curtailed it whenever possible because of the extraordinary demands on the Treasury for military expenditures. Surveys progressed in most States and Territories, however, and were begun in the new Territories of Colorado, Dakota, and Nevada. Surveys had been suspended since 1857 in Utah, and after 1862 they were discontinued in New Mexico and Arizona because of Indian hostilities and the incursions of Confederate forces. By 1861 surveying had been practically completed in Louisiana and Florida, and in that year it was completed in Missouri and Iowa. Private land claims were surveyed only at the expense of the claimants. As an economy measure, sec. 10 of the act of May 30, 1862 (cited above), permitted settlers in any township who desired a survey to make application in writing and deposit a sum sufficient to cover the survey; the surveyor general would then undertake the survey provided that the township was within the range of the regular progress of surveys.

Donaldson, Public Domain, p. 172, lists the offices of surveyors general with dates of establishments. Detailed information on New Mexico is in Victor Westphall, "The Public Domain in New Mexico, 1854-1891," New Mexico Historical Review, 33:24-52, 128-43 (Jan., Apr. 1958). Historical sketches of the offices of the surveyors general are in Survey of Federal Archives, Inventory of Federal Archives in the States, Series VIII, The Department of the Interior.

Records in Other Custody. --An act of June 12, 1840 (5 Stat. 384), authorized the transfer of the records of the surveyors general of Ohio, Indiana, Michigan, Alabama, and Mississippi--where the surveying had almost been completed--to the respective States and provided for the disposal of records of other surveyors general in the same manner. An amendatory act of Jan. 22, 1853 (10 Stat. 152), provided that deputy surveyors and other agents of the United States should have free access to the records after their transfer to the States and that records might not be transferred until the States had provided for their safekeeping. The records of the surveyors general of the States mentioned above were transferred to the States before the Civil War. The records of other surveyors general were transferred to Missouri and Wisconsin in 1866, to Iowa in 1868, to Illinois in 1869, to Kansas in 1876, to Nebraska sometime following the closing of the office in 1886, and to Minnesota about 1908.

In the public-land States of the South the records of U. S. surveyors general were taken over by the State governments early in 1861. In Arkansas, where the office of the surveyor general had been closed in 1859 and the records had been deposited in the land office at Little Rock, the records were delivered by that office to the State auditor in 1861 and have since remained in the State's possession. In Louisiana and Florida also the records of the surveyors general were delivered to State authorities. Some of the Florida land records were removed in 1861 from St. Augustine to Tallahassee and delivered to the State Register of Public Lands. The U. S. General Land Office sent a special agent, Henry C. De Ahua, to Louisiana and Florida in 1866-67 to recover, examine, and inventory the surveyors' general records and to report upon their condition. He found that the Louisiana records were in disorder but were nearly complete. When surveyors general were reappointed for Louisiana and Florida in 1869, they were instructed to regard land transactions of State governments during the war as null and void. The surveyor general of Florida found the records at Tallahassee disordered and mutilated. The Florida records were transferred to the State's Department of Agriculture in 1907, and those of Louisiana to the State Land Office in 1910. Oklahoma was still Indian land at the time of the Civil War.

Records of many of the offices of the surveyors general are described in the Survey of Federal Archives, Inventory of Federal Archives in the States, Series VIII, The Department of the Interior; and earlier descriptions of some are in American Historical Association, Annual Reports, 1904, 1905, 1908-10, 1912, and 1914.

The still operative offices of surveyors general were abolished by an act of Mar. 3, 1925 (43 Stat. 1144), and their work was transferred to the Field Surveying Service, under which public survey offices operated in 11 Far Western States. The survey work was later consolidated with other land office business in single offices for each State except California. Consequently land survey records are now maintained in the following places: Phoenix, Ariz. ; Los Angeles, Calif.; Sacramento, Calif. ; Denver, Colo. ; Boise, Idaho; Billings, Mont. ; Reno, Nev. ; Santa Fe, N. Mex. ; Portland, Oreg. ; Salt Lake City, Utah; Spokane, Wash. ; and Cheyenne, Wyo. Some records for Arizona, Colorado, and New Mexico are in the Federal Records Center at Denver, and some for Oregon and Washington are in the Center at Seattle. Records in the Centers usually consist of correspondence, lists, and registers.

The records of the offices of surveyors general, now largely in the public survey offices mentioned above, are similar for each office. They include field notes of surveys, survey plats, maps, contracts with deputy surveyors, accounts, annual reports, records of private surveys, correspondence, and records of donation claims. Most of the records of the office of the surveyor general of California were destroyed in the fire that followed the earthquake of 1906. Though the records of the old surveyors general are largely duplicated in the records of the General Land Office, some materials--including part of the correspondence and other records of a special nature--are not duplicated and are of value for studies of the States.

Records of District Land Offices

Land offices, considerably more numerous than offices of surveyors general, were scattered throughout the public-land States of the South and the Upper Mississippi Valley and in the States and Territories west of the river. These offices were staffed by registers and receivers, who dispensed information and made initial contacts with applicants for land. The registers accepted and examined applications for land and kept records of entries; the receivers accepted payments for fees and land purchases, acted as Government disbursing agents, and deposited surplus funds. These officials administered oaths, rendered decisions in contested cases, and investigated trespassing on timber lands. They corresponded frequently with the Commissioner of the General Land Office and submitted to him case papers and regular returns regarding the business of their offices. Their actions were subject to the approval of the General Land Office.

A chronological list of land offices by State and Territory, giving dates of their establishment and removal or discontinuance, is in Donaldson, The Public Domain, p. 173-176. Lists of Executive orders relating to land offices appear in the compilations prepared by the Historical Records Survey. Sketches of the land office history of each State are in the Survey of Federal Archives, Inventory of Federal Archives in the States, Series VIII, The Department of the Interior. The locations of offices in existence during the Civil War can be ascertained from the Official Register.

Like the offices of surveyors general in Southern States, the land offices came under the control of State governments early in 1861. Some of the States established their own land offices and engaged in the sale and survey of lands. Land offices were reestablished under Federal control during 1865-66; the records of the former offices were recovered from the State authorities; and the U. S. registers and receivers were instructed to consider sales of land by the States during the war as null and void but to give preference rights to actual settlers who exhibited proof of settlement and cultivation. Transcriptions of some township plats and tract books were made for the Southern States after the war to replace records lost during the war.

Records in Other Custody. --The policy of transferring records of land offices (like those of surveyors general) to the States was adopted, and the same acts of June 12, 1840, and Jan. 22, 1853, governed such transfers. When less than 100,000 acres of unsold land remained within a land district, its business and records were transferred to another land office in the same State. Finally, on completion of the land office business, the records were transferred to agencies designated by the State for their reception. Most of the records for the public-land States east of the Rocky Mountains have thus been delivered to the States.

In 11 States of the Far West where there are still public lands the records of the land offices are kept by field offices of the Bureau of Land Management. Offices of that bureau having such records are in the cities mentioned above as offices of the Field Surveying Service of the Bureau. Some records of the Los Angeles land office are in the Federal Records Center at Los Angeles; others--of Oregon and Washington--are in the Federal Records Center at Seattle. Most of the records have been retained by the specified offices of the Bureau, however, for they are needed for administration and are much consulted by Federal, State, and local officials and by the general public.

All the land offices kept certain records, and--depending upon the presence of swamp lands, mineral lands, and railroad lands--some offices maintained other records. The records include tract books, township plats, correspondence, maps, accounts, selection lists of swamp lands, lists of railroad lands, registers of entries of mining lands, abstracts of declaratory statements, registers of certificates issued, and records pertaining to land sales, preemptions, land scrip, town lots, military land warrants, homestead entries, agricultural college scrip, donation claims, Indian allotments, and land patents.

Information about records in both Federal and State custody is in Survey of Federal Archives, Inventory of Federal Archives in the States, Series VIII, The Department of the Interior. Real estate records are also in the offices of county recorders or registers of deeds. In administering the lands received from the Federal Government under acts of Congress, the States had to set up their own land offices, and records relating to these lands are in State custody. Information regarding State land records is in inventories published in the Annual Reports of the American Historical Association, from 1904 onward.

OFFICE OF INDIAN AFFAIRS

The direction of Indian affairs had been put under the War Department in 1789 and had continued there for 60 years. In 1824 a Bureau of Indian Affairs had been organized and in 1832 the newly named Office of the Commissioner of Indian Affairs had taken over the former Bureau's function of dispensing Indian annuities and the civilization fund, keeping accounts of such expenditures, and examining claims. In 1849 the Commissioner's functions were transferred to the Department of the Interior, and by the time of the Civil War the Office of the Commissioner had become known as the Office of Indian Affairs. Along with the transfer of functions to the Interior Department there were transferred the office divisions that were still in existence during the war--a Files and Records Division, a Civilization Division, a Finance Division, and a Land Division. A chief clerk had general supervision of the Office under the direction of the Commissioner.

The Commissioner of Indian Affairs had a variety of duties under acts of Congress regulating intercourse with the Indian tribes. He was concerned with negotiating treaties with the Indians, issuing instructions to

superintendents and agents and examining their accounts, supervising Indian lands, administering Indian trust funds, promoting education, paying
annuities, suppressing the liquor traffic, controlling traders, aiding missions established by religious denominations, protecting Indians on reservations from white intruders, contracting for the transportation of Indian
goods, and furnishing medical relief and supplies.

Relations with the Indians deteriorated during the Civil War owing to
the inability of the Government to keep adequate military forces on the
frontier and to delays in the payment of annuities. As a result of the withdrawal early in the war of U. S. troops from the Indian Territory, where
there was a concentration of Indians who had earlier been removed from
Southern States east of the Mississippi, and as a result also of the activities of Confederate Indian agents, most of these Indians gave their allegiance to the Confederacy. The Chickasaw and Choctaw and part of the
Seminole and Cherokee became Confederate allies. The Creeks were
sharply divided; those who remained loyal to the United States were driven
north into Kansas, accompanied by the Union faction of the Seminole. To
Kansas also fled smaller numbers of Quapaws, Seneca, Shawnee, Cherokee, Delawares, and Kickapoos. Support had to be extended to these Indians by the Federal Government, and annuities due the hostile tribes
were diverted for this purpose. Many men of these Indian tribes were enlisted in Confederate and Union military forces and participated in campaigns in the Indian Territory; these campaigns, along with guerilla activities, seriously ravaged the country.

After the war punitive measures were imposed on the principal tribes
of the Indian Territory--the Cherokee, Chickasaw, Choctaw, Creeks, and
Seminole--by treaties negotiated in 1866. The tribes were obliged to make
cessions of land on which other tribes could be located, to declare void all
treaties with the former Confederacy, to abolish slavery and allow their
former slaves the same rights as Indians, to make available part of the
proceeds from the sale of lands to reimburse loyal Indians for damages
during the war, to grant rights of way for railroads, and to declare a general amnesty for all acts committed during the war. The Government aided
the Indian refugees in Kansas to return to their homes in the Indian Territory, and also extended relief to the southern Cherokee.

Indians in other areas of the West also took to the warpath. Some tribes
were provoked to hostility by the encroachments of miners and the development of transportation lines; in Colorado the Arapahos and Cheyennes attacked mining camps and mail coaches. Raids by other tribes on emigrants
along the Santa Fe trail and the Texas border made the Government increase
its forces on the Arkansas and New Mexico frontiers. In 1863-64 a force
under Col. Kit Carson campaigned against the Apaches and Navahos, who
were finally obliged in 1865 to accept reservations. The outbreak of the
Sioux in Minnesota in 1862 resulted in extensive loss of life and property
damage.

Successive Commissioners of Indian Affairs during the war:

> Alfred B. Greenwood, May 4, 1859.
> William P. Dole, Mar. 14, 1861.
> Dennis N. Cooley, July 11, 1865.

The Annual Report of the Commissioner of Indian Affairs is in the
Report of the Secretary of the Interior, 1861-66, previously cited. See
also Annie Heloise Abel, The American Indian as Participant in the Civil

War (Cleveland, 1919), The Ameri- can Indian as Slaveholder and Seces- sionist (Cleveland, 1915), The Amer- ican Indian Under Reconstruction (Cleveland, 1925), and "The Indians in the Civil War," American Histor- ical Review, 15:281-296 (Jan. 1910); Cohen, Handbook of Federal Indian Law; Grant Foreman, A History of Oklahoma (Norman, 1942); Frederick Webb Hodge, ed. , Handbook of Amer- ican Indians North of Mexico (Bureau of American Ethnology, Bulletin 30, pts. 1 and 2. Washington, 1907, 1910); Chester M. Oehler, The Great Sioux Uprising (New York, 1959); Schmecke- bier, The Office of Indian Affairs; John R. Swanton, The Indian Tribes of North America (Bureau of American Ethnology, Bulletin 145. Washington, 1952).

Files and Records Division

This Division had charge of the correspondence and other general rec- ords of the Office of Indian Affairs. It briefed, registered, and indexed incoming letters and indexed outgoing letters.

Record Group 75. -- For the Civil War period most of the outgoing letters are recorded in letter books (vols. 65-78, Dec. 1860-Dec. 1865). Letters to superintendents and agents concern accounts, appointments of agents, agency employees, trade licenses, visits by delegations of Indians to Wash- ington, Indian spoliations, bounty land claims of Indians, Indian lands, fi- nances, erection of buildings for Indians, relief, and payments to Indians. Communications to the Secretary of the Interior contain recommendations and reports on various subjects. Appointment papers for special commis- sioners to appraise Indian lands and for special agents to purchase and dis- tribute provisions to destitute Indians are also included. Communications to the Commissioner of Pensions concern bounty lands for Indians, letters to the Commissioner of the General Land Office concern the appraisal of Indian lands and their survey, and letters to Congressmen concern spolia- tion claims against Indians and claims for the allotment of lands. Corre- spondence regarding the delivery of guns and the purchase of Indian goods is addressed to business firms. Letters to individuals concern the purchase of land from Indians, payments for services, claims of Indians for damages, employment at agencies, and other matters. General circulars and orders are also in the letters sent books. Alphabetical indexes in the volumes fa- cilitate finding letters sent to specific officials and individuals. For the letters sent there is also a series of useful abstracts, well arranged by superintendency and agency. (The letters sent by the Office of Indian Affairs, 1824-81, are available on microfilm as M 21.)

Other outgoing letters are in two smaller series. In the "Report Books" (vols. 12-14) are recorded letters to Government officials, congressional committees, and the Secretary of the Interior (available on microfilm, 1838- 81, as M 348). The letters to the Secretary relate to administrative mat- ters, claims for services, claims of Indians, claims for depredations by Indians, estimates of expenditures, the establishment of reservations, charges against agents, funds due Indian tribes, changes in appropriation bills, Indian trust funds, the employment of clerks, military reservations, and annual reports on operations. These volumes are especially important for study of the formulation of Indian policy and the administration of Indian affairs. In some "Miscellaneous Records" (vols. 8-9) are mainly letters of appointment to Indian agents and commissions of agents and superintendents, with some certificates of the Commissioner relative to payment of debts of Indian tribes and statements of payments to be made to creditors of Indian tribes.

A voluminous file of letters received during the war, comprising letters handled by all divisions of the Office, contains letters from superintendents and agents regarding accounts, annuities, buildings, claims, depredations, education, employees, health, Indian lands, progress in agriculture, subsistence, supplies, traders and licenses, treaty negotiations, and administrative matters. Included are instructions, decisions, authorizations, and other communications from the Secretary of the Interior; letters concerning accounts and other financial matters from the Second Auditor, the Second Comptroller, and other officials of the Treasury Department; letters from the General Land Office concerning Indian lands; and letters from the Secretary of War, Army officers, the President, Members of Congress, other officials, Indians, business firms, and private individuals. These letters are arranged by superintendency or agency and are therefore useful for research on particular areas of the country or on Indian tribes. Receipts for annuities are also to be found in the letters received file. Letters relating to Indian reserves sometimes follow the general file of letters received from agencies. Material on Indian schools and letters concerning miscellaneous subjects are also segregated. Registers of letters received serve as a useful index to the file. This file is of paramount importance for documenting wartime and postwar relations with the Indian tribes and is also important for the administration of the Indian service, for Territorial and local affairs, for land history, for military operations, and for the history and ethnology of the Indians. Records available on microfilm: letters received, 1824-81 (M 234), and registers of letters received, 1824-80 (M 18).

Various matters arising out of the war--such as the payment of loyal Indians' claims and of back pay, bounties, and pensions and payment for damages done to missions--were in the course of settlement for some years after the war and are documented in both letters received and letters sent.

A list of the subdivisions of the letters received file is in Van Tyne and Leland, Guide, p. 206-207. Further documentation regarding Indian affairs is in records of the Indian Division of the Office of the Secretary of the Interior (Record Group 48), records of the Office of the Secretary of War (Record Group 107), records of U. S. Army commands (Record Group 98), and domestic letters of the Department of State (Record Group 59). Much correspondence of the postwar years relating to the investigation of fraud in the settlement of problems arising out of the war is printed in H. Rept. 98, 42 Cong., 3 sess., Serial 1578.

A series of special files contains correspondence, reports, accounts, lists, affidavits, and other records relating to claims and investigations. These files, numerically arranged, contain documents relating to the settlement of the claims of Seminole (file no. 87), claims of Choctaw and Chickasaw (no. 134), claims of Creeks for reimbursement of money paid to freedmen wrongfully enrolled as Creeks (no. 284), and claims of Delawares for depredations by whites (no. 106); also papers relating to the affairs of southern Indian refugees in Kansas (no. 201). In these files also are documents relating to investigations, chiefly concerning the conduct of employees.

Documents relating to the claims of loyal Choctaw and Chickasaw are in special files nos. 134 and 142. No. 134 contains a statement of the examination of the claims reported by Commissioners E. W. Rice and A. H.

Jackson, with the claims papers. No. 142 contains a protest of the Choctaw council (Chickasaw council concurring) against the awards made by the commissioners, an amended protest, letters from James G. Blunt, the attorney for the claimants; letters from John H. B. Latrobe, attorney for the Choctaw and Chickasaw Nations; letters from the Choctaw and Chickasaw delegates and the governor of the Chickasaw Nation; letters from the Secretary of the Interior; letters from Rice and Jackson; and depositions, arguments, and briefs. Materials relating to the claims of Heald and Wright, traders, are in the foregoing files and in file no. 245. (Documents concerning these claims are also in the records of the House of Representatives, Record Group 233; and some of them are printed in H. Ex. Doc. 204, 40 Cong., 2 sess., Serial 1341.) Other records regarding the claims of the Choctaw and Chickasaw and other loyal Indians are described below under the Civilization Division.

The papers relating to the claims of loyal Seminole make up special file 87. This numerical file consists of affidavits of claimants concerning the property lost and of testimony as to the loyalty of the Indians and the claims made by them. The treaty with the Seminole of Mar. 21, 1866 (14 Stat. 757), had provided for the appointment by the Secretary of the Interior of a board of commissioners to investigate claims of loyal members of the tribe for losses sustained during the Civil War. After making an examination of the claims in the Indian country, the commissioners--J. Tyler Powell and J. W. Caldwell--submitted a report, Nov. 26, 1867, with a list of claims of loyal Seminole Indians. The commissioners considered 340 claims amounting to $214, 915. 95 and awarded the full amount. A payment of $50, 000 was made on the claims soon afterward. Much later, as a result of an agreement of Dec. 16, 1897 (30 Stat. 568), the claims were submitted to the Senate for final determination of the balance to be paid to the Seminole claimants. Finding that the commissioners had allowed the face value of every claim, the Senate reduced the amounts by 45 percent, allowed interest to 1899, and computed the balance due as $186, 000. The payment of that amount was authorized by an act of May 31, 1900 (31 Stat. 240). A special agent, James E. Jenkins, was sent to the Seminole Nation to prepare a roll of loyal Seminole and of the heirs of those who were deceased. Jenkins turned over the funds to A. J. Brown, who as administrator made the payments to the claimants.

The report of the commissioners, Nov. 26, 1867, and lists of claims are printed in S. Rept. 1875, 55 Cong., 3 sess., Serial 3741, and in S. Doc. 72, 55 Cong., 3 sess., Serial 3731. The records of the Indian Territory Division include copies of records of the U. S. Territorial Court for the Western District of Indian Territory of probate cases involving payments made by A. J. Brown to the loyal Seminole in 1901.

A file of "special cases" includes records relating to land disputes, the establishment of reservations and the survey of their boundaries, logging operations, and wagon road routes. Some letters of the Commissioner of Indian Affairs and the Secretary of the Interior relating to the establishment of Indian reservations, with endorsements by President Lincoln, are designated as "Executive Orders." With these are related letters from Indian agents and superintendents.

U. S. President, Executive Orders Relating to Indian Reservations from May 14, 1855, to July 1, 1912 (Washington, 1912).

Treaty Files

At the time of the Civil War the U. S. Government still followed its
early policy of regulating relations with the Indian tribes by treaty. Signed
by representatives of both the Government and the tribes and ratified by the
Senate, the treaties provided for cessions of land by the Indians, the payment of annuities and the allotment of land to them, the fixing of boundaries
and establishment of reservations, settlement of claims, education and
health services, regulation of trade, trust funds, establishment of military
posts, suppression of the liquor traffic, tribal government and courts, and
the use of land by missions.

The ratified treaty file contains journals of treaty commissioners; proceedings of the councils; reports and correspondence of Indian agents, superintendents, and commissioners; and copies of the treaties. Similar documents are in the unratified treaty file. The latter file contains documents
relating to the Fort Smith conference of Sept. 1865 with the Southern tribes.
Both files are arranged chronologically by date of the treaty. The treaties
and related documents are of primary importance for study of the Government's policy toward the Indians.

National Archives, List of Documents Concerning the Negotiation
of Ratified Indian Treaties, 1801-
1869, comp. by John H. Martin
(Washington, 1949), contains for
each treaty a list of documents in
the ratified treaty file and of related
instructions, correspondence, and
reports in the letters sent and letters received files of the Office of
Indian Affairs and of the Indian Division of the Secretary's Office. The
original signed and ratified treaties
and other documents are in the general records of the U. S. Government (Record Group 11). Messages
of the President and other papers
concerning Indian treaties and most
of the unratified treaties are in the
Senate records (Record Group 46).
The texts of the Indian treaties are
in the Statutes at Large and in
Charles J. Kappler, Indian Affairs,
Laws, and Treaties, vol. 2 (S.
Doc. 452, 57 Cong., 1 sess., Serial
4254; Washington, 1904). A chronological list of the treaties is in U. S.
Department of the Interior, Annual
Report, 1903, 1:469-474, and a list
arranged alphabetically by name of
tribe is in Hodge, ed., Handbook of
American Indians, 2:805-813.

Other Records

Certain records afford information on the wartime personnel of Indian
superintendencies and agencies: a record of applications for appointment,
arranged alphabetically by name; a roster of superintendents and agents,
containing information on individual appointments and terminations of appointments; and a roster of agency employees, giving data regarding persons appointed to positions at agencies, with both dates of appointment and
dates of termination. These records supplement documents relating to
personnel in the letters sent and the miscellaneous letters, described above.

The Files and Records Division of the Office of Indian Affairs accumulated an extensive collection of maps and similar materials. For the war
years these sometimes show tribal lands, land cessions, Indian and military reservations, boundary lines, wagon road and railroad rights of way,
and allotments to individual Indians. Map registers were maintained by
the Office of Indian Affairs, and a card index has been prepared by the National Archives.

National Archives, List of Cartographic Records of the Bureau of Indian Affairs, comp. by Laura E. Kelsay (Special List No. 13. Washington, 1954). Other cartographic materials useful in the study of Indian affairs during the Civil War are among the records of the Office of the Chief of Engineers (Record Group 77), the Senate (Record Group 46), and the Office of the Secretary of the Interior (Record Group 48).

Civilization Division

This Division was established in 1846, to try to civilize the Indians and enable them to support themselves. When the Indians were concentrated on reservations, agriculture became a surer way of obtaining food than hunting. An annual appropriation of $10,000, provided from 1819 onward, was used to subsidize mission schools, where vocational training was taught. These schools also received support from private sources and from tribal funds. Many of the treaties with the Indians provided funds for educating Indian youths, for teaching domestic economy to Indian maidens, for instruction in farming and stockraising, for furnishing seed and agricultural implements, for the erection and operation of gristmills and sawmills, and for the services of doctors, blacksmiths, and mechanics.

Acts of Congress regulating trade and intercourse with the Indians (adopted in 1796, 1802, and 1834) provided for reimbursing both whites and Indians for depredations upon property. An attempt was made to enforce tribal responsibility for depredations by requiring reimbursement out of tribal funds, and heavy punishment was provided for offenses committed by white men. Indian agents collected evidence on depredations by Indians and reported it to the Office of Indian Affairs; and, after examination and approval of the claims, payments were made from cash annuities due the Indians, or special appropriations were sought from Congress. An act of July 15, 1870 (16 Stat. 360), discontinued the payment of damages from the Indians' annuities and provided that Congress should make specific appropriations. The Department of the Interior was required by sec. 7 of an act of May 29, 1872 (17 Stat. 190), to investigate evidence regarding claims and to report thereon to Congress. Congress, however, did not have the time to consider the claims; and finally by an act of Mar. 3, 1891 (26 Stat. 851), it referred claims for Indian depredations to the U. S. Court of Claims. Claims accruing before July 1, 1865, were not to be considered, however, unless they had been allowed or were pending before the passage of the act.

Alice G. Fletcher, "Indian Education and Civilization," S. Ex. Doc. 95, 48 Cong., 2 sess., Serial 2264 (Washington, 1888); "Claims Arising out of Indian Treaties," June 1886, H. Rept. 3117, 49 Cong., 1 sess., Serial 2444; "Claims Arising From Indian Depredations," Mar. 26, 1890, H. Rept. 1079, 51 Cong., 1 sess., Serial 2810.

Record Group 75. --Special files relating to the civilization of the Indians include compilations prepared from the reports and other communications in the regular correspondence files of the Office. A roster of Indian schools, 1862-64, gives for each school its locality, the number of teachers, the number of students, the religious denomination by which the school was operated, the date of the treaty under which funds were applied, the population of the bands served by the school and their wealth in individual property, and the number of missionaries; and occasional remarks about contributions, farms, etc. Another compilation gives statistical data on farming operations carried on by the Indians, 1863-65. A record of licenses issued to traders shows the tribes that the traders served, the dates of the traders' licenses, the amounts of bonds and names of sureties, and the names of employees.

Claims Against Hostile Indians

Concerning depredations by Indians upon whites there are claims papers and other records begun in the Civilization Division and continued in the Depredation Division. The claims papers contain affidavits about the property lost, affidavits of witnesses on the truthfulness of the claim, reports and certificates of Indian agents, correspondence, reports of the Commissioner of Indian Affairs to the Secretary of the Interior (with the Secretary's endorsements of approval or disapproval), and powers of attorney. The claims are numerically arranged in covers bearing notations of the action taken. Registers containing alphabetical indexes by names of claimants facilitate finding the claims papers of particular persons. There is also an index to incoming correspondence concerning these claims. The investigator may also find useful an incomplete file of claims papers against the Pawnees, with related correspondence; a list of claims for depredations by the Sioux and the Chippewa of the Upper Mississippi River Valley, Apr. 1857-Oct. 1862; and a memorial of 1863 from the New Mexico legislature concerning claims for Indian depredations. (Information on wartime depredations by whites against Indians and on cheating by traders, liquor peddlers, and even Indian agents is in the regular correspondence files.)

Lists of Indian depredation claims, including some for the Civil War period, are in H. Ex. Doc. 65, 43 Cong., 2 sess., Serial 1645; H. Ex. Doc. 147, 44 Cong., 1 sess., Serial 1689; H. Ex. Doc. 135, 47 Cong., 1 sess., Serial 2030; and H. Ex. Doc. 125, 49 Cong., 1 sess., Serial 2399. Other documentation on depredation claims is in the main correspondence files of the Office of Indian Affairs and in records of the U. S. Court of Claims (Record Group 123), the House of Representatives (Record Group 233), the Senate (Record Group 46), and the Office of the Secretary of War (Record Group 107).

The Sioux outbreak in Minnesota in Aug. 1862 resulted in much loss of life, injury to individuals, the capture of women and children, and extensive loss of property. An act of Feb. 16, 1863 (12 Stat. 652), for the relief of Minnesota residents who suffered damage and injury authorized the payment of $200,000 from annuities due the Sioux and the appointment of three commissioners to ascertain the whole amount of damages and the names of the persons to whom they were due. (The provisions of the foregoing act were extended by an act of Mar. 3, 1863--12 Stat. 803--to residents of Iowa and of Dakota Territory who had suffered damages or injury by the Sioux.) A report was submitted by the commission (A. W. V. White, Eli R. Chase, and Cyrus Aldrich) on Nov. 30, 1863, allowing a total of $1,370,374 to 2,635 claimants. Payments were made for the immediate relief of families from the $200,000 already authorized, and an act of May 28, 1864 (13 Stat. 92), appropriated $1,170,374 more. Under another act of Mar. 3, 1863 (12 Stat. 819), those Sioux who had already fled from Minnesota were removed to a reservation on the Missouri River. An act of Feb. 9, 1865 (13 Stat. 427), made a small appropriation for the relief of friendly Sioux.

William Watts Folwell, A His-   Paul, 1921-30. 4 vols.); Oehler,
tory of Minnesota, 2:109-241 (Saint   Great Sioux Uprising.

The records relating to the Sioux depredation claims consist of claims papers, correspondence, and other documents giving intimate details of this interesting and important Civil War event. The claims papers contain affidavits of claimants giving the circumstances justifying the claim; the amount, character, and value of property lost; and information on the claimants' families, including their names and ages. These papers also contain transcripts of testimony of witnesses, powers of attorney, and receipts for payments received from the commissioners. Schedules (on rolls) show the payments made by the commissioners to claimants and the amounts due them; and there are correspondence, other schedules, statements of claims, and instructions to the commissioners. Besides narratives of a number of survivors, the records include depositions by Thomas J. Galbraith, Indian agent, and Stephen R. Riggs, missionary, which are valuable for the history of the outbreak. Receipts are available for payments made to claimants. There is also the record of a military commission that tried many Sioux in Sept. 1862 for murder and other outrages.

The report of the Sioux Commis-   the Finance Division (discussed be-
sion, Nov. 30, 1863, is printed in   low) and of the Office of the Secre-
H. Ex. Doc. 58, 38 Cong. , 1 sess. ,   tary of the Interior (discussed above).
Serial 1189, and in H. Rept. 42, 38   A calendar of the testimony taken by
Cong. , 1 sess. , Serial 1206. Other   the commission is in the Minnesota
records relating to the Sioux Com-   Historical Society.
mission are among the records of

At the time of the Sioux uprising an insurrection also was threatened among the Chippewa in Minnesota. The frame house of Hole-in-the-Day, the head chief of the Chippewa of the Mississippi River, was burned by troops from Fort Ripley, and in revenge the Pillager Chippewa robbed private and Government buildings at Leech Lake and took some captives. Hole-in-the-Day was not supported by other chiefs, however, and the uprising subsided. Some of the horses and other booty taken by the Chippewa were turned in at Fort Ripley. The treaty of May 7, 1864 (13 Stat. 694), stipulated that the United States would provide $20, 000 to pay claims for Chippewa depredations and $5, 000 to reimburse Hole-in-the-Day for the loss of his house and furniture. The Chippewa Indian agent made an investigation of the claims and gathered evidence relating to them. Records concerning the Chippewa depredation claims are less voluminous than the Sioux claims. They are likely, however, to throw further light on Indian attitudes during the Civil War. Submitted by the agent, 1862-69, these papers include affidavits of claimants, reports of the agent regarding the claims, transmittal letters of the agent, and lists of claims.

Claims of Loyal Indians

Numbers of the loyal Indians in the Indian Territory who had to seek refuge in Kansas during the war suffered considerable loss of property. These civilized Indians had owned good houses and farms, herds of cattle and horses, and growing crops. When they had to abandon their homes, their houses were confiscated by the hostile Indians and sold or destroyed, their fields were laid waste, and their cattle and horses were stolen, driven to Kansas, and sold there to the U. S. Army or to cattle brokers. The property lost also included household furniture and utensils, personal effects, rifles, farm equipment and tools, fences and fence rails, wagons and harness, blacksmith shops and tools, cash, and provisions. Treaties negotiated by the United States with Indian tribes before the war had usually provided that the United States would protect the persons and property of the Indians. The treaties negotiated with the Creeks, Choctaw and Chickasaw, Seminole, and Shawnee and other tribes in 1866 provided for the payment of claims of loyal tribe members for property losses suffered as a result of abandoning their homes. The treaty with the Cherokee, however, provided only for the return to the former owners of property that had been confiscated by the Cherokee Nation.

The claims papers of loyal Indians contain much information relating to the war. The affidavits of claimants and witnesses give information about the flight of the Indians, incidents of the war in the West, the service of Indians in the Union and Confederate forces, the condition of freedmen, escapes by loyal Indians from Confederate soil, the treatment of loyal Indians by hostile Indians and Confederate forces, personal histories of claimants, and the activities of Indians on behalf of the Confederacy.

The Creek treaty of June 14, 1866 (14 Stat. 787), provided for an investigation of losses sustained by Indians who enlisted in the Union Army and by loyal refugee Indians and freedmen, and it provided for the payment of awards from proceeds of the sale of Creek lands. On July 21, 1869, after an appropriation for the expenses of the investigation had been made, the Commissioner of Indian Affairs issued instructions to Gen. W. B. Hazen, Superintendent of the Southern Superintendency, in regard to taking the census required by the treaty, collecting evidence pertaining to the losses, and making awards to the claimants. On the same date instructions were sent to Capt. F. A. Field, the Creek agent, who was to prepare the census and assist the Superintendent. The report by Hazen and Field, submitted on Feb. 14, 1870, was accompanied by an abstract listing 1,523 claims amounting to $5,090,808. On these claims awards totaling $1,836,830 were eventually made. Under an act of July 15, 1870 (16 Stat. 341), $100,000 was applied pro rata on the awards, and payments were made by J. A. Williamson, a special agent of the Interior Department. In later years many bills were introduced in Congress to provide for payment of the balance due the loyal Creeks. An adverse decision on the Creek case was rendered by the U. S. Court of Claims in 1884. Finally an act of Mar. 1, 1901 (31 Stat. 869), provided for submission of the claims to the Senate for settlement. Although the award of the Senate was $1,200,000, an act of Mar. 3, 1903 (32 Stat. 994), provided a further payment of only $600,000. The Creek National Council, in accordance with the terms of the act, adopted a resolution on May 23, 1903, agreeing to accept the $600,000 as full payment and satisfaction of the claims of the loyal Creek Indians and freedmen, but in subsequent years the Creeks sought payment of the full $1,200,000. James McLaughlin, an Indian inspector, was charged with preparing the roll in order to fulfill the act of 1903; and payments provided under that act were made in 1904 by J. Blair Shoenfelt, Creek agent.

The following congressional documents contain papers relating to the history of the loyal Creek claims:

H. Ex. Doc.   217, 41 Cong. , 2 sess. , Serial 1425.
H. Misc. Doc. 38, 45 Cong. , 2 sess. , Serial 1817.
S. Doc.   67, 55 Cong. , 1 sess. , Serial 3562.
S. Doc.   3088, 57 Cong. , 2 sess. , Serial 4412.
S. Rept.   975, 60 Cong. , 2 sess. , Serial 5380.
S. Rept.   110, 76 Cong. , 1 sess. , Serial 10292.

Papers relating to the claims of loyal Creek soldiers, refugees, and freedmen (or their heirs or administrators) are in a numerically arranged file. The individual files contain affidavits of claimants setting forth the wartime circumstances under which the claims arose and the amount, character, and value of the property lost; and affidavits of witnesses as to the authenticity of the claims. An abstract lists the claims in the same order and gives the claim number, the name of claimant, sex, age, amount claimed, amount awarded, and remarks as to type of claimant.

The abstract is printed in S.Doc. 420, 57 Cong. , 1 sess. , Serial 4347, p. 18-37. The instructions to the commissioners are in Letters Sent Book 91, p. 118-121, and the report from them is in Letters Received, Creek, H 865. For the census roll see the description of the records of the Finance Division, below. Claims papers comprising affidavits establishing heirship, which were submitted to McLaughlin during 1903-4, are in Special Series A.

Articles 49 and 50 of the treaty with the Choctaw and Chickasaw, Apr. 28, 1866 (14 Stat. 780), provided that the President should appoint a commission to consider and determine the claims of loyal Indians for losses and those of licensed traders and other loyal citizens for goods or property taken or sold to members of the Choctaw Nation. In July 1866 President Johnson appointed Elliott W. Rice of Iowa and A. H. Jackson of Nebraska as commissioners, and on the 30th of that month Commissioner of Indian Affairs Cooley sent them instructions to guide their investigations. The commissioners heard and examined claims amounting to $691,095 and awarded to Choctaw claimants $109,742 and to the Chickasaw $233,008. The two nations protested the amounts of these awards, and after reexamination and presentation of additional testimony and arguments by counsel of the nations and of the claimants, Commissioner Cooley recommended on Apr. 27, 1868, the ratification of a compromise between the counsel and delegates of the nations and the counsel of the claimants. An act of Congress of July 25, 1868 (15 Stat. 177), authorized the Secretary of the Interior to adopt the agreements, by which $109,742 was to be paid to the loyal Choctaw and $150,000 to the loyal Chickasaw. Samuel S. Smoot, a special agent of the Government, made the payments, derived from funds of the nations in the hands of the Government. The $90,000 authorized for the payment of claims of traders was divided between James G. Heald and Reuben Wright (act of Apr. 10, 1869; 16 Stat. 20).

Abel, American Indian Under Reconstruction, p. 336-337; Debo, Rise and Fall of the Choctaw Republic, p. 97; "Letter of the Secretary of the Interior, Communicating . . . Information Relative to the Present Claims of the loyal Choctaw and Chickasaw Indians . . . ," June 18, 1868, S. Ex. Doc. 66, 40 Cong. , 2 sess. , Serial 1317.

The papers relating to claims of the loyal Choctaw and Chickasaw are in a numerical file, containing affidavits of claimants and witnesses and statements of the amounts awarded. There are also an alphabetical record of the names of claimants and a copy of the report of the commissioners, Dec. 31, 1866. The instructions to the commissioners, July 30, 1866, are in Letters Sent Book 81, p. 72-74. Other material is described in the discussion of special files, above.

An investigation of the losses of the Seneca, "Mixed Senecas and Shawnees," and Quapaws by a commission appointed by the Secretary of the Interior was authorized by the treaty with those tribes of Feb. 23, 1867 (15 Stat. 513). J. W. Caldwell and Landon Carter examined the claims in the Indian country in the early part of 1869 and submitted a report on Apr. 25, 1869. There were 30 Mixed Seneca and Shawnee claims for $14,757.25; 33 Shawnee claims for $18,143.85; 41 Seneca claims for $29,306.95; and 78 Quapaw claims for $48,601.85. By an act of July 15, 1870 (16 Stat. 351), Congress appropriated $90,000 to be paid personally to each claimant or his heir pro rata on the awards made by the commissioners.

These claims papers are arranged by claim number and include affidavits of claimants and transcripts of testimony of witnesses. With the papers are an original and a copy of the report of the commissioners, a copy of their instructions of Jan. 25, 1869, a letter from the Commissioner of Indian Affairs to the Secretary of the Interior, Dec. 29, 1869, and a list of the claimants. (The report of the commissioners is printed in H. Ex. Doc. 127, 41 Cong., 2 sess., Serial 1417.)

The claims of other Shawnee Indians for losses sustained during the war were investigated by Indian agents. James B. Abbott reported on some of these claims from the Shawnee Agency in Kansas on Nov. 25, 1866. Enoch Hoag, Superintendent of Indian Affairs in Kansas, submitted on Jan. 24, 1874, reports by agents on claims of the "Absentee Shawnees" and a few Delaware claims. Many years passed, however, before these claims were settled. An act of Congress of Dec. 22, 1927 (45 Stat. 18), appropriated $463,732.49 to pay the claims of loyal Shawnee and 13 Delaware Indians, their heirs, or their legal representatives. A later act, Mar. 4, 1929 (45 Stat. 155), provided $109,746.25 for payment of claims of loyal Shawnee. These payments were soon made, and in accordance with the acts receipts were taken on payrolls.

Concerning Shawnee claims there are some powers of attorney submitted by the attorney of the Shawnee in 1873. In a volume are briefs of some of the claims prepared in 1894, when the affidavits were transferred to the U. S. Court of Claims.

Other material on these claims is in the records of the Finance Division (see below), and receipts for payments made to the Indians are in the central classified files of the Office of Indian Affairs (Shawnee 260, 12475-1928)

Finance Division

Organized in 1846, the Finance Division kept ledgers of receipts and disbursements of appropriations and other funds for the Indian service, remitted funds to agents and other disbursing officers and examined accounts received from them, received bids from business firms and prepared estimates for submission to Congress, attended to the purchase and transportation of goods for the Indians, maintained records of annuity payments, and invested Indian trust funds.

Record Group 75. --The records of this Division document the Civil War and war-related financial operations of the Office of Indian Affairs. Special files of correspondence pertain to claims, financial affairs of the California Superintendency, interest on Indian trust funds, and land sales. Appropriation ledgers show the many expenditures made for fulfilling treaties with the Indians--the expenses of superintendencies, agencies, and the Civilization Division; compensation of supervisors of reservations; and payments for Indian relief, removal, and subsistence; for holding councils and negotiating treaties; for transportation and delivery of annuities and for their insurance; for erecting buildings for agencies; for contingencies; and for removal of the Sioux, losses from Sioux depredations, and the return of refugee Indians to their homes. Contracts show the terms on which goods and services were obtained. Other wartime financial records include ledgers showing receipts and disbursements of Indian agencies and superintendencies; quarterly statements from Indian agents of property returns and financial reports; amounts owed by superintendents and agents to the Government (1 vol.); a statement of the account of the United States with the Chippewa, 1854-63; files of vouchers for payments for Sioux depredations, 1863; and an account book of the Secretary of the Interior for expenditures regarding Indians, 1859-73. Records submitted by traders of the 1860's to substantiate their claims against various tribes include many account books and ledgers, which are useful for research on the Indian trade.

The annuity payrolls, in which are recorded the "treaty payments" to Indian tribes, are useful as censuses of the Indians. The payrolls are largely for years after the Civil War, but they include rolls of loyal Indians to whom payments were made for losses suffered during the war. The rolls of loyal Creek refugees, freedmen, and soldiers include the roll prepared by F. A. Field in 1870, that by F. S. Lyon in 1871, the McLaughlin roll of 1903, and the Shoenfelt rolls of 1904-5. For the loyal Seminole there is the roll prepared by James E. Jenkins in 1901. With the loyal Shawnee rolls of 1931-35 are some receipts for payments made to those Indians.

Some other records relating to freedmen resulted from the court decision in the case of Moses Whitemire, Trustee v. Cherokee Nation (30 Ct. Cl., 138, 180), Mar. 4, 1895. This suit was brought by Cherokee freedmen to recover their proportionate share of funds of the Cherokee Nation, which as citizens of the nation they regarded as due them. The court decided that the freedmen were citizens equally with the Cherokee and were equally entitled to share in the common property. The procedure for making the payments to the Cherokee freedmen involved the preparation in 1897 of "exhibits" of affidavits, containing information on the freedmen and members of their families. There are also some administration and guardianship letters, 1896-97.

For the Indian trust funds there are some special records spanning the Civil War period: books containing letters sent by the Commissioner of Indian Affairs, a general ledger, a ledger of stocks held in trust for incompetent and minor Chickasaw Indians, statements of stocks held in trust for other Indians, a journal of transactions in such stocks, and a chronological record for Sioux trust funds arising from the sale of ceded lands.

Statistical data on Indian trust funds is in the Reports of the Commissioner of Indian Affairs. The character and amounts of expenditures for 1860-61 can be ascertained from S. Ex. Doc. 31, 37 Cong., 2 sess., Serial 1121, and for 1861-62 from S. Ex. Doc. 39, 37 Cong., 3 sess., Serial 1149.

Land Division

This Division was established in 1846. It had responsibility for matters connected with Indian lands, including cessions, reservations, allotments, sales, scrip, logging, reserves, trust lands, appraisals, and titles.

The Government recognized the right of occupancy by the Indian tribes of the land they claimed as their hunting grounds. This land was held by the tribes in common; the ultimate title to it was claimed by the Government; and the Indians were not allowed to dispose of land to individuals without Government permission. The United States obtained cessions of land from the Indians by negotiating treaties until Mar. 3, 1871, and thereafter by agreements with the Indians. During the Civil War the Government continued its policy of concentrating Indians upon reservations. Some reservation lands were purchased outright; others were held in trust to be sold for the benefit of the Indians; and still others were sold to railroads for rights of way. In 1862 the Indian reservations scattered throughout the Western States comprised 175,000,000 acres of land.

Hodge, Handbook of American Indians, 1:500, 757, 2:372, 804; Schmeckebier, Office of Indian Affairs, p. 78; Royce, Indian Land Cessions in the United States. Lists of Indian reservations are in Donaldson, The Public Land, p. 240-248, 727-747.

Record Group 75. --Most of the letters received regarding Indian lands are in the central file of Indian Office letters received, in the Files and Records Division, but the Land Division also received such letters for examination and action; there is a register of these. The records of the Land Division contain, moreover, many special correspondence files. Small files of letters received, some of which cover the war years only in part, concern deeds and land titles, logging on reserves in Minnesota, Kaw land scrip, Chippewa land scrip, surveys, reservations, land claims by the Cherokee in North Carolina, claims for improvements on reserves, claims for donation or homestead land on reservations, and other subjects. More extensive is a file of correspondence concerning "Indian reserves" (tracts of land set aside for individual Indians); this file includes papers pertaining to lands of freedmen in the Indian Territory. Other records concern land allotments to Indians, Kansas trust lands and other trust lands, land certificates for land issued to various tribes, and land sales. There are also field notes of reservations and plats, maps, and sketches of Indian lands.

Military Pay and Bounty Claims

Three regiments of Indian Home Guards served with the U. S. Army in Kansas and the Indian Territory during the war. The 1st and 2d Regiments were organized in Kansas in 1862 from the refugee Indians, and after these regiments, together with white troops, invaded the Indian Territory in the summer of 1862, the 3d Regiment was recruited from other Indians who had formerly served with the Confederacy. Commanded by white officers, these Indian regiments continued in service until mustered out on May 31, 1865.

After the war provision was made for the payment of back pay, bounties, and pensions to these Indian soldiers, since they had been carried on the rolls of the Army. By a joint resolution of June 18, 1866 (14 Stat. 360), Congress authorized the payment of $100 as bounty to each enlisted man of the Indian regiments. John W. Wright, who in 1865 had presented himself to the Interior Department as attorney for all the Indian Home Guards, was appointed special agent on July 11, 1866, to assemble the claims of Indians for back pay and bounties and to pay the claims. He was to receive only such fees as were authorized by the Department and was to take receipts for payments made to claimants. George C. Whiting was appointed on Mar. 16, 1866, as the agent of the Government to settle pension claims of invalid Indian soldiers and widows and orphans of deceased soldiers. Many complaints were made against Wright, however, and an investigation of his actions was made in 1871-72. This disclosed such gross frauds that the case was referred in Mar. 1872 to the Department of Justice, and a suit against Wright was brought in the supreme court of the District of Columbia. A mass of evidence submitted to the House of Representatives on Apr. 30, 1872, was subsequently ordered to be printed.

Information on payments made to the Indian Home Guards is in various records of the Land Division; these include a schedule of pension payments giving the name of the soldier, his regiment, term of service, name of heir or representative, and remarks as to disposition; records of "admitted" (approved) pension claims of widows and heirs of soldiers; and a roll containing a record of bounty payments made to officers and men of the three regiments in 1868. For bounty payments there are also a schedule or receipts filed by J. W. Wright and a statement showing the amount of original bounty and arrears collected by Wright. Another volume shows the arrears of pay and bounty and pension claims of Indian soldiers. A record of applications for back pay and bounty (filed by widows and heirs of soldiers of the Indian Home Guards, Kansas Cavalry, and other military organizations) gives the disposition of cases and shows that their settlement extended into the 1880's. Other Indians served in the 9th Kansas Volunteer Cavalry; there is a list, 1867, of such soldiers who applied for bounty, additional bounty, back pay, and pensions.

The arrangements for making payments to the Indians through John W. Wright and George C. Whiting and the subsequent investigation of Wright's operations produced a considerable quantity of correspondence, which is grouped in a separate file. It includes letters of the Commissioner of Indian Affairs; the Secretary of the Interior; the Second Auditor; T. A. Baldwin, Seminole Indian agent; L. B. Gunckel, the commissioner appointed to investigate Wright's activities; F. E. Foster and George E. Webster, special investigators of the Pension Office; and J. W. Wright and others associated with him. With the correspondence there are also payrolls, abstracts of payments to pensioners, and lists of warrants for payments to the Cherokee. Some of the foregoing papers relate to the seizure of the Pension Office at Fort Gibson, which was shared by Wright's agent. Several lists of papers found in that office are also available. These records are useful not only for information regarding individual Indian soldiers of the Union and their families but also for the history of the Indian Home Guards and the administration of the payments. A list of claims by Indian Home Guards, submitted by Wright in Nov. 1865, is in the "Irregularly Shaped Papers."

Records Relating to Freedmen of Indian Territory

The treaties of 1866 with the tribes in the Indian Territory provided for the freeing of Negro slaves held by the Indians, for the extension to the freedmen of the rights enjoyed by the Indians, and for the freedmen's share in tribal lands. Government action in subsequent years to obtain for the freedmen their share of the land resulted in records that are valuable for genealogy and for the history of slavery among the Indians at the time of the Civil War. The Cherokee Nation, in legislating for the distribution of $300,000 paid into its treasury for lands west of the Arkansas River by an act of Mar. 3, 1883 (22 Stat. 624), did not provide for the freedmen or for Delaware and Shawnee Indians who had been incorporated in the nation. For these non-Cherokee Congress by an act of Oct. 19, 1888 (25 Stat. 609), appropriated $75,000, to be charged against the Cherokee Nation and to be distributed by the Secretary of the Interior per capita among the freedmen, according to the treaty of July 19, 1866, and among the Delawares and Shawnee. Under an act of Mar. 2, 1889 (25 Stat. 994), John W. Wallace was appointed to prepare census rolls of the Cherokee freedmen for use in making the payments authorized by the act of 1888. Another roll, to be used in distributing the proceeds of the leasing and sale of the Cherokee Strip, was prepared in 1896 by a commission composed of William Clifton, W. P. Thompson, and R. H. Kern.

The citizenship of freedmen was finally determined by the Commission to the Five Civilized Tribes (Dawes Commission). This commission was appointed under an act of Mar. 3, 1893 (27 Stat. 645), to negotiate with the Cherokee, Creeks, Chickasaw, Choctaw, and Seminole for extinguishing national or tribal titles to land either by cession to the United States or by allotment and division in severalty among the eligible Indians. The ultimate objective was the dissolution of the tribal governments and the creation of a State government for Oklahoma. The commission, which came to be known by the name of its chairman, Henry L. Dawes, was authorized by an act of June 10, 1896 (26 Stat. 339), to hear and determine applications for citizenship in any of the tribes and thereafter to prepare a complete roll of citizens of each tribe and a roll of freedmen entitled to tribal membership. The printing of the rolls was provided for by an act of June 21, 1906 (34 Stat. 325). In accordance with agreements made with the Indian Nations by the Dawes Commission, allotments of land were made to the freedmen.

Abel, American Indian Under Reconstruction, p. 273-283; Debo, Rise and Fall of the Choctaw Republic, p. 246-268; Wardell, Cherokee Nation, p. 233, 236-238, 313 ff. ; "Choctaw and Chickasaw Freedmen," Jan. 24, 1898 (S. Doc. 84, 55 Cong., 2 sess., Serial 3593. See also E. Hastain, Index to Choctaw-Chickasaw Deeds and Allottments (Muskogee, Okla., 1908), and Supplement Muskogee, Okla., 1910); "Five Civilized Tribes in Oklahoma; Reports of the Department of the Interior and Evidentiary Papers in Support of S. 7625, a Bill for the Relief of Certain Members of the Five Civilized Tribes in Oklahoma" (S. Doc. 1139, 62 Cong., 3 sess., Serial 6355; Washington, 1912); other lists in S. Docs. 472 and 478, 63 Cong., 2 sess., Serial 6597 (Washington, 1914); John B. Campbell, Campbell's Abstract of Creek Indian Census Cards and Index

(Muskogee, Okla., 1915), and Camp-   Census Cards and Index (Muskogee,
bell's Abstract of Creek Freedmen   Okla., 1915).

The rolls prescribed by the acts mentioned above are in the records of
the Land Division. A record of the names of Choctaw and Chickasaw freedmen admitted to citizenship in 1885 shows the names of all members of the
families, the nationality of the parents, and the names of owners before
emancipation. In another book are a list of the names of Choctaw and Chickasaw freedmen whose titles to citizenship were regarded as doubtful, giving
the same information; and a list of Choctaw and Chickasaw freedmen who
elected to leave the nations. The Wallace roll contains lists of authenticated and admitted freedmen of the Cherokee Nation and a list of others
whose citizenship was doubtful, showing for each the name, age, sex, and
place of residence. There is also a file of testimony taken during the preparation of the Wallace roll. Similar information is in the list of Cherokee
freedmen prepared by Clifton, Thompson, and Kern in 1896. A file of correspondence relating to the freedmen begins about 1872.

For other records pertaining to   Office of the Secretary of the Interior
the enrollment of freedmen among   (Record Group 48) and of the U. S.
the Indians, see the records of the   Court of Claims (Record Group 123).

Superintendencies and Agencies

The chief field representatives of the Office of Indian Affairs were
the Indian superintendents, who generally supervised and controlled all
field employees of the Office. Governors of Territories served ex officio
as superintendents of Indian affairs until gradually Congress set up separate superintendencies. The St. Louis Superintendency, created in 1822,
was continued by an act of June 30, 1834 (4 Stat. 735), which also authorized the Western and Michigan Superintendencies; and later the Southwestern Superintendency was established. By an act of Feb. 27, 1851 (9 Stat.
586), those three superintendencies were discontinued and Indian affairs
east of the Rocky Mountains and north of New Mexico and Texas were administered by the Central, Southern, and Northern Superintendencies. An
act of Mar. 3, 1857 (11 Stat. 185), authorized one superintendent for the
Territories of Oregon and Washington, one for the Territory of New Mexico, and one for the Territory of Utah. The California Superintendency
was divided in 1860 into northern and southern districts under superintending agents. The Oregon and Washington Superintendency was divided into
two superintendencies in 1861. On the creation of the Territories of Dakota, Colorado, and Nevada (1861), Idaho and Arizona (1863), and Montana (1864), their Governors became ex officio superintendents of Indian affairs.
The Southern, Central, and Northern Superintendencies, on the western
limits of settlement, were most affected by the Civil War. The Southern
Superintendency was responsible for the Cherokee, Creeks, Choctaw, Chickasaw, Seminole, Quapaws, Seneca, "Mixed Senecas," and Shawnee living in
the Indian Territory and for the Osage Indians in southern Kansas. The Central Superintendency had supervision of agencies concerned with the Kickapoo, Iowa, Sac and Fox, Kansas, Omaha, Delaware, Ottawa, and a few
Chippewa and Munsee Indians. The many bands of Sioux, Chippewa, and
Winnebagoes came under the Northern Superintendency.

The superintendent and the agents of the Southern Superintendency went over to the Confederacy early in 1861. A new superintendent was appointed by the U. S. Government, but because the Indian Territory was occupied by Confederate forces he made his headquarters at Leavenworth, Kans. A special agent was appointed under the superintendent in 1862 to purchase supplies for refugee Indians from the Indian Territory.

In the person of the superintendent was centered Indian administration in the field. He supervised the agents and their staffs and communicated instructions to them from the Office of Indian Affairs. He negotiated treaties with the Indians, directed the allotment of funds and supplies, provided emergency relief for Indians, issued or revoked licenses to traders, and submitted annual reports to the Office, with recommendations for the management of Indian affairs.

Indian agents, who were assigned to separate tribes or groups of tribes, came into more direct contact with the Indians. Their staffs included subagents, clerks, interpreters, teachers, blacksmiths, carpenters, farmers, millers, and physicians. Their duties included supervising employees, protecting the rights of the Indians, preserving order on the reservations and removing intruders, suppressing the liquor traffic, investigating and reporting on claims for depredations, paying annuities and issuing rations, arranging for visits of chiefs to Washington, settling intertribal disputes, disbursing money, and supervising schools and education.

Hodge, Handbook of American Indians, 1:21-23; Alban W. Hoopes, Indian Affairs and Their Administration, With Special Reference to the Far West, 1849-1860, p. 26-28 (Philadelphia, 1932). The reports of superintendents and agents, published in the Annual Report of the Commissioner of Indian Affairs, are a primary source for their activities. The Official Register, published by the U. S. Government, contains information on superintendencies and agencies, and a list of them with dates of their establishment and discontinuance is in House Committee on Interior and Insular Affairs, Report With Respect to the House Resolution Authorizing the Committee on Interior and Insular Affairs to Conduct an Investigation of the Bureau of Indian Affairs, p. 1584-1592 (H. Rept. 2503, 82 Cong., 2 sess., Serial 11582; Washington, 1953), and p. 1593 ff. for maps of tribal locations and Indian agencies. Information regarding the tribes within particular States is in Swanton, Indian Tribes of North America.

Record Group 75. --Records of Indian superintendencies for the period of the Civil War include those for the Arizona, Central, Dakota, New Mexico, Northern, Oregon, Southern, and Washington Superintendencies. These records usually include correspondence, financial records, and proceedings of treaty negotiations; and they sometimes contain contracts and proposals and property returns. The field records should be differentiated from the records of the Office of Indians Affairs itself. Though other copies of many of the papers in the records of superintendencies are also available in the records of the Office, some correspondence received by the superintendents can be found only in their own records. Records available on microfilm: Oregon Superintendency, 1848-73 (M 2); Washington Superindendency, 1853-74 (M 5).

James R. Masterson, "The Records of the Washington Superintendency of Indian Affairs, 1853-1874," Pacific Northwest Quarterly, 37:31-58 (Jan. 1946). Papers of many Territorial Governors who served ex officio as superintendents of Indian affairs are in numerous non-Federal depositories.

The records kept by the Indian agencies have been imperfectly preserved. In 1865, after the Commissioner of Indian Affairs had learned that it was customary for agents on leaving their posts to take away records properly belonging there, he issued a circular instructing them to preserve and leave as public property duplicate copies of all important papers and vouchers and a complete daily record of all transactions. Even when records were left behind, however, they were neglected in later decades by the responsible officials. The small quantity of records of Indian agencies in the National Archives for the Civil War period include letters sent, to Feb. 1864, by the Southern Apache Agency of the New Mexico Superintendency and letters sent, to May 1862, by the Winnebago Agency of the Northern Superintendency. Some Indian agency records have been transferred to Federal Records Centers. In the center at San Francisco is correspondence of the Round Valley Agency in California, 1864-70. Records of the Puget Sound area and of the Grand Ronde and Siletz Agencies of Oregon are in the center at Seattle.

Records in Other Custody. --The largest collection of Government Indian records not now in Federal custody is in the Oklahoma Historical Society, which, influenced by Grant Foreman, historian of the Oklahoma Indians, became interested in the preservation of records concerning them. In 1929 the society began a calendar of the records relating to the Five Civilized Tribes, then in the custody of the Superintendent of the Five Civilized Tribes at Muskogee, Okla. In 1932, on behalf of the society, a survey was made of the records of Indian agencies in western Oklahoma that did not deal with the Five Civilized Tribes. These records were found to have been neglected, stored under unsatisfactory conditions, and in part lost. A committee appointed by the society succeeded in obtaining an act of Congress, Mar. 27, 1934 (48 Stat. 501), which authorized the Secretary of the Interior to deposit with the Oklahoma Historical Society the records relating to the Five Civilized Tribes and of various Indian agencies in western Oklahoma. (The old records of the Union Agency had been burned on Feb. 23, 1899, in a fire that destroyed the agency building.) Other records authorized for transfer to the society were those relating to the Wichita, Kiowa, Comanche, Caddo, and Apache Indians (from the agent at Anadarko); those relating to the Arapaho and Cheyenne Indians (from the agent at Concho); those relating to the Sac and Fox, Pottawatomie, Kickapoo, and Iowa Indians (from the agent at Shawnee, Okla.); those relating to the Wyandot, Seneca, Quapaw, Peoria, Modoc, and Miami Indians (from the agent at Miami, Okla.); those relating to the Tonkawa, Ponca, Pawnee, Oto, and Kaw Indians (from the agent at Pawnee); and those of the Osage Indians (from the agent at Pawhuska). Dawes Commission records are also held by the Oklahoma Historical Society. Other manuscripts relating to the Cherokee, including papers of John Ross, Cherokee chief, are in the University of Oklahoma Library. A large collection of Ross papers, 1814-70, is in the Thomas Gilcrease Institute of American History and Art, at Tulsa.

The records of numerous agencies examined by the Survey of Federal Archives in the late 1930's are described in its published inventories of the field records of the Department of the Interior. Many agency records that agents took with them on leaving office have found their way into historical societies and libraries. Consequently the guides to depositories in the area in which a researcher is interested should be examined. See also Hamer, ed., Guide to Archives and Manuscripts; and Grant Foreman, "A Survey of Tribal Records in the Archives of the United States Government in Oklahoma," Chronicles of Oklahoma, 11:625-634 (Mar. 1933). Some documentary records of the tribal governments have been printed: see Library of Congress, Guide to the Microfilm Collection of Early State Records, and Supplement, 1951, p. 7-22; and Lester Hargrett, A Bibliography of the Constitutions and Laws of the American Indians (Cambridge, 1947).

OFFICE OF THE COMMISSIONER OF PUBLIC BUILDINGS

From 1816 the administering of Federal public buildings and grounds in the capital city had been in the charge of a Commissioner of Public Buildings, whose post had been authorized by an act of Apr. 29, 1816 (3 Stat. 324). The Commissioner had operated under the "supervisory and appellate powers" of the President until, by sec. 9 of the act of Mar. 3, 1849, establishing the Interior Department, he had been put under the supervision of the Secretary of the Interior. In matters regarding the Capitol and its police, however, the Commissioner had continued to be directed by the presiding officers of the two Houses of Congress. By an act of Aug. 4, 1854 (10 Stat. 573), he was required to submit annual reports and estimates to the Secretary of the Interior, under whose direction appropriations for repairs and improvements of public buildings, grounds, and streets were allocated.

At the beginning of the Civil War the Commissioner of Public Buildings had varied responsibilities. He had charge of the repair and maintenance of the Capitol and the White House and their grounds, superintendence of the Capitol Police, the repair of certain streets and roads, the enclosing and improving of public squares and reservations and the placing of statues in them, construction of the Patent Office Building, and the repair and operation of the "Long Bridge" over the Potomac and the bridge over the Anacostia. These duties required the Commissioner to make frequent inspection trips about the city. Arrangements for the medical treatment of transient paupers, for which an annual appropriation was made by Congress, were also under the care of the Commissioner. When the Washington Infirmary was destroyed by fire in 1861, these patients were cared for in Douglas Hospital, and after the end of Feb. 1864 in the new Providence Hospital.

The Capitol during the war housed not only Congress, but also the Supreme Court, the Library of Congress, the Commissioner of Public Buildings, the Architect of the Capitol, and the U. S. Court of Claims. For a while also the Army quartered soldiers in the Capitol, operated a bakery in the basement, and--in the emergency following the second battle of Manassas--had a hospital in the building. Because of military considerations, the Army took over control of the "Long Bridge" in 1861 and was given formal jurisdiction over it in 1863.

Besides the staff of his own Office, which included a clerk, a messenger, and a laborer, the Commissioner supervised a number of other employees. These included the Capitol Police and their captain; watchmen, gatekeepers, and gardners at the Capitol and the White House; laborers and watchmen at the public grounds and reservations and the public stables; furnace keepers at the Capitol; "draw keepers" on the bridges; and lamplighters. Commissioner French in Sept. 1861 appointed a general superintendent to oversee work in progress. The post of inspector of meters is listed for the first time in the Official Register for 1865.

The Office of Commissioner of Public Buildings was abolished by an act of Mar. 2, 1867 (14 Stat. 466), and its functions were transferred to the Office of the Chief of Engineers (War Department), in which an Office of Public Buildings and Grounds was formed.

Successive Commissioners during the war period:

John B. Blake, June 5, 1855.
William S. Wood, June 13, 1861.
Benjamin B. French, Sept. 7, 1861.

H. P. Caemmerer, Washington, the National Capital (S. Doc. 332, 71 Cong., 3 sess., Serial 9343; Washington, 1932); Fred A. Emery, "Washington's Historic Bridges," Columbia Historical Society, Records, 39:49-70 (1938); Cornelius W. Heine, A History of National Capital Parks ([Washington], 1953); U. S. Congress, Joint Select Committee to Investigate the Charities and Reformatory Institutions in the District of Columbia, Historical Sketches of Charities and Reformatory Institutions in the District of Columbia (S. Rept. 781, 55 Cong., 2 sess., Serial 3565; also H. Rept. 1092, 55 Cong., 2 sess., Serial 3723; both published in Washington, 1898).

Record Group 42. -- During the Civil War the Commissioner of Public Buildings carried on correspondence with many people. His letter books contain copies of communications to the Secretary of the Interior transmitting accounts, reports, and estimates; replying to instructions; giving information on employees and the condition of the city lot account; and making recommendations for repairs and improvements to the White House, the public grounds, and streets. The Commissioner corresponded direct with Congress concerning Capitol repairs and improvements and the management of the Capitol Police. To the police captain he sent instructions for the administration of his men. He wrote to other Government officials and (infrequently) to the President and to Mrs. Lincoln concerning the upkeep of the White House. Appointments to positions under the Commissioner's control, dismissals, acceptances of resignations, and other communications are also recorded in the letter books, as are copies of letters to business firms about materials or furnishings for the White House, to contractors about work on the White House, and to the Washington and Georgetown Railroad Co. and the Washington Gas-Light Co. about their facilities. The Commissioner often had to communicate with the mayor of Washington, the chief of the Metropolitan Police, and other local officials; and to write to private citizens about the sale of public lots or to warn against illegal occupancy of public grounds. An alphabetical index facilitates finding letters to particular persons. Letters received, which are filed numerically and indexed in registers, are largely from the same correspondents and on the same subjects. The correspondence is one of the principal sources for the history of the capital during the war. Besides the subjects already mentioned, it contains papers concerning President Lincoln's funeral, the arrangements for which were made by the Commissioner.

Two other files supply more information on people seeking jobs in the Federal District during the war. A box of applications and recommendations for employment contains letters and recommendations from Congressmen, the Secretary of the Interior, and citizens of Washington, Georgetown, the State of Virginia, and other States; and individual applications for employment in positions under the Commissioner's jurisdiction. Filed numerically, these letters give biographical data and information on the party affiliation of the applicants. A few resignations are also in this file. Easier to consult is an alphabetical file of oaths of allegiance taken by persons who were actually employed.

Some financial records give not only information about expenditures but also the names of employees under the Commissioner and those of business firms with which he dealt. The ledger lists periodically the names of employees to whom salary payments were made. In the ledger are also recorded expenditures made for other purposes, including services of various kinds; repairs and improvements of the Capitol, the White House, and the bridges; construction of the Patent Office Building; purchases of tools, supplies, furnishings, fuel, and books; and payments to hospitals for the care of paupers. Though largely duplicatory, other information about the capital city during the war can sometimes be gleaned from requisitions for funds, receipted accounts for services and supplies, canceled checks, check stubs, certificates of deposit, a statement of expenditures on the "Long Bridge" for 1836-68, invoices for furnishings and books bought for the White House, and bills and other documents concerning President Lincoln's funeral.

Records concerning the Commissioner of Public Buildings are in the records of the Senate and the House of Representatives (Record Groups 46 and 233), both of which bodies had committees on public buildings and grounds and committees on the District of Columbia.

Information on the Commissioner's expenditures is in General Accounting Office records (Record Group 217), and correspondence on his maintenance and construction operations is in the records of the Office of the Secretary of the Interior (see above).

Records in Other Custody. -- The papers of Commissioner Benjamin B. French, in the Library of Congress, contain many letters written by French to his family during the war. Although these relate largely to personal affairs, they make many references to the conduct of the Office of the Commissioner and to wartime events in Washington. Some other pertinent records are among those of the Architect of the Capitol, still in his custody.

PENSION OFFICE

The appointment of a Commissioner of Pensions under the Secretary of War had been authorized by an act of Mar. 2, 1833 (4 Stat. 688). The Commissioner had become responsible in 1840 for administering Navy as well as Army pensions and had functioned under the joint direction of the Secretaries of War and the Navy until 1849, when their "supervisory and appellate powers" over the acts of the Commissioner had been transferred to the Secretary of the Interior.

When the Civil War began, the Washington staff of the Pension Office included a chief clerk, 61 clerks, 3 messengers, 3 laborers, and a watchman; its field agents were 49 pension agents stationed throughout the States and Territories. The number of clerks was doubled within the next 2 years, and later during the war some temporary clerks and copyists were added. The clerks examined claims for different kinds of pensions, recorded or copied documents, and handled mail and filing. The pension agents, appointed by the Secretary of the Interior, served as area disbursing agents to pay pensions. Their compensation and allowances for expenses were regulated by acts of July 17, 1862, and June 30, 1864 (12 Stat. 629; 13 Stat. 325). Physicians were appointed throughout the country to examine applicants for pensions and to make biennial examinations of pensioners, and an act of July 4, 1864 (13 Stat. 387), permitted claimants to make declarations before notaries public, justices of the peace, or other duly authorized officers if the claimants lived more than 25 miles from courts of record.

Federal pension agents in the Confederate States were suspended from office in 1861, but as parts of the South came under the control of the Federal Government an attempt was made to find the former agents in order to settle their accounts. (The payment of pensions to persons in the Confederate States who had fought against the United States or had encouraged the Southern cause was suspended in 1861, and by an act of Feb. 4, 1862--12 Stat. 337--the names of such persons were stricken from the pension rolls.) Pension agencies were reestablished in the South in 1865 to restore pensions to those who could prove their continuous loyalty and to receive applications from new claimants.

At the beginning of the war pensions were granted to disabled soldiers under existing laws, but these laws did not provide for widows and orphans of deceased soldiers. Pensioners were required from 1861 onward to take an oath of allegiance in order to receive payments. An act of July 17, 1861 (12 Stat. 607), made special provision for a Navy pension fund to be established from the sale of prizes taken by the Navy. This fund amounted by 1866 to almost $12,000,000, and the interest on it was more than sufficient to pay pensions to officers, seamen, and marines.

The first and most important Civil War pension act, however, was that of July 14, 1862 (12 Stat. 566). This act made eligible for pensions officers and enlisted men of the Army, Navy, and Marines disabled after Mar. 4, 1861, by wounds inflicted or disease contracted in service and in line of duty. It also provided pensions not only for widows or children of men entitled to pensions who had died after Mar. 4, 1861, but also for their dependent mothers or orphan sisters. The liberal terms of this enactment increased the number of pension claims and proofs of claims submitted, and threw more work on the Pension Office.

Another Civil War act--that of July 4, 1864, mentioned above--still further liberalized the pension system. It authorized pensions for volunteers who had served with the armed forces and for men who had volunteered and served in engagements with "rebels" or Indians; it provided pensions for widows or other dependents of deceased volunteers; and it allowed pensions to widows of Negro soldiers without requiring other proof of marriage than that the parties had habitually lived together.

Long after the war a series of service pension laws beginning with an act of June 27, 1890 (26 Stat. 182), made increasingly liberal provisions for survivors, their widows, and their dependents. An act of Aug. 5, 1892 (27 Stat. 348), provided for the pensioning of women who had been employed by the Surgeon General of the Army as nurses during the Civil War or whose employment as nurses had been "recognized by the War Department." During the years after the war and well into the twentieth century many private laws were also passed for the relief of individuals whose claims to pensions had been rejected under the general laws.

Successive Commissioners of Pensions during the war period:

George C. Whiting, Jan. 1857.
Joseph H. Barrett, Apr. 1861.

William H. Glasson, Federal Military Pensions in the United States (New York, 1918); Gustavus A. Weber, The Bureau of Pensions; Its History, Activities, and Organization (Baltimore, 1923); Gustavus A. Weber and Laurence F. Schmeckebier, The Veterans' Administration; Its History, Activities, and Organization (Washington, 1934); "Report of the Commissioner of Pensions," 1861-65, in U. S. Department of the Interior, Annual Report, 1861-65 (Washington, 1862-66).

Record Group 15. --Now a part of the records of the Veterans Administration, the Pension Office records important to Civil War research comprise administrative records, pension case files, and financial records. Many of these records, of course, are of the postwar period but are directly related to the war. The types of records are discussed separately below.

Administrative Records

These are records accumulated by the Office of the Chief Clerk and the Pension Bureau Library. Records relating to pension appeals include registers of appeals and decisions of the Secretary of the Interior on appeals reported to the Secretary by the Commissioner of Pensions. Many such appeals and decisions concern Civil War cases. For Civil War hospitals there are indexes to records of the Adjutant General's Office pertaining to hospitals, a guide to hospitals, a list of general and post hospitals in Washington and Georgetown, D. C., and records relating to the use of the Delaney House in Washington as a field hospital. Some materials regarding National and State homes for soldiers and sailors are of interest, for they supply information about inmates who were veterans of the Civil War. Statistical items include lists and charts showing the numbers of men engaged in different wars and the numbers of pensioners. Other administrative records are a register of boards of examining surgeons, beginning in 1862; a table of U. S. bounties authorized during the Civil War, showing classes of enlistments, character of service, and limits of enlistments for bounties; a photograph of 24 employees of the Pension Office, including Commissioner Barrett; and a framed charcoal sketch of George C. Whiting.

Various items relating to the war were presented to the successor Bureau of Pensions. These include a register of patients at a convalescent camp at Vicksburg, Miss., which was kept by Dr. Joseph Speck in 1863; extracts from the diary, 1861-64, of Capt. Joseph Waldo Denny, 25th Massachusetts Volunteers; and a scrapbook of clippings from the Peoria (Ill.) Evening Star of 1917 that printed a diary, 1861-64, kept by Philip Smith of the 8th Missouri Volunteer Infantry. A printed list of officers of the Union Army and Navy imprisoned in Libby Prison, at Richmond, 1863-64, is probably available elsewhere also. A volume of reports of the special committee on volunteering for New York County, 1864, contains a list of all volunteers furnished the Army and Navy by that county, Aug. 1, 1862-May 31, 1864; and another volume labeled "Hyde Park Bounty A/C" contains a record of bounties paid to individuals in the town of Hyde Park, N. Y., for Civil War enlistments and of money paid by drafted men to their substitutes.

National Archives, Preliminary Inventory [No. 55] of the Administrative Records of the Bureau of Pensions and the Pension Service, comp. by Thayer M. Boardman, Myra R. Trever, and Louise W. Southwick (Washington, 1953). The correspondence files of the Pension Office are missing. Other records relating to pensions are in the records of the Office of the Secretary of the Interior.

In the census of 1890 an enumeration was made of the Union survivors of the Civil War or their widows. This was done to ascertain their numbers for pension legislation purposes and to provide addresses of veterans to whom their comrades could write for testimony to support pension claims. The special schedules that resulted list the names of those who served in the U. S. Army, Navy, and Marine Corps during the Civil War, and give for each man his residence, rank, company and regiment (or vessel if a Navy veteran), dates of enlistment and discharge, length of service, and any disability incurred. These schedules were transferred by an act of Apr. 21, 1894 (28 Stat. 60), to the Bureau of Pensions for the use of the Army and Navy Survivors' Division. Nearly all the schedules for the District of Columbia and the States of Alabama through Kansas and half of those for Kentucky are missing; the schedules still extant are for the States of Louisana through Wyoming.

These schedules have been microfilmed on 118 rolls (M 123), and the States and counties for which they are available are named in List of National Archives Microfilm Publications. Statistical data derived from the schedules are published in U. S. Census Office, Report on Population of the United States at the Eleventh Census: 1890, p. clxxii-clxxv (Washington, 1897). See also Evangeline Thurber, "The 1890 Census Records of Veterans of the Union Army," National Genealogical Society Quarterly, 34:7-9 (Mar. 1946).

In examining the flood of pension applications during 1861-62, the Pension Office staff became aware that attempts were being made to defraud the Government, and the Commissioner of Pensions detailed clerks to try to detect frauds. The act of July 14, 1862, provided for the appointment of a special agent in the Pension Office to assist in detecting and prosecuting fraud. Bradford Rixford became special agent on July 19, 1862, but the statutory provision for the position was repealed by the act of July 4, 1864, which authorized the temporary detail of clerks to investigate suspected fraud. This function became a regular duty of the Pension Office and eventually was put under its Law Division; after the consolidation with the Veterans' Bureau, it was assigned to the Office of the Solicitor. The pertinent records are case files of investigations made in connection with Civil War pensions; they relate to charges of malfeasance against individual attorneys, pension agents, notaries, and others. The files contain correspondence between the Commissioner of Pensions and attorneys for pensioners or claimants; and correspondence with notaries public, examining surgeons, certifying officers, and others. In cases in which infractions of the law or rules were discovered, there are also reports from special examiners, exhibits, depositions, affidavits, copies of rules and regulations, reports of indictments and of court proceedings, and appeals for reconsideration. Some files relate to the oath required of attorneys for admission to practice, powers of attorney, substitution, and consent to transfer of attorneyship; others contain forms returning information on changes of address or death. Information on the status of attorneys, firms, subagents, and organizations admitted to prosecute claims before the Bureau of Pensions is in a card file, which serves as an index to the case files.

Pension Files

The pension records that concern the Civil War period are among the following classes of case files: Civil War and later military operations, 1861-1934; the Navy, 1861-1910; Indian wars, 1817-98; and the Mexican War, 1846-48. Subgroups in each class are as follows: "survivors' originals," consisting of rejected applications and accompanying papers; "survivors' certificates," consisting of papers for cases in which pensions were granted; "widows' and dependents' originals," similar in content to the "survivors' originals"; and "widows' and dependents' certificates," similar in content to the "survivors' certificates." The typical case file contains the original application for pension, a jacket covering the claim before its allowance and another jacket covering the claim after its allowance, a brief of the case prepared by the Pension Office, a statement of the claimant's military record supplied by the War or Navy Department, affidavits and other documentary evidence supporting the claim, correspondence, a certificate of discharge, a birth certificate, a marriage certificate, a certificate of death and papers relating to claims for burial expenses (if the claim was filed by a widow), and a returned questionnaire supplying family data. A file may also contain papers giving powers of attorney, papers relating to guardianship, a medical history, personal histories of dependents, and decisions of adjudicating agencies. Materials that do not fit the case files are in a separate file; they include such items as family Bibles, diaries, account books, and photographs. The pension case files include, of course, cases of Negroes and Indians who served in the Union forces during the Civil War. Although an alphabetical card index to the files has been retained by the Veterans Administration, a microfilm of it is available.

The nature of these records is suggested by the requirements of the Pension Office that claimants submit documentation establishing their rights to receive pensions. Circulars issued by the Commissioner of Pensions, July 21, 1862, provided separate instructions to be followed in applying for Army or Navy pensions; both required declarations made before a court of record or before an authorized officer of such a court, as well as testimony taken before a justice of the peace or other officer authorized to administer oaths. The testimony was to prove a claimant's identity and, in the case of an applicant for an invalid pension, the circumstances of a wound or disability. The surgeon's certificate for discharge or, if that was lacking, the certificate of an Army or Navy surgeon or of "two respectable civil surgeons" had to be submitted. Furthermore, two credible witnesses were required to testify to the habits of the applicant. For widows, minor children, mothers, and sisters, proofs of marriage, birth, age, or relationship, as appropriate, were required; and the guardians of minor claimants had to produce evidence of their authority. The legality of a marriage could be established by the submission of the certificate of the officiating clergyman; and the ages and number of children by the mother's deposition, by the testimony of persons having knowledge of the facts, or by duly authenticated transcripts from parish or town registers.

With respect to claims of invalid veterans, they could be proved by "record" evidence only or by "record" and "parol" evidence, but never by "parol" evidence alone. The Adjutant and Surgeon Generals' reports and certificates of disability constituted what was called the "record." The Adjutant General was sole judge of all questions pertaining to enlistment, service, and discharge of a soldier. Parole evidence was testimony of any character, other than "record," tending to establish a claim. The comparable record of service of naval personnel was obtained, for officers, from the Chief of the Bureau of Navigation; for seamen, from the Fourth Auditor of the Treasury; and for marines, from the Commandant of the Marine Corps. The record of disabilities was obtained from the Surgeon General of the Navy.

Among U. S. Army general officers whose names appear in the pension case files through their widows' claims to pensions are Daniel E. Sickles (WC 785, 655); George A. Custer (WC 178, 408); U. S. Grant, whose widow was pensioned by act of Congress (WC 219, 162); William Grose (WC 525,-208), and George Gordon Meade (WC 219, 235). The file of Mary Lincoln (WC 146, 718), widow of the President, who was pensioned by an act of Congress in 1870, contains several letters written by Robert Todd Lincoln.

Case files of interest because of the kind of service rendered by the applicant include those on John L. Worden, commander of the U. S. S. Monitor at the time of its engagement with the C. S. S. Virginia (NWC 12, 948); David Baker, who assisted in the capture of John Wilkes Booth (WC 665,992); Boston Corbett, who shot Booth during his capture (SC 218, 545); Pauline Cushman ("Pauline Dickinson, now Fryer"), theatrical star and Union Spy (WC 363, 644); George Beniski, Grover Cleveland's substitute (SO 561, 108); Lemuel M. Hancock, chaplain of the 49th Indiana Volunteer Infantry (WC 582, 165); John S. Staples, alleged substitute or "representative" of Abraham Lincoln (Min C 336, 972); Emma A. Porch (née Emma Alvira Smith), who served in late 1864 as despatch bearer, guide, scout, and spy in the Department of Missouri (SC 276, 360); S. Emma E. Seelye (alias Franklin Thompson), pensioned for her service as a soldier of Co. F, 2d Mich. Volunteer Infantry (Special Act SC 282, 136); Robert Smalls, a Negro who single-handed seized the Confederate gunboat Planter and turned it over to the U. S. Navy in May 1862 (NSC 18, 992); Lewis K. Whitmore, "locomotive engineer in the military service" during the war (SC 963, 259); Feliz G. Stidger, Union spy engaged in counterespionage, 1864-65, against the Copperheads of the Northwest (C 2, 518, 210); and Timothy Webster, a detective of the U. S. Secret Service who was executed as a spy, Apr. 13, 1862, in Richmond (WC 142, 855).

The pension cases illustrate the occasional perpetration of frauds--one by a former Confederate prisoner of war who became a bounty jumper.

The pension case files may also be used to illuminate the lives of persons whose later or nonmilitary careers transcend in importance their Civil War service. Such a case is that of Benjamin F. Stephenson, a Civil War surgeon who founded the Grand Army of the Republic (WC 171, 985). The cases may also supplement regimental or company history; for example, one file (on George W. Buck, Min C 72, 980) contains what appears to be an

original muster roll of Company G, 21st Wis. Volunteers, Dec. 31, 1863-
Feb. 29, 1864, and the original monthly returns for the same company,
July-Aug. 1864. The pension claims files also throw light on the enlistment in the U. S. Army of Confederate prisoners of war, for the Frontier
Service, and the question of the eligibility of such persons for pensions (see
the cases of George W. Kirk, WC 571,150, and George W. Nelson, C 2,467,-
751).

Case files and other records relating to the provision of artificial limbs or other prosthetic devices for veterans are described under the Surgeon General's Office, War Department. Forms used in the Civil War decade in applying for pensions and instructions regarding their preparation are in Henry C. Harmon, A Manual of the Pension Laws of the United States of America . . . (Washington, 1867). Lists of pensioners on the rolls in 1883 are in S. Ex. Doc. 84, 47 Cong., 2 sess., Serials 2078-2082 (Washington, 1883). A list of the names of Indian claimants on the pension rolls in 1866 is in H. Rept. 96, 42 Cong., 2 sess., Serial 1543.

Financial Records

A number of records provide information on payments made to pensioners
or the widows of servicemen. The most extensive series is the pension agency
roll books, 1805-1912, arranged by pension agency. These roll books contain records of payments made to pensioners through the agencies, give data
concerning military service and pension payments, and sometimes provide
genealogical data. A card index to the roll books is of some help in finding
records of payments to individual pensioners. A record on cards of the
establishment and administrative history of the pension agencies facilitates
the use of the card index. A file of award cards, which in 1912 superseded
the pension roll books, is easier to use than the roll books because it is arranged alphabetically by name. There are also roll books of Army invalid
pensioners, Army widow pensioners, Navy pensioners, Navy widow pen-
sioners, and Navy invalid pensioners. "Abstracts of payments to pension-
ers," received from pension agents, cover not only payments to pensioners
but also other disbursements made by the agents. In several series arranged in different ways are records of certificates issued to pensioners.
A special record of Navy invalid and widow pensioners is available for 1857-
65. The numbers of pensioners under different laws can be ascertained
from statistical records. (Other records concerning payments to pensioners
are now in the General Accounting Office records, Record Group 217.)

PATENT OFFICE

After more than 40 years during which patents had been issued by the
Secretary of State (act of Feb. 21, 1793; 1 Stat. 318), the Patent Office had
been established in the State Department under a Commissioner of Patents
(act of July 4, 1836; 5 Stat. 117). The 1836 act required investigations of
inventions submitted for patents to determine their priority, novelty, and
utility before issuing patents for them; required fees from applicants (which
provided funds for operating the Office); and authorized the establishment
in the Office of a "library of scientific works and periodical publications."
Under an act of Aug. 29, 1842 (5 Stat. 542), the Patent Office had authority
to issue patents (for a period of 7 years) for designs of manufactured

materials, art objects, and impressions or ornaments. The registration
of trademarks was not to be provided for until 1870. By the act of Mar. 3,
1849, establishing the Department of the Interior, the Patent Office had
been transferred to the new Department, where it was to remain until its
transfer to the Department of Commerce in this century.

In the first months of the Civil War the number of applications received
by the Patent Office declined and the fees consequently decreased. As a result the examining and clerical force of the Office had to be reduced. Several employees who refused to take the prescribed oath of allegiance resigned or were removed. In Sept. 1861, according to the Official Register,
the staff comprised a chief clerk, 3 examiners in chief, 8 primary examiners, 7 assistant examiners, a librarian, 3 copiers of drawings, 18 clerks,
22 temporary clerks, a messenger, and 5 watchmen. Subsequent lists
show also a "machinist" and a disbursing clerk. As chief administrative
assistant to the Commissioner, the chief clerk received and distributed incoming mail and franked the outgoing mail. The patent examiners scruti-
nized the specifications, claims, models, and drawings to make sure that
they were consistent and searched the patent files of the office, patent publications of European governments, and other publications to determine
whether devices were patentable. From the large drawings submitted by
applicants, the copiers prepared small drawings that were engraved as il-
lustrations to accompany the Patent Office reports. The clerks recorded
letters, patents, specifications, and transfers of patents; transcribed patents onto parchments; abstracted transfers of patents; and kept accounts of
fees received. The "machinist" received, classified, and arranged the
models, which were exhibited in halls open to visitors in Washington as well
as to inventors. During the Civil War, however, the model rooms were
used as a hospital, and toward the end of 1862 they sheltered 800 wounded
soldiers.

An act of Mar. 2, 1861 (12 Stat. 246), provided for the appointment of
three examiners in chief as a board to consider appeals from applicants
whose patent applications had been rejected, to review decisions of examiners in interference cases, and--when required by the Commissioner--to
consider applications for the extension of patents. Under this provision,
which legalized a practice already developed in the Office, appeals could be
taken from the board to the Commissioner. Until 1863 decisions of the
Commissioner could be appealed to the circuit court of the District of Columbia (act of Aug. 30, 1852; 10 Stat. 75); thereafter appeals were taken to
the District's supreme court.

Though at first a brake on invention, the war soon stimulated inventors'
creative activities. By 1862 Commissioner David P. Holloway considered
it "remarkable that the inventive genius of the nation within the last few
years had taken a direction which has prepared the nation for the enormous
demands upon her men and treasures." The war, he reported, had "stimulated our creative power in every branch of industry"; for the year 1863 had
seen the patenting not only of 240 inventions in implements of war but also
of 490 inventions of agricultural implements. Commissioner Holloway, having found the "classification of inventions, by means of which the work of examination was distributed into distinct departments, and the vast collection
of drawings and models arranged for ready reference, defective in philosophical arrangement, while the development of new branches of industry exhibited the need of forming new classes," prepared a new classification. The
primary headings of this were as follows:

A. Agriculture.
B. Calorifics; Photics, Lamps, Including Lanterns, Gas, etc.
C. Carriages and Land Conveyances.
D & E. Chemical Processes; Manufacture and Compositions of Matter.
F. Engineering.
G. Fibrous and Textile Manufactures, including Looms, Sewing and Knitting Machines, etc., etc.
H. Fine Arts and Games.
I. Fire-arms and other Implements of War.
J. Household Furniture.
K. Hydraulics and Pneumatics.
L. Leather and Harness.
M. Lumber.
N. Mathematical and Philosophical Instruments, Electricity, etc.
O. Medical and Surgical Instruments.
P. Metallurgic Manufactures.
Q. Metallurgy.
R. Navigation.
S. Steam and Air Engines.
T. Glass, Stone and Clay.
U. Wearing Apparel.

In the class of "Fire-arms and other Implements of War" were included inventions for cannon, projectiles, small arms, cartridges, and tents. Rifled cannon, breech-loading rifles, and machineguns were introduced during the war but were not extensively used because of some initial imperfections and because of War Department conservatism. Patents for improvements in gunpowder were also issued during the war. Armament and revolving gun turrets for war vessels were developed, and their wartime use foredoomed the wooden ships. Patents were granted also for balloons and for telegraph and railroad instruments. Many patents in the class of "Medical and Surgical Instruments" were for artificial limbs. But, to quote further from Commissioner Holloway, "Numerous improvements in hospital beds, ambulances, stretchers, apparatus for treating fractured and bruised limbs and wounds by a constant drip of cold water, coffins and burial cases, all bear melancholy testimony to the horrors of war."
Successive Commissioners of Patents during the war period:
> Samuel T. Shugert (acting), Dec. 14, 1860.
> David P. Holloway, Mar. 28, 1861.
> Thomas C. Theaker, Aug. 16, 1865.

P. J. Federico, "Evolution of Patent Office Appeals," Patent Office Society, Journal, 22:838-864, 920-949 (Nov., Dec. 1940); Thomas B. Hudson, "A Brief History of the Development of Design Patent Protection in the United States," ibid., 30:380-400 (May 1948); Harry Kursch, Inside the U. S. Patent Office; the Story of the Men, the Laws, and the Procedures of the American Patent System (New York, 1959); Berkeley R. Lewis, Small Arms and Ammunition in the United States Service (Washington, 1956); President's Commission on Economy and Efficiency, Report of the Investigation of the United States Patent Office (H. Doc. 110, 62 Cong., 3 sess., Serial 6469; Washington, 1912); Gustavus A. Weber, The Patent Office; Its History, Activities and Organization (Baltimore, 1924); "Charges against the Commissioner of Patents," Mar. 2, 1863, H. Rept. 48, 37 Cong., 3 sess., Serial 1173. The Report of the Commissioner of Patents for each wartime year appeared as follows:

1861. H. Ex. Doc. 53, 37 Cong., 2 sess., Serials 1131-1133.
1862. H. Ex. Doc. 52, 37 Cong., 2 sess., Serials 1166, 1167.
1863. H. Ex. Doc. 60, 38 Cong., 1 sess., Serials 1191, 1192.
1864. H. Ex. Doc. 51, 38 Cong., 2 sess., Serials 1225, 1226.
1865. H. Ex. Doc. 52, 39 Cong., 1 sess., Serials 1257-1259.

Record Group 241. --Records of the Patent Office include records of patents issued, 1860-70. In that period the application for a patent included a petition, a specification, a drawing, and a model. In the specification, besides describing the invention, the inventor was required to set forth the part, improvement, or combination that he claimed as his discovery. The patent application files ("patented files"), 1836-1900, are arranged by patent number; patents granted, Jan. 1, 1861-Dec. 26, 1865, are numbers 31, 005-51, 783. The application files include the petitions, specifications and claims, reports by patent examiners accepting or rejecting the claims, rejoinders by inventors or their attorneys, oaths of invention taken by applicants, additional reports and rejoinders, printed copies of patents as granted, powers of attorney, notices of allowances and fee payments, fee receipts, and correspondence with inventors or their attorneys. The papers are folded and arranged by patent number in jackets on which are recorded the steps in the examining procedure. The amended specifications and claims of approved patents were engrossed on parchment for sending to the patentees, and record copies were made on signatures bound together in volumes for preservation in the Office. The drawings--larger than the other documents and of different sizes--are in a separate file, also arranged by patent number. Drawings for reissued patents are in another separate file, as are those for improvements to patented inventions; the latter file, however, ends in 1861, when the section of the act of 1836 that permitted the patenting of improvements was repealed. This patent extension file, 1836-61, includes patents for which rights were extended for a 7-year period beyond the original 14 years allowed by the act of 1836. All these files provide a useful starting point for the history of Civil War invention in many fields, though they seldom contain much information on the origin of the inventions. The published Subject-Matter Index cited below serves as an index to the patent application files. "Contested interference files" document the procedures used to determine conflicting or interfering applications between rival inventors or between an application and an unexpired patent for the same invention. More heavily documented than the patent application files and containing valuable information on the development and use of inventions, the "contested interference files" are an important source for the history of science and technology.

Other extensive record series, most of them dating from 1836, are in the Federal Records Center at Alexandria, Va. Registers of applications, which served as control devices during the processing of patent applications, are accompanied by index volumes. In "transfers of patents" are the documents such as deeds, transfers, assignments, and licenses, by which inventors transferred their property rights in patents and in pending applications to other persons. The documents in the "tranfers of patents" are briefed and indexed by name of inventor in "digests of assignments." Printed copies of specifications and claims in selected inactive classes and subclasses of patents and registers of design patent files, 1843-1936, containing applications and drawings of the designs, are also in the Alexandria center.

Nathan Reingold, "U. S. Patent Office Records as Sources for the History of Invention and Technological Property," Technology and Culture, 1:156-167 (Spring 1960); U. S. Patent Office, Subject-Matter Index of Patents for Inventions Issued by the United States Patent Office From 1790 to 1873, Inclusive (Washington, 1874. 3 vols.). Several special indexes have been published by the Patent Office, and digests of different kinds of patents have been issued by commercial presses. The correspondence files of the Patent Office have been destroyed (H. Doc. 577, 61 Cong., 2 sess., Serial 5836); so have the files of applications not approved for patent. Correspondence between the Commissioner of Patents and the Secretary of the Interior is in Record Group 48, which also contains applications for appointment in the Patent Office, letters of appointment, and commissions. Records relating to the construction of the Patent Office Building, which was still underway during the Civil War, are in Record Group 42. At considerable expense the Government published in the annual reports of the Commissioner of Patents abstracts of specifications and claims of patents and lists of patents and patentees. These are useful finding aids for name searches in the files and are a convenient summary of inventions during the Civil War period. Some of the models in the Patent Office were destroyed by fire in Sept. 1877. Much later, in 1925-26, after some models had been selected for preservation by the Smithsonian Institution, the rest were sold (see Donald W. Hogan, "Unwanted Treasures of the Patent Office," American Heritage, 9:16-19, 101-103; Feb. 1958).

Records in Other Custody.--Some records have been retained by the Patent Office for the use of its examiners and of the general public. In 1866 the Patent Office began to print patent specifications, claims, and drawings in order to have reference copies for its own use, to furnish other copies to the patentees, to exchange them with the British Government in return for copies of its patents, and to have copies for sale. Printing the patents provided a compact text in uniform size suitable for binding, assured an exact reproduction of the original, and precluded the possibility of alteration. The printing was gradually extended back to 1836. In the searchroom of the Patent Office are two sets of bound printed patents, one arranged numerically by patent number and the other according to the patent classification system. The patents are indexed by number, by inventor's name, and by patent classification. The numerical file of patents for Jan. 1, 1861, to Dec. 26, 1865, is printed in volumes 163 to 215 of the set of volumes in which patents are arranged numerically. The "reissue patented files" (from 1836) contain corrected patent grants necessitated by defects in the original patents. Copies of certificates issued to patentees cover 1839-87. Decisions (from 1853) of the Commissioner and the board of chief examiners on appeals from decisions of patent examiners and on petitions and motions are used as precedents by the examiners and other personnel of the Patent Office. An abstract of decisions, 1837-1917, of courts of the District of Columbia on patent appeals is available. Registers of the interference case files and the patent extension files (discussed above under Record Group 241) have been retained in the Patent Office.

"Printing of Documents by the Patent Office; Abridgment of American Patents," June 8, 1882 (H. Misc. Doc. 41, 47 Cong., 1 sess., Serial 2046). The printed reports of the circuit and supreme courts of the District of Columbia ("D. C. Reports") contain a few patent appeal cases; most of the patent decisions of these courts, however, are available only in their records. Cases involving patent infringements can also be found in records of other circuit and district courts.

Copyright Library

Copyright protection had been extended by law since 1790 to the authors or owners of books, maps, charts, musical compositions, prints, cuts, and engravings. The titles of these works had to be registered with the clerks of U. S. district courts, and copies of the works themselves had to be deposited with the clerks for yearly transmission to the Department of State. An act of Feb. 5, 1859 (11 Stat. 380), provided that the copyright deposits and the records relating to them should "be removed to, and be under the control of the Department of the Interior." Upon its transfer to the Department, the Copyright Library was assigned to the Patent Office, and during the Civil War its librarian was Edmund Flagg. At the time of the transfer in 1859 there were about 40,000 items in the copyright library. During the war more pieces were received from district court clerks, who continued to register copyrights and to receive the copies. The Librarian of Copyrights also maintained a register of copyrights. Copyright protection was extended to photographs and photographic negatives by an act of Mar. 3, 1865 (13 Stat. 540). (See Richard R. Bowker, Copyright; Its History and Its Law; Boston and New York, 1912.)

Records in Other Custody. --An act of July 8, 1870 (16 Stat. 212), transferred the administration of the copyright laws to the Library of Congress. The act also transferred to the Library of Congress the Copyright Library, together with records relating to copyrights; and it provided that thereafter copyright material should be sent direct to the Library of Congress for deposit. Copyright records in that Library include the register that was kept in the Patent Office, Jan. 10, 1860-July 5, 1870. Other copyright records transferred from the Patent Office to the Library of Congress include an index to copyrights, a letter book containing copyright correspondence of the Commissioner of Patents, 1859-70, and lists of publications, photographs, etc., which were not registered but which were kept in the Patent Office Library. The original copyright registers kept by clerks of district courts are also in the Library of Congress. Gaps in those registers can be filled from the copies of the registers sent to the Secretary of State and the Secretary of the Interior by court clerks. The copyright records are valuable for study of the state of American literature and typography during the Civil War.

U. S. Library of Congress, Records in the Copyright Office Deposited by the United States District Courts Covering the Period, 1790-1870, comp. by Martin A. Roberts (Washington, 1939).

CENSUS OFFICE

Supervision over marshals and others who took the census of the United States had been transferred in 1849, by the act establishing the Interior Department, from the Secretary of State to the Secretary of the Interior. The decennial census of 1860 was conducted as provided by an act of May 23, 1850 (9 Stat. 428). That act had put the census of 1850 under the direction of the Secretary of the Interior; but, after finishing its work on the 1850 census, the staff of the Census Office had as usual been disbanded. On June 1, 1860, Secretary of the Interior Thompson appointed Joseph C. G. Kennedy, who had been in charge of the 1850 census and who had been compiling the 1850 digest of manufactures, as superintending clerk of the Eighth

Census. An act of May 5, 1860 (12 Stat. 14), authorized the Census Office
to employ a chief clerk and such other clerks of the first class as the Secretary thought necessary. Late in 1860 the staff of the Census Office included, besides the superintendent and the chief clerk, a disbursing agent
and 125 clerks. Other clerks, messengers, laborers, and watchmen were
soon employed, but after 1862 the force was gradually reduced until the Office was abolished on May 31, 1865. The files, public property, and pending statistical compilations were transferred at that time to the General
Land Office. A few of the remaining clerks were shifted to that Office, but
Kennedy's services were discontinued. James M. Edmunds, Commissioner
of the General Land Office, succeeded him on June 6, 1865, in charge of the
census work. The organization of a permanent Census Office in the Department of the Interior was not provided for until 1902. The Census Office is
now the Bureau of the Census, in the Department of Commerce.

The enumeration of the inhabitants and the collection of statistical information in 1860 were carried on under the supervision of 64 U. S. marshals attached to the judicial districts of the country. President Buchanan
appointed a special agent to enumerate the population in the unorganized
territory west of Minnesota (Dakota), and a census was also taken of slaves
and freedmen on Indian reservations west of Arkansas. Each U. S. marshal
divided his district into subdivisions and appointed for each subdivision an
assistant, who was required to take an oath and to whom he furnished instructions, blanks, information, and supervision. The enumeration was
essentially completed by Nov. 1, 1860, and all the returns were eventually
received by the Census Office, despite the outbreak of war. The war did,
however, prevent the settlement of the accounts of some 1, 200 marshals
and assistants who had taken the census in Southern States. After the war
provision was made to pay those who could prove their loyalty to the Union
(act of June 24, 1870; 16 Stat. 167). On the basis of data compiled from the
census returns and certified by the Secretary of the Interior to the House of
Representatives, a reapportionment of the House was provided for by an act
of Mar. 4, 1862 (12 Stat. 353).

When all the census returns had been received, the staff of the Census
Office under Kennedy's direction began to compile, analyze, and interpret
them. A preliminary report summarizing the results of the census appeared
in 1862; it was followed by volumes on population and agriculture in 1864.
Two other volumes, on manufactures and statistics (of mortality, property,
etc.), were completed under Edmunds' direction and appeared in 1865 and
1866.

Successive Superintendents of the Census during the war:
Joseph C. G. Kennedy, June 1, 1860.
James M. Edmunds, June 6, 1865.

William S. Holt, The Bureau of
the Census; Its History, Activities,
and Organization (Washington, 1929);
U. S. Census Office, Eighth Census,
United States--1860; Act of Congress
of Twenty-Third May, 1850, Instructions to U. S. Marshals, Instructions
to Assistants (Washington, 1860), and
Preliminary Report on the Eighth
Census, 1860 (H. Ex. Doc. 116, 37
Cong., 2 sess., Serial 1137; Washington, 1862); Carroll D. Wright and
William C. Hunt, The History and
Growth of the United States Census
(S. Doc. 194, 56 Cong., 1 sess., Serial 3856; Washington, 1900); Report
of the House Committee on Printing,
on the memorial of Joseph C. G. Kennedy, Apr. 23, 1866 (H. Rept. 50, 39
Cong., 1 sess., Serial 1272). The

four census volumes published in
1864-66 are printed in H. Misc. Doc.
[unnumbered], 38 Cong., 1 sess.,
Serial 1176, and also separately.
In the published volume on agriculture is a table (omitted from the volume on population) giving by counties the number of slaveholders and
slaves in 1860.

Record Group 29. --Some administrative records of the Eighth Census
survive among the records of the Census Bureau. A volume containing
lists of employees of the Office gives information on each one's State of
residence, dates of appointment and dismissal, amount of salary, and com-
petence. A register of enumeration subdivisions of marshals' districts
gives descriptive data regarding each subdivision, the name of the assistant marshal serving as enumerator, his postoffice, and the amount paid
him on receipt of his returns. Besides a list, alphabetical by State, of the
names of all marshals and assistant marshals, there is a list of those who
served in the Southern States and who had not received their pay. Account
books are available for Census Office disbursements and for Interior Department payments made to marshals and their assistants.

The schedules of the Eighth Census number hundreds of volumes, of the
following classes: population (free inhabitants), 711 vols.; population (slave
inhabitants), 49 vols.; agriculture, 106 vols.; mortality, 21 vols.; manufactures, 18 vols.; and social statistics, 19 vols. (Van Tyne and Leland,
Guide, p. 238). Of these schedules only those for population are in the National Archives. The headings of the population schedules (free inhabitants)
are as follows: name of each person in family; color, sex, and age; whether
married within the year; place of birth (State, Territory, or country); profession, occupation, or trade; schooling within the year; illiteracy; physical
and mental disabilities; and value of real estate and personal property owned.
A manuscript index to the population schedules, arranged alphabetically by
State and thereunder by county, is available. The slave schedules give for
each slaveholder the number of his slaves; their age, sex, and color; those
who were fugitives; the number manumitted; those who were deaf and dumb,
blind, insane, or idiotic; and the number of slave houses.

Since the 1860 census was taken before the war, it gives information regarding both Southerners and Northerners. If the researcher knows the
names of a group of individuals--such as the members of a secession convention, a legislature, or a group of military officers--he can use the schedules for biographical data. By consolidating the information relating to an
individual or family from several schedules--e. g., the schedule of free inhabitants plus the schedule of slave inhabitants, plus the agriculture or the
manufacturing schedule and sometimes the mortality schedule--an appreci-
able amount of information can be accumulated and related. Unfortunately
the present dispersion of the schedules (see below) makes this a difficult
search. Slave schedules are available for both the 1850 and the 1860 censuses. Change and development are reflected in the data in two or more
censuses; thus some information on changes brought by the Civil War can
be ascertained by comparing the schedules of 1860 and 1870. (Indians were
not enrolled until the 1870 census.)

National Archives, Population
Schedules, 1800-1870; Volume Index
to Counties and Major Cities (Washington, 1951). The schedules of
most of the censuses are on microfilm; those of the 1860 census fill 314
rolls; see National Archives, Federal
Population Censuses, 1840-80; a Price

List of Microfilm Copies of Original Schedules (Washington, 1955). State historical societies, State archives, or State libraries usually have the microfilm for their own States and sometimes for neighboring States. The Genealogical Society of the Church of Jesus Christ of Latter-day Saints in Salt Lake City also has the microfilm for the census of 1860. See E. Kay Kirkham, A Survey of American Census Schedules; an Explanation and Description of Our Federal Census Enumeration, 1790 to 1950 (Salt Lake City, Utah, 1959); Richard W. Hale, Jr., comp., Guide to Photocopied Historical Materials in the United States and Canada (Ithaca, N. Y. 1961); George W. Kingsbury, ed., "The Census of 1860," South Dakota Historical Collections, 10:396-439 (1920). The value of census records for research and suggestions as to subjects for research are discussed in Barnes F. Lathrop, "History From the Census Returns," Southwestern Historical Quarterly, 51:293-312 (Apr. 1948); and Fabian Linden, "Economic Democracy in the Slave South; an Appraisal of Some Recent Views," Journal of Negro History, 31:140-189 (Apr. 1946).

Correspondence of 1860-79 relating to the census of 1860 and a package of papers concerning the claim of Oscar W. Streeter for compensation for taking the census in the Dakota country are in the letters received file of the Patents and Miscellaneous Division, Office of the Secretary of the Interior (Record Group 48). The report of the Senate Committee on Claims on this matter is S. Rept. 315, 48 Cong., 1 sess., Serial 2174; see also an act of Jan. 23, 1885 (23 Stat. 618), authorizing the Secretary of the Interior to investigate the claim and appropriating not more than $10,000 to compensate Streeter. Outgoing letters to the Superintendent of the Census are also in in Record Group 48.

The Federal censuses of population can be supplemented by State censuses. These frequently provide statistics not available in the Federal census for smaller geographical areas and for other than the decennial years. See U. S. Library of Congress, Census Library Project, State Censuses; an Annotated Bibliography of Censuses of Population Taken After the Year 1790 by States and Territories of the United States, comp. by Henry J. Dubester (Washington, 1948); E. Kay Kirkham, Research in American Genealogy; a Practical Approach to Genealogical Research, p. 261-267 (Salt Lake City, Utah, 1926), Noel C. Stevenson, Search and Research; the Researcher's Handbook, a Guide to Official Records and Library Sources for Investigators, Historians, Genealogists, Lawyers, and Librarians (Salt Lake City, Utah, 1959).

No statistical atlas, such as that prepared for the censuses of 1870 and later, was published for the census of 1860. At the request of the War Department, however, printed maps of the Southern States were annotated under Kennedy's direction to show population, railways, and agricultural products. On these maps are symbols showing for each county the number of whites, free colored persons, slaves, and males between the ages of 18 and 45; the number of acres of improved land; the number of horses and mules, neat cattle, and swine; and the production of wheat, corn, oats, tobacco, hay, cotton bales, and rice. These maps were used by invading Northern armies, such as that of General Sherman, when they outdistanced their supply lines, to find out where animals and foodstuffs were available. Photographic copies of the maps for Georgia and Alabama, Tennessee, Louisiana, West Virginia, Virginia, and Missouri are in the records of the Bureau of the Census.

The original annotated maps for Georgia and Alabama are in the records of the Office of the Chief of Engineers (Record Group 77); and a map for Mississippi, Louisiana, and Arkansas, and one for Illinois and Missouri (with data for Missouri counties only) are in the Geological Survey records (Record Group 57). The returns of the census of 1860 were also used for maps showing the distribution of the slave population in the Southern States and for a separate Virginia map, which were privately published in Washington in 1861.

Record Group 49.--A small quantity of incoming correspondence, received after supervision of the census was transferred to the General Land Office, is in the records of that Office. These letters relate to the claim of Charles E. Wesche, census taker for San Miguel County, New Mexico Territory; claims for taking the census of 1864 in Arizona Territory; and claims of census takers and clerks elsewhere. Other papers concern census publications and the expenditures of the Census Office.

Records in Other Custody. --The Bureau of the Census was authorized in 1918 to destroy schedules other than the population schedules of the censuses of 1850-80 (H. Doc. 921, 65 Cong., 2 sess., Serial 7447). Instead of destroying the schedules, however, the Bureau decided to give them to those historical societies and State or other libraries that were interested in them. Consequently the 1860 schedules of agriculture, mortality, manufactures, and social statistics are scattered among many repositories. Some schedules for States that refused them are in the library of the Daughters of the American Revolution, Washington, D. C. ; others are in Duke University Library.

For the places of deposit of the abovementioned schedules, see the Survey of Federal Archives, Inventory of Federal Archives in the States, Series X, the Department of Commerce; and Hamer, ed. , Guide to Archives and Manuscripts. A list of repositories of mortality schedules is in E. Kay Kirkham, The A B C's of American Genealogical Research, p. 118-120 (Salt Lake City, Utah, 1955). Information regarding repositories of Federal and State censuses is given in George B. Everton and Gunnar Rasmuson, The Handy Book for Genealogists (Logan, Utah, 1957).

Censuses were also taken in the Territories established during the Civil War. The organic acts for the Territories of Colorado, Nevada, Dakota, Arizona, Idaho, and Montana, all established during the war, authorized the Governors to have censuses taken in order to apportion members of the legislative assemblies among the counties or districts. Accordingly the Governors arranged for the enumerations, which were usually directed by the U. S. marshals. In most districts, however, these censuses seem to have been merely counts of the number of people living in settlements, mining districts, ranches, etc. , rather than lists of names and other data on the inhabitants. Some of these Territorial censuses are extant, but owing to carelessness in administering Territorial records others have been lost. The manuscript of the Arizona Territory census of 1864 is in the Arizona Department of Library and Archives. A photostatic copy of it, obtained by the Bureau of the Census, has been accessioned by the National Archives. This was a complete census; it gives for each person the name, age, sex, marital status, place of birth, period of residence in Arizona, citizenship, residence of the family, and occupation; and the value of real estate and personal property owned.

The text of the Arizona census is reproduced in Historical Records Survey, The 1864 Census of the Territory of Arizona (Phoenix, 1938). The report on the Idaho census, Sept. 1863, is in the Sixteenth Biennial Report of the State Historical Society of Idaho, 1937-38, p. 60-64 (Boise, 1938). A similar report on the Nevada census of 1861 is in the "Territorial Papers, Nevada," 1:102-112, in the State Department records (Record Group 59); and is published in the appendix to the Journal of the House of Representatives of the First Legislative Assembly of the Territory of Nevada, p. 397-403 (San Francisco, 1862). The results of the Colorado census of 1861 are in the Rocky Mountain News, July 17, 1861, and the Colorado City Journal, Aug. 1, 1861. A statistical summary of the Dakota census of 1861 is in George W. Kingsbury, History of Dakota Territory, 1:176 (Chicago, 1915. 3 vols.).

OFFICE OF THE ARCHITECT OF THE EXTENSION OF THE CAPITOL

An act of Sept. 30, 1850 (9 Stat. 538), had appropriated $100,000 for the extension of the Capitol according to a plan to be approved by the President. On June 11, 1851, President Fillmore had appointed, as Architect of the Extension of the Capitol, Thomas U. Walter, a Philadelphia architect who had won a competition with his plan providing for adding to the Capitol north and south wings as chambers for the Senate and the House. Walter had directed the work under the supervision of the Secretary of the Interior until the President in Mar. 1853 transferred the function to the Secretary of War. A later act, Mar. 3, 1855 (10 Stat. 663), had made an appropriation to build a new dome over the central part of the Capitol according to a plan designed by Walter. Although the new chambers for the Houses of Congress were in use before the Civil War, neither the exterior work nor the new dome had been completed when war began. Construction was suspended in May 1861 but was resumed in 1862 and carried on throughout the war, in spite of difficulty in getting materials and recruiting workmen. At the beginning of the war an engineer officer was still supervising the work, but by a joint resolution of Apr. 16, 1862 (12 Stat. 617), the function was returned to the Secretary of the Interior, and Walter was again put in charge of the work. He was concerned only with the new construction projects; the care and maintenance of the Capitol was the responsibility of the Commissioner of Public Buildings (see above). Secretary of the Interior Smith also assigned Walter to continue work on the Patent Office Building, to enlarge the Library of Congress, and to extend the building for the Government Printing Office. On May 23, 1865, Secretary Usher put Commissioner of Public Buildings French in charge of all work on Federal buildings in the District of Columbia. The work on the Capitol and the other buildings under Walter's supervision was then nearly completed, and he resigned his position and returned to Philadelphia. Edward Clark, who had been his assistant, succeeded him as Architect of the Capitol.

Thomas U. Walter served as Architect of the Capitol from June 11, 1851, to May 31, 1865.

Glenn Brown, History of the United States Capitol (S. Doc. 60, 56 Cong., 1 sess., Serial 3849; Washington, 1900, 1903. 2 vols.); Ihna T. Frary, They Built the Capitol (Richmond, 1940); Homer T. Rosenberger, "Thomas Ustick Walter and the Completion of the United

States Capitol," Columbia Historical Society, Records, 50:273-322
(1948-50); Documentary History of
the Construction and Development
of the United States Capitol Building
and Grounds (H. Rept. 646, 58 Cong.,
2 sess. , Serial 4585; Washington,
1904).

Records in Other Custody. --The Office of the Architect of the Capitol
has retained the records relating to construction on the Capitol in the 1850's
and 1860's. They include correspondence, contracts for art works, ledgers,
vouchers, and drawings. Walter took back to Philadelphia a great many
drawings; some 500 of these were bought from his daughters in 1910. Other
drawings that the Architect presumably stored in the Library of Congress
while it was in the Capitol are still in the Library. Also in the Library are
notebooks and diaries of Montgomery C. Meigs, superintendent of construction at the Capitol from 1853 to 1859. The Meigs collection includes some
photographs of the Capitol. Papers of Alexander B. McFarlan, a stonecut-
ter, mason, and plasterer who worked on the extension of the Capitol, are
in the Library of Congress; they include 40 letters from Meigs and notes on
materials used and wages paid. Pictures relating to the construction of the
Capitol, acquired from official sources, are in the Smithsonian Institution's
Division of Transportation.

Correspondence, including letters from Walter and Clark, and
other papers relating to the construction of the extension of the Capitol and the building of the new dome,
applications for appointment, and
letters to architects are in the records of the Office of the Secretary of
the Interior (Record Group 48). Other
materials relating to the Capitol are
in the records of the Commissioner
of Public Buildings and Public Parks
of the National Capital (Record Group
42).

WASHINGTON AQUEDUCT OFFICE

Early reports of the Secretary of the Interior recommended the introduction of an adequate water supply into Washington both for public health
and for protecting public buildings and records against fire. After a survey authorized by an act of Apr. 21, 1852 (10 Stat. 92), construction of a
9-foot conduit had been begun in 1853 under Capt. Montgomery C. Meigs of
the Corps of Engineers. The conduit, constructed from Great Falls in
Maryland to Georgetown and roughly paralleling the Chesapeake and Ohio
Canal, had to bridge the Cabin John Valley and other stream valleys. Completed in Dec. 1863, the system was opened for regular service in July
1864 after some leaks had been discovered and repaired. Large pipes
leading from the distributing reservoir in Georgetown supplied the Government buildings and were tapped by the corporations of Washington and
Georgetown, which supplied water to their residents. On July 15, 1862,
under an act of June 18 (12 Stat. 620), supervision of the aqueduct construction was transferred from the War to the Interior Department, and a civil
engineer replaced the engineer officer. The civilian staff of the Aqueduct
Office included also a principal assistant engineer, an assistant superintendent, a clerk and disbursing agent, and a supervisor of water distribution. An act of Mar. 2, 1867 (14 Stat. 466), however, returned the superintendence of the Washington Aqueduct to the Corps of Engineers.
Successive Superintendents of the Office during the war period:
　Capt. Henry W. Benham, July 17, 1860.

Lt. James St. C. Morton, Dec. 1860.
Capt. Montgomery C. Meigs, Feb. 22, 1861.
William R. Hutton, July 5, 1862.
Silas Seymour, July 21, 1863.
Theodore B. Samo, June 1865.

William T. S. Curtis, "Cabin John Bridge," Columbia Historical Society, Records, 2:293-307 (1899); Office of the Chief of Engineers, Washington Engineer District, A Historical Summary of the Work of the Corps of Engineers in Washington, D. C., and Vicinity 1852-1952 ([Washington], 1952), and History of the Washington Aqueduct ([Washington], 1953); Russell F. Weigley, Quartermaster General of the Union Army; a Biography of M. C. Meigs (New York, 1959).

Record Group 48. --In the records of the Office of the Secretary of the Interior are a press copy book of letters sent, 1862-69, and a few letters received, 1852-65 (Patents and Miscellaneous Division). Some of these letters are entered in the register mentioned below. These sources include references to the activities of soldiers who guarded the aqueduct at Great Falls and other points and to the arming of workmen employed on the aqueduct.

Record Group 77. --Other records on the construction and operation of the Washington Aqueduct are among the records of the Office of the Chief of Engineers. A letter book, July 1862-Oct. 1868, contains copies of letters sent by the Secretary of the Interior; these include letters of appointment and letters to engineers employed on the aqueduct, the Secretaries of War and Treasury, the First Comptroller of the Treasury, the Commissioner of Public Buildings, the chairman of the Senate Committee on the District of Columbia, the mayor of Washington, and officials of the Great Falls Manufacturing Co. In a register of letters received, 1862-67, are entered applications for appointment and letters and reports from the chief engineer, engineer officers, contractors, and Government counsel in a legal case involving the Great Falls Manufacturing Co. Some correspondence and reports on the aqueduct are segregated; other papers are in the regular correspondence files of the Office. Miscellaneous papers and reports of Meigs, 1853-70, are in a separate box. Title papers and other documents concern land acquired for the aqueduct. Some 60 glass-plate negatives, dated from 1857 and relating to the construction of the aqueduct, show conduit ditches, machinery, pipes, workmen, and bridges. There are also maps of the water supply system.

Records in Other Custody. --The Washington Aqueduct Office has correspondence, field survey notebooks, drawings, maps, and pictures relating to the construction of the aqueduct; and books containing transcripts of deeds for land acquired for the water system. Montgomery C. Meigs' papers in the Library of Congress contain information on the aqueduct.

OFFICE OF THE SUPERINTENDENT OF PUBLIC PRINTING

Before the Civil War public printing had been done in private plants under contract, but a beginning had been made toward the establishment of a Government printing office. An act of Aug. 26, 1852 (10 Stat. 30), had provided for the appointment of a Superintendent of Public Printing to supervise printing for the Government and to purchase paper and had authorized the election by each House of Congress of contract printers to do not only printing for Congress but also such printing for the departments as the Superintendent of Public Printing assigned to them. When the contract system had proved unsatisfactory, Congress by joint resolution of June 23, 1860 (12 Stat. 117), directed the Superintendent of Public Printing "to have executed the printing and binding" for Congress, "the executive and judicial departments," and the U. S. Court of Claims. A private printing plant, in Washington at H and North Capitol Streets, was purchased; and the Government Printing Office began operation there on Mar. 4, 1861. It was soon flooded with huge orders from Congress and the departments, some of which--especially War, Navy, and Treasury--used large quantities of blank books. The Office had to buy new presses and binding machinery; and, when space ran out, an addition to the building was erected in 1865, and still more presses and machinery were obtained.

Later acts changed the designation of the head of the Government Printing Office. An act of Feb. 22, 1867 (14 Stat. 398), provided that he was to be elected by the Senate and was to be considered an officer of that body. Though designated as the Congressional Printer, he was to superintend printing and binding not only for Congress but also for the departments, which by law had to be done at the Government Printing Office. The title of the head of the Office was again changed by an act of June 20, 1874 (18 Stat. 88), to the still current one--the Public Printer. William Towers served as chief clerk of the Government Printing Office from 1852 to 1868, and there were also a foreman and an assistant foreman of printing and a foreman and an assistant foreman of binding.

Successive Superintendents of Public Printing during the Civil War:
John Heart, May 14, 1859.
John D. Defrees, Mar. 23, 1861.

U. S. Government Printing Office, 100 GPO Years; a History of the United States Public Printing (Washington, 1961); Laurence F. Schmeckebier, The Government Printing Office; Its History, Activities and Organization (Baltimore, 1925). The Annual Reports of the Government Printing Office--containing lists of employees and data on the cost of printing, paper, engravings and lithographs, machinery, and tools--were published as follows:

1861. H. Misc. Doc. 18, 37 Cong., 2 sess., Serial 1141.
1862. H. Misc. Doc. 6, 37 Cong., 3 sess., Serial 1171.
1863. H. Misc. Doc. 21, 38 Cong., 1 sess., Serial 1199.
1864. H. Ex. Doc.   25, 38 Cong., 2 sess., Serial 1223.
1865. H. Ex. Doc.   23, 39 Cong., 1 sess., Serial 1255.

Record Group 149. --Press copies of letters sent by the Office date from 1852. They concern orders to private firms for paper and other materials, engravings, lithographs, and maps for Government publications; the printing of reports, etc., for the Executive departments and Congress; reports to congressional committees; requests to the Secretary of the Treasury for the issuance of warrants; and appointments of employees. For the period of the Civil War and later years there are special series of press copy books containing letters to the Treasury Department, to contractors, and to other business firms. The letters received for the war period are missing. Payrolls date from Mar. 4, 1861, and contain amounts paid and the signatures

of employees. Other records include paper orders, registers of paper orders, accounts current, canceled checks, and binding accounts. Personnel folders for employees, containing appointment papers, are in the Federal Records Center at St. Louis, Mo.

Some applications and recommen-   office, 1859-62, are in records of
dations regarding the appointment of   the Office of the Secretary of the In-
the Superintendent of Public Printing   terior, Appointments Division (Rec-
and a few resignations and oaths of   ord Group 48).

FEDERAL INSTITUTIONS IN THE DISTRICT OF COLUMBIA

Discussed below are five relatively small institutions that during the
Civil War were administered under the Secretary of the Interior. Two of
them--St. Elizabeths Hospital and Gallaudet College--are now under the
Department of Health, Education, and Welfare; one--the U. S. Penitentiary for the District of Columbia--no longer exists; and two--the District
Jail and the Metropolitan Police--are now directed by the District of Columbia government.

Government Hospital for the Insane (St. Elizabeths Hospital)

An act of Aug. 31, 1852 (10 Stat. 92), had provided for buying land and
building an asylum for insane persons of the District of Columbia and of the
U. S. armed forces. Situated in the southeast section of the District, on a
high plateau overlooking the Potomac and Anacostia Rivers, the hospital
had been opened in Jan. 1855. An act of Mar. 3, 1855 (10 Stat. 682), concerning the organization of the hospital, had provided for the appointment
by the President of 9 citizens of the District of Columbia as a board of visitors, who were to draw up bylaws for the management of the hospital.
This act was drafted by Dorothea Lynde Dix, whose efforts had resulted in
the passage of the earlier act. Patients from the Army and the Navy were
to be admitted on orders of the Secretaries of War and the Navy. The indigent insane of the District of Columbia were to be admitted on the authority of the Secretary of the Interior, and private patients from the District
might be admitted when there was room. Personnel of the revenue-cutter
service were also admitted to the hospital. During the war the Secretary
of the Interior was authorized (act of Jan. 28, 1864; 13 Stat. 3), to admit
transient insane persons found in the District of Columbia without means of
support, and a later act (Feb. 9, 1865; 13 Stat. 427) permitted the admission of civilian employees of the Quartermaster's Department and the Subsistence Department of the Army. Besides the Superintendent, the staff of
the hospital included in 1861 male and female supervisors and attendants
and various other workers. The name of the Government Hospital for the
Insane was changed by an act of July 1, 1916 (39 Stat. 309), to St. Elizabeths
Hospital.

During the Civil War space at the Government Hospital for the Insane
was also used for the treatment of sick and wounded U. S. soldiers and sailors and a few Confederate prisoners. A 250-bed Army hospital was opened
in the new east wing of the building in Oct. 1861 and continued in operation,
in charge of medical officers of the Army, until Apr. 1864. A smaller naval hospital, attended by naval surgeons, afforded medical care for personnel of the Potomac River Flotilla. The soldiers and sailors admitted to the

Government Hospital for the Insane suffered from mental ailments, which were described in the register mentioned below as resulting from war excitement, head wounds, the bursting of cannon, hardship in prison, heatstroke, sunstroke, intemperance, hardship and exposure, fright, nostalgia, loss of comrades, overwork, disappointed love, masturbation, or epilepsy. A factory for making artificial limbs was maintained at the hospital, and these were fitted to maimed soldiers and sailors.

The Superintendent of the hospital from 1852 to 1877 was Charles H. Nichols.

Winfred Overholser, "An Historical Sketch of Saint Elizabeths Hospital," Centennial Papers Saint Elizabeths Hospital 1855-1955 (Washington, 1956); "Reports of the Board of Visitors . . . Government Hospital for the Insane," Reports of the Secretary of the Interior, 1861-65.

Records in Other Custody. -- Many records have been preserved by the hospital. A file of admission authorizations contains court records and orders on the commitment of patients. A register of cases contains a record of admissions from Jan. 15, 1855, and shows for the years 1861-65 over 1,700 admissions. The individual entries give the patient's number, date of admission, date of discharge, the result of treatment, length of time spent in the hospital, and occupation; the number of admissions and former case numbers, if any, and the number of commitments to other hospitals; diagnosis of the disease, whether hereditary or not, and its duration on admission; the patient's color, sex, age, nativity, residence at the time of admission, education, and religion; and remarks as to his disposition and-- if deceased--whether the body was removed or buried in the hospital cemetery. The register serves as an index to the clinical files on individual patients. These sometimes contain ward notes on the patient's condition, doctor's notes on the patient, post mortem records, summaries of case histories, fever charts, photographs, and correspondence; the clinical files, however, are rather meager for the war period. The information in the clinical folders of patients is abstracted in clinical history volumes; in these the summaries of patients' medical histories and clinical notes are more easily consulted. A record of deaths supplements the register of cases, but the entries are not detailed until 1875. Letters received relate to the administration of the hospital and the procurement of materials and supplies, applications and recommendations for appointments on the staff, requests from attendants asking for changes of assignment, resignations, requests for the admission of patients and authorizations for their discharge, and instructions and blank forms from the Secretary of the Interior for administering oaths of allegiance to the staff. The file includes personal letters received by Dr. Nichols from his father and other relatives and from Dorothea L. Dix, Gen. Joseph Hooker, and Brig. Gen. William Dwight, Jr. Letters sent, from 1857, are available in press copy books. Fiscal records-- including vouchers, abstracts of disbursements, receipts for payments made for private patients, ledgers, account books, and check stubs--are available; but whether they are all extant for the Civil War period has not been ascertained. Photographs and painted portraits of Dr. Nichols and Miss Dix are available.

Records of the Office of the Secretary of the Interior (Record Group 48) contain documents on the purchase of land and the erection of hospital buildings, estimates for appropriations, letters from the superintendent, and an alphabetical file of admission papers. A press copy book contains a few letters sent to Dr. Nichols. Among the Adjutant General's records (Record Group 94) are a register of the sick and wounded at the Army hospital and carded medical records on regular soldiers. Other materials relating to the Army hospital are among the records of the Surgeon General (Record Group 112). Documents relating to the naval hospital and the admission of seamen to it are in records of the Bureau of Medicine and Surgery (Record Group 52).

Columbia Institution for the Instruction of the Deaf and Dumb (Gallaudet College)

Incorporated as the Columbia Institution for the Instruction of the Deaf and Dumb and the Blind (act of Feb. 16, 1857; 11 Stat. 161), this institution had been empowered to own land and other property and, as provided in its constitution, had been controlled by its board of directors. The Secretary of the Interior had been given authority to approve the admission of District of Columbia residents who were deaf, dumb, or blind and who lacked the means to obtain an education, to pay $150 for each such pupil yearly, and to receive and review the Institution's annual reports. An act of Feb. 23, 1865 (13 Stat. 436), authorized the removal of the few blind pupils to the Maryland Institution for the Blind, in Baltimore, and changed the Institution's name to Columbia Institution for the Instruction of the Deaf and Dumb. The school was opened on June 18, 1857, in a building and on a site donated by Amos Kendall, president of the board of directors. The act of 1857 had authorized the Institution to receive and instruct deaf, dumb, and blind persons from any State or Territory, on terms to be agreed upon. Under an act of May 29, 1858 (11 Stat. 293), the deaf, dumb, and blind children of men in U. S. military service were admitted on the same terms as residents of the District of Columbia. Though financed in part by tuition payments and contributions, the Institution has been regularly supported by appropriations by Congress. Government funds were provided in the early years for the payment of salaries and incidental expenses; for construction of buildings; for heating and lighting, a new sewer, the repair of fences, and the introduction of Potomac water; and for the purchase of additional land to be used for instruction in horticulture and agriculture and to provide sites for new shops and buildings.

Besides the head of the Institution, who was designated as superintendent until 1863 and thereafter as president, the staff included a secretary, a treasurer, instructors, a matron, an assistant matron, a master of the shop, a coachman or butler, and a gardener. A collegiate department, opened in Sept. 1864, became known as Gallaudet College in 1894. The name of the Institution was changed in 1911 to Columbia Institution for the Deaf, and in 1954 to Gallaudet College.

Edward Miner Gallaudet served as president from 1857 to 1910.

Maxine T. Boatner, Voice of the Deaf; a Biography of Edward Miner Gallaudet (Washington, 1959); Edward M. Gallaudet, "History of the Columbia Institution for the Deaf and Dumb," Columbia Historical Society, Records, 15:1-22 (1912). The annual reports of the Institution are published in the Report of the Secretary of the Interior and contain, besides narrative reports to the Secretary, statements of receipts and expenditures, rosters of pupils, and statements of subscriptions.

Records in Other Custody. --Gallaudet College has correspondence, admission records, financial records, photographs, and a survey of Kendall Green, July 9, 1864, and a contract for its purchase. Papers of Edward Miner Gallaudet, after being lent to Dr. Boatner for her biography of Gallaudet, were given to the Library of Congress. The collection includes diaries, journals of travels, and an unpublished memoir. The diary for the war period is brief and is devoted to personal data and reflections. One of the journals concerns a trip made in Apr. 1865 to Fort Sumter, where Gallaudet witnessed the raising of the U. S. flag. The memoir is valuable for the history of the college but should be checked with the published annual reports.

Maxine T. Boatner, "The Gallaudet Papers," Library of Congress, Quarterly Journal of Current Acquisitions, 17:1-12 (Nov. 1959). Correspondence in the records of the Office of the Secretary of the Interior includes letters from Gallaudet and Amos Kendall, concerning annual reports, funds, quarterly accounts, the admission of pupils, and the acquisition of land. A few outgoing letters are in a press copy book.

U. S. Penitentiary for the District of Columbia

An appropriation of $40,000 had been made for building a penitentiary for the District of Columbia by an act of May 20, 1826 (4 Stat. 178). After its opening in 1831 the institution had been used to imprison offenders against U. S. laws and laws of the District of Columbia. In Apr. 1861 there were 171 prisoners in the penitentiary, about half of them employed in broom and shoe shops and the rest sick or unemployed. There were a few women inmates, who did the housekeeping tasks. The Secretary of the Interior, who had supervised the penitentiary after 1849, recommended to President Lincoln on Apr. 10, 1861, that a more reliable warden be appointed to prevent the escape of prisoners, who might be armed by Confederate sympathizers. Besides the warden there were a board of three inspectors appointed by the President, a deputy warden, clerk, physician, chaplain, matron, guards, night wall guards, and foremen of the shops. Some of the guards left the penitentiary early in 1861 to join the secessionists. The War Department soon began to crowd the penitentiary with court-martialed soldiers, but Secretary of the Interior Smith on June 5, 1862, ordered the warden not to receive any prisoners except those sentenced by judicial tribunal. The matter was brought to the attention of Congress, and an act of July 16, 1862 (12 Stat. 589), prohibited the confinement of military personnel in the penitentiary except as punishment for certain crimes and directed the discharge of those prisoners sentenced by court-martial. By President Lincoln's order of Sept. 19, 1862, however, the penitentiary building was turned over to the War Department for use as an arsenal, and the prisoners were soon shipped on a War Department vessel to an old county jail at Albany, N. Y.

Under the provisions of an act of Jan. 16, 1863 (12 Stat. 635), the Secretary of the Interior still was responsible for the imprisonment of persons convicted of crimes in the District of Columbia. He had not only to select the places of imprisonment but also to arrange for transporting, confining, and subsisting District offenders. Secretary Usher considered this act as terminating the services of the staff of the penitentiary, since it stipulated other uses for the available funds.

574   INTERIOR DEPARTMENT

Successive wardens during the war period:
      Charles P. Sengstack, Dec. 23, 1858.
      Hiram J. King, Apr. 12, 1861-Jan. 16, 1863.

Stephen Dalsheim, "The United States Penitentiary for the District of Columbia, 1826-62," Columbia Historical Society, Records, 53-56:135-144 (1953-56; published 1959).

Record Group 48. --The records of the penitentiary are varied and almost complete for the period of its existence. Letters received include communications from business firms concerning broomcorn and leather and bills for the shipment of these materials, letters and recommendations to the President and the Secretary of the Interior regarding appointment as inspector or warden, acceptances of appointment, instructions from the Secretary of the Interior, and communications from other Government officials. With these letters are other documents such as reports on claims, descriptive rolls and lists of military prisoners, minutes of the board of inspectors, orders from the provost marshal for the transfer of prisoners to the Old Capitol Prison, and copies of certificates of officers of the penitentiary. Useful for studying the administration of the prison are the minutes of the board of inspectors and a signed register of visits by inspectors and physicians. In separate files are resolutions of the board for payments to the warden to meet the salaries of officers of the penitentiary and vouchers for expenditures, including payrolls signed by the staff for monthly salaries. Records of the shoe and broom shops show the assignments of prisoners, materials and tools supplied, time worked, output, and amounts earned. A small file of permits to visit the penitentiary, Nov. 1860-Apr. 1861, shows the names of visitors admitted and of those visited. Some requisitions from the Washington Arsenal for powder, 1861-62, indicate that the penitentiary was used as an annex to the arsenal before it was officially turned over for that purpose. Available also are annual reports and some accounting records.

Concerning the prisoners there are other records. Commitment papers, containing sentences of U. S. district courts and special orders of Army general courts-martial, show that civilians were committed for a variety of serious crimes and that soldiers from camps and fortifications in Washington and the neighborhood were committed for insubordination, forgery, and desertion. A register of prisoners contains personal information on the prisoners and their crimes, employment in the penitentiary, and dates and reasons for discharge. A record of punishments shows the penalties for prisoners who broke the rules of the penitentiary. Arranged chronologically is a file of orders, from the U. S. Marshal of the District of Columbia and the Adjutant General's Office of the War Department, for the release of prisoners.

Correspondence and reports relating to the penitentiary are in this record group among the files of the Patents and Miscellaneous Division, Office of the Secretary of the Interior. The Secretary's published annual reports contain not only reports of the board of inspectors, the warden, the matron, the physician, the chaplain, and the clerk on finances, but also a "journal of convicts," which duplicates the information given in the register of prisoners (see above) except that it gives only the initials instead of the full names of the convicts.

District of Columbia Jail

The District of Columbia Jail, which since 1842 had been at 4th and G Streets Northwest, was under the control of the U. S. Marshal of the District. Ward H. Lamon, former law partner of President Lincoln, was appointed marshal on Apr. 6, 1861, but he left the management of the jail to George W. Phillips, who continued in his post as deputy marshal. Lamon appointed John H. Wise, then crier of the court and a bailiff, as keeper of the jail, where there were 8 guards. The Senate Committee on the District of Columbia, which investigated charges against the conduct of the jail by the keeper, recommended in June 1862 that a warden should be appointed, in view of the onerous duties of the marshal. An act of Feb. 29, 1864 (13 Stat. 12), authorized President Lincoln to appoint a warden for a term of 4 years, who was to report annually to the Secretary of the Interior. The jail, which was removed to its present location at 19th and B Streets Southeast in 1872, is now under the Department of Corrections of the District of Columbia. Political or state prisoners were confined in the jail in 1861, but the last of them were removed by November of that year to the Old Capitol Prison. The District of Columbia Jail was also used to confine fugitive slaves and "contrabands" as well as criminals and persons who had committed misdemeanors.

Successive wardens during the war period:

Robert Beale, Apr. 5, 1864.
Thomas B. Brown, Aug. 12, 1865.

"Report . . . Into the Condition and Management of the Jail in the City of Washington." June 21, 1861 (S. Rept. 60, 37 Cong., 2 sess., Serial 1125). A list of 235 prisoners in the jail in Dec. 1861 is in S. Misc. Doc. 2, 37 Cong., 2 sess., Serial 1124. See also "Report of the Warden of the Jail in the District of Columbia," in Report of the Secretary of the Interior, 1865.

Records in Other Custody. --The jail still has some of its records. Jail dockets date from 1848 and are available for the Civil War period. These books give a chronological record of prisoners committed, showing for each person the name, date of commitment, by whom committed, nature of offense, date of discharge, by whom discharged, and names of witnesses. Information sometimes appears as to the sentence and transfer to other prisons. The pages for entries 365 to 379 (Apr. 18-22, 1865) in the book for Feb. 1864- Oct. 1865 have been cut out, presumably because they contained some entries relating to the imprisonment of suspects in the assassination of President Lincoln. Entry 2164 in the next book shows that John H. Surratt, another suspect in the assassination plot, was imprisoned on Feb. 19, 1867, and discharged on June 22, 1868. The jail has neither correspondence nor personnel records for the war years.

Correspondence, from 1864, with the warden and other officials regarding the jail is in the letters received file of the Patents and Miscellaneous Division, Office of the Secretary of the Interior (Record Group 48). Records concerning the trials of persons later imprisoned in the jail are among the records of the courts of the District. The papers of Ward H. Lamon are in the Henry E. Huntington Library, San Marino, Calif.

Metropolitan Police

A Federal police force was organized in the District of Columbia early in the war, to ensure better security for Federal interests and better protection for citizens against the hangers-on who followed the Army into the area. Police protection previously had been supplied by an auxiliary guard paid with Federal funds but under the control of Washington's mayor and by constables employed by the corporations of Washington and Georgetown and Washington County. Secretary of the Interior Thompson recommended to the Senate Committee on Finance on July 8, 1861, that the auxiliary guard be put under the control of the Federal Government and, more specifically, of his own Department. An act of Aug. 6, 1861 (12 Stat. 320), combined the corporations of Washington and Georgetown and Washington County in one police district, to be called the Metropolitan Police District of the District of Columbia. Control over the police district was to be exercised by a board of seven, consisting of the mayors of Washington and Georgetown and five commissioners appointed by the President. The board was empowered to appoint a Superintendent, 10 sergeants, and not more than 150 patrolmen. The Secretary of the Interior, to whom the board of commissioners was to report annually, conferred with General McClellan as to the acceptability of the men selected for commissioners; and on Aug. 15, 1861, he transmitted commissions to President Lincoln for signature. The first policemen, inducted on Sept. 11, 1861, were assigned to precincts set up by the board of commissioners. An act of July 16, 1862 (12 Stat. 579), authorized the formation of a detective force, the appointment of three police surgeons, the organization of a sanitary company, the establishment by the commissioners of stations or substations in the precincts, and the appointment of police magistrates at the stations to hear charges against persons arrested and haled to the station houses. The sanitary company, charged with enforcement of ordinances to protect public health, conveyed sick vagrants to hospitals, buried dead ones, and disposed of dead horses. Some of the police patrolled on horseback to cover the rural parts of the district, which were occupied by military camps. The metropolitan police had difficulty in getting the cooperation of the provost guard, whose function was to maintain discipline among the military forces in the District. A telegraph system connecting the police stations was installed in 1864 at a cost of $15,000. The board of police commissioners was abolished in 1878, and control over the police was transferred to the Commissioners of the District of Columbia. Successive Superintendents during the war period:

William B. Webb, 1861.
Almon C. Richards, Dec. 1, 1864.

Richard Sylvester, District of Columbia Police; a Retrospect of the Police Organizations of the Cities of Washington and Georgetown and the District of Columbia (Washington, 1894); J. Russell Young and E. C. R. Humphries, The Metropolitan Police Department, Washington, D. C., Official Illustrated History (Washington, 1908); "Report of the Board of Metropolitan Police," in Report of the Secretary of the Interior, 1861-65.

Record Group 351. -- Various records document the early years of the metropolitan police. Returns of arrests from precinct stations begin in Nov. 1861 and extend throughout the war and later years but are missing for Mar.-Apr. 1865. These are daily returns made by precinct sergeants to the Superintendent, giving detailed information on arrests, including those of soldiers and sailors, and the disposition of cases. On the backs of these printed forms are notes of the number of patrolmen attached to the precincts and some data concerning their assignments. A series of property books, the first of which covers Sept. 1861-Dec. 1875, describes lost, stolen, or missing property and its disposition if recovered. A chronological register of oaths of allegiance, on printed forms, contains signatures of members of the police force. A fragment of an order book, Feb. 1862-Jan. 1863, records sentences against erring patrolmen, laws of the corporation to be enforced by the police, and instructions to policemen. A time book, 1861-69, containing a record of leave taken by policemen, is of some value for the names of men on the force. A daily record of the police force, 1863-64, is available. The detective department blotter, or daily record, Sept. 1862-Feb. 1867, contains detailed entries on arrests, complaints of robberies, etc., assignment of detectives to investigations, and reports of investigations, reports of property recovered, and detectives appointed. In this record, for Apr. 14, 1865, and succeeding days, are entered the names of witnesses to President Lincoln's assassination, lists of articles found at Ford's Theater and of property found in the stable of John Wilkes Booth, the names of detectives who participated in the search for the assassin, and notations of the arrests of persons suspected of complicity in the assassination. Blotters kept at the precinct stations, presumably more detailed than the reports made to the Superintendent, have been destroyed. The correspondence of the Superintendent is also unavailable.

A small quantity of correspondence received by the Secretary of the Interior regarding police affairs is in the records of the Patents and Miscellaneous Division of his Office (Record Group 48).

Records in Other Custody. --The Metropolitan Police headquarters has individual personnel folders from 1861, arranged alphabetically by name. The lists of the names of patrolmen who served during the war, in the Official Register, 1863 and 1865, can be used as an index to this file.

XII. DEPARTMENT OF AGRICULTURE

In his 1860 annual report the Patent Office's Superintendent of Agricultural Affairs, Thomas G. Clemson, repeated his belief that the "requirements of the present age, and the permanent importance of the subjects embraced in its operations, demand that the powers of this agency of the Government should be enlarged." He justified the "present and contemplated" duties as follows:

1. An organized correspondence with the Agricultural Societies of the United States, and with the learned societies of the civilized world, would elicit correct statistical information which could not be collected in any other manner, and which would be of untold interest and advantage to our country and the world.

2. The publication of a Report on the subject of Agriculture, in which information could be authoritatively presented and diffused, would be of the greatest value.

3. The study of unknown indigenous plants for familiar cultivation in our own country, many of which may doubtless prove an addition of the greatest importance to our wealth.

4. Entomological investigations into the nature and history of the predatory insects which have proved so injurious to our crops of cereals, fruits, &c., and also to timber.

5. Questions of the highest moment and variety, connected with agriculture, requiring chemical aid and investigations in the field as well as the laboratory.

6. Familiar examples of special modes of culture, such as irrigation, might be put into operation and opened to the examination and study of the public, who would thus have ocular demonstrations of the methods of renovating lands, of keeping them in a constant state of fertility, and of producing crops which cannot be obtained in any other way without further outlay than by the use of water. Thousands of acres in the South, now waste and entirely unproductive, might by such means be brought to produce large crops of grass, which cannot be grown in our southern climate as the lands are now cultivated. That which is looked upon as impracticable would thus become feasible and profitable by means of irrigation.

7. The stocking of our rivers with fish such as do not live in them is a matter of great interest, and can only be carried out by the Government. We may judge of its importance when we understand that one million brood of salmon, without special attention or care, will in two years produce ten millions of pounds of the most healthful food. This subject

has not only attracted the attention of European governments, but it has been repeatedly carried into successful operation there, and, upon a limited scale, in a section of this country.

The Superintendent's rationalization of his position led him in his next annual report (1861) to the "conclusion that agriculture, manufactures, and commerce should be united under one general supervision as in France, Italy, and Prussia"; and this opinion was endorsed by Commissioner of Patents D. P. Holloway, who urged the creation of a separate Department of the Productive Arts to care for the industrial interests of the country and especially for agriculture.

A part at least of this plan was adopted by an act of May 15, 1862 (12 Stat. 387), establishing the Department of Agriculture, the "general designs and duties" of which would be "to acquire and to diffuse among the people of the United States useful information on subjects connected with agriculture in the most general and comprehensive sense of that word, and to procure, propagate, and distribute among the people new and valuable seeds and plants. " Under the provisions of the act, a Commissioner of Agriculture was to be named as the Department's "chief executive officer" whose duties would be to "acquire and preserve in his Department all information concerning agriculture which he can obtain by means of books and correspondence, and by practical and scientific experiments, (accurate records of which experiments shall be kept in his office,) by the collection of statistics, and by any other appropriate means within his power; to collect, as he may be able, new and valuable seeds and plants; to test, by cultivation, the value of such of them as may require such tests; to propagate such as may be worthy of propagation, and to distribute them among agriculturists." The Commissioner was to "receive and have charge of all the property of the agricultural division of the Patent Office in the Department of the Interior, including the fixtures and property of the propagating garden."

The new agency, though called a department, was essentially a bureau until 1889, since the organic act did not provide that the Commissioner of Agriculture should have Cabinet status. Isaac Newton, who from Apr. 1861 had been superintendent of the agricultural division of the Patent Office, was appointed on July 1, 1862, as the first Commissioner of Agriculture. He soon increased to about 50 the clerical force of the former agricultural division, engaged a chemist (Charles W. Wetherill, succeeded in 1864 by Henri Erni), established a laboratory, hired a horticulturist (William Saunders) to take charge of the propagating or experimental garden, and initiated greater activity in collecting and publicizing current agricultural data and in distributing seeds and cuttings. In his first annual report he revived the presentation of agricultural statistics, long neglected, and in 1863 he organized a statistical branch under Lewis Bollman and employed an entomologist (Townsend Glover).

In its first year, besides continuing to distribute packages of seeds to members of Congress and others, the new Department "laboriously sought" from every source information that when properly classified would "be disseminated, like the seeds, cereals, and plants, gratuitously." The Commissioner found "the space assigned . . . of a half-dozen rooms in the basement under the Patent Office . . . too limited and inconvenient for any department of this government, and . . . not only insufficient for . . . present accommodations, but . . . a positive bar to any increased operations." Not until 1867, however, was the erection of a permanent Department building to begin. This was to be constructed on Government Reservation 2, an area lying between Twelfth and Fourteenth Streets, "the canal," and B Street South, in Washington, that had been assigned to the Department for experimental agriculture in 1864.

In July 1863 Commissioner Newton began to issue the Department's series of monthly reports on current agricultural operations, in which appeared (until 1872) the meteorological tables furnished by the Smithsonian Institution. These monthly reports imparted "fresh agricultural facts" derived from the Department's correspondence and other sources, as distinguished from agricultural information of permanent value published in the annual reports. As an example of the latter, the Commissioner in 1864 instituted "a system of correspondence with our consuls abroad"--the first results of which appear in a compilation appended to the 1864 annual report. This system was designed "to elicit information concerning the character and condition of foreign agriculture, and to preserve an exchange of industrial statistics."

The postwar Chief Clerk, James M. Swank, complained that Patents Commissioner Holloway's 1861 report "did not contain one line of statistics relative to agriculture or related subjects, except some tables of milk production, nor a single letter concerning the position of the crops." He remarked that Newton's 1863 report "contained the first attempt that had been made since the days of [Patents Commissioners] Ellsworth and Burke [i. e., since 1849] to ingraft upon the census returns the statistics of the yearly progress of agricultural production." Ever conscious of the impact of the war upon agriculture, Commissioner Newton brought about an investigation of the practicability of substituting flax and hemp for cotton (see below); and in his 1863 report he described the implications of the wartime work of distributing seed, as follows:

The great, imperative, and increasing calls upon the department for seeds of all kinds, from all sections of the country, especially from the west and from the border States, where the desolations of war with the rebels and the Indians had destroyed the crops of the preceding year, gave me an early and loud warning that it would be no light labor to comply with that part of the act requiring me "to procure and distribute new and valuable seeds."

Pursuing what I regarded as the most judicious and satisfactory course, I imported from England, France, Belgium, Russia, Sweden, and other foreign countries, several hundred bushels of choice wheat and other cereal grains, and several thousand dollars' worth of the most valuable seeds for field and garden culture, including a large collection of such flower seeds as were deemed suitable for our country. These, with an assortment of the choicest varieties of the most desirable grains and vegetables grown in our own country, were spread over the country with a lavish hand.

In addition to these, about fifteen hundred bushels of cotton seed were procured, packed, and distributed mainly among the farmers of the west. There was, too, a very great demand made upon the department for tobacco seed, which was not readily found in many parts of the country, but which, fortunately, I was prepared to supply, and by which the wealth of our country was increased millions of dollars.

Isaac Newton continued as Commissioner of Agriculture until June 19, 1867.

James M. Swank, The Department of Agriculture; Its History and Objects (Washington, 1872); Francis G. Caffey, A Brief Statutory History of the Department of Agriculture (Washington, 1907); and Robert H. Cory, Jr., The United States Department of Agriculture; a History of Its Establishment, Growth, and Accomplishments Prior to Its Incorporation Into the Cabinet in 1889 (New Haven, Conn., 1936).

The annual reports of the Superintendent of Agricultural Affairs to the Commissioner of Patents in the period immediately preceding the war should be consulted, especially that for 1860 (H. Ex. Doc. 48, 36 Cong., 2 sess., Serial 1099). Printed as House documents, the four wartime annual reports of the Commissioner of Agriculture were:

1862. H. Ex. Doc. 78, 37 Cong., 3 sess., Serial 1168.
1863. H. Ex. Docs. 1 and 91, 38 Cong., 1 sess., Serials 1184 and 1196.
1864. H. Ex. Doc. 68, 38 Cong., 2 sess., Serial 1228.
1865. H. Ex. Doc. 136, 39 Cong., 1 sess., Serial 1266.

Record Groups 16, 97. --The extant records of the Department for the Civil War period are negligible. They comprise only the oaths of office of Commissioner Newton's assistants, named above (Record Group 16), and a letter book of the chemist (Record Group 97). The latter contains copies of letters received by Commissioner Newton and Chemist Wetherill, 1862-63, requesting the chemical analysis of sorghum, molasses, cane sugar, wine, minerals, and soils; and copies of reports of chemical analyses, 1864-67, by Chemist Erni and his postwar successor.

Among records of the Meteorological Division of the Smithsonian Institution (Record Group 27) are several letters, 1863-67, addressed to the Commissioner of Agriculture but sent to the Smithsonian because they dealt mainly with meteorology. Letters received in the Interior Department from the Commissioner of Agriculture during the Civil War are in the files of the Patents and Miscellaneous Division, Office of the Secretary of the Interior (Record Group 48).

COMMISSION TO INVESTIGATE FLAX AND HEMP

By an act of Feb. 25, 1863 (12 Stat. 691), Congress appropriated $20,000 for "investigations to test the practicability of cultivating and preparing flax and hemp, as a substitute for cotton," and Commissioner of Agriculture Isaac Newton proceeded to carry out these investigations as soon as the appropriation became available. He found that the people of the Middle and Western States especially "did not confine the meaning of the appropriating clause merely to the preparation of flax for cotton machinery, but took the broader view concerning the cultivation and preparation of flax generally, and with reason, growing, as they do, nearly all the flax in the country." To put the investigation "beyond all reasonable complaint or suspicion of partiality," Newton appointed as a commission to undertake the investigation three private citizens: J. K. Moorhead of Pittsburgh, William M. Bailey of Providence, and J. M. Warder of Cincinnati. (In 1864 Charles Jackson of Providence replaced Bailey on the Commission.)

The Commission met in Washington soon after its appointment and adjourned after passing a resolution that the Commissioner of Agriculture should call upon manufacturers and experimenters to send to the Department, by Nov. 20, 1863, "samples of the fibres and fabrics prepared by them, to be accompanied, in all cases, by precise statements as to the various processes, and with estimates as to the probable expense per pound of the preparation of the material, and of the proportion of fibre that may be produced from a given quantity of the stalks or straw of flax and hemp." The Commission resumed its inquiry in Dec. 1863 and on Feb. 27, 1865, submitted its report, which was printed as S. Ex. Doc. 35, 38 Cong., 2 sess., Serial 1209. The report was predicated on the assumption that Congress had intended to encourage the preparation of what was called familiarly "flax-cotton" because of "the fact that many of the extensive manufactories of our country were standing idle, in consequence of the scarcity of the product of the cotton fields, caused by the desolation of the rebellion in the southern States."

No records of the Commission as such have been found, but the original of its report is in the files of the U. S. Senate, Record Group 46 (38A-G10).

XIII. MISCELLANEOUS AGENCIES

In this section are discussed some governmental or quasigovernmental organizations of the executive branch, all well below the Cabinet level. Two of them--the Chesapeake and Ohio Canal Company and the Panama Railroad Company--began as private enterprises and were taken over by the Government; two--the U. S. Sanitary Commission and the U. S. Christian Commission--were Civil War organizations supported largely by private subscription but having close ties with the Government, especially with the War Department; one--the Commissioners of Emancipation in the District of Columbia--was an ad hoc commission set up during the war; two--the Smithsonian Institution and the National Academy of Sciences--are Government institutions partly supported by private funds (no records of the Civil War period have been transferred from either of these to the National Archives); and the last--the so-called Southern Claims Commission and various memorialization agencies--were postwar governmental bodies that created records related to the war. These agencies are discussed below in the chronological order of their establishment.

CHESAPEAKE AND OHIO CANAL COMPANY

The Chesapeake and Ohio Canal Company, successor to the Potomac Company, was incorporated by an act of the Virginia legislature on Jan. 27, 1824. The State of Maryland confirmed the incorporation on Jan. 31, 1825, and the United States did so on Mar. 3, 1825 (4 Stat. 101). Under its charter the company sought "to establish a connected navigation between the Eastern and Western waters, so as to extend and multiply the means and facilities of internal commerce and personal intercourse between two great sections of the United States; and to interweave more closely all the mutual interests and affections, that are calculated to perfect the vital principle of Union."

Construction of the canal was begun on July 4, 1828, and was completed to Cumberland in 1850. With the secession of Virginia, the canal, which ran along the northern bank of the Potomac River, was on the border between the Union and the Confederacy. In 1861 and 1862 it suffered from Southern attempts to halt its traffic. Lee's invasions of Sept. 1862 and June and July 1863 resulted in damage to some of the locks; and on occasion during the war the opposing Armies occupied some of the canal works. Moreover, the war itself reduced the coastal trade upon which canal operations depended, and the cumulative effect upon the canal's business was almost disastrous. Areas and structures belonging to the canal were occupied by the Federal Government for varying periods during the war--notably the

Potomac Aqueduct (near the present Key Bridge), which was transformed into a bridge and thus cut off the canal from its only feasible access to tidewater. The Government seized canal boats at different times, as during the panic caused by the operations of the Merrimac. AGO General Order 44, Apr. 21, 1862, ordered that the property of the canal company on the side held by Union forces be given up and restored to the president of the company.

In 1933 the Company's property was purchased by the United States and put under the jurisdiction of the National Park Service.

Walter S. Sanderlin, The Great National Project; a History of the Chesapeake and Ohio Canal (Baltimore, 1946); wartime annual reports of the company's president and directors.

Record Group 79. --The company's records in the National Archives are those that accumulated to 1889, before the company went into receivership. Series spanning the Civil War include stockholders' proceedings; proceedings of the president and directors; letters received by the president and letter books containing copies of letters sent; miscellaneous fiscal records; registers of boats and of articles transported on the canal; land, legal, and court records; and the annual reports of the president and directors. Only a detailed and laborious examination of these materials can reveal their significance to Civil War documentation, but Sanderlin's work, cited above, which uses the letters sent and received, 1861-64 and beyond, suggests their potential.

Records in Other Custody. --The University of Virginia Library has approximately 300 letters, legal documents, broadsides, etc., concerning principally the presidency of Col. Alfred Spates during the 1860's and the direct control over the canal exercised during 1861-65 by Federal military authorities.

SMITHSONIAN INSTITUTION

The Smithsonian Institution was created by an act of Congress of Aug.10, 1846 (9 Stat. 102), which directed that it be supported in perpetuity by the income from a bequest of over half a million dollars from an Englishman, James Smithson, whose will had stipulated that it was to be an "establishment for the increase & diffusion of knowledge among men." The board of regents provided for by the act met on Dec. 3, 1846, and selected Joseph Henry, then professor at Princeton, as Secretary of the Institution. The act of incorporation also provided for the construction of a building to house a museum, an art gallery, a chemical laboratory, and a library. As administered by Henry, who continued as Secretary until his death in 1878, the income from the Smithson bequest was devoted primarily to original scientific research and to the publication and distribution of the results of such research. A part of the Institution's Annual Report regularly recounted the progress of science throughout the world, and memoirs on scientific subjects were published in the Smithsonian's Contributions to Knowledge and its Miscellaneous Collections. A program for the international exchange of publications resulted in the accumulation of a large collection of journals and transactions of scientific and learned societies. The collecting of specimens of natural history and the examination and classification of minerals went on throughout the Civil War period. The Smithsonian's system of assembling weather reports by telegraph from a network of observers scattered over the country was affected during the war by the loss of observers in the South and by the U. S. Government's almost constant use of the telegraph wires.

The role of the Secretary of the Institution as the science adviser to the Government was expanded during the war. Since 1852 Henry had been a member of the Light-House Board; and during the war, as chairman of its committee on experiments, he directed tests of "lard oil" as a substitute for the scarce and expensive whale oil. Henry investigated and reported upon proposals and inventions submitted to the Government for use in the war, and he examined materials purchased by the Government to determine their quality. He advised the President and the executive departments on scientific matters. He served as a member of the Permanent Commission and the Board to Examine the Stevens Battery of the Navy Department and was a founder of the National Academy of Sciences, for which he prepared reports on war-related subjects. At the request of the Secretary of War he examined plans for balloons and participated in their testing. To meet an emergency the laboratory of the Institution prepared a disinfecting liquid for the use of Washington hospitals caring for wounded soldiers. The laboratory also investigated methods of ventilating the Capitol, where the addition of new wings had created problems.

Thomas Coulson, Joseph Henry; His Life and Work (Princeton, 1950); Paul H. Oehser, Sons of Science; the Story of the Smithsonian Institution and Its Leaders (New York, 1949). The wartime Annual Reports of the Smithsonian Institution were published as follows:

1861. H. Misc. Doc. 77, 37 Cong., 2 sess., Serial 1141.
1862. H. Misc. Doc. 25, 37 Cong., 3 sess., Serial 1172.
1863. H. Misc. Doc. 83, 38 Cong., 1 sess., Serial 1201.
1864. H. Misc. Doc. 55, 38 Cong., 2 sess., Serial 1233.
1865. H. Ex. Doc. 102, 39 Cong., 1 sess., Serial 1265.

Record Group 27. --Records relating to the Smithsonian Institution's meteorological work are now among the records of the Weather Bureau. The "meteorological letters received," 1847-67 (in 5 vols. for 1861-65), consist chiefly of letters from volunteer weather observers transmitting reports, acknowledging circulars, explaining failures to report, requesting blank forms and instructions, commenting on the weather, or offering their services. A file of meteorological reports of these unpaid observers, 1840-73, submitted monthly, is arranged alphabetically by State and thereunder by locality. A smaller file of private journals, diaries, and reports, 1720-1895 (collected by the Smithsonian Institution, the Signal Office, and the Weather Bureau), contains a few items for the war period.

National Archives, List of Climatological Records in the National Archives, comp. by Lewis J. Darter (Washington, 1942); "List of Smithsonian Meteorological Stations and Observers in North America and Adjacent Islands from 1849 up to the End of the Year 1868," in Smithsonian Institution, Annual Report, 1868, p. 68-107 (Washington, 1869).

Records in Other Custody. --A fire in the Smithsonian Building on Jan. 24, 1865, destroyed most of the letters received and sent, receipts for publications and specimens, reports on subjects referred to the Institution, records of experiments performed for the Government, and some papers of Joseph Henry, including his diaries, memorandum books, and account books (S. Rept. 129, 38 Cong., 2 sess., Serial 1211). Surviving records are still in the Smithsonian archives. Press copybooks of letters sent, from Jan. 1865, relate to meteorology and other sciences, publications, orders for materials, comments on manuscripts presented for publication, and invitations to attend meetings. Letters received that were saved from the fire include 9 volumes for the period Apr. 1863-Dec. 1865. These letters concern scientific and meteorological subjects and include offers to forward meteorological data or to serve as observers, offers of specimens for purchase or exchange, offers to deliver lectures or requests for permission to use the Smithsonian hall for public meetings, requests for information and advice on scientific subjects and inventions, and information on the preparation of publications. Letters from the Secretary of Agriculture concern weather reports, supplying observers with instruments, etc., and the examination of applicants for appointments. The correspondence of Samuel F. Baird (assistant secretary in charge of printing, exchanges of publications, and the collections of natural history) is available from 1850. His letters sent, 1861-65, are in 12 volumes, and his letters received for the same period are in 13 volumes. Other "meteorological letters received," May 1852-June 1861 and Jan.-June 1868 (11 vols.), are also in the Smithsonian archives. Considerable quantities of private correspondence of Joseph Henry, 1825-78, and Samuel F. Baird, 1850-87, are available. Henry's papers include correspondence with Alexander D. Bache, 1834-67, and other correspondence on matters concerning the Light-House Board and the Coast Survey. An account book of expenditures for meteorological apparatus, 1851-70, contains accounts for individual observers.

The Smithsonian's published Annual Reports, 1861-65, contain some correspondence, reports of the executive committee, proceedings of the board of regents, and lists of publications, lectures, specimens received, and meteorological stations and observers. See also The Smithsonian Institution; Journals of the Board of Regents, Reports of Committees, Statistics, etc. [1846-76], ed. by William J. Rhees (Smithsonian Miscellaneous Collections, vol. 18, Washington, 1879). Correspond-ence and reports by Henry are in the files of other Government departments and bureaus. See the records of the Board to Examine the Stevens Battery, the Permanent Commission, and the National Academy of Sciences, described elsewhere in this Guide. Other correspondence of Henry is in numerous depositories; for this, see Philip M. Hamer, ed., A Guide to Archives and Manuscripts in the United States (New Haven, Conn., 1961).

PANAMA RAILROAD COMPANY

The Panama Railroad Company, incorporated under the laws of New York in Apr. 1849, built and operated a railroad across the Isthmus of Panama. During the first 10 years of its operation (1855-65) the railroad carried over $700,000,000 in specie and 300,000 bags of mail. Under the treaty signed by representatives of the United States and Panama on Nov. 18, 1903, it was acquired by the U. S. Government.

Gerstle Mack, The Land Divided; a History of the Panama Canal and Other Isthmian Canal Projects (New York, 1944); Darrell H. Smith, The Panama Canal; Its History, Activities, and Organization (Institute for Government Research, Service Monographs of the U. S. Government, No. 44. Baltimore, 1927); Marshall E. Dimock, Government-Operated Enterprises in the Panama Canal Zone (Chicago, 1934).

Record Group 185.--In the Federal Records Center, New York City, is the company's correspondence during the Civil War with such U. S. officials as the Secretary of State and several consuls, with bankers and agents of steamship companies, and with representatives of Latin American governments. In addition to normal company business, the correspondence concerns Confederate plans to interfere with U. S. shipping on the Pacific Coast. Other records of the period in the Center comprise the company's annual reports, 1860-76 (2 ft.); contract files, 1861-65 (1 ft.); journals documenting fiscal operations, 1860-80 (1 ft.); and canceled stock certificates and bond coupons, 1859-70 (5 ft.).

U. S. SANITARY COMMISSION

Early in 1861 sanitarians who had been promoting the public health movement and physicians who knew of the work of the British Sanitary Commission during the Crimean War turned their attention to protecting the health of the soldiers. On the recommendation of a delegation of relief organizations in New York City, Secretary of War Stanton issued an order on June 9, 1861 (approved by Lincoln on June 13), establishing the U. S. Sanitary Commission. The original members of the commission were Henry W. Bellows (a prominent Unitarian minister of New York), Alexander Dallas Bache (Superintendent of the U. S. Coast Survey), Dr. Wolcott Gibbs, Dr. William H. Van Buren, Dr. Samuel G. Howe, Col. Robert C. Wood (Acting Surgeon General), Lt. Col. George W. Cullum, and Maj. Alexander E. Shiras. At a meeting of the commission on June 12 Bellows was elected president, and a plan of organization was adopted. The commission was to inquire into the recruiting practices, the sanitary condition of troops, and the means of preserving their health; and it was to advise the War Department on these matters. George Templeton Strong, a New York lawyer, became treasurer. As general secretary Frederick Law Olmsted, the landscape architect, directed the work of the commission from 1861 to 1863. He was succeeded in that position by Dr. J. F. Jenkins in Sept. 1863, and by J. S. Blatchford in Apr. 1865. The central office of the commission was set up in Washington in quarters supplied by the Government, which also furnished transportation for its agents in the field.

The commission developed a large organization that carried on varied activities. State branches maintained depots into which were fed supplies collected by many affiliated local aid societies. The Western Sanitary Commission was organized at St. Louis by William G. Eliot, a Congregational minister; and other commissions in the Mississippi Valley operated under the presidency of James E. Yeatman. In the same area Dr. J. S. Newberry, a member of the U. S. Sanitary Commission, organized its Western Department. Agents of the commission in the field included clerks, depot keepers, wagon drivers, relief agents, and inspectors. Their labors supplemented on a large scale the operations of the Army Medical Department in caring for soldiers. The commission's inspections of hospitals and prison camps and its agitation for their improvement resulted in better sanitary conditions. It gave massive assistance in battle areas by providing ambulance and hospital services, hospital cars and steamers, and medical supplies. The various sanitary commissions assisted in recruiting female nurses, who served chiefly in general hospitals in the North; opened gardens at hospitals to improve the patients' diets with fresh vegetables; provided convalescent homes for the further care of men discharged from hospitals; and established feeding stations along routes traveled by soldiers. Information on the latest methods of treatment and advances in medical science was compiled and disseminated, channels by which soldiers could communicate with their families were provided, and a hospital directory was issued to enable relatives and friends to locate hospitalized soldiers. Claims agencies in Washington and in the loyal States helped soldiers and sailors and their families in pressing claims for pensions, arrears of pay, bounties, and prize money and other claims on the Government. All these services were supported by contributions from private sources; in the latter part of the war large sums were raised by "sanitary fairs" held in many cities.

William Q. Maxwell, Lincoln's Fifth Wheel; the Political History of the United States Sanitary Commission (New York, 1956); Charles J. Stillé, History of the United States Sanitary Commission, Being the General Report of Its Work During the War of the Rebellion; George W. Adams, Doctors in Blue; the Medical History of the Union Army in the Civil War (New York, 1952); Howard D. Kramer, "Effect of the Civil War on the Public Health Movement," Mississippi Valley Historical Review, 35:449-462 (Dec. 1948); Roland G. Usher, "The Western Sanitary Commission," Mississippi Valley Historical Association, Proceedings, 2:218-234 (1908-9); Earl S. Fullbrook, "Relief Work in Iowa During the Civil War," Iowa Journal of History, 16:155-274 (Apr. 1918). There are also official histories of the Philadelphia branch, of the Chicago branch by Sarah E. Henshaw, of the Western Department by J. S. Newberry, and of the Western Sanitary Commission by Jacob S. Forman.

Records in Other Custody. --When terminating its activities in 1865, the U. S. Sanitary Commission directed its branches to send in their records for use in preparing an official history of the organization. Bellows held the records of the commission until they were presented in Jan. 1879 to the Astor Library, which was consolidated in 1895 with the Tilden Trust to form the New York Public Library. The records of the central office and the branches--including correspondence, reports, accounts, hospital directories, printed materials, histories, maps, and charts--were in more than a thousand books and boxes; still other boxes contained records on claims and finances. For the Washington office there are records of the medical committee, the statistical bureau, the canvass and supply department, market supply, and special inspections of Army general hospitals; there are also archives registers, a history of special relief, and condensed historical material. Records of branches and affiliated organizations include those of the New England Women's Auxiliary Association, the Boston Associates' executive committee, the California and English branches, the Philadelphia agency, the New York office and the Women's Central Relief Association of New York, and the Western Department. Battlefields, military departments, and other field agencies that are the subjects of records include the Department of the Gulf; Frederick and Sharpsburg; Annapolis and Baltimore; Army of the Potomac; Department of the Shenandoah; Department of North Carolina; and Gettysburg and Harrisburg, Pa. There are also Washington and Louisville hospital directories and records of the Army and Navy Claim Agency, the Protective War Claim Associations of New York and Philadelphia, and the American Association for the Relief of Misery on Battlefields, a successor to the Sanitary Commission.

The papers of several members and officials of the comission supplement the commission's records. Papers of Henry W. Bellows and of Samuel G. Howe are in the Massachusetts Historical Society; other Howe papers are in the Harvard University Library. Papers of Alexander D. Bache are in the Library of Congress, the Henry E. Huntington Library, and the American Philosophical Society. An extensive group of papers of Frederick Law Olmsted is in the Library of Congress. Information on the administration of the commission is in the diary of George Templeton Strong, a part of which was edited by Allan Nevins and Milton H. Thomas and published in 4 volumes in 1952. The Historical Society of Pennsylvania has papers of Charles J. Stillé that cover the war period. In the New-York Historical Society among the papers of Alfred J. Bloor, assistant secretary of the commission from July 1861 to Sept. 1864, is a letter book, Jan. -July 1864, that concerns the work of the commission. Some papers of Dr. Lewis H. Steiner, who became an inspector in 1861 and chief inspector in 1863, are in the Maryland Historical Society. The papers of another inspector, John H. Douglas, and some materials on the District of Columbia branch are in the Library of Congress.

Papers of other branches of the commission and of organizations and persons connected with it are in other depositories. Documents concerning the Buffalo branch in the Buffalo Historical Society include a hospital directory, an expense account of the soldiers' rest home at Buffalo, and other accounts for supplies and hospital stores. Records of the Cleveland branch are in the Western Reserve Historical Society. Letters and pamphlets regarding the Women's Central Association of Relief of New York are in the New-York Historical Society. Correspondence of Mrs. James P. Andrews and her aunt, Miss Kate Clark, regarding their work for the commission in Kentucky, Tennessee, Alabama, and the District of Columbia are in the Henry E. Huntington Library. Papers of William G. Eliot, organizer of the Western Sanitary Commission, are in Washington University Library, St. Louis; and among Eliot papers in the Missouri Historical Society is the order of General Frémont, Sept. 5, 1861, appointing the commission. In this society also are the minutes, Feb. 1-Aug. 5, 1864, of the Mississippi Valley sanitary fair (held at St. Louis, May 18-June 18, 1864) and the prescription book of Dr. John Green, who treated patients on the hospital ship Ella.

The U. S. Sanitary Commission published many documents concerning its work. These include circulars, statements of expenditures and receipts, compilations of papers, financial reports, instructions, orders, regulations, and rules, letters, a bulletin (Nov. 1, 1863-Aug. 1, 1864), minutes of its meetings, 1861-65, and reports of committees and branches. The records of the War Department (especially those of the Surgeon General and the Adjutant General) contain reports on relief and the improvement of medical facilities for the soldiers and many letters making suggestions. A photo-offset edition of the 135-volume hospital directory prepared by the commission was published in 1961 by G. K. Hall & Co., Boston, Mass.

U. S. CHRISTIAN COMMISSION

The U. S. Christian Commission was organized in New York City on
Nov. 15, 1861, at a meeting of the local Young Men's Christian Association,
to promote the spiritual and temporal welfare of soldiers in the Union Army
and sailors and marines in the Navy, in cooperation with chaplains and others. Its ministrations were confined chiefly though not entirely to volunteers. It brought together earlier private organizations for such welfare
and united them in one agency to collect, receive, and distribute food, clothing, and sundries; to provide religious services for the soldiers without
undue regard to particular sects; and to distribute publications, chiefly religious or moral. Its Circular No. 1, issued Nov. 16, 1861, set forth these
essential objectives and sketched a proposed organization ranging from local committees of the Y. M. C. A. and other private agencies to the central
offices and field workers.

Although the Christian Commission soon won War Department approval
it did not gain access to Army hospitals, posts, garrisons, and camps until
Jan. 24, 1863. Commission delegates and agents eventually became almost
a part of the armed forces, enjoying privileges of transportation and access
and doing many small chores, helpful especially to the Medical Department.

The evolution of the commission's functions took from Nov. 1861 to Jan.
1863, when a sizable organization was attained. At first a central office
was set up, responsible to an executive committee, which in turn reported
at intervals to the Christian Commission proper. A general committee of
three, one member of which was the treasurer, had the major administrative function of forwarding contributions of stores. Each geographical district of the commission was also governed by a committee of three, with
the same function. The Jan. 1863 organization introduced the "delegate
system" and the efficient distribution of quantities of stores sent from many
different sources throughout the North. The central office of the commission, at Philadelphia, was then composed of the commission, which had
general supervision of the work; its president, who had executive supervision; a general secretary to assist the president; and secretaries for home
and field workers respectively. Below these were 5 field agents, in charge
of "divisions" or "districts," some of whom had assistants; 300 unpaid "delegates" at stations within the Army; and about 60 women who volunteered
their services as "members of the diet kitchen." Quasi-formal "offices"
were established in the larger cities (29 at the peak) to receive contributions; "base offices" in Nashville, Louisville, and Washington; and "Army
agencies" at City Point, Fortress Monroe, New Bern (N. C.), Harper's
Ferry, and Richmond. The commission officially went out of existence in
Jan. 1866, when its activities had almost entirely ceased.

U. S. Christian Commission,
Annual Reports (Philadelphia, 1863-
66); Lemuel Moss, Annals of the
Unites States Christian Commission
(Philadelphia, 1868); The American
Annual Cyclopædia and Register of
Important Events, 4:801-803 (New
York, Appleton and Co. , 1865);
James O. Henry, "The United
States Christian Commission in the
Civil War, " Civil War History, 6:374-
388 (Dec. 1960).

Record Group 94. --Although the commission by regulations of July 22,
1864, ordered that certain field records should be kept, it seems actually
to have paid little attention to recordkeeping. The central office maintained

financial records, considerable correspondence, and scattered memoranda of minutes, lists of workers, and related records. Some field records found their way to the central office, but in general records seem to have been left in the hands of those who made them. Most of the commission's records in this record group appear to be records that were in the possession of the commission's chief benefactor and ex-president, George H. Stuart. In 1894 the collection was augmented when the Record and Pension Office received from Stuart's son a chest of commission records and family archives.

The records that can be identified as belonging to the central office include minutes of meetings of the executive committee, 1861-65 (3 in.); press copies of letters sent, 1862-66 (15 vols.); communications received, 1862-66 (1 1/2 ft.), with registers, 1864-65, and a record of inquiries, 1864-65; annual reports of the president; and delegates' reports, 1863-65 (1 ft.). The correspondence concerns contributions of money, supplies, books, and religious tracts; authorizations for delegates and agents to visit troops; the acceptance of new members and arrangements for speakers; and other matters of administration, personnel, and transportation.

Records of the individual relief department comprise letters of inquiry received (incomplete), 1864-65, concerning the whereabouts and condition of soldiers, with registers and abstracts of replies; a similar "Record of Inquiries," 1864 (1 vol.), maintained by the bureau of information at Washington; and abstracts of letters written for sick and wounded soldiers of the Army of the Potomac, 1864-65 (1 vol. and additional pieces), and for soldiers at Nashville, Tenn., 1864-65 (3 vols.).

The commission's records of accounts and contributions comprise invoices for articles furnished, order books, cash ledgers, petty-cash books, payment orders, invoices of money received from soldiers for forwarding, and cash accounts of various officials. Contributions are recorded in the "Receiving Books," 1862-65 (7 vols.); and related records include a record of contributions of Ladies' Auxiliary Christian Commissions, 1864-65 (1 vol.), and a 1-volume list of such contributors. The forwarding of items to and from soldiers is documented by receipts from the Adams Express Co., 1864-65 (2 vols.); records of express packages received at City Point, Va., 1864 (2 vols.); a record of "money expressed," 1864-65 (2 vols.); and other express books, 1864-65 (10 vols.).

Other significant records include a record of the commission's religious activities, 1864 (1 vol.); several photograph albums and scrapbooks; memoranda concerning contributors, auxiliary associations, publicity, and other office matters (11 vols.); a record of publications received and sent, 1864-65 (6 vols.); a list of religious newspapers ordered for 1865; correspondence concerning the Record of the Federal Dead, a commission publication; and copies of other commission issuances, including Christ in the Army, Information for Army Meetings, and Instructions to Delegates (1 ft.).

Records, besides those mentioned above, that are useful in identifying persons working for or cooperating with the Christian Commission include several registers of delegates and a list of delegates offering their services for general work.

The collection includes also the diaries, 1862-65, of Christian Commission officials at Nelson Station and Wild's Station, Va.; with the Fifth, Ninth, and Eighteenth Army Corps; and with the Army of the Potomac. There are also a register of prisoners at Richmond, Va., 1861-64 (apparently a record of the C. S. A., written on the unused pages of an 1842 Richmond land book), and correspondence of the New England Soldiers' Relief Association, 1862-65 (20 vols.).

National Archives, Preliminary   by Lucille H. Pendell and Elizabeth
Inventory [No. 17] of the Records of   Bethel (Washington, 1949), p. 140-
the Adjutant General's Office, comp.   147.

Records in Other Custody. --In the Library of Congress are other records of the commission, 1863-68 (5 boxes), a volume of notes kept in 1865 by an unidentified field representative in the vicinity of Norfolk, Va. , and other papers of George H. Stuart, including his correspondence with officers, officials, and other persons. The papers of the Rev. Joseph C. Thomas in the same custody relate to libraries established for the Army by the commission. A notebook kept by S. Hastings Grant while a member of the commission is in the New-York Historical Society.

COMMISSIONERS ON EMANCIPATION IN THE DISTRICT OF COLUMBIA

Under an act of Apr. 16, 1862 (12 Stat. 376), and a supplementary act of July 12, 1862 (12 Stat. 538) "for the release of certain persons held to service or labor in the District of Columbia," three Commissioners were appointed to examine petitions for compensation to the former owners of freed slaves in the District and to investigate and decide the claims to freedom of "persons held to service or labor within the District of Columbia by reason of African descent" for whom compensation had not been claimed by their former owners.

The original Commissioners were Daniel R. Goodloe, Horatio King, and Samuel F. Vinton; they met initially at the City Hall on Apr. 28, 1862; but their labors had hardly begun before Vinton died (May 11, 1862) and was replaced by John M. Brodhead, who served from June 14, 1862. Claimants for compensation were required to file their petitions by July 15, 1862; the 966 petitions presented covered 3, 100 "persons held to service or labor," for whom compensation was claimed. The Commissioners reported favorably upon 909 petitions, rejected 36 in their entirety, and rejected 21 in part. Because there were no persons available in Washington who had "the knowledge and discrimination as to the value of slaves" necessary to "a just apportionment of compensation under law," the Commissioners consulted "an experienced dealer in slaves from Baltimore," one B. M. Campbell. Their final report to the Secretary of the Treasury, Jan. 14, 1863 (H. Exec. Doc. 42, 38 Cong. , 1 sess. , Serial 1189), analyzes claims difficult of decision and includes a complete list of petitions filed showing action thereon. The supplementary act of July 12, 1862, provided not only that the Commissioners would investigate claims to freedom of persons for whom no compensation had been claimed by their owners, but also that "all persons held to service or labor under the laws of any State, and who at any time since the sixteenth day of April, anno Domini eighteen hundred and sixty-two, by the consent of the person to whom such service or labor is claimed to be owing, have been actually employed within the District of Columbia, or who shall be hereafter thus employed, are hereby declared free, and forever released from such servitude, anything in the laws of the United States or of any State to the contrary notwithstanding." Under these provisions, 161 petitions were presented, of which 139 were granted, and 22 rejected. The

Treasurer of the United States, as the disbursing officer of the Government, was authorized to pay the awards, from approximately $900,000 advanced for the purpose, and the account was settled finally by the First Auditor in 1867 (Misc. Treas. Account 158299).

Record Group 217. --Minutes of the Commissioners, Apr. 28, 1862-Jan. 14, 1863 (1 vol.), indexed; docket of petitions filed, Apr. 29-July 15, 1862 (1 vol.), indexed; the original of the Commissioners' final report; the original petitions presented, some with evidentiary documents such as wills or tax receipts (2 ft.), and a few powers of attorney. Some related records are in the files of the U. S. circuit court of the District of Columbia.

NATIONAL ACADEMY OF SCIENCES

The National Academy of Sciences was founded through the efforts of a number of Government and academic scientists. Alexander D. Bache (Superintendent of the Coast Survey), Rear Adm. Charles H. Davis (Chief of the Bureau of Navigation of the Navy Department), Benjamin A. Gould (astronomer with the Coast Survey), Louis Agassiz (the noted naturalist), and Benjamin Peirce (Harvard mathematician) met in Washington in Feb. 1863 with Senator Henry Wilson of Massachusetts to plan the establishment of the Academy. A bill introduced by Wilson and enacted into law on Mar. 3, 1863 (12 Stat. 806), named 50 incorporators of the Academy and stipulated that it was to organize itself; to fill vacancies in membership as they occurred; to hold an annual meeting; and, when called upon by the Government, to investigate, examine, and report upon any subject of science or art without compensation. At the organization meeting in New York in Apr. 1863, Bache was chosen as the first president, and thereafter semiannual meetings (in January and August) were held in Washington. Several projects of minor importance were referred to the Academy for investigation by the Departments of the Navy and the Treasury in 1863 and 1864, but no requests were received in 1865. On the whole, the advisory role of the Academy during the war was not important.

A. Hunter Dupree, Science in the Federal Government; a History of Policies and Activities to 1940 (Cambridge, Mass., 1957); Frederick W. True, ed., A History of the First Half-Century of the National Academy of Sciences, 1863-1913 (Washington, 1913). National Academy of Sciences, Annual Reports 1863/64-1866 (Cambridge, 1865-67), contain lists of officers, members of the Academy, members of committees, and foreign associates; annual reports of the president; lists of memoirs presented to the Academy; and eulogies, biographical notices, and obituaries. The series of National Academy of Sciences, Memoirs (Washington, 1866-date), contains biographical sketches of members.

Records in Other Custody. --Although the Academy has transferred its records of later years to the National Archives, it still retains its early records. For the Civil War period these are few. One thick volume contains chiefly committee reports, 1863-64, relating to investigations made by the Academy on behalf of the Navy and Treasury Departments. Besides reports, other papers (grouped by committee) consist of correspondence between Bache and Government officials and members of the committees, journals, minutes, telegrams, memoranda, drawings, extracts of addresses, and records of publications. These committees were concerned

with uniform weights and measures and coinage, protecting ship bottoms
from salt water, the magnetic deviation of the compass in iron ships,
Maury's wind and current charts and sailing directions, tests for the purity
of whisky, experiments on the expansion of steam, materials for the manufacture of pennies, and the explosion on the U. S. S. Chenango. The minutes of council, Aug. 1864, Jan. 1865, and Aug. 1865, record the proceedings of the officers of the Academy, who met just before its semiannual
meetings to decide what matters should be recommended to its attention.
The first volume of the Academy's minutes records the proceedings of the
organization meeting at New York and subsequent semiannual meetings of
the Academy. The minutes record actions of the Academy on revision and
amendment of its constitution; election of officers, council members and
academy members, and foreign associates; appointments of committees;
consideration of the reports of the investigating committees; the subjects
of scientific papers presented to the Academy; relations with other societies;
appointment of men to prepare eulogies of deceased members; announcement of social events connected with the meetings; and administration of
oaths to members. These records throw light on the Government's scientific activities, provide biographical data for members, and give information on the activities of the Academy, but they can be supplemented by records of Government agencies and the personal papers of Academy members.

    The activities of the National Academy of Sciences can be further docu-
mented by the papers of its president and other members. Sizable collections of the papers of Alexander D. Bache are in the Library of Congress
and the Henry E. Huntington Library and Art Gallery. In the latter institution and in Houghton Library of Harvard University are papers of Louis
Agassiz. Extensive groups of papers of Benjamin Peirce are in the Houghton Library and in the American Academy of Arts and Sciences, Boston,
Mass.

Reports by the president of the
Academy on its activities from 1863
to 1865, together with the reports of
the committees on the subjects mentioned above, are published in H. Misc.
Doc. 81, 38 Cong., 1 sess., Serial
1200; H. Ex. Doc. 66, 38 Cong., 2
sess., Serial 1229; and H. Ex. Doc.
72, 39 Cong., 1 sess., Serial 1256.
The printed committee reports, however, do not contain most of the accompanying papers in the manuscript committee reports.

COMMISSIONERS OF CLAIMS

    Although many types of Civil War claims had been taken care of (see
especially Court of Claims), the claims of Unionists in the Southern States
for stores, supplies, and vessels taken or used by the U. S. Army were
not provided for until adoption of an act of Mar. 3, 1871 (16 Stat. 524).
This legislation authorized the appointment of three Commissioners of
Claims (popularly called the Southern Claims Commission) to consider such
claims and report on them to Congress. On Mar. 10 the Senate approved
as Commissioners Asa Owen Aldis, a former judge of the Supreme Court
of Vermont; James B. Howell, a former U. S. Senator from Iowa; and
Orange Ferriss, a former U. S. Representative from New York. Aldis
was chosen president of the Commission, and its meetings began in Washington in March. In conducting their business the Commissioners followed
the procedures that had been developed by the Court of Claims. It held

hearings to get oral testimony from claimants and witnesses, and it studied this testimony together with evidence drawn from Government records. A supplementary act of May 11, 1872 (17 Stat. 97), authorized the appointment of special commissioners to take testimony and of agents to investigate claims, and extended the jurisdiction of the Commission to cover claims for stores and supplies taken or used during the war by the U. S. Navy. The life of the Commission was renewed for four years by an act of Mar. 3, 1873 (17 Stat. 577), and in 1877 President Hayes reappointed the Commissioners named above. The Commission was dissolved on Mar. 12, 1880.

By the last date for filing the claims (Mar. 3, 1873), 22, 298 had been presented to the Commissioners, for an aggregate amount of $60, 258, 150. Of the total number of cases 16, 991 were reported by the Commission to Congress, 5, 250 were barred because substantiating evidence was not presented before Mar. 10, 1879 (act of June 15, 1878; 20 Stat. 566), and 57 were withdrawn. The whole amount allowed was $4, 636, 920.

Frank W. Klingberg, The Southern Claims Commission (Berkeley and Los Angeles, 1955). The annual "general" reports of the Commission were published as follows:

1871. H. Misc. Doc. 16, 42 Cong., 2 sess., Serial 1524.
1872. H. Misc. Doc. 12, 42 Cong., 3 sess., Serial 1571.
1873. H. Misc. Doc. 23, 43 Cong., 1 sess., Serial 1617.
1874. H. Misc. Doc. 18, 43 Cong., 2 sess., Serial 1653.
1875. H. Misc. Doc. 30, 44 Cong., 1 sess., Serial 1698.
1876. H. Misc. Doc. 4, 44 Cong., 2 sess., Serial 1762.
1877. H. Misc. Doc. 4, 45 Cong., 2 sess., Serial 1815.
1878. H. Misc. Doc. 6, 45 Cong., 3 sess., Serial 1861.
1879. H. Misc. Doc. 10, 46 Cong., 2 sess., Serial 1928.
1880. H. Misc. Doc. 30, 46 Cong., 2 sess., Serial 1929.

Record Group 56. --The records of the Commission are more important for its activities than for the claims that it reviewed. A journal, Mar. 1871-Oct. 1872, Jan. 1878-Mar. 1880, and record books kept by the president of the Commission, Mar. 1871-Dec. 1877, contain a daily record of its activities. Bound in these large volumes are data on the cases handled, acknowledgments of the receipt of letters and reports, and petitions of claimants. They contain also entries regarding personnel matters; requisitions on the Treasury; and printed material such as rules and regulations, instructions for special commissioners, lists of questions to be asked claimants, and annual reports. Registers of claims, Mar. 22, 1871-Mar. 3, 1873 (40 vols.), record the 22, 298 claims in the order of their receipt and give information as to each claim, the claimant, and the disposition of the claim. An alphabetical index by name of claimant fills 8 volumes, and there is also a geographical list of claims arranged alphabetically by State, thereunder by county, and thereunder by name of claimant. A chronological file of miscellaneous letters received, Mar. 1871-June 30, 1880, contains letters from claimants, attorneys, informers, and Federal officials; letters of recommendation; applications for positions; lists of "disloyal" individuals and fraudulent claims; copies of letters from Confederate archives; and complaints. A file of reports and letters from special agents, Mar. 1871-Feb. 1880, arranged alphabetically by name of agent, supplies information about each agent's appointment, activities, and expenses. A small file of 57 summary reports on printed forms constitutes a sample of the reports prepared by the Commissioners for submission to Congress. The journal, the several files of letters received, the geographical list of claims, and the consolidated index cited below are all on microfilm (M 87).

U. S. Commissioners of Claims, Consolidated Index of Claims Reported by the Commissioners of Claims to the House of Representatives From 1871 to 1880, comp. under the supervision of J. B. Holloway and Walter H. French (Washington, 1892), presents all the claims in a single alphabet, with information on their disposition. The Commission's general reports, published as House documents (see above), contain lists of claims alphabetically by State and thereunder alphabetically by name of claimant. The last report (in Serial 1929) contains a complete list of all claims barred, withdrawn, or dismissed.

Not actually a part of the Commissioners' extant files are the case files they built up and sent to Congress with summary reports. The case files of disallowed claims were retained by the House Committee on War Claims and are described in this Guide under Congress. The case files of allowed claims became a part of the records of the Third Auditor of the Treasury Department and are so described elsewhere in this Guide. In the 1880's many unsettled claims were transferred to the Court of Claims for adjudication under the Bowman and Tucker Acts (see the Court of Claims) and became part of the congressional case files. In view of the dispersion of the case files and the inadvertent destruction of some 2,000 cases among the records of the Third Auditor's Office, the compilation of summary reports is especially useful; see U. S. Commissioners of Claims, Summary Reports in All Cases Reported to Congress As Disallowed under the Act of March 3, 1871 . . . [1st-9th General Report, 1871-79] (Washington, 1876-81. 4 vols.).

MEMORIALIZATION AGENCIES

Since the Civil War the Federal Government from time to time has engaged in extensive programs for setting aside historic sites, preserving or restoring battlefields, and erecting monuments, many of which memorialize the war. The planning of such activities has often required considerable research and has resulted in many records that should not be overlooked by the investigator.

Record Groups, 42, 66.--Most of the records concerning the erection of memorials to persons of prominence in the Civil War are in the records of the Office of Public Buildings and Public Parks of the National Capital (Record Group 42) and the Commission of Fine Arts (Record Group 66). In the former record group, among the records of numerous commissions that supervised the construction of memorials to individuals or to particular groups or causes, are records of commissions responsible for erecting Red Cross buildings as memorials to women of the Civil War (and World War I), 1913-30. The records of the Lincoln Memorial Commission, also in Record Group 42, happen to include a file of letters written by Isaac S. Struble, a Union soldier, to his sister, 1863-67, deposited with the commission ca. 1916 by E. Wyks of Phoenix, Ariz. , with the request that they be placed "in a fire proof v[ault] untill [sic] I call for these. " Since the

Commission of Fine Arts also was involved in the design and construction of the Lincoln Memorial, other papers about the memorial (and about the "Oldroyd collection of Lincolniana") are in Record Group 66; and in the same record group are records relating to other projects related to the Civil War: the Farragut Memorial Window (Annapolis), the Appomattox Courthouse Memorial, some of the memorials at Gettysburg, the battlefield at Manassas, many memorials in Arlington Cemetery, and the Grant and Meade Memorials in the District of Columbia.

Record Group 79.--In the records of the National Park Service are papers dating from 1890, most of which were created in the Offices of the Quartermaster General and the Chief of Engineers of the War Department, relating to plans for the establishment of military parks and monuments, the purchase of land for sites, the development of the areas, and the administration of completed projects. Much of this material concerns Civil War battle sites and some of it includes detailed studies of the battles in relation to topography and buildings.

APPENDIX

LIST OF RECORD GROUPS CONTAINING FEDERAL RECORDS RELATING TO THE CIVIL WAR

The records in the National Archives and in the Federal Records Centers are organized by record group. A record group usually consists of the records of a single agency (and its predecessors) at the bureau level in the framework of government. There are more than 300 of these record groups. The Federal records in the National Archives and the centers that are important to Civil War research are in 79 record groups. A few of these groups relate in their entirety to the Civil War--for instance, Record Group 110 (Records of the Provost Marshal General's Bureau). In most cases, however, the record groups of concern to this Guide are not confined to the Civil War in either the periods they cover or the functions they reflect.

There follows a list, arranged by record group number, of all the record groups specified in this Guide as containing records of the agencies discussed. After each record group title appear the names of the agencies concerned and the page number or numbers of this Guide on which the descriptions of their records begin.

11. General Records of the United States Government.
    General records (p. 1).
15. Records of the Veterans Administration.
    War Department: Surgeon General's Office (p. 312).
    Department of the Interior: Pension Office (p. 552).
16. General Records of the Department of Agriculture.
    Department of Agriculture (p. 581).
19. Records of the Bureau of Ships.
    Department of the Navy: Bureau of Construction, Equipment, and Repairs (p. 453); Bureau of Construction and Repair (p. 455); Bureau of Steam Engineering (p. 470); Naval Boards and Commissions (p. 482); Office of the General Superintendent of Ironclads (p. 484).
21. Records of the District Courts of the United States.
    Judiciary: U. S. District and Circuit Courts (p. 93-115 passim); Territorial Courts (p. 119-122 passim).
23. Records of the Coast and Geodetic Survey.
    Department of the Treasury: U. S. Coast Survey (p. 227).

24. Records of the Bureau of Naval Personnel.
         Department of the Navy: Bureau of Equipment and Recruiting (p.
            458); Bureau of Navigation--in general (p. 462), Office of De-
            tail (p. 463), Chaplain Corps (p. 466); Bureau of Yards and
            Docks--Naval Home (p. 473).
26. Records of the U. S. Coast Guard.
         Department of the Treasury: U. S. Revenue-Cutter Service (p. 222);
            Light-House Board (p. 231).
27. Records of the Weather Bureau.
         War Department: Topographical Bureau (p. 274); Surgeon General's
            Office (p. 312).
         Smithsonian Institution (p. 585).
28. Records of the Post Office Department.
         Post Office Department: Office of the Postmaster General (p. 431);
            Appointment Office (p. 433); Contract Office (p. 434, 435);
            Finance Office (p. 436).
29. Records of the Bureau of the Census.
         Department of the Interior: Census Office (p. 563).
36. Records of the Bureau of Customs.
         Department of the Treasury: Customs Service (p. 219).
37. Records of the Hydrographic Office.
         Department of the Navy: Bureau of Navigation--U. S. Naval Ob-
            servatory and Hydrographical Office (p. 464).
39. Records of the Bureau of Accounts (Treasury).
         Department of the Treasury: Office of the Register (p. 188).
41. Records of the Bureau of Marine Inspection and Navigation.
         Department of the Treasury: Office of the Register (p. 189); Cus-
            toms Service (p. 219); Steamboat-Inspection Service (p. 225).
42. Records of the Office of Public Buildings and Public Parks of the
         National Capital.
         Department of the Interior: Office of the Commissioner of Public
            Buildings (p. 549).
         Memorialization agencies (p. 596).
45. Naval Records Collection of the Office of Naval Records and Library.
         Department of the Navy: Secretary's Office (p. 441-453 passim);
            Bureau of Navigation--U. S. Naval Observatory and Hydrograph-
            ical Office (p. 464), Chaplain Corps (p. 466); Bureau of Ordnance
            (p. 469); Bureau of Steam Engineering (p. 471); Bureau of Yards
            and Docks (p. 471); Naval Boards and Commissions (p. 475-483
            passim); Office of the Superintendent of Ironclad Gunboats (p.
            486); Squadrons and Flotillas (p. 488-492 passim); Navy Yards
            and Naval Stations (p. 493-498 passim).
46. Records of the U. S. Senate.
         Congress: Joint Standing Committees (p. 8); Joint Select Commit-
            tees (p. 9); Senate (p. 18).
48. General Records of the Department of the Interior.
         Department of the Interior: Secretary's Office (p. 502-513 passim);
            Washington Aqueduct Office (p. 568); U. S. Penitentiary for the
            District of Columbia (p. 574).
49. Records of the Bureau of Land Management.
         Department of the Interior: General Land Office (p. 520-526 pas-
            sim); Census Office (p. 565).

50. Records of the Treasurer of the United States.
Department of the Treasury: Office of the Treasurer of the United States (p. 191).
52. Records of the Bureau of Medicine and Surgery.
Department of the Navy: Bureau of Medicine and Surgery (p. 460).
53. Records of the Bureau of the Public Debt.
Treasury Department: Office of the Register (p. 188).
56. General Records of the Department of the Treasury.
Department of the Treasury: Secretary's Office (p. 180); Special Agencies (p. 235-240 passim); U. S. Purchasing Agents (p. 241). Commissioners of Claims (p. 595).
58. Records of the Internal Revenue Service.
Department of the Treasury: Office of Internal Revenue (p. 206); State Direct Tax Commissions (p. 208-210 passim).
59. General Records of the Department of State.
Department of State: Departmental Records (p. 138-158 passim). War Department: Commissions to Investigate Political Imprisonment (p. 154, 387).
60. General Records of the Department of Justice.
Office of the Attorney General (p. 419).
Department of the Interior: Secretary's Office (p. 516).
66. Records of the Commission of Fine Arts.
Memorialization agencies (p. 596).
71. Records of the Bureau of Yards and Docks.
Department of the Navy: Bureau of Yards and Docks (p. 471); Naval Boards and Commissions (p. 479).
74. Records of the Bureau of Ordnance.
Department of the Navy: Bureau of Ordnance (p. 467, 469).
75. Records of the Bureau of Indian Affairs.
Department of the Interior: Office of Indian Affairs (p. 531-547 passim).
76. Records of Boundary and Claims Commissions and Arbitrations.
Department of State: Claims Commissions and Courts (p. 165-176 passim).
77. Records of the Office of the Chief of Engineers.
War Department: Engineer Bureau (p. 269); Topographical Bureau (p. 273); District Engineer Offices (p. 274); Defenses of Washington (p. 275); Inspector of the U. S. Military Academy (p. 277).
Department of the Interior: Secretary's Office (p. 504); Washington Aqueduct Office (p. 568).
78. Records of the Naval Observatory.
Department of the Navy: Bureau of Navigation--U. S. Naval Observatory and Hydrographical Office (p. 465), Nautical Almanac Office (p. 465).
79. Records of the National Park Service.
Chesapeake and Ohio Canal Co. (p. 584).
Memorialization agencies (p. 597).
84. Records of the Foreign Service Posts of the Department of State.
Department of State: Foreign Service Posts (p. 160).
87. Records of the United States Secret Service.
Department of the Treasury: Office of the Solicitor of the Treasury-- Secret Service Division (p. 204).

90. Records of the Public Health Service.
   Department of the Treasury: Marine Hospital Service (p. 221).
92. Records of the Office of the Quartermaster General.
   War Department: Quartermaster General's Office and Quartermaster's Department (p. 290-300 passim); Office of the Paymaster General (p. 303); Office of the Commissary General of Subsistence (p. 314); U. S. Military Telegraphs (p. 316); U. S. Military Railroads (p. 318); Cavalry Bureau (p. 339).
94. Records of the Adjutant General's Office.
   War Department: Adjutant General's Office (p. 253-266 passim); Inspector of the U. S. Military Academy (p. 276); Surgeon General's Office and the Medical Department (p. 309); Office of the Judge Advocate (p. 336); Office of the Provost Marshal (p. 337); Bureau of Refugees, Freedmen, and Abandoned Lands (p. 361); War Records Office (p. 381); Record and Pension Office (p. 383); Commission on Claims of Officers and Men, Western Department (p. 390); American Freedmen's Inquiry Commission (p. 390); Slave Claims Commissions (p. 391); Commission on Corrupt Practices in the South (p. 392); Commission on Enlistment of Germans as Substitutes (p. 393); Commission on Rewards for Apprehension of Lincoln Assassins and Others (p. 393); Territorial Commands and Armies (p. 400); Army Corps (p. 401); Volunteer Regiments (p. 404).
   Office of the Attorney General: Pardon Clerk (p. 423).
   U. S. Christian Commission (p. 590).
97. Records of the Bureau of Agricultural and Industrial Chemistry.
   Department of Agriculture (p. 581).
98. Records of the United States Army Commands.
   War Department: Arsenals (p. 285, 287); Military Prisons (p. 323-325 passim); Cavalry Bureau (p. 339); Territorial Commands and Armies (p. 398); Army Corps (p. 401); Regular Army Regiments (p. 403); Forts, Camps, and Other Army Posts (p. 406-410 passim); First--Fifth Military Districts (p. 413-417 passim).
99. Records of the Office of the Paymaster General.
   War Department: Office of the Paymaster General (p. 302).
101. Records of the Bureau of the Comptroller of the Currency.
   Department of the Treasury: Office of the Comptroller of the Currency (p. 212).
104. Records of the Bureau of the Mint.
   Department of the Treasury: U. S. Mint and Branch Mints (p. 216).
105. Records of the Bureau of Refugees, Freedmen, and Abandoned Lands.
   Department of the Treasury: Special Agencies (p. 236, 239).
   War Department: Bureau of Refugees, Freedmen, and Abandoned Lands (p. 358-379 passim).
107. Records of the Office of the Secretary of War.
   War Department: Secretary's Office (p. 246); War Department Telegraph Office (p. 249); Canby Claims Commission (p. 394).
108. Records of the Headquarters of the Army.
   War Department: Headquarters of the Army (p. 395).
109. War Department Collection of Confederate Records.
   War Department: Adjutant General's Office (p. 267); Military Prisons (p. 323-325 passim); Record and Pension Office (p. 384).
   Department of the Interior: Secretary's Office (p. 504).

110. Records of the Provost Marshal General's Bureau, 1863-66.
     War Department: Provost Marshal General's Bureau (p. 341-347
     passim).
111. Records of the Office of the Chief Signal Officer.
     War Department: Office of the Chief Signal Officer and the Signal
     Corps (p. 350-353 passim).
112. Office of the Surgeon General (War).
     War Department: Surgeon General's Office and the Medical Depart-
     ment (p. 308).
118. Records of the United States Attorneys and Marshals.
     Office of the Attorney General: U. S. Attorneys and Marshals (p.
     426).
121. Records of the Public Buildings Administration.
     Department of the Treasury: Office of the Solicitor of the Treasury
     (p. 203); Office of the Supervising Architect (p. 215).
123. Records of the United States Court of Claims.
     Judiciary: U. S. Court of Claims (p. 129).
125. Records of the Office of the Judge Advocate General (Navy).
     Department of the Navy: Secretary's Office--Office of the Solicitor
     and Naval Judge Advocate General (p. 447); Naval Boards and
     Commissions (p. 475, 476).
127. Records of the United States Marine Corps.
     Department of the Navy: U. S. Marine Corps (p. 473).
128. Records of Joint Committees of Congress.
     Congress: Joint Standing Committees (p. 8); Joint Select Commit-
     tees (p. 9).
130. Records of the White House Office.
     Presidency (p. 132).
149. Records of the Government Printing Office.
     Department of the Interior: Office of the Superintendent of Public
     Printing (p. 569).
153. Records of the Office of the Judge Advocate General (Army).
     War Department: Bureau of Military Justice (p. 327, 334); Office
     of the Assistant Judge Advocate General (p. 335).
156. Records of the Office of the Chief of Ordnance.
     War Department: Office of the Chief of Ordnance and the Ordnance
     Department (p. 278-287 passim); Military Prisons (p. 324); Com-
     mission on War Claims at St. Louis (p. 385); Commission on
     Ordnance Claims and Contracts (p. 388).
159. Records of the Office of the Inspector General.
     War Department: Office of the Inspector General (p. 354).
167. Records of the National Bureau of Standards.
     Department of the Treasury: Office of the Superintendent of Weights
     and Measures (p. 229).
181. Records of Naval Districts and Shore Establishments.
     Department of the Navy: Bureau of Navigation--U. S. Naval Acad-
     emy (p. 466); Navy Yards and Naval Stations (p. 494-498 passim).
185. Records of the Panama Canal.
     Panama Railroad Co. (p. 587).
192. Records of the Office of the Commissary General of Subsistence.
     War Department: Office of the Commissary General of Subsistence
     (p. 313).

203. Records of the Office of the Chief of Finance (War).
    War Department: Secretary's Office (p. 248).
204. Records of the Office of the Pardon Attorney.
    Office of the Attorney General: Pardon Clerk (p. 422).
205. Records of the Court of Claims Section (Justice).
    Office of the Attorney General: Assistant Attorney General for
    Claims Cases (p. 424).
206. Records of the Solicitor of the Treasury.
    Department of the Treasury: Office of the Solicitor of the Treasury
    (p. 202).
217. Records of the General Accounting Office.
    Department of the Treasury: Office of the First Comptroller (p.
    183); Office of the Second Comptroller (p. 184); Office of the
    Commissioner of Customs (p. 185); Office of the Register (p.
    188); Office of the First Auditor (p. 191); Office of the Second
    Auditor (p. 192); Office of the Third Auditor (p. 193); Office of
    the Fourth Auditor (p. 197); Office of the Fifth Auditor (p. 199);
    Office of the Auditor of the Treasury for the Post Office Depart-
    ment (p. 201); State Direct Tax Commissions (p. 208-210 pas-
    sim).
    War Department: Western Gunboat Fleet (p. 300); Office of the Pay-
    master General (p. 303); Office of the Commissary General of
    Subsistence (p. 315); Commission on War Claims at St. Louis
    (p. 385).
    Commissioners on Emancipation in the District of Columbia (p.
    593).
231. Records of the United States Soldiers Home.
    U. S. Soldiers' Home (p. 410).
233. Records of the United States House of Representatives.
    Congress: Joint Select Committees (p. 14); House of Representa-
    tives (p. 40).
241. Records of the Patent Office.
    Department of the Interior: Patent Office (p. 559).
249. Records of the Commissary General of Prisoners.
    War Department: Office of the Commissary General of Prisoners
    (p. 321); Office of the Commissioner for Exchange of Prisoners
    (p. 326).
267. Records of the Supreme Court of the United States.
    Judiciary: Supreme Court (p. 82).
318. Records of the Bureau of Engraving and Printing.
    Department of the Treasury: National Currency Bureau--First
    Division (p. 214).
351. Records of the Government of the District of Columbia.
    Department of the Interior: Metropolitan Police (p. 576).

INDEX

A One, bark, 22

Aaron Brown, U.S. revenue cutter, 223

A. McDowell, steamboat, 224

Abandoned lands, 373, 376; administered by War Dept., 244; disposition, 355; reports, 367; restored to owners, 359; sale in northern Tex., 58; to be given to veterans, 30. See also Refugees, Freedmen, and Abandoned Lands, Bureau of

Abandoned property, 239, 240, 370, 372, 374, 377, 392; Johnson impeachment report and, 52; received by U.S. Treasury agents, 233; records, 47, 182, 188, 234, 235, 236; Sea Islands, 238; to Freedmen's Bureau, 375. See also Abandoned lands, Captured and Abandoned Property, Commercial Intercourse, Property

Abbott, James B., 540

Abert, John J., 29, 273

Abolition, by border States, 4; District of Columbia, 4, 23, 52; petition re, 36, 52, 54; Territories, 4. See also Constitutional amendments

Acacia, steamboat, 224

Academy of National Sciences, papers re, 60

Acapulco, Mexico, 144

Accomack County, Va., 10

Accountability, Government depts. and, 58

Accounts, Agriculture Commr., 191; certification, 183, 184, 185; contractors, 481; Freedmen's Bureau, 372, 373, 375, 378;

J. Henry, 586; Indian Office, 531, 532; land offices, 529; marine hospitals, 221; medical, 307; Nautical Almanac Office, 465; naval, 442, 445, 468; Office of Weights and Measures, 229; opinions re, 420; pensioners, 554; quartermasters, 288, 299; Quartermaster's Dept., 388; Register's Office duties, 186; Special Agencies, 234, 236, 238, 239, 240; Steamboat-Inspection Service, 225; surgeons', 309; transportation, 294; War Records Office, 382

Accounts, House Standing Committee of, 61

Accounts Bureau, Treasury Department, 188

Adams, Charles Francis, 61, 140, 157, 163, 164

Adams, Green, 200

Adams, Henry A., 450

Adams, J. H., 19

Adams Express Co., 591

Adams Express Co. vs. Abram Kannes, 189

Addison F. Andrews, U.S. revenue cutter, 223

Adger, James, U.S.S., 489

Adjutant and Inspector, Marine Corps, 473

Adjutant General, 380, 410; adjustment of military bounties, 76; and the Commission for State Prisoners, 154; commanding generals' letters, 395; Mississippi Valley activities, 27; orders, 396-397; records, 75, 389, 390, 391, 392, 393, 394, 396

Adjutant General's Office, 250-268, 382, 384, 405; archival depository,

Cobb, George T., 66
Cobb, Howell, 179, 183
Coblens, Charles, 34
Coburn, John, 16
Cochrane, John, 63, 277
Cockburn, Sir Alexander, 164
Code of naval laws, 448
Coded correspondence, 396
Coffey, Titian J., 418
Coffins, 558
Cohen, Arthur, 164
Coinage, 216, 594
Coinage, Weights, and Measures,
House Standing Committee on a
Uniform System of, 61
Coiner, claim re, 44
Coins, assays, 217; counterfeited,
201; manufacture, 217
Colby, S. B., 188
Cold Harbor, Va., 311
Cold Spring, N.Y., 467
Cole, Cornelius, 67
Coleman, Andrew J., 210
Colfax, Schuyler, 40, 56
Colhoun, E. R., 450
Collamer, Jacob, 8, 9, 29, 31, 32,
34
Collecting Division, Sixth Auditor,
200; Third Auditor, 193
College Green Barracks, Md., 321
Colleges, occupied by U.S. Army,
125. See also Land grants
Colleton, S.C., 375
Collins, Perry M., 22, 26
Collision at sea, Supreme Court
cases, 81
Colombia, 508; claims convention,
175; transit across Panama, 142
Colón, Panama, U.S. consular
records destroyed, 162
Colonization Society, 379
Colorado, U.S.S., 453
Colorado Territory, appropriations
for, 59; Arapahos attack mining
camps, 531; censuses, 565, 566;
Cheyenne Indian massacre, 11;
courts, 119-120; Indian supt.,
545; Indian treaty in, 24; letters,
503; military force organized in,
64; mining: camps, 115, district
bylaws, 521; Mint appeals to Governor, 217; private land claims,
523, 526; records, 149; refuses

direct tax, 206; Supreme Court
judges pay, 59; surveyor general,
66, 526; township plats, 526;
troop supply, 297; volunteer regiments, 405
Colored Troops Bureau, Adjutant
General's Office, 262, 391
Colored Troops Division, Adjutant
General's Office, 263
Colt, Samuel, Co., 286
Columbia, S.C., 375; circuit court
trials, 16; claims re: expenses
for Union prisoners in, 21, prop-
erty destruction, 21; fire at in
1865, 59; freedmen's disbursing
office, 266
Columbia Barracks, Wash. Ter.,
410
Columbia Institution for the Instruc-
tion of the Deaf and Dumb, 499,
503, 572-573; grounds, 44
Columbia University Library, con-
gressional journal in, 14
Columbus, Ky., 299
Columbus, Miss., 22
Columbus, Ohio, 338; seat of district court, 108. See also Camp
Chase
Columbus, Tex., 377
Columbus Arsenal, Ohio, 283
Colvocoresses, George M., 450
Colwell, Stephen, 210
Comanche Indians, 547
Commanding generals, U.S. Army,
394, 395; records, 399; secret
service, 337
Commerce, 239; foreign: annual
report on, 152, Confederate
depredations upon, 141, flourished
in North during war, 163, history
of, 160, promoted by U.S. consuls,
47, 158, protection of, 144, 159,
statistics and reports on, 152; protection on the plains, 511; secession affects, 218; Southern: 168,
ports opened by U.S. occupation,
169; supervision, 185; with Confederate States, 44
Commerce Department, 230; Building, 232; Patent Office transferred
to, 557; transfer of Treasury functions to, 178
Commerce, House Standing Commit-

218, 219; officers, 44, 187, 218, 233, 239; regulations, 139; shipping statistics, 189-190; surveyors, 218, 221, 235. See also Tonnage duties

Customs Bureau, Treasury Department, 219

Customs cases, district courts: N. Y., 108, Pa., 110

Customs collector, 218, 223, 224, 225, 232, 236; administered loyalty oaths for passports, 147; collected seamen's tax, 220; committee papers re, 44; corresp., 181; Inspectors' pay, 24; Marine Hospital directors, 221; N. Y., 238; pay, 22; suits against, 202, 203

Customs Commissioner, 178, 181, 202, 219, 240; enemy accounts, 234; functions, 179; records, 184-186

Customs Division, Treasury Department, 219

Customs Service, Treasury Department, 178, 184, 229; records, 218-220

Cutler, O. N., 237, 241

Cuts, copyright, 561

Cutts, J. Madison, 184

Cutts, R. D., 227

Cuyler, R. R., U. S. S., 489

Dahlgren, John A., 15, 28, 450, 467, 468, 490, 498

Dahlonega, Ga., 215, 216

Daily, Samuel G., 45, 46

Dakota City, Nebr. Ter., 121

Dakota Territory, appropriations for, 59; Army posts, 406; capitol, 59; census of, 562, 564; census of 1861, 566; courts, 120-121; Indian expeditions, 406; Indian supt., 545, 546; Indian tribes in, 48; Indian War claims, 196; letters, 503; prison, 59; records of, 149; Sioux depredations, 536; surveyor general, 526; township plats, 526; wagon roads, 512

Dale, U. S. S., 490

Dallas County, Ala., 240

Damage cases, circuit court, Ohio, 108; Court of Claims, 128

Dana, Charles A., 245, 246, 248, 388

Dana, James J., 296

Dana, Richard H., Jr., 53

Daniel, Peter V., 79

D'Araujo, Marcos Antonio (Viscount d'Itajubá), 164

Darling, William A., 71

Darlington, S. C., 375

Daughters of the American Revolution Library, Washington, D. C., census schedules, 565

Davenport, Henry K., 450, 489, 492

Davenport, Richard G., 453

Davenport, Iowa, officer examining board, 263-264

Davis, Charles H., 21, 440, 450, 461, 464, 465, 478, 480, 491, 593

Davis, Charles L., 350

Davis, David, 79, 81, 85, 133, 385

Davis, Garrett, 34, 35

Davis, Henry Winter, 45, 47, 61, 68, 69, 277

Davis, J. C. Bancroft, 164

Davis, Jeff C., 369

Davis, Jefferson, 17, 25, 26, 31, 32, 51, 113, 195, 248, 254, 277, 320, 337, 393; claimants for capture reward, 43; Confederate agents' letters to, 52; imprisonment, 337; petitions for amnesty for, 423; proclamations, 449; prosecution, 420; treason trial, 53

Davis, Jefferson, C. S. S., claims re not considered, 165

Davis, Jefferson, U. S. revenue cutter, 223

Davis, John, 169

Davis, Reuben, 62

Davis, William M., 66

Davy, Joseph & Co., 286

Dawes, Henry L., 45, 63, 64, 68, 544

Dawes Commission, 544, 547

Dawson, John L., 69

Dead Letter Office, 436, 437, 438

Dead letters, 437

Deaf, care, 572

De Ahua, Henry C., 527

Deaths, Army, 255; certificates, 144, 554; consular records, 158, 161; notices, 150; Federal, 591; Govt. Hospital for the Insane, 571; Pensacola Navy Yard, 496; reports, 255

Debentures, U. S., excess, 185

230, 232; keepers, 22, 232; land titles, 420; petitions re, 44; reservations, 512, 522, 523; "scrapbooks," 232; sites, 232, 519, 521; supts., 232

Lightships, 44, 230, 231

Lincoln, Abraham, 13, 14, 19, 21, 24, 30, 48, 182, 254, 256, 328, 329, 393, 400, 407, 410, 428, 440, 443, 445, 454, 473; applications for appointments, 420; appointments: 79-80, 146, Cameron, 245, Chase, 179, military governors, 156, Negro colonization agent, 507, provost marshals, 347, Territorial officials, 116; approves: act for admission of W. Va., 114, U. S. Sanitary Commission, 587; assassination: 51, 74, 141, 393, committee to investigate, 74, conspirators in, 141-142, 407, imprisonment of suspects, 575, witnesses' names, 577; assassins: 328, apprehension, 337, prosecution, 335, trial, 329; authorized to establish Army Corps, 400; autopsy report, 256; biography of, 133; calls up: soldiers, 242, volunteers, 346; condolences on death, 139, 143, 145; directed political prisoners release, 155; direction re political prisoners, 426; Executive orders, 101-102, 533; funeral, 509, 550; issues passes to South, 157; letters received: 419, 549, Attorney General, 419, Seward, 138, State Dept., 145, Treasury Dept., 181; letters sent: 514, Attorney General, 420, Seward, 138, Stanton, 248, Treasury Dept., 181; messages to Congress, 65, 68; nomination, 93; oaths taken under pardon proclamation, 155; orders U. S. Penitentiary turned over to War Dept., 573; papers, 132, 133-134; patronage in the Territories, 149; portrait, 47; private secretaries, 133, 134; proclamations: admission of Nev., 122, amnesty, 156, blockade, 486, insurrection, 126, parole, 155, prospective citizens eligible for draft,

158, recognizes loyal govt. of Va., 156; restoration of loyal Southern govts., 156; recommendations: Court of Claims, 125, judicial reform, 89; requisitions for amnesty pardons, 156; salary to family, 24; signs ships' papers, 172; substitute, 555; summer home, 410; suspends writ of habeas corpus, 86, 103, 153; telegram files, 134, 249-250; transfers jurisdiction of political prisoners, 153; use of military telegraphs, 316; visits to telegraph office, 248. See also President

Lincoln, Mary Harlan (Mrs. Robert Todd), 504

Lincoln, Mary Todd (Mrs. Abraham), 29, 509, 549, 555

Lincoln, Robert Todd, 133, 555

Lincoln (Abraham) Association, 132, 133

Lincoln Memorial, 23, 597

Lincoln Memorial Commission, 596

Lincoln Memorial University, papers: Howard, 359, Worden, 490

Lincolniana, 597

Liquor, sale to soldiers prohibited, 329; purchases for speculation, 69; speculation in by Army officers, 69; suppression of sale among Indians, 66, 530, 534, 546; taxes, 204

Lisbon, Portugal, 159

Lithographing Division, Coast Survey, 226, 227, 228

Lithographs. See Photolithographs

Litters, 310

Little, Brown, and Co., 1

Little Rock, Ark., 235, 236, 373, 416; Army medical board, 307; captured, 93; Confederate prisoners, 322, 324; land office, 527; oaths of allegiance administered in, 155, 156

Little Rock Arsenal, Ark., 283

Liverpool, England, 140, 143, 167, 199

Livestock brands, Ariz. Ter., 118

Livingston, John W., 495

Loan, Benjamin F., 10, 68, 71

Loan and Treasury Note Branch, Treasury Department, 180

Nickel alloy, 216

Nicodemus, William J. L. , 349

Nicolay, John G. , 133

Nicolson, W. L. , 227

Niter, 145, 467, 468

Noble, Warren P. , 67

Noell, John W. , 65, 66

Noncommissioned officers, 262

Nonsupport suits for, Colo. Ter. , 119

Norfolk, Va. , 239, 390; custom-house reopened, 219; marine hospital, 221; military savings banks, 212; naval hospital, 459; paymaster, 28, 198; occupied by Federal forces, 113; seat of Federal courts, 113; U. S. Christian Commission field agent, 592

Norfolk Navy Yard, 28, 33; corresp., 470; destruction, 495-496; history, 472; hospital, 461; journal, 472; records, 495-496; supplies received, 456

Norris, Benjamin W. , 46

North Atlantic Blockading Squadron, 451, 456, 459, 486, 489

North Atlantic Ocean, 452

North Carolina, 85, 390, 451, 480, 486; Army post in, 408; Cherokee land claims, 542; colored soldiers raised in, 262; convention taxes, 26; direct tax, 208, 209; Federal judges appointed, 87; freedmen's affairs in, 48; Freedmen's Bureau, 54, 374; in Dept. of the South, 415; in Dept. of Va. , 413; lighthouses reestablished, 230; loyalty investigation, 13-14; men employed in, 270; military railroads, 317; military subdistrict, 413; police officials, 414; postwar conditions, 16, 39; public whippings of U. S. citizens in, 73; railroad to connect Ky. , Tenn. , and, 35; report re disloyal organizations in, 38; Second Congressional District, 45; Second Military District, 411; Senate seats vacated during war, 17, 18; sounds, 230; Special Agency, Treasury Dept. , 235, 238-239; tax sales halted, 207; volunteer regiments, 405

North Carolina, U. S. S. , 495

North Carolina Department of Archives and History, Taney papers, 85

North Dakota. See Dakota Territory

North Dakota (State), creation, 120

North-South differences, compromise to settle, 52

Northeast Executive Building. See Executive Building, Northeast

Northeast Ferry, N. C. , Union prisoners, 321

Northeastern Frontier. See Defenses

Northern Department, 290; medical affairs, 304; orders for artificial limbs, 312

Northern Indian Superintendency, 545, 546, 547

Northern Pacific Railroad, land sold for benefit of, 30

Northerner, U. S. revenue cutter, 219, 223

Northwestern Indian Expedition, 256

Norton, Jesse O. , 70

Norway, 159

Notaries public, administered loyalty oaths for passports, 147; charge of malfeasance against, 553; consuls serve as, 158, 161; corresp., 553; District of Columbia, 421; passport papers from Boston, 148; pension claimants' declarations, 551; political disabilities imposed on, 38; took depositions on shipping losses, 163

Note and Coupon Division, Treasury Department, 187

Note and Redemption Division, Treasury Department, 180

Nott, Charles C. , 128

Nourse, J. E. , 450

Nunn, Joseph, 167

Nurses, Army, 384; female, 305; naval, 461; pensions, 552; recruited by sanitary commissions, 588

Nye, James W. , 35, 38

Nystrom, John W. , 472

Oaths, 368; amnesty: 373, 376, violations, 423; consuls abroad administer, 44; loyalty: 369, 414, Treasury Dept. , 182; members of National

Omaha, Nebr. , court seat, 121;
district attorney records, 426
Omaha Indians, under Central Su-
perintendency, 545
O'Neill, John, 68
Opelousas, La. , court seat, 101
Operation reports, project for pub-
lication, 251-252
Opinions, Attorney General, 420
Orangeburg, S. C. , 375
Ord, Edward O. C. , 277, 373, 397,
416
Order of American Knights of the
Golden Circle, investigated, 327
Orders, Engineer Dept. , 270, 276;
War Dept. , 257-258
Ordinances, copies of State, 156
Ordnance, Army: accountability
records, 280, accounts, 184, 192,
Chief, 15, 192, 388, Chief of
Army of Potomac, 399, claims,
385, depots, 283, documents re
published, 279, experiments,
280, 281, factories, 280, inspec-
tion, 282, 283, inventions, 279,
issuance, 280, issued to Mo., 55,
procurement, 277-278, 279-280;
naval: 15, 16, inventions, 28,
public competition, 28. See also
Artillery
Ordnance, Joint Select Congressional
Committee on, 15-16
Ordnance and Hydrography Bureau,
439, 466
Ordnance Board, 282
Ordnance boards, 468
Ordnance Bureau, Navy Department,
15, 24, 439, 466-469
Ordnance Claims and Contracts
Commission, 387-388
Ordnance Department, War Department, 15, 277-283; boards, 281;
returns, 259
Ordway, Albert, 43
Ore samples, deposited at Treasury, 217
Oregon, Army posts, 408; donation
land claims, 524, 526; judicial
circuit, 89, 94; land donations,
517; Senator from, 33; surveyor
general, 526; township plats, 526;
volunteer regiments, 405; war
claims, 193, 194; war debt loan, 189

Oregon country, 175
Oregon Historical Society, Field
papers, 85
Oregon Territory, Indian superin-
tendency, 545, 546; judiciary ap-
pointments, 421
Organization Division, Treasury De-
partment, 212
Orme, W. W. , 235
Orphans, care of servicemen's, 27,
54
Orr, James L. , 19
Orth, Godlove S. , 67, 71
Orton, William, 205
Osage, U. S. S. , 491
Osage Indians, records, 547, under
Southern Superintendency, 545
Osborn, Thomas W. , 37, 367
Oswego and Erie Canal, 54
Oto Indians, 547
Otranto, Italy, U. S. consulate in,
159
Ottawa Indians, under Central Super-
intendency, 545
Otto, William T. , 501, 503
Ould, Robert, 326
Overseers of the Poor, political dis-
abilities imposed on, 38
Owen, Robert Dale, 387, 390
Oxen, 288
Ozark, U. S. S. , 491

Pacific coast, 226, 231, 587
Pacific County, Wash. Ter. , 124
Pacific Ocean, U. S. whaling vessels
captured in, 163
Pacific Ocean area, U. S. commer-
cial activities, 161; U. S. Consul
General, 199
Pacific Railroad, northern route
proposed, 67; petitions re south-
west branch, 54
Pacific Railroad, House Select Com-
mittee on the, 67-68
Pacific Railroad, House Standing
Committee on the, 61
Pacific Railroad, Senate Select Com-
mittee on the Construction of a, 33
Pacific Railroad, Senate Standing
Committee on the, 20, 31
Pacific Railroad Division, Interior
Department, 513
Pacific railroads, land grants, 499,

257; detailed to Secretary of the Treasury, 69; districts, 346-347; protection, 53; records, 400

Prussia, 254, 393, 579

Pruyn, John V. L., 69

Public buildings, accounts, 183, 191; construction, 57, 215; cost defrayed by sale of land, 517; data re guns on display, 468; District of Columbia, 502, 503; expenditures, 509; House Commerce Committee and, 44; land titles, 420; maintenance, 215; outside District of Columbia, 214; payment of rental, 516, 517; renovation of, 30; reservations, 522; seized at Charleston, 62; superintendence, 566; Territories, 499, 503; use, 27. See also Capitol

Public Buildings and Grounds, House Standing Committee on, 57, 58

Public Buildings and Grounds, Senate Standing Committee on, 20, 30

Public Buildings and Grounds, Superintendent, charges, 30, 46-47

Public Buildings and Public Parks Office of the National Capital, 596

Public Buildings Commissioner, 548-550; letters to, 568; maintenance of the Capitol, 566; papers re, 60; requisitions for funds, 503

Public Buildings Service, 203

Public debt, accounts, 183; interest payments, 190; management, 180, 188; Register's office and, 186. See also Loans Division

Public Debt Bureau, Treasury Department, 188

Public documents, congressional, 7; distribution, 515-516; handling, 499, 501

Public Health and Marine Hospital Service. See Marine Hospital Service

Public Health Service. See Marine Hospital Service

Public Lands, House Standing Committee on the, 58

Public Lands, Senate Standing Committee on, 20, 30

Public Printer, 9, 569. See also Superintendent of Public Printing

Public Printing, Joint Standing Congressional Committee, 9

Public Record Office, London, archives of Mixed Courts of Justice, 177

Public service. See Civil service, Federal employees

Public utilities, taxes, 204

Public whippings in North Carolina, 73

Public works, Washington, D. C., 57, 502

Publication Branch, War Department, 380

Publication Office, War Records, 380

Pueblo, Colo. Ter., 119

Puerto Rico, 143, 144, 176

Puget Sound Agricultural Co., 175

Pulaski, Tenn., 376

Purchasing Agents, Treasury Dept., 237, 240-241

Puritan gun carriage, 468

Quapaw Indians, 530; adjudication of claims, 540; records, 547; under Southern Superintendency, 545

Quartermaster, Freedmen's Bureau, War Dept., 363

Quartermaster, Marine Corps, 473-474

Quartermaster depots, 292, 300, 405; Alexandria, Va., 406; Commissions to Inspect, 392; investigation of inventories, 253; reports, 295

Quartermaster General, Army, 194, 234, 388, 389; examination of claims by, 126

Quartermaster General's Office, 287-299, 388

Quartermasters, Army: 393, accounts, 194, appointments, 262, Army of Potomac, 399, Hilton Head, S. C., 407; Marine Corps: accounts, 197-198

Quartermaster's Department, Army, 194, 287-299; accounts, 184, 193, 195; Cairo, Ill., 64, 388; employees admitted to Govt. Hospital for the Insane, 570; horse procurement, 338; returns, 259; use of transport

vessels, 34-35
Quebec, Canada, 143, 153, 159
Quincy, Ill. , quartermaster depot, 300

R. R. Cuyler, U. S. S. , 489
Rachel Seaman, U. S. S. , 453
Racial discrimination, 26
Radford, William, 69, 450, 489
Ragged Point, Va. , 224
Railroads, accidents, 310; approval of routes, 513; Army transportation, 385; claims, 291; destruction, 329; engineer, 512; Govt. directors, 513, 514; House Committee on, 58; Indian lands sold to, 543; instruments patented, 558; investigation of supply functions, 64; land grants, 24, 30, 73, 513, 514, 518, 520, 521, 529; letters, 83, 510, 513; loans, 189; mail contracts, 433; maps, 271, 525, 526; memorialize Senate, 36; military use, 33, 69; New York to Washington, 58, 68; petitions re, 26; photographs, 272, 352; remonstrances to Senate, 29; reports, 514; rights of way, 530; rolling stock losses, 193; routes, 514; segregation on, 23; Southern: 35, 319, 406, 564, annual reports, 73, Confederate use of, 73, debts due U.·S. , 53, Govt. relations with, 72, House investigation, 72-73, owe Va. money, 413, repair of, 53, U. S. military operations, 72, 73; Tex. , 377; wartime use of, 73. See also Military railroads, Pacific Railroad
Railway mail service, 430, 431, 434, 435
Rainey, Joseph H. , 77
Raleigh, N. C. , 374; Army post at, 408; Confederate prisoners, 324; court-martial at, 54; public whippings of U. S. citizens, 73; report re circuit court trials at, 16
Ramsey, ----, 29
Ramsey, George D. , 278
Rand, Arnold A. , 43
Randall, Alexander W. , 433
Randall, E. M. , 209

Randall, Samuel J. , 14, 68, 74
Randall, William H. , 68
Randolph Macon College, moved, 413
Ransom, George M. , 450, 453
Rappahannock, C. S. S. , 163
Rappahannock River, 226
Rathbone, Henry R. , 345
Rations, Army, 194, 195; Marines, 196
Raymond, Henry J. , 72
Rayner, Kenneth, 169
Reading, Pa. , 467
Real property, 128
Realf, Richard, 31
Rebel Archives, Bureau of, Adjutant General's Office, 266
Rebellion, assistance to, 110; petitions re suppression, 36; punishment of, 154
"Rebellion Records Division. " See War Records Office
Rebellious States, House Select Committee on the, 68
Rebels, report on use of Indians, 10
Receipts, annual report, 186, 187; ledgers, 191; records, 188
Receipts and Expenditures Division, Treasury Department, 186
Receivers of land offices, appointment, 504, 505; duties, 528; letters, 520
Receivership, banks in, 202
Receiverships, national banks, 212
Receiving ships, 458, 459; Baltimore, Md. , 494; marine guards, 473; Philadelphia Navy Yard, 497; surgeons on, 460
Reclamation Service, Interior Department, 513
Reconstruction, amnesty proclamation, 155; problems of, 76; proclamations re, 1. See also under names of States
Reconstruction, House Select Committee on, 76, 156
Reconstruction, Joint Congressional Committee on, 13, 14
Reconstruction Acts, compliance with: Ala. , 415, Ark. , 416, Fla. , 415, Ga. , 415, La. , 417, Miss. , 416, N. C. , 414, S. C. , 414, Tex. , 417, Va. , 413; enforcement of, 53;

Sanders, B. W. , 141
Sanders, George N. , 393
Sanderson, ----, 248
Sands, Benjamin F. , 450
Sandusky, Ohio, military prison, 386
Sanford, Edward S. , 315
Sanford, Henry S. , 141
Sanger, W. P. S. , 479
Sanitarians, 587
Sanitary fairs, 588
Sanitation, Army, 304; District of Columbia, 576; in South, 374
Sanpete County, Utah Ter. , court records, 124
Santa Fe, N. Mex. , land office, 525, 527
Santa Fe, N. Mex. Ter. , 123
Santa Fe trail, 530
Santee, U. S. S. , 453, 466, 490
Santo Domingo, 176
Sarah, slaver, 81
Sargent, Aaron A. , 67
Sargent, Nathan, 185, 240
Sartain pontoon bridge, 269
Sartori, Lewis C. , 450
Saunders, John, 44
Saunders, William, 579
Savannah, Ga. , 238, 240; campaign against, 21, 256; captured, 409; construction of infirmary, 48; Customhouse reopened, 219; foreign property taken at, 21; freedmen's disbursing office, 266
Savannah, Confederate privateer, 107
Savannah, U. S. S. , 462
Savannah River, 480
Sawmills, 535
Sawyer, Philetus, 73
Saxton, Rufus, 209, 375
Scandinavian ports, U. S. consuls in promoted immigration, 159
Scandinavians in South, 162
Scarburgh, George P. , 128
Schaghticoke Powder Co. , Schaghticoke, N. Y. , 467
Schenck, Robert C. , 14, 15, 53, 164
Schofield, John M. , 366, 379, 412, 413
School farm lands, S. C. , 209
Schoolcraft, Mary H. , 9
Schools, claims of before U. S. Court

of Claims, 127; District of Columbia, 23; freedmen, 361, 363, 366, 367, 369, 370, 371, 374, 376, 377, 378, 379; Indians, 511; occupied by U. S. Army, 125. See also Education
Schott, Charles A. , 226, 228
Schriver, Edmund, 353, 354
Schultz, Alexander H. , 142
Schumann, Franz, 29
Schuylkill Arsenal, Philadelphia, Pa. , 300
Schuylkill River, 479
Science, patent files a source of history, 559; Smithsonian Institution promotes, 584, 585
Scientific societies, 584, 594
Scientists, American, 227; and Coast Survey, 225; on Light-House Board, 230
Scio, Turkey, 159
Sclopis, Count Frederic, 164
Scofield, Glenni W. , 16, 70
Scofield & Co. , 448
Scots, 162
Scott, George E. , 342
Scott, John, 16, 38
Scott, Robert K. , 375
Scott, Thomas A. , 246, 315, 316, 317
Scott, Winfield, 27, 337, 394, 395, 396, 411
Scott Foundry, Reading, Pa. , 285, 467
Scouts, 29, 341
Sea Horse Key, Fla. , 231
"Sea Island Cotton," 238
Sea Islands, S. C. , 237, 238, 375
Sea letters, for whalers, 172; received by consuls, 158
Seacoast defenses, 271
Seacoasts, maps of, 272
Seaman, Rachel, U. S. S. , 453
Seamen, cave of, 199; certificates for passports, 147; claim exemption as British subjects, 139; claims for losses and unemployment, 165; consular services for, 162; crimes by, 144; Govt. equipment for, 22; medical care, 47, 218, 220, 221; protected by U. S. consuls, 158; registers of, 162; warrants for arrest of deserters, 87

126, 291; claims of Unionists, 594-596; courts, 89; denied land bounties, 518; direct tax: commrs., 207, commissions, 178, measures for collecting, 127, sales halted, 207; Federal courts inactive, 79; former Confederates elected to office, 417; govts. restored, 145, 156, 374, 411, 412; Governors: excepted from amnesty, 423, forward applications for amnesty, 423; gradual emancipation suggested in upper, 65; Homestead Act extended to, 518; Indian trust funds invested in bonds, 510; land offices, 528; land patents, 521; lend Confederate records, 383; maps, 564; marshals transfer allegiance, 426; postal service: discontinued, 429, 435, resumed, 430, 431, 435; postwar collection of taxes, 53; postwar conditions in, 16-17; postwar reorganization, 45; provisional govts.: 416, appointment, 52, 56, corresp. with Secretary of State, 156, governors, 411, 416, subservient to U. S. military, 412, 414; removal of Indians, 530; representation for, 13; Representatives readmitted, 126; Representatives withdraw, 40; republican form of govt. guaranteed to, 68; revenue collections resumed, 206; seizure of land records, 527; Senators withdraw, 17; Supreme Court resumes hearing appeals from, 81; unequal tax burden, 207. See also Confederate States, Ku Klux Klan, South

Southern States, Senate Select Committee on Alleged Outrages in the, 38, 39

Southern Steamship Co., 238

Southern sympathizers. See Confederate sympathizers

Southern war claims, jurisdiction, 127

Southerners, furnish testimony, 168; oppose division of Territories, 115; pensions, 506; petitions for removal of political disabilities, 38; requested passes to reenter South, 157; withdraw from U. S.

Army, 242

Southwest, 517; land grants, 519

Southwestern Indian Superintendency, 545

Spain, land grants, 519; U. S. Minister to, 28; U. S. salaried consuls appointed to, 159

Spalding, Rufus P., 72

Spangler, Edward, 329

Spaniards in South, 162

Spanish-American War claims, 194

Spanish colonies, 175

Spanish indemnity loan, 188

Sparrow, Jacob, 467

Spates, Alfred, 584

Spaulding, Elbridge G., 65

Speaker of the House, 40; appoints committee, 42; signs enrolled bills, 8; War Dept. report to, 393

Special Agencies, Treasury Department, 185; First: 240, arrest of agent, 396; Second: 239, 240, records, 235-236, 373; Third: 237, 238, 239, records, 236-237; Fourth: 238, records, 237; Fifth: 236, 237, records, 237-238; Sixth, records, 238-239; Seventh, records, 239-240; Eighth: 233, 238, records, 240; Ninth: 233, 238, records, 240; districts, 233; liaison with military, 239-240; records, 182, 233-240

Special agents, Commrs. of Claims, 595; Post Office Dept., 429, 430, 431; Treasury Dept.: 233, 377, conduct in New Orleans, 392, supervising, 233, 234, 235, 236, 237, 238, 239, 240. See also State Department

Specie payments, suspension of, 211

Specimens, medical, 306

Speck, Joseph, 552

Speed, James, 156, 335, 341, 418, 419

Spies, 341; arrest: 346, diplomatic despatches re, 139; female, 256; held under military arrest, 153; lists, 247; Union: 555, claims for compensation, 21, counterspies employed, 154, for General Sherman, 21, 73, in consulates, 159, report on Confederate agents in Europe, 141. See also Confederate spies